Traversing Philosophical Boundaries

Third Edition

Max O. Hallman
Merced College

Australia • Brazil • Canada • Mexico • Singapore • Spain
United Kingdom • United States

THOMSON
WADSWORTH

Philosophy Editor: Steve Wainwright
Assistant Editors: Lee McCracken, Barbara Hillaker
Editorial Assistant: Gina Kessler
Technology Project Manager: Julie Aguilar
Marketing Manager: Worth Hawes
Marketing Assistant: Alexandra Tran
Marketing Communications Manager: Stacey Purviance
Creative Director: Rob Hugel

Executive Art Director: Maria Epes
Print Buyer: Rebecca Cross
Permissions Editor: Joohee Lee
Production Service: Pre-Press Company, Inc.
Copy Editor: Debbie Prato
Cover Designer: Yvo Riezebos
Cover Image: J. A. Kraulis / Masterfile
Compositor: Pre-Press Company, Inc.
Cover and Text Printer: Malloy Incorporated

For more information about our products, contact us at:
Thomson Learning Academic Resource Center
1-800-423-0563
For permission to use material from this text or product, submit a request online at
http://www.thomsonrights.com
Any additional questions about permissions can be submitted by e-mail to
thomsonrights@thomson.com

Thomson Higher Education
10 Davis Drive
Belmont, CA 94002-3098
USA

Library of Congress Control Number: 2005938580
ISBN 0495007064

For my heart-mate, Cheryl, for teaching me to dance with the moon
For my children, Hannah, Dylan, and Aliena, for providing laughter and joy
For my mom, Neoma, for never doubting in me
For my dad, Oneal, for helping me when I most needed it
In memory of my grandmother, Addie, for supporting me in countless ways

Contents

Chapter 2

Creation and Reality 137

Chapter 3

Knowledge and Truth 223

How Do We Know What We Know? 227

Is Knowledge Really Attainable? 288

Chapter 4

Ethics 326

How Do We Determine What We Ought to Do? 331

What Are Some Reasons for Questioning Traditional Values? 367

Chapter 5

Politics 420

What Is the Basis of Our Obligations to Society? 425

Chapter 6

Religion 559

Preface

The title *Traversing Philosophical Boundaries* reflects the basic principle that guided the selection and arrangement of the diverse writings included in this anthology. More important, it captures the essence of what may be the most significant contribution the study of philosophy can make: It can help us traverse the socially determined barriers that interfere with our intellectual, psychological, and spiritual development. Finally, it suggests the joy and excitement that we, as teachers, experience when we are engaged with students who are discovering philosophy for the first time.

Unlike the introductory texts available when I began studying philosophy, *Traversing Philosophical Boundaries* is not limited to an Anglo-European canon that is based on the assumption that the philosophical enterprise began with the ancient Greeks. Nor is it limited to texts by authors who have traditionally been classified as philosophers. Rather, this is a multicultural reader; to a lesser extent, it is multidisciplinary as well. Thus, the text itself traverses philosophical boundaries between both cultures and academic disciplines.

While some scholars continue to debate the pros and cons of a "multicultural" curriculum, the current text combines a strong emphasis on the teaching of the traditional canon (there are more selections from Plato than anyone else) with an equally strong emphasis on the teaching of nontraditional writings. My reasons for adopting this approach are neither theoretical nor political—they are autobiographical and practical. Each of the three graduate schools I attended (the University of South Carolina, McGill University, and Tulane University) stressed the history of (mainly Western) philosophy. I believe that we do introductory students a disservice if we do not acquaint them with at least some of the writers who have been instrumental in the development of the Western philosophical tradition. However, since leaving graduate school, I have been fortunate to teach classes—general humanities, comparative cultures, and comparative religions—that have expanded my philosophical horizons beyond the Western tradition. Incorporating these nontraditional sources into my philosophy classes has complemented the teaching of the Western canon while enriching classroom discussion.

Another practical reason for expanding the traditional canon is that the enrollment in my classes is becoming more and more culturally diverse, and I believe that an expanded philosophical canon better serves the needs and interests of my students. Whether intended or not, teaching only the traditional Western canon often leaves students with the impression that philosophical thinking is principally the domain of European men.

Organization

My goal in this anthology is to present provocative and philosophically significant writings from a wide variety of sources. The texts have been selected from many different cultures and perspectives, and they have been taken from ancient as well as modern sources. To make the text easier to integrate into existing courses, I have grouped these writings into traditional philosophical categories, such as knowledge and truth, ethics, and politics. Each chapter is subdivided by two or three questions that indicate a principal focus of the selections included in that section. Of course, many of the selected writings cut across topics, and they usually address more than one philosophical question. Thus, my arrangement is certainly not the only possible one.

Within each chapter, I have arranged the selections in the order that best allows comparison and contrast from one to the next. For example, in the chapter "Self, Mind, and Body," I begin with five selections that focus on the question of whether we have an essential self or soul. The first selection states that we do indeed have an essential self or soul, one that survives physical death. (I begin with this because it is the view of most of my students.) The next four selections give differing reasons for doubting that an essential self or soul actually exists.

Next, I turn to the question of the nature of the body and the extent to which our bodies determine who we are. This section begins with two articles that reaffirm the position that we have an essential self or soul and that it is this self or soul, not our bodies, that determines who we are. The next four selections call this view into question and suggest reasons for considering our bodies when determining who we are.

The final section of Chapter 1 contains seven selections that address the question of *what else* determines who we are. The writers in this section offer diverse answers that represent important and interesting responses to the question. Two of the first five selections suggest that individual self-overcoming and freedom are the most important factors in deciding who we are, while three of them affirm the opposing position that the self is psychologically and/or socially determined. The final two selections discuss the role that sex and race play in determining who we are. As in Chapter 1, the selections in the other chapters are arranged in an order that will facilitate comparisons and contrasts with preceding or succeeding selections.

Features

Since many of the authors and selections found in this anthology are not included in the traditional canon, it is possible that some of them will not be familiar to you. Indeed, one of the main difficulties standing in the way of curriculum diversification is that philosophy graduate schools generally have not provided students with a multicultural education.

To help remedy this deficiency and to situate the readings for students using the text, I have included *brief biographical or historical sketches* before each selection. Also, since many of the selections contain terminology that is not part of the standard Western philosophical vocabulary, I have included an extensive *glossary* of non-Western and technical terms at the back of the text.

Moreover, to help students better understand what they are reading, I have included *introductory summaries for each selection*, as well as two sets of questions: *Questions for Reading* and *Questions for Thought*. The first set of questions, which are placed immediately before each selection, are intended to help students focus on the more important parts of what they are reading; the second set, which follows immediately after each selection, are meant to help students relate the reading to their own life experiences. These questions are also useful in helping students formulate paper topics relevant to the reading.

In addition to chapter introductions, I have provided a *general introduction to the text*. This introduction consists of several short sections that will help orient students to the study of philosophy. One section gives students an account of my first experiences in a philosophy class. Another section attempts to define philosophy, and a third section discusses the intercultural nature of philosophy. The last section provides information on how students can get the most out of this text.

Finally, since most philosophy classes require papers, I have written an *appendix on how to write philosophically* that is available to students online. My goal in this appendix is to offer students useful information on the various aspects of philosophical writing, from choosing a topic and literary form to researching, editing, and proofreading their paper.

New to the Third Edition

The third edition contains new selections from Michel Foucault, Sigmund Freud, George Herbert Mead, Elizabeth Anderson, Charles Mills, Jared Diamond, and Antony Flew. There are also new translations of the two selections from the Upanishads, the African creation myth, and the selections by Martin Buber and Albert Schweitzer. I have also reedited some of the older selections to make them more accessible to students. In addition, the glossary has been expanded, and I have added information on doing research on the Internet to the appendix on writing philosophically. This appendix has been moved online to make room for more selections in the text.

Acknowledgments

The writing, editing, and publishing of this text would not have been possible without the help, inspiration, and encouragement of many people. At Merced College, I would like to thank Susan Walsh, library director, and Dee Near and Ed Brush, research librarians, for their help in tracking down texts and biographical information. I also owe a very special debt of gratitude to Cheryl Botts, who enthusiastically embraced the text in all its dimensions and analyzed all aspects willingly.

I am indebted to the following reviewers for their insightful comments and recommendations, many of which were incorporated into the first edition of the text: Charles Brown, Emporia State University; Jeffrey R. DiLeo, Indiana University; James Doyle, University of Missouri—St. Louis; Michael Goodman, Humboldt State University; Richard Gull, University of Michigan, Flint; Joyce Henricks, Central Michigan University; Hugh Hunt, Kennesaw State College; Louisa Moon, MiraCosta College; Tom Morrow, Richland Community College; Lani Roberts, Oregon State University; Katherine Shamey, Santa Monica College; Paul Shepard, El Camino College; and Robert Sweet, Clark State Community College.

In preparing the second edition of the text, I benefited tremendously from the thoughtful analyses of the following reviewers: Mark Alfino, Gonzaga University; Jill Dieterle, Eastern Michigan University; Louisa Moon, MiraCosta College; Peter Hutcheson, Southwest Texas State University; Ted Toadvine, Emporia State University; and Lawrence Ulrich, University of Dayton.

The following reviewers contributed many useful suggestions for this edition: John M. Levasseur, Towson University; Donna Bowman, Honors College, University of Central Arkansas; Neal Vives, MiraCosta College; Todd Lekan, Muskingum College; Richard Bilsker, College of Southern Maryland; Maxine Morphis, North Central College, Lewis University; and Corrinne Bedecarre, Normandale Community College.

While I was not able to incorporate all of their suggestions, I am grateful to each of these reviewers for helping me improve upon the text.

Introduction

Beginning in Philosophy

How does one begin an introductory book in philosophy? Perhaps an appropriate way to begin is by telling you a little about my first experiences in a philosophy class. On the first day of class, I remember the professor telling us that philosophy begins in wonder. Although initially I was not too sure what he meant, after being in the class for a week I decided that the statement was a perfect description of philosophy. At that point, not only did I wonder what was going on, but I also wondered why I had signed up for the class in the first place! In high school, I had studied math, biology, and English, and thus I pretty much knew what to expect in those classes. But philosophy was entirely new— new questions, new terminology, a new way of thinking. So, as with anything new, it took me a while to orient myself.

One of the problems was that even defining philosophy seemed difficult. The professor told us that the word *philosophy* was derived from two Greek words, *philein* and *sophia,* which translate as "love" and "wisdom," respectively. He also told us that the ancient Greek philosopher Pythagoras first used the term. When asked whether he was a wise man, Pythagoras reportedly replied that he was a "lover of wisdom." Being a typical nineteen-year-old, I had no problem with the idea of being a lover, but I was not so certain about the wisdom part. I knew that I loved my mother, my girlfriend, and even my car, but I was not sure that wisdom was something one could love.

Another problem was that the philosophers we were reading had a major difficulty: They did not seem to be able to agree on anything. And, given the large and obscure words that they often used, I could easily understand why. How can you agree with someone if you are not sure exactly what he or she is saying? So there I was in my first philosophy class—confused, confused, and *more* confused.

Given this initial reaction, you may wonder why I persisted. You may be even more bewildered by the fact that I decided to devote my life to teaching this perplexing stuff to others. Why exactly does someone become a philosopher, a lover of wisdom? Perhaps the best way to respond to this question is by recalling a response that Joseph Campbell gave to Bill Moyers in an episode of that wonderful PBS series *The Power of Myth*. When

Moyers asked Campbell why he had devoted his life to the study of mythology, Campbell replied that he did not believe in studying anything just because people said that it was important and ought to be studied. On the contrary, Campbell said that one should study mythology or anything else only if it "catches you." Well, in that introductory philosophy class many years ago, I was caught. For although philosophy was definitely confusing, I noticed that it dealt with those crucial questions of human existence that most intrigued me:

Who am I?
What can I know?
What is truth?
What is real?
How should I act?
What is justice?
Am I truly free?
Does God exist?
What happens to me when I die?

In this book, which will introduce many of you to the study of philosophy, I have gathered together a varied assortment of philosophical writings that deal with many of these important questions of human existence. Although you may not (indeed cannot) agree with all of the authors' viewpoints, I believe that you will find each of these selections to be thought-provoking and personally significant. Of course, some of the selections will no doubt prove to be challenging reading, and you may initially find yourself just as confused as I was when I first began studying philosophy. But as you read the selections carefully and discuss them in class, I believe that this initial confusion will dissipate. For some of you, the confusion may suddenly disappear. For others, the process will be more like an early morning fog that is gradually burned away by the sun. Once your initial confusion dissipates, you may find yourself caught by the study of philosophy—as I was several years ago and as I still am today.

Toward a Definition of Philosophy

In the preceding section, I mentioned that one of my first impressions of philosophy was that philosophers seemed to disagree about everything. What may surprise you is that philosophers cannot even agree on an exact definition of *philosophy*. While we can trace the origin of the term to the Greek words that translate as the "love of wisdom," this definition has been interpreted in many different ways. Some philosophers believe that wisdom is best loved or attained through the use of reason; others tell us that reason is useless. Some philosophers see philosophy as being akin to religion, morality, or even art; others see it as being more akin to science. Some philosophers believe that philosophy is (and ought to be) purely speculative—that is, divorced from everyday or practical concerns; others tell us that philosophy is the most practical of studies.

Fortunately, you do not need to have a precise definition of philosophy to begin studying it. However, since this book will introduce many of you to the study of philosophy, I believe that I owe you at least an attempt at a definition. Given the controversial nature of the subject, my definition is certainly not the only way of defining *philosophy*, nor does it necessarily cover all the ways in which philosophy has been practiced.

In my own classes, after telling students about the honorific definition of philosophy derived from the ancient Greeks (*philein* + *sophia*), I offer the four following statements in an attempt to arrive at a definition:

1. Philosophy is a distinctive way of thinking.
2. Philosophy is a kind of conversation.
3. Philosophy, if taken seriously, is an agent of change.
4. Philosophy, as an agent of change, can help us traverse the socially determined boundaries that encircle us.

Of course, each of these statements requires further discussion and thought. What kind of thinking is philosophy, and how does it differ from other types of thinking? What do I mean by saying that philosophy is a "kind of conversation"? In what ways does philosophy serve as an agent of change? Finally, what kinds of boundaries limit us, and how can philosophy help us traverse them?

Let us begin with the first statement. We can distinguish types of thinking in at least two ways. We can claim that the content of one kind of thinking differs from the content of another, or we can claim that the actual process of thinking differs in the one case from other cases. The following concrete examples should make this distinction clearer. Much of our thinking is devoted to resolving practical life problems, such as what we are going to have for lunch. In this kind of thinking, we look at several factors, weigh them, and come to a decision. If the problem is what to have for lunch, we might consider how hungry we are, how much time we have, how much money we have, and the locations of potential sources of food. At other times, however, we may be called on to solve some rather abstract algebraic problem (for many of us, this occurs only when we are enrolled in an algebra class). It should be obvious that the content of our thinking in this case differs greatly from the content in first case (we are thinking about algebraic equations and not food). But it should also be clear that the kind of thinking required to do an abstract algebraic equation differs from the kind of thinking required to solve simple, practical problems of everyday life. One way of stating this difference is to say that solving algebra problems requires thinking at a higher level of abstraction than does solving simple, practical problems.

In claiming that philosophy is a distinctive kind of thinking, I am saying that philosophical thinking often differs from other kinds of thinking in both *content* and *process*. As you read the articles in this text, you will no doubt see that philosophical thinking deals with things that many types of thinking never touch. Unlike most other disciplines, philosophy deals with those large but extremely significant problems of human life—problems such as the nature of being human and the nature of ultimate reality.

However, this difference in content is not the only difference between philosophical thinking and other ways of thinking. The way in which philosophers approach these problems seems to differ from other ways of dealing with problems. The German philosopher Martin Heidegger says that the difference is that philosophers concern themselves with *meditative* thinking (or at least they ought to), whereas other types of problems require the use of *calculative* thinking. The difference between these is that calculative thinking is devoted to computing possibilities—to dealing with questions that begin with the word *how*—while meditative thinking is devoted to contemplating meaning—to dealing with questions that begin with the word *why*. Although not all philosophers would accept Heidegger's distinction between meditative thinking and calculative thinking, or agree with him that the task of philosophy is to think meditatively, most would agree that philosophical thinking differs from other types of thinking in process as well as content.

The second statement—namely, that philosophy is a kind of conversation—gives us another way of attempting to define philosophy. By saying that philosophy is a kind of conversation, I mean that philosophy provides us with a language that allows us to converse with others about many of the really important topics in our lives. In one sense, this is just another way of distinguishing the content of philosophical thinking from the content of most other types of thinking. However, by identifying philosophy as a kind of conversation, the emphasis is placed on communicating with others. Whereas you could think philosophically while alone in your room, a genuine conversation requires more than one participant. What philosophy provides is a vocabulary and various strategies of meaningful dialogue that will allow you to communicate with others on levels that may not now be possible. The study of philosophy should not only provide you with a new set of terms, but it should also help you clarify your ideas and express them in a more coherent fashion.

Turning to the third statement—that philosophy, if taken seriously, is an agent of change—what I mean to suggest is that the study of philosophy ought to make a difference in your life. Some of you may recall the remark that the musician Sting made about music at the Live Aid concert several years ago: "The purpose of music is not merely to entertain; the purpose of music is to change the world" (rough paraphrase). Of course, if the people who heard this remark had been familiar with the history of philosophy, they would have recognized that it was very similar to a statement that Karl Marx made about philosophy in the nineteenth century. As Marx said, "The philosophers have only *interpreted* the world differently; the point is, however, to *change* it." What Sting is saying about music and what Marx is saying about philosophy is that music and philosophy should not be mere pastimes; they should help change the world, it is hoped for the better.

Of course, at least in the case of philosophy, some of you may be doubtful about the accuracy of this claim. This would be especially true if you were familiar with some of the typical stereotypes about philosophers and philosophical thinking. One of the enduring stereotypes of philosophers, which can be traced back at least to the ancient Greek comedian Aristophanes, is that philosophers have their heads in the clouds and thus get nothing done. A recent example of this stereotype used for comic purposes was the *Monty Python* skit depicting Greek and German philosophers playing against one another in a soccer game. In this skit, all of the philosophers on both teams stand around rubbing their chins and contemplating who knows what, while the soccer ball rests in the middle of the field. Finally, one of the Greek philosophers (I believe it was Socrates) comes to the conclusion that he should kick the ball. After reaching this decision, he scores easily, while the German philosophers continue to rub their chins.

While this stereotype may be humorous, it does not accurately reflect the true nature of philosophy. Philosophers have almost always been interested in helping to initiate social or individual change. In the West, philosophers often defend themselves against this stereotype by pointing to the fact that Aristotle was the tutor of Alexander the Great or to the fact that modern philosophers such as Simone de Beauvoir, Bertrand Russell, Jean-Paul

Sartre, and John Dewey (among others) worked actively for social change. Outside the Western tradition, we have the equally important examples of the Chinese philosophers, such as Confucius and Mencius, who attempted to implement their political theories by becoming active in court life. Even the Buddha, who was more interested in personal or individual change than in social change, spent a large portion of his life traveling throughout India, delivering his message of self-transformation.

Of course, when I say that philosophy is an agent of change, I am not claiming that the study of philosophy will radically transform the course of history or even that it will necessarily effect wide-ranging change in the course of your own life. What I am claiming is that, if you take the study of philosophy seriously, if you carefully read and think about the selections in this text, then the *you* that emerges from this class should differ in a significant way from the *you* that entered it.

This last claim leads directly to the fourth and final statement that I make when attempting to define philosophy, the statement that philosophy can help us traverse the socially determined boundaries that encircle us. While some philosophers argue that each individual has a unique identity that is not influenced by external factors, today there seems to be little doubt that the person you currently are has developed within the confines of specific socially determined boundaries. These include cultural and religious boundaries, boundaries of language, boundaries of class, boundaries of race, and boundaries of sex and gender. Since the identities of many of the people you will encounter have developed within socially determined boundaries that differ from your own, effective communication requires that you be able to traverse your own boundaries—that is, that you not allow your boundaries to become barriers to fruitful interaction with others. Although in some cases philosophy has served to dogmatically reinforce barriers to effective communication, in its highest expression the practice of philosophy helps us overcome such barriers. One reason for this is that the domain of philosophy is not limited to a specific body of knowledge, as is the case with most of the other subjects you will study. Rather, as Socrates clearly says in Plato's *Republic,* the philosopher is a person who enthusiastically seeks knowledge of every kind, the person who loves wisdom in any shape or form. It should be obvious that to attain this diversity of knowledge and wisdom, the philosopher must be able to traverse these socially determined boundaries, not allowing them to become barriers to learning from others.

Another reason that philosophy can help us traverse the socially determined boundaries that encircle us is that an essential component of philosophical thinking, in most of its forms, is the willingness to examine and question even our most cherished beliefs. As you read the selections in this text, you will no doubt discover that many of the things you currently believe are being challenged. One common response when this happens is to become defensive, to defend dogmatically the beliefs that are being questioned, and to emotionally (or physically) attack the person or text that is challenging your beliefs. However, the study of philosophy can supply you with the tools necessary to critically discuss and analyze your beliefs, as well as the beliefs of others, on a more rational, more fruitful level. It can also help you develop the intellectual courage that will allow you to reject even your most cherished beliefs if they no longer prove tenable. In short, philosophy in its highest expression can help ensure that the socially determined boundaries that encircle you remain fluid and that they do not become impenetrable barriers to intellectual and emotional growth.

The Intercultural Nature of Philosophy

As should be obvious from the preceding discussion, philosophy is not an exclusively Western or European phenomenon. While it is true that our word *philosophy* is derived from the ancient Greeks and that philosophy classes in the West have often excluded non-Western voices, the practice of philosophy, as the term is defined here, is a global phenomenon. Centuries before the ancient Greeks, people in India, China, Egypt, and elsewhere were already pondering many of the important questions that constitute the study of philosophy. Today, although professional philosophers may not be found in every country, philosophical thinking can be.

If you reflect on the nature of philosophy, this should not be surprising. As I have already suggested, philosophy deals with those large issues of existence with which humans have been faced since the dawn of thinking. Indeed, anthropological evidence suggests that the Neanderthals, who lived on the earth from approximately 125,000 to 30,000 B.C.E., developed burial rituals that involved the use of animal bones, bear skulls, and stone tools. While this does not prove that the Neanderthals were capable of abstract philosophical inquiry, it does indicate that they had an awareness of death and that they were attempting to come to terms with it. In other words, it suggests that the Neanderthals were on the verge of the most rudimentary form of philosophical thinking.

That philosophy is indeed an intercultural phenomenon can be illustrated on a personal level if you think about one of those times you were forced to deal with some large issue of human existence. For example, like the Neanderthals, you may have had to deal with the death of someone close to you. How did you deal with this occurrence? It is likely that part of your reaction was purely emotional, but it is also likely that coming to terms with this occurrence required philosophical thinking on some level. Perhaps you were comforted by thinking that death was only a doorway to a continued existence on another level of being or that death was a necessary step toward reincarnation in this world. Perhaps you believed simply that death was the cessation of life but that the cessation of life was the cessation of suffering and pain. Perhaps in facing the death of someone close to you, you were led to ask why that death was necessary or to question the meaning of your own life. It should be obvious from the definition given here that each of these ways of coming to terms with the death of someone close to you (and countless other ways as well) involves philosophical thinking to some degree.

It should also be obvious that people in other times and places face many of the same problems of human existence that you do. Like you, they too must come to terms with the death of people close to them, and they too must do so on both an emotional and a philosophical level. Like you, they are confronted by questions of human existence and by a natural world that sometimes thwarts their goals and expectations. Like you, they must learn to live with other people and to determine their relationship to the governmental and religious structures within which they are born. It is this *commonality*, this universal need to deal with the large problems of human existence, that accounts for the intercultural nature of philosophy.

As you read the selections in this text, selections that range in time from approximately 900 B.C.E. to the twentieth century and in geographical location from Asia to Africa to the Americas, the intercultural nature of philosophy will become increasingly apparent. At times, you may be struck by the differences between another's response to one of the large problems of human existence and your own. But at other times, you will be amazed at the similarities between your own views and those of someone living in the distant past or in a distant location. Whether or not you agree with the articles you are reading, your encounter with each of them can leave you a more informed, thoughtful person—a person who is better able to traverse the socially determined boundaries that encircle you.

How to Get the Most Out of This Text

I have tried to write this text with you, the student, in mind. Two of my main criteria for selecting writings were readability and your probable level of response. That is, I wanted to find writings that raised issues of importance to you and that were not extremely difficult to read. As I suggested when describing my own first experiences in a philosophy class, philosophical writings often use unfamiliar terminology (an unflattering word for this is *jargon*), but I have tried to find writings that minimize the use of such terminology. However, since several of the selections in this book are taken from non-Western sources, it is inevitable that some of the terms will be "foreign" to you. For this reason, I have included a glossary at the back of the book containing definitions of the important non-Western and technical terms found in the selections.

I have also provided general introductions for each chapter, as well as introductions for each selection. The chapter introductions orient you to the topic covered by the chapter and identify the principal questions discussed in the chapter. The selection introductions give you biographical information about the authors as well as historical information for some of the more ancient writings. These introductions also contain a summary of the selection and two sets of questions related to it. As you will see, the first set of questions deals with the content of the reading, while the second set is intended to help you relate the reading to your own experience. Finally, I have written an appendix on writing philosophically, which is available to you online, that should help you with the paper or papers that you may be assigned. This appendix is arranged sequentially, and it is intended to provide you with tips on all of the essential components of successful philosophical writing.

Chapter 1

Self, Mind, and Body

Introductory Remarks

JUST BE YOURSELF. How many times have you heard that? What does it mean? Or you may have heard someone say, "I'm not myself today." This can be a mild complaint or even an apology. But what is the speaker really saying?

One day you are going to a job interview, and a friend tells you to be yourself. Translated, it could mean to act naturally, not showing off but not being too modest, either. Your mind is on the interview, so you just blow off the remark.

My sister, who is usually a whiz at basketball, cannot hit even the rim this morning. When I ask what is wrong, she says, "I'm just not myself today." My translation: She is feeling ill, or she is worried about her philosophy paper that is due next week. I do not give her statement much more thought—unless I am choosing up sides for a game.

At some point in your life, as happened in mine, you may pause to reflect on those statements about the self. How can you *not* be yourself? But then, why would anyone think it necessary to tell you to be yourself? If you are not feeling *yourself* today, are you feeling as if you are someone else? Just who is feeling this, anyway?

By asking these questions, you are entering the fascinating (and sometimes frustrating) land of philosophical reflection. You are, in fact, beginning an especially intriguing path in the land of philosophical reflection—a path known as the search for self-identity.

At this point, I know some of you are saying, "Is this guy for real? The land of philosophical reflection? The path of the search for self-identity? I've never been there, and I have absolutely no desire to go. Besides, my favorite show is on TV, and I have to buy groceries before going to work. So who has time for the land of philosophical reflection or the path of the search for self-identity?"

What can I say to all that? I can tell you playfully, as I sometimes tell my own students, that you ought to think about these things because someday you might be kidnapped by a mad philosopher who will tie you to a chair and refuse to let you go until you satisfactorily answer questions about the true nature of your identity. More seriously, I can tell you that, as a human being with the capacity for thought, you are destined to enter the land of philosophical reflection and to travel down the path of the search for self-identity, whether you like it or not.

1

In fact, if you think about it, you will probably realize that you have been on this path before. Psychologists tell us that as very young infants we discover that our hands and the rest of our bodies are separate from the other physical objects around us and that this seemingly insignificant discovery initiates the psychological process through which we develop the sense of self that we have today. The search for self-identity occurs when, for whatever reason, we reflect on this process—that is, when we question our self-concept and ask, "Who am I?" Interestingly, even cartoon characters (consider Popeye's oft-repeated line, "I yam what I yam") and gods (consider Yahweh's response to Moses' question about his name, "I AM; that is who I am") have not been able to avoid answering the question of self-identity.

It should not be surprising, then, to find that philosophers have also raised and attempted to answer this question. Indeed, the history of philosophy is filled with stories of philosophical "heroes" who have journeyed down the path of the search for self-identity. In Western philosophy, we have the wonderful example of Socrates, who, being guided by the oracular saying "know thyself," devoted much of his life to philosophical reflection. In fact, when given the choice of renouncing his philosophical principles or dying, Socrates chose death. In Eastern philosophy, we have the equally wonderful example of Siddhartha, a prince whose parents surrounded him with every luxury and pleasure in order to shield him from the troubles of the world. Yet, escaping one day from the palace grounds, Siddhartha saw in the public marketplace people who were sick, debilitated, and dying. At once he renounced his former life and went on a disciplined quest for self-knowledge that, after seven years, led him to experience **Nirvana** (blessedness) while seated under a tree. From that moment on, he was known as the Buddha (the Enlightened One). As this last example shows, the journey down the path of the search for self-identity is not a uniquely Western path. Since people everywhere undergo the psychological process of developing a self-image, it is not surprising that people in many different times and places have wrestled with issues of self-identity.

As you continue your own journey down the path of the search for self-identity, you will find, as have others before you, that the general question "Who am I?" can quickly divide into many others. Some of these questions might be the following:

Do I have an enduring self or soul?
If so, what is the nature of this enduring self or soul?
Is there such a thing as a universal or basic human nature?
Does the nature of being human change with time and place?
How important is my body in determining my identity?
How important is my sex or gender in determining my identity?
How important is my race or ethnicity in determining my identity?
To what extent is my identity determined by external factors?
To what extent is my identity self-created?

Overview of Selections

In this chapter, I have gathered eighteen writings, from various times and cultures, that deal with some of these questions concerning self-identity. The selections in the first part represent diverse responses to the important question of whether we have an enduring self or soul. Of these, the first selection (as well as the first two selections in the second part) strongly affirms the existence of an immortal self or soul that can exist independently from the body. In contrast, the writers of the next four selections, ranging in time and space from India in the fifth century B.C.E. to twentieth-century America, reject the existence of an immortal self or soul (although Locke, the first of the four, is somewhat ambivalent in his rejection). While their views differ in some respects, they all suggest that our identities are not fixed but are constantly changing.

Whereas the selections in the first section of this chapter deal principally with the question of whether there is an enduring self or soul, those in the second section focus on the nature of the human body and its significance in determining who we are. The authors of the first two selections in this section strongly affirm the existence of an immortal self or soul, and they suggest that this self or soul makes us who we are. While admitting that we have bodies and that our bodies interact in some way with our souls, neither Plato nor Descartes views the body as being a necessary component of our self-identity. In contrast, the authors of the next three selections in the second section claim that our bodies do play a crucial role in determining who we are. Focusing initially on the views of Plato, Elizabeth Spelman looks at the way the body has been devalued in Western culture and argues that this devaluation of the body has had negative psychological and social consequences, especially for women. Next, Derek Parfit uses certain findings of modern science to argue against what he calls the "Ego Theory": the theory that there is something about us that exists independently of the psychological continuity found in our brains and bodies. In the selection following Parfit, Michel Foucault, in discussing the history of the methods that have been used to discipline and subjugate the body, argues that the soul arose as one of the elements in this process of discipline and subjugation. Thus, for Foucault, rather than being the locus of our true identity, the soul is a product and tool of our subjugation. Last, in the final selection of the second part, Daniel Dennett uses the vehicle of science fiction to call into question some of the traditional assumptions about how our bodies are related to our minds or brains. While Dennett's story seems to undermine belief in the concept of an enduring self or soul, it also downplays the significance of the body (or at least of a particular body) in determining who we are.

Finally, the selections in the third part of this chapter examine some of the other questions concerning the nature of our identity. In the first selection, Friedrich Nietzsche introduces the concept of the superman as the goal of human existence and begins describing the journey of self-overcoming that each of us must undertake if we are to reach this goal. In the second selection, Sigmund Freud describes the complex nature of what he calls our "mental apparatus," while insisting that much of whom we are remains unconscious. Like Nietzsche, he also describes the journey by means of which we become who we are, but unlike Nietzsche, Freud focuses specifically on our childhood journey through the diverse stages of psychosexual development.

In the next two selections, the authors offer views that contrast strongly with those of both Nietzsche and Freud. First, George Herbert Mead argues that the self is essentially a social construct, a construct that is made possible by our conversation with other people. Following Mead's lead, B. F. Skinner also argues that the self is socially determined, but, unlike Mead, Skinner emphasizes the role that stimulus-response conditioning has in determining our identities.

In contrast to both Mead and Skinner, whose views seem to rule out human freedom and responsibility, Jean-Paul Sartre, in the fifth selection, argues that human existence is characterized by radical freedom. Defending the philosophy of **existentialism,** Sartre claims that we are ultimately responsible for who we are.

The last two selections in the chapter raise questions about the importance of sex and race in determining who we are. While agreeing with much of Sartre's analysis of human existence, Simone de Beauvoir argues that traditional Western philosophy, psychology, and religion have been used to deny women the same freedom to create themselves as has been afforded to men. Finally, Naomi Zack questions the concept of race, and asks—from a personal as well as a cultural perspective—what it means to be of mixed race.

Taken together, these selections raise many of the questions that have been associated with the philosophical problem of self-identity. They also show you how a small number of thoughtful people attempted to answer them. But, as I have already suggested in the introduction to the text, the goal of studying philosophy is not merely to learn what others have said on some issue of philosophical importance. Rather, one of the principal goals of studying philosophy is to develop and clarify your own beliefs about the issue being discussed. As you read these various writings, ask yourself the following questions:

What is the author telling me about who I am?
Do the author's views agree with what I already believe about my own identity?
If not, does the author give me any good reasons for changing my beliefs?

In raising such questions as you read the selections, you will discover that the path of the search for self-identity may be difficult, but it is nonetheless personally fulfilling. You may also discover, as I have, that reflecting on the nature of your identity can be more entertaining than a television show—so entertaining, in fact, that it can serve as a needed respite from those drab chores of daily existence that routinely fill our lives.

Contemporary Applications

While some of you may now be convinced of the usefulness and importance of traveling down the path of the search for self-identity (and thus of reading the selections in this chapter), others may remain skeptical. Why, after all, should you spend your precious time reading and discussing writings that were written long ago or that seem so remote from the pressing concerns of everyday life?

Perhaps the best answer to this question is that these writings and issues may not be as remote as they first seem. Take, for example, the question of whether we have an enduring self or soul. One's first response to this question could easily be "Who cares?" However, on further reflection you may realize that how you answer this question has a tremendous impact on some of your basic beliefs. Many of you, for instance, believe that after the death of your body, you (your soul?) will survive in some afterlife in which you will be either rewarded or punished for your actions on earth. You may also believe that loved ones who have died already exist in this afterlife. (While I was watching a baseball game recently, I heard one of the announcers discussing the fact that the batter's father had died earlier in the season. When the batter delivered the game-winning hit, the announcer said, "His father must really be smiling now.") But if there is no enduring self or soul, as many writers in this chapter argue, then these beliefs are obviously mistaken. Rather, as the ancient Roman philosopher Lucretius puts it, if you have no soul, "you have nothing to fear from death."

Another issue to which the question of whether we have an enduring self or soul may be relevant is the issue of abortion. While people opposing abortion have diverse reasons for doing so, one frequently cited reason is that a fetus gets its soul at the moment of conception and thus becomes fully human at that moment. Being fully human, the fetus would be entitled to the same rights as any other human, including the right to life. But if there are no souls, if humans are a bundle of perceptions or a series of processes (as some philosophers in this chapter argue), then clearly this reason for opposing abortion carries no weight.

Moreover, think of how your views on self-identity might impact the way you view and treat other people. Indeed, according to one of the writers in this chapter, a person is merely a bundle of impressions; according to another writer, each person is a manifestation of the divine presence. Can you think of two views on the nature and status of human beings that are more diametrically opposed to each other than these two? When Joseph Campbell first visited India, he was struck by the hospitality that he was shown— a hospitality that he had never experienced in the West. Campbell explains this difference in treatment by saying that in India, unlike the West, he was viewed as a visiting deity— that is, as a manifestation of the divine presence. Would he have been treated differently if he were viewed merely as a bundle of impressions? And what impact do your own views on self-identity have on the way you treat others?

Two of the things that many of us were taught rather early in life are that we live in the "land of the free and home of the brave" and that criminals are responsible for their actions. Indeed, we believe that we are justified in morally judging and legally punishing criminals precisely because they could have chosen to behave other than they did. Some of us also believe that the homeless and other economically disadvantaged people are somehow responsible for their plight and thus there is no social obligation to help them. However, several of the writers in this chapter suggest that humans are not free and so are not responsible for their actions. This suggests, at least at first glance, that talk about the "land of the free" is empty rhetoric, that our moral and legal judgments are misguided, and that the causes (and cures) of homelessness and economic disadvantage lie in the social or medical realm.

Finally, think about some of the recent discussions concerning human cloning. Although much of this discussion centers on moral issues rather than on issues of self-identity, the prospect of human cloning does raise some of the issues that are discussed in this chapter. For example, if you were cloned, which of the resulting persons would be the real you? Must this question have an answer? Does the prospect of being cloned appeal to you, or do you find this prospect unsettling for some reason? While many of the articles in this chapter have some relevance to these questions, two of them discuss the philosophical import of a person being duplicated and thus have a direct bearing on the issue of cloning.

Do We Have an Essential Self or Soul?

1   Dialogue with Death

FROM THE UPANISHADS

The **Upanishads** make up the fourth section of each of the **Vedas,** the most sacred writings of the Hindu religion. According to scholars, the origins of Hinduism can be traced to the period between 1750 and 1200 B.C.E., when Aryans migrated into the Indus valley. While there is some dispute as to the dates of the composition of the Vedas, it is generally agreed that there was a time span of several hundred years between the writing of the most ancient part of the Vedas, the hymns, or **mantras,** and the writing of the Upanishads. The latter, which consist of a collection of philosophical reflections from the classical period of Hinduism, were perhaps begun as early as 900 B.C.E. Like the following selection from the *Katha Upanishad,* many of these philosophical reflections were written in dialogue form.

Whereas earlier Hindu writings had assumed the existence of many gods, the Upanishads generally affirm the monistic view that there is one supreme reality: **Brahman.** Also, whereas earlier writings had emphasized religious ritual and sacrifice as the principal way of relating to the gods, the Upanishads suggest that a type of philosophical reflection or meditation (**Yoga**) is the most appropriate spiritual or religious path. Indeed, one of the main themes of the Upanishads is that through the practice of Yoga, you will eventually discover your enduring, eternal self, your **Atman,** and realize that your Atman is really identical to Brahman. In other words, this selection suggests that each of us has an eternal self that is one with the divine nature and that it is only illusion or false knowledge (**maya**) that prevents us from recognizing the truth of this sameness or identity. Of course, one of the assumptions of this writing, as of Hindu writings in general, is that it will take you many lifetimes to move beyond false knowledge and illusion, and thus that your Atman will be reincarnated many times into diverse physical forms. This writing promises, however, that once you truly discover your Atman and recognize its sameness with Brahman, you will escape this cycle of birth, life, death, and rebirth, thereby becoming "immortal and pure."

Questions for Reading

1. Who are the characters in this dialogue? How do they meet one another?
2. What are the three boons that Nachiketas chooses? Why is Death reluctant to fulfill the third boon?
3. What are the two paths described by Death, and where does each of them lead?
4. How is the term *Atman* used in this selection? What are some of the metaphors that are used to describe it?
5. What does the writer mean by *Brahman*? What is the relation of one's Atman to Brahman?
6. How, according to Death, can one discover Brahman? What happens when one discovers Brahman?

VAGASRAVASA, WHO HAD A SON NAMED NACHIKETAS, was desirous of heavenly rewards. In order to obtain them, he promised to sacrifice everything that he possessed. While his father was in the midst of this sacrifice, faith entered into the heart of Nachiketas, who was still a boy. Nachiketas thought to himself, "Surely the worlds are unblessed to which a man goes by sacrificing cows that have drunk water, eaten hay, given their milk, and are barren." Then, knowing that he himself was also one of the sacrifices that his father had promised to give, Nachiketas asked his father, "Dear father, to whom will you give me?" Receiving no reply, he asked this a second and a third time. Finally, his father replied angrily, "I will give you to **Yama** (Death)."

Nachiketas then said, "I go as the first, at the head of many who still have to die; I go in the midst of many who are now dying. . . . Look back to how it was with those who came before, look forward to how it will be with those who come after. A mortal ripens like corn, like corn he springs up again."

At this point, Nachiketas entered into the abode of Yama, but there was no one to receive him. . . . He dwelled there for three nights, receiving no hospitality from Yama. When Yama returned to his house, he said, "Oh venerable guest, you have dwelled in my house three nights without eating; therefore choose now three boons."

Nachiketas said, "Death, as the first of the three boons I choose that my father be pacified, kind, and free from anger towards me, that he may know and greet me, when I have been dismissed by you."

Yama replied, "Through my favor your father will know you; he will be again towards you as he was before. He will sleep peacefully through the night, and be free from anger, after having seen you freed from the mouth of death."

Nachiketas then said, "In the heaven-world there is no fear; you are not there, Death, and no one is afraid on account of old age. Leaving behind both hunger and thirst, and out of the reach of sorrow, all rejoice in the world of heaven. Those who live in the heaven-world reach immortality. You know, Death, the sacred fire that leads us to heaven. Teach it to me—this I ask as my second boon."

Yama said, "I will teach it to you; learn it from me. And when you understand that sacred fire which leads to heaven, know that it is the attainment of the endless worlds, and their firm support, and that it is hidden in the sacred place of the heart. . . . He who lights this sacred fire three times, who has been united with the three (father, mother, and teacher), and who has performed the three duties (study, sacrifice, and almsgiving), overcomes birth and death. When he has learned and understood this fire, which knows (or makes us know) all that is born of **Brahman,** the venerable and divine, then he obtains everlasting peace. . . . This is the fire which leads to heaven, and which you have chosen as your second boon. . . . Now, Nachiketas, choose your third boon."

Nachiketas replied, "There is that doubt when a man is dead. Some say that he is; others say that he is not. I would like you to teach me which opinion is right; this is the third of my boons."

Death said, "On this point even the gods have formerly doubted; it is not easy to understand. This subject is subtle. Choose another boon, Nachiketas, do not press me, and let me off that boon."

Nachiketas said, "On this point even the gods have doubted indeed, and you, Death, have declared that it is not easy to understand. Yet another teacher like you is not to be found—surely there is no other boon like this one."

Death replied, "Choose sons and grandsons who will live a hundred years, herds of cattle, elephants, gold, and horses. Choose the wide abode of the earth, and live as many years as you desire. If you can think of any boon equal to that, choose wealth and long life. Be king, Nachiketas, on the wide earth. I will make you the enjoyer of all desires. Whatever desires are difficult for mortals to attain, ask for them according to your wish. These fair maidens with their chariots and musical instruments—such indeed are not to be obtained by men. I will give them to you. Be waited on by them, but do not ask me about dying."

Nachiketas answered, "These things last until tomorrow, Death, for they wear out this vigor of all the senses. Even the whole of life is short. Keep your horses, your dance and song for yourself. No man

This is the editor's revised version of a selection from The Upanishads, Part II, *translated by Max Müller, in* The Sacred Books of the East, *Volume 15, Oxford: The Clarendon Press, 1884.*

can be made happy by wealth. Shall we possess wealth, when we see you? Shall we enjoy life, while you rule? I can only choose the boon that I have chosen.". . .

Death said, "There are two paths that attract a man—the path of goodness and the path of pleasure. It is well with him who clings to goodness; he who chooses pleasure misses his end. These two paths lie before man. The wise man examines them and distinguishes between them, preferring goodness to pleasure. The fool chooses pleasure through greed and avarice. You, Nachiketas, after pondering all the pleasures that are or seem to be delightful, have dismissed them all. You have not taken the path leading to wealth, the path on which many men perish.

"Wide apart and leading to different points are ignorance and what is known as wisdom. I believe that you, Nachiketas, are one who desires wisdom, for even many pleasures did not tempt you. Fools dwelling in darkness, conceited and puffed up with vain knowledge, go round and round, staggering to and fro, like blind men led by the blind. What lies beyond this life never rises before the eyes of the careless child, deluded by the delusion of wealth. 'This is the only world,' he thinks, 'there is no other.' Thus he falls again and again under my sway.

"Many are not able to hear of the **Atman,** the Self; many who do hear of him are unable to comprehend what they hear. Wonderful is a man, when found, who is able to teach him; wonderful is he who comprehends him, when taught by an able teacher. That Self, when taught by an inferior man, is not easily known, even though often thought upon. Unless it is taught by another, there is no way to it, for it is inconceivably smaller than what is small. That doctrine is not to be obtained by argument; but when taught by a true teacher, it is easy to understand. You have obtained it now; you are surely a man of true resolve. May we always have inquirers like you! . . .

"Though you had seen the fulfillment of all desires, the foundation of the world, the endless rewards of good deeds, the shore where there is no fear, that which is magnified by praise, the wide abode—yet being wise you have, with firm resolve, dismissed it all. The wise man who recognizes the god dwelling invisibly within and without, by means of meditation on his Self, leaves joy and sorrow far behind. A mortal rejoices who has heard this and embraced it, who has separated from it all qualities, and has thus reached the subtle Being, because he has obtained what is a cause for rejoicing. Nachiketas, a house is open for your Atman, your god."

Nachiketas replied, "Tell me what you see as neither this nor that, as neither effect nor cause, as neither past nor future."

Yama said, "That word which all the **Vedas** record, which all penances proclaim, which men desire when they live as religious students, is **OM.** That imperishable syllable means Brahman; it means that which is highest. He who knows that syllable, whatever he desires, is his. . . .

"The knowing Self, the Atman, is not born; neither does he die. He sprang from nothing, nothing sprang from him. The Atman is unborn, eternal, everlasting; he does not die when the body dies. If the killer thinks that he kills, if the killed thinks that he is killed, they do not understand; for this one does not kill, nor is that one killed.

"The Atman, which is smaller than small and greater than great, is hidden in the heart of all creatures. A man who is free from desires and from grief sees the majesty of the Self by the grace of the Creator. Though sitting still, he walks far; though lying down, he goes everywhere. Who other than my Self is able to know that god who rejoices and who rejoices not?

"The wise man who knows the Atman as bodiless within bodies, as unchanging among changing things, as great and omnipresent, transcends grief. That Self cannot be reached by studying the Vedas, by understanding, or by much learning. He whom the Self chooses, by him the Self can be reached. To his chosen, the Atman reveals his glory. But he who has not first turned away from wickedness, who is not tranquil and subdued, whose mind is not at rest, can never reach the Atman even through deep knowledge. . . .

"Know the Atman as the lord of a chariot, the body as the chariot itself, the intellect or reason as the charioteer, and the mind as the reins. The senses are like the horses, the objects of the senses like their roads. When the Highest Self is in union with the body, the senses, and the mind, then wise men call him the Enjoyer. He who has no understanding and whose mind is never steady is unable to control his senses, like a poor driver with unmanageable horses. But he who has understanding and whose mind is always steady, has his senses under control, like a good driver with well-trained horses. He who has no understanding, who is unmindful and always impure, never reaches the end of the journey, but is born again and again. But he who has understanding, who is mindful and always pure, reaches indeed that place from whence he is never born again. . . .

"Beyond the senses are their objects; beyond their objects is the mind. Beyond the mind is the intellect or reason; the Great Self is beyond the intellect or reason. Beyond the Great Self is the Undeveloped; beyond the Undeveloped is the **Purusha**. Beyond the Purusha is nothing—this is the goal, the end of the road.

"That Atman is hidden in all beings and does not shine forth, but it is seen by the seers of the subtle, when their vision is keen and clear. A wise man should surrender speech and mind; he should surrender them in the knowing Self. He should surrender the knowing Self in the Undeveloped, and the Undeveloped in the spirit of peace.

"Arise, awake! Having obtained your boons, understand them! The wise say that the path to the Atman is hard, like trying to walk along the sharp edge of a razor. But he who has perceived that which is without sound, without touch, without form, without decay, without taste, without smell, without beginning, without end, beyond the Great, eternal and unchangeable, is freed from the jaws of death.". . . .

Death continued, "Well then, I will tell you the mystery of the eternal Brahman and of what happens to the Self, after reaching death. Some enter the womb in order to have a body, as men or animals; others go into trees or plants, according to their previous work and wisdom.

"The highest being, Brahman, is awake in us while we are asleep, shaping one lovely sight after another. That indeed is the Bright; that alone is called the Immortal. All worlds are contained in it, and no one goes beyond. . . . As the one fire, after it has entered the world, becomes differentiated according to whatever it burns, thus the one Self becomes differentiated, according to whatever it enters. It exists within everything, and also exists without. As the one air, after it has entered the world, becomes differentiated according to whatever it goes into, thus the one Self becomes differentiated,

according to whatever it enters. It exists within everything, and also exists without. . . .

"There is one ruler, Brahman, within all things, who makes the one form manifold. To the wise who perceive him within their Self belongs eternal happiness; it does not belong to others. . . . To the wise who perceive him within their Self belongs eternal peace; it does not belong to others. . . . If a man does not perceive him before he dies, then he has to take body again in the worlds of creation. . . . .

"Beyond the senses is the mind, beyond the mind is the highest created Being, higher than that Being is the Great Self, higher than the Great Self is the highest Undeveloped. Beyond the Undeveloped is the Purusha, the all-pervading and entirely imperceptible. Every creature who knows him is liberated and obtains immortality.

"His form is not to be seen, no one beholds him with the eye. He is envisioned by the heart, by wisdom, by the mind. Those who know him become immortal. When the five senses and the mind stand still, when the intellect does not move, that is called the highest state. This calm stillness of the senses is what is called **Yoga**. . . .

"The Self cannot be reached by speech, by mind, or by the eye. How can it be apprehended except by one who says: 'He is?'. . . When he has been apprehended by the words 'He is,' then his reality reveals itself. When all desires that dwell in his heart cease, then the mortal becomes immortal, and obtains Brahman. When all the ties of the heart are severed here on earth, then the mortal becomes immortal—here ends the sacred teaching.

"There are a hundred and one arteries of the heart; one of them penetrates the crown of the head. Moving upwards by it, a man at death reaches the Immortal; the other arteries serve for departing in different directions.

"The Person not larger than a thumb, the inner Self, is always settled in the heart of men. Let a man withdraw that Self from his body with steadiness, as one withdraws the pith from a reed. Let him know that Self as the Bright, as the Immortal; yes, as the Bright and Immortal."

Having received this knowledge taught by Death and the whole teaching of Yoga, Nachiketas became free from passion and death, and reached Brahman. This will be true of anyone who knows his Atman, his inner Self.

Questions for Thought

1. How does the concept of Atman compare with or differ from your own views concerning your self-identity?
2. On which of the two paths described in text are you currently traveling? Can you think of any reasons for switching paths?
3. Is the notion of Brahman compatible with your own thoughts about God or divinity? Why or why not?
4. Do you think that you have lived an earthly life before this one? If you were reborn into another physical form, what form would you choose?
5. What do you think of the effectiveness of structuring this writing as a dialogue with Death? If you were to write a dialogue on self-identity, what characters would appear in your dialogue?

2   On Personal Identity

JOHN LOCKE

John Locke (1632–1704) was born in Somerset, England. Locke's father was an attorney who fought on the parliamentary side in the rebellion against the British monarchy. Embracing the liberal politics of his father, Locke was also a defender of the parliamentary side in several of the political conflicts that flared up during his lifetime. Because of this, Locke was denounced by the British crown, and he spent several years' exile in Holland.

Locke's education began at Westminster School, where he studied the classics, Arabic, and Hebrew. He began attending Christ's Church, Oxford, in 1652, earning his B.A. degree four years later. After obtaining his master's degree at Oxford, Locke lectured on Latin, Greek, and moral philosophy before receiving the first of his many political appointments in 1665.

Unhappy with the traditional education that he received at Oxford, Locke eagerly sought out and embraced the new learning that was current in Europe at the time. He learned about the new sciences from Robert Boyle, studied medicine and collaborated with the great physician Thomas Sydenham, and spent four years in France, where he befriended the Gassendists, a group of French philosophers who were harsh critics of Descartes.

Among his many political activities, Locke assisted the earl of Shaftesbury in writing the constitution for the colony of Carolina, and he participated in the plot that helped William of Orange ascend to the British throne in 1688. Because of the latter activity, he was able to return to England from his exile in Holland in 1689. Locke spent the remaining years of his life in political favor, serving as a commissioner on the Board of Trade and Plantations and enjoying the friendship of prominent citizens such as Lady Masham, who was reading to him from the Book of Psalms when he died on October 28, 1704.

Although the list of his works is not as extensive as that of many other philosophers, Locke's writings had a profound effect on the intellectual life of his time and of times to come. His lengthy *An Essay Concerning Human Understanding* (1690), from which the following selection is taken, called into question the **rationalism** of Descartes and

Spinoza and laid the foundation for what came to be known as British **empiricism.** His Letter on Toleration (1689) argued for the necessity of the separation of Church and State, greatly influencing the framers of the Constitution of the United States. And, as is well known, Locke's theory of inalienable natural rights (he cites life, liberty, and property as examples) in his *Two Treatises on Government* (1690) provided the philosophical underpinnings for Jefferson's writing of the Declaration of Independence.

Locke's lesser known writings include *Some Considerations of the Consequences of the Lowering of Interest and the Raising of the Value of Money* (1692), *Some Thoughts Concerning Education* (1693), *The Reasonableness of Christianity* (1695), and *A Paraphrase and Notes on the Epistles of St. Paul to the Galatians* (1705).

In the following selection, Locke begins by defining a person or self as a thinking being that can identity itself as itself across time and distance. In other words, personhood or selfhood is determined by the unity of consciousness—that is, by one's consciousness of being the same thinking self at different times and places. Since personal identity consists solely in this unity of consciousness, Locke leaves open the possible relationships between one's personal identity and one's body or soul. (Locke often refers to body as material **substance** and to soul as immaterial substance.) As long as the same unity of consciousness is present in two different substances, whether material or immaterial, then these two different substances will constitute the same person. Moreover, if the same body or soul were informed or inhabited by two different consciousnesses that were totally severed from each other, then that body or soul would constitute two persons.

Noting that his views conflict with the way language is commonly used, Locke draws a distinction between being the same person and being the same man. While having the same body is crucial to being the same man, it is irrelevant to being the same person. Locke explains this distinction by formulating a hypothetical case in which the consciousness of a prince inhabits the body of a cobbler after the cobbler's consciousness has departed from it. Since the body is the same body as it was before, the resulting *man* would be the cobbler (at least to everyone other than himself); however, since the consciousness inhabiting the body is that of the prince rather than the cobbler, the resulting *person* would be the prince.

Near the end of this selection, Locke briefly discusses the implications that his views on personal identity have on laws relating to reward and punishment. Since personal identity is determined by unity of consciousness, one is justified in rewarding or punishing someone only for those actions that he or she can remember doing. If, for example, an accused criminal has no consciousness of the crime for which he or she is accused, then the accused criminal should not be punished for that crime. In Locke's view, if there is no unity of consciousness, then the person who committed the crime would not be the same person as the one being punished for the crime.

Questions for Reading

1. How does Locke define the term *person?*
2. Of what, according to Locke, does personal identity consist?
3. How, according to Locke, does change of substance affect personal identity?
4. What role, if any, does the body play in determining personal identity?
5. What is Locke's example of the severed little finger intended to prove or illustrate? What is his example of Socrates waking and Socrates sleeping intended to prove or illustrate?
6. What conclusions about reward and punishment does Locke draw from his views on personal identity?

WHEREIN PERSONAL IDENTITY CONSISTS

TO FIND WHEREIN PERSONAL IDENTITY CONSISTS, we must consider what the term "person" stands for. I think that a person is a thinking, intelligent being that has reason and reflection, and that can consider itself as itself, i.e., as the same thinking thing, in different times and places. It can do this only by that consciousness which is inseparable from thinking, and which, it seems to me, is essential to it. For it is impossible for any one to perceive, without perceiving that he does perceive. When we see, hear, smell, taste, feel, meditate, or will any thing, we know that we do so. This is always the case with our present sensations and perceptions, and it is because of this that one is to himself that which he calls "self" (it not being considered, at present, whether the same self be continued in the same or diverse substances). For since consciousness always accompanies thinking, and since it is that which makes everyone to be what he calls "self," thereby distinguishing himself from all other thinking things, in this alone consists personal identity, i.e., the sameness of a rational being. As far as this consciousness can be extended backwards to any past action or thought, so far reaches the identity of that person. It is the same self now that it was then; and the past action was done by the same self as this present one that now reflects on it.

CONSCIOUSNESS MAKES PERSONAL IDENTITY

Let us further inquire whether it be the same identical substance. Few would think they had reason to doubt this, if these perceptions, with their consciousness, always remained present in the mind. For in this case the same thinking thing would be always consciously present, and one would no doubt think that it would evidently be the same to itself. But what seems to make the difficulty is the fact that this consciousness is interrupted always by forgetfulness, there being no moment of our lives wherein we have the whole train of all our past actions before our eyes in one view. Indeed, even the best memories lose the sight of one part while they are viewing

another; and sometimes, even during the greatest part of our lives, we do not reflect on our past selves, being intent on our present thoughts. Moreover, in sound sleep, we have no thoughts at all, or at least none with that consciousness that marks our waking thoughts. In all these cases in which our consciousness is interrupted and we lose sight of our past selves, doubts are raised as to whether we are the same thinking thing, i.e., the same substance. But these doubts, however reasonable or unreasonable, concern not personal identity at all. The question is what makes the same person, not whether it is the same identical substance that always thinks in the same person. In this case the latter question does not matter at all. For different substances that have the same consciousness are united into one person, just as different bodies that have the same life are united into one animal, whose identity is preserved, in that change of substance, by the unity of one continued life. Since it is the same consciousness that makes a man be himself to himself, personal identity depends on that only, whether this consciousness be annexed solely to one individual substance, or whether it can be continued in a succession of several substances. For to the extent that any intelligent being can repeat the idea of any past action with the same consciousness it had of it at first, and with the same consciousness it has of any present action, to that extent it is the same personal self. For it is by the consciousness it has of its present thoughts and actions that it is self to itself now, and so it will be the same self, as far as the same consciousness can extend to actions past or to come. Just as wearing different clothes today than he did yesterday, with a long or short sleep between, would not make a man two men, distance of time or change of substance would not make the same consciousness two persons. The same consciousness unites those distant actions into the same person, whatever substance contributed to their production.

PERSONAL IDENTITY IN CHANGE OF SUBSTANCE

That the preceding is so, we have some kind of evidence in our very bodies. When all of the particles

This is the editor's revised version of a selection from John Locke, An Essay Concerning Human Understanding, *edited by Mary Whiton Calkins, Chicago: Open Court, 1905.*

of the body are vitally united to this same thinking, conscious self—so that we feel when they are touched, and are affected by and conscious of good or harm that happens to them—they are a part of ourselves; i.e., of our thinking conscious self. Thus the limbs of his body are to everyone parts of himself; and he sympathizes and is concerned for them. However, if you cut off a hand and thereby separate it from that consciousness he had of its heat, cold, and other affections, then it is no longer a part of that which is himself, any more than the remotest part of matter. Thus we see that the bodily substance, whereof personal self consisted at one time, may be varied at another without the change of personal identity. There is no question about it being the same person, although the limbs, which a moment ago were a part of it, are cut off.

Another question, however, is what happens when the substance that thinks is changed. Will the same person still remain, or will there be different persons? To this I answer, first, that there can be no question at all to those who place thought in a purely material, animal constitution, void of an immaterial substance. For, whether their supposition is true or not, it is plain that they conceive personal identity as being preserved in something other than identity of substance, since animal identity is preserved in identity of life, and not of substance. On the other hand, those who believe that thinking is found only in immaterial substances must, in order to argue against this position, show why personal identity cannot be preserved in the change of immaterial substances . . . , just as animal identity is preserved in the change of material substances. . . . At least they must do this unless they are willing to say that it is one immaterial spirit that makes the same life in brutes, just as it is one immaterial spirit that makes the same person in men. But this is something that the Cartesians, for example, will not admit, for fear of making brutes thinking things, too.

But next, let us return to the first part of the question. If the thinking substance (supposing immaterial substances only to think) were changed, would the same person remain? I answer that this question can be resolved only by those who know what kind of substances they are that do think, and

whether the consciousness of past actions can be transferred from one thinking substance to another. I grant that if the same consciousness were the same individual act, this transference could not take place. . . . But since that which we call "the same consciousness" is not the same individual act, why one intellectual substance may not have represented to it as done by itself something it never did . . . will be difficult to conclude from the nature of things. Until we have a clearer view of the nature of thinking substances, the belief that this never happens will be best resolved into the goodness of God, who, as far as the happiness or misery of any of his sensible creatures is concerned, will not by a fatal error of theirs transfer from one to another that consciousness which draws reward or punishment with it. I leave it to be considered how far this may serve as an argument against those who would place thinking in a system of fleeting animal spirits. However, returning to the question before us, it must be allowed that if the same consciousness (which, as has been shown, is quite a different thing from the same numerical figure or motion in the body) can be transferred from one thinking substance to another, it will be possible that two thinking substances may make but one person. For the same consciousness being preserved, whether in the same or different substances, the personal identity is preserved.

WHETHER WITH THE SAME IMMATERIAL SUBSTANCE REMAINING THERE CAN BE TWO PERSONS

Looking at the issue from another perspective, we may ask whether with the same immaterial substance remaining there can be two distinct persons. This question seems to me to be built on this. Can the same immaterial being that is once conscious of its past action ever be wholly stripped of all the consciousness of its past existence, losing it beyond the power of ever retrieving it again? In other words, can it, as it were, begin a new account from a new period, having a consciousness that can never reach back beyond this new state? All those who believe in preexistence are evidently of this mind, since they allow the soul to have no remaining consciousness of what it did in that pre-existent state, either wholly separate from body, or informing any other body. And if they did not allow this, it is plain that experience would be against them. Since personal identity reaches no farther than consciousness reaches, a pre-existent spirit, not having continued so many ages in a state of silence, must needs make different persons. Suppose a Christian, Platonist, or a Pythagorean, should, upon God's having ended all his works of creation on the seventh day, think that his soul has existed ever since. Suppose also that he imagines that it has revolved in several human bodies, as I once met someone who was persuaded his had been the soul of Socrates. . . . Would anyone say that he, not being conscious of any of Socrates' actions or thoughts, could be the same person as Socrates?

Let any one reflect upon himself, and conclude that he has in himself immaterial spirit. Let him also conclude that this immaterial spirit is what thinks in him, and is what, despite the constant change of his body, keeps him the same. In other words, that it is what he calls himself. Let him also suppose it to be the same soul that was in Nestor or Thersites at the siege of Troy. (Since souls, as far as we know any thing of them, are naturally indifferent to the parcel of matter that contains them, this supposition has no apparent absurdity in it.)

However, if he now has no consciousness of any of the actions either of Nestor or Thersites, does or can he conceive himself to be the same person with either of them? Can he be concerned in either of their actions? Can he attribute them to himself, or think them his own, any more than he can the actions of any other man that ever existed? Because his present consciousness does not reach to any of the actions of either of those men, his self is no more one self with either of them, than if the soul or immaterial spirit that now informs him had been created when it began to inform his present body. Thus, even if it were true that the spirit that informed Nestor's body was numerically the same as the spirit that now informs his body, this would no more make him the same person as Nestor than would the fact that some of the particles of matter that were once a part of Nestor were now a part of this man. The same immaterial substance, without the same consciousness, does not make the same

person. . . . But let him once find himself conscious of any of the actions of Nestor, and he would then find himself the same person with Nestor.

THE BODY, AS WELL AS THE SOUL, GOES TO THE MAKING OF A MAN

Thus we may be able, without any difficulty, to conceive the same person at the resurrection, though in a body not exactly in make or parts the same as the one he had here—the same consciousness going along with the soul that inhabits it. But yet the soul alone, in the change of bodies, would scarce to any one, but to him that makes the soul the man, be enough to make the same man. For if the soul of a prince, carrying with it the consciousness of the prince's past life, enters and informs the body of a cobbler as soon as the cobbler's soul deserts it, every one can see that the resulting person would be the same person as the prince, and that he would be accountable only for the prince's actions. But who would say that it was the same man? The body too goes to the making of the man, and would to everyone, I guess, determine the man in this case, wherein the soul, with all its princely thoughts about it, would not make another man. He would, then, be the same cobbler to everyone other than himself. I know that, in the ordinary way of speaking, the same person and the same man stand for one and the same thing. And, indeed, every one will always have a liberty to speak as he pleases, and to apply any articulate sounds to the ideas he thinks fit, changing them as often as he pleases. But yet, when we will inquire what makes the same spirit, man, or person, we must fix the ideas of spirit, man, or person in our minds. Having resolved with ourselves what we mean by these ideas, it will not be hard to determine in regard to any of them, or in the case of any others, when they are the same and when they are not.

CONSCIOUSNESS ALONE UNITES ACTIONS INTO THE SAME PERSON

Thus, the same immaterial substance or soul does not by itself . . . make the same man. However, it is plain that consciousness, so far as it can ever be extended, unites existences and actions, even when very remote in time, into the same person, just as it does the existences and actions of the immediately preceding moment. So, whatever has the consciousness of present and past actions is the same person to whom they both belong. Had I the same consciousness that I saw the ark and Noah's flood, as that I saw an overflowing of the Thames last winter, or as that I write now, I could no more doubt that I who write this now, that I who saw the Thames overflow last winter, and that I who viewed the flood at the general deluge, was the same self . . . , than I could doubt that I who write this am the same self now while I write (whether I consist of the same substance, material or immaterial, or not) as I was yesterday. For, as to this point of being the same self, it matters not whether this present self is made up of the same or other substances. I am as much concerned and as justly accountable for any action that was done a thousand years ago, if that action is appropriated to me now by this self-consciousness, as I am for what I did the last moment.

We now see that self is that conscious thinking thing (whatever substance it is made up of, whether spiritual or material, simple or compounded, matters not) which is sensible or conscious of pleasure and pain, which is capable of happiness or misery, and which is concerned for itself, as far as that consciousness extends. Thus everyone finds that, while it is comprehended under one's consciousness, one's little finger is as much a part of himself as is any other part of him. Upon separation of this little finger, should one's consciousness go along with the little finger, leaving the rest of the body, it is evident that the little finger would be the person, the same person. Self would then have nothing to do with the rest of the body. In this case, it is the consciousness that goes along with the substance, when one part is separated from another, which makes the same person, and which constitutes this inseparable self. And this is also true in reference to substances distant from one another in time. That with which the consciousness of this present thinking thing can join itself makes the same person; it is

one self with it, and with nothing else. Thus, as everyone who reflects will perceive, it attributes to itself and owns all the actions of that thing as its own, as far as that consciousness reaches, and no farther.

PERSONS, NOT SUBSTANCES, ARE THE OBJECTS OF REWARD AND PUNISHMENT

In this personal identity is founded all the right and justice of reward and punishment. Happiness and misery is that for which everyone is concerned for *himself,* and it does not matter to him what becomes of any substance that is not joined to, or affected with, his consciousness. For, as is evident in the instance I gave above, if the consciousness went along with the little finger that was cut off, that would be the same self which was concerned for the whole body yesterday, as making part of itself. Since it is conscious of the past actions of this body, it must claim these actions as its own now. However, if the same body should still live, and immediately upon separating from the little finger have its own peculiar consciousness of which the little finger knew nothing, the consciousness that went along with the little finger would not at all be concerned for it, as a part of itself. Nor could it own any of its actions, or have any of them imputed to itself.

This shows us clearly wherein personal identity consists—not in the identity of substance but, as I have said, in the identity of consciousness. If Socrates and the present mayor of Queinborough have the same identity of consciousness, they are the same person. If Socrates waking and Socrates sleeping do not partake of the same consciousness, Socrates waking is not the same person as Socrates sleeping. To punish Socrates waking for what Socrates sleeping thought, i.e., for what Socrates waking was never conscious of, would not be right, just as it would not be right to punish one twin for what his brother-twin did, of which he knew nothing, simply because their outsides were so alike that they could not be distinguished.

Questions for Thought

1. How do Locke's views on personal identity compare with and differ from the views expressed in the preceding selection from the Upanishads?
2. If Locke's views are correct, then who are you?
3. On Locke's view, what makes you different from the person sitting next to you?
4. When, if ever, according to Locke, would it make sense to say that you are the same person as the person sitting next to you? That you are the same person as Socrates?
5. What, if anything, does Locke say about the soul?

3   The Questions of King Milinda on the Self

FROM THE BUDDHIST SCRIPTURES

The religion of Buddhism was founded in North India in the sixth century B.C.E. According to Buddhist teaching, the founder of this religion was a man named Siddhartha of the Gautama family, the son of a minor raja, or ruler, of ancient India. Although he reportedly was raised amid splendor and luxury, Siddhartha became dissatisfied with his life when he discovered the pain and suffering that seemed essentially to characterize human existence. After becoming aware of sickness, old age, and death, Siddhartha renounced his worldly goods, left his family, and embarked on a journey in search of spiritual enlightenment. He first sought enlightenment through the study of traditional Hindu texts and then by practicing an extreme form of asceticism. Finding both of these avenues to be fruitless, Siddhartha reportedly sat under a tree and meditated for forty days and forty nights. As a result of this intense meditation, he finally attained enlightenment. From that time forward, Siddhartha became known as the Buddha, the Awakened or Enlightened One. After attaining enlightenment, the Buddha spent the remaining years of his life teaching his religious insights to others.

The Buddha's followers organized themselves into a monastic order, or **sangha,** and the monks continued to disseminate and expand on the Buddha's teachings. The following selection is taken from one of the many Buddhist sacred scriptures. It is written in the form of a dialogue between the Buddhist monk Nagasena and the half-Greek king Milinda.

Although the literary form of this selection is similar to that of the earlier Hindu selection, the basic philosophical claims differ greatly. Whereas Death told Nachiketas that his identity consisted of an enduring, eternal self, or **atman,** the Buddhist monk Nagasena tells King Milinda that he has no enduring self at all. This Buddhist doctrine is appropriately labeled **anatman,** for the term *anatman* literally means being without an *atman,* or soul. As you might expect, King Milinda is astounded at this suggestion. However, Nagasena uses various means, including an **analogy** with a chariot, to eventually convince the king of the truth of this doctrine. The main conclusion of the dialogue is that human existence is constantly changing—that is, that it consists of continuous process and thus excludes any possibility of fixed identity.

Given that Buddhists deny the existence of an atman, or enduring self, it might seem to you that they would also have to renounce the Hindu doctrine of **reincarnation.** This, however, is not the case. In fact, Nagasena uses several other analogies to suggest that there is a causal connection that ties one incarnation to the next. This causal connection, according to Nagasena and Buddhists in general, is sufficient to explain the possibility of reincarnation, even though there is no soul or fixed identity passed from one incarnation into the next.

Questions for Reading

1. Describe the principal characters in this dialogue. How do they compare with and differ from the characters in the earlier Hindu dialogue?
2. How does Nagasena introduce himself to the king? Why is the king surprised by what Nagasena initially says?
3. What is the point of the chariot analogy?
4. The king asks the following question of Nagasena: "Does he who is born remain the same or become another?" How does Nagasena answer this question?
5. What evidence, if any, does Nagasena give in support of his belief in reincarnation?

BOOK II, CHAPTER I, SECTION I

NOW MILINDA THE KING WENT UP TO WHERE THE venerable Nagasena was. After addressing him with the greetings and compliments of friendship and courtesy, he took his seat respectfully apart. Nagasena reciprocated the king's courtesy, so that the king's heart was propitiated.

And Milinda began by asking, "How is your Reverence known? What, Sir, is your name?"

"I am known as Nagasena, O king, and it is by that name that my fellow monks address me. But although parents give such a name as Nagasena, this is only a generally understood term, a designation in common use. For there is no permanent individuality (no soul) involved in the matter."

Then Milinda called upon those in attendance to witness: "This Nagasena says there is no permanent individuality (no soul) implied in his name. Can one possibly agree with him in that?" And turning to Nagasena, he said: "If . . . there is no permanent individuality (no soul) involved in the matter, who is it, pray, who gives to you monks your robes, food, lodging, and necessaries for the sick? Who is it who enjoys such things when given? Who is it who lives a life of righteousness? Who is it who

devotes himself to meditation? Who is it who attains the goal of the Excellent Way, the goal that leads to the Nirvana of **Arhatship?** And who is it who destroys living creatures? Who is it who takes what is not his own? Who is it who lives an evil life of worldly lusts, who speaks lies, who drinks strong drink, who (in a word) commits any one of the five sins which work out their bitter fruit even in this life? If what Nagasena says is true, there is neither merit nor demerit; there is neither doer nor causer of good or evil deeds; there is neither fruit nor result of good or evil **Karma.** If, most reverend Nagasena, we were to accept that, then if a man kills you, there would be no murder. . . . You tell me that your fellow monks are in the habit of addressing you as Nagasena. Now what is that Nagasena? Do you mean to say that the hair is Nagasena?"

"I don't say that, great king."

"Or the hairs on the body, perhaps?"

"Certainly not."

"Or is it the nails, the teeth, the skin, the flesh, the nerves, the bones, the marrow, the kidneys, the heart, the liver, the abdomen, the spleen, the lungs, the larger intestines, the lower intestines, the stomach, the feces, the bile, the phlegm, the pus, the

This is the editor's revised version of a selection from The Questions of King Milinda, *translated by T. W. Rhys Davies,* *Oxford: Clarendon Press, 1874.*

blood, the sweat, the fat, the tears, the serum, the saliva, the mucus, the oil that lubricates the joints, the urine, or the brain? Is it any or all of these that is Nagasena?"

And to each of these he answered no.

"Is it the outward form then that is Nagasena, or the sensations, or the ideas, or . . . the constituent elements of character, or the consciousness, that is Nagasena?"

And to each of these also he answered no.

"Then is it all these **Skandhas** combined that are Nagasena?"

"No! great king."

"But is there anything outside the five Skandhas that is Nagasena?"

And still he answered no.

"Then, ask as I may, I can discover no Nagasena. Nagasena is a mere empty sound. Who then is the Nagasena that we see before us? It is a falsehood that your reverence has spoken, an untruth!"

At this point, the venerable Nagasena said to Milinda the king: "You, Sire, have been brought up in great luxury, as is fitting to your noble birth. If you were to walk this dry weather on the hot and sandy ground, trampling under foot the gritty, gravelly grains of the hard sand, your feet would hurt you. And as your body would be in pain, your mind would be disturbed, and you would experience a sense of bodily suffering. How then did you arrive, on foot or in a chariot?"

"I did not come, Sir, on foot. I came in a chariot."

"Then if you came, Sire, in a chariot, explain to me what that is. Is it the pole that is the chariot?"

"I did not say that."

"Is it the axle that is the chariot?"

"Certainly not."

"Is it the wheels, or the framework, or the ropes, or the yoke, or the spokes of the wheels, or the goad, that are the chariot?"

And to all these he still answered no.

"Then is it all these parts that are the chariot?"

"No, Sir."

"But is there anything outside them that is the chariot?"

And still he answered no.

"Then, ask as I may, I can discover no chariot. Chariot is a mere empty sound. What then is the chariot you say you came in? It is a falsehood that

your Majesty has spoken, an untruth! There is no such thing as a chariot!"

When he had thus spoken those in attendance shouted their applause, saying to the king: "Now let your Majesty get out of that if you can."

Milinda the king replied to Nagasena, "I have spoken no untruth, reverend Sir. It is on account of its having all these things—the pole, the axle, the wheels, the framework, the ropes, the yoke, the spokes, and the goad—that it comes under the generally understood term, the designation in common use, of 'chariot.'"

"Very good," Nagasena replied. "Your Majesty has rightly grasped the meaning of 'chariot.' And just so, it is on account of all those things you questioned me about—the thirty-two kinds of organic matter in a human body, and the five constituent elements of being—that I come under the generally understood term, the designation in common use, of 'Nagasena.' For it was said, Sire, by our Sister Vagira in the presence of the Buddha: 'Just as it is because of the co-existence of its various parts that the word "chariot" is used, just so is it that when the Skandhas are there we talk of a "being."'"

"Most wonderful, Nagasena, and most strange. The puzzle that has been put to you, most difficult though it was, has been well solved. Were the Buddha himself here, he would approve your answer. Well done, well done, Nagasena!"

BOOK II, CHAPTER 2, SECTION I

The king asked: "Does he who is born, Nagasena, remain the same or become another?"

"Neither the same nor another."

"Give me an illustration."

"Now what do you think, O king? You were once a baby, a tender thing, and small in size, lying flat on your back. Was that baby the same as you who are now grown up?"

"No. That child was one, I am another."

"If you are not that child, it will follow that you have had neither mother, father, nor teacher. You cannot have been taught learning, behavior, or wisdom. What great king, is the mother of the embryo in the first stage different from the mother of the embryo in the second stage, or the third, or the fourth? Is the mother of the baby a different person from the mother of the grown-up man? Is the person who begins school one, and the person who finishes his schooling another? Is it one who commits a crime, another who is punished by having his hands or feet cut off?"

"Certainly not. But what would you, Nagasena, say to that?"

The Elder replied: "I should say that I am the same person, now that I am grown up, as I was when I was a tender tiny baby, flat on my back. For all these states are included in one by means of this body."

"Give me an illustration."

"Suppose a man, O king, were to light a lamp, would it burn the night through?"

"Yes, it might do so."

"Now, is it the same flame that burns in the first watch of the night, Sir, and in the second?"

"No."

"Or the same that burns in the second watch and in the third?"

"No."

"Then is there one lamp in the first watch, another in the second, and another in the third?"

"No. The light comes from the same lamp all the night through."

"Just so, O king, is the continuity of a person or thing maintained. One comes into existence, another passes away; and the rebirth is, as it were, simultaneous. Thus neither as the same nor as another does a man go on to the last phase of his self-consciousness."

"Give me a further illustration."

"It is like milk. When once taken from the cow, it turns, after a lapse of time, first to curds, then from curds to butter, and then from butter to ghee. Now would it be right to say that the milk was the same thing as the curds, or the butter, or the ghee?"

"Certainly not; but they are produced out of it."

"Just so, O king, is the continuity of a person or thing maintained. One comes into existence, another passes away; and the rebirth is, as it were, simultaneous. Thus neither as the same nor as another does a man go on to the last phase of his self-consciousness."

"Well put, Nagasena."

Questions for Thought

1. Would you agree with Nagasena that you have no enduring self or soul? Why or why not?
2. Assuming that you do not have an enduring self or soul, what makes you different from your best friend?
3. Do you think that you are the same person now that you were when you were a child? Defend your answer.
4. Do you agree with Nagasena's claim that the doctrine of reincarnation makes sense even without the existence of an enduring self or soul? Why or why not?
5. How do the views expressed in this dialogue compare with and differ from the views expressed in the earlier Hindu dialogue? How do they compare with and differ from the views of Locke?

4   There Is No Personal Identity

DAVID HUME

David Hume (1711–1776) was born in Edinburgh, Scotland. His father, who died when Hume was only three, owned a small estate and was a distant cousin of the earl of Home. His mother, the daughter of the president of the Scottish court of session, came from a family of lawyers. At the urging of his maternal relatives, Hume entered the University of Edinburgh to study law. He found that he disliked legal studies, however, and he subsequently devised his own course of study.

After holding several jobs and suffering from a nervous breakdown, Hume moved to France in 1734. It was during his three years' residence in France that he wrote *A Treatise of Human Nature,* his first and longest philosophical text. He then returned to England to oversee the publication of the *Treatise,* which was issued anonymously when Hume was only twenty-eight years old.

In England and later Scotland, Hume held several minor government positions, spent a year tutoring a mad marquess, and became a librarian. However, he was never able to procure a university appointment. When he applied for the chair of moral philosophy at the University of Edinburgh in 1744, he was accused of heresy and denied the appointment. For this reason, among others, Hume became the model of the modern British philosopher—an outspoken, independent thinker who refuses to bow to authority. This image was later reinforced when Hume, who was dying from cancer, refused the last rites of the Church.

In addition to the *Treatise,* Hume's philosophical writings include *Philosophical Essays Concerning Human Understanding* (1748; retitled *An Enquiry Concerning Human Understanding* ten years later), *An Enquiry Concerning the Principles of Morals* (1751), *Political Discourses* (1752), and *Dialogues on Natural Religion* (published posthumously in 1779 but probably written in the 1750s). Hume was also known for his *History of England,* which was issued in six quatro volumes between 1754 and 1762.

In the following selection from *A Treatise on Human Nature,* Hume defends a position similar to that of Buddhism. Like the Buddhist monk Nagasena, Hume argues that the human mind is in a state of constant flux and thus that we have no basis for believing in the existence of an enduring self or soul. Claiming that all ideas must be derived from an **impression,** or sensation, Hume argues that he would be justified in believing in an enduring self or soul only if he could discover some enduring impression or sensation when he examines the contents of his thinking. When he does so, however, Hume finds only a collection of constantly changing perceptions.

Continuing in a vein that is also similar to Buddhist writings, Hume goes on to argue that the same holds true of the external world. Just as he can discover no justification for believing in the existence of an enduring self or soul, he can find no justification for believing in the existence of **substance** or the continued identity of physical objects. Rather, the concept of substance or external identity is derived from the same mistake as the concept of soul or personal identity: the tendency of the mind to overlook small or gradual changes in what is being observed. Hume concludes by saying that philosophical disputes concerning the identity of objects, as well as those concerning personal identity, result from this tendency of the mind to overlook such change and thus to mistake succession for identity. Of course, since there is no enduring self or soul, it is senseless to ask when the self or soul ceases to exist. Unlike the Buddhists, Hume believes that death, which represents the annihilation of the movement of perceptions, marks the end of one's existence.

Questions for Reading

1. What reasons does Hume give for denying the existence of an enduring self or soul?
2. How would Hume explain the apparent differences between two people?
3. Why does Hume compare the mind to a theater? What is this analogy intended to show?
4. According to Hume, what leads people to believe in personal identity?
5. What conclusions about the possibility of immortality can be drawn from Hume's position?

THERE ARE SOME PHILOSOPHERS WHO IMAGINE that at every moment we are intimately conscious of what we call *self*, that we feel its existence and its continuance in existence, and that we are certain, beyond the evidence of a demonstration, both of its perfect identity and simplicity. They say that the strongest sensation, the most violent passion, instead of distracting us from this view, only fix it the more intensely by making us consider their influence on *self*, either by their pain or pleasure. To attempt a farther proof of this would, according to these philosophers, weaken its evidence, since no proof can be derived from any fact of which we are so intimately conscious. Nor is there any thing of which we can be certain, they say, if we doubt of this.

Unluckily all these positive assertions are contrary to that very experience which is pleaded for them. Nor do we have any idea of *self*, after the manner it is here explained. For from what impression could this idea be derived? It is impossible to answer this question without a manifest contradiction and absurdity. And yet it is a question that must necessarily be answered, if we claim to have a clear and intelligible idea of self. For there must be some one impression that gives rise to every real idea. But self is not any one impression; it is that to which our several impressions and ideas are supposed to refer. If any impression gives rise to the idea of self, then that impression must continue invariably the same through the whole course of our lives, since self is supposed to exist after that manner. But there is no impression constant and invariable. Pain and pleasure, grief and joy, passions and sensations succeed each other, and never all exist at the same time. It cannot, therefore, be from any of these impressions, or from any other, that the idea of self is derived; consequently there is no such idea.

But farther, what must become of all our particular perceptions upon this hypothesis? All these are different, and distinguishable, and separable from each other. They may be separately considered, and may exist separately, and have no need of any thing to support their existence. After what manner, therefore, do they belong to self? How are they connected with it? For my part, when I enter most intimately into what I call *myself*, I always stumble on some particular perception or other, of heat or cold, light or shade, love or hatred, pain or pleasure. I never can catch *myself* at any time without a perception, and never can observe any thing but the perception. When my perceptions are removed for any time, as by sound sleep, during that time I am insensible of *myself*, and may truly be said not to exist. And were all my perceptions removed by death, and could I neither think, nor feel, nor see, nor love, nor hate after the dissolution of my body, I would be entirely annihilated. Nor do I conceive what is farther requisite to make me a perfect non-entity. If any one, upon serious and unprejudiced reflection, thinks that he has a different notion of *himself*,

This is the editor's revised version of a selection from David Hume, A Treatise of Human Nature, *edited by L. A. Selby-Bigge, London: Oxford University Press, 1888.*

I must confess that I can reason no longer with him. All I can grant him is that he may be in the right as well as I, and that we are essentially different in this particular. He may, perhaps, perceive something simple and continued, which he calls *himself,* although I am certain there is no such principle in me.

But setting aside some metaphysicians of this kind, I may venture to affirm of the rest of mankind that they are nothing but a bundle or collection of different perceptions, which succeed each other with an inconceivable rapidity, and are in a perpetual flux and movement. Our eyes cannot turn in their sockets without varying our perceptions. Our thought is still more variable than our sight; and all our other senses and faculties contribute to this change. Nor is there any single power of the soul, which remains unalterably the same, perhaps even for one moment. The mind is a kind of theatre, where several perceptions successively make their appearance; these perceptions pass, re-pass, glide away, and mingle in an infinite variety of postures and situations. There is properly no *simplicity* in the mind at one time, nor *identity* in it at different times, whatever natural propensity we may have to imagine that simplicity and identity. However, the comparison of the theatre must not mislead us. It is these successive perceptions only that constitute the mind; we do not have the most distant notion of the place where these scenes are represented, or of the materials of which it is composed.

What then gives us so great a propensity to ascribe an identity to these successive perceptions and to suppose ourselves possessed of an invariable and uninterrupted existence through the whole course of our lives? In order to answer this question, we must distinguish between personal identity as it regards our thought or imagination, and personal identity as it regards our passions or the concern we take in ourselves. The first is our present subject. To explain it perfectly we must take the matter pretty deep, and account for that identity which we attribute to plants and animals; for there is a great **analogy** between the identity of plants and animals and the identity of a self or person.

We have a distinct idea of an object that remains invariable and uninterrupted through a supposed variation of time, and we call this idea *identity* or *sameness*. We have also a distinct idea of several different objects existing in succession, which are connected together by a close relation. To an accurate view, this affords as perfect a notion of *diversity,* as if there were no manner of relation among the objects. But although these two ideas of identity and the succession of related objects are in themselves perfectly distinct, and even contrary, yet in our common way of thinking, it is certain that they are generally confounded with each other. That action of the imagination by which we consider the uninterrupted and invariable object, and that action by which we reflect on the succession of related objects, feel almost the same. Nor is there much more effort of thought required in the latter case than in the former. The relation facilitates the transition of the mind from one object to another, and renders its passage as smooth as if it contemplated one continued object. This resemblance is the cause of confusion and mistake, and makes us substitute the notion of identity instead of that of related objects. If at one moment we may consider the related succession as variable or interrupted, we are sure the next moment to ascribe to it a perfect identity, thus regarding it as invariable and uninterrupted. Our propensity to this mistake is so great . . . that we fall into it before we are aware; and although we incessantly correct ourselves by reflection and return to a more accurate method of thinking, we cannot long sustain our philosophy or remove this bias from the imagination. Our last resource is to yield to it, boldly asserting that these different related objects are in effect the same, however interrupted and variable they may be. In order to justify to ourselves this absurdity, we often feign some new and unintelligible principle that connects the objects together and prevents their interruption or variation. Thus in order to remove the interruption, we feign the continued existence of the perceptions of our senses, inventing the notions of *soul, self,* and *substance* to disguise the variation. But we may further observe that, where we do not imagine such a fiction, our propensity to confound identity with relation is so great that we are apt to imagine, in addition to their relation, something unknown and mysterious that connects the parts. This I take to be the case with regard to the identity we ascribe to plants and vegetables. Moreover, even when we do not imagine this mysterious something connecting the parts, we still feel a propensity to confound these ideas. . . . Thus the controversy concerning identity is not merely a dispute of words. For when we improperly attribute identity to variable or interrupted objects, our mistake is not confined to the expression; it is also commonly attended with a fiction, either of something invariable and uninterrupted, or of something mysterious and inexplicable, or at least with a propensity to such fictions. This hypothesis can be proved to the satisfaction of every fair inquirer if, from daily experience and observation, we can show how objects which are supposed to continue the same, actually consist of a succession of parts connected together by resemblance, contiguity, or causation. . . .

In order to do this, suppose that any mass of matter, of which the parts are contiguous and connected, is placed before us. It is plain that we must attribute a perfect identity to this mass, provided all the parts continue uninterruptedly and invariably the same, whatever motion or change of place we may observe either in the whole or in any of the parts. But suppose that some very *small* or *inconsiderable* part is added to the mass, or subtracted from it. This absolutely destroys the identity of the whole, strictly speaking; yet as we seldom think so accurately, we scruple not to pronounce the mass of matter the same, where we find so trivial an alteration. The passage of the thought from the object before the change to the object after it is so smooth and easy, that we scarce perceive the transition. For this reason, we are apt to imagine that we continue to survey the same object. . . .

This may be confirmed by another phenomenon. A change in any considerable part of a body destroys its identity; but it is remarkable that, where the change is produced *gradually* and *insensibly,* we are less apt to ascribe to it the same effect. The reason is plainly that the mind, in following the successive changes of the body, feels an easy passage from surveying its condition in one moment to viewing it in another, and at no particular time perceives any interruption in its actions. From this continued perception, it ascribes a continued existence and identity to the object.

But whatever precaution we may use in introducing the changes gradually and making them proportionate to the whole, it is certain that, where the changes are at last observed to become considerable, we make a scruple of ascribing identity to such different objects. There is, however, another artifice by which we may induce the imagination to advance a step farther. That is by producing a reference of the parts to each other and to a combination to some *common end* or purpose. A ship, of which a considerable part has been changed by frequent reparations, is thought nevertheless to be the same; nor does the difference of the materials hinder us from ascribing an identity to it. The common end, in which the parts conspire, is the same under all their variations; this affords an easy transition of the imagination from one situation of the body to another.

But this is still more remarkable when we add a *sympathy* of parts to their *common end,* and suppose that they bear the reciprocal relation of cause and effect to each other in all their actions and operations. This is the case with all animals and vegetables, where the several parts not only have a reference to some general purpose, but also have a mutual dependence on, and connection with, each other. The effect of so strong a relation is that, although every one must allow that in a very few years both vegetables and animals endure a *total* change, we still attribute identity to them, despite the fact that their form, size, and substance are entirely altered. An oak that grows from a small plant to a large tree is still the same oak, although there is not one particle of matter, or figure of its parts, that is the same. An infant becomes a man, who is sometimes fat, sometimes lean, without any change in his identity. . . .

We now proceed to explain the nature of *personal identity,* which has lately become so great a question in philosophy, especially in *England,* where all the abstruser sciences are studied with a peculiar ardor and application. And here it is evident that the same method of reasoning must be continued, which has so successfully explained the identity of plants, animals, ships, houses, and all of the compounded and changeable productions either of art or nature. The identity which we ascribe to the mind of man is only a fictitious one, of a like kind with that which we ascribe to vegetables and animal bodies. It cannot, therefore, have a different origin, but must proceed from a like operation of the imagination upon like objects. . . .

The whole of this doctrine leads us to a conclusion that is of great importance in the present affair, *viz.* that all the nice and subtle questions concerning personal identity can never possibly be decided, but are to be regarded as grammatical rather than as philosophical difficulties. Identity depends on the relations of ideas; and these relations produce identity by means of that easy transition they occasion. But as the relations and the easiness of the transition may diminish by insensible degrees, we have no just standard by which we can decide any dispute concerning the time when they acquire or lose a title to the name of identity. All the disputes concerning the identity of connected objects are merely verbal, except insofar as the relation of parts gives rise to some fiction, or imaginary principle of union, as we have already observed.

Questions for Thought

1. When you look within, can you discover a constant, unchanging impression or sensation? If not, do you think that you are justified in believing that you have an enduring self or soul? Why or why not?
2. Does Hume's comparison of the mind to a theater adequately express how you perceive your own mind? Can you think of a different metaphor for expressing this?
3. Do you believe in personal identity? If so, why?
4. Do you agree with Hume that death marks the end of your existence? If not, what arguments could you use to try to convince Hume that he is mistaken?
5. What are the basic similarities between Hume's views and the Buddhist views found in the preceding selection? What are the basic differences?

5   A Dialogue on Immortality[1]

ARTHUR SCHOPENHAUER

Arthur Schopenhauer (1788–1860) was born in Danzig, Prussia. Schopenhauer's father was a successful trader, an admirer of Voltaire, and a strong critic of absolutist government. His mother, who was well read, became a writer of popular romantic novels, essays, and travelogues. Later, after the death of her husband, she opened a literary salon in Weimar.

When Danzig was captured by the Prussians in 1793, Schopenhauer's family moved to the free city of Hamburg. In Hamburg, the young Schopenhauer was educated in a private school for three years. Later he spent two years studying in France and several months studying in London. His education was also supplemented by his family's extensive travels throughout many parts of Europe.

Although Schopenhauer showed an early interest in the study of literature, his father insisted that he pursue a career in business. Three months after apprenticing his son to a business concern, however, the elder Schopenhauer died, apparently from suicide. Out of respect for his father's wishes, Schopenhauer remained in the business world for two years before entering the University of Göttingen to study medicine. His studies were sidetracked, however, when he discovered Plato and Kant, a discovery that initiated his interest in philosophy. Since the University of Berlin was the philosophical center of Germany at the time, Schopenhauer transferred there to pursue his new interest. He then completed his studies at the University of Jena, from which he received his doctorate in philosophy in 1813.

Schopenhauer began work on his principal book, *Die Welt als Wille und Vorstellung* (*The World as Will and Idea*), shortly after finishing his doctoral thesis. This monumental work, which took four years to complete, helped him obtain a job as lecturer at the University of Berlin. However, because he intentionally scheduled his lectures at the same time as **Hegel,** the most popular German philosopher teaching at the time, Schopenhauer's academic career was short-lived.

After leaving the University of Berlin, Schopenhauer lived the solitary life of a confirmed bachelor, first in Dresden and then in Frankfurt. Although he was disappointed by the cool reception of *The World as Will and Idea* and by the failure of his academic career, Schopenhauer continued to write. His later works include *Über den Willen in der Natur* (1836; *On the Will in Nature*), *Die beiden Grundprobleme der Ethik* (1841; translated as *The Basis of Morality*), and *Parerga und Paralipomena* (1851; two volumes of essays and aphorisms). The success of the latter work brought Schopenhauer the fame that had earlier eluded him. He died of a heart attack in 1860.

In the following brief dialogue, Schopenhauer, whose views are stated by the character Philalethes, argues that human existence—indeed all existence—is a manifestation of an impersonal Will to Live. This insight, which is derived from what Schopenhauer calls **transcendental knowledge,** leads him to conclude that belief in personal identity or individuality is erroneous. In other words, my "I," like every other "I" that exists, is a manifestation of the impersonal Will to Live; and whereas the Will to Live eternally manifests itself, my "I," like all others, has only temporary existence. This leads Schopenhauer to conclude that at death "I" am everything and nothing. My "I," my personal identity or individuality, ceases to exist, but the impersonal element of my identity, the Will to Live, "never rests, but presses forward endlessly."

Questions for Reading

1. What, according to Schopenhauer, is the essential difference between transcendental knowledge and immanent knowledge?
2. At the beginning of the dialogue, Thrasymachos asks the following question: "What will I be after my death?" How does Philalethes/Schopenhauer respond to this question?
3. How does Thrasymachos react to Philalethes'/Schopenhauer's views on immortality?
4. What does Philalethes/Schopenhauer mean by the Will to Live?
5. How does the dialogue end?

Thrasymachos: Tell me now, in one word, what will I be after my death? And mind you be clear and precise.

Philalethes: All and nothing!

Thrasymachos: I thought so! I gave you a problem, and you solve it by a contradiction. That's a very stale trick.

Philalethes: Yes, but you raise transcendental questions, and you expect me to answer them in language that is only made to express **immanent knowledge.** It's no wonder that a contradiction ensues.

Thrasymachos: What do you mean by transcendental questions and immanent knowledge? I've heard these expressions before, of course; they are not new to me. The Professor was fond of using them, but only as predicates of the Deity. He never talked of anything else; which was all quite right and proper. He argued thus: if the Deity was in

This is the editor's revised version of a selection from Arthur Schopenhauer, Complete Essays of Schopenhauer, *translated by T. Bailey Saunders, New York: Wiley Book Co., 1942 (originally published in the nineteenth century).*

the world itself, he was immanent; if he was some-where outside it, he was transcendent. Nothing could be clearer and more obvious! You knew where you were. But this Kantian rigmarole won't do any more. It's antiquated and no longer applic-able to modern ideas. Why, we've had a whole row of eminent men in the metropolis of German learning—

Philalethes: (Aside.) German humbug, he means.

Thrasymachos: The mighty **Schleiermacher,** for instance, and that gigantic intellect, **Hegel.** By now, we've abandoned that nonsense. I should rather say we're so far beyond it that we can't put up with it any longer. What's the use of it then? What does it all mean?

Philalethes: Transcendental knowledge is knowl-edge that passes beyond the bounds of possible expe-rience, knowledge that strives to determine the na-ture of things as they are in themselves. Immanent knowledge, on the other hand, is knowledge that confines itself entirely within the bounds of possible experience, so that it cannot apply to anything but actual **phenomena.** As far as you are an individual, death will be the end of you. But your individuality is not your true and inmost being—it is only the out-ward manifestation of it. It is not the **thing-in-itself,** but only the phenomenon presented in the form of time, therefore having a beginning and an end. But your real being knows neither time, nor beginning, nor end, nor the limits of any given individual. It is everywhere present in every individual; and no indi-vidual can exist apart from it. So when death comes, on the one hand, you are annihilated as an individual. But, on the other hand, you are and remain every-thing. That is what I meant when I said that after your death you would be all and nothing. It is diffi-cult to find a more precise answer to your question and at the same time be brief. The answer is contra-dictory, I admit. But it is so, simply because your life is in time, while the immortal part of you is in eter-nity. The matter may also be expressed as follows: Your immortal part is something that does not last in time and yet is indestructible. But there you have an-other contradiction! You see what happens by trying to bring the transcendental within the limits of im-manent knowledge. It is, in a sense, doing violence to the latter by misusing it for ends that it was never meant to serve.

Thrasymachos: Look here, I won't give two cents for your immortality, unless I'm to remain an indi-vidual.

Philalethes: Well, perhaps I may be able to satisfy you on this point. Suppose I guarantee that after death you will remain an individual, but only on condition that you first spend three months com-pletely unconscious.

Thrasymachos: I have no objection to that.

Philalethes: But remember, if people are com-pletely unconscious, they take no account of time. So, when you are dead, it's all the same to you whether three months or ten thousand years pass in the world. In the one case as in the other, it is sim-ply a matter of believing what is told you when you awake. Thus, you can afford to be indifferent as to whether three months or ten thousand years have passed before you recover your individuality.

Thrasymachos: Yes, if it comes to that, I suppose you're right.

Philalethes: And if by chance, after those ten thousand years have gone by, no one ever thinks of awakening you, I fancy it would be no great misfor-tune. You would have become quite accustomed to non-existence after so long a spell of it—especially following upon such a very few years of life. At any rate you may be sure that you would be perfectly ignorant of the whole thing. Further, if you knew that the mysterious power which keeps you in your present state of life had never once ceased in those ten thousand years to bring forth other phenomena like yourself, and to endow them with life, it would fully console you.

Thrasymachos: Indeed! So you think you're qui-etly going to do me out of my individuality with all this fine talk. But I'm up to your tricks. I tell you that I won't exist unless I can have my individuality. I'm not going to be put off with "mysterious pow-ers," and what you call "phenomena." I can't do without my individuality, and I won't give it up.

Philalethes: You mean, I suppose, that your individ-uality is such a delightful thing—so splendid, so per-fect, and beyond compare—that you can't imagine anything better. Aren't you ready to exchange your present state for one that, if we can judge by what is told us, may possibly be superior and more endurable?

Thrasymachos: Don't you see that my individual-ity, be it what it may, is my very self? To me it is the most important thing in the world. *For God is God and I am I. I* want to exist, *I.* That's the main thing. I don't care about an existence that has to be proved to be mine, before I can believe it.

Philalethes: Think what you're doing! When you say, "I want to exist," it is not you alone who says this. Everything says it, absolutely everything that has the faintest trace of consciousness. It follows, then, that this desire of yours is just the part of you that is *not individual*—the part that is common to all things without distinction. It is the cry, not of the individual, but of existence itself. It is the intrinsic element in everything that exists; indeed, it is the cause of anything existing at all. This desire craves for (and so is satisfied with) nothing less than existence *in general*—not any definite individual existence. No! that is not its aim. It seems to be so only because this desire—this Will—attains consciousness only in the individual, and therefore looks as though it were concerned with nothing but the individual. There lies the illusion—an illusion, it is true, in which the individual is held fast. But, if he reflects, he can break the fetters and set himself free. It is only indirectly, I say, that the individual has this violent craving for existence. It is *the Will to Live* that is the real and direct aspirant, the Will to Live that is alike and identical in all things. Since, then, existence is the free work—indeed the mere reflection—of the will, where existence is, there, too, must be will. For the moment, the will finds its satisfaction in existence itself; so far, I mean, as that which never rests, but presses forward eternally, can ever find any satisfaction at all. The will is careless of the individual. The individual is not

its business, although, as I have said, this seems to be the case, because the individual has no direct consciousness of will except in himself. The effect of this is to make the individual careful to maintain his own existence; and if this were not so, there would be no surety for the preservation of the species. From all this it is clear that individuality is not a form of perfection, but rather of limitation, and to be freed from it is not loss, but gain. Trouble yourself no more about the matter. Fully recognize for once what you are, what your existence really is, namely, the universal will to live, and the whole question will seem to you childish and most ridiculous!

Thrasymachos: You're childish yourself and most ridiculous, like all philosophers! If a man of my age lets himself in for a quarter-of-an-hour's talk with such fools, it is only because it amuses me and passes the time. I've more important business to attend to, so Good-bye.

NOTE

1. The word *immortality*—*Unsterblichkeit*—does not occur in the original; nor would it, in its usual application, find a place in Schopenhauer's vocabulary. The word he uses is *Unzerstörbarkeit*—*indestructibility*. But I have preferred *immortality* because the word is commonly associated with the subject touched on in this little debate. If any critic doubts the wisdom of this preference, let me ask him to try his hand at a short, concise, and at the same time popularly intelligible rendering of the German original, which runs thus: *Zur Lehre von der Unzerstörbarkeit unseres wahren Wesens durch den Tod: kleine dialogische Schlussbelustigung.*—Trans.

Questions for Thought

1. What kinds of knowledge claims fall under the category of immanent knowledge? Can you think of any type of knowledge that corresponds to what Schopenhauer calls "transcendental knowledge"?
2. Do you agree with Schopenhauer that your existence is a manifestation of the Will to Live? Why or why not?
3. Do you think that it makes sense to believe in impersonal immortality? Defend your answer.
4. Would you categorize yourself as a unique individual? If so, what makes you unique? If not, why not?
5. Which of the earlier selections that you have read seems most compatible with the views of Schopenhauer? Which of them seems least compatible?

To What Extent Do Our Bodies Determine Who We Are?

6	The Nature of the Soul and Its Relation to the Body

PLATO

Plato (427–347 B.C.E.) was born into a wealthy, aristocratic family in Athens. After his father died when Plato was a child, Plato's mother followed Athenian tradition and married her closest kinsman. While many of the details of Plato's life are unknown, most scholars agree that he served in the Athenian military during the war with Sparta (most likely in the cavalry), that he never married, and that he was one of the close followers of the Greek philosopher Socrates. When Socrates was executed in 399, Plato traveled to Egypt and Syracuse before returning to Athens to found the Academy, a school of philosophy and scientific research that survived until the Roman emperor Justinian closed all pagan schools of philosophy in 529 C.E.

Like many members of his family, Plato was a critic of Athenian democracy. In one of his writings, the *Republic,* Plato argues that the ideal form of government is an **aristocracy** headed by a philosopher-king. However, in the same work, Plato diverges from Athenian custom by suggesting that women, as well as men, may serve as members of the ruling class of society. In addition to the *Republic,* Plato wrote many other philosophical dialogues, most of which also feature Socrates as the main character. Some of Plato's better-known dialogues include *Apology, Crito, Phaedo, Euthyphro, Gorgias, Protagoras, Meno, Symposium, Parmenides, Sophist,* and *Timaeus.*

The following selection, which is excerpted from the *Phaedo,* is set in Socrates' prison cell on the morning before his execution. In an earlier dialogue, the *Apology,* Plato had portrayed Socrates' trial, during which he had been charged with corrupting the youth of Athens and with atheism. Having found him guilty of these charges, the jury sentenced Socrates to death. Now, as he is awaiting execution, Socrates concludes his life by leading one last philosophical dialogue—a dialogue on death and the immortality of the soul.

Early in the dialogue, Socrates remarks that he is not afraid of dying. Indeed, he goes on to say that, although one should not commit suicide because it would offend the gods, a true philosopher welcomes death. This claim is based on a dualistic view of human nature—that is, a view that human beings are composed of two very distinct **substances:** body and soul. Socrates believes that death consists of the separation of the soul from the body, and he also believes that philosophy is concerned with the wisdom of the soul and not with the pleasures or comfort of the body. Since the needs of the body often interfere with the attainment of wisdom, Socrates concludes that a philosopher must neglect bodily needs and focus on the soul. Death thus represents the ideal state for philosophical reflection, a state whereby the soul, being separated from the body, is totally liberated from bodily distractions.

At this point in the dialogue, Socrates is confronted with a question about whether the soul does indeed survive the death of the body. He then proceeds to provide three arguments for the immortality of the soul. The first of these arguments is based on the assumption that it is a law of nature that opposites produce opposites—for example, being awake results from being asleep. He also notes that this process is cyclical—just as being awake results from being asleep, being asleep results from being awake. Since death is the opposite of life, Socrates argues that this cyclical process must pertain to life and death as well. Thus, just as death results from being alive, being alive must result from being dead. This latter result is possible, however, only if death is not the final state of one's existence.

Socrates' second argument is based on his assumption that we have knowledge of perfect realities—realities such as absolute equality and absolute beauty—and that this knowledge could not have been attained through the senses or other bodily means. Since this is the case, Socrates argues that such knowledge must have been obtained before we had senses *or* a body—that is, before we were born. In other words, as Plato also claims in the *Republic,* genuine knowledge is merely the soul's **recollection** of something that it learned when it existed in an unembodied state prior to its present embodiment.

The final argument for the immortality of the soul, which takes the form of an **analogy,** is also based on the assumption that perfect realities exist. Socrates claims that these perfect realities, in contrast to their sensual copies, are incomposite, invisible, unchangeable, indissoluble, grasped by reason, and akin to the divine. Noting that the soul strongly resembles these perfect realities, Socrates concludes that it must share one other property with them—namely, eternity or immortality.

The selection ends with Socrates speculating about the prospects of the soul once it leaves the body. He concludes that a pure soul will escape the necessity of rebirth and dwell eternally in the realm of the perfect realities. An impure soul, on the other hand, will be dragged to earth again and embodied in an appropriate form, perhaps even in the form of a donkey. As should be evident, Socrates' speculations on this matter are quite similar to the views expressed in the earlier selection from the **Upanishads.**

Questions for Reading

1. Why, according to Socrates/Plato, does a true philosopher not fear dying?
2. How many arguments does Socrates/Plato give for the immortality of the soul? What is the principal assumption on which the first argument is based? What is the principal assumption on which the second argument is based?
3. What, according to Cebes, is Socrates' favorite doctrine? How is this doctrine used to argue for the immortality of the soul?
4. Why does Socrates/Plato believe that the soul closely resembles perfect realities such as absolute equality and absolute beauty?
5. What, according to Socrates/Plato, are the essential differences between soul and body?
6. What, according to Socrates/Plato, happens to a pure soul when it is separated from the body? What happens to an impure soul?

Echecrates: Were you yourself, Phaedo, in the prison with Socrates on the day when he drank the poison?

Phaedo: Yes, Echecrates, I was.

Echecrates: I would very much like to hear about his death. What did he say in his last hours? We were informed that he died by taking poison. But no one from this region ever goes to Athens now, and it has been a long time since anyone from Athens has visited here. So, we have heard nothing else about Socrates' death.

Phaedo: Did you not hear about the proceedings at the trial?

The selection from Plato's Phaedo *is the editor's revised version of the translation found in* The Dialogues of Plato, *translated by Benjamin Jowett, The Macmillan Company, 1892.*

Echecrates: Yes, someone told us about the trial. But we could not understand why there was such a lengthy interval between the trial and the execution. What was the reason for this?

Phaedo: It was due to a lucky accident, Echecrates. The stern of the ship which the Athenians send to Delos happened to have been crowned on the day before he was tried.

Echecrates: What ship is this?

Phaedo: According to Athenian tradition, it is the ship in which **Theseus** went to Crete with the fourteen youths, where he saved their lives as well as his own. This tradition says that the Athenians made a vow to Apollo that if the youths were saved, they would send a yearly mission to Delos. This custom is still being followed, and the whole period of the voyage to and from Delos, which begins when the priest of Apollo crowns the stern of the ship, is a holy season. During this season, which is quite lengthy when the ship is hampered by contrary winds, the city is not allowed to be polluted by public executions. As I was saying, the ship was crowned on the day before the trial. That is the reason Socrates was in prison for such a lengthy time between his trial and his execution.

Echecrates: What about the circumstances surrounding his death, Phaedo? What was said or done? . . . If you have nothing to do, I wish that you would tell me what happened, as exactly as you can.

Phaedo: I have nothing at all to do, and will try to gratify your wish. . . . First of all, I had an unusual feeling at being in his company. Even though I was present at the death of a friend, Echecrates, I did not pity him. He died fearlessly—his words and bearing were so noble and gracious that to me he seemed blessed. I thought that in going to the other world he could not be without a divine call and that he would be happy, if any man ever was, when he arrived there. Therefore I did not feel sorrow for him as might have seemed natural at such an hour. Yet, I did not feel the degree of pleasure that I usually felt when we engaged in philosophical discourse. . . .

Echecrates: Well, what did you talk about?

Phaedo: I will begin at the beginning, and endeavor to repeat the entire conversation. On the previous days we had been in the habit of meeting early in the morning at the court in which the trial took place, which is not far from the prison. We used to wait there, talking with one another until the doors were opened, which was never very early. Then we went in and generally spent the day with Socrates. On the last morning we met earlier than usual, having heard when we left the prison the evening before that the sacred ship had returned from Delos. So we arranged to meet very early at the usual place. On our arrival at the prison, the jailer who answered the door did not let us in; instead he came out and told us to wait until he called us. "For the Eleven," he said, "are now with Socrates. They are taking off his chains and giving orders that he is to die today." He soon returned and said that we could go in. On entering we found that Socrates had just been released from his chains, and that Xanthippe, his wife, was sitting by him and holding his child in her arms. When she saw us she uttered a cry and spoke in the manner that you might expect from a woman, "Oh Socrates, this is the last time that you will converse with your friends or they with you." Socrates turned to Crito and said, "Crito, let someone take her home." She was crying out and beating herself as some of Crito's servants led her away. When she was gone, Socrates, who was sitting up on the bed, bent down to rub his leg. As he was doing so, he said: "How strange is the thing called pleasure, and how curiously related to pain, which might be thought to be the opposite of it. For they are never present to a man at the same instant, and yet he who pursues either is generally compelled to take the other. It is as if they have two bodies with a single head. I cannot help thinking that if Aesop had written about them, he would have made a fable in which god tries unsuccessfully to reconcile their strife. When he is unable to do so, he joins their heads together. This is the reason why one is always followed by the other, as my own experience clearly shows. For pleasure now follows the pain that was caused in my leg by the chain."

Upon this Cebes said, "I am glad, Socrates, that you have mentioned the name of Aesop. For it reminds me of a question that many people have asked. Only the day before yesterday Evenus the poet asked this question, and he will be sure to ask it again. If you would like me to have an answer ready for him, you must tell me how to respond. Evenus and others want to know why you were recently turning Aesop's fables into verse and composing that hymn in honor of Apollo, when you have never before written a line of poetry."

"Tell him the truth," Socrates replied. "I had no intention of rivaling him or his poems. I knew that to do so would be no easy task. But I wanted to make sure that I had not misinterpreted the meaning of certain recurring dreams that I have had, dreams that told me to 'follow the Muses and compose music.' These dreams came to me in different forms, but they always had this same message. Hitherto I had imagined that this was only intended to exhort and encourage me to pursue the study of philosophy, which is the noblest and best form of music, as I have done throughout my life. Thus I believed that the dream was bidding me do what I was already doing, in the same way that the competitor in a race is bidden by the spectators to run when he is already running. But I was not certain of this, for the dream might have meant 'music' in the popular sense of the word. Just in case this was the meaning of the dream, I decided to compose a few verses before I was executed. The festival of Apollo gave me the time to do this, and I began by writing a hymn in honor of Apollo. Then, believing that a true poet should not only put together words, but should also invent stories—a task for which I have no talent—I took some fables of Aesop that were at hand, and turned them into verse. Tell this to Evenus, Cebes, and bid him be of good cheer. Tell him also that if he is a wise man, he will follow me as soon as possible. I am likely going today, for the Athenians say that I must."

Simmias exclaimed, "What a message for such a man! Having been a frequent companion of his I can say that, from what I know of him, he will never take your advice unless forced to do so."

"Why?" asked Socrates. "Is Evenus not a philosopher?"

"I think that he is," said Simmias.

"Then he will be willing to die, like anyone else who understands the true nature of philosophy. But he will not take his own life, for that is held to be unlawful."

Here Socrates changed his position, putting his legs off the bed onto the floor. During the rest of the conversation he remained sitting.

"Why do you say," inquired Cebes, "that a man ought not to take his own life, but that the philosopher will be ready to follow the dying?"

"Cebes," said Socrates, "have you and Simmias, who are the disciples of Philolaus, never heard him speak of this?"

"Yes, but his language was obscure, Socrates."

". . . Well, as I am going to another place, it is appropriate for me to be thinking and talking of the nature of the journey which I am about to make. How could I better spend the time between now and the setting of the sun? . . . So, I want to prove to you, who will serve as my jury, that the real philosopher has reason to be happy when he is about to die, and that after death he may hope to obtain the greatest good in the other world. I will try to explain, Simmias and Cebes, how this can be. For I believe that the true follower of philosophy is likely to be misunderstood by other men, who do not perceive that he is always pursuing death and dying. But if it is true that he has looked forward to death his whole life, why, when the time of dying is at hand, should he recoil from that which he has always been pursuing and desiring?"

Simmias said laughingly, "Though I am not in a humorous mood, you have made me laugh, Socrates. For I cannot help thinking that when they hear your words the common people will say that you have accurately described philosophers. Indeed, they will say that they have discovered that what philosophers really desire while they are alive is death, and further that philosophers deserve the death they desire."

"They are right, Simmias, in thinking so, with the exception of the words 'they have discovered.' For they have not discovered either the nature of the death that the true philosopher deserves, or how he deserves or desires death. But enough about the common people. Let us rather discuss the matter among ourselves. Do we believe that there is such a thing as death?"

"To be sure," replied Simmias.

"Is dying not the separating of soul and body? And is death not the completion of this separation, when the soul is totally released from the body and the body is totally released from the soul? Is death anything but this?"

"No, it is nothing else," he replied.

"Well, see if we can also agree on the following question. If we can, it will also shed light on our present inquiry. Do you think that the philosopher should care about the so-called pleasures of eating and drinking?"

"Certainly not," answered Simmias.

"And what about the pleasures of sex and love? Should he care for them?"

"By no means."

"And will he think much of the other ways of indulging the body, for example the acquisition of costly clothing, sandals, or other adornments of the body? Rather than caring about such things, does he not despise anything in excess of the bare necessities? What do you say?"

"I would say that the true philosopher despises them."

"Would you not also say that he is principally concerned with the soul and not with the body? That he would like, as far as he can, to get away from the body and turn to the soul?"

"Quite true."

"Indeed, don't philosophers, more than other men, try to dissever the soul from communion with the body whenever possible?"

"Very true." . . .

"What again shall we say of the acquirement of knowledge? If it shares in the inquiry, is the body a hinderer or a helper? What I mean to ask is this. Are sight and hearing able to produce certainty? Are they not, as the poets are always telling us, inaccurate witnesses? But if sight and hearing, which you must admit are the most reliable of the senses, are inaccurate and indistinct, must not the other senses be even more suspect?"

"Certainly," he replied.

"Then when does the soul attain truth? It obviously cannot ever be when she attempts to do so in company with the body."

"True."

"Then must not truth be revealed to her in reasoning, if at all?"

"Yes."

"And isn't reasoning best when the soul is gathered into herself, without being distracted by sounds, sights, pain, or pleasure? In other words, isn't it best when the soul takes leave of the body, and has as little as possible to do with it, having no bodily sense or desire, but seeking true reality?"

"Certainly."

"And in doing this, doesn't the philosopher dishonor the body? Doesn't his soul avoid his body, desiring to be alone and by herself?"

"That is true."

"Well, consider the following questions, Simmias. Is there such a thing as absolute justice?"

"Assuredly there is."

"What about absolute beauty and absolute goodness?"

"Of course."

"But did you ever see any of them with your eyes?"

"Certainly not."

"Did you ever discern them with any other bodily sense? And I am asking not only about these, but also about absolute greatness, absolute health, and absolute strength—indeed about the true nature of anything that exists. Have you ever perceived the true nature of anything by means of the body? Isn't it rather the case that we can best know the true nature of something by ordering our thinking so that it is able to conceive the essence of that thing?"

"Certainly."

"Don't you think that a person would be most successful in doing this if he were to examine that thing solely with the pure light of reason, unaided by sight or any of the other senses? In other words, wouldn't that person be most successful who had gotten rid of his eyes and ears, indeed of his whole body, as far as this is possible, since eyes, ears, and body infect the soul and prevent it from acquiring truth and knowledge?"

"What you say rings true, Socrates," replied Simmias.

"When genuine philosophers consider all this, they will express themselves in words such as the following: 'Our thinking has led us to the conclusion that while we are in the body, our souls will be infected by the evils of the body, making it impossible for us to fully satisfy our greatest desire, the desire for truth. For the body is a source of endless trouble to us. It requires food and is subject to diseases— both of which interfere with the search for truth. It takes away the power of thinking by filling us with loves, lusts, fears, fancies, and endless foolery. Indeed, isn't it clear that wars, fightings, and factions are caused by the body and the lusts of the body? For wars are occasioned by the love of money, and money is acquired for the needs of the body. Because of all these impediments, we have no time to devote to philosophy. Or, worst of all, even if we do have some leisure for philosophical speculation, the body is always breaking in upon us, causing turmoil and confusion in our inquiries, and so distracting us that we are prevented from finding the truth. Experience has proven to us that if we are to have pure knowledge of anything we must get rid of the body and examine things by the soul alone. Only then will we be able to attain the wisdom we desire, the wisdom of which we say we are lovers. Obviously this cannot be attained while we live, but only after death. For if while in company with the body the soul cannot have pure knowledge, one of two things follows: either pure knowledge is not to be attained at all, or, if at all, after death. For only after death will the soul be separated from the body and exist in herself alone. In this present life, I suppose we come closest to pure knowledge when we have the least possible intercourse or communion with the body, thereby not being infected by the bodily nature, but purifying ourselves until the hour when god himself releases us. Then, having been liberated from the foolishness of the body and having become pure, we will be in the presence of others like us, and together we will know all things clearly through the light of truth. But the impure will not be there, for the impure are not permitted to approach the pure.' Aren't these the sort of words, Simmias, which the true lovers of knowledge think and say to one another?"

"Undoubtedly," Socrates.

"But if this is true, my friend, there is great reason to hope that by going where I am about to go, now that I have come to the end of my sojourn, I will attain what has been the pursuit of my life. Therefore I go on my way rejoicing, as will every man who believes that his mind has been made ready through purification."

"I agree," replied Simmias.

"But, as I asked before, isn't purification merely the separation of the soul from the body, that is, the habit of the soul avoiding contact with the body as far as possible, and gathering itself into itself so that it can dwell in its own place? Isn't purification the release of the soul from the chains of the body?"

"I believe it is," he said.

"And this separation and release of the soul from the body is termed death?"

"To be sure," he said.

"So the true philosophers, and they alone, are always seeking to release the soul. Is not the separation and release of the soul from the body their principal preoccupation?"

"That is true." . . .

"Since the true philosophers, Simmias, are always occupied in the practice of dying, they, of all men, find death to be the least alarming. . . . Many a man has been willing to go to **Hades** when motivated by the hope of there seeing and talking with an earthly love, a wife, or a son. Will he who is a true lover of wisdom, being also strongly persuaded that only in Hades can he fully enjoy her, still bemoan his death rather than departing with joy? Surely he will depart with joy, my friend, if he is a true philosopher. For he will have a firm conviction that there, and only there, can he find wisdom in her purity. And if this is true, it would be very absurd for him to be afraid of death." . . .

Cebes, who now entered the conversation, answered: "I agree, Socrates, with most of what you have said. But in matters pertaining to the soul, men are apt to be incredulous. They fear that when it has left the body its place may be nowhere, that on the very day of death the soul may perish and come to an end, that on being immediately released from the body it may be dispersed like smoke or air, vanishing away into nothingness. If it could only be collected into itself after it has obtained release from the evils of which you were speaking, Socrates, there would be good reason to hope that what you say is true. But surely much argument and many proofs are needed to show that when the man is dead his soul yet exists, and has any life force or intelligence."

"That is true, Cebes," said Socrates. "Shall we discuss the likelihood of these things happening?"

"I am sure," said Cebes, "that I would greatly like to know your opinion about them." . . .

"Let us then consider whether after death the souls of men exist in Hades. I recall an ancient doctrine that claims that they go from this world into the other world, and return again to this world, being born from the dead. Now if it is true that the living come from the dead, then our souls must exist in the other world. For if they do not, how could they have been born again? This would provide conclusive proof, if there were any real evidence that the living are born from the dead. But if this is not so, then other arguments will have to be found."

"Very true," replied Cebes.

"Then let us consider the whole question, not only in relation to man, but also in relation to animals, plants, and everything else of which there is generation. This will make the proof easier. Are not all things which have opposites generated out of their opposites? I mean things such as good and evil, just and unjust; indeed, there are innumerable other pairs of opposites which are generated out of one another. I want to show that in all opposites there is of necessity a similar alternation. For example, when anything becomes larger, must it not have first been smaller in order to become larger?"

"True."

"And must not whatever becomes smaller have first been larger in order to become smaller?"

"Yes."

"And isn't the weaker generated from the stronger, and the swifter from the slower?"

"Very true."

"And the worse from the better, and the more just from the less just?"

"Of course."

"Are we convinced that everything is generated in this way, opposites from opposites?"

"Yes."

"And in this universal pattern of generation, are there not two continuous intermediate processes marking the movement from one opposite to the other and back again? For example, between the opposites of larger and smaller, do we not find the intermediate processes of increasing and diminishing?"

"Yes," he said.

"And there are many other processes, such as separating and combining, cooling and heating, which equally involve a passage into and out of one another. Even though we do not always have names for these processes, doesn't it necessarily hold true for all opposites that they are really generated out of one another, and that there are processes marking the movement from each of them to the other?"

"Very true," he replied.

"Well, is there not an opposite to being alive, as sleeping is the opposite of waking?"

"There is," he said.

"And what is it?"

"Being dead," he answered.

"If these are opposites, are they not generated the one from the other, and do they not have their two intermediate processes also?"

"Of course."

"Now," said Socrates, "I will analyze one of the two pairs of opposites which I have mentioned to you, as well as its intermediate processes, and I will ask you to analyze the other. One of them is the opposition between sleeping and waking. The state of sleeping is the opposite of the state of waking, and sleeping is generated out of waking and waking out of sleeping. The process of generation in the first case is falling asleep, and in the other case it is waking up. Do you agree?"

"I fully agree."

"Now, you analyze life and death in the same manner. Isn't death the opposite of life?"

"Yes."

"Are they generated one from the other?"

"Yes."

"What is generated from the living?"

"The dead."

"And what from the dead?"

"In answering, I can only say the living."

"Then the living, whether things or persons, Cebes, are generated from the dead?"

"That is clear," he replied.

"Doesn't this imply that our souls must exist in the world below?"

"It does."

"And the occurrence of one of the two processes in this case is evident, is it not? For surely the process of dying is evident?"

"Surely," he said.

"What then results from this? Shall we exclude the complementary process? Shall we suppose that nature walks on one leg only? Must we not rather assign a process of generation that complements that of dying?"

"We must," he replied.

"What is that process?"

"Coming to life again."

"And if there is such a thing as coming to life, must it not be the birth of the dead into the world of the living?"

"Quite true."

"Then we arrive at the conclusion that the living come from the dead, just as the dead come from the living. But we said earlier that if this were true, it would afford a most certain proof that the souls of the dead exist in some place from which they are born again."

"Yes, Socrates," he said. "This conclusion seems to necessarily follow from what we have admitted." . . .

"Yes, Cebes, in my opinion, it is and must be so. We have not been deluded in making these admissions. I am confident that there truly is such a thing as living again, that the living spring from the dead, and that the souls of the dead do exist." . . .

"In addition, Socrates," said Cebes, "the truth of your favorite doctrine, namely that knowledge is simply **recollection,** provides another proof of the soul's immortality. For this doctrine implies a previous time in which we have learned what we now recollect, and this would be impossible if our soul had not existed in some place before taking human form."

Simmias, interposing at this point, asked: "What arguments, Cebes, are urged in favor of this doctrine of recollection? I am not very sure at the moment that I remember them."

"One excellent proof," said Cebes, "is afforded by questions. When you ask a person a question in a right way, he will give the correct answer. But how could he do this unless there were knowledge and right reason already in him?" . . .

"If you do not believe that knowledge is recollection, Simmias," said Socrates, "I would ask you whether you may not agree with me when you look at the matter in another way."

"It's not that I do not believe this doctrine of recollection," said Simmias, "but I want to have this doctrine brought to my own recollection. From what Cebes has said, I am beginning to remember and be convinced. However, I would still like to hear what you were going to say."

"This is what I would say," Socrates replied. "We would agree, if I am not mistaken, that what a man remembers he must have known at some previous time."

"Very true."

"And do we not also agree in using the term 'recollection' to refer to knowledge attained in this way? In other words, suppose that when a person sees, hears, or in any way perceives one thing, he not only knows that thing, but has a conception of something else that differs from the thing he sees, hears,

or perceives. May we not say that he recollects that of which he has the conception?"

"What do you mean?"

"What I mean may be illustrated by considering the following example. Is the knowledge of a lyre different from the knowledge of a man?"

"It is."

"Yet what do lovers feel when they recognize a lyre, or a garment, or anything else which their beloved has been in the habit of using? Does not their knowledge of the lyre lead them to form an image of the youth to whom the lyre belongs? This is recollection. Similarly, any one who sees Simmias may remember Cebes. There are endless examples of this type of thing happening."

"Endless, indeed," replied Simmias.

"Recollection is most commonly a process of recovering something that has been forgotten through time and inattention."

"Very true," he said.

"Well, may you not also remember a man from seeing a picture of a house or a lyre? Or remember Cebes from seeing a picture of Simmias?"

"You may."

"And may you not also be led to the recollection of Simmias himself?"

"Quite so."

"In all these cases, the recollection may be derived from things either like or unlike?"

"Indeed, it may."

"When the recollection is derived from like things, another consideration is sure to arise. We may ask whether the remembered likeness falls short, in any degree, of that which is recollected."

"Very true," he said.

"We can proceed a step further, and ask whether there is such a thing as equality—not the equality of one piece of wood or stone with another—but absolute equality. Do we admit that absolute equality exists?"

"Yes we do," replied Simmias. "And we swear to its existence, with utmost confidence."

"Do we know what absolute equality is?"

"We surely do," he said.

"From where did we obtain this knowledge? Did we not see equalities of material things, such as pieces of wood and stones, and gather from them an idea of an equality that differs from these equalities? For do you not see that there is a difference? Look at the matter in this way. Do not the same pieces of wood or stone appear at one time equal, and at another time unequal?"

"That is certain."

"But does it make sense to say that absolute equality admits of inequality?"

"Impossible, Socrates."

"Then these so-called equal things are not the same as absolute equality?"

"Clearly not the same, Socrates."

"And yet from these concrete things, which are not absolutely equal, you derived the knowledge of absolute equality."

"Very true," he said. . . .

"But what would you say of the equal portions of the wood or stone, or of other material things? What is the impression produced by them? Are they equal to the same degree as absolute equality is equal? Or do they fall short of this perfect equality?"

"They fall very short of it," he said.

"But when anyone looks at an object and observes that the object aims at being some other thing, but falls short of it, must not he who makes this observation have had a previous knowledge of that of which the seen object falls short?"

"Certainly."

"Does this not apply in our previous example of equal things and absolute equality?"

"It applies precisely."

"Then we must have had knowledge of absolute equality prior to the time when we first saw equal things, and reflected that they strive to attain absolute equality, but fall short of it."

"Very true."

"But don't we also recognize that we have not attained our notion of equality, nor could we have attained it, except through the medium of sight, touch, or one of the other senses?" . . .

"Yes, Socrates." . . .

"So, it must be through the senses that we derived the knowledge that all sensible things aim at an absolute equality of which they fall short."

"Yes."

"Then before we began to see, hear, or perceive in any way, we must have had a knowledge of absolute equality. Otherwise we could not have used that standard in relation to the equals known through the senses, which we claim aspire to absolute equality, but fall short of it."

"No other inference can be drawn from the previous statements."

"But did we not see, hear, and have the use of our other senses as soon as we were born?"

"Certainly."

"Then we must have acquired the knowledge of absolute equality at some previous time?"

"Yes."

"Before we were born, I suppose?"

"It seems so."

"But if we must admit that we acquired this knowledge before we were born, and were born having the use of it, we must do likewise, not only for equality and for the greater or the less, but for all absolute standards. For we are not speaking only of equality, but also of absolute beauty, goodness, justice, and piety—indeed of everything that we stamp with the name of 'essence' in our discussions. May we not say with certainty that we acquire the knowledge of all this before birth?"

"We may." . . .

"Then must we not also say, Simmias, that the existence of these absolute essences, such as absolute beauty and goodness, the knowledge of which we could only have acquired before birth, . . . implies that our souls must have had a prior existence? But if these essences do not exist, would there be any necessity to our argument? In other words, doesn't the argument that our souls must have existed before we were born logically depend on the argument that these essences must have existed before we were born, such that if the essences did not exist, we would have no reason for believing that our souls existed before our birth?"

"Yes, Socrates, I am convinced that there is precisely the same necessity for believing in the one as for believing in the other. The argument for the existence of the soul before birth cannot be separated from the argument for the existence of the essences of which you speak. But since I firmly believe that these essences of beauty, goodness, and so forth have a most real and absolute existence, I am satisfied with the proof."

"Well, but is Cebes equally satisfied? For I must convince him too."

"I think," said Simmias, "that Cebes is satisfied. Although he is the most incredulous of mortals, I believe that he is sufficiently convinced of the existence of the soul before birth. But that the soul will continue to exist after death is not yet proven even to my own satisfaction. I cannot get rid of the popular belief to which Cebes was referring, the belief that when a man dies his soul will be dispersed and thus cease to exist. For even if it existed before entering the human body . . . , why, after having entered the body and gone out again, may not the soul be destroyed and come to an end?"

"Very true, Simmias," said Cebes. "About half of what was required has been proven, namely, that ours souls existed before we were born. But the other half—that the soul will exist after death as well as before birth—must still be supplied. When that is given the demonstration will be complete."

"But if you put the two arguments together, Simmias and Cebes, the proof has been already provided," said Socrates. "I mean if you consider the argument that we just concluded, along with the earlier one in which we admitted that everything living is born of the dead. For if the soul exists before birth, and in coming to life and being born can be born only from death and dying, must she not continue to exist after death, since she has to be born again? Surely the proof which you desire has been already furnished. Still I suspect that you and Simmias would be glad to probe the argument further. Like children, you are haunted with a fear that when the soul leaves the body, the wind may really blow her away and scatter her, especially if a man happens to die in a great storm and not when the sky is calm."

Cebes smiled and said: "Then, Socrates, you must convince us that our fears are unwarranted, although, strictly speaking, they are not our fears. For there is a child within us to whom death is a sort of hobgoblin, and we must persuade him not to be afraid when he is alone in the dark." . . .

"Can we not do this," asked Socrates, "by describing the nature of a thing that is liable to be scattered, by asking for what type of thing we should fear dispersion, and for what type we should not fear dispersion? Having done this, we may proceed to inquire which type the soul resembles. Our hopes and fears about our own souls will depend upon the results of this inquiry."

"I agree," said Cebes.

"Now something composite, being compounded of parts, may be supposed to be dissoluble into the parts of which it is composed. But if anything exists which is not compounded of parts, that thing is most likely to be indissoluble."

"Yes, I should imagine so," replied Cebes.

"And the uncompounded may be assumed to be the same and unchanging, whereas the compounded is always changing and never the same."

"I agree," he said.

"Then let us now return to the previous discussion. Are those absolute essences, such as absolute equality, beauty, and so forth, ever liable to any degree of change? Or does each of them always remain what it is, having the same simple self-existence and unchanging form, never admitting of any variation whatsoever?"

"They must be always the same, Socrates," replied Cebes.

"And what would you say about the many particular instances of beauty, such as beautiful men, horses, garments, and so forth? Or about the particular instances of equality, or about the particular instances of any other of the absolute essences? Are all these particular instances unchanging and always the same, or quite the reverse? May they not rather be described as almost always changing and hardly ever the same, either with themselves or with one another?"

"The latter," replied Cebes. "They are always in a state of change."

"And these particular instances can be touched and seen and perceived with the senses, while the unchanging essences can only be perceived with the mind. Are the latter not invisible to our sight?"

"They are," said Cebes.

"Then, should we suppose that there are two sorts of existing things, one visible and the other invisible?"

"We should."

"The visible constantly changing, and the invisible unchanging?"

"That also may be supposed."

"And further, is not one part of us body, and another part soul?"

"To be sure."

"To which class is the body more alike and akin?"

"Clearly to the visible. No one can doubt that."

"And is the soul visible or invisible?" . . .

"Invisible." . . .

"Then the soul is more like the invisible, and the body more like the visible?"

"That follows necessarily," Socrates.

"But did we not admit some time ago that when it uses the body as an instrument of perception, that is to say, when it uses the sense of sight, hearing, or some other sense, the soul is then also dragged by the body into the region of the changeable? And that being corrupted by change, the soul is then confused, and wanders around like a drunkard?"

"We did."

"But when the soul reflects by itself, it passes into the other world, the region of purity, eternity, immortality, and unchangeableness, which are her kindred. When it is by itself and is not let or hindered, it ceases from its erring ways, and remains in this other world—an unchangeable being communing with the unchangeable. And this is the state of the soul that we call wisdom."

"That is well and truly said, Socrates," replied Cebes.

"So, to which class is the soul more nearly alike and akin, as far as may be inferred from this argument, as well as from the preceding one?"

"Socrates, I think that anyone who has understood the arguments, even the most dimwitted person, must admit that the soul will be infinitely more like the unchangeable."

"And the body is more like the changing?"

"Yes."

"Consider the matter from one more perspective. When the soul and the body are united, nature orders the soul to rule and govern, and the body to obey and serve. Now which of these two functions is akin to the divine and which to the mortal? Does not the divine appear to you to be that which naturally orders and rules, and the mortal to be that which is subject and serves?"

"True."

"And which does the soul resemble?"

"The soul resembles the divine, and the body the mortal. There can be no doubt about that, Socrates."

"Then, Cebes, is it not the conclusion of all we have said that the soul resembles the divine, the immortal, the intelligible, the uniform, the indissoluble and the unchangeable, whereas the body resembles the human, the mortal, the unintelligible, the multiform, the dissoluble, and the changeable? Can this, my dear Cebes, be denied?"

"It cannot."

"But if this is so, isn't the body liable to speedy dissolution and isn't the soul almost or altogether indissoluble?"

"Certainly."

"Of course you have observed that after a man is dead, the body or visible part of him, which remains in the visible world and is called a corpse, is not dissolved or decomposed at once, even though it is the nature of the body to be dissolved, decomposed and dissipated. On the contrary, if a man has a sound body and dies at the favorable season of the year, his body may remain for quite some time, or if his body is shrunk and embalmed, as is done in Egypt, it may remain almost intact through infinite ages. And even in decay, there are still some parts, such as the bones and ligaments, which are practically indestructible. Don't you agree?"

"Yes."

"Then is it likely that when the soul, which is invisible, pure, and noble, journeys to the place of the true Hades, which is also invisible, pure, and noble, on its way to the good and wise god—a journey that, if god wills, my soul will soon undertake—is it likely, if this is the nature and origin of the soul, that it will be blown away and destroyed as soon as it leaves the body, as the many say? That can never be, my dear Simmias and Cebes. The truth is rather that the soul which is pure at departing and draws after it no bodily taint, having never voluntarily had connection with the body during life, but constantly avoiding the body and keeping to itself, in other words the soul which has been a true disciple of philosophy and therefore has in fact been always engaged in the practice of dying . . . that soul, I say, departs to a world akin to itself, a world that is invisible, divine, immortal, and wise. And arriving in this world, happiness is guaranteed to it, since being released from the error and folly of men, as well as from their fears, wild passions, and other human ills, it dwells forever . . . in company with the gods. Is not this true, Cebes?"

"Yes," said Cebes, "beyond a doubt."

"But do you suppose that the soul which has been polluted by the time of its journey will depart pure and uncorrupted? I mean the soul which has become polluted by always being the companion and servant of the body, and by being in love with and fascinated by the body and its desires and pleasures, until the soul is finally led to believe that truth only exists in a material form, which a man may touch, see, taste, and use for the purposes of his lusts—in short, the soul that has been conditioned to hate, fear, and avoid whatever is dark and invisible to the senses, and is made intelligible only by philosophy."

"It is not possible that it will depart uncorrupted," he replied.

"On the contrary, it will be bound to the corporeal, which has penetrated into the soul's nature because of its continual association with and concern for the body."

"Very true."

"And this corporal element, my friend, is heavy, weighty, earthy, and oppressive. As such, it is that element by which a soul, being afraid of the invisible and of Hades, is dragged down again into the visible world, where it prowls about tombs and sepulchres. For we are told that souls which have not departed pure, but retain some element of the visible, can be seen near graveyards."

"That is very likely, Socrates."

"Yes, that is very likely, Cebes. And these must be the souls, not of the good, but of the evil, which are compelled to wander about such places in payment of the penalty of their former evil way of life. They continue to wander until their craving after the corporal, which never leaves them, finally causes them to be imprisoned in another body. And the type of their new prison is determined by the sort of nature they developed in their former lives."

"What do you mean, Socrates?"

"What I mean is that men who have practiced gluttony, wantonness, and drunkenness, having had no thought of avoiding them, would pass into asses and animals of that sort. What do you think?"

"I think such an opinion is exceedingly probable."

"And those who have chosen a life of injustice, tyranny, and violence will be reborn as wolves, hawks, or kites. Can you think of a more appropriate form?"

"No," said Cebes, "they will have such natures as these."

"And there is no difficulty," Socrates said, "in assigning to all of them bodies answering to their several natures and propensities."

"There is not," he said.

"I believe that the happiest of these souls will be the ones who have practiced the civil and social virtues, such as temperance and justice, having acquired these virtues by habit and custom without the aid of philosophy and reason."

"Why are they the happiest?"

"Because they will likely be reborn as some gentle and social creature, such as a bee, wasp, or ant. They may even pass back again into the form of a man who is just and moderate."

"Very likely."

"But only the lover of knowledge, who has studied philosophy and who is entirely pure at the time of his departure, is allowed to enter the company of the gods. This is the reason, Simmias and Cebes, why the true practitioners of philosophy abstain from all fleshly lusts, refusing to give themselves up to them. It is not because they fear poverty or the ruin of their families, like the lovers of money and the people in general. Nor is it because they dread dishonor and disgrace, like the lovers of power or honor."

"No, Socrates, that would not become them," said Cebes.

"No indeed," he replied. "Therefore they who have any care of their own souls, and do not merely live according to the dictates and desires of the body, say farewell to all this—they will not walk in the ways of the blind. But when philosophy offers them purification and release from evil, they do not resist her influence, but follow philosophy wherever it leads them."

"What do you mean, Socrates?"

"I will tell you," he said. "The lovers of knowledge are conscious that the soul was simply fastened and glued to the body. Until philosophy entered the soul, it could only view real existence through the bars of a prison, not in and through itself. It was wallowing in the mire of every sort of ignorance, and by reason of lust had become the principal accomplice in its own captivity. This was the soul's original state. Then, as I was saying, and as the lovers of knowledge are well aware, philosophy, seeing the terrible state of the soul's confinement . . . receives and gently comforts it, seeking the soul's release by pointing out that the eye, the ear, and the other senses are full of deception. Philosophy persuades the soul to withdraw from the senses, using them only when absolutely necessary. It encourages the soul to become gathered up and collected into itself, and to trust in itself and its own pure apprehension of pure existence, but to mistrust whatever comes to it through other channels and is subject to variation. For such things are visible and tangible, but what the soul sees by itself is intelligible and invisible. And the soul of the true philosopher thinks that it ought not to resist this deliverance, and therefore abstains from pleasures, desires, pains, and fears, as far as it is able. For it knows that when a man has great joys, sorrows, fears, or desires, he suffers not merely the sort of evil which might be expected—as for example, the loss of his health or property, which he has sacrificed to his lusts—but also the greatest and worst of all evils, of which he never thinks."

"What is this evil, Socrates?" asked Cebes.

"The evil is that when the feeling of pleasure or pain is most intense, the soul imagines the objects of this intense feeling to be the clearest and truest. But this is not so, since these are merely the things of sight."

"Very true."

"And is not this the state in which the soul is most enthralled by the body?"

"How so?"

"Because each pleasure and pain is like a nail which nails and rivets the soul to the body, until it becomes like the body, believing that to be true which the body affirms to be true. And from agreeing with the body and having the same delights, the soul is obliged to have the same habits and haunts, and is not likely ever to be pure when it departs to Hades. Rather, being infected by the corporeal, the soul sinks into another body, in which it germinates and grows. Therefore, it is wholly excluded from the divine, the pure, and the unchanging."

Questions for Thought

1. Do you agree with what Socrates/Plato says about the fear of dying? Do you fear your own death? Why or why not?
2. Do you agree with Socrates'/Plato's claim that everything is generated from its opposite? Can you think of any examples of generation where this is not the case?
3. Which of Socrates'/Plato's arguments for the immortality of the soul seems most convincing? Which of them seems least convincing? Explain your answers.
4. Do you agree with Socrates/Plato that there are essential differences between your soul and your body? If so, can you think of other differences that Socrates/Plato fails to mention?
5. How does what Socrates/Plato says about the destiny of the soul compare with or differ from your own views on this matter?

7 Of the Real Distinction between Mind and Body

RENÉ DESCARTES

René Descartes (1596–1650), who is often referred to as the father of modern philosophy, was born in the small town of La Haye in France. At the age of eight, Descartes was sent to the newly opened Jesuit college of La Flèche. Although he later expressed disdain for most of the education he received from the Jesuits, Descartes did develop an intense interest in mathematics while attending the college. This interest later reached fruition when Descartes discovered the fundamental principles of analytic geometry.

After leaving the college of La Flèche, Descartes went to the University of Poitiers, from which he received a law degree in 1616. This was followed by a period of travel and military adventure. In 1618, Descartes joined the army of the prince of Orange of Holland, and in 1619 he served in the army of the duke of Bavaria. During one of these military campaigns, Descartes had a visionary dream that he interpreted as a divine revelation that his true goal in life was to develop a unified science, a science that would bring together the various branches of knowledge into a comprehensive explanation of all phenomena. Descartes' first attempt to achieve this goal, the never-completed *Regulae ad Directionem Ingenii* (*Rules for the Direction of the Mind*), was written approximately ten years after his dream. Descartes spent those ten years traveling around Europe.

While residing in Paris in 1628, Descartes was involved in a famous debate about the nature of science. Later that year, he moved to Amsterdam, where, aside from a few brief excursions, he lived for the next twenty-one years. In Amsterdam, he worked further on his goal of developing a unified science while writing the books that established his reputation as a philosopher and mathematician. These included *Discours de la méthode* (1637; *Discourse on Method*), *Meditationes de Prima Philosophia* (1641; *Meditations on First Philosophy*), *Principia Philosophiae* (1644; *Principles of Philosophy*), and *Les Passions de l'âme* (1649; *The Passions of the Soul*).

In 1649, Descartes received an invitation from Queen Christina of Sweden to join her court in Stockholm as a philosophical tutor. With reluctance, Descartes accepted the queen's invitation. This decision proved tragic when he died of pneumonia in Stockholm the following winter.

In the following selections from his writings, Descartes formulates a view of human identity that is very similar to that of Plato. Like Plato, Descartes suggests that our identities consist of two very different **substances:** body and soul. One of these substances (body) is divisible and extended in space, whereas the other substance (soul) is not.

After affirming this distinction in a brief excerpt from the *Meditations on First Philosophy,* Descartes goes on to discuss some of its ramifications in the other two excerpts included here. Examining the functions of soul and body, he concludes that thinking is found only in the soul, whereas natural heat and the movement of the limbs proceed from the body. Indeed, as is evident throughout his writing, Descartes suggests that the soul is essentially a thinking thing, while the body is essentially a mechanical thing. In one place, he compares the body to a watch, arguing that human death results when the body decays or runs down, thereby causing the soul to abandon the body. In another place, he says that the human body is a machine created by God, a machine differing from those created by humans only in terms of the complexity of the workmanship involved.

Whereas Plato seems to have more or less skirted the problem of how the soul interacts with the body, Descartes is acutely aware of this problem. Saying that "we do not observe the existence of any subject that more immediately acts upon our soul than the body to which it is joined" and noting also that the soul is not situated in the body like a pilot in his ship, Descartes traces the interaction of soul and body to a gland in the center of the brain. It is in this gland that bodily motions are transformed into passions of the soul, and that actions or desires of the soul are transformed into bodily movement.

Finally, the latter of these selections also contains Descartes' well-known statement of the differences between human and nonhuman animals (or "brutes" as he calls them). Although the human body is in many respects similar to animal bodies, Descartes argues that animals act solely by nature or instinct, whereas humans are capable of using reason to deal with the diverse problems they face. Moreover, while animals may make diverse sounds, they are incapable of communicating through the use of language, as even the simplest human is able to do. In the final analysis, animals are sophisticated machines created by God, machines that lack rational souls and that thus, unlike humans, have no hope of immortality.

Questions for Reading

1. What, according to Descartes, are the essential differences between soul and body?
2. What are some of the analogies that Descartes uses in these selections? What are these analogies intended to show?
3. How does Descartes explain the interaction of soul and body?
4. What, according to Descartes, are the essential differences between humans and nonhuman animals?
5. In what ways are Descartes' views on soul and body similar to the views of Plato? In what ways are they different?

FROM *MEDITATION VI*

IN ORDER TO BEGIN THIS EXAMINATION, I SAY HERE that, in the first place, there is a great difference between mind and body. For body, by its very nature, is always divisible, while mind is entirely indivisible. As a matter of fact, when I consider the mind, that is to say myself inasmuch as I am only a thinking thing, I cannot distinguish any parts in myself; rather, I clearly apprehend myself to be one and entirely complete. Moreover, although the whole mind seems to be united to the whole body, if a foot, an arm, or some other part is separated from my body, I am aware that nothing has been taken away from my mind. In addition, the faculties of the mind, such as willing, feeling, and conceiving, cannot properly be said to be its parts, for it is one and the same mind that employs itself in willing, in feeling and in conceiving. But it is quite otherwise with corporeal or extended objects, for I can imagine none of these that cannot be easily divided into parts by my mind, which shows me clearly that such objects are divisible. This would be sufficient to teach me that the mind or soul of man is entirely different from the body, if I had not already learned it from other sources.

FROM THE PASSIONS OF THE SOUL

Next I note also that we do not observe the existence of any subject that more immediately acts upon our soul than the body to which it is joined. Consequently, we must consider that what constitutes a passion[1] in the soul is, commonly speaking, an action in the body. Thus, there is no better means of arriving at a knowledge of our passions than to examine the difference that exists between soul and body, so that we can discover to which of the two we must attribute each one of the functions which are within us.

As to this, we will not have much difficulty if we realize that all that we experience as being in us, which observation shows may exist in wholly inanimate bodies, must be attributed to our body alone. On the other hand, all that is in us, which we cannot in any way conceive as possibly pertaining to a body, must be attributed to our soul.

Thus, because we have no conception of the body as thinking in any way, we have reason to believe that every kind of thought that exists in us belongs to the soul. However, because we do not doubt either that there are inanimate bodies which

This is the editor's revised version of selections from René Descartes, The Philosophical Works of Descartes, *translated by E. S. Haldane and G. R. T. Ross, Cambridge University Press, 1911–1912.*

can move in as many or in more diverse modes than our bodies, or that such bodies can also have as much or more heat than our bodies (experience demonstrating this to us in flame, which of itself has much more heat and movement than any of our members), we must believe that all the heat and all the movements which are in us pertain only to body, since these things do not depend on thought at all.

By this means we shall avoid a very considerable error into which many have fallen. . . . It arises from the fact that from observing that all dead bodies are devoid of heat and consequently of movement, it has been thought that it was the absence of soul which caused these movements and this heat to cease, and thus, without any reason, that our natural heat and all the movements of our body depend on the soul. In fact, we ought to believe the contrary of this, namely, that the soul quits us on death only because this heat ceases, while the organs that serve to move the body disintegrate.

In order that we may avoid this error, let us consider that death never comes to pass by reason of the soul, but only because one of the principal parts of the body decays. We may judge, then, that the body of a living man differs from that of a dead man, just as a working watch . . . differs from one that is broken.

In order to render this more intelligible, I shall here explain in a few words the whole method in which the bodily machine is composed. There is no one who does not already know that there are in us a heart, a brain, a stomach, muscles, nerves, arteries, veins, and such things. We also know that the food that we eat descends into the stomach and bowels where its juice, passing into the liver and into all the veins, mingles with, and thereby increases the quantity of the blood which they contain. . . . We further know that all the movements of the members depend on the muscles, and that these muscles are so mutually related to one another that, when the one is contracted, it draws toward itself the part of the body to which it is attached, causing the opposite muscle at the same time to become elongated. . . . We know finally that all these movements of the muscles, as also all the senses, depend on the nerves, which resemble small filaments, or little tubes, which all proceed from the brain, and thus like the brain contain a certain very subtle air or wind that is called the animal spirits. . . .

After having thus considered all the functions which pertain to the body alone, it is easy to recognize that there is nothing in us that we ought to attribute to our soul except our thoughts. These are mainly of two sorts, the one being the actions of the soul, and the other its passions. Those that I call its actions are all our desires, because we find by experience that they proceed directly from our soul and appear to depend on it alone. On the other hand, we may usually call passions all those kinds of perception or forms of knowledge that are found in us, because it is often not our soul which makes them what they are. Rather, the soul always receives them from the things that are represented by them. . . .

But in order to understand all these things more perfectly, we must know that the soul is really joined to the whole body, and that we cannot, properly speaking, say that it exists in any one of its parts to the exclusion of the others. This is because the soul is one and indivisible, . . . and because it is of such a nature that it has no relation to extension, nor dimensions, nor other properties of the matter of which the body is composed. . . . This follows from the fact that we could not in any way conceive of the half or the third of a soul, nor of the space it occupies, and from the fact that it does not become smaller owing to the cutting off of some portion of the body. Rather, the soul separates itself entirely from the body when the union of the body's assembled organs is dissolved.

It is likewise necessary to know that although the soul is joined to the whole body, there is yet a certain part of the body in which the soul exercises its functions more particularly than in all the others. It is usually believed that this part of the body is the brain, or possibly the heart. . . . However, in examining this matter with care, it seems that I had clearly ascertained that the part of the body in which the soul exercises its functions immediately is neither the heart nor the whole of the brain, but merely the most inward of all its parts, namely, a certain very small gland which is situated in the middle of its substance. This small gland is so suspended above the duct whereby the animal spirits in its anterior cavities have communication with those in the posterior, that the slightest movements that take place in it may alter very greatly the course of these spirits. Reciprocally, the smallest changes that occur in the course of the spirits may do much to change the movements of this gland. . . .

Let us conclude, then, that the soul has its principal seat in the little gland that exists in the middle of the brain. From here it radiates forth through all the remainder of the body by means of the animal spirits, nerves, and even the blood, which, participating in the impressions of the spirits, can carry them by the arteries into all the members. . . . Let us here add that the small gland which is the main seat of the soul is so suspended between the cavities containing the spirits that it can be moved by them in many different ways, . . . for the nature of the soul is such that it receives in itself as many diverse impressions . . . as there are diverse movements in this gland. Reciprocally, the machine of the body is so formed that whenever this gland is diversely moved by the soul, . . . it thrusts the spirits that surround it towards the pores of the brain, and these spirits are then conducted by the nerves into the muscles, by which means it causes them to move the limbs.

FROM DISCOURSE ON METHOD

I had explained all these matters in some detail in the Treatise that I formerly intended to publish. Afterwards I had shown there what the fabric of the nerves and muscles of the human body must be, so that the animal spirits contained in it . . . can cause the members of the body to move in as many diverse ways . . . as happen in us without the direction of our free will. This will not seem strange to those who know how many different *automata* or moving machines can be made by the industry of man, even when using only a very few parts compared to the great multitude of bones, muscles, nerves, arteries, veins, and other parts that are found in the body of each animal. From this aspect the body is regarded as a machine which, having been made by the hands of God, is incomparably better arranged, and possesses in itself movements which are much more admirable, than any of those which can be invented by man. At this point, I specially stopped to show that if there had been such machines, possessing the organs and outward form of a monkey or some

other animal without reason, we should not have had any means of ascertaining that they were not of the same nature as those animals. On the other hand, if there were machines which bore a resemblance to our body and imitated our actions as far as it was morally possible to do so, we should always have two very certain means by which to recognize that, for all that, they were not real men. The first means is that they could never use speech or other signs as we do when placing our thoughts on record for the benefit of others. For we can easily understand that a machine can be constructed so that it can utter words, and even emit some responses to actions of a corporeal kind that bring about a change in its organs. For instance, if it is touched in a particular part, it may ask what we wish to say to it; if it is touched in another part, it may exclaim that it is being hurt. But it never happens that it arranges its speech in various ways, in order to reply appropriately to everything that may be said in its presence, as even the lowest type of man can do. The second means is that, although machines can perform certain things as well as or perhaps better than any of us can do, they infallibly fall short in others. Because of this, we may discover that they did not act from knowledge, but only from the disposition of their organs. For while reason is a universal instrument that is useful for all contingencies, these organs have need of some special adaptation for every particular action. From this it follows that it is impossible for there to be sufficient diversity in any machine to allow it to act, in all the events of life, in the same way as our reason causes us to act.

By these two means we may also recognize the difference that exists between men and brutes. For it is a very remarkable fact that there are none so depraved and stupid, even idiots, that they cannot arrange different words together, forming of them a statement by which they make known their thoughts. On the other hand, there is no other animal, however perfect and fortunately circumstanced it may be, that can do the same. It is not the lack of organs that causes this, for it is evident that magpies and parrots are able to utter words just like us, and yet they cannot speak as we do, that is, so as to give evidence that they think of what they say. On the other hand, men who are born deaf and dumb, and who thus lack the organs that serve others for talking . . . are in the habit of inventing certain signs by which they make themselves understood by those who, being usually in their company, have leisure to learn their language. This does not merely show that the brutes have less reason than men, but that they do not have reason at all, since it is clear that very little is required in order to be able to talk. And when we notice the inequality that exists between animals of the same species, as well as between men, and observe that some are more capable of receiving instruction than others, it is not credible that a monkey or a parrot, selected as the most perfect of its species, should not in these matters equal the stupidest child to be found . . . , unless the soul of the brute were of an entirely different nature from ours. And we ought not confound speech with natural movements that betray passions and that may be imitated by machines as well as be manifested by animals. Nor must we think, as did some of the ancients, that brutes talk and we do not understand their language. For if this were true, since they have many organs that are similar to our own, they could communicate their thoughts to us just as easily as to those of their own species. It is also a very remarkable fact that although there are many animals that exhibit more dexterity than we do in some of their actions, we at the same time observe that they do not manifest any dexterity at all in many others. Hence the fact that they do some actions better than we do does not prove that they are endowed with mind, for in this case they would have more reason than any of us, and would surpass us in all other things as well. It rather shows that they have no reason at all, and that it is nature acting in them according to the disposition of their organs. Indeed, it is similar to the case of a clock, which being composed only of wheels and weights, is able to tell the hours and measure the time more correctly than we can do with all our wisdom.

I had described after this the rational soul and shown that it could not be in any way derived from the power of matter, . . . but that it must be expressly created. I showed, too, that it is not sufficient that the soul be lodged in the human body like a pilot in his ship, unless perhaps for the moving of its members. Rather, it is necessary that it should also be joined and united more closely to the body in order to have sensations and appetites . . . and thus to form a true man.

In conclusion, I have here enlarged a little on the subject of the soul, because it is one of the greatest importance. For next to the error of those who deny God . . . , there is no belief that is more likely to lead feeble minds from the straight path of virtue, than to believe that the soul of the brute is of the same nature as our own, and that, in consequence, after this life we have no more to fear or to hope for than do flies and ants. As a matter of fact, when one comes to know how greatly they differ, one can understand much better the reasons that prove that our soul is in its nature entirely independent of the body, and in consequence that it is not liable to die with it. And then, inasmuch as we observe no other causes capable of destroying it, we are naturally inclined to judge that it is immortal.

NOTE

1. In this text, Descartes uses the term *passion* in a more general sense than is common today. Its root is from the Latin verb meaning "to suffer" or "to submit," and Descartes uses it as the opposite of *action*.

Questions for Thought

1. Assuming that you have a soul, where does your soul exist?
2. What problems, if any, result from saying that your soul is "contained in your body"?
3. Do you think that Descartes has adequately explained how the soul interacts with the body? Why or why not?
4. Can you think of any modern scientific evidence that would argue against Descartes' explanation of the principal differences between humans and nonhuman animals?
5. What might be some of the consequences of accepting Descartes' suggestion that animals are sophisticated machines?

8   Woman as Body: Ancient and Contemporary Views

ELIZABETH V. SPELMAN

Elizabeth V. Spelman (b. 1945), who received her Ph.D. from Johns Hopkins University, teaches philosophy and women's studies at Smith College in Northampton, Massachusetts. Her specialties include ethics, feminist theory, race theory, and **metaphysics.** Spelman has written several journal articles that critique the traditional philosophical distinction between mind and body. She is also the author of three books, *Inessential Woman: Problems of Exclusion in Feminist Thought* (1988), *Fruits of Sorrow: Framing Our Attention to Suffering* (1997), and *Repair: The Impulse to Restore in a Fragile World* (2002).

In the following selection, which originally appeared in the journal *Feminist Studies,* Spelman looks at the implications of the mind/body distinction in the writings of one ancient philosopher (Plato) and four contemporary feminist writers (Simone de Beauvoir, Betty Friedan, Shulamith Firestone, and Mary Daly). She notes that in the writings of each of these authors, the distinction between mind and body has been accompanied by a hierarchical ordering in which the mind has been considered to be much more important to our self-identity than has our body. She further notes that this hierarchical ordering of mind over body has been used as the basis for creating social and political hierarchies in which some humans (those who are more "mental" in nature) assume rule over other humans (those who are more "bodily" in nature). For this reason, she argues that if we are truly interested in eliminating sexism and racism, we must carefully reexamine the distinction between mind and body, as well as the hierarchical ordering that has traditionally accompanied it.

Questions for Reading

1. What, according to Spelman, have most philosophers had to say about women? Why does Spelman believe that these remarks should not be dismissed, as they usually are, as "unofficial asides"?
2. In Spelman's view, what does Plato teach us about the body and its relationship to the mind or soul?
3. How do Plato's views on the body relate to his views on women?
4. What are Spelman's main points of contention with the four feminists that she criticizes? Why does she believe that the views of Adrienne Rich are more acceptable than the views of the other feminists?
5. How, according to Spelman, are sexism and racism philosophically connected?

WHAT PHILOSOPHERS HAVE HAD TO SAY ABOUT women typically has been nasty, brutish, and short. A page or two of quotations from those considered among the great philosophers (Aristotle, Hume, and Nietzsche, for example) constitutes a veritable litany of contempt. Because philosophers have not said much about women,[1] and, when they have, it has usually been in short essays or chatty addenda which have not been considered to be part of the central body of their work, it is tempting to regard their ex-

From Feminist Studies 8, no. 1 (Spring 1982). Copyright 1982 by Feminist Studies, Inc. Reprinted by permission *of the publisher.*

pressed views about women as asystemic: their remarks on women are unofficial asides which are unrelated to the heart of their philosophical doctrines. After all, it might be thought, how could one's views about something as unimportant as women have anything to do with one's views about something as important as the nature of knowledge, truth, reality, freedom? Moreover—and this is the philosopher's move par excellence—wouldn't it be charitable to consider those opinions about women as coming merely from the *heart,* which all too easily responds to the tenor of the times, while philosophy "proper" comes from the *mind,* which resonates not with the times but with the truth?

Part of the intellectual legacy from philosophy "proper," that is, the issues that philosophers have addressed which are thought to be the serious province of philosophy, is the soul/body or mind/body distinction (differences among the various formulations are not crucial to this essay). However, this part of philosophy might have not merely accidental connections to attitudes about women. For when one recalls that the Western philosophical tradition has not been noted for its celebration of the body, and that women's nature and women's lives have long been associated with the body and bodily functions, then a question is suggested. What connection might there be between attitudes toward the body and attitudes toward women?

If one begins to reread philosophers with an eye to exploring in detail just how they made the mind/body distinction, it soon becomes apparent that in many cases the distinction reverberates throughout the philosopher's work. How a philosopher conceives of the distinction and relation between soul (or mind) and body has essential ties to how that philosopher talks about the nature of knowledge, the accessibility of reality, the possibility of freedom. This is perhaps what one would expect—systematic connections among the "proper" philosophical issues addressed by a given philosopher. But there is also clear evidence in the philosophical texts of the relationship between the mind/body distinction, on the one hand, and the scattered official and unofficial utterances about the nature of women, on the other.

In this article, I shall refer to the conceptual connections between a philosopher's views about women and his expressed metaphysical, political, and ethical views. That is, I shall refer to conceptual

relations internal to the texts themselves, and not to relations between the texts and their political and historical contexts. . . .

My focus below is on the works of Plato, to discover what connections there are between his views about women and his views about the philosophical issues for which he is regarded with such respect. . . . What I hope to show is why it is important to see the connections between what Plato says about women and other aspects of his philosophical positions. For as I shall explain in the latter part of this essay, feminist theorists frequently have wanted to reject the kinds of descriptions of woman's nature found in Plato and other philosophers, and yet at the same time have in their own theorizing continued to accept uncritically other aspects of the tradition that informs those ideas about "woman's nature." In particular, by looking at the example of Plato, I want to suggest why it is important for feminists not only to question what these philosophers have said about women, but also what philosophers have had to say about the mind/body distinction.

PLATO'S LESSONS ABOUT THE SOUL AND THE BODY

Plato's dialogues are filled with lessons about knowledge, reality, and goodness, and most of the lessons carry with them strong praise for the soul and strong indictments against the body. According to Plato, the body, with its deceptive senses, keeps us from real knowledge; it rivets us in a world of material things which is far removed from the world of reality; and it tempts us away from the virtuous life. It is in and through the soul, if at all, that we shall have knowledge, be in touch with reality, and lead a life of virtue. Only the soul can truly know, for only the soul can ascend to the real world, the world of the Forms or Ideas. That world is the perfect model to which imperfect, particular things, we find in matter merely approximate. It is a world which, like the soul, is invisible, unchanging, not subject to decay, eternal. To be good, one's soul must know the Good, that is, the Form of Goodness, and this is impossible while one is dragged down by the demands and temptations of bodily life. Hence, bodily death is nothing to be feared: immortality of the soul not only is possible, but greatly to be desired, because when one is released from the body one finally can get down to the real business of life, for this real business of life is the business of the soul. Indeed, Socrates describes his own commitment, while still on earth, to encouraging his fellow Athenians to pay attention to the real business of life:

> [I have spent] all my time going about trying to persuade you, young and old, to make your first and chief concern not for your bodies nor for your possessions, but for the highest welfare of your souls. [*Apology* 30a–b]

Plato also tells us about the nature of beauty. Beauty has nothing essentially to do with the body or with the world of material things. *Real* beauty cannot "take the form of a face, or of hands, or of anything that is of the flesh" (*Symposium* 221a). Yes, there are beautiful things, but they only are entitled to be described that way because they "partake in" the form of Beauty, which itself is not found in the material world. Real beauty has characteristics which merely beautiful *things* cannot have; real beauty

> is an everlasting loveliness which neither comes nor goes, which neither flowers nor fades, for such beauty is the same on every hand, the same then as now, here as there, this way as that way, the same to every worshiper as it is to every other. [*Symposium* 221a]

Because it is only the soul that can know the Forms, those eternal and unchanging denizens of Reality, only the soul can know real Beauty; our changing, decaying bodies can only put us in touch with changing, decaying pieces of the material world.

Plato also examines love. His famous discussion of love in the *Symposium* ends up being a celebration of the soul over the body. Attraction to and appreciation for the beauty of another's body is but a vulgar fixation unless one can use such appreciation as a stepping stone to understanding Beauty itself. One can begin to learn about Beauty, while one is still embodied, when one notices that this body is beautiful, that that body is beautiful, and so on, and then one begins to realize that Beauty itself is something beyond any particular beautiful body or thing. The kind of love between people that is to be valued is not the attraction of one body for another, but the attraction of one soul for another. There is procreation of the spirit as well as of the flesh (*Symposium* 209a). All that bodies in unison can create are more bodies—the children women bear—which are mortal, subject to change and decay. But souls in unison can create "something lovelier and less mortal than human seed," for spiritual lovers "conceive and bear the things of the spirit," that is, "wisdom and all her sister virtues" (*Symposium* 209c). Hence, spiritual love between men is preferable to physical love between men and women. . . .

So, then, one has no hope of understanding the nature of knowledge, reality, goodness, love, or beauty unless one recognizes the distinction between soul and body; and one has no hope of attaining any of these unless one works hard on freeing the soul from the lazy, vulgar, beguiling body. A philosopher is someone who is committed to doing just that, and that is why philosophers go willingly unto death; it is, after all, only the death of their bodies, and finally, once their souls are released from their bodies, these philosophical desiderata are within reach.

The offices and attributes of the body vis-a-vis the soul are on the whole interchangeable, in Plato's work, with the offices and attributes of one part of the soul vis-a-vis another part. The tug-of-war between soul and body has the same dynamics, and the same stakes, as the tug-of-war between "higher" and "lower" parts of the soul. For example, sometimes Plato speaks as if the soul should resist the desires not of the body, but of part of its very self (*Gorgias* 505b). Sometimes he describes internal conflict as the struggle between soul and body, and sometimes as the battle among the rational, the spirited, and the appetitive parts of the soul. The spirited part of the soul is supposed to help out the rational part in its constant attempt to "preside over the appetitive part which is the mass of the soul in each of us and the most insatiate by nature"; unless it is watched, the appetitive part can get "filled and infected with the so-called pleasures associated with the body" (*Republic* 442a–b).

The division among parts of the soul is intimately tied to one other central and famous aspect of Plato's philosophy that hasn't been mentioned so far: Plato's political views. His discussion of the parts of the soul and their proper relation to one another is integral to his view about the best way to set up a state. The rational part of the soul ought to rule the soul and ought to be attended by the spirited part in keeping watch over the unruly appetitive part; just so, there ought to be rulers of the state (the small minority in whom reason is dominant), who, with the aid of high-spirited guardians of order, watch over the multitudes (whose appetites need to be kept under control).

What we learn from Plato, then, about knowledge, reality, goodness, beauty, love, and statehood, is phrased in terms of a distinction between soul and body, or alternatively and roughly equivalently, in terms of a distinction between the rational and irrational. And the body, or the irrational part of the soul, is seen as an enormous and annoying obstacle to the possession of these desiderata. If the body gets the upper hand (!) over the soul, or if the irrational part of the soul overpowers the rational part, one can't have knowledge, one can't see beauty, one will be far from the highest form of love, and the state will be in utter chaos. So the soul/body distinction, or the distinction between the rational and irrational parts of the soul, is a highly charged distinction. An inquiry into the distinction is no mild metaphysical musing. It is quite clear that the distinction is heavily value-laden. Even if Plato hadn't told us outright that the soul is more valuable than the body, and the rational part of the soul is more important than the irrational part, that message rings out in page after page of his dialogues. The soul/body distinction, then, is integral to the rest of Plato's views, and the higher worth of the soul is integral to that distinction.

PLATO'S VIEW OF THE SOUL AND BODY, AND HIS ATTITUDE TOWARD WOMEN

Plato, and anyone else who conceives of the soul as something unobservable, cannot of course speak as if we could point to the soul, or hold it up for direct observation. At one point, Plato says no mere mortal can really understand the nature of the soul, but one perhaps could tell what it resembles (*Phaedrus* 246a). So it is not surprising to find Plato using many metaphors and analogies to describe what the soul is *like,* in order to describe relations between the soul and the body or relations between parts of the soul. For example, thinking, a function of the soul, is described by analogy to talking (*Theaetetus* 190a; *Sophist* 263e). The parts of the soul are likened to a team of harnessed, winged horses and their charioteer (*Phaedrus* 246a). The body's relation to the soul is such that we are to think of the body vis-a-vis the soul as a tomb (*Gorgias* 493a), a grave or prison (*Cratylus* 400c), or as barnacles or rocks holding down the soul (*Republic* 611e–612a). Plato compares

the lowest or bodylike part of the soul to a brood of beasts (*Republic* 590c).

But Plato's task is not only to tell us what the soul is like, not only to provide us with ways of getting a fix on the differences between souls and bodies, or differences between parts of the soul. As we've seen, he also wants to convince us that the soul is much more important than the body, and that it is to our peril that we let ourselves be beckoned by the rumblings of the body at the expense of harkening to the call of the soul. And he means to convince us of this by holding up for our inspection the silly and sordid lives of those who pay too much attention to their bodies and do not care enough for their souls; he wants to remind us of how unruly, how without direction, are the lives of those in whom the lower part of the soul holds sway over the higher part. Because he can't *point* to an adulterated soul, he points instead to those embodied beings whose lives are in such bad shape that we can be sure that their souls are adulterated. And whose lives exemplify the proper soul/body relationship gone haywire? The lives of women (or sometimes the lives of children, slaves, and brutes).

For example, how are we to know when the body has the upper hand over the soul, or when the lower part of the soul has managed to smother the higher part? We presumably can't see such conflict, so what do such conflicts translate into, in terms of actual human lives? Well, says Plato, look at the lives of women.[2] It is women who get hysterical at the thought of death (*Phaedo* 60a, 112d; *Apology* 35b); obviously, their emotions have overpowered their reason, and they can't control themselves. The worst possible model for young men could be "a woman, young or old or wrangling with her husband, defying heaven, loudly boasting, fortunate in her own conceit, or involved in misfortune or possessed by grief and lamentation—still less a woman that is sick, in love, or in labor" (*Republic* 395d–e). He continues:

> When in our own lives some affliction comes to us you are aware that we plume ourselves . . . on our ability to remain calm and endure, in the belief that this is the conduct of a man, and [giving in to grief] that of a woman [*Republic* 605c–d].

To have more concern for your body than your soul is to act just like a woman; hence, the most proper penalty for a soldier who surrenders to save his body, when he should be willing to die out of the courage of his soul, is for the soldier to be turned into a woman (*Laws* 944e). Plato believed that souls can go through many different embodied lifetimes. There will be certain indications, in one's life, of the kind of life one is leading now; and unless a man lives righteously now, he will as his next incarnation "pass into a woman" and if he doesn't behave then, he'll become a brute! (*Timaeus* 42b-c, 76e, 91a).

Moreover, Plato on many occasions points to women to illustrate the improper way to pursue the things for which philosophers are constantly to be searching. For example, Plato wants to explain how important and also how difficult the attainment of real knowledge is. He wants us to realize that not just anyone can have knowledge; there is a vital distinction between those who really have knowledge and those who merely think they do. Think, for example, about the question of health. If we don't make a distinction between those who know what health is, and those who merely have unfounded and confused opinions about what health is, then "in the matter of good or bad health . . . any woman or child—or animal, for that matter—knows what is wholesome for it and is capable of curing itself" (*Theaetetus* 171c). The implication is clear: if any old opinion were to count as real knowledge, then we'd have to say that women, children, and maybe even animals have knowledge. But surely *they* don't have knowledge! And why not? For one thing, because they don't recognize the difference between the material, changing world of appearance, and the invisible, eternal world of Reality. In matters of beauty, for example, they are so taken by the physical aspects of things that they assume that they can see and touch what is beautiful; they don't realize that what one knows when one has knowledge of real Beauty cannot be something that is seen or touched. Plato offers us, then, as an example of the failure to distinguish between Beauty itself, on the one hand, and beautiful things, on the other, "boys and women when they see bright-colored things" (*Republic* 557c). They don't realize that it is not through one's senses that one knows about beauty or anything else, for real beauty is eternal and unchangeable and can only be known through the soul.

So the message is that in matters of knowledge, reality, and beauty, don't follow the example of women. They are mistaken about those things. In matters of love, women's lives serve as negative examples also. Those men who are drawn by "vulgar" love, that is, love of body for body, "turn to women as the object of their love, and raise a family" (*Symposium* 208e); those men drawn by a more "heavenly" kind of love, that is, love of soul for soul, turn to other men. But there are strong sanctions against physical love between men: such physical unions, especially between older and younger men, are "unmanly." The older man isn't strong enough to resist his lust (as in woman, the irrational part of the soul has overtaken the rational part), and the younger man, "the impersonator of the female," is reproached for this "likeness to the model" (*Laws* 836e). The problem with physical love between men, then, is that men are acting like women. . . .

To anyone at all familiar with Plato's official and oft-reported views about women, the above recitation of misogynistic remarks may be quite surprising. Accounts of Plato's views about women usually are based on what he says in book 5 of the *Republic*. In that dialogue, Plato startled his contemporaries, when as part of his proposal for the constitution of an ideal state, he suggested that there is

> no pursuit of the administrators of a state that belongs to woman because she is a woman or to a man because he is a man. But the natural capacities are distributed alike among both creatures, and women naturally share in all pursuits and men in all [*Republic* 455d–e].

The only difference between men and women, Plato says at this point, is that women have weaker bodies than men, but this is no sign that something is amiss with their souls. . . .

Well now, what are we to make of this apparent double message in Plato about women? What are we to do with the fact that on the one hand, when Plato explicitly confronts the question of women's nature, in the *Republic*, he seems to affirm the equality of men and women; while on the other hand, the dialogues are riddled with misogynistic remarks? I think that understanding the centrality and importance of the soul/body distinction in Plato's work helps us to understand this contradiction in his views about women. As we've seen, Plato insists, over and over again in a variety of ways, that our souls are the most important part of us. Not only is it through our souls that we shall have access to knowledge, reality, goodness, beauty; but also, in effect we *are* our souls; when our bodies die and decay, we, that is our souls, shall live on. Our bodies are not essential to our identity; in their most benign aspect, our bodies are incidental appendages; in their most malignant aspect, they are obstacles to the smooth functioning of our souls. If we *are* our souls, and our bodies are not essential to who we are, then it doesn't make any difference, ultimately, whether we have a woman's body or a man's body. When one thinks about this emphasis in Plato's thought, his views about the equality of women and men seem integral to the rest of his views. If the only difference between women and men is that they have different bodies, and if bodies are merely incidental attachments to what constitutes one's real identity, then there is no important difference between men and women.

But as we have also seen, Plato seems to want to make very firm his insistence on the destructiveness of the body to the soul. In doing so, he holds up for our ridicule and scorn those lives devoted to bodily pursuits. Over and over again, women's lives are depicted as being such lives. His **misogyny,** then, is part of his somatophobia: the body is seen as the source of all the undesirable traits a human being could have, and women's lives are spent manifesting those traits.

So the contradictory sides of Plato's views about women are tied to the distinction he makes between soul and body and the lessons he hopes to teach his readers about their relative value. When preaching about the overwhelming importance of the soul, he can't but regard the kind of body one has as of no final significance, so there is no way for him to assess differentially the lives of women and men; but when making gloomy pronouncements about the worth of the body, he points an accusing finger at a class of people with a certain kind of body—women—because he regards them, as a class, as embodying (!) the very traits he wishes no one to have. In this way, women constitute a deviant class in Plato's philosophy, in the sense that he points to their lives as the kinds of lives that are not acceptable philosophically: they are just the kinds of lives no one, especially philosophers, ought

to live. It is true that Plato chastises certain kinds of men: **sophists,** tyrants, and cowards, for example. But he frequently puts them in their place by comparing them to women! . . .

In summary, Plato does not merely embrace a distinction between soul and body; for all the good and hopeful and desirable possibilities for human life (now and in an afterlife) are aligned with the soul, while the rather seedy and undesirable liabilities of human life are aligned with the body (alternatively, the alignment is with the higher or lower parts of the soul). There is a highly polished moral gloss to the soul/body distinction in Plato. One of his favorite devices for bringing this moral gloss to a high luster is holding up, for our contempt and ridicule, the lives of women. This is one of the ways he tries to make clear that it makes no small difference whether you lead a soul-directed or a bodily directed life.

FEMINISM AND "SOMATOPHOBIA"

There are a number of reasons why feminists should be aware of the legacy of the soul/body distinction. It is not just that the distinction has been wound up with the depreciation and degradation of women, although, as has just been shown, examining a philosopher's views of the distinction may give us a direct route to his views about women.

First of all, as the soul or mind or reason is extolled, and the body or passion is denounced by comparison, it is not just women who are both relegated to the bodily or passionate sphere of existence and then chastised for belonging to that sphere. Slaves, free laborers, children, and animals are put in "their place" on almost the same grounds as women are. The images of women, slaves, laborers, children, and animals are almost interchangeable. For example, we find Plato holding that the best born and best educated should have control over "children, women and slaves . . . and the base rabble of those who are free in name," because it is in these groups that we find "the mob of motley appetites and pleasures and pains" (*Republic* 431b–c). As we saw above, Plato lumps together women, children, and animals as ignoramuses. . . . A common way of denigrating a member of any one of these groups is to compare that member to a member of one of the other groups—women are thought to have slavish or childish appetites, slaves are said to be brutish. Recall too, that Plato's way of ridiculing male homosexuals was to say that they imitated women. It is no wonder that the images and insults are almost interchangeable, for there is a central descriptive thread holding together the images of all these groups. The members of these groups lack, for all intents and purposes, mind or the power of reason; even the humans among them are not considered fully human.

It is important for feminists to see to what extent the images and arguments used to denigrate women are similar to those used to denigrate one group of men vis-a-vis another, children vis-a-vis adults, animals vis-a-vis humans, and even—though I have not discussed it here—the natural world vis-a-vis man's will (yes, man's will). For to see this is part of understanding how the oppression of women occurs in the context of, and is related to, other forms of oppression or exploitation.

There is a second reason why feminists should be aware of the legacy of the soul/body distinction. Some feminists have quite happily adopted both the soul/body distinction and relative value attached to soul and to body. But in doing so, they may be adopting a position inimical to what on a more conscious level they are arguing for. For all her magisterial insight into the way in which the image of woman as body has been foisted upon and used against us, Simone de Beauvoir can't resist the temptation to say that woman's emancipation will come when woman, like man, is freed from this association with—according to the male wisdom of centuries—the less important aspect of human existence. According to *The Second Sex,* women's demand is "not that they be exalted in their femininity; they wish that in themselves, as in humanity in general, **transcendence** may prevail over **immanence.**"[3] But in de Beauvoir's own terms, for "transcendence" to prevail over "immanence" is for spirit or mind to prevail over matter or body, for reason to prevail over passion and desire. This means not only that the old images of women as mired in the world of "immanence"—the world of nature and physical existence—will go away. It will also happen that women won't lead lives given over mainly to their "natural" functions: "the pain of childbirth is on the

way out"; "artificial insemination is on the way in."[4] Although de Beauvoir doesn't explicitly say it, her directions for women are to find means of leaving the world of immanence and joining the men in the realm of transcendence. Men have said, de Beauvoir reminds us, that to be human is to have mind prevail over body; and no matter what disagreements she has elsewhere with men's perceptions and priorities, de Beauvoir here seems to agree with them. Explicitly de Beauvoir tells us not to be the people men have dreamt us up to be; but implicitly, she tells us to be the people men have dreamt themselves up to be.

I'm not insisting that de Beauvoir should have told us to stay where we are. The burden of her book is to describe the mixture of fear, awe, and disgust in men's attitudes toward the physical world, the body, the woman. Men have purchased one-way tickets to Transcendence in their attempt to deny, or conquer and control, the raging Immanence they see in themselves and project onto women. De Beauvoir says that this attitude toward corporeality has informed men's oppression of women, and yet her directions for women seem to be informed by just the same attitude. But can we as a species sustain negative attitudes and negative ideologies about the bodily aspects of our existence and yet keep those attitudes and ideologies from working in behalf of one group of people as it attempts to oppress other groups? Let me cite some examples to show how unlikely it is that such entrenched values can linger without doing some harm.

The first example comes from Plato. The contradiction we saw in Plato's views about women comes precisely from the source we have just been talking about. For it is just insofar as Plato continues to regard our bodily existence as cause for disappointment, embarrassment, and evil, that he finds the lives of women (and others) the occasion for scorn and ridicule—and this despite his insistence elsewhere in his writings on the equality of women and men.

A second example comes from Betty Friedan. She may seem too easy a target, but I think that something closely connected to what I'm going to point out about her thought can also be found in feminists considered much more radical than she is. Very early in *The Feminine Mystique,*[5] Friedan remarks on the absence, in women's lives, of "the world of thought and ideas, the life of the mind and spirit."[6] She wants women to be "culturally" as well as "biologically" creative—she wants us to think about spending our lives "mastering the secrets of the atoms, or the stars, composing symphonies, pioneering a new concept in government or society."[7] And she associates "mental activity" with the "professions of highest value to society."[8] Friedan thus seems to believe that men have done the more important things, the mental things; women have been relegated in the past to the less important human tasks involving bodily functions, and their liberation will come when they are allowed and encouraged to do the more important things in life.

Friedan's analysis relies on our old friend, the mind/body distinction, and Friedan, no less than Plato or de Beauvoir, quite happily assumes that mental activities are more valuable than bodily ones. Her solution to what she referred to as the "problem that has no name" is for women to leave (though not entirely) woman's sphere and "ascend" into man's. Certainly there is much pleasure and value in the "mental activities" she extols. But we can see the residue of her own negative attitude about tasks associated with the body: the bodily aspects of our existence must be attended to, but the "liberated" woman, who is on the ascendant, can't be bothered with them. There is yet another group of people to whom these tasks will devolve: servants. Woman's liberation—and of course it is no secret that by "woman," Friedan could only have meant middle-class white women—seems to require woman's dissociation and separation from those who will perform the bodily tasks which the liberated woman has left behind in pursuit of "higher," mental activity. . . .

I mentioned that feminists considered more radical than Friedan share something very close to her attitudes about the body: Shulamith Firestone is a case in point. In *The Dialectic of Sex,* Firestone traces the oppression of women to what she calls a "fundamental inequality" produced by nature: "half the human race must bear and rear the children of all of them."[9] Apart from the fact that we need some explanation of how Nature dictated that women should *rear* children, we also need to understand what it is about bearing children that Firestone finds oppressive. According to Firestone,

the fact of their childbearing capacity has been used to justify the oppression of women. But it is not just this that concerns and bothers her. She also thinks that in and of itself childbearing is dreadful; the way in which she describes pregnancy and childbirth tells us that she would find them oppressive even in the absence of oppressive institutions set up around them. She calls pregnancy "barbaric"; and says that "childbirth *hurts.*"[10] Curiously, Firestone elsewhere is angered at the male image of what women ought to look like—"Women everywhere rush to squeeze into the glass slipper, forcing and mutilating their bodies with diets and beauty programs";[11] and in fact she reminds her readers that, contrary to male myths, *human* beauty allows for "growth and flux and decay."[12] Yet she doesn't hesitate to describe pregnancy as a "deformation" of the body.[13] The disgust and fear she expressed reminds one of de Beauvoir's many descriptions of male attitudes toward specifically female and specifically physical functions. As Adrienne Rich has pointed out, "Firestone sees childbearing . . . as purely and simply the victimizing experience it has often been under **patriarchy.**"[14]

Undoubtedly, woman's body has been part of the source of our oppression in several senses. First, pregnancy and childbirth have in fact made women vulnerable, for a long time in the history of the species, and even for a short time in the history of the most economically privileged of women. Second, woman has been portrayed as essentially a bodily being, and this image has been used to deny her full status as a human being wherever and whenever mental activity as over against bodily activity has been thought to be the most human activity of all. But is the way to avoid oppression to radically change the experience of childbirth through technology, as Firestone suggested, and insist that woman *not* be seen as connected to her body at all, that is, to insist that woman's "essential self," just as man's, lies in her mind, and not in her body? If so, then we are admitting tacitly that the men—from Plato on down—have been right all along, in insisting on a distinction between mind or soul and body, and insisting that mind is to be valued more than body. They've only been wrong in ungenerously denying woman a place up there with them, among the other minds. Woman's liberation, on this view, is just a much belated version of the men's liberation that took place centuries ago, when men figured out ways both to dissociate themselves from, and/or conquer, the natural world and that part of them—their bodies—which reminds them of their place in that natural world. And one would think, reading feminists as different as de Beauvoir, Friedan, and Firestone, that indeed what woman's liberation ultimately means is liberation from our bodies—both in fact, and in definition. . . .

There is of course much more to be said about de Beauvoir, Friedan, and Firestone than my brief remarks here. And of course there is much more to feminist theory than what they have said, although their theories have been influential for different segments of the women's movement, and their works constitute important landmarks in the development of feminist theory. Even in the recent work of Mary Daly, who knows the ways of the Church "Fathers" too well to describe women's liberation simply in terms of a spirituality divorced from embodiment, it is difficult to see in any detail what women free from the shackles of patriarchy will be like: "Spinsters" appear to have none of the characteristics of personal identity which are related to embodiment: color, culture, specific histories. In her insistence on all women overcoming the barriers that have been used to divide us, Daly ends up with a general notion of woman that seems to be abstracted from any of the particular facts about us which make us different from one another. As Judith Plaskow has remarked, Daly offers "a vision of wild and ecstatic, but essentially contentless and disembodied, freedom."[15]

What I have tried to do here is bring attention to the fact that various versions of women's liberation may themselves rest on the very same assumptions that have informed the deprecation and degradation of women, and other groups, in the past. Those assumptions are that we must distinguish between soul and body, and that the physical part of our existence is to be devalued in comparison to the mental. Of course, these two assumptions alone don't mean that women or other groups have to be degraded; it's these two assumptions, along with the further assumption that woman is body, or is bound to her body, or is meant to take care of the bodily aspects of life, that have so deeply contributed to the degradation and oppression of women. And so perhaps feminists would like to keep the first two assumptions (about the difference between mind and body, and the relative worth of each of them) and somehow get rid of the last—in fact, that is what most of the feminists previously discussed have tried to do. Nothing that has been said so far has amounted to an argument against those first two assumptions: it hasn't been shown that there is no foundation for the assumptions that the mind and body are distinct and that the body is to be valued less than the mind.

There is a feminist thinker, however, who has taken it upon herself to chip away directly at the second assumption and to a certain extent at the first. Both in her poetry, and explicitly in her recent book, *Of Woman Born,* Adrienne Rich has begun to show us why use of the mind/body distinction does not give us appropriate descriptions of human experience; and she has begun to remind us of the distance we keep from ourselves when we try to keep a distance from our bodies.[16] She does this in the process of trying to redefine the dimensions of the experience of childbirth, as she tries to show us why childbirth and motherhood need not mean what they have meant under patriarchy.

We are reminded by Rich that it is possible to be alienated from our bodies not only by pretending or wishing they weren't there, but also by being "incarcerated" in them.[17] The institution of motherhood has done the latter in its insistence on seeing woman only or mainly as a reproductive machine. Defined as flesh by flesh-loathers, woman enters the most "fleshly" of her experiences with that same attitude of flesh-loathing—surely "physical self-hatred and suspicion of one's own body is scarcely a favorable emotion with which to enter an intense physical experience."[18]

But Rich insists that we don't have to experience it as a "torture rack";[19] but neither do we have to mystify it as a "peak experience." The experience of childbirth can be viewed as a way of recognizing the integrity of our experience, because pain itself is not usefully catalogued as something just our minds or just our bodies experience. Giving birth is painful, indeed; but painkillers are not necessarily the appropriate way to deal with pain, for we are no less estranged from our bodies, no less put at men's disposal, when "rescued" from our pain by drugs. The point of "natural childbirth" should be thought of not as enduring pain, but as having an active physical experience—a distinction we recognize as crucial for understanding, for example, the pleasure in athletics.

Rich recognizes that feminists have not wanted to accept patriarchal versions of female biology, of what having a female body means. It has seemed to feminists, she implies, that we must either accept that view of being female, which is, essentially, to be a body, or deny that view and insist that we are "disembodied spirits."[20] It perhaps is natural to see our alternatives that way:

> We have been perceived for too many centuries as pure Nature, exploited and raped like the earth and the solar system; small wonder if we not try to become Culture: pure spirit, mind.[21]

But we don't *have* to do that, Rich reminds us; we can appeal to the physical without denying what is called "mind." We can come to regard our physicality as "resource, rather than a destiny":

> In order to live a fully human life we require not only control of our bodies (though control is a prerequisite); we must touch the unity and resonance of our physicality, our bond with the natural order, the corporeal ground of our intelligence.[22]

Rich doesn't deny that we will have to start thinking about our lives in new ways; she even implies that we'll have to start thinking about thinking in new ways. Maybe it will give such a project a small boost to point out that philosophers for their part still squabble about mind/body dualism; the legacy of dualism is strong, but not unchallenged by any means. And in any event, as I have noted earlier, one can hardly put the blame for sexism (or any other form of oppression) on dualism itself. Indeed, the mind/body distinction can be put to progressive political ends, for example, to assert equality between human beings in the face of physical differences between them. There is nothing intrinsically sexist or otherwise oppressive about dualism, that is, about the belief that there are minds and there are bodies and that they are distinct kinds of things. But historically, the story dualists tell often ends up being a highly politicized one: although the story may be different at different historical moments, often it is said not only that there are minds (or souls) and bodies, but also that one is meant to rule and control the other. And the stage is thereby set for the soul/body distinction, now highly politicized and hierarchically ordered, to be used in a variety of ways in connection with repressive theories of the self, as well as oppressive theories of social and political relations. Among the tasks facing feminists is to think about the criteria for an adequate theory of self. Part of the value of Rich's work is that it points to the necessity of such an undertaking, and it is no criticism of her to say that she does no more than remind us of some of the questions that need to be raised.

A FINAL NOTE ABOUT THE SIGNIFICANCE OF SOMATOPHOBIA IN FEMINIST THEORY

In the history of political philosophy, the grounds given for the inferiority of women to men often are quite similar to those given for the inferiority of slaves to masters, children to fathers, animals to humans. In Plato, for example, all such subordinate groups are guilty by association with one another and each group is guilty by association with the bodily. In their eagerness to end the stereotypical association of woman and body, feminists such as de Beauvoir, Friedan, Firestone, and Daly have overlooked the significance of the connections—in theory and practice—between the derogation and oppression of women on the basis of our sexual identity and the derogation and oppression of other groups on the basis of, for example, skin color or class membership. It is as if in their eagerness to assign women a new place in the scheme of things, these feminist theorists have by implication wanted to dissociate women from other subordinate groups. One problem with this, of course, is that those other subordinate groups include women.

What is especially significant about Rich's recent work is that, in contrast to these other theorists, she both challenges the received tradition about the insignificance and indignity of bodily life and bodily tasks and explicitly focuses on racism as well as sexism as essential factors in women's oppression.

I believe that it is not merely a coincidence that someone who attends to the first also attends to the second. Rich pauses not just to recognize the significance attached to the female body, but also to re-examine that significance. "Fleshloathing" is loathing of flesh by some particular group under some particular circumstances—the loathing of women's flesh by men, but also the loathing of black flesh by whites. . . . After all, bodies are always particular bodies—they are male or female bodies (our deep confusion when we can't categorize a body in either way supports and does not belie the general point); but they are black or brown or biscuit or yellow or red bodies as well. We cannot seriously attend to the social significance attached to embodiment without recognizing this. I believe that it is Rich's recognition of this that distinguishes her work in crucial ways from that of most other major white feminists. Although the topic of feminism, sexism, and racism deserves a much fuller treatment,[23] it is important to point out in the context of the present paper that not only does Rich challenge an assumption about the nature of the bodily that has been used to oppress women, but unlike other feminists who do not challenge this assumption, she takes on the question of the ways in which sexism and racism interlock. Somatophobia historically has been symptomatic not only of sexism, but also of racism, so it is perhaps not surprising that someone who has examined that connection between flesh-loathing and sexism would undertake an examination of racism.

Feminists may find it fruitful to examine the extent to which attitudes toward and ideologies about the body have played a role not only in sexist institutions and analyses, but also in the analyses feminists themselves are developing in response to such institutions and theories. A theory of embodiment, which must include a theory of the social significance of embodiment, is part of the needed feminist theory of self referred to earlier. Such a theory might reveal some deep connections among sexism, racism, and classism. It might also help expose some of the relations between **homophobia** and racism, insofar as both historically have such strong connections to fear of sexuality. We also need to ask what theories of embodiment are presupposed by feminist analyses

of women's health. All these examinations are part of our refusal to pay homage to a long tradition of somatophobia—a tradition it has been hard for us to shake.

NOTES

1. There is no reason to think philosophers used "man" or its equivalent in other languages generically. For example, in discussing the conditions of happiness for "man," Aristotle raises the question of whether a "man's" being self-sufficient is compatible with his having a wife (*Nicomachean Ethics* 1097b11).

All references to Plato are from *Collected Dialogues of Plato*, ed. Edith Hamilton and Huntington Cairns (New York: Pantheon, 1963), and are supplied in parentheses in the text.

2. Although Plato objects to certain types of men—sophists, tyrants, and so forth—his disdain for women is always expressed as disdain for women in general and not for any subgroup of women. Moreover, one of the ways he shows his disdain for certain types of men is to compare them to women.

3. Simone de Beauvoir, *The Second Sex* (New York: Knopf, 1952), p. 123.

4. Ibid., p. 111.

5. Betty Friedan, *The Feminine Mystique* (New York: Norton, 1963).

6. Ibid., p. 36.

7. Ibid., p. 247.

8. Ibid., p. 277.

9. Shulamith Firestone, *The Dialectic of Sex* (New York: Bantam, 1970), p. 205.

10. Ibid., p. 198.

11. Ibid., p. 152.

12. Ibid., p. 155.

13. Ibid., p. 198.

14. Adrienne Rich, *Of Woman Born* (New York: Norton, 1976), p. 174.

15. Judith Plaskow, from a lecture entitled "Woman as Body: The History of an Idea," Oberlin College, Oberlin, Ohio, April 1979. I learned about this lecture long after I first entitled this essay.

16. Rich, *Of Woman Born.*

17. Ibid., p. 13.

18. Ibid., p. 163.

19. Ibid., p. 157.

20. Ibid., p. 40.

21. Ibid., p. 285.

22. Ibid., p. 39.

23. This topic is more fully covered in some of the selections in Chapter 5 of this text, especially in bell hook's "Feminism: A Transformational Politic."–ED.

Questions for Thought

1. How important is your body in determining who you are?
2. Do you believe that we can distinguish our soul or mind from our body as Plato has tried to do? Why or why not?
3. Do you agree that people who distinguish the mind or soul from the body, such as Plato, generally place more significance on the mind or soul than on the body?
4. Assuming that people who make this distinction do place more significance on the mind or soul, why do you think this happens?
5. Do you agree with Spelman that racism and sexism are often philosophically linked? Why or why not?
6. Assume for the moment that getting more in touch with your body—or becoming more "embodied," to use Spelman's term—is important. What are some of the ways in which you might accomplish this?

Divided Minds and the Nature of Persons   9

DEREK PARFIT

Derek Parfit (b. 1942) is a British philosopher who has taught at All Souls College of Oxford University for many years while also lecturing frequently in the United States. He is a fellow of both the British Academy and the American Academy of Arts and Sciences. Parfit's main areas of philosophical interest have been ethics, the nature of rationality, personal identity, and future generations. In addition to writing numerous essays like the one that follows, Parfit's philosophical insights were expressed in his influential book *Reasons and Persons,* which was published by Oxford University Press in 1984.

In the following essay, which appeared in an anthology titled *Mindwaves: Thoughts on Intelligence, Identity, and Consciousness,* Parfit discusses the implications of certain scientific experiments for the question of self-identity. Focusing specifically on experiments in which the two hemispheres of the brain were split in certain patients, Parfit argues that the separation of mental and bodily functions that resulted from these experiments is inconsistent with the *Ego Theory* of self—that is, with the theory that we have a unified self or soul that determines our identities. On the contrary, Parfit goes on to argue that these results support the opposing *Bundle Theory* of self, the theory that there are no egos or fixed identities distinct from our brains, bodies, and the mental and physiological processes that constitute them. While admitting that the Bundle Theory conflicts with certain "natural beliefs" about our self-identities, Parfit nevertheless concludes that it is much more defensible—from both a philosophical and a scientific standpoint—than is the Ego Theory.

Questions for Reading

1. What does Parfit mean by the Ego Theory of self? Which of the philosophers whom you have read subscribe to this theory?
2. How, according to Parfit, do split-brain cases undermine the Ego Theory?
3. What does Parfit mean by the Bundle Theory of self? What are his principal reasons for accepting this theory?

4. Parfit claims that "most of us . . . have false beliefs about what persons are, and about ourselves." What are some of the false beliefs that, according to Parfit, we have about ourselves?

5. What are some of the hypothetical cases that Parfit discusses in this article? Why, according to Parfit, do these cases support the Bundle Theory and not the Ego Theory?

DIVIDED MINDS AND THE "BUNDLE" THEORY OF SELF

IT WAS THE SPLIT-BRAIN CASES WHICH DREW ME into philosophy. Our knowledge of these cases depends on the results of various psychological tests, as described by Donald MacKay. These tests made use of two facts. We control each of our arms, and see what is in each half of our visual fields, with only one of our hemispheres. When someone's hemispheres have been disconnected, psychologists can thus present to this person two different written questions in the two halves of his visual field, and can receive two different answers written by this person's two hands.

Here is a simplified imaginary version of the kind of evidence that such tests provide. One of these people looks fixedly at the centre of a wide screen, whose left half is red and right half is blue. On each half in a darker shade are the words, "How many colours can you see?" With both hands the person writes, "Only one." The words are now changed to read, "Which is the only colour that you can see?" With one of his hands the person writes "Red," with the other he writes "Blue."

If this is how such a person responds, I would conclude that he is having two visual sensations—that he does, as he claims, see both red and blue. But in seeing each colour he is not aware of seeing the other. He has two streams of consciousness, in each of which he can see only one colour. In one stream he sees red, and at the same time, in his other stream, he sees blue. More generally, he could be having at the same time two series of thoughts and sensations, in having each of which he is unaware of having the other.

This conclusion has been questioned. It has been claimed by some that there are not *two* streams of consciousness, on the ground that the sub-dominant hemisphere is a part of the brain whose functioning involves no consciousness. If this were true, these cases would lose most of their interest. I believe that it is not true, chiefly because, if a person's dominant hemisphere is destroyed, this person is able to react in the way in which, in the split-brain cases, the sub-dominant hemisphere reacts, and we do not believe that such a person is just an automaton, without consciousness. The sub-dominant hemisphere is, of course, much less developed in certain ways, typically having the linguistic abilities of a three-year-old. But three-year-olds are conscious. This supports the view that, in split-brain cases, there *are* two streams of consciousness.

Another view is that, in these cases, there are two persons involved, sharing the same body. Like Professor MacKay, I believe that we should reject this view. My reason for believing this is, however, different. Professor MacKay denies that there are two persons involved because he believes that there is only one person involved. I believe that, in a sense, the number of persons involved is none.

THE EGO THEORY AND THE BUNDLE THEORY

To explain this sense I must, for a while, turn away from the split-brain cases. There are two theories about what persons are, and what is involved in a person's continued existence over time. On the *Ego Theory,* a person's continued existence cannot be explained except as the continued existence of a particular *Ego,* or *subject of experiences.* An Ego Theorist claims that, if we ask what unifies someone's consciousness at any time—what makes it

From Derek Parfit, "Divided Minds and the Nature of Persons," in Mindwaves: Thoughts on Intelligence, Identity and Consciousness, *edited by Colin Blakesmore and Susan Greenfield, Basil Blackwell, 1987. Reprinted by permission of the publisher.*

true, for example, that I can now both see what I am typing and hear the wind outside my window—the answer is that these are both experiences which are being had by me, this person, at this time. Similarly, what explains the unity of a person's whole life is the fact that all of the experiences in this life are had by the same person, or subject of experiences. In its best-known form, the *Cartesian view,* each person is a persisting purely mental thing—a soul, or spiritual **substance.**

The rival view is the *Bundle Theory.* Like most styles in art—Gothic, baroque, rococo, etc.—this theory owes its name to its critics. But the name is good enough. According to the Bundle Theory, we can't explain either the unity of consciousness at any time, or the unity of a whole life, by referring to a person. Instead we must claim that there are long series of different mental states and events—thoughts, sensations, and the like—each series being what we call one life. Each series is unified by various kinds of causal relation, such as the relations that hold between experiences and later memories of them. Each series is thus like a bundle tied up with string.

In a sense, a Bundle Theorist denies the existence of persons. An outright denial is of course absurd. As Reid protested in the eighteenth century, "I am not thought, I am not action, I am not feeling; I am something which thinks and acts and feels." I am not a series of events, but a person. A Bundle Theorist admits this fact, but claims it to be only a fact about our grammar, or our language. There are persons or subjects in this language-dependent way. If, however, persons are believed to be more than this—to be separately existing things, distinct from our brains and bodies, and the various kinds of mental states and events—the Bundle Theorist denies that there are such things.

The first Bundle Theorist was Buddha, who taught "anatta," or the *No Self view.* Buddhists concede that selves or persons have "nominal existence," by which they mean that persons are merely combinations of other elements. Only what exists by itself, as a separate element, has instead what Buddhists call "actual existence." Here are some quotations from Buddhist texts:

At the beginning of their conversation the king politely asks the monk his name, and receives the following reply: "Sir, I am known as 'Nagasena';

my fellows in the religious life address me as 'Nagasena.' Although my parents gave me the name . . . it is just an appellation, a form of speech, a description, a conventional usage. 'Nagasena' is only a name, for no person is found here."

A sentient being does exist, you think, O Mara? You are misled by a false conception. This bundle of elements is void of Self. In it there is no sentient being. Just as a set of wooden parts receives the name of carriage, so do we give to elements the name of fancied being.

Buddha has spoken thus: "O Brethren, actions do exist, and also their consequences, but the person that acts does not. There is no one to cast away this set of elements, and no one to assume a new set of them. There exists no Individual, it is only a conventional name given to a set of elements."[1]

Buddha's claims are strikingly similar to the claims advanced by several Western writers. Since these writers knew nothing of Buddha, the similarity of these claims suggests that they are not merely part of one cultural tradition, in one period. They may be, as I believe they are, true.

WHAT WE BELIEVE OURSELVES TO BE

Given the advances in psychology and neurophysiology, the Bundle Theory may now seem to be obviously true. It may seem uninteresting to deny that there are separately existing Egos, which are distinct from brains and bodies and the various kinds of mental states and events. But this is not the only issue. We may be convinced that the Ego Theory is false, or even senseless. Most of us, however, even if we are not aware of this, also have certain beliefs about what is involved in our continued existence over time. And these beliefs would only be justified if something like the Ego Theory was true. Most of us therefore have false beliefs about what persons are, and about ourselves.

These beliefs are best revealed when we consider certain imaginary cases, often drawn from science fiction. One such case is *teletransportation.* Suppose that you enter a cubicle in which, when you press a button, a scanner records the states of all of the cells in your brain and body, destroying both while doing so. This information is then transmitted at the speed of light to some other planet, where a replicator produces a perfect organic copy of you. Since the brain of your Replica is exactly like yours, it will seem to remember living your life up to the moment when you pressed the button, its character will be just like yours, and it will be in every other way psychologically continuous with you. This psychological continuity will not have its normal cause, the continued existence of your brain, since the causal chain will run through the transmission by radio of your "blueprint."

Several writers claim that, if you chose to be teletransported, believing this to be the fastest way of travelling, you would be making a terrible mistake. This would not be a way of travelling, but a way of dying. It may not, they concede, be quite as bad as ordinary death. It might be some consolation to you that, after your death, you will have this Replica, which can finish the book that you are writing, act as parent to your children, and so on. But they insist, this Replica won't be you. It will merely be someone else, who is exactly like you. This is why this prospect is nearly as bad as ordinary death.

Imagine next a whole range of cases, in each of which, in a single operation, a different proportion of the cells in your brain and body would be replaced with exact duplicates. At the near end of this range, only 1 or 2 per cent would be replaced; in the middle, 40 or 60 per cent; near the far end, 98 or 99 per cent. At the far end of this range is pure teletransportation, the case in which all of your cells would be "replaced."

When you imagine that some proportion of your cells will be replaced with exact duplicates, it is natural to have the following beliefs. First, if you ask, "Will I survive? Will the resulting person be me?" there must be an answer to this question. Either you will survive, or you are about to die. Second, the answer to this question must be either a simple "Yes" or a simple "No." The person who wakes up either will or will not be you. There cannot be a third answer, such as that the person waking up will be half you. You can imagine yourself later being half-conscious. But if the resulting person will be fully conscious, he cannot be half you. To state these beliefs together: to the question, "Will the resulting person be me?" there must always *be* an answer, which must be all-or-nothing.

There seem good grounds for believing that, in the case of teletransportation, your Replica would not be you. In a slight variant of this case, your Replica might be created while you were still alive, so that you could talk to one another. This seems to show that, if 100 per cent of your cells were replaced, the result would merely be a Replica of you. At the other end of my range of cases, where only 1 per cent would be replaced, the resulting person clearly *would* be you. It therefore seems that, in the cases in between, the resulting person must be either you, or merely a Replica. It seems that one of these must be true, and that it makes a great difference which is true.

HOW WE ARE NOT WHAT WE BELIEVE

If these beliefs were correct, there must be some critical percentage, somewhere in this range of cases, up to which the resulting person would be you, and beyond which he would merely be your Replica. Perhaps, for example, it would be you who would wake up if the proportion of cells replaced were 49 per cent, but if just a few more cells were also replaced, this would make all the difference, causing it to be someone else who would wake up.

That there must be some critical percentage follows from our natural beliefs. But this conclusion is most implausible. How could a few cells make such a difference? Moreover, if there is such a critical percentage, no one could ever discover where it came. Since in all these cases the resulting person would believe that he was you, there could never be any evidence about where, in this range of cases, he would suddenly cease to be you.

On the Bundle theory, we should reject these natural beliefs. Since you, the person, are not a separately existing entity, we can know exactly what would happen without answering the question of what will happen to you. Moreover, in the cases in the middle of my range, it is an empty question where the resulting person would be you, or would merely be someone else who is exactly like you. There are not here two different possibilities, one of which must be true. These are merely two different descriptions of the very same course of events. If 50 per cent of your cells were replaced with exact duplicates, we could call the resulting person you, or we could call him merely your Replica. But since these are not here different possibilities, this is a mere choice of words.

As Buddha claimed, the Bundle Theory is hard to believe. It is hard to accept that it could be an empty question whether one is about to die, or will instead live for many years.

What we are being asked to accept may be made clearer with this analogy. Suppose that a certain club exists for some time, holding regular meetings. The meetings then cease. Some years later, several people form a club with the same name, and the same rules. We can ask, "Did these people revive the very same club? Or did they merely start up another club which is exactly similar?" Given certain further details, this would be another empty question. We could know just what happened without answering this question. Suppose that someone said: "But there must be an answer. The club meeting later must either be, or not be, the very same club." This would show that this person didn't understand the nature of clubs.

In the same way, if we have any worries about my imagined cases, we don't understand the nature of persons. In each of my cases, you would know that the resulting person would be both psychologically and physically exactly like you, and that he would have some particular proportion of the cells in your brain and body—90 per cent, or 10 per cent, or, in the case of teletransportation, 0 per cent. Knowing this, you know everything. How could it be a real question what would happen to you, unless you are a separately existing Ego, distinct from a brain and body, and the various kinds of mental state and event? If there are no such Egos, there is nothing else to ask a real question about.

Accepting the Bundle Theory is not only hard; it may also affect our emotions. As Buddha claimed, it may undermine our concern about our own futures. This effect can be suggested by redescribing this change of view. Suppose that you are about to be destroyed, but will later have a Replica on Mars. You would naturally believe that this prospect is about as bad as ordinary death, since your Replica won't be you. On the Bundle Theory, the fact that your Replica won't be you just consists in the fact that, though it will be fully psychologically continuous with you, this continuity won't have its normal

cause. But when you object to teletransportation you are not objecting merely to the abnormality of this cause. You are objecting that this cause won't get *you* to Mars. You fear that the abnormal cause will fail to produce a further and all-important fact, which is different from the fact that your Replica will be psychologically continuous with you. You do not merely want there to be psychological continuity between you and some future person. You want to *be* this future person. On the Bundle Theory, there is no such special further fact. What you fear will not happen, in this imagined case, *never* happens. You want the person on Mars to be you in a specially intimate way in which no future person will ever be you. This means that, judged from the standpoint of your natural beliefs, even ordinary survival is about as bad as teletransportation. *Ordinary survival is about as bad as being destroyed and having a Replica.*

HOW THE SPILT-BRAIN CASES SUPPORT THE BUNDLE THEORY

The truth of the Bundle Theory seems to me, in the widest sense, as much a scientific as a philosophical conclusion. I can imagine kinds of evidence which would have justified believing in the existence of separately existing Egos, and believing that the continued existence of these Egos is what explains the continuity of each mental life. But there is in fact very little evidence in favour of this Ego Theory, and much for the alternative Bundle Theory.

Some of this evidence is provided by the split-brain cases. On the Ego Theory, to explain what unifies our experiences at any one time, we should simply claim that these are all experiences which are being had by the same person. Bundle Theorists reject this explanation. This disagreement is hard to resolve in ordinary cases. But consider the simplified split-brain case that I described. We show to my imagined patient a placard whose left half is blue and right half is red. In one of this person's two streams of consciousness, he is aware of seeing only blue, while at the same time, in his other stream, he is aware of seeing only red. Each of these two visual experiences is combined with other experiences, like that of being aware of moving one of his hands. What unifies the experiences, at any time, in each of this person's two streams of consciousness? What unifies his awareness of seeing only red with his awareness of moving one hand? The answer cannot be that these experiences are being had by the same person. This answer cannot explain the unity of each of this person's two streams of consciousness, since it ignores the disunity between these streams. This person is now having all of the experiences in both of his two streams. If this fact was what unified these experiences, this would make the two streams one.

These cases do not, I have claimed, involve two people sharing a single body. Since there is only one person involved, who has two streams of consciousness, the Ego Theorist's explanation would have to take the following form. He would have to distinguish between persons and subjects of experiences, and claim that, in split-brain cases, there are *two* of the latter. What unifies the experiences in one of the person's two streams would have to be the fact that these experiences are all being had by the same subject of experiences. What unifies the experiences in this person's other stream would have to be the fact that they are being had by another subject of experiences. When this explanation takes this form, it becomes much less plausible. While we could assume that "subject of experiences," or "Ego," simply meant "person," it was easy to believe that there are subjects of experiences. But if there can be subjects of experiences that are not persons, and if in the life of a split-brain patient there are at any time two different subjects of experiences—two different Egos—why should we believe that there really are such things? This does not amount to a refutation. But it seems to me a strong argument against the Ego Theory.

As a Bundle Theorist, I believe that these two Egos are idle cogs. There is another explanation of the unity of consciousness, both in ordinary cases and in split-brain cases. It is simply a fact that ordinary people are, at any time, aware of having several different experiences. This awareness of several different experiences can be helpfully compared with one's awareness, in short-term memory, of several different experiences. Just as there can be a single memory of just having had several experiences, such as hearing a bell strike three times, there can be a single state of awareness both of hearing the fourth striking of this bell, and of seeing, at the same time, ravens flying past the bell-tower.

Unlike the Ego Theorist's explanation, this explanation can easily be extended to cover split-brain cases. In such cases there is, at any time, not one state of awareness of several different experiences, but two such states. In the case I described, there is one state of awareness of both seeing only red and of moving one hand, and there is another state of awareness of both seeing only blue and moving the other hand. In claiming that there are two such states of awareness, we are not postulating the existence of unfamiliar entities, two separately existing Egos which are not the same as the single person whom the case involves. This explanation appeals to a pair of mental states which would have to be described anyway in a full description of this case.

I have suggested how the split-brain cases provide one argument for one view about the nature of persons. I should mention another such argument, provided by an imagined extension of these cases, first discussed at length by David Wiggins.[2]

In this imagined case a person's brain is divided, and the two halves are transplanted into a pair of different bodies. The two resulting people live quite separate lives. This imagined case shows that personal identity is not what matters. If I was about to divide, I should conclude that neither of the resulting people will be me. I will have ceased to exist. But this way of ceasing to exist is about as good— or as bad—as ordinary survival.

Some of the features of Wiggins's imagined case are likely to remain technically impossible. But the case cannot be dismissed, since its most striking feature, the division of one stream of consciousness into separate streams, has already happened. This is a second way in which the actual split-brain cases have great theoretical importance. They challenge some of our deepest assumptions about ourselves.[3]

NOTES

1. For the sources of these and similar quotations, see my *Reasons and Persons* (1984) pp. 502–3, 532. Oxford: Oxford Univ. Press.

2. At the end of his *Identity and Spatio-Temporal Continuity* (1967). Oxford: Blackwell.

3. I discuss these assumptions further in Part 3 of my *Reasons and Persons*.

Questions for Thought

Questions for Thought

1. Do you find Parfit's reasoning about split-brain cases compelling? Why or why not?
2. How many of the "false beliefs about what persons are" do you accept? Do you agree with Parfit that these are indeed "false beliefs"?
3. If a teletransporter were to create a "Replica" of you, do you think that the "Replica" would be you? Defend your answer.
4. Given what he says in this article, how do you think Parfit would respond to someone who argues for human immortality?
5. Can you think of other findings of modern science that would support the Bundle Theory? Can you think of any that might support the Ego Theory?

Disciplining the Body 10

MICHEL FOUCAULT

Michel Foucault (1926–1984), a French philosopher and historian of thought, was born in Poitiers. The son of a prominent surgeon, Foucault's father encouraged him to follow in his career footsteps, but Foucault opted to pursue an education in philosophy and psychology instead. After attending Saint-Stanislaus school and the prestigious lycée Henri-IV in Paris, he was admitted to the École Normale Supérièure, the training ground for many French intellectuals, in 1946. At the École Normale, Foucault studied with **Maurice Merleau-Ponty,** receiving his license in philosophy in 1948. This was followed two years later by a license in psychology, and in 1952 by a degree in psychopathology.

After receiving his degree, Foucault worked in a psychiatric hospital before moving to the University of Uppsala in Sweden in 1954, where he taught French for several years. During this time he also published his first book, *Maladie mentale et personalité* (*Mental Illness and Personality*), a book that he later repudiated.

After brief stints at the University of Warsaw and the University of Hamburg, Foucault returned to France to complete his doctorate. One of his required theses, *Folie et déraison: Histoire de la folie ý l'âge classique* (*Madness and Unreason: History of Madness in the Classical Age*), was published in 1961 and became his first important work. Foucault's views at this time led many to associate him with the antipsychiatry movement, a movement led by R. D. Laing and Félix Guattari that attempted to expose the hidden levels of domination in psychiatric methods and discourse.

Shortly after returning to France, Foucault acquired a position teaching philosophy at the University of Clermont-Ferrand, where he met Daniel Defert, with whom he lived in a nonmonogamous partnership for the rest of his life. When Defert was sent to Tunisia for his military service, Foucault moved to the University of Tunis and taught there for two years. Foucault and Defert returned to France in 1968, the year in which students and workers took to the streets in a major challenge to the French government. As with most French intellectuals of the time, the crushing of this revolt by the French government had a great impact on Foucault's life and thinking. Although he had briefly associated with the French Communist Party in the 1940s, Foucault's political activism became much more pronounced after the events of 1968. He became the first head of the philosophy department at the University of Vincennes, a new experimental university created by the French government. In this capacity, Foucault not only assembled a faculty of radical academics who were strongly critical of capitalism and the French government, but he also joined students in occupying administration buildings and in battling police. Foucault also helped found the *Groupe d'Information sur les Prisons* (the Prison Information Group), an organization whose purpose was to give voice to the concerns of prisoners. Despite these activities, in 1970 Foucault was elected to the Collège de France, France's most prestigious academic institution, as Professor of the History of Systems of Thought.

During the 1970s and early 1980s, Foucault's reputation grew rapidly, and he lectured in many different countries. Although he held his position at the Collège de France until his death, he frequently lectured at universities in the United States, especially at the State University of New York at Buffalo and at the University of California at Berkeley. During one of his trips to the United States in 1975, Foucault took LSD in Death Valley National Park, an experience that he would later describe as the best of his life. Also, while in the United States, Foucault actively participated in the gay culture that was flourishing in San Francisco. An early victim of HIV/AIDS, Foucault died of an AIDS-related illness in Paris in 1984.

Scholars of Foucault's philosophy generally divide his mature thinking into three distinct periods. In the mid-1960s, his thinking is associated with **structuralism,** the modern philosophical movement that replaces the focus on the subject or consciousness, found in movements such as existentialism and humanistic psychology, with a concern for the text or object. This focus of structuralism is most clearly expressed in two of Foucault's works: *Les Mots et les Choses* (1966; translated as *The Order of Things*) and *L'Archéologie du savoir* (1969; *The Archaeology of Knowledge*).

His second period, which coincided with his marked turn toward political activism, has been labeled his **poststructuralist** or **genealogical** period. During this period, Foucault focused on the ways in which power and knowledge permeate and generate each other (to capture this mutual confluence, Foucault often uses the hyphenated term **"power-knowledge"**) and on the discourse and methods of domination—the so-called "technologies of power"—that have evolved in modern societies. These themes are most clearly reflected in what is perhaps Foucault's best-known work, *Surveiller et Punir* (1975; translated as *Discipline and Punish*), and in the first volume of his *Histoire de la sexualité* (1976; *The History of Sexuality*).

Finally, in his last published works, the remaining volumes of *Histoire de la sexualité*, Foucault focused on the origin of the subject or self, a concept that he had denigrated in his earlier structuralist criticisms of existentialism and humanistic psychology. These latter works are also characterized by a more traditional philosophical style than are the works from his earlier periods.

In the following brief selection, which is excerpted from *Surveiller et Punir*, Foucault discusses the **genealogy** of the soul and its relation to the body. According to Foucault, the soul is not a **substance** as portrayed by Christian theology, but a product of the power relationships expressed in society. He specifically traces the origin of the soul to the discipline exerted upon those who are subjected to punishment or, more generally, to the techniques of control used to subjugate the subordinate members of society to those in power. In this respect, the soul serves as one of the tools of what Foucault calls the "microphysics" of power—processes and procedures through which the body is disciplined so that it becomes a reliable and controllable force of production. This analysis of the origin of the soul leads Foucault to reverse Plato's claim that the body is the prison of the soul. Rather, as one of the elements in the subjugation of the body, Foucault states that it is the soul that is the prison of the body.

This selection also contains a succinct discussion of Foucault's concept of power-knowledge. Rejecting the traditional philosophical claim that knowledge must be disinterested and thus divorced from considerations of power, Foucault argues that knowledge and power mutually interpenetrate and produce one another. As he says, "Knowledge and power directly implicate one another. There is no relation of power without the correlative constitution of a field of knowledge, nor is there knowledge that does not at the same time imply and constitute relations of power."

Questions for Reading

1. How, according to Foucault, do relationships of power affect the body?
2. What does Foucault mean by the term *microphysics of power*? What are some of the presuppositions for studying this microphysics of power?
3. How does Foucault describe the relationship of power and knowledge? What are some of the traditional claims about knowledge that Foucault calls into question?
4. What use does Foucault make of Kantorowitz's analysis of the "body of the king"? How, in Foucault's analysis, does the body of the king differ from the body of the condemned man?
5. How, according to Foucault, did the soul originate? What is the soul's relation to the body?

LONG AGO, HISTORIANS STARTED DESCRIBING THE history of the body. They have studied the body in the field of historical demography or pathology. They have viewed it as the seat of needs and appetites, as the location of physiological processes and metabolisms, as the target of bacterial and viral attacks. They have shown the extent to which historical processes have been implicated in what could be seen as the purely biological base of existence, and what place biological "occurrences," such as the circulation of bacilli or the lengthening of the life-span, should be accorded in the history of society.[1]

But the body is also directly immersed in a political field; relationships of power have an immediate grip on it. They lay siege to it, brand it, tame it, torture it, compel it to work, force it to observe ceremony, exact signs from it. This political investment of the body is linked, in accordance with complex reciprocal relations, to its economic utilization; it is, for the most part, as a force of production that the body is invested with relationships of power and domination. But, in return, its constitution as a force of labor is possible only if it is caught in a system of subjugation (where need is also a carefully arranged, calculated, and utilized political instrument); the body becomes a useful force only if it is at once a productive body and a subjugated body. This subjugation is not obtained solely by the instruments of violence or ideology; it can also very well be direct, physical, the play of force against force, bearing on material elements, and nonetheless not be violent. It may be calculated, organized, technically well-thought-out; it may be subtle, making use neither of arms nor terror, and yet remain of a physical order. That is to say, there may be a "knowledge" of the body that is not exactly the science of its functioning, and a control of its forces that is more than the ability to vanquish them. This knowledge and this control constitute what could be called the political technology of the body. Of

This is the editor's translation of a selection from Surveiller et Punir; Naissance de la prison, *by Michel Foucault, Paris: Éditions Gallimard, 1975.*

course, this technology is diffuse, rarely formulated in continuous, systematic discourse; it is frequently composed of bits and pieces. It puts into work a disparate stock of tools and procedures. Despite the coherence of its results, it is often no more than a multiform instrumentation. Further, one cannot localize it in either a definite type of institution or state apparatus. Rather institutions and state apparatuses have recourse to it; they use, value or impose certain of its procedures. However, in its mechanisms and effects, it is located on a very different level. It is a matter of a sort of microphysics of power that the apparatuses and institutions put in play, but whose field of validity is, in a sense, located between these large functionings and the bodies themselves with their materiality and their forces.

As it happens, the study of this microphysics presupposes that the power it exercises is not conceived as a property, but as a strategy, that its dominating effects are not attributed to an "appropriation," but to arrangements, maneuvers, tactics, techniques, functionings. It presupposes that one decipher in it a network of relations, always taut, always in full swing, instead of a privilege which one might possess, that one take the perpetual battle as the model of it rather than the contract governing a transfer or the conquest securing a territory. In summary, one must acknowledge that this power is exercised rather than possessed, that it is not the acquired or preserved "privilege" of the dominant class, but the combined effect of its strategic positions—an effect that manifests and sometimes extends the position of those who are dominated. On the other hand, this power is not enforced purely and simply, as an obligation or interdiction, on those who "do not have it"; it invests them, passes by them and through them. It takes hold of them, just as, in their struggle against it, they themselves in their turn resist the grip that it exerts on them. This means that these relations go far down into the depths of society, that they are not localized in the relations of the state to the citizens or on the frontier between classes, and that they are not satisfied by reproducing the general form of the law or the government at the level of individuals, bodies, gestures and behaviors. It means that while there is continuity (in fact, in this form they are well articulated through a whole series

of complex mechanisms) there is neither **analogy** nor **homology,** but a specificity of mechanism and **modality.** In short, they are not **univocal;** they define innumerable points of confrontation, fires of instability, each of which entails its own risks of conflict, of struggles, and of at least a transitory inversion of the relations of constraint. The reversal of these "micropowers" thus does not obey the law of all or nothing; it is not acquired once and for all by a new control of the apparatuses or by either a new functioning or destruction of the institutions. On the other hand, none of its localized episodes can be inscribed in history except by the effects that it induces on the whole network in which it is enmeshed.

Perhaps we should also entirely renounce a tradition which lets us imagine that knowledge can only exist where the relations of power are suspended and that knowledge can only develop outside of its injunctions, requirements, and interests. Perhaps we should renounce the belief that power makes one crazy and that, in return, the renunciation of power is one of the conditions of becoming learned. Rather we should admit that power produces knowledge (and not simply by favoring it because it is of service to power or by applying it because it is useful). Power and knowledge directly implicate one another. There is no relation of power without the correlative constitution of a field of knowledge, nor is there knowledge that does not at the same time imply and constitute relations of power. These relationships of "**power-knowledge**" are therefore not to be analyzed from the standpoint of a subject of knowledge who is or is not free in relation to the system of power; but, on the contrary, the subject who knows, the objects to be known, and the modalities of knowledge must be viewed as so many effects of these fundamental implications of power-knowledge and their historical transformations. In brief, it is not the activity of the subject of knowledge that produces knowledge, useful or resistant to power, but knowledge-power—the processes and struggles that traverse it and of which it is constituted—that determines the forms and possible domains of knowledge.

To analyze the political investment of the body and the microphysics of power thus assumes that one renounces—where power is concerned—the violence-ideology opposition, the metaphor of property, the model of the contract or that of conquest. Where knowledge is concerned one must renounce the opposition between what is "interested" and what is "disinterested," the model of knowledge, and the primacy of the subject. Laying claim to a word used by Petty,[2] but giving it a different meaning than the one given to it by Petty and his contemporaries in the seventeenth century, one might think of this as a political "anatomy." This would not be the study of a state envisioned as a "body" (with its elements, resources, and forces), nor would it be the study of the body and its surroundings envisioned as a small state. It would deal with the "political body," as an ensemble of material elements and techniques which serve as arms, as relays, as routes of communication, and as points of support for the relations of power and knowledge that invest human bodies and subjugate them by making them into objects of knowledge.

It is a matter of re-situating the techniques of punishment—whether they get hold of the body in the ritual of corporal punishment or whether they are addressed to the soul—in the history of the political body. It is a question of taking penal practices less as a consequence of judicial theories than as a chapter of political anatomy.

Kantorowitz[3] has previously given a remarkable analysis of the "body of the king"—a body double according to the juridical theology formulated in the Middle Ages, since it not only comprises the transitory element that is born and dies, but also another element that continues through time and is maintained as the physical and yet intangible support of the kingdom. Around this duality, which was initially close to the Christological model, are organized an iconography, a political theory of the monarchy, juridical mechanisms that simultaneously distinguish and link the person of the king and the demands of the crown, as well as an entire ritual that culminates in the coronation, the funeral, and the ceremonies of submission. One might imagine placing the body of the condemned man at the opposite pole. He also has his juridical status; he instigates his own ceremonial and he calls together an entire theoretical discourse, not for the purpose of laying the foundation of the "greater power" allocated to the person of the king, but in order to

encode the "lack of power" which marks those who are subjected to a punishment. In the most dismal region of the political field, the condemned man symbolizes the symmetrical but inverted figure of the king. We should analyze what, in homage to Kantorowitz, might be called the "least body of the condemned man."

If the excess power possessed by the king brings about the doubling of his body, has not the excess power exerted on the submissive body of the condemned man instigated another type of doubling? That of something incorporeal, of a "soul," as Mably[4] calls it. The history of this "microphysics" of the punitive power would then be a **genealogy,** or an item for a genealogy, of the modern "soul." Instead of seeing in this soul the reactivated remains of an ideology, one would recognize it rather as the present correlative of a certain technology of power on the body. One should not say that the soul is an illusion or an ideological effect. The soul exists; it has a reality. It is produced permanently—around, on the surface of, and within the interior of the body—by the functioning of a power that is exerted on those who are punished, and, in a more general way, on those who are watched, who are trained and corrected, on madmen, children, students, the colonized, those who are fastened to the machinery of production and who are supervised for the remainder of their lives. The historical reality of this soul, in contrast to the soul represented by Christian theology, is not born guilty and punishable; rather it is born from the procedures of punishment, of surveillance, of chastisement and constraint. This real, incorporeal soul is not a **substance;** it is the element wherein the effects of a certain type of power are articulated, the reference of a kind of knowledge, the gears through which the relations of power put in place a possible kind of knowledge and knowledge renews and reinforces the effects of power. On this reality-reference, diverse concepts have been built and domains of analysis have been carved out—psyche, subjectivity, personality, consciousness, and so on. On it, scientific techniques and discourses have been erected; from it, the moral demands of **humanism** have been emphasized. But make no mistake about it—one has not substituted a real man, the object of knowledge, philosophical reflection or technical intervention, for the soul, the illusion of the theologians. The man whom we are told about, whom we are invited to liberate, is already in himself the effect of a subjugation much more profound than him. A "soul," which is itself an item in the control that power exerts on the body, inhabits him and brings him into existence. The soul is an effect and instrument of a political anatomy; the soul is the prison of the body.

NOTES

1. Cf. E. Le Roy-Ladurie, "L'histoire immobile," *Annalles*, May–June, 1974.
2. Foucault is referring to the British scientist and philosopher William Petty, who lived from 1623 to 1687.
3. E. Kantorowitz, *The King's Two Bodies*, 1959.
4. Cf. G. de Mably, De la legislation, Oeuvres completes, IX, 1789.

Questions for Thought

1. How you think your own life has been affected by the power relations existing in the society in which you live?
2. To what extent do you believe that you have been subjected to discipline and subjugation? To what extent have you become what Foucault describes as a force of production?
3. Do you agree with Foucault's claim that power and knowledge mutually implicate one another? Why or why not?
4. What are Foucault's principal criticisms of the Christian conception of the soul? Can you think of any ways in which the Christian conception of soul could be used as a tool of control?
5. Do you agree with Foucault's claim that the soul is the prison of the body? Defend your answer.

11   Where Am I?

DANIEL C. DENNETT

Daniel C. Dennett (b. 1942) is a contemporary North American philosopher who currently teaches and serves as the director of the Center for Cognitive Studies at Tufts University in Massachusetts. Dennett, whose father was a historian and whose mother was an editor and teacher, was educated at Harvard and Oxford Universities. He has taught at a number of universities and has been a fellow at the Center for Advanced Research in the Behavioral Sciences. He has also received fellowships from the National Endowment for the Humanities and a Fulbright fellowship to attend the University of Bristol. In addition to his academic activities, Dennett has designed exhibits on computers at several museums, and he is a farmer, wine maker, and sculptor.

Dennett has contributed to numerous philosophical journals, and he has served as editorial commentator for *Behavioral and Brain Sciences*. His books include *Content and Consciousness* (1969); *Brainstorms: Philosophical Essays on Mind and Psychology* (1978); *Elbow Room: The Varieties of Free Will Worth Wanting* (1984); *The Intentional Stance* (1987); *Consciousness Explained* (1991); *Darwin's Dangerous Idea* (1995); *Kinds of Minds* (1996); *Brainchildren: A Collection of Essays 1984–1996* (1998); and *Freedom Evolves*

(2003). In addition, he was coeditor of the popular anthology *The Mind's I: Fantasies and Reflections on Self and Soul,* which was published in 1981.

In the following selection from *Brainstorms,* Dennett uses a different literary form—science fiction—to raise some of the same questions about the self and its relation to the body that Parfit and others posed in preceding selections. In the first philosophically important occurrence in the story, Dennett's brain is surgically removed from his body and placed in a vat of fluid. The brain, however, continues to control his body through the use of cerebral radio links. As his body stands in the laboratory looking at his brain, he naturally raises the question of where his true self resides. He initially decides that he is his body and not his brain, and his body goes to Tulsa, leaving his brain in Houston. This initial decision is reversed when the radio links connecting his body to his brain are severed, and his mind or consciousness shifts back to the laboratory in Houston. After Dennett's brain is electronically linked to a new body without losing its personality, the decision that he is his brain and not his body is reinforced.

Things become more complicated when Dennett discovers that scientists have built a computer duplicate of his brain and that his new body can switch back and forth between his biological brain and his computer brain with no loss of function or identity. Dennett now wonders whether his identify is located in his biological brain or in his computer brain, and he worries about the possibility of one of his brains being connected to a second body. Who, then, would be Dennett? The story concludes with a disruption in the synchronicity between the two brains and with the recognition that there are two slightly different Dennetts occupying the same body. Again he is faced with the question "Who is the real Dennett?"

Questions for Reading

1. Why and how does Dennett's brain get separated from his body?
2. Why does Dennett initially conclude that his self is where his body is and not where his brain is? What causes him to change his mind?
3. What does Dennett mean by "point of view"? Why does he believe that one's point of view differs from the content of one's beliefs or thoughts?
4. What happens to Dennett when the radio links between his body and brain are severed? What philosophical insights does he derive from this experience?
5. How does Dennett react to the creation of his computer brain? Why is Dennett upset about the prospect of one of his brains being connected to another body?
6. How does Dennett's story end? What are some of the philosophical insights that he draws from it?

NOW THAT I'VE WON MY SUIT UNDER THE Freedom of Information Act, I am at liberty to reveal for the first time a curious episode in my life that may be of interest not only to those engaged in research in the philosophy of mind, artificial intelligence, and neuroscience but also to the general public.

Several years ago I was approached by Pentagon officials who asked me to volunteer for a highly dangerous and secret mission. In collaboration with NASA and Howard Hughes, the Department of Defense was spending billions to develop a Supersonic Tunneling Underground Device, or

From Daniel Dennett, Brainstorms: Philosophical Essays on Mind and Psychology, *The MIT Press, 1978. Reprinted by permission of the publisher.*

STUD. It was supposed to tunnel through the earth's core at great speed and deliver a specially designed atomic warhead "right up the Red's missile silo," as one of the Pentagon brass put it.

The problem was that in an early test they had succeeded in lodging a warhead about a mile deep under Tulsa, Oklahoma, and they wanted me to retrieve it for them. "Why me?" I asked. Well, the mission involved some pioneering applications of current brain research, and they had heard of my interest in brains and of course my Faustian curiosity and great courage and so forth. . . . Well, how could I refuse? The difficulty that brought the Pentagon to my door was that the device I'd been asked to recover was fiercely radioactive, in a new way. According to monitoring instruments, something about the nature of the device and its complex interactions with pockets of material deep in the earth had produced radiation that could cause severe abnormalities in certain tissues of the brain. No way had been found to shield the brain from these deadly rays, which were apparently harmless to other tissues and organs of the body. So it had been decided that the person sent to recover the device should *leave his brain behind*. It would be kept in a safe place where it could execute its normal control functions by elaborate radio links. Would I submit to a surgical procedure that would completely remove my brain, which would then be placed in a life-support system at the Manned Spacecraft Center in Houston? Each input and output pathway, as it was severed, would be restored by a pair of microminiaturized radio transceivers, one attached precisely to the brain, the other to the nerve stumps in the empty cranium. No information would be lost, all the connectivity would be preserved. At first I was a bit reluctant. Would it really work? The Houston brain surgeons encouraged me. "Think of it," they said, "as a mere *stretching* of the nerves. If your brain were just moved over an *inch* in your skull, that would not alter or impair your mind. We're simply going to make the nerves indefinitely elastic by splicing radio links into them."

I was shown around the life-support lab in Houston and saw the sparkling new vat in which my brain would be placed, were I to agree. I met the large and brilliant support team of neurologists, hematologists, biophysicists, and electrical engineers, and after several days of discussions and demonstrations, I agreed to give it a try. I was subjected to an enormous array of blood tests, brains scans, experiments, interviews, and the like. They took down my autobiography at great length, recorded tedious lists of my beliefs, hopes, fears, and tastes. They even listed my favorite stereo recordings and gave me a crash session of psychoanalysis.

The day for surgery arrived at last and of course I was anesthetized and remember nothing of the operation itself. When I came out of anesthesia, I opened my eyes, looked around, and asked the inevitable, the traditional, the lamentably hackneyed postoperative question: "Where am I?" The nurse smiled down at me. "You're in Houston," she said, and I reflected that this still had a good chance of being the truth one way or another. She handed me a mirror. Sure enough, there were the tiny antennae poling up through their titanium ports cemented into my skull.

"I gather the operation was a success," I said. "I want to go see my brain." They led me (I was a bit dizzy and unsteady) down a long corridor and into the life-support lab. A cheer went up from the assembled support team, and I responded with what I hoped was a jaunty salute. Still feeling lightheaded, I was helped over to the life-support vat. I peered through the glass. There, floating in what looked like ginger ale, was undeniably a human brain, though it was almost covered with printed circuit chips, plastic tubules, electrodes, and other paraphernalia. "Is that mine?" I asked. "Hit the output transmitter switch there on the side of the vat and see for yourself," the project director replied. I moved the switch to OFF, and immediately slumped, groggy and nauseated, into the arms of the technicians, one of whom kindly restored the switch to its ON position. While I recovered my equilibrium and composure, I thought to myself: "Well, here I am sitting on a folding chair, staring through a piece of plate glass at my own brain. . . . But wait," I said to myself, "shouldn't I have thought, 'Here I am, suspended in a bubbling fluid, being stared at by my own eyes'?" I tried to think this latter thought. I tried to project it into the tank, offering it hopefully to my brain, but I failed to carry off the exercise with any conviction. I tried again. "Here am *I*, Daniel Dennett, suspended in a bubbling fluid, being stared at by my own eyes." No, it just didn't work. Most puzzling and confusing. Being a philosopher of firm **physicalist** conviction, I believed unswervingly that the token-ing of my thoughts was occurring somewhere in my brain: yet, when I thought "Here I am," where the thought occurred to me was *here,* outside the vat, where I, Dennett, was standing staring at my brain.

I tried and tried to think myself into the vat, but to no avail. I tried to build up to the task by doing mental exercises. I thought to myself, "The sun is shining *over there,*" five times in rapid succession, each time mentally ostending a different place: in order, the sunlit corner of the lab, the visible front lawn of the hospital, Houston, Mars, Jupiter. I found I had little difficulty in getting my "there's" to hop all over the celestial map with their proper references. I could loft a "there" in an instant through the farthest reaches of space, and then aim the next "there" with pinpoint accuracy at the up-per left quadrant of a freckle on my arm. Why was I having such trouble with "here?" "Here in Houston" worked well enough, and so did "here in the lab," and even "here in this part of the lab," but "here in the vat" always seemed merely an unmeant mental mouthing. I tried closing my eyes while thinking it. This seemed to help, but still I couldn't manage to pull it off, except perhaps for a fleeting instant. I couldn't be sure. The discovery that I couldn't be sure was also unsettling. How did I know *where* I meant by "here" when I thought "here?" Could I *think* I meant one place when in fact I meant another? I didn't see how that could be admitted without untying the few bonds of inti-macy between a person and his own mental life that had survived the onslaught of the brain scientists and philosophers, the physicalists and **behaviorists.** Perhaps I was incorrigible about where I *meant* when I said "here." But in my present circum-stances it seemed that either I was doomed by sheer force of mental habit to thinking systematically false indexical thoughts, or where a person is (and hence where his thoughts are tokened for purposes of semantic analysis) is not necessarily where his brain, the physical seat of his soul, resides. Nagged by confusion, I attempted to orient myself by falling back on a favorite philosopher's ploy. I began naming things.

"Yorick," I said aloud to my brain, "you are my brain. The rest of my body, seated in this chair, I dub 'Hamlet.'" So here we all are: Yorick's my brain, Hamlet's my body, and I am Dennett. *Now,* where am I? And when I think "where am I?" where's that thought tokened? Is it tokened in my brain, lounging in the vat, or right here between my ears where it *seems* to be tokened? Or nowhere? Its *temporal* coordinates give me no trouble; must it not have spatial coordinates as well? I began making a list of the alternatives.

1. *Where Hamlet goes, there goes Dennett.* This principle was easily refuted by appeal to the familiar brain-transplant thought experiments so enjoyed by philosophers. If Tom and Dick switch brains, Tom is the fellow with Dick's former body—just ask him; he'll claim to be Tom, and tell you the most inti-mate details of Tom's autobiography. It was clear enough, then, that my current body and I could part company, but not likely that I could be sepa-rated from my brain. The rule of thumb that emerged so plainly from the thought experiments was that in a brain-transplant operation, one wants to be the *donor,* not the recipient. Better to call such an operation a *body* transplant, in fact. So perhaps the truth was,

2. *Where Yorick goes, there goes Dennett.* This was not at all appealing, however. How could I be in the vat and not about to go anywhere, when I was so obviously outside the vat looking in and beginning to make guilty plans to return to my room for a substantial lunch? This begged the question I real-ized, but it still seemed to be getting at something important. Casting about for some support for my intuition, I hit upon a legalistic sort of argument that might have appealed to Locke.

Suppose, I argued to myself, I were now to fly to California, rob a bank, and be apprehended. In which state would I be tried: in California, where the robbery took place, or in Texas, where the brains of the outfit were located? Would I be a California felon with an out-of-state brain, or a Texas felon remotely controlling an accomplice of sorts in California? It seemed possible that I might beat such a rap just on the undecidability of that jurisdictional question, though perhaps it would be deemed an interstate, and hence Federal, offense. In any event, suppose I were convicted. Was it likely that California would be satisfied to throw Hamlet into the brig, knowing that Yorick was living the good life and luxuriously taking the waters in

Texas? Would Texas incarcerate Yorick, leaving Hamlet free to take the next boat to Rio? This alternative appealed to me. Barring capital punishment or other cruel and unusual punishment, the state would be obliged to maintain the life-support system for Yorick though they might move him from Houston to Leavenworth, and aside from the unpleasantness of the opprobrium, I, for one, would not mind at all and would consider myself a free man under those circumstances. If the state has an interest in forcibly relocating persons in institutions, it would fail to relocate *me* in any institution by locating Yorick there. If this were true, it suggested a third alternative.

3. *Dennett is wherever he thinks he is.* Generalized, the claim was as follows: At any given time a person has a *point of view,* and the location of the point of view (which is determined internally by the content of the point of view) is also the location of the person.

Such a proposition is not without its perplexities, but to me it seemed a step in the right direction. The only trouble was that it seemed to place one in a heads-I-win/tails-you-lose situation of unlikely infallibility as regards location. Hadn't I myself often been wrong about where I was, and at least as often uncertain? Couldn't one get lost? Of course, but getting lost *geographically* is not the only way one might get lost. If one were lost in the woods one could attempt to reassure oneself with the consolation that at least one knew where one was: one was right *here* in the familiar surroundings of one's own body. Perhaps in this case one would not have drawn one's attention to much to be thankful for. Still, there were worse plights imaginable, and I wasn't sure I wasn't in such a plight right now.

Point of view clearly had something to do with personal location, but it was itself an unclear notion. It was obvious that the content of one's point of view was not the same as or determined by the content of one's beliefs or thoughts. For example, what should we say about the point of view of the Cinerama viewer who shrieks and twists in his seat as the roller-coaster footage overcomes his psychic distancing? Has he forgotten that he is safely seated in the theater? Here I was inclined to say that the person is experiencing an illusory shift in point of view. In other cases, my inclination to call such shifts illusory was less strong. The workers in laboratories and plants who handle dangerous materials by operating feedback-controlled mechanical arms and hands undergo a shift in point of view that is crisper and more pronounced than anything Cinerama can provoke. They can feel the heft and slipperiness of the containers they manipulate with their metal fingers. They know perfectly well where they are and are not fooled into false beliefs by the experience, yet it is as if they were inside the isolation chamber they are peering into. With mental effort, they can manage to shift their point of view back and forth, rather like making a transparent Necker cube or an Escher drawing change orientation before one's eyes. It does seem extravagant to suppose that in performing this bit of mental gymnastics, they are transporting *themselves* back and forth.

Still their example gave me hope. If I was in fact in the vat in spite of my intuitions, I might be able to train myself to adopt that point of view even as a matter of habit. I should dwell on images of myself comfortably floating in my vat, beaming volitions to that familiar body *out there*. I reflected that the ease or difficulty of this task was presumably independent of the truth about the location of one's brain. Had I been practicing before the operation, I might now be finding it second nature. You might now yourself try such a *trompe l'oeil*. Imagine you have written an inflammatory letter which has been published in the *Times,* the result of which is that the government has chosen to impound your brain for a probationary period of three years in its Dangerous Brain Clinic in Bethesda, Maryland. Your body of course is allowed freedom to earn a salary and thus to continue its function of laying up income to be taxed. At this moment, however, your body is seated in an auditorium listening to a peculiar account by Daniel Dennett of his own similar experience. Try it. Think of yourself in Bethesda, and then hark back longingly to your body, far away, and yet *seeming* so near. It is only with long-distance restraint (yours? the government's?) that you can control your impulse to get those hands clapping in polite applause before navigating the old body to the rest room and a well-deserved glass of evening sherry in the lounge. The task of imagination is certainly difficult, but if you achieve your goal the results might be consoling.

Anyway, there I was in Houston, lost in thought as one might say, but not for long. My speculations were soon interrupted by the Houston doctors, who wished to test out my new prosthetic nervous system before sending me off on my hazardous mission. As I mentioned before, I was a bit dizzy at first, not surprisingly, although I soon habituated myself to my new circumstances (which were, after all, well nigh indistinguishable from my old circumstances). My accommodation was not perfect, however, and to this day I continue to be plagued by minor coordination difficulties. The speed of light is fast, but finite, and as my brain and body moved farther and farther apart, the delicate interaction of my feedback systems is thrown into disarray by the time lags. Just as one is rendered close to speechless by a delayed or echoic hearing of one's speaking voice so, for instance, I am virtually unable to track a moving object with my eyes whenever my brain and my body are more than a few miles apart. In most matters my impairment is scarcely detectable, though I can no longer hit a slow curve ball with the authority of yore. There are some compensations of course. Though liquor tastes as good as ever, and warms my gullet while corroding my liver, I can drink it in any quantity I please, without becoming the slightest bit inebriated, a curiosity some of my close friends may have noticed (though I occasionally have *feigned* inebriation, so as not to draw attention to my unusual circumstances). For similar reasons, I take aspirin orally for a sprained wrist, but if the pain persists I ask Houston to administer codeine to me *in vitro*. In times of illness the phone bill can be staggering.

But to return to my adventure. At length, both the doctors and I were satisfied that I was ready to undertake my subterranean mission. And so I left my brain in Houston and headed by helicopter for Tulsa. Well, in any case, that's the way it seemed to me. That's how I would put it, just off the top of my head as it were. On the trip I reflected further about my earlier anxieties and decided that my first postoperative speculations had been tinged with panic. The matter was not nearly as strange or **metaphysical** as I had been supposing. Where was I? In two places, clearly: both inside the vat and outside of it. Just as one can stand with one foot in Connecticut and the other in Rhode Island, I was in two places at once. I had become one of those scattered individuals we used to hear so much about. The more I considered this answer, the more obviously true it appeared. But,

strange to say, the more true it appeared, the less important the question to which it could be the true answer seemed. A sad, but not unprecedented, fate for a philosophical question to suffer. This answer did not completely satisfy me, of course. There lingered some question to which I should have liked an answer, which was neither "Where are all my various and sundry parts?" nor "What is my current point of view?" Or at least there seemed to be such a question. For it did seem undeniable that in some sense *I* and not merely *most of me* was descending into the earth under Tulsa in search of an atomic warhead.

When I found the warhead, I was certainly glad I had left my brain behind, for the pointer on the specially built Geiger counter I had brought with me was off the dial. I called Houston on my ordinary radio and told the operation control center of my position and my progress. In return, they gave me instructions for dismantling the vehicle, based upon my on-site observations. I had set to work with my cutting torch when all of a sudden a terrible thing happened. I went stone deaf. At first I thought it was only my radio earphones that had broken, but when I tapped on my helmet, I heard nothing. Apparently the auditory transceivers had gone on the fritz. I could no longer hear Houston or my own voice, but I could speak, so I started telling them what had happened. In mid-sentence, I knew something else had gone wrong. My vocal apparatus had become paralyzed. Then my right hand went limp—another transceiver had gone. I was truly in deep trouble. But worse was to follow. After a few more minutes, I went blind. I cursed my luck, and then I cursed the scientists who had led me into this grave peril. There I was, deaf, dumb, and blind, in a radioactive hole more than a mile under Tulsa. Then the last of my cerebral radio links broke, and suddenly I was faced with a new and even more shocking problem: whereas an instant before I had been buried alive in Oklahoma, now I was disembodied in Houston. My recognition of my new status was not immediate. It took me several very anxious minutes before it dawned on me that my poor body lay several hundred miles away, with heart pulsing and lungs respiring, but otherwise as dead as the body of any heart-transplant donor, its skull packed with useless, broken electronic gear. The shift in perspective I had earlier found well nigh impossible now seemed quite natural. Though I could think myself back into my body in the tunnel under Tulsa, it took some effort to sustain the illusion. For surely it was an illusion to suppose I was still in Oklahoma: I had lost all contact with that body.

It occurred to me then, with one of those rushes of revelation of which we should be suspicious, that I had stumbled upon an impressive demonstration of the immateriality of the soul based upon physicalist principles and **premises.** For as the last radio signal between Tulsa and Houston died away, had I not changed location from Tulsa to Houston at the speed of light? And had I not accomplished this without any increase in mass? What moved from A to B at such speed was surely myself, or at any rate my soul or mind—the massless center of my being and home of my consciousness. My *point of view* had lagged somewhat behind, but I had already noted the indirect bearing of point of view on personal location. I could not see how a physicalist philosopher could quarrel with this except by taking the dire and counterintuitive route of banishing all talk of persons. Yet the notion of personhood was so well entrenched in everyone's world view, or so it seemed to me, that any denial would be as curiously unconvincing, as systematically disingenuous, as the Cartesian negation, "non sum."

The joy of philosophic discovery thus tided me over some very bad minutes or perhaps hours as the helplessness and hopelessness of my situation became more apparent to me. Waves of panic and even nausea swept over me, made all the more horrible by the absence of their normal body-dependent **phenomenology.** No adrenaline rush of tingles in the arms, no pounding heart, no premonitory salivation. I did feel a dread sinking feeling in my bowels at one point, and this tricked me momentarily into the false hope that I was undergoing a reversal of the process that landed me in this fix—a gradual undisembodiment. But the isolation and uniqueness of that twinge soon convinced me that it was simply the first of a plague of phantom body hallucinations that I, like any other amputee, would be all too likely to suffer.

My mood then was chaotic. On the one hand, I was fired up with elation of my philosophic discovery and was wracking my brain (one of the few familiar things I could still do), trying to figure out how to communicate my discovery to the journals; while on the other, I was bitter, lonely, and filled with dread and uncertainty. Fortunately, this did not last long, for my technical support team sedated me into a dreamless sleep from which I awoke, hearing with magnificent fidelity the familiar opening strains of my favorite recordings! It did not take me long to realize that I was hearing the music without ears. The output from the stereo stylus was being fed through some fancy rectification circuitry directly into my auditory nerve. I was mainlining Brahms, an unforgettable experience for any stereo buff. At the end of the record it did not surprise me to hear the reassuring voice of the project director speaking into a microphone that was now my prosthetic ear. He confirmed my analysis of what had gone wrong and assured me that steps were being taken to re-embody me. He did not elaborate, and after a few more recordings, I found myself drifting off to sleep. My sleep lasted, I later learned, for the better part of a year, and when I awoke, it was to find myself fully restored to my senses. When I looked into the mirror, though, I was a bit startled to see an unfamiliar face. Bearded and a bit heavier, bearing no doubt a family resemblance to my former face, and with the same look of a spritely intelligence and resolute character, but definitely a new face. Further self-explorations of an intimate nature left me no doubt that this was a new body, and the project director confirmed my conclusions. He did not volunteer any information on the past history of my new body and I decided (wisely, I think in retrospect) not to pry. As many philosophers unfamiliar with my ordeal have more recently speculated, the acquisition of a new body leaves one's *person* intact. And after a period of adjustment to a new voice, new muscular strengths and weaknesses, and so forth, one's *personality* is by and large also preserved. More dramatic changes in personality have been routinely observed in people who have undergone extensive plastic surgery, to say nothing of sex-change operations, and I think no one contests the survival of the person in such cases. In any event I soon accommodated to my new body, to the point of being unable to recover any of its novelties to my consciousness or even memory. The view in the mirror soon became utterly familiar. That view, by the way, still revealed antennae, and so I was not surprised to learn that my brain had not been moved from its haven in the life-support lab.

I decided that good old Yorick deserved a visit. I and my new body, whom we might as well call Fortinbras, strode into the familiar lab to another round of applause from the technicians, who were of course congratulating themselves, not me. Once more I stood before the vat and contemplated poor Yorick, and on a whim I once again cavalierly flicked off the output transmitter switch. Imagine my surprise when nothing unusual happened. No fainting spell, no nausea, no noticeable change. A technician hurried to restore the switch to ON, but still I felt nothing. I demanded an explanation, which the project director hastened to provide. It seems that before they had even operated on the first occasion, they had constructed a computer duplicate of my brain, reproducing both the complete information-processing structure and the computational speed of my brain in a giant computer program. After the operation, but before they had dared to send me off on my mission to Oklahoma, they had run this computer system and Yorick side by side. The incoming signals from Hamlet were sent simultaneously to Yorick's transceivers and to the computer's array of inputs. And the outputs from Yorick were not only beamed back to Hamlet, my body; they were recorded and checked against the simultaneous output of the computer program, which was called "Hubert" for reasons obscure to me. Over days and even weeks, the outputs were identical and synchronous, which of course did not *prove* that they had succeeded in copying the brain's functional structure, but the **empirical** support was greatly encouraging.

Hubert's input, and hence activity, had been kept parallel with Yorick's during my disembodied days. And now, to demonstrate this, they had actually thrown the master switch that put Hubert for the first time in on-line control of my body—not Hamlet, of course, but Fortinbras. (Hamlet, I learned, had never been recovered from its underground tomb and could be assumed by this time to have largely returned to dust. At the head of my grave still lay the magnificent bulk of the abandoned device, with the word STUD emblazoned on its side in large letters—a circumstance which may provide archeologists of the next century with a curious insight into the burial rites of their ancestors.)

The laboratory technicians now showed me the master switch, which had two positions, labeled B, for Brain (they didn't know my brain's name was Yorick) and H, for Hubert. The switch did indeed point to H, and they explained to me that if I wished, I could switch it back to B. With my heart in my mouth (and my brain in its vat), I did this. Nothing happened. A click, that was all. To test their claim, and with the master switch now set at B, I hit Yorick's output transmitter switch on the vat and sure enough, I began to faint. Once the output switch was turned back on and I had recovered my wits, so to speak, I continued to play with the master switch, flipping it back and forth. I found that with the exception of the transitional click, I could detect no trace of difference. I could switch in mid-utterance, and the sentence I had begun speaking under the control of Yorick was finished without a pause or hitch of any kind under the control of Hubert. I had a spare brain, a prosthetic device which might some day stand me in very good stead, were some mishap to befall Yorick. Or alternatively, I could keep Yorick as a spare and use Hubert. It didn't seem to make any difference which I chose, for the wear and tear and fatigue on my body did not have any debilitating effect on either brain, whether or not it was actually causing the motions of my body, or merely spilling its output into thin air.

The one truly unsettling aspect of this new development was the prospect, which was not long in dawning on me, of someone detaching the spare—Hubert or Yorick, as the case might be—from Fortinbras and hitching it to yet another body—some Johnny-come-lately Rosencrantz or Guildenstern. Then (if not before) there would be *two* people, that much was clear. One would be me, and the other would be a sort of super-twin brother. If there were two bodies, one under the control of Hubert and the other being controlled by Yorick, then which would the world recognize as the true Dennett? And whatever the rest of the world decided, which one would be *me*? Would I be the Yorick-brained one, in virtue of Yorick's causal priority and former intimate relationship with the original Dennett body, Hamlet? That seemed a bit legalistic, a bit too redolent of the arbitrariness of consanguinity and legal possession, to be convincing at the metaphysical level. For suppose that before the arrival of the second body on the scene, I had been keeping

Yorick as the spare for years, and letting Hubert's output drive my body—that is, Fortinbras—all the time. The Hubert-Fortinbras couple would seem then by squatter's rights (to combat one legal intuition with another) to be the true Dennett and lawful inheritor of everything that was Dennett's. This was an interesting question, certainly, but not nearly so pressing as another question that bothered me. My strongest intuition was that in such an eventuality *I* would survive so long as *either* brain-body couple remained intact, but I had mixed emotions about whether I should want both to survive.

I discussed my worries with the technicians and the project director. The prospect of two Dennetts was abhorrent to me, I explained, largely for social reasons. I didn't want to be my own rival for the affections of my wife, nor did I like the prospect of two Dennetts sharing my modest professor's salary. Still more vertiginous and distasteful, was the idea of knowing *that much* about another person, while he had the very same goods on me. How could we ever face each other? My colleagues in the lab argued that I was ignoring the bright side of the matter. Weren't there many things I wanted to do but, being only one person, had been unable to do? Now one Dennett could stay at home and be the professor and family man, while the other could strike out on a life of travel and adventure—missing the family of course, but happy in the knowledge that the other Dennett was keeping the home fires burning. I could be faithful and adulterous at the same time. I could even cuckold myself—to say nothing of other more lurid possibilities my colleagues were all too ready to force upon my overtaxed imagination. But my ordeal in Oklahoma (or was it Houston?) had made me less adventurous, and I shrank from this opportunity that was being offered (though of course I was never quite sure it was being offered to *me* in the first place).

There was another prospect even more disagreeable: that the spare, Hubert or Yorick as the case might be, would be detached from any input from Fortinbras and just left detached. Then, as in the other case, there would be two Dennetts, or at least two claimants to my name and possessions, one embodied in Fortinbras, and the other sadly, miserably disembodied. Both selfishness and altruism bade me take steps to prevent this from happening. So I asked that measures be taken to ensure that no one could ever tamper with the transceiver connections or the master switch without my (our? no *my*)

knowledge and consent. Since I had no desire to spend my life guarding the equipment in Houston, it was mutually decided that all the electronic connections in the lab would be carefully locked. Both those that controlled the life-support system for Yorick and those that controlled the power supply for Hubert would be guarded with fail-safe devices, and I would take the only master switch, outfitted for radio remote control, with me wherever I went. I carry it strapped around my waist and—wait a moment—*here it is*. Every few months I reconnoiter the situation by switching channels. I do this only in the presence of friends, of course, for if the other channel were, heaven forbid, either dead or otherwise occupied, there would have to be somebody who had my interests at heart to switch it back, to bring me back from the void. For while I could feel, see, hear, and otherwise sense whatever befell my body, subsequent to such a switch, I'd be unable to control it. By the way, the two positions on the switch are intentionally unmarked, so I never have the faintest idea whether I am switching from Hubert to Yorick or vice versa. (Some of you may think that in this case I really don't know *who* I am, let alone where I am. But such reflections no longer make much of a dent on my essential Dennettness, on my own sense of who I am. If it is true that in one sense I don't know who I am then that's another one of your philosophical truths of underwhelming significance.)

In any case, every time I've flipped the switch so far, nothing has happened. *So let's give it a try. . . .*

"THANK GOD! I THOUGHT YOU'D NEVER FLIP THAT SWITCH! You can't imagine how horrible it's been these last two weeks—but now you know; it's your turn in purgatory. How I've longed for this moment! You see, about two weeks ago—excuse me, ladies and gentlemen, but I've got to explain this to my . . . um, brother, I guess you could say, but he's just told you the facts, so you'll understand—about two weeks ago our two brains drifted just a bit out of synch. I don't know whether *my* brain is now Hubert or Yorick, any more than you do, but in any case, the two brains drifted apart, and of course once the process started, it snowballed, for I was in a slightly different receptive state for the input we both received, a difference that was soon magnified. In no time at all the illusion that I was in control of my body—our body—was completely dissipated. There was nothing I could do—no way to call you. YOU DIDN'T EVEN KNOW I EXISTED! It's been like being carried around in a cage, or better, like being possessed—hearing my own voice say things I didn't mean to say, watching in frustration as my own hands performed deeds I hadn't intended. You'd scratch our itches, but not the way I would have, and you kept me awake, with your tossing and turning. I've been totally exhausted, on the verge of a nervous breakdown, carried around helplessly by your frantic round of activities, sustained only by the knowledge that some day you'd throw the switch.

"Now it's your turn, but at least you'll have the comfort of knowing *I* know you're in there. Like an expectant mother, I'm eating—or at any rate tasting, smelling, seeing—for *two* now, and I'll try to make it easy for you. Don't worry. Just as soon as this colloquium is over, you and I will fly to Houston, and we'll see what can be done to get one of us another body. You can have a female body—your body could be any color you like. But let's think it over. I tell you what—to be fair, if we both want this body, I promise I'll let the director flip a coin to settle which of us gets to keep it and which then gets to choose a new body. That should guarantee justice, shouldn't it? In any case, I'll take care of you, I promise. These people are my witnesses.

"Ladies and gentlemen, this talk we have just heard is not exactly the talk *I* would have given, but I assure you that everything he said was perfectly true. And now if you'll excuse me, I think I'd—we'd—better sit down."

Questions for Thought

1. Assuming that you have a self, where do you think your self is located? What is the connection, if any, between your self and your brain?
2. Do you think that your self could exist outside your body? Why or why not?
3. Dennett concludes at one point that he would still be himself even if he had another body. Do you think you would still be yourself if you had a different body? Explain your answer.
4. Assume for the moment that you have two brains that could be connected to two different bodies (or that it was possible to create an exact clone of yourself). Would you find this prospect upsetting? Why or why not?
5. How effective is Dennett's use of science fiction in stating and defending his views? Do you find this approach to be more effective or less effective than the approaches used in the earlier selections that you have read?
6. How do you think Dennett would respond to someone like Plato, who claimed that human beings have souls?

What Else Determines Who I Am?

Zarathustra's Prologue and Three Speeches   12

FRIEDRICH NIETZSCHE

Friedrich Nietzsche (1844–1900), one of the most influential modern German philosophers, was born in Röcken, Prussia. Interestingly, Nietzsche, who was to become one of the most outspoken critics of Christianity, was the son of a Lutheran minister.

Nietzsche's paternal grandfather, himself also a Lutheran minister, had written several books defending the faith, and Nietzsche's mother was the daughter of a Lutheran minister.

After Nietzsche's father died from "softening of the brain" in 1849 and his younger brother died the following year, his mother moved the family to Naumburg. In Naumburg, Nietzsche lived with his mother, sister, paternal grandmother, and two aunts in a predominantly female household. In 1858, he was awarded a scholarship to attend Schulpforta, Germany's leading Protestant boarding school, which was near Naumburg. An excellent student, Nietzsche graduated from Schulpforta in 1864 and went to the University of Bonn to study theology and philology. He soon became disenchanted with theology and transferred to the University of Leipzig in 1865. At Leipzig, Nietzsche discovered the philosophical writings of Schopenhauer, met Richard Wagner, wrote several prize-winning papers, and composed some musical pieces. However, Nietzsche's studies were interrupted in 1867 when he began his military service in the Prussian cavalry. This interruption ended the following year when a horse-riding accident led to his discharge, and he returned to Leipzig.

In 1869, at age twenty-four, Nietzsche's academic promise was publicly recognized when he was appointed associate professor in philology at the University of Basel in Switzerland without having completed his doctoral degree. His degree was awarded the same year without thesis or examination, and Nietzsche became a full professor the following year.

When the Franco-Prussian War broke out in 1870, Nietzsche volunteered as a medical orderly. While working with injured soldiers, he contracted dysentery and diphtheria—both of which contributed to his poor health in later life. He returned to the University of Basel but was forced to take a leave of absence for health reasons in 1876 and finally to resign in 1879. Living on the small pension that he received from the university, Nietzsche then embarked on an ascetic life of writing, moving among boardinghouses in Switzerland, Italy, and the French Riviera. Nietzsche's often frenzied literary activity further contributed to his poor health, and he suffered an irreversible mental collapse in Turin in 1889, reportedly while hugging a horse that had just been beaten by a coachman. After a brief stay in a Basel asylum, Nietzsche spent the last years of his life living first with his mother and then with his sister. He died in Weimar on August 25, 1900.

Although the bulk of Nietzsche's writings were accomplished during a period of less than twenty years, his literary output was prolific. His published works include *Die Geburt der Tragödie* (1872; *The Birth of Tragedy*), *Unzeitgemässe Betrachtungen* (4 vols., 1873–1876; *Untimely Meditations*), *Menschliches, Allzumenschliches* (2 vols., 1878–1879; *Human, All Too Human*), *Der Wanderer und sein Schatten* (1880; *The Wanderer and His Shadow*), *Die Morgenröte* (1881; *The Dawn*), *Die fröhliche Wissenschaft* (1882; *The Gay Science*), *Also sprach Zarathustra* (1883–1885; *Thus Spoke Zarathustra*), *Jenseits von Gut und Böse* (1886; *Beyond Good and Evil*), *Zur Genealogie der Moral* (1887; *On the Genealogy of Morals*), *Der Fall Wagner* (1888; *The Case of Wagner*), *Die Götzen-Dämmerung* (1889; *The Twilight of the Idols*), and *Der Antichrist* (written 1888–1889, published 1895; *The Antichrist*).

In the following excerpt from *Thus Spoke Zarathustra*, Nietzsche uses poetic language in the context of a journey toward self-discovery to raise many of the questions concerning human identity that were mentioned in the introduction to this chapter. This journey toward self-discovery begins when Zarathustra, the ancient Persian priest who founded the religion of **Zoroastrianism,** emerges from his mountain cave after ten years of philosophical reflection. Deciding that the time is ripe to share the fruits of his reflection with all humanity, Zarathustra descends to the marketplace, the gathering spot of humanity. Along the way, he encounters the last saint, probably an allusion to St. Francis of Assisi, who has fled to the forest in search of God. This encounter leads Zarathustra to state one of Nietzsche's best-known claims—namely, that "God is dead."

Zarathustra continues to the marketplace, where he proclaims his doctrine of the superman, the creative individual who fashions his or her own destiny. Misunderstood and mocked by the people, Zarathustra then describes the last man, the paradigm of human impotency who follows the crowd and is incapable of authentic existence. After his speech is interrupted by the episode of the rope-dancer, whose death symbolizes the dangers associated with the attempt to overcome one's present existence and to become the superman, Zarathustra leaves the marketplace carrying the corpse of the rope-dancer with him.

Disillusioned by his rejection in the marketplace, Zarathustra then wanders aimlessly, looking for a proper place to bury the corpse. During the course of his wandering, he seeks food from an old man, an encounter that gives him the opportunity to state one of his many differences with the teachings of Jesus ("He who feeds the hungry refreshes his own soul" versus Jesus' "And if anyone give so much as a cup of cold water to one of these little ones, because he is a disciple of mine, I tell you this: that man will assuredly not go unrewarded"). Exhausted from his wandering, Zarathustra falls into a deep sleep and awakens with a new insight—that he should come not as a shepherd of the herd (another obvious allusion to Jesus) but as a seeker and teacher of the creative individual.

Much of the remainder of *Thus Spoke Zarathustra* consists of a series of speeches in which Zarathustra describes the path leading to the creative individual and critiques those philosophical and cultural views that serve as barriers to this path. In the first of the three speeches included in this selection, Zarathustra describes the process of self-overcoming, the "three metamorphoses," that one must move through in order to become creative. In the last two speeches, he critiques those traditions that focus on transcendent or otherworldly concerns and thus divorce us from our bodies and the earth. Like Sartre in a later selection, Nietzsche claims that belief in God and other-worldly beings serves to limit human freedom and creativity; and like Spelman, in an earlier selection, he suggests that to be liberated, we must not only acknowledge our bodily nature but also become fully embodied.

Questions for Reading

1. Why does Zarathustra decide to leave his mountain cave?
2. What is the point of Zarathustra's encounter with the saint in the forest? Why does he not tell the saint that God is dead?
3. What are the essential differences between the "superman" and the "last man"?
4. What is the significance of the episode of the rope-dancer? What sort of person does the rope-dancer symbolize? Whom or what does the buffoon symbolize?
5. What new truth does Zarathustra discover near the end of the Prologue?
6. What are the essential differences between the camel, the lion, and the child? Why, according to Zarathustra/Nietzsche, must one become the child?
7. How does Zarathustra/Nietzsche view the body?

ZARATHUSTRA'S PROLOGUE

1

WHEN ZARATHUSTRA WAS THIRTY YEARS OLD, HE left his home and the lake of his home, and went into the mountains. There he enjoyed his spirit and his solitude, and for ten years did not become weary of it. But finally he had a change of heart. Arising one morning with the rosy dawn, he stood before the sun, and spoke to it thus:

"You great star! What would be your happiness if you did not have those for whom you shine!

"For ten years you have climbed hither to my cave: you would have wearied of your light and of this journey had it not been for me, my eagle, and my serpent.

"But we awaited you every morning, took from you your overflow, and blessed you for it.

"Lo! I am weary of my wisdom, like the bee that has gathered too much honey; I need hands outstretched to take it.

"I would bestow and distribute, until the wise have once more become joyous in their folly, and the poor happy in their riches.

"To do so, I must descend into the deep—as you do in the evening when you go behind the sea, and still bring light to the underworld, you exuberant star! Like you, I must *go under*,[1] as man, to whom I will descend, calls it.

"Bless me, then, you tranquil eye that can behold even the greatest happiness without envy! Bless the cup that is about to overflow, that the water may flow golden out of it, and carry everywhere the reflection of your bliss!

"Lo! This cup will become empty again, and Zarathustra will become man again."

Thus began Zarathustra's going under.

2

Zarathustra met no one as he went down the mountain alone. However, when he entered the forest, there suddenly stood before him an old man, who had left his holy cottage to seek roots. And the old man spoke to Zarathustra:

"No stranger to me is this wanderer—he passed by many years ago. He was called Zarathustra, but he has changed. Then you carried your ashes into the mountains. Will you now carry your fire into the valleys? Do you not fear being punished as a firebug?

"Yes, I recognize Zarathustra. Pure are his eyes, and no loathing lurks about his mouth. Does he not move like a dancer? Zarathustra is changed—he has become a child, an awakened one. What will you now do in the land of the sleepers? You have floated on the sea of solitude. Alas, will you now go ashore? Will you again haul your own body?"

Zarathustra answered: "I love mankind."

"Why," asked the saint, "did I go into the forest and the desert? Was it not because I loved humans far too well? Now I love God—I do not love humans. Mankind is a thing too imperfect for me. Love of humanity would be fatal to me."

Zarathustra answered: "Was it of love that I spoke? I am bringing humans a gift."

"Give them nothing," said the saint. "Take rather part of their load and carry it for them—that will be most agreeable to them, if only it is agreeable to you! If, however, you give something to them, give them only alms, and make them beg for that!"

"No," replied Zarathustra, "I do not give alms. I am not poor enough for that."

The saint laughed at Zarathustra and spoke thus: "Then see to it that they accept your treasures! They are distrustful of hermits, and do not believe that we come with gifts. Our footsteps through their streets sound too solitary. They ask of us, 'Where goes the thief?,' just as they do of other men whom they hear walking by late at night while they are lying in their beds. Go not to men, but stay in the forest! Go rather to the animals! Why not be like me—a bear among bears, a bird among birds?"

"And what is the saint doing in the forest?" asked Zarathustra.

The saint answered: "I make hymns and sing them; and in making hymns, I laugh, weep, and grumble—thus do I praise God. With singing, weeping, laughing, and grumbling, I praise the God who is my God. But what do you bring us as a gift?"

The selection from Nietzsche's Thus Spoke Zarathustra *is the editor's revised version of the translation by Thomas Common, Edinburgh: T. N. Foulis, 1947.*

When Zarathustra had heard these words, he bowed to the saint and said: "What could I have to give you? Let me rather leave hurriedly lest I take something away from you!" And thus they parted from one another, the old man and Zarathustra, laughing like schoolboys.

When Zarathustra was alone, however, he said to his heart: "Could it be possible? This old saint in his forest has still heard nothing of this, that *God is dead!*"

3

When Zarathustra arrived at the town nearest the forest, he found many people assembled in the marketplace; for it had been announced that a ropedancer would give a performance. And Zarathustra spoke thus to the people:

"*I teach you the superman.*[2] Man is something that must be overcome. What have you done to overcome man?

"All beings hitherto have created something beyond themselves. Do you want to be the ebb of that great tide? Would you rather go back to being beasts rather than overcoming man? What is the ape to man? A laughing-stock, a thing of shame. To the superman, man will be just the same—a laughing-stock, a thing of shame. You have made your way from the worm to man, and much within you is still worm. Once you were apes, and man is still more of an ape than any of the apes.

"Even the wisest among you is only a disharmony, a hybrid of plant and ghost. But do I bid you become ghosts or plants?

"Lo, I teach you the superman. The superman is the meaning of the earth. Let your will say, 'The superman *shall be* the meaning of the earth!'

"I implore you, my brothers, *remain loyal to the earth*, and believe not those who speak to you of superearthly hopes! They are poisoners, whether they know it or not. They are despisers of life, themselves decaying and poisoned, of whom the earth is weary. So away with them!

"Once blasphemy against God was the greatest blasphemy; but God died, and those blasphemers also died with him. To blaspheme the earth, to value the bowels of the unknowable more than the meaning of the earth, is now the most dreadful sin.

"Once the soul looked contemptuously on the body, and then that contempt was the supreme thing—the soul wished the body meager, ghastly, and famished. Thus it thought to escape from the body and the earth. Oh, that soul was itself meager, ghastly, and famished—cruelty was the delight of that soul!

"But tell me, also, my brothers: What does your body say about your soul? Is your soul not poverty and pollution and wretched complacency?

"Verily, a polluted stream is man. One must be a sea in order to receive a polluted stream without becoming impure. Lo, I teach you the superman—he is that sea. In him your great contempt can submerge.

"What is the greatest thing you can experience? It is the hour of great contempt. The hour in which even your happiness becomes loathsome to you, as does your reason and virtue.

"The hour when you say, 'What good is my happiness? It is poverty and pollution and wretched complacency. But my happiness should justify existence itself!'

"The hour when you say, 'What good is my reason? Does it long for knowledge as the lion longs for his food? It is poverty and pollution and wretched complacency!'

"The hour when you say, 'What good is my virtue? As yet it has not filled me with passion. How weary I am of my good and my evil! It is all poverty and pollution and wretched complacency!'

"The hour when you say, 'What good is my justice? I do not see that I am a glowing fire and fuel! The just, however, are a glowing fire and fuel!'

"The hour when you say, 'What good is my pity? Is pity not the cross on which he is nailed who loves man? But my pity is not a crucifixion.'

"Have you ever spoken thus? Have you ever cried thus? Ah, would that I had heard you crying thus!

"It is not your sin but your self-satisfaction that cries to heaven; your short-coming, even in sin, cries to heaven!

"Where is the lightning to lick you with its tongue? Where is the frenzy with which you should be inoculated?

"Lo, I teach you the superman—he is that lightning, he is that frenzy!"

When Zarathustra had thus spoken, one of the people called out: "We have heard enough about the rope-dancer; it is time now for us to see him!" And all the people laughed at Zarathustra. But the rope-dancer, who thought the words applied to him, began his performance.

4

Zarathustra, however, looked at the people and wondered. Then he spoke thus:

"Man is a rope stretched between the animal and the superman—a rope over an abyss. A dangerous crossing, a dangerous on-the-way, a dangerous looking-back, a dangerous trembling and halting. What is great in man is that he is a bridge and not a goal; what is lovable in man is that he is a *transition* and a *going under*.

"I love those that know not how to live except by going under, for they are the ones who go over.

"I love the great despisers, because they are the great adorers and arrows of longing for the other shore.

"I love those who do not first seek a reason beyond the stars for going under and for being sacrifices, but who sacrifice themselves to the earth so that the earth of the superman may become possible.

"I love him who lives in order to know, and who seeks to know so that the superman may one day live. Thus he seeks his own going under.

"I love him who labors and invents so that he may build the house for the superman, and prepare earth, animal, and plant for him. Thereby he seeks his own going under.

"I love him who loves his virtue, for virtue is the will to go under and an arrow of longing.

"I love him who reserves no share of spirit for himself, but who wants to be wholly the spirit of his virtue. Thus he walks as spirit over the bridge.

"I love him who makes his virtue his inclination and his destiny. Thus, for the sake of his virtue, he is willing to live on and to live no more.

"I love him who does not desire too many virtues. One virtue is more of a virtue than two, because it is more of a noose for one's fate to hang itself.

"I love him whose soul is lavish, who wants no thanks and gives none: for he always bestows and desires not to preserve himself.

"I love him who is ashamed when the dice fall in his favor, and who then asks "Am I a dishonest player?" For he is willing to succumb.

"I love him who scatters golden words in advance of his deeds, and always does more than he promises: for he seeks his own going under.

"I love him who justifies the future and redeems the past: for he is willing to succumb in the present.

"I love him who chastens his God because he loves his God: for he must succumb through the wrath of his God.

"I love him whose soul is deep even when injured, and who may succumb through a small matter: thus he goes willingly over the bridge.

"I love him whose soul is so overfull that he forgets himself, and all things are in him: thus all things become his going under.

"I love him who has a free spirit and a free heart: thus his head is only the bowels of his heart; his heart, however, causes his going under.

"I love all who are like heavy drops falling one by one out of the dark cloud that hovers over man: they herald the coming of the lightning, and, as heralds, they succumb.

"Lo, I am a herald of the lightning, and a heavy drop out of the cloud; the lightning, however, is called *superman*."

5

When Zarathustra had spoken these words, he again looked at the people and was silent. "There they stand," he said to his heart; "there they laugh. They do not understand me; I am not the mouth for these ears.

"Must one first batter their ears so that they may learn to hear with their eyes? Must one clatter like kettledrums and preachers of fire and brimstone? Or do they believe only the stammerer?

"They have something of which they are proud. What do they call that which makes them proud? Good breeding, they call it; it distinguishes them from the goatherds. Therefore, they dislike hearing the word *contempt* applied to them. So I will appeal to their pride. I will tell them about the most contemptible thing: that, however, is *the last man!*"

And Zarathustra spoke thusly to the people: "It is time for man to fix his goal. It is time for man to plant the germ of his highest hope. His soil is still rich enough for this. But that soil will one day be poor and exhausted, and no longer will a lofty tree be able to grow in it. Alas! the time is coming when man will no longer launch the arrow of his longing beyond man—and the string of his bow will have forgotten how to whizz!

"I tell you: one must still have chaos in oneself in order to give birth to a dancing star. I tell you: you have still chaos in yourself.

"Alas! The time will come when man will no longer give birth to any star. Alas! The time of the most despicable man will come, the man who can no longer despise himself. Behold! I show you *the last man*.

"'What is love? What is creation? What is longing? What is a star?'—so asks the last man and he blinks.

"Then the earth has become small, and on it hops the last man, who makes everything small. His species is ineradicable like that of the ground-flea; the last man lives longest.

"'We have discovered happiness,' say the last men, and they blink.

"They have left the regions where it is hard to live; for they need warmth. One still loves one's neighbor and rubs against him, for one needs warmth. They consider becoming ill and being distrustful as sinful; they walk warily. He is a fool who still stumbles over stones or men!

"A little poison now and then—that produces pleasant dreams. And much poison, finally, for a pleasant death. One still works, for work is a pastime. But one is careful lest the pastime prove too exhausting. One no longer becomes poor or rich—both are too burdensome. Who still wants to rule? Who still wants to obey? Both are too burdensome.

"No shepherd and one herd! Everyone wants the same; everyone is the same. He who feels otherwise goes voluntarily into the madhouse. 'Formerly all the world was insane,' say the subtlest of them, and they blink.

"They are clever and know all that has happened; so there is no end to their mocking. People still quarrel, but they are soon reconciled—otherwise it upsets their stomachs. They have their little pleasures for the day and their little pleasures for the night, but they have a regard for health.

"'We have discovered happiness,' say the last men, and they blink."

And here ended Zarathustra's first discourse, which is also called "The Prologue," for at this point the shouting and mirth of the multitude interrupted him. "Give us this last man, O Zarathustra," they called out. "Make us into these last men! Then will we make you a present of the superman!" And all the people exulted and smacked their lips.

Zarathustra, however, became sad, and said to his heart: "They do not understand me; I am not the mouth for these ears. Perhaps I have lived too long in the mountains. I have hearkened too much to the brooks and trees; now I speak to them as to goatherds. My soul is calm and clear, like the mountains in the morning. But they think I am cold, and a mocker with terrible jests. Now they look at me and laugh; and while laughing, they hate me too. There is ice in their laughter."

6

Then, however, something happened which made every mouth mute and every eye fixed. For in the meantime the rope-dancer had commenced his performance. He had come out at a little door and was going along the rope, which was stretched between two towers so that it hung above the marketplace and the people. When he was exactly midway across, the little door opened once more. A gaudily dressed fellow, who looked like a buffoon, sprang out, and walked rapidly after the first one. "Go on, slow poke," cried his frightful voice, "go on, lazy-bones, swindler, pale-face—lest I tickle you with my heel! What are you doing here between the towers? Your place is in the tower. You should be locked up; you are blocking the way of one better than yourself!" And with every word he came nearer and nearer to the first one. When he was but a step behind, the frightful thing happened which made every mouth mute and every eye fixed—he uttered a yell like a devil, and jumped over the other who was in his way. However, when he saw his rival triumph, the man who had first come out of the door lost his head and his footing on the rope at the same time. He threw his pole away, falling into the depth faster than it, like an eddy of arms and legs. The marketplace and the people were like the sea when buffeted by a storm: they fled over and under each other, especially from where the body was about to fall.

Zarathustra, however, remained standing where he was; and it was right beside him that the body fell, badly injured and disfigured, but not yet dead. After a while the shattered man regained consciousness, and he saw Zarathustra kneeling beside him. "What are you doing here?" he finally asked. "I knew long ago that the devil would trip me up; now he will drag me to hell. Will you prevent him?"

"On my honor, my friend," answered Zarathustra, "there is nothing to that of which you are speaking: there is no devil and no hell. Your soul will be dead even sooner than your body. There is nothing more to fear!"

The man looked up distrustfully. "If you are speaking the truth," he said, "I lose nothing when I lose my life. I am not much more than an animal that has been taught to dance by blows and a few scraps of food."

"Not at all," said Zarathustra, "you have made danger your calling; there is nothing contemptible about that. Now you perish by your calling: for this I will bury you with my own hands." When Zarathustra had said this, the dying one did not reply further. But he moved his hand as if seeking Zarathustra's hand in gratitude.

7

Meanwhile the evening arrived, and the marketplace veiled itself in darkness. Then the people dispersed, for even curiosity and terror become fatigued. Zarathustra, however, still sat beside the dead man on the ground, so absorbed in thought that he forgot the time. But at last it became night, and a cold wind blew upon the lonely one.

Then Zarathustra arose and said to his heart: "Verily, a fine catch of fish has Zarathustra made today! It is not a man that he has caught, but a corpse. Human existence is absurd, and as yet without meaning: a buffoon may become its fate. I want to teach men the meaning of their existence, that is, the superman, the lightning out of the dark cloud of man. But I am still far from them, and my sense does not speak to their sense. To men I am still something between a fool and a corpse. Obscure is the night, obscure are the ways of Zarathustra. Come, you cold and stiff companion! I will carry you to the place where I can bury you with my own hands."

8

When Zarathustra had said this to his heart, he put the corpse upon his shoulders and set out on his way. Yet he had not gone a hundred steps when a man crept up to him and whispered in his ear—and lo! he that spoke was the buffoon from the tower. "Leave this town, O Zarathustra," he said, "there are many here who hate you. The good and the just hate you; they call you their enemy and despiser.

The orthodox believers hate you; they call you a danger to the multitude. It was your good fortune to be laughed at; and verily you spoke like a buffoon. It was your good fortune to associate with the dead dog; by so humbling yourself, you saved your life today. Leave, however, from this town, or tomorrow I shall jump over you, a living man over a dead one."

When he had said this the buffoon vanished; Zarathustra, however, went on through the dark streets. At the gate of the town the grave-diggers met him: they shined their torch on his face, and, recognizing Zarathustra, they sorely ridiculed him. "Zarathustra is carrying away the dead dog: a fine thing that Zarathustra has become a grave-digger! For our hands are too clean for that roast. Will Zarathustra steal this bite from the devil? Well then, have a good meal! If only the devil were not a better thief than Zarathustra!—he will steal and eat them both!" And they laughed among themselves, and put their heads together.

Zarathustra did not answer them, but went on his way. When he had walked for two hours, past forests and swamps, he had heard much of the hungry howling of the wolves, and he himself became hungry. So he halted at a lonely house in which a light was burning.

"Hunger attacks me like a robber," said Zarathustra. "Among forests and swamps my hunger attacks me, and late at night. My hunger is unpredictable. Often it comes to me only after a meal, and today it did not come to me at all. Where has my hunger been?"

Thereupon Zarathustra knocked at the door of the house. An old man carrying a light appeared. He asked, "Who comes unto me and my bad sleep?"

"A living man and a dead one," said Zarathustra. "Give me something to eat and drink; I forgot it during the day. He that feeds the hungry refreshes his own soul, thus says wisdom."

The old man withdrew, but came back immediately and offered Zarathustra bread and wine. "This is a bad country for the hungry," he said. "That is why I live here. Animal and man come to me, the religious hermit. But bid your companion eat and drink also, for he is wearier than you."

Zarathustra answered, "My companion is dead; I shall hardly be able to persuade him to eat."

"That does not concern me," said the old man sullenly. "He that knocks at my door must take what I offer him. Eat and be on your way!"

Thereafter Zarathustra walked for two more hours, trusting to the path and the light of the stars. For he was an experienced night-walker, and liked to look into the face of all that slept. When the morning dawned, however, Zarathustra found himself in a thick forest, and no path was any longer visible. He then put the dead man in a hollow tree at his head—for he wanted to protect him from the wolves—and laid himself down on the ground and moss. Immediately he fell asleep; his body was weary, but his soul was tranquil.

9

Zarathustra slept for a long time. Not only did the rosy dawn pass over his head, but the morning did so as well. At last, however, his eyes opened, and he gazed amazedly into the forest and the stillness; he gazed amazedly into himself. Then he arose quickly, like a seafarer who all at once sees land. He shouted for joy, for he saw a new truth. And he spoke thus to his heart:

"A light has dawned upon me. I need living companions, not dead companions and corpses, which I carry with me where I will. I need living companions, who will follow me because they want to follow themselves—to the place where I will. A light has dawned upon me. Let me not speak to the people, but to companions! Zarathustra shall not be the herd's shepherd and sheepdog!

"To allure many from the herd—for that purpose I have come. The people and the herd will be angry with me: Zarathustra will be called a robber by the shepherds. Shepherds, I say, but they call themselves the good and just. Shepherds, I say, but they call themselves the orthodox believers.

"Behold the good and just! Whom do they hate most? One who breaks up their tablets of values, the breaker, the law-breaker; that one, however, is the creator.

"Behold the believers of all beliefs! Whom do they hate most? One who breaks up their tablets of values, the breaker, the law-breaker; that one, however, is the creator.

"The creator seeks companions, not corpses—and not herds or believers either. The creator seeks fellow-creators—those who engrave new values on new tablets.

"The creator seeks companions and fellow-reapers, for everything is ripe for the harvest with him. But he lacks the hundred sickles; so he plucks the ears of corn and is vexed. The creator seeks companions who know how to whet their sickles. They will be called destroyers, and despisers of good and evil. But they are the reapers and rejoicers. Zarathustra seeks fellow-creators, fellow-reapers and fellow-rejoicers. What could he create with herds and shepherds and corpses?

"And you, my first companion, rest in peace! I have buried you well in your hollow tree; I have hid you well from the wolves. But I part from you; the time has arrived. Between rosy dawn and rosy dawn a new truth came to me. I am not to be a shepherd; I am not to be a grave-digger. No longer will I talk to the people; for the last time have I spoken to the dead.

"I will join the creators, the reapers, and the rejoicers; I will show them the rainbow, and all the stairs to the superman. I will sing my song to the lone-dwellers and the twain-dwellers; and heavy with my happiness will I make the heart of anyone who still has ears for the unheard.

"Toward my goal, I will follow my own way; I will leap over the loiterers and those who hesitate. Thus let my going be their going under!"

10

This Zarathustra had spoken to his heart when the sun stood at midday. Then he looked inquiringly upward, for he heard above him the sharp call of a bird. And behold! An eagle soared through the air in wide circles, and on him hung a serpent, not like a prey, but like a friend; for she kept herself coiled around his neck.

"They are my animals," said Zarathustra, rejoicing in his heart. "The proudest animal under the sun, and the wisest animal under the sun—they are exhausted from their search. They want to know whether Zarathustra still lives. Verily, do I still live? I found it to be more dangerous among men than among animals; on dangerous paths goes Zarathustra. Let my animals lead me!"

When Zarathustra had said this, he remembered the words of the saint in the forest. Then he sighed and spoke thus to his heart: "Would that I were wiser! Would that I were thoroughly wise, like my serpent! But I am asking the impossible. Therefore I ask my pride to go always with my wisdom! And if my wisdom should some day forsake me—alas, it loves to fly away—may my pride then fly with my folly!"

Thus began Zarathustra's going under.

ZARATHUSTRA'S SPEECHES

On the Three Metamorphoses

THREE METAMORPHOSES OF THE SPIRIT DO I designate to you: how the spirit becomes a camel, the camel a lion, and the lion, at last, a child.

Many hard things are there for the spirit, the strong load-bearing spirit in which reverence dwells: its strength demands the hard and the hardest.

What is hard? asks the load-bearing spirit, who kneels down like a camel, wanting to be well loaded.

What is the hardest thing, you heroes? asks the load-bearing spirit, that I may take it upon myself and rejoice in my strength.

Is it not this: To humble oneself in order to mortify one's pride? To exhibit one's folly in order to mock one's wisdom?

Or is it this: To desert our cause when it celebrates its triumph? To ascend high mountains to tempt the tempter?

Or is it this: To feed on the acorns and grass of knowledge, and for the sake of truth to suffer hunger in one's soul?

Or is it this: To be sick and dismiss comforters, and make friends with the deaf, who never hear your requests?

Or is it this: To go into foul water when it is the water of truth, and not disclaim cold frogs and hot toads?

Or is it this: To love those who despise us, and give our hand to the phantom that would frighten us?

All these heaviest things the load-bearing spirit takes upon itself: and like the camel, which, when laden, hastens into the desert, so hastens the spirit into its desert.

But in the loneliest desert the second metamorphosis takes place: here the spirit becomes a lion which will seize its freedom and be lord in its own desert. Here it seeks its last master: it will become enemies with him, and with his last god; for victory the lion will wrestle with the great dragon.

What is the great dragon which the spirit is no longer inclined to call Lord and God? The great dragon is called "Thou shalt." But the spirit of the lion says, "I will."

"Thou shalt" lies in its path, sparkling with gold—a scale-covered beast; and on every scale glitters a golden "Thou shalt!"

Thousand-year-old values glitter on those scales; and thus speaks the mightiest of all dragons: "The worth of all things glitters on me. All values have already been created, and I represent all created values. Verily, there shall be no more 'I will.'" Thus speaks the dragon.

My brothers, why is there need of the lion in the spirit? Why does not the beast of burden, which renounces and is reverent, suffice?

To create new values—that even the lion cannot yet do: but to create for itself the freedom for new creating—that is within the power of the lion. To create for itself freedom, saying a holy "No" even to duty: for that, my brothers, there is need of the lion.

To assume the right to new values—that is the most formidable assumption for a load-bearing and reverent spirit. Verily, unto such a spirit it is preying, and the work of a beast of prey. It once loved "Thou shalt" as being most sacred: now it is forced to find illusion and arbitrariness even in the most sacred things, so that it may seize its freedom from its love. The lion is needed for this seizing.

But tell me, my brothers, what can the child do that even the lion could not do? Why must the preying lion still become a child?

The child is innocence, forgetfulness, a new beginning, a game, a self-rolling wheel, a first movement, a sacred "Yes-saying." For the game of creating, my brothers, there is needed a sacred "Yes-saying," whereby the spirit wills *its own* will, and, no longer lost in the world, wins *its own* world.

I have spoken to you of three metamorphoses of the spirit: how the spirit became a camel, the camel a lion, and the lion, at last, a child. . . .

On Believers in Worlds Beyond

Once Zarathustra also cast his delusion beyond man, like all believers in worlds beyond. The work of a suffering and tortured god, the world then seemed to me. It then seemed to me to be a dream and the fiction of a god—colored smoke before the eyes of a divinely dissatisfied one. Good and evil, and joy and woe, and I and you—to me they seemed to be colored smoke before creative eyes. The creator wished to look away from himself—thus he created the world. It is drunken joy for the sufferer to look away from his suffering and to forget himself. Drunken joy and self-forgetting, the world once seemed to me. This world, eternally imperfect, an eternally contradictory and imperfect image, a drunken joy to its imperfect creator—thus the world once seemed to me.

Thus I also once cast my delusion beyond man, like all believers in worlds beyond. In truth, beyond man?

Ah, my brothers, that god whom I created was human-made and human madness, like all gods! He was human, and only a poor fragment of a human being and ego. Out of my own ashes and ardor that specter came to me. Verily, it did not come to me from the beyond!

What happened, my brothers? I, the suffering one, overcame myself; I carried my own ashes to the mountain; I invented a brighter flame for myself. And lo! Thereupon the specter *went away* from me! Now it would be suffering for me, and torment for the recovered to believe in such specters. Now it would be suffering for me and humiliation. Thus I speak to believers in worlds beyond.

It was suffering and impotence that created all worlds beyond, as well as that brief madness of bliss, which only the greatest sufferer experiences. Weariness, which wants to get to the ultimate with one leap, with a death-leap, a poor ignorant weariness, unwilling even to will any longer—this created all gods and worlds beyond.

Believe me, my brothers! It was the body that despaired of the body—with the fingers of the infatuated spirit, it groped at the ultimate walls. Believe me, my brothers! It was the body that despaired of the earth—it heard the bowels of being speaking to it. And then it sought to get through the ultimate walls with its head—and not only with its head—into "that world." But "that world" is well hidden from humans, that dehumanized, inhuman world, which is a heavenly nothing; and the bowels of being do not speak to humans at all, except as human.

Verily, all being is difficult to prove and to bring to speech. Tell me, my brothers, is not yet the oddest of all things best proved?

Yes, this ego, with its contradiction and confusion, still speaks most honestly of its being—this creating, willing, valuing ego, which is the measure and value of things. And this most honest being, the ego, speaks of the body and still desires the body, even when it muses and revels and flutters with broken wings. The ego learns to speak ever more honestly; and the more it learns, the more words and honors it finds for body and earth.

My ego taught me a new pride, which I teach humans: no longer to stick one's head into the sand of heavenly things, but to carry it freely, an earthly head, which creates meaning for the earth.

A new will I teach humans: to will that path which humans have followed blindly, and to approve of it—no longer sneaking away from it, like the sick and dying.

It was the sick and dying who despised body and earth, and invented the heavenly world and the redemptive blood-drops; but they took even those sweet and depressing poisons from body and earth. They wanted to run away from their misery, and the stars were too remote for them. So they sighed: "Oh, if only there were heavenly paths by which to steal into another existence and happiness!" Then they invented for themselves their secret paths and bloody potions. Those ungrateful ones now fancied themselves removed from their bodies and from this earth. Yet to what did they owe the convulsion and rapture of their removal? To their bodies and to this earth.

Zarathustra is gentle with the sick. Verily, he is not angry about their kinds of consolation and ingratitude. May they become convalescents and overcomers, and create higher bodies for themselves! Neither is Zarathustra angry at a convalescent who glances lovingly towards his delusions, and at midnight steals around the grave of his God; but to me, sickness and a sick body still remain in his tears.

There have always been many sick people among those who are poetizers and God-addicts; furiously they hate the perceptive ones, and that most recent of virtues, which is called "honesty." They always glance backwards toward dark ages: then, of course, delusion and faith were something different. God-likeness was the rage of reason, and doubt was sin.

I know these godlike ones all too well: they want to be believed in, and want doubt to be sin. I also know all too well what they themselves most believe in. Verily, not in worlds beyond and redemptive blood-drops—they also most believe in the body; their own body is for them their thing-in-itself. But it is a sickly thing to them, and willingly they would get out of their skin. Therefore they listen to the preachers of death, and themselves preach worlds beyond.

Listen rather to me, my brothers, to the voice of the healthy body; this is a more honest and clearer voice. More honestly and clearly speaks the healthy body that is perfect and right-angled; and it speaks of the meaning of the earth.

Thus spoke Zarathustra.

On the Despisers of the Body

To the despisers of the body I will speak my word. I would not have them learn afresh or teach anew, but only to bid farewell to their own bodies—and thus become silent.

"Body am I, and soul"—so speaks the child. And why should one not speak like children?

But the awakened one, the knowing one, says: "Body am I entirely, and nothing more; and soul is only a word for something in the body."

The body is a great reason, a plurality with one sense, a war and a peace, a flock and a shepherd.

An instrument of your body is also your little reason, my brother, which you call "spirit"—a little instrument and plaything of your great reason.

You say "I," and are proud of that word. But the greater thing is that in which you are unwilling to believe—your body with its great reason. It does not say "I," but does "I."

What the sense feels, what the spirit discerns, never has its end in itself. But sense and spirit are so vain that they would persuade you that they are the end of all things.

Instruments and playthings are sense and spirit: behind them there is still the self. The self seeks with the eyes of the senses; it also listens with the ears of the spirit. Always listening and seeking, the self compares, overcomes, conquers, destroys. It rules and is also the ego's ruler.

Behind your thoughts and feelings, my brother, stands a mighty lord, an unknown sage—it is called self. It dwells in your body, it is your body.

There is more reason in your body than in your best wisdom. And who knows then why your body needs just your best wisdom?

Your self laughs at your ego and its proud prancings. "What are these prancings and flights of thought to me?" it says to itself. "A roundabout way to my purpose. I am the leading-strings of the ego, and the prompter of its ideas."

The self says to the ego, "Feel pain here!" And thereupon it suffers, and thinks how it might suffer no more—and for that very purpose it is *made* to think.

The self says to the ego, "Feel pleasure here!" Thereupon it rejoices, and thinks how it may rejoice again and again—and for that very purpose it is *made* to think.

To the despisers of the body I will speak a word. Their despising is caused by their esteem. What is it that created esteeming and despising and worth and will? The creating self created for itself esteeming and despising; it created for itself joy and woe. The creating body created for itself spirit, as a hand of its will.

Even in your folly and despising you serve your self, you despisers of the body. Your very self wants to die and turns away from life. It can no longer do what it most desires: to create beyond itself. That is what it most desires; that is its entire fervor.

But it is now too late for it to do this: so your self wants to go under, you despisers of the body. Your self wants to go under; and therefore you have become despisers of the body. For you can no longer create beyond yourselves.

And that is why you are now angry with life and with the earth. An unconscious envy is in the squint-eyed glance of your contempt.

I go not your way, you despisers of the body! You are no bridges for me to the superman!

Thus spoke Zarathustra.

NOTES

1. The German term here is *untergehen*. Following the lead of Walter Kaufmann, I have rendered this term as "going under." However, it should be noted that the astronomical use of the term means "to set," as the sun

sets in the evening. One of Nietzsche's points is that, seen from a limited human perspective, when the sun sets its light is extinguished. However, Zarathustra's wisdom tells him that when the sun sets it continues to overflow and to bring light to the underworld, like Zarathustra himself wishes to do.—ED.

2. I have chosen to use the English word *superman* to translate the German term *Übermensch.* In the first English translation of *Thus Spoke Zarathustra,* the German term was translated as "Superman." However because of negative associations attached to this word arising from its use by the Nazis, Walter Kaufmann, in a later translation, substituted *overman* for "superman." Now that these negative associations have weakened, I believe that it is safe to return to the translation of the term found in most German dictionaries. As Kaufmann and others have clearly shown, Nietzsche's notion of the superman—which may be roughly defined as the authentic, creative individual—differs greatly from the notion of the superman used by the Nazis.—ED.

Questions for Thought

1. What do you think Zarathustra means when he says, "God is dead"? Would you agree with this statement? Why or why not?
2. What does the marketplace symbolize in this selection? Why do you think Zarathustra takes his message to the marketplace? What lessons does Zarathustra learn there?
3. To what extent is your life like that of the last man? To what extent is it like that of the superman?
4. What two animals does Zarathustra identify as his own? Why do you think he chooses these two? If you were to identify in some way with an animal, which one would you choose and why?
5. Given how Zarathustra describes them, would you categorize yourself as a camel, a lion, or a child? Explain your answer.
6. What is Zarathustra's/Nietzsche's attitude toward the "believers in worlds beyond"? What do you think about such people?
7. I have suggested one difference between the teachings of Zarathustra and the teachings of Jesus. Can you identify other differences?

The Question of Lay Analysis   13

SIGMUND FREUD

Sigmund Freud (1856–1939), the founder of **psychoanalysis**, was born in Freiburg, Moravia, a region which is now part of Czech Republic. However, a year after Austria abolished legal restrictions on Jews in 1860, the Freud family moved to Vienna. Living in a family that included eight children, of which he was the eldest, Freud's childhood was marked by extreme poverty.

In 1873, Freud received financial support from a Jewish philanthropic society, and he entered the University of Vienna as a medical student. After graduating with his medical degree in 1881, he became a resident physician at the General Hospital of Vienna the following year. However, it was the year 1885 that marked an important turning point in Freud's career. That year he went to Paris to study with the neurologist Jean Martin Charcot, who was experimenting with the use of hypnosis to treat mentally ill patients. Although Freud later rejected hypnosis as a useful therapeutic tool, it was during his work with Charcot that he arrived at his belief that at least some mental illnesses had psychological rather than physiological causes. Returning to Vienna in 1886, where he specialized in the study and treatment of hysterical patients, Freud gradually developed his theories concerning the unconscious, **repression,** and the psychological stages of sexual development that would make him one of the most controversial intellectual figures of the twentieth century. It was also soon after his return to Vienna that Freud married Martha Bernays, a friend of his sisters, with whom he had fallen in love four years earlier. This marriage, which has been described by some commentators as one of "unalloyed happiness," produced six children. One of these children, Anna Freud, became a distinguished practitioner and defender of the psychoanalytic method founded by her father.

While still a resident at the General Hospital of Vienna, Freud had published a series of papers on the medicinal uses of cocaine. When he returned to Vienna in 1886, he entered into a collaborative partnership with the physician Josef Breuer, a partnership that culminated in a joint publication, *Studien über Hysterie* (*Studies in Hysteria*), in 1895. This work, which presented key elements of Freud's psychoanalytic method, was followed in 1899 by the publication of Freud's seminal study of dreams, *Die Traumdeutung* (*The Interpretation of Dreams*), and in 1905 by his study of psychosexual development, *Drei Abhandlungen zur Sexualtheorie* (*Three Essays on the Theory of Sexuality*). It was in the latter work that Freud unveiled two of his most controversial concepts, the concept of **infantile sexuality** and the concept of the **Oedipus complex.** By claiming that children not only had sexual impulses but that their earliest sexual impulses were directed toward their parent of the opposite sex, Freud shocked the sensibilities of many of his contemporaries.

A highly cultivated person who had a deep appreciation and understanding of Greek mythology, classical literature, and many of the arts, Freud wrote prolifically during his many years of practice in Vienna (the English edition of Freud's works numbers twenty-three volumes). While a large part of this writing consists of clinical papers dealing with intricate problems of psychoanalysis that were originally published in psychoanalytic journals founded by Freud, he also wrote numerous works of more general interest. Indeed, in 1912 Freud founded a periodical, *Imago*, which was devoted specifically to the application of his findings to areas outside the medical realm. This was followed by several lengthy essays and books that pursued the same purpose. Two of his most influential writings in this vein were *Totem and Tabu* (1913; *Totem and Taboo*), which dealt with the origin and development of religion, and *Das Unbehagen in der Kultur* (1930; *Civilization and Its Discontents*), which analyzed modern civilization from a psychoanalytical standpoint.

Having lived at the same address in Vienna for over forty years—19 Berggasse, which is today a museum devoted to his life and work—Freud reluctantly immigrated to London in 1938 to escape the Nazi occupation of Austria. Although he had been diagnosed with cancer of the mouth in 1923, Freud fought its effects for many years, suffering through a series of painful operations. Throughout the ordeal, Freud continued treating his patients and writing, activities that ended only a month before his death. He finally succumbed to cancer on September 23, 1939.

In the following selection from a work entitled *Die Frage der Laienanalyse* (1926; *The Question of Lay Analysis*), a dialogue in which Freud tries to convince his adversary that a medical degree is not necessary to successfully practice psychoanalysis, Freud presents a summary of many of his theories and concepts. After first stressing the importance of dreams in providing access to our unconscious thoughts—the existence of which he later defends—Freud goes on to describe what he refers to as "the structure of the mental apparatus." According to Freud this apparatus, which stands between our bodily needs or desires and the acts through which we attempt to fulfill them, consists of three agencies or regions. Freud intentionally uses the simple German pronouns "*es*" ("it"), "*Ich*" ("I"), and "*Über-Ich*" ("over-I") to label these agencies, although most English translations have used the technical terms "id," "ego," and "super-ego" to translate them.

Freud describes the "it" as the most extensive and obscure of these agencies and states that the "it" contains the drives or instincts that motivate our actions. The "it," according to Freud, remains forever unconscious. On the other hand, the "I," much of which rises to the level of consciousness, mediates between these unconscious drives or instincts and the external world. In other words, although both the "it" and the "I" seek to gratify our bodily needs, the "it" does so without regard for the external world whereas the "I" takes both the opportunities and dangers of the external world into account. Freud characterizes this difference by saying that the "it" operates according to the **pleasure principle**, whereas the "I" operates according to the **reality principle**.

Before describing the third agency or region of the mental apparatus, Freud provides an explanation of how mental problems or neuroses can arise. This leads Freud to not only explain his concept of repression, but also to elaborate several of his findings concerning human sexual development. Repression, which marks the origin of the mental problem, occurs when an "I" that is not yet sufficiently developed must deal with a drive or instinct of the "it" that, if followed, would lead to a disastrous conflict with external reality. Since the "I" is not strong enough to moderate this drive or instinct, it represses the drive or instinct in order to avoid conflict. However, once a drive or instinct is repressed, the "I" loses all influence over it. The drive or instinct submerges into the depths of the "it," where it is free to take revenge on the "I" for denying it gratification, eventually resurfacing as a neurotic symptom. The goal of psychoanalytic treatment, according to Freud, is to bring this repressed material to the level of consciousness so that a more mature and strengthened "I" can deal with it.

Freud goes on to say that since the decisive repressions all take place in early childhood, it is this period of a patient's life that is of chief interest to the analyst. Also, since repressions are instituted to combat drives or instincts associated with the various stages of sexual development, Freud elaborates his important findings concerning this development. After introducing and defending his concept of infantile sexuality, Freud describes the two-stage process that characterizes this development. He also briefly describes the male fear of castration, the female envy of the penis, and the child's desire for his or her parent of the opposite sex—the so-called "Oedipus complex."

It is from these stages of sexual development, specifically from the working through of the Oedipus complex, that, according to Freud, the third agency or region of the mental apparatus, the "over-I," emerges. This agency, which Freud says is "the carrier of the phenomenon that we call 'conscience,'" develops much later than the "I" and stands between the "I" and the "it." If one's sexual development has been smoothly traversed, the "over-I" works harmoniously with the "I" in its attempt to mediate between the "it" and external reality. However, if this development has not gone smoothly, then conflicts between the "I" and the "over-I" can arise, conflicts that are just as problematic as those between the "I" and the "it."

Freud concludes his dialogue by trying to explain to his adversary why psychoanalytic treatment takes so long. He does so by describing several resistances in the patient that the psychoanalyst must overcome. Using a military metaphor, Freud says that "a route that in peacetime can be traversed by a train in a couple of hours can delay an army for several weeks, if it has to overcome the enemy's resistance there." Like the military strategist, the analyst must figure out how combat this resistance.

To make the following dialogue easier to read, the words of Freud's adversary are set off by quotation marks, whereas the words of Freud are not.

Questions for Reading

1. What, according to Freud, are the essential differences between what he calls "academic psychology" and psychoanalysis?
2. How does Freud describe the mental apparatus? Why does he believe that the construction of the mental apparatus is not of psychological interest?
3. In what ways does the "I" differ from the "it"? Why does Freud use common pronouns to name these agencies?
4. What spatial metaphors does Freud use to explain psychological processes or interactions?
5. What are the two forces that, according to Freud, drive the mental apparatus?
6. How does the pleasure principle differ from the reality principle?
7. What, according to Freud, is repression, and under what conditions does it arise?
8. How does Freud describe the therapeutic aim of psychoanalysis? What techniques are used to reach this aim?
9. What, according to Freud, are the most surprising things that psychoanalysts have learned about the sex life of children?
10. How does Freud describe the "over-I?" How does the "over-I" of a neurotic differ from the "over-I" of a normal or well-adjusted person?

IF I AM TO SAY ANYTHING COMPREHENSIBLE TO you, then I must communicate something of a psychological doctrine that, outside of analytical circles, is neither known nor appreciated. From this theory, you will be able to easily derive what it is that we want from our patients and the way in which we achieve it. Although I will recite it to you dogmatically, as if it were a finished set of doctrines, you should not believe that it arose as such, like a philosophical system. We have developed it very slowly, wrestled for a long time with each small piece; in constant contact with observation, we have modified it continually, until it has finally gained a form that seems to suffice for our purposes. Several years ago, I would have had to clothe this doctrine in other terms. Of course, I cannot vouch to you that the form of expression in use today will remain the definitive form. As you know, science is no revelation; it still lacks, long after its beginnings, the characteristics of certainty, constancy, and infallibility for which human thinking so strongly yearns. But such as it is, it is all that we can have. If you add that our science is very young, scarcely as old as the century, and that it is engaged with what is probably the most difficult material for which human research can be presented, then you will easily be able to assume the right attitude towards my discourse. Interrupt me at your discretion, however, if you cannot follow me or if you would like further clarification.

"I will interrupt you before you even begin. You say that you will present to me a new psychology, but I would have thought that psychology is not a new science. There have been enough psychologies and psychologists; and while in school, I heard of great achievements in this field."

I would not think of arguing with them. But if you examine the matter more closely, these great achievements would be better classified as belonging to the physiology of the senses. The doctrine of mental life could not be developed, because it was inhibited by a single essential misconception. What does it involve today, as it is taught in the schools? Outside of these worthwhile discernments of the

This is the editor's translation of selections from Gesammelte Werke, *Bd. 14 by Sigmund Freud, Frankfurt am Main: S. Fischer Verlag, 1948.*

physiology of the senses, only a number of classifications and definitions of our mental processes that, thanks to linguistic usage, have become the common property of everyone who has been educated. Clearly that does not suffice as a conception of our mental life. Have you not noticed that every philosopher, writer, historian and biographer invents for himself his own psychology, producing his own particular suppositions about the connections and purposes of mental acts, all of them more or less appealing and all equally unreliable? Obviously a common foundation is lacking. And that is also why there is, so to speak, no respect or authority in the domain of psychology. There every person can run wild at will. If you raise a question in physics or chemistry, a person who knows that he does not possess the specialized knowledge will remain silent. However, if you dare to make a psychological assertion, you must brace yourself for judgment and contradiction from everyone. Apparently there is no specialized knowledge in this field. Everyone has his own mental life, and for that reason everyone thinks of himself as a psychologist. But that seems to me not to be an adequate title of right. It is told that a person who was applying as a nanny was asked whether she understood how to care for toddlers. "Certainly," she answered, "after all, I was once a toddler myself."

"And you have discovered this 'common foundation' of mental life, which has been overlooked by all psychologists, through the observation of sick people?"

I do not think that this origin devalues our findings. Embryology, for example, would deserve no trust, if it could not plainly explain the origin of congenital deformities. But I have told you of persons whose thoughts go their own way, so that they are forced to brood over problems to which they are totally indifferent. Do you think that academic psychology could make any contribution whatsoever to the explanation of such an abnormality? Further, it happens to all of us nightly that our thoughts go their own way and create things that we do not understand, that appear strange to us, and that remind us in alarming ways of pathological products. I mean our dreams. The common people have always held firmly to the belief that dreams have a meaning, a value, that they signify something. This meaning of dreams has never been specified by academic psychology. It did not know what to make of dreams. If it did attempt to provide explanations, they were non-psychological. . . . But one may say that a psychology which cannot explain dreams is also not useful for understanding normal mental life; it has no claim to be called a science.

"You are becoming aggressive; thus you have obviously touched upon a sensitive point. I have heard, to be sure, that in analysis great value is put upon dreams, that they are interpreted, that memories of real occurrences are sought behind them, et cetera. But I have also heard that the interpretation of dreams depends upon the arbitrariness of the analyst, and that analysts themselves have not finished disputing over how to interpret dreams and the conclusions that can be drawn from them. If that is so, then you must not so strongly emphasize the advantage that psychoanalysis has over academic psychology."

What you say really is quite accurate. It is true that the interpretation of dreams for both the theory and practice of analysis has gained an unmatched importance. If I seem to be aggressive, for me that is only a means of defense. But when I think of all the mischief that some analysts have done with the interpretation of dreams, I could become disheartened and repeat the pessimistic saying . . . that every step forward is always only half as large as it first seems to be. . . . But with a bit of foresight and self-discipline, most of the dangers associated with the interpretation of dreams can surely be avoided. However, you must agree that I will never complete my exposition if we allow ourselves to be distracted like this.

"Yes, you wanted to relate to me the fundamental supposition of the new psychology, if I understood you correctly."

That was not what I wanted to do initially. My intent was to let you hear about the conceptions of the structure of the mental apparatus that we have formed during the course of our analytic studies.

"If I may ask, what do you mean by the mental apparatus, and from what is it constructed?"

What the mental apparatus is will shortly become clear; but please do not ask from what material it is constructed. That is not of psychological interest. Psychology can be as indifferent to this as optics is to the question of whether the walls of telescopes are made from metal or from cardboard. We will completely put aside the material point of view, but not the spatial point of view. For we perceive the unknown apparatus as performing mental activities, that is to say, really as an instrument that is constructed of several parts that we call "agencies." Each of these performs a specific function, and they have a fixed spatial relation to each other. In other words, the spatial relation—"in front of" and "behind," "shallow" and "deep"—is only a way of representing the regular succession of the functions. Am I still intelligible?

"Hardly. Perhaps I will understand it later. But, in any case, this is a curious anatomy of the soul, which, moreover, no longer exists at all for the naturalist."

What do you desire? This is a helpful conception, like so many others in the sciences. The very first of these have always been rather crude. *Open to revision*—we can say in such cases. . . . The value of such a conception—such a "fiction" as the philosopher **Vaihinger** would call it—depends upon how much one can accomplish with it. So let us proceed.

We place ourselves on the soil of everyday wisdom and acknowledge in human beings a mental organization that is interpolated between their sensory stimuli and the perception of their bodily needs on the one hand, and their motor acts on the other, an organization that mediates between them for a definite purpose. We call this organization their "I."[1] Now this is not news. Each of us makes this assumption even if he is not a philosopher, and some do so in spite of the fact that they are philosophers. However, we do not believe that with this we have exhausted the description of the mental apparatus. Besides this "I" we discern another mental zone—more extensive, more grandiose, and more obscure than the "I." This we call the "it." The relation between the two should be our immediate concern.

You will likely object to the fact that we have chosen simple pronouns in order to designate our two mental agencies or provinces, instead of labeling them with impressive sounding Greek names. But in psychoanalysis we like remain in contact with the popular way of thinking; we prefer to make its concepts scientifically usable, rather than dismissing them. There is no merit in this. We have to go in this direction, since we want our doctrines to be understood by our patients, who are often very intelligent, but not always learned. The impersonal "it" is directly connected with certain sayings used by ordinary people. "It shot through me," people say, "there was something in me at that moment which was stronger than I was.". . .

In psychology we can only describe with the help of analogies. This is not unusual; it is the same elsewhere as well. But we must constantly revise these analogies; none of them lasts us long enough. Thus if I am to make the relation between the "I" and the "it" clear, I must request that you picture the "I" as a kind of facade of the "it," as a foreground, similar to an outer cortical layer, of the "it." We can hold on to the last analogy. We know that cortical layers owe their distinctive features to the modifying influence of the external medium to which they abut. Thus we suggest that the "I" is the layer of the mental apparatus, of the "it," that has been modified by the influence of the outer world (of reality). You can see thereby in what way we take spatial views seriously in psychoanalysis. For us, the "I" is really more superficial, the "it" is deeper—considered from the outside of course. The "I" lies between reality and the "it," which is really mental.

"I will not now ask you how one can know all this. First, why don't you tell me what this separation of an "I" and an "it" does for you? Why do you need it?"

Your question shows me the right way to continue. What is important and valuable to know is that the "I" and the "it" differ greatly from one another in many respects. There are different rules that govern the course of mental acts in the "I" than in the "it"; the "I" pursues different purposes and with other means. A good deal could be said about this. But will you perhaps be satisfied by a new analogy and an example? Think of the difference that had developed during the war between the front lines and the area behind the lines. It did not surprise us then that on the front lines many things took place that did not occur behind the lines, and that in the area behind the lines many things were allowed that had to be forbidden at the front. The determining factor was, of course, the nearness of the enemy; for mental life it is the nearness of the external world. Outside, alien, and hostile were at one time identical concepts. And now the example:

in the "it" there are no conflicts; contradictions and oppositions stand unperturbed next to each other and often are balanced by the formation of compromises. However, in such cases the "I" feels a conflict that must be resolved, and the resolution consists of one urge being forsaken in favor of the other. The "I" is an organization that is distinguished by a very remarkable striving towards harmonization, towards synthesis. This characteristic is lacking in the "it." The "it" is, so to speak, scatterbrained; its discrete urges follow their own purposes independently and without regard for one another.

"And if a mental area behind the lines of such importance exists, explain to me how it has been overlooked until the time of analysis."

That takes us back to one of your earlier questions. Psychology has barred itself from access to the region of the "it" by adhering to one assumption that is obvious enough but still not tenable. This assumption is namely that all mental acts are conscious, that being conscious is the mark of the mental, and that if there are processes in our brain which are not conscious, they do not deserve to be called mental acts and are not the concern of psychology.

"Yet, it seems to me that this is self-evident."

Yes, psychologists also think so. However, it is easy to show that this assumption is false, that is to say, that it is a wholly inexpedient hypothesis. The slightest self-observation teaches that one can have ideas that could not have come about without preparation. But you experienced nothing of these preliminary steps of your thinking, steps that also must have certainly been of a mental nature; only the finished result appears in your consciousness. Occasionally you are able to make these preliminary steps conscious *in retrospect*, as in a reconstruction.

"It was probably the case that one's attention was distracted, so that one did not notice these preliminary steps."

Excuses! You cannot thereby get around the fact that acts of a mental nature—often very complicated ones—can proceed within you, of which your consciousness experiences nothing and of which you know nothing. Or are you willing to assume that a tad more or less of your "attention" suffices to convert an act that is not mental into one that is? But what's the point of quarreling? There are hypnotic

experiments in which the existence of such nonconscious thoughts is irrefutably demonstrated for everyone who would like to learn.

"I will not disavow what I've said; but I believe that I finally understand you. What you call the 'I' is consciousness, and your 'it' is the so-called subconscious, which is currently talked about so much. But why the masquerade through the new names?"

It is no masquerade; those other names are useless. And do not attempt to give me literature instead of science. When someone speaks of the subconscious, I do not know whether he means it topically, as something that lies in the mind beneath consciousness, or qualitatively, as another consciousness, a subterranean one as it were. He himself is probably not clear about this. The only admissible antithesis is that between conscious and unconscious. However, it would be a serious error to believe that this antithesis coincides with the separation of "I" and "it." It would certainly be wonderful if it were so simple; then our theory would have smooth sailing. But it is not that simple. What is true is that everything that takes place in the "it" is and remains unconscious, and that what takes place in the "I," and it alone, *can* become conscious. But not everything is, or is always, or is necessarily, conscious; and large portions of the "I" can remain perpetually unconscious. . . .

"I expect that you will want to explain to me how the origin of nervous maladies can be conceived according to psychoanalytical theories."

I will try to do so. But for that purpose, we must study our "I" and our "it" from a new point of view, from the *dynamic* one, that is, with regard to the forces at play within them and between them. Up to this point, we have been content with the description of the mental apparatus.

"If only it would not become so incomprehensible again!"

I hope not. You will soon get your bearings. Well then, we assume that the forces which drive the mental apparatus to action are generated in the organs of the body as an expression of the great bodily needs. You may remember the words of our poet-philosopher: hunger and love. Incidentally, quite a respectable pair of forces! We call these bodily needs, insofar as they constitute the stimulus for mental action, *Triebe*,[2] a word for which we are envied by many modern languages. Now these drives or impulses fill the "it"; we can say, to put it briefly, that all of the energy in the "it" originates from them. Moreover, the forces in the "I" have no other origin; they are derived from those in the "it." What, then, do these drives or impulses want? Gratification, that is to say, the establishment of situations in which the bodily needs can be extinguished. The reduction of the tension caused by need is felt by our organ of consciousness as pleasure; an increase of it is soon felt as irritating. From these fluctuations there arises the succession of feelings of pleasure-irritation according to which the whole mental apparatus regulates its actions. We speak of this as a "dominion of the pleasure principle."

Unbearable conditions come about, if the demands of "it's" drives or impulses find no gratification. Experience soon indicates that these situations of gratification can only be produced with the help of the external world. Therewith the portion of the "it" that is turned towards the external world, namely the "I," starts to function. If all the horsepower that starts the vehicle moving is provided by the "it," it is the "I," so to speak, that takes over the steering that is required if a destination is be reached. The drives or impulses in the "it" recklessly urge immediate gratification, which cannot be obtained in this manner, and which may even bring about perceptible damage. Now it is the task of the "I" to prevent these failures, to mediate between the demands of the "it" and the concrete opposition of the external world. This activity of the "I" unfolds in two directions. On the one hand, the "I" observes, with the help of its sense organs, its system of consciousness, the external world in order to catch the most favorable moment for harmless gratification. On the other hand, the "I" sways the "it," bridles its "passions," induces the drives or impulses to postpone their gratification and, indeed, if it is perceived to be necessary, to modify their aims or to give them up for other compensation. By subduing the motions of the "it" in this way, the "I" replaces the pleasure principle, which had formerly been solely authoritative, with the so-called *reality principle*, which, it is true, pursues the same final aims, but which soberly takes into account the conditions of the real external world. Later the "I" learns that there is still another way to assure gratification other than the *adaptation* to the external world that was just described. One can also intervene in the external world by *modifying* it and

by purposefully producing in it those conditions which make gratification possible. This activity then becomes the highest function of the "I." Deciding when it is more expedient to control one's passions and bow to reality, or to take sides with them and lay siege against the external world—that is the long and short of worldly wisdom.

"And does the 'it' acquiesce to such domination by the 'I,' even though it is, if I understand you correctly, the stronger part?"

Yes, it goes well, if the "I" possesses its entire organization and effectiveness, if it has access to all parts of the "it" and can exercise its influence on them. Indeed, there is no natural opposition between the "I" and the "it." They belong together and, in healthy cases, they cannot be practically separated from each other.

"All of this sounds fine, but I do not see where there can be the slightest opening for a pathological disorder in such an ideal relationship."

You are right. As long as the "I" and its relations with the "it" fulfill these ideal conditions, there will be no nervous disorder. The irruption point of the illness lies in an unexpected place, although one who appreciates general pathology will not be surprised to find verification that it is the significant developments and differentiations that carry within them the germ of illness, of the breakdown of function.

"You are becoming too scholarly; I cannot understand you."

I must go back a little further. Is it not true that a small creature is quite a wretched, powerless thing compared to the overpowering external world, which is full of destructive influences? A primitive creature that has developed no "I"-organization is exposed to all these "traumas." It lives by the "blind" gratification of the wishes of its drives or impulses and is frequently destroyed by this. The differentiation of an "I" is above all a step toward the preservation of life. To be sure, nothing can be learned from one's demise; but if one has luckily survived a trauma, one pays attention to the approach of similar situations and signalizes the danger through an abbreviated re-enactment of the impressions that one experienced with the trauma, by an *affect of anxiety*. This reaction to the perception of the danger now induces an attempt to escape, which acts as a lifesaving mechanism, until one is strong enough to meet the dangers of the external world in a more active manner, perhaps even through aggression.

"This is all very far removed from what you have promised."

You don't suspect how close I am to the fulfillment of my promise. Even with creatures that later develop an effective "I"-organization, during their childhood years the "I" is initially frail and barely differentiated from the "it." Now imagine what will happen if this powerless "I" experiences a demand from the drives or impulses of the "it" that it would already like to resist—because the "I" guesses that the gratification of it is dangerous and would evoke a traumatic situation, a clash with the external world— but which the "I" cannot control, since it does not yet possess the strength to do so. In such a case, the "I" handles the danger of the drive or impulse as if it were an external danger; it attempts an escape, withdraws from this portion of the "it," and abandons it to its fate, having withheld from the "it" all the contributions that it normally makes to the movement of the drives or impulses. We say that the "I" carries out a *repression* of these movements of the drives or impulses. For the moment this succeeds in defending against the danger, but one cannot confuse the inner and the outer with impunity. One cannot run away from oneself. By repression, the "I" is following the pleasure principle, which it usually is in the custom of correcting; and it is bound to suffer harm for this. This consists in the fact that the "I" has now permanently limited its zone of influence. The repressed movement of the drive or impulse is now isolated, left to itself, inaccessible, but also not subject to influence. It goes its own way. Even later, when the "I" has grown stronger, most of the time it can not nullify the repression; its synthesis is impaired, a portion of the "it" remains forbidden ground for the "I." However, the isolated movement of desire or impulse does not remain idle; it knows how to make up for the fact that its normal gratification is denied. To compensate for this, it produces psychical dispensations; it places itself in alliance with other processes which, through its influence, it likewise wrests from the "I." Finally, in an unrecognizable, warped form, it breaks through into the "I" and into consciousness, creating thereby what we refer to as a symptom. All of a sudden the facts in the case of a nervous disorder become obvious to us: an "I" which is obstructed in its synthesis, which has no influence over parts of the "it," which must forego some of its activities in order to avoid a new clash with what has been repressed, which exhausts itself in what are mostly futile defensive actions against the symptoms that are dispensations of the suppressed movements, and an "it," in which individual drives and impulses have made themselves autonomous, pursuing their goals without concern for the interests of the whole person and, moreover, obeying only the rules of a primitive psychology that holds sway in the depths of the "it." When we survey the entire situation, a straightforward formula for the origin of a neurosis manifests itself to us—that the "I" has attempted to suppress certain portions of the "it" in an *unsuitable* manner, that this has failed, and that the "it" has taken its revenge for that. Thus, the neurosis is the result of a conflict between the "I" and the "it," which the "I" has begun because, as in-depth investigation shows, it wants by all means to hold on to its pliancy towards the real external world. The antagonism runs between the external world and the "it," but because the "I," loyal to its innermost nature, takes sides with the external world, it comes into conflict with its "it." But note well that it is not the fact of this conflict that creates the condition of being sick—for such oppositions between reality and the "it" are inevitable and it is one of the standing tasks of the "I" to mediate in them—but the circumstance that the "I" has employed the inefficient means of repression in order to settle this conflict. However, this was itself caused by the fact that at the time it was presented with this task, the "I" was undeveloped and impotent. Indeed, the crucial repressions all take place in early childhood.

"What a strange path! I will follow your advice not to criticize, since you only want to show me what psychoanalysis believes about the origin of neurosis, so that you can go on to describe how psychoanalysis undertakes the battle against it. I have various things to ask, some of which will be raised later. For now, I feel the temptation to build further upon the base of your train of thought and to venture a theory of my own. You have developed the relation between external world, 'I,' and 'it,' and have claimed that the determinant of a neurosis is the fact that the 'I' in its subjection to the external world struggles with the 'it.' Is not another case also conceivable, that the 'I' in such a conflict allows itself to be swept away by the 'it,' and disowns its concern for the external world? What happens in such a case? According to my unprofessional ideas about the nature of a mental illness, this decision of the 'I' could be the cause of mental illness. After all, such an aversion to reality seems to be the essential element in mental illness."

Yes, I myself have thought of that, and it actually holds true, although to prove this conjecture would require a discussion of quite complicated considerations. Neuroses and psychoses are apparently intimately related, but they must still differ from each other at a crucial point. This point could well be the side the "I" takes in such a conflict. The "it" would, in both cases, keep its character of blind intransigence.

"Well, continue. What tips does your theory give for the treatment of neurotic illnesses?"

Our therapeutic aim is now easy to describe. We want to rebuild the "I," to liberate it from its retrenchments, to give it back its mastery over the "it," which it has forfeited as a result of its early repressions. It is only for this purpose that we undertake the analysis; our entire technique is directed to this goal. We have to seek out the repressions that have occurred and to induce the "I" to now correct them with our help, and to take care of conflicts better than by an attempt to escape. Since these repressions belong to very early childhood years, analytical work also leads us back to that time of life. The path to these mostly forgotten situations of conflict, which we want to revive in the patient's memory, is pointed out to us by the symptoms, dreams, and free associations of the patient. These, however, must first be interpreted or translated, for, under the influence of the psychology of the "it," they have assumed unfamiliar forms of expression that we do not understand. We may assume that the associations, thoughts and memories that the patient can only communicate to us with inner struggles are somehow connected with the repressions or are descendents of them. By impelling the patient to disregard his resistances to the disclosure of these things, we are nurturing his "I" to overcome the attempt to escape and to tolerate the approach of the repressed material. In the end, if the situation of the repression is successfully reproduced in his memory, his pliancy will be splendidly rewarded. The whole passage of time between then and now runs in his favor; and that from which his childish "I" fled in panic-stricken terror will often

seem to the adult and strengthened "I" mere child's play.

"Everything that you have told me up to now has been psychology. It often has sounded strange, brittle, opaque; but it was nevertheless, if I may say so, 'pure.' No doubt I have hitherto known very little about your psychoanalysis; yet the rumor has gotten to me that you are chiefly engaged with things that have no claim to that predicate. . . . It is commonly said that in analyses the most intimate— and the nastiest—affairs of sex life, with all their details, come up.". . .

The sex life is not just something spicy, but it is also a serious scientific problem. There were many new things to find out about it, many strange things to explain. I have already told you that analysis must go back to the early childhood years of the patient, because it is at that time, during the weakness of the "I," that the crucial repressions take place. But surely in childhood there is no sex life? Surely that first arises in puberty? On the contrary, we have made the discovery that the movement of the sexual drives or impulses accompanies life from birth, and that it is just to defend against those drives or impulses that the infantile "I" carries out repressions. A noteworthy coincidence, is it not, that the small child is already struggling against the power of sexuality? . . .

The discovery of infantile sexuality belongs to those findings which make us blush. It seems that a few pediatricians have always known about it, as well as a few children's nurses. Intellectual men, who call themselves child psychologists, have nevertheless spoken in a reproachful tone of a "denigration of childhood innocence." Time and again, sentiment in the place of argument! . . .

Naturally the sex life of children is different from that of adults. The sexual function, from its beginnings to the form that is so familiar to us, goes through a complicated development. It grows out of numerous component drives or impulses with several distinct aims, passing through many phases of organization, until it finally comes into the service of reproduction. Not all the component drives or impulses are equally useful for the end result; they must be diverted, restructured, and in part subdued. Such a circuitous development is not always passed through flawlessly. Inhibitions of development arise, partial fixations at early developmental stages. Later where obstacles to the exercise of the sexual function occur, the sexual urge—the **libido,** as we call it—is likely to revert back to these earlier points of fixation.

"After all that, I still can not form any image of the sex life of children."

Then I will linger a bit longer on this subject; anyhow it is not easy for me to break away from it. I will tell you that the most noteworthy thing about the sex life of children, it seems to me, is that it runs through its whole, very extensive development in the first five years of the child's life; the so-called latency period extends from then on until puberty. During the period of latency—normally—sexuality makes no progress; on the contrary, the sexual urges die down in strength and many things are given up and forgotten that the child formerly did and knew. In this latency period, after the early blooming of the sex life has withered, attitudes of the "I," such as shame, disgust, and morality, develop; later these attitudes will stand their ground against the storm of puberty and point the way to newly awakening sexual desires. This so-called *two-stage onset of sexual life* has a great deal to do with the origin of nervous disorders. It seems to be found only in human beings; perhaps it is one of the conditions of the human prerogative of becoming neurotic. Before psychoanalysis, the developmental history of the sex life was overlooked just as in another area the background of conscious mental life was overlooked. You are also correct in presuming that the two are intimately connected.

Of the contents, alterations and performances of this early period of sexuality, there is very much to be related, for which our expectations are not prepared. For example, you will certainly be astonished to hear that little boys are commonly frightened of being devoured by their father. (And do you also wonder why I include this fear among the characteristics of sexual life?) But I may remind you of the mythological story, which perhaps you have still not forgotten from your years in school, of how the god **Chronos** swallowed his children. How fantastic this myth must have appeared to you when you first heard it! I suppose, however, that at the time none of us gave it much thought. Today we can also think of many a fairy tale in which a ravenous beast, such as the wolf, appears, and we will be able to discern in

this a disguise of the father. Anyway I will take this opportunity to assure you that mythology and the world of fairy tales first became comprehensible through the knowledge of infantile sexuality. So, this is an added benefit of analytic studies.

You will be no less astonished to hear that the male child suffers from the fear of being deprived of his sex member by the father, so that this castration anxiety has the most powerful influence on his character development and on determining the direction that his sexuality takes. Here also mythology may give you the courage to believe psychoanalysis. The same Chronos, who swallowed his children, had also emasculated his father, and was in turn emasculated by his son **Zeus,** who had been rescued through the trickery of his mother. If you have been inclined to assume that everything that psychoanalysis related about the early sexuality of children stemmed from the confused imagination of the analyst, still you must at least acknowledge that this imagination has created the same products as the imaginative activity of primitive man, from which myths and fairy tales precipitate. The alternative view—friendlier and also likely more appropriate—would be that in the mental life of children today the same archaic momentums are detectable, that once generally governed human civilization in primitive times. In its mental development the child would be repeating **phylogony** in an abbreviated way, just as **embryology** long ago recognized was the case with embryonic development.

Another characteristic of early infantile sexuality is that the female sex organ does not yet actually play any role in it—the child has still not discovered it. All of the emphasis falls upon the male member; all of the interest is thereupon directed to whether it is present or not. Of the sex life of little girls, we know less that we do of that of little boys. We do not need to be ashamed of this difference, for the sex lives of adult women is also still a "dark continent"[3] for psychology. However, we have discerned that girls feel deeply the lack of a sex organ which is equal in value to the male sex member, regarding themselves therefore as inferior, and that this "penis envy" is the source of an entire array of characteristic female reactions.

It is also peculiar to children that the two excretory needs are filled with sexual interest. Later on, upbringing enforces a sharp divorce from this, which the practice of joking again cancels. That may seem unsavory to us, but it is known that a long time is needed for a child to acquire a sense of disgust. That is not even denied by those who otherwise advocate the seraphic chasteness of the child's mind.

No other fact, however, requires more attention than the fact that the sexual desires of the child are regularly directed toward his or her closest relative, thus first and foremost towards the father and mother, and secondarily towards brothers and sisters. The mother is the first love object for boys; the father is the first love object for girls—so far as there is not a bisexual disposition that favors the contrary focus at the same time. The other parent is felt as a troubling rival and is not infrequently considered with intense hostility. You must understand me correctly; I am not saying that the child merely wants that type of affection which we adults often like to see as the essence of the parent-child relationship. No, analysis leaves no doubt about this; the wishes of the child aspire for something beyond this affection. They aspire for what we understand as sensual gratification, as far, that is, as the powers of imagination of the child reaches. It is easy to understand that the child never guesses the actual facts of sexual intercourse; in place of these facts the child inserts other ideas derived from his experiences and feelings. Ordinarily his or her wishes culminate in the intent to bear, or in some indeterminable way to sire, a child. In their ignorance, boys also do not exclude themselves from the wish to bear a child. We name this entire mental structure after the well-known Greek sage, calling it the "Oedipus complex." Under normal conditions, it should be left behind at the end of the early sexual period; it should be thoroughly dismantled and become transformed, and the results of this transformation are destined for large-scale functions in later mental life. However, as a rule this does not happen thoroughly enough and then puberty evokes a reanimation of this complex, which can have serious consequences. . . .

"Go on with your narration. A bit more theory does not matter now."

When I explained the relation of the "I" and the "it" to you, I suppressed an important part of the doctrine of the mental apparatus. That is to say, we have been impelled to assume that in the "I" itself a peculiar authority has been differentiated, which we call the "over-I."+ This "over-I" occupies a special position between the "I" and the "it." It belongs to the "I," sharing its advanced psychological organization; however, it has an especially intimate relation with the "it." In actuality, it is the precipitate of the first **object-cathexes** of the "it," the legacy of the Oedipus complex after its cessation. This "over-I" can oppose the "I," treating it as an object and often treating it very severely. It is just as important for the "I" to remain in agreement with the "over-I" as it is for the "I" to remain in agreement with the "it." Disharmony between the "I" and the "over-I" has great significance for mental life. You will have already guessed that the "over-I" is the carrier of the phenomenon that we call "conscience." For mental health, it is very important that the "over-I" has developed normally, that it has become sufficiently impersonal. With neurotics, in whom the Oedipus complex has not experienced the proper transformation, this is precisely not the case. Their "over-I" still continually confronts the "I" as the strict father confronts the child, and their morality operates in such a primitive manner that the "I" lets itself be punished by the "over-I." The illness is used as a vehicle for this "self-punishment"; neurotics have to so behave, as though they were ruled by a sense of guilt which, in order to be gratified, needs the sickness as punishment.

"That really sounds very mysterious. The strangest thing about it is that even the patient is not aware of this power of his conscience."

Yes, we are just now beginning to appreciate the significance of all these momentous affairs. For this reason, my depiction was bound to end up so opaque. I can now proceed. We refer to all the powers that defy the work of recovery as the patient's "resistances." The gain from illness is the source of one such resistance. The "unconscious feeling of guilt" represents the resistance of the "over-I"; it is the most powerful factor, the one that we most dread. We encounter still other related resistances during the course of treatment. If during the early period the "I" has instituted a repression out of fear, this fear now still exists and manifests itself as a resistance, when the "I" approaches what has been repressed. Finally you can conceive that it is not without difficulty if the movement of a drive or impulse, which has been going along a certain path for decades, is suddenly expected to take a new path that has been opened to it. That might be called the resistance of the "it." The struggle against all these resistances is our principal work during analytical treatment; the job of interpretation pales in comparison with it. However, through this struggle and the overcoming of the resistances, the "I" of the patient is so modified and strengthened that we may calmly look forward to the patient's future behavior after completion of the treatment. On the other hand, you can now understand why such a long duration of therapy is needed. The length of the path of development and the wealth of material are not the crucial factors. It comes down to the question of whether the path is clear. A route that in peacetime can be traversed by train in a couple of hours can delay an army for several weeks, if it has to overcome the enemy's resistance there. Such struggles also consume time in mental life. Alas, I must confirm that every effort to substantially accelerate analytical treatment has so far failed. The best way to shorten it seems to be to correctly implement it.

NOTES

1. Freud uses common German pronouns for the parts of the mental organization—for example, the pronoun *Ich* for the part named here. He explains why he does so later in *The Question of Lay Analysis*. Despite this, previous English translations have used technical terms—"ego," "id," and "super-ego"—to name the parts of the mental organization. I am following Freud's lead and using common English pronouns to name these parts.

2. The German word *Triebe* is difficult to translate using a single English word. While *Triebe* has been translated as "instincts," I believe that this translation fails to adequately capture the dynamism that is expressed by the German term. Thus, I have decided to translate *Triebe* with two English words, "drives" and "impulses."

3. Freud uses the English words "dark continent" here.

4. The German term here is *Über-Ich*. *Über*, which is prefixed to many German words, is translated as "over," "above," "across," and sometimes as "super." In earlier English translations, *Über-Ich* is rendered as "super-ego." However, in continuing to comply with Freud's stated desire to avoid technical language, I have decided to translate the term as "over-I." I believe that this translation nicely captures the relation of the "over-I" to the "I," since the former stands over or oversees the latter and frequently judges it.

Questions for Thought

1. What does Freud say about the significance of dreams? Do you agree with Freud's position on dreams? Why or why not?

2. Do you believe that Freud has correctly described the nature of the mental apparatus? Defend your answer.

3. Do you agree with Freud's claim that hunger and love are the driving forces of our mental life? If not, how would you describe these driving forces?

4. Can you think of any times in your life when you have acted according to what Freud calls the "pleasure principle"? What about the reality principle?

5. Do you remember any events or experiences in your life that Freud would label "traumatic"? If so, what effect did these events or experiences have on your life?

6. Which of Freud's claims about infantile sexuality do you find most believable? Which of them do you find least believable? Explain your answers.

7. Can you think of any evidence from your own mental life that would affirm the existence of what Freud calls the "over-I"? How does Freud describe the relationship between the "I" and the "over-I"?

14   The Social Self

GEORGE HERBERT MEAD

George Herbert Mead (1863–1931), the son of a clergyman, was born in South Hadley, Massachusetts. When Mead was seven, his family moved to Oberlin, Ohio, and he spent the remainder of his youth there. At age sixteen Mead entered Oberlin College, receiving his A.B. four years later. After graduation from Oberlin, he spent two years doing graduate work at Harvard University, where his professors included Josiah Royce and William James. In 1888, Mead moved to Berlin, where he continued his studies in philosophy and psychology for the next three years.

Returning from Europe in 1891, Mead married and then obtained a position as instructor at the University of Michigan, where he became a colleague of John Dewey. Two years later Mead followed Dewey to the University of Chicago and eventually became chairperson of the department of philosophy. Mead remained a member of the faculty at the University of Chicago until his death on April 26, 1931.

Although Mead was an original, influential thinker who was a major figure in the development of the philosophy of **pragmatism**, he published no books during his lifetime. After his death, however, four books based on his unfinished manuscripts and on students' notes taken during his lectures were published. These were *The Philosophy of the Present* (1932); *Mind, Self and Society* (1934); *Movements of Thought in the Nineteenth Century* (1936); and *Philosophy of the Act* (1938). In addition, several of Mead's published articles were collected by Andrew Reck and published in 1964.

In the following selection from *Mind, Self and Society*, Mead offers an analysis of the self that is in many respects diametrically opposed to both Nietzsche and Freud. Whereas Nietzsche emphasizes the role of individual creativity in the process of self-development, Mead claims that the self can only develop within the context of social experience. And whereas Freud claims that much of our psychic life remains unconscious, Mead subscribes to the view of **behaviorism,** which totally denies the existence of unconscious thinking or experience.

Indeed, starting from a scientific, evolutionary standpoint, Mead argues that many human actions, like those of nonhuman animals, can take place without the accompaniment of self. However, he believes that in order to act rationally or intelligently, a human must be able to "take an objective, impersonal attitude toward himself"—that is, he must be able to view himself from the perspective of other individuals with whom he is interacting. According to Mead, this process of self-objectification is only possible through the act of communication, the beginning of which lies in what Mead refers to as the **"conversation of gestures."** In the conversation of gestures, as in more complex communication, one not only reacts instinctively to what one hears, but one "talks and replies to himself as truly as the other person replies to him." In other words, when one is engaged in conversation with others, one necessarily becomes aware of himself or herself. Thus, it is only within this social context that the self arises, and Mead claims that if a person were isolated from all social contact from birth on, the person would never develop a concept of self.

Toward the end of this selection Mead notes that the unity of the self depends on the unity of the society in which one lives. However, since all societies are fragmented into diverse social groups, and since each of us is called upon to play many different roles in society, it is highly unlikely that a unified self would evolve. On the contrary, given the social conditions under which we live, Mead claims that "a multiple personality is in a certain sense normal."

Questions for Reading

1. Why, according to Mead, does one not have a self at birth?
2. Mead claims that "the self is not necessarily involved in the life of the organism." What does Mead mean by this claim? What evidence does he provide for it?
3. How, according to Mead, does the self differ from the body and from other objects? What reasons does Mead give for claiming that the self can be distinguished from the body?
4. How does Mead describe what he calls the "conversation of gestures"? What significance does the conversation of gestures have for the development of the self?
5. Why does Mead claim that "a multiple personality is in a certain sense normal"? How does he explain the origin of a multiple personality?

IN OUR STATEMENT OF THE DEVELOPMENT OF intelligence we have already suggested that the language process is essential for the development of the self. The self has a character which is different from that of the physiological organism proper. The self is something which has a development; it is not initially there, at birth, but arises in the process of social experience and activity, that is, develops in the given individual as a result of his relations to that process as a whole and to other individuals within that process. The intelligence of the lower forms of animal life, like a great deal of human intelligence, does not involve a self. In our habitual actions, for example, in our moving about in a world that is simply there and to which we are so adjusted that no thinking is involved, there is a certain amount of sensuous experience such as persons have when they are just waking up, a bare thereness of the world. Such characters about us may exist in experience without taking their place in relationship to the self. One must, of course, under those conditions, distinguish between the experience that immediately takes place and our own organization of it into the experience of the self. One says upon analysis that a certain item had its place in his experience, in the experience of his self. We do inevitably tend at a certain level of sophistication to organize all experience into that of a self. We do so intimately identify our experiences, especially our affective experiences, with the self that it takes a moment's abstraction to realize that pain and pleasure can be there without being the experience of the self. Similarly, we normally organize our memories upon the string of our self. If we date things we always date them from the point of view of our past experiences. We frequently have memories that we cannot date, that we cannot place. A picture comes before us suddenly and we are at a loss to explain when that experience originally took place. We remember perfectly distinctly the picture, but we do not have it definitely placed, and until we can place it in terms of our past experience we are not satisfied. Nevertheless, I think it is obvious when one comes to consider it that the self is not necessarily involved in the life of the organism, nor involved in what we term our sensuous experience, that is, experience in a world about us for which we have habitual reactions.

We can distinguish very definitely between the self and the body. The body can be there and can operate in a very intelligent fashion without there being a self involved in the experience. The self has the characteristic that it is an object to itself, and that characteristic distinguishes it from other objects

From *George Herbert Mead,* Mind, Self, and Society, *Morris (Ed.), section 18, pp. 134–144. Reprinted by permission of* The University of Chicago Press.

and from the body. It is perfectly true that the eye can see the foot, but it does not see the body as a whole. We cannot see our backs; we can feel certain portions of them, if we are agile, but we cannot get an experience of our whole body. There are, of course, experiences which are somewhat vague and difficult of location, but the bodily experiences are for us organized about a self. The foot and hand belong to the self. We can see our feet, especially if we look at them from the wrong end of an opera glass, as strange things which we have difficulty in recognizing as our own. The parts of the body are quite distinguishable from the self. We can lose parts of the body without any serious invasion of the self. The mere ability to experience different parts of the body is not different from the experience of a table. The table presents a different feel from what the hand does when one hand feels another, but it is an experience of something with which we come definitely into contact. The body does not experience itself as a whole, in the sense in which the self in some way enters into the experience of the self.

It is the characteristic of the self as an object to itself that I want to bring out. This characteristic is represented in the word "self," which is a reflexive, and indicates that which can be both subject and object. This type of object is essentially different from other objects, and in the past it has been distinguished as conscious, a term which indicates an experience with, an experience of, one's self. It was assumed that consciousness in some way carried this capacity of being an object to itself. In giving a behavioristic statement of consciousness we have to look for some sort of experience in which the physical organism can become an object to itself.[1]

When one is running to get away from someone who is chasing him, he is entirely occupied in this action, and his experience may be swallowed up in the objects about him, so that he has, at the time being, no consciousness of self at all. We must be, of course, very completely occupied to have that take place, but we can, I think, recognize that sort of a possible experience in which the self does not enter. We can, perhaps, get some light on that situation through those experiences in which in very intense action there appear in the experience of the individual, back of this intense action, memories and anticipations. Tolstoi as an officer in the war gives an account of having pictures of his past experience in the midst of his most intense action. There are also the pictures that flash into a person's mind when he is drowning. In such instances there is a contrast between an experience that is absolutely wound up in outside activity in which the self as an object does not enter, and an activity of memory and imagination in which the self is the principal object. The self is then entirely distinguishable from an organism that is surrounded by things and acts with reference to things, including parts of its own body. These latter may be objects like other objects, but they are just objects out there in the field, and they do not involve a self that is an object to the organism. This is, I think, frequently overlooked. It is that fact which makes our anthropomorphic reconstructions of animal life so fallacious. How can an individual get outside himself (experientially) in such a way as to become an object to himself? This is the essential psychological problem of selfhood or of self-consciousness; and its solution is to be found by referring to the process of social conduct or activity in which the given person or individual is implicated. The apparatus of reason would not be complete unless it swept itself into its own analysis of the field of experience; or unless the individual brought himself into the same experiential field as that of the other individual selves in relation to whom he acts in any given social situation. Reason cannot become impersonal unless it takes an objective, non-affective attitude toward itself; otherwise we have just consciousness, not *self*-consciousness. And it is necessary to rational conduct that the individual should thus take an objective, impersonal attitude toward himself, that he should become an object to himself. For the individual organism is obviously an essential and important fact or constituent element of the empirical situation in which it acts; and without taking objective account of itself as such, it cannot act intelligently, or rationally.

The individual experiences himself as such, not directly, but only indirectly, from the particular standpoints of other individual members of the same social group, or from the generalized standpoint of the social group as a whole to which he belongs. For he enters his own experience as a self or individual, not directly or immediately, not by becoming a subject to himself, but only in so far as he first becomes an object to himself just as other individuals are objects to him or in his experience; and he becomes an object to himself only by taking the attitudes of other individuals toward himself within a social environment or context of experience and behavior in which both he and they are involved.

The importance of what we term "communication" lies in the fact that it provides a form of behavior in which the organism or the individual may become an object to himself. It is that sort of communication which we have been discussing—not communication in the sense of the cluck of the hen to the chickens, or the bark of a wolf to the pack, or the lowing of a cow, but communication in the sense of significant symbols, communication which is directed not only to others but also to the individual himself. So far as that type of communication is a part of behavior it at least introduces a self. Of course, one may hear without listening; one may see things that he does not realize; do things that he is not really aware of. But it is where one does respond to that which he addresses to another and where that response of his own becomes a part of his conduct, where he not only hears himself but responds to himself, talks and replies to himself as truly as the other person replies to him, that we have behavior in which the individuals become objects to themselves.

Such a self is not, I would say, primarily the physiological organism. The physiological organism is essential to it, but we are at least able to think of a self without it. Persons who believe in immortality, or believe in ghosts, or in the possibility of the self leaving the body, assume a self which is quite distinguishable from the body. How successfully they can hold these conceptions is an open question, but we do, as a fact, separate the self and the organism. It is fair to say that the beginning of the self as an object, so far as we can see, is to be found in the experiences of people that lead to the conception of a "double." Primitive people assume that there is a double, located presumably in the diaphragm, that leaves the body temporarily in sleep and completely in death. It can be enticed out of the body of one's enemy and perhaps killed. It is represented in infancy by the imaginary playmates which children set up, and through which they come to control their experiences in their play.

The self, as that which can be an object to itself, is essentially a social structure, and it arises in social experience. After a self has arisen, it in a certain sense provides for itself its social experiences, and so we can conceive of an absolutely solitary self. But it is impossible to conceive of a self arising outside of social experience. When it has arisen we can think of a person in solitary confinement for the rest of his life, but who still has himself as a companion, and is able to think and to converse with himself as he had communicated with others. That process to which I have just referred, of responding to one's self as another responds to it, taking part in one's own conversation with others, being aware of what one is saying and using that awareness of what one is saying to determine what one is going to say thereafter—that is a process with which we are all familiar. We are continually following up on our own address to other persons by an understanding of what we are saying, and using that understanding in the direction of our continued speech. We are finding out what we are going to say, what we are going to do, by saying and doing, and in the process we are continually controlling the process itself. In the conversation of gestures what we say calls out a certain response in another and that in turn changes our own action, so that we shift from what we started to do because of the reply the other makes. The conversation of gestures is the beginning of communication. The individual comes to carry on a conversation of gestures with himself. He says something, and that calls out a certain reply in himself which makes him change what he was going to say. One starts to say something, we will presume an unpleasant something, but when he starts to say it he realizes it is cruel. The effect on himself of what he is saying checks him; there is here a conversation of gestures between the individual and himself. We mean by significant speech that the action is one that affects the individual himself, and that the effect upon the individual himself is part of the intelligent carrying-out of the conversation with others. Now we, so to speak, amputate that social phase and dispense with it for the time being, so that one is talking to one's self as one would talk to another person.

This process of abstraction cannot be carried on indefinitely. One inevitably seeks an audience, has to pour himself out to somebody. In reflective intelligence one thinks to act, and to act solely so that this action remains a part of a social process. Thinking becomes preparatory to social action. The very process of thinking is, of course, simply an inner conversation that goes on, but it is a conversation of gestures which in its completion implies the expression of that which one thinks to an audience. One separates the significance of what he is saying to others from the actual speech and gets it ready before saying it. He thinks it out, and perhaps writes it in the form of a book; but it is still a part of social intercourse in which one is addressing other persons and at the same time addressing one's self, and in which one controls the address to other persons by the response made to one's own gesture. That the person should be responding to himself is necessary to the self, and it is this sort of social conduct which provides behavior within which that self appears. I know of no other form of behavior than the linguistic in which the individual is an object to himself, and, so far as I can see, the individual is not a self in the reflexive sense unless he is an object to himself. It is this fact that gives a critical importance to communication, since this is a type of behavior in which the individual does so respond to himself.

We realize in everyday conduct and experience that an individual does not mean a great deal of what he is doing and saying. We frequently say that such an individual is not himself. We come away from an interview with a realization that we have left out important things, that there are parts of the self that did not get into what was said. What determines the amount of the self that gets into communication is the social experience itself. Of course, a good deal of the self does not need to get expression. We carry on a whole series of different relationships to different people. We are one thing to one man and another thing to another. There are parts of the self which exist only for the self in relationship to itself. We divide ourselves up in all sorts of different selves with reference to our acquaintances. We discuss politics with one and religion with another. There are all sorts of different selves answering to all sorts of different social reactions. It is the social process itself that is responsible for the appearance of the self; it is not there as a self apart from this type of experience.

A multiple personality is in a certain sense normal, as I have just pointed out. There is usually an organization of the whole self with reference to the community to which we belong, and the situation in which we find ourselves. What the society is,

whether we are living with people of the present, people of our own imaginations, or people of the past, varies, of course, with different individuals. Normally, within the sort of community as a whole to which we belong, there is a unified self, but that may be broken up. To a person who is somewhat unstable nervously and in whom there is a line of cleavage, certain activities become impossible, and that set of activities may separate and evolve another self. Two separate "me's" and "I's," two different selves, result, and that is the condition under which there is a tendency to break up the personality. There is an account of a professor of education who disappeared, was lost to the community, and later turned up in a logging camp in the West. He freed himself of his occupation and turned to the woods where he felt, if you like, more at home. The pathological side of it was the forgetting, the leaving out of the rest of the self. This result involved getting rid of certain bodily memories which would identify the individual to himself. We often recognize the lines of cleavage that run through us. We would be glad to forget certain things, get rid of things the self is bound up with in past experiences. What we have here is a situation in which there can be different selves, and it is dependent upon the set of social reactions that is involved as to which self we are going to be. If we can forget everything involved in one set of activities, obviously we relinquish that part of the self. Take a person who is unstable, get him occupied by speech, and at the same time get his eye on something you are writing so that he is carrying on two separate lines of communication, and if you go about it in the right way you can get those two currents going so that they do not run into each other. You can get two entirely different sets of activities going on. You can bring about in that way the dissociation of a person's self. It is a process of setting up two sorts of communication which separate the behavior of the individual. For one individual it is this thing said and heard, and for the other individual there exists only that which he sees written. You must, of course, keep one experience out of the field of the other. Dissociations are apt to take place when an event leads to emotional upheavals. That which is separated goes on in its own way.

The unity and structure of the complete self reflects the unity and structure of the social process as a whole; and each of the elementary selves of which it is composed reflects the unity and structure of one of the various aspects of that process in which the individual is implicated. In other words, the various elementary selves which constitute, or are organized into, a complete self are the various aspects of the structure of that complete self answering to the various aspects of the structure of the social process as a whole; the structure of the complete self is thus a reflection of the complete social process. The organization and unification of a social group is identical with the organization and unification of any one of the selves arising within the social process in which that group is engaged, or which it is carrying on.

The phenomenon of dissociation of personality is caused by a breaking up of the complete, unitary self into the component selves of which it is composed, and which respectively correspond to different aspects of the social process in which the person is involved, and within which his complete or unitary self has arisen; these aspects being the different social groups to which he belongs within that process.

NOTE

1. Man's behavior is such in his social group that he is able to become an object to himself, a fact that constitutes him a more advanced product of evolutionary development than are the lower animals. Fundamentally it is this social fact—and not his alleged possession of a soul or mind with which he, as an individual, has been mysteriously and supernaturally endowed, and with which the lower animals have not been endowed—that differentiates him from them.

Questions for Thought

1. Do you agree with Mead's claim that your self did not exist at birth? Why or why not?
2. Assuming that Mead is wrong in saying that the self arises in social experience, from where else could it have arisen?
3. Can you describe a recent encounter in which you engaged in what Mead refers to as the "conversation of gestures"?
4. Do you believe that you have a multiple personality as Mead suggests? Why or why not?
5. What implications do you think Mead's position on the self would have on the debate about the morality or immorality of abortion? Explain your answer.

The Illusion of Human Freedom   15

B. F. SKINNER

Burrhus Fredric Skinner (1904–1990), the leading proponent of the behaviorist school of psychology, was born in Susquehanna, Pennsylvania. After growing up in what most commentators describe as a typical all-American small-town environment, Skinner majored in English at Hamilton College. Receiving his B.A. in 1926, he lived at his parents' home for a year and attempted to earn his living as a writer of fiction. When this failed, he turned his attention to psychology, entering the Harvard Graduate School in 1928.

On earning his doctorate in psychology in 1931, Skinner remained on fellowship at Harvard for the next five years. Then, in 1936, he obtained his first faculty appointment at the University of Minnesota, where he remained until 1945. It was during his tenure at Minnesota that Skinner wrote and published the first of his many books, *The Behavior of Organisms: An Experimental Analysis* (1938).

After a three-year sojourn as professor of psychology at Indiana University, Skinner returned to Harvard University in 1948, where he was to remain for the rest of his teaching career. Also in 1948, he published one of his most controversial works, *Walden Two.* Skinner's literary background is clearly evident in this work, which takes the form of a novel chronicling life in a utopian community founded on behaviorist principles.

In addition to being a prolific writer and a tireless defender of **behaviorism,** Skinner was an inventor, an educational innovator, and a noted social critic. While still at Indiana University, he invented the "Air-Crib," a large, soundproof, germ-free, air-conditioned box that was designed to provide the optimal environment for growth during the first two years of a child's life. Skinner employed this device in raising his second child. Later, he developed the so-called Skinner box, a device in which animal learning behavior could be strictly controlled and measured. He is also credited with the invention of programmed instruction and with several teaching machines that employ its principles.

As a social critic, Skinner remained an outspoken proponent of behaviorist techniques throughout his life. His defense of the use of behaviorist techniques in social and educational settings led to the writing of another of his controversial works, *Beyond Freedom and Dignity* (1971). In this book, Skinner argues that the concepts of freedom and human dignity are counterproductive and that they should be displaced by a thoroughgoing science of behavior comparable to that of the physical sciences.

A prolific writer throughout his life, Skinner published nineteen books and more than 150 articles and essays. The last of his books, *Recent Issues in the Analysis of Behavior* (1989), was published the year before he died from leukemia. Skinner's other important works include *Science and Human Behavior* (1953), *Verbal Behavior* (1957), *Schedules of Reinforcement* (1957), *The Technology of Teaching* (1968), *About Behaviorism* (1974), *Reflections on Behaviorism and Society* (1978), and *Upon Further Reflection* (1987). Skinner also wrote an autobiography in three parts: *Particulars of My Life* (1976), *The Shaping of a Behaviorist* (1979), and *A Matter of Consequences* (1983).

In the following selection from *Walden Two,* Skinner (whose views are represented by the character Frazier) briefly describes some of the basic assumptions of behaviorism. In arguing against Castle, a defender of human freedom, Frazier claims that belief in human freedom is incompatible with a science of human behavior. Indeed, if humans were free, their behaviors would not be subject to the laws of science, and neither would their actions be determined by these laws.

Frazier goes on to argue that there are in fact three things that wholly determine human behavior: force, the threat of force, and positive reinforcement. While the first two are obvious and often lead to rebellion, positive reinforcement (the technique whereby desired behavior is rewarded in some sense) is subtle and does not give rise to the question of freedom. Indeed, Skinner claims that although behavior determined by positive reinforcement is not free, it is compatible with a feeling of freedom.

Based on these principles, Walden Two is a planned utopian community in which force and the threat of force have been eliminated. The science of behavior has been used to create a blueprint for social harmony, and the people living there have been conditioned to act as they do through the use of positive reinforcement. While their behavior has been wholly determined, they are nevertheless left with a strong sense of personal freedom.

Questions for Reading

1. Who are the three characters in the dialogue? Which one of them can be categorized as a behaviorist?

2. What exactly does it mean to be a behaviorist?
3. Frazier asks Castle the following question: "What would you do if you found yourself in possession of an effective science of behavior?" How does Castle respond to this question? Why does Castle respond in the way he does?
4. What, according to Frazier/Skinner, are the three ways in which a person can be controlled? Which of these ways does he consider to be the most effective and why?
5. What are the essential differences between positive reinforcement and negative reinforcement (or punishment)? Why does Frazier/Skinner reject the use of negative reinforcement?

"EACH OF US," FRAZIER BEGAN, "IS ENGAGED IN A pitched battle with the rest of mankind."

"A curious premise for a Utopia," said Castle. "Even a pessimist like myself takes a more hopeful view than that."

"You do, you do," said Frazier. "But let's be realistic. Each of us has interests which conflict with the interests of everybody else. That's our original sin, and it can't be helped. Now, 'everybody else,' we call 'society.' It's a powerful opponent, and it always wins. Oh, here and there an individual prevails for a while and gets what he wants. Sometimes he storms the culture of a society and changes it slightly to his own advantage. But society wins in the long run, for it has the advantage of numbers and of age. Many prevail against one, and men against a baby. Society attacks early, when the individual is helpless. It enslaves him almost before he has tasted freedom. The 'ologies' will tell you how its done. Theology calls it building a conscience or developing a spirit of selflessness. Psychology calls it the growth of the super-ego.

"Considering how long society has been at it, you'd expect a better job. But the campaigns have been badly planned and the victory has never been secure. The behavior of the individual has been shaped according to revelations of 'good conduct,' never as the result of experimental study. But why not experiment? The questions are simple enough. What's the best behavior for the individual so far as the group is concerned? And how can the individual be induced to behave in that way? Why not explore these questions in a scientific spirit?

"We could do just that in Walden Two. We had already worked out a code of conduct—subject, of course, to experimental modification. The code would keep things running smoothly if everybody lived up to it. Our job was to see that everybody did. Now, you can't get people to follow a useful code by making them into so many jacks-in-the-box. You can't foresee all future circumstances, and you can't specify adequate future conduct. You don't know what will be required. Instead you have to set up certain behavioral processes which will lead the individual to design his own 'good' conduct when the time comes. We call that sort of thing 'self-control.' But don't be misled, the control always rests in the last analysis in the hands of society." . . .

"Mr. Castle," said Frazier very earnestly, "let me ask you a question. I warn you, it will be the most terrifying question of your life. *What would you do if you found yourself in possession of an effective science of behavior?* Suppose you suddenly found it possible to control the behavior of men as you wished. What would you do?"

"That's an assumption."

"Take it as you like. *I* take it as a fact. And apparently you accept it as a fact too. I can hardly be as despotic as you claim unless I hold the key to an extensive practical control."

"What would I do?" said Castle thoughtfully. "I think I would dump your science of behavior in the ocean."

"And deny men all the help you could otherwise give them?"

"And give them the freedom they would otherwise lose forever!"

"How could you give them freedom?"

"By refusing to control them!"

"But you would only be leaving the control in other hands."

"Whose?"

"The charlatan, the demagogue, the salesman, the ward heeler, the bully, the cheat, the educator, the priest—all who are now in possession of the techniques of behavioral engineering."

"A pretty good share of the control would remain in the hands of the individual himself."

"That's an assumption, too, and it's your only hope. It's your only possible chance to avoid the implications of a science of behavior. If man is free, then a technology of behavior is impossible. But I'm asking you to consider the other case."

"Then my answer is that your assumption is contrary to fact and any further consideration idle." . . .

Frazier sighed dramatically.

"It's a little late to be proving that a behavioral technology is well advanced. How can you deny it? Many of its methods and techniques are really as old as the hills. Look at their frightful misuse in the hands of the Nazis! And what about the techniques of the psychological clinic? What about education? Or religion? Or practical politics? Or advertising and salesmanship? Bring them all together and you have a sort of rule-of-thumb technology of vast power. No, Mr. Castle, the science is there for the asking. But its techniques and methods are in the wrong hands—they are used for personal aggrandizement in a competitive world or, in the case of the psychologist and educator, for futilely corrective purposes. My question is, have you the courage to take up and wield the science of behavior for the good of mankind? You answer that you would dump it in the ocean!"

"I'd want to take it out of the hands of the politicians and advertisers and salesmen, too."

"And the psychologists and educators? You see, Mr. Castle, you can't have that kind of cake. The fact is, we not only *can* control human behavior, we *must*. But who's to do it, and what's to be done?"

"So long as a trace of personal freedom survives, I'll stick to my position," said Castle, very much out of countenance.

"Isn't it time we talked about freedom?" I said. "We parted a day or so ago on an agreement to let the question of freedom ring. It's time to answer, don't you think?"

"My answer is simple enough," said Frazier. "I deny that freedom exists at all. I must deny it—or my program would be absurd. You can't have a science about a subject matter which hops capriciously about. Perhaps we can never *prove* that man isn't free; it's an assumption. But the increasing success of a science of behavior makes it more and more plausible."

"On the contrary, a simple personal experience makes it untenable," said Castle. "The experience of freedom. I *know* that I'm free."

"It must be quite consoling," said Frazier.

"And what's more—you do, too," said Castle hotly. "When you deny your own freedom for the sake of playing with a science of behavior, you're acting in plain bad faith. That's the only way I can explain it." He tried to recover himself and shrugged his shoulders. "At least you'll grant that you *feel* free."

"The 'feeling of freedom' should deceive no one," said Frazier. "Give me a concrete case."

"Well, right now," Castle said. He picked up a book of matches. "I'm free to hold or drop these matches."

"You will, of course, do one or the other," said Frazier. "Linguistically or logically there seem to be two possibilities, but I submit that there's only one in fact. The determining forces may be subtle but they are inexorable. I suggest that as an orderly person you will probably hold—ah! you drop them! Well, you see, that's all part of your behavior with respect to me. You couldn't resist the temptation to prove me wrong. It was all lawful. You had no choice. The deciding factor entered rather late, and naturally you couldn't foresee the result when you first held them up. There was no strong likelihood that you would act in either direction, and so you said you were free."

"That's entirely too glib," said Castle. "It's easy to argue lawfulness after the fact. But let's see you predict what I will do in advance. Then I'll agree there's law."

"I didn't say that behavior is always predictable, any more than the weather is always predictable. There are often too many factors to be taken into account. We can't measure them all accurately, and we couldn't perform the mathematical operations needed to make a prediction if we had the measurements. The legality is usually an assumption—but none the less important in judging the issue at hand."

"Take a case where there's no choice, then," said Castle. "Certainly a man in jail isn't free in the sense in which I am free now."

"Good! That's an excellent start. Let us classify the kinds of determiners of human behavior. One class, as you suggest, is physical restraint—handcuffs, iron bars, forcible coercion. These are ways in which we shape human behavior according to our wishes. They're crude, and they sacrifice the affection of the controllee, but they often work. Now, what other ways are there of limiting freedom?"

Frazier had adopted a professorial tone and Castle refused to answer.

"The threat of force would be one," I said.

"Right. And here again we shan't encourage any loyalty on the part of the controllee. He has perhaps a shade more of the feeling of freedom, since he can always 'choose to act and accept the consequences,' but he doesn't feel exactly free. He knows his behavior is being coerced. Now what else?"

I had no answer.

"Force or the threat of force—I see no other possibility," said Castle after a moment.

"Precisely," said Frazier.

"But certainly a large part of my behavior has no connection with force at all. There's my freedom!" said Castle.

"I wasn't agreeing that there was no other possibility—merely that *you* could see no other. Not being a good behaviorist—or a good Christian, for that matter—you have no feeling for a tremendous power of a different sort."

"What's that?"

"I shall have to be technical," said Frazier. "But only for a moment. It's what the science of behavior calls 'reinforcement theory.' The things that can happen to us fall into three classes. To some things we are indifferent. Other things we like—we want them to happen, and we take steps to make them happen again. Still other things we don't like—we don't want them to happen and we take steps to get rid of them or keep them from happening again.

"*Now,*" Frazier continued earnestly, "if it's in our power to create any of the situations which a person likes or to remove any situation he doesn't like, we can control his behavior. When he behaves as we want him to behave, we simply create a situation he likes, or remove one he doesn't like. As a result, the probability that he will behave that way again goes up, which is what we want. Technically it's called 'positive reinforcement.'

"The old school made the amazing mistake of supposing that the reverse was true, that by removing a situation a person likes or setting up one he doesn't like—in other words by punishing him—it was possible to *reduce* the probability that he would behave in a given way again. That simply doesn't hold. It has been established beyond question. What is emerging at this critical stage in the evolution of society is a behavioral and cultural technology based on positive reinforcement alone. We are gradually discovering—at an untold cost in human suffering—that in the long run punishment doesn't reduce the probability that an act will occur. We have been so preoccupied with the contrary that we always take 'force' to mean punishment. We don't say we're using force when we send shiploads of food into a starving country, though we're displaying quite as much *power* as if we were sending troops and guns."

"I'm certainly not an advocate of force," said Castle. "But I can't agree that it's not effective."

"It's *temporarily* effective, that's the worst of it. That explains several thousand years of bloodshed. Even nature has been fooled. We 'instinctively' punish a person who doesn't behave as we like—we spank him if he's a child or strike him if he's a man. A nice distinction! The immediate effect of the blow teaches us to strike again. Retribution and revenge are the most natural things on earth. But in the long run the man we strike is no less likely to repeat his act."

"But he won't repeat it if we hit him hard enough," said Castle.

"He'll still *tend* to repeat it. He'll *want* to repeat it. We haven't really altered his potential behavior at all. That's the pity of it. If he doesn't repeat it in our presence, he will in the presence of someone else. Or it will be repeated in the disguise of a neurotic symptom. If we hit him hard enough, we clear a little place for ourselves in the wilderness of civilization, but we make the rest of the wilderness still more terrible.

"Now, early forms of government are naturally based on punishment. It's the obvious technique when the physically strong control the weak. But we're in the throes of a great change to positive reinforcement—from a competitive society in which one man's reward is another man's punishment, to a cooperative society in which no one gains at the expense of anyone else." . . .

"But what has all this got to do with freedom?" I asked hastily.

Frazier took time to reorganize his behavior. He looked steadily toward the window, against which the rain was beating heavily.

"Now that we *know* how positive reinforcement works and why negative doesn't," he said at last, "we can be more deliberate, and hence more successful, in our cultural design. We can achieve a sort of control under which the controlled, though they are following a code much more scrupulously than was ever the case under the old system, nevertheless *feel free*. They are doing what they want to do, not what they are forced to do. That's the source of the tremendous power of positive reinforcement— there's no restraint and no revolt. By a careful cultural design, we control not the final behavior, but the *inclination* to behave—the motives, the desires, the wishes.

"The curious thing is that in that case *the question of freedom never arises*. Mr. Castle was free to drop the matchbook in the sense that nothing was preventing him. If it had been securely bound to his hand he wouldn't have been free. Nor would he have been quite free if I'd covered him with a gun and threatened to shoot him if he let it fall. The question of freedom arises when there is restraint— either physical or psychological.

"But restraint is only one sort of control, and absence of restraint isn't freedom. It's not control that's lacking when one feels 'free,' but the objectionable control of force. Mr. Castle felt free to hold or drop the matches in the sense that he felt no restraint—no threat of punishment in taking either course of action. He neglected to examine his positive reasons for holding or letting go, in spite of the fact that these were more compelling in this instance than any threat of force.

"We have no vocabulary of freedom in dealing with what we want to do," Frazier went on. "The question never arises. When men strike for freedom, they strike against jails and the police, or the threat of them—against oppression. They never strike against forces which make them want to act the way they do. Yet, it seems to be understood that governments will operate only through force or the threat of force, and that all other principles of control will be left to education, religion, and commerce. If this continues to be the case, we may as well give up. A government can never create a free people with the techniques now allotted to it.

"The question is: Can men live in freedom and peace? And the answer is: Yes, if we can build a social structure which will satisfy the needs of everyone and in which everyone will want to observe the supporting code. But so far this has been achieved only in Walden Two. Your ruthless accusations to the contrary, Mr. Castle, this is the freest place on earth. And it is free precisely because we make no use of force or the threat of force. Every bit of our research, from the nursery through the psychological management of our adult membership, is directed toward that end—to exploit every alternative to forcible control. By skillful planning, by a wise choice of techniques we *increase* the feeling of freedom.

"It's not planning which infringes upon freedom, but planning which uses force. A sense of freedom was practically unknown in the planned society of Nazi Germany, because the planners made a fantastic use of force and the threat of force.

"No, Mr. Castle, when a science of behavior has once been achieved, there's no alternative to a planned society. We can't leave mankind to an accidental or biased control. But by using the principle of positive reinforcement—carefully avoiding force or the threat of force—we can preserve a personal sense of freedom." . . .

Questions for Thought

1. To what extent do you believe that your behavior is controlled? What are some of the techniques that have been used to control your behavior?
2. What seems to be Frazier's attitude toward religion, education, and advertising? How does your own attitude toward these things compare with or differ from that of Frazier?
3. How would you answer the question that Frazier asks of Castle: "What would you do if you found yourself in possession of an effective science of behavior?"

4. What is Castle's dropping of the matchbook intended to prove? How does Frazier respond to Castle's "proof"?
5. From what you have read, would you want to live in Walden Two? Why or why not?

Existentialism Is a Humanism 16

JEAN-PAUL SARTRE

Jean-Paul Sartre (1905–1980), the best-known proponent of the philosophy of **existentialism,** was born in Paris. Sartre's father, who was a naval officer, died when he was a young boy, and he was reared in the home of his maternal grandfather, a professor of German at the Sorbonne and the uncle of Albert Schweitzer.

After studying at the École Normale Supérieure from 1924 to 1928, Sartre taught in a number of lycées in Le Havre, Lyon, and then Paris. His teaching career was suspended between 1933 and 1935, when he traveled to Germany as a research student in Berlin and at the University of Freiburg. While in Germany, Sartre studied with Edmund Husserl and Martin Heidegger, two philosophers whose work had a profound impact on his early philosophical writings. Sartre's career was again suspended in 1939, when he was drafted into the French army. Captured by the Germans in 1940, he spent nine months in a prisoner-of-war camp before being released. Returning to Paris on his release, Sartre resumed his teaching career and began work on his massive philosophical statement of the principles of existentialism, *L'être et le néant* (*Being and Nothingness*), which was published during the German occupation of France. Sartre also became active in the French resistance during this time, writing for its underground newspapers *Combat* and *Les Lettres Françaises.*

At the end of World War II, Sartre was one of the cofounders (with Simone de Beauvoir and Maurice Merleau-Ponty) of *Les Temps Modernes,* an existentialist literary/political journal. In 1951, he attempted to found a leftist, non-Communist political party, and he was active in workers' struggles throughout his life. An outspoken critic of both the Algerian and the Vietnam wars, Sartre participated in an international war crimes tribunal in 1967 that indicted the U.S. government for war crimes committed in Vietnam.

Because of his philosophical rejection of the institution of marriage and of bourgeois culture in general, Sartre never married. He did, however, maintain an intimate relationship with Simone de Beauvoir, whom he met in college, until the end of his life. Sartre's critique of bourgeois institutions also led him to reject the 1964 Nobel Prize for literature, along with its $53,000 in prize money.

A writer of short stories, plays, novels, essays, and journals, as well as philosophical treatises, Sartre was prolific in many areas of literature. The bibliography of his writing is extensive. The following is a list of his important philosophical writings: *L'imagination* (1936; translated as *Imagination: A Psychological Critique*), *Esquisse d'une théorie des émotions* (1939; translated as *The Emotions: Outline of a Theory*), *L'imaginaire: Psychologie phénoménologique de l'imagination* (1940; translated as *The Psychology of the Imagination*),

L'être et le néant: Essai d'ontologie phénoménologique (1943; *Being and Nothingness: An Essay on Phenomenological Ontology*), *L'existentialisme est un humanisme* (1946; translated as *Existentialism*), *Questions de méthode* (1960; translated as *The Problem of Method*), and *Critique de la raison dialectique* (1960; *Critique of Dialectical Reason*).

Some of his better-known literary writings include *La nausée* (1938; *Nausea*), *Les mouches* (1943; *The Flies*), *Le sursis* (1945; *The Reprieve*), *L'age de raison* (1945; *The Age of Reason*), *La putain respectueuse* (1946; *The Respectful Prostitute*), *Baudelaire* (1947), *Huis clos* (1947; *No Exit*), *La mort dans l'âme* (1949; translated as *Troubled Sleep*), *Le diable et le bon Dieu* (1951; *The Devil and the Good Lord*), *Saint Genet: Comédien et martyr* (1952; *Saint Genet, Actor and Martyr*), *Les séquestres d'Altona* (1961; translated as *The Condemned of Altona*), and *Les mots* (1963; *The Words*).

In the following selection, which is excerpted from *L'existentialisme est un humanisme*, Sartre defends existentialism against certain criticisms. In so doing, he provides one of his clearest statements of what existentialism means. In opposition to the claim that it leads to apathy, Sartre suggests that existentialism encourages action because it teaches that "existence precedes essence"—that is, that we are only what we make of ourselves. And rejecting belief in God and in human nature as limitations of human possibility, he argues that we are radically free—indeed, that "man is freedom."

Sartre acknowledges that the price of radical freedom is total responsibility for our own existence and indirectly for the existence of all humanity. He also acknowledges that this responsibility entails such existential burdens as anguish, forlornness, and despair. Anguish results from the sheer weight of our responsibility, from knowing that in choosing ourselves we choose a blueprint for all others. Forlornness is a consequence of our knowing the true significance of God's nonexistence—namely, that there is no external authority to which we can appeal to justify our choices—and despair arises from the recognition that the success of our undertakings depends on probabilities and not certainties.

Sartre concludes by reaffirming that we are constantly in the process of creating our self-identities, constantly transcending or "passing-beyond" ourselves. Never able to transcend the human realm into one that is nonhuman, never able to offer excuses or to blame others for what we have become, we are, to use Sartre's phrase, "condemned to be free."

Questions for Reading

1. What, according to Sartre, is an existentialist?
2. What are some of the criticisms of existentialism that Sartre identifies? How does he respond to these criticisms?
3. What is Sartre's purpose in using the analogy of the letter opener?
4. How, according to Sartre, does belief in God limit human freedom?
5. Why, according to Sartre, do anguish, forlornness, and despair fundamentally characterize human existence?
6. How does Sartre define the term *humanism*? What do humanism and existentialism have in common?

AT THIS TIME, I WOULD LIKE TO DEFEND EXISTEN-TIALISM against a certain number of reproaches that people have lodged against it. First, some have reproached it for inviting people to remain in a quietism of hopelessness, because it rules out all final solutions. This being the case, they claim that it makes action in this world totally impossible, resulting ultimately in a contemplative philosophy.

This is the editor's translation of selections from L'existentialisme est un humanisme *by Jean-Paul Sartre, New York: French and European Publications, 1970.*

Moreover, since contemplation is a luxury, we end up with a bourgeois philosophy. This has especially been the accusation of the communists.

On the other hand, we have been reproached for emphasizing human ignominy, for showing everywhere the sordid, the shady, the slimy, while neglecting the pleasing and beautiful, the luminous side of human nature. For example, Mlle. Mercier, the Catholic critic, accuses us of having forgotten the smile of the child.

Both sides reproach us for having lost human solidarity, for considering man to be isolated. The communists say that, for the most part, this is because we start from pure subjectivity, from the Cartesian *I think,* that is to say, from the moment when man becomes fully aware of his solitude. From this standpoint, we are incapable of returning to solidarity with other men, for such solidarity cannot be reached out of the *cogito.*

And from the Christian side, we are reproached for denying the reality and the seriousness of human undertakings, because if we reject God's commandments and eternal values, nothing remains but pure caprice. Everyone can do as he wishes, and everyone is incapable, from his point of view, of condemning the points of view and the acts of others.

Today, I will attempt to respond to these different reproaches. This is why I have entitled this short exposition "Existentialism is a Humanism." Many people are going to be astonished by what is said here about **humanism.** We will try to see in what sense this term is to be understood. In any case, what we can say in the beginning is that by existentialism we intend a doctrine that makes human life possible and, in addition, we declare that every truth and every action implies human surroundings and a human subjectivity.

The essential reproach against us, as one knows, is that we put the accent on the unpleasant side of human life. Someone recently told me of a woman who blurted out a vulgar word in a moment of irritation, and who excused herself by saying, "I believe I'm becoming existentialist." In consequence, existentialism is associated with ugliness; that is why people say that we are naturalists. But if we are, it is surprising that we frighten and scandalize people today much more so than does what can be properly called **naturalism.** A person who can easily stomach one of Zola's novels, such as *The Earth,* is nauseated when he reads an existentialist novel. A person

who finds use for traditional wisdom—which is extremely sad—finds us sadder still. However, what can be more disillusioning than saying "true charity is directed toward oneself," or better still, "once a scoundrel, always a scoundrel." One knows the commonplace things that are said on this subject, things that always demonstrate the same thing—we shouldn't fight the powers-that-be; we shouldn't struggle against authority; we shouldn't attempt to rise above our station; every action that isn't grounded in tradition is mere romanticism; every endeavor that isn't based on proven experience is certain to fail; experience shows that man always tends toward baseness, that unless a firm hand restrains him, there will be anarchy. There are still people who repeat these sad proverbs over and over again, people who say, "It's only human," each time someone points out an act that is more or less repugnant to them, people who feast on "realistic songs." These are the very people who reproach existentialism for being too somber, and to such an extent that I wonder if their grievance against existentialism is not that it is too pessimistic, but rather that it is too optimistic. Can it be that what frightens them about the doctrine that I am attempting to explain to you is the fact that it leaves a possibility of choice to man? In order to know, we must look at this question from a strictly philosophical standpoint. What exactly does the term *existentialism* mean?

Most people who use this word would be quite embarrassed if called upon to explain it, since today it has become so fashionable that even the work of a musician or a painter is being proclaimed to be "existentialist." A gossip columnist for the *Clartés* signs his column *The Existentialist;* and today this word is used so broadly and has been stretched so far that at bottom it no longer means anything at all. It seems that, for want of an avant-garde doctrine analogous to **surrealism,** people who relish scandal and commotion embrace this philosophy, which in other respects cannot supply what they are seeking. In reality, it is the doctrine that is the least scandalous, the most austere; it is reserved strictly for specialists and philosophers. Nevertheless, it can be easily defined. What complicates things is that there are two kinds of existentialists—first, those who are Christian, among whom I would rank Jaspers and Gabriel Marcel; . . . on the other hand, the atheistic existentialists, among whom I would list Heidegger and also the French existentialists including myself. What they have in common is simply the fact that they deem that existence precedes essence or, if you prefer, that one must start from subjectivity.

But just what does this mean? Let us consider a manufactured object, such as a book or a letter opener. Such an object has been manufactured by an artisan whose inspiration has been drawn from a concept. He referred to the concept of the letter opener, and likewise to a pre-established production technique which is part of the concept, and which is at bottom a blueprint. Thus, the letter opener is at once an object that is produced in a fixed manner and that, on the other hand, has a specific use. One cannot imagine someone making a letter opener without knowing what it is going to be used for. We can say, therefore, that the essence of the letter opener—that is to say, the collection of blueprints, production techniques, and definitions needed to produce it—precedes the existence of the letter opener. Thus, the presence of this letter opener or this book in front of me is determined. What we have here is a technical view of the world, a view of which it can be said that production precedes existence.

When we conceive of a creator God, this God is compared most of the time to a superior artisan. Whatever the doctrine we may be considering, whether it is a doctrine like that of Descartes or a doctrine like that of Leibniz, we always admit that will more or less follows understanding, or at least accompanies it, and that when God creates, He knows precisely what he is creating. Thus, the concept of man in the mind of God is similar to the concept of the letter opener in the mind of the manufacturer; and God follows certain techniques and a definition in making man just as the artisan does in making a letter opener. The individual man, therefore, is the realization of a specific concept in the divine understanding.

In the eighteenth century, with the atheism of the *philosophes,* the concept of God was rejected, but not so much because of the idea that essence precedes existence. We find this idea, to a certain extent, everywhere—we find it in Diderot, in Voltaire, and even in Kant. Man is the possessor of a human nature; this human nature, which is the human concept, is found in all men, which means that each

man is a particular example of a universal concept—man. In Kant, the result of this universality is that the man of the forest, the man of nature, along with the bourgeois, is subject to the same definition and possesses the same basic qualities. Thus, here the essence of man still precedes that historical existence that we discover in nature.

Atheistic existentialism, which I represent, is more coherent. It declares that if God does not exist, there exists at least one being in whom existence precedes essence, a being who exists before he is defined by any concept. That being is man, or as Heidegger says, human reality. What do we mean here in saying that existence precedes essence? What we mean is that man exists first of all, he is met with, surges up in the world, and defines himself afterward. If man, as the existentialist conceives him, is not definable, it is because initially he is nothing. He will only become something afterward, and he will become what he has made himself become. Thus, there is no human nature, since there is no God to conceive it. Man is solely—not solely what he conceives himself to be, but what he chooses; and just as his self-conception follows after his existence, so does he choose himself after being thrust into existence. Man is nothing other than what he makes of himself. Such is the first principle of existentialism.

This is also what is called subjectivity, a name that people have attached to us and for which we have been criticized. But what do we mean by this, if not that man has a greater dignity than a stone or a table? Indeed, we mean that man exists first, that is to say, that man first flings himself toward the future, and is conscious of projecting himself into the future. At the start, man is a self-conscious project, instead of being moss, rot, or a cauliflower; nothing exists prior to this project. There is nothing in an intelligible heaven, and man will be what he has projected himself to be. Not what he wishes to be; because when we speak of wishing, we usually mean a conscious decision that for the most part is subsequent to what we have already made of ourselves. I can wish to join a political party, to write a book, to get married—but all of this is only a manifestation of a more primitive, more spontaneous choice that is called "will."

But if existence truly precedes essence, man is responsible for what he is. Thus, the first step of existentialism is to put every man in possession of what he is, to place on him total responsibility for his existence. And, when we say that man is responsible for himself, we mean that he is not only responsible for his own existence, but that he is responsible for all men.

There are two senses of the word "subjectivism," and our opponents play on these two senses. Subjectivism can mean, on the one hand, that the individual subject chooses himself; on the other hand, it can refer to the impossibility of man surpassing human subjectivity. It is the second sense that is the profound sense of existentialism. When we say that man chooses himself, we mean that each of us chooses himself; but by this we also mean that in choosing himself, each of us chooses all men. Indeed, there is not one of our acts, in creating the man we wish to be, that does not at the same time create an image of man as we deem he ought to be. In choosing to be this or that, we simultaneously affirm the value of what we choose, because we can never choose evil. We always choose the good, and nothing can be good for us without being good for all.

On the other hand, if existence precedes essence, and if we grant that in choosing our existence we simultaneously mold our image, this image is valid for everyone and for our entire epoch. Thus, our responsibility is much greater than we might have supposed, for it engages all humanity. If I am a worker who chooses to join a Christian trade-union rather than being communist, and if by this action I wish to show that resignation is at bottom the solution which best suits man, that man's kingdom is not of this earth, I am not only engaged in my own case. Rather, I want to be resigned for everyone; consequently my action has engaged humanity in its entirety. And if, on a more personal level, I want to get married, to have children—even if this marriage depends solely on my situation, my passion or my desire—I engage not only myself, but all humanity, on the path of monogamy. Thus, I am responsible for myself and for everyone else. I am choosing and creating a specific image of man—in choosing myself, I choose man.

This allows us to understand what lies hidden in such grandiloquent words as anguish, forlornness, and despair. As you will see, it's extremely simple. First, what is meant by anguish? The existentialist willingly declares that man is anguish. What he

means by this is that the man who engages himself and who realizes that he is not only choosing his own being, but that he is simultaneously choosing what he wants all humanity to be, cannot escape the feeling of his total and profound responsibility. Of course, there are many people who are not anxious. But we maintain that they are masking their anxiety, that they are fleeing from it. Certainly, many people believe that in acting they are only engaging themselves. When someone asks them, "What if everyone acted like that?" they shrug their shoulders and respond, "Everyone doesn't act like that." But in truth, one must always ask oneself, "What would happen if everyone were to act like that?" One can only escape this disturbing thought through a kind of **bad faith.** Someone who lies and who excuses himself by saying, "Everyone doesn't act like that," is someone who is ill at ease with his conscience, for the act of lying implies that a universal value is being conferred upon the lie.

However, anguish becomes visible even when it masks itself. This is the anguish that Kierkegaard referred to as the "anguish of Abraham." You know the story: an angel has ordered Abraham to sacrifice his son. Everything would be well if it were truly an angel who had come and said: "You are Abraham, you will sacrifice your son." But everyone might ask himself, at the start, whether this is really an angel, and whether I am really Abraham. What proof do I have? There was a madwoman who had hallucinations—someone would speak to her on the telephone and give her orders. Her doctor asked her, "But who is it who speaks to you?" She replied, "He says he's God." What proof did she have, in fact, that it was God? If an angel appears to me, what proof do I have that it is an angel? And if I hear voices, what proves that they come from heaven and not from hell, or from the unconscious, or from a pathological state? What proves that they are addressed to me? What proves that I have been surely designated to impose my conception of man and my choice on humanity? I will never find any proof, any sign, to convince me of that. If I hear a voice, I am always the one who will decide whether this voice is the voice of an angel; if I believe that an act is good, I am the one who will choose to say that this act is good rather than bad. Nothing denotes me as being Abraham, and nevertheless at each moment I am obligated to perform exemplary acts.

Everything happens as if, for every man, all humanity has their eyes fixed on what he does, guiding themselves by his actions. And each man ought to ask himself, "Am I really the type who has the right to act in such a way that humanity can guide itself by my actions?" And if he does not say this to himself, he is masking his anguish.

Here there is no question of an anguish that would lead to quietism, to inaction. It is a question of a simple anguish, an anguish that is well known to those who have been in a position of responsibility. When, for example, a military officer takes the responsibility for an attack and dispatches a certain number of men to their death, he chooses to do so, and at bottom only he chooses. Undoubtedly, there are orders that come from above, but they are quite broad and he interprets them. And the lives of ten or fourteen or twenty men depend on his interpretation. In making this decision, he cannot avoid having a certain anguish. All leaders know this anguish. This doesn't stop them from acting; on the contrary, it is the very condition of their action. For it implies that they envision a plurality of possibilities, and that, in choosing one, they realize that it only has value because it is chosen. Besides, we will see that this type of anguish, which is the type that existentialism describes, is explained by a direct responsibility to the other men whom it engages. It is not a curtain that separates us from action; it is part of action itself.

When we speak of forlornness, an expression dear to Heidegger, we mean only that God does not exist, and that one must draw all of the consequences of this. The existentialist is strongly opposed to a certain type of secular ethics that would like to get rid of God with the least possible cost. Around 1880, some French professors tried to establish a secular ethics which they expressed roughly as follows: God is a useless and costly hypothesis which we are abolishing; but, nevertheless, in order for there to be an ethics, a society, a civilized world, it is necessary that certain values be taken seriously and be considered as existing *a priori*. It must be obligatory, *a priori*, to be honest, not to lie, not to beat your wife, to have children, and so on. Thus, with a little work we will be able to show that these values exist all the same, inscribed in an intelligible heaven, even though God does not exist. In other words—and this, I believe, is the tendency of everything that is

called "radicalism" in France—nothing will be changed if God does not exist. We will still find the same norms of honesty, of progress, of humanism; and we will have made of God an out-of-date hypothesis that will quietly die of itself.

The existentialist, on the contrary, thinks that it is very troublesome that God does not exist, because along with God, every possibility of finding values in an intelligible heaven disappears as well. There can no longer be an *a priori* good, since there is no infinite and perfect consciousness to think it. Nowhere is it written that this good exists—that one must be honest, that one must not lie—precisely because we exist on a plane where there are only men. Dostoevsky has written, "If God didn't exist, everything would be permitted." This is the starting point of existentialism. In effect, everything is permissible if God doesn't exist, and consequently man is forlorn, because he can't find, either within himself or without, anything to latch onto. He can discover no excuses. Indeed, if existence precedes essence, one can never explain things by referring to a given and fixed human nature. In other words, there is no determinism—man is free, man is freedom.

Moreover, if God does not exist, we do not find before us any values or commands that legitimize our conduct. Thus, we do not have, either behind us or in front of us, in the bright domain of values, justifications or excuses. We are alone, without excuses. This is what I am trying to express when I say that man is condemned to be free. Condemned, because he did not give birth to himself, but in other respects he is still free, for once thrown into the world, he is responsible for everything that he does.

The existentialist does not believe in the power of passion. He never thinks that a beautiful passion is a destructive torrent that inevitably leads man to certain acts, and which, in consequence, is an excuse. He believes that man is responsible for his passion. Moreover, the existentialist does not think that man will be able to find on earth any kind of omen that will help him find his bearings, because he thinks that man will decipher the omen to please himself. He thinks, therefore, that man, without any prop and without any help, is condemned at each moment to invent man. Ponge has said, in an excellent article, "Man is the future of man." That's completely correct. But if one means by this that this future is written in heaven, that God sees it, then the statement is false, because that would amount to saying that one no longer had a future. However, if one means by it that whatever man may appear to be, there is a future to be made, a virgin future awaiting him, then the statement is legitimate. But then, we are forlorn. . . .

When I was a prisoner, I knew a rather remarkable young man who had become a Jesuit. He had entered the Jesuit order in the following manner. He had suffered a certain number of rather sharp blows. His father had died when he was a child, leaving him in poverty; and he had been a student on scholarship at a religious institution, where he was constantly made to feel that he was a charity case. In addition, he was unsuccessful in winning any of the distinctions of honor that are pleasing to children. Later, when he was around eighteen, he had failed in an affair of the heart; finally, at twenty-two, he flunked his military training. While the latter was a rather childish matter, it was the final drop of water that made the vase overflow. This young man could have thus thought that he had screwed up everything. It was an omen, but an omen of what? He could have taken refuge in bitterness or in despair. But he judged, very cleverly for himself, that this was an omen that he was not made for secular triumphs, but that only the triumphs of religion, of the sacred, of faith, were accessible to him. Thus, he saw in all of this a word from God, and he entered the order. Who can fail to see that the decision concerning the meaning of the omen had come solely from himself? One could have concluded something else from this series of blows—for example, that he was intended to be a carpenter or a revolutionary. He bears, therefore, the entire responsibility of deciphering it. Forlornness implies that we ourselves choose our being. Forlornness and anguish go together.

With regard to despair, the meaning of this term is extremely simple. It means that we are limited to counting on what depends on our will, or on the ensemble of probabilities that makes our action possible. When we want something, we are always faced with probabilities. I am counting on the arrival of a friend. This friend is coming by train or by trolley car. This supposes that the train will arrive on time, or that the trolley car will not derail. I remain in the realm of possibilities; but possibilities count only to the point where our action requires the ensemble of these possibilities. From the moment when the possibilities I am considering are not rigorously engaged by my action, I am bound to disengage myself from them, for no God, no design, can adapt the world and its possibilities to my will. At bottom, when Descartes said, "Conquer yourself rather than the world," he meant the same thing—act without hope.

The Marxists, to whom I have spoken, respond to me, "Even though your action will obviously be limited by your death, you can count on the support of others. This means counting both on what others elsewhere are now doing to help you, in China, in Russia, and on what they will do later after your death to further the action and to bring it to fruition, which will be the revolution. You must count on that, otherwise you are not being moral."

I reply at once that I will always count on comrades in the struggle to the extent that these comrades are concretely engaged with me in a common struggle. I will always count on the unity of a party or a grouping that I can more or less put my stamp on, that is to say, one in which I am militantly engaged and of which I know the movements at each moment. In such a case, counting on the unity and the will of the party is precisely like counting on the fact that the train will arrive on time, or that the trolley car will not derail. However, given that man is free and that there is no human nature on which I can depend, I cannot count on men that I do not know, or rely on human goodness or on man's concern for the well-being of society. . . . Given that men are free and that they will freely decide tomorrow what man will be, I cannot be sure that my comrades in the struggle will carry on my work after my death in order to bring it to its maximum perfection. Tomorrow, after my death, some men may decide to establish fascism, and the others may be too cowardly and helpless to stop them. At that moment, fascism will be the human truth, and so much the worse for us.

In reality, things will be the way man will have decided they are to be. Does that mean that I should abandon myself to quietism? No. First, I should engage myself, then I should act on the old adage, "It is not necessary to hope in order to act." This doesn't mean that I shouldn't belong to a cause, but that I should be without illusion and that I should do what I can. For example, what if I were to ask myself, "Will **collectivism,** as such, ever come about?" I know nothing about this; I only know that I will do everything in my power to make it happen—I will do what I can. Outside of that, I can count on nothing. Quietism is the attitude of people who say, "The others can do what I can't do." The doctrine that I am presenting is precisely the opposite of quietism, since it declares, "There is no reality except in action." Moreover, it goes further since it adds, "Man is nothing other than his project; he exists only to the extent that he realizes himself; thus he is nothing other than the ensemble of his acts, nothing other than his life."

After this, we can understand why a certain number of people are horrified by our doctrine. Because often the only means they have of enduring their misery is to think: "Circumstances have been against me, I am worth much more than what I am. Of course, I've not had a great love, or a great friendship, but that's because I've never found a man or a woman who was worthy of it. I haven't written very good books, but that's because I've not had the spare time to write them. I haven't had children to whom I could devote myself, but that's because I haven't found the man with whom I could have shared my life. Thus there remains in me, unused and wholly viable, a multitude of dispositions, of inclinations, of possibilities, that gives me a worth that cannot be inferred simply from the series of my acts."

Well, for the existentialist, there is in reality no love other than that which fashions itself, no possibility of love other than that which manifests itself in the act of loving. There is no genius other than that which expresses itself in works of art—the genius of Proust is the totality of Proust's works; the genius of Racine is the series of his tragedies. There is nothing outside of that. Why attribute to Racine the possibility of writing an additional tragedy, since it is a fact that he didn't write it? A man is engaged in life, makes his mark, and outside of this mark there is nothing. Obviously, this thought may seem harsh to someone who has not accomplished much in life. But on the other hand, it disposes people to realize that only reality counts, that dreams, expectations, and hopes merely permit a man to be defined as a disappointed dream, as miscarried hopes, as useless expectations. That is to say, they allow him to be defined negatively and not positively.

However, when we say, "You are nothing other than your life," this does not imply that the artist will be judged solely by his works of art. There are a thousand other things that contribute equally to defining him. What we mean is that a man is nothing other than a series of undertakings, that he is the total, the summing-up, the ensemble of the relations that constitute these undertakings. . . .

People have reproached me for asking whether existentialism is a humanism. They have said, "But you wrote in *Nausea* that the humanists were wrong; you mocked a certain type of humanism. Why return to it now?" In reality, the word "humanism" has two different meanings. By humanism one can mean a theory that takes man as an end and as a higher value. This is the meaning of humanism found in Cocteau, when, for example, in his story *Around the World in Eighty Hours* a character who is flying over some mountains in an airplane declares, "How wonderful is man." What this means is that even though I did not personally build the airplanes, I will profit from this particular invention, and that I, like all men, will be able to personally consider myself responsible for, and honored by, the particular acts of a few men. This presupposes that we can ascribe a value to man according to the highest acts of certain men. This humanism is absurd, because only the dog or the horse would be able to make an over-all judgment about man, to declare that man is a wonder, and, at least to my knowledge, they have refrained from doing this. But it cannot be admitted that man can make a judgment about man. Existentialism exempts him from all judgments of this nature. The existentialist will never take man as an end, because he is always in the making. And we should not believe that there is a humanity for which we could produce a cult, in the manner of Auguste Comte. The cult of humanity results in the self-closed humanism of Comte, and, it must be said, in fascism. This is a humanism for which we have no desire.

But there is another meaning of humanism, which at bottom means this: man is constantly outside of himself. It is by projecting himself beyond himself, by losing himself outside himself, that he makes himself exist as man. Stated another way, it is by pursuing transcendent goals that he is able to exist. Man, who is this surpassing and who takes hold of things only as they profit this surpassing, is at the heart, at the center, of this surpassing. There is no other universe than a human universe, the universe of human subjectivity. This joining of transcendence, as constitutive of man—not in the sense that God is transcendent, but in the sense of surpassing—with subjectivity, in the sense that man is not closed within himself but is always present in a human universe, is what we call "existentialist humanism." Humanism, because we remind man that there is no other legislator than himself, and that he will decide by himself, in his forlornness. Humanism, because we point out that man will realize himself exactly as human, not by recoiling within himself, but always by seeking outside himself a goal, which is just this liberation, just this particular realization.

One can see, from these few reflections, that nothing is more unjust than the objections that have been made against us. Existentialism is nothing other than an effort to draw all the consequences of a coherent atheistic position. It isn't at all seeking to plunge man into despair. But if, like the Christians, one calls every attitude of unbelief "despair," one has strayed from the original meaning of the term. Existentialism isn't so much of an atheism that it exhausts itself in demonstrating that God does not exist. It declares, rather, that even if God existed, that would change nothing; that's our point of view. Not that we believe that God exists, but we think that the crucial problem is not that of his existence. What's more valuable than a proof of the existence of God is helping man find himself again, and persuading him that nothing can save himself from himself. In this sense, existentialism is optimistic, it is a doctrine of action; and it is solely in bad faith that, confounding their own despair with ours, the Christians can call us despairing.

Questions for Thought

1. Would you categorize yourself as an existentialist? Why or why not?
2. To what extent do you believe that human beings are free? Explain your answer.
3. Do you agree with Sartre's claim that belief in God necessarily limits human freedom? Do you think that belief in God is compatible with belief in human freedom? Defend your answers.
4. Have you experienced any of the existential states (anguish, forlornness, or despair) that Sartre describes? If so, under what circumstances?
5. What do you think the term *humanism* means? How does your definition compare with or differ from that of Sartre?
6. Do you agree with Sartre that existentialism is an optimistic and not a pessimistic philosophy? Why or why not?
7. What are the essential ways in which Sartre's views differ from Skinner's views? On what points, if any, do they agree?

Woman as The Second Sex   17

SIMONE DE BEAUVOIR

Simone de Beauvoir (1908–1986), the older of two daughters of a respectable bourgeois family, was born in Paris. After having decided to become a writer at an early age, de Beauvoir attended the Sorbonne, where, to the dismay of her parents, she studied philosophy. After receiving her degree in 1929, she taught philosophy at a number of lycées in Marseilles, Rouen, and eventually Paris. She retired from teaching in 1943 to devote all her energies to writing. She also became very active in the **existentialist** movement that was growing in Paris during and after World War II, serving as cofounder (with Jean-Paul Sartre and Maurice Merleau-Ponty) of *Les Temps Modernes,* a journal devoted to the analysis of political and literary questions from an existentialist perspective.

Like Sartre, with whom she had an intimate relationship for over fifty years, de Beauvoir expressed her ideas in both philosophical and literary writings. One of her philosophical writings, *Le deuxieme sexe* (1949; *The Second Sex* [1952]), has become a classic of modern feminism, and her literary writings often focus on existentialist and feminist themes. Her other writings include *L'invitée* (1943; translated as *She Came to Stay*), *Pyrrhus et Cinéas* (1944), *Le sang des autres* (1945; *The Blood of Others*), *Pour une morale de l'ambiguité* (1947; *The Ethics of Ambiguity*), *Les Mandarins* (1954; *The Mandarins*), *Memoires d'une jeune fille rangée* (1958; *Memoirs of a Dutiful Daughter*), *La force de l'age* (1960; translated as *The Prime of Life*), *Une mort très douce* (1964; *A Very Easy Death*), *La vieillesse* (1970; translated as *The Coming of Age* [1972]), *Tout compte fait* (1972; translated as *All Said and Done*), and *Adieux: A Farewell to Sartre* (1984).

Also like Sartre and many of the other existentialists, de Beauvoir was socially committed and thus participated in the various protest movements of her time. In a number of speeches and articles, she supported the rights of workers and the elderly and attacked the colonialist policies of France and other Western nations. She also participated in an important march for abortion rights that took place in Paris in 1970. De Beauvoir died of a respiratory ailment one day before the sixth anniversary of Sartre's death.

In the following selection, which is excerpted from the introduction and the conclusion to *The Second Sex,* de Beauvoir raises the question of what it means to be a woman. While observing that the answer to this question is often linked to the notion of femininity, she denies that femininity represents a fixed concept or essence. Indeed, like Sartre in the last selection, she denies the existence of any universal human essence and claims that the concept of femininity, like the concept of humanity, is socially and historically determined.

Adopting the standpoint of existentialist ethics, de Beauvoir argues that human beings have the capacity to freely determine their own destinies. In other words, she claims that human existence is characterized by **transcendence**—that is, by the possibility of choosing one's own goals and projects. However, she believes that realizing one's transcendence is limited by both internal and external obstacles. Internally, there is a tendency to absolve ourselves of responsibility and the difficulty of decision by allowing others to control our lives. And externally, there are others who, in pursuing their own transcendence, willingly dominate and oppress us.

While all human beings encounter these obstacles to realizing their transcendence, de Beauvoir argues that women have been especially limited by external obstacles and their internalization. Indeed, using many examples from philosophy, theology, and literature, she claims that women have been relegated to the position of the Other, or the inessential, in Western society. As such, woman's transcendence has been blocked not only by the existential obstacles faced by all human beings but also by a wide range of legal, social, theological, and scientific barricades.

Toward the end of this selection, de Beauvoir specifically addresses the obstacle to women's freedom that results from traditional male dominance in erotic experience. After noting that some modern women reject this subordinate position by dominating their partners, she says that others have responded by displacing the idea that the erotic experience is a victory or defeat with the idea that it is an equal exchange between partners. De Beauvoir then suggests that this latter idea of equal exchange may come to characterize the overall relationship between women and men. Once they accept their existential standing in the world, women and men will be able to recognize their mutual need for each other, and "fraternity between them could then come into existence."

Questions for Reading

1. What does de Beauvoir mean by the term *femininity*?
2. Who, according to de Beauvoir, are some of the thinkers that have viewed women as inferior to men? What are some of their justifications for doing so?
3. Why does de Beauvoir believe that the story of creation found in Genesis makes women subordinate to men?
4. Why, according to de Beauvoir, has the subordination of women been so hard to overcome? Does she believe that this subordination can be overcome? If so, how? If not, why not?
5. How does de Beauvoir describe the erotic experience between women and men? In what ways, if any, has this experience changed over time?

FOR A LONG TIME I HAVE HESITATED TO WRITE A book on woman. The subject is irritating, especially to women; and it is not new. The quarrel over feminism has caused enough ink to flow. At present it is nearly over, and perhaps we should not talk about it any longer. However, people still talk about it—it does not seem that the voluminous nonsense uttered during the last century has done much to clarify the problem. Besides, is there a problem? And what exactly is it? Are there even women? Certainly the theory of the eternal feminine still has its followers who whisper, "Even in Russia, women still remain *women*." But other well-informed persons—sometimes the very same ones—sigh, "Woman is losing her way, woman is lost." One might well wonder if women still exist, if they will always exist, if it is desirable or not that they should, what their place in this world is, what their place should be. "Where are the women?" was recently asked in a periodic magazine.

Before answering this question, we must ask what it means to be a woman. "*Tota mulier in utero*—woman is a womb," someone says. However, in talking about certain women, the connoisseurs decree, "They are not women," even though they have a uterus like the others. Everyone recognizes that there are females in the human species; they constitute, today as always, approximately half of humanity. Nevertheless we are told that "femininity is in peril." We are exhorted to "Be women, remain women, become women." All this suggests that to be a human female is not necessarily to be a woman; to be a woman, one must participate in that mysterious and threatened reality called femininity. But is femininity something secreted by the ovaries? Or has it been conjured up as an essence of a Platonic heaven? Will a rustling petticoat suffice to bring it down to earth? While certain women have zealously striven to incarnate it, the pattern of femininity has never been captured. It has been loosely described in vague and shimmering terms that seem to have been borrowed from the vocabulary of the seers. In the time of Saint Thomas, it was taken to be an essence as surely defined as the dormitive virtue of the poppy. But conceptualism has lost ground. The biological and social sciences no longer posit the existence of immutably fixed entities that determine the given character of something, such as woman, the Jew or the Negro. Character is considered to be a secondary reaction to a *situation*. If femininity no longer exists today, then it never existed.

This is the editor's translation of selections from Le Deuxième Sexe, *vols. I and II, by Simone de Beauvoir, Paris: Éditions Gallimard, 1949.*

But then does the word *woman* not have a singular meaning? This is vigorously affirmed by the partisans of the philosophy of the enlightenment, of **rationalism,** and of **nominalism.** To them, women are only those human beings who have been arbitrarily designated by the word *woman*. American women, in particular, freely think that woman no longer has any place; and if a backward-thinking person still views herself as a woman, her friends recommend that she be psychoanalyzed in order to free herself of this obsession. In the work, *Modern Woman: A Lost Sex*—a work that is extremely irritating in many other respects—Dorothy Parker has written: "I cannot be fair to books that treat woman as woman. . . . My belief is all of us, men as well as women, should be considered human beings."

However, nominalism is a rather limited doctrine, and the antifeminists have had great sport in showing that women *are not* men. Certainly woman is, like man, a human being; but such an affirmation is abstract. The fact is that every concrete human being is always singularly situated. To refuse the notions of the eternal feminine, the black soul, the Jewish character is not to deny that today there are Jews, Negroes, or women. This negation does not represent liberation for those concerned, but rather an inauthentic evasion. It is clear that no woman can claim, without being in **bad faith,** to place herself outside of her sex. A well-known woman writer refused, several years ago, to let her portrait appear in a series of photographs dedicated solely to women writers—she wished to be included among the men. But she used the influence of her *husband* to obtain this privilege. Women who affirm that they are men still crave masculine respect and acknowledgment. I remember this young Trotskyite getting up on a stage in the middle of a rowdy meeting, and who, despite her evident fragility, was getting ready to come to blows. She denied her feminine weakness, but she did so because of her love for a militant male of whom she wished to be the equal. The defiant attitude found in so many American women proves that they are haunted by the feeling of their femininity. And in truth, walking around with open eyes suffices to prove that humanity is divided into two categories of individuals, whose clothes, faces, bodies, smiles, bearing,

interests, and occupations are manifestly different. Perhaps these differences are superficial; perhaps they are destined to disappear. What is certain is that for the moment they do evidently and strikingly exist.

If functioning as a female does not suffice to define woman, if we also refuse to explain her by "the eternal feminine," and if, moreover, we admit that, at least provisionally, there are women on earth, then we must ask ourselves the following question: What is a woman?

The statement of the problem itself already suggests to me an initial response. It is significant that I ask the question. A man would not think of writing a book on the peculiar situation or place of the human male. However, if I want to define myself, I must begin by stating that, "I am a woman." This truth constitutes the ground on which all other affirmations must be based. A man never begins by identifying himself as an individual of a certain sex; that he is a man goes without saying. It is only in a formal way, as on marriage certificates and identification papers, that the rubric of masculine and feminine becomes symmetrical. The connection of the two sexes is not like the circuit between two electrical poles—man represents at once both the positive and the neutral. In the French language this is shown by the fact that the term *man* is used for human beings in general, as well as for individual males. The term *woman*, on the other hand, appears only as the negative, so that everything about her is seen as a limitation without reciprocity. Occasionally, in the course of abstract discussions, I have been irritated when hearing men say to me, "You think such things because you are a woman." But I know that my only defense is to respond, "I think these things because they are true," thereby eliminating my subjectivity from the matter. It would be out of the question to reply, "And you think the opposite because you are a man." This is because it is understood that there is nothing peculiar in the fact that one is a man—a man is within his rights in being a man, it is woman who is in the wrong.[1] In a practical way, just as for the ancients there was an absolute vertical with reference to which the oblique was defined, so there is an absolute human type, which is the masculine. Woman has ovaries, a uterus; these are the peculiar conditions that lock her up in her subjectivity. It is often said that she thinks with her glands. Man arrogantly forgets that his anatomy also requires hormones, that he has glands like the testicles. He understands his body as having a direct, a normal relation to the world, which he believes he apprehends objectively, whereas he considers the body of a woman to be weighed down by its peculiarities, to be an obstacle, a prison. "The female is female by virtue of a certain *lack* of qualities," said Aristotle. He adds, "We should consider the character of women as suffering from a natural defectiveness." And Saint Thomas for his part decreed that woman is an "incomplete man," a "supplementary" being. This is symbolized in the story from Genesis where Eve is created from, in the words of Bossuet, a "supernumary bone" extracted from Adam. Humanity is male, and man defines woman not in herself but in relation to him; she is not considered as an autonomous being. "Woman, the relative being," writes Michelet. In his *Rapport d'Uriel,* Benda affirms in the same manner that, "The body of man has a meaning in itself, when abstracted from that of woman, whereas the body of woman seems stripped of meaning if it is not connected in some way with the male. . . . Man can think of himself without woman. She cannot think of herself without man." And she is nothing other than what man determines her to be. Thus she is called "the sex," which is to say that she appears to the male essentially as a sexual being. For him, she is sex—nothing but sex to be sure. She is determined and defined in relation to man, while he is not determined and defined in relation to her. She is the inessential opposite the essential. He is the Subject, the Absolute—she is the Other. . . .

Woman has always been, if not the slave of man, at least his vassal. The two sexes have never shared the world in equality; and still today, even though her condition is evolving, woman is heavily handicapped. In most countries her legal status is not identical to that of man, and frequently this is a considerable disadvantage to her. Even when her rights are legally recognized in the abstract, long-standing customs prevent them from finding concrete expression in the **mores.** Economically, men and women almost constitute two castes—all things being equal, men have better jobs, higher salaries, and more chances for success than their recent rivals. In industry, politics, etc., men occupy a much greater number of positions, and they hold the most important ones. In addition to these concrete advantages that they possess, men have traditionally been endowed with a prestige that the entire education of children supports. The present encompasses the past; and in the past, all history has been created by men. Now women are beginning to take part in the elaboration of the world, but this world is still a world that belongs to men—men have no doubt whatsoever about this, and women have little doubt. To refuse to be the Other, to refuse complicity with men, would require that women renounce all the advantages that alliance with the superior cast confers upon them. The sovereign-man will materially protect the woman-liege, and he will take upon himself the justification of her existence. Along with the economic risk, she also eludes the metaphysical risk of a freedom that must invent its own ends without help. Indeed, beside the urge of every individual to affirm himself as subject, which is an ethical urge, there is also the temptation to flee one's freedom and to become an object. This is a disastrous path—passive, alienated, lost; on it one becomes prey to someone else's will, cut off from one's transcendence, defrauded of all worth. But it is an easy path. On it one evades the anguish and the stress of taking upon oneself an authentic existence. The man who tries to constitute woman as the *Other* will, therefore, meet with a profound complicity in her. Thus, woman does not affirm herself as subject because she does not have the material resources, because she feels that the bond that ties her to the man is necessary even if it lacks reciprocity, and because she is often pleased with her role as the *Other.*

But a question immediately presents itself: How did all this history begin? One can understand that the duality of the sexes, like any duality, might lead to conflict. One can also understand that if one of the two succeeds in imposing its superiority, then it would establish itself as absolute. But what remains to be explained is why man should have won from the start. It seems that women could have won the victory, or that the struggle might never have been resolved. How did it come to be that this world has always belonged to the men and that only nowadays have things begun to change? Is this change good? Will it lead to an equal sharing of the world between men and women?

These questions are not new; there have already been many responses to them. But it is precisely the bare fact that woman is *Other* that casts an odor over all the justifications that men have hitherto provided. It is quite evident that these justifications have been dictated by men's interests. "Everything that has been written by men about women should be suspect, because men are at once judge and litigant," wrote Poulain de la Barre, a little-known feminist of the seventeenth century. Everywhere, at all times, males have experienced great satisfaction in feeling that they are the lords of creation. "Blessed be God, our Lord and the Lord of the whole world, that he did not make me a woman," say the Jews in their morning prayers; however, their wives whisper with resignation, "Blessed be the Lord, who created me according to his will." Among the blessings for which Plato thanked the gods, the first was that they had created him free and not a slave, the second was that they had made him a man and not a woman. But the males would not have been able to fully revel in this privilege, if they did not consider it as having been founded on something absolute and eternal. Thus, they tried to transform the fact of their supremacy into a right. "Those who have made and compiled the laws, being men, have favored their own sex, and the legal experts have turned the laws into principles," Poulain de la Barre adds. Legislators, priests, philosophers, writers, and scholars have been bent upon showing that the subordinate rank of woman has been willed in heaven and advantageous on earth. The religions created by men reflect this will to dominate—in the myths of Eve, of Pandora, they have taken up arms. That they have philosophy and theology at their service is shown by the previous quotations from Aristotle and Saint Thomas. . . .

But for proving the inferiority of woman, the antifeminists not only have the contributions of religion, philosophy, and theology from which to draw, they also have the recent findings of science—biology, experimental psychology, etc. The most that these have been willing to grant to the *other* sex is "equality in difference." This formula, which has had much success, is very significant; it is exactly like the formula that is used with respect to the Jim Crow laws of the Negroes in the United States. This so-called egalitarian segregation has served to introduce the most extreme discrimination. This similarity is not incidental. For whether it is the matter of a race, a caste, a class, or a sex that is reduced to a condition of inferiority, the processes of justification are the same. "The eternal feminine" is analogous to the "black soul" and to the "Jewish character." Granted, the Jewish problem is on the whole very different from the other two—for the anti-Semite, the Jew is not so much an inferior as an enemy, an enemy for whom there is no place on earth, for whom annihilation is desired. But there are profound similarities between the situation of women and that of Negroes. Today both are freeing themselves from a like paternalism, and the formerly dominant class wants them to stay in "their place," which is to say the place that this class has chosen for them. In both cases, those who would keep them in their place spew out eulogies, more or less sincerely, on the virtues of the "good Negro" with his passive, childish, laughing soul, of the submissive Negro, and of the "truly feminine" woman, that is to say, of the woman who is frivolous, juvenile, and irresponsible, the woman who submits herself to the man. In both cases, they get their argument from the state of affairs that they have created. One understands the witticism of Bernard Shaw. "The white American," he says, in substance, "has relegated the Negro to the rank of shoeshine boy, and he concludes from this that the Negro is only good at shining shoes." One finds this vicious circle in all similar circumstances—when an individual (or a group of individuals) is kept in a position of inferiority, the fact is that he *is* inferior. But the import of the word *to be* must be correctly understood. One acts in bad faith if one gives it a fixed value when it actually has the dynamic Hegelian sense—*to be* is to have become. It is this having been made so, that manifests itself. Yes, on the whole women today *are* inferior to men; that is to say, their situation offers fewer possibilities to them. The problem is knowing whether this state of affairs should continue.

Many men hope so; all have not yet given up the battle. The conservative bourgeoisie continues to see a danger in the emancipation of woman, a danger that threatens its morals and interests. Certain males fear female competition. The other day in the *Hebdo-Latin* a male student wrote, "Every female student who takes a position in medicine or law *steals* a job from us." That student had no question whatsoever about his rights on this earth. And economic interests are not the only ones at stake. One of the benefits that oppression gives to the oppressors is that it makes the most humble among them feel *superior*. A "poor white" in the Southern states has the consolation of saying to himself that he is not a "dirty nigger," and the wealthier whites cleverly exploit this pride. In the same way, when compared to women, the most mediocre male can think of himself as a demi-god. . . .

However, we should not consider the arguments of the feminists with any less suspicion than we do those of the antifeminists. For often the polemical nature of these arguments robs them of all value. If the "woman question" is so trifling, it is because masculine arrogance has made of it a "quarrel," and when one quarrels, one no longer reasons well. Different people have tirelessly tried to prove that woman is superior, inferior or equal to men. Created after Adam, she is evidently a secondary being, some say. Others say that, on the contrary, Adam was only a rough draft and that God succeeded in creating the perfect human being when he created Eve. Her brain is smaller; yes, but it is relatively larger. Christ was made a man; yes, but perhaps to make him more humble. Each argument immediately calls to mind its opposite, and both of them are usually fallacious. If we want to try to see clearly, we must get out of these ruts. We must reject the vague notions of superiority, inferiority, and equality that have perverted these discussions and start anew.

But, then, how shall we pose the question? And in the first place, who are we to pose it? Men are judges and litigants, but so are women. Where can we find an angel? In truth, an angel would be poorly qualified to speak, for an angel would be ignorant of all the given facts of the problem. With regard to the hermaphrodite, the case would be most peculiar, for the hermaphrodite is not simultaneously man and woman, but rather neither man nor woman. Besides, I believe that certain women are best placed to elucidate the situation of woman. . . . It is not some mysterious essence that dictates

good or bad faith to men and women; it is their situation that more or less disposes them toward the search for truth. Many women today, having had the opportunity of seeing all the privileges of a human being restored to them, can afford the luxury of impartiality—we even feel the necessity of it. We are no longer like our embattled elders; for the most part we have won the match. In recent discussions on the status of woman, the United Nations has persistently and forcefully proclaimed that the equality of the sexes is being realized, and already a number of us have never had to experience our femininity as a constraint or as an obstacle. Many problems seem to us to be more essential than those which singularly concern us. This detachment even permits us to hope that our attitude will be objective. However, we know the feminine world more intimately than men do because we have our roots in it. We understand more immediately what it means for a human being to be feminine, and we are more concerned with such knowledge. I have said that there are more essential problems; but this does not prevent us from seeing some importance in asking the following: How will the fact that we are women affect our lives? Precisely what opportunities have been given to us, and what opportunities have been refused? What destiny awaits our younger sisters, and in what direction should they be oriented? It is striking that, on the whole, feminine literature of our day is animated much less by a will to vindicate than by an effort toward lucidity. We leave behind an era of excessive polemics, and this book is one attempt among others to prove this point.

But it is, without doubt, impossible to discuss any human problem without a set purpose. Even the manner in which the questions are posed, as well as the assumed perspectives, presuppose a hierarchy of interests. All qualifications are wrapped in values; so-called objective descriptions presuppose an ethical background. Rather than trying to conceal principles that are more or less clearly implied, one should state them openly at the start. In doing so, it will not be necessary to specify on each page the meaning given to the words *superior, inferior, better, worse, progress, regression,* etc. If we review some of the works devoted to woman, we see that one of the points of view most frequently adopted is that of the public good, of the general interest. In truth, by the interest of society everyone means the manner in which they wish society to be maintained or set up. To us, the only public good that has value is one that assures the private good of the citizens. It is from the point of view of giving concrete opportunities to individuals that we judge institutions. But we do not confuse the idea of private interest with that of happiness, although from another point of view, these ideas are frequently conjoined. Are not women living in a harem happier than women voters? Is not the housewife happier than the working woman? One scarcely knows what the word *happiness* means, and still less what positive values it may hide. It is impossible for anyone to measure the happiness of another, and it is always easy to state that happiness lies in the situation that one wishes to force on them. Those who are condemned to stagnation, in particular, are declared happy on the pretext that happiness is immobility. However, this is a notion to which we do not subscribe. Indeed, the perspective that we adopt is that of existentialist ethics. Every subject, as transcendence, realizes himself concretely only through his projects; he realizes his freedom only through his perpetual surpassing toward other freedoms. There is no other justification for present existence than its expansion towards an indefinitely open future. Each time transcendence falls back into **immanence,** there is a degradation of existence into the "**en-soi,**" of freedom into **facticity.** If it is consented to by the subject, this fall represents a moral fault; if it is imposed upon him, it takes the form of frustration or oppression. In both cases, it is an absolute evil.

Every individual, then, feels the anxiety of justifying his existence as an unlimited need to transcend himself. But what peculiarly defines the situation of woman is that, being free and autonomous like all humans, she opens up and chooses herself in a world where men compel her to assume the role of the Other. They attempt to congeal her into an object and to condemn her to immanence, since her transcendence is to be continually transcended by another consciousness that is essential and sovereign. The drama of woman is acted out within this conflict between the fundamental claim of every subject to always affirm itself as the essential, and the demands of a situation in which she is constituted as the inessential. How can one in the feminine condition realize oneself as a human being? Which paths are open to us? Which ones are blocked? How can one regain independence after being in a state of dependency? What are the circumstances limiting the freedom of woman, and how can she surpass them? . . .

Now, woman is not the victim of a mysterious fatality. The peculiarities that specify her as woman get their importance from the significance placed upon them. They can be surpassed when they are viewed from new perspectives. . . . Thus, for example, through her erotic experience woman feels—and frequently detests—the domination of the male; but there is no reason to conclude that her ovaries condemn her to live eternally on her knees. Virile aggressiveness seems like a lordly privilege only within a system that conspires, in its entirety, to affirm masculine sovereignty. And woman *feels* herself so profoundly passive in the sexual act only because she already *thinks* of herself as such. Claiming their dignity as human beings, many modern women still understand their erotic life from the perspective of a tradition of slavery; thus, finding it humiliating to lie beneath the man, to be penetrated by him, they shrivel up in frigidity. But if the reality were different, the meaning symbolically expressed in amorous gestures and postures would also be different. For example, a woman who pays, who dominates her lover can take pride in her superb idleness and feel that she is conquering the male who actively exerts himself; and here and there many sexually well-balanced couples exist, for whom the notions of victory and defeat have been displaced by an idea of exchange.

In truth, man, like woman, is flesh, and consequently a passivity, the plaything of his hormones and of the species, restless prey of his desires; and like him, she is, in the midst of the carnal fever, a consenting, voluntary gift, an activity. They each live, in their own manner, the strange ambiguity of existence made body. In those battles where they think that they are confronting one another, they are only struggling against themselves, projecting that part of themselves that they repudiate into their partner. Instead of living the ambiguity of his condition, each strives to make the other bear his abjection, while reserving for himself the honor. If, however, both assume their ambiguity with a lucid modesty, along with an authentic pride, they would see themselves as equals and live the erotic drama in amity. The fact that one is a human being is infinitely more important than all the peculiarities that distinguish human beings from one another. It is never the given that confers superiorities— "virtue," as the ancients called it, is defined at the level of "that which depends on us." The same drama of the flesh and the spirit, of finitude and transcendence, is played out in both sexes. Time consumes both of them and death lays in wait. They have the same essential need for each other; and they can both gain from their freedom the same glory. If they knew the taste of this, they would no longer be tempted to argue about fallacious privileges and fraternity between them could then be born.

NOTE

1. It is especially interesting to read this in light of the remarks that Georges de Beauvoir, Simone's father, often made about her: "Simone has a man's brain. She thinks like a man; she is a man."—ED.

Questions for Thought

1. Do you agree with de Beauvoir's claim that women have been traditionally subordinated to men in Western culture? Do you think that this is still true today?
2. De Beauvoir says that women and men are conditioned to be different from birth on. Do you agree with this statement? Provide specific examples from your own life that could serve to either support or refute this claim.
3. Evaluate de Beauvoir's interpretation of the creation story from Genesis. Do you think that religion has generally supported the subordination of women? Support your answer.
4. How does de Beauvoir's description of the erotic experience between women and men compare with or differ from what you have experienced in your own relationships?
5. De Beauvoir raises the following questions: "What opportunities precisely have been given to us [women] and what opportunities have been refused? What destiny awaits our younger sisters, and in what direction should they be oriented?" How would you answer these questions?

An Autobiographical View of Mixed Race and Deracination 18

NAOMI ZACK

Naomi Zack (b. 1944) now teaches philosophy at the University of Oregon. However, after receiving her Ph.D. from Columbia University in 1970, she began a twenty-year odyssey outside the domain of academia. During this time, she made films, ran a small business, and did freelance writing. She also gained the depth of experience on issues of race and race relations that is reflected in the following article and in many of her other writings.

Since obtaining her first position within academia at the State University of New York at Albany, Zack has become a prolific writer. In addition to numerous articles and chapters in books written by others, Zack has published several books of her own. These include *Race and Mixed Race* (1993), *Bachelors of Science: Seventeenth Century Identity, Then and Now* (1996), *Thinking About Race* (1998), and *Philosophy of Science and Race* (2002). She has also edited several important anthologies, such as *American Mixed Race: Constructing Microdiversity* (1995); *RACE/SEX: Their Sameness, Difference and Interplay* (1997); and *Women of Color: A Critical Reader* (2000).

Zack begins the following article by noting that in American society, racial categories are disjunctive—that is, one must be of one race or another (in this case, either black or white) but not both. However, as de Beauvoir noted concerning the relationship of male to female, the two disjunctive categories are not reciprocal. As Zack suggests in several places in her article, in American society being white has traditionally been viewed as being preferable to being black. Moreover, one was considered white only if one had all white ancestors; anyone with even one nonwhite ancestor was considered nonwhite and therefore nondesirable. Such a schema or system of racial designation, according to Zack, is obviously both racist and unjust. It is also scientifically indefensible, for Zack points out that this system of racial classification lacks any basis in physiology or biology. Rather, as de Beauvoir suggested concerning the concept of femininity, Zack claims that the concept of race is socially and historically determined. Since it is both racist and unjust and since it has no defensible theoretical basis, Zack suggests that the concept of race should be rejected, a move that she calls "deracination."

One of the remarkable things about Zack's article is that she combines this rather theoretical analysis of the concept of race (an analysis that she refers to as the "problematization" of race) with personal reflections on her own self-identity. Being of mixed race—an African-American father and a Jewish mother—Zack finds that the traditional schema of racial classification, especially given its disjunctive nature, interferes with her own self-development or self-emancipation. While she notes that self-development or self-emancipation begins with self-respect, she does not believe that it can be fully attained in isolation. On the contrary, Zack believes that an essential component of self-development or self-emancipation depends on what others think about us—our self-respect must be complemented by the respect of others. However, given the traditional schema of racial classification found in American society, Zack believes that a person of mixed race is not likely to receive this respect from others. Thus, her call for deracination, her refusal to have anything to do with the concept of race, has personal as well as theoretical implications.

Questions for Reading

1. How does Zack define the concept of race?
2. What factors in her own life have made this concept problematic?
3. What does Zack mean by *self-emancipation*? How does one go about emancipating oneself?
4. What form, according to Zack, does the kinship schema take in the United States? Why does she believe that this kinship schema is both racist and unjust?
5. How does Zack define the term *deracination*? What arguments does she give in favor of becoming deracinated?

THE SUBJECT

AMERICAN RACIAL CATEGORIES ARE EXCLUSIVELY disjunctive: Thou shalt have a race, and, thy race must be black or white, but not both! As a result of this imperative disjunction, the person of mixed black and white race may pose a problem for others. The mixed-race person may also encounter contradictory identities in her view of herself. These contradictory identities do not admit of any easeful resolution.

In racial matters self-emancipation may be a last recourse. But self-emancipation can lead the person of mixed race to conclusions which are jarring in their ahistoricality, and unacceptable to people whose racial identities are not self-contradictory. I will call the awareness of the problem of mixed race, by a person of mixed race, the problematization of mixed race. And I will call the solution of the problematization of mixed race, deracination. Deracination is a problem for people with black or white racial identities. An awareness of the problem of deracination by a deracinated person could be called the problematization of deracination. These distinctions between problems and problematizations are merely a preliminary way of demarcating racial existence, which includes experience, values and ideology, from racial theory. Problematization is on the side of theory.

THE FIRST PERSON

I am going to begin by describing some facts about myself which it has taken me many years to be able to describe evenly. It has taken me a long time to be able to even describe these facts, publicly, because of warps in my psychology, warps which I do not consider it irresponsible to insist are the effects of warps in external social reality.

My mother was a Jew whose parents came to this country from Lithuania, in 1903. My father was an African-American whose father was born a slave and whose mother claimed Sioux (Native American) descent. My parents were never married to each other and only my mother raised me. My mother was ashamed of her relationship with my father and she encouraged me to deny my black ancestry. She was not an observant Jew and neither am I. But she saw the world through (what I take to be) Jewish eyes and felt the world with (what I take to be) Jewish fears, and I have never been able to avoid (what I take to be) the same apperceptions. In other words, I believe I "identify" with my mother.

My mother knew herself to be a Jew, totally. Many Jews believe that if one's mother is a Jew, then one is a Jew oneself and it does not matter what one's father is. In American society, Jews are classified as white racially. For these reasons, I have usually been designated as white on official documents, especially those documents which do not have a category of undesignated "other."

I do not like to explicitly say that I am white because that is a lie—in American society, if one has a black parent, then one is black. I am black. There are known to be blacks in the USA who have become Jews by religious conversion, but there is no widely recognized category of hereditary Jews who are racially black. Until recently, the American Jews I have known, have, with varying degrees of (slight) **skepticism,** accepted me as a Jew, with the understanding that my father was not a Jew—they have not been specially concerned with how he was not a Jew.[1] But my husbands and the close friends of my adult life have been white gentiles, for the most part. After I have told them that my father was black, a veil has often dropped over any understanding they had about how one inherits a Jewish identity. They have often made the judgment that I have been passing (for white), and that I cannot be a Jew because my father was black. This judgment has been echoed by some blacks I have known. In a way that I intuitively understand, the judgment by blacks that I have been passing (for white) has sometimes been accompanied by resentment and implied moral condemnation.

I am a Jew and therefore I am white. I am black and therefore I am not white. This contradiction is very difficult to think about without momentum from self-emancipation. Self-emancipation is a movement of values.

This article appeared in an American Philosophical Association Newsletter on Philosophy and the Black Experience (Issue no. 91:1, Spring 1992). Copyright 1992, The American Philosophical Association. *Reprinted by permission of the American Philosophical Association and the author.*

SELF-EMANCIPATION AND VALUATION

What am I? The racial and ethnic answers to this question can have a direct bearing on how I feel and whether my life, in general, is bearable to me. This question, What am I? as a question about racial and ethnic identity, divides into three categories: what I think I am; what others think I am; what I want others to think I am. The answers have value-neutral, value-positive, and value-negative, first-, second- and third-person aspects. The goal of self-emancipation is to unite a value-positive answer to the question What do I think I am? with a value-positive answer to the question What do others think I am? This movement from a value-positive, first-person description of myself, to a value-positive second- and third-person description of me, is contained in how I *want* others to value me. Thus, first I aim to feel good about myself and then I aim to get others to have good feelings toward me; although at stake is something more stringent than feelings, more than a matter of being liked, something which at least involves respect. Self-emancipation is thereby a social activity which begins with positive self-valuation. Oppression is also a social activity, although it need not begin in value-negative, third-person judgments; oppression may begin with self-interest, for example.

Self-emancipation is difficult to get started because the self which needs to be positively revalued in order to overcome oppression has already been identified by negative valuations from others. Every step up in value will be resisted by those who not only devalue me but consider it their right to do so. Solitary acts of self-revaluation may at the outset be indistinguishable from delusions of grandeur and other alienated and isolated anti-social expressions of inner life, which have little to do with freedom. Positive self-valuation about race and ethnicity requires that negative valuations which express racism and ethnocentricity be somehow overcome. There are few forms of negative valuation in the USA which are more oppressive than racial designations. American racial designations are based on a kinship schema of black and white racial inheritance. A person of mixed race must begin with this schema in order to answer the question, What am I?

THE KINSHIP SCHEMA OF BLACK AND WHITE RACIAL INHERITANCE

There is a strong asymmetry between black and white racial inheritance.

If a person has a black parent, a black grandparent or black great "n" grandparents (where n is indeterminate, in principle), then that person is considered black. But if a person has a white parent, or three white grandparents, or X white great "n" grandparents (where X is any odd number and n is still indeterminate, in principle), then that person is not thereby considered white. This is a kinship schema and it means that whiteness is nothing more than the absence of any black forebears, and blackness is nothing more than the presence of one black forebear. Apart from this cultural schema, there is no natural black or white racial substratum or essence which anyone can identify in physiological terms. Nevertheless, the kinship schema of racial inheritance is so widely accepted that it is assumed to have a physiological basis. It is assumed that if one refers to a person's race according to this schema, then one is referring to some objective and universal-to-that-race characteristic of the person. As a social entity, the black race in America is perceived to have an ethnic cohesion based on family affiliation; the recognition of black people by white people and other black people; the general negative value of being black; and the shared cultural practices, preferences, aspirations and experiences of black people. This entire social situation contributes to black ethnicity or black identity.[2] Given the false identification of race with a physiological substratum, an analogy could be drawn between race and ethnicity, and sex and gender. But the analogy breaks down insofar as there is now less tolerance of critiques of ethnicity than critiques of gender.

In contrast to black ethnic identity, white ethnic identity in the USA is usually based on differences in the national origins of the forebears of white people. Thus, while black ethnic identity is believed to be racial, white ethnic identity refers to foreign nationality. Two exceptions to this rule come to mind, however: White supremacists appear to base their ethnicity solely on the absence of non-white forebears in their heredity. And some white ethnic groups, such as Jews, and perhaps Roman Catholics, seem to base their ethnic identity primarily on their religion.

The above sketch of the schema of black and white racial inheritance and the description of racial ethnicity in the USA is not new and neither does it contradict the common sense racial and ethnic categorizations which most American people make. If one adds the negative valuation of blacks in comparison to whites, to the strong asymmetry in the schema of black and white racial inheritance, it is impossible to escape the conclusion that the schema is both racist in favor of whites and unjust. The schema is racist in favor of whites because it automatically excludes some people, who have white ancestors, from membership in the white race, while others with white ancestry are not thereby excluded. This exclusionary force of the schema reinforces social beliefs about the superiority of whites in comparison to blacks. The schema is unjust because it denies individuals with black forebears the right to claim anything of positive racial value on the basis of having white forebears. Thus, the schema discriminates against people with black forebears, with respect to their having white forebears, solely because they have black forebears.

THE PROBLEMATIZATION OF MIXED RACE

I mean to distinguish between the problem of mixed race and the problematization of mixed race. The problem of mixed race is a problem for white people, mainly, because historically sexual relations between white people and black people were socially taboo—they were also illegal for long periods of American history. The existence of an individual of mixed race was, and still is, proof that these taboos had been violated, and it was proof which many proponents of the prohibitions valued negatively in social and moral spheres. The problematization of mixed race is formulated by a person of mixed race when she thinks about the schema of racial inheritance and the prevailing attitudes about race and ethnicity. Except in cases of extreme despair, the person of mixed race does not have a problem with mixed race because she does not have a problem with the bare fact of her own existence.

The first part of the problematization of mixed race is in the designation of the term "mixed race" for someone who has both black and white forebears. Strictly speaking, the designation should never be made and fails to make sense. According to the accepted schema of racial inheritance, everyone with at least one black forebear is black and everyone with all white forebears is white. Therefore everyone is either black or white. There are no people of mixed race.

Black people are likely to perceive the person who is culturally and ethnically white, but racially black, as an inauthentic black person, someone who is disloyal to other black people or who evades or denies racial discrimination by attempting to pass (for white). From a black ethnic perspective it is not plausible that someone who is designated as of mixed race in white contexts, might have spent so much of her life in white contexts that she does not have a black ethnic identity. The (authentic) racial and ethnic black person will hold the person of mixed race responsible for not having had the courage (and good faith) to acquire a black ethnic identity, as soon as she became aware of the injustice of racism and racial discrimination against black people. There is a moral injunction here that one ought not to benefit from a loophole in what one knows to be an unjust situation. The black person, who functions as a white person in white contexts, under the honorarium of a mixed race designation, has an obligation, supererogatory though it may be, to insist that her skills be recognized by white people as the skills of a black person. If this person of mixed race does not do that, then it can only be because she agrees with the negative valuation of black people by white people. This, then, is how I understand the implied moral argument.

I think that the argument is persuasive up to a point. The argument is only persuasive as long as one accepts the strongly asymmetrical kinship schema of racial designation. The argument ceases to be persuasive when one's racial existence does not support this schema. If one spent one's formative years with white people and failed to realign one's ethnic identity in adolescence, when it may still have been possible, then the moral argument may not so much be a spur to action as the cause of bad conscience. My bad conscience is not assuaged by claims of Jewish ethnic identity because the difficulty of the Jewish experience is not immediate in contemporary American society. While I do not think that it can be conclusively argued that in a conflict between two allegiances, morality is always on the side of the claim which represents the greater present suffering, if present action is called for, one is obligated to respond to the present situation. Any bad conscience can be a spur to an intellectual and moral position which has merits in spite of its origins. The bad conscience which has grown out of my problematization of mixed race, has at times led me to a position of deracination. But regardless of my conscience, the position of deracination has strong merits.

DERACINATION

This is the position of deracination: The schema of racial inheritance in the USA is racist and unjust. As a rational woman with both black and white forebears, I do not accept this schema. I refuse to be pressured into denying the existence of black forebears to please whites, and I refuse to be pressured into denying my white ethnicity and my white forebears, to please blacks. There is no biological foundation of the concept of race. The concept of race is an oppressive cultural invention and convention, and I refuse to have anything to do with it. I refuse to be reasonable in order to placate either blacks or whites who retain nonempirical and irrational categorizations. Therefore, I have no racial affiliation and will accept no racial designations. If more people joined me in refusing to play the unfair game of race, fewer injustices based on the concept of race would be perpetrated.

The literal meaning of the term "deracination" is "to be plucked up by the roots." What is it in me that is supposed to have roots? What is the "soil" in which these "roots" have a natural and not-to-be-disturbed location? Affiliations with others in the present, mental reconstructions of the past and plans for the future based on my "roots," and their "soil," especially plans which I would have to impose on my children, are all active, deliberate doings, which require choices and expenditures of energy in the present and future. There is no automatic "claim" exerted by "roots." I am not a fish out of water, a cat up a tree, or any kind

of plant. If I cannot follow the imperative disjunction, Thou shalt have a race, and, thy race shall be black or white!, then perhaps I can construct a racial identity of mixed race. Failing that construction, perhaps there are some shreds of benign universalism with which I can cover my deracinated self, or maybe there is still some humanistic soil in which an aracial self can be "implanted."

Even if I had a black ethnic identity from childhood or had developed one as an adult, any attempt to synthesize black and white ethnic identities would be doomed to fail as soon as I confronted the racial antagonisms and tensions in wider social reality. Any attempt to base my identity on membership in both black and white races could only take place on a level not subject to racial tensions and antagonisms. The level on which I could be both black and white would be culturally isolated.[3] If racial identity is based on wider group membership, then a black and white racial identity would be but another form of deracination, and perhaps a needlessly complicated one.

The new use of the term "of color" may represent an effort to bypass some of the contradictions and bitterness in racial categorization. Anyone who is not white is a person of color. But to say that I am a person of color is merely to say what I am not racially, i.e., not white. This categorization glides over my diverse ethnic experiences and cannot even begin to describe the ways in which I am not white. Using the term "of color" in effect deracinates non-whites within the category of non-white. It is but another instance of the tendency of whites to assign race itself to non-whites, perhaps analogously to the way in which men assign sex itself to members of the female gender. What is needed is a term which will deracinate people who are white, as well as non-white, some racial analogue to the designation "no religious affiliation."

The position of deracination could lead to conflicts at the intersection of racial identity and family membership. If a person is deracinated because she has both black and white forebears, her relatives may not have the same racial heredity, or if they do, they may not share her position of deracination. But the insistence on racial uniformity within a family is no more or less worthy of fulfillment than other forms of family uniformity, such as political or religious sameness, for example. If people who are biologically related have divisive differences, then those differences ought to be addressed on their own merits (as they often are during times of rapid social change).

THE PROBLEMATIZATION
OF DERACINATION

Again, I want to distinguish between the problem and the problematization. Deracination is a problem for people who belong to races and wish to categorize everyone else in racial terms as well. The problematization of deracination, as I have proposed it, has to do with the viewpoint of a deracinated person.

In ordinary, walking-around reality, the deracinated person will not have solved anything. People will still insist on categorizing her racially and her explicit refusal to participate in their (racializing) attempts will only add to their scorn and dislike of her. In her own mind she will be relieved from many contentious dialogues and ambivalent impulses. But as soon as she puts her position into plain language, she will have a problem with others.

Intellectually, deracination is not in harmony with the spirit of the times. For the past two or three decades, there has been an intensification of ethnicity and in expressions of pride in the culture of forebears, among different groups in America. This has its correlative in the critiques by feminists and other marginal spokespersons of the perceived white, upper class, heterosexist, male tradition in Philosophy. Continental Philosophy, since Martin Heidegger, as well as deconstructionist literary theory, has been increasingly preoccupied with the limitations imposed on thought by different European languages, and with the question of whether translation is even possible. In Philosophy of Science, the idea that competing theories may be incommensurable has unsettled much contemporary discussion. Politically, nationalism has probably never been as insistent a theme in any other period of world peace as it has in recent years. These generalities about diversities, as well as practical considerations, make it unlikely that a case for universalism of any kind can be formulated in a convincing manner at this time. But this is not to say that the case cannot be formulated at all—a philosophic analysis of American concepts of race might leave no rational alternative.

With deracination, one may come full circle to an old ideal of universalism within the refuge of abstract thought. This is a treacherous place because the universalism may once more conceal a bias in favor of certain groups. In this new universalism the bias would be in favor of raceless races— it would be a bias of antirace. But unlike racism, which is an asymmetrical privileging of race, antirace would be a theoretical move that blocks the privileging of race by undermining racial designations. Furthermore, the risk of this antirace bias may be outweighed by the gains of self-emancipation. In self-emancipation, it may be necessary to deracinate oneself in order to understand the problems and problematizations of race and ethnicity, and to address them evenly. It may also be necessary to remove everything concerning race from oneself, in order to feel good about being the self who is obliged to ask and answer the question, What am I?

NOTES

1. American concepts of race and ethnic identity are not stable over time. In recent years, I have noticed that some American Jews have become more insistent on their racial whiteness. Furthermore, it is by no means a forgone conclusion that a majority of Jews accept someone who does not have two Jewish parents as a Jew.

2. It is important to remember that these generalizations only hold true in American society. In European society there is a longer history of the identification of race with ethnicity, especially by anti-Semites. The French anti-Semite, for example, bases both his own racial identity and his ethnic pride on the fact that his forebears originated in the same place where he lives. See Jean-Paul Sartre's analysis in *Anti-Semite and Jew* (New York: Schocken Books, 1948), especially pp. 7–30.

3. There have always been isolated individuals and small groups without voices of authority who have refused to be pressured into identities of black or white racial designations. See for example, *Interrace,* a magazine that features interracial heterosexual relationships and persons of mixed race in the entertainment industry.

Questions for Thought

1. To what extent, if any, does your race determine your self-identity?
2. Do you agree with Zack's claim that self-development or self-emancipation depends on the valuation of others? Why or why not?
3. Why do you think that sexual relations between black and white people have been taboo in American society? Can you think of any justification whatsoever that would support this taboo?
4. Do you agree with Zack that deracination is desirable? If so, to what extent do you consider yourself to be deracinated?
5. I have pointed out a couple of similarities between Zack's views and those of de Beauvoir. Can you think of other similarities?

Chapter 2

Creation and Reality

Introductory Remarks

IN THE INTRODUCTION TO THE LAST CHAPTER, I asked you how many times someone had told you to just be yourself and whether you had heard someone say, "I'm not myself today." These questions led us to the path of the search for self-identity, a path found in the land of philosophical reflection. However, in journeying down this particular path, you may have noticed signposts for several other paths, marked by different questions. For example, in thinking about whom you are, you may have been led to question how you got here. And in thinking about how you got here, you may also have wondered how other things got here. Or, to take another example, in thinking about the nature of your identity, you may have been led to questions about the identity of other persons or things. Put somewhat differently, in thinking about your own existence, you may have been led to consider the existence or nonexistence of other persons or things.

If you were led to any of these other questions, then you were on the verge of another philosophical journey, the journey down the path of reflecting on creation and reality (otherwise known as the path of metaphysical thinking). However, even if none of these questions occurred to you in reading the last chapter, it is likely that you have encountered this path before. For just as people have told you to be yourself, they may also have told you to "be real." Of course, you might initially think (as I did when people said this to me) that this was just another way of telling you to be yourself. But is this all that was involved? If we think about this statement philosophically, we might ask ourselves what it means to be "real." Did this statement imply that you were somehow being "unreal" and that the person was telling you to come more fully into reality? Assuming that this is what the statement meant, you might wonder how you or anyone else could bring about this movement from unreality to reality. If you were not already fully real, how could you make yourself more real?

But even if no one has ever told you to be real, even if you have never thought about the nature of reality and unreality, it is likely that you have still been on the verge of metaphysical thinking. Indeed, you may have heard the following question, or some version of it, used as a way of proving the existence of God: "If God doesn't exist, how did we get here?" Of course, by bringing up God, this question could point to another philosophical path that we will examine later: the path of thinking about religion. But it can also direct us toward thinking about creation and reality. Indeed, when you consider this question, you discover that it is actually making several claims about the nature of creation and reality. First, it is obviously suggesting that God exists—that is to say, that God is *real.* Second, it is claiming that the existence or reality of God explains our own existence or reality. Or, put in terms of creation rather than existence and reality, this question is implying that we are here because God created us.

Of course, not all of you believe in God. Even if you do believe in God, it does not necessarily follow that you believe such a being created you. Nevertheless, as a thinking human being, it is very likely that you have, at some point in your life, raised the two principal questions of this chapter:

What is the nature of reality?
How did what is real come into being (assuming, of course, that it did not always exist)?

Indeed, some people raise these or similar questions quite early in life, as did one kindergartener in a school in Louisiana. The pupil had been absent from school for a few days. When he returned, his teacher asked him if he missed "being at school." The pupil replied with a question of his own: "What is being?" There he was, at age five, already beginning his journey down the path of metaphysical thinking.

Overview of Selections

In this chapter, as in the last one, I have collected several articles from various times and cultures to help you on your own journey down this path. The seven selections in the first part deal principally with the question of how we (and other things) got here. Four of these selections consist of creation stories. Each of these stories represents an attempt by a certain group of people (one story is African, one is from India, one is from the Middle East, and the other is Native American) to explain mythically how they and the universe came into being. The last three selections in the first section are modern scientific writings. In the first of the three, Stephen Hawking explains the big bang theory of the origin of the universe; in the second of the three, Charles Darwin formulates and defends the theory of evolution as a scientific alternative to religious accounts of the origin of life; and in the last of the three, Jared Diamond offers an explanation of why history has developed very differently for peoples inhabiting different parts of the earth.

The selections in the second section grapple with the somewhat broader question of the nature of reality. In the first selection, the ancient Greek philosopher Plato argues that ultimate reality consists of invisible, unchanging entities that he calls **Forms,** entities of which we are unaware in our everyday existence. In the second selection, from ancient China, we are told that ultimate reality consists of the **Tao,** an unnamable and mysterious force that is the source of all life and all movement. The next two selections, in contrast, suggest that ultimate reality is bodily or material rather than nonphysical or mystical. Wang Chung argues that what is ultimately real are materialistic fluids that come together to produce everything that exists, while Lucretius tells us that reality consists of an infinite number of materialistic seeds or atoms that combine with the void to produce everything in the universe. In the fifth selection in this second part, the German philosopher Leibniz rejects this materialistic turn in philosophy and claims that ultimate reality consists of spiritual atoms, which he calls **Monads,** that do not physically interact with one another.

While the final three writings in the second section deal less directly with the nature of reality than do the first five, they critique one of the fundamental notions of Western **metaphysics**—the notion of a fixed, objective reality that exists independently of the knowing subject. Bergson appeals to absolute knowledge or **intuition** to show us that the entity that we can most directly grasp—namely, our own self-existence—is marked by a continuous flow, or "pure duration," that excludes all fixity. In a similar vein, Nishida claims that the notion of a fixed, objective reality results from a distortion of what he calls "immediate reality" or "pure experience." Both Bergson and Nishida also argue that knowledge gained through the natural sciences does not provide us with the best description of the true nature of reality. Finally, Marilyn Frye critiques the dominant conception of reality from a feminist perspective. She argues that the dominant conception has relegated women to the background and that it must be displaced by a conception of reality that recognizes and includes the perspectives of women.

Contemporary Applications

Ancient myths, Forms, the Tao, Monads—you may wonder what relevance the discussion of these things could possibly have for your everyday life. However, as with the questions and concepts found in the preceding chapter, a little reflection may reveal that these things are not as foreign to your life as they initially seem to be.

First of all, it is likely that you hold some opinion about how the universe came into being. It is also likely that your opinion on this matter was derived from some religious text, such as the Bible, or from the teachings of modern science. If your view is derived from a religious text, then two important questions immediately present themselves: What exactly does the text mean? Why accept the account in this text and not some other text? On the other hand, if you accept a scientific account, such as the big bang theory and/or the theory of evolution, what exactly do you believe, and what evidence do you have that these scientific accounts are accurate?

Moreover, the account of creation that you accept may have important implications about how you view yourself and other people. For example, the African creation story in the text says that you are the vomitus of the god, Bumba, whereas one of the creation stories found in the Bible says that you are created in "the image of God." The theory of evolution, by way of contrast, says that you are a complex life form that has evolved from less complex life forms. Which, if either, of these claims is correct? Your answer to this question will obviously impact the way you view yourself and other people.

Another issue that is addressed in some of these stories is the relationship between humans and nonhuman animals. For instance, the African creation story in the text affirms the common origin of humans and animals, and the Cherokee story describes human cruelties toward animals, while one of the biblical stories grants humans "dominion" over the animals. Such statements are clearly relevant to the modern debate about how nonhuman animals are to be treated. If we think of animals as our equals, we would probably treat them quite differently than we would if we think of them as subhuman creatures over which we have dominion. If animals are our equals, would we still allow the kinds of animal research that are presently allowed? Would we still hunt them for sport or eat them for food?

When I taught philosophy at Loyola University in New Orleans, I would always begin the discussion of the nature of reality by asking my students to name the things that they considered to be most real. Each semester I would get answers such as the following: "the person sitting next to me," "the desk in which I am sitting," "the book on my desk," and so on. Surprisingly, no one ever said that God was most real. (This was especially surprising, since Loyola is a Catholic university and most of my students believed in God.) What this suggests is that, despite our religious or philosophical beliefs, most of us tend to be commonsense realists; that is, most of us find it easier to accept the reality of sensible or physical objects than we do the reality of nonsensible or spiritual entities such as God. This commonsense assumption, however, immediately suggests several important questions:

Are tables and chairs more real than God?
What exactly are tables and chairs?
What does science tell us about the reality of physical objects?
If we assert that God is more real than tables and chairs, what exactly are we claiming?
What does it mean to say that God or any other nonphysical entity is real?

Noticing that certain of our commonsense assumptions about the nature of reality are open to question may lead us to ask deeper, more basic questions about what we believe to be real. In other words, if our faith in commonsense realism is shattered, we may raise questions such as the following:

Is reality something fixed that we can discover?
Or is our conception of reality socially or culturally determined?
Does our dominant conception of reality privilege certain people while relegating others to the background?
If our dominant conception of reality does privilege certain people, should it be displaced by a conception of reality that is more egalitarian?
How can one conception of reality be displaced by another?

Some of these deeper questions may be suggested by comparing and contrasting the accounts of creation in the first section of the chapter or by examining statements about the nature of reality found in any of the selections in the second section. Moreover, both Bergson and Nishida explicitly raise the first two of these questions, while Frye focuses attention on the latter three.

How Did We Get Here?

An African Creation Story   1

FROM THE SACRED STORYTELLING OF THE BOSHONGO PEOPLE

The following creation story comes to us from the **Boshongo,** one of the Bantu peoples of central and southern Africa. Like most African myths, this story was originally told in oral form, and it is impossible to determine exactly when the story originated.

For those of you familiar with other creation stories, especially those found in Genesis, this myth may seem a bit shocking. But the story does answer one question that the stories in Genesis fail to address: It provides a reason why the creator god began creation. According to this African story, the process of creation began when **Bumba,** the first creator god, became sick and started vomiting. The sun, the moon, the stars, and the first living creatures were Bumba's vomitus. The first humans were also produced in this manner (a beginning far removed from the claim made in Genesis that humans were created in the "image" of God). Interestingly, once he gets over his initial sickness, Bumba turns the act of creating over to others. The first living creatures produced all the other creatures, except for the white ants and the kite, which were created by Bumba's sons. Another of Bumba's sons created the first plant, from which all other plants evolved. This creation story ends with Bumba walking through the villages of men and telling them that these marvelous things that he has created belong to them.

Questions for Reading

1. How is Bumba, the chief creator god, described in this story?
2. Why and how does Bumba begin the process of creation?
3. What are the creative forces in the story other than Bumba?
4. What specific role does each of Bumba's sons play?
5. How does the story end?

IN THE BEGINNING THERE WAS ONLY DARKNESS and nothing existed on the earth except water. In this chaos, Bumba, the Chembe (God), reigned alone. Bumba had the form of a man, but of enormous size and white in color. One day he felt a great pain in his stomach and he began to vomit. First of all he vomited up the sun, followed by the moon, and then the stars; it was thus that light was

This is the editor's translation of a selection from "Notes ethnographiques sur les peuples communément appelés Bakuba, ainsi que sur les peuplades apparentées. Les Bushongo," by E. Torday and T.A. Joyce, Bruxelles: Ministère des colonies, 1910.

born. Following this, under the influence of the sun, the water began to evaporate and the sandbanks appeared on the surface. But these sandbanks, like the water from which they emerged, were completely devoid of all life, animal as well as plant.

Bumba began to vomit again and this time he gave birth to the following order of things: to the leopard, Koy Bumba; to the crested eagle, Pongo Bumba; to the crocodile, Ganda Bumba; to a small fish, Yo Bumba; to the tortoise, Kono Bumba; to the *foudre*[1] (an animal that was similar to a leopard except that it was black), Tsetse Bumba; to a white heron, Nyanyi Bumba; to a beetle; and to the goat, Budi Bumba. Next Bumba vomited up men, a great number of them, but there was only one who was white like him. He was called Loko Yima.

The animals which had been created in this way embarked upon the work of populating the world. The white heron vomited all the birds except the kite; the crocodile, all the serpents and the iguana (Lebeme Gandu); the goat vomited all the animals with horns; the fish Yo, all the fish; and the beetle, all the insects. Then the serpents vomited the grasshoppers (Minye) and the iguana all the animals without horns.

After this, one of Bumba's sons, Nyonye Ngana, vomited the white ants, but the effort was too considerable for him and he died from it. The white ants, in thankfulness for their creation, went searching for all the black soil in the bowels of the earth and covered the sterile sandbanks with it in order to bury their creator. Another of Bumba's sons, Chonganda, vomited a plant from which all the vegetation sprang, while still another son named Chedi Bumba tried to vomit forth some new creatures. He succeeded in producing the kite, but nothing else.

Such is the story of the creation of the world as we now know it. But when the work of creation was finished, Bumba walked through all the villages of men and said to them: "Look at these marvelous things that I have created; everything belongs to you."

NOTES

1. In this version of the myth, the foudre is a black leopard-like animal—possibly a panther—as the following parenthetical remark clearly shows. However, in a later variation of the myth, the foudre is associated with the lightning. The later version claims that "the foudre, Tsetse Bumba, began to make much mischief; therefore Bumba chased her and she took refuge in the sky. But this brought about a difficulty, because men could no longer procure fire. So Bumba allows the foudre to return from time to time, but every time she visits the earth she causes some damage."

Questions for Thought

1. How does this story compare with or differ from other creation myths with which you are familiar?
2. In what ways, if any, is this story similar to modern scientific views about the origin of life?
3. What do you think about the role that Bumba's sons play in the story? In what ways do they differ from their father?
4. How do you think the ending of the story should be interpreted?
5. If you were to write a creation myth, how would you begin?

Creation of the World from the Self   2

FROM THE UPANISHADS

As mentioned earlier, the **Upanishads** make up the fourth section of the **Vedas,** the most sacred writings of the religion of Hinduism. It is generally believed that the earliest of the Upanishads was written around 900 B.C.E., but most of them were written hundreds of years later. Whereas the first three sections of the Vedas were written in the form of hymns and ritual chants, the Upanishads take the form of philosophical dialogues and myth. For these stylistic reasons, as well as for the many similarities in content, the Upanishads can be fruitfully compared with the writings of Plato. The following creation story is from the *Brhad-aranyaka-Upanishad,* which many scholars view as the most important of the Upanishads.

In this creation myth, unlike the **Bumba** story, there is only one being prior to creation—the self in the form of a person. Fear arises within this self, but the self realizes this fear is unfounded, since there is nothing outside itself that could possibly harm it. However, in coming to this realization, the self discovers its aloneness. To overcome this aloneness, the self expands and splits into male and female. The two halves unite, and human beings are born. However, the female half is bothered by the semi-incestuous nature of the relationship ("How can he mate with me after engendering me from himself?"), and she takes many female animal forms as disguises. But the male half takes the corresponding male form in each case and mates with her. The various types of animals are produced in this manner. The creator self then produces fire, food, the gods, and all the separate forms found within the universe. Once this creation is complete, the self enters into everything that exists. The selection ends by identifying this creative self with *Brahman* and by saying that the goal of knowledge is to discover the ultimate identity between one's own self and Brahman.

Questions for Reading

1. What, according to this story, existed in the beginning?
2. Why is the self initially afraid? What allows the self to overcome this fear?
3. How does the writer of this story account for the origin of humans? What happens when male and female are separated?
4. What does the writer mean by *Brahman?* What role does Brahman play in the story?
5. What seems to be the role of the gods in this myth? What is the relation of humans to the gods?

1. IN THE BEGINNING, THERE WAS ONLY THE self in the shape of a person (purusha). Looking around, he saw nothing other than his Self. He first said, "This is I," and thus the name "I" was born. Thus even now when a man identifies himself he first says, "This is I," before saying the other name that he has. . . .

This is the editor's revised version of a selection from The Upanishads, *translated by Max Müller, in* The Sacred Books of the East, *Volume 15, Oxford University Press (1884).*

2. Fear arose within him; thus anyone who is alone is afraid. However, he then thought to himself, "Since there is nothing other than myself, what do I fear?" Thus his fear passed away. For what should he have feared? Verily it is only from a second that fear arises.

3. Yet, he felt no delight. Therefore one who is alone feels no delight. He wished for a second, and he became as large as a man and woman together. He then divided in two. From this, there arose husband and wife. As Yajnavalkya says, "When we are alone, we are like half of a seashell." Thus the void that was there was filled by the wife. He mated with her, and human beings were born.

4. She thought to herself, "How can he mate with me after engendering me from himself? I will conceal myself." She then became a cow, but the other became a bull and mated with her; hence cows were born. She became a mare, he a stallion; she a female ass, he a male ass. He mated with her, and hence one-hoofed animals were born. She became a she-goat, he a he-goat; she became a ewe, he a ram. He mated with her, and hence goats and sheep were born. And thus he created everything that exists in pairs, down to the ants.

5. He knew, "I indeed am this creation, for I created all this." Hence he became the creation. Whoever knows this is born in that creation of his.

6. Next he produced fire by blowing on his hands while rubbing them together. Thus both the mouth and the hands are hairless on the inside, for the source of fire is hairless on the inside. When people say, "Sacrifice to this or to that god," each god is but his own manifestation, for he is himself all gods. Now, he created everything moist from his semen, which is also **Soma**. Verily, everything in this universe is either food or the eater of food. Soma indeed is food, and **Agni** is the eater of food. This is the highest creation of **Brahma**, for he created the gods who are superior to him. Although he was mortal, he created the immortals. Therefore it was the highest creation. Whoever knows this becomes a creator himself in this highest creation.

7. At this time nothing was differentiated. It became differentiated by name and form, so that one could say, "He, who is called so and so, has such a form." Now everything is differentiated by name and form, so that one can still say, "He, who is called so and so, has such a form." The Self (Brahman) entered into everything, to the very tips of the finger-nails, as a razor might be fitted into a razor-case, or as fire into a fire-place. He cannot be seen, yet he is manifested throughout. When one breathes, he is the breath; when one speaks, he is the voice; when one sees, he is the eye; when one hears, he is the ear; when one thinks, he is the mind. All of these, however, are merely the names of his acts. Anyone who regards him as one or another of these acts does not know him, for regarded as such he is incomplete. Let men therefore meditate upon the Self, for in the Self all these are one. The Self is the footprint of everything, for through the Self one knows everything. Just as from footsteps one can find again what was lost, one who knows this finds glory and praise.

8. This Self, which is nearer to us than anything, is dearer than a son, dearer than wealth, dearer than all else. If someone declared anything other than the Self to be dear, you would be correct in telling him that he will lose what is dear to him. One should meditate on the Self alone as dear. He who does so will never lose what he holds dear.

9. People ask, "If men think that by knowledge of Brahman they will become all, what then did Brahman know by which he became all?"

10. Verily in the beginning Brahman knew its Self only, saying, "I am Brahman." From this it became all. Thus, whatever god was awakened to know Brahman, he indeed became all. The same is true in the case of seers and in the case of men. The seer Vamadeva saw and understood this, singing, "I was Manu (moon), I was the sun." Therefore anyone who knows that he is Brahman becomes all; even the gods cannot prevent it, for he becomes their Self. So, if a man worships another deity, thinking the deity is one and he is another, he does not know. He is like a beast to the gods. For verily, as many beasts serve a man, thus does each man serve the gods. If only one beast is taken away, it is not pleasant; how much more so when many are taken! Thus, it is not pleasant to the gods that men should know this. . . .

15. Now if a man departs this life without having seen his true Self, then that Self, not being known, does not receive and bless him. It is as if the **Vedas** had not been read, or as if a good work had not been done. Indeed, even if one who does not know that Self should perform here on earth some great holy work, it will perish for him in the end. Let a man worship the Self only as his true state. If a man worships the Self only as his true state, his work does not perish; for whatever he desires, he gets from that Self.

Questions for Thought

1. What do you think of the claim that the original being who created the universe was a self in the form of a person? Is this claim compatible with your own views about the origin of the universe?
2. Do you think the female half of the self was justified in trying to avoid the male half? What is this motif intended to explain?
3. The last sentence of section 6 ("Whoever knows this becomes a creator himself in this highest creation.") has been taken as a statement of humanity's place in the universe. What do you think this statement means?
4. Do you agree that Brahman or the creative force of the universe is to be found in everything that exists? Why or why not?
5. If you were to write a creation myth, how would it end?

The Creation and the Fall   3

FROM THE BIBLE

The following selection is taken from the sacred writings of the religion of Judaism. Most scholars agree that the selection actually consists of at least two stories that were transmitted orally for many years before being written down. While the canonization of the Jewish Bible was a lengthy process, probably beginning with the priest Ezra in the fifth century B.C.E. and culminating with the meeting of a council of Jewish leaders near the end of the first century C.E., many of the writings predated the time of Ezra by several centuries. One of the stories found in this selection, the first creation story, is believed to be derived from the most ancient source of Jewish religious writing, probably dating from the tenth century B.C.E.

The selection is found at the beginning of the first book of Jewish scriptures, the book of *Bereshith*. Christianity, which was originally considered to be a sect of Judaism, also claims these stories as part of its sacred literature. In the Christian Bible, the book of *Bereshith* is referred to as *Genesis*.

Since Judaism is a monotheistic religion, both creation stories claim that the work of creation was performed by one god, **Yahweh** (translated in the following selection simply as "God"). In the first creation story, Yahweh completes creation in six days before resting on the seventh day. During the first four days, Yahweh creates light, heaven, dry land, plants, and the sun, moon, and stars. On the next two days, he creates living creatures. He begins with water animals and birds, then turns to land animals, and concludes by creating humans, both male and female. Near the end of this story we find the well-known claim that Yahweh created humans "in his own image."

In the second creation story, Yahweh creates heaven and earth. Realizing that it is barren, he then creates a male human being from dust and breathes life into his nostrils. Next, Yahweh plants a garden in Eden and places the man in it, warning him not to eat from one tree in the garden, the "tree of the knowledge of good and evil." At this point, Yahweh realizes that the man is alone and that such aloneness is undesirable. So he creates wild animals and birds as companions for the man. When these prove to be inadequate companions, he creates a female human being from one of the ribs of the man. While the male is initially happy with the female, this happiness ceases when the serpent, the cleverest animal in the garden, convinces the woman to eat some of the fruit from the forbidden tree, and she in turn convinces the man to eat the fruit. Discovering these acts of disobedience, Yahweh curses the serpent, the woman, and the man and then expels the man and woman from the garden.

Questions for Reading

1. How does the first creation story in this selection differ from the second one?
2. What are the essential differences between these creation stories and the preceding story from the Upanishads?
3. How are human beings viewed in these stories? What is their relationship to nonhuman animals?
4. What role does woman play in each story?
5. Why, according to the second story, are humans ejected from the garden in Eden? What is this story intended to explain?
6. What are the three curses intended to explain? What do the woman's curse and the man's curse tell us about the relationship of women and men? What does the man's curse tell us about the relationship of man and nature?

THE CREATION OF THE WORLD

IN THE BEGINNING OF CREATION, WHEN GOD made heaven and earth, the earth was without form and void, with darkness over the face of the abyss, and a mighty wind that swept over the surface of the waters. God said, "Let there be light," and there was light; and God saw that the light was good, and he separated light from darkness. He called the light day, and the darkness night. So evening came, and morning came, the first day.

God said, "Let there be a vault between the waters, to separate water from water." So God made the vault, and separated the water under the vault from the water above it, and so it was; and God called the vault heaven. Evening came, and morning came, a second day.

God said, "Let the waters under heaven be gathered into one place, so that dry land may appear"; and so it was. God called the dry land earth, and the gathering of the waters he called seas; and God saw that it was good. Then God said, "Let the earth produce fresh growth, let there be on the earth plants bearing seed, fruit-trees bearing fruit each with seed according to its kind." So it was; the earth yielded fresh growth, plants bearing seed according to their kind and trees bearing fruit each with seed according to its kind; and God saw that it was good. Evening came, and morning came, a third day.

God said, "Let there be lights in the vault of heaven to separate day from night, and let them serve as signs both for festivals and for seasons and years. Let them also shine in the vault of heaven to give light on earth." So it was; God made the two great lights, the greater to govern the day and the lesser to govern the night; and with them he made the stars. God put these lights in the vault of heaven to give light on earth, to govern day and night, and to separate light from darkness; and God saw that it was good. Evening came, and morning came, a fourth day.

God said, "Let the waters teem with countless living creatures, and let birds fly above the earth across the vault of heaven." God then created the great sea-monsters and all living creatures that move and swarm in the waters, according to their kind, and every kind of bird; and God saw that it was good. So he blessed them and said, "Be fruitful and increase, fill the waters of the seas; and let the birds increase on land." Evening came, and morning came, a fifth day.

God said, "Let the earth bring forth living creatures, according to their kind: cattle, reptiles, and wild animals, all according to their kind." So it was; God made wild animals, cattle, and all reptiles, each according to its kind; and he saw that it was good. Then God said, "Let us make man in our image and likeness to rule the fish in the sea, the birds of heaven, the cattle, all wild animals on earth, and all reptiles that crawl upon the earth." So God created man in his own image; in the image of God he created him; male and female he created them. God blessed them and said to them, "Be fruitful and increase, fill the earth and subdue it, rule over the fish in the sea, the birds of heaven, and every living thing that moves upon the earth." God also said, "I give you all plants that bear seed everywhere on earth, and every tree bearing fruit which yields seed: they shall be yours for food. All green plants I give for food to the wild animals, to all the birds of heaven, and to all reptiles on earth, every living creature." So it was; and God saw all that he had made, and it was very good. Evening came, and morning came, a sixth day.

Thus heaven and earth were completed with all their mighty throng. On the sixth day God completed all the work he had been doing, and on the seventh day he ceased from all his work. God blessed the seventh day and made it holy, because on that day he ceased from all the work he had set himself to do.

This is the story of the making of heaven and earth when they were created.

THE BEGINNINGS OF HISTORY

When the Lord God made earth and heaven, there was neither shrub nor plant growing wild upon the earth, because the Lord God had sent no rain on the earth; nor was there any man to till the ground. A flood used to rise out of the earth and water all the surface of the ground. Then the Lord God formed a man from the dust of the ground and breathed into his nostrils the breath of life. Thus the man became a living creature. Then the Lord God planted a garden in Eden away to the east, and there he put the man whom he had formed. The Lord God made trees spring from the ground, all trees pleasant to look at and good for food; and in the middle of the garden he set the tree of life and the tree of the knowledge of good and evil.

There was a river flowing from Eden to water the garden, and when it left the garden it branched into four streams. The name of the first is Pishon; that is the river which encircles all the land of Havilah, where the gold is. The gold of that land is good; bdellium and cornelians are also to be found there. The name of the second river is Gihon; this is the one which encircles all the land of Cush. The name of the third is Tigris; this is the river which runs east of Asshur. The fourth river is the Euphrates.

The Lord God took the man and put him in the garden of Eden to till it and care for it. He told the man, "You may eat from every tree in the garden, but not from the tree of the knowledge of good and evil; for on the day that you eat from it, you will certainly die." Then the Lord God said, "It is not good for the man to be alone. I will provide a partner for him." So God formed out of the ground all the wild animals and all the birds of heaven. He brought them to the man to see what he would call them, and whatever the man called each living creature, that was its name. Thus the man gave names to all cattle, to the birds of heaven, and to every wild animal; but for the man himself no partner had yet been found. And so the Lord God put the man into a trance, and while he slept, he took one of his ribs and closed the flesh over the place. The Lord God then built up the rib, which he had taken out of the man, into a woman. He brought her to the man, and the man said:

> "Now this, at last—
> bone from my bones,
> flesh from my flesh!—
> this shall be called woman,
> for from man was this taken."

That is why a man leaves his father and mother and is united to his wife, and the two become one flesh. Now they were both naked, the man and his wife, but they had no feeling of shame towards one another.

The serpent was more crafty than any wild creature that the Lord God had made. He said to the woman, "Is it true that God has forbidden you to eat from any tree in the garden?" The woman answered the serpent, "We may eat the fruit of any tree in the garden, except for the tree in the middle of the garden; God has forbidden us either to eat or to touch the fruit of that; if we do, we shall die." The serpent said, "Of course you will not die. God knows that as soon as you eat it, your eyes will be opened and you will be like gods knowing both good and evil." When the woman saw that the fruit of the tree was good to eat, and that it was pleasing to the eye and tempting to contemplate, she took some and ate it. She also gave her husband some and he ate it. Then the eyes of both of them were opened and they discovered that they were naked; so they stitched fig-leaves together and made themselves loinclothes.

The man and his wife heard the sound of the Lord God walking in the garden at the time of the evening breeze and hid from the Lord God among the trees of the garden. But the Lord God called to the man and said to him, "Where are you?" He replied, "I heard the sound as you were walking in the garden, and I was afraid because I was naked,

and I hid myself." God answered, "Who told you that you were naked? Have you eaten from the tree which I forbade you?" The man said, "The woman you gave me for a companion, she gave me fruit from the tree and I ate it." Then the Lord God said to the woman, "What is this that you have done?" The woman said, "The serpent tricked me, and I ate." Then the Lord God said to the serpent:

> "Because you have done this you are accursed
> more than all cattle and all wild creatures.
> On your belly you shall crawl, and dust you shall eat
> all the days of your life.
> I will put enmity between you and the woman,
> between your brood and hers.
> They shall strike at your head,
> and you shall strike at their heel."

To the woman he said:

> "I will increase your labour and your groaning,
> and in labour you shall bear children.
> You shall be eager for your husband,
> and he shall be your master."

And to the man he said:

> "Because you have listened to your wife
> and have eaten from the tree which I forbade you,
> accursed shall be the ground on your account.
> With labour you shall win your food from it
> all the days of your life.
> It will grow thorns and thistles for you,
> none but wild plants for you to eat.
> You shall gain your bread by the sweat of
>   your brow
> until you return to the ground;
> for from it you were taken.
> Dust you are, to dust you shall return."

The man called his wife Eve because she was the mother of all who live. The Lord God made tunics of skins for the man and his wife and clothed them. He said, "The man has become like one of us, knowing good and evil; what if he now reaches out his hand and takes fruit from the tree of life also, eats it and lives for ever?" So the Lord God drove him out of the garden of Eden to till the ground from which he had been taken. He cast him out, and to the east of

the garden of Eden he stationed the cherubim and a
sword whirling and flashing to guard the way to the
tree of life.

Questions for Thought

1. Do you think the differences between the two stories can be reconciled? If so, how?
2. What do you think it means to say that humans are created in the "image of god"? Do you think you are created in the image of god? Why or why not?
3. Do you think it makes sense to say that woman was created from the rib of man? If this claim is true, what does it tell us about male/female relationships?
4. What do you think the serpent represents in the second story? What does the tree of the knowledge of good and evil represent?
5. Do you believe that these stories are compatible with the findings of modern science? Why or why not?

How the World Was Made and the Origin of Disease and Medicine   4

FROM THE SACRED STORYTELLING OF THE CHEROKEE

The Cherokee, or Yûñ'wiyǎ (literally "real people"), are a Native American people of Iroquoian lineage. Once inhabitants of the Great Lakes region, they moved to the southern Allegheny and Great Smoky Mountains region prior to the arrival of European immigrants. It has been estimated that in 1650, about 22,500 Cherokee lived in this area that today covers parts of eight states. Prior to the early 1700s, the Cherokee lived in small, autonomous villages that were ruled by two political entities—a White organization that ruled in times of peace and a Red organization that ruled in times of conflict or war. However, in the early 1700s, the Cherokee formed a tribal state that eventually became known as the Cherokee Nation.

During the 1700s, a series of treaties deprived the Cherokee of much of their land, and there were numerous skirmishes with European settlers. But, by the early 1800s, the Cherokee were rapidly assimilating many aspects of European culture, including certain methods of agriculture, weaving, and house building. Then, after developing a syllabic alphabet, the Cherokee began publishing the first Native American newspaper in 1828. However, in this same year, gold was discovered on Cherokee land in Georgia, a discovery that had ominous implications for the Cherokee Nation. Following several years of land grabbing by European immigrants, the state of Georgia negotiated the Treaty of

New Echota, which was signed by seventy-nine Cherokee in 1835. This treaty gave up all claims to land east of the Mississippi River. Although almost 16,000 Cherokee signed a letter rejecting the treaty, which was subsequently invalidated by the Supreme Court, the state of Georgia ignored the court decision. When President Andrew Jackson refused to enforce this decision, troops were sent to force the Cherokee (numbering more than 17,000) to undertake a 116-day march to Indian Territory in what is now Oklahoma. During this march, which has become known as the "Trail of Tears," the Cherokee were provided with inadequate clothing, food, and medical attention. As a result, about 4,000 people died during the harsh journey.

The Cherokee who made it to Indian Territory set up their government in what is today Tahlequah, Oklahoma. In 1984, Wilma Mankiller became the first female principal chief of this group, which is known as the Western Band. Today the Western Band has over 50,000 members. Sixty families who refused to move were later joined by about 1,200 Cherokee who escaped during the forced march. They formed the Eastern Band and eventually reacquired 56,000 acres of the 7 million acres that had been fraudulently seized from them. Today the Eastern Band numbers about 9,000, and many of them live in or near Cherokee, North Carolina. The following stories were told by members of the Eastern Band during the late nineteenth century.

The first story, "How the World Was Made," contains a fairly common creation motif about the earth being originally covered with water. However, unlike similar stories from other cultures, the creation of land is not the work of a god or gods but the work of animals. The Water-beetle brings mud to the surface, and the Great Buzzard creates mountains and valleys. The animal conjurers then set the sun in its place in the sky. The first two humans, a brother and a sister, arrive on the scene after the plants and animals. The brother impregnates his sister by hitting her with a fish, and human pro-creation begins.

The second story, as the title indicates, is an account of how disease and medicine came into the world. Like certain African stories, this story takes a dim view of humans. Whereas humans were originally few in number and peaceful, they eventually overpopulate the earth and begin to kill animals. The various animals meet to decide how to defend themselves against the humans, and they create a number of diseases that can kill humans. Only the intervention of the plants, which side with the humans and offer themselves as medicine, prevents the extermination of the human species.

Questions for Reading

1. How many levels of existence are described in the first story? What is the explanatory function of each level?
2. Who creates the earth in the first story? Who creates mountains and valleys?
3. What is the role of humans in these stories? How does the role of humans compare with or differ from the role of nonhuman animals?
4. How, according to the first story, did the first two humans procreate? Why were the earliest human procreations problematic?
5. According to the second story, why and how were diseases created? What was the origin of medicine?

HOW THE WORLD WAS MADE

THE EARTH IS A GREAT ISLAND FLOATING IN A SEA of water, and suspended at each of the four cardinal points by a cord hanging down from the sky vault, which is of solid rock. When the world grows old and worn out, the people will die and the cords will break and let the earth sink down into the ocean, and all will be water again. . . .

When all was water, the animals were above in Gălûñ'lătĭ, beyond the arch; but it was very much crowded, and they were wanting more room. They wondered what was below the water, and at last Dâyuni'sĭ, "Beaver's Grandchild," the little Water-beetle, offered to go and see if it could learn. It darted in every direction over the surface of the water, but could find no firm place to rest. Then it dived to the bottom and came up with some soft mud, which began to grow and spread on every side until it became the island which we call the earth. It was afterward fastened to the sky with four cords, but no one remembers who did this.

At first the earth was flat and very soft and wet. The animals were anxious to get down, and sent out different birds to see if it was yet dry, but they found no place to alight and came back again to Gălûñ'lătĭ. At last it seemed to be time, and they sent out the Buzzard and told him to go and make ready for them. This was the Great Buzzard, the father of all the buzzards we see now. He flew all over the earth, low down near the ground, and it was still soft. When he reached the Cherokee country, he was very tired, and his wings began to flap and strike the ground, and wherever they struck the earth there was a valley, and where he turned up again there was a mountain. When the animals above saw this, they were afraid that the whole world would be mountains, so they called him back, but the Cherokee country remains full of mountains to this day.

When the earth was dry and the animals came down, it was still dark, so they got the sun and set it in a track to go every day across the island from east to west, just overhead. It was too hot this way, and Tsiska'gĭlĭ', the Red Crawfish, had his shell scorched a bright red, so that his meat was spoiled; and the Cherokee do not eat it. The conjurers put the sun another handbreadth higher in the air, but it was still too hot. They raised it another time, and another, until it was seven handbreadths high and just under the arch. Then it was right, and they left it so. This is why the conjurers call the highest place Gûlkwâ'gine Di'gălûñ'lătiyûñ', "the seventh height," because it is seven handbreadths above the earth. Every day the sun goes along under this arch, and returns at night on the upper side to the starting place.

There is another world under this, and it is like ours in everything—animals, plants, and people—save that the seasons are different. The streams that come down from the mountains are the trails by which we reach this underworld, and the springs at their heads are the doorways by which we enter it, but to do this one must fast and go to water and have one of the underground people for a guide. We know that the seasons in the underworld are different from ours, because the water in the springs is always warmer in winter and cooler in summer than the outer air.

When the animals and plants were first made—we do not know by whom—they were told to watch and keep awake for seven nights, just as young men now fast and keep awake when they pray to their medicine. They tried to do this, and nearly all were awake through the first night, but the next night several dropped off to sleep, and the third night others were asleep, and then others, until, on the seventh night, of all the animals only the owl, the panther, and one or two more were still awake. To these were given the power to see and to go about in the dark, and to make prey of the birds and animals which must sleep at night. Of the trees only the cedar, the pine, the spruce, the holly, and the laurel were awake to the end, and to them it was given to be always green and to be greatest for medicine, but to others it was said: "Because you have not endured to the end you shall lose your hair every winter."

From James Moody, Myths of the Cherokee, 19th Annual Report of the Bureau of American Ethnology, 1897–1898, *Part I, Washington, 1900. Reprinted in Frederick Turner, ed.,* The Portable North American Indian Reader, *Viking Press, 1973.*

Men came after the animals and plants. At first there were only a brother and sister until he struck her with a fish and told her to multiply, and so it was. In seven days a child was born to her, and thereafter every seven days another, and they increased very fast until there was danger that the world could not keep them. Then it was made that a woman should have only one child in a year, and it has been so ever since. . . .

THE ORIGIN OF DISEASE
AND MEDICINE

In the old days the beasts, birds, fishes, insects, and plants could all talk, and they and the people lived together in peace and friendship. But as time went on the people increased so rapidly that their settlements spread over the whole earth, and the poor animals found themselves beginning to be cramped for room. This was bad enough, but to make it worse Man invented bows, knives, blowguns, spears, and hooks, and began to slaughter the larger animals, birds, and fishes for their flesh or their skins, while the smaller creatures, such as the frogs and worms, were crushed and trodden upon without thought, out of pure carelessness or contempt. So the animals resolved to consult upon measures for their common safety.

The Bears were the first to meet in council in their townhouse under Kuwâ'hǐ mountain, the "Mulberry Place," and the old White Bear chief presided. After each in turn had complained of the way in which Man killed their friends, ate their flesh, and used their skins for his own purposes, it was decided to begin war at once against him. Someone asked what weapons Man used to destroy them. "Bows and arrows, of course," cried all the Bears in chorus. "And what are they made of?" was the next question. "The bow of wood, and the string of our entrails," replied one of the Bears. It was then proposed that they make a bow and some arrows and see if they could not use the same weapons against Man himself. So one Bear got a nice piece of locust wood and another sacrificed himself for the good of the rest in order to furnish a piece of his entrails for the string. But when everything was ready and the first Bear stepped up to make the trial, it was found

that in letting the arrow fly after drawing back the bow, his long claws caught the string and spoiled the shot. This was annoying, but someone suggested that they might trim his claws, which was accordingly done, and on a second trial it was found that the arrow went straight to the mark. But here the chief, the old White Bear, objected, saying it was necessary that they should have long claws in order to be able to climb trees. "One of us has already died to furnish the bowstring, and if we now cut off our claws we must all starve together. It is better to trust to the teeth and claws that nature gave us, for it is plain that Man's weapons were not intended for us."

No one could think of any better plan, so the old chief dismissed the council and the Bears dispersed to the woods and thickets without having concerted any way to prevent the increase of the human race. Had the result of the council been otherwise, we should now be at war with the Bears, but as it is, the hunter does not even ask the Bear's pardon when he kills one.

The Deer next held a council under their chief, the Little Deer, and after some talk decided to send rheumatism to every hunter who should kill one of them unless he took care to ask their pardon for the offense. They sent notice of their decision to the nearest settlement of humans and told them at the same time what to do when necessity forced them to kill one of the Deer tribe. Now, whenever the hunter shoots a Deer, the Little Deer, who is swift as the wind and cannot be wounded, runs quickly up to the spot and, bending over the bloodstains, asks the spirit of the Deer if it has heard the prayer of the hunter for pardon. If the reply be "Yes," all is well, and the Little Deer goes on his way; but if the reply be "No," he follows on the trail of the hunter, guided by the drops of blood on the ground, until he arrives at his cabin in the settlement, when the Little Deer enters invisibly and strikes the hunter with rheumatism, so that he becomes at once a helpless cripple. No hunter who has regard for his health ever fails to ask pardon of the Deer for killing it, although some hunters who have not learned the prayer may try to turn aside the Little Deer from his pursuit by building a fire behind them in the trail.

Next came the Fishes and Reptiles, who had their own complaints against Man. They held their council together and determined to make their victims dream of snakes twining about them in slimy folds and blowing foul breath in their faces, or to make them dream of eating raw or decaying fish, so that they would lose appetite, sicken, and die. This is why people dream about snakes and fish.

Finally the Birds, Insects, and smaller animals came together for the same purpose, and the Grubworm was chief of the council. It was decided that each in turn should give an opinion, and then they would vote on the question as to whether or not Man was guilty. Seven votes should be enough to condemn him. One after another denounced Man's cruelty and injustice toward the other animals and voted in favor of his death. The Frog spoke first, saying: "We must do something to check the increase of the race, or people will become so numerous that we shall be crowded from off the earth. See how they have kicked me about because I'm ugly, as they say, until my back is covered with sores"; and here he showed the spots on his skin. Next came the Bird—no one remembers now which one it was—who condemned Man "because he burns my feet off," meaning the way in which the hunter barbecues birds by impaling them on a stick set over the fire, so that their feathers and tender feet are singed off. Others followed in the same strain. The Ground-squirrel alone ventured to say a good word for Man, who seldom hurt him because he was so small, but this made the others so angry that they fell upon the Ground-squirrel and tore him with their claws, and the stripes are on his back to this day.

They began to devise and name so many new diseases, one after another, that had not their invention at last failed them, no one of the human race would have been able to survive. The Grubworm grew constantly more pleased as the name of each disease was called off, until at last they reached the end of the list, when someone proposed to make menstruation sometimes fatal to women. On this he rose up in his place and cried: "Wadâñ'! [Thanks] I'm glad some more of them will die, for they are getting so thick that they tread on me." The thought fairly made him shake with joy, so that he fell over backward and could not get on his feet again, but had to wriggle off on his back, as the Grubworm has done ever since.

When the Plants, who were friendly to Man, heard what had been done by the animals, they determined to defeat the latter's evil designs. Each Tree, Shrub, and Herb, down even to the Grasses and Mosses, agreed to furnish a cure for some one of the diseases named, and each said: "I shall appear to help Man when he calls upon me in his need." Thus came medicine; and the plants, every one of which has its use if we only knew it, furnish the remedy to counteract the evil wrought by the revengeful animals. Even weeds were made for some good purpose, which we must find out ourselves. When the doctor does not know what medicine to use for a sick man the spirit of the plant tells him.

Questions for Thought

1. What do you make of the fact that the earth was created by the water-beetle?
2. What do these stories tell you about the relationship between the Cherokee and the animals? How does this compare with or differ from traditional European attitudes toward animals?
3. Do you agree with the Cherokee belief about the standing of the human species in the natural world? Why or why not?
4. Do you find the Cherokee account of the origin of disease believable? If not, how would you explain the existence of disease?
5. What are the principal differences between the Cherokee account of creation and the stories found in the Bible? Can you find any similarities between the Cherokee account and the biblical stories?
6. In what ways, if any, is the Cherokee account of the origin of the earth similar to modern scientific accounts?

5   Origin and Fate of the Universe

STEPHEN W. HAWKING

Stephen W. Hawking (b. 1942), a British theoretical physicist and mathematician, was born in Oxford, England. Showing exceptional talent in mathematics and physics at an early age, Hawking entered Oxford University in 1958. After earning his bachelor's degree in physics four years later, Hawking enrolled in the department of applied mathematics and theoretical physics at the University of Cambridge. He earned his Ph.D. from Cambridge in 1966. After receiving his doctorate, Hawking remained at Cambridge to do postgraduate work. In 1977, he was appointed professor of physics at Cambridge, and two years later he was named Lucasian Professor of Mathematics, a position that was founded at Cambridge in 1663 and was once held by Isaac Newton.

While he was in the postgraduate program at Cambridge, Hawking was diagnosed as having amyotrophic lateral sclerosis (ALS), a rare, incurable disease that progressively destroys a person's ability to move and speak. Early in its history, this disease made Hawking wheelchair dependent, and an operation in 1985 made it impossible for him to speak. However, computer and voice synthesizer technology allowed Hawking to continue his writing and to give numerous scientific and popular talks. Of his disease, Hawking wrote, "I have had motor neurone disease for practically all my adult life. Yet it has not prevented me from having a very attractive family, and being successful in my work. This is thanks to the help I have received from Jane [his wife], my children, and a large number of other people and organizations. I have been lucky, that my condition has progressed more slowly than is often the case. But it shows that one need not lose hope."

Hawking is the author of numerous studies and articles dealing with specific scientific problems, such as the properties of space-time, the nature of black holes, and the beginnings of the universe. He also wrote two books, *A Brief History of Time* (1988) and *Black Holes and Baby Universes and Other Essays* (1993), that are intended to make the results of modern scientific research accessible to the general public. In 1992, *A Brief History of Time* was made into a film about Hawking's life and work.

In the following excerpt from *A Brief History of Time*, Hawking explains the modern scientific theory of the origin of the universe. This theory, which is usually referred to as the "big bang theory," suggests that at the big bang the universe had zero size and was infinitely hot. After the big bang, the universe gradually cooled and expanded in size. Once sufficient cooling had occurred, the rapidly moving subatomic particles, which initially consisted principally of photons, electrons, neutrinos, and their antiparticles, combined to produce the first nuclei of atoms. These would further combine to produce the first elements, such as hydrogen and helium.

After more cooling had occurred, galaxies were formed, and nuclear fusion reactions appeared within them. These nuclear fusion reactions constituted the first stars, which burned hydrogen into helium, thus producing heat and light for a long period of time. Gradually, some of these stars depleted their supply of hydrogen; this then caused them to contract and to begin converting helium into heavier elements, such as carbon and oxygen. When this process was completed, some of these stars further contracted, eventually producing a condition in which their center collapsed into a very dense state (forming a neutron star or a black hole), while their outer regions were blown off by a tremendous explosion referred to as a supernova.

These explosions provided some of the material for later generations of stars, one such star being our sun. Also, some of the heavier elements from these explosions collected together to form planets, such as the earth, as well as other bodies that orbit the suns.

In its initial state, the earth was extremely hot and without an atmosphere. As it cooled, the earth acquired an atmosphere, and the first primitive life forms appeared. Then a process of evolution began in which changes in atmospheric conditions were accompanied by changes in the life forms inhabiting the earth. As atmospheric conditions became more hospitable, diverse complex life forms developed from the primitive life forms.

One of the more surprising claims that Hawking makes in this selection concerns the timing of the big bang itself. While the big bang is often referred to as the moment of creation (and could thus be interpreted as the work of God), Hawking suggests that "space-time was finite but had no boundary." For him this means that the universe had no beginning and thus that the big bang cannot be described as the moment of creation. Perhaps Hawking's claim can be better understood if viewed in light of the answer that Carl Sagan, another prominent contemporary scientist who wrote the introduction to *A Brief History of Time,* gave to someone who asked him how the universe got here if God did not create it. Sagan responded by asking the person how God got here, to which the person replied that God was eternal. Sagan then suggested that it would be simpler to assume that the universe itself was eternal, thus eliminating the necessity of postulating the existence of God. Thus, while the big bang initiated the process that eventually gave birth to stars, galaxies, and life as we know it, the universe in some form has always existed.

Questions for Reading

1. What does Hawking mean by the "big bang singularity"? What does he mean by "quantum effects"?
2. What was the nature of the conference that Hawking attended at the Vatican? Why was he happy that the pope was unaware of the subject of the talk he had given at the conference?
3. What, according to Hawking, was the universe like at the moment of the big bang? What was it like one second later? One hundred seconds later?
4. When, according to Hawking, did our sun come into existence? What conditions were necessary to produce it?
5. Under what conditions did life first appear on earth? What was the nature of the earliest life forms? How were humans first produced?

EINSTEIN'S GENERAL THEORY OF RELATIVITY, ON its own, predicted that space-time began at the big bang singularity and would come to an end either at the big crunch singularity (if the whole universe recollapsed), or at a singularity inside a black hole (if a local region, such as a star, were to collapse). Any matter that fell into the hole would be destroyed at the singularity, and only the gravitational effect of its mass would continue to be felt outside. On the other hand, when quantum effects were taken into account, it seemed that the mass of energy of the matter would eventually be returned to the rest of the universe, and that the black hole, along with any singularity inside it, would evaporate away and finally disappear. Could **quantum mechanics** have an equally dramatic effect on the big bang and big crunch singularities? What really happens during the very early or late stages of the universe, when gravitational fields are so strong that quantum effects cannot be ignored? Does the universe in fact have a beginning or an end? And if so, what are they like?

Throughout the 1970s, I had been mainly studying black holes, but in 1981 my interest in questions about the origin and fate of the universe was reawakened when I attended a conference on **cosmology** organized by the Jesuits in the Vatican. The Catholic Church had made a bad mistake with Galileo when it tried to lay down the law on a question of science, declaring that the sun went round the earth. Now, centuries later, it had decided to invite a number of experts to advise it on cosmology. At the end of the conference the participants were granted an audience with the pope. He told us that it was all right to study the evolution of the universe after the big bang, but we should not inquire into the big bang itself because that was the moment of Creation and therefore the work of God. I was glad then that he did not know the subject of the talk I had just given at the conference—the possibility that space-time was finite but had no boundary, which means it had no beginning, no moment of Creation. I had no desire to share the fate of Galileo, with whom I feel a strong sense of identity, partly because of the coincidence of having been born exactly 300 years after his death!

In order to explain the ideas that I and other people have had about how quantum mechanics may affect the origin and fate of the universe, it is necessary first to understand the generally accepted history of the universe, according to what is known as the "hot big bang model." This assumes that the universe is described by a Friedmann model, right back to the big bang. In such models one finds that as the universe expands, any matter or radiation gets cooler. (When the universe doubles in size, its temperature falls by half.) Since temperature is simply a measure of the average energy—or speed—of the particles, this cooling of the universe would have a major effect on the matter in it. At very high temperatures, particles would be moving around so fast that they could escape any attraction toward each other due to nuclear or electromagnetic forces, but as they cooled off one would expect particles that attract each other to start to clump together. Moreover, even the types of particles that exist in the universe would depend on the temperature. At high enough temperatures, particles have so much energy that whenever they collide many different particle/antiparticle pairs would be produced—and although some of these particles would annihilate on hitting antiparticles, they would be produced more rapidly than they could annihilate. At lower temperatures, however, when colliding particles have less energy, particle/antiparticle pairs would be produced less quickly—and annihilation would become faster than production.

At the big bang itself, the universe is thought to have had zero size, and so to have been infinitely hot. But as the universe expanded, the temperature of the radiation decreased. One second after the big bang, it would have fallen about ten thousand million degrees. This is about a thousand times the temperature at the center of the sun, but temperatures as high as this are reached in H-bomb explosions. At this time the universe would have contained mostly photons, electrons, and neutrinos (extremely light particles that are affected only by the weak force and gravity) and their antiparticles, together with some protons and neutrons. As the universe continued to expand and the temperature to drop, the rate at which electron/antielectron pairs were being produced in collisions would have fallen below the rate at which they were being destroyed by annihilation. So most of the electrons and antielectrons would have annihilated with each other to produce more photons, leaving only a few electrons left over. The neutrinos and antineutrinos, however, would not have annihilated with each other, because these particles interact with themselves and with other particles only very weakly. So they should still be around today. If we could observe them, it would provide a good test of this picture of a very hot early stage of the universe. Unfortunately, their energies nowadays would be too low for us to observe them directly. However, if neutrinos are not massless, but have a small mass of their own, as suggested by an unconfirmed Russian experiment performed in 1981, we might be able to detect them indirectly: they could be a form of "dark matter," . . . with sufficient gravitational attraction to stop the expansion of the universe and cause it to collapse again.

About one hundred seconds after the big bang, the temperature would have fallen to one thousand million degrees, the temperature inside the hottest stars. At this temperature protons and neutrons would no longer have sufficient energy to escape the attraction of the strong nuclear force, and would have started to combine together to produce the nuclei of atoms of deuterium (heavy hydrogen), which contain one proton and one neutron. The deuterium nuclei then would have combined with more protons and neutrons to make helium nuclei, which contain two protons and two neutrons, and also small amounts of a couple of heavier elements, lithium and beryllium. One can calculate that in the hot big bang model about a quarter of the protons and neutrons would have converted into helium nuclei, along with a small amount of heavy hydrogen and other elements. The remaining neutrons would have decayed into protons, which are the nuclei of ordinary hydrogen atoms.

This picture of a hot early stage of the universe was first put forward by the scientist George Gamow in a famous paper written in 1948 with a student of his, Ralph Alpher. Gamow had quite a sense of humor—he persuaded the nuclear scientist Hans Bethe to add his name to the paper to make the list of authors "Alpher, Bethe, Gamow," like the first three letters of the Greek alphabet, alpha, beta, gamma: particularly appropriate for a paper on the beginning of the universe! In this paper they made the remarkable prediction that radiation (in the form of protons) from the very hot early stages of the universe should still be around today, but with its temperature reduced to only a few degrees above absolute zero ($-273°C$). It was this radiation that Penzias and Wilson found in 1965. At the time that Alpher, Bethe, and Gamow wrote their paper, not much was known about the nuclear reactions of protons and neutrons. Predictions made for the proportions of various elements in the early universe were therefore rather inaccurate, but these calculations have been repeated in the light of better knowledge and now agree very well with what we observe. It is, more-

over, very difficult to explain in any other way why there should be so much helium in the universe. We are therefore fairly confident that we have the right picture, at least back to about one second after the big bang.

Within only a few hours of the big bang, the production of helium and other elements would have stopped. And after that, for the next million years or so, the universe would have just continued expanding, without anything much happening. Eventually, once the temperature had dropped to a few thousand degrees, and electrons and nuclei no longer had enough energy to overcome the electromagnetic attraction between them, they would have started combining to form atoms. The universe as a whole would have continued expanding and cooling, but in regions that were slightly denser than average, the expansion would have been slowed down by the extra gravitational attraction. This would eventually stop expansion in some regions and cause them to start to recollapse. As they were collapsing, the gravitational pull of matter outside these regions might start them rotating slightly. As the collapsing region got smaller, it would spin faster—just as skaters spinning on ice spin faster as they draw in their arms. Eventually, when the region got small enough, it would be spinning fast enough to balance the attraction of gravity, and in this way disklike rotating galaxies were born. Other regions, which did not happen to pick up a rotation, would become oval-shaped objects called elliptical galaxies. In these, the region would stop collapsing because individual parts of the galaxy would be orbiting stably round its center, but the galaxy would have no overall rotation.

As time went on, the hydrogen and helium gas in the galaxies would break up into smaller clouds that would collapse under their own gravity. As these contracted, and the atoms within them collided with one another, the temperature of the gas would increase, until eventually it became hot enough to start nuclear fusion reactions. These would convert the hydrogen into more helium, and the heat given off would raise the pressure, and so stop the clouds from contracting any further. They would remain stable in this state for a long time as stars like our sun, burning hydrogen into helium and radiating the resulting energy as heat and light. More massive stars would need to be hotter to balance their stronger gravitational attraction, making the nuclear fusion reactions proceed so much more rapidly that they would use up their hydrogen in as little as a hundred million years. They would then contract slightly, and as they heated up further, would start to convert helium into heavier elements like carbon or oxygen. This, however, would not release much more energy, so a crisis would occur. . . . What happens next is not completely clear, but it seems likely that the central regions of the star would collapse to a very dense state, such as a neutron star or black hole. The outer regions of the star may sometimes get blown off in a tremendous explosion called a supernova, which would outshine all the other stars in its galaxy. Some of the heavier elements produced near the end of the star's life would be flung back into the gas in the galaxy, and would provide some of the raw material for the next generation of stars. Our own sun contains about 2 percent of these heavier elements because it is a second- or third-generation star, formed some five thousand million years ago out of a cloud of rotating gas containing the debris of earlier supernovas. Most of the gas in that cloud went to form the sun or got blown away, but a small amount of the heavier elements collected together to form the bodies that now orbit the sun as planets like the earth.

The earth was initially very hot and without an atmosphere. In the course of time it cooled and acquired an atmosphere from the emission of gases from the rocks. This early atmosphere was not one in which we could have survived. It contained no oxygen, but a lot of other gases that are poisonous to us, such as hydrogen sulfide (the gas that gives rotten eggs their smell). There are, however, other primitive forms of life that can flourish under such conditions. It is thought that they developed in the oceans, possibly as a result of chance combinations of atoms into large structures, called macromolecules, which were capable of assembling other atoms in the ocean into similar structures. They would thus have reproduced themselves and multiplied. In some cases there would be errors in the reproduction. Mostly these errors would have been such that the new macromolecule could not reproduce itself and eventually would have been destroyed. However, a few of the errors would have produced new macromolecules that were even better at reproducing themselves. They would have therefore had an advantage and would have tended to replace the original macromolecules. In this way a process of evolution was started that led to the development of more and more complicated, self-reproducing organisms. The first primitive forms of life consumed various materials, including hydrogen sulfide, and released oxygen. This gradually changed the atmosphere to the composition that it has today and allowed the development of higher forms of life such as fish, reptiles, mammals, and ultimately the human race.

Questions for Thought

1. Hawking asks the following question: "Does the universe in fact have a beginning or an end?" How does he answer this question? How would you answer it?
2. How would you describe the "big bang"? Do you think the big bang theory adequately explains the origin of the universe? Why or why not?
3. Why does Hawking compare himself with Galileo? Why did the Catholic Church censure Galileo? Do you think the Church was justified in censuring him? Defend your answer.
4. What evidence does Hawking provide to support his account of the origin and development of the universe?
5. Which of the earlier creation myths seems most compatible with Hawking's description of the origin of the universe? Which of them seems least compatible with his description?

The Origin of the Species   6

CHARLES DARWIN

Charles Robert Darwin (1809–1882), a naturalist best known for his formulation of the theory of evolution, was born in Shrewsbury, England. The son of a prominent provincial family (both his father and his paternal grandfather were physicians, while his maternal grandfather was the founder of a pottery firm), Darwin was freed from the necessity of earning a living. He attended the University of Edinburgh and Cambridge University, first studying medicine and then theology. Finding neither of these to his liking and having formed a friendship with a professor of botany, Darwin turned his attention to the scientific investigation of nature.

In 1831, Darwin signed on as an unpaid naturalist aboard the HMS *Beagle,* a ship whose mission was to explore the wildlife of the west coast of South America and some of the Pacific islands. During this five-year voyage, Darwin made many of the observations that later led to his formulation of the theory of evolution. Some historians also believe that bacteria from a bug bite that Darwin suffered during this trip was the source of the chronic health problems that he experienced later in life.

On returning to England in 1836, he lived in London for the next six years. During this time, Darwin wrote a journal of his researches and married his cousin Emma. In 1842, he moved to Down, an isolated village in Kent, where he lived for the remaining forty years of his life. In this small village, Darwin continued his research and wrote the books that brought him fame. These include *Geological Observations on the Volcanic Islands, Visited During the Voyage of the H.M.S. Beagle* (1844), *A Monograph on the Sub-Class Cirripedia, with Figures of All the Species* (2 vols., 1851–1854), *On the Origin of the Species* (1859), *The Various Contrivances by Which Orchids Are Fertilized by Insects* (1862), *The Movements and Habits of Climbing Plants* (1865), *The Variation of Animals and Plants Under Domestication* (1868), *The Descent of Man and Selection in Relation to Sex* (1871), *The Expression of the Emotions in Man and Animals* (1872), *Insectivorous Plants* (1875), *Autobiography of Charles Darwin* (1876), *The Different Forms of Flowers on Plants of the Same Species* (1877), *The Power of Movement in Plants* (1877), and *The Formation of Vegetable Mold Through the Action of Worms* (1881). As the variety of his writings clearly shows, Darwin contributed to many areas of natural science.

In the following selection from *The Origin of the Species,* Darwin formulates and defends his version of the theory of evolution, or, as he refers to it, "the theory of descent with modification through variation and natural selection." Although Darwin is often misrepresented as claiming that humans are derived from apes, what he does claim is that members of the same species, as well as all species of the same genus, are derived from common ancestors. The correct formulation of Darwin's claim, therefore, is not that humans are derived from apes but rather that humans and apes have common biological ancestors that are not yet either human or ape. Humans and apes, as well as other species, develop from these common ancestors through a process of modification that occurs gradually over an immense period of time. This modification is determined largely, though not wholly, by natural selection—that is, by a struggle for continued existence after which only the best-adapted individuals and species survive.

After acknowledging and responding to some of the difficulties that arise from accepting his theory, Darwin offers positive evidence that both supports his theory and raises questions concerning the competing theory that wholly perfected species were produced by special acts of creation. He claims that the modifications produced through the breeding and domestication of animals are analogous to the modifications produced in nature through the process of natural selection. He also argues that the theory of evolution is better able than the competing theory to explain why there is no fixed line of demarcation between species and variations and why there is so much diversity and imperfection found in the natural world. Finally, he claims that the theory of evolution is supported by the facts of geographical distribution, by the geological record, by certain anatomical similarities in different organisms, and by the similarities found in the embryos of mammals, birds, reptiles, and fishes.

Near the end of this selection, Darwin responds to the moral and religious criticisms that were directed at his theory. In the nineteenth century, as is still the case in certain religious circles today, the theory of evolution was attacked for being inconsistent with the biblical account of creation (reprinted earlier) and for denying human dignity. Darwin counters that he can see no reason why the theory, properly understood, should shock religious feelings or why it should be deemed incompatible with human dignity. Indeed, using near-poetic language, he concludes *The Origin of the Species* by saying, "There is grandeur in this view of life, with its several powers, having been originally breathed by the Creator into a few forms or into one; and that, whilst this planet has gone cycling on according to the fixed law of gravity, from so simple a beginning endless forms most beautiful and most wonderful have been, and are being, evolved."

Questions for Reading

1. What exactly does Darwin mean by evolution? What, according to Darwin, is the evolutionary relationship of humans and apes?
2. How, according to Darwin, does the theory of evolution differ from the competing theory that he rejects?
3. What evidence does Darwin present in defense of the theory of evolution? What evidence does he provide against the competing theory?
4. How does Darwin define *natural selection*? What role does natural selection play in evolutionary development?
5. Does Darwin seem to believe in the existence of a divine being? If so, how does he describe this being?

AS THIS WHOLE VOLUME [*The Origin of Species*] IS one long argument, it may be convenient to the reader to have the leading facts and inferences briefly recapitulated.

That many and serious objections may be advanced against the theory of descent with modification through variation and natural selection, I do not deny. I have endeavored to give them their full force. Nothing at first can appear more difficult to believe than that the more complex organs and instincts have been perfected, not by means superior to, though analogous with, human reason, but by

From Charles Robert Darwin, On The Origin of the Species by means of Natural Selection, or the Preservation of Favoured Races in the Struggle for Life, *London, 1859.*

the accumulation of innumerable slight variations, each good for the individual possessor. Nevertheless, this difficulty, though appearing to our imagination insuperably great, cannot be considered real if we admit the following propositions: all parts of the organization and instincts offer, at least, individual differences; there is a struggle for existence leading to the preservation of profitable deviations of structure or instinct; and gradations in the state of perfection of each organ may have existed, each good of its kind. The truth of these propositions cannot, I think, be disputed.

It is, no doubt, extremely difficult even to conjecture by what gradations many structures have been perfected, especially amongst broken and failing groups of organic beings, which have suffered much extinction. But we see so many strange gradations in nature that we ought to be extremely cautious in saying that any organ or instinct, or any whole structure, could not have arrived at its present state by many graduated steps. . . .

Turning to geographical distribution, the difficulties encountered on the theory of descent with modification are serious enough. All the individuals of the same species, and all the species of the same genus, or even higher group, are descended from common parents. Therefore, in however distant and isolated parts of the world they may now be found, they must in the course of successive generations have traveled from some point to all the others. We are often wholly unable even to conjecture how this could have been effected. Yet, as we have reason to believe that some species have retained the same specific form for very long periods of time, immensely long as measured by years, too much stress ought not to be laid on the occasional wide diffusion of the same species. For during very long periods there will always have been a good chance for wide migration by many means. A broken or interrupted range may often be accounted for by the extinction of the species in the intermediate regions. It cannot be denied that we are as yet very ignorant as to the full extent of the various climatic and geographical changes that have affected the earth during modern periods; and such changes will often have facilitated migration. As an example, I have attempted to show how potent has been the influence of the Glacial period on the distribution of the same and of allied species throughout the world. We are as yet profoundly ignorant of the many occasional means of transport.

With respect to distinct species of the same genus inhabiting distant and isolated regions, as the process of modification has necessarily been slow, all the means of migration will have been possible during a very long period. Consequently, the difficulty of the wide diffusion of the species of the same genus is in some degree lessened.

As according to the theory of natural selection an indeterminable number of intermediate forms must have existed, linking together all the species in each group by gradations as fine as are our existing varieties, it may be asked: Why do we not see these linking forms all around us? Why are not all organic beings blended together in an inextricable chaos? With respect to existing forms, we should remember that we have no right to expect (excepting in rare cases) to discover *directly* connecting links between them, but only between each and some extinct and supplanted form. Even in a wide area . . . in which the climatic and other conditions of life change insensibly from a district occupied by one species into another district occupied by a closely allied species, we have no just right to expect often to find intermediate varieties in the intermediate zones. For we have reason to believe that only a few species of a genus ever undergo change, and that the other species become utterly extinct and leave no modified progeny. Of the species that do change, only a few within the same country change at the same time; and all modifications are slowly effected. I have also shown that the intermediate varieties that probably at first existed in the intermediate zones would be liable to be supplanted by the allied forms on either hand. For the latter, from existing in greater numbers, would generally be modified and improved at a quicker rate than the intermediate varieties, which existed in lesser numbers. So, the intermediate varieties would, in the long run, be supplanted and exterminated.

On this doctrine of the extermination of an infinitude of connecting links between the living and extinct inhabitants of the world, and at each successive period between the extinct and still older species, why is not every geological formation charged with such links? Why does not every collection of fossil remains afford plain evidence of the gradation and mutation of the forms of life? Although geological research has undoubtedly revealed the former existence of many links, bringing numerous forms of life much closer together, it does not yield the infinitely many fine gradations between past and present species required on the theory. This is the most obvious of the many objections that may be urged against it. Why, again, do whole groups of allied species appear, though this appearance is often false, to have come in suddenly on the successive geological stages? Although we now know that organic beings appeared on this globe, at a period incalculably remote, long before the lowest bed of the Cambrian system was deposited, why do we not find beneath this system great piles of strata stored with the remains of the progenitors of the Cambrian fossils? For on the theory, such strata must somewhere have been deposited at these ancient and utterly unknown epochs of the world's history.

I can answer these questions and objections only on the supposition that the geological record is far more imperfect than most geologists believe. The number of specimens in all our museums is almost nothing when compared with the countless generations of countless species that have certainly existed. . . . We should not be able to recognize a species as the parent of another and modified species, if we were to examine the two ever so closely, unless we possessed most of the intermediate links. However, owing to the imperfection of the geological record, we have no just right to expect to find so many links. . . . Only a small portion of the world has been geologically explored. Only organic beings of certain classes can be presented in a fossil condition, at least in any great number. Many species when once formed never undergo any further change but become extinct without leaving modified descendants. And the periods, during which species have undergone modification, though long as measured by years, have probably been short in comparison with the periods during which they retain the same form. . . . Most formations have been intermittent in their accumulation; and their duration has probably been shorter than the average duration of specific forms. Successive formations are in most cases separated from each other by blank intervals of time of great length; for fossiliferous formations thick enough to resist future degradations can as a general rule be accumulated only where much sediment is deposited on the subsiding bed of the sea. During the alternate periods of elevation and of stationary level the record will generally be blank. During these latter periods there will probably be more variability in the forms of life; during periods of subsidence, more extinction. . . .

That the geological record is imperfect all will admit; but that it is imperfect to the degree required by our theory, few will be inclined to admit. If we look to long enough intervals of time, geology plainly declares that species have all changed; and they have changed in the manner required by the theory, for they have changed slowly and in a graduated manner. We clearly see this in the fossil remains from consecutive formations invariably being much more closely related to each other, than are the fossils from widely separated formations.

Such is the sum of the several chief objections and difficulties which may be justly urged against the theory. I have now briefly recapitulated the answers and explanations that, as far as I can see, may be given. I have felt these difficulties far too heavily during many years to doubt their weight. But one must not fail to notice that the more important objections relate to questions on which we are confessedly ignorant; nor do we know how ignorant we are. We do not know all the possible transitional gradations between the simplest and the most perfect organs; it cannot be pretended that we know all the varied means of Distribution during the long lapse of years, or that we know how imperfect the Geological Record is. Serious as these several objections are, in my judgment they are by no means sufficient to overthrow the theory of descent with subsequent modification.

Now let us turn to the other side of the argument. Under domestication we see much variability, caused, or at least excited, by changed conditions of life, but often in so obscure a manner that we are tempted to consider the variations as spontaneous. Variability is determined by many complex laws—by correlated growth, compensation, the increased use and disuse of parts, and the definite action of the surrounding conditions. There is much difficulty in ascertaining how largely our domestic productions have been modified; but we may safely infer that the amount has been large, and that modifications can be inherited for long periods. As long as the conditions of life remain the same, we have reason to believe that a modification, which has already been inherited for an almost infinite number of generations, may continue to be inherited for an almost infinite number of generations. On the other hand, we have evidence that when variability has once come into play, it does not cease under domestication for a very long period. Nor do we know that it ever ceases, for new varieties are still occasionally produced by our oldest domesticated productions.

Variability is not actually caused by man; he only unintentionally exposes organic beings to new conditions of life. Then nature acts on the organization and causes it to vary. But man can and does select the variations given to him by nature, and thus accumulates them in any desired manner. He thus adapts animals and plants for his own benefit or pleasure. He may do this methodically, or he may do it unconsciously by preserving the individuals most useful or pleasing to him without any intention of altering the breed. It is certain that he can largely influence the character of a breed by selecting, in each successive generation, individual differences so slight as to be inappreciable except by an educated eye. This unconscious process of selection has been the great agency in the formation of the most distinct and useful domestic breeds. . . .

There is no reason why the principles that have acted so efficiently under domestication should not have acted under nature. In the survival of favored individuals and species, during the constantly recurring Struggle for Existence, we see a powerful and ever-acting form of Selection. The struggle for existence inevitably follows from the high geometrical ratio of increase that is common to all organic beings. This high rate of increase is proved by calculation—by the rapid increase of many animals and plants during a succession of peculiar seasons, and when naturalized in new countries. More individuals are born than can possibly survive. A grain in the balance may determine which individuals shall live and which shall die, as well as which variety or species shall increase in number, and which shall decrease or finally become extinct. As the individuals of the same species come into the closest competition with each other in all respects, the struggle will generally be most severe between them. It will be almost equally severe between the varieties of the same species, and next in severity between the species of the same genus. On the other hand, the struggle will often be severe between beings remote in the scale of nature. The slightest advantage in certain individuals, at any age or during any season, over those with which they come into competition, or better adaptation in however slight a degree to the surrounding physical conditions, will, in the long run, turn the balance. . . .

If then, animals and plants do vary, let it be ever so slightly or slowly, why should not variations or individual differences, which are in any way beneficial, be preserved and accumulated through natural selection or the survival of the fittest? If man can by patience select variations useful to him, why, under changing and complex conditions of life, should not variations useful to nature's living products often arise, and be preserved or selected? What limit can be put to this power, acting during long ages and rigidly scrutinizing the whole constitution, structure, and habits of each creature, favoring the good and rejecting the bad? I can see no limit to this power, in slowly and beautifully adapting each form to the most complex relations of life. The theory of natural selection, even if we look no farther than this, seems to be in the highest degree probable. I have already recapitulated, as fairly as I could, the opposed difficulties and objections. Now let us turn to the special facts and arguments in favor of the theory.

Given that species are only strongly marked, permanent varieties, and that each species first existed as a variety, we can see why no line of demarcation can be drawn between species, which are commonly supposed to have been produced by special acts of creation, and varieties, which are acknowledged to have been produced by secondary laws. On this same view we can understand how it is that in a region where many species of a genus have been produced, and where they now flourish, these same species should present many varieties. For where the manufactory of species has been active, we might expect, as a general rule, to find it still in action; and this is the case if varieties be incipient species. . . .

As natural selection acts solely by accumulating slight, successive, favorable variations, it can produce no great or sudden modifications; it can act only by short and slow steps. . . . We can see why throughout nature the same general end is gained by an almost infinite diversity of means, for every peculiarity when once acquired is long inherited, and structures already modified in many different ways have to be adapted for the same general purpose. We can, in short, see why nature is prodigal in variety, though niggard in innovation. But why this should be a law of nature if each species has been independently created no man can explain.

Many other facts are, it seems to me, explicable on this theory. How strange it is that a bird with the form of a woodpecker should prey on insects on the ground, that upland geese, which rarely or never swim, should possess webbed feet, that a thrush-like bird should dive and feed on sub-aquatic insects, that a petrel should have the habits and structure fitting it for the life of an awk, and so in endless other cases. But on the view that each species is constantly trying to increase in number, with natural selection always ready to adapt the slowly varying descendants of each to any unoccupied or ill-occupied place in nature, these facts cease to be strange, or might even have been anticipated.

We can to a certain extent understand how it is that there is so much beauty throughout nature, for this may be largely attributed to the agency of selection. That beauty, according to our sense of it, is not universal, must be admitted by every one who looks at some venomous snakes, at some fishes, and at certain hideous bats with a distorted resemblance to the human face. Sexual selection has given the most brilliant colors, elegant patterns, and other ornaments to the males, and sometimes to both sexes of many birds, butterflies, and other animals. With birds it has often rendered the voice of the male musical to the female, as well as to our ears. Flowers and fruit have been rendered conspicuous by brilliant colors in contrast with the green foliage, in order that the flowers may be readily seen, visited and fertilized by insects, and the seeds disseminated by birds. . . .

As natural selection acts by competition, it adapts and improves the inhabitants of each country only in relation to their co-inhabitants. For this reason, we need feel no surprise at the species of any one country, although on the ordinary view supposed to have been created and specially adapted for that country, being beaten and supplanted by the naturalized productions from another land. Nor ought we to marvel if all the contrivances in nature are not, as far as we can judge, absolutely perfect (as is the case even of the human eye), or if some of them be abhorrent to our ideas of fitness. We need not marvel at the sting of the bee, when used against an enemy, causing the bee's own death, at drones being produced in such great numbers for one single act, and then being slaughtered by their sterile sisters, at the astonishing waste of pollen by our fir-trees, at the instinctive hatred of the queen-bee for her own fertile daughters, at the ich-neumonidae feeding within the living bodies of caterpillars, or at other such cases. The wonder indeed is, on the theory of natural selection, that more cases of the want of absolute perfection have not been detected. . . .

If we admit that the geological record is imperfect to an extreme degree, then the facts, which the record does give, strongly support the theory of descent with modification. New species have come on the stage slowly and at successive intervals; and the amount of change, after equal intervals of time, is widely different in different groups. The extinction of species and of whole groups of species which has played so conspicuous a part in the history of the organic world, almost inevitably follows from the principle of natural selection; for old forms are supplanted by new and improved forms. . . .

Let us now look to geographical distribution. If we admit that there has been much migration from one part of the world to another throughout the long course of ages, migration owing to former climatic and geographical changes and to the many occasional and unknown means of dispersal, then the theory of descent with modification can explain most of the leading facts of Distribution. We can see why there should be so striking a parallelism in the distribution of organic beings throughout space, and in their geological succession throughout time. For in both cases the beings have been connected by the bond of ordinary generation, and the means of modification have been the same. We see the full meaning of the wonderful fact that has struck every traveler, namely, that on the same continent, under the most diverse conditions, under heat and cold, on mountain and lowland, on deserts and marshes, most of the inhabitants within each great class are plainly related. For they are the descendants of the same progenitors and early colonists. On this same principle of former migration, combined in most cases with modification, we can understand, by the aid of the Glacial period, the identity of some few plants, and the close alliance of many others, on the most distant mountains, and in the northern and southern temperate zones. Likewise we can understand the close alliance of some of the inhabitants of the sea in the northern and southern temperate latitudes, even though they are separated by the whole intertropical ocean. . . .

On this view of migration, with subsequent modification, we see why oceanic islands are inhabited by only a few species, but why many of these are peculiar or endemic forms. We clearly see why species belonging to those groups of animals which cannot cross wide spaces of the ocean, such as frogs and terrestrial mammals, do not inhabit oceanic islands. On the other hand, we also see why new and peculiar species of bats, animals that can traverse the ocean, are found on islands far distant from any continent. Cases such as the presence of peculiar species of bats on oceanic islands and the absence of all other terrestrial mammals are facts that are utterly inexplicable on the theory of independent acts of creation. . . .

The similar framework of bones in the hand of a man, the wing of a bat, the fin of the porpoise, and the leg of the horse, the fact that the same number of vertebrae are found in the neck of the giraffe and the neck of the elephant, and innumerable other such facts, can be easily explained by the theory of descent with slow and slight successive modifications. The similarity of pattern in the wing and in the leg of a bat, though used for such different purposes, in the jaws and legs of a crab, and in the petals, stamens, and pistils of a flower are likewise intelligible on the view of the gradual modification of parts or organs that were aboriginally alike in an early progenitor in each of these classes. On the principle of successive variations not always supervening at an early age, and being inherited at a corresponding not early period of life, we clearly see why the embryos of mammals, birds, reptiles, and fishes should be so closely similar, and so unlike the adult forms. We may cease marveling at the embryo of an air-breathing mammal or bird having branchial slits and arteries running in loops, like those of a fish that has to breathe the air dissolved in water by the aid of well-developed branchiae.

Disuse, aided sometimes by natural selection, will often have reduced organs when rendered useless under changed habits or conditions of life; and we can understand on this view the meaning of rudimentary organs. Disuse and selection will generally act on each creature, when it has come to maturity and has to play its full part in the struggle for exis-

tence. But they will have little power on an organ during early life; hence the organ will not be reduced or rendered rudimentary at this early age. . . . On the view of each organism with all its separate parts having been specially created, how utterly inexplicable is it that organs bearing the plain stamp of inutility, such as the teeth in the embryonic calf or the shriveled wings under the soldered wing-covers of many beetles, should so frequently occur. Nature may be said to have taken pains to reveal her scheme of modification, by means of rudimentary organs, of embryological and homologous structures, but we are too blind to understand her meaning.

I have now recapitulated the facts and considerations which have thoroughly convinced me that species have been modified during a long course of descent. This modification has been effected chiefly through the natural selection of numerous successive, slight, favorable variations, a process that has been aided in an important manner by the inherited effects of the use and disuse of parts, and in an unimportant manner, that is in relation to adaptive structures, whether past or present, by the direct action of external conditions, and by variations that seem to us in our ignorance to arise spontaneously. . . .

It can hardly be supposed that a false theory would explain, in so satisfactory a manner as does the theory of natural selection, the several large classes of facts above specified. It has recently been objected that this is an unsafe method of arguing. But it is a method used in judging of the common events of life that has also often been used by the greatest natural philosophers. The undulatory theory of light has thus been arrived at; and the belief in the revolution of the earth on its own axis was until lately supported by hardly any direct evidence. It is no valid objection that science as yet throws no light on the far higher problem of the essence or origin of life. Who can explain what is the essence of the attraction of gravity? No one now objects to following out results based on this unknown element of attraction, notwithstanding the fact that Leibniz formerly accused Newton of introducing "occult qualities and miracles into philosophy."

I see no good reason why the views given in this volume should shock the religious feelings of any one. It is satisfactory, as showing how transient such impressions are, to remember that the greatest discovery ever made by man, namely the law of the attraction of gravity, was also attacked by Leibniz as being "subversive of natural, and inferentially of revealed religion." A celebrated author and divine has written to me that "he has gradually learned to see that it is just as noble a conception of the Deity to believe that He created a few original forms capable of self-development into other and needful forms as it is to believe that He required a fresh act of creation to supply the voids caused by the action of His laws." . . .

Authors of the highest eminence seem to be fully satisfied with the view that each species has been independently created. To my mind, however, it is more in accord with what we know of the laws impressed on matter by the Creator to believe that the production and extinction of the past and present inhabitants of the world should have been due to secondary causes, like those determining the birth and death of the individual. When I view all beings not as special creations, but as the lineal descendants of some beings which lived long before the first bed of the Cambrian system was deposited, they seem to me to become ennobled. Judging from the past, we may safely infer that not one living species will transmit its unaltered likeness to a distant futurity. And of the species now living, very few will transmit progeny of any kind to a far distant futurity. For the manner in which all organic beings are grouped shows that the greater number of species in each genus, and all the species in many genera, have left no descendants, but have become utterly extinct. We can so far take a prophetic glance into futurity as to foretell that it will be the common and widely spread species, belonging to the larger and dominant groups within each class, which will ultimately prevail and procreate new and dominant species. As all the living forms of life are the lineal descendants of those which lived long before the Cambrian epoch, we may feel certain that the ordinary succession by generation has never once been broken, and that no cataclysm has desolated the whole world. Hence we may look with some confidence to a secure future of great length. And as natural selection works solely by and for the good of each being, all corporeal and mental endowments will tend to progress towards perfection.

It is interesting to contemplate a tangled bank, clothed with many plants of many kinds, with birds singing on the bushes, with various insects flitting about, and with worms crawling through the damp earth. It is even more interesting to realize that these elaborately constructed forms, so different from each other, and dependent upon each other in so complex a manner, have all been produced by laws acting around us. These laws, taken in the largest sense, are Growth with Reproduction, Inheritance that is almost implied by reproduction, Variability from the indirect and direct action of the conditions of life, and from use and disuse. The working of these laws has resulted in a Ratio of Increase so high as to lead to a Struggle for Life, and as a consequence to Natural Selection, entailing Divergence of Character and the Extinction of less-improved forms. Thus, from the war of nature, from famine and death, the most exalted object that we are capable of conceiving, namely, the production of the higher animals, directly follows. There is grandeur in this view that life, with its several powers, has been originally breathed by the Creator into a few forms or into one, and that, while this planet has continued cycling according to the fixed law of gravity, from so simple a beginning, endless forms most beautiful and most wonderful have been, and are still being evolved.

Questions for Thought

1. What are the essential differences between Darwin's account of creation and the preceding creation stories? Can you find any similarities between Darwin's account and the accounts found in the Bible?
2. Do you find the evidence that Darwin presents convincing? Why or why not?
3. What evidence, if any, is provided for the earlier creation stories? If no evidence is provided, on what basis might one accept one of these accounts while rejecting the others?
4. Do you think that the process of natural selection is adequate to explain biological diversity? Defend your answer.
5. Do you agree with Darwin that there is "grandeur" in his account and that it should not shock religious feelings? Why or why not?

Yali's Question   7

JARED DIAMOND

Jared Diamond (b. 1937), who was born in Boston to a physician father and a teacher/musician/linguist mother, received his Ph.D. from Cambridge University in England in 1966. Shortly after receiving his doctorate, he obtained a position at the University of California, Los Angeles, where he still teaches. He currently holds the position of Professor of Geography and Physiology.

While in his twenties, Diamond developed a keen interest in the study of the birds of New Guinea, and he has led numerous expeditions to explore the ecological and evolutionary history of New Guinea and nearby islands. The following selection was inspired by a conversation he had with a New Guinean named Yali while on one of those expeditions.

Diamond speaks a dozen languages, and he has written prolifically. His writings include a number of popular science works in which he combines the findings of biology, anthropology, genetics, linguistics, and history. The best known of these works is his Pulitzer Prize–winning book *Gun, Germs and Steel: The Fates of Human Societies* (1997), from which the following selection is taken. Diamond has also published three other books, *The Third Chimpanzee: The Evolution and Future of the Human Animal* (1992), *Why Is Sex Fun?: The Evolution of Human Sexuality* (1998), and *Collapse: How Societies Choose to Fail or Succeed* (2004).

In describing his work in *Guns, Germs and Steel* and elsewhere, Diamond says, "I've set myself the modest task of trying to explain the broad pattern of human history, on all the continents, for the last 13,000 years. Why did history take such different evolutionary courses for peoples of different continents? This problem has fascinated me for a long time, but it's now ripe for a new synthesis because of recent advances in many fields seemingly remote from history, including molecular biology, plant and animal genetics and biogeography, archaeology, and linguistics." This is the task on which Diamond focuses in the following selection.

As just mentioned, the inspiration for the selection came from a meeting with Yali, a New Guinean man. During their conversation, Yali asks Diamond why it is that white people have so much, while the black people of New Guinea have so little. When expanded beyond the confines of New Guinea, this question asks about the inequities that exist between different peoples currently inhabiting the earth. Why is it that "peoples of Eurasian origin, especially those still living in Europe and eastern Asia, plus those transplanted to North America, dominate the modern world in wealth and power?" Why did wealth and power become distributed in the ways they did?

While Diamond believes that this is a difficult question to answer, he notes that many people do not. They believe that differences in wealth and power are easily explained by genetic or biological differences that exist between peoples. In its simplest version, this view would be that peoples of Eurasian origin dominate other peoples because Eurasians are more intelligent.

In countering such explanations, which he considers to be racist, Diamond offers two responses. First, he argues that "modern 'Stone Age' peoples are on average probably more intelligent, not less intelligent, than industrialized peoples." Second, he argues that the differences between the long-term histories of peoples on different continents are due to environmental factors rather than to innate differences. Thus, the dominance by peoples of Eurasian origin is not due to superior intelligence, creativity, or inventiveness. Rather, as Diamond concludes, "All human societies contain inventive people. It's just that some environments provide more starting materials, and more favorable conditions for utilizing inventions, than do other environments."

Questions for Reading

1. Who was Yali, and what was Yali's question?
2. What were some of the traditional answers to Yali's question? How does Diamond characterize these answers?
3. What evidence does Diamond provide for his claim that modern "Stone Age" peoples are more intelligent than industrialized peoples?
4. How does Diamond describe the legacies of colonialism?
5. What are the three objections to discussing Yali's question that Diamond says might be raised? How does he respond to these objections?
6. What are some of the nongenetic answers to Yali's question that Diamond dismisses? How does his own answer to Yali's question differ from these other nongenetic answers?

WE ALL KNOW THAT HISTORY HAS PROCEEDED very differently for peoples from different parts of the globe. In the 13,000 years since the end of the last Ice Age, some parts of the world developed literate industrial societies with metal tools, other parts developed only nonliterate farming societies, and still others retained societies of hunter-gatherers with stone tools. Those historical inequalities have cast long shadows on the modern world, because the literate societies with metal tools have conquered or exterminated the other societies. While those differences constitute the most basic fact of world history, the reasons for them remain uncertain and controversial. This puzzling question of their origins was posed to me twenty-five years ago in a simple, personal form.

In July 1972 I was walking along a beach on the tropical island of New Guinea, where as a biologist I study bird evolution. I had already heard about a remarkable local politician named Yali, who was touring the district then. By chance, Yali and I were walking in the same direction on that day, and he overtook me. We walked together for an hour, talking during the whole time.

Yali radiated charisma and energy. His eyes flashed in a mesmerizing way. He talked confidently about himself, but he also asked lots of probing questions and listened intently. Our conversation began with a subject then on every New Guinean's mind—the rapid pace of political developments. Papua New Guinea, as Yali's nation is now called, was at that time still administered by Australia as a mandate of the United Nations, but independence was in the air. Yali explained to me his role in getting local people to prepare for self-government.

After a while, Yali turned the conversation and began to quiz me. He had never been outside New Guinea and had not been educated beyond high school, but his curiosity was insatiable. First, he wanted to know about my work on New Guinea birds (including how much I got paid for it). I explained to him how different groups of birds had colonized New Guinea over the course of millions of years. He then asked how the ancestors of his own people had reached New Guinea over the last tens of thousands of years, and how white Europeans had colonized New Guinea within the last 200 years.

The conversation remained friendly, even though the tension between the two societies that Yali and I represented was familiar to both of us. Two centuries ago, all New Guineans were still "living in the Stone Age." That is, they still used stone tools similar to those superseded in Europe by metal tools thousands of years ago, and they dwelt in villages not organized under any centralized political authority. Whites had arrived, imposed centralized government, and brought material goods whose value New Guineans instantly recognized, ranging from steel axes, matches, and medicines to clothing, soft drinks, and umbrellas. In New Guinea all these goods were referred to collectively as "cargo."

Many of the white colonialists openly despised New Guineans as "primitive." Even the least able of New Guinea's white "masters," as they were still called in 1972, enjoyed a far higher standard of living than New Guineans, higher even than charismatic politicians like Yali. Yet Yali had quizzed lots of whites as he was then quizzing me, and I had quizzed lots of New Guineans. He and I both knew perfectly well that New Guineans are on the average at least as smart as Europeans. All those things must have been on Yali's mind when, with yet another penetrating glance of his flashing eyes, he asked me, "Why is it that you white people developed so much cargo and brought it to New Guinea, but we black people had little cargo of our own?"

It was a simple question that went to the heart of life as Yali experienced it. Yes, there still is a huge difference between the lifestyle of the average New Guinean and that of the average European or American. Comparable differences separate the lifestyles of other peoples of the world as well. Those huge disparities must have potent causes that one might think would be obvious.

Yet Yali's apparently simple question is a difficult one to answer. I didn't have an answer then. Professional historians still disagree about the solution; most are no longer even asking the question. In the years since Yali and I had that conversation, I have studied and written about other aspects of human evolution, history, and language. This book, written twenty-five years later, attempts to answer Yali.

Although Yali's question concerned only the contrasting lifestyles of New Guineans and of European whites, it can be extended to a larger set of contrasts within the modern world. Peoples of Eurasian origin, especially those still living in Europe and eastern Asia, plus those transplanted to North America, dominate the modern world in wealth and power. Other peoples, including most Africans, have thrown off European colonial domination but remain far behind in wealth and power. Still other peoples, such as the aboriginal inhabitants of Australia, the Americas, and southernmost Africa, are no longer even masters of their own lands but have been decimated, subjugated, and in some cases even exterminated by European colonialists.

Thus, questions about inequality in the modern world can be reformulated as follows. Why did wealth and power become distributed as they now are, rather than in some other way? For instance, why weren't Native Americans, Africans, and Aboriginal Australians the ones who decimated, subjugated, or exterminated Europeans and Asians?

We can easily push this question back one step. As of the year A.D. 1500, when Europe's worldwide colonial expansion was just beginning, peoples on different continents already differed greatly in technology and political organization. Much of Europe, Asia, and North Africa was the site of metal-equipped states or empires, some of them on the threshold of industrialization. Two Native American peoples, the Aztecs and the Incas, ruled over empires with stone tools. Parts of sub-Saharan Africa were divided among small states or chiefdoms with iron tools. Most other peoples—including all those of Australia and New Guinea, many Pacific islands, much of the Americas, and small parts of sub-Saharan Africa—lived as farming tribes or even still as hunter-gatherer bands using stone tools.

Of course, those technological and political differences as of A.D. 1500 were the immediate cause of the modern world's inequalities. Empires with steel weapons were able to conquer or exterminate tribes with weapons of stone and wood. How, though, did the world get to be the way it was in A.D. 1500?

Once again, we can easily push this question back one step further, by drawing on written histories and archaeological discoveries. Until the end of the last Ice Age, around 11,000 B.C., all peoples on all continents were still hunter-gatherers. Different rates of development on different continents, from 11,000 B.C. to A.D. 1500, were what led to the technological and political inequalities of A.D. 1500. While Aboriginal Australians and many Native

Americans remained hunter-gatherers, most of Eurasia and much of the Americas and sub-Saharan Africa gradually developed agriculture, herding, metallurgy, and complex political organization. Parts of Eurasia, and one area of the Americas, independently developed writing as well. However, each of these new developments appeared earlier in Eurasia than elsewhere. For instance, the mass production of bronze tools, which was just beginning in the South American Andes in the centuries before A.D. 1500, was already established in parts of Eurasia over 4,000 years earlier. The stone technology of the Tasmanians, when first encountered by European explorers in A.D. 1642, was simpler than that prevalent in parts of Upper Paleolithic Europe tens of thousands of years earlier.

Thus, we can finally rephrase the question about the modern world's inequalities as follows: why did human development proceed at such different rates on different continents? Those disparate rates constitute history's broadest pattern and my book's subject.

While this book is thus ultimately about history and prehistory, its subject is not of just academic interest but also of overwhelming practical and political importance. The history of interactions among disparate peoples is what shaped the modern world through conquest, epidemics, and genocide. Those collisions created reverberations that have still not died down after many centuries, and that are actively continuing in some of the world's most troubled areas today.

For example, much of Africa is still struggling with its legacies from recent colonialism. In other regions—including much of Central America, Mexico, Peru, New Caledonia, the former Soviet Union, and parts of Indonesia—civil unrest or guerrilla warfare pits still-numerous indigenous populations against governments dominated by descendants of invading conquerors. Many other indigenous populations—such as native Hawaiians, Aboriginal Australians, native Siberians, and Indians in the United States, Canada, Brazil, Argentina, and Chile—became so reduced in numbers by genocide and disease that they are now greatly outnumbered by the descendants of invaders. Although thus incapable of mounting a civil war, they are nevertheless increasingly asserting their rights.

In addition to these current political and economic reverberations of past collisions among peoples, there are current linguistic reverberations—especially the impending disappearance of most of the modern world's 6,000 surviving languages, becoming replaced by English, Chinese, Russian, and a few other languages whose numbers of speakers have increased enormously in recent centuries. All these problems of the modern world result from the different historical trajectories implicit in Yali's question.

Before seeking answers to Yali's question, we should pause to consider some objections to discussing it at all. Some people take offense at the mere posing of the question, for several reasons.

One objection goes as follows. If we succeed in explaining how some people came to dominate other people, may this not seem to justify the domination? Doesn't it seem to say that the outcome was inevitable, and that it would therefore be futile to try to change the outcome today? This objection rests on a common tendency to confuse an explanation of causes with a justification or acceptance of results. What use one makes of a historical explanation is a question separate from the explanation itself. Understanding is more often used to try to alter an outcome than to repeat or perpetuate it. That's why psychologists try to understand the minds of murderers and rapists, why social historians try to understand genocide, and why physicians try to understand the causes of human disease. Those investigators do not seek to justify murder, rape, genocide, and illness. Instead, they seek to use their understanding of a chain of causes to interrupt the chain.

Second, doesn't addressing Yali's question automatically involve a Eurocentric approach to history, a glorification of western Europeans, and an obsession with the prominence of Western Europe and Europeanized America in the modern world? Isn't that prominence just an ephemeral phenomenon of the last few centuries, now fading behind the prominence of Japan and Southeast Asia? In fact, most of this book will deal with peoples other than Europeans. Rather than focus solely on interactions between Europeans and non-Europeans, we shall also examine interactions between different non-European peoples—especially those that took place within sub-Saharan Africa, Southeast Asia, Indonesia, and New Guinea, among peoples native to those areas. Far from glorifying peoples of Western European origin, we shall see that most basic elements of their civilization were developed by other peoples living elsewhere and were then imported to Western Europe.

Third, don't words such as "civilization," and phrases such as "rise of civilization," convey the false impression that civilization is good, tribal hunter-gatherers are miserable, and history for the past 13,000 years has involved progress toward greater human happiness? In fact, I do not assume that industrialized states are "better" than hunter-gatherer tribes, or that the abandonment of the hunter-gatherer lifestyle for iron-based statehood represents "progress," or that it has led to an increase in human happiness. My own impression, from having divided my life between United States cities and New Guinea villages, is that the so-called blessings of civilization are mixed. For example, compared with hunter-gatherers, citizens of modern industrialized states enjoy better medical care, lower risk of death by homicide, and a longer life span, but receive much less social support from friendships and extended families. My motive for investigating these geographic differences in human societies is not to celebrate one type of society over another but simply to understand what happened in history.

Does Yali's question really need another book to answer it? Don't we already know the answer? If so, what is it?

Probably the commonest explanation involves implicitly or explicitly assuming biological differences among peoples. In the centuries after A.D. 1500, as European explorers became aware of the wide differences among the world's peoples in technology and political organization, they assumed that those differences arose from differences in innate ability. With the rise of Darwinian theory, explanations were recast in terms of natural selection and of evolutionary descent. Technologically primitive peoples were considered evolutionary vestiges of human descent from apelike ancestors. The displacement of such peoples by colonists from industrialized societies exemplified the survival of the fittest. With the later rise of genetics, the explanations were recast once again, in genetic terms. Europeans became considered genetically more intelligent than Africans, and especially more so than Aboriginal Australians.

Today, segments of Western society publicly repudiate racism. Yet many (perhaps most!) Westerners continue to accept racist explanations privately or subconsciously. In Japan and many other countries, such explanations are still advanced publicly and without apology. Even educated white Americans, Europeans, and Australians, when the subject of Australian Aborigines comes up, assume that there is something primitive about the Aborigines themselves. They certainly look different from whites. Many of the living descendants of those Aborigines who survived the era of European colonization are now finding it difficult to succeed economically in white Australian society.

A seemingly compelling argument goes as follows. White immigrants to Australia built a literate, industrialized, politically centralized, democratic state based on metal tools and on food production, all within a century of colonizing a continent where the Aborigines had been living as tribal hunter-gatherers without metal for at least 40,000 years. Here were two successive experiments in human development, in which the environment was identical and the sole variable was the people occupying that environment. What further proof could be wanted to establish that the differences between Aboriginal Australian and European societies arose from differences between the peoples themselves?

The objection to such racist explanations is not just that they are loathsome, but also that they are wrong. Sound evidence for the existence of human differences in intelligence that parallel human differences in technology is lacking. In fact, as I shall explain in a moment, modern "Stone Age" peoples are on the average probably more intelligent, not less intelligent, than industrialized peoples. Paradoxical as it may sound, . . . white immigrants to Australia do not deserve the credit usually accorded to them for building a literate industrialized society with the other virtues mentioned above. In addition, peoples who until recently were technologically primitive—such as Aboriginal Australians and New Guineans—routinely master industrial technologies when given opportunities to do so.

An enormous effort by cognitive psychologists has gone into the search for differences in IQ between peoples of different geographic origins now living in the same country. In particular, numerous white American psychologists have been trying for decades to demonstrate that black Americans of African origins are innately less intelligent than white

Americans of European origins. However, as is well known, the peoples compared differ greatly in their social environment and educational opportunities. This fact creates double difficulties for efforts to test the hypothesis that intellectual differences underlie technological differences. First, even our cognitive abilities as adults are heavily influenced by the social environment that we experienced during childhood, making it hard to discern any influence of preexisting genetic differences. Second, tests of cognitive ability (like IQ tests) tend to measure cultural learning and not pure innate intelligence, whatever that is. Because of those undoubted effects of childhood environment and learned knowledge on IQ test results, the psychologists' efforts to date have not succeeded in convincingly establishing the postulated genetic deficiency in IQs of nonwhite peoples.

My perspective on this controversy comes from thirty-three years of working with New Guineans in their own intact societies. From the very beginning of my work with New Guineans, they impressed me as being on the average more intelligent, more alert, more expressive, and more interested in things and people around them than the average European or American is. At some tasks that one might reasonably suppose to reflect aspects of brain function, such as the ability to form a mental map of unfamiliar surroundings, they appear considerably more adept than Westerners. Of course, New Guineans tend to perform poorly at tasks that Westerners have been trained to perform since childhood and that New Guineans have not. Hence when unschooled New Guineans from remote villages visit towns, they look stupid to Westerners. Conversely, I am constantly aware of how stupid I look to New Guineans when I'm with them in the jungle, displaying my incompetence at simple tasks (such as following a jungle trail or erecting a shelter) at which New Guineans have been trained since childhood and I have not.

It's easy to recognize two reasons why my impression that New Guineans are smarter than Westerners may be correct. First, Europeans have for thousands of years been living in densely populated societies with central governments, police, and judiciaries. In those societies, infectious epidemic diseases of dense populations (such as smallpox) were historically the major cause of death, while murders were relatively uncommon and a state of war was the exception

rather than the rule. Most Europeans who escaped fatal infections also escaped other potential causes of death and proceeded to pass on their genes. Today, most live-born Western infants survive fatal infections as well and reproduce themselves, regardless of their intelligence and the genes they bear. In contrast, New Guineans have been living in societies where human numbers were too low for epidemic diseases of dense populations to evolve. Instead, traditional New Guineans suffered high mortality from murder, chronic tribal warfare, accidents, and problems in procuring food.

Intelligent people are likelier than less intelligent ones to escape those causes of high mortality in traditional New Guinea societies. However, the differential mortality from epidemic diseases in traditional European societies had little to do with intelligence, and instead involved genetic resistance dependent on details of body chemistry. For example, people with blood group B or O have a greater resistance to smallpox than do people with blood group A. That is, natural selection promoting genes for intelligence has probably been far more ruthless in New Guinea than in more densely populated, politically complex societies, where natural selection for body chemistry was instead more potent.

Besides this genetic reason, there is also a second reason why New Guineans may have come to be smarter than Westerners. Modern European and American children spend much of their time being passively entertained by television, radio, and movies. In the average American household, the TV set is on for seven hours per day. In contrast, traditional New Guinea children have virtually no such opportunities for passive entertainment and instead spend almost all of their waking hours actively doing something, such as talking or playing with other children or adults. Almost all studies of child development emphasize the role of childhood stimulation and activity in promoting mental development, and stress the irreversible mental stunting associated with reduced childhood stimulation. This effect surely contributes a non-genetic component to the superior average mental function displayed by New Guineans.

That is, in mental ability New Guineans are probably genetically superior to Westerners, and they surely are superior in escaping the devastating developmental disadvantages under which most children in industrialized societies now grow up. Certainly, there is no hint at all of any intellectual disadvantage of New Guineans that could serve to answer Yali's question. The same two genetic and childhood developmental factors are likely to distinguish not only New Guineans from Westerners, but also hunter-gatherers and other members of technologically primitive societies from members of technologically advanced societies in general. Thus, the usual racist assumption has to be turned on its head. Why is it that Europeans, despite their likely genetic disadvantage and (in modern times) their undoubted developmental disadvantage, ended up with much more of the cargo? Why did New Guineans wind up technologically primitive, despite what I believe to be their superior intelligence?

A genetic explanation isn't the only possible answer to Yali's question. Another one, popular with inhabitants of northern Europe, invokes the supposed stimulatory effects of their homeland's cold climate and the inhibitory effects of hot, humid, tropical climates on human creativity and energy. Perhaps the seasonally variable climate at high latitudes poses more diverse challenges than does a seasonally constant tropical climate. Perhaps cold climates require one to be more technologically inventive to survive, because one must build a warm home and make warm clothing, whereas one can survive in the tropics with simpler housing and no clothing. Or the argument can be reversed to reach the same conclusion: the long winters at high latitudes leave people with much time in which to sit indoors and invent.

Although formerly popular, this type of explanation, too, fails to survive scrutiny. As we shall see, the peoples of northern Europe contributed nothing of fundamental importance to Eurasian civilization until the last thousand years; they simply had the good luck to live at a geographic location where they were likely to receive advances (such as agriculture, wheels, writing, and metallurgy) developed in warmer parts of Eurasia. In the New World the cold regions at high latitude were even more of a human backwater. The sole Native American societies to develop writing arose in Mexico south of the Tropic of Cancer; the oldest New World pottery comes from near the equator in tropical South America; and the New World society generally considered the most advanced in art, astronomy, and other respects was

the Classic Maya society of the tropical Yucatan and Guatemala in the first millennium A.D.

Still a third type of answer to Yali invokes the supposed importance of lowland river valleys in dry climates, where highly productive agriculture depended on large-scale irrigation systems that in turn required centralized bureaucracies. This explanation was suggested by the undoubted fact that the earliest known empires and writing systems arose in the Tigris and Euphrates Valleys of the Fertile Crescent and in the Nile Valley of Egypt. Water control systems also appear to have been associated with centralized political organization in some other areas of the world, including the Indus Valley of the Indian subcontinent, the Yellow and Yangtze Valleys of China, the Maya lowlands of Mesoamerica, and the coastal desert of Peru.

However, detailed archaeological studies have shown that complex irrigation systems did not *accompany* the rise of centralized bureaucracies but *followed* after a considerable lag. That is, political centralization arose for some other reason and then permitted construction of complex irrigation systems. None of the crucial developments preceding political centralization in those same parts of the world were associated with river valleys or with complex irrigation systems. For example, in the Fertile Crescent food production and village life originated in hills and mountains, not in lowland river valleys. The Nile Valley remained a cultural backwater for about 3,000 years after village food production began to flourish in the hills of the Fertile Crescent. River valleys of the southwestern United States eventually came to support irrigation agriculture and complex societies, but only after many of the developments on which those societies rested had been imported from Mexico. The river valleys of southeastern Australia remained occupied by tribal societies without agriculture.

Yet another type of explanation lists the immediate factors that enabled Europeans to kill or conquer other peoples—especially European guns, infectious diseases, steel tools, and manufactured products. Such an explanation is on the right track, as those factors demonstrably *were* directly responsible for European conquests. However, this hypothesis is incomplete, because it still offers only a proximate (first-stage) explanation identifying immediate causes. It invites a search for ultimate causes: why were Europeans, rather than Africans or Native Americans, the ones to end up with guns, the nastiest germs, and steel?

While some progress has been made in identifying those ultimate causes in the case of Europe's conquest of the New World, Africa remains a big puzzle. Africa is the continent where protohumans evolved for the longest time, where anatomically modern humans may also have arisen, and where native diseases like malaria and yellow fever killed European explorers. If a long head start counts for anything, why didn't guns and steel arise first in Africa, permitting Africans and their germs to conquer Europe? And what accounts for the failure of Aboriginal Australians to pass beyond the stage of hunter-gatherers with stone tools?

Questions that emerge from worldwide comparisons of human societies formerly attracted much attention from historians and geographers. The best-known modern example of such an effort was Arnold Toynbee's twelve-volume *Study of History*. Toynbee was especially interested in the internal dynamics of twenty-three advanced civilizations, of which twenty-two were literate and nineteen were Eurasian. He was less interested in prehistory and in simpler, nonliterate societies. Yet the roots of inequality in the modern world lie far back in prehistory. Hence Toynbee did not pose Yali's question, nor did he come to grips with what I see as history's broadest pattern. Other available books on world history similarly tend to focus on advanced literate Eurasian civilizations of the last 5,000 years; they have a very brief treatment of pre-Columbian Native American civilizations, and an even briefer discussion of the rest of the world except for its recent interactions with Eurasian civilizations. Since Toynbee's attempt, worldwide syntheses of historical causation have fallen into disfavor among most historians, as posing an apparently intractable problem.

Specialists from several disciplines have provided global syntheses of their subjects. Especially useful contributions have been made by ecological geographers, cultural anthropologists, biologists studying plant and animal domestication, and scholars concerned with the impact of infectious diseases on history. These studies have called attention to parts of the puzzle, but they provide only pieces of the needed broad synthesis that has been missing.

Thus, there is no generally accepted answer to Yali's question. On the one hand, the proximate explanations are clear: some peoples developed guns, germs, steel, and other factors conferring political and economic power before others did; and some peoples never developed these power factors at all. On the other hand, the ultimate explanations—for example, why bronze tools appeared early in parts of Eurasia, late and only locally in the New World, and never in Aboriginal Australia—remain unclear.

Our present lack of such ultimate explanations leaves a big intellectual gap, since the broadest pattern of history thus remains unexplained. Much more serious, though, is the moral gap left unfilled. It is perfectly obvious to everyone, whether an overt racist or not, that different peoples have fared differently in history. The modern United States is a European-molded society, occupying lands conquered from Native Americans and incorporating the descendants of millions of sub-Saharan black Africans brought to America as slaves. Modern Europe is not a society molded by sub-Saharan black Africans who brought millions of Native Americans as slaves.

These results are completely lopsided: it was not the case that 51 percent of the Americas, Australia, and Africa was conquered by Europeans, while 49 percent of Europe was conquered by Native Americans, Aboriginal Australians, or Africans. The whole modern world has been shaped by lopsided outcomes. Hence they must have inexorable explanations, ones more basic than mere details concerning who happened to win some battle or develop some invention on one occasion a few thousand years ago.

It *seems* logical to suppose that history's pattern reflects innate differences among people themselves. Of course, we're taught that it's not polite to say so in public. We read of technical studies claiming to demonstrate inborn differences, and we also read rebuttals claiming that those studies suffer from technical flaws. We see in our daily lives that some of the conquered peoples continue to form an underclass, centuries after the conquests or slave imports took place. We're told that this too is to be attributed not to any biological shortcomings but to social disadvantages and limited opportunities.

Nevertheless, we have to wonder. We keep seeing all those glaring, persistent differences in peoples' status. We're assured that the seemingly transparent biological explanation for the world's inequalities as of A.D. 1500 is wrong, but we're not told what the correct explanation is. Until we have some convincing, detailed, agreed-upon explanation for the broad pattern of history, most people will continue to suspect that the racist biological explanation is correct after all. . . .

Yali's question went to the heart of the current human condition, and of post-Pleistocene human history. . . . How shall we answer Yali?

I would say to Yali: the striking differences between the long-term histories of peoples of the different continents have been due not to innate differences in the peoples themselves but to differences in their environments. I expect that if the populations of Aboriginal Australia and Eurasia could have been interchanged during the Late Pleistocene, the original Aboriginal Australians would now be the ones occupying most of the Americas and Australia, as well as Eurasia, while the original Aboriginal Eurasians would be the ones now reduced to downtrodden population fragments in Australia. One might at first be inclined to dismiss this assertion as meaningless, because the experiment is imaginary and my claim about its outcome cannot be verified. But historians are nevertheless able to evaluate related hypotheses by retrospective tests. For instance, one can examine what did happen when European farmers were transplanted to Greenland or the U.S. Great Plains, and when farmers stemming ultimately from China emigrated to the Chatham Islands, the rain forests of Borneo, or the volcanic soils of Java or Hawaii. These tests confirm that the same ancestral peoples either ended up extinct, or returned to living as hunter-gatherers, or went on to build complex states, depending on their environments. Similarly, Aboriginal Australian hunter-gatherers, variously transplanted to Flinders Island, Tasmania, or southeastern Australia, ended up extinct, or as hunter-gatherers with the modern world's simplest technology, or as canal builders intensively managing a productive fishery, depending on their environments.

Of course, the continents differ in innumerable environmental features affecting trajectories of human societies. But a mere laundry list of every possible difference does not constitute an answer to Yali's question. Just four sets of differences appear to me to be the most important ones.

The first set consists of continental differences in the wild plant and animal species available as starting materials for domestication. That's because food production was critical for the accumulation of food surpluses that could feed non-food-producing specialists, and for the buildup of large populations enjoying a military advantage through mere numbers even before they had developed any technological or political advantage. For both of those reasons, all developments of economically complex, socially stratified, politically centralized societies beyond the level of small nascent chiefdoms were based on food production.

But most wild animal and plant species have proved unsuitable for domestication: food production has been based on relatively few species of livestock and crops. It turns out that the number of wild candidate species for domestication varied greatly among the continents, because of differences in continental areas and also (in the case of big mammals) in Late Pleistocene extinctions. These extinctions were much more severe in Australia and the Americas than in Eurasia or Africa. As a result, Africa ended up biologically somewhat less well endowed than the much larger Eurasia, the Americas still less so, and Australia even less so, as did Yali's New Guinea (with one-seventieth of Eurasia's area and with all of its original big mammals extinct in the Late Pleistocene).

On each continent, animal and plant domestication was concentrated in a few especially favorable homelands accounting for only a small fraction of the continent's total area. In the case of technological innovations and political institutions as well, most societies acquire much more from other societies than they invent themselves. Thus, diffusion and migration within a continent contribute importantly to the development of its societies, which tend in the long run to share each other's developments (insofar as environments permit). . . . That is, societies initially lacking an advantage either acquire it from societies possessing it or (if they fail to do so) are replaced by those other societies.

Hence a second set of factors consists of those affecting rates of diffusion and migration, which differed greatly among continents. They were most rapid in Eurasia, because of its east-west major axis and its relatively modest ecological and geographical barriers. The reasoning is straightforward for movements of crops and livestock, which depend strongly on climate and hence on latitude. But similar reasoning also applies to the diffusion of technological innovations, insofar as they are best suited without modification to specific environments. Diffusion was slower in Africa and especially in the Americas, because of those continents' north-south major axes and geographic and ecological barriers. It was also difficult in traditional New Guinea, where rugged terrain and the long backbone of high mountains prevented any significant progress toward political and linguistic unification.

Related to these factors affecting diffusion *within* continents is a third set of factors influencing diffusion *between* continents, which may also help build up a local pool of domesticates and technology. Ease of intercontinental diffusion has varied, because some continents are more isolated than others. Within the last 6,000 years it has been easiest from Eurasia to sub-Saharan Africa, supplying most of Africa's species of livestock. But interhemispheric diffusion made no contribution to Native America's complex societies, isolated from Eurasia at low latitudes by broad oceans, and at high latitudes by geography and by a climate suitable just for hunting-gathering. To Aboriginal Australia, isolated from Eurasia by the water barriers of the Indonesian Archipelago, Eurasia's sole proven contribution was the dingo.

The fourth and last set of factors consists of continental differences in area or total population size. A larger area or population means more potential inventors, more competing societies, more innovations available to adopt—and more pressure to adopt and retain innovations—because societies failing to do so will tend to be eliminated by competing societies. That fate befell African pygmies and many other hunter-gatherer populations displaced by farmers. Conversely, it also befell the stubborn, conservative Greenland Norse farmers, replaced by Eskimo hunter-gatherers whose subsistence methods and technology were far superior to those of the Norse under Greenland conditions. Among the world's landmasses, area and the number of competing societies were largest for Eurasia, much smaller for Australia and New Guinea and especially for Tasmania. The Americas, despite their large aggregate area, were fragmented by geography and ecology and functioned effectively as several poorly connected smaller continents.

Those four sets of factors constitute big environmental differences that can be quantified objectively and that are not subject to dispute. While one can contest my subjective impression that New Guineans are on the average smarter than Eurasians, one cannot deny that New Guinea has a much smaller area and far fewer big animal species than Eurasia. But mention of these environmental differences invites among historians the label "geographic determinism," which raises hackles. The label seems to have unpleasant connotations, such as that human creativity counts for nothing, or that we humans are passive robots helplessly programmed by climate, fauna, and flora. Of course these fears are misplaced. Without human inventiveness, all of us today would still be cutting our meat with stone tools and eating it raw, like our ancestors of a million years ago. All human societies contain inventive people. It's just that some environments provide more starting materials, and more favorable conditions for utilizing inventions, than do other environments.

Questions for Thought

1. How do you think you would have responded to Yali's question before reading Diamond's article? Has your answer changed now that you have read the article?
2. Do you agree with Diamond's claim that "Stone Age" peoples are probably more intelligent than industrialized peoples? Why or why not?
3. What have you learned about the legacies of colonialism? What, if anything, do you think should be done to address these legacies?
4. Do you believe that Diamond has correctly answered Yali's question? Defend your answer.
5. What does Diamond say about the belief in "progress?" How do your own views about "progress" compare with and differ from the views of Diamond?
6. Which of Darwin's views do you think Diamond might reject? What would likely be his reasons for rejecting them?

What Is the Nature of Reality?

The Myth of the Cave   8

PLATO

Plato (427–347 B.C.E.) was born into a wealthy, aristocratic family in Athens. After Plato's father died when Plato was a child, Plato's mother followed Athenian tradition and married her closest kinsman. While many of the details of Plato's life are unknown, most scholars agree that Plato served in the Athenian military during the war with Sparta (most likely in the cavalry), that he never married, and that he was one of the close followers of the Greek philosopher Socrates. When Socrates was executed in 399, Plato traveled to Egypt and Syracuse before returning to Athens to found the Academy, a school of philosophy and scientific research that survived until the Roman emperor Justinian closed all pagan schools of philosophy in 529 C.E.

Like many members of his family, Plato was a critic of Athenian **democracy.** In one of his writings, the *Republic,* Plato argues that the ideal form of government is an **aristocracy** headed by a philosopher-king. However, in the same work, Plato diverges from Athenian custom by suggesting that women, as well as men, may serve as members of the ruling class of society.

In addition to the *Republic,* from which the following selection is excerpted, Plato wrote many other philosophical dialogues. The names of several of these are found in the introduction to the selection from the *Phaedo* (see Chapter 1). As in that dialogue, Socrates appears as the principal character in the following selection.

In this selection, Plato offers a succinct account of his views on the nature of reality and on the human condition. He begins by suggesting that we are born into a world of illusion, a world that he likens to a subterranean cave in which we are chained and forced to view shadows projected on its rear wall. Having seen nothing but these shadows during the course of our life, we naturally assume that they constitute reality. While Plato relies on the somewhat complicated mechanism of a low wall, carried objects, and a fire to account for the origin of the shadows on the rear wall of the cave, modern technology allows us a more concise metaphor. Plato is asking you to imagine that you have spent your entire life in a movie theater, chained to your seat so that you are able to see only the images projected on the screen in front of you. Wouldn't you, of necessity, assume that the images on the screen were real?

However, if you were able to break the chains and turn toward the light of the projector (the fire), you would be blinded by the intensity of what you now saw. The temptation would be to return immediately to your seat and to warn others about leaving theirs. But, if your eyes became accustomed to the fire or light, you would realize that what you are now seeing is the source of the projected shadows and that it is more real than what you saw before. And, if you gradually ascended out of the cave (or slowly found your way out of the theater), you would discover a world outside that differed radically from the world of the cave or theater. You would discover new objects with even greater reality. Finally, you would be able to look on the sun or the **Form** of the Good. This Form, as Plato says, is "the universal author of all things beautiful and right, . . . the origin of the source of light in the visible world, and the immediate source of reason and truth in the intelligible world."

As should be evident from this statement, Plato believes that there are two levels of reality. The first level, the level represented by the cave or theater, is the level of everyday existence, a level that we know through the evidence of our senses. The other level, the level outside the cave or theater, is the intelligible world, a world that cannot be discovered by the senses but must be ascertained through reason. As we saw in the selection from Plato in Chapter 1, the world of the senses is constantly changing, and the objects in it are shadowy copies of the realities found in the intelligible world. These latter realities, which Plato calls *Forms,* are invisible, eternal, unchanging, and fully real.

Questions for Reading

1. What does Plato's "Myth of the Cave" tell us about the human condition?
2. What do the prisoners in the cave believe about the nature of reality? What happens when a prisoner escapes from his or her chains?
3. How does the world outside the cave differ from the world within the cave?
4. What happens when someone reenters the cave? Why, according to Plato, must people be forced to reenter?
5. What does Plato mean by "the Form of the Good"? How does one gain knowledge of this Form?

Socrates: And now, let me give a parable to show how far our nature is enlightened or unenlightened. Imagine human beings living in an underground cave with an opening upward towards the light, which filters into the depths of the cave. These human beings have been here since birth, and their legs and necks have been chained so that they cannot move. They can only see what is directly in front of them, since they are prevented by the chains from turning their heads to either side. At a distance above and behind them is a blazing fire, and between the fire and the prisoners there is a raised path. And if you look closely, you will see a low wall built along the path, like the screen used by marionette players to conceal themselves from the audience while they show their puppets.

Glaucon: I see.

Socrates: And do you see men passing behind the wall carrying all sorts of objects, such as figures of animals and humans made of wood, stone, and various materials, which they are holding above the wall? Some of the men carrying these objects are talking, while others are silent.

Glaucon: You have shown me a strange image, and these are strange prisoners.

Socrates: They are similar to us. For, initially, how could they see anything but their own shadows, or the shadows of each other, which the fire projects on the wall of the cave in front of them?

Glaucon: That is true. How could they see anything but the shadows if they were never allowed to turn their heads?

Socrates: And wouldn't they also see only the shadows of the objects that are being carried by the men?

Glaucon: Obviously.

Socrates: And if these prisoners were able to talk to each other, would they not suppose that the words they used referred only to the shadows that they saw on the wall in front of them?

The selection from Plato is the editor's revised version of the translation found in The Dialogues of Plato, *translated by Benjamin Jowett, The Macmillan Company, 1892.*

Glaucon: Undoubtedly.

Socrates: And suppose further that the prison had an echo which came from the wall in front of them. When one of the men passing behind them spoke, would they not surely believe that the voice came from one of the shadows on this wall?

Glaucon: Without question.

Socrates: To them, the truth would be literally nothing but the shadows of themselves and of the objects being carried behind them.

Glaucon: That is certain.

Socrates: Now look again, and see what will naturally follow if the prisoners are suddenly released. . . . At first, when one of them is liberated and forced to stand up, to turn his neck, and to look and walk towards the light, he will suffer sharp pains. The glare will hurt his eyes, and he will be unable to see the objects that had been the cause of the shadows he had formerly seen. Suppose someone saying to him at this point that what he had formerly seen was an illusion, and that now he was approaching nearer to being, that now his eye was turned towards more real existence, that now he had a clearer vision. What would be his reply? And suppose further what would happen if someone pointed to the passing objects and asked him to name them. Would he not be confused? Would he not believe that the shadows which he formerly saw were truer than the objects now being shown to him?

Glaucon: Far truer.

Socrates: And if he were forced to look straight at the light, would not the pain in his eyes make him turn away from it? Would it not make him take refuge in those things that he could see? Would it not make him believe that what was now being presented to him was less clear than what he had previously seen?

Glaucon: Certainly.

Socrates: And suppose further that he were dragged reluctantly up the steep and rugged ascent, being finally forced into the presence of the sun itself. Would he not likely be pained and irritated? When he approached the light his eyes would be dazzled, and he would not be able to see anything at all of the realities outside the cave.

Glaucon: Not immediately.

Socrates: He would have to grow accustomed to the sights of the upper world. First he would be able to see the shadows best, next the reflections of men and other things in the water, and then the things

themselves. Afterwards he would be able to gaze upon the light of the moon, the stars, and the spangled heaven. Would it not be easier at first for him to look upon the sky and the stars by night than upon the sun or the light of the sun by day?

Glaucon: Certainly.

Socrates: Last of all he would be able to see the sun, not merely as it is reflected in the water, but in its true nature and in its own proper place.

Glaucon: Absolutely.

Socrates: He will then begin to conclude that it is the sun which causes the seasons and the years, which is the guardian of everything in the visible world, and which, in a certain way, is the cause of all the things that he and his fellows have formerly seen.

Glaucon: It is evident that he would first see the sun and then reason about it.

Socrates: And when he remembered his old habitation, and the wisdom of the cave and of his fellow-prisoners, do you not suppose that he would be happy about his change and pity those who were still prisoners?

Glaucon: Certainly, he would.

Socrates: And if they were in the habit of honoring those who could most quickly observe the passing shadows and decide which of them went before others, which came after, or which occurred simultaneously—being therefore best able to draw conclusions about the future—do you think that he would care for such honors or envy the possessors of them? Would he not say with Homer, "Better to be the poor servant of a poor master," and to endure anything, rather than think as they do and live after their manner?

Glaucon: Yes, I think that he would rather suffer anything than accept these false notions and live in this miserable manner.

Socrates: Indeed, imagine what it would be like for him to come suddenly out of the sun and to return to his old place in the cave. Would he not be certain to have his eyes full of darkness?

Glaucon: Most assuredly.

Socrates: And while his eyes were filled with darkness and his sight still weak (and the time needed to become re-accustomed to the cave might be very considerable), if there were a contest in which he had to compete in measuring the shadows with the prisoners who had never been out of the cave, would he not be ridiculous? Men would say of him that his ascent and descent had destroyed his eyesight, and thus that it was better not even to think of ascending. And if they caught anyone trying to free another and lead him up to the light, they would put the offender to death.

Glaucon: Without question.

Socrates: You may append this entire allegory, dear Glaucon, to what I have said before. The prisonhouse or cave is the world of sight; the light of the fire within the cave is the sun. And you will not misapprehend me if you interpret the journey upwards to be the ascent of the soul into the intelligible world, which, at your request, I have described. Only the god knows whether or not my description is accurate.

But, whether true or false, my opinion is that in the world of knowledge the Form of the Good appears last of all, and is seen only with an effort. When seen, however, it can only lead us to the **conclusion** that it is the universal author of all things beautiful and right, that it is the origin of the source of light in the visible world, and the immediate source of reason and truth in the intelligible world. Without having seen the Form of the Good and having fixed his eye upon it, one will not be able to act wisely either in public affairs or in private life.

Glaucon: I agree, as far as I am able to understand you.

Questions for Thought

1. Do you think Plato's myth is an accurate metaphor for everyday existence? Why or why not?
2. Can you think of other philosophies or religious views that suggest our everyday experience does not represent genuine reality? If so, how do these other views compare with or differ from the position of Plato?
3. Can you think of events in your own life that would be analogous to one of the prisoners escaping from his or her chains?
4. Do you think that the Form of the Good, or something like it, exists? Why or why not?
5. Would you agree with Plato's claim that there are two levels of reality? If so, how would you describe the differences between the two levels? If not, why not?
6. If you were to write a myth about the nature of reality, what setting would you use? How would your myth end?

9   The Way of the Universe

LAO-TZU

Lao-tzu (ca. 551–479 B.C.E.) is traditionally identified as the author of the *Tao Tê Ching* and thus as the founder of **Taoism.** Although there is very little in the way of historical knowledge about the life of Lao-tzu, frequently repeated legends suggest that he was the keeper of the royal archives during the time when the Chou dynasty was disintegrating. Dissatisfied with his job and court life, Lao-tzu reportedly left his post for the life of a mountain hermit. Before heading off into anonymity, he was stopped by the guard at a mountain pass and coerced into writing down his views on the nature of the universe, human existence, and government. The resulting text was the *Tao Tê Ching*, from which the following excerpts are taken.

The principal concept in the *Tao Tê Ching* is the **Tao,** a term that is often translated as "the Way." However, as the following excerpts clearly show, the Tao, which is the ultimate source of all life, cannot be adequately described or even named. Its mystery can be approached only through metaphor and **paradox.** Metaphorically, it is "the door of all spiritual awareness," the "mother of the universe." Elsewhere in the *Tao Tê Ching,* it is likened to water, which is ever flowing, ever changing. Paradoxically, it is "formless form," "imageless image." But one message in the *Tao Tê Ching* does come across clearly: Human wisdom and happiness are attainable only if one harmonizes one's life with the movement of the Tao. Living in harmony with the Tao is expressed by the term *wu wei,* a term that is often translated as "actionless activity." Thus, in following the Tao, the sage or wise person "gets things done by doing nothing, teaches things by saying nothing."

Questions for Reading

1. What does the author mean by "the Tao"?
2. What are some metaphors that are used to represent the Tao? What are some of the paradoxes that are used to represent it?
3. How, according to the author, can one gain an awareness of the Tao?
4. How is the sage described in this selection?
5. What does the author mean by "heaven"?

I

The Tao that can be spoken of is not the eternal Tao;
The name that can be named is not the eternal
   Name.
The Nameless is the source of heaven and earth;
The namable gives birth to individual things.

Therefore it is said:

"He who is without desire gains insight into the inner workings of life, but he who is bound by desire sees only its outer manifestations."

The inner workings of life and its outer manifestations spring from the same source, but they differ in name. We can only say of this common source that it is a mystery. Indeed, it is the mystery of mysteries, the door of all spiritual awareness.

2

To recognize beauty, one must be aware of ugliness;
To recognize goodness, one must be aware of
   badness.
One cannot have being without nonbeing,
The easy without the difficult,
The long without the short,
Above without below,
Before without after.

Therefore the sage gets things done by doing nothing, teaches things by saying nothing. When things happen, he resists them not. Creating without possessing, acting without appropriating, the sage accomplishes much, but claims credit for nothing. Since he takes credit for nothing, he has nothing to lose.

. . . .

The selection from the Tao Tê Ching *is the editor's revised version of the translation by Paul Carus, Open Court Publishing Company, 1913.*

4

The Tao appears empty, but its fullness cannot be
    exhausted; Like a bottomless bowl, it is the
    grandfather of everything that is.
The Tao blunts all sharpness, loosens all knots;
It dims all radiance, settles all dust.[1]
Yet, how calm it seems to remain.
I know not whose son it is.
Apparently it existed even before God.

. . . .

14

The Tao is not visible;
thus when we look for it, we do not see it.
The Tao makes no sound;
thus when we listen for it, we do not hear it.
The Tao is not tangible;
thus when we grope for it, we do not grasp it.

Invisible, soundless, intangible—these three things
cannot be differentiated. Combined and conceived as
a unity, they remain obscure. Thus the Tao remains
forever unnamable; again and again it returns to nothingness.

The Tao is called the formless form, the imageless
    image.
It is called that which transcends comprehension.
Standing in front of it, you will not discover its be-
    ginning.
Standing behind it, you will not discover its end.
But standing within it, you will master the moment.
By mastering the moment, you will understand the
    origin of the past.

. . . .

25

There is something wondrous and complete.
It existed before Heaven and Earth.
How calm it is! How mysterious!
It stands alone, and changes not;
It moves around, and suffers not;
It is the mother of the universe.
I do not know its name,
But I refer to it as Tao.
Forced to give it a name,
I call it the great.

To be great is to depart,
To depart is to pass beyond,
To pass beyond is to return to the source.

The saying goes: "The Tao is great, heaven is great,
earth is great, and royalty is great." Man's standard is
the earth. The earth's standard is heaven. Heaven's
standard is the Tao. The Tao has no standard beyond
itself.

. . . .

32

The eternal Tao is unnamable.
In its simplest aspect, it seems insignificant,
but the whole world cannot subdue it.
If princes and kings could capture it,
everything would pay homage to them.
Heaven and earth would unite in dripping sweet dew,
and the people would naturally follow righteousness.

As soon as the Tao creates order,
it becomes namable.
Whenever the namable acquires existence,
one learns when to stop.

By learning when to stop one avoids danger.
The Tao flows through the world
like a stream flows into a river,
like a river flows into the sea.

. . . .

34

How all-pervading is the Tao!
It flows to the left and to the right.
All things depend on the Tao for their life,
and it refuses them not.
When it accomplishes something,
it does not take credit for it.
It lovingly nourishes all things
without trying to possess them.
Ever desireless,
it can be classed with the small.
Yet, all things return home to it,
and it plays not the lord.
Thus it can be classed with the great.
Because the sage does not claim greatness,
he, too, may become great.

. . . .

40

Returning unto itself is the Tao's course,
Not resisting is the Tao's force.
Heaven, Earth and particular things come from be-
  ing,
But being comes from non-being.

. . . .

51

The Tao gives life to all creatures.
Virtue feeds them.
Matter forms them.
The forces of nature complete them.
Therefore all things esteem the Tao and honor
  virtue.

Esteeming the Tao and honoring virtue are not
  commanded;
They spontaneously flow from the nature of
  things.
The Tao gives life to all creatures.
Virtue feeds them.
They are raised, nurtured, completed,
They are matured, reared, protected.
Giving life without owning,
Creating without possessing,
Raising without controlling,
This is profound Virtue.

NOTE

1. In Chinese thinking, dust often symbolizes the
mental pollution of desire, fear, attachment, and aggression.—ED.

Questions for Thought

1. What are the essential differences between the Tao and Plato's "Form of the Good"? Can
   you think of any similarities between the two concepts?
2. In section 4, it is said that the Tao "existed even before God." Does it make sense to say
   that something existed before God? Why or why not?
3. Why do you think the author considers it important to harmonize one's life with the
   movement of the Tao? Do you think your life is in harmony with the Tao?
4. What does the author mean by saying that the sage "gets things done by doing nothing,
   teaches things by saying nothing"? Can you think of examples that might illustrate these
   claims?
5. Why, according to the author, might it be pointless (or even counterproductive) to ask
   and/or to answer these questions?

10   The Nature of Reality

WANG CHUNG

Wang Chung (ca. 27–97 C.E.) studied at the Imperial College at Loyang, where he was reportedly an avid reader. After completing his studies, he lived a life of relative poverty and obscurity as a teacher and minor government official. However, he did write several books on a wide variety of topics: ethics, macrobiotics, **metaphysics,** and government. Only his *Lun-Hêng,* from which the following selection was taken, has survived. His translator, Alfred Forke, refers to Wang Chung as a heterodox philosopher, a materialist and eclectic, "whose views do not agree with the current ideas of either Confucianists or Taoists."

Wang Chung's **materialism** is evident in the following selection, which is excerpted from chapters titled "Spontaneity" and "The Nature of Things." Throughout this selection, it is claimed that everything in the universe is produced from the spontaneous mixture of "the fluids of Heaven and Earth." The materialistic nature of these fluids is demonstrated by the example used to explain how the creative process works—the mixture of male and female fluids to produce a child. Another aspect of Wang's materialism that is emphasized in this selection is his rejection of purpose in the workings of nature. In contrast to the traditional Chinese claim that everything happens because of the design of Heaven (or according to God's will, to use a more Western phrasing), Wang claims that the spontaneous movement of nature is devoid of intention. As he bluntly says, "Heaven does not act and thus it does not speak." Rather, borrowing the Taoist concept of *wu wei,* Wang says that the way of nature is the way of "inactive action," or actionless activity. The final aspect of Wang's materialism that comes across in this selection is his identification of human actions with the processes of nature. Virtue or righteousness is determined not by good intentions but by the amount of heavenly fluid one possesses. And the way of the wise man, like the way of nature, is the way of inactive action, the way of spontaneous creation.

Questions for Reading

1. Of what, according to Wang, are all things composed? How does he explain change?
2. What are some of the examples that he uses to illustrate his views?
3. What does Wang mean by "spontaneous action"? Why does he believe that natural changes are produced spontaneously?
4. How does Wang explain righteousness or virtue? How does he explain criminal behavior?
5. How is the concept of Heaven used in this selection?

BY THE FUSION OF THE FLUIDS OF HEAVEN AND Earth all things of the world are produced spontaneously, just as by the mixture of the fluids of husband and wife children are born spontaneously. Among the things thus produced, creatures with blood in their veins are sensitive of hunger and cold. Seeing that grain can be eaten, they use it as food, and discovering that silk and hemp can be worn, they take it as raiment. Some people are of the opinion that Heaven produces grain for the purpose of

From Lun-Hêng: The Philosophical Essays of Wang Chung, *translated by Alfred Forke, Paragon Book Gallery, 1962.*

feeding mankind, and silk and hemp to cloth them. That would be tantamount to making Heaven the farmer of man or his mulberry girl;[1] it would not be in accordance with spontaneity. Therefore this opinion is very questionable and unacceptable.

Reasoning on Taoist principles we find that Heaven emits its fluid everywhere. Among the many things of this world grain dispels hunger, and silk and hemp protect from cold. For that reason man eats grain, and wears silk and hemp. That Heaven does not produce grain, silk, and hemp purposely, in order to feed and cloth mankind, follows from the fact that by calamitous changes it does not intend to reprove man. Things are produced spontaneously, and man wears and eats them; the fluid changes spontaneously, and man is frightened by it, for the usual theory is disheartening. Where would be spontaneity, if the heavenly signs were intentional, and where inaction?[2]

Why must we assume that Heaven acts spontaneously? Because it has neither mouth nor eyes. Activity is connected with the mouth and the eyes: the mouth wishes to eat, and the eyes to see. These desires within manifest themselves without. That the mouth and the eyes are craving for something, which is considered an advantage, is due to those desires. Now, provided that the mouth and the eyes do not affect things, there is nothing which they might long for; why should there be activity then?

How do we know that Heaven possesses neither mouth nor eyes? From Earth. The body of the Earth is formed of earth, and earth has neither mouth nor eyes. Heaven and Earth are like husband and wife. Since the body of the Earth is not provided with a mouth or eyes, we know that Heaven has no mouth or eyes either. Supposing that Heaven has a body, then it must be like that of the Earth, and should it be air only, this air would be like clouds and fog. How can a cloudy or nebular **substance** have a mouth or an eye?

Someone might argue that every movement is originally inaction. There is desire provoking the movement, and, as soon as there is motion, there is action. The movements of Heaven are similar to those of man, how could they be inactive? I reply that, when Heaven moves, it emits its fluid. Its body moves, the fluid comes forth, and things are produced. When man moves his fluid, his body moves, his fluid then comes forth, and a child is produced. Man emitting his fluid does not intend to beget a child, yet the fluid being emitted, the child is born of itself. When Heaven is moving, it does not desire to produce things thereby, but things are produced of their own accord. That is spontaneity. Letting out its fluid it does not desire to create things, but things are created of themselves. That is inaction.

But how is the fluid of Heaven, which we credit with spontaneity and inaction? It is placid, tranquil, desireless, inactive, and unbusied. . . . In the State of Sung a man carved a mulberry-leaf of wood, and it took him three years to complete it. Confucius said, "If the Earth required three years to complete one leaf, few plants would have leaves." According to this dictum of Confucius the leaves of plants grow spontaneously, and for that reason they can grow simultaneously. If Heaven made them, their growth would be as much delayed as the carving of the mulberry-leaf by the man of the Sung State.

Let us look at the hair and feathers of animals and birds, and their various colors. Can they all have been made? If so, animals and birds would never be quite finished. In spring we see the plants growing, and in autumn we see them full-grown. Can Heaven and Earth have done this, or do things grow spontaneously? If we may say that Heaven and Earth have done it, they must have used hands for the purpose. Do Heaven and Earth possess many thousand or many ten thousand hands to produce thousands and ten thousands of things at the same time?

The things between Heaven and Earth are like a child in his mother's womb. After ten months pregnancy the mother gives birth to the child. Are his nose, his mouth, his ears, his hair, his eyes, his skin with down, the arteries, the fat, the bones, the joints, the nails, and the teeth grown of themselves in the womb, or has the mother made them?

Why is a dummy never called a man? Because it has a nose, a mouth, ears, and eyes, but not a spontaneous nature. Wu Ti was very fond of his consort Wang. When she had died, he pondered whether he could not see her figure again. The Taoists made an artificial figure of the lady.[3] When it was ready, it passed through the palace gate. Wu Ti, greatly alarmed, rose to meet her, but, all of a sudden, she was not seen any more. Since it was not a real, spontaneous being, but a semblance, artificially made by jugglers, it became diffuse at first sight, dispersed, and vanished. Everything that has been made does not last long, like the image of the empress, which appeared only for a short while.

The Taoist school argues on spontaneity, but it does not know how to substantiate its cause by evidence. Therefore their theory of spontaneity has not yet found credence. However, in spite of spontaneity there may be activity for a while in support of it. Plowing, tilling, weeding, and sowing in spring are human actions. But as soon as the grain has entered the soil, it begins growing by day and night. Man can do nothing for it, or if he does, he spoils the thing.

A man of Sung was sorry that his sprouts were not high enough; therefore he pulled them out. But, on the following day, they were dry, and died. He who wishes to do what is spontaneous, is on a par with this man of Sung.

The following question may be raised: "Man is born from Heaven and Earth. Since Heaven and Earth are inactive, man, who has received the fluid of Heaven, ought to be inactive likewise. Why does he act nevertheless?"

For the following reason. A man with the highest, purest, and fullest virtue has been endowed with a large quantity of the heavenly fluid; therefore he can follow the example of Heaven, and be spontaneous and inactive like it. He who has received but a small quota of the fluid, does not live in accordance with righteousness and virtue, and does not resemble Heaven and Earth. Hence he is called unlike, which means that he does not resemble Heaven and Earth. Not resembling Heaven and Earth, he cannot be accounted a wise man or a sage. Therefore he is active.

Heaven and Earth are the furnace, and the creating is the melting process. How can all be wise, since the fluid of which they are formed is not the same? Huang and Lao were truly wise. Huang is Huang Ti and Lao is Lao-tzu. Huang and Lao's conduct was such, that their bodies were in a state of quietude and indifference. Their government consisted in inaction. They took care of their persons, and behaved with reverence, hence *Yin* and *Yang* were in harmony. They did not long for action, and things were produced of themselves; they did not think of creating anything, and things were completed spontaneously. . . .

The principle of Heaven is inaction. Accordingly in spring it does not do the germinating, in summer the growing, in autumn the ripening, or in winter the hiding of the seeds. When the *Yang* fluid comes forth spontaneously, plants will germinate and grow of themselves, and, when the *Yin* fluid rises, they ripen and disappear of their own accord.

When we irrigate garden land with water drawn from wells or drained from ponds, plants germinate and grow also, but, when showers of rain come down, the stalks, leaves, and roots are all abundantly soaked. Natural moisture is much more copious than artificial irrigation from wells and ponds. Thus inactive action brings the greatest results. By not seeking it, merit is acquired, and by not affecting it, fame is obtained. Rain-showers, merit, and fame are something great, yet Heaven and Earth do not work for them. When the fluid harmonizes, rain gathers spontaneously. . . .

Heaven expands above, and Earth below. When the fluid from below rises, and the fluid on high descends, all things are created in the middle. While they are growing, it is not necessary that Heaven should still care for them, just as the father does not know the embryo, after it is in the mother's womb. Things grow spontaneously, and the child is formed of itself. Heaven and Earth, and father and mother, can take no further cognizance of it. But after birth, the way of man is instruction and teaching, the way of Heaven, inaction and yielding to nature. Therefore Heaven allows the fish to swim in the rivers, and the wild beasts to roam in the mountains, following their natural propensities. It does not drive the fish up the hills, or the wild beasts into the water. Why? Because that would be an outrage upon their nature, and a complete disregard of what suits them. The people resemble fish and beasts. High virtue governs them as easily, as one fries small fish, and as Heaven and Earth would act. . . .

Those who believe in reprimands, refer to human ways as a proof. Among men a sovereign reprimands his minister, and high Heaven reprimands the sovereign. It does so by means of calamitous events, they say. However, among men it also happens that the minister remonstrates with his sovereign. When Heaven reprimands an emperor by visiting him with calamities, and the latter wishes at the same time to remonstrate with high Heaven, how can he do it? If they say that Heaven's virtue is so perfect, that man cannot remonstrate with it, then Heaven possessed of such virtue, ought likewise to keep quiet, and ought not to reprimand. When the sovereign of Wan Shih did wrong, the latter did not say a word, but at table he did not eat, which showed his perfection.

An excellent man can remain silent, and august Heaven with his sublime virtue should reprimand? Heaven does not act, therefore it does not speak. The disasters, which so frequently occur, are the work of the spontaneous fluid.

Heaven and Earth cannot act, nor do they possess any knowledge. When there is a cold in the stomach, it aches. This is not caused by man, but the spontaneous working of the fluid. The space between Heaven and Earth is like that between the back and the stomach.[4]

If Heaven is regarded as the author of every calamity, are all abnormalities, great and small, complicated and simple, caused by Heaven also? A cow may give birth to a horse, and on a cherry-tree a plum may grow. Does, according to the theory under discussion, the spirit of Heaven enter the belly of the cow to create the horse, or stick a plum upon a cherry-tree? . . .

Lao[5] said, "The Master said, 'Having no official employment, I acquired many arts,' and he said, 'When I was young, my condition was low, and therefore I acquired my ability in many things, but they were mean matters.'" What is low in people, such as ability and skillfulness, is not practiced by the great ones. How could Heaven, which is so majestic and sublime, choose to bring about catastrophes with a view to reprimanding people?

Moreover, auspicious and inauspicious events are like the flushed color appearing on the face. Man cannot produce it, the color comes out of itself. Heaven and Earth are like the human body, the transformation of their fluid, like the flushed color. How can Heaven and Earth cause the sudden change of their fluid, since man cannot produce the flushed color? The change of the fluid is spontaneous, it appears of itself, as the color comes out of itself. . . .

The literati declare that Heaven and Earth produce man on purpose. This assertion is preposterous, for, when Heaven and Earth mix up their fluids, man is born as a matter of course unintentionally. In just the same manner a child is produced spontaneously, when the essences of husband and wife are harmoniously blended. At the time of such an intercourse, the couple does not intend to beget a child. Their passionate love being roused, they unite, and out of this union a child is born. From the fact that husband and wife do not purposely beget a child one may infer that Heaven and Earth do not produce man on purpose either.

However, man is produced by Heaven and Earth just as fish in a pond, or lice on man. They grow in response to a peculiar force, each species reproducing itself. This holds good for all the things which come into being between Heaven and Earth.

NOTES

1. Who feeds the silkworms.
2. Inaction does not mean motionlessness, but spontaneous action without any aim or purpose. It is more or less mechanical, and not inspired by a conscious spirit.
3. The apparition of the lady was evoked by the court magician Shao Wêng in 121 B.C.E.
4. And it is likewise filled with the fluid.
5. One of Confucius' disciples, not Lao-tzu.

Questions for Thought

1. How does Wang's view on the nature of things compare with or differ from the view found in the *Tao Tê Ching*? Which of these two views is closer to your beliefs about the nature of reality?
2. Do you agree that spontaneity characterizes the way of the universe? Why or why not?
3. What might be some of the consequences of what Wang says about the origin of righteousness or virtue? Do you agree with his analysis of righteousness? Do you think Plato would agree?
4. Does the concept of "inactive action" make sense to you? How does Wang try to explain it?
5. Do you consider yourself to be a spontaneous person? If not, would you like to be? Why or why not?

11   On the Nature of Things

LUCRETIUS

Lucretius (ca. 99–55 B.C.E.), whose full name is Titus Lucretius Carus, was an ancient Roman poet-philosopher. While there is little outside testimony concerning the life of Lucretius, scholars have surmised from his writings that he was from an aristocratic family, that he was well educated, and that he traveled at least as far as Sicily. An uncorroborated statement from St. Jerome, one of the early Church Fathers who was philosophically opposed to Lucretius' metaphysical position, claims that Lucretius was poisoned by a love potion that eventually drove him to suicide.

The only extant writing of Lucretius, *De Rerum Natura* (*On the Nature of Things*), consists of a long poem composed in Latin. Although the poem was probably unfinished, it still amounts to over 7,000 hexameter lines divided into six books. Lucretius claims that his work is merely a poetical statement of the philosophical views of the ancient Greek philosopher **Epicurus;** however, scholars believe that certain aspects of the poem, especially his attitude toward religion, diverged from the Epicurean position. At any rate, in being one of the first Western philosophers to write in Latin as opposed to Greek, Lucretius created his own vocabulary to express Epicurean views.

In the following selection from Book I of *On the Nature of Things,* Lucretius describes the universe from a naturalistic standpoint. He begins by arguing against the religious belief that things were created out of nothing by divine power. Noting that nature operates in an orderly and predictable manner, Lucretius claims that this is best explained if we recognize that everything in nature is produced by "fixed seeds" and not by separate acts of creation.

In obvious contrast to both Plato's **Forms** and Lao-tzu's **Tao**, Lucretius goes on to argue that these fixed seeds are bodily in nature. Indeed, he tells us that everything that exists is composed of tiny, invisible, solid particles that are in constant motion and are indestructible. (While the term *seeds* is used in the selection to name these particles, other ancient philosophers used the term *atom*.) These indestructible seeds or atoms, which are constantly moving through the void or space, are conjoined with each other by what Lucretius calls "mutual entanglement" to form the things that we see. Death or destruction results when these entangled seeds meet with a force strong enough to disentangle them. Of course, since the seeds themselves cannot be destroyed, they fly off through space until they become mutually entangled again, thereby becoming part of another visible object.

Lucretius goes on to draw two other philosophically interesting conclusions about the nature of the universe in this selection. First, he argues that since everything in the universe is composed of a combination of the void and the material seeds, there can be no other types of being in the universe. While he uses this **conclusion** here to suggest that time has no separate existence (time being simply the measure of bodily movement), it should be obvious, as he argues elsewhere, that this also rules out the existence of spiritual beings such as souls or God. Second, Lucretius argues that since there is nothing outside the universe that could possibly limit it, the universe must be limitless in all directions. This being the case, the universe has no center (or perhaps we could say that the center of the universe is wherever we are). As he says, "And it does not matter in which of its regions you take your stand. Invariably, in whatever position one is, one leaves the universe just as infinite as before in all directions."

Questions for Reading

1. Of what, according to Lucretius, are all things composed?
2. How does Lucretius explain change? Does he believe that there is anything in the universe that remains changeless?
3. What exactly does Lucretius mean by *void*? What reasons does he give for believing that void exists?
4. How does Lucretius view religion in this selection?
5. Why, according to Lucretius, must the universe be infinite in all directions?

BOOK I

I WILL DESCRIBE FOR YOU THE MOST HIGH SYSTEM of heaven and the gods, and open up the first beginnings of things, out of which nature gives birth, increase, and nourishment to all things, and into which nature likewise dissolves them back after their destruction. In explaining these things, we customarily call them "matter," "the begetting bodies of things," "the seeds of things" or "first bodies," because they are the first element from which all things come into being.

When human life lay foully prostrate upon earth, crushed down under the weight of religion, . . . a man of Greece[1] first ventured to lift up his mortal eyes and to confront religion face to face. Neither the story of gods or thunderbolts or heaven with threatening roar could quell him—they only inflamed the eager courage of his soul, filling him with desire to be the first to burst through the fast bars of nature's portals. Thus, the vivacity of his soul gained the day. He passed on far beyond the flaming walls of the world and traversed throughout the immeasurable universe in mind and spirit. From this journey, he returned a conqueror to tell us what can, and what cannot, come into being; in short, he returned to tell us on what principle each thing has its powers defined, its deepest boundary mark. Therefore religion is put under foot and trampled upon, and his victory brings us level with heaven. . . .

This terror of religion and darkness of mind must not be dispelled by the rays of the sun and glittering shafts of day. Rather, it must be dispelled by the aspect and the law of nature, the warp of whose design we shall begin to describe with this first principle, namely, that nothing is ever produced out of nothing by divine power. It is true that fear holds all mortals so in check, because they see many operations happening on earth and in heaven, the causes of which they can in no way understand. Because of this, they believe that these operations are done by divine power. However, when we see that nothing can be produced from nothing, we will then more correctly ascertain that which we are seeking, both the elements out of which every thing can be produced, and the manner in which all things occur without the hand of the gods.

If things came from nothing, any kind of thing could be born of any other thing, nothing would require matter or seed. Men for instance might rise out of the sea, the scaly race out of the earth, and birds might burst out of the sky. . . . Nor would the same fruits keep constant to trees, but would change; any tree might bear any fruit. For if there were not begetting bodies for each, how could things have a fixed unvarying mother? But in fact, since all things are produced from fixed seeds, each thing is born and goes forth into the borders of light out of that in which resides its matter and first bodies. For this reason all things cannot be gotten out of

This is the editor's revised version of the translation found in Lucretius, On the Nature of Things, *translated by H. A. J. Munro, Cambridge, 1864–1886.*

all things, because a distinct power resides in particular things. Moreover, why do we see the rose bloom in spring, corn in the summer, vines in autumn? Is this not because, when the fixed seeds of things have streamed together at the proper time, whatever is born discloses itself in its due season? . . . But if things came from nothing, they would rise up suddenly at uncertain periods and unsuitable times of year, inasmuch as there would be no first-beginnings to be kept from a begetting union by the unpropitious season. No, nor would time be required for the growth of things after the meeting of the seed, if they could increase out of nothing. Little babies would at once grow into men and trees in a moment would rise and spring out of the ground. But it is plain that none of these events ever come to pass, since all things grow step by step at a fixed time, as is natural, since they all grow from a fixed seed and in growing preserve their kind. So, you can be sure that all things increase in size and are fed out of their own matter. Furthermore, without fixed seasons of rain the earth is unable to put forth its gladdening produce, without which the nature of living things could not continue its kind and sustain life. So, you may hold with greater truth that many bodies are common to many things, as we see letters common to different words, than that any thing could come into being without first-beginnings. . . .

Moreover, nature dissolves every thing back into its first bodies and does not annihilate things. For if anything were mortal in all its parts alike, the thing would immediately be snatched away to destruction from before our eyes, since no force would be needed to produce disruption among its parts and undo their fastenings. Whereas in fact, as all things consist of an imperishable seed, nature suffers the destruction of nothing, until it encounters a force sufficient to dash things to pieces by a blow, or to pierce the void places within it and break it up. Again if time, which wears things down through age, utterly destroys them and eats up all their matter, out of what are new things created? Or, when they are created, out of what does earth . . . give them nourishment and increase, furnishing them with food each after its kind? Out of what do its own native fountains and extraneous rivers from far and wide keep full the sea? Out of what does ether feed the stars? For infinite time gone by and the lapse of days

would have eaten up all things that are of mortal body. Now if in that period of time gone by those things have existed, of which this sum of things is composed and recruited, they are possessed no doubt of an imperishable body, which cannot therefore return to nothing. Again, the same force and cause would destroy all things without distinction, unless indestructible matter held them together, matter that is more or less closely linked in mutual entanglement. If this were not the case, a touch would be the sufficient cause of death, inasmuch as any amount of force must undo the texture of things in which no parts at all were of an imperishable body. But in fact, because the fastenings of first-beginnings one with the other are unlike and matter is everlasting, things continue with body uninjured, until they encounter a force strong enough to overpower the texture of each. A thing therefore never returns to nothing, but all things after disruption go back into the first bodies of matter. . . . None of the things therefore which seem to be lost is utterly lost, since nature replenishes one thing out of another, and does not suffer any thing to be begotten without the death of some other.

Now mark me, I have taught that things cannot be born from nothing, and cannot when begotten be reduced to nothing. However, since the first-beginnings of things cannot be seen by the eyes, you may mistrust my words. To see how this would be mistaken, look at the list of bodies that you must yourself admit to exist, although they cannot be seen. First of all, at times the force of the wind beats on the harbor, overwhelms huge ships, and scatters clouds. Sometimes in swift whirling eddy it scours the plains and strews them with large trees, or scourges the mountain summits with forest-rending blasts. So fiercely does the wind rave with a shrill howling and rage with threatening roar. Winds therefore are surely unseen bodies that sweep the seas, the lands, and the clouds of heaven, tormenting them and catching them up in sudden whirls. . . . Then again we perceive the different smells of things, yet we never see them coming to our nostrils. Neither do we behold heats, observe cold with the eyes, or see voices. Yet all things must consist of a bodily nature, since they are able to move the senses. For nothing but body can touch and be touched. Again clothes hung up on a shore which waves break upon become moist, and then get dry if spread out in the sun. Yet it has not been seen in what way the moisture of water has sunk into them nor again in what way this has been dispelled by heat. The moisture therefore is dispersed into small particles that the eyes are quite unable to see. . . . Lastly the bodies that time and nature add to things little by little, constraining them to grow in due measure, no exertion of the eyesight can behold. So too wherever things grow old by age and decay, e.g., when rocks hanging over the sea are eaten away by the gnawing salt spray, you cannot see what they lose at any given moment. Nature therefore works by unseen bodies.

And yet all things are not on all sides jammed together and kept in by body; there is also void in things. . . . If there were not void, things could not move at all. For that which is the property of body, to let and hinder, would be present to all things at all times. Nothing therefore could move, since no other thing would be the first to give way. But in fact, throughout seas, lands and the heights of heaven, we see before our eyes many things move in many ways for various reasons, which could not happen without void. Indeed, these things never would have been begotten at all, since matter jammed on all sides would have been at rest. Again however solid things are thought to be, you may yet learn from this that they are of rare body. In rocks and caverns, the moisture of water oozes through; food distributes itself through the whole body of living things; trees grow and yield fruit in season, because food is diffused through the whole from the very roots over the stem and all the boughs. Voices pass through walls and fly through houses shut, stiffening frost pierces to the bones. Now if there are no void parts, how can the bodies pass through one another? You would see it to be quite impossible. Once more, why do we see one thing surpass another in weight though not larger in size? For if there is just as much body in a ball of wool as there is in a lump of lead of the same size, they should weigh the same, since the property of body is to weigh all things downwards, while the nature of void is ever without weight. Therefore when a thing is just as large as another thing, yet is found to be lighter that it, we can conclude that the first thing has more of void in it. On the other hand, the thing that is heavier has more of body and much less of void. Therefore that which we are seeking with keen

reason surely exists, mixed up in things; and we call it void. . . .

[A]ll nature then, as it exists by itself, is founded on two things: There are bodies and there is void in which these bodies are placed and through which they move. For the general feeling of mankind declares that body exists by itself; and unless belief in this be firmly grounded at the start, there will be nothing to which we can appeal to prove anything about the nature of things by reasoning of mind. Then again, if room and space, which we call void, did not exist, bodies could not be placed anywhere, nor could they move about in any direction, as we have demonstrated above. Moreover, you cannot discover a third nature that is at once separate from all body and quite distinct from void. For whatever exists must be something or other. Now if it admits of touch, in however slight and small a measure, it will increase the amount of body and join the sum, whether what it adds be large or small. But if it is intangible and unable to hinder any thing from passing through it on any side, then it will be what we call empty void. Again whatever shall exist by itself, will either do something or will itself suffer by the action of other things, or will be of such a nature as things are able to exist and move in. But no thing can do or suffer anything without body, nor can anything furnish room except void and vacancy. Therefore beside void and bodies, there can be no third nature left in the number of things, either such as fall at any time under the ken of our senses, or such as any one can grasp by the reason of his mind.

Moreover, any things that can be named will either be properties linked to these two things or they will be accidents of these things. A property of something is that which can never be disjoined and separated from it without utterly destroying it, such as the weight of a stone, the heat of fire, or the fluidity of water. Slavery on the other hand, as well as poverty and riches, liberty, war, concord, and all other things that may come and go while the nature of the thing remains unharmed, are properly called accidents. Time also does not exist in itself, but is rather the apprehension of the movement of the things that have happened in time past, as well as the apprehension of what is present and what is to follow afterwards. And we must admit that no one feels time by itself, abstracted from the motion and calm rest of things. . . .

Bodies again are partly first-beginnings of things, and partly those that are formed of a union of first-beginnings. But no force can quench or destroy those bodies that are the first-beginnings of things, and this is better assured if they are thought of as having a solid body, even though it seems difficult to believe that anything can be found with a solid body. For the lightning of heaven passes through the walls of houses, as does noise and voices. Iron grows red-hot in the fire and stones burn with fierce heat and burst asunder. The hardness of gold is broken up and dissolved by heat; the ice of brass melts vanquished by the flame. Warmth and piercing cold ooze through silver, since we have felt both, as we held cups in our hands in which hot and cold water were poured. So universally there seems to be found nothing solid in things. However, as true reason and the nature of things teaches us, there are such things as consist of solid and everlasting body, which we have claimed to be the seeds of things and first-beginnings, out of which the whole sum of things which now exists has been produced.

First of all, since there has been found to exist a two-fold and widely dissimilar nature of two things, that is to say of body and of place in which things severally move, each of the two must exist for and by itself, quite unmixed. For wherever there is empty space that we call void, body is not there; wherever again body maintains itself, empty void does not exist there. First bodies, therefore, are solid and without void. Again since there is void in created things, solid matter must exist around this void. No thing can be proved by true reason to have void within its body, unless you choose to allow that that which holds it in is solid. Again that can be nothing but a union of matter which can keep in the void of things. Matter, therefore, which consists of a solid body, may be everlasting, although all other things are dissolved. Moreover if there were no empty void, the universe would be solid; and if there were not bodies to fill up whatever places they occupied, the existing universe would be empty and void space. Therefore surely body and void are marked off in alternate layers, since the universe is neither perfectly full nor perfectly void. There are therefore certain bodies that are solid and thus contain no void space. These can neither be broken in pieces by the stroke of blows

from without, nor can they have their texture undone by anything piercing to their core, nor can they give way before any other kind of assault, as we have proved above. For without void nothing seems to admit of being crushed in, broken up, split in two by cutting, or of taking in wet, permeating cold or penetrating fire, or of being destroyed in any other way. And the more void that anything contains within it, the more thoroughly it gives way to the assault of these things. Therefore if first bodies are solid and without void, as I have shown, they must be everlasting. Again unless matter is eternal, all things before now would have utterly returned to nothing, and whatever things we now see would have been born anew from nothing. But since I have proved above both that nothing can be produced from nothing and that what is begotten cannot be recalled to nothing, first-beginnings must be of an imperishable body. It is into these first-beginnings that all things are dissolved at their last hour, so that there may be a supply of matter for the reproduction of things. Therefore first-beginnings are of solid singleness, for in no other way could they have been preserved through infinite time past in order to reproduce things.

Again if nature had set no limit to the breaking of things, by this time the bodies of matter would have been so far reduced by the breaking of past ages that nothing could, within a fixed time, be conceived out of them. . . . For we see that anything is more quickly destroyed than renewed again. Therefore, whatever the long, infinite duration of all bygone time had broken up, demolished and destroyed, could never be reproduced in all remaining time. So surely a fixed limit to their breaking has been set, since we see each thing renewed, and at the same time definite periods fixed wherein things reach the flower of their age. Moreover while the bodies of matter are most solid, we can still explain how all things that are formed soft, such as air, water, earth, and fire, are so formed and by what force they severally move, since there is void mixed up in things. But on the other hand, if the first-beginnings of things were soft, it cannot be explained from what enduring basalt and iron is produced, for their whole nature will utterly lack a first foundation from which to begin. First-beginnings therefore are strong in solid singleness, and by a denser combination they can be closely packed so that they exhibit enduring strength. . . .

But since I have taught that solid bodies of matter fly about unvanquished through all time, let us examine whether there is or is not any limit to their sum. Likewise let us clearly see whether void (or room and space), in which things severally move, is finite, or whether it stretches without limits to an unfathomable depth.

Well, it appears that the existing universe is bounded in none of its dimensions; for if it were, then it must have had an outside. Again it is seen that there can be an outside of nothing, unless there be something beyond to bound it. . . . Now since we must admit that there is nothing outside the sum, it has nothing to bound it and therefore is without end or limit. And it does not matter in which of its regions you take your stand. Invariably, in whatever position one is, one leaves the universe just as infinite as before in all directions. Suppose for the moment that all existing space is bounded, and that a man runs forward to its outside borders, stands on the utmost verge and throws a winged javelin. Do you believe that when hurled with vigorous force the javelin will advance to the point to which it has been sent and keep flying, or do you believe that something can get in its way and stop it? You must admit and adopt one of these two suppositions, either of which compels you to grant that the universe stretches without end. For whether there is something to get in its way, preventing its forward movement, or whether it is carried forward, in either case the end has not been reached. This being the case, I will continue to press the issue, and, wherever you have placed the outside borders, I will ask what then becomes of the javelin when thrown from that point. The result will be that an end can nowhere be fixed, and that the room given for flight will still prolong the power of flight. Although one thing is seen by the eyes to end another thing, e.g., air bounds off hills, mountains bound air, earth limits sea, and sea limits all lands, there is nothing outside that can limit the universe.

Again, if all the space of the whole sum were enclosed within fixed borders and bounded, then the store of matter by its solid weight would have streamed together from all sides to the lowest point.

Nor could anything have gone on under the canopy of heaven, nor would there even have been a heaven or sunlight at all, inasmuch as all matter, settling down through infinite time past, would lie together in a heap. But as it stands, it is evident that no rest is given to the bodies of the first-beginnings, because there is no lowest point at all to which they might stream together and where they might take up their positions. All things are ever moving in ceaseless motion on all sides, and bodies of matter stirred to action are supplied from beneath out of infinite space. Therefore, the nature of the unfathomable void is such that bright thunderbolts cannot race through and complete their course, even given an endless tract of time, nor will the distance they have already traveled lessen the journey that remains ahead of them by one jot. This is true because the void or room in which things move is spread out on all sides, without bounds in any direction.

Furthermore, nature keeps the sum of things from setting any limit to itself, because she compels body to be ended by void and void in turn by body. Since this is the case, it follows that either she renders the universe infinite by this alternation of body and void, or else by the one of the two, which, in case the other does not bound it, stretches immeasurably with its single nature. But since I have already proved that void is infinite, matter must be infinite. If void were infinite, but matter finite, neither sea nor earth nor the glittering quarters of heaven . . . could hold their ground one brief passing hour, since forced asunder from its union, the store of matter would be dissolved and carried along the mighty void. Or rather, I should say that matter would never have combined to produce any thing, since scattered throughout infinite void it could never have been brought together. For it was not by design guided by keen intelligence that the first-beginnings of things stationed themselves each in its right place. Nor did some intelligence determine what motions each should assume. But many in number and shifting about in many ways throughout the universe, they are driven and tormented by blows during infinite time past. After trying motions and unions of every kind, they eventually fall into arrangements such as those out of which this our sum of things has been formed, and by which it is preserved through many great years when once it has been thrown into the appropriate motions. It is this that causes the streams to replenish the greedy sea with copious river waters, the earth, fostered by the heat of the sun, to renew its produce, the race of living things to come up and flourish, and the gliding fires of ether to live. None of this could occur, unless a store of matter could rise up from infinite space, out of which store things are able to replenish in due season whatever has been lost. For, just as it is the nature of living things robbed of food to lose substance and waste away, all other things must be broken up as soon as matter has ceased to be supplied, being diverted in any way from its proper course.

NOTE

1. Lucretius is referring to the Greek philosopher Epicurus (341 B.C.E.–270 B.C.E.).

Questions for Thought

1. What are the basic differences between Plato's view of reality and the view of Lucretius? Can you think of any similarities between the two positions?
2. Why does Lucretius deny that things are created out of nothing by divine power? Do you find his arguments convincing? How do his arguments compare with or differ from those of Darwin?
3. How does Lucretius' attitude toward religion compare with or differ from your own views?
4. Do you find Lucretius' reasoning concerning the existence of the void compelling? Why or why not?
5. Does it make sense to you to say that the universe is infinite in all directions? Can you think of other reasons that might support this claim? Can you think of any reasons for denying it?
6. Assuming that the universe is infinite in all directions, what can we conclude about the nature of being human? How do you think Lucretius would characterize human existence?

12   The Monadology

GOTTFRIED WILHELM LEIBNIZ

Gottfried Wilhelm Leibniz (1646–1716), a German philosopher who also made significant contributions to mathematics, science, history, and diplomacy, was born in Leipzig. His father, who died when Leibniz was only six, was a professor at the University of Leipzig, and his mother was the daughter of a professor. Leibniz's early formal education was in the Nicolai school, but he was informally educated by reading in his father's private library.

Leibniz entered the University of Leipzig in 1661 to study law but quickly became interested in the writings of modern science and philosophy. Nevertheless, Leibniz persisted in working toward his doctorate in law. When he completed his legal studies in 1666, however, he was denied his doctorate on the grounds that he was too young. This occurrence precipitated Leibniz's departure from his native city, and he never returned.

Leibniz then went to Nürnberg, where, at the University of Altdorf, he immediately earned his doctorate degree and was offered a professor's chair. Refusing this offer, he became secretary of the Rosicrucian Society and then secretary to the elector of Mainz, for whom he composed several political papers. In 1672, the elector sent Leibniz on a mission to Paris, where he resided for the next four years. Part of Leibniz's mission was to try to reunite Catholicism and Protestantism. Although this mission was to result in failure, Leibniz invented a calculating machine and laid the foundations of both integral and differential calculus during his stay in Paris.

In 1676, Leibniz moved to Hanover, where he was granted a position by the reigning duke. Starting out as a librarian, he was promoted to the post of councilor in 1678. In this post, Leibniz was free to develop his work in many directions. He continued his work in mathematics and diplomacy, proposed educational reforms, developed and improved numerous mechanical devices, experimented with phosphorus, and even served as a mining engineer. Later, while serving in other political posts, Leibniz wrote a history of the house of Brunswick and made contributions to historical scholarship in several other areas. In 1700, with the help of Sophie Charlotte, daughter of the duke of Hanover and soon to become the first queen of Prussia, Leibniz founded the German Academy of Sciences in Berlin. Because of his important contributions to so many fields of endeavor, Leibniz has been referred to as "the last of the universal geniuses." He died in Hanover in 1716 after being confined to his bed for several months by a severe case of gout.

Leibniz's writings include *De Arte Combinatoria* (1666; *On the Art of Combination*), *Hypothesis Physica Nova* (1671; *New Physical Hypothesis*), *Discours de métaphysique* (1686; *Discourse on Metaphysics*), *Système nouveau* (1695; *New System*), *De Ipsa Natura* (1698; *On Nature Itself*), *Nouveaux essais sur l'entendement human* (1704; *New Essays on Human Understanding*), and *Essais de Thèodicee sur la bonte de Dieu, la liberte de l'homme et l'origine du mal* (1710; translated as *Theodicy*). The following selection is taken from a paper that Leibniz wrote in 1714, near the end of his life.

In this paper, Leibniz claims that the universe consists of simple **substances** called **Monads**. Although Leibniz also refers to these Monads as atoms, it should be obvious that Leibniz's worldview differs radically from that of Lucretius. Whereas Lucretius' seeds are material, Leibniz tells us that the Monads are spiritual. Moreover, whereas Lucretius claims that change occurs when the seeds become mutually entangled and disentangled (the latter occurring when the seeds are struck by an external force sufficient to dislodge them), Leibniz argues that no external force can impact the Monads and thus that all change must be internally produced. Finally, whereas Lucretius claims that the seeds have always existed, Leibniz suggests that the Monads were created by God.

In reading this selection, you will discover several other interesting claims about the nature of reality. First, although Leibniz says that Monads differ in their degree of perception (with the highest degree of perception belonging to the Rational Soul or Mind, which is able to understand "eternal and necessary truths"), he argues that everything that exists has some level of awareness. Second, Leibniz argues that there must be a sufficient reason—that is, an explanation from necessity—for everything that happens in the universe. This claim serves as the foundation both for one of Leibniz's arguments for the existence of God and for his suggestion that this is the best of all possible worlds. Finally, Leibniz argues that since God has created each Monad so that it is adapted to all other Monads, any change in one Monad will be reflected in all the others. Thus, while there is no physical interaction between Monads, there is harmonious change, with each Monad being "a perpetual living mirror of the universe."

Questions for Reading

1. What, according to Leibniz, is a Monad? How is one Monad related to the other Monads?
2. How does a simple Monad differ from the type of Monad that Leibniz refers to as a Rational Soul or Mind? When, according to Leibniz, does a Rational Soul most resemble a simple Monad?
3. How does Leibniz describe God? What role does God play in this selection?
4. What arguments does Leibniz use to prove the existence of God?
5. Why, according to Leibniz, must this be the best of all possible worlds?

1. THE MONAD, OF WHICH WE SPEAK HERE, IS nothing else than a simple **substance** that goes to make up composites; by simple, we mean something without parts.

2. There must be simple substances because there are composites; for a composite is nothing but a collection or aggregation of simple substances.

3. Now, where there are no constituent parts, there cannot possibly be extension, form, or divisibility. These Monads are the true Atoms of nature; in fact, they are the Elements of things.

4. Their dissolution, therefore, is not to be feared, for there is no way conceivable by which a simple substance can perish through natural means.

5. For the same reason, there is no way conceivable by which a simple substance might, through natural means, come into existence, since it cannot be formed by composition.

6. We may say, then, that the existence of Monads can begin or end only all at once, that is to say, the Monad can begin only through creation and end only through annihilation. Composites, however, begin or end gradually.

7. There is also no way of explaining how a Monad can be altered or changed in its inner being by any other created thing, since there is no possibility of transposition within it. Nor can we conceive of any internal movement—such as can take place in composites where changes can occur among the parts—being produced, directed, increased or diminished within a Monad. The Monads have no windows through which anything may come in or go out. The Attributes are not liable to detach themselves and make an excursion outside the substance. . . . In the same way external substances and attributes cannot enter into a Monad.

8. Still, Monads must have some qualities, otherwise they would not even be existences. And if simple substances did not differ at all in their qualities, there would be no means of perceiving any change in things. Whatever is in a composite can come into it only through its simple elements; and if the Monads, which are the simple elements that do not differ at all in quantity were without qualities, things would be indistinguishable one from another. For instance, if we imagine a *plenum* or completely filled space, where each part receives only the equivalent of its own previous motion, one state of things would not be distinguishable from another.

9. Each Monad, indeed, must be different from every other Monad. For in nature there are never two beings that are exactly alike, that is, two beings in which it is not possible to find a difference of some sort.

10. I assume it as admitted that every created being, and consequently the created Monad, is subject to change, and indeed that this change is continuous.

11. It follows from what has just been said that the natural changes of the Monad come from an internal principle, because an external cause can have no influence upon its inner being.

12. Now besides this principle of change, there must also be in the Monad a manifoldness which changes. This manifoldness constitutes, so to speak, the specific nature and the variety of the simple substances.

13. This manifoldness must involve a multiplicity in the unity or in that which is simple. For since

This is the editor's revised version of a selection from Gottfried Wilhelm Leibniz, Monadology, *translated by George R. Montgomery, Open Court Publishing Company, 1902.*

every natural change takes place by degrees, there must be something which changes and something which remains unchanged, and consequently there must be in the simple substance a plurality of conditions and relations, even though it has no parts.

14. The passing condition that involves and represents a multiplicity in the unity, or in the simple substance, is nothing else than what is called Perception. This should be carefully distinguished from **Apperception** or Consciousness, as will appear in what follows. In this matter the Cartesians have fallen into a serious error, in that they treat as nonexistent those perceptions of which we are not conscious. It is this also that has led them to believe that spirits alone are Monads and that there are no souls of animals or other **Entelechies**. . . .

15. The action of the internal principle that brings about the change or the passing from one perception to another may be called Appetition. It is true that the desire (*l'appetit*) is not always able to attain to the whole of the perception for which it strives, but it always attains a portion of it and reaches new perceptions.

16. We, ourselves, experience a multiplicity in a simple substance, when we find that the most trifling thought of which we are conscious involves a variety in the object. Therefore all those who acknowledge that the soul is a simple substance ought to grant this multiplicity in the Monad. . . .

17. It must be confessed, however, that Perception and everything that depends upon it are inexplicable by mechanical causes, that is to say, by figures and motions. Suppose that there were a machine whose structure produced thought, sensation, and perception. We could conceive of it as being large enough for one to enter into its interior, as he would into a mill. Now, when he entered it, he would find only pieces working upon one another, but he would never find anything to explain Perception. It is accordingly in the simple substance, and not in the composite or in a machine, that the Perception must be sought. Furthermore, there is nothing besides perceptions and their changes to be found in the simple substance. It is in these alone that all the internal activities of the simple substance can consist.

18. All simple substances or created Monads may be called Entelechies, because they have in themselves a certain perfection. . . . There is in them a sufficiency . . . that renders them, so to speak, incorporeal Automatons.

19. If we wish to designate as soul everything that has perceptions and desires in the general sense that I have just explained, all simple substances or created Monads could be called souls. But since feeling is something more than a mere perception, I think that the general name of *Monad* or *Entelechy* should suffice for simple substances which have only perception, while we may reserve the term *Soul* for those whose perception is more distinct and is accompanied by memory.

20. We experience in ourselves a state where we remember nothing and where we have no distinct perception, as in periods of fainting, or when we are overcome by a profound, dreamless sleep. In such a state the soul does not sensibly differ in any respect from a simple Monad. As this state, however, is not permanent, the soul can recover from it. Thus, the soul is something more.

21. Nevertheless it does not follow at all that the simple substance is without perception. This is so because of the reasons given above. For it cannot perish, nor would it exist without some affection; and the affection is nothing else than its perception. When, however, there are a great number of weak perceptions where nothing stands out distinctively, we are stunned. For example, if one turns around and around in the same direction, a dizziness comes on. This makes him swoon, and he is unable to distinguish one thing from another. Among animals, death can occasion this state for quite some time.

22. Every present state of a simple substance is a natural consequence of its preceding state, in such a way that its present is big with its future.

23. Therefore, since when we awaken after a period of unconsciousness we become conscious of our perceptions, we must, without having been conscious of them, have had perceptions immediately before. For one perception can by nature derive only from another perception, just as a motion can by nature derive only from a motion.

24. It is evident from this that if we were to have nothing distinctive, prominent, or of a higher flavor in our perceptions, we would be in a continual state of stupor. This is the condition of Monads which do not have anything distinctive in their perceptions.

25. We see that nature has given heightened perceptions to animals, having provided them with organs that collect and effectively combine numerous rays of light or numerous waves of air. Something similar to this takes place in the case of smell, of taste, of touch, and perhaps in many other senses that are unknown to us. I will soon explain how that which occurs in the soul represents that which goes on in the sense-organs.

26. The memory furnishes a sort of consecutiveness that imitates reason but that is to be distinguished from it. We see that when animals have the perception of something that they notice, of which they have had a similar previous perception, they are led by the representation of their memory to expect that which was associated in the preceding perception. Thus, they come to have feelings like those that they had before. For instance, if a stick is shown to a dog that has been hit by one, he remembers the pain the stick has caused him and he whines or runs away.

27. The vividness of the picture that comes to him and moves him is derived either from the magnitude or from the number of the previous perceptions. For, oftentimes, a strong **impression** brings about, all at once, the same effect that is brought about by a long-continued habit, or by the repetition of a great many moderate perceptions.

28. Men act similarly to animals when the sequence of their perceptions is determined only by the law of memory, and thus they resemble the *empirical physicians* who practice simply, without any theory. Indeed, we are empiricists in three-fourths of our actions. For instance, when we expect that there will be daylight tomorrow, we do so empirically, because it has always happened so up to the present time. It is only the astronomer who uses his reason in making such an affirmation.

29. But the knowledge of eternal and necessary truths is that which distinguishes us from mere animals and which gives us reason and the sciences. It is this that raises us to a knowledge of ourselves and of God. This is what is called in us the Rational Soul or the Mind.

30. It is also through the knowledge of necessary truths and through abstractions from them that we come to perform Reflective Acts, acts that cause us to think of what is called the I, and to decide that this or that is within us. It is thus that in thinking upon ourselves we think of *being,* of *substance,* of the *simple* and *composite,* of a *material* and of *God* himself, conceiving that what is limited in us is unlimited in him. These Reflective Acts furnish the principal objects of our reasoning.

31. Our reasoning is based upon two great principles. First is the principle of Contradiction, by means of which we decide that to be false which involves contradiction, and that to be true which contradicts or is opposed to the false.

32. Second is the principle of Sufficient Reason, in virtue of which we believe that no fact can be real or existing, and no statement true, unless it has a sufficient reason why it should be thus and not otherwise. Most frequently, however, these reasons cannot be known by us.

33. There are also two kinds of Truths: those of Reasoning and those of Fact. The Truths of Reasoning are necessary and their opposite is impossible. Those of Fact, however, are contingent and their opposite is possible. When a truth is necessary, the reason can be found by analysis in resolving it into simpler ideas and into simple truths until we reach those that are primary.

34. It is thus that in mathematics, the Speculative Theorems and the practical Canons are reduced by analysis to Definitions, Axioms, and Postulates. . . .

36. But there must also be a sufficient reason for contingent truths or truths of fact, that is to say, for the sequence of the things that extend throughout the universe of created beings. Here, the analysis into more particular reasons can be continued into greater detail without limit, because of the immense variety of the things in nature and because of the infinite division of bodies. There is an infinity of figures and of movements, present and past, that enter into the **efficient cause** of my present writing; and in its **final cause,** there are an infinity of slight tendencies and dispositions of my soul, present and past.

37. And as all this detail again involves other and more detailed contingencies, each of which again has need of a similar analysis in order to find its explanation, no real advance has been made. Therefore, the sufficient or ultimate reason must be outside of the sequence or series of these details of contingencies, however infinite they may be.

38. It is thus that the ultimate reason for things must be a necessary substance, in which the detail of the changes will be present merely potentially, as in the fountain-head. This substance we call *God*.

39. Now, since this substance is a sufficient reason for all of the above-mentioned details, which are linked together throughout, *there is but one God, and this God is sufficient*.

40. We hold that the supreme substance, which is unique, universal and necessary, with nothing independent outside of it, which is further a pure sequence of possible being, must be incapable of limitation and must contain as much reality as possible.

41. Whence it follows that God is absolutely perfect, perfection being understood in the strict sense as the magnitude of positive reality remaining when the limitations or bounds of those things that have them are removed. Where there are no limits, that is to say, in God, perfection is absolutely infinite.

42. It follows also that created things derive their perfection from the influence of God, but their imperfections come from their own natures, which cannot exist without limits. It is in this latter sense that they are distinguished from God. An example of this original imperfection of created things is to be found in the natural inertia of bodies.

43. It is true, furthermore, that not only is the source of existences found in God, but so is the source of essences, in so far as they are real. In other words, he is the source of everything that is real in the possible. This is because the Understanding of God is in the region of eternal truths or of the ideas upon which they depend, and because without him there would be nothing real in the possibilities of things. Not only would nothing exist, nothing would even be possible.

44. For it must be that if there is a reality in essences, in possibilities, or indeed in the eternal truths, this reality is based upon something existent and actual. In other words, it is based upon the existence of the necessary Being, in whom essence includes existence, and in whom possibility is sufficient to produce actuality.

45. Therefore it is true only of God (or the Necessary Being) that if he is possible, he must necessarily exist. And, since nothing is able to prevent the possibility of that which involves no bounds, no negation, and consequently, no contradiction, this alone is sufficient to establish *a priori* his existence. We have, therefore, proved his existence through the reality of eternal truths. But a little while ago we also proved it *a posteriori*, because contingent beings exist, which can have their ultimate and sufficient reason only in the necessary being which, in turn, has the reason for existence in itself. . . .

47. God alone is the ultimate unity or the original simple substance, of which all created or derivative Monads are the products. The latter arise, so to speak, through the continual outflashings of the divinity from moment to moment, limited by the receptivity of the creature in whom limitation is an essential.

48. In God we find the following: *Power,* which is the source of everything; *Knowledge,* which contains the details of the ideas; and, finally, *Will,* which produces or effects changes in accordance with the principle of the greatest good. In the created Monad, these correspond to what forms the subject or basis, the faculty of perception and the faculty of appetition. In God these attributes are absolutely infinite or perfect, while in the created Monads or in the entelechies, . . . they are imitations that approach God in proportion to their perfection.

49. A created thing is said to act outwardly in so far as it has perfection, and to suffer from another in so far as it is imperfect. Thus action is attributed to the Monad in so far as it has distinct perceptions, and passion or passivity is attributed to it in so far as it has confused perceptions.

50. One created thing is more perfect than another created thing when we find in the first that which gives an *a priori* reason for what occurs in the second. This is why we say that one acts upon the other.

51. In the case of simple substances, the influence that one Monad has upon another is purely ideal. It can have its effect only through the mediation of God, inasmuch as in the ideas of God each Monad can demand with reason that God, in regulating the others from the beginning of things, should have regarded it also. For, since one created Monad cannot have a physical influence upon the inner being of

another, it is only through this primal regulation of God that one can have dependence upon another. . . .

53. Now since there is an infinity of possible universes in the Ideas of God, and since only one of them can exist, there must be a sufficient reason for the choice of God that determines him to select one rather than another.

54. And this reason is to be found only in the fitness or in the degree of perfection which these worlds possess, each possible world having the right to claim existence in proportion to the perfection that it possesses.

55. This is the cause for the existence of the greatest good; namely, that his wisdom permits God to know it, his goodness causes him to choose it, and his power enables him to produce it.

56. Now, this interconnection, relationship, or this adaptation of all things to each particular one, and of each one to all the rest, brings it about that every simple substance has relations which express all the others. Consequently, every simple substance is a perpetual living mirror of the universe.

57. As the same city regarded from different sides appears entirely different, and is, as it were, multiplied perspectively, it also happens that, because of the infinite number of simple substances, there are a similar infinite number of universes that are, nevertheless, only the aspects of a single universe, as seen from the special point of view of each Monad.

58. Through this means has been obtained the greatest possible variety, together with the greatest order that may be; that is to say, through this means has been obtained the greatest possible perfection.

Questions for Thought

1. What are the essential differences between Leibniz's views on the nature of reality and those of Lucretius? Can you find any similarities between their views?
2. Do you think that Monads exist? Why or why not?
3. Do you agree with Leibniz's claim that there must be a sufficient reason for everything that happens? Defend your answer.
4. Do you find either of Leibniz's arguments for the existence of God convincing? Can you think of other arguments that might prove the existence of God?
5. Can you think of any reasons for believing that this is the best of all possible worlds? Can you think of any reasons for believing that it is not?

13   An Introduction to Metaphysics

HENRI BERGSON

Henri Bergson (1859–1941), one of the first proponents of **process philosophy,** was born in Paris. His father, who was a talented musician, came from a rich Polish Jewish family and his mother from a well-to-do English Jewish family. The affluence and intelligence of his parents assured that Bergson received an excellent early education. For his formal education, he attended the Lycée Condorcet in Paris and then studied at the École Normale Supérieure. At both institutions, he proved to be an outstanding student, being equally at home in the humanities and in the sciences.

Bergson began teaching at various lycées in 1881, an occupation that he held for the next sixteen years. During this time he wrote his first book, *Essai sur les données immédiates de la conscience* (1889; translated as *Time and Free Will: An Essay on the Immediate*

Data of Consciousness), received his doctorate, and married Louise Neuburger, a cousin of the novelist Marcel Proust. With the publication of his second book, *Matière et mémoire: Essai sur la relation du corps à l'esprit* (1896; *Matter and Memory: Essay on the Relation of the Body to the Spirit*), Bergson was well on the way to being recognized as one of the most popular lecturers and writers of his time. This recognition resulted in his appointment as a professor of philosophy at the École Normale Supérieure in 1897 and at the Collège de France three years later. Bergson held the latter position until poor health forced him to retire in 1921. Bergson, who had been named to the Académie Française in 1915, was awarded the Nobel Prize for literature in 1927. Having observed the horrors of World War I, Bergson spent much of his time from the end of the war until his death promoting international cooperation and peace. However, when Bergson died in 1941, World War II had already begun. France was occupied by the Nazis, and the Vichy government had just passed a law requiring that Jews be registered. Although Bergson's influence and health exempted him from this requirement, he arose from his sickbed to register, thereby showing his solidarity with those "who tomorrow were to be persecuted."

Bergson's other writings include *Le rire: Essai sur la significance du comique* (1900; *Laughter: An Essay on the Meaning of the Comic*), *Introduction à la métaphysique* (1903; *Introduction to Metaphysics*), *L'Évolution créatrice* (1907; *Creative Evolution*), and *Les deux sources de la morale et de la religion* (1932; *The Two Sources of Morality and Religion*).

In the following selection from Bergson's essay "Introduction to Metaphysics," he summarizes some of his important views on the nature of knowledge and reality. Unlike Leibniz, who describes the nature of the Monads, or ultimate reality, before discussing the types of knowledge, Bergson opens his essay by noting that there are two types of knowledge: relative knowledge and absolute knowledge. Relative knowledge, according to Bergson, consists of viewing an object from the outside, expressing what one learns in a variety of symbols or concepts, and comparing the object to other objects. Bergson also tells us that relative knowledge, which is produced by the natural sciences, is analytical and necessarily incomplete.

On the other hand, absolute knowledge, which is the goal of **metaphysics,** is both simple and complete. Rather than analyzing the object from an external perspective, absolute knowledge allows us to grasp intuitively something from within, without the use of symbols. Bergson explains this intuitive grasp as a kind of sympathy by which "one is transported into the interior of an object in order to coincide with what there is unique and consequently inexpressible in it." He goes on to add that concepts are extremely useful in the natural sciences but that they are totally inadequate to communicate this intuitive grasp. While Bergson believes that images are more useful to metaphysics than are concepts, images have value only insofar as they are able to stimulate **intuition.**

After describing these two kinds of knowledge, Bergson turns to the nature of reality. Since the natural sciences depend on conceptual analysis, they can never provide us with a complete picture of anything that exists. However, Bergson claims that at least one complete existence can be revealed to us through intuition—our own self as it flows through time. Although he refers to this experience as "pure duration," Bergson warns us again that words and symbols are inadequate to express what we know of ourselves through intuition. Interestingly, Bergson's metaphysics does not lead us to either the material seeds of Lucretius or the spiritual Monads of Leibniz but rather to "an absolute internal knowledge of the duration of the self by the self."

Questions for Reading

1. What are the two types of knowledge recognized by Bergson? How do these compare with or differ from the types of knowledge recognized by Leibniz?
2. What does Bergson mean by "intuition"? Why, according to Bergson, can an absolute only be given in an intuition?
3. How does Bergson define the term *metaphysics*?
4. Why, according to Bergson, are concepts inadequate to express intuitive knowledge? Why are images inadequate?
5. What images does Bergson use to try to approximate the experience of pure duration?

IF WE COMPARE THE VARIOUS WAYS OF DEFIN-ing metaphysics and of conceiving the absolute, we shall find, despite apparent discrepancies, that philosophers agree in making a deep distinction between two ways of knowing a thing. The first implies going all around it, the second entering into it. The first depends on the viewpoint chosen and the symbols employed, while the second is taken from no viewpoint and rests on no symbol. Of the first kind of knowledge we shall say that it stops at the *relative;* of the second that, wherever possible, it attains the *absolute*.

Take, for example, the movement of an object in space. I perceive it differently according to the point of view from which I look at it, whether from that of mobility or of immobility. I express it differently, furthermore as I relate it to the system of axes or reference points, that is to say, according to the symbols by which I translate it. And I call it *relative* for this double reason: in either case, I place myself outside the object itself. When I speak of an absolute movement, it means that I attribute to the mobile an inner being and, as it were, states of soul; it also means that I am in harmony with these states and enter into them by an effort of imagination. Therefore, according to whether the object is mobile or immobile, whether it adopts one movement or another, I shall not have the same feeling about it. And what I feel will depend neither on the point of view I adopt toward the object, since I am in the object itself, nor on the symbols by which I translate it, since I have renounced all translation in order to possess the original. In short, the movement will

not be grasped from without and, as it were, from where I am, but from within, inside it, in what it is in itself. I shall have hold of an absolute.

Or again, take a character whose adventures make up the subject of a novel. The novelist may multiply traits of character, make his hero speak and act as much as he likes: all this has not the same value as the simple and indivisible feeling I should experience if I were to coincide for a single moment with the personage himself. The actions, gestures and words would then appear to flow naturally, as though from their source. They would no longer be accidents making up the idea I had of the character, constantly enriching this idea without ever succeeding in completing it. The character would be given to me all at once in its entirety, and the thousand and one incidents which make it manifest, instead of adding to the idea and enriching it, would, on the contrary, seem to me to fall away from it without in any way exhausting or impoverishing its essence. I get a different point of view regarding the person with every added detail I am given. All the traits which describe it to me, yet which can only enable me to know it by comparisons with persons or things I already know, are signs by which it is more or less symbolically expressed. Symbols and points of view then place me outside it; they give me only what it has in common with others and what does not belong properly to it. But what is properly itself, what constitutes its essence, cannot be perceived from without, being internal by definition, nor be expressed by symbols, being incommensurable with everything else. Description, history and analysis in

From Henri Bergson, The Creative Mind, *translated by Mabelle L. Addison, Philosophical Library, 1946. Reprinted by permission of Philosophical Library.*

this case leave me in the relative. Only by coinciding with the person itself would I possess the absolute.

It is in this sense, and in this sense alone, that *absolute* is synonymous with *perfection*. Though all the photographs of a city taken from all possible points of view indefinitely complete one another, they will never equal in value that dimensional object, the city along whose streets one walks. All the translations of a poem in all possible languages may add nuance to nuance and, by a kind of mutual retouching, by correcting one another, may give an increasingly faithful picture of the poem they translate, yet they will never give the inner meaning of the original. A representation taken from a certain point of view, a translation made with certain symbols still remain imperfect in comparison with the object whose picture has been taken or which the symbols seek to express. But the absolute is perfect in that it is perfectly what it is.

It is probably for the same reason that the *absolute* and the *infinite* are often taken as identical. If I wish to explain to someone who does not know Greek the simple impression that a line of Homer leaves upon me, I shall give the translation of the line, then comment on my translation, then I shall develop my commentary, and from explanation to explanation I shall get closer to what I wish to express; but I shall never quite reach it. When you lift your arm you accomplish a movement the simple perception of which you have inwardly; but outwardly, for me, the person who sees it, your arm passes through one point, then through another, and between these two points there will be still other points, so that if I begin to count them, the operation will continue indefinitely. Seen from within, an absolute is then a simple thing; but considered from without, that is to say relative to something else, it becomes, with relation to those signs which express it, the piece of gold for which one can never make up the change. Now what lends itself at the same time to an indivisible apprehension and to an inexhaustible enumeration is, by definition, an infinite.

It follows that an absolute can only be given in an *intuition*, while all the rest has to do with *analysis*. We call intuition here the *sympathy* by which one is transported into the interior of an object in order to coincide with what there is unique and consequently inexpressible in it. Analysis, on the contrary, is the operation which reduces the object to elements already known, that is, common to that object and to others. Analyzing then consists in expressing a thing in terms of what is not it. All analysis is thus a translation, a development into symbols, a representation taken from successive points of view from which are noted a corresponding number of contacts between the new object under consideration and others believed to be already known. In its eternally unsatisfied desire to embrace the object around which it is condemned to turn, analysis multiplies endlessly the points of view in order to complete the ever incomplete representation, varies interminably the symbols with the hope of perfecting the always imperfect translation. It is analysis ad infinitum. But intuition, if it is possible, is a simple act.

This being granted, it would be easy to see that for positive science analysis is its habitual function. It works above all with symbols. Even the most concrete of the sciences of nature, the sciences of life, confine themselves to the visible form of living beings, their organs, their anatomical elements. They compare these forms with one another, reduce the more complex to the more simple, in fact they study the functioning of life in what is, so to speak, its visual symbol. If there exists a means of possessing a reality absolutely, instead of knowing it relatively, of placing oneself within it instead of adopting points of view toward it, of having the intuition of it instead of making the analysis of it, in short, of grasping it over and above all expression, translation or symbolical representation, metaphysics is that very means. *Metaphysics is therefore the science which claims to dispense with symbols.*

There is at least one reality which we all seize from within, by intuition and not by simple analysis. It is our own person in its flowing through time, the self which endures. With no other thing can we sympathize intellectually, or if you like, spiritually. But one thing is sure: we sympathize with ourselves. When, with the inner regard of my consciousness, I examine my person in its passivity, like some superficial encrustment, first I perceive all the perceptions which come to it from the material world. These perceptions are clear-cut, distinct, juxtaposed or mutually juxtaposable; they seek to group themselves into objects. Next I perceive memories more or less adherent to these perceptions and which serve to interpret them; these memories are, so to speak, as if detached from the depth of my person and drawn to the periphery by perceptions resembling them; they are fastened on me without being absolutely myself. And finally, I become aware of tendencies, motor habits, a crowd of virtual actions more or less solidly bound to those perceptions and these memories. All these elements with their well-defined forms appear to me to be all the more distinct from myself the more they are distinct from one another. Turned outwards from within, together they constitute the surface of a sphere which tends to expand and loose itself in the external world. But if I pull myself in from the periphery toward the center, if I seek deep down within me what is the most uniformly, the most constantly and durably myself, I find something altogether different.

What I find beneath these clear-cut crystals and this superficial congelation is a continuity of flow comparable to no other flowing I have ever seen. It is a succession of states each one of which announces what follows and contains what precedes. Strictly speaking they do not constitute multiple states until I have already got beyond them, and turn around to observe their trail. While I was experiencing them they were so solidly organized, so profoundly animated with a common life, that I could never have said where any one of them finished or the next one began. In reality, none of them do begin or end; they all dove-tail into one another.

It is, if you like, the unrolling of a spool, for there is no living being who does not feel himself coming little by little to the end of his span; and living consists in growing old. But it is just as much a continual winding, like that of thread into a ball, for our past follows us, becoming larger and larger with the present it picks up on its way; and consciousness means memory.

To tell the truth, it is neither a winding nor an unwinding, for these two images evoke the representation of lines or surfaces whose parts are homogeneous to and superposable on one another. Now, no two moments are identical in a conscious being. Take for example the simplest feeling, suppose it to be constant, absorb the whole personality in it: the consciousness which will accompany this feeling will not be able to remain identical with itself for two consecutive moments, since the following moment always contains, over and above the preceding one,

the memory the latter has left it. A consciousness which had two identical moments would be a consciousness without memory. It would therefore die and be re-born continually. How otherwise can unconsciousness be described?

We must therefore evoke a spectrum of a thousand shades, with imperceptible gradations leading from one shade to another. A current of feeling running through the spectrum, becoming tinted with each of these shades in turn, would suffer gradual changes, each of which would announce the following and sum up within itself the preceding ones. Even then the successive shades of the spectrum will always remain external to each other. They are juxtaposed. They occupy space. On the contrary, what is pure duration excludes all idea of juxtaposition, reciprocal exteriority and extension.

Instead, let us imagine an infinitely small piece of elastic, contracted, if that were possible, to a mathematical point. Let us draw it out gradually in such a way as to bring out of the point a line which will grow progressively longer. Let us fix our attention not on the line as line, but on the action which traces it. Let us consider that this action, in spite of its duration, is indivisible if one supposes that it goes on without stopping; that, if we intercalate a stop in it, we make two actions of it instead of one and that each of these actions will then be the indivisible of which we speak; that it is not the moving act itself which is never indivisible, but the motionless line it lays down beneath it like a track in space. Let us take our mind off the space subtending the movement and concentrate solely on the movement itself, on the act of tension or extension, in short, on pure mobility. This time we shall have a more exact image of our development in duration.

And yet that image will still be incomplete, and all comparison furthermore will be inadequate, because the unrolling of our duration in certain aspects resembles the unity of a movement which progresses, in others, a multiplicity of states spreading out, and because no metaphor can express one of the two aspects without sacrificing the other. If I evoke a spectrum of a thousand shades, I have before me a complete thing, whereas duration is the state of completing itself. If I think of an elastic being stretched, of a spring being wound or unwound, I forget the wealth of coloring characteristic of duration as something lived and see only the simple movement by which consciousness goes from one shade to the other. The inner life is all that at once, variety of qualities, continuity of progress, unity of direction. It cannot be represented by images.

But still less could it be represented by *concepts*, that is, by abstract ideas, whether general or simple. Doubtless no image will quite answer to the original feeling I have of the flowing of myself. But neither is it necessary for me to try to express it. To him who is not capable of giving himself the intuition of the duration constitutive of his being, nothing will ever give it, neither concepts nor images. In this regard, the philosopher's sole aim should be to start up a certain effort which the utilitarian habits of mind of everyday life tend, in most men, to discourage. Now the image has at least the advantage of keeping us in the concrete. No image will replace the intuition of duration, but many different images, taken from quite different orders of things, will be able, through the convergence of their action, to direct the consciousness to the precise point where there is a certain intuition to seize on. By choosing images as dissimilar as possible, any one of them will be prevented from usurping the place of the intuition it is instructed to call forth, since it would then be driven out immediately by its rivals. By seeing that in spite of their differences in aspect they all demand of our mind the same kind of attention and, as it were, the same degree of tension, one will gradually accustom the consciousness to a particular and definitely determined disposition, precisely the one it will have to adopt in order to appear unveiled to itself. But even then the consciousness must acquiesce in this effort; for we shall have shown it nothing. We shall simply have placed it in the attitude it must take to produce the desired effort and, by itself, to arrive at the intuition. On the other hand the disadvantage of too simple concepts is that they are really symbols which take the place of the object they symbolize and which do not demand any effort on our part. Upon close examination one would see that each of them retains of the object only what is common to that object and to others. Each of them is seen to express, even more than does the image, a *comparison* between the object and those objects resembling it. But as the comparison has brought out a resemblance, and as the resemblance is a property of the object, and as a

property seems very much as though it were a *part* of the object possessing it, we are easily persuaded that by juxtaposing concepts to concepts we shall recompose the whole of the object with its parts and obtain from it, so to speak, an intellectual equivalent. We shall in this way think we are forming a faithful representation of duration by lining up the concepts of unity, multiplicity, continuity, finite or infinite divisibility, etc. That is precisely the illusion. And that, also, is the danger. In so far as abstract ideas can render service to analysis, that is, to a scientific study of the object in its relations with all others, to that very extent are they incapable of replacing intuition, that is to say, the metaphysical investigation of the object in what essentially belongs to it. On the one hand, indeed, these concepts placed end to end will never give us anything more than an artificial recomposition of the object of which they can symbolize only certain general and, as it were, impersonal aspects: therefore it is vain to believe that through them one can grasp a reality when all they present is its shadow. But on the other hand, alongside the illusion, there is also a very grave danger. For the concept generalizes at the same time that it abstracts. The concept can symbolize a particular property only by making it common to an infinity of things. Therefore it always more or less distorts this property by the extension it gives to it. A property put back into the metaphysical object to which it belongs coincides with the object, at least molds itself on it, adopting the same contours. Extracted from the metaphysical object and represented in a concept, it extends itself indefinitely, surpassing the object since it must henceforth contain it along with others. The various concepts we form of the properties of a thing are so many much larger circles drawn round it, not one of which fits it exactly. And yet, in the thing itself, the properties coincided with it and therefore with each other. We have no alternative then but to resort to some artifice in order to re-establish the coincidence. We shall take any one of these concepts and with it try to rejoin the others. But the junction will be brought about in a different way, depending upon the concept we start from. According to whether we start, for example, from unity or from multiplicity, we shall form a different conception of the multiple unity of duration. Everything will depend on the weight we assign to this or that concept, and this weight will always be arbitrary, since the concept, extracted from the object, has no weight, being nothing more than the shadow of a body. Thus a multiplicity of different *systems* will arise, as many systems as there are external viewpoints on the reality one is examining or as there are larger circles in which to enclose it. The simple concepts, therefore, not only have the disadvantage of dividing the concrete unity of the object into so many symbolical expressions; they also divide philosophy into distinct schools, each of which reserves its place, chooses its chips, and begins with the others a game that will never end. Either metaphysics is only this game of ideas, or else, if it is a serious occupation of the mind, it must transcend concepts to arrive at intuition. To be sure, concepts are indispensable to it, for all the other sciences ordinarily work with concepts, and metaphysics cannot get along without the other sciences. But it is strictly itself only when it goes beyond the concept, or at least when it frees itself of the inflexible and ready-made concepts and creates others very different from those we usually handle, I mean flexible, mobile, almost fluid representations, always ready to mold themselves on the fleeting forms of intuition. . . . [O]ur duration can be presented to us directly in an intuition, . . . it can be suggested indirectly to us by images, but . . . it cannot—if we give to the word *concept* its proper meaning—be enclosed in a conceptual representation.

Let us for an instant try to break it up into parts. We must add that the terms of these parts, instead of being distinguished like those of any multiplicity, encroach upon one another; that we can, no doubt, by an effort of imagination, solidify this duration once it has passed by, divide it into pieces set side by side and count all the pieces; but that this operation is achieved on the fixed memory of the duration, on the immobile track the mobility of the duration leaves behind it, not on the duration itself. Let us therefore admit that, if there is a multiplicity here, this multiplicity resembles no other. Shall we say then that this duration has unity? Undoubtedly a continuity of elements prolonged into one another partakes of unity as much as it does of multiplicity, but this moving, changing, colored and living unity scarcely resembles the abstract unity, empty and motionless, which the concept of pure unity circumscribes. Are we to conclude from this that duration must be defined by both unity and multiplicity at the same time? But curiously enough, no matter how I manipulate the two concepts, apportion them, combine them in various ways, practice on them the most delicate operations of mental chemistry, I shall never obtain anything which resembles the simple intuition I have of duration; instead of which, if I place myself back in duration by an effort of intuition, I perceive immediately how it is unity, multiplicity and many other things besides. These various concepts were therefore just so many external points of view on duration. Neither separated nor reunited have they made us penetrate duration itself.

We penetrate it, nevertheless, and the only way possible is by an intuition. In this sense, an absolute internal knowledge of the duration of the self by the self is possible.

Questions for Thought

1. Do you think you have ever had intuitive knowledge of the type that Bergson describes? If so, what was the object of this knowledge?
2. Can you think of other images that might be used to approximate the experience of pure duration?
3. How does Bergson's description of the nature of the self differ from Lucretius' description? How do you think Bergson would respond to Lucretius' claim that everything consists of material seeds in motion?
4. At one point, Bergson compares the experience of human living to the "unrolling of a spool." What exactly does Bergson mean by this comparison? Do you think that this comparison captures the experience of living? Why or why not?
5. Why, according to Bergson, do the natural sciences never give us a complete picture of anything? Do you think that this is true? Explain your answer.

The True Features of Reality 14

KITARŌ NISHIDA

Kitarō Nishida (1875–1945) taught at Kanazawa Higher School and then at Kyoto University as a professor of philosophy. On retiring from Kyoto University, he devoted much of his time to writing. Among his many published works are *Ippansha no jikakuteki taikei* (1930; *The Self-Conscious System of the Universal*), *Mu no jikakuteki gentei* (1932; *The Self-Conscious Determination of Nothingness*), *Tetsugaku no konponmondai* (1933–1934; *The Fundamental Problems of Philosophy*), and *Tetsugaku ronbunshu* (7 vols., 1935–1946; *A Collection of Philosophical Essays*).

Nishida is perhaps best known as a philosophical precursor of the Kyoto school of philosophy, a group of Japanese scholars who attempted to fuse Eastern and Western concepts into a world philosophy. Nishida's contribution to this movement has been described by Masao Abe as follows: "Realizing the uniqueness of the Eastern way of thinking, Nishida took absolute nothingness as ultimate reality and tried to give it a logical foundation through his confrontation with Western philosophy. Forming his synthesis on the basis of historical life innate in human existence, which is neither Eastern nor Western, he neither established a new Eastern philosophy nor reconstructed Western philosophy but created a new world philosophy."

In this selection from a short work titled *An Inquiry into the Good,* Nishida critiques traditional conceptions of reality and knowledge. His main criticism is that in traditional philosophy, reality and knowledge are often divorced from the practical demands of life. In this divorce, knowledge is portrayed as the objective description of a fixed reality that exists independently of the knowing subject. It is also traditionally claimed that science is the vehicle best suited for discovering such knowledge.

In opposition to this traditional conception of knowledge and reality, Nishida describes what he calls immediate reality or pure experience. In immediate reality or pure experience, there is no opposition between subject and object and no separation of knowledge, feeling, and volition. As his example of the listener who is enraptured by exquisite music is intended to show, immediate reality or pure experience is a unified activity. In language that parallels Bergson's description of intuitive knowledge, Nishida says that in such a state we are one with the music, or, more accurately, in such a state the separation between listener and music does not yet exist. All separation (including the separation between subject and object and the separation between knowing, feeling, and willing) represents a movement away from and distortion of immediate reality. Nishida says that separation results in abstract concepts, which are the subject matter of scholars and scientists. However, immediate reality, which is undivided and includes feeling and willing as well as knowing, is the proper domain of art, religion, and philosophy. As Nishida says, "A scientist's way of explanation is slanted toward just one aspect of knowledge, whereas in a complete explanation of reality we must satisfy intellectual demands as well as the demands of feeling and the will."

Questions for Reading

1. What, according to Nishida, should be the relation between philosophical views of the world and practical demands of living?
2. What does Nishida mean by "immediate reality"? How does he define "pure experience"?
3. How, according to Nishida, do people often view scientific inquiry? What are his views on the nature and value of scientific inquiry?
4. Nishida says that "it is not that the individual possesses feeling and the will, but rather that feeling and the will create the individual." What exactly does Nishida mean by this statement?
5. What does Nishida say about the Greeks near the end of this selection? How does what he says about the Greeks relate to his own views?

THE STARTING POINT OF THE INQUIRY

PHILOSOPHICAL VIEWS OF THE WORLD AND of human life relate closely to the practical demands of morality and religion, which dictate how people should act and where they can find peace of mind. People are never satisfied with intellectual convictions and practical demands that contradict each other. Those with high spiritual demands fail to find satisfaction in **materialism,** and those who believe in materialism come to harbor doubts about spiritual demands. Fundamentally, truth is singular. Intellectual truth and practical truth must be one and the same. Those who think deeply or are genuinely serious inevitably seek congruence between knowledge and the practical realm of feeling and willing. We must now investigate what we ought to do and where we ought to find peace of mind, but this calls first for clarification of the nature of the universe, human life, and true reality.

The Indian religio-philosophical tradition, which provides the most highly developed congruence of philosophy and religion, holds that knowledge is good and delusion is evil. The fundamental reality of the universe is **Brahman,** which is our soul, our **Atman.** Knowledge of this identity of Brahman and Atman is the culmination of Indian philosophy and religion. Christianity was entirely practical at its inception, but because the human mind insistently demands intellectual satisfaction, Christian philosophy was developed in the Middle Ages. In the Chinese tradition, the system of morality at first lacked philosophical elaboration, but since the Sung period this dimension has predominated. Such historical trends in the Indian, Christian, and Chinese traditions attest to the basic human demand for congruence between our knowledge and our feeling and will.

In classical Western philosophy beginning with Socrates and Plato, didactic goals were central, whereas in modern times knowledge has assumed a prominent position, making the unity of the intellectual and the emotional-volitional aspects more difficult. In fact, the two dimensions now tend to diverge, and this in no way satisfies the fundamental demands of the human mind.

To understand true reality and to know the true nature of the universe and human life, we must discard all artificial assumptions, doubt whatever can be doubted, and proceed on the basis of direct and indubitable knowledge. From the perspective of common sense, we think that things exist in the external world apart from consciousness and that in the back of consciousness there is something called the mind, which performs various functions. Our assumption that mind and matter exist independently constitutes the basis of our conduct and is

Kitarō Nishida, An Inquiry into the Good, *translated by Masao Abe and Christopher Ives, Yale University Press, 1990. Reprinted by permission of Yale University Press.*

itself based on the demands posed by our thinking. This assumption leaves much room for doubt. Science, which does not take the most profound explanation of reality as its goal, is constructed on such hypothetical knowledge. But insufficiently critical thinking is also found in philosophy, which does take that explanation as its goal. Many philosophers base their thinking on existing assumptions and hence fail to engage in penetrating doubt. . . .

THE TRUE FEATURES OF REALITY

What is immediate reality before we have added the fabrications of thinking? In other words, what is a fact of truly pure experience? At the time of pure experience, there is still no opposition between subject and object and no separation of knowledge, feeling, and volition; there is only an independent, self-sufficient, pure activity.

Intellectualist psychologists regard sensations and ideas as the requisite elements of mental **phenomena** and hold that all mental phenomena are constituted by their union. From this perspective, they construe a fact of pure experience to be the most passive state of consciousness, namely, sensation. But this approach confuses the results of academic analysis with the facts of direct experience. In facts of direct experience, there is no pure sensation. What we term pure sensation is already a simple perception, but no matter how simple, perception is not at all passive: it necessarily includes active—constructive—elements. (This is obvious when we consider examples of spatial perception.)

The characterization of pure experience as active becomes clearer when we examine such complex cognitive activities as association and thinking. Though association is usually deemed passive, the direction of the linkage of ideas in association is determined not only by circumstances in the external world, but also by the internal qualities of consciousness. Association and thinking thus differ only in degree. Moreover, people divide the phenomena of consciousness into knowledge, but in actuality we do not find these three types of phenomena. In fact, each and every phenomena of consciousness possesses all three aspects. (For instance, although

academic research is considered a purely intellectual activity, it can never exist apart from feeling and will.) Of these three aspects the will is the most fundamental form of consciousness. As voluntarist psychologists assert, our consciousness is always active: it begins with an impulse and ends with the will. However simple, the most direct phenomena of consciousness takes the form of the will—that is, the will is a fact of pure experience. . . .

In pure experience, our thinking, feeling, and willing are still undivided; there is a single activity, with no opposition between subject and object. Such opposition arises from the demands of thinking, so it is not a fact of direct experience. In direct experience there is only an independent, self-sufficient event, with neither a subject that sees nor an object that is seen. Just [as] when we become enraptured by exquisite music, forget ourselves and everything around us, and experience the universe as one melodious sound, true reality presents itself in the moment of direct experience. Should the thought arise that the music is the vibration of air or that one is listening to music, at that point one has already separated oneself from the true reality because that thought derives from the reflection and thinking divorced from the true state of the reality of the music.

It is usually thought that subject and object are realities that can exist independently of each other and that phenomena of consciousness arise through their activity, which leads to the idea that there are two realities: mind and matter. This is a total mistake. The notions of subject and object derive from two different ways of looking at a single fact, as does the distinction between mind and matter. But these dichotomies are not inherent in the fact itself. As a concrete fact, a flower is not at all like the purely material flower of scientists; it is pleasing with a beauty of color, shape, and scent. Heine gazed at the stars in a quiet night sky and called them golden tracks in the azure.[1] Though astronomers would laugh at his words as the folly of a poet, the true nature of stars may very well be expressed in his phrase.

In the independent, self-sufficient true reality prior to the separation of subject and object, our knowledge, feeling, and volition are one. Contrary to popular belief, true reality is not the subject matter of dispassionate knowledge; it is established through our feeling and willing. It is not simply an existence but something with meaning. If we were to remove our feelings and the will from this world of actuality, it would no longer be a concrete fact— it would become an abstract concept. The world described by physicists, like a line without width and a plane without thickness, is not something that actually exists. In this respect, it is the artist, not the scholar, who arrives at the true nature of reality. Each and every thing we see or hear contains our individuality. Though we might speak of identical consciousness, our consciousnesses are not truly the same. When viewing a cow, for example, farmers, zoologists, and artists have different mental images. Depending on one's feeling at the moment, the same scenery can appear resplendently beautiful or depressingly gloomy. Buddhist thought holds that according to one's mood the world becomes either heaven or hell. Thus our world is constructed upon our feeling and volition. However much we talk about the objective world as the subject matter of pure knowledge, it cannot escape its relation to our feelings.

People think that the world seen scientifically is most objective in that it exists independently of our feeling and volition. But it is in no way divorced from the demands of feeling and the will because scientific inquiry derives from actual demands in our struggle for survival. As especially Jerusalem has said, the idea that a power in the external world performs various activities—this idea being the fundamental principle of the scientific world view—is generated by analogical inference from one's will.[2] Ancient explanations of things in the universe were anthropomorphic, and they are the springboard from which contemporary scientific explanations developed.

Taking the distinction between subject and object as fundamental, some think that objective elements are included only in knowledge and that idiosyncratic, subjective events constitute feeling and volition. This view is mistaken in its basic assumptions. If we argue that phenomena arise by means of the mutual activity of subject and object, then even such content of knowledge as color or form can be seen as subjective or individual. If we argue further that there is a quality in the external world that gives rise to feeling and volition, then they come to possess an objective base, and it is therefore an error to say they are totally individual. Our feeling and volition allow for communication and sympathy between individuals; they have a trans-individual element.

Because we think that such emotional and volitional entities as joy, anger, love, and desire arise in individual people, we also think that feeling and the will are purely individual. Yet it is not that the individual possesses feeling and the will, but rather that feeling and the will create the individual. Feeling and the will are facts of direct experience.

The anthropomorphic explanation of the myriad things in the universe is the way of explanation used by ancient people and naive children in all eras. Although scientists might laugh it away—indeed, it is infantile—from a certain perspective this is the true way of explaining reality. A scientist's way of explanation is slanted toward just one aspect of knowledge, whereas in a complete explanation of reality we must satisfy intellectual demands as well as the demands of feeling and the will.

To the Greeks, all of nature was alive. Thunder and lightning were the wrath of Zeus on Mount Olympus, the voice of the cuckoo was Philamela's lament of the past.[3] To the natural eye of a Greek, the true meaning of the present appeared just as it was. Contemporary art, religion, and philosophy all strive to express this true meaning.

NOTES

1. Heinrich Heine (1797–1856) was a German poet and critic who was heavily influenced by German romanticism.

2. K. W. Jerusalem, *Einleitung in die Philosophie*, 6, Aufl. 27.

3. Friedrich Schiller, *Die Götter Griechenlands*. An English translation of Schiller's poem, "The Gods of Greece," can be found in J. G. Fischer, ed., *Schiller's Works,* vol. 1 (Philadelphia: George Barrie, 1883), p. 36.

Questions for Thought

1. Do you believe you have access to immediate reality? Why or why not?
2. How effective is Nishida's example of the person enraptured by music in illustrating his claim that immediate reality exists? Can you think of other examples that might support the existence of immediate reality?
3. Do you agree with Nishida's claim that knowledge must not be divorced from feeling and will? Why or why not?
4. Nishida claims that scientific descriptions of reality are not as satisfying as artistic descriptions. On what basis does he make this claim? Do you agree with him on this point?
5. What would you consider to be an adequate description of a flower? What would you consider to be an adequate description of love?
6. In what ways are Nishida's views on the nature of knowledge and reality similar to those of Bergson? In what ways are they different?

The Politics of Reality 15

MARILYN FRYE

Marilyn Frye (b. 1941) was born in Tulsa, Oklahoma. The younger of two daughters, she grew up in a traditional, devoutly Christian family. Frye studied philosophy as an undergraduate at Stanford University, receiving her bachelor's degree in 1963. Six years later she earned her doctorate in philosophy from Cornell University. After teaching philosophy for several years at the University of Pittsburgh, Frye obtained a position at Michigan State University, where she currently teaches.

In addition to teaching philosophy, Frye has helped run a bookstore, been a partner in a small press, worked in women's studies, and helped run a lesbian center. She has lived on both coasts of the United States and in western Canada. She has also written several articles on feminist philosophy and the philosophy of language, as well as two books, *The Politics of Reality: Essays in Feminist Theory* (1983) and *Willful Virgin: Essays in Feminism* (1992). More recently, Frye coedited the book *Feminist Interpretations of Mary Daly* (2000).

In the following selection from *The Politics of Reality*, Frye discusses recent claims about the possibility of there being a lesbian **epistemology**. Frye argues that the traditional conceptual scheme, the traditional way of viewing reality, has been decidedly "phallocratic"; that is, it has excluded women in general and lesbians in particular. Indeed, in examining dictionary definitions of the term *lesbian*, she concludes that such definitions typically make lesbians "*naturally* impossible as well as *logically* impossible."

Frye goes on to argue that while women in general have been excluded from the traditional conceptual scheme and have suffered much as a result of this exclusion, their exclusion has not been absolute. Rather, realizing that women are necessary to the dominant reality, Frye says that the traditional conceptual scheme acknowledges the existence of women but relegates them to the background. Frye's point here can perhaps best be understood if we reflect on the once-popular saying, "*Behind* every great man is a great woman" (my italics).

While many contemporary women are beginning to question this placement of women in the background, Frye claims that lesbians are specially positioned to do so. For while women in general have been given a supporting role in the traditional conceptual scheme, lesbians have been totally excluded from it. Because they are operating from a perspective outside the dominant conception of reality, lesbians are better situated to recognize the inadequacies of the dominant scheme, such as its relegation of women to the background. Moreover, having no loyalties whatsoever to a scheme that totally excludes them, lesbians are also best positioned to undermine the authority of this scheme. Speaking of the dominant conception of reality, Frye says that a lesbian "is not committed to its maintenance and the maintenance of those who maintain it, and worse, her mode of disloyalty threatens its utter dissolution in the mere flick of an eye." Of course, in using the word *worse* here, she is saying that this is "worse" for those who wish to maintain the dominant scheme, for those who wish to keep women in the background.

Questions for Reading

1. What does the term *lesbian epistemology* mean? What were some of the responses to the suggestion that lesbians occupied a special epistemic position?
2. What is the point that Frye is trying to make in section II of her paper? What strategy does she use to make this point?
3. How, according to Frye, is the term *lesbian* defined? Why does she believe that the various dictionary definitions make lesbians "*naturally* impossible as well as *logically* impossible?"
4. Why does Frye include the quotation from John Langshaw Austin? What, according to Frye, does this quotation tell us about the dominant conception of reality?
5. What are the two kinds of erasure of women that are associated with or activated by the dominant conception of reality? Why does Frye believe that the erasure or exclusion of lesbians in particular is more radical than that of women in general?
6. What extended metaphor does Frye use to illustrate the place of women in the dominant conception of reality? In terms of this metaphor, what are some of the strategies that are used to keep women in the background?
7. Why, according to Frye, do lesbians pose such a challenge or threat to the maintenance of the dominant conception of reality?

I

IN THE SPRING OF 1978, AT A MEETING OF THE Midwestern Division of the Society for Women in Philosophy, Sarah Hoagland read a paper entitled "Lesbian Epistemology," in which she sketched the following picture:

In the conceptual schemes of phallocracies there is no category of woman-identified-woman, woman-loving-woman, or woman-centered-woman; that is, there is no such thing as a lesbian. This puts a lesbian in the interesting and peculiar position of being something that doesn't exist, and this position is a singular vantage point

Marilyn Frye, The Politics of Reality: Essays in Feminist Theory, *The Crossing Press, 1984. Reprinted by permission of The Crossing Press.*

with respect to the reality which does not include her. It affords her a certain freedom from constraints of the conceptual system; it gives her access to knowledge which is inaccessible to those whose existence is countenanced by the system. Lesbians can therefore undertake kinds of criticism and description, and kinds of intellectual invention, hitherto unimagined.

Hoagland was urging lesbian-feminists to begin this work, and she did not try to say in advance what could be seen from that exceptional epistemic position.

Some critics of that paper, bridling at the suggestion that lesbians might be blessed with any exotic powers or special opportunities, were quick to demand a definition of the word "lesbian." They knew that if a definition of "lesbian" featured certain patterns of physical contacts as definitive, then the claim that **phallocratic** conceptual schemes do not include lesbians would be obviously false, since phallocrats obviously can and do wrap their rapacious minds around verbal and visual images of females so positioned physically, with respect to each other. And they knew also, on the other hand, that any definition which is more "spiritual," such as *woman-identified-woman,* will be flexible enough to permit almost any woman to count herself a lesbian and claim for herself these exciting epistemological privileges.

Other critics, who found Hoagland's picture engaging but were loathe to glorify the conditions of exile, pressed for a definition of "lesbian" which would be both accurate and illuminating—a definition which would shed light on what it means to say lesbians are excluded from phallocratic conceptual schemes, and which might even provide some clue as to what lesbians might see from this strange nonlocation beyond the pale.

These pressures combined with the philosopher's constitutional propensity to view all orderly procedure as beginning with definitions, and the assembly was irresistibly drawn into trying to define the term "lesbian." But to no avail. That term is extraordinarily resistant to standard procedures of semantic analysis. It finally dawned on me that the elusiveness of the meaning of the term was itself a clue that Hoagland's picture was right. If indeed lesbians' existence is not countenanced by the dominant conceptual scheme, it would follow that we could not construct a defini-

tion of the term "lesbian" of the sort we might recommend to well-intentioned editors of dictionaries. If a conceptual scheme excludes something, the standard vocabulary of those whose scheme it is will not be adequate to the defining of a term which denotes it. If Hoagland's picture is right, then whatever we eventually do by way of defining the word "lesbian," that definition will evolve within a larger enterprise and cannot be the *beginning* of understanding and assessing that picture.

Another way of beginning is suggested by the observation that women of all stripes and colors, including lesbians but also including nonlesbians, suffer erasure. This is true, but it also seems to me that Hoagland is right: the exclusion of lesbians from phallocratic reality is different and is related to unusual knowing. The difficulty lies in trying to say just what this *means*. In order to get a handle on this we need to explore the differences and the connections between the erasure of women generally and the erasure of lesbians.

This inquiry, about what is *not* encompassed by a conceptual scheme, presents problems which arise because the scheme in question is, at least in the large, the inquirer's own scheme. The resources for the inquiry are, in the main, drawn from the very scheme whose limits we are already looking beyond in order to conceive the project. This undertaking therefore engages me in a sort of flirtation with meaninglessness—dancing about a region of cognitive gaps and negative semantic spaces,[1] kept aloft only by the rhythm and momentum of my own motion, trying to plumb abysses which are generally agreed not to exist and to map the tensions which create them. The danger is of falling into incoherence. But conceptual schemes have saving complexities such that their structures and substructures imitate and reflect each other and one thus can locate holes and gaps indirectly which cannot, in the nature of the thing, be directly named.

I start with a semantic reminder.

II

Reality is that which is.
The English word "real" stems from a word which
    meant regal, of or pertaining to the king.

"Real" in Spanish means *royal*.

Real property is that which is proper to the king.

Reality is that which pertains to the one in power,
    is that over which he has power, is his domain,
    his estate, is proper to him.

The ideal king reigns over everything as far as the
    eye can see.

His eye. What he cannot see is not royal, not real.

He sees what is proper to him.

To be real is to be visible to the king.

The king is in his counting house.

III

I say, "I am a lesbian. The king does not count lesbians. Lesbians are not real. There are no lesbians." To say this, I use the word "lesbian," and hence one might think that there is a word for this thing, and thus that the thing must have a place in the conceptual scheme. But this is not so. Let me take you on a guided tour of a few standard dictionaries, to display some reasons for saying that lesbians are not named in the lexicon of the King's English.

If you look up the word "lesbian" in *The Oxford English Dictionary,* you find an entry that says it is an adjective that means *of or pertaining to the island of Lesbos,* and an entry describing at length and favorably an implement called a lesbian rule, which is a flexible measuring device used by carpenters. Period.

Webster's Third International offers a more pertinent definition. It tells us that a lesbian is a homosexual female. And going on, one finds that "homosexual" means *of or pertaining to the same sex.*

The elucidating example provided is the phrase "homosexual twins" which means *same-sex twins.* The alert scholar can conclude that a lesbian is a same-sex female.

A recent edition of *Webster's Collegiate Dictionary* tells us that a lesbian is a woman who has sex, or sexual relations, with other women. Such a definition would be accepted by many speakers of the language and at least seems to be coherent, even if too narrow. But the appearance is deceptive, for this account collapses into nonsense, too. The key word in this definition is "sex": having sex or having sexual relations. But what is having sex? It is worthwhile to follow this up because the pertinent dictionary entries obscure an important point about the logic of sex. Getting clear about that point helps one see that there is a semantic closure against recognition of the existence of lesbians, and it also prepares the way for understanding the connection between the place of *woman* and the place of *lesbian* with respect to the phallocentric scheme of things.[2]

Dictionaries generally agree that "sexual" means something on the order of *pertaining to the genital union of a female and a male animal,* and thus that "having sex" is having intercourse—intercourse being defined as the penetration of a vagina by a penis, with ejaculation. My own observation of usage leads me to think these accounts are inadequate and misleading. Some uses of these terms do fit this dictionary account. For instance, parents and counselors standardly remind young women that if they are going to be sexually active they must deal responsibly with the possibility of becoming pregnant. In this context, the word "sexually" is pretty clearly being used in a way that accords with the given definition. But many activities and events fall under the rubric "sexual," apparently without semantic deviance, though they do not involve penile penetration of the vagina of a female human being. Penile penetration of almost anything, especially if it is accompanied by ejaculation, counts as having sex or being sexual. Moreover, events which cannot plausibly be seen as pertaining to penile erection, penetration and ejaculation will, in general, not be counted as sexual, and events that do not involve penile penetration or ejaculation will not be counted as having sex. For instance, if a girlfriend is fondled and aroused by a man, and comes to orgasm, but the man refrains from penetration and ejaculation, the man can say, and speakers of English will generally agree, that he did not have sex with her. No matter what is going on, or (it must be mentioned) *not* going on, with respect to female arousal or orgasm, or in connection with the vagina, a pair can be said without semantic deviance to have had sex, or not to have had sex; the use of that term turns entirely on what is going on with respect to the penis.

When one first considers the dictionary definitions of "sex" and "sexual," it seems that all sexuality is heterosexuality, by definition, and that the term "homosexual" would be internally contradictory. There are uses of the term according to which this is exactly so. But in the usual and standard use, there is nothing semantically odd in describing two men as having sex with each other. According to that usage, any situation in which one or more penises are present is one in which something could happen that could be called having sex. But on this apparently "broader" definition there is nothing women could do in the absence of men that could, without semantic oddity, be called "having sex." Speaking of women who have sex with other women is like speaking of ducks who engage in arm wrestling.

When the dictionary defines lesbians as women who have sex or sexual relations with other women, it defines lesbians as logically impossible.

Looking for other words in the lexicon that might denote these beings which are non-named "lesbians," one thinks of terms in the vernacular, like "dyke," "bulldagger" and so on. Perhaps it is just as well that standard dictionaries do not pretend to provide relevant definitions of such terms. Generally, these two terms are used to denote women who are perceived as imitating, dressing up like, or trying to be men. Whatever the extent of the class of women who are perceived to do such things, it obviously is not coextensive with the class of lesbians. Nearly every feminist, and many other women as well, have been perceived as wishing to be men, and a great many lesbians are not so perceived. The term "dyke" has been appropriated by some lesbians as a term of pride and solidarity, but in that use it is unintelligible to most speakers of English.

One of the current definitions of "lesbianism" among lesbians is *woman-loving*—the polar opposite of **misogyny.** Several dictionaries I checked have entries for "misogyny" (hatred of women), but not for "philogyny" (love of women). I found one which defines "philogyny" as *fondness for women,* and another dictionary defines "philogyny" as *Don Juanism.* Obviously neither of these means *love of women* as it is intended by lesbians combing the vocabulary for ways to refer to themselves. According to the dictionaries, there is no term in English for the polar opposite of misogyny nor for persons whose characteristic orientation toward women is the polar opposite of misogyny.

Flinging the net wider, one can look up the more Victorian words, like sapphism and sapphist. In

Webster's Collegiate, "sapphism" is defined just as *lesbianism.* But *The Oxford English Dictionary* introduces another twist. Under the heading of "sapphism" is an entry for "sapphist" according to which sapphists are those addicted to unnatural sexual relations between women. The fact that these relations are characterized as unnatural is revealing. For what is unnatural is contrary to the laws of nature, or contrary to the nature of the **substance** of the entity in question. But what is contrary to the laws of nature cannot happen: that is what it means to call these laws the laws of nature. And I cannot do what is contrary to my nature, for if I could do it, it would be in my nature to do it. To call something "unnatural" is to say it cannot be. This definition defines sapphists, that is lesbians, as *naturally* impossible as well as *logically* impossible.

The notion that lesbianism is not possible in nature, that it is nobody's nature to be a lesbian, has a life of its own even among some people who do know factually that there are certain women who do and are inclined to do certain things with other women and who sincerely avow certain feelings and attitudes toward women. Lesbianism can be seen as not natural in that if someone lives as a lesbian, it is not assumed that that is just who, or how, she *is.* Rather, it is presumed to be some sort of affliction, or is a result of failed attempts to solve some sort of problem or resolve some sort of conflict (and if she could find another way, she would take it, and then would not be a lesbian). Being a lesbian is understood as something which could be nobody's natural configuration but must be a configuration one is twisted into by some sort of force which is in some basic sense "external" to one. "Being a lesbian" is understood here as certain sorts of people understand "being a delinquent," or "being an alcoholic." It is not of one's nature the way illness is not of one's nature. To see this sense of "unnatural," one can contrast it with the presumed "naturalness" of the heterosexuality of women. As most people see it, being heterosexual is just being. It is not *interpreted.* It is not understood as a consequence of anything. It is not viewed as possibly a solution to some problem, or as a way of acting and feeling which one worked out or was pushed to by circumstances. On this sort of view, all women *are* heterosexual, and some women somehow come to *act* otherwise. On this view, no one *is,* in the same sense, a lesbian.

There are people who do believe in the real existence of perverts and deviants. What they share with those who do not is the view that the behaviors and attitudes in question are not natural to *humans.* One's choice then, when confronted with someone who says she is a lesbian, is to believe her and class her as not fully or really human, or to class her as fully and really human and not believe that she is a lesbian.

Lesbian.
One of the people of the Isle of Lesbos.

It is bizarre that when I try to name myself and explain myself, my native tongue provides me with a word that is so foreign, so false, so hopelessly inappropriate. Why am I referred to by a term which means *one of the people of Lesbos?*

The use of the word "lesbian" to name us is a quadrifold evasion, a laminated euphemism. To name us, one goes by way of a reference to the island of Lesbos, which in turn is an indirect reference to the poet Sappho (who used to live there, they say), which in turn is itself an indirect reference to what fragments of her poetry have survived a few millennia of **patriarchy,** and this in turn (if we have not lost you by now) is a prophylactic avoidance of direct mention of the sort of creature who would write such poems or to whom such poems would be written . . . assuming you happen to know what is in those poems written in a dialect of Greek over two thousand five hundred years ago on some small island somewhere in the wine dark Aegean Sea.

This is a truly remarkable feat of silence.

The philosopher John Langshaw Austin, commenting on the connection between language and conceptions of reality, said the following: "Our common stock of words embodies all the distinctions men have found worth drawing, and the connections they have found worth marking, in the lifetimes of many generations."[3]

our

common stock of words

men have found

distinction is not worth drawing

connection is not worth marking

Revealing as this is, it still dissembles. It is not that the connections and distinctions are not worth drawing and marking, it is that men do not want to draw and mark them, or do not dare to.

IV

When one says that some thing or some class is not countenanced by a certain conceptual scheme, or that it is not "among the values over which the variables of the system range," or that it is not among the ontological commitments of the system, there are at least three things this can mean. One is just that there is no simple direct term in the system for the thing or class, and no very satisfactory way to explain it. For example, it is in this sense that Western conceptual schemes do not countenance the forces or arrangements called "**karma.**" Indeed, I don't know whether it is suitable to say "forces or arrangements" here, and that is part of the point. A second thing that can be meant when it is said that something is not in the scope of the concepts of the scheme is that the term which ostensibly denotes the thing is internally self-contradictory, as in the case of round squares. Nothing can be in both the class denoted by "round" and the class denoted by "square," given what those words mean. A third thing one can mean when one says a scheme does not encompass a certain thing is that according to principles which are fundamental to the most general picture of how things are in the world, the thing could not exist in nature. An example of this is the denial that there could be a beast which was a cross between a dog and a cat. The belief that such a thing could exist would be inconsistent with beliefs about the nature of the world and of animals which underlie vast chunks of the rest of our world view.

Lesbian is the only class I have ever set out to define, the only concept I have ever set out to explain, that seemed to be shut out in more than one of these ways. As the considerations reviewed here seem to show, it is shut out in all three. You can "not believe in lesbians" as you don't believe in the possibility of "doggie-cats" or as you don't believe in round squares; or you can be just unable to accommodate lesbianism in the way I cannot accommodate the notion of karma—it doesn't articulate suitably with the rest of my concepts; it can't be worked into my active conceptual repertoire.

The redundancy of the devices of closure which are in place here is one of the things which leads me to say that lesbians are *excluded* from the scheme. The overdetermination, the metaphysical overkill, signals a manipulation, a scurrying to erase, to divert the eye, the attention, the mind. Where there is manipulation there is motivation, and it does not seem plausible to me that the reason lies with the physical details of certain women's private lives. The meaning of this erasure and of the totality and conclusiveness of it has to do, I think, with the maintenance of phallocratic reality as a whole, and with the situation of women generally *a propos* that reality.

V

At the outset I said lesbians are not real, that there are no lesbians. I want to say also that women in general are not countenanced by the phallocratic scheme, are not real; there are no women. But the predicament of women *a propos* the dominant reality is complex and paradoxical, as is revealed in women's mundane experience of the seesaw of demand and neglect, of being romanced and assaulted, of being courted and being ignored. The observations which lead me to say there are no women in phallocratic reality themselves also begin to reveal the elements of the **paradox.** These observations are familiar to feminists; they are among the things we come back to again and again as new layers of their meanings become accessible to our understanding.

There are two kinds of erasure of women which have by now become "often noted." One is the conception of human history as a history of the acts and organizations of men, and the other is a long and sordid record in western civilization of the murder and mutilation of women. Both of these erasures are extended into the future, the one in fiction and speculation, the other in the technological projects of sperm selection for increasing the proportion of male babies, of extrauterine gestation, of cloning, of male to female transsexual reconstruction. Both sorts of erasure seem entwined in the pitched religious and political battle between males who want centralized male control of female reproductive functions, and males who want individualized male control of female reproductive functions. (I speak of the fights about abortion, forced sterilization, the conditions of birthing, etc.)

A reasonable person might think that these efforts to erase women reveal an all-too-vivid recognition that there *are* women—that the projects of ideological and material elimination of women presuppose belief in the existence of the objects to be eliminated. In a way, I agree. But also, there is a peculiar mode of relating belief and action which I think is characteristic of the construction of phallocratic reality, according to which a project of annihilation can be seen to presuppose the nonexistence of the objects being eliminated. This mode is an insane reversal of the reasonable procedure of adjusting one's views so that they accord with reality as actively discovered: it is a mode according to which one begins with a firmly held view, composed from fabulous images of oneself, and adopts as one's project the alteration of the world to bring it into accord with that view.

A powerful example of this strange practice was brought to my attention by Harriet Desmoines who had been reading about the United States' expansion across the North American continent. It seems that the white men, upon encountering the vast and rich midcontinental prairie, called the prairie a *desert*. They conceived a desert, they took it to be a desert, and a century later it is a desert (a fact which is presently somewhat obscured by the annual use of megatons of chemical fertilizers). Did they *really* believe that what they were seeing was a desert? It is a matter of record that that is what they *said* they saw.

There is another example of this sort of practice to be found in the scientific and medical realm, which was brought to my attention by the work of Eileen Van Tassell. It is a standard assumption in the disciplines of human biology and human medicine that the species consists of two sexes, male and female. Concrete physical evidence that there are individuals of indeterminate sex and that "sex-characteristics" occur in spectrums and not as all-or-nothing phenomena is not acknowledged as existent evidence but is removed, erased, through chemical and surgical "cures" and "corrections." In this case, as in the case of the rich and living prairie, erasure of fact and destruction of concrete objects does not demonstrate recognition of the fact or object; it is, on the contrary, direct manifestation of the belief that those are not the facts and the belief that no such individual objects exist.

If it is true that this mode of connection of belief and action is characteristic of phallocentric culture, then one can construct or reconstruct beliefs which are fundamental to that culture's conceptual/scientific system by inspecting the culture's projects and reasoning that what is believed is what the projects would make to be true. As noted before, there are and have long been ongoing projects whose end will be a world with no women in it. Reasoning back, one can conclude that those whose projects these are believe there are no women.

For many of us, the idea that there are no women, that we do not exist, began to dawn when we first grasped the point about the nongeneric so-called "generic," "man." The word "woman" was supposed to mean *female of the species,* but the name of the species is "Man." The term "female man" has a tension of logical impossibility about it that is absent from parallel terms like "female cat" and "female terrier." It makes one suspect that the concept of the species which is operative here is one according to which there are no females of the species. I think one can begin to get a handle on what this means by seeing how it meshes with another interesting phenomenon, namely the remarkable fact that so many men from so many stations in life have so often declared that women are unintelligible to them.

Reading or hearing the speeches of men on the unintelligibility of women, I imagine these men are like people who for some reason can see everything but automobiles and are constantly and painfully perplexed by blasts and roars, thumps and bumps, which they cannot avoid, control or explain. But it is not quite like that, for such men do seem to recognize our physical existence, or at least the existence of some of our parts. What they do not see is our souls.

The phallocratic scheme does not admit women as authors of perception, as seers. Man understands his own perception as simultaneously generating and being generated by a point of view. Man is understood to author names; men have a certain status as points of intellectual and perceptual origin. Insofar as the phallocratic scheme permits the understanding that women perceive at all, it features women's perceptions as passive, repetitive of men's perception, nonauthoritative. Aristotle said it

outright: Women are rational, but do not have authority.[4]

Imagine two people looking at a statue, one from the front, the other from the back, and imagine that the one in front thinks the one in back must be seeing exactly what he is seeing. He cannot fathom how the other can come up with a description so different from his own. It is as though women are assumed to be robots hooked up to the senses of men—not using senses of our own, not authoring perception, not having and generating a point of view. And then they cannot fathom how we must be wired inside, that we could produce the output we produce from the input they assume to be identical with their own. The hypothesis that we are seeing from a different point of view, and hence simply seeing something he cannot see, is not available to a man, is not in his repertoire, so long as his total conception of the situation includes a conception of women as not authoritative perceivers like himself, that is, so long as he does not count women as men. And no wonder such a man finds women incomprehensible.

VI

For the reasons given, and in the ways indicated, I think there is much truth in the claim that the phallocratic scheme does not include women. But while women are erased in history and in speculation, physically liquidated in gynocidal purges and banished from the community of those with perceptual and semantic authority, we are on the other hand regularly and systematically invited, seduced, cajoled, coerced and even paid to be in intimate and constant association with men and their projects. In this, the situation of women generally is radically different from the situation of lesbians. Lesbians are not invited to join—the family, the party, the project, the procession, the war effort. There is a place for a woman in every game. Wife, secretary, servant, prostitute, daughter, assistant, babysitter, mistress, seamstress, proof-reader, nurse, confidante, masseuse, indexer, typist, mother. Any of these is a place for a woman, and women are much encouraged to fill them. None of these is a place for a lesbian.

The exclusion of women from the phallocratic scheme is not simple and absolute. Women's existence is both absolutely necessary to and irresolvably problematic for the dominant reality and those committed to it, for our existence is *presupposed* by phallocratic reality, but it is not and cannot be *encompassed* by or countenanced by that reality. Women's existence is a background against which phallocratic reality is a foreground.

A foreground scene is created by the motion of foreground figures against a static background. Foreground figures are perceptible, are defined, have identity, only in virtue of their movement against a background. The space in which the motion of foreground figures takes place is created and defined by their movement with respect to each other and against the background. But nothing of the background is *in* or is *part of* or is *encompassed by* the foreground scene and space. The background is unseen by the eye which is focused on foreground figures, and if anything somehow draws the eye to the background, the foreground dissolves. What would draw the eye to the background would be any sudden or well-defined motion in the background. Hence there must be either no motion at all in the background, or an unchanging buzz of small, regular and repetitive motions. The background must be utterly un*event*ful if the foreground is to continue to hang together, that is, if it is to endure as *a space* within which there are discrete *objects* in relation to each other.

I imagine phallocratic reality to be the space and figures and motion which constitute the foreground, and the constant repetitive uneventful activities of women to constitute and maintain the background against which this foreground plays. It is essential to the maintenance of the foreground reality that nothing within it refer in any way to anything in the background, and yet it depends absolutely upon the existence of the background. It is useful to carry this metaphor on in a more concrete mode—thinking of phallocratic reality as a dramatic production on a stage.

The motions of the actors against the stage settings and backdrop constitute and maintain the existence and identities of the characters in the play. The stage setting, props, lights and so forth are created, provided, maintained and occasionally rearranged (according to the script) by stagehands. The stagehands, their motions and the products of

those motions, are neither in nor part of the play, are neither in nor part of the reality of the characters. The reality in the framework of which Hamlet's actions have their meaning would be rent or shattered if anything Hamlet did or thought referred in any way to the stagehands or their activities, or if that background blur of activity were in any way to be resolved into attention-catching events.

The situation of the actors is desperately paradoxical. The actors are absolutely committed to the maintenance of the characters and the characters' reality: participation as characters in the ongoing creation of Reality is their **raison d'être.** The reality of the character must be lived with fierce concentration. The actor must be immersed in the play and undistracted by any thought for the scenery, props or stagehands, lest the continuity of the characters and the integrity of their reality be dissolved or broken. But if the character must be lived so intently, who will supervise the stagehands to make sure they don't get rowdy, leave early, fall asleep or walk off the job? (Alas, there is no god nor heavenly host to serve as Director and Stage Managers.) Those with the most intense commitment to the maintenance of the reality of the play are precisely those most interested in the proper deportment of the stagehands, and this interest competes directly with that commitment. There is nothing the actor would like better than that there be no such thing as stagehands, posing as they do a constant threat to the very existence, the very life, of the character and hence to the meaning of the life of the actor; and yet the actor is irrevocably tied to the stagehands by his commitment to the play. Hamlet, of course, has no such problems; there are no stagehands in the play.

To escape his dilemma, the actor may throw caution to the wind and lose himself in the character, whereupon stagehands are unthinkable, hence unproblematic. Or he may construct and embrace the belief that the stagehands share exactly his own perceptions and interests and that they are as committed to the play as he—that they are like robots. On such a hypothesis he can assume them to be absolutely dependable and go on about his business single-mindedly and without existential anxiety. A third strategy, which is in a macabre way more sane, is that of trying to solve the problem technologically by constructing actual robots to serve as stagehands.[5]

Given the primacy of this commitment to the play, all solutions must involve one form or another of annihilation of the stagehands. Yet all three require the existence of stagehands; the third, he would hope, requiring it only for a while longer.

The solution to the actor's problem which will appear most benign with respect to the stagehands because it erases the erasure, is that of training, persuading and seducing the stagehands into *loving* the actors and taking the actors' interests and commitments unto themselves as their own. One significant advantage to this solution is that the actors can carry on without the guilt or confusion that might come with annihilating, replacing or falsely forgetting the stagehands. As it turns out, of course, even this is a less than perfect solution. Stagehands, in the thrall of their commitment, can become confused and think of themselves as actors—and then they may disturb the play by trying to enter it as characters, by trying to participate in the creation and maintenance of Reality. But there are various well-known ways to handle these intrusions and this seems to be, generally speaking, the most popular solution to the actor's dilemma.

VII

All eyes, all attention, all attachment must be focused on the play, which is Phallocratic Reality. Any notice of the stagehands must be oblique and filtered through the interest in the play. Anything which threatens the fixation of attention on the play threatens a cataclysmic dissolution of Reality into Chaos. Even the thought of the possibility of a distraction is a distraction. It is necessary to devise devices and construct systems which will lock out the thought-crime of conceiving the possibility of a direct and attentive focus on anything but Reality.

The ever-present potential for cosmological disaster lies with the background. There is nothing in the nature of the background that disposes it to be appropriately tame: it is not made to serve the foreground, it is just there. It therefore is part of the vocation of phallocratic loyalists to police *attention*. They must make it radically impossible to attend to anything in the background; they must make it impossible to think it possible to fasten one's eye on anything in the background.

We can deduce from this understanding of their motivation *what it is* that phallocratic loyalists are motivated to forbid conceiving. What must not be conceived is *a seer* for whom the background is eventful, dramatic, compelling—whose attention fastens upon stagehands and their projects. The loyalists cannot just identify such seers and kill them, for that would focus the loyalists' own attention on the criminal, hence the crime, hence the object of the crime, and that would interrupt the loyalists' own attention to Reality.

The king is in his counting house. The king is greedy and will count for himself everything he dares to. But his greed itself imposes limits on what he dares to count.

VIII

What the king cannot count is a seer whose perception passes the plane of the foreground Reality and focuses upon the background. A seer whose eye is attracted to the ones working as stagehands—the women. A seer in whose eye the woman has authority, has interests of her own, is not a robot. A seer who has no motive for wanting there to be no women; a seer who is not loyal to Reality. We can take the account of the seer who must be unthinkable if Reality is to be kept afloat as the beginning of an account of what a lesbian is. One might try saying that a lesbian is one who, by virtue of her focus, her attention, her attachment, is disloyal to phallocratic reality. She is not committed to its maintenance and the maintenance of those who maintain it, and worse, her mode of disloyalty threatens its utter dissolution in the mere flick of an eye. This sounds extreme, of course, perhaps even hysterical. But listening carefully to the rhetoric of the fanatic fringe of the phallocratic loyalists, one hears that they do think that feminists, whom they fairly reasonably judge to be lesbians, have the power to bring down civilization, to dissolve the social order as we know it, to cause the demise of the species, by our mere existence.

Even the fanatics do not really believe that a lone maverick lesbian can in a flick of her evil eye atomize civilization, of course. Given the collectivity of conceptual schemes, the way they rest on agreement, a maverick perceiver does not have the power to bring one tumbling down—a point also verified by my own existence as a not-so-powerful maverick. What the loyalists fear, and in this I think they are more-or-less right, is a contagion of the maverick perception to the point where the agreement in perception which keeps Reality afloat begins to disintegrate.

The event of becoming a lesbian is a reorientation of attention in a kind of ontological conversion. It is characterized by a feeling of a world dissolving, and by a feeling of disengagement and re-engagement of one's power as a perceiver. That such a conversion happens signals its possibility to others.

Heterosexuality for women is not simply a matter of sexual preference, any more than lesbianism is. It is a matter of orientation of attention, as is lesbianism, in a metaphysical context controlled by neither heterosexual nor lesbian women. Attention is a kind of passion. When one's attention is on something, one is present in a particular way with respect to that thing. This presence is, among other things, an element of erotic presence. The orientation of one's attention is also what fixes and directs the application of one's physical and emotional work.

If the lesbian sees the woman, the woman may see the lesbian seeing her. With this, there is a flowering of possibilities. The woman, feeling herself seen, may learn that she *can be* seen; she may also be able to know that a woman can see, that is, can author perception. With this, there enters for the woman the logical possibility of assuming her authority as a perceiver and of shifting her own attention. With that there is the dawn of choice, and it opens out over the whole world of women. The lesbian's seeing undercuts the mechanism by which the production and constant reproduction of heterosexuality for women was to be rendered *automatic*. The nonexistence of lesbians is a piece in the mechanism which is supposed to cut off the possibility of choice or alternative at the root, namely at the point of conception.

The maintenance of phallocratic reality requires that the attention of women be focused on men and men's projects—the play; and that attention not be focused on women—the stagehands. Woman-loving, as a spontaneous and habitual orientation of attention is then, both directly and indirectly, inimical

to the maintenance of that reality. And therein lies the reason for the thoroughness of the ontological closure against lesbians, the power of those closed out, and perhaps the key to the liberation of women from oppression in a male-dominated culture.

IX

My primary goal here has not been to state and prove some rigid thesis, but simply to *say* something clearly enough, intelligibly enough, so that it can be understood and thought about. Lesbians are outside the conceptual scheme, and this is something done, not just the way things are. One can begin to see that lesbians are excluded by the scheme, and that this is *motivated*, when one begins to see what purpose the exclusion might serve in connection with keeping women generally in their metaphysical place. It is also true that lesbians and their seeing is why they have to be excluded. Lesbians are woman-seers. When one is suspected of seeing women, one is spat summarily out of reality, through the cognitive gap and into the negative semantic space. If you ask what became of such a woman, you may be told she became a lesbian, and if you try to find out what a lesbian is, you will be told there is no such thing.

But there is.

NOTES

1. Phrase due to Julia Penelope Stanley.
2. The analysis that follows is my own rendering of an account developed by Carolyn Shafer. My version of it is informed also by my reading of "Sex and Reference," by Janice Moulton, *Philosophy and Sex,* edited by Robert Baker and Frederick Elliston (Prometheus Books, Buffalo, New York, 1975).
3. From "A Plea for Excuses," *Philosophical Papers* (Oxford University Press, 1961).
4. *Politics* I 13, 1260a13. My attention was first brought to this by a paper, "Aristotle's Views on Women in the *Politics,*" presented at the meetings of the Western Division of the Society for Women in Philosophy, Fall 1974, by Jan Bidwell, Susan Ekstrom, Sue Hildebrand, and Rhoda H. Kotzin.
5. This solution is discussed in *The Transsexual Empire: The Making of the She-Male,* by Janice G. Raymond (Beacon Press, Boston, 1979).

Questions for Thought

1. How would you define the term *lesbian?* Do you think that Frye would find your definition to be problematic? Why or why not?
2. To what extent do you believe that the dominant conception of reality in our society is phallocratic? Assuming for the moment that it is phallocratic, why do you think that this is the case?
3. Can you think of specific examples of what Frye refers to as the "erasure of women"?
4. How does Frye explain the fact that so many men have claimed that women are unintelligible? What do such claims reveal?
5. Do you think that Frye's extended metaphor accurately represents the place of men and women in the dominant conception of reality? Defend your answer.
6. You have probably heard the popular saying "Behind every great man is a great woman." How do you think Frye would respond to this saying? What is your response to it?
7. Do you agree with Frye's claim that lesbians occupy a special epistemic position? Why or why not?

Chapter 3

Knowledge and Truth

Introductory Remarks

WHILE READING THE SELECTIONS IN THE LAST CHAPTER, you may have wondered how the authors knew what they claimed to know and whether some of their claims were true. Did Bumba really vomit up the sun and moon? Is this statement to be taken literally? If it is, how did the originator of this myth know that Bumba threw up the sun and moon? Indeed, how did he or she even know that Bumba existed? In later selections, you were told that originally there was only the one self in the form of a person and that the ultimate components of reality are windowless, spiritual entities called **Monads.** One does not have to be extremely skeptical to wonder whether these statements are true. And even if you believe they are true, you might still wonder how the author came to know them.

If any of these questions occurred to you as you were reading earlier selections, then you were, like it or not, on the verge of traversing yet another philosophical path. We can call this path the path of reflecting on knowledge and truth, known in Western philosophy as the path of epistemological thinking. Indeed, in traditional Western philosophy, especially during the seventeenth and eighteenth centuries, this was a favorite path of philosophers. Reacting against the metaphysical claims that were commonly heard in his day, the British philosopher John Locke reportedly commented to one of his friends, "You and I have had enough of this kind of fiddling." Even though Locke's *An Essay Concerning Human Understanding* contains some metaphysical fiddling itself, his principal purpose in writing the book was to examine human mental faculties and to establish the boundaries and limitations of human knowledge. Of course, Locke was just one of many traditional Western philosophers who traveled down the path of epistemological thinking.

The quest to define and understand the nature of truth has an equally long history. While earlier Greek philosophers, including Plato and Aristotle, had already addressed this problem, it was a Roman government official named Pontius Pilate who gave voice to one of the simplest and best-known formulations of the question itself. During his examination of Jesus of Nazareth, Pilate reportedly asked, "What is truth?" Moreover, in ancient China as in ancient Greece, philosophers not only pondered this question but also attempted to formulate the rules of disputation—that is, rules that could be used to distinguish true statements from false ones.

Overview of Selections

The selections in this chapter represent philosophical attempts, from a wide array of sources, to determine the nature and limitations of knowledge and truth. All the writers of the selections in the first part affirm that knowledge and truth are obtainable, but they often disagree over what can be known and how we go about knowing it. While the writers of the selections in the second part sometimes address these issues as well, they focus primarily on the limitations of what we can know. This focus leads them to question the possibility of certain types of knowledge claims and, in some cases, to maintain that the search for truth and knowledge is futile.

In the first selection, the French philosopher René Descartes defends the position known as **rationalism.** The rationalist position is that certain indubitable truths, discovered through "rational **intuition,**" provide the foundation for all other knowledge claims. In the next two selections, John Locke and George Berkeley, two British empiricists, reject the rationalist position and argue that all knowledge comes from experience. Interestingly, Berkeley's **empiricism,** unlike that of Locke, leads him to deny the commonsense belief in the existence of physical objects.

The fourth and fifth selections in the first section are written, respectively, by two American philosophers, Charles Sanders Peirce and William James. Peirce discusses the various methods by which people arrive at the beliefs they hold, while arguing that the modern scientific method is the most reliable way of fixing belief. Following Peirce, James denies the existence of fixed or eternal truths, while specifically defending the pragmatic conception of truth. In James' formulation, the pragmatic conception of truth maintains that a statement is true if it "works"—that is, if it allows us to overcome a difficulty and to enhance our lives.

The final four selections in the first part all suggest, at least implicitly, that these traditional Western ways of viewing the nature of knowledge and truth are inadequate. The Mexican philosopher José Vasconcelos argues that traditional Western philosophical thinking about knowledge has overemphasized the value of reason and analytical judgments, thereby failing to recognize the importance of **aesthetic** judgments. Next, Karl Jaspers identifies and describes four modes of being human and claims that a different conception of truth is operative for each mode. He believes that one of these conceptions of truth, the conception that is operative at the level of *Existenz* (or authentic existence), has been overlooked by most philosophers. Third, the Navajo philosopher Herbert John Benally also describes four types of knowledge that are necessary for human life, while suggesting that some of these ways of knowing have been lost in modern secular society. Finally, Jorge Valadez examines the social and political implications of certain epistemological claims, while arguing that certain assumptions of Western epistemological thinking have led to **metaphysical imperialism,** an imperialism that can be overcome only if we adopt a multicultural perspective.

The selections in the second part of the chapter raise doubts about the possibility of attaining knowledge. The first three, which are taken from diverse times and cultures, suggest that the universe is constantly changing and, thus, theoretical knowledge of the universe is impossible. Each of these selections also warns us that philosophical disputation is divisive and ultimately fruitless. While the next three selections also raise questions concerning the possibility of knowledge, they use different routes to do so. The Scottish philosopher David Hume examines the nature of our knowledge claims and argues that all knowledge falls into two categories. He then argues that the line of reasoning associated with the category that gives us information about the world, the category that he calls "matters of fact," cannot be theoretically justified. Next, Alfred Jules Ayer adopts Hume's division of knowledge claims into two categories before arguing that metaphysical statements do not fall into either of the categories. This leads Ayer to conclude that such statements are utterly meaningless. Finally, Elizabeth Anderson discusses how feminist epistemologists have called attention to the ways in which knowers are situated in relation to what is known and to other knowers. While not ruling out the possibility of objective knowledge, Anderson claims that once the situatedness of the knower is taken into account, the possibility of objective knowledge becomes much more problematic.

Reading these selections can help you on your own journey down the path of epistemological thinking, but they cannot serve as substitutes for your own reflections. You will find this chapter much more meaningful if you compare and contrast your beliefs with those of the authors. In short, the most important questions are the following:

What do you believe to be true?
How do you know that what you believe to be true is indeed true?

Contemporary Applications

While the topics in the first two chapters may have initially seemed somewhat esoteric, somewhat removed from the concerns of everyday life, we are constantly confronted by issues that require us to think about questions concerning knowledge and truth. If you doubt the *truth* of this claim, just turn on your television to the evening news and look at what is being presented. In the course of the program, you will no doubt be presented with numerous statements of fact. Some of these statements of fact will be fairly straightforward and noncontroversial. For example, you may be told that a bus collided with a truck on Interstate 5. The pictures that usually accompany such reports serve as evidence that such an accident did in fact occur, and you normally believe that what the reporter is saying is true.

However, other things that you hear on the news may not be so straightforward and simple. The reporter mentions that a foreign news agency has reported that a missile fired by a U.S. warplane has missed its intended target, hit a hospital, and killed seven people. The reporter then adds that the number of casualties has not been "independently verified." What exactly does that mean? Why do we not simply accept the report of the foreign news agency as we did the report of the accident on Interstate 5? One answer to this question is that perhaps the foreign news agency is biased, perhaps it is distorting the facts (either intentionally or unintentionally) to make the United States look bad.

In thinking about this answer, however, you may come up with even more questions. If the reporting of foreign news agencies can be biased, might not news reporting in the

United States or Canada be biased as well? (This doubt will take on added substance if you are familiar with any of the past fabrications found in the media, such as reports after the Japanese attack on Pearl Harbor that stated only one U.S. battleship had been sunk, whereas the Japanese had suffered heavy casualties.) The news media allegedly report the facts. But what exactly is a fact? The philosopher Friedrich Nietzsche once said that there are no facts, only "interpretations." What do you think Nietzsche meant by that? Is he right?

Thinking further about the news example, you may wonder what "independently verified" means. If you look up the word *verify* in your dictionary, you will find that it means "to show that something is true." But how exactly does one go about showing that something is true? Consider the following statements:

"The lights are on in the room in which you are reading this sentence."
"The lights are not on in the room in which you are reading this sentence."
"Intelligent life exists elsewhere in the universe."
"Intelligent life exists only on the planet Earth."
"Abortion is morally wrong."
"Abortion is not morally wrong."
"God exists."
"God does not exist."

Which of these statements do you think are true? Can they all be true? If not, why not? How do you know that the true ones are indeed true? How would you go about verifying them? Almost all the selections in this chapter have some bearing on these questions.

Let's consider a couple of examples of a more personal nature. When I was a student at the University of South Carolina, I was walking across the quad one day, when I spotted a friend whom I had not seen for quite some time. I waved joyously and picked up my pace, wondering why my friend did not wave back. When I got closer, however, I saw that it was not my friend but a total stranger. Yet, until that moment, I had no doubt that the person I saw was my friend.

Throughout my life, I have been very fortunate in being able to remember many of my dreams. One night, while I was having one of my scarier dreams, I asked myself, "Is this only a dream?" Then I answered myself that I was indeed dreaming. The dream continued, but I was no longer afraid. However, I often wonder what would have happened if I had answered that it was *not* a dream.

I have also had dreams that I was a child playing in a store in the Old West and that I was an infantryman fighting the Nazis during World War II. How do I know that these images were only dreams? Some people might believe that they were memories from former lives. For that matter, how do I know that some of the memories of things I have done in my present life represent things I have actually done and not things that I have only dreamed of doing?

Have you had experiences such as these, experiences that lead you to question the reliability of your senses, experiences that cause you to wonder whether it is possible to always know when you are dreaming and when you are not? If you think about it, you will probably be able to remember at least one occasion on which you were mistaken about something, an occasion on which you felt just as foolish as I did when I mistook a stranger for my friend. Or are you only remembering an occurrence that happened in a dream?

How Do We Know What We Know?

Meditations on the Nature of Knowledge   1

RENÉ DESCARTES

René Descartes (1596–1650), who is often referred to as the father of modern philosophy, was born in the small town of La Haye in France. At the age of eight, Descartes was sent to the newly opened Jesuit college of La Flèche. Although he later expressed disdain for most of the education he received from the Jesuits, Descartes did develop an intense interest in mathematics while attending the college. This interest later reached fruition when Descartes discovered the fundamental principles of analytic geometry.

After leaving the college of La Flèche, Descartes went to the University of Poitiers, from which he received a law degree in 1616. This was followed by a period of travel and military adventure. In 1618, he joined the army of the prince of Orange of Holland, and in 1619 he served in the army of the duke of Bavaria. During one of his military campaigns, Descartes had a dream, which he interpreted as a divine revelation, that his true goal in life was to develop a unified science, a science that would bring together the various branches of knowledge into a comprehensive explanation of all phenomena. Descartes' first written attempt to achieve this goal, the never-completed *Regulae ad Directionem Ingenii* (*Rules for the Direction of the Mind*), was written approximately ten years after this dream. Descartes spent those ten years, like the immediately preceding ones, traveling around Europe.

In 1628, Descartes was residing in Paris when he was involved in a famous debate about the nature of science. Later that year, he moved to Amsterdam, and, aside from a few brief excursions, he lived there for the next twenty-one years. In Amsterdam, he worked further on his goal of developing a unified science while writing the books that established his reputation as a philosopher and mathematician. These included the *Discours de la méthode* (1637; *Discourse on Method*), the *Meditationes de prima Philosophia* (1641; *Meditations on First Philosophy*), the *Principia philosophiae* (1644; *Principles of Philosophy*), and *Les passions de l'âme* (1649; *The Passions of the Soul*).

In 1649, Descartes received an invitation from Queen Christina of Sweden to join her court in Stockholm as a philosophical tutor. With reluctance, he accepted the queen's invitation. This decision proved tragic when he died of pneumonia in Stockholm the following winter.

In the following selection from his *Meditations,* Descartes advocates the philosophical position known as **rationalism**—that is, the position that we know reality by means of reason and not by means of sense experience. Rather than immediately arguing for this position, Descartes begins by attempting methodically to doubt everything that he believes. Noting that all his knowledge claims are based on either sense experience or reason, Descartes offers several arguments to call each of these sources of knowledge into question. First, he argues that since his senses have sometimes deceived him in the past, he cannot be absolutely certain that they are not deceiving him now. Then after briefly mentioning the possibility that his sense experiences could merely be the delusions of a madman, Descartes concludes his questioning of sense experience by formulating his well-known dream argument. In this argument, Descartes claims that since he cannot discover any way in which waking experience can be absolutely distinguished from sleeping experience, it is possible that what he is now experiencing is merely a dream.

While Descartes believes that these arguments suffice to make him doubt all his knowledge claims derived from sense experience, they are not powerful enough to make him doubt simple truths of reason, such as the claim that a square must have four sides. In order to show the doubtfulness of these types of claims, Descartes raises the possibility that he was created by a God who formed him so that his reasoning is always mistaken. Indeed, he goes on to suggest that perhaps he was not created by a divine being at all but rather by an all-powerful evil genius who receives great pleasure in deceiving him. He also argues that rejecting the belief that he was created by an all-powerful being does not eliminate the possibility that his reasoning is mistaken, for the less powerful his creator, the more likely it is that his reasoning is fallible. With these final arguments Descartes believes that he has succeeded in raising doubts concerning all his former beliefs, and he concludes Meditation I in a state of extreme uncertainty.

In Meditation II, Descartes looks for and finds a truth that he believes he cannot doubt: the truth of his own existence. Descartes argues that even if an all-powerful evil genius were deceiving him about everything else, he must exist in order to be deceived. As he says, "The proposition, 'I am, I exist,' is necessarily true each time I pronounce or mentally conceive it."

Having discovered his first truth, Descartes then proceeds to examine the nature of his being and the nature of knowledge. Since he is not yet sure that he has a body, he argues that he is justified only in believing that he is a thinking thing—that is, that he is a mind or soul. Finally, near the end of Meditation II, Descartes defends the rationalist position that knowledge results from reason, or what he calls an **"intuition** of the mind." Using a piece of wax as an example, he argues that even physical bodies cannot be known by sense experience or by the imagination but only by the understanding.

Questions for Reading

1. Why does Descartes resolve to doubt everything that he knows?
2. What arguments does Descartes give for doubting knowledge claims derived from sense experience? What is the basic supposition of his famous dream argument?
3. What arguments does Descartes give for doubting knowledge claims derived from reason? Why does he introduce the supposition of the evil genius?
4. What is Descartes' first truth, and how does he discover it? On what grounds does he claim that this truth is indubitable?
5. What happens to the piece of wax in Meditation II? What is this intended to prove?

MEDITATION I

SOME YEARS HAVE PASSED SINCE I FIRST DE-
tected how many of the beliefs that I had held to be
true from an early age were actually false, and how
doubtful everything was that I had since
constructed on their basis. From that time, I was
convinced that if I wanted to establish any firm and
permanent structure in the sciences, I must seriously undertake to rid myself of all the opinions
that I had formerly accepted, and begin to build
anew from the foundation. But as this appeared to
be a very great undertaking, I waited until I had
reached an age so mature that I could not hope to
be better fitted to execute my design at any later
date. This reason caused me such a delay that I feel
I would be acting improperly if I were to spend the
time that yet remains to me in deliberation rather
than in action. Today, very favorably for the plan I
have in view, I have freed my mind from every care,
and have procured for myself an assured and peaceable leisure. Thus, I will at last seriously and openly
address myself to the general upheaval of all my former opinions. Now for this purpose it is not necessary that I show that all of these opinions are false,
for I would perhaps never arrive at this end. But
since reason already persuades me that I should
withhold my assent from matters which are not entirely certain and indubitable just as carefully as I
do from those which appear manifestly to be false,
finding in each one some reason to doubt will suffice to justify my rejecting the whole. For that end
it will not be necessary for me to examine each particular belief, which would be an endless undertaking. Owing to the fact that the destruction of the
foundations necessarily brings with it the downfall
of the rest of the edifice, I will only attack those
principles upon which all my former opinions
rested.

All that I have so far accepted as most true and
certain, I have learned either from the senses or
through the senses. However, it is sometimes
proved to me that these senses are deceptive, and it
is wiser not to entirely trust any thing by which we
have once been deceived.

But it may be that although the senses sometimes deceive us concerning things which are
barely perceptible or very far away, there are yet
many others of which we cannot reasonably have
any doubt, although we recognize them through
the senses. For example, there is the fact that I am
here, seated by the fire, attired in a dressing gown,
having this paper in my hands, and so on. How
could I deny that these hands and this body are
mine? Perhaps I could only do so by comparing
myself to certain persons, devoid of sense, whose
cerebella are so troubled and clouded by the violent vapors of black bile that they constantly assure
us that they are kings when they are really quite
poor, or that they are clothed in purple when they
are really naked, or that they have an earthenware
head, or that they are nothing but pumpkins, or
that they are made of glass. But they are mad, and
I would be just as insane were I to follow examples
so extravagant.

At the same time I must remember that I am a
man, and that consequently I am in the habit of
sleeping and of representing to myself in dreams the
same things, or sometimes even less probable
things, than do those who are insane in their waking
moments. How often in the night have I dreamed
that I found myself in this particular place, dressed
and seated near the fire, while in reality I was lying
undressed in bed! At this moment it does indeed
seem to me that I am awake and looking at this
paper, that this head which I move is not asleep,
that I extend my hand deliberately and perceive it.
What happens in sleep does not appear so clearly or
so distinctly as does all this. However, in thinking
about this, I remind myself that on many occasions
I have in sleep been deceived by similar illusions.
Dwelling carefully on this reflection, I see so manifestly that there are no certain indications by which
we may clearly distinguish wakefulness from sleep
that I am lost in astonishment, an astonishment so

This Selection from Descartes' Meditations *is the editor's revised version of the translation found in* The Philosophical
Works of Descartes, *translated by H. S. Haldane and G. R. T. Ross, Cambridge University Press, 1911–1912.*

great that it is almost capable of persuading me that I now dream.

So let us assume that we are asleep and that all these particulars, such as opening our eyes, shaking our head, extending our hands, and so on, are but false delusions. Let us also assume that possibly neither our hands nor our whole body are such as they appear to us to be. At the same time we must at least confess that the things which appear to us in sleep are like painted representations that can only have been formed as the counterparts of something real and true, and that those general things at least, i.e., eyes, a head, hands, and a whole body, are not imaginary but really exist. For, as a matter of fact, even when painters with the greatest skill try to represent sirens and satyrs by the most strange and extraordinary forms, they cannot give them natures which are entirely new, but merely make a certain medley of the members of different animals. Or, even if their imagination is extravagant enough to invent something so novel that nothing similar has ever been seen, even if they represent a thing that is purely fictitious and absolutely false, it is certain that the colors of which this is composed are necessarily real. For the same reason, although these general things, i.e., eyes, a head, and so on, may be imaginary, we are bound to admit that there are some other more simple, more universal objects which are real and true. And just as the inventions of the artist are composed of certain real colors, these objects form all the images of things, whether true and real or false and fantastic, that dwell in our thoughts. To this class of objects belongs corporeal nature in general, its extension, the figure of extended things, their quantity or magnitude and number, the place in which they exist, the time which measures their duration, and so on.

That is possibly why our reasoning is not wrong when we conclude that physics, astronomy, medicine, and all other sciences that examine composite things are very dubious and uncertain, whereas arithmetic, geometry and other sciences which only deal with things that are very simple and very general, without taking great trouble to ascertain whether or not they actually exist, contain some measure of certainty and indubitability. For whether I am awake or asleep, two and three together always

form five, and the square can never have more than four sides. It does not seem possible that truths so clear and apparent can be suspected of any falsity.

Yet, I have long believed that an all-powerful God existed by whom I have been created the way I am. How do I know that He has not brought it to pass that there is no earth, no heaven, no extended body, no magnitude, no place, and that nonetheless they seem to me to exist just exactly as I now see them? Besides, as I sometimes imagine that others deceive themselves in the things which they think they know best, how do I know that I am not deceived every time I add two and three, or count the sides of a square, or judge of things yet simpler, if anything simpler can be imagined? Possibly God has not desired that I should be thus deceived, for He is said to be supremely good. If, however, it is contrary to His goodness to permit me to constantly deceive myself, it would also appear to be contrary to His goodness to permit me to be sometimes deceived. Nevertheless, I cannot doubt that He does permit this.

There may indeed be those who would prefer to deny the existence of a God so powerful, rather than believe that all other things are uncertain. Let us not oppose them for the present, but grant that everything that is said of a God is a fable. Nevertheless, in whatever way they suppose that I have arrived at my present state of being—whether they attribute it to fate, or to accident, or to a continual succession of antecedents, or to some other means—it is clear that, since to err and deceive oneself is a defect, the less powerful the author to whom they assign my origin, the greater will be the probability of my being so imperfect that I always deceive myself. I have nothing to reply to this line of reasoning, and I must confess that there is nothing that I formerly believed to be true which cannot in some measure be doubted, not merely through want of thought or through levity, but for reasons that are very powerful and maturely considered. Hence, if I desire to arrive at any certainty, I ought to carefully refrain from giving credence to these doubtful opinions just as I refrain from giving credence to those which are obviously false.

But it is not enough to have made these remarks; we must also be careful to keep them in mind. For my mind frequently reverts to these ancient and commonly held opinions, long and familiar custom having given them the right to occupy my mind against my inclination, rendering them almost masters of my belief. Nor will I ever lose the habit of accepting or believing in them as long as I view them in terms of what I have just shown them to be, i.e., opinions in some measure doubtful, but at the same time highly probable, so that there is much more reason to believe them than to deny them. Thus, I will not be acting amiss if, for a period of time, I purposely accept a contrary belief, allowing myself to be deceived and pretending that all these opinions are entirely false and imaginary, until at last I have counterbalanced my former opinions. In this way, my judgment will no longer be dominated by bad usage or turned away from the way things really are. For I know that in following this course I will not be led to either peril or error, and that it is impossible for me to be overly distrustful, since I an not now considering the question of action, but only the question of knowledge.

Thus, I will suppose, not that God who is supremely good and the fountain of truth, but some evil genius who is as powerful as he is deceitful, and who has employed his whole energies in deceiving me. I will suppose that the heavens, the earth, colors, figures, sound, and all other external things are nothing but the illusions and dreams that this genius has used to lay traps for my credulity. I will suppose myself as having no hands, eyes, flesh, blood, or senses, yet falsely believing that I have all these things. I will remain obstinately attached to these suppositions, and if by this means it is not in my power to gain knowledge of any truth, I may at least avoid giving credence to any falsity or being fooled by this arch deceiver, however powerful and deceptive he may be. But this is a difficult task, and a certain weariness leads me back to my everyday concerns. Just as a prisoner who enjoys imaginary liberty fears to awaken when he begins to suspect that his liberty is but a dream, conspiring with these agreeable illusions to prolong the deception, so insensibly of my own accord I revert to my former opinions. I dread awakening from this tranquil slumber, lest the laborious wakefulness which would follow it should have to be spent not in daylight, but in the excessive darkness of the difficulties which have just been discussed.

MEDITATION II

The meditation of yesterday filled my mind with so many doubts that it is no longer in my power to forget them. Yet I do not see how they can be resolved. Just as if I had suddenly fallen into very deep water, I am so disconcerted that I can neither make certain of setting my feet on the bottom, nor swim and remain on the surface. I will nevertheless try by following again the same path that I entered yesterday, i.e., I will proceed by setting aside everything for which there is the least doubt, just as if I had discovered that it was absolutely false. I will follow on this path until I have found something which is certain, or, if I can do nothing else, at least until I have learned for certain that there is nothing in the world that is certain. In order that he might draw the terrestrial globe out of its place and transport it elsewhere, Archimedes demanded only that one point should be fixed and immovable. In the same way I will be justified in having high hopes if I am happy enough to discover a single thing which is certain and indubitable.

I suppose, then, that all the things that I see are false. I persuade myself that nothing that my fallacious memory represents to me has ever existed. I suppose that I possess no senses; and I imagine that body, figure, extension, movement, and place are but the fictions of my mind. What, then, can be accepted as true? Perhaps nothing at all, unless it is that there is nothing in the world that is certain.

But how can I know there is not something different from the things that I have just considered, of which one cannot have the slightest doubt? Is there not some God, or some other being by whatever name we call it, who puts these reflections into my mind? That is not necessary. For is it not possible that I am capable of producing them myself? Yet, am I myself not at least something? I have already denied that I had senses and body. But I hesitate, for what follows from that? Am I so dependent on body and senses that I cannot exist without these? I supposed that there was nothing in all the world—no heaven, no earth, no minds, no bodies. Was I not then persuaded that I did not exist? Not at all. Since I persuaded myself of something, I surely did exist. I supposed that there is some deceiver, very powerful and very cunning, who continuously employs his ingenuity in deceiving me. To be deceived, however, I must necessarily exist. Let him deceive me as much as he will, he can never cause me to be nothing as long as I think that I am something. Thus, after having carefully and deliberately examined all these things, we must conclude with certainty that the proposition, "I am, I exist," is necessarily true each time I pronounce or mentally conceive it. Although I am certain that I exist, I do not yet know clearly enough what I am. Hence, I must be careful not to imprudently mistake some other object for myself, and thus misconceive what I hold to be the most certain and most evident of all that I have formerly learned. That is why I will now consider again what I believed I was before I embarked upon these meditations; and I will eliminate all of my former opinions that might be invalidated, even in a small degree, by the reasons that I have just brought forward. In this way, there will be nothing left that is not absolutely certain and indubitable.

What then did I formerly believe myself to be? Undoubtedly I believed myself to be a man. But what is a man? Shall I say a rational animal? Certainly not. For then I would have to inquire what an animal is, and what it means to be rational; and thus from a single question I would be led to an infinitude of more difficult ones. I do not want to waste the little time and leisure that I have left trying to unravel subtleties like these. Rather, I will stop here to consider the thoughts which involuntarily appeared in my mind, and which were not inspired by anything beyond my own nature, when I examined my being. In the first place, I considered myself as having a face, hands, arms, and everything else designated by the term "body," i.e., the whole system of members made of bones and flesh as seen in a corpse. In addition to this, I considered that I was nourished, that I walked, that I felt, and that I thought. I referred all these actions to the soul, but I did not stop to consider what the soul was, or if I did stop, I imagined that it was something extremely rare and subtle,

like a wind, flame, or ether, dispersed throughout the grosser parts of my body. I had no doubts about the nature of my body, but thought I had a very clear understanding of it. If I had desired to explain it according to what I then thought, I would have said the following: By "body" I mean that which can be defined by a certain figure, which can occupy a particular place, which can fill a given space in such a way that every other body will be excluded from it, which can be perceived either by touch, sight, hearing, taste, or smell, and which can be bumped and moved in many ways by things outside of itself. I did not think it could move itself, for I did not believe that the power of self-movement, or the power of feeling or thinking, belonged to the nature of body. On the contrary, I was rather astonished to find that powers similar to these existed in some bodies. However, now that I assume the existence of a certain extremely powerful and malicious genius who employs all his powers to deceive me, what can I say that I am? Can I affirm that I possess even the least of those things which I have just said pertain to the nature of body? Thinking carefully about the nature of these things, I find that I cannot definitely say that any of them pertains to me. It would be tedious to stop to enumerate them. So, let us move on to the attributes of soul and see if there is any one which is in me. What of nutrition or walking? If it is true that I have no body, it is also true that I cannot walk or take nourishment. Another attribute is sensation. But one cannot feel without a body. Besides I have thought I perceived many things during sleep that, when awake, I realized I had not perceived at all. What of thinking? Now I find that thinking is an attribute that belongs to me; it alone cannot be separated from me. I am, I exist, that is certain. But how often? Just when I think. For it might possibly be the case that if I stopped thinking entirely, I would totally cease to exist. Since I do not now admit anything which is not necessarily true, I conclude that I am nothing more than a thing which thinks. In other words, I am a "mind," a "soul," an "understanding," or a "reason"—terms whose significance was formerly unknown to me. I am indeed a real thing that exists. But what thing? As I have already said, I am a thing which thinks.

But is this all? Let me think about this further. I am not a collection of members that we call the human body. I am not a subtle air dispersed through these members. I am not a wind, fire, vapor, breath, or anything that I can imagine or conceive, because I have assumed that all these were nothing. On the basis of this assumption, I find that I leave myself only certain of the bare fact that I exist. Perhaps it is true that these other things which I have assumed to be nothing are not really different from the "I" that I know. I am not sure about this, and I will not argue about it now. I can only judge about things that I know. I know that I exist, and I inquire what I am. It is very certain that the knowledge of my existence, in its most basic sense, does not depend on things of whose existence I do not yet know. Consequently, it does not depend on things which I can feign in imagination. Indeed the very term "feign in imagination" proves to me my error. Since imagining is nothing else than contemplating the figure or image of a corporeal thing, in feigning myself in imagination, I necessarily imagine myself to be corporeal. Yet, I already know for certain that I exist, while it is possible that all these images, and generally speaking all things pertaining to the nature of body, are nothing but dreams. I thus see clearly that I would have as little reason to say, "I will stimulate my imagination in order to know more distinctly what I am," as I would to say, "I am now awake, and perceive something that is real and true; however, since I do not yet perceive it distinctly enough, I will intentionally go to sleep so that my dreams may represent it with greatest truth and evidence." Therefore, I know for certain that nothing that I can imagine belongs to this knowledge I have of myself, and that it is necessary to diligently keep the mind from imagining if it is to understand its own nature with perfect distinctness.

But what then am I? A thing that thinks. What is a thing that thinks? It is a thing that doubts, understands, affirms, denies, wills, refuses, imagines, and feels.

Certainly it is no small matter if all these things pertain to my nature. And why should they not so pertain? Am I not that being who now doubts nearly everything, who nevertheless understands certain things, who affirms that only one is true, who denies all the others, who desires to know more, who tries not to be deceived, who imagines many things (sometimes despite his will), and who also perceives many things, seemingly by means of the bodily organs? Is not all this just as certain as the fact that I exist, even if I am always sleeping, and even if he who has created me has employed all his ingenuity in deceiving me? Can any one of these attributes be distinguished from my thought, or be separated from myself? For it is so self-evident that it is I who doubts, who understands, and who desires, that no additional reasons are needed to explain it. It is also certain that I have the power of imagining. For although it may happen, as I formerly supposed, that none of the things that I imagine are true, this power of imagining nevertheless does not cease to comprise a part of my thinking. Finally, it is true that I feel or perceive certain things, seemingly by the organs of sense, since I see light, hear noise, and feel heat. But it will be said that these phenomena are false and that I am dreaming. Let it be so. Still it is at least evident that it seems to me that I see light, hear noise, and feel heat. That cannot be false. Properly speaking this is what is called "feeling" in me; and used in this precise sense, it is nothing but thinking.

I am now beginning to know what I am a little more clearly and distinctly than I did before. Nevertheless I still cannot prevent myself from thinking that corporeal things, whose images are framed by thought and tested by the senses, are much more distinctly known than that obscure part of me which does not come under the imagination. Yet, it really would be very strange if I were to better know and understand these things, whose existence seems to me dubious, and which are unknown to me and not part of my nature, than other things, of whose truth I am convinced, and which are known to me and pertain to my real nature—in other words, better than I know myself. But I see clearly what happens. My mind loves to wander, and cannot yet restrain itself within the appropriate limits of truth. Very well, let us once more give it the freest rein, so that, when afterwards we seize the proper moment for pulling in the reins, it may be regulated and controlled more easily.

Let us begin by considering those matters that we commonly believe to be the most distinctly comprehended, namely, the bodies that we touch and see. We will not start with bodies in general, for these general ideas are usually a little more confused, but with one body in particular. Take, for example, this piece of wax. It has been recently taken from the hive, and has not yet lost the sweetness of the honey it contains. It still retains some of the odor of the flowers from which it has been culled. Its color, figure, and size are apparent. It is hard, cold, easily handled, and if you strike it with the finger, it will emit a sound. Finally, everything necessary to cause us to distinctly recognize a body is found in it. Notice, however, that while I speak and approach the fire, what remained of the taste is exhaled, the smell evaporates, the color alters, the figure is destroyed, and the size increases. It becomes liquid, and heats so much that one can hardly handle it. Finally, when one strikes it, no sound is emitted. Does the same wax remain after these changes? We must confess that it does— none would judge otherwise. What then did I know so distinctly in this piece of wax? It could certainly be nothing of which the senses informed me, since everything falling under taste, smell, sight, touch, and hearing have changed, while the same wax remains.

Perhaps the wax was what I now think it is, not that sweetness of honey, nor that agreeable scent of flowers, nor that particular whiteness, nor that figure, nor that sound, but simply a body that I had earlier perceived under certain forms and now perceive under others. But what precisely is it that I imagine in this manner? Focusing on this question, let us abstract from the wax everything that does not belong to it and see what remains. Surely nothing remains except a certain extended thing that is flexible and movable. But what does it mean to be flexible and movable? Is it not that I imagine that this round piece of wax is capable of becoming square, and then of passing from a square to a triangle? No, certainly it is not that, since I see that it admits of an infinitude of similar changes, and these cannot be encompassed by my finite imagination. Consequently, this perception that I have of the wax is not derived from the faculty of imagination. What now does it mean for the wax to be extended? Is this not also unknown? For the extension becomes greater when the wax is melted, even greater when it is boiled, and greater still when the heat increases. I would not truly perceive what wax is, if I did not think that this piece under consideration were capable of undergoing more variations in extension than I have ever imagined. We must thus admit that my imagination could not lead me to an understanding of what this piece of wax is, and that it is my mind alone which perceives it. And it is even clearer that what I have said about this particular piece of wax applies to wax in general. So, what is this piece of wax that can only be perceived by the mind? It is certainly the same as what I see, touch, and imagine; indeed, it is what I have always believed it to be. But what must be carefully noted is that its perception is neither an act of vision, nor of touch, nor of imagination, and has never been so. Although this may once have appeared to be the case, I now know that the wax is perceived through an intuition of the mind, which may be as imperfect and confused as it was formerly, or as clear and distinct as it is at present, depending upon the degree of attention that I direct to the elements of which it is composed.

Yet, I am still greatly astonished by my mind's proneness to fall into error. Even when I am merely considering all this in my mind without speaking, I am often impeded by words, almost to the point of being deceived by the common usage of language. For if a piece of wax remains before us, we say that we "see" the same wax, and not simply that we "judge" it to remain the same from its having a constant color and figure. This might have led me to conclude that I knew the wax by means of vision and not simply by an intuition of the mind, if I had not remembered that when I look from a window and say I see men passing in the street, just as when I say I see wax, I do not actually see men, but only infer their existence. For what do I see from the window but hats and coats that might cover automatic machines? Yet I judge these to be men. It is only the faculty of judgment, which rests in my mind, that allows me to comprehend what I believed I saw with my eyes.

A man who aims to raise his knowledge above what is commonly accepted should be ashamed to allow the common usage of language to lead him to doubts. I prefer to bypass such doubts and to ask the following: Did I have a more evident and perfect perception of what the wax was when I first encountered it, i.e., when I believed I knew it by means of the external senses (or by common sense, as it is called, or by the imaginative faculty)? Or is my present perception clearer now that I have very carefully examined what the wax is, and in what way it can be known? The answer to this should be obvious. For what was there in the first perception that was distinct? What was there that might not have also been perceived by any animal? But in order to distinguish the wax from its external forms, in order to remove its clothing, as it were, and consider it quite naked, a human mind, although still liable to some error in judgment, is needed.

Finally, what can I say about this mind, that is, about myself? For up to this point I do not admit that I am anything but mind. Do I, who seem to perceive this piece of wax distinctly, not only know myself with much more truth and certainty, but also with much more distinctness and clearness? For if I judge that the wax exists from the fact that I see it, it certainly follows much more evidently from this fact that I myself exist. For it may be that what I see is not really wax. It may also be that I do not possess eyes with which to see anything. But it cannot be that when I see or think I see (for I no longer make a distinction here), I who think am nothing. So if I judge that the wax exists from the fact that I touch it, it will follow that I exist. If I judge that my imagination, or any other cause whatsoever, persuades me that the wax exists, I will still conclude that I exist. What I have said here about the wax may be applied to all other external things. Moreover, if the perception of the wax has been made clearer and more distinct, not only by sight and touch, but also by many other causes, it must be said that I now know myself even more clearly and distinctly. For anything that contributes to the knowledge of wax, or of any other body, provides even better evidence as to the nature of my mind. But since there are so many other things in the mind itself that allow us to know its nature, these things that depend on body are hardly worth mentioning.

I have finally reached the point I desired. Since I now realize that even bodies are known solely by the understanding and not by the senses or the faculty of imagination, i.e., they are known by being understood and not by being seen or touched, I see clearly that nothing is easier for me to know than my mind. But because it is difficult to quickly eliminate a belief that one has held for so long, it will be appropriate for me to pause here and reflect, so that I may more deeply imprint this new knowledge on my memory.

Questions for Thought

1. Which of your knowledge claims, if any, do you think are absolutely certain? Why do you believe that these claims are certain?
2. Do you agree with Descartes' claim that "there are no certain indications by which we may clearly distinguish wakefulness from sleep"? Why or why not?
3. Can you think of any arguments, other than those of Descartes, that might lead you to question the certainty of your beliefs?
4. Do you agree with Descartes that the truth of your own existence cannot be doubted? Defend your answer.
5. How does Descartes' use of the term *intuition* compare with or differ from the way that Bergson uses the term in the selection from the preceding chapter?

2   The Source of Our Knowledge

JOHN LOCKE

John Locke (1632–1704) was born in Somerset, England. Locke's father was an attorney who fought on the parliamentary side in the rebellion against the British monarchy. Embracing the liberal politics of his father, Locke was also a defender of the parliamentary side in several of the political conflicts that flared up during his lifetime. Because of this, Locke was denounced by the British crown, and he spent several years' exile in Holland.

Locke's education began at Westminster School, where he studied the classics, Arabic, and Hebrew. He began attending Christ's Church, Oxford, in 1652, earning his B.A. degree four years later. After obtaining his master's degree at Oxford, Locke lectured on Latin, Greek, and moral philosophy before receiving the first of his many political appointments in 1665. Unhappy with the traditional education that he received at Oxford, Locke eagerly sought out and embraced the new learning that was current in Europe at the time. He learned about the new sciences from Robert Boyle, studied medicine and collaborated with the great physician Thomas Sydenham, and spent four years in France, where he befriended the Gassendists, a group of French philosophers who were harsh critics of Descartes.

Among his many political activities, Locke assisted the earl of Shaftesbury in writing the constitution for the colony of Carolina, and he participated in the plot that helped William of Orange ascend to the British throne in 1688. Because of the latter activity, he was able to return to England in 1689. Locke spent the remaining years of his life in political favor, serving as a commissioner on the Board of Trade and Plantations and enjoying the friendship of prominent citizens such as Lady Masham, who was reading to him from the Book of Psalms when he died on October 28, 1704.

While the list of his writings is not as extensive as that of many other philosophers, Locke's writings had a profound effect on the intellectual life of his time and of times to come. His lengthy *An Essay Concerning Human Understanding* (1690), from which the following selection is taken, called into question the **rationalism** of Descartes and Spinoza and laid the foundation for what came to be known as British **empiricism.** His *Letter on Toleration* (1689) argued for the necessity of the separation of Church and State, greatly influencing the framers of the Constitution of the United States. And, as is well known, Locke's theory of inalienable natural rights (he cites life, liberty, and property as examples) in his *Two Treatises on Government* (1690) provided the philosophical underpinnings for Jefferson's writing of the Declaration of Independence. A list of some of Locke's lesser-known writings can be found in the introduction to the Locke selection found in Chapter 1.

In the following selection from his *Essay,* Locke states and explains several of the fundamental tenets of the empiricist theory of knowledge. After referring to his earlier rejection of the existence of **innate ideas,** Locke claims that all our simple ideas must derive from two kinds of experience: from sensation—the perception of external objects—and from reflection—the perception of our internal thought processes. He then goes on to explain how sensation works, an explanation in which he introduces his well-known distinction between primary qualities and secondary qualities. According to Locke, the process of sensation begins when small, imperceptible particles of matter travel through space and strike one of our sense organs. The force of this impact initiates an internal physiological process whereby the motion is conveyed from the sense organ to the mind, and an idea is ultimately produced. Whereas some of the ideas in our mind resemble the qualities or powers in the objects that produce them, most do not. Locke gives the name of "primary qualities" or "real qualities" to those qualities or powers, such as extension and figure, which produce ideas that resemble them. He gives the name of "secondary qualities" to the qualities or powers that produce ideas, such as color and smell, that have no resemblance to what produces them. In other words, Locke believes that something resembling our idea of extension exists in the external world, whereas there is nothing like color or smell to be found outside our minds.

Questions for Reading

1. What does Locke mean by the term *idea?* From where are our ideas derived?
2. How does Locke distinguish between a simple idea and a complex idea? Give two examples of simple ideas and two examples of complex ideas.
3. What does Locke mean when he claims that positive ideas can be derived from privative causes? Can you think of an example, other than the ones used by Locke, in which this might happen?
4. How does a primary quality differ from a secondary quality? Which of our ideas, according to Locke, are derived from primary qualities and which are derived from secondary qualities?
5. What are the essential differences between Locke's theory of knowledge and Descartes' theory of knowledge? On which points, if any, do they agree?

IDEAS IN GENERAL, AND THEIR ORIGIN

1. *AN IDEA IS THE OBJECT OF THINKING.*—EVERY man is conscious to himself that he thinks, and that while thinking, it is to the ideas in his mind that the mind is applied. It is past doubt, therefore, that men have in their minds several ideas, such as those expressed by the words whiteness, hardness, sweetness, thinking, motion, man, elephant, army, drunkenness, and so on. In the first place, then, we must inquire, How does he come by these ideas?

I know that it is a received doctrine that men have innate ideas and original characters stamped upon their minds in their very first being. I have already examined this opinion in an earlier chapter. And I suppose that my claim that there are no such ideas or characters will be much more easily admitted, when I have shown how the understanding may get all the ideas it has, that is, by what ways and degrees they may come into the mind. In order to show this, I will appeal to every one's own observation and experience.

2. *All Ideas come from Sensation or Reflection.*—Let us suppose that the mind is, as we say, white paper, void of all characters, without any ideas. How does it come to be furnished? From where does it come by that vast store that the busy and boundless

This is the editor's revised version of a selection from John Locke, An Essay Concerning Human Understanding, *edited by Mary Whiton Calkins, Chicago: Open Court, 1905.*

fancy of man has painted on it with an almost end-less variety? From where does it derive all the *mate-rials* of reason and knowledge? To this I answer, in one word, from EXPERIENCE. In that all our knowledge is founded; and from that, it ultimately derives itself. Our observation, employed either about external sensible objects or about the internal operations of our minds as perceived and reflected on by ourselves, is what supplies our understandings with all the *materials* of thinking. These two types of observation are the fountains of knowledge, from whence all the ideas we have, or can naturally have, do spring.

3. *The Objects of Sensation.*—First, our Senses, conversant about particular sensible objects, con-vey into the mind several distinct perceptions of things, according to those various ways wherein those objects affect them. It is through this means that we come by those *ideas* we have of *yellow, white, heat, cold, soft, hard, bitter, sweet,* and all those that we call sensible qualities. When I say that these are conveyed into the mind by the senses, I mean that from external objects the sen-ses convey into the mind what produces there those perceptions. This great source of most of the ideas we have, depending wholly upon our senses, and derived by them to the understanding, I call SENSATION.

4. *The Operations of Our Minds Is the Other Source of Ideas.*—Secondly, the other fountain from which experience furnishes the understanding with ideas is the perception of the operations of our own mind within us, as it is employed about the ideas it has got. These operations, when the soul comes to reflect on and to consider them, furnish the under-standing with another set of ideas, which could not be derived from external things. Such are the ideas of *perception, thinking, doubting, believing, reason-ing, knowing, willing,* and all the different actings of our own minds. Being conscious of these, and observing them in ourselves, we receive into our un-derstanding ideas of them that are as distinct as the ideas we receive from bodies affecting our senses. This source of ideas every man has wholly in him-self. And although it is not sense, as it has nothing to do with external objects, yet it is very much like it, and might properly enough be called *internal*

sense. But as I call the other Sensation, I will call this REFLECTION, since the ideas it affords are such only as the mind gets by reflecting on its own oper-ations within itself. By reflection then, . . . I mean that notice which the mind takes of its own opera-tions, and the manner of them, by reason whereof there come to be ideas of these operations in the understanding. These two, I say, namely external material things as the objects of SENSATION, and the operations of our own minds within as the objects of REFLECTION, are to me the only ori-gins from whence all our ideas take their begin-nings. The term *operations* I use here in a broad sense, as comprehending not merely the actions of the mind about its ideas, but some sort of passions arising sometimes from them, such as is the satisfac-tion or uneasiness arising from any thought.

5. *All Our Ideas Are of One or the Other of These.*—The understanding seems to me not to have the least glimmering of any ideas which it does not receive from one of these two. *External objects* fur-nish the mind with the ideas of sensible qualities, which are all those different perceptions they pro-duce in us; and *the mind* furnishes the understand-ing with ideas of its own operations.

When we have taken a full survey of these, along with their several modes, combinations, and relations, we shall find them to contain all our whole stock of ideas, and that we have nothing in our minds that did not come in one of these two ways. Let anyone examine his own thoughts, and thoroughly search into his understanding; and then let him tell me whether all the original ideas he has there, are of anything other than the objects of his senses or of the operations of his mind considered as objects of his reflection. No matter how great a mass of knowledge he imagines to be lodged there, he will, upon taking a strict view, see that he does not have any idea in his mind that was not im-printed by one of these two. . . .

OF SIMPLE IDEAS

1. *Uncompounded Appearances.*—To better under-stand the nature, manner, and extent of our know-ledge, one thing must be carefully observed

concerning the ideas we have. This is that some of the ideas we have are *simple* and some are *complex.*

Although the qualities that affect our senses are, in the things themselves, so united and blended that there is no separation, no distance between them, yet it is plain that the ideas they produce in the mind enter by the senses simple and unmixed. For whereas sight and touch often take in from the same object, at the same time, different ideas—as, for example, a man sees at once motion and color, or the hand feels softness and warmth in the same piece of wax—the simple ideas thus united in the same subject are as perfectly distinct as those that come in by different senses. The coldness and hardness that a man feels in a piece of ice are distinct ideas in the mind, as are the smell and whiteness of a lily, or the taste of sugar and the smell of a rose. And nothing can be plainer to a man than the clear and distinct perception he has of those simple ideas, each of which is in itself uncompounded, containing in itself nothing but *one uniform appearance or conception in the mind,* which is not distinguishable into different ideas.

2. *The Mind Can Neither Make nor Destroy Simple Ideas.*—These simple ideas, the materials of all our knowledge, are suggested and furnished to the mind only by those two ways above mentioned, that is, by sensation and reflection. When the understanding is once stored with these simple ideas, it has the power to repeat, compare, and unite them, even to an almost infinite variety, and so can make at pleasure new complex ideas. But it is not in the power of the exalted wit or the enlarged understanding, by any quickness or variety of thought, to *invent* or *frame* one new simple idea in the mind that is not taken in by the ways before mentioned. Nor can any force of the understanding *destroy* those that are already there. The dominion of man, in this little world of his own understanding, is much the same as it is in the great world of visible things. In both worlds, his power, however managed by art and skill, reaches no farther than to compound and divide the materials that he finds at hand; he can do nothing towards making the least particle of new matter or destroying one atom of what is already in being. Everyone will find the same inability in himself who tries to fashion in his understanding one simple idea, that is not received in by his senses from external objects or by reflection from the operations of his own mind about them. I would have anyone try to fancy any taste that had never affected his palate, or to frame the idea of a scent he had never smelled. If he could do this, I would also conclude that a blind man has ideas of colors, and a deaf man has true distinct notions of sounds. . . .

SOME FARTHER CONSIDERATIONS CONCERNING OUR SIMPLE IDEAS OF SENSATION

1. *Positive Ideas from Privative Causes.*—Concerning the simple ideas of sensation, it is to be noted that anything in nature, which is so constituted as to be able to cause any perception in the mind by affecting the senses, will be able to produce a simple idea in the understanding. Regardless of the external cause of it, when such an idea comes to be taken notice of by our discerning faculty, the mind considers it to be a real positive idea in the understanding, as real as any other whatsoever, even if the cause of it is but a privation in the subject.

2. *Ideas in the Mind Can Be Distinguished from the Things that Cause Them.*—Thus the ideas of heat and cold, light and darkness, white and black, motion and rest, are equally clear and positive ideas in the mind, although perhaps some of the causes that produce them are merely privations in those subjects from whence our senses derive those ideas. In its view, the understanding considers all of them as distinct positive ideas without taking notice of the causes that produce them. Indeed, an inquiry into their causes does not belong to the ideas as they exist in the understanding, but to the nature of the things existing without us. These are two very different things, and they must be carefully distinguished. For it is one thing to perceive and know the idea of white or black, and quite another to examine what kind of particles they must be, and how they must be arranged, to make any object appear white or black.

3. *We May Have Ideas Even If We Are Ignorant of Their External Causes.*—A painter or dyer who has

never inquired into their causes, has the ideas of white, black, and other colors as clearly, perfectly, and distinctly in his understanding, and perhaps more distinctly, than the philosopher who has busied himself in considering their natures, and who thinks that he knows how far either of them is in its cause positive or privative. Indeed, the idea of black is no less positive in his mind than that of white, even though the cause of the color black in the external object may be only a privation.

4. *Why a Privative Cause in Nature May Produce a Positive Idea.*—If it were the design of my present undertaking to inquire into the natural causes and manner of perception, I should offer this as a reason why a privative cause might, at least in some cases, produce a positive idea. Since all sensation is produced in us only by different degrees and modes of motion in our animal spirits, variously agitated by external objects, the abatement of any former motion must as necessarily produce a new sensation as the variation or increase of it. This new sensation will produce a new idea that depends only on a different motion of the animal spirits in that organ. . . .

6. *Positive Ideas Derived from Privative Causes.*— And thus one may truly be said to see darkness. For, supposing a hole perfectly dark, from whence no light is reflected, it is certain one may see the figure of it, and that it may be painted. . . . The privative causes of positive ideas that I have discussed here accord with common opinion; but, in truth, it will be hard to determine whether there really are any ideas from a privative cause, until it is determined whether rest is any more of a privation than is motion.

7. *Ideas Are in the Mind, Qualities Are in Bodies.*—To better discover the nature of our *ideas,* and to discourse of them intelligibly, it will be convenient to distinguish the *ideas or perceptions in our minds* from the *modifications of matter in the bodies that cause such perceptions in us.* By so doing, we may not think (as perhaps usually is done) that our ideas are exactly the images and resemblances of something inherent in external bodies. Indeed, most of the ideas of sensation in the mind no more resemble something existing without us than the names that stand for them resemble our ideas. . . .

8. *Ideas Further Distinguished from Qualities.*— Whatever the mind perceives in itself, or is the immediate object of perception, thought, or understanding, I call "idea." And the power to produce any idea in our mind, I call "quality" of the body wherein that power is. Thus a snowball has the power to produce in us the ideas of white, cold, and round; and the powers to produce those ideas in us as they are in the snowball, I call "qualities." However, as the sensations or perceptions of white, cold, and round are in our understanding, I call them "ideas." If at times I speak of these as in the things themselves, I would be understood to mean those qualities in the objects that produce them in us.

9. *On Primary Qualities.*—When we consider qualities in bodies, we find first such qualities as are utterly inseparable from the body, in whatever state it be. These are qualities that, in all the alterations and changes a body suffers, in all the force that can be used upon it, it constantly keeps. They are qualities that sense constantly finds in every particle of matter that has bulk enough to be perceived, qualities that the mind finds inseparable from every particle of matter, though less than to make itself singly be perceived by our senses. Take, for example, a grain of wheat, and divide it into two parts. Each part has still solidity, extension, figure, and mobility; divide it again, and it retains still the same qualities. And so divide it on until the parts become insensible, each of them must retain still all those qualities. For division (which is all that a mill or pestle or any other body does upon another, in reducing it to insensible parts) can never take away either solidity, extension, figure, or mobility from any body. . . . These I call *original* or *primary* qualities of body, which I think we may observe to produce simple ideas in us, that is, solidity, extension, figure, motion or rest, and number.

10. *On Secondary Qualities.*—Secondly, when considering qualities in bodies, we find qualities that in truth are nothing in the objects themselves. Rather, they are powers to produce various sensations in us by their primary qualities, i.e., by the bulk, figure, texture, and motion of their insensible parts, as colors, sounds, tastes, etc. These I call *secondary* qualities. . . .

11. *How Primary Qualities Produce Their Ideas.*—The next thing to be considered is how bodies produce ideas in us. That must manifestly be by impulse, for this is the only way in which we can conceive bodies to operate.

12. *Further Explanation of This.*—If, then, external objects are not united to our minds when they produce ideas in them, and yet we perceive the original qualities in those objects that singly fall under our senses, it is evident that some motion must be continued by our nerves, animal spirits, or some parts of our bodies, to the brain or the seat of sensation, there to produce in our minds the particular ideas we have of them. And since we may perceive the extension, figure, number, and motion of sensible bodies that are at a distance from us, it is evident that some imperceptible bodies must come to the eyes from these sensible bodies. These imperceptible bodies convey to the brain some motion that produces the ideas that we have in us.

13. *How Secondary Qualities Produce Their Ideas.*—In the same manner that the ideas of these original qualities are produced in us, we may conceive that the ideas of secondary qualities are also produced, that is, by the operation of insensible particles on our senses. For it is manifest that there are many bodies, each of which is so small that we cannot by any of our senses discover either its bulk, figure, or motion (as is evident in the particles of the air and water, and other extremely smaller particles than those, perhaps as much smaller than the particles of air or water are smaller than peas or hailstones). Let us suppose at present that the different motions and figures, bulk and number, of such particles, effecting several organs of our senses, produce in us those different sensations that we have from the colors and smells of bodies. For example, a violet, by the impulse of such insensible particles of matter of peculiar figures and bulks, and in different degrees and modifications of their motions, causes the idea of the blue color and the sweet scent of that flower that is produced in our minds. It is no more impossible to conceive that God should annex such ideas to such motions, with which they have no similitude, than that he should annex the idea of pain to the motion of a piece of steel dividing our flesh, with which the idea has no resemblance.

14. *Further Examples of This.*—What I have said concerning colors and smells may be understood also of tastes and sounds, and other like sensible qualities. Whatever reality we by mistake attribute to them, they are in truth nothing in the objects themselves but powers to produce various sensations in us, and thus they depend on those primary qualities, that is, on bulk, figure, texture, and motion of parts.

15. *Ideas of Primary Qualities Are Resemblances; Those of Secondary Qualities Are Not.*—From this I think it is easy to draw the **conclusion** that the ideas of primary qualities of bodies are resemblances of them, and that their patterns do really exist in the bodies themselves. However, the ideas produced in us by these secondary qualities have no resemblance of them at all. In other words, there is nothing like our ideas existing in the bodies themselves. There is, in the bodies we denominate from them, only a power to produce those sensations in us; and what is sweet, blue, or warm in idea, is but the certain bulk, figure, and motion of the insensible parts in the bodies themselves. . . .

16. *Still More Examples.*—Flame is denominated *hot* and *light;* snow is denominated *white* and *cold,* and manna is denominated *white* and *sweet,* from the ideas they produce in us. These qualities are commonly thought to be the same in those bodies as those ideas are in us, the one the perfect resemblance of the other, as they are in a mirror. Indeed, most men would judge it to be very extravagant if one should say otherwise. And yet, if one considers that the same fire, which at one distance produces in us the sensation of warmth, but at a nearer approach produces in us the far different sensation of pain, ought to ask himself what reason he has to say that this idea of warmth, which is produced in him the same way as the ideas of hot and light, is not in the fire. Why is whiteness and coldness in snow and pain not, when it produces all of these ideas, and can produce neither but by the bulk, figure, number, and motion of its solid parts?

17. *Primary Qualities May Be Called Real Qualities.*—The particular bulk, number, figure, and motion of the parts of fire or snow are really in them, whether any one's senses perceive them or not; and therefore they may be called *real* qualities, because

they really exist in those bodies. But light, heat, whiteness, and coldness are no more really in them than is sickness or pain. Take away the sensation of them. Let not the eyes see light or colors nor the ears hear sounds, let not the palate taste nor the nose smell, and all colors, tastes, odors, and sounds, as they are such particular ideas, vanish and cease. They are reduced to their causes, *i.e.,* to bulk, figure, and motion of parts.

Questions for Thought

1. Do you agree with Locke's claim that all knowledge is derived from experience? Which of your ideas, if any, were not derived from experience?
2. If Locke is correct, do you think a person could have knowledge of God? Defend your answer.
3. Locke's account of how our ideas of sensation are produced has been referred to as the "Spectator Theory of Knowledge." Do you think that this is a fitting name for Locke's theory? Why or why not?
4. On Locke's views, what can we say about the nature of the external world? How do Locke's views about the nature of the external world compare with or differ from your own views?
5. One of Locke's contemporaries was the English physicist Isaac Newton. Can you think of any similarities between Locke's views and those of Newton?

3   Principles of Human Knowledge

GEORGE BERKELEY

George Berkeley (1685–1753), a British empiricist whose metaphysical views are known as subjective **idealism,** was born in Kilkenny, Ireland. The son of a British gentleman, Berkeley spent his early years at Dysert Castle. After studying for four years at Kilkenny College, which he entered in 1700, Berkeley transferred to Trinity College, Dublin. He received his A.B. degree from Trinity College in 1704 and became a fellow of the college three years later. While at Trinity, where he taught courses in theology, Hebrew, and Greek, Berkeley published his first important works, *An Essay Towards a New Theory of Vision* (1709) and part I of *A Treatise Concerning the Principles of Human Knowledge* (1710). In the same year in which the latter work appeared, Berkeley was ordained as an Anglican priest.

In 1713, Berkeley traveled to London, where he published his *Three Dialogues Between Hylas and Philonous,* before moving on to continental Europe. He toured on the Continent, mainly in Italy, during the years 1713 and 1714 and again from 1716 to 1720. During this latter sojourn, Berkeley worked on and lost the manuscript of what was to be the second part of his *Treatise Concerning the Principles of Human Knowledge.* Discouraged by this occurrence, he never completed the text.

Returning to Britain, Berkeley worked at Trinity College for three more years before being appointed dean of Derry in 1724. During this time, he became disillusioned with

British life, as evidenced by his *Essay Towards Preventing the Ruin of Great-Britain* (1721), and he looked longingly toward the Americas. He proposed building a college in Bermuda for training priests and converting Native Americans. Expecting to receive government funding for his project, Berkeley married Anne Forster in 1728 and moved to Newport, Rhode Island. However, the grant never arrived, and the Berkeleys returned to London three years later.

Back in London, Berkeley authored a series of writings directed against those thinkers of his day who opposed certain doctrines of the Church. These writings were no doubt partly responsible for his being named bishop of Cloyne, Ireland, in 1734. Taking his duties seriously, Berkeley turned his attention to the practical problems facing the people residing in his diocese. These problems provided the focus of his most prominent later writings, *The Querist* (1735–1737) and *A Chain of Philosophical Reflexions and Inquiries Concerning the Virtues of Tar-Water, and Divers other Subjects Connected Together and Arising from One Another* (1744). In August 1752, Berkeley took leave of his ecclesiastical duties and moved with his wife and children to Oxford. He died there the following January.

The following selection from Berkeley's *Treatise Concerning the Principles of Human Knowledge* is a response to certain claims about the nature of knowledge that had been earlier formulated by the British philosopher John Locke. As we saw in the preceding selection, Locke had rejected Cartesian **rationalism** and argued that all knowledge comes from experience. Accepting the atomism of the physicist Isaac Newton, Locke believed that there were physical objects in the world and that these objects had certain properties, such as size and shape. When these physical objects, which are constantly in motion, strike our sense organs, they produce simple ideas in our minds. While some of our simple ideas resemble properties in the physical objects that cause them, Locke believed that others, such as texture and color, do not. Of course, once experience equips our minds with simple ideas, we are capable of ordering these ideas in various ways to produce what Locke calls compound ideas. For example, from the simple idea of a certain shade of redness, a certain size, and a certain shape, we may produce the idea of an apple.

Berkeley begins the following selection by affirming Locke's claim that all knowledge comes from experience. Like Locke, Berkeley also views knowledge in terms of ideas perceived by a mind or spirit. Unlike Locke, however, Berkeley goes on to deny the existence of physical objects. While agreeing with Locke that the compound idea of an apple is produced by the mind from simple ideas, he rejects Locke's claim that certain characteristics of the apple resemble properties found in objects existing independently of the mind. (In other words, Berkeley denies Locke's distinction between primary qualities and secondary qualities.) For Berkeley, what we normally take to be physical objects are only collections of ideas designated by a common term. He thus concludes that only minds and ideas exist.

Having argued this point, Berkeley notes that his ideas are constantly changing and that he has control over some of these changes through acts of will or volition. In other words, he believes that his fancies and daydreams are his own creation. However, he notes that he does not have the same power of will or volition over the ideas perceived through the senses. As he says, "When in broad daylight I open my eyes, it is not in my power to choose whether I shall see or no, or to determine what particular objects shall present themselves to my view." While common sense might tell us that this is caused by the existence of external physical objects over which we have no control, Berkeley has denied that such objects exist. Rather than appealing to the existence of physical objects to explain this phenomenon, Berkeley appeals to "the Author of Nature," or God. God, according to Berkeley, is an infinite mind that imprints the ideas of "real things" on our senses. Thus, again departing from a commonsense view of the world, Berkeley concludes that "real things" are actually ideas existing in the mind of God. Given this conclusion, it further follows that "laws of nature" are not principles explaining the movements of external physical objects but explanations of the patterns of God's thinking.

Questions for Reading

1. How do Berkeley's views on the nature of knowledge compare with or differ from the views of Locke?
2. What, according to Berkeley, is an apple? How would Locke describe an apple?
3. What are Berkeley's reasons for rejecting the existence of physical objects?
4. How does Berkeley describe mind or spirit? Why does he believe that we cannot have an idea of mind or spirit?
5. What function does God play in Berkeley's theory? How does he know that God exists?

PART I

1. IT IS EVIDENT TO ANYONE WHO SURVEYS the *objects* of human knowledge that they are either ideas actually imprinted on the senses, ideas that are perceived by attending to the passions and operations of the mind, or lastly, ideas formed by help of memory and imagination—either compounding, dividing, or barely representing ideas originally perceived in the first two ways. Sight gives me the ideas of light and colors, with their several degrees and variations. By touch I perceive, for example, hard and soft, heat and cold, motion and resistance, and of all these more and less either as to quantity or degree. Smelling furnishes me with odors, the palate with tastes, and hearing conveys sounds to the mind in all their variety of tone and composition. And as several ideas are observed to accompany each other, they come to be marked by one name, and so are taken to be one thing. Thus, for example, a certain color, taste, smell, figure, and consistency are observed to go together, and they are accounted one distinct thing signified by the name "apple." Other collections of ideas constitute a stone, a tree, a book, and like sensible things—which may be either pleasing or disagreeable, and thereby may excite the passions of love, hatred, joy, grief, and so forth.

2. But, in addition to all that endless variety of ideas or objects of knowledge, there is also something that knows or perceives them and that exercises diverse operations upon them, such as willing, imagining, and remembering. This perceiving, active being is what I call "mind," "spirit," "soul," or "myself." By such words I do not denote any one of my ideas, but something entirely distinct from them, wherein they exist or, in other words, whereby they are perceived. For the existence of an idea consists in being perceived.

3. Everyone will admit that our thoughts, our passions, and the ideas formed by our imagination do not exist outside the mind. And it seems no less evident that the various sensations or ideas imprinted on the senses, however blended or combined together (that is, whatever objects they compose), cannot exist otherwise than in a mind perceiving them. I think that an intuitive knowledge of this may be obtained by anyone who will examine what is meant by the term "exist" when it is applied to sensible things. I say that the table I write on exists, that is, I see and feel it. And if I were out of my study

This is the editor's revised version of a selection from George Berkeley, A Treatise Concerning the Principles of Human Knowledge, *2nd ed., Dublin, 1734.*

I would say the table existed—meaning thereby that if I were in my study I might perceive it, or that some other spirit actually does perceive it. There was an odor, that is, it was smelled; there was a sound, that is to say, it was heard; there was a color or figure, which means that it was perceived by sight or touch. This is all that I can understand by these and similar expressions. For it seems perfectly unintelligible to speak of the absolute existence of unthinking things without any relation to their being perceived. Their *esse* is *percipi,* nor is it possible that they should have any existence outside the minds or thinking things that perceive them.

4. Certainly an opinion strangely prevails amongst men that houses, mountains, rivers, and, in a word, all sensible objects have an existence, natural or real, distinct from their being perceived by the understanding. But even though this principle may be widely accepted with the greatest assurance, yet whoever finds it in his heart to call this principle into question may, if I am not mistaken, perceive that it involves a manifest contradiction. For what are the aforementioned objects but things we perceive by sense? And what do we perceive other than our own ideas or sensations? And is it not plainly inconceivable that any one of these, or any combination of them, can exist unperceived?

5. If we thoroughly examine this principle it will, perhaps, ultimately be found to depend on the doctrine of *abstract ideas.* For can there be a nicer strain of abstraction than to distinguish the existence of sensible objects from their being perceived, so as to conceive of them existing unperceived? Light and colors, heat and cold, extension and figures—in a word, the things we see and feel—what are they but so many sensations, notions, ideas, or impressions on the sense? And is it possible to separate, even in thought, any of these from perception? For my part, I might as easily divide a thing from itself. I may, indeed, divide in my thoughts, or conceive apart from each other, those things which, perhaps, I never perceived by sense so divided. Thus I can imagine the trunk of a human body without the limbs, or conceive the smell of a rose without thinking on the rose itself. I will not deny that I can abstract to this extent—if separating in thought such objects that may really exist or be actually perceived asunder can be properly called "abstraction." But my conceiving or imagining power does not extend beyond the

possibility of real existence or perception. Hence, just as it is impossible for me to see or feel anything without an actual sensation of that thing, it is likewise impossible for me to conceive in my thoughts any sensible thing or object distinct from the sensation or perception of it.

6. Some truths are so near and obvious to the mind that a man need only open his eyes to see them. Such I take this important truth to be, namely, that all the choir of heaven and all the furniture of the earth, in a word, all those bodies that compose the mighty frame of the world, have not any subsistence without a mind. Their *being* is to be perceived or known. Consequently, as long as they are not actually perceived by me, or do not exist in my mind or that of any other created spirit, they must either have no existence at all or else they must subsist in the mind of some eternal spirit. For it is perfectly unintelligible, and involves all the absurdity of abstraction, to attribute to any single part of them an existence independent of a spirit. To be convinced of this, the reader need only reflect, and try to separate in his own thoughts, the *being* of a sensible thing from its *being perceived.*

7. From what has been said it follows that there is not any other *substance* than *spirit,* or that which perceives. But, for the fuller proof of this point, let us consider the sensible qualities of color, figure, motion, smell, taste, and such like—that is, the ideas perceived by sense. Now, it is a manifest contradiction for an idea to exist in an unperceiving thing, for to have an idea is the same thing as to perceive. So the substance, wherein color, figure, and like qualities exist, must perceive them. Hence, it is clear there can be no unthinking substance or *substratum* of those ideas.

8. But, say you, though the ideas themselves do not exist outside the mind, there may yet be things like them, of which they are copies or resemblances, that do exist outside the mind in an unthinking substance. I answer that an idea can be like nothing but an idea; a color or figure can be like nothing but another color or figure. If we look but ever so little into our thoughts, we shall find it impossible for us to conceive a likeness except only between our ideas. Again, I ask whether those supposed originals or external things, of which our ideas are the pictures or representations, are themselves perceivable or not? If they are perceivable, then they are ideas and we have

gained our point. But if you say they are not perceivable, I ask whether it makes sense to assert that a color is like something which is invisible, that hard or soft is like something which is intangible, and so of the rest. . . .

23. But, say you, surely nothing is easier than to imagine trees, for instance, in a park, or books existing in a closet, with nobody there to perceive them. I answer that you may do so; there is no difficulty in it. But what more is all this, I ask you, than framing in your mind certain ideas that you call books and trees, and at the same time omitting to frame the idea of anyone that may perceive them? But do not you yourself perceive or think of them all the while? This therefore proves nothing; it only shows that you have the power of imagining or forming ideas in your mind. It does not show that you can possibly conceive the objects of your thought existing without the mind. To prove this, it would be necessary for you to conceive them existing unconceived or unthought of, which is a manifest contradiction. When we do our utmost to conceive the existence of external bodies, we are all the while only contemplating our own ideas. But the mind, taking no notice of itself, is deluded to think that it can and does conceive bodies existing unthought of or without the mind, although at the same time they are apprehended by or exist in the mind itself. A little attention will show to anyone the truth and evidence of what is said here, making it unnecessary to insist on any other proofs calling into question the existence of *material substance.*

24. It is very easy, upon the least inquiry into our own thoughts, to know whether it is possible for us to understand what is meant by "the absolute existence of sensible objects in themselves, or without the mind." To me it is evident that these words mark out either a direct contradiction or else nothing at all. And to convince others of this, I know of no readier or fairer way than to ask them to examine their own thoughts calmly. If from this examination, they discover the emptiness or inconsistency of those expressions, then surely nothing more is requisite for their conviction. It is on this, therefore, that I insist, namely, that the words "the absolute existence of unthinking things" are words without a meaning, or words that involve a contradiction.

This is what I repeat and inculcate, earnestly recommending it to the attentive thoughts of the reader.

25. All our ideas, sensations, or the things that we perceive, by whatsoever names they may be differentiated, are visibly inactive. There is nothing of power or agency included in them. So that one idea or object of thought cannot produce or make any alteration in another. To be satisfied of the truth of this, nothing else is requisite but a bare observation of our ideas. For since they and every part of them exist only in the mind, it follows that there is nothing in them but what is perceived. But whoever shall attend to his ideas, whether of sense or reflection, will not perceive in them any power or activity; there is, therefore, no such thing contained in them. A little attention will show us that the very being of an idea implies passiveness and inertness in it, so much so that it is impossible for an idea to do anything or, strictly speaking, to be the cause of anything. Neither can it be the resemblance or pattern of any active being, as was shown in sec. 8 above. From this, it plainly follows that extension, figure, and motion cannot be the cause of our sensations. To say, therefore, that these are the effects of powers resulting from the configuration, number, motion, and size of minute particles of matter must certainly be false.

26. We perceive a continual succession of ideas; some are excited anew, others are changed or totally disappear. There is, therefore, some cause of these ideas, whereon they depend and which produces and changes them. That this cause cannot be any quality or idea or combination of ideas is clear from the preceding section. It must therefore be a substance. However, it has been shown that there is no corporeal or material substance; therefore, the cause of ideas can only be an incorporeal, active substance or spirit.

27. A spirit is one simple, undivided, active being. As it perceives ideas, it is called "the understanding"; as it produces or otherwise operates upon them, it is called "the will." Hence there can be no *idea* formed of a soul or spirit. For since all ideas whatsoever are passive and inert (see sec. 25 above), they cannot represent unto us, by way of image or likeness, that which acts. A little attention will make it plain to anyone that to have an idea of the active principle of motion and change of ideas is absolutely impossible. Such is the nature of *spirit,* of that which acts, that it

cannot be perceived in itself; it can only be perceived by the effects that it produces. If any man doubts the truth of what is here stated, let him reflect and try to frame the idea of any power or active being. Let him also see whether he has ideas of two principal powers marked by the names "will" and "understanding," ideas that are distinct from each other, as well as from a third idea of substance or being in general—which may be called by the name "soul" or "spirit"—that supports or is the subject of the aforesaid powers. This is what some hold. But, as far as I can see, the words "will," "soul," and "spirit" do not stand for different ideas or, in truth, for any idea at all. Rather, they stand for something that is very different from ideas, something that, being an agent, cannot be similar to, or represented by, any idea whatsoever. However, it must be admitted at the same time that we have some notion of soul, spirit, and the operations of the mind, such as willing, loving, and hating, inasmuch as we know or understand the meaning of those words.

28. I find that I can excite ideas in my mind whenever I please, and that I can vary and shift the scene as often as I think fit. Simply through willing, this or that idea immediately arises in my fancy; and by the same power, it is obliterated and makes way for another. This making and unmaking of ideas does very properly denominate the mind active. This much is certain and grounded on experience. But when we talk of unthinking agents or of exciting ideas exclusive of willing, we only amuse ourselves with words.

29. But, whatever power I may have over my own thoughts, I find that the ideas actually perceived by the senses do not have a like dependence on my will. When in broad daylight I open my eyes, it is not in my power to choose whether I shall see or not, or to determine what particular objects shall present themselves to my view. This applies likewise in the case of hearing and the other senses; the ideas imprinted on them are not creatures of my will. There is therefore some *other* will or spirit that produces them.

30. The ideas of sense are stronger, livelier, and more distinct than are those of the imagination. They have likewise a steadiness, order, and coherence; they are not excited at random, as those that are the effects of human wills often are. Rather, they appear in a regular train or series, the admirable connection of which sufficiently testifies to the wisdom and benevolence of its Author. Now the set rules or established methods, by which the mind we depend on excites in us the ideas of sense, are called "the laws of nature." We learn these by experience, which teaches us that such and such ideas are attended with such and such other ideas in the ordinary course of things.

31. This gives us a sort of foresight that enables us to regulate our actions for the benefit of life. Without this we should be eternally at a loss; we could not know how to do anything that might procure us the least pleasure or remove the least pain of sensation. We know that food nourishes, that sleep refreshes, that fire warms us, that to sow in the planting season is the way to reap in the harvest, and that generally such or such means are conducive to bringing about such or such ends. And we know all this, not by discovering any necessary connection between our ideas, but only by the observation of the settled laws of nature. Without such observation, we would be completely uncertain and confused, and a grown man would no more know how to manage himself in the affairs of life than a newborn infant.

32. And yet this consistent, uniform working, which so evidently displays the goodness and wisdom of that Governing Spirit whose Will constitutes the laws of nature, is far from leading our thoughts to Him. On the contrary, it rather sends our thoughts searching after secondary causes. For when we perceive certain ideas of sense constantly followed by other ideas, and we know this is not of our own doing, we forthwith attribute power and agency to the ideas themselves, making one the cause of another. Nothing can be more absurd and unintelligible than this. Thus, for example, having observed that when we perceive by sight a certain round, luminous figure, we at the same time perceive by touch the idea or sensation called "heat," from this we conclude that the sun is the cause of heat. And in like manner, perceiving the motion and collision of bodies to be attended with sound, we are inclined to think the latter an effect of the former.

33. The ideas imprinted on the senses by the Author of Nature are called "real things"; those ideas

excited in the imagination, being less regular, vivid, and constant, are more properly termed "ideas" or "images of things" which they copy and represent. But then our sensations, even when they are ever so vivid and distinct, are nevertheless ideas; they exist in the mind, or are perceived by it, as truly as the ideas of its own framing. The ideas of sense are allowed to have more reality in them, that is, to be more strong, orderly, and coherent than the creations of the mind; but this is no argument that they exist outside the mind. They are also less dependent on the spirit, or thinking substance that perceives them, in that they are excited by the will of another and more powerful spirit. Still they are *ideas;* and it is certain that no idea, whether faint or strong, can exist otherwise than in a mind perceiving it.

Questions for Thought

1. When you eat an apple, how would *you* describe what you are eating? How does your description compare with or differ from Berkeley's description of an apple?
2. Do you find Berkeley's arguments for rejecting the existence of physical objects convincing? If not, how would you try to convince him that physical objects exist?
3. Someone once tried to refute Berkeley by kicking a rock. How is this action relevant to refuting Berkeley's position? Why would Berkeley not be convinced by it?
4. Do you agree with Berkeley that we cannot have an idea of mind or spirit? Why or why not?
5. How do your own views about God compare with or differ from Berkeley's views about God? Do you think you have an idea of God? If so, how did you get this idea?

4   The Fixation of Belief

CHARLES SANDERS PEIRCE

Charles Sanders Peirce (1839–1914), who was one of the most original American philosophers, was born in Cambridge, Massachusetts. The son of the mathematician Benjamin Peirce, the younger Peirce was educated by his father to be a scientist. He attended Harvard University, where his studies focused on mathematics and the physical sciences, before earning a degree in chemistry from the Lawrence Scientific School in 1863. After graduation, Peirce held several different jobs. He worked as an astronomer at the Harvard Observatory and as a physicist for the U.S. Coast and Geodetic Survey before being appointed lecturer at Johns Hopkins University in 1879. Peirce's academic career, however, was short-circuited in 1884. Reasons given for his departure from Johns Hopkins include his "highly independent nature" and his marital difficulties and subsequent divorce.

In 1887, Peirce inherited a small sum of money, and he went into semiretirement in Milford, Pennsylvania. There he continued to work intermittently for the Geodetic Survey (until 1891) and to further develop his earlier studies in philosophy and logic. Unable to find a publisher for his writings, Peirce died in relative obscurity and poverty in 1914. Peirce published several journal articles in the years 1867–1869 and again in 1877–1879. These, along with his numerous unpublished manuscripts, were later published in *The Collected Papers of Charles Sanders Peirce* (1931–1935). Today Peirce is recognized as the founder of **pragmatism,** a term that he first used in one of his journal articles in 1878, as well as the originator of the modern form of semiotics.

In the following selection, which is excerpted from an essay first published in *Popular Science Monthly* in November 1877, Peirce explains the differences between doubt and belief before going on to describe the process of inquiry. He says that belief produces a comfortable state of mind that carries a propensity to action, whereas doubt produces an unsettled state of mind that leads to inquiry—the process whereby the irritation of doubt is transformed into belief.

Peirce goes on to say that although we would like to believe that the purpose of inquiry is to seek truth, in fact inquiry ends as soon as we reach firm belief, whether that firm belief be true or false. In other words, if the belief that we reach satisfies our desires, one of which is to escape from the unsettling effects of doubt, then inquiry comes to an end.

Having said this, Peirce examines the various ways in which belief may be attained or fixed, and he argues that some of these ways are more effective than others. The first method that he describes, the method of tenacity, is the simplest to employ. It consists of choosing the answer that we like and repeating this answer over and over to ourselves until we come to believe it. While this method may succeed in initially settling doubt, Peirce says that it will ultimately be destroyed by our social impulse. As we come to realize that other people hold beliefs that are contrary to our own and that at least some of their beliefs are just as good as our own, we will be led to abandon the radical individualism on which this method is based.

The second method of fixing belief that Peirce discusses, the method of authority, is firmly grounded in social impulse. In this method, an institution is created that has the power to determine and to teach socially sanctioned doctrines and to persecute anyone who questions them. While Peirce admits that this method is superior to the method of tenacity, he argues that it too has serious shortcomings. First, unlike the method of tenacity, it sanctions the oppression of anyone holding contrary opinions, and this oppression often leads to unspeakable cruelties. Moreover, as with the method of tenacity, thoughtful people will eventually come to see that different social institutions affirm different beliefs and that there is no rational way to justify the beliefs that they accept on authority against contrary beliefs that others accept on authority.

Realizing this, many people turn to the third method of fixing belief, the method that Peirce refers to as the *a priori* method. This is the method of fixing belief employed by metaphysicians who claim that their beliefs are based on reason rather than authority. However, since diverse metaphysical systems have been created by this method, Peirce argues that in the final analysis, this method is based on sentiment. In other words, the system that one embraces has to do more with taste than with reason.

The failure of this third method of fixing belief leads to a discussion of the method that Peirce finds most effective, the method of science. This method, as Peirce notes, assumes that there is an external world that exists independently of human perception. It also maintains that through observation and inductive thinking, we can formulate and test hypotheses about this world. With the scientific method, the hypothesis that we ultimately accept is the hypothesis that most successfully resolves the problem with which we are faced. Since our chosen hypothesis can then be tested by others, Peirce claims that this is the only one of the four methods of fixing belief that is neither subjective nor arbitrary.

Questions for Reading

1. How does Peirce describe the state of doubt? Why does doubt initiate inquiry?
2. What, according to Peirce, is the method of tenacity? How does it allow a person to overcome doubt?
3. What is the method of authority, and why does it often supplant the method of tenacity? What are some of the beliefs that, according to Peirce, are derived from the method of authority?
4. How does the third method of fixing belief differ from the first two?
5. What exactly does Peirce mean by scientific investigation? Why does he believe that it is the superior method of fixing belief?

REASONING, BELIEVING, AND DOUBTING

THE OBJECT OF REASONING IS TO FIND OUT, from the consideration of what we already know, something that we do not know. Consequently, reasoning is good if it gives a true **conclusion** from true **premises,** and not otherwise. Thus, the question of its validity is purely one of fact and not of thinking. *A* being the premises and *B* being the conclusion, the question is, whether these facts are really so related that if *A* is, *B* is. If so, the inference is valid; if not, the inference is not valid. The question is not in the least whether, if the premises are accepted by the mind, we feel an impulse to accept the conclusion also. It is true that we do generally reason correctly by nature. But that is an accident. The true conclusion would remain true if we had no impulse to accept it; and the false one would remain false, though we could not resist the tendency to believe it.

In the main, we are doubtless rational animals, but we are not perfectly so. . . . Logicality in regard to practical matters is the most useful quality an animal can possess, and might, therefore, result from the action of natural selection. But outside of these practical matters, it is probably of more advantage to the animal to have his mind filled with pleasing and encouraging visions, independently of their truth; and thus, upon unpractical subjects, natural selection might occasion a fallacious tendency of thought. . . .

We generally know when we wish to ask a question and when we wish to pronounce a judgment, for there is a dissimilarity between the sensation of doubting and that of believing. But this is not all that distinguishes doubt from belief. There is a practical difference. Our beliefs guide our desires and shape our actions. The Assassins, or followers of the Old Man of the Mountain, used to rush into death at his least command, because they believed that obedience to him would insure everlasting felicity. Had they doubted this, they would not have acted as they did. So it is with every belief, according to its degree. The feeling of believing is a more or less sure indication that some habit has been established in our nature that will determine our actions. Doubt never has such an effect.

Nor must we overlook a third point of difference. Doubt is an uneasy and dissatisfied state from which we struggle to free ourselves and to pass into the state of belief. Belief, on the other hand, is a calm and satisfactory state that we do not wish to avoid, or to change to a belief in anything else. On the contrary, we cling tenaciously, not merely to believing, but to believing just what we do believe.

Thus, both doubt and belief have positive effects upon us, though very different ones. Belief does not make us act at once, but puts us into such a condition that we shall behave in some certain way, when the occasion arises. Doubt has not the least effect of this sort, but stimulates us to inquiry until it is destroyed. . . .

From *Charles Sanders Peirce, "The Fixation of Belief,"* Popular Science Monthly 12 *(November 1877), pp. 1–15.*

THE END OF INQUIRY

The irritation of doubt causes a struggle to attain a state of belief. I shall term this struggle *inquiry*, though it must be admitted that this is sometimes not a very apt designation. The irritation of doubt is the only immediate motive for the struggle to attain belief. It is certainly best for us that our beliefs should be such as may truly guide our actions so as to satisfy our desires; and this reflection will make us reject every belief that does not seem to have been so formed as to insure this result. But it will only do so by creating a doubt in the place of that belief. With the doubt, therefore, the struggle begins; with the cessation of doubt, it ends. Hence, the sole object of inquiry is the settlement of opinion. We may fancy that this is not enough for us, and that we seek, not merely an opinion, but a true opinion. But put this fancy to the test, and it proves groundless. For as soon as a firm belief is reached we are entirely satisfied, whether that belief is true or false. And it is clear that nothing out of the sphere of our knowledge can be our object, for nothing that does not affect the mind can be the motive for mental effort. The most that can be maintained is that we seek for a belief that we *think* is true. But we think each one of our beliefs is true, and indeed, it is merely a **tautology** to say so.

That the settlement of opinion is the sole end of inquiry is a very important proposition. It sweeps away, at once, various vague and erroneous conceptions of proof. A few of these may be listed here.

1. Some philosophers have imagined that to start an inquiry it was only necessary to utter a question, whether orally or by setting it down upon paper. They have even recommended that we begin our studies by questioning everything! But the mere putting of a proposition into the interrogative form does not stimulate the mind to any struggle after belief. There must be a real and living doubt, and without this all discussion is idle.

2. It is a very common idea that a demonstration must rest on some ultimate and absolutely indubitable propositions. These, according to one school, are first principles of a general nature; according to another school, they are first sensations. But, in point of fact, for an inquiry to have that completely satisfactory result called demonstration, it need only start with propositions perfectly free from all actual doubt. If the premises are not in fact doubted at all, they cannot be more satisfactory than they are.

3. Some people seem to love to argue a point after everyone in the world is fully convinced of it. But no further advance can be made. When doubt ceases, mental action on the subject comes to an end; and, if it did go on, it would be without a purpose.

METHODS OF FIXING BELIEF

If the settlement of opinion is the sole object of inquiry, and if belief is of the nature of a habit, why should we not attain the desired end by taking, as the answer to a question, anything we fancy, constantly reiterating it to ourselves and dwelling on all that supports it, while learning contempt and hatred for anything that might disturb it? This simple and direct method is really pursued by many men. I remember once being entreated not to read a certain newspaper lest it might change my opinion upon free-trade. "Lest I might be entrapped by its fallacies and misstatements," was the form of expression. "You are not," my friend said, "a special student of political economy. You might, therefore, easily be deceived by fallacious arguments upon the subject. You might, then, if you read this paper, be led to believe in protection. But you admit that free-trade is the true doctrine; and you do not wish to believe what is not true." I have often known this system to be deliberately adopted. Still oftener, the instinctive dislike of an undecided state of mind, exaggerated into a vague dread of doubt, makes men cling spasmodically to the views they already have. The man feels that, if he only holds to his belief without wavering, it will be entirely satisfactory. Nor can it be denied that a steady and immovable faith yields great peace of mind. It may, indeed, give rise to inconveniences, as if a man should resolutely continue to believe that fire would not burn him, or that he would be eternally damned if he received his *ingesta* otherwise than through a stomach-pump. But then the man who adopts this method will not allow that its inconveniences are greater than its advantages. He will say, "I hold steadfastly to the truth, and the truth is always wholesome." And in many cases it may very well be that the pleasure he derives from his calm faith overbalances any inconveniences resulting from its deceptive character. Thus, if it is true that death is annihilation, then the man who believes that he will certainly go straight to heaven when he dies, provided he has fulfilled certain simple observances in his life, has a cheap pleasure that will not be followed by the least disappointment. A similar consideration seems to have weight with many persons in religious topics, for we frequently hear it said, "Oh, I could not believe so-and-so, because I should be wretched if I did." When an ostrich buries its head in the sand as danger approaches, it very likely takes the happiest course. It hides the danger, and then calmly says there is no danger. And, if it feels perfectly sure there is none, why should it raise its head to see? A man may go through life, systematically keeping out of view all that might cause a change in his opinions, and if he only succeeds—basing his method, as he does, on two fundamental psychological laws—I do not see what can be said against his doing so. It would be an egotistical impertinence to object that his procedure is irrational, for that only amounts to saying that his method of settling belief is not ours. He does not propose to himself to be rational, and, indeed, will often talk with scorn of man's weak and illusive reason. So let him think as he pleases.

But this method of fixing belief, which may be called the method of tenacity, will be unable to hold its ground in practice. The social impulse is against it. The man who adopts it will find that other men think differently from him, and it will likely occur to him, in some saner moment, that their opinions are quite as good as his own, and this will shake his confidence in his belief. This conception, that another man's thought or sentiment may be equivalent to one's own, is a distinctly new step, and a highly important one. It arises from an impulse too strong in man to be suppressed, without danger of destroying the human species. Unless we make ourselves hermits, we shall necessarily influence each other's opinions, so that the problem becomes how to fix belief, not merely in the individual, but in the community.

Let the will of the state act, then, instead of that of the individual. Let an institution be created whose object will be to keep correct doctrines before the attention of the people, to reiterate them perpetually, and to teach them to the young; having at the same time power to prevent contrary doctrines from being taught, advocated, or expressed. Let all possible causes of a change of mind be removed from men's apprehensions. Let them be kept ignorant, lest they should learn of some reason to think otherwise than they do. Let their passions be enlisted, so that they may regard private and unusual opinions with hatred and horror. Then, let all men who reject the established belief be terrified into silence. Let the people turn out and tar-and-feather such men. Or let inquisitions be made into the manner of thinking of suspected persons; and when they are found guilty of forbidden beliefs, let them be subjected to some signal punishment. When complete agreement could not otherwise be reached, a general massacre of all those who have not thought in a certain way has proved a very effective means of settling opinion in a country. If the power to do this be wanting, let a list of opinions be drawn up, to which no man of the least independence of thought can assent. Let the faithful then be required to accept all these propositions, in order to segregate them as radically as possible from the influence of the rest of the world.

This method has, from the earliest times, been one of the chief means of upholding correct theological and political doctrines, and of preserving their universal or catholic character. In Rome, especially, it has been practiced from the days of Numa Pompilius to those of Pius Nonus. This is the most perfect example in history; but wherever there is a priesthood—and no religion has been without one—this method has been more or less used. Wherever there is an **aristocracy,** or a guild, or any association of a class of men whose interests depend or are supposed to depend on certain propositions, there will be inevitably found some traces of this natural product of social feeling. Cruelties always accompany this system; and when it is consistently carried out, they become atrocities of the most horrible kind in the eyes of any rational man. Nor should this surprise anyone, for the officer of a society does not feel justified in surrendering the interests of that society for the sake of mercy, as he might his own private interests. It is natural, therefore, that sympathy and fellowship should thus produce a most ruthless power.

In judging this method of fixing belief, which may be called the method of authority, we must, in the first place, allow its immeasurable mental and moral superiority to the method of tenacity. Its success is proportionately greater; and, in fact, it has over and over again worked the most majestic results. The mere structures of stone which it has caused to be put together—in Siam, for example, in Egypt, and in Europe—have many of them a sublimity that has rivaled the greatest works of Nature. And, except for the geological epochs, there are no periods of time that are as vast as those measured by some of these organized faiths. If we scrutinize the matter closely, we shall find that there has not been one of their creeds which has remained always the same; yet the change is so slow as to be imperceptible during one person's life, so that individual belief remains sensibly fixed. For the mass of mankind, then, there is perhaps no better method than this. If it is their highest impulse to be intellectual slaves, then slaves they ought to remain.

But no institution can undertake to regulate opinions upon every subject. Only the most important ones can be attended to, and on the rest men's minds must be left to the action of natural causes. This imperfection will be no source of weakness as long as men are in such a state of culture that one opinion does not influence another, that is, as long as they cannot put two and two together. But even in the most priest-ridden states, some individuals will be found who are raised above that condition. These men possess a wider sort of social feeling; they see that men in other countries and in other ages have held to very different doctrines than those they themselves have been brought up to believe. And they cannot help seeing that it is the mere accident of their having been taught as they have, and of their having been surrounded with the manners and associations they have, that has caused them to believe as they do and not far differently. Nor can their candor resist the reflection that there is no reason to rate their own views at a higher value than those of other nations and other centuries, thus giving rise to doubts in their minds.

They will further perceive that such doubts as these must exist in their minds with reference to every belief that seems to be determined by the caprice either of themselves or of those who originated the popular opinions. Therefore, the willful adherence to a belief, and the arbitrary forcing of it upon others, must both be given up. A new and different method of settling opinions must be adopted, a method that will not only produce an impulse to believe, but that will also decide what proposition is to be believed. Let the action of natural preferences be unimpeded, then, and under their influence let men, conversing together and regarding matters in different lights, gradually develop beliefs in harmony with natural causes. This method resembles that by which conceptions of art have been brought to maturity. The most perfect example of this is to be found in the history of metaphysical philosophy. Systems of this sort have not usually rested upon any observed facts, at least not to any great degree. They have been chiefly adopted because their fundamental propositions seemed "agreeable to reason." This is an apt expression; it does not mean that which agrees with experience, but that which we find ourselves inclined to believe. Plato, for example, finds it agreeable to reason that the distances of the celestial spheres from one another should be proportional to the different lengths of strings that produce harmonious chords. Many philosophers have been led to their main **conclusions** by considerations like this. But this is the lowest and least developed form that the method takes, for it is clear that another man might find Kepler's theory that the celestial spheres are proportional to the inscribed and circumscribed spheres of the different regular solids more agreeable to *his* reason. But the shock of opinions will soon lead men to rest on preferences of a far more universal nature. Take, for example, the doctrine that man only acts selfishly, that is, from the consideration that acting in one way will afford him more pleasure than acting in another. This rests on no fact in the world, but it has had a wide acceptance as being the only reasonable theory.

This method is far more intellectual and respectable from the point of view of reason than either of the others we have discussed. Indeed, as long as no better method can be applied, this method ought to be followed. . . . However, its failure has been the most manifest. It makes of inquiry something similar to the development of taste, but taste, unfortunately, is always more or less a matter of fashion. Accordingly, metaphysicians have never come to any fixed agreement, but the pendulum has swung backward and forward between a more material and a more spiritual philosophy, from the earliest times to the latest. . . .

To satisfy our doubts, therefore, it is necessary that a method should be found by which our beliefs are determined by nothing human, but by some external permanency—by something upon which our thinking has no effect. Some mystics imagine that they have such a method in a private inspiration from on high. But that is only a form of the method of tenacity, in which the conception of truth as something public is not yet developed. Our external permanency would not be external, in our sense, if it was restricted in its influence to one individual. It must be something that affects, or might affect, every man. And, though these affections are necessarily as various as are individual conditions, yet the method must be such that the ultimate conclusion of every man shall be the same. Such is the method of science. Its fundamental hypothesis, restated in more familiar language, is this: There are real things, whose characters are entirely independent of our opinions about them; those realities affect our senses according to regular laws, and, though our sensations are as different as are our relations to the objects, yet, by taking advantage of the laws of perception, we can ascertain by reasoning how things really and truly are; and any man, if he has sufficient experience and reasons enough about it, will be led to the one true conclusion. The new conception here involved is that of reality. It may be asked how I know that there are any realities. If this hypothesis is the sole support of my method of inquiry, my method of inquiry must not be used to support my hypothesis. The reply is this: (1) If investigation cannot be regarded as proving that there are real things, it at least does not lead to a contrary conclusion; but the method and the conception on which it is based remain ever in harmony. No doubts of the method, therefore, necessarily arise from its practice, as is the case with all the others. (2) The feeling which gives rise to any method of fixing belief is a dissatisfaction at two repugnant propositions. But here already is a vague concession that there is some *one* thing which a proposition should represent. Nobody, therefore, can really doubt that there are realities, for, if he did, doubt would not be a source of dissatisfaction. The hypothesis, therefore, is one that every mind admits, so that the social impulse does not cause men to doubt it. (3) Everybody uses the scientific method about a great many things, and only ceases to use it when he does not know how to apply it. (4) Experience of the method has not led us to doubt it, but, on the contrary, scientific investigation has had the most wonderful triumphs in the way of settling opinion. These afford the explanation of my not doubting the method or the hypothesis that it supposes; and not having any doubt, nor believing that anybody else whom I could influence has, it would be the merest babble for me to say more about it. If there is anybody with a living doubt upon the subject, let him consider it.

To describe the method of scientific investigation is the object of this series of papers. At present I have only room to notice some points of contrast between it and other methods of fixing belief.

This is the only one of the four methods that presents any distinction of a right and a wrong way. If I adopt the method of tenacity, and shut myself out from all influences, whatever I think necessary to doing this is necessary according to that method. So with the method of authority: the state may try to put down heresy by means that, from a scientific point of view, seem very ill-calculated to accomplish its purposes; but the only test *on that method* is what the state thinks; so that it cannot pursue the method wrongly. This is also the case with the *a priori* method. The very essence of it is to think as one is inclined to think. All metaphysicians will be sure to do that, however, they may be inclined to judge each other to be perversely wrong. . . . But with the scientific method the case is different. I may start with known and observed facts to proceed to the unknown; and yet the rules which I follow in doing so may not be such as investigation would approve. The test of whether I am truly following the method is not an immediate appeal to my feelings and purposes, but, on the contrary, itself involves the application of the method. Hence it is that bad reasoning as well as good reasoning is possible; and this fact is the foundation of the practical side of logic.

It is not to be supposed that the first three methods of settling opinion present no advantage whatever over the scientific method. On the contrary, each has some peculiar convenience of its own. The *a priori* method is distinguished for its comfortable conclusions. It is the nature of the process to adopt whatever belief we are inclined to, and there are certain flatteries to the vanity of man that we all believe by nature, until we are awakened from our pleasing dream by rough facts. The method of authority will always govern the mass of mankind; and those who wield the various forms of organized force in the state will never be convinced that dangerous reasoning ought not to be suppressed in some way. If liberty of speech is to be untrammeled from the grosser forms of constraint, then uniformity of opinion will be secured by a moral terrorism to which the respectability of society will give its thorough approval. Following the method of authority is the path of peace. Certain non-conformities are permitted; certain others (considered unsafe) are forbidden. These are different in different countries and in different ages; but, wherever you are, let it be known that you seriously hold a tabooed belief, and you may be perfectly sure of being treated with a cruelty less brutal but more refined than hunting you like a wolf. Thus, the greatest intellectual benefactors of mankind have never dared, and dare not now, to utter the whole of their thought; and thus a shade of *prima facie* doubt is cast upon every proposition that is considered essential to the security of society. Singularly enough, the persecution does not all come from without; but a man torments himself and is oftentimes most distressed at finding himself

believing propositions which he has been brought up to regard with aversion. The peaceful and sympathetic man will, therefore, find it hard to resist the temptation to submit his opinions to authority. But most of all I admire the method of tenacity for its strength, simplicity, and directness. Men who pursue it are distinguished for their decision of character, which becomes very easy with such a mental rule. They do not waste time in trying to make up their minds what they want, but, fastening like lightning upon whatever alternative comes first, they hold to it to the end, whatever happens, without an instant's irresolution. This is one of the splendid qualities which generally accompany brilliant, unlasting success. It is impossible not to envy the man who can dismiss reason, although we know how it must turn out at last.

Such are the advantages that the other methods of settling opinion have over scientific investigation. A man should consider well of them; and then he should consider that, after all, he wishes his opinions to coincide with the fact, and that there is no reason why the results of these three methods should do so. To bring about this effect is the prerogative of the method of science. Upon such considerations he has to make his choice—a choice that is far more than the adoption of any intellectual opinion, a choice that is one of the ruling decisions of his life, to which, when once made, he is bound to adhere. The force of habit will sometimes cause a man to hold on to old beliefs, after he is in a condition to see that they have no sound basis. But reflection upon the state of the case will overcome these habits, and he ought to allow reflection its full weight. . . .

Yes, the other methods do have their merits: a clear logical conscience does cost something—just as any virtue, just as all that we cherish, costs us dearly. But we should not desire it to be otherwise. The genius of a man's logical method should be loved and reverenced as his bride, whom he has chosen from everyone else in the world. He need not condemn the others; on the contrary, he may honor them deeply, and in doing so he only honors her the more. But she is the one that he has chosen, and he knows that he was right in making that choice. And having made it, he will work and fight for her. He will not complain that there are blows to take, hoping that there may be as many and as hard to give, and he will strive to be the worthy knight and champion of her, from the blaze of whose splendors he draws his inspiration and his courage.

Questions for Thought

1. What are some of the doubts that have plagued you in recent times? Were you able to resolve these doubts? If so, how?
2. Which of your beliefs, if any, are based on the method of tenacity? Which of them are based on the method of authority?
3. Do you subscribe to any philosophical or theological system? If so, how does this system of belief deal with doubt?
4. Do you agree with Peirce that scientific investigation is more reliable than the other three methods of fixing belief? Why or why not?
5. What seems to be Peirce's attitude toward social norms and religious beliefs? How does your own attitude toward social norms and religious beliefs compare with or differ from Peirce's attitude?

5   Pragmatism's Conception of Truth

WILLIAM JAMES

William James (1842–1910), the brother of novelist Henry James, was born in New York City. James' father, often described as an eccentric follower of the Swiss mystic Emanuel Swedenborg, was a true proponent of self-development who left his children free to make their own decisions on matters of belief. Although much of James' education was provided informally by his father and his father's friends (who included such **transcendentalist** writers as Ralph Waldo Emerson), he intermittently attended a variety of private educational institutions in the United States and abroad.

Because his family's wealth freed James from the necessity of seeking immediate employment (his grandfather had become rich by investing in the Erie Canal), he was able to pursue a variety of interests. In 1860, James studied painting for a year before deciding that his talents lay elsewhere. The following year, he entered the Lawrence Scientific School at Harvard University, where he studied chemistry, anatomy, and physiology. In 1864, he transferred to the Harvard Medical School, although he had no intention of practicing medicine. In 1865–1866, James volunteered for an expedition to Brazil with the well-known naturalist Louis Agassiz. Unfortunately, during this expedition he contracted smallpox, the first of a series of health problems that were to plague him in later life. After returning to medical school for a term, he spent the years 1867–1868 in Germany, recuperating and studying physiology.

James returned to the United States in 1868 and received his M.D. from Harvard the following year. However, still ill and suffering from an emotional crisis precipitated by doubts about human freedom, he spent the next three years living in his father's house. Then, in 1872, he was offered a job teaching physiology at Harvard. Displaying the breadth of his learning, he began teaching psychology in 1875 and philosophy in 1879. James remained affiliated with Harvard until 1907. After marrying Alice Gibbens in 1878, James' health problems seemed to diminish, and he turned wholeheartedly to writing and lecturing. Contracting to write a textbook on psychology in 1880, James instead wrote a large two-volume work in theoretical psychology, *The Principles of Psychology,* which was published ten years later. Having written this definitive work in psychology, James then turned his attention to religion, writing diverse essays and lectures on the subject between 1893 and 1903. A collection of these were published in the widely read work *The Will To Believe and Other Essays in Popular Philosophy,* published in 1897. However, the culmination of James' focus on religion came in 1901–1902, when he delivered the Gifford Lectures at the University of Edinburgh in Scotland. These were published in 1902 under the title *The Varieties of Religious Experience.*

From this point to the end of his life, James devoted his energies more and more to describing and defending the views of **pragmatism,** a method of philosophy that he had first identified in a lecture at the University of California in 1898. (While lecturing on pragmatism at Stanford University in 1906, James experienced the great earthquake that destroyed much of San Francisco.) When health problems returned, James was forced to give up lecturing in 1908. After unsuccessfully seeking a cure in Europe, he returned to the United States. He died at his country home in New Hampshire in 1910.

In the following lecture, James, who sees himself as following the lead of Peirce and Dewey, explains and defends the pragmatic theory of truth. Rejecting the theory of certain philosophers that the truth or falsity of an idea is determined by whether it is an accurate copy of reality—this theory is usually referred to as the correspondence theory of truth—James claims that the truth of an idea depends on its usefulness or expediency. Although he does admit that an idea may sometimes copy some aspect of reality, he does not believe that an idea must meet this criterion in order to be considered true. Indeed, like Peirce and Dewey, James believes that both reality and our ideas are constantly changing; thus, any correspondence between an idea and some aspect of reality could be only a temporary phenomenon.

Rather than thinking of knowledge in terms of adapting our ideas to a fixed, independent reality, James says that we must seek ideas that will work—that is, ideas that will lead to desirable consequences. We should ask ourselves what difference, if any, a certain idea will make in our lives. If the idea leads us to other experiences that are worthwhile, then we are justified in saying the idea is true. However, since truth is neither stagnant nor eternal, further experience may reveal that the idea is no longer useful and thus that it has become false. While James focuses on examples related to everyday problem solving in much of this selection, near the end he notes that the pragmatic conception of truth applies to scientific thinking as well. In science, as in everyday problem solving, the theory that is true is the theory that works, the theory that gives us "the maximum possible sum of satisfactions."

Questions for Reading

1. What exactly does James mean by the "pragmatic conception of truth"? How does the pragmatic conception of truth differ from the intellectualist conception of truth?
2. What is James' example of the house at the end of the cow path intended to show?

3. What does James mean by verification? How, according to James, does one go about verifying an idea?
4. Why does James reject the possibility of absolute truths?
5. How does James distinguish "scientific" ideas from "nonscientific" ideas? What, according to James, does a scientific idea have in common with a nonscientific idea?

PRAGMATISM'S CONCEPTION OF TRUTH

WHEN CLERK-MAXWELL WAS A CHILD IT IS written that he had a mania for having everything explained to him, and that when people put him off with vague verbal accounts of any phenomenon he would interrupt them impatiently by saying, "Yes; but I want you to tell me the *particular go* of it!" Had his question been about truth, only a pragmatist could have told him the particular go of it. I believe that our contemporary pragmatists, especially Messrs. Schiller and Dewey, have given the only tenable account of this subject. It is a very ticklish subject, sending subtle rootlets into all kinds of crannies, and hard to treat in the sketchy way that alone befits a public lecture. But the Schiller-Dewey view of truth has been so ferociously attacked by rationalistic philosophers, and so abominably misunderstood, that here, if anywhere, is the point where a clear and simple statement should be made.

I fully expect to see the pragmatist view of truth run through the classic stages of a theory's career. First, you know, a new theory is attacked as absurd; then it is admitted to be true, but obvious and insignificant; finally it is seen to be so important that its adversaries claim that they themselves discovered it. Our doctrine of truth is at present in the first of these three stages, with symptoms of the second stage having begun in certain quarters. I wish that this lecture might help it beyond the first stage in the eyes of many of you.

Truth, as any dictionary will tell you, is a property of certain of our ideas. It means their "agreement," as falsity means their disagreement, with "reality." Pragmatists and intellectualists both accept this definition as a matter of course. They begin to quarrel only after the question is raised as to what may precisely be meant by the term "agreement," and what by the term "reality," when reality is taken as something for our ideas to agree with.

In answering these questions the pragmatists are more analytic and painstaking, the intellectualists more offhand and irreflective. The popular notion is that a true idea must copy its reality. Like other popular views, this one follows the **analogy** of the most usual experience. Our true ideas of sensible things do indeed copy them. Shut your eyes and think of yonder clock on the wall, and you get just such a true picture or copy of its dial. But your idea of its "works" (unless you are a clockmaker) is much less of a copy, yet it passes muster, for it in no way clashes with the reality. Even though it should shrink to the mere word "works," that word still serves you truly; and when you speak of the "timekeeping function" of the clock, or of its spring's "elasticity," it is hard to see exactly what your ideas can copy.

You perceive that there is a problem here. Where our ideas cannot copy definitely their object, what does agreement with that object mean? Some idealists seem to say that they are true whenever they are what God means that we ought to think about that object. Others hold the copy view all through, and speak as if our ideas possessed truth just in proportion as they approach to being copies of the Absolute's eternal way of thinking.

These views, you see, invite pragmatistic discussion. But the great assumption of the intellectualists is that truth means essentially an inert static relation. When you've got your rule idea of anything, there's an end of the matter. You're in possession; you *know;* you have fulfilled your thinking destiny. You are where you ought to be mentally; you have obeyed your categorical imperative; and nothing more need follow on that climax of your rational destiny. Epistemologically you are in stable equilibrium.

From William James, Pragmatism: A New Name for Some Old Ways of Thinking, *New York, 1907.*

Pragmatism, on the other hand, asks its usual question. "Grant an idea or belief to be true," it says, "what concrete difference will its being true make in any one's actual life? How will the truth be realized? What experiences will be different from those which would obtain if the belief were false? What, in short, is the truth's cash value in experiential terms?"

The moment pragmatism asks this question, it sees the answer: *True ideas are those that we can assimilate, validate, corroborate and verify. False ideas are those that we can not.* That is the practical difference it makes to us to have true ideas; that, therefore, is the meaning of truth, for it is all that truth is known-as.

This thesis is what I have to defend. The truth of an idea is not a stagnant property inherent in it. Truth *happens* to an idea. It *becomes* true, is *made* true by events. Its verity *is* in fact an event, a process: the process namely of its verifying itself, its veri-*fication*. Its validity is the process of its valid-*ation*.

But what do the words verification and validation themselves pragmatically mean? They again signify certain practical consequences of the verified and validated idea. It is hard to find any one phrase that characterizes these consequences better than the ordinary agreement formula—just such consequences being what we have in mind whenever we say that our ideas "agree" with reality. They lead us, namely, through the acts and other ideas which they instigate, into or up to, or toward, other parts of experience with which we feel all the while—such feeling being among our potentialities—that the original ideas remain in agreement. The connections and transitions come to us from point to point as being progressive, harmonious, satisfactory. This function of agreeable leading is what we mean by an idea's verification. Such an account is vague and it sounds at first quite trivial, but it has results which it will take the rest of my hour to explain.

Let me begin by reminding you of the fact that the possession of true thoughts means everywhere the possession of invaluable instruments of action; and that our duty to gain truth, so far from being a blank command from out of the blue, or a "stunt" self-imposed by our intellect, can account for itself by excellent practical reasons.

The importance to human life of having true beliefs about matters of fact is a thing too notorious. We live in a world of realities that can be infinitely useful or infinitely harmful. Ideas that tell us which of them to expect count as the true ideas in all this primary sphere of verification, and the pursuit of such ideas is a primary human duty. The possession of truth, so far from being here an end in itself, is only a preliminary means towards other vital satisfactions. If I am lost in the woods and starved, and find what looks like a cow path, it is of the utmost importance that I should think of a human habitation at the end of it, for if I do so and follow it, I save myself. The true thought is useful here because the house which is its object is useful. The practical value of true ideas is thus primarily derived from the practical importance of their objects to us. Their objects are, indeed, not important at all times. I may on another occasion have no use for the house; and then my idea of it, however verifiable, will be practically irrelevant and had better remain latent. Yet since almost any object may some day become temporarily important, the advantage of having a general stock of *extra* truths, of ideas that shall be true of merely possible situations, is obvious. We store such extra truths away in our memories, and with the overflow we fill our books of reference. Whenever such an extra truth becomes practically relevant to one of our emergencies, it passes from cold storage to do work in the world and our belief in it grows active. You can say of it then either that "it is useful because it is true" or that "it is true because it is useful." Both these phrases mean exactly the same thing, namely that here is an idea that gets fulfilled and can be verified. True is the name for whatever idea starts the verification process, useful is the name for its completed function in experience. True ideas would never have been singled out as such, would never have acquired a class name, least of all a name suggesting value, unless they had been useful from the outset in this way.

From this simple cue pragmatism gets her general notion of truth as something essentially bound up with the way in which one moment in our experience may lead us towards other moments which it will be worth while to have been led to. Primarily, and on the commonsense level, the truth of a state of mind means this function of *a leading that is worth while*. When a moment in our experience, of any kind whatever, inspires us with a thought that is true, that means that sooner or later we dip by that thought's guidance into the particulars of experience again and make advantageous connection with them. This is a vague enough statement, but I beg you to retain it, for it is essential.

Our experience meanwhile is all shot through with regularities. One bit of it can warn us to get ready for another bit, can "intend" or be "significant of" that remoter object. The object's advent is the significance's verification. Truth, in these cases, meaning nothing but eventual verification, is manifestly incompatible with waywardness on our part. Woe to him whose beliefs play fast and loose with the order which realities follow in his experience; they will lead him nowhere or else make false connections.

By "realities" or "objects" here, we mean either things of common sense, sensibly present, or else commonsense relations, such as dates, places, distances, kinds, activities. Following our mental image of a house along the cow path, we actually come to see the house; we get the image's full verification. *Such simply and fully verified leadings are certainly the originals and prototypes of the truth process.* Experience offers indeed other forms of truth process, but they are all conceivable as being primary verifications arrested, multiplied or substituted one for another.

Take, for instance, yonder object on the wall. You and I consider it to be a "clock," although no one of us has seen the hidden works that make it one. We let our notion pass for true without attempting to verify. If truths mean verification process essentially, ought we then to call such unverified truths as this abortive? No, for they form the overwhelmingly large number of the truths we live by. Indirect as well as direct verifications pass muster. Where circumstantial evidence is sufficient, we can go without eyewitnessing. Just as we here assume Japan to exist without ever having been there, because it *works* to do so, everything we know conspiring with the belief, and nothing interfering, so we assume that thing to be a clock. We *use* it as a clock, regulating the length of our lecture by it. The verification of the assumption here means its leading to no frustration or contradiction. Verifi*ability* of wheels and weights and pendulum is as good as verification. For one truth process completed there are a million in our lives that function in this state of nascency. They turn us *toward* direct verification; lead us into the *surroundings* of the objects they envisage; and then, if everything runs on harmoniously, we are so sure that verification is possible that we omit it, and are usually justified by all that happens.

Truth lives, in fact, for the most part on a credit system. Our thoughts and beliefs "pass," so long as nothing challenges them, just as bank notes pass so long as nobody refuses them. But this all points to direct face-to-face verifications somewhere, without which the fabric of truth collapses like a financial system with no cash basis whatever. You accept my verification of one thing, I yours of another. We trade on each other's truth. But beliefs verified concretely by *somebody* are the posts of the whole superstructure. Another great reason—beside economy of time—for waiving complete verification in the usual business of life is that all things exist in kinds and not singly. Our world is found once for all to have that peculiarity. So that when we have once directly verified our ideas about one specimen of a kind, we consider ourselves free to apply them to other specimens without verification. A mind that habitually discerns the kind of thing before it, and acts by the law of the kind immediately, without pausing to verify, will be a "true" mind in ninety-nine out of a hundred emergencies, proved so by its conduct fitting everything it meets, and getting no refutation.

Indirectly or only potentially verifying processes may thus be true as well as full verification processes. They work as true processes would work, give us the same advantages, and claim our recognition for the same reasons. All this on the commonsense level of matters of fact, which we are alone considering.

But matters of fact are not our only stock in trade. *Relations among purely mental ideas* form another sphere where true and false beliefs obtain, and here the beliefs are absolute, or unconditional. When they are true they bear the name either of definitions or of principles. It is either a principle or a definition that 1 and 1 make 2, that 2 and 1 make 3, and so on; that white differs less from gray than it does from black; that when the cause begins to act the effect also commences. Such propositions hold of all possible "ones," of all conceivable "whites" and "grays" and "causes." The objects here are mental objects. Their relations are perceptually obvious at a glance, and no sense verification is necessary. Moreover, once true, always true, of those same mental objects. Truth here has an "eternal" character. If you can find a concrete thing anywhere that is "one" or "white" or "gray" or an "effect," then your principles will everlastingly apply to it. It is but a case of ascertaining the kind, and then applying the law of its kind to the particular object. You are sure to get truth if you can but name the kind rightly, for your mental relations hold good of everything of that kind without exception. If you then, nevertheless, failed to get truth concretely, you would say that you had classed your real objects wrongly.

In this realm of mental relations, truth again is an affair of leading. We relate one abstract idea with another, framing in the end great systems of logical and mathematical truth, under the respective terms of which the sensible facts of experience eventually arrange themselves, so that our eternal truths hold good of realities also. This marriage of fact and theory is endlessly fertile. What we say is here already true in advance of special verification, *if we have subsumed our objects rightly.* Our ready-made ideal framework for all sorts of possible objects follows from the very structure of our thinking. We can no more play fast and loose with these abstract relations than we can do so with our sense experiences. They coerce us; we must treat them consistently, whether or not we like the results. The rules of addition apply to our debts as rigorously as to our assets. The hundredth decimal of π, the ratio of the circumference to its diameter, is predetermined ideally now, though no one may have computed it. If we should ever need the figure in our dealings with an actual circle we should need to have it given rightly, calculated by the usual rules; for it is the same kind of truth that those rules elsewhere calculate.

Between the coercions of the sensible order and those of the ideal order, our mind is thus wedged tightly. Our ideas must agree with realities, be such realities concrete or abstract, be they facts or be they principles, under penalty of endless inconsistency and frustration.

So far, intellectualists can raise no protest. They can only say that we have barely touched the skin of the matter.

Realities mean, then, either concrete facts, or abstract kinds of thing and relations perceived intuitively between them. They furthermore and thirdly mean, as things that new ideas of ours must no less take account of, the whole body of other truths already in our possession. But what now does "agreement" with such threefold realities mean?— to use again the definition that is current.

Here it is that pragmatism and intellectualism begin to part company. Primarily, no doubt, to agree means to copy, but we saw that the mere word "clock" would do instead of a mental picture of its works, and that of many realities our ideas can only be symbols and not copies. "Past time," "power," "spontaneity"—how can our mind copy such realities?

To "agree" in the widest sense with a reality can only mean to be guided either straight up to it or into its surroundings, or to be put into such working touch with it as to handle either it or something connected with it better than if we disagreed. Better either intellectually or practically! And often agreement will only mean the negative fact that nothing contradictory from the quarter of that reality comes to interfere with the way in which our ideas guide us elsewhere. To copy a reality is, indeed, one very important way of agreeing with it, but it is far from being essential. The essential thing is the process of being guided. Any idea that helps us to *deal*, whether practically or intellectually, with either the reality or its belongings, that doesn't entangle our progress in frustrations, that *fits*, in fact, and adapts our life to the reality's whole setting, will agree sufficiently to meet the requirement. It will hold true of that reality.

Thus, *names* are just as "true" or "false" as definite mental pictures are. They set up similar verification processes, and lead to fully equivalent practical results.

All human thinking gets discursified; we exchange ideas; we lend and borrow verifications, get them from one another by means of social intercourse. All truth thus gets verbally built out, stored up, and made available for every one. Hence, we must *talk* consistently just as we must *think* consistently: for both in talk and thought we deal with kinds. Names are arbitrary, but once understood they must be kept to. We mustn't now call Abel "Cain" or Cain "Abel."

If we do, we ungear ourselves from the whole book of Genesis, and from all its connections with the universe of speech and fact down to the present time. We throw ourselves out of whatever truth that entire system of speech and fact may embody.

The overwhelming majority of our true ideas admit of no direct or face-to-face verification—those of past history, for example, as of Cain and Abel. The stream of time can be remounted only verbally, or verified indirectly by the present prolongations or effects of what the past harbored. Yet if they agree with these verbalities and effects, we can know that our ideas of the past are true. *As true as past time itself was,* so true was Julius Caesar, so true were antediluvian monsters, all in their proper dates and settings. That past time itself was, is guaranteed by its coherence with everything that's present. True as the present *is,* the past *was* also.

Agreement thus turns out to be essentially an affair of leading—leading that is useful because it is into quarters that contain objects that are important. True ideas lead us into useful verbal and conceptual quarters as well as directly up to useful sensible termini. They lead to consistency, stability and flowing human intercourse. They lead away from eccentricity and isolation, from foiled and barren thinking. The untrammeled flowing of the leading process, its general freedom from clash and contradiction, passes for its indirect verification; but all roads lead to Rome, and in the end and eventually, all true processes must lead to the face of directly verifying sensible experiences *somewhere,* which somebody's ideas have copied.

Such is the large loose way in which the pragmatist interprets the word *agreement.* He treats it altogether practically. He lets it cover any process of conduction from a present idea to a future terminus, provided only it run prosperously. It is only thus that "scientific" ideas, flying as they do beyond common sense, can be said to agree with their realities. It is, as I have already said, *as if* reality were made of ether, atoms or electrons, but we mustn't think so literally. The term "energy" doesn't even pretend to stand for anything "objective." It is only a way of measuring the surface of phenomena so as to string their changes on a simple formula.

Yet in the choice of these man-made formulas we can not be capricious with impunity any more than we can be capricious on the commonsense practical level. We must find a theory that will *work;* and that means something extremely difficult; for our theory must mediate between all previous truths and certain new experiences. It must derange common sense and previous belief as little as possible, and it must lead to some sensible terminus or other that can be verified exactly. To "work" means both these things; and the squeeze is so tight that there is little loose play for any hypothesis. Our theories are wedged and controlled as nothing else is. Yet sometimes alternative theoretic formulas are equally compatible with all the truths we know, and then we choose

between them for subjective reasons. We choose the kind of theory to which we are already partial; we follow "elegance" or "economy." Clerk-Maxwell somewhere says it would be "poor scientific taste" to choose the more complicated of two equally well-evidenced conceptions; and you will all agree with him. Truth in science is what gives us the maximum possible sum of satisfactions, taste included, but consistency both with previous truth and with novel fact is always the most imperious claimant.

I have led you through a very sandy desert. But now, if I may be allowed so vulgar an expression, we begin to taste the milk in the coconut. . . .

Our account of truth is an account of truths in the plural, of processes of leading, realized *in rebus,* and having only this quality in common, that they *pay.* They pay by guiding us into or towards some part of a system that dips at numerous points into sense percepts, which we may copy mentally or not, but with which at any rate we are now in the kind of commerce vaguely designated as verification. Truth for us is simply a collective name for verification processes, just as health, wealth, strength, etc., are names for other processes connected with life, and also pursued because it pays to pursue them. Truth is *made,* just as health, wealth, and strength are made, in the course of experience. . . .

"The true," to put it very briefly, *is only the expedient in the way of our thinking, just as "the right" is only the expedient in the way of our behaving.* Expedient in almost any fashion; and expedient in the long run and on the whole of course; for what meets expediently all the experience in sight won't necessarily meet all farther experiences equally satisfactorily. Experience, as we know, has ways of *boiling over,* and making us correct our present formulas.

The "absolutely" true, meaning what no further experience will ever alter, is that ideal vanishing point towards which we imagine that all our temporary truths will some day converge. It runs on all fours with the perfectly wise man, and with the absolutely complete experience; and, if these ideals are ever realized, they will all be realized together. Meanwhile we have to live today by what truth we can get today, and be ready tomorrow to call it falsehood. Ptolemaic astronomy, euclidean space, aristotelian logic, scholastic **metaphysics,** were expedient for centuries, but human experience has boiled over those limits, and we now call these things only relatively true, or true within those borders of experience. "Absolutely" they are false; for we know that those limits were casual, and might have been transcended by past theorists just as they are by present thinkers.

Questions for Thought

1. Would you consider yourself to be a pragmatist in James' sense? Why or why not?
2. Can you think of other examples that would illustrate the point that James makes with his example of the house at the end of the cow path?
3. Assuming that James' conception of truth is accurate, do you think it would justify belief in a divine being? Why or why not?
4. Do you think that there are absolute truths? If so, what are they? If not, why not?
5. What are some of the similarities between what James says in this selection and what Peirce says in the preceding one? Can you discern any differences between the two positions?

Methods and Modes of Knowing   6

JOSÉ VASCONCELOS

José Vasconcelos (1882–1959) was born in Oaxaca, Mexico. During his very active life, he participated in the Mexican Revolution, was instrumental in Mexican educational reform, and ran unsuccessfully for the presidency in 1929. In addition to serving as rector of the National University of Mexico, he also served as visiting professor at the University of Chicago and as director of the Biblioteca Nacional de México. Despite his preoccupation with political and educational reform, Vasconcelos still managed to find time to develop a sophisticated philosophical system, a system he named "**aesthetic** monism." Unfortunately, most of his writings have not been translated into English.

In the following selection from his *Tratado de metafísica,* Vasconcelos discusses the nature and types of knowledge. He argues that although each discipline has its own form of knowledge with a distinct methodology and subject matter, these varied forms of knowledge are linked to each other by a common connection or movement—the movement toward liberation or **transcendence.** However, he notes that traditional Western thinking has often overlooked this common connection for two reasons: (1) It has taken thought to be synonymous with knowledge, and (2) in so doing, it has excluded emotions and aesthetic experience as possible sources of knowledge. The result is that the search for knowledge has emphasized reason or analytical judgment to the exclusion of art.

While Vasconcelos does not totally reject the value of reason and analytical judgment, he argues that by making them the sole source of knowledge, Western thinking has become fixated on rigid concepts, on abstract logical formulas that do not allow for creative transformation. In opposition to such rigid concepts, Vasconcelos praises the fluidity of aesthetic judgments, especially the judgments of music and poetry. As he so poetically says, such judgments are "an open sesame that elevates us, with soul rejuvenated, to an improved and **transcendental** creation." Despite his praise for such judgments, Vasconcelos warns us that we must be careful not to allow ourselves to move so far in the direction of emotional and aesthetic experience that we deny the importance of reason and analytical judgment. The goal of philosophy is to combine all the varied forms of knowledge, to "interlace" reason and passion, analytical judgment and aesthetic judgment. Only by achieving this balance in our own lives can we become the creative, harmonious beings that we are capable of becoming.

Questions for Reading

1. What are Vasconcelos' principal criticisms of traditional Western views on the nature of knowledge?
2. What, according to Vasconcelos, can aesthetic judgments and emotions reveal to us that analytical judgments cannot?
3. What does Vasconcelos mean when he says that "reason is to the soul what body is to the spirit"?
4. How does Vasconcelos conceive art and the artist?
5. What, according to Vasconcelos, is the proper nature of philosophy?

IT IS OF SPECIAL INTEREST TO NOTE THAT EACH series of particular disciplines is made up of common elements, and that the only thing distinguishing one from another is an intrinsic distinctive characteristic in the orientation of movement. In the areas of reality, from the atom to grace, there is a series of broad and concentrated fields, but there is always a substantial unity, a community of existence, and the possibility of their concurrence in the final goal of redemption.

The sensible world, the intelligible, and transcendental reversion—here are the three fundamental categories; the methodological problem is to determine the common connection that allows them to coexist without conflict and, moreover, to concur in a common direction toward liberation. To define the relationship and the manner of transition among the diverse manifestations of existence is one of the purposes of the philosophy sketched in these pages, and our method, as well, must be in accord with this purpose. To show, at the same time, that not only the soul but also nature suffers and rejoices because of this eagerness to transcend itself, is another of the fundamental goals of our doctrine.

Necessary agreement between method and subject matter can only result from the comparison of the reality which is being dealt with and the system which interprets it and orders it. We have already stated that **aesthetics** gives us a type of dialectic exclusively its own; its aim is to create suprasensible realities and at the same time transmute its external energy. Whether it derives an image from reality or whether it envelopes the object itself in an aura of beauty, aesthetic emotion imposes upon existence its own order and logic, which has always been recognized in old sayings as "logic of the heart," "the heart has its reasons that reason does not understand," etc.

Its standards—alogical logic, free rhythm, the passion of becoming—go beyond the objective law but without being alien to it, without ceasing to move it and modify it in a fundamental fashion; on the contrary, beauty frequently transfigures the object and raises it to the plane of emotion. According to aesthetic standards, the object enters the realm of the spirit, by dint of the combined witchery of beauty's image, the affinity, and the **pathos.** At this point, analytical judgment and the image itself become fused in a dynamism of the emotions, which is creative of beauty, just as structure becomes one with energy and maintains it in the atom, and as the body maintains and nourishes conscious life. Reason is to the soul what the body is to the spirit, a framework of fixed movements; we must go beyond it in order to delve into its infinite profundities.

For example, with music the judgment plunges itself into the abyss, where it is dissolved; I am referring to logical judgment; but on the other hand,

Excerpt from pp. 78–84, from "Appendix C: Some Representative Selections from Writings of Jose Vasconcelos," translated by John M. Sharp and John H. Haddox, in Vasconcelos of Mexico: Philosopher and Prophet *by John H. Haddox,* © *1967. Reprinted by permission of University of Texas Press.*

another model makes its appearance which is, as it were, a sort of more flexible skeleton, a framework accommodated to the new nature, the angelic nature, which one needs in order to live beauty. That other logic is the logic of aesthetic judgment, which unlike the syllogism inclines us to hope for, obliges us to demand, the miracle, the exception, salvation. A similar thing occurs in every poetic judgment, and shines forth in all its splendid power in the enlightenment of those who are profoundly inspired, and even in that of those who are less inspired, as one may note in the first verse of some chapters of the Koran: "In the name of mild and merciful God"—a sovereign cry that thunders as if a golden drum were deafening heaven with its music; wondrous rings expand; celestial trumpets tremble; and their echoes expand space limitlessly. Overhead, the abyss is enraptured with brightness, like an infinity which is but poorly imitated by the domes of the greatest mosques. The air is filled with fragrances, as if the gardens of paradise had opened their gates. "Mild and merciful God"—the resounding vibrancy of these magic words re-echoes, bringing into harmony with themselves all the echoes of creation. . . . True art is always thus, an open sesame that elevates us, with soul rejuvenated, to an improved and transcendental creation.

It has not thus far been possible to formulate the basis for an exact philosophy in which the subject and the object, science and religion, may be brought into harmony rather than into mutual opposition, simply because the aesthetic problem has stood in our way. We still have not been able to define the significance of this problem within the general process of knowing; nor even less, to show how it is a means to grace for the object itself. Therefore, we have frequently been in like error in judging aesthetics either as the goal of the living process or as a simple variant of biological energy. Hence, currently we have applied to it constantly the first logical method, the biological; but never its own, superior because it is genuinely spiritual.

Furthermore, we have time and again, in the case of art, confused form and content; holy creative inspiration needs forms in order to make itself apparent to our nature; but inspiration passes and the form remains; inspiration frequently remains unfulfilled; at other times, inspiration does not succeed in giving life, in transforming its mold, and then the mold reverts to its parallel, the intellectual form

subject to the logic of reason, which is the logic of the object. Thus we see, for example, that in the classical Spanish theater the characters frequently discuss their love until they turn it into a dialectic; in the French theater it is even worse, for pathos becomes the golden mean, and one must turn to Shakespeare again to find the lyric tide which elevates the soul and the world beyond the mean, reason, and form.

The problem here is one of form as well as of essence, since emotion does not take on a fully material form, is not realized, except in concrete manifestations which emotion itself determines. Every river delves and slowly defines its own bed; each flood leaves its mark along the banks and its own particular channel on the bottom; just so does emotion constantly forge and alter its motifs; but never will the particular motif or the limited form be enough to retain all the contents of the emotion. Light cannot penetrate the cracks through which water may leak away; but in a cave the flow of water may be recognized by its mysterious music; light, in contrast, dances where not even clouds may ascend. None of the aspects of the object, none of its elements, no sensible impression, none of the senses, none of the forms of reason, no thought, no partial reality, will succeed in containing or capturing the entire course of the rivers and whirlpools of emotion which give birth to aesthetic creation. Only wonder accompanies the endless beauty of earth and heaven.

It is not a simple task to follow art's own law; creative artists are rare, and even they, if they allow themselves to be enthralled by their aesthetic emotion, run the risk of falling prey to passions, dances and orgies, until they are blinded and become as incapable of progress as a Persian Sufi or a howling dervish, despite the fact that their point of departure is sublime emotion. This means that in the human condition one has no right to delay for a long time, and that, hence, to achieve precise philosophical knowledge one must employ a method based upon attentive observation as well as upon a constant motivation toward higher conditions.

At any rate, the world of the philosopher is to be distinguished from the methodology of experimental science and from all specialized approaches, in that it is not limited to a single criterion but must combine all of them: a philosopher requires a super-criterion. He must constantly compare the discoveries of the mind with those of the senses, and with that which the emotions teach him.

Philosophy cannot disregard universal ancient knowledge without falling into the childishness of contemporary empirical systems; neither may it ignore contemporary discoveries relating to the material world and to our dealings with material things; but the supreme law must not be sought in a physical world. As soon as one affirms that practical convenience establishes the law, the instinct to transcend it is destroyed, and the greatest of the powers at philosophy's disposal is precisely the instinct to transcend the material world.

No philosophy, then, is valid unless it is based upon the harmony of all facets of universal knowledge, and it is up to the philosopher alone to establish the values and hierarchies which give meaning to that harmony; the method to achieve such a task must be, accordingly, multifold, and not isolated, but interrelated—both an interlacement of the cosmos and a sign of the spirit that transcends it.

In order to begin to conceive a system, it is fundamental that we recall that each one of the realms into which existence can be broken down possesses its own rhythm of development and perfection, and yet that none of them can by itself explain the universal process. To join the spokes to the hubs one must first observe how the change from one order to another takes place. Reality viewed from within by a judgment participating in its rhythms, but transcending them, reveals to us regular processes and leaps. Whenever existence passes from power to will, from will to enjoyment, and vice versa, judgment is filled with astonishment as if it were in the presence of something that lies without its realm; but emotion understands, and becomes intoxicated with miraculous power; then, under the full power of its own nature, it ascends a scale, the scale of emotions, and sees how, within a single essence, the object is clothed, as it were, in light, in the oppositions of different types of energy; the biological impulse is fulfilled and realized in pleasure, and the feeling of the soul is overwhelmed with divine joy. Here we have a glimpse of unity in the heterogeneous, a unity which takes in the three primary orders: object, intelligence, will.

Since emotion embraces more than intelligence, it is of prime necessity to assign it a place of honor among the means of knowledge. Thus we shall continue investigating and penetrating until we find a supreme unity, which can gather in all the currents without obliterating their identity, in order to bring into being by their means a new mode of existence. One word defines our method: concurrent. . . .

Let us now try this definition: emotional knowledge manifests itself when things and processes reveal a sudden identity or disparity with our innermost nature. When we perceive certain processes taking place in the outer world, such as the flow of melody, we feel arising in our consciousness as well a parallel flow, intangible but real, flexible, and almost free. At the same time we become aware that the flow within becomes more closely joined to the flow without, that one can influence the other. Moreover, rational knowledge works upon a **substance** that is a matter of indifference to me and whose development depends on its own nature, without my being able to change it fundamentally. On the other hand, the flow that I perceive with an internal sense of identity to it seems subject to my free will, and offers me at least the possibility of exerting my free will upon the thing and of affecting it in a parallel fashion.

A certain opposition between the two modes of knowledge, rational and emotional, that is, the one that discovers the rules of a process and the one that inquires into its nature and purpose, is no obstacle to their working cooperatively in the task of research. Pythagoras, without distinguishing the two modes, achieves their synthesis when, after defining the relationships of the triangle and the squares derived from it, and after finding the numerical combinations of the triad, the square, and so forth, he moves on to music to follow in it the development of the numerical rhythms; but it is necessary to note clearly that in the same instant that the move is made from numbers to music, one enters the field of aesthetics and one's judgment is no longer rational but emotional when one enters a realm of knowing through sympathies and differences based on emotion. By difference or by similarity of essence or of goal the two dramatic poles of every aesthetic contemplation are engendered: the subject and the object, no longer confronted for measurement by the rules of logical judgment, but suspended in the mutual mystery that separates them in a sort of morphological reality, while joining them through their involvement with the Absolute. . . .

It is evident, accordingly, that besides rational knowledge, which is a result of the exercise of the intelligence on the data of the internal and external sensitivity, or the sensitivity produced by both, we possess another means for penetrating reality, that is, another mode of knowing. The **intuition** of color as a scale of beauty, of sound as melody and mystery, the emotion of the presence and correspondence to us of things that are intimately related to us, although superficially farther from us than the water we drink or the air that replenishes our blood, all these experiences constitute a source of a specific type of knowledge that cannot be transferred to another category, but is closely linked to us in a sort of instinctive coordination and existential harmony. Accordingly knowledge is not a synonym for thought but something still more inclusive than thought; that is, it involves bringing into the terms of consciousness elements that are most extraneous to it, making them part of our lives according to their affinities to the various powers of our personality so that all become joined in an awareness of super-existence and transcendence in which dissimilar elements are combined for the total achievement of harmony. Of course we are not proposing a type of harmony that will respect each unit of reality; on the contrary [we are proposing] a great, perhaps catastrophic, series of deep emotions and changes that will keep changing things, beings, and goals.

Questions for Thought

1. Do you think that Vasconcelos' criticisms of traditional Western views on the nature of knowledge apply to the views of Descartes and Berkeley? Defend your answer.
2. What, if anything, have you learned from your emotions?
3. Do you agree with Vasconcelos' conception of art and the artist? Why or why not?
4. How important is art in your life? Do you consider yourself to be a creative individual?
5. Now that you have read the works of several philosophers, how would you describe the proper nature of philosophy? How do your views on the proper nature of philosophy compare with or differ from the views of Vasconcelos?

Truth and Existence 7

KARL JASPERS

Karl Jaspers (1883–1969), an important existentialist philosopher, was born in Oldenburg, Germany. Jaspers' father was a lawyer who served as high constable of his district and later as the director of a bank. Following in his father's footsteps, Jaspers began the study of law at the University of Heidelberg in 1901. The following year, he transferred to the University of Munich, where he continued to study law. However, not finding law to his liking, Jaspers moved to the University of Berlin, where he began the study of medicine. After continuing his medical studies at the University of Göttingen, Jaspers ended his round of German universities by returning to the University of Heidelberg. He completed his medical studies at Heidelberg and was registered as an M.D. in 1909. In 1910, he married Gertrud Meyer, the sister of Ernst Meyer, a good friend who became his philosophical collaborator during the 1920s.

Jaspers' first medical position was that of volunteer research assistant in the psychiatric clinic at the University of Heidelberg. This, along with his publication of an influential critique of clinical methodology, led to his appointment to a professorship in psychology at Heidelberg in 1916. After the publication of another work that fused psychological and philosophical concerns, Jaspers was offered a professorship in philosophy, also at Heidelberg, in 1921. Then, devoting his attention almost exclusively to philosophy, Jaspers completed his first important philosophical writings, *Die geistige Situation der Zeit* (*Man in the Modern Age*) and the three-volume *Philosophie* (*Philosophy*) in the early 1930s.

However, because his wife was Jewish and because he refused to collaborate in any way with the Nazi regime, Jaspers was carefully watched and eventually relieved of his teaching duties in 1937. The next several years were anxiety filled, as Jaspers and his wife were forced into hiding. Having made a suicide pact in the event of capture, they managed to elude the Nazis until Heidelberg was liberated by Allied forces in 1945. After World War II, Jaspers returned to teaching and writing. He focused on the collective guilt of the German people in works such as *Die Schuldfrage* (1946; translated as *The Question of German Guilt*) and on formulating a world philosophy in works such as *Der philosophische Glaube* (1949; translated as *The Perennial Scope of Philosophy*). Fusing politics and his global orientation, Jaspers called for the formation of a world government in his book *Die Atombombe und die Zukunft des Menschen* (1958; translated as *The Future of Mankind*). This latter work earned him the German Peace Prize in 1958. Jaspers died of a stroke on February 26, 1969, in Basel, Switzerland, where he had lived and taught since 1948.

In the following essay, Jaspers describes four different levels or modes of being human and suggests that a different meaning of truth is associated with each level. Moreover, he claims that each type of truth is marked by a distinctive form of communication and by a distinctive limitation that prevents it from being fully satisfying.

At one level of being human, a level that Jaspers refers to as "consciousness-in-general," truth is defined as cogent correctness. Its governing concepts are validity, universality, and objectivity. In short, it is the arena of logical or rational thinking, the arena that was the home of Descartes and many other Western philosophers.

The second level of being human that Jaspers describes, the level of existence, is almost the mirror image of the first. At this level, truth is particular rather than universal, subjective rather than objective. The goal of thinking is not validity but the enhancement of one's life, the fulfillment of one's needs. Truth is thus defined as that which works. As Jaspers clearly indicates, this is the level marked by the pragmatic conception of truth, the conception defended by James in an earlier selection in this chapter.

The third level of being human is the level of spirit, the level where we think in terms of the systematic relation of ideas. At this level, truth is not defined either as universal validity or as that which works; it is defined as coherence, as that which produces wholeness. (Jaspers is alluding here to the coherence theory of truth, the theory that a claim is true if it coheres with a system of other statements and false if it does not.)

The final level of being human is the level of *Existenz,* the level of the authentic self. Jaspers believes that this level of being human and the type of truth associated with it allow us to clearly appreciate the nature and limitations of the other levels and types. In becoming aware of our authentic selves, we realize that we are not merely consciousness-in-general, existence, or spirit and thus that the types of truth associated with these levels of being human are incomplete. However, we also discover that the possibility of knowing the complete truth lies beyond our horizons, since the truth of *Existenz* cannot be known. As Jaspers says, "My authentic self can never become my possession; it remains my potentiality. . . . *Existenz* experiences truth in faith." Although the truth of *Existenz* is crucial for being human, it cannot be adequately expressed and has thus been overlooked by most philosophers. To fully appreciate this type of truth, Jaspers claims that philosophers must realize that philosophy cannot ultimately provide knowledge—it can only point in the direction of authentic selfhood. To emphasize this point, Jaspers uses the term *philosophizing*, a term that indicates that doing philosophy is an activity, a becoming, not a state of being or body of knowledge.

Questions for Reading

1. What are the four levels of being human described by Jaspers?
2. What is the meaning of truth attached to each level of being human? Why, according to Jaspers, can we not know the truth of *Existenz*?
3. How does communication differ at each level of being human?
4. How does Jaspers use the term *the encompassing*?
5. What, according to Jaspers, is the function of philosophy (or, to use his term, "philosophizing")?

TRUTH—THE WORD HAS AN INCOMPARABLE magic. It seems to promise what really matters to us. The violation of truth poisons everything gained by the violation.

Truth can cause pain, and can drive one to despair. But it is capable—merely in virtue of being truth, regardless of content—of giving deep satisfaction: there is truth after all.

Truth gives courage: if I have grasped it at any point, the urge grows to pursue it relentlessly.

Truth gives support: here *is* something indestructible, something linked to being.

But what this truth might be that so powerfully attracts us—not particular determinate truths but truth itself—that is the question.

There is truth, we think, as if that were self-evident. We hear and speak truths about things, events, and realities that are unquestionable to us. We even are confident that truth will ultimately triumph in the world.

But here we stop short: Little can be seen of a reliable presence of truth. For example, common opinions are for the most part expressions of the need for some support: one would much rather hold to something firm in order to spare himself further thought than face the danger and trouble of incessantly thinking further. Moreover, most of what people say is imprecise, and in its apparent clarity is primarily the expression of hidden practical interests. In public affairs, there is so little reliance on truth among men that one cannot do without an attorney in order to make a truth prevail. The claim to truth is turned into a weapon even of falsehood. Whether truth will prevail seems to depend on favorable chance events, not on truth as such. And in the end, everything succumbs to the unexpected.

All such examples of the lack of truth in psychological and sociological situations need not affect truth itself if truth is self-subsistent and separable from its realization. Yet even the existence of truth in itself can become doubtful. The experience of being unable to agree about truth—despite a relentless will to clarity and open readiness—especially where the content of this truth is so essential to us that everything seems to depend on it because it is the basis of our faith—can cause us to doubt truth in the familiar sense of something extant. It could be that the truth that matters is by its very nature not amenable to univocal and unanimous statement. The unquestioned truth that governs my life appears false to others. In our Western world we hear conflicting claims coming from essentially different sources, and the deafening noise that echoes through the centuries as they explode into mass-occurrences.

From Karl Jaspers, Philosophy of Existence, *translated by Richard F. Grabau, University of Pennsylvania Press, 1971.*
Reprinted by permission of University of Pennsylvania Press.

In the face of this situation, one is inclined to accept the proposition that there is no truth. One does not allow truth to be self-sustaining; one derives it from something else as the condition on which alone truth is truth.

In consequence, thought has vacillated throughout its history: first the claim to absolute truth, then doubt about all truth, and along with both the sophistically arbitrary use of pseudo-truth.

The question of truth is one of the dizzying questions of philosophizing. As we think through this question, the magic gleam of truth is obscured.

Confronted by this confusion, we quickly imagine ourselves to have a secure foundation: we conceive unequivocal truth to lie in the *validity of statements* made on the ground of visual experience and logical evidence. Despite all the skeptical subtleties, we nevertheless find the objects of the methodologically purified sciences. Through our understanding we discover cogent intelligibility and, corresponding to it, the in fact universal assent to its results on the part of every rational being who understands them. There is a realm of established correctness for consciousness-in-general, a narrow but vaguely limited realm of valid truth.

Our highly developed insight into the logical connections between the meanings of statements—a field of scientific investigation all the more intensive in proportion as it is more and more subjected to mathematical techniques (in logistics)—yet always finds that logical stringency stops when we come to the facts themselves. The truth lies in the *presuppositions* of this logical analysis; truth becomes real only on the strength of their *content*.

This content is either empirical—evident as something perceivable, measurable, and so on—in which case it is logically something that we can only accept, or it lacks this compelling power to impress itself upon everybody, having instead grown from roots which are different in essence and are the sources of those absolute contents that uphold man's life—though not every life in the same way—and that are then also communicated in statements.

Although "consciousness in general," this realm of the sciences, is also the realm where matters become clear for us because they can be stated, yet its compelling correctness is by no means ever in itself alone the absolute truth. Rather, truth emerges from *all* modes of the **encompassing.**

Truth that is vitally important to us begins precisely where the cogency of "consciousness in general" ends. We encounter a limit where our existence and another's existence, though both are aiming at truth as something that is one and universally valid, yet do not acknowledge that truth as one and the same. At this limit we either come into conflict, where force and cunning decide matters, or else sources of faith are communicated which approach each other without ever being capable of becoming one and identical.

At these boundaries another truth speaks. A peculiar meaning of truth emerges from every mode of the encompassing that we are, not only from consciousness-in-general, which is the locus of cogent insight, but from existence, spirit, and *Existenz* as well.

We shall present this multiplicity of truth: of existence, of spirit, of *Existenz.*

As knowledge and volition at the level of *existence,* truth has neither universal validity nor compelling certainty.

Existence is always particular, and wills *to preserve* and extend *itself;* Truth is what furthers existence (life), what works; falsity is what harms, limits, paralyzes it.

Existence wills *its own happiness: Truth* is the satisfaction of existence resulting from its creative interaction with its environment.

Existence, as consciousness or soul, manifests and expresses itself. *Truth* is the adequacy with which the inwardness of existence is manifested, and the adequacy of the expression and of consciousness to the unconscious.

In sum: existence grasps truth as suitable conduct, suitable first for the preservation and enhancement of existence, second for lasting satisfaction, and third for the adequacy of expression and of consciousness to the unconscious.

This is the pragmatic concept of truth. Everything that is, is in that it can be perceived and used, is raw material, is means and ends without a final end. Truth does not lie in something permanent and already known, or in something knowable, or in something unconditioned; it lies in whatever arises here and now in the immediate situation, and in what results.

Just as existence itself changes in accordance with differences in its make-up and in the course of changing time, so there is only changing, relative truth.

As spirit, truth is again not universally valid for the evidence of the understanding.

Truth of the spirit exists by virtue of membership in a self-elucidating and self-contained whole. This whole does not become objectively knowable; it can be grasped only in the action of the membership which endows it with existence and knowability.

In its understanding of being, spirit follows the ideas of wholeness which stand imaged before it, serving as impulses to move it, and as methodical system bringing coherence to its thought. *Truth* is what produces wholeness.

Although we, being consciousness-in-general, think in terms of cogent correctness; being existence, in terms of the advantageous and threatening; and being spirit, in terms of what produces wholeness—none of this occurs in us with the certainty of a natural event. Rather, most of the time we end up in a bewildering hodgepodge. Actually, we grasp each given meaning of truth resolutely, and with an awareness of the limits of every meaning of truth, only *to the extent that we are truly ourselves.* In other words: truth that comes from any other source derives purity only from the truth of *Existenz.*

Existenz appears to itself as consciousness-in-general, existence and spirit; and it can contrast itself with their modes. But it can never take a position outside itself, cannot know itself and at the same time be identical with what it knows.

What I myself am, therefore, always remains a question, and yet is the certainty that supports and fulfills everything else. My authentic self can never become my possession; it remains my potentiality. If I knew it, I would no longer be it, since I become inwardly aware of myself in temporal existence only as a task. The truth of *Existenz* can therefore rest simply and unconditionally on itself, without wanting to know itself. In the most powerful *Existenzen* one feels this parsimony and resignation—that attains no image, no visible representation of its own nature.

This short presentation points up the plurality of meanings of truth. We shall now *compare* these *meanings,* each of which, seen in this light, has its appropriate source in a particular mode of the encompassing.

1. Truth at the level of *existence* is a *function* of the preservation and extension of existence. It proves itself by its usefulness in practice.

Truth at the level of *consciousness-in-general* has validity as *compelling correctness.* It is by virtue of itself, and does not depend on anything else to which it would be a means. It proves itself by evidence.

Truth at the level of *spirit* is *conviction.* It *proves* itself in actuality through existence and thought, to the extent to which it submits to the wholeness of ideas, thereby confirming their truth.

Existenz experiences truth in *faith.* Where I am no longer sheltered by a certifying effectiveness of pragmatic truth, by a demonstrable certainty of the understanding, or by a protective totality of spirit, there I have come upon a truth in which I break out of all worldly immanence. Only from this experience of transcendence do I return to the world, now living both in it and beyond it, and only now for the first time myself. The truth of Existenz *proves* itself as authentic consciousness of reality.

2. Each mode of truth is characterized by him *who speaks in it* at any time. The mode of truth is given along with the encompassing within which we stand in communication.

In *existence* a purposefully and limitlessly self-interested life speaks. It subjects everything to the condition that it must enhance its own existence. It feels sympathy and antipathy in this sense only, and enters into community only on the basis of this interest.

Communication at this level is either conflict or expression of an identity of interests. It is not unlimited communication, but breaks off to suit its own purposes and uses cunning against the enemy, and against the possible enemy in the friends. It is constantly concerned with the practical effects of what is said. It wants to persuade and suggest, to strengthen or weaken.

In *consciousness-in-general* an interchangeable point of mere thought speaks. It is thought-in-general, not that of a particular individual or the selfhood of Existenz.

Its communication proceeds by rational argument. It aims at the universal, and seeks formal validity and compelling correctness.

At the level of *spirit,* communication occurs in the atmosphere of a concrete and self-rounding totality to which both speaker and listener belong.

In the selection, emphasis, and relevance of what is said, its communication is guided by the idea—in constant connection with the meaning of the totality.

In *Existenz,* the man who is himself present speaks. He speaks to another Existenz as one irreplaceable individual to another.

Their communication takes place in a loving struggle—not for power but for openness—in which all weapons are surrendered but all modes of the encompassing appear.

3. In each mode of the encompassing that we are, *truth is opposed to untruth,* and in each a *specific dissatisfaction* finally arises, that presses on to another, deeper truth:

In *existence,* there is the exultation of self-fulfilling life and the pain of being lost. Arising *in opposition to both,* however, is the dissatisfaction with mere existence, the boredom of repetition, and the dread in the boundary-situation of utter failure: all existence contains the seeds of its destruction. Happiness at the level of existence cannot be concretely imagined or even thought as a noncontradictory possibility. There is no happiness in duration and permanence, no happiness which, when it becomes clear to itself, continues to satisfy.

In *consciousness-in-general,* there is the compelling power of cogent correctness, the unwillingness to tolerate, and thus the repudiation of incorrectness. *Opposed to both* is the tedium of correctness, because it is endless and in itself unessential.

In *spirit,* there is the deep satisfaction in the whole and the torment of continual incompleteness. Arising *in opposition to both* is dissatisfaction with harmony and the perplexity that results when totalities are broken.

In *Existenz* there is faith and despair. *Opposed to both* stands the desire for the peace of eternity, where despair is impossible and faith becomes the vision, that is to say, the perfect presence of perfect reality.

Thus far in our discussion of the various modes of the meaning of truth, the different modes simply stand side by side, and nowhere do we find truth itself.

But the modes of the meaning of truth are in no sense an unrelated aggregate. They are in *conflict:* in possible reciprocal assaults upon each other.

Each truth falls into untruth when it violates the integrity of its own meaning and comes to be dependent upon and distorted by another truth.

One example must suffice: the question of the extent to which the truth of consciousness-in-general—the compelling certainty in knowledge of all that can be experienced—is useful, that is, true, for existence. If knowledge of this universally valid truth always also had beneficial consequences in existence, there would be no division, and thus no possible conflict, between the truth of existence and the truth of universally valid knowledge. But in fact, *existence constantly subverts universally valid truth* by concealing, displacing, and suppressing it. It is by no means clear whether doing this in the long run serves the interests of existence or brings about its ultimate destruction. In any case, complete acceptance and communication of the truth of universally valid knowledge is at first almost always also a threat to one's own existence. The truth of cogent correctness becomes untruth in existence. To a self-isolating will-to-existence, truth can appear as a doom to be rejected. Conversely, practical interests become a source of falsehood, in that in the medium of consciousness-in-general they deceive me into thinking that things are the way I would like them to be.

From these conflicts we acquire a feeling for the uniqueness of each individual meaning of truth— and in each conflict we apprehend a particular source of possible falsehood. If we now try to go beyond these conflicts and seek for *truth itself,* we never find it by giving *precedence to one mode* of the encompassing as authentic truth. We alternately succumb to prejudices that absolutize *one* encompassing. Thus we absolutize existence as if furthering life were the last word and could be taken as absolutely unconditioned; or we absolutize *consciousness-in-general,* the understanding, as if we could possess being itself in correct knowledge and not merely reach a perspective—a beam of light in the darkness—within the encompassing reality; or we absolutize *spirit,* as if an idea were real and self-sufficient; or we absolutize *Existenz,* as if selfhood could exist in isolation, whereas to the extent that it is itself, it comes from an other, and sees itself in relation to the other. Truth can no longer remain truth in the isolation of a single one of its meanings.

The fact that all modes of the meaning of truth *come together* in actual human life, and that man thus exists within all the sources of all the modes, urges us on to the *one* truth in which no mode of the encompassing is lost. And only clarity about the multiplicity of meanings of truth brings the question of the one truth to that point where breadth of view becomes possible, and an easy answer—in the presence of an intense urgency of the One—becomes impossible.

If the one truth were present to us, it would have to permeate all modes of the encompassing and join them all together in a present unity.

It is a *fundamental condition* of our reality that for us this unity is not attained by means of a conceivable harmony of the whole, in which every mode of the encompassing would have its sufficient as well as limited place. Instead, we remain in motion, we see every fixed harmonious form of truth once again destroyed, and we must therefore always be *seeking* further for this unity. Our knowledge would sometimes mislead us *into secluding ourselves within the consciousness* of what we at any given time systematically hold to be real and true. But in the course of time new experiences and facts befall us. Our knowing consciousness, too, must change in unforeseeable ways. For—as Hegel said—truth is in league with reality against consciousness.

The *one* truth would be accessible only in conjunction with its content—not as one kind of formal truth—and consequently in a form that binds all the modes of the encompassing together.

We cannot, therefore, directly grasp the one truth in a known whole. Grasped directly, truth is expressed formally, perhaps as the manifestness of the other that comes to meet us, then further as the being that is what it can be only through its manifestation; that is, as a manifestation that is simultaneously the realization of that being: selfhood.

But this formally expressed truth becomes *the* truth for us only along with the *content* of the realization of being. And because of the nature of our temporal existence this content becomes accessible to us as one and whole only in *historical* form. . . .

If in philosophizing I desire a known content to which I can cling, if I want knowledge *instead* of faith, technical recipes for everything *instead* of an Existenz based on the whole of all the modes of the encompassing, if I want psychotherapeutic instructions *instead* of the freedom of selfhood—then philosophy leaves me in the lurch. It speaks only where knowledge and technique fail. It points, but does not give. It moves with illuminating beams of light, but produces nothing.

Just as in our description of the encompassing we ended with no more than the *broad realms* where we encounter possible being, so in the description of truth we attain nothing but *avenues* to such possibilities.

But the intent of our philosophical impulse goes much further. We do not want possibilities; we want reality.

Philosophy, of course, neither produces reality nor gives it to anyone suffering from a lack of it. But the philosopher relentlessly presses on in thought with his whole being to catch sight of reality, and to realize himself.

Questions for Thought

1. Do you believe that Jaspers' description of being human is accurate? Can you think of other modes of being human that Jaspers overlooks?
2. Can you identify times in your life when you have communicated on each of the levels that are described by Jaspers?
3. What are Jaspers' principal criticisms of James' conception of truth? Do you think these criticisms are warranted? Why or why not?
4. How does Jaspers' conception of philosophy differ from the conception of Descartes? How does it differ from the conception of Vasconcelos?
5. Have you experienced what Jaspers calls authentic selfhood? If so, how would you describe this experience?

8   Navajo Ways of Knowing

HERBERT JOHN BENALLY

Herbert John Benally (b. 1944) lives in Sweetwater, Arizona, on the Navajo Reservation. While many members of his family have sought to preserve native traditions by following the path of the medicine man, he has attempted to achieve the same goal through teaching and curriculum reform. Currently, he teaches courses in Navajo history, culture, and philosophy at Diné College (formerly Navajo Community College) in Shiprock, New Mexico. In addition, his writings on Navajo ways of learning have been used as the basis for curriculum reform at Diné College and in several of the K–12 schools on the reservation. They have also provided the philosophical foundation for a program to combat substance abuse among students in grades K–12. Benally has presented his views on educational reform in workshops at several national and international conferences, and his essays on Navajo philosophy and culture have appeared in many publications, including *Photographing Navajos: John Collier Jr. on the Reservation 1948–1953* (2002).

The following selection, which was published in *Tribal College*, was originally titled "Spiritual Knowledge for a Secular Society." In this essay, Benally discusses the intimate connection between spirituality and knowledge in Navajo thinking. He describes four types of sacred knowledge—"that which gives direction to life," "sustenance," "the gathering of family," and "rest, contentment and respect for creation"—and explains why each of these types of sacred knowledge was traditionally associated with a part of the day and with one of the four cardinal directions. Benally argues that to achieve a harmonious life, we must focus on each of these four areas of knowledge and maintain a balance among them. In doing so, we will not only achieve harmony within the family and the human community but we will also find harmony between the human and the natural world. On the other hand, failure to recognize the importance of each type of knowledge or to maintain a balance between them will produce dire consequences. As Benally says, "When we are not taught in this way, drawing on all four areas of knowledge, we become spiritually, emotionally, socially, physically, and environmentally impoverished."

Questions for Reading

1. What are the four types of knowledge found in traditional Navajo thinking? Why is each of them associated with a specific part of the day?
2. What is the purpose of prayer in Navajo life?
3. How does Benally view the relationship of competition and community? Under what conditions is competition allowed in Navajo society?
4. What are the basic features of the traditional Navajo family system?
5. How is the natural world viewed in Navajo thinking? How do Navajos attain their knowledge of the natural world?

TRADITIONAL NAVAJO WISDOM RECOGNIZES spirituality as the foundation of all knowledge necessary for achieving harmony, or *hózhǫ́,* the Beauty Way of Life. This foundation is as relevant today as it ever was, and could serve as the basis of an approach to teaching which avoids the separation of secular and spiritual knowledge that characterizes Western society. The connection between that separation and the problems of contemporary life is apparent, and calls for a close re-examination of this traditional wisdom. The Navajo organized their knowledge, as well as their life activities, around the parts of the day and the four cardinal directions. This system of organization was placed by the Holy People in the primordial era. At that time the gods laid the foundation of this world with grandfathers and grandmothers fire, water, air, and soil. Around that foundation they placed the four different lights and four forms of sacred knowledge which would regulate man and all life's activities. With the dawn they placed "that which gives direction to life" (*bik'ehgo da'iináanii*) and with the blue twilight they placed "sustenance" (*nihigáál*). "The gathering of family" (*aha'ná'oo'níil*) was placed with the yellow evening twilight and "rest, contentment and respect for creation" (*háá'áyį́į́h, sihasin dóó hodílzin*) was placed with the darkness. "All of these things placed will direct all lives from here on," it was said.

I. BIK'EHGO DA'IINÁANII

The first area of knowledge, "that which gives direction to life," emphasizes character development, particularly excellence of heart and mind. This encompasses all knowledge which enables the individual to make intelligent decisions whenever a choice involving values is to be made. Just as dawn brings light, this area of knowledge brings clarity and perspective to the mind, permeating all aspects of one's life. This area of learning includes beliefs, self-discipline, and values that provide standards of behavior and give meaning to life.

The Navajo believe that the gods pass over the country at dawn. If an individual is up and about he will be blessed by them with health and prosperity. Corn pollen is usually offered to these gods and a petition extended to them at this time. It was believed that the things which they petitioned for became part of one's thoughts, planning, teaching and life. In time the petitioner becomes one with his prayer. It was important to pray. It helped one to organize the priorities in his life and to clarify his thinking. His spirituality was recognized as the source of both his strength and his enlightenment.

It was also believed that one should get up at dawn and run. To the elders this was not just a physical exercise but an activity that brought about physical, mental and spiritual well-being. By running at dawn one disciplines and strengthens his mind in order to be in control in all situations. With a well-developed constitution he can overcome any adversity that may arise.

Another way of establishing a strong foundation is by listening to the wisdom of the elders and keeping their words close to one's heart. "If things are to be it's up to you," "remember the young and the old and those yet to be born," and "stability comes from a clear purpose for being" are some of the teachings that have survived. This wisdom has been passed from generation to generation and finds roots in one's being, becoming the source of strength throughout one's life.

The dawn provides the blueprint for building a good life. It is the source of fortitude, sound teaching, standards of conduct and appreciation for life. Without the guiding principles provided by the dawn there would be no standards by which people could evaluate the effectiveness of their thoughts and actions. They would be unable to fully experience life or to develop a genuine appreciation for themselves, others and nature. They would run the risk of falling into great disharmony, hunger, illness, poverty and other social ills which are so prevalent today.

II. NIHIGÁÁL

The second area of knowledge, associated with the blue twilight, is sustenance. This area focuses on

This article appeared in Tribal College *(Volume III:4, Spring 1992) under the title "Spiritual Knowledge for a Secular Society." Reprinted by permission of* Tribal College: Journal of American Indian Higher Education.

obtaining self-reliance, providing for the family and being a contributing member of the community. To achieve these goals one must recognize work in all its dimensions including the ethical, vocational, social and environmental. All of these areas are connected and interdependent. For instance, traditional Navajo wisdom views objects of material wealth as having spirit and personality. There is a Navajo saying, *"Yódí dóó nitl'iz soosą́ądoo,"* "May the spirit of all good things show favor upon me." Attracting these good spirits requires a certain attitude and personality. They come to the person who exercises prudence, order, industry, patience and kindness, and most importantly, to one who is prayerful. These qualities are all founded on the principle of receiving and giving. Sharing promotes happiness, while excessiveness inclines one toward evil. Conversely, when one sleeps late he attracts the being of poverty and his cousins—hunger, shame, apathy, disorder and ignorance. The good spirits will avoid a house that is disorganized, where vulgar and abusive language is used and where there is idleness.

Another aspect of sustenance involves learning how to work and becoming responsible. Children learn specific skills "on the job" well before they are able to understand the nature of the work or the responsibility involved. It was said that the livestock teach the child dependability, resourcefulness and responsibility. For example, when a sheep is lost the child is sent back to find it. The job was not considered complete until every sheep was accounted for. This might sometimes be a hard lesson but was absolutely necessary for adult life. Elders would advise parents to "Teach the children while they are yet tender and when their minds can still be bent and shaped like a young willow" and remind them that "It is harder when their minds have formed. Instill in them appropriate habits and they will discover reasons for their behavior when they come of age."

Cooperation was the basis of Navajo communal existence. On the other hand, competition was never foreign to the Navajo—in fact, it was the basis of their traditional games. However, making competition a part of one's life was frowned upon because it led to pride, which was considered an evil. Everyone was expected to come to the aid of their neighbors in time of need. "My people are my insurance" was how one woman put it when describing the events surrounding the loss of a loved one. Her people had come from miles around to console her and to help her with the substantial expenses with which she was faced. Helping in Navajo society was an opportunity to show the person being helped respect and regard.

The elders watch the stars, particularly Pleiades, the . . . "seeds of all kinds." They were instructed to watch this constellation in order to know when to start planting. The community performs a blessing on the seeds when . . . the "seeds of all kinds" set in the west. During the seed blessing ceremony, offerings are made at sacred places to the gods for moisture and for a good harvest. The seeds which had been blessed are then planted. Everyone worked together as a single unit to plant and harvest. When the harvest and winter storage were completed a special ceremony of thanksgiving was made to the gods.

Work, which is central to the blue twilight, is a life-sustaining principle. It is essential for obtaining and preserving one's dignity. Dignity and respectability are not possible unless a person is able to provide for his family and help those that need assistance. The worker understands that material possessions are based upon the principles of giving and receiving, and of industry and integrity. He is a skilled provider who understands the forces of nature and is able to use them to his benefit. He understands that cooperation within the community is the key to assuring the general welfare of the community. In order to maintain prosperity he continues to offer prayers for blessings and thanksgiving to the creators, who are the source of sustenance. A person who is ignorant or neglectful of these principles invites poverty, apathy, health problems and discord in the family and community.

III. AHA'ÁNAÁ'OO'NÍÍL

The third category of knowledge is associated with the yellow evening twilight. It focuses on *k'é,* a term which encompasses emotional ties and relationships associated with the family, extended family, community, nation as a whole, and the natural environment. The term *k'é* in Navajo conveys love, cherishing, caring, esteem, as well as the simple acknowledgment of the inherent value of others.

This learning begins at home. One of the teachings within our tribe centers on the relationship between husband and wife. A primary source for this teaching comes from the relationship between Father Sky and Mother Earth. When the plants, animals, seasons and constellations were completed and ready to be put into motion, Mother Earth is said to have asked, "Who will be responsible for all of these creations and their movements?" The Holy People replied that this responsibility will be placed in the hands of Sky Father. He will awake and put all things in motion. In the spring he will awaken you with thunder from your rest and with his help you will make all things grow and mature. In the fall he will once again sound the thunder, his scepter of leadership, at which time your work will be completed and you will rest. Father Sky then covers Mother Earth with a white blanket for the winter months. His primary work begins and woe to those who have been lazy and unprepared. Cold and hunger will find them and teach them the value of industry and preparation.

Mother Earth, the prototypical mother, is gentle and kind—no one who truly understands the nature of things must suffer from cold or hunger during the summer months. She nurtures and strengthens all living things and prepares them for the future. She follows the lead of her husband Father Sky. Father Sky exemplifies fatherhood, which includes unwavering leadership, tenderness toward Mother Earth, sternness in teaching, and gentleness to those of his children who are industrious and prepared.

Our elders taught that a man carries his shield on his left arm, protecting his family, his beliefs, his land and his freedom. The mother carries her cooking utensils in her right hand to represent her shield against hunger, illness and other adversities. Between the two parents a great deal of security is provided to the children from which they can achieve maturity. It is the weak, undisciplined and immature parent who does not understand what is required in the role of a parent who leaves the children in darkness, hunger, cold, to be ravaged by all manner of afflictions.

Appreciation for all that is included in the concept of *k'é* originates within the home where kinship terms, rather than names, are generally used to address family members. It is very difficult to translate the expression of endearment that these terms convey into another tongue. Kinship relationship terms communicate and reinforce an acceptance and a sense of belonging and caring to the person to whom they are directed. For example, the word that the mother uses with her children is *shee'awee shiyazhi,* my dear little one. Notice in these kinship expressions the word "my": my child, my sister, my mother, my grandfather, etc. The kinship terms are not just empty expressions, but living words that lie at the foundation of self-esteem. When terms of endearment are absent a gray area of doubt emerges in the mind of the young person regarding acceptance and belonging. The loneliness, alienation and rejection felt by the young person may become contributing factors in the young person trying to seek acceptance in negative ways.

The use of appropriate kinship terms between siblings and other family members defines their respective roles and encourages positive family ties. I have personally observed that children in a family that uses kinship terms to address each other tend to get along much better than children in families where personal names are used. The Navajo family system employs a hierarchical structure in which people are recognized according to their age. With maturity comes the responsibility to care, to teach and to set an example for those that are younger. The younger were obligated to respect and obey those that were older. It reflected very poorly on both the older and younger sibling when they argued. This system of relating remained with the individual throughout his life. One is not necessarily respected simply on the basis of how much he may have or what he can do. Respect is primarily based on age. When we use personal names we become equals, and being at the same level seems to encourage competition and bickering. The two systems can be compared by observing that one encourages respect and cooperation and the other conflict and competition.

A child's identity is based on his immediate family and clan membership. He represents his family wherever he goes, and in whatever he does. A person is never alone; he carries with him his family's reputation and their expectations. Any behavior contrary to that expected behavior reflects negatively both on that individual and his family. An individual can never divorce himself from his family. As long as parents and grandparents are living, it is expected that their positions in the family hierarchy will be honored.

Another major element involved in establishing relations among Navajos is the clan system. One is born *into* the mother's clan and is born *for* the father's clan. The maternal and paternal grandfathers usually are of different clans. One addresses a member of his clan as brother and sister. Members of the father's clan are addressed as paternal aunts and uncles and are thought of as the father's relatives. Individuals who are members of one's maternal or paternal grandfather's clans are thought of as that grandfather's relative and treated accordingly. The Navajo people function like one large extended family according to the clan system. The knowledge and use of the clan system in our tribe is therefore very important. It is the basis for holding each other in high regard and for dealing with each other as family. The interpersonal relationships learned in the home are thus lived out in the community. Family relationships are the foundation of all social interaction on the reservation.

Our elders are constantly reminding us to question the aims of schools and churches operating on the reservation. What is the point of having schools and churches if they do not teach compassion for the elders and for those who are less fortunate? We see on the reservation senior citizens alone during the winter without anyone to take care of them, to take them to the hospital or to the store to buy food. Frequently, their children had been educated or baptized and moved away, leaving their families behind. "Where is the compassion, concern, and kindness that we thought were being taught in the classroom and in the churches?" they often inquire. The old way was to care for the elders who occupied positions of honor in the community. We are losing respect for this great source of moral support as well as a vital link with our heritage. Learning must be sought which will increase our level of concern for the welfare of our children, youth and elders.

IV. HÁÁ'ÁYÍÍH, SIHASIN DÓÓ HODÍLZIN

The fourth area of knowledge is associated with darkness. The focus in this area is on reverence and respect for nature. The Navajo sees the world full of life and intelligence. He learns to interact with the intelligence around him with appropriate respect and dignity. There is a great natural order to the universe of which man is an integral part. Man is endowed with the ability to observe and imitate this order. For example, the Navajo have found that certain birds mate for life and have become symbols of fidelity in marriage. Proper interaction with this order requires knowledge of one's position and moving from there with reverence or, as a Navajo would put it, with *k'é*.

There is tremendous power in the natural order. We move with this power interdependently. We follow a course that is followed by all intelligence, or creation—a world of order and prosperity. As one recognizes his being as a part of a great circle manifested in the seasons, including birth and old age and the movement of the celestial bodies, he finds renewing power and strength. To the Navajo people all creation is endowed with great powers and the ability to bestow blessings in each of their respective seasons.

To understand this power we must return to the time of the placement of all things. The mountains, for example, were endowed with thinking, planning, prayer, teaching and material things. They were placed and dressed in that way for our benefit. As the clouds rest upon the mountains and the rains fall, the water begins to flow, taking with it the blessings of the mountains. When we utilize this water it unfolds the gifts of prayer, thinking, planning, teaching, and prosperity that it carries from the mountains. We may either use this blessing that was provided by the Holy People for our benefit, or destroy it through improper or disrespectful use.

All creation is connected and interdependent. If any part of the system is upset, the whole system is affected, creating an imbalance. The contemporary threats of pollution, toxicity and destruction of our ozone attest to this connection and interdependence. I believe we are only now finally beginning to understand this circle of connection.

Gratitude is at the very heart of respect and reverence for nature. Gratitude is directed to the water, the trees, plants and animals that nourish and shelter, and especially to the creators, that their blessings would never diminish. In this way the great law of receiving and giving is recognized.

In the Navajo world spiritual understanding is that which gives vitality and meaning to all life. The Western educational system requires us to separate the religious from the secular. Native Americans prefer to maintain their spiritually holistic perspective. When they are forced to put holism aside they find their lives and the values that give them meaning disintegrating or diminishing, and replaced with a fragmented and incoherent philosophy that leads into the mire of social disintegration.

FINDING A BALANCE

The essence of the Navajo philosophy is holism and the goal it sets for life is peace and harmony. By balancing the four cardinal areas of Navajo knowledge the individual will develop sound beliefs and values and be prepared to make responsible decisions. He will develop knowledge and skills so that he will be able to provide for his family, demonstrate good leadership within the family and community, and retain a sense of reverence for all things, both those on the earth and in the heavens. There is a great central focus where all forms of knowledge converge. In Navajo, this point of convergence is the synthesis of knowledge obtained from the cardinal points that find expression in appreciation, reverence, and love for harmony.

The Navajo organized their lives according to these four areas of knowledge. It seems that if we were all educated in this way we would find balance. This "balance" is similar to the way a nutritionist would speak about a balanced diet. If a person does not eat properly he will not have vitality and general good health. When we are not taught in this way, drawing on all four areas of knowledge, we become spiritually, emotionally, socially, physically and environmentally impoverished. We become narrow in our views and cannot see the connection between all knowledge. We wind up perpetuating the imbalance within and between ourselves, other people and the natural world.

This traditional wisdom is not only relevant today, but is even necessary to restore the balance which many of us have lost along with our most cherished traditions. Understanding and practicing the essence of the principles placed in each of the four directions will give us a strong foundation to make wise decisions for ourselves, our families and our communities. The internalization of these principles immunizes us from many of the adversities of life. When we recognize and become one with the divine power of the circle of creation we experience the Beauty Way of Life, or *hózhǫ*.

Questions for Thought

1. If you were to categorize the types of human knowledge, how many categories would you list, and what would these categories be?
2. What is the purpose of prayer, if any, in your own life? How does your own attitude toward prayer compare with or differ from that of Benally?
3. In what ways, if any, do your views on the relationship of competition and community differ from the views of Benally?
4. How does the Navajo tribal system compare with or differ from the characteristics of your own family system?
5. In what ways are Benally's views on the nature of knowledge and truth similar to those of Jaspers? In what ways are they different?

9   The Metaphysics of Oppression

JORGE VALADEZ

Jorge Valadez (b. 1951) was born in Nuevo Laredo, Mexico. His family immigrated to the United States when he was five, and they settled in Laredo, Texas, a town on the U.S.-Mexican border. During some of his high school years, Valadez was a migrant farmworker, traveling to Wisconsin, Nebraska, and Minnesota to work the fields with other members of his family.

The only person in his family to graduate from high school in the United States, Valadez earned his B.A. in philosophy from the University of Texas. He then attended Yale University, from which he obtained both his M.A. and his Ph.D. He currently teaches philosophy at Our Lady of the Lake University in San Antonio, Texas.

Valadez's special interests are in social and political philosophy and multiculturalism, and he has published several articles in these areas. He was also the author of the chapter on Latin American philosophy in the text *World Philosophy* (1995), and he recently published his first book, *Deliberative Democracy, Political Legitimacy, and Self-Determination in Multicultural Societies* (2000).

One of the distinguishing features of Valadez's thinking and writing is that he has been able to reexamine the function and nature of philosophical thinking, at least in part because of his working-class and minority background. As he says, "Issues of social justice, racism, and poverty have been prominent in my thinking. I believe that philosophy should concern itself with the most serious problems that confront society, and that it should be an enterprise that should not detach itself from concrete problems."

In the following essay, Valadez argues that questions of **epistemology,** or of how one perceives reality, are not purely theoretical questions. On the contrary, he claims that the way in which one perceives reality has profound economic and political implications.

To show that this is indeed the case, Valadez describes the poverty and oppression that exist in Guatemala and other Latin American countries and demonstrates how this poverty and oppression is supported by the foreign policy of the United States. He further shows how American foreign policy is grounded in what he calls "**metaphysical imperialism**"—that is, in the assumed right to impose one's views of reality on others. According to the tenets of metaphysical imperialism, the intellectual and philosophical traditions of Western Europe and the United States are superior to the traditions found in Third World countries, and this superiority gives the United States the right to intervene in the political and economic affairs of those countries. However, this intervention has had dire consequences for the lives of most of the people living there.

Because of this, Valadez argues that metaphysical imperialism is indefensible on both epistemological and moral grounds and that it must be supplanted by what he calls "the multicultural perspective." The multicultural perspective requires that all cultural bias or blindness be overcome and that all the interested parties in a discussion enter into an open, mutually liberated dialogue with one another. In doing so, the voices of all the participants can be heard, and the poverty and oppression that currently exists can be displaced.

While admitting that this may sound somewhat unrealistic, Valadez believes that with great effort, it can be realized. To make it a reality, however, all the participants in the dialogue must receive a level of education that is roughly equal to that of all other participants, and the tremendous economic and class differences that divide people must be bridged. Embracing the multicultural perspective may be a small step toward eliminating poverty and oppression, but it is an important and necessary step.

Questions for Reading

1. Who was Consuelo? Why does Valadez begin his essay by recounting her story?
2. How does Valadez describe life in Guatemala? What are some of the statistics that he cites in support of his description?
3. What does Valadez mean by "metaphysical imperialism"? How is metaphysical imperialism related to political oppression?
4. What, according to Valadez, is the foreign policy of the United States toward Latin American countries? How has this policy changed since the end of the Cold War?
5. How does the multicultural perspective differ from what Valadez calls **ontocentrism**? What are some of the steps that are necessary for the development of the multicultural perspective?

CONSUELO HAD BEEN LIVING AT A FRANTIC PACE for months. She was deeply involved in an organization of mothers who were demanding that the Guatemalan government account for their sons and daughters who had disappeared. Many of the mothers believed that their sons or daughters had probably already been killed by the government security forces, but they continued to hope that perhaps they might be alive and jailed with other political prisoners. The crimes of their loved ones consisted of their having protested and opposed the policies of the militarily controlled government. In Guatemala the degree of poverty and human suffering is staggering and many of the people from the poor and disenfranchised classes had finally decided that it was necessary to speak up against the government, even if it meant placing themselves in danger.

Consuelo knew all of this, and she also knew that the bloated bodies of some of the disappeared were sometimes found floating in a river or buried in shallow graves. But despite it all she felt that it was preferable for her to know what had happened to her twenty-year-old son. Even the knowledge that he was dead was better than the insufferable uncertainty that haunted her dreams. At least the body could then receive a proper burial.

Early on in her life Consuelo had learned about responsibility and about hardship, and the latter she had come to accept as an inevitable aspect of her existence. She was the eldest child, and by age twelve she had assumed the duties of an adult. She had married while still an adolescent. Later, in her tenth year of marriage her husband left to seek work in the United States. Whether he actually ever made it across the border she never knew, since she had not heard from him since. Through the years, she had convinced herself that it was best to think of him only as part of those joyful scenes that she stored in her memory like precious jewels.

From Jorge Valadez, "The Metaphysics of Oppression," in Thirteen Questions in Ethics and Social Philosophy, *edited by G. Lee Bowie, Kathleen M. Higgins, and Meredith Michaels, Harcourt, 1994. Reprinted by permission of the author.*

Nothing in her life, however, had prepared her for what occurred that warm Sunday evening when the four armed men broke into her house. The organization of mothers which she headed had been particularly vocal during the last few months and the government wanted to set an example. While two of the men held her, the others grabbed her six-year-old child. One of them took out a pointed pair of pliers and in a savagely methodical motion pulled out the fingernail from one of the horrified child's fingers. The image of her son's contorted face and the sound of his uncontrolled screams pierced and bored into her brain. The child kicked and twisted his whole body in a crazed effort to get free, but the butchers had had practice. One of them put his knee on the boy's chest and pinned him against the floor, while holding down the other small flailing arm. His partner then completed the gruesome task.

The event just described actually occurred, and incidents of this degree of brutality are not rare in Guatemala and other Central American countries. During the 1980s the United States provided tens of millions of dollars in military aid to the Guatemalan government. Even though Guatemala has an elected civilian president, the military wields a great deal of power. Death squads and special security forces play a crucial role in the maintenance of power by the military and wealthy elites. In Guatemala approximately 2 percent of the population own about 75 percent of the country's land and resources. It is a country where great inequalities of wealth exist between the privileged few and the mostly poor Indian population. About 73 percent of all children under the age of five are malnourished and, for every 1,000 births, 270 will die before reaching the age of five. The national illiteracy rate is 65 percent. Government violence has been responsible for more than 100,000 deaths in the last 30 years.[1]

The problems faced by the Guatemalan people are not unique; they are shared by people in other Third World countries. These problems could no doubt be analyzed from a variety of perspectives, including the sociological, political, anthropological, etcetera. A question that I want to consider here is whether there are certain insights that a distinctively philosophical perspective could give

us into the problem of oppression. Are there some elements of this problem that could be elucidated by taking the peculiarly general and abstract position of the philosopher? I believe the answer is yes. In what follows, I will try to show that some philosophical orientations dominant in our culture limit our understanding of Third World oppression and contribute to the acceptance of oppressive policies.

In my analyses I will distinguish between two forms of oppression, namely, the economic and the political. I will identify the philosophical orientations that underpin each of these forms of oppression, and will articulate the interconnections that exist between them. I begin by analyzing political forms of oppression.

METAPHYSICAL IMPERIALISM AND POLITICAL OPPRESSION

One of the important assumptions of our cultural worldview is that Americans have the right to interfere with and determine the internal politics of Latin American countries. The last century provides us with numerous examples of such interference, including the overthrow of established, elected governments (for example, Chile under Allende) and the invasion of countries like Nicaragua and Mexico. What is important to note here is that this assumption of the right of interference is an expression of our supposed right to impose our visions of reality on Latin America. It is our perception of the world that counts. It is Americans who should determine how other people are to live, how they are to organize their governments, and how they are to choose their values and priorities. This perspective is in effect a kind of **metaphysical imperialism** that involves the forced imposition of a dominant culture's vision of reality on another culture.

Most Americans are so convinced of the metaphysical imperialist perspective that it is almost impossible for us to question the basis of this perspective or to think of entering into a real and equal dialogue with the people of Latin America. Instead of engaging in an egalitarian effort to understand the world from their point of view, our attitude is that we have the right to impose our own visions of reality (through armed invasion if necessary). When dealing with underdeveloped countries, the notion that political truth is something that emerges as the result of a negotiated, open interchange of perspectives and ideas is foreign to most of us. And the belief that we have the right to impose our way of looking at the world on others is based on an even more deeply rooted philosophical view, namely, that those who are economically, technologically, and militarily superior, and are assumed to be intellectually and morally superior, have the right to control those who are deemed inferior in these same respects. The history of Latin America can be seen as an example of the concrete implementation of this philosophical principle, first at the hands of Western European countries and then at the hands of the United States.

It is difficult to overemphasize the importance and influence of this last philosophical principle for understanding the historical relationships between Latin America and Western Europe, and in contemporary times, between Latin America and the United States. America has, to a large extent, inherited its intellectual and philosophical traditions from Western Europe, including its attitudes toward underdeveloped or Third World nations. A common thread running through these attempts is not only the metaphysical imperialist appropriation of the "truth" but also the above mentioned principle that those who are in possession of this "truth" have the moral right, and in some cases (like that of Christianity), even the moral obligation to impose their vision of reality on others. This principle works by assigning an inferior status to those who fail to meet our criteria of intellectual and moral worth. And once they have been categorized as inferior, it is an easy step toward the attitude that it is the task of their "superiors" either to subjugate them or to transform their perspectives of reality to conform with the ideals of their "superiors."

Examples of the oppression of other cultures, and of the forced imposition of a view of reality on them, can be readily acknowledged: the conquest of Mexico, which involved not only a military conquest, but also the destruction of an indigenous metaphysical and religious worldview; the long and well-documented history of racial subjugation of blacks and Native Americans in the United States; the oppression of women and their categorization

as secondary and marginal beings, etc. We can elaborate briefly on one of these cases. The refusal to recognize that women have a status equal to that of men is a phenomenon that is deeply entrenched within our historical and cultural traditions. Aristotle, one of the most influential philosophers in Western intellectual history, thought that slaves completely lacked deliberative faculties, while women had such faculties but in an incomplete or imperfect sense. He believed that women's rational capacity was not equal to that of men, that is, that it lacked full legitimacy or authority.

It can be said without fear of exaggeration that understanding the phenomenon of oppression is crucial for an adequate understanding of Western history and civilization. Unfortunately, such an analysis is usually neglected especially at the metaphysical level. A philosophical approach to the phenomenon of oppression helps us to see its scope as well as its deep roots within our intellectual traditions.

Probably all cultures are, to some degree, **ethnocentric** and even predisposed to believe that others see the world as they do. But what makes the Western European culture distinctive is its excessive emphasis on control and its systematic attempts to prove the alleged inferiority of various oppressed groups. Even though in most of these attempts to prove inferiority there may have been no conscious intention to justify oppression, nevertheless the actual impact of several prominent Western theoretical traditions has been to reinforce attitudes which make oppressive behavior toward these groups appear reasonable and justifiable. The above mentioned Aristotelian view of women, the early views of some Spanish conquistadores that Indians did not possess souls, and the pseudo-scientific attempts throughout history to establish the "natural" inferiority of blacks are all examples of theories which have complemented and sometimes justified the control, subjugation, and/or indoctrination of these groups.

The set of philosophical assumptions we have discussed has been used to justify our foreign policies in Latin America. The position taken by the United States during the Cold War years was that we had to keep the armies of the presumably "democratically" elected governments of Latin America strong so that they could repel externally instigated Communist threats.

The idea was that the demands that the people of El Salvador or Guatemala, for example, made of their governments for better living conditions and respect of their human rights were the result of external Communist interference and not the result of the poverty and oppression that they suffered. Democracy is so far superior to a Communist system of government, so the argument went, that no price was too high to pay to keep Communism away from this hemisphere. Thus we supported elected leaders in Latin American countries even when they reached office through electoral fraud and even when they were controlled by military and wealthy elites. This foreign policy position was bolstered by the alleged threat posed by Communism to our own national security. Further, our continued support of these military regimes was justified by either denying or de-emphasizing the human rights abuses which these governments perpetrated.

In the current post–Cold War era, the emphasis has shifted from fighting Communist infiltration to supporting democratic reforms. The United States supports these democratic reforms, however, only when they are done on our own terms. Time and again the United States has interfered with the rights of Latin American countries for democratic self-determination by giving money to parties that support U.S. political and economic policies. A case in point involves the ten million dollars that the U.S. gave in 1988 to Guillermo Endara's campaign fund to assist his candidacy for president of Panama.[2] Endara was the "U.S. candidate" because he upheld U.S. economic and political interests in Panama. Endara was leading in the presidential elections and appeared to be the certain winner when Manuel Noriega forfeited the elections. This action by Noriega was later used by the United States as a rationale for invading Panama and installing Endara as the "legitimate" president of Panama. Endara was sworn in as president in a U.S. military base.

Imagine for a moment a scenario in which a foreign country gave a U.S. candidate for president one hundred million dollars for his or her campaign (the latter figure is the approximate equivalent of the ten million given to Endara). Suppose further that this candidate won the election. Without a doubt, such an "election" would be universally condemned in the United States as fraudulent and would be declared invalid. Yet we believe that it is acceptable for us to meddle in the internal democratic processes of Latin America and expect U.S.-influenced elections to be recognized as legitimate by the international community and the people of Latin America. More often than not, which elections are recognized as legitimate is determined by whether the successful party or candidate supports our financial and political interests in the region. Similarly, the United States tends to overlook human rights abuses (such as the widespread abuses in Guatemala and El Salvador) of regimes that are friendly to the United States. In the post–Cold War era, freedom and democracy have become code words for democratization that is conditioned on U.S. concerns.

THE INTERNATIONAL ECONOMIC SYSTEM AND ECONOMIC OPPRESSION

In order to understand economic oppression, we must see how the international economic system contributes to the economic oppression of Latin American and other Third World countries. Countries like Guatemala, Mexico, Brazil, Peru, and Argentina have collective foreign debts that total in the hundreds of billions of dollars. These foreign debts are primarily the result of an inequitable system of international trade. During the colonial period, Third World countries were forced to use their most fertile land to grow export crops for the colonial powers like England and Spain and to mine their minerals for export to these same countries. Thus, many Third World countries are now largely dependent on export crops and minerals for their income. But the industrialized countries have implemented a system of import duties that are higher for manufactured or processed goods and lower for raw materials and unprocessed goods. The manufactured/raw goods exchange created conditions of trade that put Third World countries at an economic disadvantage. In addition, the industrialized countries give large subsidies to their domestic agriculture and as a result poor farmers in Third World countries cannot compete with the large-scale subsidized agriculture of the Western countries.[3]

In order to buy the needed manufactured goods (such as tractors, factory machinery, etcetera) that they need to attain a higher level of technological and industrial development, Third World countries have had to borrow from the industrialized countries and from organizations like the International Monetary Fund. They had to pay interest on these loans, but the inequitable terms of international trade made it practically impossible for them to keep up the interest payments without borrowing more to do so. In the last fifteen years the foreign debt of Third World countries has been steadily rising. In 1990 it was well over four hundred billion for Latin American countries alone.[4]

The result of this degree of indebtedness is that much needed resources that could be used for health care, education, etcetera, are channeled into the payment of foreign debt. This in turn creates more misery and poverty for the majority of the population, who remain undernourished, illiterate, and with inadequate medical care. And it gets worse. The dire conditions under which the people are forced to live create an atmosphere of political instability which is exacerbated by the realization that the wealth in their countries is concentrated in a few hands. The wealthy classes and the high-ranking military and government officials who benefit from the unjust distribution of resources want to maintain the status quo. In order to suppress the demands of the populace for better wages, improved working conditions, etc., the governments of many of these countries use a significant portion of their economic resources to strengthen the military and to create specialized security forces trained in intelligence and internal security operations (intimidation techniques, torture, etcetera). Thus more of these countries' funds are used in areas that do not improve the living conditions of the people. The vicious cycle of poverty and oppression is reinforced—the demands of the poor for the alleviation of their misery lead to their political oppression, and the mechanisms that implement this oppression in turn increase their poverty.

What are the philosophical assumptions of our worldview that underpin the policies of economic oppression that are imposed on Latin American and other Third World countries? The answer to this question emerges from an analysis of the neoliberal economic policies that have been proposed as solutions to the economic dilemmas of these underdeveloped countries. The conventional proposals are another indication of the **ontocentrism**[5] that is so characteristic of our cultural worldview. The neoliberal solution involves greater foreign investment and ownership of businesses in Latin America, privatization of public services, the lifting of trade restrictions, greater reliance on export-based economic systems, and structural economic adjustments that involve reductions in government services to the people. No mention is made of encouraging economic self-sufficiency for Third World countries, of dismantling the military units that help perpetuate corruption and oppression, of a more equitable distribution of resources, of the need to provide better health care, or of the importance of respecting human rights.

In suggesting solutions to the problems of poverty and oppression, these proposals ignore the need of Latin Americans to live in a manner that respects their values and traditions; instead, these solutions call for their greater integration and dependence on the international economic system that has undermined their traditional ways of life. Adopting the industrial technocratic ways of life and the consumption patterns of Western countries will invariably entail a weakening of their cultural heritage and values. To be sure, there are some technological advances that all Third World countries would benefit from, especially regarding medical care and education, but Third World nations can enjoy these advances without having to transform their value system into one which prizes materialism, depersonalization, hierarchical rigidity, abuse of nature, and individualism over community relationships, rootedness in history and cultural tradition, economic decentralization and self-sufficiency, and an integrated approach to life. The assumption that people of a different culture can deal with the problems of poverty and economic development only by adopting our values and way of life again betrays the ontocentrism of our conceptual framework. . . .

MULTICULTURALISM—A CHANCE FOR RENEWAL

Just as the philosophical point of view has deepened our understanding of oppression, can it now offer us some insights that can serve as a starting point for resolving the problem of oppression in Latin America and the Third World? Even though philosophical reflection by itself will certainly not resolve this problem, philosophy can nevertheless help us to formulate a useful approach to deal with this issue. The approach I want to propose can be called the multicultural perspective. According to this perspective, an adequate understanding of reality is one which emerges as the result of an open, mutually liberated dialogue between the participants of the different cultural traditions making up a society. This multicultural context of dialogue and interaction would make possible the recognition and removal of the cultural blinders of each of the participants. Thus, one of the first goals of this dialogue would be for the participants to understand and appreciate the perspectives from which the others perceive reality. The articulation and negotiation of their different needs and interests would be based on this prior understanding. None of the perspectives would have an initial or *a priori* privileged status, nor would there be an initial hierarchical differentiation between perspectives or between the elements of the perspectives.

It is important to note that there would be certain normative principles implicit in the adoption of this multicultural perspective. The liberated dialogue would in essence be free from ideological distortions; its participants would have an equal access to information (and would have developed the critical thinking skills necessary for evaluating that information); and there would be a lack of hierarchical controls in the exchange of information. The practical and political implications of these principles are profound and wide-ranging. Consider the second of the conditions just mentioned. If the participants in the dialogue are to have equal access to, as well as a critical understanding of, any information that may be relevant for the negotiation of a case at hand, then this implies at least an approximate parity in the educational preparation of the

participants, as well as the elimination of economic restrictions that would impose arbitrary limitations on the use of available information. Furthermore, a critical understanding of this information presupposes an awareness of sexist, racist, classist, and other ideological factors that may distort its meaning and interpretation. It is important to note that putting these normative principles into practice will take work and effort, and that we should not be discouraged by the realization that these principles will not be implemented simply by adopting the multicultural perspective. Attaining educational parity, for example, or developing modes of communication that are free of ideological distortions and biases, will take strong political efforts to achieve.

The satisfaction of these conditions for liberated dialogue implies the elimination of substantial differences in the economic and educational status of the participants. In the multicultural perspective the connection between the socioeconomic position of the participants of a political community and their capacity to participate meaningfully in the decision-making processes of that community are emphasized. This perspective thus avoids the naïve viewpoint of classical liberal political theory that severs the connection between political power and economic power and the capacity to equally exercise one's civil rights in real political settings.

Finally, I want to clarify the multicultural perspective by indicating what it is not. It is not a relativistic or perspectival approach according to which all cultural perspectives are "equally valid." It is entirely possible that the participants in the open liberated dialogue may determine that certain cultural practices are oppressive or unethical (traditional views of women are a case in point). Thus we do not naively idealize or romanticize other cultures. This perspective does not tell us ahead of time which practices of what culture are oppressive or not. Instead, what it does is to give us a methodology by which the identification of such practices is to be achieved. Also, the multicultural perspective is not a Marxist perspective, because, although it recognizes the important role of economic factors in oppression, it leaves as an open question whether it is in the best interests of the members of a community (either local, national, or global) to adopt a capitalist, socialist, Communist, or mixed economic system. It is certainly logically possible that one or another of these systems may be more effective and desirable to different communities at different points in time.

It is unlikely that we will be able to deal adequately with the issues of poverty and oppression in the Third World until we recognize the philosophical assumptions which shape the way in which we understand these issues. In our dealings with the Third World and in our own domestic policies we should have the moral courage to strive for economic and social justice, for this is the ethically correct thing to do. But in addition to this compelling moral reason, we have strong practical reasons to do so. We can no longer afford not to do so. The facts that the population of the United States is becoming increasingly multicultural and that we live in an increasingly interdependent world, make it necessary for us to adopt the multicultural perspective in order to function effectively, at a political and economic level, in the future. We must reevaluate the philosophy of **egoism** and ontocentrism that is so central to our conceptual orientations. And, most importantly, we must realize that refusing to deal with oppression involves an alienation from our own humanity and compassion. The struggle with the problem of oppression is not to be taken lightly, for ultimately the battle is to reclaim our own souls.

NOTES

1. Guatemala Health Rights Support Project, *Guatemala Health Rights Support Project* (Washington, D.C.: Guatemala Health Rights Support Project, 1987).

2. The Independent Commission of Inquiry on the U.S. Invasion of Panama, *The U.S. Invasion of Panama: The Truth behind Operation "Just Cause"* (Boston: South End Press, 1991), p. 132.

3. Paul Vallely, *Bad Samaritans* (Maryknoll, N.Y.: Orbis Books, 1990), pp. 105–108.

4. Scott B. MacDonald, Jane Hughes, and Uwe Bott, *Latin American Debt in the 1990s* (New York: Praeger, 1991), p. 4.

5. "Ontocentrism" is the belief that the vision of reality of one's culture or society is superior to all others.

Questions for Thought

1. In what ways does your life differ from the life of Consuelo? What, if anything, can you do to improve the lives of people like Consuelo?

2. Under what conditions do you think the United States would be justified in intervening in other countries? What reasons could you give to justify such intervention?

3. How does Valadez explain the origin of Third World debt? What do you think should be done about Third World indebtedness?

4. To what extent have you developed a multicultural perspective? Do you agree with Valadez about the value of developing a multicultural perspective? Why or why not?

5. How do Valadez's views on the nature of knowledge compare with and differ from the views of Benally?

Is Knowledge Really Attainable?

10   A Dialogue on Dogmatism and Truth

FROM THE BUDDHIST SCRIPTURES

As stated in the introduction to the Buddhist selection in Chapter 1, Buddhism arose in northern India in the sixth century B.C.E. Its founder, Siddhartha of the Gautama family, reportedly left a life of great luxury—which he considered to be a life of illusion—to seek the true meaning of human existence. This act in itself clearly illustrates that Siddhartha, who was later known as the Buddha, had recognized one of the basic epistemological distinctions, the distinction between truth and illusion.

After trying to attain the true meaning of human existence by studying the traditional Hindu teachings and then by practicing extreme **asceticism,** Siddhartha achieved enlightenment by intensely meditating for forty days. On achieving enlightenment, he became a wandering teacher, an enlightened figure, who attempted to impart what he had learned and accomplished to others. No doubt because of his own failure to attain enlightenment through the study of theological teachings and dogmas, the Buddha is often portrayed in Buddhist literature as warning his disciples to avoid dogmatic statements and metaphysical speculations. This is one of the dominant themes in these two brief selections. The first selection is from the *Sutta-Nipata*. The second selection, the well-known "Parable of the Arrow," is from the *Majjhima-nikaya*. Like many other Buddhist writings, the first selection is written in the form of a dialogue between the Buddha and one of his followers. The second selection is written in parable form—that is, in the form of a story that illustrates a religious or philosophical point.

In the first selection, the Buddha (the Lord) says that dogmatic assertions can lead only to dissension and not to truth. True knowledge or wisdom can be attained only by freeing oneself from earthly worries and disputes. In the second selection, the Buddha tells the story of a man who has been shot by a poisoned arrow. In typical scholarly fashion, the man seeks to know the nature of the arrow and the bow used to shoot it, the name of the man who shot it, and the kind of poison used. In seeking such knowledge, however, the man overlooks the obvious: If he does not remove the arrow, he will die. The point again is that we should not waste precious time trying to understand useless theories and dogmas but, rather, we should concentrate on what is really important in life and take steps to expunge the poison in our life that is killing us. In Buddhist philosophy, this poison is *tanha* (desire).

Questions for Reading

1. Who does the Enquirer represent in the first selection? With what problem does he approach the Buddha?
2. What are the Buddha's principal reasons for rejecting dogmatism?

3. Why does the Buddha introduce the parable of the arrow?
4. What happens in the parable of the arrow? What is this parable intended to show?
5. What, according to the parable of the arrow, are the Buddha's principal teachings?

TRUTH IS ABOVE SECTARIAN DOGMATISM

The Enquirer: Fixed in their pet beliefs, these divers wranglers bawl—"Hold this, and truth is yours"; "Reject it, and you're lost." Thus they contend, and dub opponents "dolts" and "fools." Which of the lot is right, when all as experts pose?

The Lord: Well, if dissent denotes a "fool" and stupid "dolt," then all are fools and dolts—since each has his own view. Or, if each rival creed proves lore and brains and wit, no "dolts" exist—since all alike are on a par. I count not that as true which those affirm, who call each other "fools." They call each other so, because each deems his own view "Truth."

The Enquirer: What some style "truth," the rest call empty lies; strife reigns. Pray why do anchorites (religious hermits) not speak in unison?

The Lord: There's one sole "Truth" (not two), to know which bars men's strife. But such a motley crowd of "truths" have they evolved, that anchorites, perforce, speak not in full accord.

The Enquirer: What makes these "experts" preach "truths" so diverse? Is each inherited? Or just a view they've framed themselves?

The Lord: Apart from consciousness, no diverse truths exist. Mere sophistry declares this [view] "true," and that view "false." The senses' evidence, and works, inspire such scorn for others, and such smug conviction *he* is right, that all rivals rank as "sorry, brainless fools." When he admits himself to "expert's" rank and style, this fires his scorn anew and off he starts again. Chock-full of error, drunk with pride and arrogance, he consecrates himself a "sage"—so grand in his perfected "view." . . . Delight in their dear views makes sectaries assert that all who disagree "miss Purity and err." These divers sectaries—these sturdy advocates of private paths to bliss—claim Purity as theirs alone, not found elsewhere. Whom should the sturdiest venture to call a "fool," when this invites the like retort upon himself? Stubborn in theories which they themselves devised, these wrangle on through life. Leave then dogmatic views and their attendant strife!

The Enquirer: Take those who dogmatize and lay sole claim to Truth. Is blame their constant fate? Are they not praised as well?

The Lord: Yes, though a trifling thing is all of this . . . and it does not lead to Peace. Wherefore one should shun strife and aim at Peace, which knows no strife. No vulgar theories engage the wise. Why should the free seek bondage, when phenomena of sense appeal to them no more? They that place practice first, deeming that regimen wins Purity, take vows to practice only what their "master taught as pure"—experts self-styled who cling to mere phenomena! . . .

The Enquirer: The doctrine some vaunt "best," others term "low." Which states the fact? . . .

The Lord: Ah! It is her own dear creed which each proclaims as "rare." His rival's creed is "low." And so they squabble on, each claiming truth as *his!* If other's criticisms could make a doctrine "low," then none is excellent. For all unite to damn all doctrines, save their own. As they extol their "Way," so they revere their creeds. Their tune is still the same: "Our purity" is its theme.

The true Brahmin adopts nothing from others, owes nothing to others' views; immune from strife, he deems no theory "the Truth." . . . No true Brahmin attains the goal by mere research; no partisan is he, nor brother-sectary; all vulgar theories—which others toil to learn—he knows, but heeds them not. From earthly trammels freed, aloof from

"A Dialogue on Dogmatism and Truth" is from Buddha's Teachings, *translated by Lord Chalmers, Harvard University Press, 1932. "The Parable of the Arrow" is from* Buddhist Scriptures, *translated by E. J. Thomas, John Murray Publishers, 1913.*

party broils, at peace where peace has fled, the un-heeding sage ignores what others toil to learn. From whilom cankers purged, with no fresh growths afoot, from lusts and dogmas free, quit too of theories, he goes his stainless way, devoid of self-reproach.

THE PARABLE OF THE ARROW

I have heard that the Lord was once dwelling near Sāvatthi, at Jetavana in the park of Anātha-pindika. Now the elder Mālunkyāputta had retired from the world. As he meditated the thought arose: "These theories have been left unexplained by the Lord; they have been set aside and rejected—whether the world is eternal or not eternal, whether the world is finite or not, whether the soul (life) is the same as the body or whether the soul is one thing and the body another, whether a Buddha (**Tathāgata**) ex-ists after death or does not exist after death, whether a Buddha both exists and does not exist after death, and whether a Buddha is non-existent and not non-existent after death. These things the Lord does not explain to me. That he does not explain them to me does not please me; it does not suit me. I will approach the Lord, and ask about this matter. . . . If the Lord does not explain them to me, I will give up the training and return to a worldly life." [When Mālunkyāputta had approached and put his questions, the Lord replied:] "Now did I ever say to you, 'Come Mālunkyāputta, lead a religious life with me, and I will explain to you whether the world is eternal or not eternal, whether the world is finite or not, whether the soul is the same as the body, or whether the soul is one thing and the body another, whether a Buddha exists after death or does not ex-ist after death, whether a Buddha both exists and does not exist after death, and whether a Buddha is non-existent and not non-existent after death?'"

"You did not, reverend sir."

"Anyone, Mālunkyāputta, who says, 'I will not lead a religious life with the Lord, until the Lord explains to me whether the world is eternal or not eternal, whether the world is finite or not, whether the soul is the same as the body, or whether the soul is one thing and the body another, whether a Buddha exists after death or does not exist after death, whether a Buddha both exists and does not

exist after death, and whether a Buddha is non-existent and not non-existent after death,' that per-son will die without its being explained. Suppose that there was a man who had been wounded by an arrow thickly smeared with poison. Suppose also that when his friends, companions, relatives, and kins-men brought a surgeon to heal him, he said, 'I will not have this arrow pulled out, until I know by what man I was wounded, whether he is of the warrior caste, or a brahmin, or of the agricultural caste, or of the lowest caste.' Or suppose he said, 'I will not have this arrow pulled out until I know of what name or family the man is . . . or whether he is tall, short, or of middle height . . . or whether he is black, dark, or yellowish . . . or whether he comes from such and such a village, town, or city . . . or until I know whether the bow with which I was wounded was a chāpa or a kondanda, or until I know whether the bow-string was of swallow-wort, bamboo-fiber, sinew, hemp, or milk-sap tree, or until I know whether the shaft was from a wild or cultivated plant . . . or whether it was feathered from the wing of a vulture, heron, hawk, peacock, or a sithilahanu-bird . . . or whether it was wrapped round with the sinew of an ox, buffalo, ruru-deer, or monkey . . . or until I know whether it was an ordinary arrow, a razor arrow, a vekanda, an iron arrow, a calf-tooth arrow, or a karavira leaf arrow.' That man would die, Mālunkyāputta, without knowing all this.

"It is not on the view that the world is eternal that a religious life depends; it is not on the view that the world is not eternal that a religious life de-pends. Whether the view is held that the world is eternal or that the world is not eternal, there is still re-birth, old age, and death, as well as grief, lamentation, suffering, sorrow, and despair, the destruction of which even in this life I announce. It is not on the view that the world is finite. . . . It is not on the view that a Tathāgata exists after death. . . . Therefore, Mālunkyāputta, consider as unexplained what I have not explained, and con-sider as explained what I have explained. And what have I not explained? I have not explained whether the world is eternal or whether it is not eternal. . . . I have not explained whether a Tathāgata is born non-existent and not non-existent after death. And why have I not explained this? Because this, Mālunkyāputta, is not useful; it is not concerned with the principle of a religious life. It does not conduce to aversion, absence of passion, cessation, tranquility, supernatural faculty, perfect knowledge, and **Nirvana.** Thus I have not explained it.

"And what have I explained? I have explained suffering, the cause of suffering, the destruction of suffering, and the path that leads to the destruction of suffering. For this is useful; this is concerned with the principle of a religious life. This conduces to aversion, absence of passion, cessation, tranquility, supernatural faculty, perfect knowledge, Nirvana; and thus have I explained it. Therefore, Mālunkyāputta, consider as unexplained what I have not explained, and consider as explained what I have explained."

Thus spoke the Lord, and with joy the elder Mālunkyāputta applauded the words of the Lord.

Questions for Thought

1. Do you agree with the Buddha's rejection of dogmatism? Why or why not?
2. Can you think of any of your own views that might be classified as dogmatic?
3. How effective is the parable of the arrow in illustrating the Buddha's point?
4. Are you familiar with other religious or philosophical parables? If so, how do they compare with or differ from the parable of the arrow?
5. Can you create a brief parable of your own that could be used to illustrate something that you believe to be true?

The Identity of Contraries   11

CHUANG-TZU

Chuang-tzu (ca. 369–275 B.C.E.) was a follower of Lao-tzu, a semi-legendary figure who lived in China in the sixth century B.C.E. Lao-tzu is credited with having written the *Tao Te Ching,* the book that contains the philosophical foundation of **Taoism.** Chuang-tzu spread the teachings of Lao-tzu and urged the Chinese rulers and people to accept Lao-tzu as their master teacher. As is the case with Lao-tzu, very little is known about Chuang-tzu's life, except that he once served as a minor government official and later refused a more prominent government position (the position of prime minister of the province of Ch'u) in order to maintain his political and philosophical independence. Although the *Chuang-tzu,* from which the following selection is taken, is credited solely to Chuang-tzu, most scholars agree that it consists of a collection of Taoist writings from various authors.

Like the preceding Buddhist selections, this Taoist selection begins by commenting on the doctrinal differences among humans. Chuang-tzu compares these differences to wind blowing through the hollows of trees, each making its own discordant sound. He notes that the disciples of the various philosophers use language to refute the doctrines of their opponents but that their opponents do the same. The result is continuous disputation without the possibility of agreement or solution. Unlike these scholars, the sage refuses to argue; that is, the sage refuses to use language to discriminate or divide what is into this reality or that. Rather, the sage realizes that what is (the Way, or **Tao**) cannot be reached by division or discrimination but only by immersing oneself in a unity or oneness that transcends all distinction.

Near the end of this selection, Chuang-tzu says that accepting our ignorance is perhaps the highest knowledge that we can attain in this life. He compares life to a dream and says that the sage realizes that this life *is* only a dream. However, one who is not a sage mistakenly believes that he or she can clearly distinguish between waking experience and dreamed experience. In opposition to such people, Chuang-tzu says that after having once dreamed that he was a butterfly, he is unable to determine whether he was a human being who had dreamed he was a butterfly or a butterfly who is now dreaming that he is a human being.

Questions for Reading

1. Why does Chuang-tzu believe that disputation or argument is useless?
2. What exactly does Chuang-tzu mean by "the identity of contraries"?
3. Does Chuang-tzu believe that it is possible for humans to know the true nature of reality? If not, why not? If so, how?
4. What does Chuang-tzu mean by the Way (Tao)? How does he know that the Way exists?
5. How is the sage described in this selection?
6. Why does Chuang-tzu think he might be a butterfly? What is his discussion of the butterfly intended to show?

TZU CH'I OF NAN-KUO SAT LEANING ON A table. Looking up to heaven, he sighed and stared vacantly, as though his body and soul had separated. Tzu Yu, who was standing beside him, exclaimed, "What are you thinking about that your body should become still like dry wood, that your mind should become like dead ashes? Surely the man now leaning on the table is not the one who was just here."

"My friend," replied Tzu Ch'i, "your question is timely. *Today I have lost myself.* . . . Do you understand? . . . Ah! perhaps you only know the music of man, and not that of earth. Or even if you have heard the music of earth, perhaps you have not heard the music of heaven."

"Please explain," said Tzu Yu.

"The breath of the universe," continued Tzu Ch'i, "is called wind. At times it is inactive. But when active, every aperture resounds to the blast. Have you never listened to its growing roar? Caves and dells of hill and forest, hollows in huge trees of great expanse—these are like nostrils, mouths, ears, sockets, goblets, mortars, ditches, and bogs. And the wind goes rushing through them, sniffing, snoring, singing, sighing, puffing, wailing, whistling, and whirring—now shrilly treble, now deeply bass, now soft, now hard. Until, with a lull, silence reigns supreme. Have you never witnessed such a disturbance as this among the trees?"

"Well," inquired Tzu Yu, "if the music of earth consists of nothing more than such hollows, and the music of man consists of things such as pipes and flutes, of what, then, consists the music of heaven?"

"The effect of the wind upon these various apertures," replied Tzu Ch'i, "is not uniform. But what is it that gives to each its individuality, and to everything the potentiality of sound? Great knowledge embraces the whole; small knowledge embraces only a part. Great speech is universal; small speech is particular.

"Whether we are sleeping or waking, we are subject to daily mental disturbances—to indecision, to lack of insight, to concealment, to fretting fear and trembling terror. Today the mind flies forth like a javelin, the arbiter of right and wrong. Today, it

This is the editor's revised version of a selection from Chuang Tzu: Taoist Philosopher and Chinese Mystic, *translated by Herbert A. Giles, London: George Allen & Unwin, 1889.*

remains firm like a solemn knight, the guardian of truths gained. But tomorrow, as if from autumn and winter's blight, comes gradual decay, a passing away, like the flow of water, never to return. Finally, when it is all clogged up like an old drain, the failing mind will not see light again.

"Joy and anger, sorrow and happiness, light heartedness and remorse, come upon us in turns. Like music from the hollows and mushrooms from the damp, our moods are ever-changing. Night and day alternate within us, but we do not know from whence they spring. Can we then hope to lay our finger upon their very cause?

"If not for these emotions *I* would not be. But if not for me, *they* would have no scope. That much we can say. But we do not know what it is that brings them into play. It would seem to be a *soul*; but the clue to its existence is lacking. That such a power operates is credible enough, even if we cannot see its form. Perhaps it has functions without form. . . .

"But whether or not we ascertain what the functions of the soul are, it matters but little to the soul itself. For coming into existence with this mortal body of mine, its mandate will also be exhausted when the body becomes exhausted. To be harassed by the wear and tear of life, to pass rapidly through life without the possibility of arresting one's course—is not this pitiful indeed? To labor without ceasing, and then, worn out, without living to enjoy the fruit of one's labor, to depart suddenly, knowing not whither—is not this just cause for grief?

"What advantage is there in what men call immortality? The body decomposes, and the mind goes with it. This is our real cause for sorrow. Can everyone in the world be so dull as not to see this? Or is it I who am dull, and not the others?

"If we are to be guided by criteria found in our own minds, who will be without a guide? Why do we need to be taught about the alternations of emotion, when the mind, even the mind of a fool, knows that this is so? However, for a mind without criteria to admit the idea of contraries, is like saying, *I went to Yueh today, and got there yesterday.* Or it is like placing nowhere somewhere—topography that even the great Yu would fail to understand. How much more so I?

"Speech is not mere breath. It is differentiated by meaning. Take away meaning, and you cannot say

whether it is speech or not. Can you then even distinguish it from the chirping of young birds? But how can **Tao** be so obscured that we speak of it as true and false? And how can speech be so obscured that it admits the idea of contraries? How can Tao go away and yet not remain? How can speech exist and yet be impossible? Tao is obscured by our lack of grasp; speech is obscured by the gloss of this world. Hence the affirmations and negations of the **Confucians** and **Mohists**—each denies what the other affirms, and affirms what the other denies. But he who would reconcile affirmative with negative and negative with affirmative must do so by the light of nature.

"There is nothing which is not objective; there is nothing which is not subjective. But it is impossible to start from the objective. Only from subjective knowledge is it possible to proceed to objective knowledge. Hence it has been said, 'The objective emanates from the subjective; the subjective is consequent upon the objective. This is the *Alternation Theory*.' Nevertheless, when one is born, the other one dies. When one is possible, the other one is impossible. When one is affirmative, the other one is negative. This being the case, the true sage rejects all distinctions of this and that. He takes refuge in the Tao, and places himself in subjective relation to all things.

"And inasmuch as the subjective is also objective, and the objective also subjective, and as the contraries under each are indistinguishably blended, does it not become impossible for us to say whether subjective and objective really exist at all?

"When subjective and objective are both without their correlates, that is the very axis of Tao. And when that axis passes through the center at which all infinities converge, positive and negative, subjective and objective, blend into an infinite oneness. . . .

"Using a finger to show that something is not a finger, is not as good as using something that is not a finger. Using a horse to show that something is not a horse, is not as good as using something that is not a horse. So with the universe and all that is in it. These things are but fingers and horses in this sense. The possible is possible; the impossible is impossible. Tao operates, and given results follow. Things receive names like 'finger' or 'horse,' and they are what they are. They achieve this by their natural affinity for what they are and their natural antagonism to what they are not. For all things have their own particular constitutions and potentialities. Nothing can exist without these.

"But viewed from the standpoint of Tao, horizontal and vertical are identical. So are ugliness and beauty, greatness and smallness, wickedness and goodness. Dividing is the same as uniting; construction is the same as destruction. Nothing is subject to either construction or destruction, for these conditions are brought together into one.

"Only the true sage understands this principle of the identity of all things. He does not view things objectively as an impartial subject existing separately from them, but he projects himself into the place of the things viewed. And viewing them thus, he is able to comprehend them, even to master them—he who can master things, must be near. So it is that by *not* placing oneself in subjective relation to externals, that is, by transcending the duality between subjectivity and objectivity, that one is able to view things from the standpoint of Tao. But to wear out one's intellect by stubbornly adhering to the individuality of things, thus not recognizing the fact that all things are one—this is called *Three in the Morning*."

"Why is it called *Three in the Morning?*" asked Tzu Yu.

"A keeper of monkeys," replied Tzu Ch'i, "said that, in their ration of chestnuts, each monkey could have three in the morning and four at night. But this proposal made the monkeys very angry; so the keeper said that they could have four in the morning and three at night. The monkeys were very happy with this new arrangement. The actual number of chestnuts remained the same, but there was an adaptation to the likes and dislikes of those concerned. Such is the principle of placing oneself in subjective relation to externals, of stubbornly adhering to the individuality of things. The true sage, however, regards contraries as identical, adapting himself to the laws of heaven. This is called *following two courses at once*. . . . Therefore what the true sage aims at is the light that comes out of darkness. He does not view things as apprehended by himself, subjectively, but transfers himself into the place of the things viewed. This called *using the light*.

"There remains, however, the question of speech. Does not speech presuppose that contraries

exist? And if this is so, how can I use speech to affirm the identity of contraries? . . . If there is existence, there must have been non-existence. And if there was a time when nothing existed, then there must have been a time before that—a time when even nothing did not exist. When nothing suddenly came into existence, could one really say whether it belonged to the category of existence or of non-existence? Even the very words I have just now uttered—I cannot say whether they have really been uttered or not.

"There is nothing under the canopy of heaven greater than the tip of an autumn blade of grass. A mountain is a small thing. Neither is there any age greater than that of a child cut off in infancy. . . . The universe and I came into being together; and I, and everything therein, are one.

"But if then all things are one, what place is there for speech? On the other hand, since I can utter these words, how can speech not exist? If it does exist, we have the one and speech, which equals two; and two and the one equals three. From this point, even the best mathematicians will fail to reach the Tao. How much more so, then, will ordinary people fail? . . .

"Before contraries existed, Tao was. Before definitions existed, speech was. Subjectively, we are conscious of certain delimitations—of right and left, relationship and obligation, division and discrimination, emulation and contention. These are called the *Eight Predicables*. For the true sage, beyond the limits of an external world, they exist but are not recognized. For the true sage, within the limits of an external world, they are recognized but not assigned. Even when the true sage assigns, he does not justify by argument. And thus, classifying, he does not classify; arguing, he does not argue."

"How can that be?" asked Tzu Yu.

"The true sage," answered Tzu Ch'i, "keeps his knowledge within him, while other men set forth theirs in argument, in order to convince each other. And therefore it is said that in argument the true sage does not manifest himself. Perfect Tao does not declare itself. Neither does perfect argument express itself in words, nor perfect charity show itself in act. . . . For the Tao which shines forth is not Tao. Speech that argues falls short of its aim. Charity which has fixed points loses its scope. . . . Thus it is that knowledge which stops at what it does not know is the highest knowledge."

II

Chu Ch'iao said to Chang Wu Tzu, "I heard Confucius say that the following were crazy words: 'The true sage pays no heed to worldly affairs. He neither seeks gain nor avoids injury. He asks nothing at the hands of man. He adheres, without questioning, to Tao. Without speaking, he can speak; and he can speak and yet say nothing. And so he roams beyond the limits of this dusty world.' To me, however, these words are the skillful embodiment of Tao. What, Sir, is your opinion?"

Chang Wu Tzu replied, "How should Confucius know something that even the Yellow Emperor doubted? I would say to Confucius, 'You are going too fast. You see your egg, and expect to hear it crow. You look at your cross-bow, and expect to have boiled-pigeon before you. I will say a few words to you at random, so please listen at random.'

"How does the sage seat himself by the sun and moon, and hold the universe in his grasp? He blends everything into one harmonious whole, rejecting the confusion of this and that. Rank and privilege, which the vulgar prize, the sage stolidly ignores. The revolutions of ten thousand years leave his unity unscathed. The universe itself may pass away, but he will still flourish.

"How do I know that love of life is not a delusion after all? How do I know that he who dreads death is not like a child who has lost the way and cannot find his home? The Lady Li Chi was the daughter of the border chieftain Ai Feng. The Duke of Chin carried her off. When he first got her, she wept until the bosom of her dress was drenched with tears. But when she came to the royal palace, where she lived with the Duke and ate rich food, she repented of having wept. How do I know that the dead do not repent of having previously clung to life?

"Those who dream of the banquet wake to lamentation and sorrow. Those who dream of lamentation and sorrow wake to join the hunt. While they dream, they do not know that they dream. Some will even interpret the very dream that they are dreaming; and only when they awaken will they know that it was a dream. By and by comes the great awakening, when we find out that this life is really a great dream. Fools think that they are now awake, and flatter themselves that they know whether they are really princes or peasants. However, Confucius and you are both dreams; and I who say that you are dreams—I am a dream myself. Such is the **paradox.** Tomorrow a sage may arise to explain it; but that tomorrow will not come until unlimited tomorrows have passed.

"Let us suppose that you and I argue. If you beat me and not I you, are you necessarily right and I wrong? Or if I beat you and not you me, am I necessarily right and you wrong? Or are we both partly right and partly wrong? Or are we both wholly right and wholly wrong? You and I cannot know this, and neither can anyone else in the world. For who shall serve as arbiter between us? If it is someone who takes your view, he will side with you; if it is someone who takes my view, he will side with me. How can such a person arbitrate between us? And if it is someone who either differs from both of us, or agrees with both of us, he will be equally unable to decide between us. Since neither you nor I nor anyone else can decide, must we not depend upon something else? Such dependence is as though it were not dependence. We are embraced in the obliterating unity of Tao. In it, we are perfectly adapted to whatever may eventuate, and so we complete our allotted span. . . . Take no heed of time, or of right and wrong. But passing into the realm of the infinite, take your final rest therein."

III

Once upon a time, I, Chuang-tzu, dreamed that I was a butterfly, fluttering hither and thither, having all the intents and purposes of a butterfly. I was conscious only of following my fancies as a butterfly; I had no consciousness of my individuality as a man. Suddenly, I awakened, and there I lay, myself again. Now I do not know whether I was then a man dreaming that I was a butterfly, or whether I am now a butterfly dreaming that I am a man.

Questions for Thought

1. Do you agree with Chuang-tzu that disputation, or argument, is useless? If so, why? If not, when do you think it might be useful?
2. Do you think that you know the true nature of reality? Defend your answer.
3. How would you describe a sage, or wise person? How does your description of a sage compare with or differ from the description of Chuang-tzu?
4. Have you ever dreamed that you were someone other than you now believe you are? If so, how do you know who you really are now?
5. How does Chuang-tzu's use of the dream example compare with and differ from Descartes' dream argument in Meditation I (earlier in this chapter)?

12   Circles

RALPH WALDO EMERSON

Ralph Waldo Emerson (1803–1882) was one of the leading proponents of the **transcendentalist** movement in literature and philosophy that flourished in the United States during the middle years of the nineteenth century. Emerson was born in Boston, the son of a Unitarian minister who served as chaplain of the Massachusetts state senate. When Emerson's father died in 1811, his mother supported the family by keeping a boardinghouse. After attending Boston Latin School, Emerson entered Harvard College in 1817. At Harvard, he began keeping the journal that became the source of much of his published writing while also winning prizes for several of his essays.

After graduating from Harvard, Emerson taught at his brother's school for young ladies in Boston before entering Harvard Divinity School. However, he was forced to take a hiatus from his studies to travel to Georgia and Florida for health reasons. Returning to Boston, Emerson was ordained pastor of the Second Church in 1829. That same year, he married Ellen Tucker, who died of tuberculosis two years later. Depressed about his wife's death and troubled by doubts about certain religious dogmas, Emerson resigned his pastorate and traveled to England, where he visited the poets Coleridge and Wordsworth and initiated a lifelong friendship with the essayist and historian Thomas Carlyle.

When Emerson returned to the United States, he took up residence in Concord, where he remarried and became a leader in the transcendentalist movement. He served as editor of the transcendentalist journal *The Dial,* to which he made several literary contributions. Emerson's first book, *Nature,* was published in 1836. The first series of his widely read essays appeared in 1841, followed by a second series three years later. The success of Emerson's writings was matched by his success as a speaker, and he became a popular lecturer on the lecture circuits that had become an important part of intellectual life in the United States during the latter half of the nineteenth century. Emerson continued to write and to lecture extensively until senility gradually overcame him in the late 1870s. He died in Concord on April 27, 1882. Some of Emerson's later writings include *Poems* (1846), *Representative Men* (1850), *English Traits* (1856), *The Conduct of Life*

(1860), *Mad-Day and Other Pieces* (1867), *Society and Solitude* (1870), and *Letters and Social Aims* (1876).

In the following essay, Emerson affirms many of the skeptical **conclusions** found in the two preceding selections. Beginning with the claim that nature is ever changing, Emerson suggests that human existence, as well as human knowledge, must be continually revised if it is to mirror the process of nature. However, the necessity of constant revision rules out the possibility that one could ever arrive at a truth that would be final or complete. As Emerson says, "Every ultimate fact is only the first of a new series."

Emerson's doubts about the possibility of discovering ultimate facts or final truths about the natural world led him to ethical and aesthetic **relativism** as well. Just as there are no ultimate facts about nature, there are no absolute moral or **aesthetic** values. In a classical statement of moral and aesthetic relativism, Emerson tells us that "one man's justice is another's injustice; one man's beauty another's ugliness; one man's wisdom another's folly."

Questions for Reading

1. What are Emerson's principal reasons for denying that we can know the true nature of reality?
2. What does the concept of the circle represent in Emerson's essay? What does he mean by saying that conversation is a "game of circles"?
3. Why does Emerson believe that "every ultimate fact is only the first of a new series"? What exactly does he mean by this statement?
4. Why does Emerson value the poet more than the scientist?
5. How are values viewed in this essay? How is nature viewed?

CIRCLES

Nature centers into balls,
And her proud ephemerals,
Fast to surface and outside,
Scan the profile of the sphere;
Knew they what that signified,
A new genesis were here.

THE EYE IS THE FIRST CIRCLE; THE HORIZON which it forms is the second; and throughout nature this primary figure is repeated without end. It is the highest emblem in the cipher of the world. St. Augustine described the nature of God as a circle whose center was everywhere and whose circumference was nowhere. All our lifetime we are reading the copious sense of this first of forms. In considering the circular or compensatory character of every human action, we have already deduced one moral from this. We shall now trace another **analogy**, namely, that every action admits of being outdone. Our life is an apprenticeship to the truth that around every circle another circle can be drawn. There is no end in nature, but every end is a beginning; there is always another dawn risen on mid-noon, and under every deep a lower deep opens. . . .

There are no fixtures in nature. The universe is fluid and volatile. Permanence is but a word of degrees. Our globe seen by God is a transparent law, not a mass of facts. The law dissolves the fact and holds it fluid. Our culture is the predominance of an idea which draws after it this train of cities and institutions. Let us rise into another idea; they will disappear. The Greek sculpture is all melted away, as if

This is the editor's revised version of a selection from Ralph Waldo Emerson, Essays, *1841–1842.*

it had been statues of ice; here and there a solitary figure or fragment remains, as we see flecks and scraps of snow left in cold dells and mountain clefts in June and July. For the genius that created it now creates something else. The Greek letters last a little longer, but they are already passing under the same sentence and tumbling into the inevitable pit which the creation of new thought opens for all that is old. The new continents are built out of the ruins of an old planet; the new races fed out of the decomposition of the foregoing. New arts destroy the old. See the investment of capital in aqueducts, made useless by hydraulics; fortifications, by gunpowder; roads and canals, by railways; sails, by steam; steam, by electricity.

You admire this tower of granite, weathering the hurts of so many ages. Yet a little waving hand built this huge wall, and that which builds is better than that which is built. The hand that built it can topple it down much faster. However, better and nimbler than the hand was the invisible thought which wrought through it; and thus ever, behind the coarse effect is a fine cause that, being narrowly seen, is itself the effect of a finer cause. Everything looks permanent until its secret is known. A rich estate appears to women a firm and lasting fact; to a merchant, it appears as something easily created out of any materials, and easily lost. To an ordinary citizen an orchard, good tillage, and good grounds seem to be a fixture, like a gold mine or a river; but to a large farmer, these things seem not much more fixed than the state of the crop. Nature looks provokingly stable and secular, but it has a cause like all the rest. When once I comprehend that, will these fields stretch so immovably wide, these leaves hang so individually considerable? Permanence is a word of degrees. Every thing is medial. Moons are no more bounds to spiritual power than bat-balls. . . .

The life of man is a self-evolving circle, which, from a ring imperceptibly small, rushes on all sides outwards to new and larger circles, without end. The extent to which this generation of circles, wheel without wheel, will go, depends on the force or truth of the individual soul. For it is the inert effort of each thought, having formed itself into a circular wave of circumstance—as for instance an empire, rules of an art, a local usage, a religious rite—to heap itself on that ridge, where it solidifies and hems in life. But if the soul is quick and strong it bursts over that boundary on all sides and expands another orbit on the great deep. But this also runs up into a high wave and attempts again to stop and to bind. However, the heart refuses to be imprisoned; in its first and narrowest pulses, it already tends outward with a vast force to immense and innumerable expansions.

Every ultimate fact is only the first of a new series. Every general law is only a particular fact of some more general law presently to disclose itself. There is no outside, no inclosing wall, no circumference to us. The man finishes his story. How good! How final! How it puts a new face on all things! He fills the sky. Yet, on the other side also rises a man who draws a circle around the circle that we had just pronounced to be the outline of the sphere. Then already our first speaker is not man, but only a first speaker. His only redress is forthwith to draw a circle outside of his antagonist. And thus men do so by themselves. The result of today, which haunts the mind and cannot be escaped, will presently be abridged into a word; the principle that seemed to explain nature will itself be included as one example of a bolder generalization. In the thought of tomorrow there is a power to upheave all your creed—indeed, all the creeds and all the literatures of the nations—and to marshal thee to a heaven which no epic dream has yet depicted. Every man is not so much a workman in the world as he is a suggestion of what he should be. Men walk as prophecies of the next age.

Step by step we scale this mysterious ladder; the steps are actions, the new prospect is power. Every result is threatened and judged by that which follows. Every result seems to be contradicted by the new, but it is only limited by the new. The new statement is always hated by the old, and to those dwelling in the old, it comes like an abyss of **skepticism.** But the eye soon gets accustomed to it, for the eye and it are effects of one cause; then its innocency and benefit appear, until finally, all its energy spent, it pales and dwindles before the revelation of the new hour. . . .

There are no fixtures to men, if we appeal to consciousness. Every man supposes himself not to be fully understood; and if there is any truth in him, if he rests at last on the divine soul, I do not see how it can be otherwise. He must feel that the last chamber, the last closet, was never opened; there is always a residuum, unknown and unanalyzable. That is, every man believes that he has a greater possibility.

Our moods do not believe in each other. Today I am full of thoughts and can write what I please. I see no reason why I should not have the same power of expression tomorrow. While I write it, what I write seems the most natural thing in the world; but yesterday I saw a dreary vacuity in this direction in which now I see so much. A month hence, I doubt not, I shall wonder who he was that wrote so many continuous pages. Alas for this infirm faith, this will not strenuous, this vast ebb of a vast flow! I am God in nature; I am a weed by the wall. . . .

Each new step we take in thought reconciles twenty seemingly discordant facts, as expressions of one law. Aristotle and Plato are reckoned the respective heads of two schools. A wise man will see that Aristotle platonizes. By going one step farther back in thought, discordant opinions are reconciled by being seen to be two extremes of one principle, and we can never go so far back as to preclude a still higher vision.

Beware when the great God lets loose a thinker on this planet. Then all things are at risk. It is as if a conflagration has broken out in a great city, and no man knows what is safe, or where it will end. There is not a piece of science but its flank may be turned tomorrow; there is not any literary reputation, not the so-called eternal names of fame, which may not be revised and condemned. The very hopes of man, the thoughts of his heart, the religion of nations, the manners and morals of mankind, are all at the mercy of a new generalization. Generalization is always a new influx of the divinity into the mind. Hence the thrill that attends it.

Valor consists in the power of self-recovery, so that a man cannot have his flank turned, cannot be out-generalled. Put him where you will, he stands. This can only be because he prefers truth to his past apprehension of truth, because of his alert acceptance of truth from whatever quarter, because of the intrepid conviction that his laws, his relations to society, his Christianity, his world, can be superseded and decease at any time.

There are degrees in **idealism.** We learn first to play with it academically, as the magnet was once a toy. Then in the heyday of youth and poetry we see that it may be true, that it is true in gleams and fragments. Then its countenance waxes stern and grand, and we see that it must be true. It now shows itself ethical and practical. We learn that God IS, that he is

in me, and that all things are shadows of him. The idealism of Berkeley is only a crude statement of the idealism of Jesus, and that again is a crude statement of the fact that all nature is the rapid efflux of goodness executing and organizing itself. It is much more obvious that history and the state of the world are, at any one time, directly dependent on the intellectual classification then existing in the minds of men. The things which are dear to men at this hour are so on account of the ideas that have emerged on their mental horizon, ideas that cause the present order of things, as a tree bears its apples. A new degree of culture would instantly revolutionize the entire system of human pursuits.

Conversation is a game of circles. In conversation we pluck up the *termini* which bound the common silence on every side. The parties are not to be judged by the spirit they partake and even express under this Pentecost. Tomorrow they will have receded from this high-water mark. Tomorrow you shall find them stooping under the old pack-saddles. Yet let us enjoy the cloven flame while it glows on our walls. When each new speaker strikes a new light, emancipating us from the last speaker who oppressed us with the greatness and exclusiveness of his own thought, thereby yielding us to another redeemer, we seem to recover our rights, to become men. . . . In common hours, society sits cold and statuesque. We all stand waiting, empty—knowing, possibly, that we can be full, surrounded by mighty symbols which are not symbols to us, but prose and trivial toys. Then the god comes and converts the statues into fiery men, and by a flash of his eye burns up the veil that shrouded all things. The meaning of the very furniture, of cup and saucer, of chair and clock and tester, is manifest. The facts that loomed so large in the fogs of yesterday—property, climate, breeding, personal beauty and the like—have strangely changed their proportions. All that we reckoned to be settled, shakes and rattles; and literatures, cities, climates, religions, leave their foundations and dance before our eyes. And yet here again see the swift circumscription! Good as discourse is, silence is better and shames it. The length of the discourse indicates the distance of thought between the speaker and the hearer. If they were at a perfect understanding on any point, no words on that point would be necessary. If they were at a perfect understanding on all points, no words would be suffered.

Literature is a point outside of our **hodiernal** circle through which a new one may be described. The use of literature is to afford us a platform from where we may command a view of our present life, a purchase by which we may move it. We fill ourselves with ancient learning, installing ourselves as best we can in Greek, Punic, and Roman houses, only so that we may see, with greater wisdom, French, English and American houses and modes of living. In like manner we see literature best from the midst of wild nature, or from the din of affairs, or from a high religion. The field cannot be well seen from within the field. The astronomer must have his diameter of the earth's orbit as a base to find the parallax of any star.

Therefore we value the poet. All argument and all wisdom is not in the encyclopedia, the treatise on **metaphysics,** or the Body of Divinity, but in the sonnet or the play. In my daily work I am inclined to repeat my old steps; I do not believe in remedial force, in the power of change and reform. But some **Petrarch** or **Ariosto,** filled with the new wine of his imagination, writes me an ode or a brisk romance, full of daring thought and action. He smites and arouses me with his shrill tones, breaks up my whole chain of habits, and I open my eyes on my own possibilities. He claps wings to the sides of all the solid old lumber of the world, and I am capable once more of choosing a straight path in theory and practice.

We have the same need to command such a view of the religion of the world. We can never see Christianity from the catechism—from the pastures, from a boat in the pond, from amidst the songs of wood-birds, we possibly may. Cleansed by elemental light and wind, steeped in the sea of beautiful forms which the field offers us, we may chance to cast a right glance back upon biography. Christianity is rightly dear to the best of mankind; yet there was never a young philosopher whose breeding had fallen into the Christian church by whom that brave text of Paul's was not specially prized: "Then shall also the Son be subject unto Him who put all things under him, that God may be all in all." Let the claims and virtues of persons be never so great and welcome, still the instinct of man presses eagerly onward to the impersonal and illimitable, gladly arming itself against the dogmatism of bigots with this generous word out of the book itself.

The natural world may be conceived of as a system of concentric circles. Now and then we detect in nature slight dislocations which apprise us that this surface on which we now stand is not fixed, but sliding. These manifold tenacious qualities, this chemistry and vegetation, these metals and animals, which seem to stand there for their own sake, are means and methods only—they are words of God, as fugitive as other words. Has the naturalist or chemist who has explored the gravity of atoms and the elective affinities learned his craft, if he has not yet discerned the deeper law of which this is only a partial or approximate statement, namely the law that like draws to like, that the goods which belong to you gravitate to you and need not be pursued with pains and cost? Yet that statement is also approximate and not final. Omnipresence is a higher fact. Not through subtle subterranean channels need friend and fact be drawn to their counterpart, but, rightly considered, these things proceed from the eternal generation of the soul. Cause and effect are two sides of one fact.

The same law of eternal procession applies to all that we call the virtues, and extinguishes each in the light of a better. The great man will not be prudent in the popular sense; all his prudence will be so much deduction from his grandeur. But when he sacrifices prudence, it behooves each to see to what god he devotes it; if to ease and pleasure, he had better be prudent still; if to a great trust, he who has a winged chariot can well spare his mule and saddle bags. . . .

One man's justice is another's injustice; one man's beauty is another's ugliness; one man's wisdom is another's folly—as one beholds the same objects from a higher point. One man thinks justice consists in paying debts, and he has no measure in his abhorrence of another who is very remiss in this duty and makes the creditor wait tediously. But that second man has his own way of looking at things. He asks himself, "Which debt must I pay first, the debt to the rich, or the debt to the poor? The debt of money, or the debt of thought to mankind, of genius to nature?" For you, O broker, there is no other principle but arithmetic. For me, commerce is of trivial import; love, faith, truth of character, the aspiration of man, these are sacred. Nor can I detach one duty, like you, from all other duties, and concentrate my forces mechanically on the payment of moneys. . . .

There is no virtue which is final; all virtues are initial. The virtues of society are vices of the saint. The terror of reform is the discovery that we must cast away our virtues, or what we have always esteemed as such, into the same pit that has consumed our grosser vices:—

"Forgive his crimes, forgive his virtues too,
Those smaller faults, half converts to the right.". . .

And thus, O circular philosopher, I hear some reader exclaim that I have arrived at a fine **Pyrrhonism,** at an equivalence and indifferency of all actions, that I happily teach that *if we are true,* then our crimes may be lively stones out of which we shall construct the temple of the true God!

I am not careful to justify myself. I admit that I am gladdened by seeing the predominance of the saccharine principle throughout vegetable nature, and not less by beholding in morals that unrestrained inundation of the principle of good into every chink and hole that selfishness has left open, even into selfishness and sin itself, so that no evil is pure and hell itself is not without its extreme satisfactions. But so as not to mislead anyone when I have my own head and obey my own whims, let me remind the reader that I am only an experimenter. Do not set the least value on what I do, or the least discredit on what I do not do, as if I pretended to settle any thing as true or false. I unsettle all things. No facts are sacred to me; none are profane. I simply experiment; I am an endless seeker with no past at my back.

Yet this incessant movement and progression in which all things partake could never become sensible to us but by contrast to some principle of fixture or stability in the soul. While the eternal generation of circles proceeds, the eternal generator abides. That central life is somewhat superior to creation, superior to knowledge and thought, and contains all its circles. Forever it labors to create a life and thought as large and excellent as itself, but in vain, for that which is made instructs how to make a better.

Thus there is no sleep, no pause, no preservation, but all things renew, germinate and spring. Why should we import rags and relics into the new hour? Nature abhors the old, and old age seems the only disease; all others run into this one. We call it by many names—fever, intemperance, insanity, stupidity and crime—they are all forms of old age. They are rest, conservatism, appropriation, inertia;

they are not newness, not the way onward. We grizzle every day. I see no need of it. As long as we converse with what is above us, we do not grow old, we grow young. Infancy, youth, receptive, aspiring, with religious eye looking upward, counts itself nothing and abandons itself to the instruction flowing from all sides. But if the man and woman of seventy assume to know all, they have outlived hope; they have renounced aspiration, accepted the actual for the necessary and talked down to the young. Let them then become organs of the Holy Ghost; let them be lovers; let them behold truth. With their eyes uplifted, their wrinkles smoothed, they are perfumed again with hope and power. This old age ought not to creep on a human mind. In nature every moment is new; the past is always swallowed and forgotten; the coming only is sacred. Nothing is secure but life, transition, the energizing spirit. No love can be bound by oath or covenant to secure it against a higher love. No truth is so sublime that it may not be trivial tomorrow in the light of new thoughts. People wish to be settled; only as far as they are unsettled is there any hope for them.

Life is a series of surprises. We do not guess today the mood, the pleasure, the power of tomorrow. . . . Of lower states, of acts of routine and sense, we can tell somewhat; but the masterpieces of God, the total growths and universal movements of the soul, are hidden; they are incalculable. I can know that truth is divine and helpful; but how it shall help me I can have no guess, for *so to be* is the sole inlet of *so to know.* The new position of the advancing man has all the powers of the old, yet has them all new. It carries in its bosom all the energies of the past, yet is itself an exhalation of the morning. I cast away in this new moment all my once hoarded knowledge, as vacant and vain. Now, for the first time, do I seem to know anything rightly. The simplest words—we do not know what they mean except when we love and aspire. . . .

The great man is not convulsible or tormentable; events pass over him without much impression. People say sometimes, "See what I have overcome; see how cheerful I am; see how completely I have triumphed over these black events." Not if they still remember them as black events. True conquest causes the calamity to fade and disappear as an early cloud of insignificant result in a history so large and advancing.

The one thing that we seek with insatiable desire is to forget ourselves, to be surprised out of our propriety, to lose our enduring memory and to do something without knowing how or why; in short to draw a new circle. Nothing great was ever achieved without enthusiasm. The way of life is wonderful; it is by abandonment. . . . "A man," said Oliver Cromwell, "never rises so high as when he knows not whither he is going." Dreams and drunkenness, the use of opium and alcohol are the semblance and counterfeit of this oracular genius, and hence their dangerous attraction for men. For the same reason they ask the aid of wild passions, as in gaming and war, to ape in some manner these flames and generosities of the heart.

Questions for Thought

1. Do you find Emerson's reasons for denying that we can know the true nature of reality convincing? Why or why not?
2. How do you think Jaspers would respond to Emerson's claim about the nature of conversation?
3. Do you agree with Emerson's statement that "one man's justice is another's injustice"? Why or why not?
4. What might be some of the negative consequences of accepting Emerson's position that values are relative? What might be some of the positive consequences?
5. What do you think Emerson means when he says that there is "some principle of fixture or stability in the soul"? Is this statement consistent with his claim that there are no ultimate facts? Defend your answer.

13   Doubts Concerning the Possibility of Knowledge

DAVID HUME

As mentioned in the introduction to the Hume selection in Chapter 1, David Hume (1711–1776) was born in Edinburgh, Scotland. Hume's father owned a small estate, and his mother was the daughter of the president of the Scottish court of session. Hume entered the University of Edinburgh to study law, but when he found that the study of law was not to his liking, he devised his own course of study. After leaving the university and holding several jobs, Hume moved to France in 1734 and wrote his first and longest philosophical text, *A Treatise of Human Nature*. This monumental work was published when he was only twenty-eight years old.

Returning to England and then Scotland, Hume held several minor government positions, spent a year tutoring a mad marquess, and worked as a librarian. He was never able to procure a university appointment, however. When he applied for the chair of moral philosophy at the University of Edinburgh in 1744, he was accused of heresy and denied the appointment. For this reason, among others, Hume became the model of the modern British philosopher—an outspoken, independent thinker who refuses to bow to authority. This image was later reinforced when Hume, who was dying of cancer, refused the last rites of the Church.

Hume produced several important philosophical writings in addition to his *Treatise.* A list of several of these can be found in the introduction to the Hume selection in Chapter 1.

In the following excerpt from *An Inquiry Concerning Human Understanding,* Hume provides a more complex argument for doubting the possibility of knowledge than does Emerson. Hume raises his doubts by examining the ways in which we come to know things and by showing that there is no rational or philosophical justification for accepting knowledge claims about anything that goes beyond our immediate experiences.

Hume begins by dividing all knowledge claims into two types: relations of ideas and matters of fact. Relations of ideas, such as mathematical claims, are produced by demonstrative reasoning. Since they are only statements expressing the necessary relations between ideas or concepts, they are "demonstratively or intuitively certain." However, they make no factual claims about the world in which we live. Matters of fact, on the other hand, are not statements that express the necessary relations between ideas or concepts. Rather, they are either reports about something that we are presently experiencing or else claims about some state of affairs that lies outside our present experiences. Matter-of-fact statements cannot be known by demonstrative reasoning, and they are not certain; however, they are crucial for our continued survival. Without knowledge such as "fire burns" and "milk nourishes," we would not live very long.

Having made this distinction between two kinds of knowledge, Hume examines the reasoning behind matter-of-fact claims. He first argues that all our reasoning concerning matters of fact is based on the relation of cause and effect. This relation allows us to explain how certain events are connected to other events. For example, if our car will not start, we automatically assume that there must be some causal explanation for this occurrence. We then check out several possible reasons why the car will not start, until we find the right one (or we let a mechanic do it for us).

Hume's next step is to ask how we arrive at the knowledge of cause and effect. Since the idea of the effect is in no way necessarily connected to the idea of the cause, it follows that the knowledge of cause and effect cannot be merely a relation of ideas. In other words, the cause cannot be known by demonstrative reasoning; it can be discovered only by experience. This is why in cases where the causal reasoning may be quite complex, as in the case of a car not starting, we often rely on the help of someone who has more experience in such matters.

Having established that knowledge of cause and effect is derived from experience, Hume then seeks the foundation for **conclusions** based on experience. He argues that all such conclusions depend on the belief that the future will resemble the past. If we did not believe this, then we would have no basis for using our past experiences of cause and effect in our present causal reasoning. But how do we know that the future will resemble the past? Hume argues that this belief, like the knowledge of cause and effect, cannot be based on demonstrative reasoning; it cannot be a relation of ideas. Thus, it must be a matter of fact derived from experience. In other words, we believe that the future will resemble the past because in the past the future has resembled the past. With this latter claim, however, Hume thinks he has taken his inquiry into our reasoning concerning matters of fact as far as he possibly can, for he has now reached what philosophers call a **vicious circle.** Our belief in any matter of fact is based on cause and effect, which is based on experience. So far, there is no circle. However, our reliance on experience is based on the belief that the future will resemble the past, which is itself based on experience. For Hume, this vicious circle indicates that there is no rational or theoretical justification for accepting any matter-of-fact knowledge claim. But since matter-of-fact knowledge claims are the only ones that give us information concerning the world around us, Hume concludes that **skepticism** is the only defensible philosophical position. As he says, "The recognition of human blindness and weakness is the result of all philosophy, and this recognition meets us, at every turn, in spite of our endeavors to elude or avoid it."

Questions for Reading

1. What is the difference between a relation of ideas and a matter of fact?
2. What does Hume mean by the relation of cause and effect? Why does he think that all our knowledge of the world is based on this relation?
3. Why does Hume believe that the relation between cause and effect is not a relation of ideas?
4. What is Hume's example of the billiard balls intended to show?
5. How does Hume the philosopher differ from Hume the agent? Why does he distinguish between these two aspects of his life?

DOUBTS CONCERNING THE POSSIBILITY OF KNOWLEDGE

PART I

ALL THE OBJECTS OF HUMAN REASON OR INQUIRY may naturally be divided into two kinds, namely, "Relations of Ideas," and "Matters of Fact." The sciences of Geometry, Algebra, and Arithmetic are of the first kind, as is, in short, every affirmation that is either intuitively or demonstratively certain. *That the square of the hypotenuse is equal to the square of the two sides* is a proposition that expresses a relation between these figures. *That three times five is equal to half of thirty* expresses a relation between these numbers. Propositions of this kind are discoverable by the mere operation of thought, without dependence on what is anywhere existent in the universe. Even if a circle or triangle never existed in nature, the truths demonstrated by Euclid would still forever retain their certainty and evidence.

Matters of fact, which are the second objects of human reason, are not ascertained in the same manner. Nor is our evidence of their truth, however great, of a like nature with the foregoing. The contrary of every matter of fact is still possible, because it can never imply a contradiction and is conceived by the mind with the same facility and distinctness as if ever so conformable to reality. *That the sun will not rise tomorrow* is no less intelligible a proposition and implies no more contradiction than the affirmation *that it will rise*. Thus, it would be useless to attempt to demonstrate its falsehood. Were it demonstratively false, it would imply a contradiction and could never be distinctly conceived by the mind.

It may, therefore, be a subject worthy of curiosity to inquire into the nature of the evidence that assures us of any real existence and matter of fact that goes beyond the present testimony of our senses or the records of our memory. This part of philosophy, it may be noted, has been little cultivated either by the ancients or moderns. Therefore, our doubts and errors in the prosecution of so important an inquiry may be the more excusable while we march through such difficult paths without any guide or direction. They may even prove useful by exciting curiosity and destroying the implicit faith and security that is the bane of all reasoning and free inquiry. The discovery of defects in the common philosophy, if there be such, will not, I presume, be a discouragement. Rather, it will be an incitement, as is usual, to attempt something more full and satisfactory than has yet been proposed to the public.

This is the editor's revised version of a selection from David Hume, An Inquiry Concerning Human Understanding, *Oxford, Clarendon Press, 1777.*

All reasonings concerning matter of fact seem to be founded on the relation of *cause* and *effect*. It is by means of that relation alone that we can go beyond the evidence of our memory and senses. If you were to ask a man why he believes any matter of fact that is absent—for instance, that his friend is in the country or in France—he would give you a reason, and this reason would consist of some other fact, such as a letter received from his friend or the knowledge of his friend's former resolutions and promises. A man finding a watch or any other machine on a desert island would conclude that there had once been men on that island. All our reasonings concerning fact are of the same nature. And here it is constantly supposed that there is a connection between the present fact and whatever is inferred from it. Were there nothing to bind them together, the inference would be entirely precarious. Hearing an articulate voice and rational discourse in the dark assures us of the presence of some person. Why? Because these are effects of the human make and fabric, and they are closely connected with it. If we anatomize all the other reasonings of this nature, we shall find that they are founded on the relation of cause and effect, and that this relation is either near or remote, either direct or collateral. Heat and light are collateral effects of fire, and the one effect may justly be inferred from the other.

If we would satisfy ourselves, therefore, concerning the nature of the evidence that assures us of matters of fact, we must inquire how we arrive at the knowledge of cause and effect.

I shall venture to affirm, as a general proposition that admits of no exception, that the knowledge of this relation is never attained by reasonings *a priori,* but arises entirely from experience, when we find that any particular objects are constantly conjoined with each other. Let an object be presented to a man with the strongest natural reason and abilities—if that object is entirely new to him, he will not be able, by the most accurate examination of its sensible qualities, to discover any of its causes or effects. Adam, though his rational faculties are supposed at first to be entirely perfect, could not have inferred from the fluidity and transparency of water that it would suffocate him, or from the light and warmth of fire that it would consume him. No object ever shows, by the qualities that appear to the senses, either the causes that produced it or the effects that will arise from it. Nor can our reason, unassisted by experience, ever draw any inference concerning real existence and matter of fact.

This proposition—*that causes and effects are discoverable, not by reason, but by experience*—will readily be admitted with regard to objects that we remember as having once been altogether unknown to us. For in such cases we would remember our utter inability to foretell, upon our first contact with those objects, what would arise from them. Present two smooth pieces of marble to a man who has no tincture of natural philosophy, and he will not discern that they will adhere together in such a manner as to require great force to separate them in a direct line, while making so small a resistance to a lateral pressure. Events that bear little **analogy** to the common course of nature are also generally admitted to be known only by experience. For example, no man imagines that the explosion of gunpowder or the attraction of a loadstone could ever be discovered by arguments *a priori*. In like manner, when an effect is supposed to depend upon an intricate machinery or secret structure of parts, we make no difficulty in attributing all our knowledge of it to experience. Who will assert that he can give the ultimate reason why milk or bread is proper nourishment for a man, but not for a lion or tiger?

But at first sight it may not appear that this truth holds for those events that have become familiar to us from our first appearance in the world, or which bear a close analogy to the whole course of nature, or which are supposed to depend on the simple qualities of objects without any secret structure of parts. We are apt to imagine that we could discover these effects by the mere operation of our reason without experience. We fancy that, were we suddenly brought into this world, we could immediately infer that one billiard ball would communicate motion to another upon striking it, and that we do not need to wait for the event in order to pronounce with certainty concerning it. Such is the influence of custom. Where it is strongest it not only covers our natural ignorance, but it even conceals itself, thus seeming not to occur, merely because it is found in the highest degree.

But the following reflections may suffice to convince us that all the laws of nature and all the operations of bodies, without exception, are known only by experience. Were any object presented to us, and were we required to pronounce concerning the effect that will result from it without consulting past observation, in what manner, I ask you, could the mind proceed in this operation? It must invent or imagine some event that it ascribes to the object as its effect; and it is plain that this invention must be entirely arbitrary. The mind can never possibly find the effect in the supposed cause, even by the most accurate scrutiny and examination. For the effect is totally different from the cause and consequently can never be discovered in it. Motion in the second billiard ball is a quite distinct event from motion in the first, and there is nothing in the one to suggest the smallest hint of the other. A stone or piece of metal raised into the air and left without any support immediately falls. But considering the matter *a priori,* is there anything we discover in this situation that can beget the idea of a downward rather than an upward motion, or indeed any other motion, in the stone or metal?

Since the first imagination or invention of a particular effect in all natural operations is arbitrary where we do not consult experience, it is also obvious that the supposed tie or connection between the cause and effect—a tie that would bind them together and render it impossible that any effect other than the imagined one could result from the operation of that cause—is also arbitrary. For instance, when I see a billiard ball moving in a straight line toward another ball, even if motion in the second ball should by accident be suggested to me as the result of their contact or impulse, may I not conceive that a hundred different events could just as well follow from that cause? May not both these balls remain at absolute rest? May not the first ball return in a straight line or leap off from the second in any line or direction? All these suppositions are consistent and conceivable. Why, then, should we give the preference to one that is no more consistent or conceivable than the rest? All our reasonings *a priori* will never be able to show us any foundation for this preference.

In a word, then, every effect is a distinct event from its cause. The effect could not, therefore, be discovered in the cause, and the first invention or conception of the effect, *a priori,* must be entirely arbitrary. And even after it is suggested, the conjunction of it with the cause must appear equally arbitrary, since there are always many other effects which,

to reason, must seem fully as consistent and natural. In vain, therefore, should we pretend to determine any single event, or to infer any cause or effect, without the assistance of observation and experience.

Hence we have discovered the reason why no philosopher who is rational and modest has ever pretended to assign the ultimate cause of any natural operation, or to show distinctly the action of that power which produces any single effect in the universe. It must be confessed that the most that human reason can do is to reduce the principles productive of natural phenomena to a greater simplicity, and to resolve the many particular effects into a few general causes, by means of reasonings from analogy, experience, and observation. But as to the causes of these general causes, we should in vain attempt to discover them, nor will we ever be able to satisfy ourselves by any particular explication of them. These ultimate springs and principles are totally hidden from human curiosity and inquiry. Elasticity, gravity, cohesion of parts, communication of motion by impulse—these are probably the ultimate causes and principles that we will ever discover in nature. And we may esteem ourselves sufficiently happy if, by accurate inquiry and reasoning, we can trace up the particular phenomena to, or near to, these general principles. The most perfect philosophy of the natural kind only staves off our ignorance a little longer, as perhaps the most perfect philosophy of the moral or metaphysical kind serves only to discover larger portions of it. Thus the recognition of human blindness and weakness is the result of all philosophy, and this recognition meets us, at every turn, in spite of our endeavors to elude or avoid it. . . .

PART II

But we have not yet attained any tolerable satisfaction with regard to the question first proposed. Each solution gives rise to a new question as difficult as the foregoing and thus leads us on to further inquiries. When we ask about *the nature of all our reasonings concerning matter of fact,* the proper answer seems to be that they are founded on the relation of cause and effect. When we again ask about *the foundation of all our reasonings and conclusions concerning that relation,* the answer may be stated in one word, *experience.* But if we carry our inquisitiveness further and ask about *the foundation of all conclusions from experience,* this implies a new question that may be even more difficult to solve or explain. Philosophers that give themselves airs of superior wisdom and sufficiency have a hard task when they encounter persons of inquisitive dispositions, persons who push them from every corner to which they retreat, and who are sure at last to bring them to some dangerous dilemma. The best expedient to prevent this confusion is to be modest in our pretensions and even to discover the difficulty ourselves before it is objected to us. By this means we may make a kind of merit of our very ignorance.

I shall content myself in this section with an easy task and shall pretend only to give a negative answer to the question here proposed. I say, then, that even after we have experience of the operations of cause and effect, our conclusions from that experience are *not* founded on reasoning or any process of the understanding. We must endeavor both to explain and to defend this answer.

It must certainly be allowed that nature has kept us at a great distance from all her secrets and has afforded us only the knowledge of a few superficial qualities of objects, while concealing from us those powers and principles on which the influence of these objects entirely depends. Our senses inform us of the color, weight, and consistency of bread, but neither sense nor reason can ever inform us of those qualities that make it fit for the nourishment and support of the human body. Sight or feeling conveys an idea of the actual motion of bodies, but we cannot form the most distant conception of the wonderful force or power that carries on a moving body forever in a continued change of place, and which bodies never lose except by communicating it to others. But notwithstanding this ignorance of natural powers and principles, we always presume when we see like sensible qualities that they have like secret powers, and we expect that effects similar to those that we have experienced will follow from them. If a body of like color and consistency with bread that we have formerly eaten is presented to us, we make no scruple of repeating the experiment and foresee with certainty like nourishment and support. Now this is a process of the mind or thought of which I would willingly know the foundation. It is allowed on all hands that there is no known connection between the sensible qualities and the secret

powers, and, consequently, that the mind is not led to form such a conclusion concerning their constant and regular conjunction by anything which it knows of their nature. As to past *experience,* it can be allowed to give *direct* and *certain* information of those precise objects only, and of the precise period of time that fell under its cognizance. But why this experience should be extended to future times and to other objects which, for all we know, may be only in appearance similar, this is the main question on which I would insist. The bread that I formerly ate nourished me; that is, a body of such sensible qualities was, at that time, endued with such secret powers. But does it follow that other bread must also nourish me at another time, and that like sensible qualities must always be attended with like secret powers? This consequence seems in no way necessary. At least, it must be acknowledged that here a consequence has been drawn by the mind, that a certain step or process of thought has been taken, that an inference has been made that needs to be explained. These two propositions are far from being the same: *I have found that such an object has always been attended with such an effect,* and *I foresee that other objects which are in appearance similar will be attended with similar effects.* I shall allow, if you please, that the one proposition may justly be inferred from the other. I know, in fact, that it always is inferred. But if you insist that the inference is made by a chain of reasoning, I desire you to produce that reasoning. The connection between these propositions is not intuitive. A medium would be required to allow the mind to draw such an inference, if indeed it is to be drawn by reasoning and argument. However, I must confess that the nature of such a medium is beyond my comprehension; and it is incumbent on those who assert that it really exists and is the origin of all our conclusions concerning matter of fact to produce it.

This negative argument must certainly, in process of time, become altogether convincing if many penetrating and able philosophers turn their inquiries this way, and no one is ever able to discover any connecting proposition or intermediate step which supports the understanding in this conclusion. But as the question is still new, a reader must not trust his own penetration so far as to conclude that, because an argument escapes his inquiry, it does not really exist. For this reason it may be necessary to venture upon a more difficult task, and, enumerating all the branches of human knowledge, to try to show that none of them can afford such an argument.

All reasonings may be divided into two kinds, namely, demonstrative reasoning, or that concerning the relation of ideas, and moral reasoning, or that concerning matter of fact and existence. That there are no demonstrative arguments in the case seems evident, since no contradiction is implied in the claim that the course of nature may change and that an object, seemingly like those that we have experienced, may be attended with different or contrary effects. May I not clearly and distinctly conceive that a body, falling from the clouds and which in all other respects resembles snow, has yet the taste of salt or feeling of fire? Is there a more intelligible proposition than to affirm that all the trees will flourish in December and January, and that they will decay in May and June? Now, whatever is intelligible and can be distinctly conceived implies no contradiction, and can never be proved false by any demonstrative argument or abstract reasoning *a priori*.

Therefore, if we are engaged by arguments to put trust in past experience and make it the standard of our future judgment, these arguments must be probable only, that is, such as regard matter of fact and real existence, according to the division mentioned above. But we must recognize that there is no argument of this kind either, if our explication of this species of reasoning be admitted as solid and satisfactory. We have said that all arguments concerning existence are founded on the relation of cause and effect, that our knowledge of that relation is derived entirely from experience, and that all our experimental conclusions proceed upon the supposition that the future will be conformable to the past. To endeavor, therefore, to prove this last supposition by probable arguments, that is, by arguments regarding existence, must be evidently going in a circle and taking that for granted which is the very point in question.

In reality, all arguments from experience are founded on the similarity that we discover among natural objects, a similarity that induces us to expect effects similar to those that we have found to follow from such objects. Although no one but a fool or madman would ever pretend to dispute the authority of experience or to reject this great guide of human life, a philosopher may surely be allowed to have at least enough curiosity to examine the principle of human nature that gives to experience this mighty authority, and that makes us draw advantage from the similarity that nature has placed among different objects. From causes that appear similar, we expect similar effects. This is the sum of all our experimental conclusions. Now it seems evident that, if this conclusion were formed by reason, it would be as perfect at first, and upon one instance, as after a very long course of experience; but the case is far otherwise. Nothing is so alike as eggs are to each other, yet no one, on account of this appearing similarity, expects the same taste and relish in all of them. In the case of any event, it is only after a long course of uniform experiments that we attain a firm reliance and security with regard to that particular event. Now, where is the process of reasoning that, from one instance, draws a conclusion so different from that which it infers from a hundred instances differing in no way from that single one? I propose this question as much for the sake of information as with an intention of raising difficulties. I cannot find, I cannot imagine any such reasoning. But I keep my mind still open to instruction if anyone will vouchsafe to show me what it is.

Should it be said that, from a number of uniform experiments, we *infer* a connection between the sensible qualities and the secret powers, I must confess that this seems the same difficulty, only couched in different terms. The question still occurs, On what process of argument is this *inference* founded? Where is the medium, or the interposing ideas, joining propositions so very different from each other? It is admitted that the color, consistency, and other sensible qualities of bread do not appear, in themselves, to have any connection with the secret powers of nourishment and support. For otherwise we could infer these secret powers from the first appearance of these sensible qualities without the aid of experience, contrary to the belief of all philosophers, and contrary to plain matter of fact. Here, then, is our natural state of ignorance with regard to the powers and influence of all objects. How is this remedied by experience? It only shows us a number of uniform effects resulting from certain objects, and teaches us that those particular objects, at that particular time, were endowed with such powers and forces. When a new object endowed with similar sensible qualities is produced, we expect similar powers and forces, and look for a like effect. From a body of like color and consistency with bread, we expect like nourishment and support. But this surely is a step or progress of the mind that needs to be explained. When a man says, *I have found, in all past instances, such sensible qualities, conjoined with such secret powers,* and when he says, *similar sensible qualities will always be conjoined with similar secret powers,* he is not guilty of a **tautology,** nor are these propositions in any respect the same. You say that the one proposition is an inference from the other; but you must confess that the inference is neither intuitive nor demonstrative. Of what nature is it then? To say that it is experimental is begging the question. For all inferences from experience suppose, as their foundation, that the future will resemble the past and that similar powers will be conjoined with similar sensible qualities. If there be any suspicion that the course of nature may change, and that the past may not be a rule for the future, all experience becomes useless and can give rise to no inference or conclusion. It is impossible, therefore, that any arguments from experience can prove this resemblance of the past to the future, since all these arguments are founded on the supposition of that resemblance. Even though in the past the course of things is ever so regular, that fact alone, without some new argument or inference, does not prove that in the future it will continue to be so. In vain do you pretend to have learned the nature of bodies from your past experience. The secret nature of bodies, and consequently all their effects and influence, may change without any change in their sensible qualities. This happens sometimes, and with regard to some objects. Why may it not happen always, and with regard to all objects? What logic, what process of argument, secures you against this supposition? My practice, you say, refutes my doubts. But you mistake the purport of my question. As an everyday person who acts, I am quite satisfied in the point; but as a philosopher, who has some share of curiosity, I will not say skepticism, I want to learn the foundation of this inference. No reading or inquiry has yet been able to remove my difficulty or to give me satisfaction in a matter of such importance. Can I do better than propose the difficulty to the public, even though, perhaps, I have

small hopes of obtaining a solution? We shall at least, by this means, be sensible of our ignorance, even if we do not augment our knowledge.

I must confess that a man is guilty of unpardonable arrogance if he concludes that, because an argument has escaped his own investigation, it does not really exist. I must also confess that although all the learned for several ages have employed themselves in a fruitless search upon any subject, it may still, perhaps, be rash to conclude positively that the subject must therefore transcend all human comprehension. Even if we examine all the sources of our knowledge and conclude them unfit for such a subject, there may still remain a suspicion that the enumeration is not complete or that the examination is not accurate. But with regard to the present subject, there are some considerations that seem to remove all this accusation of arrogance or suspicion of mistake.

It is certain that the most ignorant and stupid peasants, as well as infants and even brute beasts, improve by experience and learn the qualities of natural objects by observing the effects that result from them. When a child has felt the sensation of pain from touching the flame of a candle, he will be careful not to put his hand near any candle, expecting a similar effect from a cause that is similar in its sensible qualities and appearance. If you assert, therefore, that the understanding of the child is led into this conclusion by any process of argument or ratiocination, I must justly require you to produce that argument, and you cannot have any pretense to refuse so equitable a demand. You cannot say that the argument is abstruse and may possibly escape your inquiry, since you confess that it is obvious to a mere infant. Therefore, if you hesitate a moment, or if, after reflection, you produce an intricate or profound argument, you thereby give up the question, confessing that it is not reasoning that engages us to suppose that the past resembles the future, or to expect similar effects from causes that appear similar. This is the proposition that I intended to enforce in the present section. If I am right, I do not pretend to have made any mighty discovery. And if I am wrong, I must indeed acknowledge myself to be a very backward scholar, since I cannot now discover an argument that, it seems, was perfectly familiar to me long before I was out of my cradle.

Questions for Thought

1. Can you think of examples of knowledge claims that would be classified as matters of fact? What about ones that would be classified as relations of ideas?
2. Do you find Hume's argument about cause and effect persuasive? If not, how would you go about showing him that he was wrong?
3. Can you provide an example, other than the billiard ball example, that would support Hume's position?
4. How do you think Hume would respond to the claim that God necessarily exists?
5. How would you define the term *skeptic*? To what extent would you describe yourself as a skeptic?

14   The Elimination of Metaphysics

ALFRED JULES AYER

Alfred Jules Ayer (1910–1989), the leading proponent of **logical positivism** in Britain, was born in London. The son of a timber merchant, Ayer attended Eton College and Oxford University. After graduation in 1932, he spent some time at the University of Vienna, where he became familiar with the logical positivist movement. Returning to Britain in 1933, Ayer taught at Oxford University for several years before working in military intelligence during World War II.

After the war, Ayer served briefly as dean of Wadham College at Oxford before being named Grote Professor of the Philosophy of Mind and Logic at the University of London. Ayer held this position for thirteen years before returning to Oxford in 1959, where he was named Wykeham Professor of Logic. He remained at Oxford until his retirement in 1983. Ayer, who had been made a fellow of the British Academy in 1952, was knighted in 1970. He died in London after a long respiratory ailment on June 27, 1989. Ayer's book *Language, Truth, and Logic,* from which the following selection is taken, brought him international recognition when it was published in 1936. His later writings include *The Foundations of Empirical Knowledge* (1940), *The Problems of Knowledge* (1956), *The Origins of Pragmatism* (1968), *Russell and Moore: The Analytical Heritage* (1971), *The Central Questions of Philosophy* (1973), *Part of My Life* (1977), *More of My Life* (1984), and *Wittgenstein* (1985).

In the following selection, Ayer uses a different route than Hume, the route of the logical analysis of statements, to call certain of our knowledge claims into question. While his **skepticism** is not as extensive as Hume's, he argues that certain knowledge claims, what he calls metaphysical statements or **"pseudo-propositions,"** are meaningless.

Underlying Ayer's argument is Hume's belief that all genuine knowledge claims can be divided into two types: tautologies (Hume calls these *relations of ideas*) and empirical statements (Hume's matter-of-fact statements). A tautology, as we saw when discussing Hume's relations of ideas, is a statement that is logically and necessarily true. Empirical statements, on the other hand, are not known by logical reasoning. Referring to such statements as hypotheses, Ayer claims that no empirical statement can be conclusively proven. To say that an empirical statement is true is to assert probability and not necessity.

This latter claim about the nature of empirical statements leads to a crucial concept in Ayer's argument, the concept of verifiability. If empirical statements cannot be proven true or false by logical reasoning, how are we able to distinguish true empirical statements from false ones? Ayer says that a true empirical statement is one that has been verified by experience, by observations of some kind, whereas a false empirical statement is one that cannot be verified. He then goes on to argue that if any statement is to qualify as an empirical statement, it must be potentially, if not actually, verifiable; that is, the person making the statement must know "what observations would lead him, under certain conditions, to accept the proposition as being true, or reject it as being false."

Having argued that a genuine knowledge claim must be either a tautology or an empirical statement, Ayer examines the nature of metaphysical statements, such as "the Absolute enters into, but is itself incapable of, evolution and progress." He first notes that such statements seem to be making claims about some actually existing thing, in this case the "Absolute," and thus they are not tautologies. Yet, since such statements are not even potentially verifiable, they do not seem to qualify as empirical statements, either. This leads Ayer to conclude that such statements are meaningless. They are pseudo-propositions, propositions that seem to be making a factual claim but are in fact nonsensical.

Toward the end of this selection, Ayer suggests that many metaphysical statements are the result of linguistic confusion. For example, he believes that the metaphysical beliefs in **substance** and Being arose from the mistaken assumption that there must be an actually existing entity corresponding to every word that can be used grammatically as the subject of a sentence. Like many other modern philosophers, Ayer suggests that if we eliminate linguistic confusion, we will eliminate many of the concepts and problems that have traditionally plagued philosophical thinking.

Questions for Reading

1. What does Ayer mean by "metaphysics"? Why does he think metaphysics ought to be eliminated?
2. What, according to Ayer, is the essential difference between a genuine proposition and a pseudo-proposition? What examples of pseudo-propositions does Ayer provide?
3. How does Ayer explain the concept of verifiability?
4. What is Ayer's example of mountains on the moon intended to show? Why would this example no longer work to demonstrate his point?
5. What, according to Ayer, is the origin of most metaphysical assertions? How does a metaphysician differ from a poet?

THE ELIMINATION OF METAPHYSICS

THE TRADITIONAL DISPUTES OF PHILOSOPHERS are, for the most part, as unwarranted as they are unfruitful. The surest way to end them is to establish beyond question what should be the purpose and method of a philosophical enquiry. And this is by no means so difficult a task as the history of philosophy would lead one to suppose. For if there are any questions which science leaves it to philosophy to answer, a straightforward process of elimination must lead to their discovery.

We may begin by criticising the metaphysical thesis that philosophy affords us knowledge of a reality

From Alfred Jules Ayer, Language, Truth and Logic, *Dover Publications, 1952. Reprinted by permission of Dover Publications.*

transcending the world of science and common sense. Later on, when we come to define **metaphysics** and account for its existence, we shall find that it is possible to be a metaphysician without believing in a transcendent reality; for we shall see that many metaphysical utterances are due to the commission of logical errors, rather than to a conscious desire on the part of their authors to go beyond the limits of experience. But it is convenient for us to take the case of those who believe that it is possible to have knowledge of a transcendent reality as a starting-point for our discussion. The arguments which we use to refute them will subsequently be found to apply to the whole of metaphysics.

One way of attacking a metaphysician who claimed to have knowledge of a reality which transcended the phenomenal world would be to enquire from what **premises** his propositions were deduced. Must he not begin, as other men do, with the evidence of his senses? And if so, what valid process of reasoning can possibly lead him to the conception of a transcendent reality? Surely from empirical premises nothing whatsoever concerning the properties, or even the existence, of anything superempirical can legitimately be inferred. But this objection would be met by a denial on the part of the metaphysician that his assertions were ultimately based on the evidence of his senses. He would say that he was endowed with a faculty of intellectual **intuition** which enabled him to know facts that could not be known through sense-experience. And even if it could be shown that he was relying on empirical premises, and that his venture into a non-empirical world was therefore logically unjustified, it would not follow that the assertions which he made concerning this non-empirical world could not be true. For the fact that a **conclusion** does not follow from its putative premise is not sufficient to show that it is false. Consequently one cannot overthrow a system of transcendent metaphysics merely by criticising the way in which it comes into being. What is required is rather a criticism of the nature of the actual statements which comprise it. And this is the line of argument which we shall, in fact, pursue. For we shall maintain that no statement which refers to a "reality" transcending the limits of all possible sense-experience can possibly have any literal significance; from which it must follow that the labours of those

who have striven to describe such a reality have all been devoted to the production of nonsense.

It may be suggested that this is a proposition which has already been proved by Kant. But although Kant also condemned transcendent metaphysics, he did so on different grounds. For he said that the human understanding was so constituted that it lost itself in contradictions when it ventured out beyond the limits of possible experience and attempted to deal with things in themselves. And thus he made the impossibility of a transcendent metaphysic not, as we do, a matter of logic, but a matter of fact. He asserted, not that our minds could not conceivably have had the power of penetrating beyond the phenomenal world, but merely that they were in fact devoid of it. And this leads the critic to ask how, if it is possible to know only what lies within the bounds of sense-experience, the author can be justified in asserting that real things do exist beyond, and how he can tell what are the boundaries beyond which the human understanding may not venture, unless he succeeds in passing them himself. As Wittgenstein says, "in order to draw a limit to thinking, we should have to think both sides of this limit,"[1] a truth to which Bradley gives a special twist in maintaining that the man who is ready to prove that metaphysics is impossible is a brother metaphysician with a rival theory of his own.[2]

Whatever force these objections may have against the Kantian doctrine, they have none whatsoever against the thesis that I am about to set forth. It cannot here be said that the author is himself overstepping the barrier he maintains to be impassable. For the fruitlessness of attempting to transcend the limits of possible sense-experience will be deduced, not from a psychological hypothesis concerning the actual constitution of the human mind, but from the rule which determines the literal significance of language. Our charge against the metaphysician is not that he attempts to employ the understanding in a field where it cannot profitably venture, but that he produces sentences which fail to conform to the conditions under which alone a sentence can be literally significant. Nor are we ourselves obliged to talk nonsense in order to show that all sentences of a certain type are necessarily devoid of literal significance. We need only formulate the criterion which enables us to test whether a sentence expresses a genuine proposition about a matter of fact, and then point out that the sentences under consideration fail to satisfy it. And this we shall now proceed to do. We shall first of all formulate the criterion in somewhat vague terms, and then give the explanations which are necessary to render it precise. The criterion which we use to test the genuineness of apparent statements of fact is the criterion of verifiability. We say that a sentence is factually significant to any given person, if, and only if, he knows how to verify the proposition which it purports to express—that is, if he knows what observations would lead him, under certain conditions, to accept the proposition as being true, or reject it as being false. If, on the other hand, the putative proposition is of such a character that the assumption of its truth, or falsehood, is consistent with any assumption whatsoever concerning the nature of his future experience, then, as far as he is concerned, it is, if not a tautology, a mere pseudo-proposition. The sentence expressing it may be emotionally significant to him; but it is not literally significant. And with regard to questions the procedure is the same. We enquire in every case what observations would lead us to answer the question, one way or the other; and, if none can be discovered, we must conclude that the sentence under consideration does not, as far as we are concerned, express a genuine question, however strongly its grammatical appearance may suggest that it does.

As the adoption of this procedure is an essential factor in the argument of this book, it needs to be examined in detail.

In the first place, it is necessary to draw a distinction between practical verifiability, and verifiability in principle. Plainly we all understand, in many cases believe, propositions which we have not in fact taken steps to verify. Many of these are propositions which we could verify if we took enough trouble. But there remain a number of significant propositions, concerning matters of fact, which we could not verify even if we chose; simply because we lack the practical means of placing ourselves in the situation where the relevant observations could be made. A simple and familiar example of such a proposition is the proposition that there are mountains on the farther side of the moon.[3] No rocket has yet been invented which would enable me to go and look at the farther side of the moon, so that I am unable to decide the matter by actual

observation. But I do know what observations would decide it for me, if, as is theoretically conceivable, I were once in a position to make them. And therefore I say that the proposition is verifiable in principle, if not in practice, and is accordingly significant. On the other hand, such a metaphysical pseudo-proposition as "the Absolute enters into, but is itself incapable of, evolution and progress,"[4] is not even in principle verifiable. For one cannot conceive of an observation which would enable one to determine whether the Absolute did, or did not, enter into evolution and progress. Of course it is possible that the author of such a remark is using English words in a way in which they are not commonly used by English-speaking people, and that he does, in fact, intend to assert something which could be empirically verified. But until he makes us understand how the proposition that he wishes to express would be verified, he fails to communicate anything to us. And if he admits, as I think the author of the remark in question would have admitted, that his words were not intended to express either a tautology or a proposition which was capable, at least in principle, of being verified, then it follows that he has made an utterance which has no literal significance even for himself.

A further distinction which we must make is the distinction between the "strong" and the "weak" sense of the term "verifiable." A proposition is said to be verifiable, in the strong sense of the term, if, and only if, its truth could be conclusively established in experience. But it is verifiable, in the weak sense, if it is possible for experience to render it probable. In which sense are we using the term when we say that a putative proposition is genuine only if it is verifiable?

It seems to me that if we adopt conclusive verifiability as our criterion of significance, as some positivists have proposed,[5] our argument will prove too much. Consider, for example, the case of general propositions of law—such propositions, namely, as "arsenic is poisonous"; "all men are mortal"; "a body tends to expand when it is heated." It is of the very nature of these propositions that their truth cannot be established with certainty by any finite series of observations. But if it is recognised that such general propositions of law are designed to cover an infinite number of cases, then it must be admitted that they cannot, even in principle, be verified conclusively. And then, if we adopt conclusive verifiability as our criterion of significance, we are logically obliged to treat these general propositions of law in the same fashion as we treat the statements of the metaphysician.

In face of this difficulty, some positivists[6] have adopted the heroic course of saying that these general propositions are indeed pieces of nonsense, albeit an essentially important type of nonsense. But here the introduction of the term "important" is simply an attempt to hedge. It serves only to mark the authors' recognition that their view is somewhat too paradoxical, without in any way removing the **paradox.** Besides, the difficulty is not confined to the case of general propositions of law, though it is there revealed most plainly. It is hardly less obvious in the case of propositions about the remote past. For it must surely be admitted that, however strong the evidence in favour of historical statements may be, their truth can never become more than highly probable. And to maintain that they also constituted an important, or unimportant, type of nonsense would be unplausible, to say the very least. Indeed, it will be our contention that no proposition, other than a tautology, can possibly be anything more than a probable hypothesis. And if this is correct, the principle that a sentence can be factually significant only if it expresses what is conclusively verifiable is self-stultifying as a criterion of significance. For it leads to the conclusion that it is impossible to make a significant statement of fact at all.

Nor can we accept the suggestion that a sentence should be allowed to be factually significant if, and only if, it expresses something which is definitely confutable by experience.[7] Those who adopt this course assume that, although no finite series of observations is ever sufficient to establish the truth of a hypothesis beyond all possibility of doubt, there are crucial cases in which a single observation, or series of observations, can definitely confute it. But, as we shall show later on, this assumption is false. A hypothesis cannot be conclusively confuted any more than it can be conclusively verified. For when we take the occurrence of certain observations as proof that a given hypothesis is false, we presuppose the existence of certain conditions. And though, in any given case, it may be extremely improbable that

this assumption is false, it is not logically impossible. We shall see that there need be no self-contradiction in holding that some of the relevant circumstances are other than we have taken them to be, and consequently that the hypothesis has not really broken down. And if it is not the case that any hypothesis can be definitely confuted, we cannot hold that the genuineness of a proposition depends on the possibility of its definite confutation.

Accordingly, we fall back on the weaker sense of verification. We say that the question that must be asked about any putative statement of fact is not, Would any observations make its truth or falsehood logically certain? but simply, Would any observations be relevant to the determination of its truth or falsehood? And it is only if a negative answer is given to this second question that we conclude that the statement under consideration is nonsensical. . . .

This criterion seems liberal enough. In contrast to the principle of conclusive verifiability, it clearly does not deny significance to general propositions or to propositions about the past. Let us see what kinds of assertion it rules out.

A good example of the kind of utterance that is condemned by our criterion as being not even false but nonsensical would be the assertion that the world of sense-experience was altogether unreal. It must, of course, be admitted that our senses do sometimes deceive us. We may, as the result of having certain sensations, expect certain other sensations to be obtainable which are, in fact, not obtainable. But, in all such cases, it is further sense-experience that informs us of the mistakes that arise out of sense-experience. We say that the senses sometimes deceive us, just because the expectations to which our sense-experience give rise do not always accord with what we subsequently experience. That is, we rely on our senses to substantiate or confute the judgements which are based on our sensations. And therefore the fact that our perceptual judgments are sometimes found to be erroneous has not the slightest tendency to show that the world of sense-experience is unreal. And, indeed, it is plain that no conceivable observation, or series of observations, could have any tendency to show that the world revealed to us by sense-experience was unreal. Consequently, anyone who condemns the sensible world as a world of mere appearance, as opposed to reality, is saying something which, according to our criterion of significance, is literally nonsensical.

An example of a controversy which the application of our criterion obliges us to condemn as fictitious is provided by those who dispute concerning the number of **substances** that there are in the world. For it is admitted both by monists, who maintain that reality is one substance, and by pluralists, who maintain that reality is many, that it is impossible to imagine any empirical situation which would be relevant to the solution of their dispute. But if we are told that no possible observation could give any probability either to the assertion that reality was one substance or to the assertion that it was many, then we must conclude that neither assertion is significant. . . .

There is no need for us to give further examples of the operation of our criterion of significance. For our object is merely to show that philosophy, as a genuine branch of knowledge, must be distinguished from metaphysics. We are not now concerned with the historical question how much of what has traditionally passed for philosophy is actually metaphysical. We shall, however, point out later on that the majority of the "great philosophers" of the past were not essentially metaphysicians, and thus reassure those who would otherwise be prevented from adopting our criterion by considerations of piety. . . .

It should be mentioned here that the fact that the utterances of the metaphysician are nonsensical does not follow simply from the fact that they are devoid of factual content. It follows from that fact, together with the fact that they are not *a priori* propositions. . . . [A] *priori* propositions, which have always been attractive to philosophers on account of their certainty, owe this certainty to the fact that they are tautologies. We may accordingly define a metaphysical sentence as a sentence which purports to express a genuine proposition, but does, in fact, express neither a tautology nor an empirical hypothesis. And as tautologies and empirical hypotheses form the entire class of significant propositions, we are justified in concluding that all metaphysical assertions are nonsensical. Our next task is to show how they come to be made. The use

of the term "substance," to which we have already referred, provides us with a good example of the way in which metaphysics mostly comes to be written. It happens to be the case that we cannot, in our language, refer to the sensible properties of a thing without introducing a word or phrase which appears to stand for the thing itself as opposed to anything which may be said about it. And, as a result of this, those who are infected by the primitive superstition that to every name a single real entity must correspond assume that it is necessary to distinguish logically between the thing itself and any, or all, of its sensible properties. And so they employ the term "substance" to refer to the thing itself. But from the fact that we happen to employ a single word to refer to a thing, and make that word the grammatical subject of the sentences in which we refer to the sensible appearances of the thing, it does not by any means follow that the thing itself is a "simple entity," or that it cannot be defined in terms of the totality of its appearances. It is true that in talking of "its" appearances we appear to distinguish the thing from the appearances, but that is simply an accident of linguistic usage. Logical analysis shows that what makes these "appearances" the "appearances of" the same thing is not their relationship to an entity other than themselves, but their relationship to one another. The metaphysician fails to see this because he is misled by a superficial grammatical feature of his language.

A simpler and clearer instance of the way in which a consideration of grammar leads to metaphysics is the case of the metaphysical concept of Being. The origin of our temptation to raise questions about Being, which no conceivable experience would enable us to answer, lies in the fact that, in our language, sentences which express existential propositions and sentences which express attributive propositions may be of the same grammatical form. For instance, the sentences "Martyrs exist" and "Martyrs suffer" both consist of a noun followed by an intransitive verb, and the fact that they have grammatically the same appearance leads one to assume that they are of the same logical type. It is seen that in the proposition "Martyrs suffer," the members of a certain species are credited with a certain attribute, and it is sometimes assumed that the same thing is true of such a proposition as "Martyrs exist." If this were actually the case, it would, indeed, be as legitimate to speculate about the Being of martyrs as it is to speculate about their suffering. But, as Kant pointed out,[8] existence is not an attribute. For, when we ascribe an attribute to a thing, we covertly assert that it exists: so that if existence were itself an attribute, it would follow that all positive existential propositions were tautologies, and all negative existential propositions self-contradictory; and this is not the case.[9] So that those who raise questions about Being which are based on the assumption that existence is an attribute are guilty of following grammar beyond the boundaries of sense.

A similar mistake has been made in connection with such propositions as "Unicorns are fictitious." Here again the fact that there is a superficial grammatical resemblance between the English sentences "Dogs are faithful" and "Unicorns are fictitious," and between the corresponding sentences in other languages, creates the assumption that they are of the same logical type. Dogs must exist in order to have the property of being faithful, and so it is held that unless unicorns in some way existed they could not have the property of being fictitious. But, as it is plainly self-contradictory to say that fictitious objects exist, the device is adopted of saying that they are real in some non-empirical sense—that they have a mode of real being which is different from the mode of being of existent things. But since there is no way of testing whether an object is real in this sense, as there is for testing whether it is real in the ordinary sense, the assertion that fictitious objects have a special non-empirical mode of real being is devoid of all literal significance. It comes to be made as a result of the assumption that being fictitious is an attribute. And this is a fallacy of the same order as the fallacy of supposing that existence is an attribute, and it can be exposed in the same way.

In general, the postulation of real non-existent entities results from the superstition, just now referred to, that, to every word or phrase that can be the grammatical subject of a sentence, there must somewhere be a real entity corresponding. For as there is no place in the empirical world for many of these "entities," a special non-empirical world is invoked to house them. To this error must be attributed, not only the utterances of a Heidegger, who

bases his metaphysics on the assumption that "Nothing" is a name which is used to denote something peculiarly mysterious,[10] but also the prevalence of such problems as those concerning the reality of propositions and universals whose senselessness, though less obvious, is no less complete.

These few examples afford a sufficient indication of the way in which most metaphysical assertions come to be formulated. They show how easy it is to write sentences which are literally nonsensical without seeing that they are nonsensical. And thus we see that the view that a number of the traditional "problems of philosophy" are metaphysical, and consequently fictitious, does not involve any incredible assumptions about the psychology of philosophers.

Among those who recognise that if philosophy is to be accounted a genuine branch of knowledge it must be defined in such a way as to distinguish it from metaphysics, it is fashionable to speak of the metaphysician as a kind of misplaced poet. As his statements have no literal meaning, they are not subject to any criteria of truth or falsehood: but they may still serve to express, or arouse, emotion, and thus be subject to ethical or **aesthetic** standards. And it is suggested that they may have considerable value, as means of moral inspiration, or even as works of art. In this way, an attempt is made to compensate the metaphysician for his extrusion from philosophy.[11]

I am afraid that this compensation is hardly in accordance with his deserts. The view that the metaphysician is to be reckoned among the poets appears to rest on the assumption that both talk nonsense. But this assumption is false. In the vast majority of cases the sentences which are produced by poets do have literal meaning. The difference between the man who uses language scientifically and the man who uses it emotively is not that the one produces sentences which are incapable of arousing emotion, and the other sentences which have no sense, but that the one is primarily concerned with the expression of true propositions, the other with the creation of a work of art. Thus, if a work of science contains true and important propositions, its value as a work of science will hardly be diminished by the fact that they are inelegantly expressed. And similarly, a work of art is not necessarily the worse for the fact that all the propositions comprising it are literally false. But to say that many literary works are largely composed of falsehoods, is not to say that they are composed of pseudo-propositions. It is, in fact, very rare for a literary artist to produce sentences which have no literal meaning. And where this does occur, the sentences are carefully chosen for their rhythm and balance. If the author writes nonsense, it is because he considers it most suitable for bringing about the effects for which his writing is designed.

The metaphysician, on the other hand, does not intend to write nonsense. He lapses into it through being deceived by grammar, or through committing errors of reasoning, such as that which leads to the view that the sensible world is unreal. But it is not the mark of a poet simply to make mistakes of this sort. There are some, indeed, who would see in the fact that the metaphysician's utterances are senseless a reason against the view that they have aesthetic value. And, without going so far as this, we may safely say that it does not constitute a reason for it.

It is true, however, that although the greater part of metaphysics is merely the embodiment of humdrum errors, there remain a number of metaphysical passages which are the work of genuine mystical feeling; and they may more plausibly be held to have moral or aesthetic value. But, as far as we are concerned, the distinction between the kind of metaphysics that is produced by a philosopher who has been duped by grammar, and the kind that is produced by a mystic who is trying to express the inexpressible, is of no great importance: what is important to us is to realise that even the utterances of the metaphysician who is attempting to expound a vision are literally senseless; so that henceforth we may pursue our philosophical researches with as little regard for them as for the more inglorious kind of metaphysics which comes from a failure to understand the workings of our language.

NOTES

1. *Tractatus Logico-Philosophicus,* preface.
2. Bradley, *Appearance and Reality,* 2nd ed., p. 1.
3. This example has been used by Professor Schlick to illustrate the same point.
4. A remark taken at random from *Appearance and Reality,* by F. H. Bradley.
5. E.g., M. Schlick, "Positivismus und Realismus," *Erkenntnis,* vol. 1, 1930. F. Waismann, "Logische Analyse des Warscheinlichkeitsbegriffs," *Erkenntnis,* vol. 1, 1930.
6. E.g., M. Schlick, "Die Kausalität in der gegenwärtigen Physik," *Naturwissenschaft,* vol. 19, 1931.
7. This has been proposed by Karl Popper in his *Logik der Forschung.*
8. Vide *The Critique of Pure Reason,* "Transcendental Dialectic," book 2, chap. 3, sec. 4.
9. This argument is well stated by John Wisdom, *Interpretation and Analysis,* pp. 62, 63.
10. Vide *Was ist Metaphysik,* by Heidegger: criticized by Rudolf Carnap in his "Überwindung der Metaphysik durch logische Analyse der Sprache," *Erkenntnis,* vol. 2, 1932.
11. For a discussion of this point, see also C. A. Mace, "Representation and Expression," *Analysis,* vol. 1, no. 3; and "Metaphysics and Emotive Language," *Analysis,* vol. 2, nos. 1 and 2.

Questions for Thought

1. How would you define *metaphysics*? Do you believe that metaphysical knowledge is possible? Why or why not?
2. Can you think of any examples of pseudo-propositions other than the ones mentioned by Ayer?
3. Do you agree with Ayer that in order to be meaningful, a proposition must be verifiable? Defend your answer.
4. Does Ayer's account of the origin of metaphysical assertions seem plausible? Why or why not?
5. Do you accept any propositions as true that, according to Ayer's criterion, could be classified as metaphysical? If so, on what grounds do you accept these propositions?

15   Situated Knowers

ELIZABETH ANDERSON

Elizabeth Anderson (b. 1959), who is the John Rawls Professor of Philosophy and Women's Studies at the University of Michigan, Ann Arbor, was born in Boston. She received her B.A. in philosophy from Swarthmore College in 1981 and her Ph.D. in philosophy from Harvard University in 1987. Her research interests include democratic theory, equality in political philosophy and American law, the ethical limits of markets, theories of value and rational choice, the philosophy of John Stuart Mill, and feminist epistemology and philosophy of science.

Anderson has presented papers at numerous conferences in the United States and abroad, and she has appeared as a guest speaker on public radio. In addition, she is the author of *Values in Ethics and in Economics*, which was published by Harvard University Press in 1993, as well as various articles on value theory, democratic theory, philosophy of law, and feminist epistemology and philosophy of science.

In the following excerpt from a lengthy article published in the *Stanford Encyclopedia of Philosophy*, Anderson clearly summarizes many of the questions that feminist epistemologists have raised about the possibility of objective knowledge. Focusing on the different ways in which we are situated to what we know and to other knowers, Anderson points out that our situatedness has a definite impact on what we claim to know. As she says, "What is known, and the way it is known, . . . reflects the situation or perspective of the knower."

Although some of the ways in which knowledge is situated are not gender specific—such as the knower's physical location in relation to what he or she claims to know and the knower's background beliefs and worldviews—Anderson points out ways that are. She notes that men and women are not only assigned to distinct social roles but they are also expected to follow different norms of behavior and bodily comportment.

After describing the various gender differences that exist in the world in which we live, Anderson raises numerous questions about how these differences situate the knower in relation to what he or she knows. In other words, just as a person's perspective of an object depends on the viewer's physical location in relation to the object, might not the same be true about gender differences? Given that women and men are assigned different social roles and are expected to follow different norms of behavior and "body language," might not these gender differences also impact the knowledge claims that women and men make about the world around them?

Toward the end of the selection, Anderson says that feminist epistemologists do not claim that simple propositional statements, such as "2 + 2 = 4," are gendered. However, she also points out that although such simple statements are often taken as the paradigm of knowledge by mainstream epistemologists, they do not comprise the totality—or even the most important—of the knowledge claims that we make. And in the case of these other, more important claims, gender differences must be taken into account. When we do take them into account, the claim that one's knowledge is "objective" becomes much more problematic. As Anderson concludes, "Feminist epistemology does not rule out in advance the possibility or desirability of objective knowledge. It does raise new questions about objectivity."

Questions for Reading

1. What, according to Anderson, does it means to say that a knower is situated?
2. What are some of the ways in which people in general are situated in relation to what is known and to other knowers?
3. How does Anderson explain the difference between one's sex and one's gender?
4. What are some of the differences between the gender roles and the gender norms for men and women? How do these differences affect what and how one knows?
5. What, according to Anderson, is the difference between an "androcentric" representation and a "gynocentric" representation? What examples does she use to illustrate this difference?
6. Which type of knowledge claims does Anderson not take to be gendered? Why does she think that examining such claims is not particularly helpful?
7. What does it mean to say that knowledge is objective? What are some of the questions that feminist epistemology raises concerning the possibility of objective knowledge?

FEMINIST EPISTEMOLOGY CONCEIVES OF KNOWERS as situated in particular relations to what is known and to other knowers. What is known, and the way that it is known, thereby reflects the situation or perspective of the knower. Here we are concerned with *claims* to know, temporarily bracketing the question of which claims are true or warranted.

SITUATED KNOWLEDGE IN GENERAL

Consider how people may understand the same object in different ways that reflect the distinct relations in which they stand to it.

Embodiment. People experience the world by using their bodies, which have different constitutions and are differently located in space and time. In virtue of their different physical locations, observers who stand in front of an object have different information about it than observers who have a distant but bird's eye view of it.

First-person vs. third-person knowledge. People have first-personal access to some of their own bodily and mental states, yielding direct knowledge of phenomenological facts about what it is like for them to be in these states. Third parties may know these states only by interpreting external symptoms, imaginative

projection, or obtaining their testimony. People also have knowledge *de se* about themselves, expressed in the form "*I* am F *here, now.*" This is distinct in character and inferential role from propositional knowledge having the same content, which does not use indexicals.

Emotions, attitudes, interests, and values. People often represent objects in relation to their emotions, attitudes and interests. A thief represents a lock as a frustrating obstacle while its owner represents the lock as a comforting source of security.

Personal knowledge of others. People have different knowledge of others, in virtue of their different personal relationships to them. Such knowledge is often tacit, incompletely articulated, and intuitive. Like the knowledge it takes to get a joke, it is more an interpretive skill in making sense of a person than a set of propositions. (The German language usefully marks this as the distinction between *Erkenntnis* and *Wissenschaft.*) Because people behave differently toward others, and others interpret their behavior differently, depending on their personal relationships, what others know of them depends on these relationships.

Know-how. People have different skills, which may also be a source of different propositional knowledge. An expert dog handler knows how to elicit more interesting behavior from a dog than a novice

From Elizabeth Anderson, "Feminist Epistemology and Philosophy of Science," The Stanford Encyclopedia of Philosophy (Summer 2004 Edition), Edward N. Zalta (ed.). Reprinted by permission of Elizabeth S. Anderson, John Rawls Professor of Philosophy, University of Michigan, Ann Arbor.

does. Such know-how expresses a more sophisticated understanding of dogs on the part of the expert, and also generates new phenomena about dogs for investigation.

Cognitive Styles. People have different styles of investigation and representation. What looks like one phenomenon to a lumper may look like three to a splitter.

Background beliefs and worldviews. People form different beliefs about an object, in virtue of different background beliefs. In virtue of the different background beliefs against which they interpret a patient's symptoms, a patient may think he is having a heart attack while his doctor believes he just has heartburn. Differences in global metaphysical or political worldviews (**naturalism,** theism, liberalism, Marxism) may also generate different beliefs about particulars on a more comprehensive scale.

Relations to other inquirers. People may stand in different epistemic relations to other inquirers—for example, as informants, interlocutors, students—which affects their access to relevant information and their ability to convey their beliefs to others.

These kinds of situatedness affect knowledge in several ways. They influence knowers' access to information and the terms in which they represent what they know. They bear on the form of their knowledge (articulate/implicit, formal/informal, by acquaintance or description, and so forth). They affect their attitudes toward their beliefs (certainty/doubt, dogmatic/open to revision), their standards of justification (relative weights they give to different epistemic values such as predictive power and consilience, amount, sources, and kinds of evidence they require before they accept a claim, etc.), and the authority with which they lay claim to their beliefs and can offer them to others. Finally, they affect knowers' assessment of which claims are significant or important.

SOCIAL SITUATION

Many of these ways in which knowers' physical and psychological relations to the world affect what and how they know are familiar and extensively studied by cognitive psychology, naturalized epistemology, and philosophy of science. Feminist epistemology takes such studies a further step by considering how the social location of the knower affects what and how she knows. It can thus be seen as a branch of social epistemology. An individual's social locations consist of her ascribed social identities (gender, race, sexual orientation, ethnicity, caste, kinship status, etc.) and social roles and relationships (occupation, political party membership, etc.). Partly in virtue of their different ascribed identities, individuals occupy different social roles that accord them different powers, duties, and role-given goals and interests. They are subject to different norms that prescribe different virtues, habits, emotions, and skills that are thought to be appropriate for these roles. They also acquire different subjective identities. Subjective identification with one's social groups can take several forms. One may simply know oneself to have certain ascribed identities. One may accept or endorse these identities, actively affirming the norms and roles associated with them. Or one may regard one's social identities as oppressive (if, say, one's identity is cast by society as evil, contemptible, or disgusting), yet see one's fate as tied with the groups with which one is identified, and commit oneself to collective action with other members of those groups to overcome that oppression.

GENDER AS A MODE OF SOCIAL SITUATION

Most feminist theorists distinguish between sex and gender. Sex comprises the biological differences between males and females. Gender is what societies make of sexual differences: the different roles, norms, and meanings they assign to men and women and the things associated with them on account of their real or imagined sexual characteristics. Gender thus has several dimensions.

Gender roles. Men and women are assigned to distinct social roles. For example, most societies reserve political and military offices mostly for men, and assign women most childrearing responsibilities.

Gender norms. Men and women are expected to comply with different norms of behavior and bodily comportment. For example, men are expected to be assertive and athletic; women, deferential and modest. Gender norms are tailored to gender roles: men and women are expected to conform to those norms that make them fit for their gender roles (whether or not they actually occupy those roles).

Gendered traits and virtues. Psychological traits are considered "masculine" and "feminine" if they dispose their bearers to comply with the gender norms assigned to men and women, respectively. "Masculine" traits are therefore regarded as virtues in men and (often) vices in women, while "feminine" traits are regarded as vices in men and virtues in women.

Gendered performance/behavior. Many feminist theorists, often influenced by **postmodernism,** have come to stress the contextual and performative aspects of gender. Rather than viewing masculinity and femininity as fixed traits, expressed in every social context, these theorists represent human beings as more flexible and disposed to enact both "masculine" and "feminine" behaviors in different contexts. The man who avoids tenderly comforting a crying baby in the presence of women may do so when alone. Rather than viewing masculinity and femininity as manifested only in behavior within fixed, distinct gender roles, they can be seen as contrasting styles of performance in almost any role. Female body builders strive to show off their muscles in a "feminine" way.

Gender identity. A person's ascribed gender identity—how others identify him or her—may not match his or her subjective gender identity—the sense that one is "really" a man or a woman. Subjective gender identity includes all of the ways one might understand oneself to be a man or a woman. One could identify with any subset of gender norms, roles, and traits ascribed to the gender of which one sees oneself as a member, while repudiating others. One could even repudiate them all, but still identify oneself as a man or a women in terms of what one sees as distinct roles men and women ought to play in bringing about a just future (one that may or may not include gender distinctions). One could, as many feminists do, understand one's gender identity as a predicament shared by all with the same ascribed identity, and thus as a basis for collective action to change the very basis of one's gender identity. One could embrace an **"androcentric"** identity, including both "feminine" and "masculine" roles, norms, and traits, decline to view oneself in gender polarized terms at all, or play with gender identities in a postmodernist spirit.

Gender symbolism. Animals and inanimate objects may be placed in a gendered field of representation through conventional association, imaginative projection, and metaphorical thinking. Thus, the garage is regarded as "male" space, the kitchen, "female"; male deer are said to have "harems"; pears are seen as "womanly," assault rifles as "manly."

GENDERED KNOWLEDGE

By bringing together the general account of situated knowledge with the account of gender as a kind of social situation, we can now generate a catalogue of ways in which what people know, or think they know, can be influenced by their own gender (roles, norms, traits, performance, identities), other people's genders, or by ideas about gender (symbolism). Each mode of gendered knowledge raises new questions for epistemology.

*The **phenomenology** of gendered bodies.* People's bodies are not just differently sexed; they are differently gendered. Early child socialization trains boys' and girls' bodies to different norms of bodily comportment. In the U.S., these norms stress physical freedom, aggressive play, large motor skills, informal and relaxed posture, and indifference to clothing, neatness and appearance in boys; physical constraint, subdued play, small motor skills, formal and modest posture, and self-consciousness about clothing, neatness and appearance for girls. Once internalized, such norms profoundly affect the phenomenology of embodiment. They inform men's and women's distinct first-personal knowledge of what it is like to inhabit a body, to express capacities unique to one sex or another (e.g., breast feeding), and to have experiences that are manifested through different body parts in differently sexed bodies (e.g., orgasm). They also cause men's and women's experiences of gendered behaviors that both can perform to differ—in comfort, fluidity, feelings of "naturalness" or novelty, self-consciousness, confidence, awkwardness, shame, and so forth. One question these facts raise for feminist epistemology is to what extent dominant models of the world, especially of the relation between minds and bodies, have seemed compelling because they conform to a male or masculine phenomenology.

Gendered first-personal knowledge de se. It is one thing to know what sexual harassment is, and how to identify it in a case described in third-personal terms. It is another to come to the recognition "*I* have been sexually harassed." Many women who are able to see that women in general are disadvantaged have difficulty recognizing themselves as sharing women's predicament. The problems of *de se* knowledge are particularly pressing for feminist theory, because it is committed to theorizing in ways that women can use to improve their lives. This entails that women be able to recognize themselves and their lives in feminist accounts of women's predicament. Feminist epistemology is therefore particularly concerned with investigating the conditions of feminist self-understanding and the social settings in which it may arise—feminist consciousness-raising sessions, men's studies classes, and so forth.

Gendered emotions, attitudes, interests, and values. Feminist theory defines a representation as *androcentric* if it depicts the world in relation to male or masculine interests, emotions, attitudes or values. A "male" interest is an interest a man has, in virtue of the goals given to him by social roles that are designated as especially appropriate for men to occupy, or in virtue of his subjective gender identity. A "masculine" interest is an interest a man has in virtue of attitudes or psychological dispositions that are thought specifically appropriate to men. Such attitudes and interests structure the cognition of those who have them. For example, a representational scheme that classifies women as either "babes," "dogs," "whores," or (grand)mothers reflects the androcentric attitudes, interests, and values of single heterosexual adolescent men who view women in terms of their fantasized eligibility for sexual intercourse with them. A representation is *gynocentric* if it depicts the world in relation to female or feminine interests, emotions, attitudes or values. When a man is described as an "eligible bachelor," this reflects the gynocentric perspective of a heterosexual, single woman interested in marriage. An interest, emotion, attitude, or value might be symbolically gendered even if men and women do not manifest it differently. For example the ethics

of care represents moral problems in terms of symbolically feminine values—values culturally associated with women's gender roles. It thus can qualify as a symbolically gynocentric perspective, even if men and women do not differ in their propensity to represent moral problems in its terms, and are equally able to act accordingly. From a performative perspective, this shows that men can behave in "feminine" ways, too. Feminist epistemology raises numerous questions about these phenomena. Can situated emotional responses to things be a valid source of knowledge about them? Do dominant practices and conceptions of science and scientific method reflect an androcentric perspective, or a perspective that reflects other dominant positions, as of race and colonial rule? Do mainstream philosophical conceptions of objectivity, knowledge, and reason reflect an androcentric perspective? How would the conceptual frameworks of particular sciences change if they reflected women's interests?

Knowledge of others in gendered relationships. Gender norms differentially structure the social spaces to which men and women are admitted, as well as the presentation of self to others. As performative theories of gender stress, men manifest their male identity, and women their female identity, differently alone than in mixed company, and differently in these settings than in gender-segregated contexts. Male and female inquirers therefore have access to different information about others. Male and female ethnographers may be admitted to different social spaces. Even when admitted to the same social spaces, their presence has different effects on those being observed, because they do not stand in the same social relationships to their subjects. Physical objects do not behave differently depending on whether a man or a woman is observing them. But human beings do behave differently according to their beliefs about the gender of who is observing them. Research that elicits information about others through personal contact between the researchers and the research subjects therefore raises the question of how findings might be influenced by the gendered relations between researchers and subjects, and whether gender-inclusive research teams are in a better position to detect this. **Ethnography,** which derives propositional knowledge of others from personal knowledge of native informants in long-term, often intimate relationships, raises these issues most acutely. Similar issues arise in survey research, clinical research, and human experimentation.

Gendered skills. Some skills are labeled masculine or feminine because men and women need them specifically to perform their respective gender roles, and they are not generically useful for almost any role (as walking, talking, and seeing are). It takes a particular knowledge of small children to know how to comfort them, a particular knowledge of soldiers to know how to whip up their morale. Although men and women alike may acquire and exercise these skills, they are considered the peculiar responsibility of one or the other gender. Men and women may therefore have differential access to such skill-based knowledge. To the extent that the skill is perceived by the agent as the proper province of the "other" gender, he or she may have a difficult time seeing himself or herself perform it confidently and fluidly, and this inability to self-identify with the task can impair performance. The feedback effects of the phenomenology of gendered embodiment and *de se* knowledge of one's own subjective gender identity can therefore influence the exercise of gendered skills. To the extent that a skill is perceived by others as the proper province of one gender, others may grant or withhold acknowledgment of an agent's expertise. If the successful exercise of the skill requires that others be willing to accept it as a competent performance—as in the cases of comforting children or raising soldiers' morale—others' gender-based readiness or refusal to grant expertise to an agent in exercising that skill can be a self-fulfilling prophecy. These phenomena raise various questions for epistemology. Does the "masculine" symbolism of certain scientific skills, such as of assuming an "objective" stance toward nature, interfere with the integration of women into science? Do actually or symbolically "feminine" skills aid the acquisition of scientific knowledge?

Gendered cognitive styles. Some theorists believe that men and women have different cognitive styles. Whether or not this is true, cognitive styles are gender symbolized. Deductive, analytic, atomistic, acontextual, and quantitative cognitive styles are labeled "masculine," while intuitive, synthetic, holistic, contextual and qualitative cognitive styles

are labeled "feminine." Such associations are not wholly arbitrary, the way blue is gendered male and pink, female. For example, it is seen as masculine to make one's point by means of argument, feminine to make one's point by means of narrative. Argument is commonly cast as an adversarial mode of discourse, in which one side claims vindication by vanquishing the opposition. Such pursuit of dominance follows the competitive pattern of male gender roles in combat, athletics, and business. Narrative is a seductive mode of discourse, persuading by an enticing invitation to take up the perspective of the narrator, which excites one's imagination and feeling. Its operations are more like love than war, and thereby follow a mode of persuasion thought more suitable for women. These phenomena raise numerous epistemological questions: does the quest for "masculine" prestige by using "masculine" methods distort practices of knowledge acquisition? Are some kinds of sound research unfairly ignored because of their association with "feminine" cognitive styles? Do "feminine" cognitive styles yield knowledge that is inaccessible or harder to achieve by "masculine" means?

Gendered background beliefs and worldviews. We have seen above how men and women have access to different phenomenological knowledge, *de se* knowledge, know-how, and personal knowledge of others, in virtue of their gender. They also tend to represent the world in different terms, in virtue of their gendered interests, attitudes, emotions and values, and perhaps also (although this is a matter of controversy among feminist theorists) in virtue of different cognitive styles. These differences create different background webs of belief against which information to which men and women have in principle equal access may be processed. Representational schemes that are functional for different gender roles and gendered attitudes make different kinds of information salient. In traditional domestic settings, women tend to notice dirt that men don't. This is not because women have an especially sensitive sensory apparatus. It is because they have a role which designates the females of the household as the ones who have to clean up. Male surgeons have no difficulty maintaining much higher degrees of vigilance about contamination in an operating room than would ever be warranted in housecleaning. Besides making different kinds of information salient to men and women, their different background knowledge may lead them to interpret commonly accessed information differently. A man might read a woman's demure smile as a coy come-on, where another woman may interpret it as her polite and defensive reaction to unwanted attention from him. Such differences can spring from differential access to phenomenological knowledge. The male and female observers imaginatively project themselves into her situation, inferring her feelings from the feelings they think underlie her body language. Because men's and women's phenomenologies of embodiment are different—most men are not in the habit of smiling as a defense against unwanted attention from women—the man may narcissistically imagine the smile as relaxed and spontaneous, whereas the woman may suspect it is forced. Here are a few epistemological questions raised by these phenomena. Are there epistemic obstacles to men's ability to know when they are raping or sexually harassing women, or to legal institutions recognizing this, insofar as they confine their thinking within a "masculine" perspective? More generally, do the unexamined sexist or androcentric background beliefs of scientists cause them to generate sexist theories about women, despite their adherence to ostensibly objective scientific methods? More generally still, how might the social practices of science be organized so that variations in background beliefs of inquirers function as a resource rather than an obstacle to scientific success?

Relations to other inquirers. Gender differences in knowledge and background beliefs can be reduced if men and women participate in inquiry together. Each gender can take on testimony what the other can acquire through direct experience. Each may also learn how to exercise imaginative projection more effectively, and to take up the perspective of the other gender. However, gender norms influence the terms on which men and women communicate. In many contexts, women are not allowed to speak or even show up, or their questions, comments, and challenges are ignored, interrupted, and systematically distorted, or they aren't accepted as experts. Gendered norms of conversational interaction and epistemic authority thus influence the ability of knowledge practices to incorporate the knowledge

and experience of men and women into their processes of discovery and justification. Feminist epistemologists are therefore interested in exploring how gender norms distort the dissemination of testimony and relations of cognitive authority among inquirers and how the social relations of inquirers could be reformed, especially with regard to the allocation of epistemic authority, so as to enable more successful practices of inquiry.

PROBLEMS OF AND APPROACHES TO GENDERED SITUATED KNOWLEDGE

Mainstream epistemology takes as paradigms of knowledge simple propositional knowledge about matters in principle equally accessible to anyone with basic cognitive and sensory apparatus: "2 + 2 = 4"; "grass is green"; "water quenches thirst." Feminist epistemology does not claim that such knowledge is gendered. But examination of such examples is not particularly helpful for answering the epistemological problems that arise specifically in feminist theory and practice. What is it to know that I am a woman? What is it like to be sexually objectified? Why is it that men and women so often have dramatically divergent understandings of what happened in their sexual encounters? How can we arrange scientific practices so that science and technology serve women's interests? These kinds of questions make other kinds of knowledge salient for feminist epistemology: phenomenological knowledge, *de se* knowledge, knowledge of persons, know-how, moral knowledge, knowledge informed by emotions, attitudes, and interests. These kinds of knowledge are often gendered, and they can influence the propositional claims people are disposed to form and accept. This has critical implications for mainstream epistemological conceptions of knowledge, insofar as the latter are based on false generalizations drawing only from examples of ungendered knowledge.

Feminist epistemologists stress the situatedness or perspective-relativity of much knowledge. They do not thereby embrace epistemological **relativism.** To regard some knowledge claim or form of understanding as situated in a perspective is not to claim that the perspective yields true beliefs or satisfactory understandings (not even "for" those taking up the perspective). It is not to claim that perspectives can only be judged in their own terms, or that no perspectives are better than others, or that one cannot take a more objective view of the phenomena than that taken up in one or another perspective. It is not to claim that all knowledge necessarily reflects some peculiar non-universalizable relation of a subset of knowers to the object of knowledge. What attention to situated knowledge does do is enable questions to be raised and addressed that are difficult even to frame in epistemologies that simply assume that gender, and the social situation of the knower more generally, is irrelevant to knowledge. How are the knowledge claims generated by gendered perspectives related to one another? Can men take up a gynocentric perspective, and women, an androcentric perspective? Or are there epistemological barriers to such perspective crossing? Are certain perspectives epistemically privileged? Is there any way to construct a more objective perspective out of differently gendered perspectives? What is the relation of an objective perspective, if one is possible, to gendered perspectives? What would be the point of achieving such a perspective? Would the achievement of such an objective perspective make possible or desirable the elimination of gendered perspectives? Feminist epistemology does not rule out in advance the possibility or desirability of objective knowledge. It does raise new questions about objectivity.

Questions for Thought

1. How are the ways that you are a situated knower different from those of your best friend as a situated knower?
2. To what extent do you think your background beliefs and worldviews affect your assessment of what is going on in the world around you?
3. Do you agree with what Anderson says about the differences between gender roles and norms? Defend your answer.
4. How much of what you say or believe could be classified as "androcentric"? How much of it could be classified as "gynocentric"?
5. Do you believe that men and women have different cognitive styles? Why or why not?
6. How would you define the concept of "objectivity"? How much of what you know would you classify as "objective knowledge"?

Chapter 4

Ethics

Introductory Remarks

WHILE YOUR JOURNEY DOWN THE PATH of thinking about self-identity could easily have led you to the path of thinking about creation and reality, it could also have led you to the path that we are about to consider: the path of ethical or moral thinking. It is easy to see that thinking about who you are can lead to questions about what you ought to do. Indeed, in the history of philosophy, deliberations about the nature of human existence have frequently led to deliberations about the nature of morality.

Whether or not you were led to this path during your earlier journey down the path of thinking about self-identity, you have no doubt been on the path of moral thinking many times. At a very early age, you were most likely taught a set of rules about how you were expected to act in certain situations. For example, your parents may have told you not to hit your little sister or brother. Or they may have told you to share your toys with friends who came to your house to play. In addition to moral rules dealing with individual types of activity or with particular people, you were probably also taught more general ethical rules and moral principles. In Western society, some of the best-known general moral rules include the Ten Commandments, while the Golden Rule, "Do unto others as you would have them do unto you," is one of the best-known moral principles.

As a child, you may have merely accepted these moral rules or principles because of the authority of the person who taught them. (Of course, that did not mean you always followed them.) At some point in your life, however, you probably asked yourself why you should follow these rules and not others. For example, you may have asked yourself *why* you should not hit your little brother, especially if he were really bugging you. You might have even reasoned that a better moral rule would be "Never hit your little brother unless he really deserves it."

Even if you never engaged in such moral reasoning, you probably had occasion to observe that not everyone was taught the same set of moral rules that you were. Your first reaction to this discovery may have been to claim that your moral rules were obviously the right ones and that the other person's rules were obviously wrong; however,

326

deeper reflection may have shaken this initial confidence. You might have wondered exactly what it was that made your moral rules right and the rules that differed from yours wrong.

Questions such as these have been as important in the history of philosophy as have questions about the nature of self-identity, the nature of creation and reality, and the nature of knowledge and truth. For example, the ancient Greek philosopher Socrates, who was mentioned in the introduction to Chapter 1 of this book, was extremely interested in the nature of morality. In Plato's dialogues, in which he often appears, Socrates is portrayed as the Athenian gadfly who goes about stinging his fellow citizens out of their moral complacency. In addition, we are also told that Socrates' quest for the good life, the only type of life that he considered worth living, ultimately led to his arrest, trial, and execution. (Of course, being the philosophical hero that he was, Socrates remained loyal to his philosophical and moral principles to the very end.)

But this concern with moral questions and principles, which has been a major focus of Western thinking, did not originate with Socrates. It was already evident in the earlier writings of Judaism and **Zoroastrianism,** two religions often characterized by their concern with ethical principles. One has only to glance at the so-called priestly writings—the last part of Exodus and all of Leviticus, Numbers, and Deuteronomy— to discover a host of moral commandments and regulations. And the sacred writings of Zoroastrianism include a fully developed code of ethics that requires a righteous person to practice good thoughts, good words, and good deeds. Likewise, a cursory reading of the Sermon on the Mount shows that this Judeo-Zoroastrian-Socratic concern with the ethical dimension of human existence was just as important to Jesus as it was to Socrates and earlier religious writers. A similarly cursory reading of the history of Western philosophy shows that the concern with moral rules and principles preoccupied most of the major philosophical writers. From Aristotle's golden mean to Kant's **categorical imperative,** from Ayer's emotivism to Singer's call for animal liberation, traditional Western philosophers have attempted to formulate ethical theories and/or to resolve moral problems. This concern with the ethical dimension of human existence was, moreover, not limited to Western religious and philosophical traditions. The Jain notion of *ahimsa* (noninjury), the Buddha's call for his disciples to follow a Middle Way between **asceticism** and **hedonism,** the Confucian formulation of a code regulating proper behavior among members of society, and Radhakrishnan's claim that ethics must be grounded in religious insight—these are just a few examples of ethical or moral thinking from non-Western sources.

Overview of Selections

In this chapter, I have included fourteen selections from diverse times and cultures that deal with ethical or moral issues. The selections in the first part focus on the important question of how we determine what we ought to do. Each of these writers attempts to describe the source and nature of moral action or behavior. In so doing, most of them formulate and defend what they claim to be the most basic moral rule or principle.

While the selections in the second part focus on many of the same issues, what distinguishes these latter selections is that each of them constitutes a radical critique of traditional Western moral theories. The first three selections suggest that traditional Western theories have erred in limiting the sphere of moral concern, the next two argue that traditional theories have ignored the moral insights of women, and the final selection calls into question the very concept of moral responsibility.

In the first selection of the chapter, the ancient Greek philosopher Aristotle argues that the ultimate human good is *eudaimonia* (living well or happiness) and that in order to live well, we must act in accordance with rational principle. For Aristotle, this is possible only if we possess certain virtues—intellectual virtues that we are taught and moral virtues that we acquire through habit. In the second selection, the ancient Chinese philosopher Mencius agrees with Aristotle that human morality consists of acting in accordance with virtue, but he believes that virtue is neither taught nor acquired through habit. Rather, Mencius believes that human beings are born with certain innate moral qualities, such as a sense of right and wrong. These innate qualities will naturally lead one to act or behave morally, unless they are perverted by external influences.

In the third selection, the German philosopher Immanuel Kant disputes Aristotle's claim that the ultimate human good is living well or happiness, while arguing that consequences are totally irrelevant in determining the moral worth of an action. Rather, Kant claims that good will is not only the ultimate human good but also the factor that determines whether an action has moral worth. For Kant, this means that in order to be moral, an act must be universalizable; that is, it must be motivated by what he calls the *categorical imperative.*

The British philosopher Jeremy Bentham, in the fourth selection, offers an account of the origin and nature of morality that differs significantly from all the previous accounts. Bentham argues that the moral value of an action is determined solely by its consequences, specifically by whether it increases pleasure or decreases pain. For Bentham, *utility* is the most basic moral principle.

In the next selection, the Cuban philosopher Enrique José Varona stresses the communal nature of morality by arguing that morality is based on a feeling of solidarity that one develops through one's interaction with other people. This analysis of the nature of morality leads Varona to claim that the morality or immorality of an action is determined by the principle of social solidarity: An action is moral if it is in conformity with social solidarity; it is immoral if it is not.

In the sixth selection, Sarvepalli Radhakrishnan, a modern Indian philosopher, argues that morality cannot be divorced from **metaphysics**—that is, from a philosophical conception of the ultimate nature of reality. He then argues that all attempts to ground ethics in a this-worldly, humanistic metaphysics (of the sort endorsed by Aristotle, Bentham, and Varona) are destined to fail because they do not take into account the true nature of human existence. In opposition to all the preceding philosophers, Radhakrishnan believes that true morality must be based on certain universal religious insights.

The final selection of the first part emphasizes the importance of extending moral concern beyond the realm of human interests. The Alsatian philosopher and religious thinker Albert Schweitzer claims that the highest moral values are compassion and reverence for life. For Schweitzer, the good is that which preserves and advances life (in any form), while evil is whatever destroys or hinders life.

The selections in the second part, as mentioned earlier, constitute radical critiques of much of traditional Western moral thinking. First, whereas traditional thinking (especially Christian and Kantian thinking) has often affirmed the existence of absolute moral values, the first two selections in this section claim that there is no single universally valid moral code or set of values. David Wong, a Chinese-American philosopher, argues that extreme **relativism** (namely, the view that all moral values have equal worth and that one is never justified in judging others) is self-defeating, but he does argue in favor of adopting a qualified moral relativism. Friedrich Nietzsche, a nineteenth-century German philosopher, traces the history or **genealogy** of morality and notes that every great people has created and followed its own moral system. He claims that all these systems can be classified into two basic categories—**master morality** and **slave morality**—while also claiming that modern Western moral thinking is essentially a slave morality, that is, a morality that encourages herd mentality rather than self-affirmation and creativity.

Second, whereas traditional moral thinking has often been *anthropocentric*—that is, it has focused principally on humans as subjects of moral concern—the third and fourth selections in the second part of this chapter suggest that moral concern should be extended to all living things. Although Schweitzer reached a similar conclusion in the last selection of the first section, these readings seem to go beyond Schweitzer by extending moral concern to the earth itself. They also introduce important moral principles that are not generally found in traditional Western thinking. Ed (Eagle Man) McGaa discusses the Native American concept of *Mitakuye Oyasin,* a concept that stresses the brotherhood and sisterhood of everything that lives. He also contrasts the Native American attitude toward the earth with the attitude of the European settlers who came to North America. Aldo Leopold agrees with McGaa that ethical concern should be extended to the land. However, whereas McGaa's extension of moral concern to the earth is based on Native American spirituality, Leopold justifies this extension by appealing to the discoveries of the science of ecology.

The next two selections, those by Gilligan and Daly, consist of critiques of traditional Western morality from the standpoint of women. Each of these writers also offers her own vision of the type of morality that should displace the male-dominated, or patriarchal, morality that currently exists. Gilligan argues that traditional Western morality has emphasized moral values typically associated with men, such as **autonomy** and equality, while devaluing other desirable moral traits, such as concern, caring, and community, that have been typically associated with women. However, in giving voice to the moral experience of women, Gilligan asserts that the moral insights of women complement the moral insights of men. In contrast to Gilligan, Daly argues that traditional Western morality is beyond redemption—indeed, that it is inextricably linked to rape, genocide, and war. For this reason, she calls for a transformation of human consciousness and experience, a transformation that will allow us to displace traditional morality with a morality free from domination or oppression.

Finally, in the last selection of the chapter, John Hospers examines several criteria of moral responsibility that have been offered by philosophers. After concluding that none of these criteria is wholly adequate, Hospers argues that there are good reasons to believe that people are never responsible for what they do. This conclusion, of course, represents the broadest possible challenge to morality. For, if Hospers is right, all moral principles, from Kant's categorical imperative to Leopold's land ethic, would ultimately be ineffective in altering human behavior. Indeed, if Hospers is right, the path of thinking about morality would be, to a large extent, a dead-end path.

Contemporary Applications

In thinking about contemporary applications for this chapter, I am faced with a different problem than with earlier chapters. There, the principal problem was thinking of examples of how rather abstract philosophical issues were related to everyday life. Here, the problem is choosing which of the numerous moral issues confronting us to discuss.

Let's begin with a rather simple issue: whether you should cheat on a test. In thinking about this issue, you decide to ask one of your friends what he believes. He tells you that you should act on the basis of the following rule: "One should cheat only when it is highly probable that one won't get caught." If you choose to adopt your friend's rule, then your decisions about whether to cheat on specific tests will be based on your assessment of the likelihood of getting caught. If the likelihood of getting caught is low, you will feel justified in cheating; if the likelihood of getting caught is high, you will refrain from cheating. In the latter case, what motivates your decision not to cheat is simply the fear of getting caught. As should be obvious, whether to cheat on tests is not a moral issue for your friend.

However, you have some qualms about your friend's rule, and you decide to ask another friend what she believes. She tells you that you should not cheat on a test because "cheating is always wrong." Think about how the word *wrong* is used in this friend's rule about cheating. Unlike your first friend's rule, her rule is clearly intended to make a moral claim. Think also about how these two friends would likely react to an admission that you had cheated on a test. The first friend probably would ask you whether you got caught cheating. Hearing that you did not, he would likely give you a high five and say, "Way to go!" On the other hand, the second friend would probably judge that you had done something wrong, and she may decide that she has a moral obligation to report what you have done. But whether she reports you or not, it is likely that she will have negative feelings about you. Her verbal response could well be "I'm really disappointed in you."

While this moral issue may seem somewhat trivial, many of the other moral issues that you face clearly are not. Consider, for example, the serious moral issues revolving around the question of when, if ever, killing is justified. As I am writing this, abortion (at least in the first two trimesters of a pregnancy) and capital punishment are both legally permissible in the United States. However, there is strong disagreement over whether either of them is *morally* right. Indeed, using arguments involving legal, moral, and/or theological reasoning, many groups are trying desperately to have either or both of these things outlawed.

What exactly is your position on the issues of abortion and capital punishment?

More important, what are your reasons for believing what you believe on these issues?

These are difficult issues, indeed. Unfortunately, there are many more moral issues that are just as difficult as these two. Limiting our discussion solely to issues involving justified killing, other issues immediately come to mind. One such issue is euthanasia, or assisted suicide. In 1939, after suffering from throat cancer for more than fifteen years, Sigmund Freud asked his doctor to give him a lethal dose of morphine. The doctor complied, and Freud ended his life. But was what Freud's doctor did morally right?

Being a typical American meat eater, I must confess that I have a fondness for burgers and steaks. However, my daughter Hannah has been a strict vegetarian (for essentially moral reasons) since she was in the fourth grade. My son Dylan, who is in high school and who also loves burgers and steaks, recently asked me if I had ever killed anything. I told him that when I was about his age, I killed rabbits, squirrels, and birds for food. He was shocked that I had done such a thing, but it did make him feel better. What motivated him to ask this question was that he was feeling guilty about the cells that he had accidentally killed during an experiment in his biology class. While many of our moral debates about justified killing are limited to the discussion of the justified killing of humans, these examples show that this discussion can easily be extended to issues involving animals as well. When, if ever, are we justified in intentionally killing animals?

Although the writers in this chapter do not focus on such specific moral issues, several of them do describe general moral principles, such as the categorical imperative and the **principle of utility,** that can help us decide how to deal with these and other moral issues. Moreover, other writers discuss related problems—for example, whether moral values are relative—that have a bearing on how we respond to particular moral issues.

How Do We Determine What We Ought to Do?

The Proper Function of Man and Its Relation to the Good Life

1

ARISTOTLE

Aristotle (384–322 B.C.E.), who was born in northern Greece in the city of Stagira, was the son of the court physician to Amyntas II, the king of Macedon. His father died when Aristotle was a young boy, and he was placed under the control of a guardian. At the age of seventeen, Aristotle was sent to Athens to study at Plato's Academy, and he remained there until Plato's death in 347 B.C.E. After Plato's death, Aristotle moved to

Assos, where he lived under the protection of the tyrant Hermias of Atarneus and where he married Pythias, Hermias' niece and adopted daughter.

In 345 B.C.E., Aristotle went to the island of Lesbos, and he remained there for the next three years. During this time, he did much of the research that was to make him the most important biological scientist until the Renaissance. He left the island of Lesbos when he was summoned to the Macedonian court at Pella to become the tutor to the king's son, the future Alexander the Great. After this three-year appointment, Aristotle lived in his hometown of Stagira for several years before returning to Athens around 335 B.C.E. While in Athens, he founded his own school of philosophy, the Lyceum. When Alexander died in 323 B.C.E., however, political conditions in Athens forced Aristotle to flee to Chalcis on the island of Euboea. He died there the following year.

Aristotle made important contributions to many areas of philosophy and science. His writings include *Physica* (*Physics*), *De Caelo* (*On the Heavens*), *De Generatione et Corruptione* (*On Generation and Corruption*), *De Anima* (*On the Soul*), *Historia Animalium* (*The History of Animals*), *De Partibus Animalium* (*On the Parts of Animals*), *De Generatione Animalium* (*On the Generation of Animals*), *Metaphysica* (*Metaphysics*), *Ethica Nicomachea* (*Nicomachean Ethics*), *Politica* (*Politics*), *Rhetorica* (*Rhetoric*), *De Poetica* (*Poetics*), and several treatises on logic collectively referred to as the *Organon*.

In the following selection from his *Nicomachean Ethics,* Aristotle examines several important questions concerning the nature of morality. After noting that the good is defined as that at which things aim, he attempts to discover the highest good of human existence. He argues that this highest good must be something that is desired for its own sake. Then, after examining several possibilities, Aristotle claims that this highest good is happiness, or "living well" (the Greek word is *eudaimonia*). Unlike goods such as honor, wealth, and pleasure, which are desired at least in part as a means to happiness, happiness has no end beyond itself.

Having argued that happiness is the highest good of human existence, Aristotle turns to the question of the nature of happiness. In what exactly does happiness consist? Observing that the goodness of anything is connected to its function (for example, the goodness of a sculptor is to sculpt, while the goodness of an eye is to see), Aristotle attempts to determine the function of man. Since he believes that the function of man must be something uniquely human, he denies that this function can be either the life of nutrition and growth (which even plants possess) or the life of sensation (which man shares with animals). Rather, it lies in a life lived according to reason—that is, "an activity of soul in accordance with rational principle, or at least not without it." Arguing further that excellence consists of performing one's function well (for example, the excellence of a flute player consists of playing the flute well), Aristotle claims that human excellence consists of living fully in accord with rational principle. In other words, human excellence is defined as "an activity of the soul in accordance with virtue." One must be careful, however, not to be misled by this definition. Although Aristotle defines human excellence as an activity of the soul, he makes it clear that one cannot achieve excellence without having certain external aids as well. Noble birth, family prosperity, and even personal beauty are prerequisites of human goodness.

Aristotle concludes the present selection by examining the nature of virtue and asking how one becomes virtuous. First, after noting that the soul can be distinguished into three aspects—one wholly irrational, one wholly rational, and one capable of following the commands of reason—Aristotle says that two types of virtues can also be distinguished. The first type is what he calls intellectual virtues. Intellectual virtues, such as intelligence and wisdom, are fostered by teaching and must be developed over a long period of time. The second type is the moral virtues, such as generosity and self-control. Like intellectual virtues, moral virtues are not implanted by nature but must be developed over time. However, rather than being the direct outcome of teaching, moral virtues are formed by habit. One develops the virtue of generosity by acting generously, the virtue of courage by acting courageously. Given the importance of habituation for developing the moral virtues, Aristotle ends by stressing the importance of one's early childhood environment. As he forcefully says, "Thus it is no small matter which habits are instilled in us in early childhood; on the contrary, this makes a considerable difference, or rather all the difference."

Questions for Reading

1. What, according to Aristotle, is the highest good of human existence?
2. What are the three basic types of human life identified by Aristotle? How do the three basic types of human life differ from one another?
3. What, according to Aristotle, is the function of being human? Why does he choose this function rather than another?
4. How does Aristotle use the term *soul*? What are the three aspects of the soul that he identifies?
5. What are the basic differences between intellectual virtues and moral virtues? What are the examples of each type that Aristotle provides?
6. How, according to Aristotle, do we develop moral virtues? Why is early childhood so important?

BOOK I

EVERY ART AND EVERY SCIENTIFIC INQUIRY, as well as every action and purpose, may be said to aim at some good. Hence the good has been rightly defined as that at which all things aim. But it is clear that there is a difference in the ends at which things aim. In some cases the activity is the end; in other cases the end is some result beyond the activity. . . .

As there are various actions, arts, and sciences, it follows that their ends are also various. Thus the end of medicine is health, the end of shipbuilding is a ship, the end of strategy is victory, and the end of economics is wealth. . . .

If it is true in the sphere of action that there is an end which we desire for its own sake, an end for the sake of which we desire everything else, . . . it is clear that this end will be the good, indeed the highest good. Does it not follow then that the knowledge of this highest good is of great importance for the conduct of life? With knowledge of this good, wouldn't we, like archers who have a target at which to aim, be more likely to hit upon what is right? But, if this is the case, we must endeavor to comprehend, at least in outline, what this highest good is. . . .

This is the editor's revised version of a selection from Aristotle, The Nicomachean Ethics, *translated by J. E. C. Welldon, P.D., reprinted by Prometheus Books, 1987.*

All knowledge and every activity aims at some good. . . . But what is the highest good that can be obtained by action? As for its name there is, I believe, general agreement. The masses and the cultured classes agree in calling it happiness, and believe that "to live well" or "to do well" is the same thing as "to be happy." But as to the nature of happiness, they do not agree. The masses do not give the same account of it as do the philosophers. The masses define happiness as something visible and palpable, such as pleasure, wealth, or honor. Different people give different definitions of it, and often the same person gives different definitions at different times. For example, when a person has been ill, he says that it is health; when he is poor, he says that it is wealth. And if the person is conscious of his own ignorance, he envies people who proclaim grand ideas that he cannot comprehend. Some *philosophers*,[1] on the other hand, have held that, besides these various goods, there is an absolute good that is the cause of the goodness in them all. . . .

[I]t does not seem unreasonable that people should derive their conception of the good or of happiness from men's lives. Thus ordinary or vulgar people conceive it to be pleasure, and this explains why they approve a life of enjoyment. For there are basically three types of life—the sensual life, the political life, and the speculative life. Now the masses are absolutely slavish in their tastes, preferring the life of brute beasts. However, they meet with consideration because so many persons in authority share the tastes of Sardanapalus.[2] Cultivated and politically active people, on the other hand, identify happiness with honor, as honor is the general end of political life. But honor seems too superficial to be the highest good that we are seeking. For honor seems to depend more upon the people who pay it, than it does upon the person to whom it is paid. And we have an intuitive feeling that the good is something that is proper to a man himself, something that cannot easily be taken away from him. It seems too that the reason why men seek honor is that they may be confident of their own goodness. Accordingly they seek it at the hands of the wise and of those who know them well, and

they seek it on the ground of virtue. Hence it is clear that in their judgment, at any rate, virtue is superior to honor. It would perhaps be right then to look upon virtue rather than honor as being the end of the political life. Yet it appears that virtue also lacks completeness. For it seems that a man may possess virtue and yet be asleep or inactive throughout life, or also that he may experience the greatest calamities and misfortunes. But nobody would call such a life happy, unless he were maintaining a **paradox**. . . .

The life of making money is in a sense a life of constraint, and it is clear that wealth is not the good for which we are looking. For money is useful in part as a means for obtaining something else. It would be more reasonable therefore to view the things mentioned before, that is, sensual pleasure, honor and virtue, as ends, since they are valued for their own sake. . . .

As it appears that there are more ends than one and that some of these, such as wealth, flutes, and instruments generally, are desired as a means to something else, it is evident that not all of them are final ends. But the highest good is clearly something final. Hence if there is only one final end, this will be what we are seeking, and if there are more than one, the most final of them will satisfy our quest. We speak of that which is desired for its own sake as being more final than that which is desired as a means to something else. We speak of that which is never desired as a means to something else as being more final than that which is desired both in itself and as a means to something else. And we speak of a thing as absolutely final, if it is always desired in itself and never as a means to anything else.

Now happiness, above all else, fits the description of what we are seeking, for we always desire happiness for its own sake and never as a means to something else. On the other hand, we desire honor, pleasure, intellect, and every virtue, partly for their own sakes (for we should desire them independently of what might result from them), but partly also as being means to happiness, because we suppose they will lead to happiness. On the other hand, nobody desires happiness for the sake of these things, nor indeed as a means to anything else at all. . . .

Since it seems to be generally accepted as true that happiness is the highest good, what we now need to do is to define its nature a little more clearly. The best way of arriving at such a definition will probably be to ascertain the function of man. For just as the goodness or excellence of a flute-player, a sculptor, an artisan, or in fact anybody who has a definite function and action seems to lie in his function, so it would seem to be the case for man, if indeed man has a definite function. Can it be said, then, that a carpenter and a cobbler have definite functions and actions, but that man, unlike them, is naturally functionless? The reasonable view is that just as the eye, the hand, the foot, and similarly each other part of the body has a definite function, so man may be regarded as having a definite function apart from all these. What, then, can this function be? It is not life, for life is apparently something that man shares with the plants. And we are looking for something peculiar to man. We must exclude therefore the life of nutrition and growth. There is next what may be called the life of sensation. But man also apparently shares this life with horses, cattle, and all other animals. There remains what I will call the life of living in accordance with rational principle. But living in accordance with rational principle might mean being obedient to rational principle, or it might mean exercising thought and conceiving rational principle. In other words, the life of living in accordance with rational principle can be viewed either as a state of being or as an activity.[3] But since the latter is the more proper sense of the term, the latter seems to have a greater claim to be the function of man than does the former.

The function of man then is an activity of soul in accordance with rational principle, or at least not without it. In speaking of the proper function of a certain type of person (e.g., a lyre-player) we recognize that it is the same in kind as the function of that type of person who excels in what he does (e.g., a good lyre-player). This applies to any and every type of person. The full attainment of excellence is merely added to the function. The function

of a lyre-player is to play the lyre; the function of a good lyre-player is to play it well. This being so, if we define the function of man as a kind of life, and this life as an activity of soul operating in accordance with reason, the function of a good man is the good and noble performance of this kind of life. In other words, the good of man is an activity of the soul in accordance with virtue or, if there are more virtues than one, in accordance with the best and most complete virtue. But it is necessary to add the words "in a complete life." For just as one swallow or one day does not make spring, one day or a short time does not make a blessed or happy man. . . .

It appears too that the requisite characteristics of happiness are all contained in this definition. For some people hold that happiness is virtue, others that it is prudence, others that it is wisdom of some kind, others that it is these things or one of them conjoined with pleasure (or at least not disassociated from it), others again include external prosperity. . . .

Now this definition is in harmony with the view of those who hold that happiness is virtue or excellence of some sort, for activity in accordance with virtue implies virtue. But it would seem that there is a considerable difference between taking the highest good to consist in acquisition or in use, that is, to be a moral state or a moral activity. For a moral state, although it exists, may produce nothing good, e.g., if a person is asleep, or has in any other way become inactive. But this cannot be the case with an activity, as activity implies action and good action. Just as it is not the most beautiful and strongest persons who receive the crown in the Olympian games, but they who actually enter the contests as competitors (for it is some of these who become victors), so it is they who act rightly that achieve what is noble and good in life. Again, their life is pleasant in itself. For pleasure is a psychical fact, and whatever a man is said to be fond of is pleasant to him. For example, a horse is pleasant to one who is fond of horses, a spectacle is pleasant to one who is fond of spectacles, just actions are pleasant to a lover of justice, as are virtuous actions to a lover of virtue. Now most men find a sense of discord in their pleasures, because their pleasures are not of the type that are naturally pleasant. But lovers of nobleness do not experience this discord, since actions in accordance with virtue are naturally pleasant. Such actions thus are pleasant both relatively to these persons and in themselves. Nor does their life require that pleasure be attached to it as a sort of amulet; it possesses pleasure in itself. For it may be added that a person is not good if he does not take delight in noble actions, nor would anyone call a person just if he did not take delight in just actions or liberal if he did not take delight in liberal actions and so on. But if this is so, it follows that actions in accordance with virtue are pleasant in themselves. But they are also good and noble, and good and noble in the highest degree, if the judgment of the virtuous man upon them is right, his judgment being such as we have described. Happiness then is the best, noblest, most pleasant thing in the world. . . .

Still it is clear that happiness requires the addition of external goods. . . . For it is impossible, or at least difficult, for a person to do what is noble unless he is furnished with external means. There are many things that can be done through the instrumentality of friends or wealth or political power, and there are some things that, if missing, would mar felicity, e.g., noble birth, a prosperous family, and personal beauty. For a person is incapable of happiness if he is absolutely ugly in appearance, low born, or solitary and childless, and perhaps still more so if he has exceedingly bad children or friends, or has had good children or friends who have died. . . .

Another question concerns whether happiness is something that can be learned or acquired by habit or discipline of any other kind, or whether it comes by some divine dispensation or even by chance.

Now if there is anything in the world that is a gift of the gods to men, it is reasonable to suppose that happiness is a divine gift, especially since it is the best thing that humans can possess. . . . But even if happiness is not sent by the gods but is the result of virtue and of some process of learning or discipline, it is apparently one of the most divine things in the world. For it would appear that that which is the prize and end of virtue is the highest good and is in its nature divine and blessed. Moreover, if it depends on excellence, happiness will be shared by many people. For it will be capable of being produced in all persons, except those who are morally deformed, by a process of study and effort. And if it is better that happiness should be produced in this way than by chance, it may reasonably be supposed that it is so produced. For in nature things are arranged in the best possible way, as they are in art and in any kind of causation, especially causation of the highest kind. It would be altogether inconsistent to leave what is greatest and noblest to chance. Indeed, the very definition of *happiness* helps clear up this question, for happiness has been defined as a certain kind of activity of the soul in accordance with virtue. Of the other goods, i.e. of goods besides those of the soul, some are necessary as antecedent conditions of happiness, while others are in their nature co-operative and serviceable as instruments of happiness. . . .

It is not reasonable then to speak of an ox, or a horse, or any other animal as happy, as none of them is capable of participating in activity as so defined. For the same reason no child can be happy, since the age of a child makes it impossible for him to display this activity at present. If a child is ever said to be happy, the ground of the felicitation is his promise, rather than his actual performance. For happiness demands, as we have said, a complete virtue and a complete life. As there are all sorts of changes and chances in life, it is possible that the most prosperous of men will, in his old age, fall into extreme calamities. . . . But if a person has experienced such chances, and has died a miserable death, nobody calls him happy. . . .

We may safely then define a happy man as one whose activity accords with perfect virtue and who is adequately furnished with external goods, not for a short period of time but for a complete or perfect lifetime. . . .

Yet since happiness is an activity of soul in accordance with complete or perfect virtue, it is necessary to consider virtue, as this will perhaps be the best way of studying happiness. . . . It is clear that it is human virtue which we have to consider; for the good which we are seeking is, as we said, human good, and the happiness, human happiness. By human virtue or excellence we mean not that of the body, but that of the soul, and by happiness we mean an activity of the soul. . . .

There are some facts concerning the soul which are adequately stated in the popular or exoterical discourses, and these we may rightly adopt. It is stated, for example, that the soul has two parts, one irrational and the other possessing reason. But whether these parts are distinguished like the parts of the body and like everything that is itself divisible, or whether they are theoretically distinct, but in fact inseparable, as convex and concave in the circumference of a circle, is of no importance to the present inquiry. Again, it seems that of the irrational part of the soul one part is common (i.e., shared by man with all living things) and vegetative; I mean the part which is the cause of nutrition and growth. For we may assume such a faculty of the soul to exist in all things that receive nutrition, in embryos as well as in things that are full grown, as it is more reasonable to suppose that it is the same faculty than that it is different. It is clear then that the virtue or excellence of this faculty is not distinctively human but is shared by man with all living things. In humans it seems that this faculty is especially active in sleep, because good and bad people are never so little distinguishable as in sleep. Thus it is said that there is no difference between the happy and the miserable during half their lifetime. And this is only natural; for sleep is an inactivity of the soul in respect of its virtue or vice, except in so far as certain impulses affect it to a slight extent, and make the dreams of the virtuous better than those of ordinary people. But enough has been said on this point, and we must now leave the principle of nutrition, as it possesses no natural share in human virtue.

In addition to this faculty, it seems that there is another natural principle of the soul which is irrational and yet in a sense partakes of reason. For in both a morally strong and a morally weak person, we praise reason and that part of the soul which possesses reason, because it exhorts men rightly and exhorts them to the best conduct. But it is clear that there is in them another principle which is naturally different from reason and fights and contends against reason. For just as when we attempt to move the paralyzed parts of the body to the right, we find that they are drawn away in the contrary direction to the left, so it is with the soul. The impulses of morally weak people run counter to reason. But there is this difference, however, that in the body we see the part which is drawn astray, whereas in the soul we do not see it. But it still seems equally certain that there is in the soul something different from reason, which opposes and thwarts it, although the sense in which it is distinct from reason is immaterial. It appears that this part also partakes in reason, as we have said; at all events in a morally strong person it obeys reason, and is perhaps even more obedient in a person who is self-controlled and courageous. For in the latter sort of person, it always speaks with the same voice as the rational principle.

It appears then that the irrational part of the soul is itself twofold; for the vegetative faculty does not participate at all in reason, while the faculty of the appetites and of desire in general participates in it more or less, in so far as it is submissive and obedient to reason. But it is obedient in the sense in which we speak of "paying attention to a father" or "to friends," not in the sense in which we speak of "paying attention to mathematics." All correction, rebuke and exhortation is a witness that the irrational part of the soul is in a sense subject to the influence of reason. Thus if we were to say that this part too possesses reason, then the rational part of the soul would have two divisions, one possessing reason absolutely and in itself, the other listening to reason as a child listens to its father.

Virtue or excellence also admits of a distinction which depends on this difference. For we speak of some virtues as intellectual, such as wisdom, intelligence, and prudence, and other virtues as moral, such as generosity and self-control. When we describe a person's moral character, we do not say that he is wise or intelligent but that he is gentle or self-controlled. Yet we praise a wise man too in respect of his mental state, and we refer to mental states that deserve praise as being virtuous.[4]

BOOK II

Virtue or excellence is twofold, being partly intellectual and partly moral. Intellectual virtue is both originated and fostered mainly by teaching; it therefore requires experience and time. Moral virtue, on the other hand, is the outcome of habit, and accordingly its name *ethike* is derived by a slight deflexion from habit (*ethos*). From this fact it is clear that no moral virtue is implanted in us by nature; a law of nature cannot be altered by habituation. Thus a stone naturally tends to fall downwards, and it cannot be habituated or trained to rise upwards, even if we were to throw it upwards ten thousand times. Nor again can fire be trained to sink downwards, nor can anything else that follows one natural law be habituated or trained to follow another. It is neither by nature then nor in defiance of nature that virtues are implanted in us. Nature gives us the capacity of receiving them, and that capacity is perfected by habit.

Again, if we take the various natural powers which belong to us, we first acquire the proper faculties and afterwards display the activities. It is clearly so with the senses. It was not by seeing frequently or hearing frequently that we acquired the senses of seeing or hearing. On the contrary, it was because we possessed the senses that we made use of them, not by making use of them that we obtained them. But as is the case with all the arts, virtues are acquired by first exercising them. The things which we have to learn before we can do them are learned by doing. We become shipbuilders by building ships and lyre-players by playing the lyre. Similarly it is by acting justly that we become just, by acting with self-control that we become

self-controlled, by acting courageously that we become courageous. . . .

Again, the causes and means by which any virtue is produced and by which it is destroyed are the same, just as it is with any art. For it is by playing the lyre that both good and bad lyre-players are produced. And this applies to builders and all other artisans. Men will become good or bad builders by building well or badly. If this were not so, there would be no need of anyone to teach them; they would all be born good or bad in their several trades. The case of the virtues is the same. It is by interacting with other men that we become either just or unjust. It is by acting in the face of danger and by habituating ourselves to fear or to courage that we become either cowardly or courageous. It is much the same with our desires and passions. Some people become self-controlled and gentle, others become licentious and irascible, according to how they conduct themselves in particular circumstances. In short, states of character are produced by corresponding activities. This is why our activities must be of a certain kind, for different activities will produce different states of character. Thus it is no small matter which habits are instilled in us in early childhood; on the contrary, this makes a considerable difference, or rather all the difference.

NOTES

1. Aristotle is alluding to Plato's **Forms,** especially the Form of the Good. This concept is discussed in the Plato selection found in Chapter 2 of this text.—ED.

2. The most luxury-loving, and the last, Assyrian monarch.

3. In other words, life may be taken to mean either the mere possession of certain faculties or their active exercise.

4. The student of Aristotle must familiarize himself with the conception of intellectual as well as of moral virtues, although it is not the rule in modern philosophy to speak of the "virtues" of the intellect.

Questions for Thought

1. What do you consider to be the highest good of human existence? How do your views on this subject compare with or differ from the views of Aristotle?
2. Can you think of an important type of life that Aristotle has overlooked?

3. Do you think that humans have a function? If so, how would you describe it?

4. Do you agree with Aristotle's claim that certain external aids, such as noble birth, family prosperity, and personal beauty, are prerequisites of human goodness? Why or why not?

5. Can you think of some other examples of intellectual virtue? What about moral virtue?

6. Do you agree with Aristotle's account of how we obtain moral virtues or principles? If so, why? If not, how do you think we obtain such virtues?

On Human Goodness 2

MENCIUS

Mencius (372–289 B.C.E.) was Confucius' most famous disciple. Like Confucius, Mencius was reportedly the only child of a poor widow who had to work very hard to support and educate him. Other traditions say that Mencius studied under the disciples of Tzu Ssu, the grandson of Confucius, and that, like Confucius, Mencius became a political adviser to some of the rulers of his time. His views on human nature are often contrasted with the views of Hsun Tzu, another of the disciples of Confucius, who claimed that human nature was basically evil. However, it was in his arguments with Kao Tzu, about whom little is known, that Mencius' views on the nature of human goodness were stated in greatest detail.

In the following sections from the *Book of Mencius,* a collection of dialogues and sayings probably compiled by Mencius' pupils after his death, Mencius argues against two of Kao Tzu's closely related claims. The first is the claim that at birth human beings are neither good nor evil; the second is the claim that a person becomes good or just because of external input. After reading the preceding selection from Aristotle, it should be evident that Mencius' criticisms apply to the views of Aristotle as well as to those of Kao Tzu. In opposition to both Kao Tzu and Aristotle, Mencius insists that all humans are endowed with certain natural qualities: a sense of pity, of shame, of respect, and of right and wrong. Because of these natural qualities, the source of goodness or justice lies within. In other words, unless a person's development is perverted by some external force, that person will naturally become good and just. As in many other Chinese writings, the principal arguments of both Kao Tzu and Mencius take the form of **analogies** or comparisons—in this case analogies or comparisons between human nature and the nature of other things, such as wood and water.

Questions for Reading

1. What is Kao Tzu's position on human nature? What are some of the metaphors that he uses to support his position?

2. How does Mencius' position differ from that of Kao Tzu? What evidence does he give to show that his view is the correct view?

3. According to Mencius, what are the four things with which all men are naturally endowed?

4. What are the moral or ethical implications of each of these four things?

5. Who was Yi Ya, and why does Mencius mention him in this selection?

BOOK SIX, PART I

6A : 1

KAO TZU SAID: "THE NATURE OF MAN IS comparable to the nature of the wood of the willow tree. Such things as Justice and Humanity are comparable to cups and bowls carved in willow wood. To make man's nature Humane or Just is comparable to making cups and bowls from willow wood."

Mencius replied: "But when the wood is carved into a bowl, is its nature left unscarred? No! It becomes a bowl only at the price of suffering damage to its original nature. If that is so, then must a man suffer damage to his original nature in order to become Humane and Just? In such a view, to make men Humane and Just is to violate their nature. From what you say, one would be forced to such a **conclusion.**"

6A : 2

Kao Tzu said: "The nature of man is comparable to water trapped in a whirlpool. Open a channel for it on the east side and it will flow away to the east. Open a channel for it on the west side and it will flow away to the west. This is because man's nature is neither inherently good nor bad, just as it is not inherently in the nature of water to flow to the east or to the west."

Mencius replied: "It is assuredly not in the nature of water to flow to the east or to the west; but can one say that it is not in the nature of water to flow upwards or downwards? Man's nature is inherently good, just as it is the nature of water to flow downwards. As there is no water that flows upwards, so there are no men whose natures inherently are bad. Now you may strike forcefully upon water, and it will splash above your head. With a series of dams, you may force it uphill. But this is surely nothing to

do with the nature of water; it happens only after the intrusion of some exterior force. A man can be made to do evil, but this is nothing to do with his nature. It happens only after the intrusion of some exterior force."

6A : 3

Kao Tzu said: "What I mean by nature is the thing that gives life."

Mencius asked: "Do you mean that in the sense that you would say that whiteness is the thing that whitens?"

Kao Tzu said: "Yes, certainly!"

Mencius continued: "Then it would follow that the whiteness of a white feather and the whiteness of white snow are comparable, and similarly that the whiteness of white snow and the whiteness of white jade are comparable?"

Kao Tzu said: "Yes, certainly."

Mencius replied: "With that line of reasoning would you not have to say that the nature of a dog and the nature of an ox are comparable, and so the nature of an ox and the nature of a man are comparable?"

6A : 4

Kao Tzu said: "What I mean by nature is food and color (the taste and senses). I regard Humanity as pertaining to these senses and not external to them. Justice, on the other hand, is something external; it does not pertain to the senses."

Mencius said: "How can you say that the one is inherent and the other external?"

Kao Tzu said: "To a man who is my senior I pay, in Justice, the deference due to his seniority. This is not because paying such deference is an intrinsic part of *me;* I react to the stimulus of his seniority just as I see a white thing as white, since I am

From Mencius, *translated by W. A. C. H. Dobson, University of Toronto Press, 1963. Reprinted by permission of University of Toronto Press.*

actuated by its whiteness, which is external to myself. It is for this reason that I say such things are external."

Mencius said: "If in speaking of the whiteness of a white horse, we say that it differs in no way from the whiteness of a white man, I suppose we must say that the 'seniority' (old age) of an old horse differs in no way from the 'seniority' of an old man. In which case, in what does Justice repose? In 'seniority' itself or in him who responds to seniority as he, in Justice, should?"

Kao Tzu said: "I feel love for my younger brother, but I feel no love for the younger brother of a man of Ch'in. My brother provokes a feeling of pleasure within me, and so I say it is inherent. To a man from Ch'in who is my senior I pay the deference due to his seniority, just as I would pay deference to a senior of my own family. My doing so provokes a feeling of pleasure within my seniors. So accordingly I say that Justice is an external thing."

Mencius said: "My enjoyment of a dish cooked by a man of Ch'in differs in no way from my enjoyment of a similar dish cooked by my own people. This is true of a number of similar material things. Since it is so, would you still assert that the enjoyment of food is something external?"[1]

. . .

6A : 6

Kung-tu Tzu said: "Kao Tzu says, 'Man's nature is neither good nor bad.' Others say man's nature may tend in either direction. They say in the reigns of the good kings Wen and Wu[2] the people were disposed to do good. In the reigns of the bad kings Yu and Li[3] the people were disposed to do evil. Still others say some men's natures are good while others are bad. These say that, under a good sovereign like Yao,[4] a bad man like Hsiang appeared, and that, to a bad father like Ku-sou, a good son Shun[5] was born. . . . Now, Sir, you say, 'Man's nature is good.' I suppose that these others are wrong?"

Mencius said: "It is of the essence of man's nature that he do good. That is what I mean by

good. If a man does what is evil he is guilty of the sin of denying his natural endowment. Every man has a sense of pity, a sense of shame, a sense of respect, a sense of right and wrong. From his sense of pity comes *jen* (Humanity); from his sense of shame comes *yi* (Justice); from his sense of respect, *li* (the observance of rites); from his sense of right and wrong, *chih* (wisdom). *Jen, yi, li,* and *chih* do not soak in from without; we have them within ourselves. It is simply that we are not always consciously thinking about them. So I say, 'Seek them and you have them. Disregard them and you lose them.' Men differ, some by twice, some by five times, and some by an incalculable amount, in their inability to exploit this endowment. The *Book of Songs*[6] says,

> Heaven gave birth to all mankind
> Gave them life and gave them laws.
> In holding to them
> They lean towards the virtue of excellence.

Confucius said, 'This poet really understood the Way.' Thus, to possess life is to possess laws. These are to be laid hold upon by the people, and thus they will love the virtue of excellence."

6A : 7

Mencius said: "When the harvest is good, the younger people are for the most part amenable, but when the harvest is lean, they are obstreperous. Their reacting differently under these differing circumstances is not due to the nature with which Heaven has endowed them but to those who create these overwhelming conditions. Sow the barley and cover it with soil. Providing that the ground is uniform and the barley is sown at one time, it will spring to life, and in due time all the barley will ripen. However, differing circumstances do arise; some ground is rich, some is poor; some well watered, some not; not all is equally well-tended. Even so, things of a kind resemble each other. And can we doubt that human beings are any different? The Sages and we ourselves are things of a kind. Lung Tzu[7] said, 'The sandal-maker may not know beforehand the size of his customer's feet, but we can be sure that he will not make the sandals the size of baskets.' Sandals resemble each other; men's feet are things of a kind. All men relish flavorings in their food. But it took a Yi Ya[8] first to discover those flavorings. Suppose Yi Ya's nature differed in kind from those of other men, just as the nature of horses and hounds differs from that of a man. How could it have happened that, whatever flavorings humans like, all derive from Yi Ya? As far as flavorings are concerned, the world is indebted to Yi Ya, but this could only happen because all men's palates are similar.

"This, too, is true of the ear. For music, the world in indebted to K'uang the Music Master.[9] But this could only happen because all men's ears are similar. This, too, is true of the eyes. No one would deny that Tzu-tu[10] was handsome, unless he was blind.

"Therefore, the human mouth enjoys its flavorings, the ear its music, the eye its beauty. These things are all alike. And is this not true of the things of the heart? What are those things that all hearts have in common? I say, 'the underlying principle, the essential Justice.'

"The Sages (differ from us only) in being the first to discover those things which all hearts have in common. The underlying principle and the essential Justice evoke joy in our hearts just as rich meat delights our palate."

NOTES

1. The dialogue between Mencius and Kao Tzu ends at this point. The remaining subsections record dialogues between Mencius and his disciples.

2. The first two rulers of the Chou dynasty, who are often cited as ideal examples of wise and beneficent rule.

3. Kings who ruled in the eighth and ninth centuries B.C.E. and who often serve as examples of wicked rulers.

4. Mythical sage-emperor who supposedly ruled in the third millennium B.C.E. According to tradition, he lived the simple life of a common farmer.

5. The mythical sage-emperor who supposedly succeeded Yao.

6. An anthology of early Chinese poetry.

7. An ancient wise man.

8. Chef of Duke Huan of Ch'i.

9. Concert master for Duke P'ing of Chin.

10. An ancient person who was known for his handsome features.

Questions for Thought

1. Do you believe that there is an essential human nature? Why or why not?
2. Are human beings really born with a propensity for goodness, as Mencius claims? How would Aristotle respond to this claim?
3. Assuming that Mencius is correct, why is there so much violence and injustice in the world today?
4. How effective do you think Mencius' analogies or comparisons are in supporting his claims?
5. Can you think of a different analogy or comparison that would also support Mencius' position? Can you think of one that would weaken his position?

The Good Will and Morality   3

IMMANUEL KANT

Immanuel Kant (1724–1804), the son of a saddler, was born in Königsberg, Prussia. Both of Kant's parents belonged to the Pietist branch of the Lutheran Church, and Kant received his early education at a Pietist school run by his pastor. In 1740, Kant entered the University of Königsberg to study theology, but he soon found that physics and mathematics were more to his liking. When his father died in 1746, Kant was forced to suspend his formal studies and to take employment as a tutor. During the next nine years, he tutored for three different families while continuing his studies on an informal level. Finally, in 1755, aided by the financial help of a friend, Kant was able to return to the university and complete his degree.

From 1755 to 1770, Kant worked as a poorly paid lecturer at the University of Königsberg. During this time, he taught courses in mathematics, physics, geography, and philosophy and wrote several scientific treatises. Kant's financial fortunes improved in 1770, when he was given the chair of logic and **metaphysics** at the university. However, his scholarly output declined as he spent the next ten years working on his first truly important philosophical work: the *Kritik der reinen Vernunft* (*Critique of Pure Reason*), which was published in 1781. Once this work was published, Kant's literary output picked up again, and he published a series of important philosophical works during the next decade. These included *Prolegomena zur einer jeden künftigen Metaphysik die als Wissenschaft wird auftreten können* (1783; *Prolegomena to Any Future Metaphysics*), *Grundlegung zur Metaphysik der Sitten* (1785; *Fundamental Principles of the Metaphysic of Morals*), *Metaphysiche Anfangsgründe der Wissenschaft* (1786; *Metaphysical Foundations of Natural Science*), *Critik der practischen Vernunft* (1788; *Critique of Practical Reason*), and *Critik der Urteilskraft* (1790; *Critique of Judgment*).

Kant's personal life is often used as an example of methodical regularity. Kant, who never married, had few if any romantic involvements, and he never traveled more than sixty miles from Königsberg. One legend even suggests that Kant's life was so routine that local villagers set their clocks according to the time Kant passed their houses on his daily walk. Kant died in 1804 in the city in which he was born.

In the following excerpt from his *Fundamental Principles of the Metaphysic of Morals,* Kant is concerned with the same problem that Aristotle examined in the first selection of this chapter, the problem of determining the highest good of human existence. Indeed, one of Kant's principal purposes in this selection is to argue against Aristotle's claim that the highest good lies in human happiness. For Kant, human happiness, as well as the intellectual and moral virtues that Aristotle saw as necessary components of the good life, are good only if they are accompanied by what Kant calls *good will*. In direct contrast to Aristotle's position, Kant argues that good will is the only thing that is good without qualification and that good will is "the indispensable condition even of being worthy of happiness."

After arguing that good will is the highest human good, Kant goes on to claim that an action has true moral worth only if it is motivated *solely* by good will, without regard to consequences or results. In other words, Kant is telling us that the moral worth of an action is determined by the nature of the intention that motivates the action and not by any external factor. Even if the outcome of an action were disastrous, the action would have moral worth provided that it was motivated by good will—that is, by a resolve to do what was right solely because one had a duty to do so. On the other hand, if an action had wonderful consequences, it would have no moral worth if it was done from selfish inclinations or even from more praiseworthy inclinations, such as the feeling of compassion for others. Thus, in another statement that is directly opposed to Aristotle's position, Kant concludes that an act of generosity done by a person who has been habituated to act generously—that is, who has developed an inclination toward generous behavior—has less moral worth than an act of generosity done by someone who has not been so habituated. The same holds for any other act that we normally praise as having moral value.

Given that the moral worth of an act derives from the fact that it is motivated solely by good will, by duty absolutely divorced from inclination, Kant says that the value of the act depends on the principle of volition, or the **maxim,** that motivates the act. Moreover, he argues that the only time an act is wholly divorced from inclination is when the act is motivated by respect for the moral law itself—the moral law that, according to Kant, all rational beings can discover and follow. Finally, Kant adds that this respect for the moral law, this attempt to act so that our actions are motivated solely by duty divorced from inclination, leads to the recognition that the only truly moral acts are acts that we can universalize. In other words, as Kant says, "I am never to act otherwise than so that *I could also will that my maxim should become a universal law.*" It should be obvious that this moral principle, which Kant elsewhere calls the *categorical imperative,* is an abstract statement of the Golden Rule: "Do unto others as you would have them do unto you." Only by acting according to the dictates of this general moral principle do we achieve the highest good; only then are we truly worthy of happiness.

Questions for Reading

1. What does Kant mean by *good will*? Why does he believe that only acts motivated by good will have true moral worth?
2. What is Kant's attitude toward utility?
3. What is the fundamental principle that Kant assumes at the beginning of section 2? Why does he introduce this principle?
4. How does an action done from inclination differ from an action done from duty?
5. What is Kant's example of the merchant or tradesman intended to show?
6. What does Kant mean when he says that "I am never to act otherwise than so that I could also will that my maxim should become a universal law"?

FIRST SECTION

Transition from the Common Rational Knowledge of Morality to the Philosophical

1 NOTHING CAN POSSIBLY BE CONCEIVED IN the world, or even out of it, that can be called good without qualification, except a Good Will.

Intelligence, wit, judgment, and the other *talents* of the mind, whatever they may be called, as well as courage, resolution, perseverance, and other qualities of temperament, are undoubtedly good and desirable in many respects. However, these gifts of nature may also become extremely bad and mischievous if the will or character that puts them to use is not good. The same can be said of the *gifts of fortune*. Power, riches, honor, and even health, as

This is the editor's revised version of a selection from Immanuel Kant, Fundamental Principles of the Metaphysic of Morals, *translated by T. K. Abbott, London, 1873.*

well as the general well-being and contentment with one's condition that promotes happiness, often inspire pride and presumption, unless there is a good will to correct their influence on the mind, and thereby to direct the principle of acting to its proper end. The sight of a person who shows no trace of a pure and good will, and who yet enjoys unbroken prosperity, can never give pleasure to an impartial rational observer. Thus a good will appears to constitute the indispensable condition of even being worthy of happiness.

There are some personal qualities that are of service to good will and that may facilitate its action. Yet these qualities presuppose a good will, and thus they have no intrinsic unconditional value in themselves. This qualifies the esteem that we rightly have for them and does not permit us to regard them as absolutely good. For example, moderation in the affections and passions, self-control and calm deliberation are not only good in many respects, but they even seem to constitute part of the intrinsic worth of the person. However, although they have been praised unconditionally by the ancients, they are far from deserving to be called good without qualification. For without the principles of a good will, they may become extremely bad. Cold-bloodedness in a villain not only makes him far more dangerous, but it also makes him more abominable in our eyes than he would have been without it.

A good will is not good because of what it performs or effects. Nor is it good because of its aptness for the attainment of some proposed end. Rather, a good will is good simply by virtue of its volition, that is, it is good in itself. It is to be esteemed much higher than anything that can be accomplished by means of it. . . .

Suppose that a special disfavor of fortune or the niggardly provision of a stepmotherly nature made it such that, despite one's greatest efforts, one's good will wholly lacked the power to accomplish its purpose and thus achieved nothing, leaving only the good will itself. Nevertheless, it would still shine like a jewel with its own light, as a thing that is the source of its own value. Its usefulness or fruitfulness can neither add to nor take away anything from this value. . . .

There is, however, something very strange in this idea of the absolute value of the will, which takes no account of its utility. Notwithstanding that the idea has the thorough assent of common sense, still a suspicion could arise that this idea is merely the product of high-flown fancy, and that we have misunderstood the purpose of nature in claiming that it is reason, not utility, that governs our will. Therefore we will examine this idea from this point of view.

2 We assume as a fundamental principle that the physical constitution of an organized being, that is, a being adapted suitably to the purposes of life, contains no organ for any purpose that is not the fittest and best adapted for that purpose. Now if nature gave reason and a will to a being in order to guarantee its conservation and welfare, in short to secure its happiness, then nature would have chosen a very bad arrangement in selecting the reason of the creature to carry out this purpose. For all the actions that the creature has to perform to secure its happiness would be far more surely prescribed to it by instinct, and thus happiness would be more certainly guaranteed by instinct than by reason. Should reason have been given to this favored creature over and above instinct, it would only have allowed the creature to contemplate the happy constitution of its nature, to admire it, to congratulate itself thereon, and to feel thankful for it to the beneficent cause. However, nature would not have made the creature's desires subject to the weak and delusive guidance of reason, for reason meddles bunglingly with the purpose of nature. In a word, nature would have made certain that reason would never be translated into action. Nor would it have allowed reason, with its weak insight, to presume to map out the plan of the creature's happiness or the means of attaining it. Nature herself would not only have determined the choice of the ends, but also of the means; and with wise foresight she would have entrusted both to instinct.

In fact, we find that the more a cultivated reason deliberately applies itself to the enjoyment of life and happiness, the more it misses true satisfaction. Because of this, there arises in many, if they are candid enough to admit it, a certain degree of misology or disgust with reason, especially in the case of those who are most experienced in using it. For after weighing all the advantages and disadvantages that they derive from reason, they find that they have, in fact, brought more trouble on their shoulders and that they have not increased their happiness. They end up envying, rather than despising, the more common lot of men who keep closer to the guidance of instinct and who do not allow their reason to influence their conduct very much. We must admit, however, that those who would very much like to tone down or even to eliminate lofty eulogies to reason, for the happiness and satisfaction it supposedly affords, are by no means morose or ungrateful for the goodness with which the world is governed. What lies at the root of these judgments is the idea that our existence has a different and far nobler end than happiness, and that it is for this nobler end that reason is properly intended. This nobler end is the supreme condition to which the private ends of man must, for the most part, be subordinated.

For we have seen that reason is not competent to guide the will to its objects or to the satisfaction of all of man's wants (which to some extent it even multiplies), this being an end to which an implanted instinct would have led with much greater certainty. Nevertheless, since reason is given to us as a practical faculty that can influence the will, and since we must admit that nature has generally adapted the means to the end in the distribution of her faculties, the true purpose of reason, for which it was absolutely necessary, is to produce a will that is good in itself and not merely as a means to something else. While this will is not the sole and complete good, it must be the supreme good that is the condition of every other good, even of the desire of happiness. Under these circumstances, there is nothing inconsistent with the wisdom of nature in that the cultivation of the reason, which is necessary for the first and unconditional purpose, interferes in many ways, at least in this life, with the attainment of the second purpose, namely happiness, which is always conditional. Indeed, happiness may even be reduced to nothing, without nature thereby failing of her purpose. For the establishment of a good will is the highest practical function of reason, and only in attaining this purpose does reason realize its own proper kind of satisfaction, the satisfaction of fulfilling a wholly rational purpose, even if this runs counter to one's own inclinations.

3 We must, then, develop the notion of a will that in itself deserves to be highly esteemed, a will that is good without a view to anything further. This notion already exists in the sound natural understanding, and it requires rather to be cleared up than to be taught. It is always of prime importance in estimating the value of our actions, constituting the condition of everything else. In order to clear up this notion, let us look at the idea of duty, which includes a good will, although it also contains certain subjective restrictions and hindrances. However, far from concealing it or rendering it unrecognizable, this notion is brought out more clearly, made to shine forth so much brighter, by contrast with these restrictions and hindrances.

I omit here all actions that are already recognized as inconsistent with duty. Although such actions may be useful for this or that purpose, the question whether or not they are done *from duty* cannot arise at all, since they are in conflict with it. I also set aside those actions that conform to duty, but to which men have no direct *inclination,* performing them only because they are impelled to do so by some other motivation. For in this case we can readily distinguish whether the action that agrees with duty is done *from duty,* or whether it is motivated by self-interest. It is much harder to make this distinction when the action accords with duty, and the subject has in addition a *direct* inclination to do it. For example, it is always a matter of duty for a seller not to overcharge an inexperienced buyer. Wherever there is much commerce, the prudent seller does not overcharge, keeping rather a fixed price for everyone, so that a child buys of him at the same rate as anyone else. Men are thus honestly served. However, this is not enough to make us believe that the seller has acted this way from duty and from principles of honesty. His own advantage required it; and there is no reason to suppose that he did it because he also had a direct inclination in favor of all buyers, loving them all equally and thus refusing to give advantage to one buyer over another. Accordingly the action was done neither from duty nor from direct inclination; it was motivated solely by self-interest.

On the other hand, self-preservation is a duty. And, in addition, everyone also has a direct inclination to do so. But this is why the anxious care that most men usually take in order to preserve themselves has no intrinsic worth; it is why the maxim of their action has no moral import. They preserve their lives *as duty requires,* no doubt, but not *because duty requires.* On the other hand, adversity and hopeless sorrow may completely take away the joy of life, and an unfortunate person, strong in mind and indignant at his fate may, rather than being depressed or dejected, wish for death. Yet, if he nevertheless preserves his life without loving it—not from inclination or fear, but from duty—then the maxim of his action has moral worth.

To help others when we can is a duty. Besides, there are many people who are so sympathetic that, without any other motive of vanity or self-interest, they find pleasure in spreading joy around them, taking delight in personally bringing about satisfaction in others. Yet, in such a case I maintain that an action of this kind, however proper and amiable it may be, has nevertheless no true moral worth. Rather, it is on a level with other inclinations, *e.g.,* the desire for honor, which, if it is directed to actions of public utility that are in accord with duty, deserves praise and encouragement, but not esteem. This is because the maxim in this case lacks moral import, for to have moral import actions must be done *from duty,* not from inclination.

Consider the case of a philanthropist whose mind is clouded by sorrow of his own, thereby extinguishing all sympathy with the lot of others. Although he still has the power to help others in distress, he is not touched by their trouble because he is absorbed with his own. Now suppose that he tears himself out of this dead insensibility, and helps another without any inclination to do so, being motivated simply from duty. It is then that his action first has genuine moral worth.

Further still, suppose that nature has put little sympathy in the heart of a certain upright man thereby making him cold and indifferent to the suffering of others. Perhaps this is because nature has also provided him with the special gift of patience and fortitude, and because he presumes, or even requires, that others should have the same. Such a man would certainly not be the meanest product of nature. But even though nature has not specially framed him to be a philanthropist, could he not still find in himself a source through which he could give himself a far higher moral worth than could someone that nature had framed to be a philanthropist? Without doubt, he could. For the highest moral worth of an action—in this case being helpful to others—comes from doing good, not from inclination, but from duty. . . .

The second[1] proposition is that an action done from duty derives its moral worth, not from the purpose for which it was done, but from the maxim that motivated or governed it. Therefore, the moral worth of an action does not depend upon the successful result of the action; it is determined solely by the principle of volition or the maxim that guides the action. It is clear from what precedes that actions do not attain any unconditional moral worth from the purposes or the intended effects regarded as motivations for them. Where does the moral worth of an action lie, then, if it does not lie in the relation of will to its expected effect? It cannot lie anywhere else than in the principle or maxim of the will, without reference to the ends that can be attained by the action. For the will stands between its *à priori* principle, which is formal, and its *à posteriori* motivation, which is material, as between two roads. And since the will must be determined by something, when an action is done from duty the will is determined solely by its formal principle of volition, from which every material motivation has been eliminated.

4   The third proposition is a consequence of the two preceding ones. I would express it as follows: *Duty is the necessity of acting from respect for the law.* If I have inclination for an object of my proposed action, I cannot have respect for it. This is because such an action, while being an effect of my will, is not determined by my will alone. Similarly, I cannot have respect for inclination, whether my own or another's. At most, if it is my own, I can approve it; if it is another's, sometimes I can even love it, *i.e.,* I can view it as being favorable to my own interest. Something can be an object of respect and hence a duty only if it is connected with my will as a principle, never as an effect. This means that rather than being subservient to inclination, it overpowers it, or at least in the case of choice excludes it from its calculation. Thus, an action done from duty must wholly exclude the

influence of inclination, and with it every object of the will, so that nothing remains to determine the will except objectively the *law* and subjectively *pure respect* for this practical law. Consequently it is a maxim[2] that I should obey this law even if it thwarts all my personal inclinations.

The moral worth of an action, therefore, does not lie in the effect expected from it, nor in any principle of action that is motivated by this expected effect. For any effects, such as agreeableness of one's condition or even the promotion of the happiness of others, could have been brought about by other causes, and there would have been no need of the will of a rational being. However, the supreme and unconditional good can only be found in such a will. Therefore, the pre-eminent good, which we call moral, can consist in nothing but the conception of law in itself, and admittedly this occurs only in a rational being whose will is determined solely by this conception and not by any expected effect.

But by what sort of law can the will be called good absolutely and without qualification? In other words, what sort of law, by its conception alone and without any reference to expected effects, can determine the will? Since I have deprived the will of all motivation arising from obedience to any particular law, there remains nothing but the universal conformity of its actions to law in general that could serve the will as a principle. In other words, *I ought never to act unless I can will that the maxim of my action should become a universal law.* In this case, it is simple conformity to law in general, without assuming any particular law applicable to certain actions, that serves the will as its principle, and that must so serve it, if duty is not to be a vain delusion or chimerical notion. In practice, common sense agrees with this and always keeps this principle handy.

To see that this is so, let us consider the following question. When I am in trouble, is it acceptable for me to make a promise that I do not intend to keep? I can clearly distinguish here between two senses of this question. The first sense is whether or not it is prudent to make a false promise; the second sense is whether or not it is morally right to do so. Undoubtedly, it may often seem prudent to make a false promise. However, I see clearly that escaping from a present difficulty by means of such a promise is not the sole consideration; I must also carefully consider whether this lie may not cause a much greater problem later than the one from which I now free myself. Since the consequences of a lie cannot be easily foreseen, and since lost credibility may be much more harmful to me than any present trouble that I seek to avoid, I should consider whether it would not be more prudent to act according to a universal maxim, making it a habit to make no promises that I do not intend to keep. But it is soon clear to me that such a maxim will still be based only on the fear of consequences.

Now it is a wholly different thing to be truthful from duty than it is to be truthful from apprehension of harmful consequences. In the first case, the very notion of the action already implies a law for me; in the second case, I must first look around to see what the consequences would be for me. For to deviate from the principle of duty is undoubtedly wicked; but to be unfaithful to my maxim of prudence may often be very advantageous to me, although it is certainly safer to abide by it. However, the shortest, surest way to discover the answer to the question of whether a lying promise is consistent with duty, is to ask myself the following question. Should I be content that my maxim—that it is acceptable to get out of trouble by making a false promise—serve as a universal law for myself as well as for others? Could I tell myself that everyone may make a deceitful promise whenever he finds himself in a difficulty from which he cannot otherwise escape? Suddenly I become aware that while I can will to lie, I can by no means will that lying should be a universal law. Indeed, with such a law, there could be no promises at all. For it would be in vain to state my intention in regard to my future actions, since no one would believe what I said, or if they over-hastily did so, they would pay me back in my own coin. Hence my maxim, as soon as it became a universal law, would necessarily destroy itself.

No far-reaching insight is needed to discern what I have to do to make my will morally good. Even if I am inexperienced in worldly ways and incapable of preparing for all contingencies, I need only ask myself: Can I will that my maxim become a universal law? If not, then it must be rejected. Not because it is disadvantageous to me or even to others, but rather because it cannot serve as a principle of a possible universal legislation, a legislation that would rationally demand immediate respect from me. I do not indeed yet know the source of this respect (of this the philosopher may inquire), but at least I understand that this respect warrants an estimation of worth that far outweighs the worth of anything motivated by inclination. I also know that the necessity of acting from pure respect for the practical law is what constitutes duty and that every other motive must give way to this. Indeed, acting from duty is the condition of a will being good in itself, and such a will is worth more than anything else.

NOTES

1. The first proposition was that in order to have moral worth, an action must be done from duty.

2. A *maxim* is the subjective principle of volition or willing. In other words, it is the rule or intention that governs an act. The objective principle, which would also serve subjectively as a practical principle to all rational beings if reason had full power over the faculty of desire, is the practical *law*.

Questions for Thought

1. What are Kant's main criticisms of Aristotle? How do you think he would respond to Mencius' claim that human beings are born with certain natural moral qualities, such as a sense of right and wrong?

2. Do you think that acting from a good will is more important than what Aristotle calls "happiness"? If so, why? If not, why not?

3. Can you think of an example other than that of the merchant or tradesman that might support the point that Kant is trying to make?

4. How does Kant use the term *maxim*? If you were to think back to the last difficult moral decision you made, how would you describe the maxim that determined your action?

5. To what extent do you think your actions are motivated by what Kant calls "good will"?

6. Do you agree that what Kant calls the "categorical imperative" is the highest moral principle? Why or why not?

The Principle of Utility   4

JEREMY BENTHAM

Jeremy Bentham (1748–1832), the earliest proponent of the philosophy of **Utilitarianism,** was born in London. Something of a child prodigy, Bentham was already an eager reader when he began studying Latin at age four. He won high praise for his writing of Greek and Latin verse at the Westminster School, and he entered Queen's College, Oxford, when he was only twelve years old. He graduated from Queen's College three years later and went to Lincoln's Inn to study law. Although Bentham obtained his law degree in 1767, he never practiced law. Instead, he devoted his time to performing chemical experiments and to working for political and legal reform. To promote reform, Bentham published a number of pamphlets on a wide variety of subjects, and he founded the *Westminster Review.* He also maintained an active correspondence with many of the leading thinkers in Europe and the United States. Because of his advocacy of radical democratic theory, Bentham was made a citizen of the newly formed French republic in 1792. While he was a prolific writer, Bentham failed to see most of his writings through to publication. His *Introduction to the Principles of Morals and Legislation* (1789), from which the following selection is taken, was the only major theoretical work that he himself published. Fortunately, Bentham enjoyed the friendship of many prominent intellectuals, and his friends edited many of his rough manuscripts into publishable form. These included *The Book of Fallacies* (1824; prepared and edited by Peregrine Bingham) and *Rationale of Judicial Evidence* (1827; edited by J. S. Mill). His friends also saw to it that his rather unusual last wishes were followed. After his death, Bentham's head was severed from his body and mummified. His embalmed body was then dressed in his favorite clothes, provided with a wax head, and displayed in a glass case. Both the embalmed body and the mummified head are still on display at University College in London.

In the following selection, Bentham formulates and defends what he calls the *principle of utility*. He begins his argument by claiming that pain and pleasure are the determining factors of human behavior and that any realistic moral theory must take this into account. Bentham then goes on to argue that the only moral principle that adequately accounts for this fact of human nature is the principle of utility, the principle that bases moral judgments on the tendency of an action to either increase or decrease happiness. According to the principle of utility, the act of an individual is good if it adds to the sum total of his or her pleasures or diminishes the sum total of his or her pains; it is bad if it has opposite results. Similarly, a law or government program is justified depending on "the tendency which it appears to have to augment or diminish the happiness of the party whose interest is in question . . . or . . . to promote or to oppose that happiness."

Bentham's account of the origin and nature of morality differs in important respects from all the earlier views in this chapter. First, although Bentham (like Aristotle) says that the ultimate goal of morality is happiness, Bentham's use of the term *happiness* is narrower than Aristotle's use of the term. For Bentham, happiness is simply the increase of pleasure or the decrease of pain, an increase or decrease that lends itself to quantitative or mathematical calculation. Indeed, elsewhere in his writings, Bentham devises a **"hedonistic calculus"** that he believes can be used in making moral decisions. Second, there seems to be little room in Bentham's conception of human nature for those natural moral qualities with which Mencius believes all humans are born. For Bentham, all human action, including moral behavior, springs from the desire to gain pleasure and/or to avoid pain. Finally, Bentham's principle of utility is diametrically opposed to Kant's **categorical imperative.** Whereas Kant argues that in order to have moral worth an action cannot be motivated by any sort of inclination, Bentham says that our natural inclinations to seek pleasure and to avoid pain are the very foundation of morality. Moreover, whereas Kant claims that consequences are totally irrelevant to the moral worth of an action, the principle of utility requires that one compare the projected outcomes of possible actions and choose the one that will bring about the greatest increase in pleasure or the greatest decrease in pain.

Questions for Reading

1. What, according to Bentham, motivates human behavior?
2. What exactly does Bentham mean by the "principle of utility"? Why does he believe that it represents the only acceptable moral principle?
3. How does Bentham use the term *happiness*?
4. According to Bentham, what does it mean to say that something is "in the interest of the community"? How is the interest of the community related to the interest of the individual?
5. What are the principal questions that Bentham submits to someone who happens not to "relish" the principle of utility?

OF THE PRINCIPLE OF UTILITY

I.   Nature has placed mankind under the governance of two sovereign masters, *pain* and *pleasure*. It is for them alone to point out what we ought to do, as well as to determine what we shall do. On the one hand the standard of right and wrong, on the other the chain of causes and effects, are fastened to their throne. They govern us in all we do, in all we say, in all we think: every effort we can make to throw off our subjection, will serve but to demonstrate and confirm it. In words a man may pretend to abjure their empire: but in reality he will remain subject to it all the while. The *principle of utility* recognizes this subjection, and assumes it for the foundation of that system, the object of which is to rear the fabric of felicity by the hands of reason and of law. Systems which attempt to question it, deal in sounds instead of sense, in caprice instead of reason, in darkness instead of light.

But enough of metaphor and declamation: it is not by such means that moral science is to be improved.

II.   The principle of utility is the foundation of the present work: it will be proper therefore at the outset to give an explicit and determinate account of what is meant by it. By the principle of utility is meant that principle which approves or disapproves of every action whatsoever, according to the tendency which it appears to have to augment or diminish the happiness of the party whose interest is in question: or, what is the same thing in other words, to promote or to oppose that happiness. I say of every action whatsoever; and therefore not only of every action of a private individual, but of every measure of government.

III.   By utility is meant that property in any object, whereby it tends to produce benefit, advantage, pleasure, good, or happiness, (all this in the present case comes to the same thing) or (what comes again to the same thing) to prevent the happening of mischief, pain, evil, or unhappiness to the party whose interest is considered: if that party be the community in general, then the happiness of the community: if a particular individual, then the happiness of that individual.

IV.   The interest of the community is one of the most general expressions that can occur in the phraseology of morals: no wonder that the meaning of it is often lost. When it has a meaning, it is this. The community is a fictitious *body,* composed of the individual persons who are considered as constituting as it were its *members.* The interest of the community then is, what?—the sum of the interests of the several members who compose it.

V.   It is in vain to talk of the interest of the community, without understanding what is the interest of the individual. A thing is said to promote the interest, or to be *for* the interest, of an individual, when it tends to add to the sum total of his pleasures: or, what comes to the same thing, to diminish the sum total of his pains.

VI.   An action then may be said to be conformable to the principle of utility, or, for shortness sake, to utility (meaning with respect to the community at large), when the tendency it has to augment the happiness of the community is greater than any it has to diminish it.

VII.   A measure of government (which is but a particular kind of action, performed by a particular person or persons) may be said to be conformable to or dictated by the principle of utility, when in like manner the tendency which it has to augment the happiness of the community is greater than any which it has to diminish it.

VIII.   When an action, or in particular a measure of government, is supposed by a man to be conformable to the principle of utility, it may be convenient, for the purposes of discourse, to imagine a kind of law or dictate, called a law or dictate of utility; and to speak of the action in question, as being conformable to such law or dictate.

IX.   A man may be said to be a partizan of the principle of utility, when the approbation or disapprobation he annexes to any action, or to any measure, is determined by and proportioned to the tendency which he conceives it to have to augment

From Jeremy Bentham, An Introduction to the Principles of Morals and Legislation, *London, 1789.*

or to diminish the happiness of the community: or in other words, to its conformity or unconformity to the laws or dictates of utility.

X.   Of an action that is conformable to the principle of utility one may always say either that it is one that ought to be done, or at least that it is not one that ought not to be done. One may say also, that it is right it should be done; at least that it is not wrong it should be done; that it is a right action; at least that it is not a wrong action. When thus interpreted, the words *ought,* and *right* and *wrong,* and others of that stamp, have a meaning: when otherwise, they have none.

XI.   Has the rectitude of this principle been ever formally contested? It should seem that it had, by those who have not known what they have been meaning. Is it susceptible of any direct proof? It should seem not: for that which is used to prove every thing else, cannot itself be proved: a chain of proofs must have their commencement somewhere. To give such proof is as impossible as it is needless.

XII.   Not that there is or ever has been that human creature breathing, however stupid or perverse, who has not on many, perhaps on most occasions of his life, deferred to it. By the natural constitution of the human frame, on most occasions of their lives men in general embrace this principle, without thinking of it: if not for the ordering of their own actions, yet for the trying of their own actions, as well as of those of other men. There have been, at the same time, not many, perhaps, even of the most intelligent, who have been disposed to embrace it purely and without reserve. There are even few who have not taken some occasion or other to quarrel with it, either on account of their not understanding always how to apply it, or on account of some prejudice or other which they were afraid to examine into, or could not bear to part with. For such is the stuff that man is made of: in principle and in practice, in a right track and in a wrong one, the rarest of all human qualities is consistency.

XIII.   When a man attempts to combat the principle of utility, it is with reasons drawn, without his being aware of it, from that very principle itself. His arguments, if they prove any thing, prove not that the principle is *wrong,* but that, according to the applications he supposes to be made of it, it is *misapplied.* Is it possible for a man to move the earth? Yes; but he must first find out another earth to stand upon.

XIV.   To disprove the propriety of it by arguments is impossible; but, from the causes that have been mentioned, or from some confused or partial view of it, a man may happen to be disposed not to relish it. Where this is the case, if he thinks the settling of his opinions on such a subject worth the trouble, let him take the following steps and at length, perhaps, he may come to reconcile himself to it.

1.   Let him settle with himself, whether he would wish to discard this principle altogether; if so, let him consider what it is that all his reasonings (in matters of politics especially) can amount to?

2.   If he would, let him settle with himself, whether he would judge and act without any principle, or whether there is any other he would judge and act by?

3.   If there be, let him examine and satisfy himself whether the principle he thinks he has found is really any separate intelligible principle; or whether it be not a mere principle in words, a kind of phrase, which at bottom expresses neither more nor less than the mere averment of his own unfounded sentiments; that is, what in another person he might be apt to call caprice?

4.   If he is inclined to think that his own approbation or disapprobation, annexed to the idea of an act, without any regard to its consequences, is a sufficient foundation for him to judge and act upon, let him ask himself whether his sentiment is to be a standard of right and wrong, with respect to every other man, or whether every man's sentiment has the same privilege of being a standard to itself?

5.   In the first case, let him ask himself whether his principle is not despotical, and hostile to all the rest of the human race?

6.   In the second case, whether it is not anarchical, and whether at this rate there are not as many different standards of right and wrong as there are men? and whether even to the same man, the same thing, which is right to-day, may not (without the least change in its nature) be wrong to-morrow? and whether the same thing is not right and wrong in the same place at the same time? and in either case, whether all argument is not at an end? and whether, when two men have said, 'I like this,' and 'I don't

like it,' they can (upon such a principle) have any thing more to say?

7.   If he should have said to himself, No: for that the sentiment which he proposes as a standard must be grounded on reflection, let him say on what particulars the reflection is to turn? if on particulars having relation to the utility of the act, then let him say whether this is not deserting his own principle, and borrowing assistance from that very one in opposition to which he sets it up: or if not on those particulars, on what other particulars?

8.   If he should be for compounding the matter, and adopting his own principle in part, and the principle of utility in part, let him say how far he will adopt it?

9.   When he has settled with himself where he will stop, then let him ask himself how he justifies to himself the adopting it so far? and why he will not adopt it any farther?

10.   Admitting any other principle than the principle of utility to be a right principle, a principle that it is right for a man to pursue; admitting (what is not true) that the word *right* can have a meaning without reference to utility, let him say whether there is any such thing as a *motive* that a man can have to pursue the dictates of it: if there is, let him say what that motive is, and how it is to be distinguished from those which enforce the dictates of utility: if not, then lastly let him say what it is this other principle can be good for?

Questions for Thought

1. Do you agree with Bentham's claim that human behavior is determined by the desire to increase pleasure or to decrease pain? What evidence, if any, does Bentham offer for this claim? Can you think of additional evidence that might support it?
2. How does Bentham's use of the term *happiness* differ from Aristotle's use of the term?
3. How do Bentham's views on the origin and nature of morality differ from the views of Kant? Which of these views is closest to your own position?
4. Bentham claims that the value of both individual actions and governmental measures or laws is determined by the principle of utility. Do you think that the morality or immorality of governmental measures or laws can be determined by the same principle that determines the morality or immorality of individual actions? Why or why not?
5. Can you think of any currently existing laws or governmental policies that might not be justified by the principle of utility? If so, do you think these laws or policies should be repealed?

The Sentiment of Solidarity as the Foundation of Ethics   5

ENRIQUE JOSÉ VARONA

Enrique José Varona (1849–1933) was born in Puerto Príncipe, Cuba. After studying at the local university and earning his doctorate in philosophy, Varona eventually obtained a teaching position at the University of Havana. A writer of both literature and philosophy, Varona dominated Cuban intellectual life for over fifty years. He was founding editor of the journal *Revista Cuba*, and he was a fierce defender of Cuban independence from Spain. First representing his province in the Spanish *Cortes*, Varona later fought beside the great revolutionary José Martí in the war for independence. A considerable portion of his writing is devoted to condemning Spanish colonial rule and thus justifying the revolutionary uprising.

After Cuba won its independence in 1898, Varona held many important offices in the new government. As secretary of education, he was instrumental in structuring the public education system; and in 1913, he was elected vice president of Cuba. Often described as a skeptic and pessimist, Varona never allowed his **skepticism** or pessimism to interfere with his commitment to public service. Saying that Varona's attitude toward life might be summed up in the formula "I know the worst and I do my best," one scholar described him as a person who "never lost his faith that the human will, led on by the illusion of its freedom, could change the world and make it better."

As is the case with most other Latin American philosophers, little of Varona's writing has been translated into English. His principal works include *Conferencias filosóficas. Primera serie: Lógica* (1880), *Estudios literarios y filosóficos* (1883), *Seis conferencias* (1887), *Conferencias filosóficas. Segunda serie: Psicología* (1888), *Conferencias filosóficas. Tercera serie: Moral* (1888), *Nociones de Lógica* (1902), *Curso de Psicología* (1905), and *Con el eslabón* (1927).

In the following selection from the third volume of his *Conferencias filosóficas,* Varona claims that morality is based on the feeling of social solidarity that one develops through one's interaction with other people. He defends this contention by first saying that one cannot conceive of a human being outside a social context and by then adding that our thoughts and actions are determined by the social context within which we live. After noting that the social context of our thoughts and actions is reflected in our religious beliefs as well, Varona concludes by defining a moral action as one that is in conformity with social solidarity and an immoral action as one that is not.

Questions for Reading

1. What does Varona mean by the "sentiment of solidarity"?
2. How does Varona view the relationship of the individual to society? What is his example of Robinson Crusoe intended to show?
3. In what ways are Varona's remarks about religion relevant to the rest of his essay? What value judgments does he make about different types of religious belief?
4. How does Varona view psychological change? How does he view social change?
5. What, according to Varona, is the essential difference between an act that is moral and one that is immoral?

MORALITY IS NOTHING BUT THE INDIVIDUAL'S more or less clear sentiment of his dependence upon the social body—in a word, of social solidarity.

We have . . . attentively studied and observed the thousand ties by which man is subjugated to the social body; no action takes place in the latter which does not affect him in one way or another. His reactions, in turn, influence the mass to a greater or lesser degree. Solidarity is the permanent form of this relation between the individual and the social ambient, as necessary as that which exists between the organism and the cosmic ambient. Just as his acts, which are the exterior revelations of his interior states, tend to adapt themselves to the social circumstances, by a process of which we are clearly aware only in serious cases; so do his subjective states pattern themselves after his objective impressions of the social order. And it is not at all surprising that in the majority of cases we are not aware of this dependence, just as we are generally not aware of the fact that we are breathing.

In these analyses it is not possible to conceive of man outside the social state, because that would be

From Contemporary Latin-American Philosophy, *edited by Anibal Sanchez Reulet and translated by Willard R. Trask,* University of New Mexico Press, 1954. Reprinted by permission of University of New Mexico Press.

an abstraction without meaning. He has always been in it and his whole inner life has been shaped accordingly. It is of great importance that we attend to this point. The majority of men can lack even the most remote idea of what solidarity is, yet all their emotions, images, ideas, and judgments with respect to their fellows will nevertheless be comprised within this supreme sentiment. Imitating Kant's language, we may say that this is a category of sentiment within which all our relations with other men take place. Robinson Crusoe on his desert island was formed by society and continued to live for society. Even more! Man's thought itself has been cast in a mold that is the product of society, since its most common form is language. Too powerful geniuses, men endowed with too exquisite a sensibility, the Swifts, the Leopardis, who isolate themselves from the world, do so because their concept of society is too perfect for their time. But whence did they draw the elements of their ideal? All its elements came from the very social life that they disdain and desire to improve. At the other extreme, completely abnormal persons possessed by destructive instincts, such as congenital criminals, separate themselves to a certain degree from properly constituted society but form among themselves associations consonant with the rudimentary condition of their morals. When as a result of various circumstances, definite portions of the population of a State find themselves in more or less pronounced disagreement with the rest, they tend to group themselves in more or less secret partial associations, where they create an artificial ambient for themselves. We find this phenomenon occurring even among the semi-savage peoples of the west and the interior of Africa.

Given our physical and mental organization, this special form of relations that are so necessary and so constant must have as its result an accommodation of subject to object; and the influence of this accommodation cannot but be felt in all our inner life. Through habit, happiness or unhappiness, pleasure or pain, it cannot but govern our reactions, our movements, our acts, and our entire conduct. A decisive proof of this subjective conformation to the state of society is found in man's way of conceiving his contact with the beings that he regards as supernatural. From the grossest fetishism to the purist **Deism** all the relations between man and his gods are cast in the social mode. When interest and fear are the motors of the religious sentiment, the savage conceives of his fetish as a more powerful man who can protect him or annihilate him, and he acts accordingly. When the moral element penetrates into religions, in what form does it do so? As a conception of a just and impartial judge who will weigh human acts and examine consciences to reward each according to his works in another world, in another society. And if we turn to the most beautiful conception, to the most beautiful picture yet presented of a future life as the end and prize of all mortal efforts—a conception that is a product at once of the most refined religious sentiment and of the most complete philosophical learning in its epoch—we find the type of a perfect society realized in the ideal *City of God* of St. Augustine.

Even in those forms of association which depart the furthest from the normal type we have conceived—as those constituted by conquest or slavery—all the power of solidarity is to be found. After a certain time the sentiments and ideas of the conquerors and conquered, of masters and servants, bear the impress of their mutual influence, whether that has been exercised in the direction of progress or of regression.

This, furthermore, calls our attention to the fact that the action of this powerful sentiment extends to the sphere of time. The social emotions, once experienced, have produced this modification, which then enters as a factor into all new mental combinations. The various acts and the various situations of the life of an individual are not and cannot be isolated facts; their consequences, even their merely psychic consequences, vibrate through all his subjective states, their traces can be found in his ultimate acts or in his ultimate appetites and desires. How many times a scene, a picture, a thought, an image has sufficed to act as a solvent in a consciousness! We need but remember certain celebrated conversions, such as that of the Marquis of Lombay. The sight of the disfigured corpse of his protectress, the Empress Elizabeth, fills him with such horror and produces in his soul an impression so enduring that it finally estranges him from the life of the world and fills the consciousness of a courtier with mystical thoughts.

Some equivalent takes place in the life of the social collectivity. All the events which occur within it leave their more or less profound trace, and determine to a greater or lesser extent the successive trends in that society's manner of feeling, judging, and acting. In this fashion the acts of one generation operate upon those of others, and solidarity reveals to us one of the most important aspects of the law of historical continuity. The people, the nation, the group, form a whole in space and time. The movement imparted, the vibration begun in one part is extended, ramifies, is communicated with more or less intensity to the whole. There may be—indeed there are—numerous and constant collisions and conflicts, real interferences; but even these are modifications. A movement that ceases in the face of a contrary force of equal intensity is a result, a new result, that in its turn influences those which follow. In the life of an organism, ceasing to act is sometimes as important as acting. While one body suspends its activity, the others continue their movements; and when the suspended effect is produced in the former, the position of the surrounding objects is different,

and hence the result of their mutual actions and reactions is different too.

We see, then, that, individually and collectively, solidarity binds us, and that it would be vain for us to take refuge in our inmost selves. For even there we would be followed by the images, the ideas, and the emotions that we owe to our perpetual contact with other human beings. From this we derive an important and incontestable **conclusion.** There must be a disposition of mind, a mode of feeling and thinking, and a manner of acting, which are favorable to this predominant sentiment and which therefore contribute powerfully to the accommodation of the individual to the social milieu; as there must be others which oppose and prejudice this accommodation. The former are precisely the disposition, the feelings, the judgments, and the acts, which we call moral; the latter those which we designate immoral. We can now establish this proposition: the acts of individuals who live in a society are moral if they conform to solidarity.

Questions for Thought

1. To what extent do you feel the sentiment of solidarity that Varona describes?
2. Do you agree with Varona's claim that "it is not possible to conceive of man outside the social state"? Why or why not?
3. How do Varona's views on religion compare with or differ from your own views?
4. What problems, if any, might arise from deriving one's moral values from the sentiment of social solidarity?
5. What are the essential differences between Varona's views on the origin and nature of morality and the views of Kant?

6   Mysticism and Ethics in Hindu Thought

SARVEPALLI RADHAKRISHNAN

Sarvepalli Radhakrishnan (1888–1975), who was born in southern India, held chairs in philosophy at the University of Mysore, at the University of Calcutta, and at Benares Hindu University. In addition, Radhakrishnan taught for many years at Oxford. On returning to India after its independence was obtained in 1947, he became very active in Indian political affairs. His political offices included ambassador to the Soviet Union and vice president and then president of India.

Radhakrishnan was also a prolific writer. In his various writings, he championed the philosophy of Hinduism and became a strong advocate of the philosophical dialogue between Eastern and Western philosophical traditions. His better-known writings include *Indian Philosophy* (2 vols., 1923–1927), *The Hindu View of Life* (1926), and *Eastern Religions and Western Thought* (1939). Radhakrishnan also translated and wrote commentaries for several Hindu religious texts, and he was the coeditor of *A Sourcebook in Indian Philosophy,* which was published by Princeton University Press in 1957.

In the following selection, taken from *Eastern Religions and Western Thought,* Radhakrishnan begins by arguing that an ethical theory must be grounded on a certain view of the nature of knowledge and reality. However, in opposition to Bentham, Varona, and most other moral philosophers, Radhakrishnan goes on to argue that all attempts to ground ethics in a this-worldly, humanistic **metaphysics** are destined to fail because they do not take account of the true nature of human existence. Adopting the Hindu conception of self-identity (expressed in the selection from the Upanishads in Chapter 1 of this text), Radhakrishnan claims that human beings contain a divine spark that links them to a reality higher than the reality of the everyday, **empirical** world. It is our connection to this higher, otherworldly reality that allows us to attain our highest moral ideals. As Radhakrishnan states, "If goodwill, pure love, and disinterestedness are our ideals [and he thinks they should be], then our ethics must be rooted in other-worldliness." While claiming that this need not lead to either the neglect or the negation of this-worldly life, Radhakrishnan does argue that the empirical world has value only insofar as it is the reflection of the higher spiritual universe. For this reason, the higher moral life requires that we liberate ourselves from "sense addiction" and see the historical process as a "succession of spiritual opportunities."

Questions for Reading

1. How would you describe Radhakrishnan's metaphysics? Why does he believe that ethical theory must be grounded in metaphysics?
2. What is Radhakrishnan's attitude toward material possessions? How does he perceive the nature of man?
3. What are Radhakrishnan's principal reasons for claiming that a this-worldly ethics will ultimately prove unsatisfactory?
4. What, according to Radhakrishnan, is the doctrine that is most characteristic of Hindu thought? What does this doctrine tell us about how we are to interact with other people?
5. How does Radhakrishnan view the world of our everyday experience? How is the spiritual world related to this world?

ANY ETHICAL THEORY MUST BE GROUNDED IN metaphysics, in a philosophical conception of the relation between human conduct and ultimate reality. As we think ultimate reality to be, so we behave. Vision and action go together. If we believe absurdities, we shall commit atrocities. A self-sufficient **humanism** has its own metaphysical presuppositions. It requires us to confine our attention to the immediate world of space and time and argues that moral duty consists in conforming to nature and modeling our behavior in accordance with the principles of her working. It attempts to perfect the causes of human life by purely natural means. The subject of ethics is treated as a branch of sociology or a department of psychology. Scientific **materialism** and mystical nationalism are two types of humanist ethics, interpreted in a narrow sense. They look upon man as a purely natural phenomenon whose outlook is rigorously confined by space and time. They encourage a cynical subservience to nature and historical process and an acquiescence in the merely practicable. Renunciation, self-sacrifice, disinterested service of humanity are not stimulated by the workings of natural law.

An abundance of material things will not help to make life more interesting. The rich of the world are among those who find life stale, flat, and unprofitable. Even the social conscience that urges us to extend the benefits of a material civilization cannot be accounted for by the principles of scientific **naturalism.** The material basis, while essential, is still too narrow for real living. The collective myths of Nazism, Fascism, and Communism propose to make life seem rich and significant by asking us to banish all considerations of reason and humanity and to worship the State. Man is not merely an emotional being. The Nation-State falls short of the human and the universal in man which is postulated with increasing force by the advance of science and which the well-being of human society demands.

The question has its center in the nature of man. Is he only a body which can be fed, clothed, and housed, or is he also a spirit that can aspire? The feeling of frustration experienced even by those who are provided with all the comforts and conveniences which a material civilization can supply indicates that man does not live by bread or emotional excitement alone. Besides, progress is not its own end. If it is the ultimate reality, it cannot ever be completed. We can draw nearer and nearer the goal, but cannot reach it. Its process has neither a beginning nor an end. It starts nowhere and leads nowhere. It has no issue, no goal. Senseless cycles of repetition cannot give meaning to life. It may be argued that, although the universe may have no purpose, items in the universe such as nations and individuals may have their purposes. The rise and fall of nations, the growth and crash of individuals may be quite interesting, and the universe may be viewed as an infinite succession of finite purposes. But this cannot be regarded as a satisfactory goal of ethics. Does not the humanist hope to build a terrestrial paradise inhabited by a perfect race of artists and thinkers? What is the good of telling us that though our sun, moon, and stars will share in the destruction of earthly life, other suns, moons, and stars will arise? We long for a good which is never left behind and never superseded. Man's incapacity to be satisfied with what is merely relative and remain permanently within the boundaries of the finite and empirical reality cannot be denied. Man stands before the shrine of his own mystery. He enters it the moment he becomes aware of his own eternity. Apart from eternity there is nothing that can, strictly speaking, be called human. A meaningful ethical ideal must be transcendent to the immediate flow of events.

Again, in view of the enigmatic character of the actual, is moral life possible? There are some thinkers who exhort us to do what is right even though we may not know whether it can be realized or not. Moral enthusiasm is possible only if our motive includes the expectation of being able to contribute to the achievement of moral ideals. If we are not certain that active service of the ideals will further their actualization, we cannot be sure of their worthwhileness.

We cannot help asking ourselves whether our ideals are mere private dreams of our own or bonds created by society, or even aspirations characteristic of the human species. Only a philosophy which affirms that they are rooted in the universal nature of things can give depth and fervor to moral life, courage and confidence in moral difficulties. We need to be fortified by the conviction that the service of the ideals is what the cosmic scheme demands of us, that our loyalty or disloyalty to them is a matter of the deepest moment not only to ourselves or to society, or even to the human species, but to the nature of things. If ethical thought is profound, it will give a cosmic motive to morality. Moral consciousness must include a conviction of the reality of ideals. If the latter is religion, then ethical humanism is acted religion. When man realizes his essential unity with the whole of being, he expresses this unity in his life. Mysticism and ethics, otherworldliness and worldly work go together. In the primitive religions we have this combination. Otherworldliness appears as *mana,* which the savage derives from an innate sense of some mysterious power within the phenomena and behind the events of the visible world, and morality appears as taboo, and the sense of sacredness in things and persons, which with its inhibitions controls the whole range of his conduct. In the higher religions of mankind, belief in the transcendent and work in the natural have grown together in close intimacy and interaction. Religion is the soul's attitude, response, and adjustment in the presence of the supreme realities of the transcendent order; ethics deal with the right adjustment of life on earth, especially in human society. Both are motivated by a desire to live in the light of ideals. If we are satisfied with what exists, there is no meaning in "ought"; if we are a species of passing phenomena, there is no meaning in religion. Religion springs from the conviction that there is another world beyond the visible and the temporal with which man has dealings, and ethics require us to act in this world with the compelling vision of another. With our minds anchored in the beyond we are to strive to make the actual more nearly like what it ought to be. Religion alone can give assurance and wider reference to ethics and a new meaning to human life. We make moral judgments about individual lives and societies simply because we are spiritual beings, not merely social animals.

If there is one doctrine more than another which is characteristic of Hindu thought, it is the belief that there is an interior depth to the human soul, which, in its essence, is uncreated and deathless and absolutely real. The spirit in man is different from the individual ego; it is that which animates and exercises the individual, the vast background of his being in which all individuals lie. It is the core of all being, the inner thread by being strung on which the world exists. In the soul of man are conflicting tendencies: the attraction of the infinite, which abides for ever, changeless, unqualified, untouched by the world; and the fascination of the finite, that which like the wind-beaten surface of the waters is never for a moment the same. Every human being is a potential spirit and represents, as has been well said, a hope of God and is not a mere fortuitous concourse of episodes like the changing forms of clouds or the patterns of a kaleidoscope. If the feeling for God were not in man, we could not implant it any more than we could squeeze blood from a stone. The heart of religion is that man truly belongs to another order, and the meaning of man's life is to be found not in this world but in more than historical reality. His highest aim is release from the historical succession denoted by birth and death. So long as he is lost in the historical process without a realization of the super-historical goal, he is only "once born" and is liable to sorrow. God and not the world of history is the true environment of our soul. If we overlook this important fact, and make

our ethics or world affirmation independent of religion or world negation, our life and thought become condescending, though this condescension may take the form of social service or philanthropy. But it is essentially a form of self-assertion and not real concern for the well-being of others. If goodwill, pure love, and disinterestedness are our ideals, then our ethics must be rooted in other-worldliness. This is the great classical tradition of spiritual wisdom. The mystery cults of Greece had for their central doctrine that man's soul is of divine origin and is akin to the spirit of God. The influence of these mystery cults on Socrates and Plato is unmistakable. When Jesus tells Nicodemus that until a man is begotten from above he cannot see or enter the Kingdom of God, when Paul declares that "he that soweth to the flesh shall of the flesh reap corruption; but he that soweth to the spirit shall of the spirit reap everlasting life," they are implying that our natural life is mortal and it is invaded by sin and death, and that the life of spirit is immortal. St. John in the First Epistle says: "the world passeth away, and the lust thereof: but he that doeth the will of God abideth for ever." We are amphibious beings, according to Plotinus. We live on earth and in a world of spirit.

Although the view about the coexistence of the human and the divine in close intimacy and interpenetration may be true, does not Hindu thought declare that life is empty and unreal, and that it has no purpose or meaning? Schweitzer tells us that for the **Upanishads** "the world of the senses is a magic play staged by the universal soul for itself. The individual soul is brought into this magic play under a spell. By reflection about itself it must become capable of seeing through the deception. Thereupon it gives up taking part in the play. It waits quietly and enjoys its identity with the universal soul until, at death, the magic play for it ceases to be." "Man cannot engage in ethical activity in a world with no meaning." "For any believer in the *maya* doctrine ethics can have only a quite relative importance." This account is by no means a fair representation of the position of the Upanishads. The long theistic tradition interprets the doctrine of the Upanishads in a way directly opposed to this account. . . . Religious experience, by its affirmation that the basic fact in the universe is spiritual, implies that the world of sound and sense is not final. All existence finds its source and support in a supreme reality whose nature is spirit. The visible world is the symbol of a more real world. It is the reflection of a spiritual universe which gives to it its life and significance.

What is the relation of absolute being to historical becoming, of eternity to time? Is succession, history, progress, real and sufficient in its own right, or does man's deep instinct for the unchanging point to an eternal perfection which alone gives the world meaning and worth? Is the inescapable flux all, or is there anything which abides? Religious consciousness bears testimony to the reality of something behind the visible, a haunting beyond, which both attracts and disturbs, in the light of which the world of change is said to be unreal. The Hebrews contrasted the abidingness of God with the swift flow of human generations. "Before the mountains were brought forth or ever Thou hadst formed the earth and the world even from everlasting to everlasting, Thou art God." The psalmist cries to his God: "They [i.e., heaven and earth] shall be changed: but Thou art the same, and Thy years shall have no end." The Christian exclaims: "The things which are seen are temporal; but the things which are not seen are eternal." The mutability of things which is part of the connotation of the word *"maya"* is a well-known theme in the world's literature. The saying that "time and chance happeneth to them all" of Ecclesiastes is the refrain we hear often.

Gaudapāda argues that "whatever is non-existent at the beginning and in the end is non-existent in the middle also." In other words, the things of the world are not eternal. The world is *maya,* i.e., passes away, but God is eternal. Change, causality, activity are finite categories and the Eternal is lifted above them. God is not a mere means to explain the universe or improve human society.

Śaṁkara, who is rightly credited with the systematic formulation of the doctrine of *maya,* tells us that the highest reality is unchangeable, and therefore that changing existence such as human history has not ultimate reality (*pāramārthika sattā*). He warns us, however, against the temptation to regard what is not completely real as utterly illusory. The world has empirical being (*vyāvahārika sattā*) which is quite different from illusory existence (*prātibhāsika sattā*). Human experience is neither ultimately real nor completely illusory. Simply because the world of experience is not the perfect form of reality, it does not follow that it is a delusion, without any significance. The world is not a phantom, though it is not real. **Brahman** is said to be the real of the real, *satyasyasatyam.* In all objective consciousness, we are in a sense aware of the real.

Similarly, all knowledge presupposes the knower who is constant, while the known is unsteady. When Plato tells us that we bring universal ideas with us from the world in which we lived before our birth, he is referring to the non-phenomenal, time-transcending power in us which belongs to a different world from the observed phenomena. The **"nous"** which organizes the facts of experience and interprets them is not itself a fact of experience. It must have had its origin in and belong to another world. It beholds by virtue of its own nature eternal realities. This presence in us is an assurance that we are in touch with reality. Spirit is real being and the rest its limited activity. The spirit is pure existence, self-aware, timeless, spaceless, unconditioned, not dependent for its being on its sense of objects, not dependent for its delight on the gross or subtle touches of outward things. It is not divided in the multitude of beings. Śaṁkara's **advaita** or non-duality has for its central thesis the non-difference between the individual self and Brahman. As for difference or multiplicity (*nānātva*), it is not real. Its self-discrepant character shows that it is only an appearance of the real. All schools of *advaita* are agreed on these two propositions. Differences arise when the nature of the actuality of the manifold world as distinct from the reality is described. Śaṁkara accepts the empirical reality of the world, which is negated only when perfect insight or intuition of the oneness of all is attained. Until then it has empirical validity or pragmatic justification. There are *advaitins* who argue that the world of difference has not even empirical validity. Śaṁkara, however, tells us that so long as we are in the world of *maya* and occupy a dualistic standpoint, the world is there, standing over against us, determining our perceptions and conduct.

Besides, the world we see and touch is not independent and self-sufficing. It carries no explanation of itself. It is a world reflecting the condition of our minds, a partial construction made from insufficient data under the stress of self-conscious individuality with its cravings and desires. What is perceived and shaped into meaning depends on the powers of apprehension we employ and the interests we possess. Our passion-limited apprehension gives us the world of common sense. Take the apparent facts of the universe. Matter is not primal. It is a thing made, not self-existent. It is not unreal, but is being as it forms itself to sense. It is not a baseless fiction, but at the lowest it is a misrepresentation of truth; at the highest it is an imperfect representation or translation of the truth into a lower plane. Even as our knowledge implies the presence of a constant consciousness, the object of our knowledge implies the reality of pure being. Our conceptions of the universe answer to our degrees of consciousness. As our consciousness increases in its scope, we see more clearly. We now see partly as an animal and partly as a human being. Sometimes the world is viewed as one of self-satisfaction, at other times as an object of curiosity and contemplation. To see it in truth, one has to free oneself from sense addiction and concentrate the whole energy of one's consciousness on the nature of reality. It is the only way by which we can attain a clear consciousness of reality as it is and get a true picture of the world instead of partial sketches. Knowledge which we now obtain through senses and reason cannot be regarded as complete or perfect. It is flawed with antinomies and contradictions. Through the force of *avidya* (not knowing) we impose on the reality of the one the multiplicity of the world. Being which is one only appears to the soul as manifoldness, and the soul beholds itself as entangled in the world of *samsara,* in the chain of birth and death. This *avidya* is natural (*naisargika*) to the human mind, and the world is organically connected with it. It is not therefore mere waking dream.

Maya is not solipsism. It does not say that suns and universes are the invention of the solitary mind. Śaṁkara proclaims his opposition to **Vijñānavāda** or mentalism. He argues that waking experiences are distinct from dreamstates, though neither can be regarded as real metaphysically. Our world of waking experience is not the ultimate reality, but neither is it a shadow-show. We are surrounded by something other than ourselves, which cannot be reduced to states of our own consciousness. Though the world is always changing, it has a unity and a meaning. These are revealed by the reality present all through it. This reality lies not in the facts but in the principle which makes them into a whole. We are able to know that the world is imperfect, finite, and changing, because we have a consciousness of the eternal and the perfect. It is by the light of this consciousness that we criticize ourselves or condemn the world. Even as the human individual is a complex of the eternal and the temporal, the world which confronts him contains both. It is for Śaṁkara a mixture of truth and illusion. It partakes of the characteristics of being and non-being (*sadasadātmaka*). Although, therefore, it has a lower form of reality than pure spirit, it is not non-existence. While Śaṁkara refuses to acquiesce in the seeming reality of the actual, he does not dismiss it as an unreal phantasmagoria. It is not determinable either as real or unreal. Its truth is in being, reality, truth (*sat*); its multiplicity and division, its dispersal in space and time is untrue (*an-ṛtam*). In the world itself we have change. Śaṁkara does not tell us that the process of the world is perpetual recurrence, in which events of past cycles are repeated in all their details. If everything is recurrent, perpetually rotating, and governed by a law of cyclic motion, there is nothing new, no meaning in history. But there is an historical fulfillment and destiny for the cosmic process. Mankind is engaged in a pursuit that tends towards a definite goal. Truth will be victorious on earth, and it is the nature of the cosmic process that the finite individual is called upon to work through the exercise of his freedom for that goal through ages of struggle and effort. The soul has risen from the sleep of matter, through plant and animal life, to the human level, and is battling with ignorance and imperfection to take possession of its infinite kingdom. It is absolute not in its actual empirical condition but in its potentiality, in its capacity to appropriate the Absolute. The historical process is not a mere external chain of events, but offers a succession of spiritual opportunities. Man has to attain a mastery over it and reveal the higher world operating in it. The world is not therefore an empty dream or an eternal delirium.

Questions for Thought

1. What is the foundation of your own moral views? In what ways, if any, is your foundation similar to that of Radhakrishnan?
2. What are the essential differences between Varona's views and those of Radhakrishnan? Which of them comes closest to your own position?
3. How does your own attitude about the nature of material possessions compare with or differ from that of Radhakrishnan?
4. Do you agree with Radhakrishnan's critique of this-worldly ethics? How do you think Bentham would have reacted to his critique?
5. Do you think Radhakrishnan would agree with Aristotle's claim that the highest human good is happiness? What would be his reasons for either accepting or rejecting this claim?

7   Compassion and the Reverence for Life

ALBERT SCHWEITZER

Albert Schweitzer (1875–1965), the eldest son of a Lutheran pastor, was a philosopher, theologian, medical doctor, and accomplished musician. He studied both philosophy and theology at the University of Strasbourg, receiving his doctorate in philosophy in 1899 and his doctorate in theology the following year. While studying at Strasbourg, Schweitzer also found time to practice music, becoming an organist in 1893. Especially interested in the music of Bach, Schweitzer wrote a study of the composer's life, *J. S. Bach: Le musicien-poète,* which was published in 1905. That same year, Schweitzer announced his plans to become a mission doctor, and he spent the next eight years working toward his medical degree.

In 1913, Schweitzer and his wife, Hélène Bresslau, a nurse, traveled to the Gabon province of French Equatorial Africa to establish a hospital to serve the native population. His mission work was interrupted during World War I, when Schweitzer, who was German, was incarcerated as a prisoner of war by the French forces. However, in 1924, he returned to the same region of Africa to rebuild his hospital. He later added a leper colony to the hospital, and these institutions were still serving hundreds of people when Schweitzer died in 1965. In addition to his book on Bach, Schweitzer wrote several other influential works. His book *Von Reimarus zu Wrede* (1906; translated as *The Quest for the Historical Jesus*) was widely read in theological circles, and his *Kulturphilosophie* (1923; *Philosophy of Civilization*) represented an attempt to deal with world problems by extending moral consideration to all living things. Not content to limit himself to mission work and writing, Schweitzer was also a tireless lecturer and performer, giving lectures and organ recitals throughout Europe. His efforts on behalf of world peace won him the Nobel Peace Prize in 1952.

In the following selection, which was delivered at a Sunday morning church service on February 23, 1919, Schweitzer examines the nature and origin of morality. Given that Schweitzer presented his views in the form and context of a sermon, one might expect that he would follow Radhakrishnan and argue that morality is based on certain religious or spiritual insights. However, despite the fact that Schweitzer begins his sermon with a quotation from the biblical book of Romans, he does not base morality on religion or on the sort of otherworldly metaphysics endorsed by Radhakrishnan. Rather, Schweitzer claims that the ground of moral behavior is compassionate reverence for everything that lives. He says that "in the final analysis the good consists in the elemental reverence of the mystery that we call life, in reverence for all of its appearances, the smallest as well as the greatest. The good is whatever conserves and furthers life; evil is whatever inhibits and destroys life."

Schweitzer goes on to contrast the human possibility of compassion with the egotistical, compassionless struggle that characterizes the rest of nature. He also points out that several factors conspire to eliminate the capacity for compassion, thereby reducing human action to the level of nonhuman nature. Observing the tremendous quantity of suffering in the world that we are powerless to prevent, Schweitzer notes that we are tempted to give up, to become unfeeling like everyone else. This temptation is strengthened when we realize the psychological truth that compassion for the suffering of others causes us to suffer as well—that it reduces or even eliminates our potentiality for happiness. However, as we have already seen, Schweitzer does not believe that the highest human good lies in happiness, as do Aristotle and Bentham. Rather, Schweitzer believes that in preserving life and in sharing the sorrows of others, we will experience a kind of joy that is missing from the lives of those who have lost the capacity for compassion.

Questions for Reading

1. Who is Schweitzer addressing in this selection?
2. What, according to Schweitzer, is the basis of morality?
3. What does Schweitzer identify as "the great enemy of morality"? How is this enemy to be overcome?
4. How, according to Schweitzer, does human existence differ from the existence of other creatures of nature?
5. Toward the middle of the selection, Schweitzer asks the following question: "Why is the God who manifests himself in nature the negation of everything that we perceive to be moral?" How does Schweitzer answer this question?
6. What does Schweitzer say about the nature and desirability of human happiness? What, if anything, does he consider to be more important than happiness?

For no one of us lives, and equally no one of us dies, for himself alone.

ROMANS 14:7

AS I SAID LAST SUNDAY, WE WOULD DEAL FURTHER with the problem of morality in our next devotions.

In connection with the question about the greatest commandment in the Old Testament, Jesus responded to the inquiring scribes by combining two commandments—the commandment to love God and the commandment to love one's neighbor.

In our last devotions, this led us to the question of the essence of ethics, to the question of the ultimate grounding principle of morality. We were not content with the conventional answer that the essence of ethics consisted of love, but we went further and asked: Then what is love? What is the love of God that compels us to be good to others? What is it to love our neighbors?

And we asked not only the heart, but also the reason, about the ethical. For we saw then that the weakness of our time resides in the lack of

This is the editor's translation of a selection from Predigten 1898–1948, *by Albert Schweitzer, München: Verlag C.H. Beck, 2001.*

reasoning, in the fact that morality can be destroyed through prejudices and passions. Although we cannot at all assume that reason and heart walk side by side without bumping one another, the true heart deliberates and the true reason feels. We found that the both of them, reason and heart, concur that in the final analysis the good consists in the elemental reverence of the mystery that we call life, in reverence for all of its appearances, the smallest as well as the greatest. The good is whatever conserves and furthers life; evil is whatever inhibits and destroys life.

We are ethical when we step out of our solitariness, when we shed our alienation from other beings and share in the experiences and suffering that takes place around us. It is this quality that first makes us truly human; in it we possess an undetachable, continuously developing, self-oriented morality that is properly ours.

These universal expressions—"reverence for life," "shedding alienation," "the urge toward the conservation of the life around us"—sound cold and empty. But even if they are unimpressive words, they may nonetheless be prolific. The seed is also unimpressive, and yet it carries within itself the germ from which things grow. Just so, in these unimpressive words lies the basic conception from which all of morality develops, whether the individual is aware of it or not.

The presupposition of morality is thus that we share in the experience of everything around us, not only in the case of human life, but of all beings that we encounter. This constrains us to do everything that we can do to conserve and to further life.

The great enemy of morality is desensitization. As children, so far as our understanding for things went, we had an elementary capacity for compassion. But this capacity did not grow over the years; it did not keep pace with the growing intellect. It was something uncomfortable and confusing to us. We saw so many people who were no longer compassionate. Then we too suppressed our sensitiveness in order to be like the others, in order not to be apart from them, and because we did not know what else to do. In this way many people become like houses, in which one room after another has been emptied, and which thus look cold and strange along the street.

To stay good means to stay awake! We are all like men walking outdoors in the cold and snow. Woe to him who sits down, giving in to fatigue, and falls asleep. He will never wake up. Just so, the moral man within us dies when we become too weary to share the life-experiences of the other beings around us, to suffer with them. Woe to us if our sensitiveness is deadened—our conscience in the broadest sense of the word, our consciousness of how we should act, dies along with it.

Reverence for life and compassion for other lives is the great happening for us and the great happening for the world. Nature knows no such reverence for life. It brings into existence a thousandfold life in the most meaningful way, and yet destroys this thousandfold life in the most meaningless way. Throughout all the levels of life up to the human sphere, terrible ignorance pours out of all beings. They have only the will to live, but not the capacity for compassion toward other beings; they suffer, but they cannot share the suffering of others. The great will to life, by which nature is preserved, is in mysterious disunion with itself.

Beings live at the expense of the life of other beings. Nature permits the most dreadful cruelties to be committed. Through instinct it guides insects to bore holes into other insects with their stingers and to lay their eggs in them, so that the egg develops and lives off the caterpillar, thus causing its agonizing death. Nature lets ants band together and prey upon poor little beings, badgering them to death. Look at the spider! How ghastly is the craft that nature taught it!

Nature is beautiful and magnificent when looked at from a distance, but when read as a book, it is horrid. And its cruelty is so senseless! The most precious life is sacrificed to the lowliest. Once a child inhales tuberculosis bacteria, he grows up and thrives, but is subject to suffering and an early death because these lowly beings multiply in his vital organs. How often in Africa I have been stricken with terror when I examined the blood of a patient with sleeping sickness. Why did this man sit there, his face distorted by suffering, and moan, "Oh, my head, my head!"? Why must he weep night after night and die miserably? Because there, under the microscope, were delicate, tiny, pale corpuscles, ten to fifteen-thousandths of a millimeter long—oh, not very many, often so few that one would sometimes have to search for hours in order to discover any of them.

Such then is the mysterious disunion in the will to live—life against life, creating suffering and death for others, both guiltless and guilty. Nature teaches horrible egoism, only interrupted for a short time by the urge it has implanted in beings to bring offspring to life and to offer, as long as it is necessary, love and aid to them. Indeed, animals love their young ones with such self-sacrifice that they are willing to die for them. Thus, here they are able to feel compassion; yet this makes their lack of compassion for those beings that are unrelated to them even more abominable.

The world, handed over to ignorant egoism, is like a valley shrouded in darkness; there is brightness only up in the heights. All must live in the dark; only the highest being, man, can ascend and look for the light. He can attain the knowledge of the reverence for life; he can reach the knowledge of shared experience and compassion, thus transcending the ignorance in which the rest of the creatures languish.

And this knowledge is the great event in the evolution of life. Here truth and the good appear in the world, light shines over the dark, and the most profound concept of life is reached—life sharing experience together, where, in one existence, the wash of the waves of the whole world is felt, where, in one existence, life as such becomes conscious of itself. Isolated existence ceases; the experience of outside beings floods into us.

We live in the world and the world lives in us. Around this knowledge itself enigmas arise. Why is the law of nature so far asunder from the moral law? Why cannot our reason simply adopt and build upon the utterances that it discovers in the life of nature, rather than coming into such monstrous opposition with everything it sees in the natural world? Why must it find that the law it discovers within itself is totally different than the laws governing the world? Why must it divorce itself from the world when it reaches the concept of the good? Why must we experience this antagonism without hope of ever being able to resolve it? Why, instead of harmony, is there rupture?

Furthermore, God is the power that conceives everything. Why is the God who manifests himself in nature the negation of everything that we perceive to be moral? How can he be a power who meaningfully creates life while senselessly destroying life? How can we bring into reconciliation God, the power of nature, with the God of moral will, the God of love, as we must extol him when we have risen to a higher knowledge of life, to reverence for life, to compassion and the sharing of experience?

Several Sundays ago, when we were trying to get straight about optimistic and pessimistic world views, I told you that it was a great calamity for humanity that there is no closure, that we cannot offer a simple philosophy of life, because the more knowledge advances, the more it leads us away from such a possibility. And this is not only because it becomes ever clearer how little we can actually apprehend in knowledge, but also because the contradictions in life become more deeply felt. "Our knowledge is partial," says the Apostle Paul (I Corinthians, 13, 9). But that is saying it much too mildly. A still greater difficulty is that our knowledge allows us a glimpse into irresolvable contradictions—all of which can be traced back to the one fundamental contradiction, namely that the law, according to which everything happens in the world, has in itself nothing that we recognize and feel to be moral.

Instead of being able to attach our morality to a coherent worldview and a uniform concept of God, we must constantly defend our morality against the contradictions arising from our worldview that crash against it like a raging surf. We must construct a dike—but will it hold?

Something else that threatens our ability and our will to feel compassion is the ever-recurring, intruding thought—it is useless! Whatever you do, whatever you are able to do in order to prevent and mitigate suffering and to conserve life—all this is nothing when compared to the suffering that occurs in the world around you, suffering about which you cannot do anything.

It is certainly terrible to be reminded of the extent of our powerlessness; yet how much suffering we ourselves bring about in other beings without being able to prevent it. You go for a walk on a trail in the woods; the sun is shining in bright splotches through the tree tops. Birds are singing, and thousands of insects buzz cheerily in the air. But your path, without you knowing anything about it, is deadly. Here an ant, which you trod upon, lies in agony; there lies a beetle that you squashed; and there squirms a worm that you unknowingly stepped on. In the midst of the magnificent song of life rings the melody of pain and death, a melody that you compose; you are guilty, yet nonetheless innocent. And so above all you feel, despite the good that you are able to do, the terrible powerlessness to help as much as you would like. Then comes the voice of the tempters who say to you: Then why torture yourself? It cannot be helped. Give up! Become indifferent, thoughtless, and unfeeling like the others.

Still another temptation arises. Compassion includes suffering.[1] Anyone who experiences the woes of the world within himself can no longer become happy in the sense that humans would like. He is not able to give himself unreservedly to the hours that bring him happiness and joy, because of the woes that he has shared with others. What he has seen weighs upon him. He thinks of the poor that he has come across, of the sick that he has seen, of the men whose grave destiny he has read about—and darkness shuts out the light of his joy. And so it goes.

In the merriest of company, he suddenly is absent-minded. And once more the tempter says to him: one must not live like this. One must be able to disregard what goes on around them. One must not be so highly sensitive. Teach yourself the requisite insensibility, put on armor, become thoughtless like the others, if you want to live sensibly. Then in the end, we move so far in this direction that we feel ashamed to know the great sharing of experience and the great compassion. We hide it from one another and act as if it is something foolish to us, as if it is something that one sheds when one starts to become a more reasonable human being.

These are the three great temptations that subtly ruin the prerequisite on which the good depends. Be on guard against them.

Meet the first one by saying that, for you, sharing experience and helping is an inner necessity. In view of what needs to be done, everything that you are able to do will always be only a drop of water rather than a stream; however, it is this that gives your life the only meaning that it can have, that makes it worthwhile. Wherever you are, so far as you can, you should bring about redemption, redemption from the misery that is itself brought into the world by the self-contradictory will to life, redemption that only

the human being who is aware can bring. The few things that you are able to do are much—if only you somewhere take the pain, suffering and anxiety from a living being, be it human or be it any other creature. Conserving life is the sole happiness.

As for the other temptation, that compassion for those around you will cause you suffering, meet it by becoming aware that compassion gives you the ability to share joy as well as sorrow. With the deadening of compassion you lose, at the same time, the capacity to share the happiness of others. And however little the happiness is that we see in the world, still the sharing of the happiness around us, along with the good that we ourselves are able to create, provides the sole happiness that makes our life bearable.

And lastly, you do not at all have the right to say: I will be one way or another, because it seems to me that being so will make me happier than other ways. Rather you must be what you must be—a truly aware human being, a human being who lives with the world, who experiences the world within himself. Whether thereby you are happier or not, according to the customary conception of happiness, makes no difference. It is not being happy, but being good, that the mysterious hour requires of us—to obey her is the only thing that can satisfy.

Thus, I say to you: do not let yourself grow deadened. Remain awake! Your soul is at stake. If by these words, in which I am revealing my innermost thoughts, I could only compel you who are here now with me to disrupt the delusion with which the world would lull us to sleep, so that none of you would any longer be thoughtless, so that you would no longer thereby escape from learning reverence for life and the great sharing of experience—then I would be content. I would look at my work as consecrated, even if I knew that tomorrow my preaching would be forbidden, or that I had accomplished nothing with my preaching up to now and would accomplish nothing else in the future.

I, who usually have grave anxiety when it comes to influencing others because of the responsibility that one assumes in doing so, would like to have the power to enchant you so that you became sympathetic, until each of you experienced the great sorrow from which one can not escape when one becomes compassionately aware. Then I could say to myself that you are on the path to goodness and that you will never lose your way again.

"No one of us lives for himself"—may these words pursue us. May they never become silent until we are embedded in our graves.

NOTE

1. In German, the word for compassion, "Mitleiden," includes the word for suffering, "leiden," within it. The prefix "mit" is translated as "with"; thus compassion literally means to suffer with others. (translator's note)

Questions for Thought

1. What do you think the quotation from Romans means? Why do you think Schweitzer began his sermon with this particular quotation?
2. How do Schweitzer's views on the nature of morality compare with or differ from the views of Radhakrishnan?
3. Do you believe that Schweitzer has accurately described the difference between humans and other creatures of nature? If not, how would you describe this difference?
4. Do you agree with Schweitzer's views on happiness? Which of the other philosophers whom you have read would most likely agree with Schweitzer's views? Which of them would most likely disagree?
5. Do you think that human beings have the capacity to feel a compassionate reverence for life? To what extent do you have a compassionate reverence for life?

What Are Some Reasons for Questioning Traditional Values?

Relativism   8

DAVID B. WONG

David B. Wong (b. 1949), who received his Ph.D. in philosophy from Princeton University in 1977, is professor of philosophy at Duke University. Before his recent appointment at Duke, Wong taught philosophy for many years at Brandeis University in Waltham, Massachusetts. His teaching and research interests include ethical theory, comparative ethics, Chinese philosophy, and other areas of the history of philosophy.

In addition to performing his teaching duties, Wong has delivered numerous papers, written more than thirty articles and reviews, and appeared on the PBS television series *The Examined Life*. He is also the author of the influential book *Moral Relativity* (1984) and is currently working on another book dealing with ethical theory. Recently Wong served as coeditor of an anthology of comparative essays on Confucianism and Western philosophy entitled *Confucian Ethics: A Comparative Study of Self, Autonomy, and Community* (2004).

In the following essay, Wong describes and defends moral **relativism,** the doctrine that there is no single universally valid moral code or set of values. After contrasting relativism with moral absolutism, or what he calls "universalism," Wong distinguishes between two types of moral relativism. The first type, meta-ethical relativism, maintains that no single moral code is valid in all times and places; the second type, normative moral relativism, maintains that it is wrong to judge others according to our own moral values and/or to coerce them into adopting our values. Wong then goes on to discuss some of the reasons that have been used to defend either or both of these types of relativism. One of the principal reasons that has frequently been cited is the fact that widely differing moral codes are found to exist in diverse cultures, a fact that has been noted both by ancient authors and by modern cultural anthropologists.

Regardless of the reason given for moral relativism, Wong argues that the extreme version of normative relativism—namely, that one should never judge others (or never try to make them conform to one's values)—is self-defeating. For in making this claim, a person is implicitly affirming a value, the value of tolerance, and suggesting that others adopt it.

While extreme normative relativism is not defensible, Wong argues that there are good reasons for rejecting universalism and adopting a qualified relativism. This qualified relativism would allow us to both acknowledge the diversity found in competing moral codes and to embrace tolerance while still making it possible for us to judge the actions of others in certain cases. For example, we could morally condemn a reprehensible action, such as human torture, while still admitting that there is no single moral code that everyone must follow. Since much of Western thinking about morality, such as that found in both Kantian and Christian ethics, has been absolutist, Wong's position obviously represents a challenge to such thinking.

Questions for Reading

1. What exactly does Wong mean by "moral relativism"? How does it differ from what he calls "universalism"?
2. What are the two types of relativism identified by Wong? How do these types of relativism compare with or differ from one another?
3. What are some of the reasons that have led people to endorse moral relativism? Why is Darius' experiment relevant to this question? What role has anthropology played in the debate over relativism?
4. How, according to Wong, does Confucian ethics differ from the ethical culture of the modern West?
5. Why does Wong believe that extreme normative relativism is indefensible? How does Wong's own position compare with or differ from extreme normative relativism?
6. What is Wong's discussion of abortion intended to show?

INTRODUCTION

MORAL RELATIVISM IS A COMMON RESPONSE to the deepest conflicts we face in our ethical lives. Some of these conflicts are quite public and political, such as the apparently intractable disagreement in the United States over the moral and legal permissibility of abortion. Other conflicts inviting the relativistic response are of a less dramatic but more recurrent nature. This author's experience as a first-generation

From A Companion to Ethics, *edited by Peter Singer, Basil Blackwell, 1991. Reprinted by permission.*

Chinese American exemplifies a kind of conflict that others have faced: that between inherited values and the values of the adopted country. As a child I had to grapple with the differences between what was expected of me as a good Chinese son and what was expected of my non-Chinese friends. Not only did they seem bound by duties that were much less rigorous in the matter of honoring parents and upholding the family name, but I was supposed to feel superior to them because of that. It added to my confusion that I sometimes felt envy at their freedom.

Moral relativism, as a common response to such conflicts, often takes the form of a denial that any single moral code has universal validity, and an assertion that moral truth and justifiability, if there are any such things, are in some way relative to factors that are culturally and historically contingent. This doctrine is *meta-ethical* **relativism,** because it is about the relativity of moral truth and justifiability. Another kind of moral relativism, also a common response to deep moral conflict, is a doctrine about how one ought to act toward those who accept values very different from one's own. This *normative* **moral relativism** holds that it is wrong to pass judgment on others who have substantially different values, or to try to make them conform to one's values, for the reason that their values are as valid as one's own. Another common response to deep moral conflict, however, contradicts moral relativism in its two major forms. It is the universalist or absolutist position that both sides of a moral conflict cannot be equally right, that there can be only one truth about the matter at issue. This position is so common, in fact, that William James was led to call us "absolutists by instinct." The term **"universalism"** will be used hereafter, because "absolutism" is used not only to refer to the denial of moral relativism, but also to the view that some moral rules or duties are absolutely without exception.

META-ETHICAL RELATIVISM

The debate between moral relativism and universalism accounts for a significant proportion of philosophical reflection in ethics. In ancient Greece at least some of the **"Sophists"** defended a version of moral relativism, which Plato attempted to refute. Plato attributes to the first great Sophist, Protagoras, the argument that human custom determines what is fine and ugly, just and unjust. Whatever is communally judged to be the case, the argument goes, actually comes to be the case (*Theaetetus,* 172AB; it is unclear, however, whether the real Protagoras actually argued in this manner). Now the Greeks, through trade, travel, and war, were fully aware of wide variation in customs, and so the argument concludes with the relativity of morality. The question with this argument, however, is whether we can accept that custom determines in a strong sense what is fine and ugly, just and unjust. It may influence what people *think* is fine and just. But it is quite another thing for custom to determine what *is* fine and just. Customs sometimes change under the pressure of moral criticism, and the argument seems to rely on a **premise** that contradicts this phenomenon.

Another kind of argument given for relativism is premised on the view that the customary ethical beliefs in any given society are functionally necessary for that society. Therefore, the argument concludes, the beliefs are true for that society, but not necessarily in another. The sixteenth-century essayist, Michel de Montaigne, sometimes makes this argument ("Of custom, and not easily changing an accepted law," 1595), but it has had its greatest acceptance among anthropologists of the twentieth century who emphasize the importance of studying societies as organic wholes of which the parts are functionally interdependent. . . . The problem with the functional argument, however, is that moral beliefs are not justified merely on the grounds that they are necessary for a society's existence in anything like its present form. Even if a society's institutions and practices crucially depend on the acceptance of certain beliefs, the justifiability of those beliefs depends on the moral acceptability of the institutions and practices. To show that certain beliefs are necessary for maintaining a fascist society, for instance, is not to justify those beliefs.

Despite the weaknesses of these arguments for moral relativism, the doctrine has always had its adherents. Its continuing strength has always been rooted in the impressiveness of the variation in ethical belief to be found across human history and culture. In an ancient text (*Dissoi Logoi* or the *Contrasting Arguments*) associated with the Sophists, it is pointed out that for the Lacedaemonians, it was fine for girls to exercise without tunics, and for children not to learn music and letters, while for the Ionians, these things were foul. Montaigne assembled a catalogue of exotic customs, such as male prostitution, cannibalism, women warriors, killing one's father at a certain age as an act of piety, and recites from the Greek historian Herodotus the experiment of Darius. Darius asked Greeks how much they would have to be paid before they would eat the bodies of their deceased fathers. They replied that no sum of money could get them to do such a thing. He then asked certain Indians who customarily ate the bodies of their deceased fathers what they would have to be paid to burn the bodies of their fathers. Amidst loud exclamations, they bade him not to speak of such a thing (Montaigne's "Of Custom," 1595, and Herodotus, *Persian Wars,* Book III, 38).

But while many have been moved by such examples to adopt moral relativism, the argument from diversity does not support relativism in any simple or direct way. As the Socrates of Plato's dialogues observed, we have reason to listen only to the wise among us (*Crito,* 44CD). The simple fact of diversity in belief is no disproof of the possibility that there are some beliefs better to have than the others because they are truer or more justified than the rest. If half the world still believed that the sun, the moon, and the planets revolved around the earth, that would be no disproof of the possibility of a unique truth about the structure of the universe. Diversity in belief, after all, may result from varying degrees of wisdom. Or it may be that different people have their own limited perspectives of the truth, each perspective being distorted in its own way.

It is sometimes thought that the extent and depth of disagreement in ethics indicates that moral judgments are simply not judgments about facts, that they assert nothing true or false about the world but straightforwardly express our own subjective reactions to certain facts and happenings, whether these be collective or individual reactions (e.g., see C. L. Stevenson, *Ethics and Language,* 1944). A more complicated view is that moral judgments purport to report objective matters of fact, but that there are no such matters of fact (see J. L. Mackie, *Ethics: Inventing Right and Wrong,* 1977). The success of modern science in producing a remarkable degree of convergence of belief about the basic structure of the physical world probably reinforces these varieties of **skepticism** about the objectivity of moral beliefs. It is hard to deny that there is a significant difference in the degree of convergence of belief in ethics and in science. Yet there are possible explanations for that difference that are compatible with claiming that moral judgments are ultimately about facts in the world. These explanations might stress, for instance, the special difficulties of acquiring knowledge of subjects that pertain to moral knowledge.

An understanding of human nature and human affairs is necessary for formulating an adequate moral code. The enormously difficult and complex task of reaching such an understanding could be a major reason for differences in moral belief. Furthermore, the subject matter of ethics is such that people have the most intense practical interest in what is established as truth about it, and surely this interest engenders the passions that becloud judgment. Universalists could point out that many apparently exotic moral beliefs presuppose certain religious and metaphysical beliefs, and that these beliefs, rather than any difference in fundamental values, explain the apparent strangeness. Consider, for example, the way our view of Darius' Indians would change if we were to attribute to them the belief that eating the body of one's deceased father is a way of preserving his spiritual **substance.** Finally, some of the striking differences in moral belief across societies may not be rooted in differences in fundamental values but in the fact that these values may have to be implemented in different ways given the varying conditions that obtain across societies. If one society contains many more women than men (say, because men are killing each other off in warfare), it would not be surprising if polygamy were acceptable there, while in another society, where the proportion of women to men is equal, monogamy is required. The difference in accepted marriage practice may come down to that difference in the proportion of women to men, and not to any difference in basic moral ideals of marriage or of the proper relationships between women and men.

The mere existence of deep and wide disagreements in ethics, therefore, does not disprove the possibility that moral judgments can be objectively correct or incorrect judgments about certain facts. Moral relativists must chart some other more complicated path from the existence of diversity to the **conclusion** that there is no single true or most justified morality. I believe (and have argued in *Moral Relativity,* 1984) that the relativist argument is best conducted by pointing to particular kinds of differences in moral belief, and then by claiming that these particular differences are best explained under a theory that denies the existence of a single true morality. This would involve denying that the various ways that universalists have for explaining ethical disagreement are sufficient for explaining the particular differences in question. . . .

One apparent and striking ethical difference that would be a good candidate for this sort of argument concerns the emphasis on individual rights that is embodied in the ethical culture of the modern West and that seems absent in traditional cultures found in Africa, China, Japan and India. The content of duties in such traditional cultures instead seems organized around the central value of a common good that consists in a certain sort of ideal community life, but imperfectly embodied in ongoing existing practice. The ideal for members is composed of various virtues that enable them, given their place in the network of relationships, to promote and sustain the common good.

Confucianism, for instance, makes the family and kinship groups the models for the common good, with larger social and political units taking on certain of their features, such as benevolent leaders who rule with the aim of cultivating virtue and harmony among their subjects. . . . Moralities centered on such values would seem to differ significantly from ones centered on individual rights to liberty and to other goods, if the basis for attributing such rights to persons does not seem to lie in their conduciveness to the common good of a shared life, but in a moral worth independently attributed to each individual. By contrast a theme frequently found in ethics of the common good is that individuals find their realization as human beings in promoting and sustaining the common good. Given this assumption of the fundamental harmony between the highest good of individuals and the common good, one might expect the constraints on freedom to have greater scope and to be more pervasive when compared to a tradition in which no such fundamental harmony between individual and common goods is assumed.

If the contrast between the two types of morality is real, it raises the question of whether one or the other type is truer or more justified than the other. The argument for a relativistic answer may start with the claim that each type focuses on a good that may reasonably occupy the center of an ethical ideal for human life. On the one hand, there is the good of belonging to and contributing to a community; on the other, there is the good of respect for the individual apart from any potential contribution to community. It would be surprising, the argument goes, if there were just one justifiable way of setting a priority with respect to the two goods. It should not be surprising, after all, if the range of human goods is simply too rich and diverse to be reconciled in just a single moral ideal.

Such an argument could be supplemented by an explanation of why human beings have such a thing as a morality. Morality serves two universal human needs. It regulates conflicts of interest between people, and it regulates conflicts of interest within the individual born of different desires and drives that cannot all be satisfied at the same time. Ways of dealing with those two kinds of conflict develop in anything recognizable as human society. To the extent that these ways crystallize in the form of rules for conduct and ideals for persons, we have the core of a morality. Now in order to perform its practical functions adequately, it may be that a morality will have to possess certain general features. A relatively enduring and stable system for the resolution of conflict between people, for instance, will not permit the torture of persons at whim.

But given this picture of the origin and functions of morality, it would not be surprising if significantly different moralities were to perform the practical functions equally well, at least according to standards of performance that were common to these moralities. Moralities, on this picture, are social creations that evolve to meet certain needs. The needs place conditions on what could be an adequate morality, and if human nature has a definite structure, one would expect further constraining conditions on an adequate morality to derive from our nature. But the complexity of our nature makes it possible for us to prize a variety of goods and to order them in different ways, and this opens the way for a substantial relativism to be true.

The picture sketched above has the advantage of leaving it open as to how strong a version of relativism is true. That is, it holds that there is no single true morality, yet does not deny that some moralities might be false and inadequate for the functions they all must perform. Almost all polemics against moral relativism are directed at its most extreme versions: those holding that all moralities are equally true (or equally false, or equally lacking in cognitive content). Yet a substantial relativism need not be so radically egalitarian. Besides ruling out moralities that would aggravate interpersonal conflict, such as the one described above, relativists could also recognize that adequate moralities must promote the production of persons capable of considering the interests of others. Such persons would need to have received a certain kind of nurturing and care from others. An adequate morality, then, whatever else its content, would have to prescribe and promote the sorts of upbringing and continuing interpersonal relationships that produce such persons.

A moral relativism that would allow for this kind of constraint on what could be a true or most justified morality might not fit the stereotype of relativism, but would be a reasonable position to hold. One reason, in fact, that not much progress has been made in the debate between relativists and universalists is that each side has tended to define the opponent as holding the most extreme position possible. While this makes the debating easier, it does nothing to shed light on the vast middle ground where the truth indeed may lie. Many of the same conclusions could be drawn about the debate over normative moral relativism: much heat, and frequent identification of the opponent with the most extreme position possible.

NORMATIVE RELATIVISM

The most extreme possible position for the normative relativist is that no one should ever pass judgment on others with substantially different values, or try to make them conform to one's own values.

Such a definition of normative relativism is usually given by its opponents, because it is an indefensible position. It requires self-condemnation by those who act according to it. If I pass judgment on those who pass judgment, I must condemn myself. I am trying to impose a value of tolerance on everyone, when not everyone has that value, but this is not what I am supposed to be doing under the most extreme version of normative relativism. Philosophers are usually content with such easy dismissals of the most extreme version of normative relativism, but there is reason to consider whether more moderate versions might be more tenable. The reason is that normative relativism is not just a philosophical doctrine but a stance adopted toward morally troubling situations.

Anthropologists are sometimes identified with this stance, and it is instructive to understand how this identification emerged from a historical and sociological context. The birth of cultural anthropology in the late nineteenth century was in part subsidized by colonizing governments needing to know more about the nature and status of "primitive" peoples. Influenced by Darwinian theory, early anthropological theory tended to arrange the peoples and social institutions of the world in an evolutionary series, from primordial man to the civilized human being of nineteenth-century Europe. Many anthropologists eventually reacted against the imperialism of their governments and to its rationalization supplied by their predecessors. More importantly, they came to see the peoples they studied as intelligent men and women whose lives had meaning and integrity. And this led to questioning the basis for implicit judgments of the inferiority of their ways of life, especially after the spectacle of the civilized nations in brutal struggle with one another in the First World War (see, for example, Ruth Benedict, *Patterns of Culture*, 1934, and more recently, Melville Herskovits, *Cultural Relativism: Perspectives in Cultural Pluralism*, 1972).

The normative relativism of some of the anthropologists of that period, then, was a response to real moral problems concerning the justifiability of colonization and more generally concerning intervention in another society so as to cause major changes in previously accepted values or in people's ability to act on those values. No simple version of

normative relativism is the answer to these problems, as was illustrated by the fact that an ethic of
non-judgmental tolerance would self-destruct when
used to condemn the intolerant. The inadequacy of
the simple versions also is illustrated by the swing in
anthropology on the question of normative relativism after the Second World War. That war, many
realized, was a battle against enormous evil. Such a
realization brought vividly to the forefront the
necessity of passing judgment at least sometimes
and of acting on one's judgment. And accordingly
there was a new trend within cultural anthropology
toward finding a basis for making judgments that
would depend on criteria to be applied to all moral
codes.

A more reasonable version of normative relativism would have to permit us to pass judgment on
others with substantially different values. Even if
these different values are as justified as our own
from some neutral perspective, we still are entitled
to call bad or evil or monstrous what contradicts
our most important values. What we are entitled to
do in light of such judgments, however, is another
matter. Many of us who are likely to read this book
would be reluctant to intervene in the affairs of
others who have values substantially different from
ours, when the reason for intervention is the
enforcement of our own values, and when we think
that we have no more of an objective case for our
moral outlook than the others have for theirs. The
source of this reluctance is a feature of our morality.
A liberal, **contractualist** outlook is very much part
of our ethical life in the postmodern West, whether
we acknowledge it or not. . . . We want to act toward
others in such a way that our actions could be seen
as justified by them if they were fully reasonable and
informed of all relevant facts. If we hold a meta-
ethical moral relativism, however, then we must
recognize that there will be occasions when some
otherwise desirable course of action toward others
with different values will violate this feature of our
morality.

At that point, there is no general rule that will
tell us what to do. It would seem to depend on what
other values of ours are at stake. If a practice
performed by others were to involve human sacrifice, for example, then the value of tolerance might
indeed be outweighed, and we may decide to intervene to prevent it. The disagreement over the legal

permissibility of abortion demonstrates how difficult the weighing can be, however. Consider the
position of those who believe that abortion is
morally wrong because it is the taking of life that has
moral status. Within this group some seem undis-
turbed by the fact that there is deep disagreement
over the moral status of the fetus. They wish to
prohibit abortion. But others in this group, while
holding that abortion is wrong, admit that reasonable persons could disagree with them and that
human reason seems unable to resolve the question.
For this reason they oppose legal prohibitions of
abortion. The former believe that the latter do not
take the value of human life seriously, while the
latter believe that the former fail to recognize the
depth and seriousness of the disagreement between
reasonable persons. . . .

Each position has some force, and clearly normative relativism offers no simple solution to the
dilemma. What the doctrine provides, however, is a
set of reasons for tolerance and non-intervention
that must be weighed against other reasons. The
doctrine applies not only to proposed interventions
by one society in another, but also, in the case of
abortion, to deep moral disagreements within
pluralistic societies containing diverse moral traditions. If meta-ethical relativism is true, even if only
with respect to a limited set of moral conflicts such
as abortion, then our moral condition is immeasurably complicated. We must strive to find what will
be for us the right or the best thing to do, and also
deal with the feelings of unease caused by the recognition that there is no single right or best thing to
do. This task, no matter how difficult, is not the end
of moral reflection. It instead may be the beginning
of a different sort of reflection that involves on the
one hand an effort to reach an understanding with
those who have substantially different values, and on
the other the effort to stay true to one's own values.
Some of those who believe that abortion is the
taking of a life with moral status, for instance, have
chosen to oppose it by placing their efforts into
organizations that aim to lessen the perceived need
for abortion, organizations that aid unwed mothers,
for example.

One final issue regarding relativism needs
addressing. Relativism has a bad name in some
quarters because it is associated with a lack of moral
conviction, with a tendency toward **nihilism.** Part

of the reason for the bad name may be the identification of relativism with its most extreme forms. If these forms are true, then everything is permitted, on someone's morality. But another reason for the bad name is the assumption that one's moral confidence, one's commitment to act on one's values, is somehow dependent on maintaining the belief that one's morality is the only true or the most justified one. But surely some reflection will reveal that such a belief alone would not guarantee a commitment to act. The commitment to act involves a conception of what one's morality means to the self, whether it be the only true one or not. It involves making a connection between what one desires, what one aspires to, and the substantive content of one's moral values. It is being able to see morality as important to us in these ways that allows us to avoid nihilism. The belief that our morality is the only true or most justified one does not automatically create this kind of importance, nor is it a necessary condition for this kind of importance, because the values I may see as important and part of what makes life most meaningful to me may not have to be values that all reasonable persons would accept or recognize to be true.

Here, as in other matters concerning relativism, the emotion provoked by the mere name tends to muddle the issues and to polarize unnecessarily. When we get through defending and attacking what most people conceive as relativism or what they associate with it, then most of the real work remains to be done. What is left is a moral reality that is quite messy and immune to neat solutions. But why should we have expected anything else?

Questions for Thought

1. How would you define moral relativism? Do you consider yourself to be a moral relativist? Why or why not?
2. Under what conditions, if any, do you think you would be justified in intervening in another person's life?
3. Can you think of any reasons not mentioned by Wong that would support moral relativism? Can you think of any reasons that would support universalism?
4. To what extent do you think individual rights should be protected?
5. How, according to Wong, was anthropology used to justify colonialism? Do you think that colonialism can ever be morally justified? Defend your answer.
6. What are your moral views on the issue of abortion? What judgments, if any, do you make about people who hold opposing views on this issue?

9   Master Morality and Slave Morality

FRIEDRICH NIETZSCHE

Friedrich Nietzsche (1844–1900), one of the most influential modern German philosophers, was born in Röcken, Prussia. Interestingly, Nietzsche, who was to become one of the most outspoken critics of Christianity, was the son of a Lutheran minister. Nietzsche's paternal grandfather, himself also a Lutheran minister, had written several books defending the faith, and Nietzsche's mother was the daughter of a Lutheran minister.

After Nietzsche's father died from "softening of the brain" in 1849 and his younger brother died the following year, his mother moved the family to Naumburg. In Naumburg, Nietzsche lived with his mother, sister, paternal grandmother, and two aunts in a predominantly female household. In 1858, he was awarded a scholarship to attend Schulpforta, Germany's leading Protestant boarding school, which was near Naumburg. An excellent student, Nietzsche graduated from Schulpforta in 1864 and went to the University of Bonn to study theology and philology. He soon became disenchanted with theology and transferred to the University of Leipzig in 1865. At Leipzig, Nietzsche discovered the philosophical writings of Schopenhauer, met Richard Wagner, wrote several prize-winning papers, and composed some musical pieces. However, Nietzsche's studies were interrupted in 1867 when he began his military service in the Prussian cavalry. This interruption ended the following year when a horse-riding accident led to his discharge, and he returned to Leipzig.

In 1869, at age twenty-four, Nietzsche's academic promise was publicly recognized when he was appointed associate professor in philology at the University of Basel in Switzerland without having completed his doctoral degree. His degree was awarded the same year without thesis or examination, and Nietzsche became a full professor the following year.

When the Franco-Prussian War broke out in 1870, Nietzsche volunteered as a medical orderly. While working with injured soldiers, he contracted dysentery and diphtheria—both of which contributed to his poor health in later life. He returned to the University of Basel but was forced to take a leave of absence for health reasons in 1876 and finally to resign in 1879. Living on the small pension that he received from the university, Nietzsche then embarked on an ascetic life of writing, moving among boardinghouses in Switzerland, Italy, and the French Riviera. Nietzsche's often frenzied literary activity further contributed to his poor health, and he suffered an irreversible mental collapse in Turin in 1889, reportedly while hugging a horse that had just been beaten by a coachman. After a brief stay in a Basel asylum, Nietzsche spent the last years of his life living first with his mother and then with his sister. He died in Weimar on August 25, 1900.

Although the bulk of Nietzsche's works was written during a span of less than twenty years, his literary output was prolific. A list of his most important published works can be found in the introduction to the Nietzsche selection in Chapter 1.

In the following excerpt from *Beyond Good and Evil*, Nietzsche discusses the nature and history of morality, a topic that he discusses in more detail in his later work *On the Genealogy of Morals*. In this brief selection, he claims that while there have been many moral systems—elsewhere he remarks that every great people has become great by creating and following its own distinctive moral system—all these can be reduced to two fundamental types, **master-morality** and **slave-morality.** Master-morality is created by those who occupy positions of power in aristocratic societies, societies that, according to Nietzsche, have produced every advancement of the human type. The essential moral distinction in master-morality is the distinction between "good" and "bad," where "good" is identified with that which is noble (that is, with the personal traits of the masters), while "bad" refers to that which is ignoble or base (that is, with the personal traits of those who are ruled). Master-morality is a morality that values difference, honor, self-control, courage, vitality, and overflowing. It is a morality that encourages people to help others, not out of a sense of pity or compassion but simply because helping others is one way in which one's vitality or overflowing can be expressed. In this selection and elsewhere, Nietzsche introduces the term *Will to Power* to refer to the vitality or overflowing that characterizes the life of the master—indeed that characterizes healthy life in all its forms.

In contrast to this type of morality, there is slave-morality. Slave-morality is created by those in whom the Will to Power has decayed, by those who are oppressed by others. Its chief moral distinction is the distinction between "good" and "evil." In this case, the term *good* refers to the traits of the oppressed—that is, to meekness, humility, powerlessness, and servility—while the term *evil* is applied to everything that characterizes those who possess power. It should be obvious from Nietzsche's description that the "evil" of slave-morality is the "good" of master-morality. Also, in contrast to master-morality, slave-morality is a morality that values pity and compassion; it is a morality that emphasizes utility while discouraging creativity.

In light of this discussion, we can see that Nietzsche's answer to the question of how one determines what one ought to do will depend on the type of morality to which one subscribes. If one is a follower of slave-morality (and the word *follower* should be emphasized), one's moral decisions will be based on sympathy for others and on utility. However, if one acts from the standpoint of master-morality—something that, according to Nietzsche, is extremely difficult in the modern world—one will be no longer a follower but rather the creator of one's own values.

Questions for Reading

1. Why does Nietzsche believe that every advancement of the human type has been produced by an aristocratic society?
2. What, according to Nietzsche, is the function of a healthy aristocratic society?
3. How does Nietzsche define the *Will to Power*?
4. How does Nietzsche view exploitation? What is the relationship between Will to Power and exploitation?
5. What are the essential differences between master-morality and slave-morality?

257

EVERY ELEVATION OF THE TYPE "MAN" HAS thus far been the work of an aristocratic society, that is, of a society that believes in a long scale of gradations of rank and differences of worth among human beings, a society that requires slavery in some form or other. And this will always be the case. Without the ***pathos of distance***—the pathos that grows out of the deep-seated differences between classes, out of the constant outlooking and downlooking of the ruling class on subordinates and instruments, out of their equally constant practice of obeying and commanding, of keeping down and keeping at a distance—that other more mysterious pathos could never have arisen, the pathos marked by a longing for an ever-new widening of distance within the soul itself, by the formation of ever higher, rarer, further-reaching, more extended, more comprehensive states, in short, by the elevation of the type "man," the continued "self-surmounting of man," to use a moral formula in a supermoral sense. To be sure, one must not resign oneself to any humanitarian illusions about the history of the origins of an aristocratic society (that is to say, of the preliminary condition for the elevation

---

This is the editor's revised version of a selection from Friedrich Nietzsche, Beyond Good and Evil, *in* The Complete Works of Friedrich Nietzsche, *edited by Oscar Levy (1910).*

of the type "man"): truth is hard. Let us speak honestly, without self-deception, about how every higher civilization that has existed on earth thus far has *originated*! Men whose nature was still natural, barbarians in every terrible sense of the word, men of prey still in possession of unbroken strength of will and desire for power—such men threw themselves upon weaker, more civilized, more peaceful races (perhaps those engaged in trading or cattle-rearing), or upon old mellow civilizations in which the final vital force was flickering out in brilliant fireworks of wit and corruption. At the beginning, the noble caste was always the barbarian caste. Their superiority did not consist primarily in their physical power, but in their mental power—they were more *complete* men (which on every level also implies that they were "more complete beasts").

258

Corruption is the indication that anarchy threatens to break out among the instincts, and that the foundation of the emotions, which is called "life," has been shaken; and it is something radically different according to the organization in which it manifests itself. When, for instance, an **aristocracy,** like that of France at the beginning of the Revolution, flung away its privileges with a sublime disgust and sacrificed itself to an excess of its moral sentiments, that was a type of corruption. But it was really only the closing act of a corruption that had existed for centuries, a corruption by virtue of which that aristocracy had abdicated step by step its lordly prerogatives and lowered itself to a *function* of royalty (in the end even to its decoration and parade-dress). The essential thing, however, in a good and healthy aristocracy is that it should *not* regard itself as a function either of the kingship or the commonwealth, but as the *significance* and highest justification thereof. It should, therefore, accept with a good conscience the sacrifice of a legion of individuals, who, *for its sake,* must be suppressed and reduced to imperfect men, to slaves, to instruments. The healthy aristocracy's fundamental belief must be precisely that society is *not* allowed to exist for its own sake. Rather, society is to serve as a foundation and scaffolding by means of which

a select class of beings can elevate themselves to their higher tasks, and, in general, to a higher *existence*—a class of beings like those sun-seeking climbing plants in Java . . . that continuously encircle an oak with their tendrils until at last, high above it but still supported by it, they can unfold their tops in the open light and exhibit their happiness.

259

Refraining mutually from injury, from violence, from exploitation, and putting one's will on a par with that of others, may become good behavior, in a certain rough sense, among individuals, as long as the necessary conditions are present (namely, the actual similarity of the individuals in amount of force and degree of worth, and their co-relation within one organization). As soon, however, as one wants to extend this principle more generally, and if possible even to make it *the fundamental principle of society,* it would immediately disclose what it really is—namely, a Will to the *denial* of life, a principle of dissolution and decay. Here one must think profoundly, not superficially, resisting all sentimental weakness. Life itself is *essentially* appropriation, injury, overpowering of the strange and weak, suppression, hardness, imposing one's own forms, incorporation. Or, to express it in the mildest manner, life is exploitation. But why exactly should we continue to use these words which, for ages, have had a negative slant stamped upon them?

Even the organization mentioned above, the organization within which individuals treat each other as equal (and this takes place in every healthy aristocracy) must, if it is a living and not a dying organization, do to other organizations everything that the individuals within it refrain from doing to each other. It will have to be an incarnate Will to Power, that is, it will endeavor to grow, to gain ground, to attract others to itself, to acquire ascendancy—not owing to any morality or immorality, but because it *lives,* and because life simply *is* Will to Power. On no point, however, is the ordinary consciousness of Europeans more unwilling to be corrected than on this matter; people now rave everywhere, even under the guise of science, about the coming conditions of society in which there is to be no more "exploitation." To my ears, this sounds as if they promised to invent a mode of life that would refrain from all organic functions. "Exploitation" does not belong to a depraved, imperfect, or primitive society. It belongs to the *nature* of the living being as a primary organic function; it is a consequence of the intrinsic Will to Power, which is precisely the Will to Life. It may be granted that this is a novelty as a theory. However, as a reality, it is the *fundamental fact* of all history. Let us be honest with ourselves—at least that far!

260

Wandering through the many finer and coarser moralities which previously prevailed or which still prevail on earth, I found certain traits that recurred regularly together, certain traits that were bound up with one another. Finally, two primary types revealed themselves to me and a radical distinction was brought to light. There is *master-morality* and *slave-morality*. I would add at once, however, that in all higher and mixed civilizations, there are also attempts to reconcile the two moralities—indeed they are sometimes closely juxtaposed, even in the psyche of a single human being. Yet in such cases one usually finds the confusion and mutual misunderstanding of both of them. The differentiation of moral values has originated either in a ruling type, which took conscious delight in being different from the ruled, or among those who were ruled, that is, among slaves and dependents of all sorts. In the first case, when the rulers determine what is "good," it is the exalted, proud disposition that is regarded as the distinguishing feature that determines the order of rank. The noble type of man distances himself from the people who display the opposite of this exalted, proud disposition: he despises them. Let it at once be noted that in this first kind of morality, the antithesis "good" and "bad" means practically the same thing as "noble" and "despicable." . . . The cowardly, the timid, the insignificant, and those thinking merely of narrow utility are despised; moreover, so are the distrustful

with their suspicious glances, the self-abasing, the dog-like kind of men who let themselves be abused, the mendicant flatterers, and above all the liars. It is a fundamental belief of all aristocrats that the common people are untruthful. "We truthful ones"—the nobility in ancient Greece called themselves. It is obvious that everywhere the designations of moral value were at first applied to *men,* and were only derivatively and at a later period applied to *actions.* It is a gross mistake, therefore, when historians of morals start with questions like, "Why have sympathetic actions been praised?" The noble type of man regards *himself* as a determiner of values; he does not require to be approved of; he passes the judgment, "What is injurious to me is injurious in itself." He knows that it is only he himself who confers honor on things; he is a *creator of values.* He honors whatever he recognizes in himself; thus, such morality is self-glorification. In the foreground there is the feeling of plenitude, of power that seeks to overflow, the happiness of high tension, the consciousness of a wealth that would give and bestow. The noble man also helps the unfortunate, but not—or at least not mainly—out of pity, but rather from an impulse generated by the superabundance of power. The noble man honors in himself the powerful one, the one who has power over himself, who knows how to speak and how to keep silent, who takes pleasure in subjecting himself to severity and hardness, and who has reverence for all that is severe and hard. "**Wotan** placed a hard heart in my breast," says an old Scandinavian Saga—an appropriate poetic expression from the soul of a proud Viking. Such a type of man is even proud of *not* being made for sympathy. The hero of the Saga therefore adds warningly, "he who has not a hard heart when young, will never have one." The noble and brave who think thus are the furthest removed from that morality which places the distinguishing feature of that which is moral in sympathy, in acting for the good of others, or in *désintéressment.* Faith in oneself, pride in oneself, a radical enmity and irony towards "selflessness"—these belong as definitely to noble morality, as do a slight disdain and cautious attitude in presence of sympathy and the "warm heart." It is the powerful who *know* how to honor; it is their art, their domain for invention. The profound reverence for age and for tradition (all law rests on this double reverence), the belief and prejudice in favor of ancestors and unfavorable to those yet to come, is typical in the morality of the powerful. If, contrary to this, men of "modern ideas" believe almost instinctively in "progress" and the "future," if they have less and less respect for old age, this in itself would clearly betray the ignoble origin of these "ideas."

Yet, a morality of the ruling class is especially foreign and irritating to present-day taste in the severity of its principle that one has duties only to one's equals, while one may act towards beings of a lower rank, towards all that is foreign, just as seems good to one, "as the heart desires," or, in any case, "beyond good and evil." . . . The ability and obligation to exercise prolonged gratitude and prolonged revenge (both only within the circle of equals), artfulness in retaliation, a subtly refined idea in friendship, a certain necessity to have enemies as outlets for the emotions of envy, quarrelsomeness, arrogance (in fact, in order to be a good *friend*)—all of these are typical characteristics of the noble morality. Since, as has been pointed out, this is not the morality of "modern ideas," at present it is difficult to empathize with this morality, just as it is difficult to unearth and to disclose it.

It is otherwise with the second type of morality, *slave-morality.* Supposing that the abused, the oppressed, the suffering, the unemancipated, the weary, and those uncertain of themselves should moralize, what will be the common element in their moral estimates? Probably a pessimistic suspicion with regard to the entire situation of man will find expression, perhaps a condemnation of man, together with his situation. The slave has an unfavorable eye for the virtues of the powerful; he is skeptical and distrustful, especially distrustful of everything "good" that is honored there. Indeed, he would finally persuade himself that the very happiness of the powerful is not genuine. On the other hand, *those* qualities that serve to alleviate the existence of sufferers are brought into prominence and flooded with light; it is here that sympathy, the kind, helping hand, the warm heart, patience, diligence, humility, and friendliness attain honor. For here these are the most useful qualities and almost the only means of supporting the burden of existence. Slave-morality is essentially the morality of utility. Here lies the origin of the famous antithesis "good vs. evil." Power and dangerousness are assumed to reside in the evil, as are a certain dreadfulness, subtlety, and strength. . . . According to slave-morality, therefore, the "evil" man arouses fear; according to master-morality, it is precisely the "good" man who arouses fear and seeks to arouse it, while the bad man is regarded as the despicable being. This antithesis reaches its climax when, in accordance with the logical consequences of slave-morality, a touch of disdain . . . at last attaches itself to the "good" man of this morality. While this disdain may be slight and well-intended, it arises because, according to the servile mode of thought, the good man must always be the *safe* man. He must be good-natured, easily deceived, perhaps a little stupid, *un bonhomme.* Everywhere that slave-morality gains the ascendancy, language shows a tendency to approximate the signification of the words "good" and "stupid." A final essential difference is that the desire for *freedom,* the instinct for happiness, and the subtleties of the feeling of freedom, belong just as necessarily to slave-morals and morality, as skill and enthusiasm in reverence and devotion belong to an aristocratic mode of thinking and estimating. Hence we can understand without further detail why love *as a passion,* which is our European specialty, must absolutely be of noble origin. As is well known, its invention is due to Provençal poet-cavaliers, those brilliant, ingenious men of the "*gai saber,*" to whom Europe owes so much, and almost owes itself.[1]

NOTE

1. Nietzsche is referring to a group of wandering lyric poets, often known as "troubadours," who lived mainly in southern France from the eleventh through the thirteenth centuries. Their songs and poems, which were written in *langue d'oc,* focused on the theme of courtly love. Like Nietzsche, many scholars trace the origin of the modern notion of romantic love to the art of the troubadours. This art was often called the "*gai saber*" ("gay science"), a term that Nietzsche himself used in the title of one of his books.—ED.

Questions for Thought

1. How would you describe the nature and function of an aristocracy? How do your views compare with or differ from the views of Nietzsche on this matter?
2. What do you think Nietzsche's attitude toward democracy would be? Defend your answer.
3. Do you agree with what Nietzsche says about exploitation? Why or why not?
4. How would you characterize your own moral values in terms of Nietzsche's distinction between master-morality and slave-morality?
5. To what extent were your moral values self-chosen?

10   Mitakuye Oyasin: We Are All Related

ED (EAGLE MAN) McGAA

Ed (Eagle Man) McGaa (b. 1936), who is a registered tribal member of the **Oglala** Sioux, was born on the Pine Ridge Reservation. After getting his early education in missionary schools, McGaa received his bachelor's degree in biology from St. John's University, earned his law degree from the University of South Dakota, and studied under the Sioux holy men Chief Eagle Feather and Chief Fool's Crow. McGaa also served as a fighter pilot in Vietnam, flying in over 100 combat missions, and he is honored by the Sioux for having participated six times in the Sun Dance ceremony.

In *Mother Earth Spirituality: Native American Paths to Healing Ourselves and Our World,* from which the following selection is taken, McGaa gives this account of how he acquired his natural name: "Ben Black Elk, the interpreter of *Black Elk Speaks,* named me as a boy, *Wanblee Hoksila* (Eagle Boy). Later, when I became a fighter pilot and a warrior who returned to dance the Sun Dance, Ben, Bill Eagle Feather, and the Sun Dance chief, Fool's Crow, named me *Wanblee Wichasha* (Eagle Man)."

Shortly after returning from Vietnam, Eagle Man wrote a children's biography of the Oglala chief Red Cloud. Since 1990, when *Mother Earth Spirituality* was published, he has been a leading proponent of Native American spiritualism. Mixing natural spirituality, the belief that humanity is rooted in a living, feeling earth, and an awareness of scientific ecological principles, Eagle Man has drawn on centuries of Native American wisdom to offer ceremonies and practices that help one reestablish a nurturing relationship with nature. His other books include *Rainbow Tribe: Ordinary People Journeying on the Red Road* (1992), *Native Wisdom: Perceptions of the Natural Way* (1995), *Eagle Vision: Return of the Hoop* (1998), and *Nature's Way: Native Wisdom for Living in Balance with the Earth* (2004). Eagle Man has also interpreted Black Elk's wisdom on a recording entitled *Black Elk's Prayer and Vision* (1998).

Throughout this selection, Eagle Man contrasts the value system of the European immigrants who came to America with the value system of the Native Americans. He notes that the European value system was based on conquest and acquisition, whereas the Native American value system was based on respect and sharing. As in the Benally selection reprinted in Chapter 3 of this text, Eagle Man discusses the importance of the four cardinal directions and the good things that come from each of them. Tied in with the goods derived from the four directions are the four ethical commandments given by the Great Spirit: respect for the earth, for the Great Spirit, for our fellow humans, and for individual freedom. These four commandments are summarized in the concept of *Mitakuye Oyasin,* a concept that implies that we are interrelated to all living things as an extended family.

Questions for Reading

1. What are Eagle Man's main criticisms of European culture and values? What, if anything, does he praise about European culture?
2. According to Eagle Man, what are the four ethical commandments given by the Great Spirit? How are these commandments related to each other?
3. Why, according to Eagle Man, is it crucial that humans accept some of the values taught by Native Americans?
4. What is Eagle Man's attitude toward possessions? How is this attitude reflected in his actions?
5. What exactly does the concept of *Mitakuye Oyasin* mean?

THE PLIGHT OF THE NON-INDIAN WORLD IS that it has lost respect for Mother Earth, from whom and where we all come.

We all start out in this world as tiny seeds—no different from our animal brothers and sisters, the deer, the bear, the buffalo, or the trees, the flowers, the winged people. Every particle of our bodies comes from the good things Mother Earth has put forth. Mother Earth is our real mother, because every bit of us truly comes from her, and daily she takes care of us.

The tiny seed takes on the minerals and the waters of Mother Earth. It is fueled by *Wiyo,* the sun, and given spirit by *Wakan Tanka.*

This morning at breakfast we took from Mother Earth to live, as we have done every day of our lives. But did we thank her for giving us the means to live? The old Indian did. When he drove his horse in close to a buffalo running at full speed across the prairie, he drew his bowstring back and said as he did so, "Forgive me, brother, but my people must live." After he butchered the buffalo, he took the skull and faced it toward the setting sun as a thanksgiving and an acknowledgment that all things come from Mother Earth. He brought the meat back to camp and gave it first to the old, the widowed, and the weak. For thousands of years great herds thrived

across the continent because the Indian never took more than he needed. Today, the buffalo is gone.

You say *ecology.* We think the words *Mother Earth* have a deeper meaning. If we wish to survive, we must respect her. It is very late, but there is still time to revive and discover the old American Indian value of respect for Mother Earth. She is very beautiful, and already she is showing us signs that she may punish us for not respecting her. Also, we must remember she has been placed in this universe by the one who is the All Powerful, the Great Spirit Above, or *Wakan Tanka*—God. But a few years ago, there lived on the North American continent people, the American Indians, who knew a respect and value system that enabled them to live on their native grounds without having to migrate, in contrast to the white brothers and sisters who migrated by the thousands from their homelands because they had developed a value system different from that of the American Indian. There is no place now to which we can migrate, which means we can no longer ignore the red man's value system.

Carbon-dating techniques say that the American Indian has lived on the North American continent for thousands upon thousands of years. If we did migrate, it was because of a natural phenomenon— a glacier. We did not migrate because of a social system, value system, and spiritual system that neglected its responsibility to the land and all living things. We Indian people say we were always here.

We, the American Indian, had a way of living that enabled us to live within the great, complete beauty that only the natural environment can provide. The Indian tribes had a common value system and a commonality of religion, without religious animosity, that preserved that great beauty that the two-leggeds definitely need. Our four commandments from the Great Spirit are: (1) respect for Mother Earth, (2) respect for the Great Spirit, (3) respect for our fellow man and woman, and (4) respect for individual freedom (provided that individual freedom does not threaten the tribe or the people or Mother Earth).

We who respect the great vision of Black Elk see the four sacred colors as red, yellow, black, and white. They stand for the four directions—red for the east, yellow for the south, black for the west, and white for the north.

From the east comes the rising sun and new knowledge from a new day.

From the south will come the warming south winds that will cause our Mother to bring forth the good foods and grasses so that we may live.

To the west where the sun goes down, the day will end, and we will sleep; and we will hold our spirit ceremonies at night, from where we will communicate with the spirit world beyond. The sacred color of the west is black; it stands for the deep intellect that we will receive from the spirit ceremonies. From the west come the lifegiving rains.

From the north will come the white winter snow that will cleanse Mother Earth and put her to sleep, so that she may rest and store up energy to provide the beauty and bounty of springtime. We will prepare for aging by learning to create, through our arts and crafts, during the long winter season. Truth, honesty, strength, endurance, and courage also are represented by the white of the north. Truth and honesty in our relationships bring forth harmony.

All good things come from these sacred directions. These sacred directions, or four sacred colors, also stand for the four races of humanity: red, yellow, black, and white. We cannot be a prejudiced people, because all men and women are brothers and sisters and because we all have the same mother—Mother Earth. One who is prejudiced, who hates another because of that person's color, hates what the Great Spirit has put here. Such a one hates that which is holy and will be punished, even during this lifetime, as humanity will be punished for violating Mother Earth. Worse, one's conscience will follow into the spirit world, where it will be discovered that all beings are equal. This is what we Indian people believe.

We, the Indian people, also believe that the Great Spirit placed many people throughout this planet: red, yellow, black, and white. What about the brown people? The brown people evolved from the sacred colors coming together. Look at our Mother Earth. She, too, is brown because the four directions have come together. After the Great Spirit, *Wakan Tanka,* placed them in their respective areas, the *Wakan Tanka* appeared to each people in a different manner and taught them ways so that they might live in harmony and true beauty. Some men, some tribes, some nations have still retained the teachings of the Great Spirit. Others have not. Unfortunately, many good and peaceful religions have been assailed by narrow-minded zealots. Our religious beliefs and our traditional Indian people have suffered the stereotype that we are pagans, savages, or heathens; but we do not believe that only one religion controls the way to the spirit world that lies beyond. We believe that *Wakan Tanka* loves all of its children equally, although the Great Spirit must be disturbed at times with those children who have destroyed proven value systems that practiced sharing and generosity and kept Mother Earth viable down through time. We kept Mother Earth viable because we did not sell her or our spirituality!

Brothers and sisters, we must go back to some of the old ways if we are going to truly save our Mother Earth and bring back the natural beauty that every person seriously needs, especially in this day of vanishing species, vanishing rain forests, overpopulation, poisoned waters, acid rain, a thinning ozone layer, drought, rising temperatures, and weapons of complete annihilation.

Weapons of complete annihilation? Yes, that is how far the obsession with war has taken us. These weapons are not only hydraheaded; they are hydro-headed as well, meaning that they are the ultimate in hydrogen bomb destruction. We will have to divert our obsession with defense and wasteful, all-life-ending weapons of war to reviving our environment. . . .

The quest for peace can be more efficiently pursued through communication and knowledge than by stealth and unending superior weaponry. If the nations of the world scale back their budgets for weaponry, we will have wealth to spend to solve our serious environmental problems. Our home planet is under attack. It is not an imagined problem. This calamity is upon us now. We are in a real war with the polluting, violating blue man of Black Elk's vision.

Chief Sitting Bull advised us to take the best of the white man's ways and to take the best of the old Indian ways. He also said, "When you find something that is bad, or turns out bad, drop it and leave it alone."[1]

The fomenting of fear and hatred is something that has turned out very badly. This can continue no longer; it is a governmental luxury maintained in order to support pork-barrel appropriations to the Department of Defense, with its admirals and generals who have substituted their patriotism for a defense contractor paycheck after retirement. War has become a business for profit. In the last two wars, we frontline warriors—mostly poor whites and minorities—were never allowed to win our wars, which were endlessly prolonged by the politicians and profiteers, who had their warrior-aged sons hidden safely away or who used their powers, bordering on treason, to keep their offspring out of danger. The wrong was that the patriotic American or the poor had to be the replacement. The way to end wars in this day and age is to do like the Indian: put the chiefs and their sons on the front lines.

Sitting Bull answered a relative, "Go ahead and follow the white man's road and do whatever the [Indian] agent tells you. But I cannot so easily give up my old ways and Indian habits; they are too deeply ingrained in me."[2]

My friends, I will never cease to be an Indian. I will never cease respecting the old Indian values, especially our four cardinal commandments and our values of generosity and sharing. It is true that many who came to our shores brought a great amount of good to this world. Modern medicine, transportation, communication, and food production are but a few of the great achievements that we should all appreciate. But it is also true that too many of those who migrated to North America became so greedy and excessively materialistic that great harm has been caused. We have seen good ways and bad ways. The good way of the non-Indian way I am going to keep. The very fact that we can hold peace-seeking communication and that world leaders meet and communicate for peace shows the wisdom of the brothers and sisters of this time. By all means, good technology should not be curtailed, but care must be taken lest our water, air, and earth become irreparably harmed. The good ways I will always respect and support. But, my brothers and sisters, I say we must give up this obsession with excess consumption and materialism, especially when it causes the harming of the skies surrounding our Mother and the pollution of the waters upon her. *She is beginning to warn us!*

Keep those material goods that you need to exist, but be a more sharing and generous person. You will find that you can do with less. Replace this empty lifestyle of hollow impressing of the shallow ones with active participation for your Mother Earth. At least then, when you depart into the spirit world, you can look back with pride and fulfillment. Other spirit beings will gather around you, other spirits of your own higher consciousness will gather around you and share your satisfaction with you. The eternal satisfaction of knowing you did not overuse your Mother Earth and that you were here to protect her will be a powerful satisfaction when you reach the spirit world.

Indian people do not like to say that the Great Mystery is exactly this or exactly that, but we do know there is a spirit world that lies beyond. We are allowed to know that through our ceremonies. We know nothing of hell-fire and eternal damnation from some kind of unloving power that placed us here as little children. None of that has ever been shown to us in our powerful ceremonies, conducted by kind, considerate, proven, and very nonmaterialistic leaders. We do know that everything the Great Mystery makes is in the form of a circle. Our Mother Earth is a very large, powerful circle.

Therefore, we conclude that our life does not end. A part of it is within that great circle. If there is a hell, then our concept of hell would be an eternal knowing that one violated or took and robbed from Mother Earth and caused this suffering that is being bestowed upon the generations unborn. This then, if it were to be imprinted upon one's eternal conscience, this would surely be a terrible, spiritual, mental hell. Worse, to have harmed and hurt one's innocent fellow beings, and be unable to alter (or conceal) the harmful actions would also be a great hell. Truth in the spirit world will not be concealed, nor will it be for sale. Lastly, we must realize that the generations unborn will also come into the spirit world. Let us be the ones that they wish to thank and congratulate, rather than eternally scorn.

While we are shedding our overabundant possessions, and linking up with those of like minds, and advancing spiritual and environmental appreciations, we should develop a respect for the aged and for family-centered traditions, even those who are single warriors, fighting for the revitalization of our Mother on a lone, solitary, but vital front. We should have more respect for an extended family, which extends beyond a son or daughter, goes beyond to grandparents and aunts and uncles, goes beyond to brothers, sisters, aunts, and uncles that we have adopted or made as relatives—and further beyond, to the animal or plant world as our brothers and sisters, to Mother Earth and Father Sky and then above to *Wakan Tanka*, the *Unci/Tankashilah*, the Grandparent of us all. When we pray directly to the Great Spirit, we say *Unci* (Grandmother) or *Tankashilah* (Grandfather) because we are so family-minded that we think of the Great Power above as a grandparent, and we are the grandchildren. Of course, this is so because every particle of our being is from Mother Earth, and our energy and life force are fueled by Father Sky. This is a vital part of the great, deep feeling and spiritual psychology that we have as Indian people. It is why we preserved and respected our ecological environment for such a long period. *Mitakuye oyasin!* We are all related!

In conclusion, our survival is dependent on the realization that Mother Earth is a truly holy being, that all things in this world are holy and must not be violated, and that we must share and be generous with one another. You may call this thought by whatever fancy words you wish—psychology, theology, sociology, or philosophy—but you must think of Mother Earth as a living being. Think of your fellow men and women as holy people who were put here by the Great Spirit. Think of being related to all things! With this philosophy in mind as we go on with our environmental ecology efforts, our search for spirituality, and our quest for peace, we will be far more successful when we truly understand the Indians' respect for Mother Earth.

NOTES

1. John F. McBride, *Modern Indian Psychology* (Vermillion, SD: University of South Dakota, Indian Studies Department, 1971), p. 1.

2. David Humphreys Miller, *Ghost Dance* (Lincoln, NE: University of Nebraska Press, 1959), p. 65.

Questions for Thought

1. How do the four commandments given by the Great Spirit compare with or differ from the Ten Commandments given by Yahweh or God?

2. Do you agree with Eagle Man's claim that it is crucial that humans accept some of the values taught by Native Americans? Defend your answer.

3. How do Eagle Man's views on possessions compare with or differ from the views of Schweitzer? How do they compare with or differ from your own views?

4. Do you think that *Mitakuye Oyasin* is an important ethical concept? Why or why not?

5. What do you think is the most important moral value? What makes this value so important?

The Land Ethic   11

ALDO LEOPOLD

Aldo Leopold (1887–1948), who is often called the father of wildlife conservation in the United States, was born in Burlington, Iowa. After receiving his early education in prep schools in Burlington and New Jersey, Leopold studied at the Sheffield Scientific School of Yale University. He then enrolled in the Yale Forestry School, receiving his master's degree in 1909. After graduation, Leopold went to work for the U.S. Forestry Service, and he remained with the Forestry Service until 1933. That year he obtained a position at the University of Wisconsin, being named to the newly created chair in game management. Leopold, who also served as an adviser on conservation to the United Nations, remained in this position until his death.

Leopold was the author of over 350 articles dealing with scientific and policy matters as well as a classic textbook titled *Game Management*. He also wrote the popular work on conservation, *A Sand County Almanac* (1949), from which the following selection is taken. In a death perhaps befitting a champion of conservation, Leopold died of a heart attack while helping fight a grass fire. He was named posthumously to the National Wildlife Federation's Conservation Hall of Fame.

Leopold begins the following selection by recounting the story of the slave girls who were hanged by their master Odysseus when he returned from his long journey. While most of us would find this behavior morally reprehensible, Odysseus was acting properly according to the ethical criteria of his time. For, according to those criteria, slaves were property and not persons, and there were no moral prohibitions concerning the disposal of property. Today, however, our moral sensibility suggests that human beings cannot be property and that all human beings have moral value and certain moral rights. Leopold claims that this modern moral sensibility is the result of a long process of development, one characterized by an extension of moral concern to wider and wider areas. Whereas the earliest moral theories limited moral concern to certain humans, later theories extended such concern to more and more humans and finally to all humans. Moreover, whereas the earliest moral theories dealt exclusively with the relations obtaining between individuals, later ones dealt with the relation of the individual to society.

Leopold goes on to argue that we are now on the verge of an even wider extension of moral concern, an extension that would include the land itself within the sphere of moral consideration. Labeling this new extension of moral concern "the land ethic," Leopold claims that the land ethic is both "an evolutionary possibility and an ecological necessity." Since he believes that we can have moral concern only for something that we can relate to on a personal level, Leopold spends several pages developing the view of land as a biotic organism. He suggests that land is most accurately viewed as a biotic pyramid consisting of a complex series of food chains or energy transfers. The position of a species in the land pyramid is determined by what the species eats; thus, since human beings eat both meat and vegetables, they occupy an intermediate level with bears, raccoons, and squirrels. Thus, one of the implications of the land ethic, as

Leopold clearly says, is to change "the role of *Homo sapiens* from conqueror of the land-community to plain member and citizen of it." Once this occurs, the value of other members of the land-community can no longer be determined by human interests, such as whether they have economic worth. Rather, we must recognize that each member of the land-community has intrinsic value, that each member of the land-community is properly the object of moral concern. Indeed, Leopold concludes that the land ethic suggests a moral principle that differs significantly from earlier moral principles. He states this moral principle as follows: "A thing is right when it tends to preserve the integrity, stability, and beauty of the biotic community. It is wrong when it tends otherwise."

Questions for Reading

1. With what story does Leopold open this selection? How does this story relate to what he says later?
2. How does Leopold use the term *symbiosis*? Why does he believe that ethics represents a type of symbiosis?
3. What does Leopold mean when he says that "plant succession steered the course of history"? What evidence does he use to support this claim?
4. How does Leopold describe the land pyramid? Why does he choose this particular model to illustrate the workings of nature?
5. How are right and wrong defined in the context of the land ethic?

THE LAND ETHIC

WHEN GOD-LIKE ODYSSEUS RETURNED FROM the wars in Troy, he hanged all on one rope a dozen slave-girls of his household whom he suspected of misbehavior during his absence.

This hanging involved no question of propriety. The girls were property. The disposal of property was then, as now, a matter of expediency, not of right and wrong.

Concepts of right and wrong were not lacking from Odysseus' Greece: witness the fidelity of his wife through the long years before at last his black-prowed galleys clove the wine-dark seas for home. The ethical structure of that day covered wives, but had not yet been extended to human chattels. During the three thousand years which have since elapsed, ethical criteria have been extended to many fields of conduct, with corresponding shrinkages in those judged by expediency only.

The Ethical Sequence

This extension of ethics, so far studied only by philosophers, is actually a process in ecological evolution. Its sequences may be described in ecological as well as in philosophical terms. An ethic, ecologically, is a limitation on freedom of action in the struggle for existence. An ethic, philosophically, is a differentiation of social from anti-social conduct. These are two definitions of one thing. The thing has its origin in the tendency of interdependent individuals or groups to evolve modes of co-operation. The ecologist calls these symbioses. Politics and economics are advanced symbioses in which the original free-for-all competition has been replaced, in part, by co-operative mechanisms with an ethical content.

The complexity of co-operative mechanisms has increased with population density, and with the efficiency of tools. It was simpler, for example, to define the anti-social uses of sticks and stones in the days of the mastodons than of bullets and billboards in the age of motors.

The first ethics dealt with the relation between individuals; the Mosaic Decalogue is an example. Later accretions dealt with the relation between the individual and society. The Golden Rule tries to integrate the individual to society; **democracy** to integrate social organization to the individual.

There is as yet no ethic dealing with man's relation to land and to the animals and plants which grow upon it. Land, like Odysseus' slave-girls, is still property. The land-relation is still strictly economic, entailing privileges but not obligations.

The extension of ethics to this third element in human environment is, if I read the evidence correctly, an evolutionary possibility and an ecological necessity. It is the third step in a sequence. The first two have already been taken. Individual thinkers since the days of Ezekiel and Isaiah have asserted that the despoliation of land is not only inexpedient but wrong. Society, however, has not yet affirmed their belief. I regard the present conservation movement as the embryo of such an affirmation.

An ethic may be regarded as a mode of guidance for meeting ecological situations so new or intricate, or involving such deferred reactions, that the path of social expediency is not discernible to the average individual. Animal instincts are modes of guidance for the individual in meeting such situations. Ethics are possibly a kind of community instinct in-the-making.

The Community Concept

All ethics so far evolved rest upon a single **premise:** that the individual is a member of a community of interdependent parts. His instincts prompt him to compete for his place in that community, but his ethics prompt him also to co-operate (perhaps in order that there may be a place to compete for).

The land ethic simply enlarges the boundaries of the community to include soils, waters, plants, and animals, or collectively: the land.

This sounds simple: do we not already sing our love for and obligation to the land of the free and the home of the brave? Yes, but just what and whom do we love? Certainly not the soil, which we are sending helter-skelter downriver. Certainly not the waters, which we assume have no function except to turn turbines, float barges, and carry off sewage. Certainly not the plants, of which we exterminate whole communities without batting an eye. Certainly not the animals, of which we have already extirpated many of the largest and most beautiful species. A land ethic of course cannot prevent the alteration, management, and use of these "resources," but it does affirm their right to continued existence, and, at least in spots, their continued existence in a natural state.

In short, a land ethic changes the role of *Homo sapiens* from conqueror of the land-community to plain member and citizen of it. It implies respect for his fellow-members, and also respect for the community as such.

In human history, we have learned (I hope) that the conqueror role is eventually self-defeating. Why? Because it is implicit in such a role that the conqueror knows, *ex cathedra,* just what makes the community clock tick, and just what and who is valuable, and what and who is worthless, in community life. It always turns out that he knows neither, and this is why his conquests eventually defeat themselves.

In the biotic community, a parallel situation exists. Abraham knew exactly what the land was for: it was to drip milk and honey into Abraham's mouth. At the present moment, the assurance with which we regard this assumption is inverse to the degree of our education.

The ordinary citizen today assumes that science knows what makes the community clock tick; the scientist is equally sure that he does not. He knows that the biotic mechanism is so complex that its workings may never be fully understood.

That man is, in fact, only a member of a biotic team is shown by an ecological interpretation of history. Many historical events, hitherto explained solely in terms of human enterprise, were actually biotic interactions between people and land. The characteristics of the land determined the facts quite as potently as the characteristics of the men who lived on it.

Consider, for example, the settlement of the Mississippi valley. In the years following the Revolution, three groups were contending for its control: the native Indian, the French and English traders, and the American settlers. Historians wonder what would have happened if the English at Detroit had thrown a little more weight into the Indian side of those tipsy scales which decided the outcome of the colonial migration into the cane-lands of Kentucky. It is time now to ponder the fact that the cane-lands, when subjected to the particular mixture of forces represented by the cow, plow, fire, and axe of the pioneer, became bluegrass. What if the plant succession inherent in this dark and bloody ground had, under the impact of these forces, given us some worthless sedge, shrub, or weed? Would Boone and Kenton have held out? Would there have been any overflow into Ohio, Indiana, Illinois, and Missouri? Any Louisiana Purchase? Any transcontinental union of new states? Any Civil War?

Kentucky was one sentence in the drama of history. We are commonly told what the human actors in this drama tried to do, but we are seldom told that their success, or the lack of it, hung in large degree on the reaction of particular soils to the impact of the particular forces exerted by their occupancy. In the case of Kentucky, we do not even know where the bluegrass came from—whether it is a native species, or a stowaway from Europe.

Contrast the cane-lands with what hindsight tells us about the Southwest, where the pioneers were equally brave, resourceful, and persevering. The impact of occupancy here brought no bluegrass, or other plant fitted to withstand the bumps and buffetings of hard use. This region, when grazed by livestock, reverted through a series of more and more worthless grasses, shrubs, and weeds to a condition of unstable equilibrium. Each recession of plant types bred erosion; each increment to erosion bred a further recession of plants. The result today is a progressive and mutual deterioration, not only of plants and soils, but of the animal community subsisting thereon. The early settlers did not expect this: on the *ciénegas* of New Mexico some even cut ditches to hasten it. So subtle has been its progress that few residents of the region are aware of it. It is quite invisible to the tourist who finds this wrecked landscape colorful and charming (as indeed it is, but it bears scant resemblance to what it was in 1848).

This same landscape was "developed" once before, but with quite different results. The Pueblo Indians settled the Southwest in pre-Columbian times, but they happened *not* to be equipped with range livestock. Their civilization expired, but not because their land expired.

In India, regions devoid of any sod-forming grass have been settled, apparently without wrecking the land, by the simple expedient of carrying the grass to the cow, rather than vice versa. (Was this the result of some deep wisdom, or was it just good luck? I do not know.)

In short, the plant succession steered the course of history; the pioneer simply demonstrated, for good or ill, what successions inhered in the land. Is history taught in this spirit? It will be, once the concept of land as a community really penetrates our intellectual life.

The Ecological Conscience

Conservation is a state of harmony between men and land. Despite nearly a century of propaganda, conservation still proceeds at a snail's pace; progress still consists largely of letterhead pieties and convention oratory. On the back forty we still slip two steps backward for each forward stride.

The usual answer to this dilemma is "more conservation education." No one will debate this, but is it certain that only the *volume* of education needs stepping up? Is something lacking in the *content* as well?

It is difficult to give a fair summary of its content in brief form, but, as I understand it, the content is substantially this: obey the law, vote right, join some organizations, and practice what conservation is profitable on your own land; the government will do the rest.

Is not this formula too easy to accomplish anything worth-while? It defines no right or wrong, assigns no obligation, calls for no sacrifice, implies no change in the current philosophy of values. In respect of land-use, it urges only enlightened self-interest. Just how far will such education take us? . . .

No important change in ethics was ever accomplished without an internal change in our intellectual emphasis, loyalties, affections, and convictions. The proof that conservation has not yet touched these foundations of conduct lies in the fact that philosophy and religion have not yet heard of it. In our attempt to make conservation easy, we have made it trivial.

Substitutes for a Land Ethic

When the logic of history hungers for bread and we hand out a stone, we are at pains to explain how much the stone resembles bread. I now describe some of the stones which serve in lieu of a land ethic.

One basic weakness in a conservation system based wholly on economic motives is that most members of the land community have no economic value. Wildflowers and songbirds are examples. Of the 22,000 higher plants and animals native to Wisconsin, it is doubtful whether more than 5 per cent can be sold, fed, eaten, or otherwise put to economic use. Yet these creatures are members of the biotic community, and if (as I believe) its stability depends on its integrity, they are entitled to continuance.

When one of these non-economic categories is threatened, and if we happen to love it, we invent subterfuges to give it economic importance. At the beginning of the century songbirds were supposed to be disappearing. Ornithologists jumped to the rescue with some distinctly shaky evidence to the effect that insects would eat us up if birds failed to control them. The evidence had to be economic in order to be valid. It is painful to read these circumlocutions today. We have no land ethic yet, but we have at least drawn nearer the point of admitting that birds should continue as a matter of biotic right, regardless of the presence or absence of economic advantage to us.

A parallel situation exists in respect of predatory mammals, raptorial birds, and fish-eating birds. Time was when biologists somewhat overworked the evidence that these creatures preserve the health of game by killing weaklings, or that they control rodents for the farmer, or that they prey only on "worthless" species. Here again, the evidence had to be economic in order to be valid. It is only in recent years that we hear the more honest argument that predators are members of the community, and that no special interest has the right to exterminate them for the sake of a benefit, real or fancied, to itself. . . .

Some species of trees have been "read out of the party" by economics-minded foresters because they grow too slowly, or have too low a sale value to pay as timber crops: white cedar, tamarack, cypress, beech, and hemlock are examples. In Europe, where forestry is ecologically more advanced, the noncommercial tree species are recognized as members of the native forest community, to be preserved as such, within reason. Moreover some (like beech) have been found to have a valuable function in building up soil fertility. The interdependence of the forest and its constituent tree species, ground flora, and fauna is taken for granted.

Lack of economic value is sometimes a character not only of species or groups, but of entire biotic communities: marshes, bogs, dunes, and "deserts" are examples. Our formula in such cases is to relegate their conservation to government as refuges, monuments, or parks. The difficulty is that these communities are usually interspersed with more valuable private lands; the government cannot possibly own or control such scattered parcels. The net effect is that we have relegated some of them to ultimate extinction over large areas. If the private owner were ecologically minded, he would be proud to be the custodian of a reasonable proportion of such areas, which add diversity and beauty to his farm and to his community. . . .

There is a clear tendency in American conservation to relegate to government all necessary jobs that private landowners fail to perform. Government ownership, operation, subsidy, or regulation is now widely prevalent in forestry, range management, soil and watershed management, park and wilderness conservation, fisheries management, and migratory bird management, with more to come. Most of this growth in governmental conservation is proper and logical, some of it is inevitable. That I imply no disapproval of it is implicit in the fact that I have spent most of my life working for it. Nevertheless the question arises: What is the ultimate magnitude of the enterprise? Will the tax base carry its eventual ramifications? At what point will governmental conservation, like the mastodon, become handicapped by its own dimensions? The answer, if there is any, seems to be in a land ethic, or some other force which assigns more obligation to the private landowner.

Industrial landowners and users, especially lumbermen and stockmen, are inclined to wail long and loudly about the extension of government ownership and regulation to land, but (with notable exceptions) they show little disposition to develop the only visible alternative: the voluntary practice of conservation on their own lands. . . .

To sum up: a system of conservation based solely on economic self-interest is hopelessly lopsided. It tends to ignore, and thus eventually to eliminate, many elements in the land community that lack commercial value, but that are (as far as we know) essential to its healthy functioning. It assumes, falsely, I think, that the economic parts of the biotic clock will function without the uneconomic parts. It tends to relegate to government many functions eventually too large, too complex, or too widely dispersed to be performed by government.

An ethical obligation on the part of the private owner is the only visible remedy for these situations.

The Land Pyramid

An ethic to supplement and guide the economic relation to land presupposes the existence of some mental image of land as a biotic mechanism. We can be ethical only in relation to something we can see, feel, understand, love, or otherwise have faith in.

The image commonly employed in conservation education is "the balance of nature." For reasons too lengthy to detail here, this figure of speech fails to describe accurately what little we know about the land mechanism. A much truer image is the one employed in ecology: the biotic pyramid. I shall first sketch the pyramid as a symbol of land, and later develop some of its implications in terms of land-use.

Plants absorb energy from the sun. This energy flows through a circuit called the biota, which may be represented by a pyramid consisting of layers. The bottom layer is the soil. A plant layer rests on the soil, an insect layer on the plants, a bird and rodent layer on the insects, and so on up through various animal groups to the apex layer, which consists of the larger carnivores.

The species of a layer are alike not in where they came from, or in what they look like, but rather in what they eat. Each successive layer depends on those below it for food and often for other services, and each in turn furnishes food and services to those above. Proceeding upward, each successive layer decreases in numerical abundance. Thus, for every carnivore there are hundreds of his prey, thousands of their prey, millions of insects, uncountable plants. The pyramidal form of the system reflects this numerical progression from apex to base. Man shares an intermediate layer with the bears, raccoons, and squirrels which eat both meat and vegetables.

The lines of dependency for food and other services are called food chains. Thus soil-oak-deer-Indian is a chain that has now been largely converted to soil-corn-cow-farmer. Each species, including ourselves, is a link in many chains. The deer eats a hundred plants other than oak, and the cow a hundred plants other than corn. Both, then, are links in a hundred chains. The pyramid is a tangle of chains so complex as to seem disorderly, yet the stability of the system proves it to be a highly organized structure. Its functioning depends on the co-operation and competition of its diverse parts.

In the beginning, the pyramid of life was low and squat; the food chains short and simple. Evolution has added layer after layer, link after link. Man is one of thousands of accretions to the height and complexity of the pyramid. Science has given us many doubts, but it has given us at least one certainty: the trend of evolution is to elaborate and diversify the biota.

Land, then, is not merely soil; it is a fountain of energy flowing through a circuit of soils, plants, and animals. Food chains are the living channels which conduct energy upward; death and decay return it to the soil. The circuit is not closed; some energy is dissipated in decay, some is added by absorption from the air, some is stored in soils, peats, and long-lived forests; but it is a sustained circuit, like a slowly augmented revolving fund of life. There is always a net loss by downhill wash, but this is normally small and offset by the decay of rocks. It is deposited in the ocean and, in the course of geological time, raised to form new lands and new pyramids.

The velocity and character of the upward flow of energy depend on the complex structure of the plant and animal community, much as the upward flow of sap in a tree depends on its complex cellular organization. Without this complexity, normal circulation would presumably not occur. Structure means the characteristic numbers, as well as the characteristic kinds and functions, of the component species. This interdependence between the complex structure of the land and its smooth functioning as an energy unit is one of its basic attributes.

When a change occurs in one part of the circuit, many other parts must adjust themselves to it. Change does not necessarily obstruct or divert the flow of energy; evolution is a long series of self-induced changes, the net result of which has been to elaborate the flow mechanism and to lengthen the circuit. Evolutionary changes, however, are usually slow and local. Man's invention of tools has enabled him to make changes of unprecedented violence, rapidity, and scope.

One change is in the composition of floras and faunas. The larger predators are lopped off the apex of the pyramid; food chains, for the first time in history, become shorter rather than longer. Domesticated species from other lands are substituted for wild ones, and wild ones are moved to new habitats. In this world-wide pooling of faunas and floras, some species get out of bounds as pests and diseases, others are extinguished. Such effects are seldom intended or foreseen; they represent unpredicted and often untraceable readjustments in the structure. Agricultural science is largely a race between the emergence of new pests and the emergence of new techniques for their control.

Another change touches the flow of energy through plants and animals and its return to the soil. Fertility is the ability of soil to receive, store, and release energy. Agriculture, by overdrafts on the soil, or by too radical a substitution of domestic for native species in the superstructure, may derange the channels of flow or deplete storage. Soils depleted of their storage, or of the organic matter which anchors it, wash away faster than they form. This is erosion.

Waters, like soil, are part of the energy circuit. Industry, by polluting waters or obstructing them with dams, may exclude the plants and animals necessary to keep energy in circulation.

Transportation brings about another basic change: the plants or animals grown in one region are now consumed and returned to the soil in another. Transportation taps the energy stored in rocks, and in the air, and uses it elsewhere; thus we fertilize the garden with nitrogen gleaned by the guano birds from the fishes of seas on the other side of the Equator. Thus the formerly localized and self-contained circuits are pooled on a world-wide scale.

The process of altering the pyramid for human occupation releases stored energy, and this often gives rise, during the pioneering period, to a deceptive exuberance of plant and animal life, both wild and tame. These releases of biotic capital tend to becloud or postpone the penalties of violence.

This thumbnail sketch of land as an energy circuit conveys three basic ideas:

1. That land is not merely soil.
2. That the native plants and animals kept the energy circuit open; others may or may not.
3. That man-made changes are of a different order than evolutionary changes, and have effects more comprehensive than is intended or foreseen.

These ideas, collectively, raise two basic issues: Can the land adjust itself to the new order? Can the desired alternations be accomplished with less violence?

Biotas seem to differ in their capacity to sustain violent conversion. Western Europe, for example, carries a far different pyramid than Caesar found there. Some large animals are lost; swampy forests have become meadows or plowland; many new plants and animals are introduced, some of which escape as pests; the remaining natives are greatly changed in distribution and abundance. Yet the soil is still there and, with the help of imported nutrients, still fertile; the waters flow normally; the new structure seems to function and to persist. There is no visible stoppage or derangement of the circuit.

Western Europe, then, has a resistant biota. Its inner processes are tough, elastic, resistant to strain. No matter how violent the alterations, the pyramid, so far, has developed some new *modus vivendi* which preserves its habitability for man, and for most of the other natives.

Japan seems to present another instance of radical conversion without disorganization.

Most other civilized regions, and some as yet barely touched by civilization, display various stages of disorganization, varying from initial symptoms to advanced wastage. In Asia Minor and North Africa diagnosis is confused by climatic changes, which may have been either the cause or the effect of advanced wastage. In the United States the degree of disorganization varies locally; it is worst in the Southwest, the Ozarks, and parts of the South, and least in New England and the Northwest. Better land-uses may still arrest it in the less advanced regions. In parts of Mexico, South America, South Africa, and Australia a violent and accelerating wastage is in progress, but I cannot assess the prospects.

This almost world-wide display of disorganization in the land seems to be similar to disease in an animal, except that it never culminates in complete disorganization or death. The land recovers, but at some reduced level of complexity, and with a reduced carrying capacity for people, plants, and animals. Many biotas currently regarded as "lands of opportunity" are in fact already subsisting on exploitative agriculture, i.e., they have already exceeded their sustained carrying capacity. Most of South America is overpopulated in this sense. . . .

The combined evidence of history and ecology seems to support one general deduction: the less violent the man-made changes, the greater the probability of successful readjustment in the pyramid. Violence, in turn, varies with human population density; a dense population requires a more violent conversion. In this respect, North America has a better chance for permanence than Europe, if she can contrive to limit her density.

This deduction runs counter to our current philosophy, which assumes that because a small increase in density enriched human life, that an indefinite increase will enrich it indefinitely. Ecology knows of no density relationship that holds for indefinitely wide limits. All gains from density are subject to a law of diminishing returns. . . .

Land Health and the A-B Cleavage

A land ethic, then, reflects the existence of an ecological conscience, and this in turn reflects a conviction of individual responsibility for the health of the land. Health is the capacity of the land for self-renewal. Conservation is our effort to understand and preserve this capacity.

Conservationists are notorious for their dissensions. Superficially these seem to add up to mere confusion, but a more careful scrutiny reveals a single plane of cleavage common to many specialized fields. In each field one group (A) regards the land as soil, and its function as commodity-production; another group (B) regards the land as a biota, and its function as something broader. How much broader is admittedly in a state of doubt and confusion.

In my own field, forestry, group A is quite content to grow trees like cabbages, with cellulose as the basic forest commodity. It feels no inhibition against violence; its ideology is agronomic. Group B, on the other hand, sees forestry as fundamentally different from agronomy because it employs natural species, and manages a natural environment rather than creating an artificial one. Group B prefers natural reproduction on principle. It worries on biotic as well as economic grounds about the loss of species like chestnut, and the threatened loss of the white pines. It worries about a whole series of secondary forest functions: wildlife, recreation, watersheds, wilderness areas. To my mind, Group B feels the stirrings of an ecological conscience.

In the wildlife field, a parallel cleavage exists. For Group A the basic commodities are sport and meat; the yardsticks of production are ciphers of take in pheasants and trout. Artificial propagation is acceptable as a permanent as well as a temporary recourse—if its unit costs permit. Group B, on the other hand, worries about a whole series of biotic side-issues. What is the cost in predators of producing a game crop? Should we have further recourse to exotics? How can management restore the shrinking species, like prairie grouse, already hopeless as shootable game? How can management restore the threatened rarities, like trumpeter swan and whooping crane? Can management principles be extended to wildflowers? Here again it is clear to me that we have the same A-B cleavage as in forestry. . . .

In all of these cleavages, we see repeated the same basic paradoxes: man the conqueror *versus* man the biotic citizen; science the sharpener of his sword *versus* science the searchlight on his universe; land the slave and servant *versus* land the collective organism. Robinson's injunction to Tristram may well be applied, at this juncture, to *Homo sapiens* as a species in geological time:

Whether you will or not
You are a King, Tristram, for you are one
Of the time-tested few that leave the world,
When they are gone, not the same place it was.
Mark what you leave.

The Outlook

It is inconceivable to me that an ethical relation to land can exist without love, respect, and admiration for land, and a high regard for its value. By value, I of course mean something far broader than mere economic value; I mean value in the philosophical sense.

Perhaps the most serious obstacle impeding the evolution of a land ethic is the fact that our educational and economic system is headed away from, rather than toward, an intense consciousness of land. Your true modern is separated from the land by many middlemen, and by innumerable physical gadgets. He has no vital relation to it; to him it is the space between cities on which crops grow. Turn him loose for a day on the land, and if the spot does not happen to be a golf links or a "scenic" area, he is bored stiff. If crops could be raised by hydroponics instead of farming, it would suit him very well. Synthetic substitutes for wood, leather, wool, and other natural land products suit him better than the originals. In short, land is something he has "outgrown." . . . One of the requisites for an ecological comprehension of land is an understanding of ecology, and this is by no means co-extensive with "education"; in fact, much higher education seems deliberately to avoid ecological concepts. An understanding of ecology does not necessarily originate in courses bearing ecological labels; it is quite as likely to be labeled geography, botany, agronomy, history, or economics. This is as it should be, but whatever the label, ecological training is scarce.

The case for a land ethic would appear hopeless but for the minority which is in obvious revolt against these "modern" trends.

The "key-log" which must be moved to release the evolutionary process for an ethic is simply this: quit thinking about decent land-use as solely an economic problem. Examine each question in terms of what is ethically and esthetically right, as well as what is economically expedient. A thing is right when it tends to preserve the integrity, stability, and beauty of the biotic community. It is wrong when it tends otherwise. . . .

I have purposely presented the land ethic as a product of social evolution because nothing so important as an ethic is ever "written." Only the most superficial study of history supposes that Moses "wrote" the Decalogue; it evolved in the minds of a thinking community, and Moses wrote a tentative summary of it for a "seminar." I say tentative because evolution never stops.

The evolution of a land ethic is an intellectual as well as emotional process. Conservation is paved with good intentions which prove to be futile, or even dangerous, because they are devoid of critical understanding either of the land, or of economic land-use. I think it is a truism that as the ethical frontier advances from the individual to the community, its intellectual content increases.

The mechanism of operation is the same for any ethic: social approbation for right actions; social disapproval for wrong actions.

By and large, our present problem is one of attitudes and implements. We are remodeling the Alhambra with a steam-shovel, and we are proud of our yardage. We shall hardly relinquish the shovel, which after all has many good points, but we are in need of gentler and more objective criteria for its successful use.

Questions for Thought

1. What is the point of the story about Odysseus and the slave girls? Can you think of other stories or historical events that would illustrate Leopold's point?
2. What exactly does it mean to view nature in "ecological" terms? To what extent do you view nature in this manner?
3. Do you think that the land pyramid is an accurate representation of the natural world? Why or why not?
4. If you were to accept Leopold's definition of right and wrong, how might your moral decisions change?
5. In what ways are Leopold's views similar to those of Eagle Man? In what ways are they different?

12   In a Different Voice

CAROL GILLIGAN

Carol Gilligan (b. 1936), who earned a B.A. in English literature and an M.A. in clinical psychology before receiving her Ph.D. in social psychology in 1964, was a professor at Harvard University for over thirty years. As an assistant professor at Harvard in the 1970s, Gilligan realized that most studies of psychological and moral development involved only privileged white men. This realization led her to focus her research on women and girls, research that ultimately led her to conclude that women's psychological and moral development differed in important ways from the psychological and moral development of men. By introducing and validating research on women, Gilligan undermined the commonly held belief that men represented the standard of human behavior. Her insights were published in the influential work *In a Different Voice: Psychological Theory and Women's Development* (1982). Because of her work, Gilligan was awarded the 1997 Heinz Award in the Human Condition. She received this award, in the words of the Awards Committee, for "courageously challenging long-held assumptions about human development in a way that has transformed the paradigm of what it means to be human."

While still at Harvard, Gilligan also published several articles on developmental psychology, and coauthored or edited five books with her students: *Mapping the Moral Domain* (1988); *Making Connections: The Relational Worlds of Adolescent Girls at Emma Willard School* (1990); *Women, Girls, and Psychotherapy: Reframing Resistance* (1991); *Meeting at the Crossroads: Women's Psychology and Girls' Development* (1992); and *Between Voice and Silence: Women and Girls, Race and Relationships* (1995).

In 2002, Gilligan left her position at Harvard and joined the faculty of New York University. She splits her time between the Graduate School of Education and the School of Law. Her most recent book, *Birth of Pleasure: A New Map of Love*, was published in 2003. Gilligan's play *The Scarlet Letter* was produced by Shakespeare and Company in 2002.

In the following selection from *In a Different Voice*, Gilligan discusses the values that inform the moral thinking of modern women, along with the conflict or dilemma that such women often experience in their moral development. According to Gilligan, women's moral values have traditionally centered on such concepts as self-sacrifice and compassion for others (elsewhere she says that the traditional moral values of women constitute an ethic of care). However, in struggling for liberation, women have found it necessary to embrace certain values that have been traditionally associated with men, values such as **autonomy** and equality (elsewhere she says that such traditional masculine values form an ethic of rights). Since these two sets of values have usually been taken to be incompatible, women find themselves torn between two moral worlds.

Gilligan argues, however, that the dichotomy between these two ethics has been the result of flawed thinking—thinking in which women have been viewed as inferior, sexually passive, and incapable of moral choice and responsibility. Because of this thinking, the ethic of care has been subordinated to the ethic of rights, and women's moral development has been seen as being stunted in comparison with the moral development of men.

To overcome such flawed thinking (and the flawed research on which it was based), Gilligan suggests that the moral voice of women must be heard. And once it is heard, she believes that the traditional prejudices against women and women's moral development can be overcome. Then the ethic of care will be seen as complementing, rather than conflicting with, the ethic of rights; and the importance of both of these ethics, for the moral development of both women and men, will be recognized.

Questions for Reading

1. What is the nature of the moral conflict that is revealed in the responses that Gilligan quotes? What, according to Gilligan, is the common thread that runs through all of them?
2. Why, according to Gilligan, were most of the women interviewed unwilling to take a moral stand?
3. What is the gist of the story of the middle-aged divorced woman? What insights does Gilligan derive from her story?
4. Who are the two fictional characters whom Gilligan discusses? What points does she make in discussing these two characters?
5. What psychological significance does Gilligan attribute to women's access to birth control and abortion?
6. What, according to Gilligan, traditionally distinguishes the moral thinking of women from the moral thinking of men?

A COLLEGE STUDENT, RESPONDING TO THE question "If you had to say what morality meant to you, how would you sum it up?" replies:

> When I think of the word *morality*, I think of obligations. I usually think of it as conflicts between personal desires and social things, social considerations, or personal desires of yourself versus personal desires of another person or people or whatever. Morality is that whole realm of how you decide these conflicts. A moral person is one who would decide by placing themselves more often than not as equals. A truly moral person would always consider another person as their equal. . . . In a situation of social interaction, something is morally wrong where the individual ends up screwing a lot of people. And it is morally right when everyone comes out better off.

Yet when asked if she can think of someone whom she considers a genuinely moral person, she replies, "Well, immediately I think of Albert Schweitzer, because he has obviously given his life to help others." Obligation and sacrifice override the ideal of equality, setting up a basic contradiction in her thought.

Another undergraduate responds to the question "What does it mean to say something is morally right or wrong?" by also speaking first of responsibilities and obligations:

> It has to do with responsibilities and obligations and values, mainly values. . . . In my life situation I relate morality with interpersonal relationships that have to do with respect for the other person and myself. (*Why respect other people?*) Because they have a consciousness or feelings that can be hurt, an awareness that can be hurt.

The concern about hurting others persists as a major theme in the responses of two other women students to the question "Why be moral?"

Millions of people have to live together peacefully. I personally don't want to hurt other people. That's a real criterion, a main criterion for me. It underlies my sense of justice. It isn't nice to inflict pain. I empathize with anyone in pain. Not hurting others is important in my own private morals. Years ago I would have jumped out of a window not to hurt my boyfriend. That was pathological. Even today, though, I want approval and love, and I don't want enemies. Maybe that's why there is morality—so people can win approval, love, and friendship.

My main principle is not hurting other people as long as you aren't going against your own conscience and as long as you remain true to yourself. . . . There are many moral issues, such as abortion, the draft, killing, stealing, monogamy. If something is a controversial issue like these, then I always say it is up to the individual. The individual has to decide and then follow his own conscience. There are no moral absolutes. Laws are pragmatic instruments, but they are not absolutes. A viable society can't make exceptions all the time, but I would personally. . . . I'm afraid I'm heading for some big crisis with my boyfriend someday, and someone will get hurt, and he'll get more hurt than I will. I feel an obligation not to hurt him, but also an obligation not to lie. I don't know if it is possible not to lie and not to hurt.

The common thread that runs through these statements is the wish not to hurt others and the hope that in morality lies a way of solving conflicts so that no one will be hurt. This theme is independently introduced by each of the four women as the most specific item in their response to a most general question. The moral person is one who helps others; goodness is service, meeting one's obligations and responsibilities to others, if possible without sacrificing oneself. While the first of the four women ends by denying the conflict she initially introduced, the last woman anticipates a conflict between remaining true to herself and adhering to her principle of not hurting others. The dilemma that would test the limits of this judgment would be one where helping others is seen to be at the price of hurting the self.

The reticence about taking stands on "controversial issues," a willingness to "make exceptions all the time," is echoed repeatedly by other college women:

I never feel that I can condemn anyone else. I have a very relativistic position. The basic idea that I cling to is the sanctity of human life. I am inhibited about impressing my beliefs on others.

I could never argue that my belief on a moral question is anything that another person should accept. I don't believe in absolutes. If there is an absolute for moral decisions, it is human life.

Or as a thirty-one-year-old graduate student says when explaining why she would find it difficult to steal a drug to save her own life, despite her belief that it would be right to steal for another: "It's just very hard to defend yourself against the rules. I mean, we live by consensus, and if you take an action simply for yourself, by yourself, there's no consensus there, and that is relatively indefensible in this society now."

What emerges in these voices is a sense of vulnerability that impedes these women from taking a stand, what George Eliot regards as the girl's "susceptibility" to adverse judgments by others, which stems from her lack of power and consequent inability "to do something in the world" (p. 365). The unwillingness to make moral decisions that Kohlberg and Kramer (1969) and Kohlberg and Gilligan (1971) associate with the adolescent crisis of identity and belief takes the form in men of calling into question the concept of morality itself. But these women's reluctance to judge stems rather from their uncertainty about their right to make moral statements, or perhaps from the price for them that such judgment seems to entail.

When women feel excluded from direct participation in society, they see themselves as subject to a consensus or judgment made and enforced by men on whose protection and support they depend and by whose names they are known. A divorced middle-aged woman, mother of adolescent daughters, resident of a sophisticated university community, tells the story:

As a woman, I feel I never understood that I was a person, that I could make decisions and I had a right to make decisions. I always felt that that belonged to my father or my husband in some way, or church, which was always represented by a male clergyman. They were the three men in my life: father, husband, and clergyman, and they had much more to say about what I should or shouldn't do. They were really authority figures which I accepted. It only lately has occurred to me that I never even rebelled against it, and my girls are much more conscious of this, not in the militant sense, but just in the recognizing sense. . . . I still let things happen to me rather than make them happen, than make choices, although I know all about choices. I know the procedures and the steps and all. (*Do you have any clues about why this might be true?*) Well, I think in one sense there is less responsibility involved. Because if you make a dumb decision, you have to take the rap. If it happens to you, well, you can complain about it. I think that if you don't grow up feeling that you ever have any choices, you don't have the sense that you have emotional responsibility. With this sense of choice comes this sense of responsibility.

The essence of moral decision is the exercise of choice and the willingness to accept responsibility for that choice. To the extent that women perceive themselves as having no choice, they correspondingly excuse themselves from the responsibility that decision entails. Childlike in the vulnerability of their dependence and consequent fear of abandonment, they claim to wish only to please, but in return for their goodness they expect to be loved and cared for. This, then, is an "altruism" always at risk, for it presupposes an innocence constantly in danger of being compromised by an awareness of the tradeoff that has been made. Asked to describe herself, a college senior responds:

I have heard of the onion-skin theory. I see myself as an onion, as a block of different layers. The external layers are for people that I don't know that well, the agreeable, the social, and as you go inward, there are more sides for people I know that I show. I am not sure about the innermost, whether there is a core, or whether I have just picked up everything as I was growing up,

these different influences. I think I have a neutral attitude toward myself, but I do think in terms of good and bad. Good—I try to be considerate and thoughtful of other people, and I try to be fair in situations and be tolerant. I use the words, but I try and work them out practically. Bad things I am not sure if they are bad, if they are altruistic or I am doing them basically for approval of other people. (*Which things are these?*) The values that I try to act out. They deal mostly with interpersonal relations. . . . If I were doing things for approval, it would be a very tenuous thing. If I didn't get the right feedback, there might go all my values.

Ibsen's play *A Doll's House* depicts the explosion of just such a world through the eruption of a moral dilemma that calls into question the notion of goodness which lies at its center. Nora, the "squirrel wife," living with her husband as she lived with her father, puts into action this conception of goodness as sacrifice and, with the best intentions, takes the law into her own hands. The crisis that ensues, most painfully for her in the repudiation of that goodness by the very person who was its recipient and beneficiary, causes her to reject the suicide that she initially saw as its ultimate expression and to choose instead to seek new and firmer answers to questions of identity and moral belief.

The availability of choice, and with it the onus of responsibility, has now invaded the most private sector of the woman's domain and threatens a similar explosion. For centuries, women's sexuality anchored them in passivity, in a receptive rather than an active stance, where the events of conception and childbirth could be controlled only by a withholding in which their own sexual needs were either denied or sacrificed. That such a sacrifice entailed a cost to their intelligence as well was seen by Freud (1908) when he tied the "undoubted intellectual inferiority of so many women" to "the inhibition of thought necessitated by sexual suppression" (p. 199). The strategies of withholding and denial that women have employed in the politics of sexual relations appear similar to their evasion or withholding of judgment in the moral realm. The hesitance of college students to assert a belief even in the value of human life, like the reluctance to claim one's sexuality, bespeaks a self uncertain of its strength, unwilling to deal with choice, and avoiding confrontation.

Thus women have traditionally deferred to the judgment of men, although often while intimating a sensibility of their own which is at variance with that judgment. Maggie Tulliver in *The Mill on the Floss* responds to the accusations that ensue from the discovery of her secretly continued relationship with Phillip Wakeham by acceding to her brother's moral judgment, while at the same time asserting a different set of standards by which she attests to her own superiority:

> I don't want to defend myself. . . . I know I've been wrong—often continually. But yet, sometimes when I have done wrong, it has been because I have feelings that you would be the better for if you had them. If *you* were in fault ever, if you had done anything very wrong, I should be sorry for the pain it brought you; I should not want punishment to be heaped on you.

Maggie's protest is an eloquent assertion of the age-old split between thinking and feeling, justice and mercy, that underlies many of the clichés and stereotypes concerning the difference between the sexes. But considered from another point of view, her protest signifies a moment of confrontation, replacing a former evasion. This confrontation reveals two modes of judging, two different constructions of the moral domain—one traditionally associated with masculinity and the public world of social power, the other with femininity and the privacy of domestic interchange. The developmental ordering of these two points of view has been to consider the masculine as more adequate than the feminine and thus as replacing the feminine when the individual moves toward maturity. The reconciliation of these two modes, however, is not clear.

Norma Haan's (1975) research on college students and Constance Holstein's (1976) three-year study of adolescents and their parents indicate that the moral judgments of women differ from those of men in the greater extent to which women's judgments are tied to feelings of empathy and compassion and are concerned with the resolution of real as opposed to hypothetical dilemmas. However, as long as the categories by which development is assessed are derived from research on men, divergence from the masculine standard can be seen only as a failure of development. As a result, the thinking of women is often classified with that of children. The absence of alternative criteria that might better encompass the development of women, however, points not only to the limitations of theories framed by men and validated by research samples disproportionately male and adolescent, but also to the diffidence prevalent among women, their reluctance to speak publicly in their own voice, given the constraints imposed on them by their lack of power and the politics of relations between the sexes.

In order to go beyond the question, "How much like men do women think, how capable are they of engaging in the abstract and hypothetical construction of reality?" it is necessary to identify and define developmental criteria that encompass the categories of women's thought. Haan points out the necessity to derive such criteria from the resolution of the "more frequently occurring, real-life moral dilemmas of interpersonal, empathic, fellow-feeling concerns" (p. 34) which have long been the center of women's moral concern. But to derive developmental criteria from the language of women's moral discourse, it is necessary first to see whether women's construction of the moral domain relies on a language different from that of men and one that deserves equal credence in the definition of development. This in turn requires finding places where women have the power to choose and thus are willing to speak in their own voice.

When birth control and abortion provide women with effective means for controlling their fertility, the dilemma of choice enters a central arena of women's lives. Then the relationships that have traditionally defined women's identities and framed their moral judgments no longer flow inevitably from their reproductive capacity but become matters of decision over which they have control. Released from the passivity and reticence of a sexuality that binds them in dependence, women can question with Freud what it is that they want and can assert their own answers to that question. However, while society may affirm publicly the woman's right to choose for herself, the exercise of such choice brings her privately into conflict with the conventions of femininity, particularly the moral equation of goodness with sacrifice. Although independent assertion in judgment and action is considered to be the hallmark of adulthood, it is rather in their care and concern for others that women have both judged themselves and been judged.

The conflict between self and other thus constitutes the central moral problem for women, posing a dilemma whose resolution requires a reconciliation between femininity and adulthood. In the absence of such a reconciliation, the moral problem cannot be resolved. The "good woman" masks assertion in evasion, denying responsibility by claiming only to meet the needs of others, while the "bad woman" forgoes or renounces the commitments that bind her in self-deception and betrayal. It is precisely this dilemma—the conflict between compassion and autonomy, between virtue and power—which the feminine voice struggles to resolve in its effort to reclaim the self and to solve the moral problem in such a way that no one is hurt.

Questions for Thought

1. What moral rights do you think you have? Can you think of a case in which compassion could justify suspending or overriding a moral right?

2. Do you think that self-sacrifice is a moral virtue? Why or why not?

3. With which of the women interviewed do you most identify? With which of them do you least identify? Explain your answers.

4. Do you agree with what Gilligan says about the psychological significance of birth control and abortion? Why or why not?

5. Do you think that there are any essential differences between the moral judgments of women and the moral judgments of men? If so, what are these differences, and how would you explain them?

Transvaluation of Values: The End of Phallic Morality   13

MARY DALY

Mary Daly (b. 1928) has been a critic of the male supremacy found in organized Christianity since her book *The Church and the Second Sex* was published in 1968. And she has been a leading spokesperson for radical feminism since her provocative text *Beyond God the Father* was published in 1973. Daly has expanded on and supplemented the ideas found in the latter text in two equally provocative works, *Gyn/Ecology: The Metaethics of Radical Feminism* (1978) and *Pure Lust: Elemental Feminist Philosophy* (1984). More recent publications include *Websters' First New Intergalactic Wickedary of the English Language* (1987), which was coauthored by Jane Caputi; *Outercourse: The Bedazzling Voyage* (1992); and *Quintessence: Realizing the Outrageous Contagious Courage of Women. A Radical Elemental Feminist Manifesto* (1998). In addition to her books, Daly has written numerous articles, and she has presented lectures at more than 300 colleges, universities, and public gatherings throughout the United States, Canada, Europe, and Australia.

After receiving her Ph.D. in religion at St. Mary's College in Notre Dame, Indiana, Daly planned to pursue a doctoral degree in Catholic theology. However, since women were excluded from such study in the United States at that time, Daly traveled to Switzerland, where she attended the University of Feibourg. She became the first woman to earn a Ph.D. in Catholic theology from the University of Freibourg. Daly remained at the university and earned her doctorate in philosophy shortly thereafter.

Returning to the United States, Daly obtained a professorship at Boston College, where she taught for twenty-five years. However, in 1999, the university administration ousted Daly for refusing to admit male students into her classes. Although Daly taught male students in independent study courses, she argued that admitting male students into her regular classes created a dynamic that inhibited women. Words that Daly wrote in her autobiographical book *Outercourse* may well apply to this and the numerous other conflicts that she had with her employers over the years: "There are and will be those who think I have gone overboard. Let them rest assured that this assessment is correct, probably beyond their wildest imagination, and that I will continue to do so."

Since her departure from Boston College, Daly has continued lecturing on radical feminism. Having settled a lawsuit for wrongful termination against Boston College in 2001, Daly now refers to herself as a "Professor-at-Large." She also continues to work on her eighth book, *Amazon Grace*.

In the following selection, taken from *Beyond God the Father,* Daly describes the re-creation of values that she believes will result from radical feminism. Unlike Gilligan, who sees some value in traditional rights-oriented ethics, Daly offers a thoroughgoing critique of traditional Western morality, a morality that she describes as "phallocentric" and "patriarchal." She argues that this traditional morality was based on a dualism of stereotypical sexual roles, the eternal masculine and the eternal feminine, and that its main values, such as chastity, meekness, humility, and selflessness, resulted from a reaction to stereotypically male excesses. Moreover, this traditional Western emphasis on "feminine" or passive virtues has served to reinforce the oppression of women and to mask the real motives behind aggressive male behavior. As she shows through her analysis of historical and literary examples, it has also been intimately connected with the "Most Unholy Trinity"—that is, with rape, genocide, and war.

Daly believes that the only philosophy that is capable of moral transvaluation, of overcoming the oppression of this Most Unholy Trinity, is radical feminism. Since traditional morality has been "feminine" in nature, Daly claims that feminists, who have suffered most from the effects of such a passive morality, are best suited to see through the logic of oppression that is embedded in it. In freeing themselves from this logic of oppression (or in "castrating the phallic ethic," as Daly says elsewhere), women will be able to realize a new type of existence that is no longer characterized by psychic, sexual, or social alienation. This new type of existence, which will transcend the stereotypical sex roles of traditional morality, will allow women to eliminate oppression in all its forms. Most important, it will allow women to truly comprehend and to actualize the "Most Holy and Whole Trinity of Power, Justice, and Love" and thus to overcome rape, genocide, and war.

Questions for Reading

1. What does Daly mean by "phallic morality"? Why does she believe that traditional Western morality has been phallic?
2. In what ways, according to Daly, has traditional morality been hypocritical?

3. How are the terms *Apollonian* and *Dionysian* used in this selection?
4. Which biblical passages does Daly quote in this selection? What is Daly's point in quoting these particular passages?
5. What, according to Daly, constitutes the "Most Unholy Trinity"? What constitutes the "Most Holy and Whole Trinity"? How can the former be transformed into the latter?

If the first woman God ever made was strong enough to turn the world upside down, all alone—these together ought to be able to turn it back and get it rightside up again: and they is asking to do it. The men better let 'em.

SOJOURNER TRUTH (1851)

*See
That no matter what you have done
I am still here.
And it has made me dangerous, and wise.
And brother,
You cannot whore, perfume and suppress me anymore.
I have my own business in this skin
And on this planet.*

GAIL MURRAY (1970)

A transvaluation of values can only be accomplished when there is a tension of new needs, and a new set of needy people who feel all old values as painful— although they are not conscious of what is wrong.

FRIEDRICH NIETZSCHE

IN ORDER TO UNDERSTAND THE POTENTIAL impact of radical feminism upon phallocentric morality it is important to see the problem of structures of alienation on a wide scale. Some contemporary social critics of course have seen a need for deep psychic change. Herbert Marcuse, for example, encourages the building of a society in which a new type of human being emerges. He recognizes that unless this transformation takes place, the transition from capitalism to socialism would only mean replacing one form of domination by another. The human being of the future envisaged by Marcuse would have a new sensibility and sensitivity, and would be physiologically incapable of tolerating an ugly, noisy, and polluted universe.[1] Norman O. Brown, recognizing that the problem of human oppression is deeply linked with the prevalence of the phallic personality, quotes King James who in 1603 said: "I am the husband and the whole island is my lawful wife."[2] The statement calls to mind the traditional insistence of ecclesiastics that the church is "the bride of Christ." For Theodore Roszak, such imagery poses a dilemma:

> Does social privilege generate the erotic symbolism? Does the erotic symbolism generate social privilege? . . . Politically, it poses the question of how our liberation is to be achieved. How shall we rid ourselves of the king or his dominating surrogates?[3]

The point is not missed by any of these authors that the desired psychic change is related to overcoming sexual alienation. What is lacking is adequate recognition of the key role of women's becoming in the process of human liberation. When this crucial role is understood and experienced, it can be seen that there are ways of grappling with the problems of psychic/social change that are concrete and real. As distinct from the speculations of Marcuse, Brown, and other social philosophers, the analysis developing out of feminism has a compelling power deriving from its concreteness and specificity. It speaks precisely out of and to the experience of the sexually oppressed and has an awakening force that is emotional, intellectual, and moral. It changes the fabric of lives, affecting also the consciousness of the men related to the women whose consciousness it is changing.

The dynamics of the psychic/social revolution of feminism involve a twofold rejection of patriarchal society's assumptions about "women's role." First, there is a basic rejection of what Alice Rossi calls the pluralist model of sex roles, which involves a rigid "equal but different" ideology and socialization of the sexes.[4] The assumption of such "pluralism" is that there is and should be "complementarity," based not upon individual differences but upon sex stereotyping. Feminists universally see through the fallaciousness and oppressiveness of the "complementarity" theme at least to some degree. However, there are "levels and levels" of perception of this, and permitting oneself to have deep insight is threatening to the self. Thus, it is possible to stop at a rather surface level of denying this stereotypic pluralism, by reducing the problem to one of "equal pay for equal work," or (in the past) acquisition of the right to vote, or passage of the Equal Rights Amendment. In the present wave of feminism, a second and deeper rejection of patriarchal assumptions is widespread. This is rejection of what Rossi calls the "assimilation model." Radical feminists know that "50/50 equality" within patriarchal space is an absurd notion, neither possible nor desirable. The values perpetuated within such space are seen as questionable. When the myth of the eternal feminine is seen through, then the brutalization implied in the eternal masculine also becomes evident. Just as "unveiling" the eternal feminine logically entails revealing the true face of the eternal masculine, the whole process, if carried through to its logical **conclusion,** involves refusal of uncritical assimilation into structures that depend upon this polarization. The notion of a fifty percent female army, for example, is alien to the basic insights of radical feminism.

Intrinsic to the re-creative potential of the women's movement, then, is a new naming of values as these have been incarnated in society's laws, customs, and arrangements. This means that there will be a renaming of morality which has been false because phallocentric, denying half the species the possibility not only of naming but even of *hearing* our own experience with our own ears.

HYPOCRISY OF THE TRADITIONAL MORALITY

Much of traditional morality in our society appears to be the product of reactions on the part of men—perhaps guilty reactions—to the behavioral excesses of the stereotypic male. There has been a *theoretical* one-sided emphasis upon charity, meekness, obedience, humility, self-abnegation, sacrifice, service. Part of the problem with this moral ideology is that it became accepted not by men but by women, who hardly have been helped by an ethic which reinforces the abject female situation. Of course, oppressed males are forced to act out these qualities in the presence of their "superiors." However, in the presence of females of the oppressed racial or economic class, the mask is dropped. Basically, then, the traditional morality of our culture has been "feminine" in the sense of hypocritically idealizing some of the qualities imposed upon the oppressed.

A basic irony in the phenomenon of this "feminine" ethic of selflessness and sacrificial love is the fact that the qualities that are *really* lived out and valued by those in dominant roles, and esteemed by those in subservient roles, are not overtly held up as values but rather are acted out under pretense of doing something else. Ambitious prelates who have achieved ecclesiastical power have been praised not for their ambition but for "humility." Avaricious and ruthless politicians often speak unctuously of sacrifice, service and dedication. Not uncommonly such pronouncements are "sincere," for self-deceit is encouraged by a common assumption that the simple fact of having an office proves that the incumbent truly merits it. The Judeo-Christian ethic has tended to support rather than challenge this self-legitimating facticity, by its obsession with obedience and respect for authority. Since the general effect of Christian morality has been to distort the real motivations and values operative in society, it hinders confrontation with the problems of unjust acquisition and use of power and the destructive effects of social conditioning. Since it fails to develop an understanding and respect for the aggressive and creative virtues, it offers no alternative to the hypocrisy-condoning situation fostered by its one-sided and unrealistic ethic.

A mark of the duplicity of this situation is the fact that women, who according to the fables of our culture (the favorable ones, as opposed to those that stress the "evil" side of the stereotype) should be living embodiments of the virtues it extols, are rarely admitted to positions of leadership. It is perhaps partial insight into the inconsistency of this situation that has prompted Christian theologians to justify it not only by the myth of feminine evil but also by finding a kind of tragic flaw in women's natural equipment. Commonly this flaw has been seen as an inherent feebleness of the reasoning power, linked, of course, to emotional instability. Typically, Thomas Aquinas argued that women should be subject to men because "in man the discretion of reason predominates."[5] This denial of rationality in women by Christian theologians has been a basic tactic for confining them to the condition of moral imbecility. Inconsistently, women have been blamed for most of the evil in the world, while at the same time full capacity for moral responsibility has been denied to females.

FEMINISM VERSUS THE "FEMININE" ETHIC

While Christian morality has tended to deny responsibility and self-actualization to women by definition, it has also stifled honesty in men. I have pointed out that the pseudo-feminine ethic—which I also call the passive ethic—conceals the motivations and values that are actually operative in society. While it is true that there has been an emphasis upon some of the aspects of the masculine stereotype, for example, control of emotions by "reason" and the practice of courage in defense of the prevailing political structure or of a powerful ideology (the courage of soldiers and martyrs), these have been tailored to serve mechanisms that oppress, rather than to liberate the self. The passive ethic, then, whether stressing the so-called feminine qualities or the so-called masculine qualities does not challenge exploitativeness but supports it. This kind of morality lowers consciousness so that "sin" is basically equated with an offense against those in power, and the structures of oppression are not recognized as evil.

Feminism has a unique potential for providing the insight needed to undercut the prevailing moral ideology. Striving for freedom involves an awakening process in which layer upon layer of society's deceptiveness is ripped away. The process has its own dynamics: after one piece of deception is seen through the pattern can be recognized elsewhere, again and again. What is equally important, women build up a refusal of self-deception. The support

group, which is the cognitive minority going through the same process, gains in its power to correlate information and refute opposing arguments. Nietzsche, the prophet whose prophecy was short-circuited by his own misogynism, wanted to transvaluate Judeo-Christian morality, but in fact it is women who will confront patriarchal morality as *patriarchal*. It is radical feminism that can unveil the "feminine" ethic, revealing it to be a phallic ethic.

EXISTENTIAL COURAGE AND TRANSVALUATION

The Aristotelian theory of moral virtue, which was assumed into Christian theology, centered around the virtue of prudence, the "queen" of the moral virtues. Prudence presumably is "right reason about things to be done," enabling one to judge the right and virtuous course.[6] Since moral virtue was understood as the mean between two extremes, prudence was understood as a virtue in the intellect which enabled one to steer between two opposed vices.

As Sam Keen and others have pointed out, a theory of moral virtue so dominated by the motif of prudence is basically Apollonian. It presupposes a view of human life in which the emotions are considered inferior to "reason," which is at the summit of the hierarchy of human faculties. Aquinas, following Aristotle, believed that prudence involved a kind of practical knowledge by which one was enabled to judge in a particular set of circumstances what would be the best course of action. Since prudential knowledge was understood to be connatural and nonideological, it would seem that there should have been hope for an ethic thus envisaged to be free of subservience to authoritarian structures. However, it did not work out this way. In the opinion of Aquinas and of all "main line" Catholic moralists the prudent person would accept guidance from the moral teachings of the church and attempt to apply these in the given situation. Ecclesiastical ideology, then, did work itself into one's prudential decision about how to act.

A major difficulty with all of this arises from the fact that the moral teachings designed to guide the Christian in making prudential decisions have to a large extent been the products of technical reason, that is, the capacity for "reasoning" about means for achieving ends, cut off from the **aesthetic,** intuitive, and practical functions of the mind. As Tillich realized, when the reasoning process about means is cut off from the deep sources of awareness in the human mind (ontological reason), then the ends to which the means are uncritically directed are provided by other nonrational forces external to the self.[7] These may be traditions or authoritarian structures or ideologies that have become so embedded in the psyche that they have rendered themselves invisible. In any case the result is blindness concerning the ends or goals which are actually behind the whole reasoning process and which are motivating the selection of certain **premises** that will determine what other data, that is, what other possible premises, will be excluded from consideration in the reasoning process.

It is precisely this unconsciousness of ends and motivations which makes so much of Christian doctrine about morality suspect. While Tillich and others have seen the problem of **heteronomy** conflicting with **autonomy** in a general way, it is feminist women who now are gaining insights about *specific* ways in which prudential ethics has lent itself to the service of patriarchal power and about *specific* issues that have been clouded by this. Patriarchal systems demand precisely this: cautious execution of means on the part of those who are in bondage to such systems, without application of the mind's powers to the work of criticizing their purposes. This blotting out of critical power involves a desensitizing to elements in human experience which, if heeded, would challenge the "reasonableness" of the dominant ethic.

Classical and medieval moralists did of course put a great deal of emphasis upon the role of the end or goal in determining the morality of a human act. However, in Christian scholastic ethics especially, the greatest attention was paid to the *ultimate* end of human acts, that is, "eternal happiness." Intermediate ends did not receive the kind of scrutiny that a revolutionary morality requires. The built-in assumption was that these goals should be determined by authority and receive unquestioning assent from subordinates. Such assumptions still dominate a great deal of "modern" ethical theory. . . . The potential that radical feminism has for breaking their demonic power has its source in the awakening

of existential courage in women, which can give rise to a Dionysian feminist ethic.

Although repudiation of the passive and Apollonian ethic of authoritarian religion is not entirely new, there is a qualitative newness arising from the fact that women are beginning to *live* this repudiation personally, corporately, and politically. Those who have been socialized most profoundly to live out the passive ethic are renouncing it and starting to affirm a style of human existence that has existential courage as its dominant motif.

It may be asked what this qualitative newness means. In what does it consist? Aren't there "situation ethicists" around already challenging the Old Morality? . . .

Clues to fundamental differences between the Dionysian feminist ethic that is beginning to be lived and spoken about by some women and the "New Morality" of situation ethics can be found in the work of Joseph Fletcher, author of *Situation Ethics.* Fletcher insists upon labeling what he is doing as "Christian situation ethics."[8] One may well ask why the label "Christian" is necessary. What does it add to "situation ethics"? Fletcher himself responds to this question by saying that what makes it different from other moralities is a theological factor, "the faith affirmation that God himself suffered for man's sake to reconcile the world in Christ."[9] This means that, however valuable many of the author's insights may be, there is here a basic affirmation of sacrificial love morality. Fletcher feels constrained to give priority to "the desire to satisfy the neighbor's need, not one's own."[10] As the primordial victims of this kind of unrealistic and destructive moral ideal, women—once consciousness has been liberated— can see that this kind of "New Morality" is very much like the old. It does not move us beyond the good and evil of **patriarchy** because it does not get us out of the bind of scapegoat psychology. Those who have actually been scapegoats and have said No to being victims any longer are in a position to say NO to this modernized Christolatrous morality, in which "love" is always privatized and lacking a specific social context, and in which the structures of oppression are left uncriticized.

Out of this "No" to the morality of victimization, which women share with all the oppressed, comes a "Yes" to an ethic which transcends the most basic role stereotypes, those of masculine/feminine. Janice Raymond points out that this ethic upholds as its ideal "a dynamic metaphysical process of becoming, in which what has been traditionally circumscribed as masculine and feminine is divested of its sex-typing and categorization and is brought together into a new reality of being, a new wholeness of personhood." Far from being "unisex," in the sense of universal sameness, it involves a revolt against standardization.[11] As another feminist writer has pointed out, terms such as "masculinize" or "feminize" would then come to mean a process of warping children to develop only half of their potentialities. In these terms a man of our culture now seen as "masculine" would be seen to have been masculinized, that is, to have lost half of himself.[12]

Before the androgynous world can begin to appear, however (a world in which even the term "androgynous" itself would be rendered meaningless because the word reflects the archaic heritage of psycho-sexual dualism), women will have to assume the burden of castrating the phallic ethic (which "appears" as a feminine ethic or a passive ethic) by calling forth out of our experience a new naming in the realm of morality. To do this it will be necessary to understand the dynamics of the false naming in the realm of ethics that has been encased in patriarchy's definitions of good and evil. . . .

THE MOST UNHOLY TRINITY: RAPE, GENOCIDE, AND WAR

The first dimension of what I have baptized as The Most Unholy Trinity is rape. It is clear that there has always been a connection between the mentality of rape and the phenomenon of war, although there is much unseeing of this connection when the war is perceived as "just." An example within recent times was the horrible treatment of the women of Bangladesh. Many horrendous stories came out at the time of the civil war between East and West Pakistan, but scant reference was made to "the heartbreaking reports that as many as 200,000 Bengali women, victims of rape by West Pakistani soldiers, had been abandoned by their husbands, because no Moslem will live with a wife who has been touched by another man."[13] Joyce Goldman, a

writer who discovered such a reference buried in a postwar "return to normality" article, decided that if male reporters would not investigate, she would attempt to do so. The experience of reading her account is unforgettable. A Pakistani officer is quoted as saying: "We used the girls until they died." Many of the women imprisoned in barracks (to be used by soldiers as "cigarette machines," as one government official described it), tried to commit suicide. Goldman cites reports of a town named Camilla, near Dacca, where women were raped and then thrown from the rooftops like rubbish. "One eight-year-old girl who was found too child-small for the soldiers' purposes was slit to accommodate them, and raped until she died."[14] Goldman points to the obvious cruel irony in the fact that these victims were then abandoned by their husbands as unclean, which is an obvious corollary of looking upon women as objects and possessions, for then they must have only one possessor. Most significantly she shows that the concept of a raped woman as damaged is only a morbid exaggeration of "our" own attitudes, for the women of Bangladesh have suffered "collectively, exaggeratedly what individual women in this and other 'advanced' countries know from their own experience. . . ."[15]

"Informed" Christians and Jews may protest that rape and brutality are alien to our own heritage. The reader, then, should refer to biblical passages which tell a different story, namely that there is precedent for looking upon women as spoils of war. In the book of *Numbers,* Moses, after the campaign against Midian, is described as enraged against the commanders of the army for having spared the lives of all the women:

> So kill all the male children. Kill also all the women who have slept with a man. Spare the lives only of the young girls who have not slept with a man, and take them for yourselves. (Numbers 31:17–18)

The story continues:

> Moses and Eleazar the priest did as **Yahweh** had ordered Moses. The spoils, the remainder of the booty captured by the soldiers, came to six hundred and seventy-five thousand head of small stock, seventy-two thousand head of cattle, sixty-one thousand donkeys, and in persons,

women who had never slept with a man, thirty-two thousand in all. (Numbers 31:31–35)

In *Deuteronomy*, the advice given to the Hebrews is that when they go to war and Yahweh delivers the enemy into their power, they may choose a wife from among them.

> Should she cease to please you, you will let her go where she wishes, not selling her for money: you are not to make any profit out of her, since you have had the use of her. (Deuteronomy 21:14)

Even outside the context of war (if such a context is imaginable in a patriarchal world), the value placed upon women in the Old Testament is illustrated in the story of the crime of the men of Gibeah. A man who was giving hospitality to a Levite and his concubine was having dinner with them. Scoundrels came to the house demanding to have the guest, in order to abuse him. The response of the host was to offer them his daughter as substitute for the guest. The devoted father is reported to have said:

> Here is my daughter; she is a virgin; I will give her to you. Possess her, do what you please with her, but do not commit such an infamy against this man. (Judges 19:24)

Since the visitors refused this offer, the guest gallantly offered them his concubine as a replacement for himself. They raped her all night and she died. Tastefully the guest, when he had returned home with her, cut her into twelve pieces and sent all these around Israel with a message about the crime. The text offers no negative judgment upon the host or his guest. The crime was seen as an offense against men, not against their female property.

The second dimension of The Most Unholy Trinity is genocide. It should require no great imaginative leap to perceive a deep relationship between the mentality of rape and genocide. The socialization of male sexual violence in our culture forms the basis for corporate and military interests to train a vicious military force. It would be a mistake to think that rape is reducible to the physical act of a few men who are rapists. This ignores the existence of the countless armchair rapists who vicariously enjoy the act through reading pornography or news stories about it. It also overlooks the fact that all men have their power enhanced by rape, since this instills in women a need for protection. Rape is a way of life. Since this is the case, police do not feel obliged to "believe" women who report rape. Typical of police attitudes was the statement of Police Captain Vincent O'Connell of Providence, Rhode Island, concerning women who attempt to report rape: "We are very skeptical when we first interview them. We feel there's a tendency for women not to tell the truth."[16] The politics of domination are everywhere. E. Ionesco wrote:

> The world of the concentration camps . . . was not an exceptionally monstrous society. What we saw there was the image, and in a sense the quintessence, of the infernal society in which we are plunged every day.[17]

This "everyday world" is fundamentally a world of sexual dominance and violation.

The logical extension of the mentality of rape is the objectification of all who can be cast into the role of victims of violence. Rape is the primordial act of violation but it is more than an individual act. It is expressive of a basic alienation within the psyche and of structures of alienation within society. Rape is an act of group against group: male against female. As I have pointed out, it is also an act of male against male, in which the latter is attacked by the pollution of his property. Rape is expressive of group-think, and group-think is at the core of racial prejudice whose logical conclusion and final solution is genocide.

Writing of Vietnam, Paul Mayer pointed out that the United States [conducted] the same kind of genocide against the Indochinese as the Nazis once ordered against European Jewry. "The method has changed from the gas chambers of Auschwitz to those crematoria that rain burning death and terror from the skies, particularly on civilians."[18] Mr. Mayer's dismay that American Catholics and Jews [did] not see the parallel [appeared] to spring from his not seeing the fundamental patriarchal character of these traditions. The record of the church in Nazi Germany is well known. Guenter Lewy writes:

When thousands of German anti-Nazis were tortured to death in Hitler's concentration camps, when the Polish intelligentsia was slaughtered, when hundreds of thousands of Russians died as a result of being treated as Slavic *Untermenschen*, and when 6,000,000 human beings were murdered for being "non-Aryan," Catholic Church officials in Germany bolstered the regime perpetrating these crimes.[19]

With characteristic insight, Lewy points out that the hold of the church upon the faithful is precarious and that this prevents it from risking confrontation with a state that tramples upon human dignity and freedom. Lewy asserts that the situation is worsened when the clergy are infected with an alien creed. I would point out that the creed of totalitarian governments is not all that "alien." As Lewy himself notes, theologians such as Michael Schmaus and Joseph Lortz saw basic similarities between the Nazi and the Catholic *Weltanschauung*.[20] At any rate, whether one wishes to call the affinity an infection or a recognition of some dimension of secret sameness, the alliance of hierarchical Catholicism with the demonic forces is a familiar pattern. . . .

Silence in the face of genocide or open support of this is hardly foreign to Protestant Christianity. In Nazi Germany, there was the Nazi-approved National Church, or *Reich* church, co-opted by Hitler. This fact is not obliterated by the compensatory fact that there existed also the "Confessing Church," which refused to cooperate with the Nazis, nor is it wiped out by the lives of Protestant heroes such as Dietrich Bonhoeffer, who was hanged by the Nazis. For that matter, there were also Catholic heroes and martyrs such as Franz Jägerstätter, the peasant who was beheaded, and Alfred Delp, a priest killed by the Nazis. The fact is that the United States, at the peak of its genocidal mania, was a predominantly Protestant nation. Nor should it be forgotten that Christianity, Catholic and Protestant, has deep roots in the Judaic tradition, in which the people of Yahweh were able to see themselves as different from "the Other"—the worshipers of "false gods." If, then, many American Jews have allowed themselves not to see the parallels between American genocide and Auschwitz, this phenomenon is not totally contradictory, for the mentality of rape is also embedded in the Hebrew tradition itself.

The third dimension of The Most Unholy Trinity is war. Theodore Roszak writes of "the full and hideous flowering of the politics of masculine dominance" which from the late nineteenth to the mid-twentieth centuries became more candid than ever before.[21] Such diverse figures as Teddy Roosevelt, General Homer Lea, Patrick Pearse, and the Spanish political philosopher Juan Donoso-Cortés agreed in associating war with "the manly and adventurous virtues" and the civilized horror of war with loss of manhood. This masculine metaphysical madness was lived out in Nazism and Fascism. It is being lived out today to an even greater extent, but the language of violence has become disguised, mathematized, and computerized. There are occasional linguistic lapses that are gross enough to make tragic absurdity visible, as when a military officer made the famous statement that it was necessary to destroy a (Vietnamese) village in order to save it. Such lapses briefly jolt the consciences of a few, but the majority, drugged by the perpetual presence of the politics of rape on the TV screen, sees it all but sees nothing. The horrors of a phallocentric world have simultaneously become more visible and more invisible. . . .

The Most Unholy Trinity of Rape, Genocide, and War is a logical expression of phallocentric power. These are structures of alienation that are self-perpetuating, eternally breeding further estrangement. The circle of destruction generated by the Most Unholy Trinity and reflected in the Unwhole Trinitarian symbol of Christianity will be broken when women, who are by patriarchal definition objects of rape, externalize and internalize a new self-definition whose compelling power is rooted in the power of being. The casting out of the demonic Trinities *is* female becoming. . . .

THE MOST HOLY AND WHOLE TRINITY: POWER, JUSTICE, AND LOVE

Tillich has rightly shown that "all problems of love, power, and justice drive us to an ontological analysis."[22] What his analysis leaves out is the essential fact that division by socialization into sex roles divides the human psyche itself, so that love cut off from power and justice is pseudo-love, power isolated from love and justice is inauthentic power of dominance, and justice is a meaningless facade of legalism split off from love and real power of being. Without a perception of the demonic divisiveness of sex role socialization, an "ontological" analysis of these problems remains hopelessly sterile and removed from the concrete conditions of existence. It is not really ontological.

Given this multiple dividedness, "love" is restricted to a private sphere. The theory of the "two kingdoms," according to which "love" holds a prominent place in the private order whereas power reigns in the political order, has been a common idea in Lutheran theology. Expressed in other "language systems" than that of the "two kingdoms," this is a common idea in our whole culture. The idea that these realities can be separated and still be real is, of course, a mirage. Women's movement theorists have shown that "the personal is political," that the power structures get into the fabric of one's psyche and personal relationships: this is "sexual politics." Power split off from love makes an obscenity out of what we call love, forcing us unwillingly to destroy ourselves and each other. R. D. Laing has given us a terrible insight into the destructiveness of this privatized love which is ultimately public, reflecting the alienated consciousness shared by all. He writes of the menace to those trying to break out of alienated consciousness coming precisely from those who "love" them:

> And because they are humane, and concerned, and even love us, and are very frightened, they will try to cure us. They may succeed, but there is still hope that they will fail.[23]

When extended outside the sphere of familial and personal relationships the "love" that serves patriarchal power sometimes is the impotent do-gooder quality that is conveyed by such expressions as "charity bazaar" or "charity case." Sometimes it is the mask of absolute violence, as in the case of the American "love" for the people of South Vietnam who [were] being "protected."

Genuine love, which is not blindly manipulable by political power of domination, seeks to overcome such power by healing the divided self. Sexist society maintains its grasp over the psyche by keeping it divided against itself. Through stereotyping it harnesses the power of human becoming. It is

commonly perceived that on the deepest ontological level love is a striving toward unity, but the implications of this unity have not been understood by the philosophers of patriarchy. It means the becoming of new human beings, brought forth out of the unharnessed energy of psychically androgynous women, whose primary concern is not giving birth to others but to ourselves.

A qualitatively different understanding of justice also emerges when the peculiar rigidities of the stereotypic male no longer dominate the scene. Tillich has written of transforming or creative justice, which goes beyond calculating in fixed proportions. Unfortunately, he tries to uphold the idea that "the religious symbol for this is the kingdom of God."[24] I suggest that as long as we are under the shadow of a *kingdom*, real or symbolic, there will be no creative justice. The transforming and creative element in justice has been intuited and dimly expressed by the term "equity." Aristotle defined this as a correction of law where it is defective owing to its "universality."[25] What this leaves out is the dynamic and changing quality of justice which does not presuppose that there are fixed and universal essences, but which is open to new data of experience.

The falsely universal and static quality of patriarchal thought which allows no breakthrough beyond "equity" reaches the ultimate state of sclerotic rigidity when the subject under consideration is the female half of the species. An example of this sclerosis which has prevented anything like creative justice in relation to women from emerging in Christian thought is the approach of renowned theologian Helmut Thielicke who, in his *The Ethics of Sex*, writes:

> It is, so to speak, the "vocation" of the woman to be lover, companion, and mother. And even the unmarried woman fulfills her calling in accord with the essential image of herself only when these fundamental characteristics, which are designed for wifehood and motherhood, undergo a sublimating transformation, but still remain discernible. . . .[26]

Further on, Thielicke gets even worse, opining that "woman" is oriented monogamously because she is profoundly stamped by the sexual encounter, insisting that she is marked by the first man who "possesses" her:

One must go even further and say that even the first meeting with this first man possesses the faculty of engraving and marking the women's being, that it has, as it were, the character of a *monos* and thus tends toward monogamy.[27]

For Thielicke, clearly, the male is God in relation to women. His language betrays him at every step. He claims that numerous psychopathological symptoms are "determined" by this "structure" of feminine sexuality. A woman's "frigidity" as well as the "vampire insatiability of the strumpet" are traced to her first sexual encounter. Creative justice, which could break through this dualistic sort of ethics, is not likely to come from those whose status benefits so totally from stereotypic rigidity.

The sterility and rigidity of noncreative justice that classifies and remains closed to change is reflected not only in ethics but also in legal systems as well as in the attitudes of those who interpret the law. Patriarchal rigidity expressed in law, moreover, carries over from women to other disadvantaged groups (and it is important to remember that over fifty percent of all of these segments of humanity—for example, blacks, the Third World—are women). Gunnar Myrdal, in his famous Appendix Five of *An American Dilemma*, wrote:

> In the earlier common law, women and children were placed under the jurisdiction of the paternal power. When a legal status had to be found for the imported Negro servants in the seventeenth century, the nearest and most natural **analogy** was the status of women and children.[28]

Myrdal cites George Fitzhugh, who in his *Sociology for the South* (1854) categorizes together wives, apprentices, lunatics, and idiots, asserting that a man's wife and children are his slaves.

As marginal beings whose authentic personal interest is not served by the rigidities of patriarchal power, women have the potential to see through these. Some men have seen this, of course, but the tendency has been to capture the insight into stereotypes which reinforce the separation of love and justice and therefore support the demonic usages of political power. This can be seen in the cliche: "Man is the head, woman is the heart." At least one renowned legal authority, however, tried (very timidly) to suggest the possibility of overcoming the dichotomy by bringing more women into the legal profession. Justice Jerome Frank suggested that there might be a connection between the inflexibility of the Roman legal system and the fact that the power of the father (*patria potestas*) was a dominant characteristic of Roman society. He points out that in Greek society, in which the power of the father had diminished, the legal system was more flexible:

> I suggest that it is barely possible that, as a result, the role of the mother emerged as an influence on Greek legal attitudes, so that equity, greater lenience, more attention to "circumstances that alter cases" in the application of rules, became an accepted legal ideal.[29]

Although Frank had tendencies to be both apologetic and stereotypic in his exposition of his opinion that women could bring flexibility into the legal system, his view is hardly totally bereft of insight. In support of it, he cited Henry Adams' passages about the role of Mary in the twelfth and thirteenth centuries. Adams saw Mary as functioning symbolically as the only court of equity capable of overruling strict law (symbolized in the Trinity):

> The mother alone was human, imperfect, and could love. . . . The Mother alone could represent whatever was not Unity; whatever was irregular, exceptional, *outlawed* [emphasis mine]; and this was the whole human race. . . .[30]

The church has harnessed (but not succeeded in destroying) this power of diversity, irregularity, and exceptionality by standardizing it into its bland and monolithic image of Mary. It has captured this power of diversity and imprisoned it in a symbol. The real diversity and *insight* into diversity is in existing rebellious women, whose awareness of power of being is emerging in refusal to be cast into a mold. The primordial experiencers of powerlessness and victims of phallic injustice, fixed in the role of practitioners of servile and impotent "love," having been aroused from our numbness, have something to say about the Most Holy and Whole Trinity of Power, Justice, and Love. Grounded in ontological unity this Trinity can overcome Rape, Genocide, and their offspring, the Unholy Spirit of War, which together they spirate in mutual hate.

Women are beginning to be able to say this because of our conspiracy—our breathing together. It is being said with individuality and diversity, in the manner of *outlaws*—which is exactly what radical feminists are. It is being said in the diverse words of our lives, which are just now being spoken.

NOTES

1. Herbert Marcuse, "Marxism and the New Humanity: An Unfinished Revolution," *Marxism and Radical Religion,* ed. by John C. Raines and Thomas Dean (Philadelphia: Temple University Press, 1970), pp. 7–9.

2. Norman O. Brown, *Love's Body* (New York: Random House, 1966), pp. 132–133.

3. Theodore Roszak, *The Making of the Counter Culture* (New York: Doubleday, 1969), p. 86.

4. Alice Rossi, "Sex Equality: The Beginning of Ideology," *Masculine/Feminine,* ed. by Betty Roszak and Theodore Roszak, Harper Colophon Books (New York: Harper and Row, 1969), pp. 173–186.

5. Thomas Aquinas, *Summa theologiae* I, q. 92, a. 1, a. 2. For Aquinas, this inferiority was so inherent in female nature that women even would have been in a state of subjection before the Fall, which he understood as an historical event of the past.

6. Ibid., II–II, q. 47, a. 2. See Aristotle, *Nichomachean Ethics* vi, 5.

7. See Tillich, *Systematic Theology* I, pp. 72–73.

8. Joseph Fletcher, *Situation Ethics* (Philadelphia: Westminster Press, 1966), p. 59.

9. Ibid., p. 156.

10. Ibid., p. 104.

11. Janice Raymond, "Beyond Male Morality," a paper delivered at the International Congress of Learned Societies in the Field of Religion, Los Angeles, September 1–5, 1972. Published by the American Academy of Religion (University of Montana) in *Proceedings of the Working Group on Women and Religion,* 1972, ed. by Judith Plaskow Goldenberg, pp. 83–93.

12. Linda Thurston, "On Male and Female Principle," *The Second Wave* I (summer 1971), p. 39.

13. See Joyce Goldman, "The Women of Bangladesh," *Ms.* 1 (August 1972), p. 84.

14. Ibid., p. 88. While Daly cites atrocities that were committed against women in a war that happened over twenty years ago, similar atrocities are still occurring. Recent reports from Bosnia graphically illustrate this point.—ED.

15. Ibid.

16. Quoted in *The Providence Sunday Journal,* January 16, 1972, p. E-1.

17. E. Ionesco, in *Nouvelle Revue Française,* July 1956, as quoted in Herbert Marcuse, *One Dimensional Man* (Boston: Beacon Press, 1964), p. 80.

18. Paul Mayer, "Jeremiah and Jesus," *American Report,* October 23, 1972, p. 2.

19. Guenter Lewy, *The Catholic Church and Nazi Germany* (New York: McGraw-Hill, 1964), p. 341.

20. Ibid., p. 107.

21. Theodore Roszak, "The Hard and the Soft," in *Masculine/Feminine,* pp. 91–92.

22. Paul Tillich, *Love, Power, and Justice: Ontological Analyses and Ethical Applications* (New York: Oxford University Press, 1960), p. 18.

23. R. D. Laing, *The Politics of Experience* (New York: Ballantine Books, 1968), p. 168.

24. Tillich, *Love, Power, and Justice,* p. 65.

25. Aristotle, *Nichomachean Ethics,* book 5, chap. 10.

26. Helmut Thielicke, *The Ethics of Sex,* trans. by John W. Doberstein (New York: Harper and Row, 1964), p. 81.

27. Ibid., p. 84.

28. Gunnar Myrdal, app. 5, "A Parallel to the Negro Problem," *An American Dilemma* (New York: Harper and Row, 1944, 1962), p. 1073.

29. Jerome Frank, *Courts on Trial: Myth and Reality in American Justice* (New York: Atheneum, 1971), pp. 384–85.

30. Henry Adams, *Mont Saint-Michel and Chartres* (New York: Collier Books, 1963), p. 260.

Questions for Thought

1. Do you think that traditional Western morality has been phallic? Why or why not?

2. Can you think of any examples from your own experience that might substantiate Daly's claim that traditional morality has been hypocritical?

3. How would you interpret the biblical passages that Daly cites? Do you agree with her that the Bible has condoned or promoted rape, genocide, and war? Defend your answer.

4. Do you agree with Daly's claim that we need a transvaluation of values? Why or why not? Do you think Gilligan would agree with this claim?

5. How does Daly envision the new type of human being that emerges from the overcoming of phallocentric morality? In what ways, if any, does this new type of human existence differ from your own existence?

What Means This Freedom?   14

JOHN HOSPERS

John Hospers (b. 1918) was born in Pella, Iowa. He received his A.B. from Central College in 1939, his M.A. from the University of Iowa in 1941, and his Ph.D. from Columbia University in 1946. Hospers held teaching positions at Columbia University and the University of Minnesota before spending a year in London on a Fulbright research scholarship in 1954–1955. On returning to the United States, Hospers taught philosophy at Brooklyn College before moving to California in 1966. He taught for two years at California State University, Los Angeles, before spending the last twenty years of his teaching career at the University of Southern California. Hospers retired from teaching in 1988.

During his long academic career, he served as the editor for three philosophical journals and was president of the American Society of **Aesthetics.** He has also authored works in several areas of philosophy and edited a number of philosophical anthologies. These include *Meaning and Truth in the Arts* (1946), *Introduction to Philosophical Analysis* (1953), *Human Conduct* (1961), *Readings in Introductory Philosophical Analysis* (1968), *Introductory Readings in Aesthetics* (1969), *Artistic Expression* (1971), *The Long Search* (1971), *Libertarianism, a Political Philosophy for Tomorrow* (1971), *Will Capitalism Survive?* (1980), and *Understanding the Arts* (1982).

Outside the academic domain, Hospers was a close friend of the novelist-philosopher Ayn Rand in the 1960s, a film reviewer for a journal from 1974 to 1982, and an early leader in the libertarian movement. He was the Libertarian Party's first presidential candidate in 1972, and the Libertarian Party candidate for governor of California in 1974. In 2002, an hour-long video about Hospers' life, work, and philosophy was released by the Liberty Fund of Indianapolis as part of its *Classics of Liberty* series.

In the following selection, Hospers raises another question about traditional moral theories, the question of whether the concept of responsibility makes sense. Going back to Aristotle, philosophers have argued that there is a necessary connection between moral approbation or condemnation, responsibility, and genuine choice. In order to praise or blame a person for an action, we normally believe that the person must be responsible for the action; and in order to hold the person responsible, we generally agree that the person must have had the capability of acting otherwise. However, Hospers uses a series of examples to suggest that much (if not all) of our behavior is motivated by complex psychological factors over which we have no control, factors that make it reasonable to say that we really cannot act differently than we do. Not being able to act differently, we are not responsible for our actions and thus cannot be held morally accountable for them.

Hospers begins his argument by examining several possible criteria for determining when a person is to be held morally responsible for an action. These include whether the act is premeditated, whether it can be defended with reasons, whether it is the result of "unconscious forces," and whether it is compelled. Finding all these criteria inadequate, Hospers says that a better criterion would be the degree to which an action is responsive to reason. Under this criterion, we would be responsible for an action if we are (or would have been) able to stop from doing the action if we are (or would have been) given good reasons for not doing it.

Given this criterion of responsibility, Hospers asks whether we are ever responsible for any action. He asks, "How can anyone be responsible for his actions, since they grow out of his character, which is shaped and molded and made what it is by influences— some hereditary, but most of them stemming from early parental environment—that were not of his own making or choosing?" Agreeing with Aristotle's and Freud's claim about the importance of the early childhood environment for determining later behavior, Hospers argues that a person's actions are produced by a series of causes over which he or she has no control. Hospers thus suggests that a criminal's aggressive actions are like "the wriggling of a worm on a fisherman's hook," and he goes on to claim that normal behavior is just as psychologically determined as is criminal behavior. Once we recognize this, Hospers believes that we should stop morally condemning others for criminal behavior, realizing that "there, but for the grace of God and a fortunate early environment, go we."

Questions for Reading

1. What are the five criteria for responsibility that are discussed by Hospers? Which of the five does he consider most nearly adequate?
2. Why does Hospers believe that we may not be responsible for any of our actions? What examples does he use to try to prove this?
3. Which findings of psychiatry does Hospers allude to in this selection? How are these findings used to bolster his position?
4. Hospers claims that the more we know about the causal factors leading to behavior, the more we tend to exempt people from responsibility. Why does Hospers believe that this is true? What hypothetical examples does he provide to support this claim?
5. How, according to Hospers, does a normal person compare with and differ from a neurotic person? What leads him to discuss the similarities and differences between the two?

WHAT MEANS THIS FREEDOM?

I AM IN AGREEMENT TO A VERY LARGE EXTENT with the conclusions of Professor Edwards' paper, and am happy in these days of "soft determinism" to hear the other view so forcefully and fearlessly stated. As a preparation for developing my own views on the subject, I want to mention a factor that I think is of enormous importance and relevance: namely, unconscious motivation. There are many actions— not those of an insane person (however the term "insane" be defined), nor of a person ignorant of the effects of his action, nor ignorant of some relevant fact about the situation, nor in any obvious way

mentally deranged—for which human beings in general and the courts in particular are inclined to hold the doer responsible, and for which, I would say, he should not be held responsible. The deed may be planned, it may be carried out in cold calculation, it may spring from the agent's character and be continuous with the rest of his behavior, and it may be perfectly true that he could have done differently *if* he had wanted to; nonetheless his behavior was brought about by unconscious conflicts developed in infancy, over which he had no control and of which (without training in psychiatry) he does not even have knowledge. He may even *think* he knows why he acted as he did, he may *think* he has

From Determinism and Freedom in the Age of Modern Science, *edited by Sidney Hook, New York University Press, 1958. Reprinted by permission of New York University Press.*

conscious control over his actions, he may even *think* he is fully responsible for them; but he is not. Psychiatric casebooks provide hundreds of examples. The law and common sense, though puzzled sometimes by such cases, are gradually becoming aware that they exist; but at this early stage countless tragic blunders still occur because neither the law nor the public in general is aware of the genesis of criminal actions. The mother blames her daughter for choosing the wrong men as candidates for husbands; but though the daughter thinks she is choosing freely and spends a considerable amount of time "deciding" among them, the identification with her sick father, resulting from Oedipal fantasies in early childhood, prevents her from caring for any but sick men, twenty or thirty years older than herself. Blaming her is beside the point; she cannot help it, and she cannot change it. Countless criminal acts are thought out in great detail; yet the participants are (without their own knowledge) acting out fantasies, fears, and defenses from early childhood, over whose coming and going they have no conscious control.

Now, I am not saying that none of these persons should be in jails or asylums. Often society must be protected against them. Nor am I saying that people should cease the practices of blaming and praising, punishing and rewarding; in general these devices are justified by the results—although very often they have practically no effect; the deeds are done from inner compulsion, which is not lessened when the threat of punishment is great. I am only saying that frequently persons we think responsible are not properly to be called so; we mistakenly think them responsible because we assume they are like those in whom no unconscious drive (toward this type of behavior) is present, and that their behavior can be changed by reasoning, exhorting, or threatening.

I

I have said that these persons are not responsible. But what is the criterion for responsibility? Under precisely what conditions is a person to be held morally responsible for an action? Disregarding here those conditions that have to do with a person's *ignorance* of the situation or the effects of his action, let us concentrate on those having to do with his "inner state." There are several criteria that might be suggested:

1. The first idea that comes to mind is that responsibility is determined by the presence or absence of *premeditation*—the opposite of "premeditated" being, presumably, "unthinking" or "impulsive." But this will not do—both because some acts are not premeditated but responsible, and because some are premeditated and not responsible.

Many acts we call responsible can be as unthinking or impulsive as you please. If you rush across the street to help the victim of an automobile collision, you are (at least so we would ordinarily say) acting responsibly, but you did not do so out of premeditation; you saw the accident, you didn't think, you rushed to the scene without hesitation. It was like a reflex action. But you acted responsibly: unlike the knee jerk, the act was the result of past training and past thought about situations of this kind; that is why you ran to help instead of ignoring the incident or running away. When something done originally from conviction or training becomes habitual, it becomes *like* a reflex action. As Aristotle said, virtue should become second nature through habit: a virtuous act should be performed *as if* by instinct; this, far from detracting from its moral worth, testifies to one's mastery of the desired type of behavior; one does not have to make a moral effort each time it is repeated.

There are also premeditated acts for which, I would say, the person is not responsible. Premeditation, especially when it is so exaggerated as to issue in no action at all, can be the result of neurotic disturbance or what we sometimes call an emotional "block," which the person inherits from long-past situations. In Hamlet's revenge on his uncle (I use this example because it is familiar to all of us), there was no lack, but rather a surfeit, of premeditation; his actions were so exquisitely premeditated as to make Freud and Dr. Ernest Jones look more closely to find out what lay behind them. The very premeditation camouflaged unconscious motives of which Hamlet himself was not aware. I think this is an important point, since it seems that the courts often assume that premeditation is a criterion of responsibility. If failure to kill his uncle had been considered a crime, every court in the land would have convicted Hamlet. Again: a woman's decision to stay with her husband in spite of endless "mental cruelty" is, if she is the victim of an unconscious masochistic "will to punishment," one for which she is not responsible; she is the victim and not the agent, no matter how profound her conviction that she is the agent; she is caught in a masochistic web (of complicated genesis) dating back to babyhood, perhaps a repetition of a comparable situation involving her own parents, a repetition-compulsion that, as Freud said, goes "beyond the pleasure principle." Again: a criminal whose crime was carefully planned step by step is usually considered responsible, but as we shall see in later examples, the overwhelming impulse toward it, stemming from an unusually humiliating ego defeat in early childhood, was as compulsive as any can be.

2. Shall we say, then, that a person is not responsible for his act unless he can *defend it with reasons*? I am afraid that this criterion is no better than the previous one. First, intellectuals are usually better at giving reasons than nonintellectuals, and according to this criterion would be more responsible than persons acting from moral conviction not implemented by reasoning; yet it is very doubtful whether we should want to say that the [former] are the more responsible. Second, the giving of reasons itself may be suspect. The reasons may be rationalizations camouflaging unconscious motives of which the agent knows nothing. Hamlet gave many reasons for not doing what he felt it was his duty to do: the time was not right, his uncle's soul might go to heaven, etc. His various "reasons" contradicted one another, and if an overpowering compulsion had not been present, the highly intellectual Hamlet would not have been taken in for a moment by these rationalizations. The real reason, the Oedipal conflict that made his uncle's crime the accomplishment of his own deepest desire, binding their fates into one and paralyzing him into inaction, was unconscious and of course unknown to him. One's intelligence and reasoning power do not enable one to escape from unconsciously motivated behavior; it only gives one greater facility in rationalizing that behavior; one's intelligence is simply used in the interests of the neurosis—it is pressed into service to justify with reasons what one does quite independently of the reasons.

If these two criteria are inadequate, let us seek others.

3. Shall we say that a person is responsible for his action unless it is the *result of unconscious forces* of which he knows nothing? Many psychoanalysts would probably accept this criterion. If it is not largely reflected in the language of responsibility as ordinarily used, this may be due to ignorance of fact: most people do not know that there are such things as unconscious motives and unconscious conflicts causing human beings to act. But it may be that if they did, perhaps they would refrain from holding persons responsible for certain actions.

I do not wish here to quarrel with this criterion of responsibility. I only want to point out the fact that if this criterion is employed a far greater number of actions will be excluded from the domain of responsibility than we might at first suppose. Whether we are neat or untidy, whether we are selfish or unselfish, whether we provoke scenes or avoid them, even whether we can exert our powers of will to change our behavior—all these may, and often do, have their source in our unconscious life.

4. Shall we say that a person is responsible for his act unless it is *compelled*? Here we are reminded of Aristotle's assertion (*Nicomachean Ethics*, Book III) that a person is responsible for his act except for reasons of either ignorance or compulsion. Ignorance is not part of our problem here (unless it is unconsciously induced ignorance of facts previously remembered and selectively forgotten—in which case the forgetting is again compulsive), but compulsion is. How will compulsion do as a criterion? The difficulty is to state just what it means. When we say an act is compelled in a psychological sense, our language is metaphorical—which is not to say that there is no point in it or that, properly interpreted, it is not true. Our actions are compelled in a literal sense if someone has us in chains or is controlling our bodily movements. When we say that the storm compelled us to jettison the cargo of the ship (Aristotle's example), we have a less literal sense of compulsion, for at least it is open to us to go down with the ship. When psychoanalysts say that a man was compelled by unconscious conflicts to wash his hands constantly, this is also not a literal sense of "compel"; for nobody forced his hands under the tap. Still, it is a typical example of what psychologists call *compulsive* behavior: it has unconscious causes inaccessible to introspection, and moreover nothing can change it—it is as inevitable for him to do it as it would be if someone were forcing his

hands under the tap. In this it is exactly like the action of a powerful external force; it is just as little within one's conscious control.

In its area of application this interpretation of responsibility comes to much the same as the previous one. And this area is very great indeed. For if we cannot be held responsible for the infantile situations (in which we were after all passive victims), then neither, it would seem, can we be held responsible for compulsive actions occurring in adulthood that are inevitable consequences of those infantile situations. And, psychiatrists and psychoanalysts tell us, actions fulfilling this description are characteristic of all people some of the time and some people most of the time. Their occurrence, once the infantile events have taken place, is inevitable, just as the explosion is inevitable once the fuse has been lighted; there is simply more "delayed action" in the psychological explosions than there is in the physical ones. . . .

5. There is still another criterion, which I prefer to the previous ones, by which a man's responsibility for an act can be measured: the degree to which that act can (or could have been) *changed by the use of reasons.* Suppose that the man who washes his hands constantly does so, he says, for hygienic reasons, believing that if he doesn't do so he will be poisoned by germs. We now convince him, on the best medical authority, that his belief is groundless. Now, the test of his responsibility is whether the changed belief will result in changed behavior. If it does not, as with the compulsive hand washer, he is not acting responsibly, but if it does, he is. It is not the *use* of reasons, but their *efficacy in changing behavior,* that is being made the criterion of responsibility. And clearly in neurotic cases no such change occurs; in fact, this is often made the defining characteristic of neurotic behavior: it is unchangeable by any rational considerations.

II

I have suggested these criteria to distinguish actions for which we can call the agent responsible from those for which we cannot. Even persons with extensive knowledge of psychiatry do not, I think, use any one of these criteria to the exclusion of the others; a conjunction of two or more may be used at once. But however they may be combined or selected in actual application, I believe we can make the distinction along some such lines as we have suggested.

But is there not still another possible meaning of "responsibility" that we have not yet mentioned? Even after we have made all the above distinctions, there remains a question in our minds whether we are, in the final analysis, *responsible for any of our actions at all.* The issue may be put this way: How can anyone be responsible for his actions, since they grow out of his character, which is shaped and molded and made what it is by influences—some hereditary, but most of them stemming from early parental environment—that were not of his own making or choosing? This question, I believe, still troubles many people who would agree to all the distinctions we have just made but still have the feeling that "this isn't all." They have the uneasy suspicion that there is a more ultimate sense, a "deeper" sense, in which we are *not* responsible for our actions, since we are not responsible for the character out of which those actions spring. . . .

Let us take as an example a criminal who, let us say, strangled several persons and is himself now condemned to die in the electric chair. Jury and public alike hold him fully responsible (at least they utter the words "he is responsible"), for the murders were planned down to the minutest detail, and the defendant tells the jury exactly how he planned them. But now we find out how it all came about; we learn of parents who rejected him from babyhood, of the childhood spent in one foster home after another, where it was always plain to him that he was not wanted; of the constantly frustrated early desire for affection, the hard shell of nonchalance and bitterness that he assumed to cover the painful and humiliating fact of being unwanted, and his subsequent attempts to heal these wounds to his shattered ego through defensive aggression.

> The criminal is the most passive person in this world, helpless as a baby in his motorically inexpressible fury. Not only does he try to wreak revenge on the mother of the earliest period of his babyhood; his criminality is based on the inner feeling of being incapable of making the mother even feel that the child seeks revenge on her. The situation is that of a dwarf trying to annoy a giant who superciliously refuses to see these

attempts. . . . Because of his inner feeling of being a dwarf, the criminotic uses, so to speak, dynamite. Of that the giant must take cognizance. True, the "revenge" harms the avenger. He may be legally executed. However, the primary inner aim of forcing the giant to acknowledge the dwarf's fury is fulfilled.[1]

The poor victim is not conscious of the inner forces that exact from him this ghastly toll; he battles, he schemes, he revels in pseudo-aggression, he is miserable, but he does not know what works within him to produce these catastrophic acts of crime. His aggressive actions are the wriggling of a worm on a fisherman's hook. And if this is so, it seems difficult to say any longer, "He is responsible." Rather, we shall put him behind bars for the protection of society, but we shall no longer flatter our feeling of moral superiority by calling him personally responsible for what he did.

Let us suppose it were established that a man commits murder only if, sometime during the previous week, he has eaten a certain combination of foods—say, tuna fish salad at a meal also including peas, mushroom soup, and blueberry pie. What if we were to track down the factors common to all murders committed in this country during the last twenty years and found this factor present in all of them, and only in them? The example is of course empirically absurd; but may it not be that there is *some* combination of factors that regularly leads to homicide, factors such as are described in general terms in the above quotation? (Indeed the situation in the quotation is less fortunate than in our hypothetical example, for it is easy to avoid certain foods once we have been warned about them, but the situation of the infant is thrust on him; something has already happened to him once and for all, before he knows it has happened.) When such specific factors are discovered, won't they make it clear that it is foolish and pointless, as well as immoral, to hold human beings responsible for crimes? Or, if one prefers biological to psychological factors, suppose a neurologist is called in to testify at a murder trial and produces X-ray pictures of the brain of the criminal; anyone can see, he argues, that the *cella turcica* was already calcified at the age of nineteen; it should be a flexible bone, growing, enabling the gland to grow.[2] All the defendant's disorders might have

resulted from this early calcification. Now, this particular explanation may be empirically false; but who can say that no such factors, far more complex, to be sure, exist?

When we know such things as these, we no longer feel so much tempted to say that the criminal is responsible for his crime; and we tend also (do we not?) to excuse him—not legally (we still confine him to prison) but morally; we no longer call him a monster or hold him personally responsible for what he did. Moreover, we do this in general, not merely in the case of crime: "You must excuse Grandmother for being irritable; she's really quite ill and is suffering some pain all the time." Or: "The dog always bites children after she's had a litter of pups; you can't blame her for it: she's not feeling well, and besides she naturally wants to defend them." Or: "She's nervous and jumpy, but do excuse her: she has a severe glandular disturbance."

Let us note that the more *thoroughly* and *in detail* we know the causal factors leading a person to behave as he does, the more we tend to exempt him from responsibility. When we know nothing of the man except what we see him do, we say he is an ungrateful cad who expects much of other people and does nothing in return, and we are usually indignant. When we learn that his parents were the same way and, having no guilt feelings about this mode of behavior themselves, brought him up to be greedy and avaricious, we see that we could hardly expect him to have developed moral feelings in this direction. When we learn, in addition, that he is not aware of being ungrateful or selfish, but unconsciously represses the memory of events unfavorable to himself, we feel that the situation is unfortunate but "not really his fault." When we know that this behavior of his, which makes others angry, occurs more constantly when he feels tense or insecure, and that he now feels tense and insecure, and that relief from pressure will diminish it, then we tend to "feel sorry for the poor guy" and say he's more to be pitied than censured. We no longer want to say that he is personally responsible; we might rather blame nature or his parents for having given him an unfortunate constitution or temperament. . . .

"But," a critic complains, "it's immoral to exonerate people indiscriminately in this way. I might have thought it fit to excuse somebody because he was born on the other side of the tracks, if I didn't know so many bank presidents who were also born on the other side of the tracks." Now, I submit that the most immoral thing in this situation is the critic's caricature of the conditions of the excuse. Nobody is excused merely because he was born on the other side of the tracks. But if he was born on the other side of the tracks *and* was a highly narcissistic infant to begin with *and* was repudiated or neglected by his parents *and* . . . (here we list a finite number of conditions), and if this complex of factors is *regularly* followed by certain behavior traits in adulthood, and moreover *unavoidably* so—that is, they occur no matter what he or anyone else tries to do—then we excuse him morally and say he is not responsible for his deed. If he is not responsible for *A*, a series of events occurring in his babyhood, then neither is he responsible for *B*, a series of things he does in adulthood, provided that *B* inevitably—that is, unavoidably—follows upon the occurrence of *A*. And according to psychiatrists and psychoanalysts, this often happens.

But one may still object that so far we have talked only about neurotic behavior. Isn't nonneurotic or normal or not unconsciously motivated (or whatever you want to call it) behavior still within the area of responsibility? There are reasons for answering "No" even here, for the normal person no more than the neurotic one has caused his own character, which makes him what he is. Granted that neurotics are not responsible for their behavior (that part of it which we call neurotic) because it stems from undigested infantile conflicts that they had no part in bringing about, and that are external to them just as surely as if their behavior had been forced on them by a malevolent deity (which is indeed one theory on the subject); but the so-called normal person is equally the product of causes in which his volition took no part. And if, unlike the neurotic's, his behavior is changeable by rational considerations, and if he has the will power to overcome the effects of an unfortunate early environment, this again is no credit to him; he is just lucky. If energy is available to him in a form in which it can be mobilized for constructive purposes, this is no credit to him, for this too is part of his psychic legacy. Those of us who can discipline ourselves and develop habits of concentration of purpose tend to

blame those who cannot, and call them lazy and weak-willed; but what we fail to see is that they literally *cannot* do what we expect; if their psyches were structured like ours, they could, but as they are burdened with a tyrannical superego (to use psychoanalytic jargon for the moment), and a weak defenseless ego whose energies are constantly consumed in fighting endless charges of the superego, they simply cannot do it, and it is irrational to expect it of them. We cannot with justification blame them for their inability, any more than we can congratulate ourselves for our ability. This lesson is hard to learn, for we constantly and naïvely assume that other people are constructed as we ourselves are.

For example: A child raised under slum conditions, whose parents are socially ambitious and envy families with money, but who nevertheless squander the little they have on drink, may simply be unable in later life to mobilize a drive sufficient to overcome these early conditions. Common sense would expect that he would develop the virtue of thrift; he would make quite sure that he would never again endure the grinding poverty he had experienced as a child. But in fact it is not so: the exact conditions are too complex to be specified in detail here, but when certain conditions are fulfilled (concerning the subject's early life), he will always thereafter be a spendthrift, and no rational considerations will be able to change this. He will listen to the rational considerations and see the force of these, but they will not be able to change him, even if he tries; he cannot change his wasteful habits any more than he can lift the Empire State Building with his bare hands. We moralize and plead with him to be thrifty, but we do not see how strong, how utterly overpowering, and how constantly with him, is the opposite drive, which is so easily manageable with us. But he is possessed by the all-consuming, all-encompassing urge to make the world see that he belongs, that he has arrived, that he is just as well off as anyone else, that the awful humiliations were not real, that they never actually occurred, for isn't he now able to spend and spend? The humiliation must be blotted out; and conspicuous, flashy, expensive, and wasteful buying will do this; it shows the world what the world must know! True, it is only for the moment; true, it is in the end self-defeating, for wasteful consumption is the best way to bring poverty back again; but the person with an over-powering drive to mend a lesion to his narcissism cannot resist the avalanche of that drive with this puny rational consideration. A man with his back against the wall and a gun at this throat doesn't think of what may happen ten years hence. (Consciously, of course, he knows nothing of this drive; all that appears to consciousness is its shattering effects; he knows only that he must keep on spend-ing—not why—and that he is unable to resist.) He hasn't in him the psychic capacity, the energy to stem the tide of a drive that at that moment is all-powerful. We, seated comfortably away from this flood, sit in judgment on him and blame him and exhort him and criticize him; but he, carried along by the flood, can-not do otherwise than he does. He may fight with all the strength of which he is capable, but it is not enough. And we, who are rational enough at least to exonerate a man in a situation of "overpowering im-pulse" when we recognize it to be one, do not even recognize this as an example of it; and so, in addition to being swept away in the flood that childhood con-ditions rendered inevitable, he must also endure our lectures, our criticisms, and our moral excoriation.

But, one will say, he could have overcome his spendthrift tendencies; some people do. Quite true: some people do. They are lucky. They have it in them to overcome early deficiencies by exerting great effort, and they are capable of exerting the effort. Some of us, luckier still, can overcome them with but little effort; and a few, the luckiest, haven't the deficiencies to overcome. It's all a matter of luck. The least lucky are those who can't overcome them, even with great effort, and those who haven't the ability to exert the effort.

But, one persists, it isn't a matter simply of luck; it *is* a matter of effort. Very well then, it's a matter of effort; without exerting the effort you may not overcome the deficiency. But whether or not you are the kind of person who has it in him to exert the effort is a matter of luck.

All this is well known to psychoanalysts. They can predict, from minimal clues that most of us don't notice, whether a person is going to turn out to be lucky or not. "The analyst," they say, "must be able to use the residue of the patient's uncon-scious guilt so as to remove the symptom or char-acter trait that creates the guilt. The guilt must not only be present, but *available* for use, *mobilizable*.

If it is used up (absorbed) in criminal activity, or in an excessive amount of self-damaging tendencies, then it cannot be used for therapeutic purposes, and the prognosis is negative." Not all philoso-phers will relish the analyst's way of putting the matter, but at least as a physician he can soon de-tect whether the patient is lucky or unlucky—and he knows that whichever it is, it *isn't the patient's fault*. The patient's conscious volition cannot remedy the deficiency. Even whether he will co-operate with the analyst is really out of the patient's hands: if he continually projects the denying-mother fantasy on the analyst and unconsciously identifies him always with the cruel, harsh forbid-der of the nursery, thus frustrating any attempt at impersonal observation, the sessions are useless; yet if it happens that way, he can't help that either. That fatal projection is not under his control; whether it occurs or not depends on how his un-conscious identifications have developed since his infancy. He can try, yes—but the ability to try enough for the therapy to have effect is also be-yond his control; the capacity to try more than just so much is either there or it isn't—and either way "it's in the lap of the gods."

The position, then, is this: if we *can* overcome the effects of early environment, the ability to do so is itself a product of the early environment. We did not give ourselves this ability; and if we lack it we cannot be blamed for not having it. Sometimes, to be sure, moral exhortation brings out an ability that is there but not being used, and in this lies its *occa-sional* utility; but very often its use is pointless, be-cause the ability is not there. The only thing that can overcome a desire, as Spinoza said, is a stronger contrary desire; and many times there simply is no wherewithal for producing a stronger contrary de-sire. Those of us who do have the wherewithal are lucky.

There is one possible practical advantage in re-membering this. It may prevent us (unless we are compulsive blamers) from indulging in righteous in-dignation and committing the sin of spiritual pride, thanking God that we are not as this publican here. And it will protect from our useless moralizings those who are least equipped by nature for enduring them.

As with responsibility, so with deserts. Someone commits a crime and is punished by the state; "he deserved it," we say self-righteously—as if we were moral and he immoral, when in fact we are lucky and he is unlucky—forgetting that there, but for the grace of God and a fortunate early environment, go we.

NOTES

1. Edmund Bergler, *The Basic Neurosis* (New York: Grune and Stratton, 1949), p. 305.

2. Meyer Levin, *Compulsion* (New York: Simon and Schuster, 1956), p. 403.

Questions for Thought

1. Under what conditions do you think a person should be held morally responsible for an action? Under what conditions should a person not be held responsible?
2. Can you think of other examples that show that we are not responsible for what we do?
3. Supposing that Hospers' criminal example is accurate, do you think the criminal should be held responsible for his crimes? What punishment, if any, should the criminal receive?
4. Do you think people have the ability to change their characters? Do you think you could radically change your character if you decided to do so?
5. What do you think Kant would say about Hospers' position? How do you think Hospers would respond?

Chapter 5

Politics

Introductory Remarks

HAVING COMPLETED OUR JOURNEY DOWN THE TREACHEROUS PATH of thinking about morality, we are now ready to embark on what might be an even more perilous path: the path of thinking about politics. As you are no doubt well aware, this path is marked by many dangers. First, there is the danger of disagreement—that is, the danger that the path of thinking about politics may end up like one of those political talk shows on CNN. On such shows, the guests and commentators (usually divided into those from the left and those from the right) cannot seem to agree on anything. Second, there is the danger of disloyalty, the danger that the path of thinking about politics may lead to conflict with some of the patriotic beliefs that you have been taught to accept without question. Third, there is the danger of dullness. While you may be one of those rare individuals who find political discussion and argument fascinating, it is more likely that you are among those countless others who prefer to amuse themselves in almost any other way.

Why, then, should you be forced to journey down this path? Perhaps I could convince you by appealing to Thomas Jefferson's claim that a **democracy** cannot thrive without well-informed and politically active citizens. Since you live in a democracy, it is your duty to become well informed and politically active. Or I might use the more ancient argument of Aristotle that man (this now includes women as well, even if Aristotle saw fit to exclude them) is a political animal. Since being political is part of being human, you have no choice but to journey down the path of political thinking.

Despite the fact that Americans are often viewed as being apolitical, you have likely already begun this journey. In reading the preceding paragraph, you no doubt knew who Thomas Jefferson was, and it is likely that you have read at least a portion of his Declaration of Independence. (In case you have not, it is included as one of the selections in this chapter.) Also, you probably knew what a democracy was; and while you may have disagreed with Jefferson's claim that you have a duty to become well informed and politically active, you no doubt had some idea of what it means to have a social duty.

Overview of Selections

We could explore numerous topics on the path of thinking about politics, but I have selected writings that focus on two basic questions. The selections in the first part deal with the fundamental question of the origin of our obligations to society. Although you may be confused about what they are, you probably do believe that you have certain social duties or obligations. But have you ever asked yourself *why* this is the case? Many philosophers have pondered this question, and the selections in the first section represent various responses to it.

The question raised by the selections in the second part is closely related to the question addressed in the first part. Given that we have social duties or obligations, another important question immediately arises: the question concerning the extent of our duties or obligations to society. Each of the selections in the second part attempts to determine, in some manner, the boundary between governmental authority and individual liberty. Interestingly, all the writers in this section suggest that government often infringes on individual freedom, but they by no means agree on where the boundary between governmental authority and individual freedom is to be drawn.

The first four selections in the first part represent either formulations or critiques of what has been called the contract theory of the origin of government. The contract theory maintains that one's obligations to society are derived from some sort of initial agreement between various individuals to form a society, or between an individual and the existing society in which he or she lives. In what is perhaps the earliest formulation of this theory, Plato argues in the first selection that one who freely chooses to live in a state and to receive the benefits of doing so enters into an implicit contract to uphold the laws of that state. For Plato, this implicit agreement is sacrosanct and cannot be broken even to save one's life. In the second selection, the French philosopher Jean-Jacques Rousseau hypothesizes a state of nature in which individuals are endowed with natural freedom. At some point, however, this natural freedom proves insufficient to ensure the continued existence of those living in the state of nature. When this happens, the individuals enter into a social contract whereby each of them gives up his or her natural freedom to become part of a collective body governed by what Rousseau calls the "general will." In the following selection, Thomas Jefferson claims that all men are created equal and have certain inalienable rights. Government is formed by the consent of the governed for the purpose of protecting these inalienable rights. When a government fails to fulfill its purpose, Jefferson argues that the citizens have the right to render the contract void and to create a new government. In the last of these four selections, Charles Mills argues that in Europe and the United States there is another contract—the "racial contract"—underlying the social contract discussed in Western political theory. This unspoken racial contract has undermined the promises of liberty and equality that are contained in the social contract, giving rise to discrimination and white supremacy. According to Mills, this racial contract must be acknowledged and ultimately broken if these promises of liberty and equality are to be realized.

The next five selections offer other explanations of the origin and extent of governmental authority. In *The Communist Manifesto*, Karl Marx and Friedrich Engels suggest that the form of government in a society is produced by the economic conditions that exist in that society. They also claim that governments produced by economic capitalism are extremely repressive and that capitalism will ultimately be overthrown. Once capitalism is destroyed, the repressive governments associated with it will be replaced by a classless society characterized by social harmony and economic justice. In *We Are Practical Revolutionaries,* Che Guevara accepts the account of the origin of government formulated by Marx and Engels and argues that the Cuban Revolution represents one example in which a repressive government has been overthrown by armed revolt. John Dewey, in the next selection, suggests that government originated as a means to an end, the end being to facilitate social interaction and thus to ensure human well-being and happiness. He also argues that democracy, both as a form of government and as a way of life, represents the best means of social interaction thus far devised. Next, in contrast to Marx, Engels, Guevara, and Dewey, Abu'l A'la Maududi claims that government receives its legitimacy from **Allah** (God). He believes that political leaders are vice-regents of God and that the purpose of government is to establish God's laws on earth. Finally, in *Who Is Your Mother? Red Roots of White Feminism,* Paula Gunn Allen contrasts European-derived models of government with traditional tribal systems of government. She argues that European-derived models were patriarchal and inherently repressive in many respects, whereas most tribal systems were **gynocratic** and "provided the basis for all the dreams of liberation that characterize the modern world." For these reasons, Allen says that in order to be just, a government must incorporate many of the political principles found in traditional tribal systems.

As mentioned previously, all the selections in the second part deal with the question of the boundary between governmental authority and individual liberty. In the first selection, the British philosopher John Stuart Mill explicitly raises the question of where our obligations to society end, noting that philosophers have, for the most part, avoided this question. To fill this void, Mill introduces and defends the principle that, in the case of consenting adults, governmental authority extends only to those actions that directly harm other people. On the other hand, he believes that an individual has sovereignty over all of his or her other actions, even if such actions prove harmful to the individual who engages in them. Mill also argues that, even in democracies, governments often overstep the limits of their legitimate authority.

The next four selections all question the legitimacy of certain governmental policies, while affirming the value of rebellion or protest in defending human freedom and dignity against governmental oppression. Mohandas K. Gandhi, the modern Indian philosopher and social reformer, describes the concept of *satyagraha* (nonviolence) and claims that *satyagraha* is often needed to bring about individual and social change. Gandhi insists, however, that *satyagraha* is inconsistent with violence or the use of physical force, and he rejects these as legitimate tools for bringing about social change. In his "Letter from Birmingham Jail," Martin Luther King Jr., like Gandhi, defends the philosophy of nonviolence in his attempt to combat certain social evils (elsewhere he lists these as racism, economic exploitation, and militarism) that exist in the United States. He also distinguishes between just and unjust laws, while arguing that one is morally justified in breaking unjust laws. Stokely Carmichael, in the next selection, explains the history and philosophy of black power, and he provides a stinging indictment of racism and economic exploitation in the United States. In opposition to Gandhi and King, however, Carmichael rejects the claim that *satyagraha,* or nonviolence, is the only justifiable means of bringing about social change. Next, bell hooks agrees with Carmichael's indictment of the racial and economic inequalities that exist in the United States, and she also rejects the claim that the only legitimate means of bringing about social change is nonviolence. But unlike Carmichael, hooks believes that it is feminism, not the politics of black power, that holds the promise of self-transformation and social change.

The final three selections in the second part represent the position that legitimate governmental authority is either severely limited or nonexistent. In the first of these, Nellie Wong, like both Carmichael and hooks, points out the racial and economic inequalities that exist under capitalism, and she calls for a socialist feminist revolution. Until such a revolution takes place, Wong suggests that governmental authority is necessarily tied to capitalist oppression and is therefore illegitimate. In the next-to-last selection, Henry David Thoreau argues that individual conscience is a higher law than governmental statutes. He claims that individuals have a duty not to contribute to any governmental action that conflicts with the dictates of conscience. Citing several examples of such actions in the United States in the nineteenth century, Thoreau believes that civil disobedience is often necessary to slow such injustices perpetrated by governments. Finally, Emma Goldman takes Thoreau's indictment of government one step further. She argues that governmental authority necessarily requires violence against the individual and that, for this reason, governmental authority is never legitimate. Goldman calls for the overthrow of governmental authority and for the subsequent formation of a society based on the political principles of **anarchism.**

Although the questions covered in this chapter are only two of the many found on the path of thinking about politics, it seems to me that they are important and interesting ones—ones that at least avoid the danger of dullness. Whether they also avoid the dangers of disagreement and disloyalty only you can decide. Keep in mind, however, that both autonomous thinking and personal growth involve a certain amount of risk and danger and that a life without them is precisely what many of the writers in this chapter were struggling to overcome.

Contemporary Applications

When it comes to the topic of political thinking, I am faced with the same problem that I was faced with in the last chapter. There are so many interesting issues that it is difficult to decide where to begin. After much reflection, it occurred to me that a good place to start is to recite a political creed that most of you (at least those of you who have grown up in the United States) have been saying since you were in kindergarten:

> I pledge allegiance to the flag of the United States of America, and to the Republic for which it stands, one nation under God, indivisible, with liberty and justice for all.

This is, of course, the text of the Pledge of Allegiance, a text that is regularly repeated in schools and at public functions throughout the United States. But what exactly does this pledge mean? When you recite it, what exactly are you saying?

If we think about the pledge philosophically, certain key words merit examination. Take the word *allegiance,* for example. When you pledge allegiance to the flag or to your country, what precisely are you promising to do? Does allegiance require that you accept, without question, everything that your country (or the government of your country) does? Some people seem to think so. During the Vietnam War, a popular bumper sticker simply stated, "America: Love It or Leave It." Many people who displayed this sticker on their cars believed that those who were protesting the war were unpatriotic, and some believed that these protestors should be forced to leave the country.

Martin Luther King Jr. and others who were struggling for civil rights in the United States were often confronted by people who held similar beliefs about civil rights activities. King was accused of being disloyal or unpatriotic, and the FBI closely monitored his activities. Indeed, King's "Letter from Birmingham Jail," which is included in this chapter, represents one of his many attempts to deal with such accusations.

But does allegiance to one's country rule out disagreement or protest? Were the people who were protesting the Vietnam War and civil rights abuses in the 1960s being disloyal or unpatriotic? Most of them did not think so. Indeed, while King did not go as far as George Bernard Shaw, who referred to patriotism as the "last refuge of a scoundrel," he did warn against the dangers of "superficial patriotism." He also argued that it was the civil rights workers, not their critics, who represented the American ideal. For, like Thomas Jefferson (whose Declaration of Independence is included in this chapter), the civil rights activists were struggling to overcome oppression and to implement the creed that all men are created equal. In a similar manner, the antiwar demonstrators often saw themselves as descendants of Jefferson or Henry David Thoreau, a nineteenth-century American writer who also protested the injustices of his time. (In his essay on civil disobedience, which is also included in this chapter, Thoreau lists slavery and the treatment of Native Americans as two such injustices.) In response to the previously mentioned bumper sticker, the demonstrators coined their own slogan: "America: Stay and Change It."

Recently, the president of the United States, in response to the events of September 11, 2001, declared a "war on terrorism." As I write this chapter introduction, the U.S. military is currently deployed in both Afghanistan and Iraq, and Congress is debating the issue of whether certain civil liberties will have to be curtailed in order to combat the threat of terrorism. While many people support the military operations that were undertaken in this new war, voices of dissent are already making themselves heard. And while there are numerous calls for the curtailment of civil liberties, civil libertarians are arguing that such calls are either unconstitutional or un-American. Questions similar to those raised in the 1960s are once again being debated on college campuses:

Was the invasion of Afghanistan and/or Iraq justified?

What other military actions are justified in the fight against terrorism and/or in the defense of U.S. interests around the world?

Do we really want to curtail our civil liberties to combat the threat of terrorism or for any other reason?

If so, which liberties are to be curtailed, and to what extent are they to be curtailed?

Should we even be asking these sorts of questions?

Isn't someone who asks these questions being disloyal or unpatriotic?

These are difficult questions indeed. And all of them arose simply from thinking philosophically about the first important word in the Pledge of Allegiance. But what about those other important words in the pledge? What happens when we think about words like *Republic, God, liberty,* and *justice*? Thinking about these words, which seem to be broader or much less concrete than the word *allegiance,* will no doubt lead to many other interesting philosophical questions. Here are just a few of the questions that spring to mind:

What is a republic?

Is a republic the same thing as a democracy?

Is a republic (or a democracy) the best form of government?

Why does the word *God* appear in the Pledge of Allegiance of a country in which the doctrine of the separation of church and state is an avowed political principle?

What exactly does the word *liberty* mean?

Is liberty the same thing as freedom?

When, if ever, are governments justified in curtailing individual liberty or freedom?

How are we to understand the word *justice*?

What distinguishes a just act or governmental policy from an unjust act or governmental policy?

Does the word *justice* refer only to laws or rules governing criminal behavior, or is there such a thing as economic justice?

If there is such a thing as economic justice, how is it to be determined?

Of course, these are only a few of the many questions that we might ask concerning those other important words in the Pledge of Allegiance.

All the selections contained in this chapter bear on one or more of these questions. Thus, it would be useful for you to keep them in mind as you read. Moreover, during the course of your reading, other questions will no doubt occur to you, and you will perhaps learn (if you have not already) one of the most important lessons of political and/or philosophical thinking: Asking the right questions is just as, if not more, important than providing answers.

What Is the Basis of Our Obligations to Society?

Crito   1

PLATO

Plato (427–347 B.C.E.) was born into a wealthy, aristocratic family in Athens. While many of the details of his life are unknown, it is generally agreed that Plato served in the Athenian military during the war with Sparta and that he never married. He was also a close follower of the philosopher Socrates, who serves as the main character in most of Plato's dialogues, including the following one. When Socrates was executed in 399 B.C.E., Plato traveled to Egypt and Syracuse before returning to Athens to found the Academy, one of the earliest schools of philosophy and scientific research. Plato wrote many philosophical dialogues, several of which are mentioned in the introduction to the selection from Plato in Chapter 1.

The following dialogue takes place in Socrates' prison cell shortly before he was to be executed. Several months earlier, Socrates had been sentenced to death for atheism and for corrupting the youth of Athens. According to Athenian custom, however, no executions could take place while a certain sacred ship was out of port. At the beginning of this dialogue, Crito, one of his close friends, tells Socrates that the ship had been sighted in a nearby city and that its return and Socrates' execution are imminent. Crito then attempts to persuade Socrates that he should try to avoid death by escaping from prison. Socrates agrees to listen to Crito, but he says that he will agree to escape only if there are good reasons for doing so. If, however, there are stronger reasons for not escaping, Socrates says he must remain in prison even though it will cost him his life.

Crito's main reasons as to why Socrates should escape are that people will think harshly of his friends for not helping him to escape and that Socrates has a duty to see that his children are cared for and educated. Socrates replies, however, that there are stronger moral and political reasons for not escaping. He introduces the moral principle that one is never justified in returning injury for injury. (You may recognize this as closely akin to a principle attributed to Jesus, the principle that when you receive a blow you should "turn the other cheek.") He also introduces the political principle that by living in a society and benefiting from the goods of that society, one enters into an implicit contract to uphold the laws of that society. Indeed, Socrates claims that this obligation is stronger than any other, including obligations to one's family. If he were to escape, Socrates says that he would be intentionally injuring the laws of Athens and the state itself, thereby violating the moral principle that one should not return injury for injury. Moreover, he would be failing to fulfill the terms of his contract with the state, a contract into which he freely entered. Given the strength of these reasons, Socrates concludes that it would be wrong for him to attempt to escape. According to the accounts in Plato's dialogues, Socrates was executed two days later.

Questions for Reading

1. What is the setting of the dialogue? Who are the characters in it?
2. What are Crito's main reasons as to why Socrates should escape from prison? How does Socrates respond to Crito's entreaty?
3. What are Socrates' principal reasons for refusing to escape?
4. Why does Socrates discount the opinion of the multitude?
5. What, according to Socrates, is the source and extent of our obligations to the state? Why does he think that his obligations to the state are stronger than his obligations to his family?
6. How does the dialogue end?

Socrates: Why have you come at this hour? Isn't it quite early?

Crito: Yes, it is.

Socrates: What is the exact time?

Crito: The dawn is breaking.

Socrates: I am surprised that the keeper of the prison let you in.

Crito: He knows me, Socrates, because I often come. Besides, I have done him a kindness.

Socrates: And have you just arrived?

Crito: No, I came some time ago.

Socrates: Then why did you sit silently, instead of awakening me at once?

Crito: . . . I have been watching your peaceful slumbers with amazement. I did not awaken you, because I wished to minimize the pain. I have always thought that you had a happy disposition; but I have never seen anything like the easy, tranquil manner with which you face your calamity.

This selection from the Crito *is the editor's revised version of the translation found in* The Dialogues of Plato, *The Macmillan Company, 1892.*

Socrates: When a man has reached my age, Crito, he ought not to fret at the approach of death.

Crito: Yet in the case of other old men who face a similar misfortune, age does not prevent them from fretting.

Socrates: That is true. But you have not told me why you came at this early hour.

Crito: I have come to bring you a message that is sad and painful, perhaps not to yourself, but to all of your friends, especially to me.

Socrates: What? Has the ship arrived from Delos, the ship on the arrival of which I am to die?

Crito: No, the ship has not yet arrived, but it will probably be here today. Persons who have come from Sunium tell me that the ship was there when they left. Therefore, Socrates, tomorrow will be the last day of your life.

Socrates: Very well, Crito. If such is the will of the gods, I am willing. But my belief is that there will be a delay of a day.

Crito: Why do you think so?

Socrates: I will tell you. Am I not to die on the day after the arrival of the ship?

Crito: Yes, that is what the authorities say.

Socrates: But I do not think that the ship will be here until tomorrow. I infer this from a vision which I had last night, or rather only moments ago, when you fortunately allowed me to sleep.

Crito: And what was the nature of your vision?

Socrates: There appeared to me the likeness of a woman, fair and beautiful, clothed in bright garments. She called to me and said, "O Socrates, you will go to fertile Phthia on the third day hence."

Crito: What an unusual dream, Socrates!

Socrates: I think that there can be no doubt about its meaning, Crito.

Crito: Yes, the meaning is only too clear. But dear beloved Socrates, let me entreat you once more to take my advice and escape. For if you die, I will not only lose an irreplaceable friend, there is another evil. People who do not know you and me will believe that I might have saved you if I had been willing to give money, but that I did not care. Now, can there be a worse disgrace than this—that I should be thought to value money more than the life of a friend? For the multitude will not be persuaded that I wanted you to escape, and that you refused.

Socrates: But why, my dear Crito, should we care about the opinion of the multitude? Good men (and they are the only persons whose opinions matter) will think of these things as they truly occurred.

Crito: But you see, Socrates, that the opinion of the multitude must be considered, for what is now happening shows that they can do the greatest evil to any one who has lost their good opinion.

Socrates: I only wish it were true, Crito, that the multitude could do the greatest evil. For then they would also be able to do the greatest good. . . . But in reality they can do neither. For they cannot make a man either wise or foolish; and whatever they do is the result of chance.

Crito: Well, I will not argue with you. But please tell me, Socrates, whether you are acting out of regard for me and your other friends. Are you afraid that if you escape from prison we will get into trouble with the informers for having helped you escape, that we will lose either the whole or a great part of our property, or that something worse may happen to us? Now, if you are afraid on our account, be at ease. For in order to save you we ought surely run this risk, and even a greater risk. Be persuaded, then, and do as I say.

Socrates: Yes, Crito, that is one fear that I have, but by no means the only one.

Crito: Fear not, for there are persons who are willing to get you out of prison at no great cost. And as for the informers, they are far from being exorbitant in their demands. A little money will satisfy them. My ample means are at your service; and if you have a scruple about spending all my money, there are strangers here who will give you the use of theirs. One of them, Simmias the Theban, has brought a large sum of money for this very purpose. And Cebes and many others are prepared to spend their money in helping you to escape. Therefore, do not hesitate because of us, and do not say, as you did in court, that you will have difficulty in knowing what to do with yourself anywhere else. For men will love you in other places to which you may go, not only in Athens. There are friends of mine in Thessaly, if you would like to go there, who will value and protect you, so that no Thessalian will give you any trouble. Nor can I think that you are at all justified, Socrates, in betraying your own life when you might be saved. In acting thus you are playing into the hands of your enemies, who are hurrying you to your death. And further you are deserting your own children; for you might bring them up and educate them. Instead, you go away and leave them, and they will have to take their chance. If they do not meet with the usual fate of orphans, there will be no small thanks to you. No man should bring children into the world who is unwilling to persevere to the end in their nurture and education. But you appear to be choosing the easier path, not the better and manlier, which would have been more appropriate to someone, like yourself, who professes to care for virtue in all his actions. Indeed, I am ashamed not only of you, but of all us who are your friends, when I think that the whole business will be attributed entirely to our lack of courage. The trial need never have taken place, or it might have been handled differently. And this last act, this crowning folly, will seem to have occurred through our negligence and cowardice. . . . See now, Socrates, how sad and discreditable are the consequences, both to you and to those of us who might have saved you. Make up your mind, then. Or rather have your mind already made up, for the time for deliberation is over. There is only one thing to be done, and it must be done this very night. If we wait any longer, it will not be practicable or possible. Therefore, I beseech you, Socrates, be persuaded by me. Do as I say!

Socrates: Dear Crito, your zeal is priceless, if it is rightly directed. However, if wrongly directed, the greater the zeal the greater the danger. Therefore, we ought to consider whether I should or should not do as you say. For I am and always have been one of those persons who must be guided by reason, that is, by whatever reason reflection shows me to be the best. I cannot repudiate my own words now that this chance has happened to me. I still honor the principles that I have hitherto honored and revered; and unless we can now find other better principles, I am certain not to agree with you. No, not even if the power of the multitude could inflict many more imprisonments, confiscations, and deaths, or frighten us like children with hobgoblin terrors. What will be the fairest way of considering the question? Should I return to your old argument about the opinions of men? We said before that some of them are to be considered, while others are not. Now, were we right in maintaining this before I was condemned? And has the argument, which was good once, now proved to be talk for the sake of talking, or mere childish nonsense?

What I want to consider with your help, Crito, is whether or not, under my present circumstances, the argument appears to be in any way different. Is it to be allowed by me or disallowed? That argument, which is maintained by many persons of authority, is, as I was saying, that the opinions of some men are to be considered, but those of other men are not to be considered. Now you, Crito, are not going to die tomorrow (at least it is probable that you are not). You therefore are disinterested, and are not liable to be deceived by the circumstances in which you are placed. Tell me, then, whether I am right in saying that only some men and their opinions are to be valued, while other men and their opinions are not to be valued. Was I right in maintaining this?

Crito: Certainly.

Socrates: The good are to be valued, not the bad.

Crito: Yes.

Socrates: And the opinions of the wise are good, and the opinions of the unwise are evil.

Crito: Certainly.

Socrates: Consider the matter this way. Is the pupil who devotes himself to the practice of gymnastics supposed to attend to the praise and blame and opinion of every man, or only that of one man, his physician or trainer?

Crito: Of one man only. . . .

Socrates: And he ought to act and train, and eat and drink in the way which seems good to his single master who has understanding, rather than according to the opinion of all other men put together.

Crito: True.

Socrates: And if he disobeys and disregards the opinion and approval of the one, and regards the opinion of the multitude who have no understanding, will he not suffer evil?

Crito: Certainly he will.

Socrates: And what will the evil affect in the disobedient person?

Crito: It will clearly affect the body. That is what is destroyed by this type of evil.

Socrates: Very good. But is this not true, Crito, of other things that we need not separately enumerate? In questions of justice and injustice, fairness and unfairness, good and evil, . . . ought we to follow the opinions of the multitude or to fear them? Or should we follow the opinion of the one man who has understanding? Shouldn't we fear and revere him more than all the rest of the world? If we desert him, will we not injure and destroy that principle in us which may be assumed to be improved by justice and deteriorated by injustice? There is such a principle, isn't there?

Crito: Certainly there is, Socrates.

Socrates: Consider an analogous example. If, acting under the advice of those who have no understanding, we destroy that which is improved by health and deteriorated by disease, would life be worth having? And what would be destroyed in this case would be the body.

Crito: Yes.

Socrates: Could we live with an evil and corrupted body?

Crito: Certainly not.

Socrates: And will life be worth having, if that higher part of man is destroyed, that part which is improved by justice and depraved by injustice? Do we suppose that the principle in man, whatever it is, that has to do with justice and injustice is inferior to the body?

Crito: Certainly not.

Socrates: Is it more valuable than the body?

Crito: Far more.

Socrates: Then, my friend, we must not consider what the multitude says about us, but only what the one man who has understanding of the just and the unjust will say, only what the truth will say. Therefore, you begin in error when you suggest that we should consider the opinion of the multitude about the just and the unjust, or about good and evil, or about what is honorable and dishonorable. But won't some people respond to us that the multitude can kill us?

Crito: Yes, Socrates, that will clearly be some people's response.

Socrates: And they would be right in saying this. But surprisingly I still find that the old argument is as unshaken as ever. And I would like to know whether I can say the same of another proposition, the proposition that not life, but a good life, is worth living?

Crito: Yes, that principle also remains unshaken.

Socrates: And does the claim that a good life is equivalent to a just and honorable one still hold?

Crito: Yes, it does.

Socrates: Given these premises, I will critically analyze the question of whether or not I ought to try

to escape without the consent of the Athenians. If I am right to escape, then I will make the attempt. However, if I am not right, I will abstain. The other considerations that you mention, such as loss of money and character, and the duty of educating one's children, are, I fear, only doctrines of the multitude, who would be as ready to restore people to life, if they were able, as they now are to put them to death—and with as little reason. But now that the argument has proceeded this far, the only question that remains to be answered is whether or not we will be acting rightly in escaping or in allowing others to help us escape. . . . If doing so is not acting rightly, then death or any other calamity that may follow upon my remaining here must not be allowed to enter into the argument.

Crito: I think you are right, Socrates. How shall we proceed?

Socrates: Let us consider the matter together. Refute my argument if you can, my dear friend, and I will be convinced; or else stop from repeating to me that I ought to escape against the wishes of the Athenians. Although I highly value your attempt to persuade me to do so, I will not be persuaded against my own better judgment. Now consider my first position, and try to refute me as best you can.

Crito: I will.

Socrates: Should we say that we are never intentionally to do wrong, or rather that sometimes we ought to do wrong and sometimes not? Is doing wrong always evil and dishonorable, as we have said before? Are all the conclusions that we reached in the last few days to be thrown away? Have we, at our age, been earnestly discoursing with one another all our life, only to discover that we are no better than children? Or, in spite of the opinion of the multitude, in spite of consequences whether better or worse, shall we insist on the truth of what was then said, namely, that injustice is always an evil and dishonor to him who acts unjustly? Shall we say so or not?

Crito: We shall.

Socrates: Then we must do no wrong?

Crito: Certainly not.

Socrates: Nor shall we return injury when we are injured, as the multitude believes, for we must injure no one at all.

Crito: Clearly not.

Socrates: Again, Crito, may we do evil?

Crito: Surely not, Socrates.

Socrates: And what about doing evil in return for evil, which is the morality of the multitude? Is that just or not?

Crito: Not just.

Socrates: For isn't doing evil to another the same as injuring him?

Crito: Yes, it is.

Socrates: Then we ought not to retaliate or render evil for evil to any one, whatever evil we may have suffered from him. But consider carefully, Crito, whether you really mean what you are saying. For this opinion has never been held, and never will be held, by any considerable number of people. And those who are agreed and those who are not agreed on this point have no common ground, and can only despise one another when they see how widely they differ. Tell me, then, whether you truly agree with and assent to my first principle, that neither injury, retaliation, nor warding off evil by evil is ever right. Shall we accept this as the **premise** of our argument? Or do you decline and dissent from this? For I have always thought this and continue to do so. But if you are of another opinion, let me hear what you have to say. If, however, you remain of the same mind as formerly, I will proceed to the next step.

Crito: You may proceed, for I have not changed my mind.

Socrates: Then I will go on to the next point, which may be put in the form of a question. Should a man live up to his agreements, if they are just, or should he betray them?

Crito: He ought to live up to his agreements.

Socrates: But if this is true, how should it be applied in the present case? In leaving the prison against the will of the Athenians, do I wrong any one? Or rather do I not wrong those whom I ought least to wrong? Do I not desert the principles that were acknowledged by us to be just? What do you say?

Crito: I cannot tell, Socrates; I do not know.

Socrates: Then consider the matter in this way. Imagine that I am about to play truant (or call it by whatever name you like), when the laws and the government come and interrogate me. "Tell us, Socrates," they say, "what are you about to do? Is not your act an attempt to do whatever is in your power to overturn us, the laws and the whole state?

Do you think that a state can subsist and not be overthrown, in which the decisions of law have no power, but are set aside and trampled on by individuals?" What will be our answer, Crito, to these and like questions? Anyone, especially a rhetorician, will have a good deal to say on behalf of the law that requires a sentence to be carried out. He will argue that this law should not be disobeyed. Shall we reply, "Yes, but the state has injured us and given us an unjust sentence?" Suppose we say that?

Crito: Very good, Socrates.

Socrates: "And was that our agreement with you?" the laws would answer. "Or were you to abide by the sentence of the state?" And if I were to express my astonishment at these words, the laws would probably add: "Answer, Socrates, instead of raising your eyebrows, you who are in the habit of asking and answering questions. Tell us what complaint you have to make against us that justifies you in attempting to destroy us and the state. In the first place, did we not bring you into existence? Your father married your mother by our aid and begat you. Do you have any objection to urge against those of us who regulate marriage?" None, I would reply. "Or against those of us who after birth regulate the nurture and education of children, by which you were also trained? Were not the laws which have the charge of education right in commanding your father to train you in music and gymnastics?" They were right, I would reply. "Well then, since you were brought into the world and nurtured and educated by us, can you deny in the first place that you are our child and slave, as your fathers were before you? And if this is true, you are not on equal terms with us. Nor can you think that you have a right to do to us what we are doing to you. Would you have any right to strike or revile or do any other evil to your father or your master, if you had one, because you have been struck or reviled by him, or received some other evil at his hands? You would not say that you would. But because we think it right to destroy you, do you think that you have any right to try to destroy us and your country in return? Will you, O professor of true virtue, pretend that you are justified in this? Has a philosopher like you failed to discover that our country is far more to be valued, far higher and holier, than is mother or father or any ancestor? That our country is to be more highly regarded in the eyes of the gods and of men of understanding? That even more than a father, it is to be soothed, and gently and reverently entreated when angry, either to be persuaded, or if not persuaded, then obeyed? And when we are punished by her, whether with imprisonment or stripes, the punishment is to be endured in silence. If she leads us to wounds or death in battle, we must rightly follow her. No one must either yield or retreat or leave his rank. But whether in battle or in a court of law, or in any other place, one must do what his city and his country order him; or he must change their view of what is just. If he may do no violence to his father or mother, much less may he do violence to his country." How shall we answer all this, Crito? Do the laws speak truly, or do they not?

Crito: I think that they do.

Socrates: Then the laws will say, "Consider, Socrates, whether we are speaking truly when we say that in attempting to escape you would be doing us an injury. For, after bringing you into the world, nurturing, and educating you, and giving you and every other citizen a share in every good which we have to give, we further proclaim to any Athenian, by the liberty which we allow him, that if he does not like us when he has become of age, seen the ways of the city, and made our acquaintance, he may go where he pleases and take his goods with him. Any one who does not like us and the city, and who wants to emigrate to a colony or to any other city, may go where he likes, retaining his property. But whoever has experience of the manner in which we order justice and administer the state, and still remains, has entered into an implied contract that he will do as we command him. And he who disobeys us is, as we maintain, thrice wrong. First, because in disobeying us he is disobeying his parents. Secondly, because we are the authors of his education. Thirdly, because he has made an agreement with us that he will duly obey our commands. But he neither obeys them nor convinces us that our commands are unjust. . . . These are the sort of accusations to which you, above all Athenians, will be exposed, Socrates, if you accomplish your intentions."

If I now ask why these accusations would apply to me above all other Athenians, they will justly reply that I above all other men have acknowledged the agreement. "There is clear proof, Socrates," they will say, "that we and the city were not displeasing to you. Of all Athenians you have been the most constant resident in the city, which, as you never leave, you may be supposed to love. For you never went out of the city either to see the games (except once when you went to the Isthmus), or to any other place, except when you were on military duty. Nor did you travel as other men do. You had no curiosity to know other states or their laws; your affections did not go beyond us and our state. We were your special favorites, and you acquiesced in our government of you. Here in this city you begat your children, which is a proof of your satisfaction. Moreover, in the course of the trial, if you had liked, you could have fixed the penalty at banishment. The state which refuses to let you go now would have let you go then. But you pretended that you preferred death to exile, and that you were not unwilling to die. And now you have forgotten these fine sentiments, and pay no respect to us the laws, of whom you are the destroyer. You are doing what only a miserable slave would do, running away and turning your back on the compacts and agreements that you made as a citizen. But first answer this important question. Are we right in saying that you agreed to be governed according to us in deed, and not in word only? Is that true or not?" How shall we answer, Crito? Must we not assent?

Crito: We cannot help it, Socrates.

Socrates: Then will they not say: "You, Socrates, are breaking the covenants and agreements which you made with us at your leisure, not in any haste or under any compulsion or deception. You have had seventy years to think about them, during which time you were at liberty to leave the city, if we were not to your liking, or if our covenants appeared to you to be unfair. You had your choice, and might have gone either to Lacedaemon or Crete, both of which states are often praised by you for their good government, or to some other Hellenic or foreign state. But you, above all other Athenians, seemed to be so fond of the state, or, in other words, of us her laws, . . . that you never stirred out of her. The lame, the blind, the maimed were not more stationary in her than you were. And now you run away and forsake your agreements. You will not do so, Socrates, if you take our advice. Do not make yourself ridiculous by escaping out of the city.

"For ask yourself what good you will do to either yourself or your friends if you transgress and err in this sort of way. It is tolerably certain that your friends will be driven into exile and deprived of citizenship, or will lose their property. And if you flee to one of the neighboring cities, such as Thebes or Megara, both of which are well governed, you will come to them as an enemy, Socrates. Their government will be against you, and all patriotic citizens will cast an evil eye upon you as a subverter of the laws; and you will confirm in the minds of the judges the justice of their own condemnation of you. For he who is a corrupter of the laws is more than likely to be a corrupter of the young and foolish portion of mankind. Will you then flee from well-ordered cities and virtuous men? Is existence worth having on these terms? Or will you go to them without shame, and talk to them, Socrates? What will you say to them? What you say here about virtue and justice and institutions and laws being the best things among men? Would that be decent of you? Surely not. But if you go away from well-governed states to Crito's friends in Thessaly, where there is great disorder and license, they will be charmed to hear the tale of your escape from prison, set off with ludicrous particulars of the manner in which you were wrapped in a goatskin or some other disguise, and metamorphosed like other runaways. But will there be no one to remind you that in your old age you were not ashamed to violate the most sacred laws from a miserable desire for a little more life? Perhaps not, if you keep them in a good temper. But if they are out of temper you will hear many degrading things. You will live, but how? As the flatterer of all men, as the servant of all men? And doing what? Eating and drinking in Thessaly, having gone abroad in order that you may get a dinner? Where will be your fine sentiments about justice and virtue? If you say that you wish to live for the sake of your children, to bring them up and educate them, will you take them into Thessaly and deprive them of Athenian citizenship? Is this the benefit you will confer upon them? Or are you under the impression that they will be better cared for and educated by your friends here if you are still alive, but absent from them? Do you fancy that if you are an inhabitant of Thessaly your friends will take care of them, but if you are an inhabitant of the other world they will not take care of them? No, if they who call themselves friends are good for anything, they will take care of them when you are in the other world.

"Listen, then, Socrates, to us who have brought you up. Think not of life and children first, and of justice afterwards. Think of justice first, so that you may be justified before the princes of the world below. For neither will you or any that belong to you be happier or holier or juster in this life, or happier in another life, if you do as Crito bids. Now you depart in innocence, a sufferer and not a doer of evil, a victim, not of the laws, but of men. But if you go forth, returning evil for evil, injury for injury, breaking the covenants and agreements which you have made with us, and wronging those whom you ought least of all to wrong, that is to say, yourself, your friends, your country, and us, we will be angry with you while you live, and our brethren, the laws in the world below, will receive you as an enemy. For they will know that you have done your best to destroy us. Listen, then, to us and not to Crito."

This, dear Crito, is the voice that I seem to hear murmuring in my ears, like the sound of the flute in the ears of the mystic. That voice is humming in my ears, preventing me from hearing any other. I know that anything more that you may say will be in vain. Yet speak, if you have anything to say.

Crito: I have nothing to say, Socrates.

Socrates: Leave me then, Crito, to fulfill the will of the gods, and to follow wherever they lead.

Questions for Thought

1. If you were trying to convince Socrates to escape from prison, what reasons would you use to try to convince him?
2. Do you think that the opinion of the multitude has value? To what extent are your beliefs determined by the opinion of the multitude?
3. One of the principles that Socrates states in this dialogue is that it is not just life but a *good* life that is worth living. What do you think this principle means? What might be some of the consequences of accepting this principle?

4. Do you agree with Socrates (and Jesus) that we should never return injury for injury? Can you think of any good reasons for rejecting this principle? What might be some reasons for accepting it?

5. Do you believe that your obligations to your country are stronger than your obligations to your family? Why or why not?

6. If you were sentenced to death by the state in which you live and had the opportunity to escape execution, would you choose to do so? If so, why? If not, why not?

The Social Contract 2

JEAN-JACQUES ROUSSEAU

Jean-Jacques Rousseau (1712–1778), the son of a watchmaker, was born in Geneva, Switzerland. His mother died a few days after his birth, and Rousseau was raised by his father and an aunt. When he was ten, however, his father fled France to avoid a prison sentence, and Rousseau was placed in the care of a country priest at Boissy. He later returned to Geneva, where he lived with an uncle before being apprenticed to a notary and then to an engraver. Mistreated by the latter, Rousseau ran away at age sixteen.

Having little formal education, Rousseau went to the province of Savoy, where he obtained a job as steward in the home of a wealthy noblewoman, Mme. de Warens, who converted Rousseau to Catholicism, provided him with a first-rate education, and eventually became his lover. She also provided him with important letters of introduction when he left Savoy for Paris in 1741. In Paris, Rousseau became part of a group of young radical intellectuals, later known as **"Philosophes,"** and he met Thérèse Levasseur, a servant in the boardinghouse where he lived, who became his lover. During this time, Rousseau also became a successful writer of both prose and music. Rousseau's essay *Discours sur les sciences et les arts* (1750; *A Discourse on the Sciences and the Arts*) won a prize from the Academy of Dijon. His opera *Le devin du village* (1752; *The Cunning-Man*) was greatly admired by King Louis XIV, and it later became the basis for an operetta by Mozart.

After the publication of his *Discours sur l'origine de l'inegalité* (1755; *Discourse on the Origin of Inequality*), Rousseau left Paris to be closer to nature. Settling in a country cottage, he wrote the three works for which he is best known: *Julie: ou, la nouvelle Héloïse* (1761; *Julie: or, The New Eloise*), *Du contrat social* (1762; *The Social Contract*), and *Émile: ou, de l'éducation* (1762; *Emile: or, On Education*). When the last work drew the ire of the French priesthood, Rousseau was forced to flee France. After meeting a similar fate in Switzerland, he was invited to England by the Scottish philosopher David Hume. Rousseau lived there for a short time before returning incognito to France in 1767. A year later, Rousseau married Thérèse Levasseur, who cared for him the remaining ten years of his life. During these years, he completed a series of autobiographical writings that were published shortly after his death. These included *Les rêveries du promeneur solitaire* (1782; *Reveries of a Solitary Walker*) and *Les confessions* (1782–1789; *The Confessions*). He died suddenly on July 2, 1778.

In the following excerpt from *The Social Contract,* Rousseau examines the question of the legitimacy of government. Beginning with the assumption that humans are born free, Rousseau tries to discover the process whereby this natural freedom can be legitimately displaced or alienated. In other words, he tries to discover the justification of the social order, an order in which one's natural liberty gives way to conventional liberty. Rousseau begins his search by ruling out one possible justification of the social order, justification by force. Contrary to the popular saying, he argues that might can never make right, that physical power cannot produce a moral or social obligation. During the course of the discussion, Rousseau also forcefully argues that slavery can never be justified. For while we may legitimately give up our natural freedom for conventional freedom, we cannot willingly become a slave.

Having ruled out force as the justification for the social order, Rousseau describes what he considers to be the legitimate origin of our obligations to society. He hypothesizes that a time arose when the natural freedom of individuals became inadequate to preserve them and that these individuals realized that only by forming an association with other individuals could they survive. Moreover, they recognized that only by means of what Rousseau calls a *social contract* could they create a common force for the protection of each individual without at the same time sacrificing their freedom. In entering into this contract, each individual gives up his natural freedom and all his natural rights to become part of a "moral collective body," a body in which natural liberty is displaced by civil liberty. This moral collective body will be ruled by what Rousseau calls the "general will," which is not determined by some external authority but by each person acting as citizen and sovereign. While Rousseau believes that the general will always reflects the common good, he recognizes that an individual, who is not acting in the capacity of citizen, may have a particular will that is contrary to the general will. When this happens, Rousseau says that the individual must be "forced to be free"; that is, he or she must be forced to assume the duties that are an essential component of the social freedom that is connected with citizenship. Rousseau concludes this selection by lavishly praising the virtues of citizenship and by claiming that the advantages of social freedom greatly outweigh those of natural freedom.

Questions for Reading

1. What does Rousseau mean when he says that "man is born free; and everywhere he is in chains"? What evidence, if any, does he give to support these claims?
2. Why does Rousseau reject force as the source of moral and political obligation?
3. What are the arguments in favor of slavery that Rousseau discusses? How does he go about refuting them?
4. What does Rousseau mean by the "social contract"? What circumstances led to the formulation of this contract?
5. How does Rousseau use the terms *citizen* and *subject*?
6. What exactly does Rousseau mean when he says that some people must be "forced to be free"? Why does he believe that this is true?

BOOK I

IN THIS TREATISE, I INTEND TO INQUIRE WHETHER or not there can be any sure and just rule for the administration of the civil order, given the way men are and the way laws might be. In the course of my inquiry, I will endeavor to unite right sanctions with what is prescribed by interest, in order that justice and utility may never be divorced.

I begin my task without proving the importance of the subject. If I am asked whether I am a prince or a legislator, in that I write on politics, I will answer that I am neither. Indeed, it is because I am neither a prince nor a legislator that I can be a political theorist. For if I were a prince or a legislator, I would not waste time theorizing about what needs to be done. I would do it, or else remain silent.

I was born a citizen of a free state, and am thus a member of its sovereign body. For this reason, I believe that, however feeble the influence of my voice is on public affairs, the right of voting on them makes it my duty to study them. And whenever I reflect upon governments, I am happy to find that my inquiries always furnish me with new reasons for admiring the government of my own country.

I: Subject of the First Book

Man is born free, and yet we see him everywhere in chains. People who believe that they are the masters of others are less free than those whom they would enslave. How did it happen that some people have come to govern others? I do not know. What can justify such a state of affairs? That is a question I think I can answer.

If I considered only force and the effects derived from it, I would have to say the following: "As long as a people is compelled to obey, and does so obey, it does well. However, as soon as it can get rid of its yoke, and does so get rid of it, it does still better. For it uses the same right to regain its liberty as was used to take away its liberty. Thus, either it is justified in regaining its liberty, or else there was no justification for those who took it away in the first place." But the

social order is a sacred right that is the basis of all other rights. Nevertheless, this right does not come from nature; it must therefore be founded on conventions. However, before discussing that point, I must first prove what I have just asserted.

II: The First Societies

The most ancient of all societies—indeed the only society that is natural—is the family. Yet, even here the children remain attached to the father only as long as they need his protection. As soon as this need ceases, the natural bond is dissolved. The children, being then released from the obedience they owe to the father, and the father, being then released from the care he owes to his children, return equally to independence. If the father and children remain together, they do so as the result of a voluntary rather than a natural union. At this point, the family itself is maintained only by convention.

This common liberty results from the nature of man. His first law is that of self-preservation; his first cares are the ones that he owes to himself. And as soon as he reaches the age of reason, he is the sole judge of the proper means of preserving himself, thus becoming his own master.

The family may then be viewed as the first model of a political society. The ruler corresponds to the father; the people correspond to the children. And being all born free and equal, they alienate their liberty only when it is advantageous for them to do so. The only difference between the two is that in the family the father's love for his children repays him for the care he takes of them, while in the state the pleasure of commanding replaces this love, which the ruler cannot feel for his people.

Grotius denies that all human power is established for the benefit of those who are governed, and he uses the example of slavery as evidence of this. But his usual method of reasoning is to establish right by fact. It would be possible to employ a more logical method. However, one cannot find a method more favorable to tyrants.

This is the editor's revised version of a selection from Jean-Jacques Rousseau, The Social Contract, *translated by G. D. H. Cole, P.D., and reprinted by Prometheus Books, 1988.*

According to Grotius, one cannot be certain whether the human race belongs to a hundred men, or whether these hundred men belong to the human race. However, throughout his book, he seems to incline to the former alternative, which is also the view of Hobbes. On this view, the human species is divided into herds of cattle, with each herd having its own ruler who keeps guard over his herd so that he can devour it.

As a shepherd is naturally superior to his flock, so are the shepherds of men, i.e. the rulers, naturally superior to the people under them. According to Philo, this was the manner in which the Emperor Caligula reasoned, concluding that either kings were gods or that men were beasts.

The reasoning of Caligula agrees with that of Hobbes and Grotius. However, before any of them, Aristotle had already said that men are not equal by nature, but that some men are born for slavery while others are born for dominion.

Aristotle was right; but he mistook the effect for the cause. Nothing can be more certain than that every man who is born in slavery is born for slavery. Slaves are so debased by their chains that they even lose the desire of escaping from them; they love their servitude, as the comrades of Ulysses loved their brutish condition. If then there are men who are slaves by nature, it is only because they have been enslaved against nature. Force made the first slaves, and slavery, by debasing its victims, perpetuated their bondage. . . .

III: The Right of the Strongest

The strongest person is never strong enough to be always the master, unless he is able to transform strength into right and obedience into duty. In this way the right of the strongest—which is usually taken ironically—is established as a fundamental principle. But are we never to have an explanation of the phrase, "the right of the strongest"? Force is a physical power and I fail to see what moral effect it can have. To yield to force is an act of necessity, not of will—at most, it is an act of prudence. In what sense, then, can it be a duty to yield to force?

Suppose for a moment that this so-called "right of the strongest" exists. I maintain that the sole result is a mass of inexplicable nonsense. If force creates right, then the effect changes with the cause. For every force that is greater than the first succeeds to its right; and as soon as it is possible to disobey with impunity, disobedience is legitimate. If the strongest is always in the right, then the only thing that matters is to act so as to become the strongest. But what kind of right is it that perishes when force fails? If we are compelled to obey by force, there is no need to obey because of duty. Thus when the force ceases, our obligation ceases as well. Clearly, then, the word *right* adds nothing to force, and, in this context, it is merely an empty term.

People say that we should obey the powers that be. If by this they mean that we should yield to force, it is a good precept. However, it is superfluous, for it can never be violated. I will admit that all power comes from God, but so does all sickness. Does this mean that we should never call a doctor? If a robber surprises me at the edge of a forest, I may be forced to surrender my purse. However, if I am in a position to escape, am I still obligated by conscience to give him my purse? For it is certainly the case that the pistol he holds is also a power. Let us grant, therefore, that force does not create right, and that we are obligated to obey only legitimate powers. In that case, we must return to my original question.

IV: Slavery

Since no man has any natural authority over his fellow men, and since force does not create any right to authority, we must conclude that conventions form the basis of all legitimate authority among men.

After assuming that an individual can alienate his liberty and make himself the slave of a master, Grotius asks why a whole people could not do the same and make itself subject to a king? While there are several ambiguous words in this claim that need explaining, let us focus on the word *alienate*. To alienate is to give or to sell. Now, a man who becomes the slave of another does not give himself; he sells himself, at least for his subsistence. But for what would a people sell itself? A king is so far from furnishing his subjects with their subsistence that he gets his subsistence only from them. . . . Do subjects then give their persons on condition that the king takes their goods also? I fail to see what they have left to preserve.

It will be said that the despot assures his subjects civil tranquillity. This may be granted. But what do they gain if the wars caused by his ambition, as well as his insatiable greed and the vexations of his ministers, bring about more harm than their own discord would ever have done? What do they gain, if the very tranquillity they enjoy is one of their miseries? Tranquillity is found also in dungeons. But is that enough to make them desirable places in which to live? The Greeks imprisoned in the cave of the Cyclops lived there very tranquilly while they were waiting their turn to be devoured.

To say that a man would freely become the slave of another is to say something absurd and inconceivable. Such an act would be null and illegitimate, from the mere fact that he who does it would be out of his mind. To say the same of a whole people would be to suppose a people of madmen; and madness creates no right.

Even if each individual could alienate himself, he could not alienate his children. For, being born men and free, their liberty belongs to them; and only they have the right to dispose of it. Before they reach the age of reason, their father can, in their name, lay down conditions for their preservation and well being; but he cannot give them irrevocably and without conditions. For such a gift is contrary to the ends of nature, and exceeds the rights of paternity. In order to legitimize an arbitrary government, it would therefore be necessary that the people in every generation be at liberty to accept or reject it. But if this were the case, the government would be no longer arbitrary.

To renounce liberty is to renounce being a man, that is, it would amount to surrendering all human rights and duties. No compensation would ever be adequate to justify such a sacrifice. Indeed, such a renunciation is incompatible with human nature, for to remove all liberty from one's will is to remove all morality from one's acts. Finally, it is an empty and contradictory convention that sets up, on the one side, absolute authority, and, on the other side, unlimited obedience. Is it not clear that we can be under no obligation to a person from whom we have the right to exact everything? Is not the absence of equivalence or exchange by itself sufficient to nullify the act? For what right can my slave have against me, when all that he has belongs to me? In such a case, his right is my right, and this right of mine against myself is utter nonsense.

Grotius and others derive from war another origin for the so-called right of slavery. They hold that the victor has the right to kill the vanquished, and that the latter can buy back his life at the price of his liberty. Moreover, they claim that this convention is even more legitimate because it is to the advantage of both parties.

But it is clear that this supposed right to kill the vanquished is by no means deducible from the state of war. For while they are living in their primitive independence, men have no mutual relations stable enough to constitute either the state of peace or the state of war, and thus cannot be natural enemies. War results from a relation between things, and not from personal relations between individuals. However, since the state of war cannot arise out of simple personal relations, but only out of real relations, private war, or war of man with man, can exist neither in the state of nature, where there is no constant property, nor in the social state, where everything is under the authority of the laws. . . .

War then is a relation, not between man and man, but between State and State. Because of this, individuals are enemies only accidentally, not as men or even as citizens, but as soldiers, that is, as defenders of their country. Finally, each State can have for enemies only other States, and not men; for there can be no real relation between things so different in nature.

Furthermore, this principle is in conformity with the established rules of all times and is the constant practice of all civilized peoples. . . . Since the object of the war is the destruction of the hostile State, the other side has a right to kill a State's defenders while they are bearing arms. But as soon as they lay them down and surrender, they cease to be enemies or instruments of the enemy, and become once more merely men, whose life no one has any right to take.

Sometimes it is possible to kill the State without killing a single one of its members; and war gives no right that is not necessary to the gaining of its object. These principles are not those of Grotius; neither are they based on the authority of poets. Rather, they are derived from the nature of reality and are based on reason.

The right of conquest has no foundation other than the right of the strongest. If war does not give the conqueror the right to massacre the conquered peoples, then the right to enslave them cannot be based upon a right that does not exist. No one has a right to kill an enemy when he cannot make him a slave, and the right to enslave him cannot therefore be derived from the right to kill him. It is accordingly an unfair exchange to make him buy his life, over which the victor holds no right, at the price of his liberty. Is it not clear that there is a **vicious circle** in founding the right of life and death on the right of slavery, and the right of slavery on the right of life and death?

Even if we assume this terrible right of massacring everybody, I maintain that a slave made in war, or a conquered people, is under no obligation to a master. Such a slave would only obey the master as along as he is compelled to do so. By requiring his service in exchange for his life, the victor has not done him a favor; instead of killing him without profit, he has in effect killed him usefully. Indeed, the conqueror is so far from acquiring over the vanquished any authority other than that of force that the state of war continues to subsist between them. Their relation results from this state of war, and is thus based on the rights of war. For this reason, no peace treaty can exist between them. While one might say that a convention has been made between them, it is a convention that, rather than destroying the state of war, presupposes its continuance.

So, from whatever angle we examine the question, the right of slavery is null and void. It is not only illegitimate; it is absurd and meaningless as well. The terms *slave* and *right* contradict each other and are mutually exclusive. Whether speaking to a man or to a people, it would always be foolish for someone to say: "I make a convention with you wholly at your expense and wholly to my advantage.

I will keep it as long as I like, and you will also keep it as long as I like."

V: That We Must Always Go Back to a First Convention

Even if I granted all that I have been refuting, the friends of despotism would be no better off. There will always be a great difference between subduing a multitude and ruling a society. If one man successively enslaves a number of scattered individuals, I would still see nothing but a master and his slaves, no matter how large the number is. I would certainly not see a people and its ruler. While this relation may be called an aggregation, it could never be called an association, for there is as yet neither public good nor body politic. The man in question, even if he has enslaved half the world, is still only an individual; his interest, apart from that of others, is still purely private interest. If this same man were to die, his empire, after him, remains scattered and without unity, as an oak falls and dissolves into a heap of ashes when the fire has consumed it.

A people, says Grotius, can give itself to a king. According to Grotius, then, a people already exists prior to giving itself. The gift is a civil act, and thus implies public deliberation. Before examining the act by which a people gives itself to a king, it would be better to examine the act by which it has become a people. For this act, being necessarily prior to the other, is the true foundation of society.

In fact, if there were no prior convention, where would be the obligation on the minority (unless the election were unanimous) to submit to the choice of the majority? How could a hundred men who wish for a master have the right to vote on behalf of ten who do not? The law of majority voting is itself something established by convention; it presupposes unanimity, at least on one occasion.

VI: The Social Contract

I will suppose that in the state of nature men have reached the point at which the strength of individuals no longer suffices to preserve them from the obstacles that stand in the way of their continued existence. At this point, that primitive condition can no longer subsist; and the human race would perish unless it changed its manner of existence. But, since men cannot create new forces—being able only to unite and direct existing ones—they cannot preserve themselves except by forming an aggregation of forces that is strong enough to overcome the resistance. This aggregation must be brought into play by means of a single motive power, a motive power that makes it possible for the forces to act in concert.

This sum of forces can arise only where several persons come together. However, since the force and liberty of each man are the chief instruments of his self-preservation, how can he pledge them to others without harming his own interests and neglecting the care he owes to himself? This difficulty, as it relates to my present subject, may be stated in the following terms:

"The problem is to find a form of association that will defend and protect the person and goods of each associate with the whole common force, a form of association in which each, while uniting himself with all, may still obey himself alone, remaining as free as before." This is the fundamental problem of which the *Social Contract* provides the solution.

The articles of this contract are so definitively fixed by the nature of the act that the slightest modification would make them null and void. For this reason, these articles are the same everywhere, and they are tacitly admitted and recognized everywhere, although perhaps they have never been formally set forth. They remain in effect until the social contract is violated, in which case each man regains his original rights and resumes his natural liberty, while losing the conventional liberty for which he renounced it.

These articles, properly understood, may be reduced to one—the total alienation of each associate, together with all his rights, to the whole community. In such a case, since each associate gives up himself entirely, the conditions are the same for everyone; and, this being so, no one has any interest in making these conditions burdensome to others.

Moreover, since the alienation is without reserve, the union is as perfect as it can be and no associate has any further claim to anything. For if the individuals retained certain rights not shared by all, as there would be no common superior to decide between them and the public, on these points each person would be his own judge, and would ask to be so on all. The state of nature would thus continue, and the association would necessarily become inoperative or tyrannical.

Finally, in giving himself to all, each man gives himself to no one in particular. And as there is no associate over whom he does not acquire the same right that he yields to others over himself, he gains an equivalent for everything he loses, as well as an increase of force for the preservation of what he has.

If, therefore, we eliminate everything from the social contract that is not essential, we find that it can be reduced to the following terms:

"Each of us places in common his person and all his power under the absolute direction of the general will; and, as a unified body, we all receive each member as an indivisible part of the whole."

In place of the individual personality of each contracting party, this act of association creates at once a moral and collective body composed of as many members as the assembly contains voters, a body that receives from this act its unity, its common identity, its life, and its will. This public person that is formed from the union of all other persons formerly took the name of *city;* now it is known as a *Republic* or *body politic.* Its members call it *State* when it is passive, *Sovereign* when it is active, and *Power* when it is compared with others like itself. Those who are associated in it take collectively the name of *people.* They are called *citizens,* insofar as they share in the sovereign power, and *subjects,* insofar as they are governed by the laws of the State. But these terms are often confused and used interchangeably. It suffices if one knows how to distinguish them when they are being used with precision.

VII: The Sovereign

This formula shows us that the act of association comprises a reciprocal undertaking between the public and the individuals. In making a contract with himself, as it were, each individual is bound in a double capacity; as a member of the Sovereign he is bound to the individuals, and as a member of the State he is bound to the Sovereign. Because of this, the maxim of civil right which states that no one is bound by undertakings made to himself does not apply in this case. For there is a great difference between incurring an obligation to yourself and incurring one to a collective body of which you form a part.

It must also be noted here that this public deliberation, which can bind all the subjects to the Sovereign because of the two different capacities in which each of them may be regarded, cannot, for the opposite reason, bind the Sovereign to itself. Consequently, it is against the nature of the body politic for the Sovereign to impose on itself a law that it cannot infringe. Being able to regard itself in only one capacity, it is in the position of an individual who makes a contract with himself. This makes it clear that there neither is nor can be any kind of fundamental law binding on the body of the people — not even the social contract itself. This does not mean that the body politic cannot enter into undertakings with others, provided that the contract is not infringed by these undertakings. Indeed, in relation to what is external to it, the body politic becomes a simple being, an individual.

However, the body politic or the Sovereign, which derives its existence wholly from the sanctity of the contract, can never bind itself, even to an outsider, to do anything derogatory to the original act. For example, it can never agree to alienate any part of itself or to submit to another Sovereign. To violate the contract by which it exists would amount to self-annihilation; and that which is itself nothing can create nothing. . . .

Furthermore, the Sovereign, being formed wholly of the individuals who compose it, neither has nor can have any interest contrary to theirs. For this reason, the sovereign power need give no guarantee to its subjects, because it is impossible for the body to wish to hurt all its members. We shall also see later on that it cannot harm any particular individual. The Sovereign, solely by virtue of what it is, is always what it should be.

This, however, is not the case with the relation of the subjects to the Sovereign, which, despite the common interest, would have no way of guaranteeing that the subjects would fulfil their obligations unless it found means to assure itself of their fidelity. In fact, each individual, as a man, may have a particular will contrary or dissimilar to the general will that he has as a citizen. His particular interest may dictate to him something quite different from what is dictated by the common interest. His absolute and naturally independent existence may make him regard what he owes to the common cause as a gratuitous contribution, the loss of which would do less harm to others than would the payment be burdensome to himself. And, regarding the moral person that constitutes the State as a fictitious being, because it is not a man, he may wish to enjoy the rights of citizenship without being ready to fulfill the duties of a subject. The continuance of such an injustice would surely prove to be the undoing of the body politic.

In order then to prevent the social contract from becoming an empty formula, it will tacitly include the article, which alone can give force to the rest, that whoever refuses to obey the general will must be compelled to do so by the whole body. This in fact means simply that he will be forced to be free; for this is the condition which, by giving each citizen to his country, secures him against all personal dependence. In this lies the key to the working of the political machine. This alone legitimizes civil undertakings, which, without it, would be absurd, tyrannical, and liable to the most frightful abuses.

VIII: *The Civil State*

Passing from the state of nature to the civil state produces a very remarkable change in man. Justice is substituted for instinct in his actions, giving them the morality they had formerly lacked. Only then, when the voice of duty takes the place of physical impulses and appetites, does man, who had thus far acted solely from self-interest, find that he is forced to act on different principles and to consult his reason before listening to his inclinations. Although in this state he deprives himself of some advantages derived from nature, he gains others in return that far surpass what he has given up. Indeed, his faculties are so stimulated and developed, his ideas are so broadened, his feelings are so ennobled, and his whole soul is so uplifted that he would continually bless this happy moment, if he did not sometimes sink below the state he had left by abusing his new condition. For it was this happy moment that made him an intelligent being and a man, instead of a stupid and unimaginative animal.

To further illustrate this, let us state the advantages and disadvantages of his new situation in terms that can easily be compared. By the social contract man loses his natural liberty and an unlimited right to everything he tries to get and succeeds in getting; but he gains civil liberty and the proprietorship of all he possesses. If we are to accurately weigh one of these against the other, we must clearly distinguish natural liberty, which is limited only by the strength of the individual, from civil liberty, which is limited by the general will. We must also distinguish possession, which is merely the effect of force or the right of the first occupier, from property, which is founded on a positive title.

Beyond all this, we might add moral liberty to what man acquires in the civil state, while noting that it is moral liberty that alone makes man truly master of himself. For the mere impulse of appetite is slavery, while obedience to a law that we prescribe to ourselves is liberty. But I have already said too much on this topic, and the philosophical meaning of the word *liberty* is not my present subject.

Questions for Thought

1. Rousseau says, "Man is born free; and everywhere he is in chains." Do you think that these claims are true today? Defend your answer.
2. Can you think of any cases in which the statement "might makes right" could be true? If so, how would you try to convince Rousseau that this is indeed the case?
3. Can you think of other arguments that have been, or might be, used to justify slavery? How would you respond to such arguments?
4. How does Rousseau's concept of the social contract compare with or differ from the implied contract that Socrates describes in Plato's *Crito*?
5. Would you categorize yourself as a citizen of the state in which you live? If so, what does it mean to you to be a citizen?
6. Do you agree with Rousseau that some people must be "forced to be free"? Why or why not?

The Declaration of Independence   3

THOMAS JEFFERSON

Thomas Jefferson (1743–1826), the best-known representative of enlightenment thinking in the United States, was born in Albemarle County, Virginia. Jefferson's father, who died in 1757, was a surveyor who left his son with a sizable inheritance. After childhood studies in local grammar and classical schools, Jefferson entered the College of William and Mary in 1760 and graduated two years later. He then studied law with George Wythe of the Virginia bar for five years before being admitted to the bar in 1767. Two years later, Jefferson took a seat in the Virginia House of Burgesses, and his political career began. He quickly became a leading spokesperson for the radical element in colonial politics that opposed British rule in the colonies. In addition to being the principal author of the Declaration of Independence (1776), Jefferson authored two earlier essays that opposed British rule, *A Summary View of the Rights of British America* (1774) and *Declaration of the Causes and Necessity for Taking Up Arms* (1775).

In 1776, Jefferson returned to Virginia to work for reform in his home state. He sought to fashion laws to prevent the accumulation of property in the hands of the few, arguing that no society can be just in which some people live in poverty while others live in luxury. He also proposed a system of universal public education and fought for a statute guaranteeing religious freedom to all Virginians. Although Jefferson served as governor of Virginia from 1779 to 1781, he was unable to win passage of these far-reaching reforms during his tenure in office. His statute on religious freedom was, however, finally enacted in 1786, and it became a landmark document in the political ideal of the separation of church and state.

After a two-year retirement from politics, during which Jefferson cared for his fatally ill wife and worked on his only book, he returned to public service during the latter part of 1782 as a member of the Virginia delegation to the Continental Congress. During the next few years, he helped write the Northwest Ordinance, served as the U.S. minister to France, and became secretary of state in George Washington's first cabinet. He was elected vice president in 1797 and became the third president of the United States four years later. After serving two terms as president, Jefferson retired to his country estate, Monticello, in 1809. While best known for his political accomplishments, Jefferson was a Renaissance man. He knew six languages in addition to English, was conversant in mathematics and the natural sciences, conducted a large number of experiments in scientific farming, designed his house and tomb, and carried on a lively correspondence with many of the outstanding thinkers of his day. He was also the principal architect of the University of Virginia, an accomplishment of which he was particularly proud. Jefferson died on July 4, 1826, the fiftieth anniversary of the signing of the Declaration of Independence.

In his Declaration of Independence, which is one of the best-known political documents from the period of the American Revolution, Jefferson attempts to justify the colonies' separation from Great Britain. He begins his argument by stating several important philosophical principles. First, he claims that all men are created equal and that they have certain "unalienable" natural rights, such as life, liberty, and the pursuit of happiness. Second, he says that the purpose of government is to protect these rights and that the legitimacy of government is derived from "the consent of the governed." Third, he argues that when a government no longer protects these natural rights, the governed have the right to alter or abolish that government and to replace it with any new form of government that they believe will be more effective in securing their natural rights.

Having stated these principles, Jefferson goes on to list many instances in which he believed George III, the king of Great Britain, had violated the natural rights of the colonists. Among these, Jefferson says that the king failed to approve needed laws and interfered with and dissolved legislative bodies. He restricted immigration, obstructed the judicial system, and sent a multitude of government officials and a standing army to harass the colonists. He limited trade and imposed taxes without the consent of those taxed. He waged war against the colonists and encouraged "the merciless Indian Savages" to do so as well. In a statement that seems to summarize many of these alleged abuses, Jefferson says that the king "plundered our seas, ravaged our Coasts, burnt our towns, and destroyed the lives of our people." Interestingly, Jefferson's list of grievances against the king originally included the following condemnation of slavery: "He has waged cruel war against human nature itself, violating its most sacred rights of life and liberty in the persons of a distant people who never offended him, captivating and carrying them into slavery in another hemisphere, or to incur miserable death in their transportation thither." In his autobiography, Jefferson says that this clause was omitted because of objections from the representatives of South Carolina and Georgia, "who had never attempted to restrain the importation of slaves, and who, on the contrary, still wished to continue it." Jefferson adds that this clause was unsettling to northern representatives as well, for "though their people had very few slaves themselves, yet they had been pretty considerable carriers of them to others." He concludes by claiming that these tyrannical acts of the king are sufficient justification for breaking political ties with Great Britain.

Questions for Reading

1. What do you think Jefferson meant when he said that "all men are created equal"?
2. What are the three "unalienable" rights listed by Jefferson? What privileges does each of these rights entail?
3. What, according to Jefferson, is the principal purpose of government?
4. Under what circumstances does Jefferson think a government can be abolished?
5. What are the principal charges that Jefferson leveled against the king of Great Britain? Why does he believe that the king's actions justified revolution?

WHEN IN THE COURSE OF HUMAN EVENTS IT becomes necessary for one people to dissolve the political bonds which have connected them with another, and to assume among the powers of the earth, the separate and equal station to which the Laws of Nature and of Nature's God entitle them, a decent respect to the opinions of mankind requires that they should declare the causes which impel them to the separation.

We hold these truths to be self-evident, that all men are created equal, that they are endowed by their Creator with certain unalienable Rights, that among these are Life, Liberty and the pursuit of Happiness.—That to secure these rights, Governments are instituted among Men, deriving their just powers from the consent of the governed.—That whenever any Form of Government becomes destructive of these ends, it is the Right of the People to alter or to abolish it, and to institute new Government, laying its foundation on such principles, and organizing its powers in such form, as to them shall seem most likely to effect their Safety and Happiness. Prudence, indeed, will dictate that Governments long established should not be changed for light and transient causes; and accordingly all experience hath shewn, that mankind are more disposed to suffer, while evils are sufferable, than to right themselves by abolishing the forms to which they are accustomed. But when a long train of abuses and usurpations, pursuing invariably the same Object, evinces a design to reduce them under absolute Despotism, it is their right, it is their duty, to throw off such Government, and to provide new Guards for their future security.—Such has been the patient sufferance of these Colonies; and such is now the necessity which constrains them to alter their former Systems of Government. The history of the present King of Great Britain is a history of repeated injuries and usurpations, all having in direct object the establishment of an absolute Tyranny over these States. To prove this, let Facts be submitted to a candid world.

He has refused his Assent to Laws, the most wholesome and necessary for the public good.

He has forbidden his Governors to pass Laws of immediate and pressing importance, unless suspended in their operation till his Assent should be obtained; and when so suspended, he has utterly neglected to attend to them.

He has refused to pass other Laws for the accommodation of large districts of people, unless those people would relinquish the right of Representation in the Legislature, a right inestimable to them and formidable to tyrants only.

He has called together legislative bodies at places unusual, uncomfortable, and distant from the depository of their public Records, for the sole purpose of fatiguing them into compliance with his measures.

He has dissolved Representative Houses repeatedly, for opposing with manly firmness his invasions on the rights of the people.

He has refused for a long time, after such dissolutions, to cause others to be elected; whereby the Legislative powers, incapable of Annihilation, have returned to the People at large for their exercise; the State remaining in the mean time exposed to all the dangers of invasion from without, and convulsions within.

He has endeavoured to prevent the population of these States; for that purpose obstructing the Laws for Naturalization of Foreigners; refusing to pass others to encourage their migrations hither, and raising the conditions of new Appropriations of Lands.

He has obstructed the Administration of Justice, by refusing his Assent to Laws for establishing Judiciary powers.

He has made Judges dependent on his Will alone, for the tenure of their offices, and the amount and payment of their salaries.

He has erected a multitude of New Offices, and sent hither swarms of Officers to harass our people, and eat out their substance.

He has kept among us, in times of peace, Standing Armies without the Consent of our legislatures.

He has affected to render the Military independent of and superior to the Civil power.

He has combined with others to subject us to a jurisdiction foreign to our constitution, and unacknowledged by our laws; giving his Assent to their Acts of pretended Legislation:

For quartering large bodies of armed troops among us:

For protecting them, by a mock Trial, from punishment for any Murders which they should commit on the Inhabitants of these States:

For cutting off our Trade with all parts of the world:

For imposing Taxes on us without our Consent:

For depriving us in many cases, of the benefits of Trial by Jury:

For transporting us beyond Seas to be tried for pretended offences:

For abolishing the free System of English Laws in a neighbouring Province, establishing therein an Arbitrary government, and enlarging its Boundaries so as to render it at once an example and fit instrument for introducing the same absolute rule into these Colonies:

For taking away our Charters, abolishing our most valuable Laws, and altering fundamentally the Forms of our Governments:

For suspending our own Legislatures, and declaring themselves invested with power to legislate for us in all cases whatsoever.

He has abdicated Government here, by declaring us out of his Protection and waging War against us.

He has plundered our seas, ravaged our Coasts, burnt our towns, and destroyed the lives of our people.

He is at this time transporting large Armies of foreign Mercenaries to complete the works of death, desolation and tyranny, already begun with circumstances of cruelty and perfidy scarcely paralleled in the most barbarous ages, and totally unworthy the Head of a civilized nation.

He has constrained our fellow Citizens taken Captive on the high Seas to bear Arms against their Country, to become the executioners of their friends and Brethren, or to fall themselves by their Hands.

He has excited domestic insurrections amongst us, and has endeavoured to bring on the inhabitants of our frontiers; the merciless Indian Savages, whose known rule of warfare, is an undistinguished destruction of all ages, sexes and conditions.

In every stage of these Oppressions We have Petitioned for Redress in the most humble terms:

Our repeated Petitions have been answered only by repeated injury. A Prince, whose character is thus marked by every act which may define a Tyrant, is unfit to be the ruler of a free people.

Nor have we been wanting in attentions to our British brethren. We have warned them from time to time of attempts by their legislature to extend an unwarrantable jurisdiction over us. We have reminded them of the circumstances of our emigration and settlement here. We have appealed to their native justice and magnanimity, and we have conjured them by the ties of our common kindred to disavow these usurpations, which would inevitably interrupt our connections and correspondence. They too have been deaf to the voice of justice and of consanguinity. We must, therefore, acquiesce in the necessity, which denounces our Separation, and hold them, as we hold the rest of mankind, Enemies in War, in Peace Friends.

We, therefore, the Representatives of the United States of America, in General Congress, Assembled, appealing to the Supreme Judge of the world for the rectitude of our intentions, do, in the Name, and by Authority of the good People of these Colonies solemnly publish and declare, That these United Colonies are, and of Right ought to be Free and Independent States; that they are Absolved from all Allegiance to the British Crown, and that all political connection between them and the State of Great Britain, is and ought to be totally dissolved; and that as Free and Independent States, they have full Power to levy War, conclude Peace, contract Alliances, establish Commerce, and to do all other Acts and Things which Independent States may of right do.

And for the support of this Declaration, with a firm reliance on the protection of divine Providence, we mutually pledge to each other our Lives, our Fortunes and our sacred Honor.

Questions for Thought

1. Do you agree with Jefferson that "all men are created equal"? If so, do you think this statement includes women as well as men? Do you think Jefferson intended this statement to include women?
2. What do you think is the principal purpose of government? How do your views compare with or differ from the views of Jefferson on this point?
3. In what ways are Jefferson's views on the origin and legitimacy of government similar to the views of Rousseau? Can you find any differences between their views?
4. Under what conditions, if any, do you think a government ought to be abolished?
5. Do you think the charges leveled against the king of Great Britain were sufficient justification for dissolving political ties with Great Britain? How do you think the king might have responded to some of these charges?
6. What do you make of Jefferson's deletion of the clause concerning slavery? How do you think Rousseau would have responded to this deletion?

4   The Racial Contract

CHARLES MILLS

Charles Mills (b. 1951), a Jamaican-American philosopher who currently teaches at the University of Illinois at Chicago, was born in England of Jamaican parents. During the first year of his life, his parents returned to Jamaica, and Mills grew up there. He received a B.S. in physics from the University of the West Indies in 1971 and an M.A. (1976) and Ph.D. (1985) in philosophy, both from the University of Toronto. His principal research interests are in radical and oppositional political theory, particularly concerning issues of class, gender, and race.

After receiving his degree in physics, Mills worked as a physics lecturer at the College of Arts, Science and Technology in Kingston, Jamaica for two years before moving to Toronto to pursue his studies in philosophy. Upon completing his M.A., he went back to Kingston to teach physics at Campion College for a year before returning to Toronto to work on his doctorate. He obtained his first professorship of philosophy at the University of Oklahoma in 1987, where he taught for three years before moving to his present position at the University of Illinois at Chicago.

Over the years Mills has been a prolific writer and presenter. He has published over fifty essays in a wide variety of journals and books, and he has done presentations in Canada, Venezuela, Mexico, England, South Africa, the United States, and throughout the Caribbean. He has also authored three books: *The Racial Contract* (1997); *Blackness Visible: Essays on Philosophy and Race* (1998); and *From Class to Race: Essays in White Marxism and Black Radicalism* (2003). He is currently working on two projects: a collection of Caribbean essays and a joint book with Carole Pateman, tentatively titled *Contract and Domination*. More information about Mills's life and work can be found in the essay "Red Shift: Politically Embodied/Embodied Politics," which he wrote for the anthology *The Philosophical I: Personal Reflections on Life in Philosophy* (2002).

In the following excerpts from *The Racial Contract*, Mills examines the social contract theory of government that lies at the heart of Western political theory in light of actual historical events that occurred in Europe and the United States. While he notes that the contractarian theory as formulated by Rousseau, Kant, Locke, Hobbes, and others is associated with the ideals of equality and justice for all, those ideals have not in fact been realized in Western societies. On the contrary, Western societies have not only condoned and supported discrimination within their own borders, but most of them have also engaged in imperialist colonial policies that have discriminated against indigenous populations in areas beyond their borders that they have conquered and controlled.

This disparity between the stated ideals of **contractarianism** and historical reality leads Mills to suggest that the social contract has been largely displaced by a different kind of contract, a Racial Contract, whereby certain peoples (whites) have entered into an implicit agreement to treat other peoples (nonwhites) as subordinate and unequal. Like the social contract, the Racial Contract has been used to found or justify a certain political system—in this case the political system of white supremacy. Moreover, in addition to the political implications associated with this system, the Racial Contract, like the social contract, has moral and epistemological implications as well. In other words, both the social contract and the Racial Contract not only establish certain political institutions and practices, but they also provide the grounds or justification for certain moral principles and knowledge claims about the world. Of course, as Mills points out, the political, moral, and epistemological implications of the Racial Contract are incompatible with those universal ideals espoused by the proponents of the social contract theory of the origin of government.

One of Mills's main reasons for introducing the notion of the Racial Contract is to provide a conceptual framework for discussing the inequalities that we find in the world around us. He argues at the beginning of the selection that philosophers have been largely silent about the system of white supremacy, preferring instead to discuss abstract theories that have little basis in reality. And he further suggests at the end of the selection that this silence reveals "at best, a disturbing **provincialism** and an ahistoricity profoundly at odds with the radically foundational questioning on which philosophy prides itself and, at worst, a complicity with the terms of the Racial Contract itself."

Questions for Reading

1. Why, according to Mills, has the concept of white supremacy not been discussed in undergraduate philosophy courses?
2. How does Mills describe the social contract? What are the main differences between the social contract and the Racial Contract?
3. What is a nonideal or "naturalized" contract? How is this concept used by Rousseau?
4. What, according to Mills, are the political implications of the Racial Contract? What are the moral implications?
5. What does Mills mean when he says that the Racial Contract "prescribes for its signatories an inverted **epistemology**"? Why does he believe that this is so?
6. What evidence does Mills give for his claim that "the modern world was expressly created as a *racially hierarchical* polity, globally dominated by Europeans"?
7. How does Mills describe the world in which we currently live? Does he believe that the Racial Contract still holds?

INTRODUCTION

White supremacy is the unnamed political system that has made the modern world what it is today. You will not find this term in introductory, or even advanced, texts in political theory. A standard undergraduate philosophy course will . . . introduce you to notions of **aristocracy, democracy,** absolutism, liberalism, representative government, **socialism,** welfare capitalism, and **libertarianism.** But though it covers more than two thousand years of Western political thought and runs the ostensible gamut of political systems, there will be no mention of the basic political system that has shaped the world for the past several hundred years. And this omission is not accidental. Rather, it reflects the fact that standard textbooks and courses have for the most part been written and designed by whites, who take their racial privilege so much for granted that they do not even see it as *political*, as a form of domination. Ironically, the most important political system of recent global history—the system of domination by which white people have historically ruled over and, in certain important ways, continue to rule over nonwhite people—is not seen as a political system at all. It is just taken for granted; it is the background against which other systems, which we *are* to see as political, are highlighted. . . .

What is needed is a global theoretical framework for situating discussions of race and white racism, and thereby challenging the assumptions of white political philosophy, which would correspond to feminist theorists' articulation of the centrality of gender, **patriarchy,** and sexism to traditional moral and political theory. What is needed, in other words, is a recognition that racism (or, as I will argue, global white supremacy) is *itself* a political system, a particular power structure of formal or informal rule, socioeconomic privilege, and norms for the differential distribution of material wealth and opportunities, benefits and burdens, rights and duties. The notion of the Racial Contract is, I suggest, one possible way of making this connection with mainstream theory, since it uses the vocabulary and apparatus already developed for **contractarianism** to map this unacknowledged system. Contract talk is, after all, the political **lingua franca** of our times.

We all understand the idea of a "contract," an agreement between two or more people to do something. The "social contract" just extends this idea. If we think of human beings as starting off in a "state of nature," it suggests that they then *decide* to establish civil society and a government. What we have, then, is a theory that founds government on the popular consent of individuals taken as equals.

But the peculiar contract to which I am referring, though based on the social contract tradition that has been central to Western political theory, is not a contract between everybody ("we the people"), but between just the people who count, the people who really are people ("we the white people"). So it is a Racial Contract.

The social contract, whether in its original or in its contemporary version, constitutes a powerful set of lenses for looking at society and the government. But in its obfuscation of the ugly realities of group power and domination, it is, if unsupplemented, a profoundly misleading account of the way the modern world actually is and came to be. The "Racial Contract" as a theory—I use quotation marks to indicate when I am talking about the theory of the Racial Contract, as against the Racial Contract itself—will explain that the Racial Contract is real

and that apparent racist violations of the terms of the social contract in fact *uphold* the terms of the Racial Contract.

The "Racial Contract," then, is intended as a conceptual bridge between two areas now largely segregated from each other: on the one hand, the world of mainstream (i.e., white) ethics and political philosophy, preoccupied with discussions of justice and rights in the abstract; on the other hand, the world of Native American, African American, and Third and **Fourth World** political thought, historically focused on issues of conquest, imperialism, colonialism, white settlement, land rights, race and racism, slavery, jim crow, reparations, apartheid, cultural authenticity, national identity, *indigenismo,* Afrocentrism, etc. These issues hardly appear in mainstream political philosophy, but they have been central to the political struggles of the majority of the world's population. Their absence from what is considered serious philosophy is a reflection not of their lack of seriousness but of the color of the vast majority of Western academic philosophers (and perhaps *their* lack of seriousness).

The great virtue of traditional social contract theory was that it provided seemingly straightforward answers both to factual questions about the origins and workings of society and government and to normative questions about the justification of socioeconomic structures and political institutions. Moreover, the "contract" was very versatile, depending on how different theorists viewed the state of nature, human motivation, the rights and liberties people gave up or retained, the particular details of the agreement, and the resulting character of the government. In the modern **Rawlsian** version of the contract, this flexibility continues to be illustrated, since Rawls dispenses with the historical claims of classic contractarianism and focuses instead on the justification of the basic structure of society. From its 1650–1800 heyday as a grand quasi-anthropological account of the origins and development of society and the state, the contract has now become just a normative tool, a conceptual device to elicit our intuitions about justice.

But my usage is different. The "Racial Contract" I employ is in a sense more in keeping with the spirit of the classic contractarians—Hobbes, Locke, Rousseau, and Kant. I use it not merely normatively, to generate judgments about social justice and injustice, but descriptively, to *explain* the actual genesis of the society and the state, the way society is structured, the way the government functions, and people's moral psychology. The most famous case in which the contract is used to explain a manifestly *non*ideal society—what would be termed in current philosophical jargon a "naturalized" account—is Rousseau's *Discourse on Inequality* (1755). Rousseau argues that technological development in the state of nature brings into existence a nascent society of growing divisions in wealth between rich and poor, which are then consolidated and made permanent by a deceitful "social contract." Whereas the ideal contract explains how a just society would be formed, ruled by a moral government, and regulated by a defensible moral code, this nonideal/naturalized contract explains how an unjust, *exploitative* society, ruled by an *oppressive* government and regulated by an *immoral* code, comes into existence. If the ideal contract is to be endorsed and emulated, this nonideal/naturalized contract is to be demystified and condemned. So the point of analyzing the nonideal contract is not to ratify it but to use it to explain and expose the inequities of the actual nonideal polity and to help us to see through the theories and moral justifications offered in defense of them. It gives us a kind of X-ray vision into the real internal logic of the sociopolitical system. Thus it does normative work for us not through its own values, which are detestable, but by enabling us to understand the polity's actual history and how these values and concepts have functioned to rationalize oppression, so as to reform them. . . .

My aim here is to adopt a nonideal contract as a rhetorical **trope** and theoretical method for understanding the inner logic of *racial* domination and how it structures the polities of the West and elsewhere. The ideal "social contract" has been a central concept of Western political theory for understanding and evaluating the social world. And concepts are crucial to cognition: cognitive scientists point out that they help us to categorize, learn, remember, infer, explain, problem-solve, generalize, analogize. Correspondingly, the *lack* of

appropriate concepts can hinder learning, interfere with memory, block inferences, obstruct explanation, and perpetuate problems. I am suggesting, then, that as a central concept the notion of a Racial Contract might be more revealing of the real character of the world we are living in, and the corresponding historical deficiencies of its normative theories and practices, than the raceless notions currently dominant in political theory. Both at the primary level of an alternative conceptualization of the facts and at the secondary (reflexive) level of a critical analysis of the orthodox theories themselves, the "Racial Contract" enables us to engage with mainstream Western political theory to bring in race. Insofar as contractarianism is thought of as a useful way to do political philosophy, to theorize about how the polity was created and what values should guide our prescriptions for making it more just, it is obviously crucial to understand what the original and continuing "contract" actually was and is, so that we can correct for it in constructing the ideal "contract.". . .

OVERVIEW

I will start with an overview of the Racial Contract, highlighting its differences from, as well as its similarities to, the classical and contemporary social contract. The Racial Contract is political, moral, and **epistemological;** the Racial Contract is real; and economically, in determining who gets what, the Racial Contract is an exploitation contract.

The Racial Contract is political, moral, and epistemological.

The "social contract" is actually several contracts in one. Contemporary contractarians usually distinguish, to begin with, between the *political* contract and the *moral* contract, before going on to make (subsidiary) distinctions within both. I contend, however, that the orthodox social contract also tacitly presupposes an "epistemological" contract, and that for the Racial Contract it is crucial to make this explicit. . . .

Now the Racial Contract—and the "Racial Contract" as a theory, that is, the distanced, critical examination of the Racial Contract—follows the classical model in being both sociopolitical and moral. It explains how society was created or crucially transformed, how the individuals in that society were reconstituted, how the state was established, and how a particular moral code and a certain moral psychology were brought into existence. (As I have emphasized, the "Racial Contract" seeks to account for the way things are and how they came to be that way—the descriptive—*as well as* the way they should be—the normative—since indeed one of its complaints about white political philosophy is precisely its otherworldliness, its ignoring of basic political realities.) But the Racial Contract, as we will see, is also epistemological, prescribing norms for cognition to which its signatories must adhere. A preliminary characterization would run something like this:

The Racial Contract is that set of formal or informal agreements or meta-agreements (higher-level contracts *about* contracts, which set the limits of the contracts' validity) between the members of one subset of humans, henceforth designated by (shifting) "racial" (phenotypical/genealogical/cultural) criteria C_1, C_2, C_3 . . . as "white," and coextensive (making due allowance for gender differentiation) with the class of full persons, to categorize the remaining subset of humans as "nonwhite" and of a different and inferior moral status, subpersons, so that they have a subordinate civil standing in the white or white-ruled polities the whites either already inhabit or establish. . . . The general purpose of the Contract is always the differential privileging of the whites as a group with respect to the nonwhites as a group, the exploitation of their bodies, land, and resources, and the denial of equal socioeconomic opportunities to them. All whites are *beneficiaries* of the Contract, though some whites are not *signatories* to it.

It will be obvious, therefore, that the Racial Contract is not a contract to which the nonwhite subset of humans can be a genuinely consenting party (though, depending again on the circumstances, it may sometimes be politic to pretend that this is the case). Rather, it is a contract between those categorized as white *over* the nonwhites, who are thus the objects rather than the subjects of the agreement.

The logic of the classic social contract, political, moral, and epistemological, then undergoes a corresponding refraction with shifts, accordingly, in the key terms and principles.

Politically, the contract to establish society and the government, thereby transforming abstract raceless "men" from denizens of the state of nature into social creatures who are politically obligated to a neutral state, becomes the founding of a *racial polity*, whether white settler states (where preexisting populations already are or can be made sparse) or what are sometimes called "sojourner colonies," the establishment of a white presence and colonial rule over existing societies (which are somewhat more populous, or whose inhabitants are more resistant to being made sparse). In addition, the colonizing mother country is also changed by its relation to these new polities, so that its own citizens are altered.

In the social contract, the crucial human metamorphosis is from "natural" man to "civil/political" man, from the resident of the state of nature to the citizen of the created society. This change can be more or less extreme, depending on the theorist involved. For Rousseau it is a dramatic transformation, by which animal-like creatures of appetite and instinct become citizens bound by justice and self-prescribed laws. For Hobbes it is a somewhat more laid-back affair by which people who look out primarily for themselves learn to constrain their self-interest for their own good. But in all cases the original "state of nature" supposedly indicates the condition of *all* men, and the social metamorphosis affects them all in the same way.

In the Racial Contract, by contrast, the crucial metamorphosis is the preliminary conceptual partitioning and corresponding transformation of human populations into "white" and "nonwhite" men. The role played by the "state of nature" then becomes radically different. In the white settler state, its role is not primarily to demarcate the (temporarily) prepolitical state of "all" men (who are really *white* men), but rather the permanently prepolitical state or, perhaps better, nonpolitical state (insofar as "pre-" suggests eventual internal movement toward) of *nonwhite* men. The *establishment* of society thus implies the denial that a society already existed; the creation of society *requires* the intervention of white men, who are thereby positioned as *already* sociopolitical beings. White men who are (definitionally) already part of society encounter nonwhites who are not, who are "savage" residents of a state of nature characterized in terms of wilderness, jungle, wasteland. These the white men bring partially into society as subordinate citizens or exclude on reservations or deny the existence of or exterminate. In the colonial case, admittedly preexisting but (for one reason or another) deficient societies (decadent, stagnant, corrupt) are taken over and run for the "benefit" of the nonwhite natives, who are deemed childlike, incapable of self-rule and handling their own affairs, and thus appropriately wards of the state. Here the natives are usually characterized as "barbarians" rather than "savages," their state of nature being somewhat farther away (though not, of course, as remote and lost in the past—if it ever existed in the first place—as the Europeans' state of nature). But in times of crisis the conceptual distance between the two, barbarian and savage, tends to shrink or collapse, for this technical distinction within the nonwhite population is vastly less important than the *central* distinction between whites and nonwhites.

In both cases, then, though in different ways, the Racial Contract establishes a racial polity, a racial state, and a racial juridical system, where the status of whites and nonwhites is clearly demarcated, whether by law or custom. And the purpose of this state, by contrast with the neutral state of classic contractarianism, is, **inter alia**, specifically to maintain and reproduce this racial order, securing the privileges and advantages of the full white citizens and maintaining the subordination of nonwhites. Correspondingly, the "consent" expected of the white citizens is in part conceptualized as a consent, whether explicit or tacit, to the racial order, to white supremacy, what could be called Whiteness. To the extent that those phenotypically/genealogically/ culturally categorized as white fail to live up to the civic and political responsibilities of Whiteness, they are in dereliction of their duties as citizens. From the inception, then, race is in no way an "afterthought," a "deviation" from ostensibly raceless

Western ideals, but rather a central shaping constituent of those ideals.

In the social contract tradition, there are two main possible relations between the moral contract and the political contract. On the first view, the moral contract represents *preexisting* objectivist morality (theological or secular) and thus constrains the terms of the political contract. This is the view found in Locke and Kant. In other words, there is an objective moral code in the state of nature itself, even if there are no policemen and judges to enforce it. So any society, government, and legal system that are established should be based on that moral code. On the second view, the political contract *creates* morality as a conventionalist set of rules. So there is no independent objective moral criterion for judging one moral code to be superior to another or for indicting a society's established morality as unjust. On this conception, which is famously attributed to Hobbes, morality is just a set of rules for expediting the rational pursuit and coordination of our own interests without conflict with those other people who are doing the same thing.

The Racial Contract can accommodate both versions, but as it is the former version (the contract as described in Locke and Kant) rather than the latter version (the contract as described in Hobbes) which represents the mainstream of the contract tradition, I focus on that one. Here, the good polity is taken to rest on a preexisting moral foundation. Obviously, this is a far more attractive conception of a political system than Hobbes's view. The ideal of an objectively just polis to which we should aspire in our political activism goes back in the Western tradition all the way to Plato. In the medieval Christian worldview which continued to influence contractarianism well into the modern period, there is a "natural law" immanent in the structure of the universe which is supposed to direct us morally in striving for this ideal. (For the later, secular versions of contractarianism, the idea would simply be that people have rights and duties even in the state of nature because of their nature as human beings.) So it is wrong to steal, rape, kill in the state of nature even if there are no human laws written down saying it is wrong. These moral principles must constrain the human laws that are made and the civil rights that are assigned once the polity is established. In part, then, the political contract simply *codifies* a morality that already exists, writing it down and filling in the details, so we don't have to rely on a divinely implanted moral sense, or conscience, whose perceptions may on occasion be distorted by self-interest. What is right and wrong, just and unjust, in society will largely be determined by what is right and wrong, just and unjust, in the state of nature.

The character of this objective moral foundation is therefore obviously crucial. For the mainstream of the contractarian tradition, it is the *freedom and equality of all men in the state of nature*. As Locke writes in the *Second Treatise*, "To understand Political Power right, and derive it from its Original, we must consider what State all Men are naturally in, and that is, a *State of perfect Freedom* to order their Actions. . . . A *State* also *of Equality*, wherein all the Power and Jurisdiction is reciprocal, no one having more than another."[1] For Kant, similarly, it is our equal moral personhood.[2] Contractarianism is (supposedly) committed to moral egalitarianism, the moral equality of all men, the notion that the interests of all men matter equally and all men must have equal rights. Thus, contractarianism is also committed to a principled and foundational opposition to the traditionalist hierarchical ideology of the old feudal order, the ideology of inherent ascribed status and natural subordination. It is this language of equality which echoes in the American and French Revolutions, the Declaration of Independence, and the Declaration of the Rights of Man. And it is this moral egalitarianism that must be retained in the allocation of rights and liberties in civil society. When in a modern Western society people insist on their rights and freedoms and express their outrage at not being treated equally, it is to these classic ideas that, whether they know it or not, they are appealing.

But . . . the color-coded morality of the Racial Contract restricts the possession of this natural freedom and equality to *white* men. By virtue of their complete nonrecognition, or at best inadequate, myopic recognition, of the duties of natural law, nonwhites are appropriately relegated to a lower rung on the moral ladder (the Great Chain of Being). They are designated as born *unfree* and unequal. A partitioned social **ontology** is therefore created, a universe divided between persons and racial subpersons, *Untermenschen,* who may variously be black, red, brown, yellow—slaves, aborigines, colonial populations—but who are collectively appropriately known as "subject races." And these subpersons—niggers, injuns, chinks, wogs, greasers, blackfellows, kaffirs, coolies, abos, dinks, googoos, gooks—are biologically destined never to penetrate the normative rights ceiling established for them below white persons. Henceforth, then, whether openly admitted or not, it is taken for granted that the grand ethical theories propounded in the development of Western moral and political thought are of restricted scope, explicitly or implicitly intended by their proponents to be restricted to persons, whites. The terms of the Racial Contract set the parameters for white morality as a whole, so that competing Lockean and Kantian contractarian theories of natural rights and duties, or later anticontractarian theories such as nineteenth-century utilitarianism, are all limited by its stipulations.

Finally, the Racial Contract requires its own peculiar moral and empirical epistemology, its norms and procedures for determining what counts as moral and factual knowledge of the world. In the standard accounts of contractarianism it is not usual to speak of there being an "epistemological" contract, but there *is* an epistemology associated with contractarianism, in the form of natural law. This provides us with a moral compass, whether in the traditional version of Locke—the light of reason implanted in us by God so we can discern objective right and wrong—or in the revisionist version of Hobbes—the ability to assess the objectively optimal prudential course of action and what it requires of us for self-interested cooperation with others. So through our natural faculties we come to know reality in both its factual and its valuational aspects, the way things objectively are and what is objectively good or bad about them. I suggest we can think of this as an idealized consensus about cognitive norms and, in this respect, an agreement or "contract" of sorts. There is an understanding about what counts as a correct, objective interpretation of the world, and for agreeing to this view, one is ("contractually") granted full cognitive standing in the polity, the official epistemic community.

But for the Racial Contract things are necessarily more complicated. The requirements of "objective" cognition, factual and moral, in a racial polity are in a sense more demanding in that officially sanctioned reality is divergent from actual reality. So here, it could be said, one has an agreement to misinterpret the world. One has to learn to see the world wrongly, but with the assurance that this set of mistaken perceptions will be validated by white epistemic authority, whether religious or secular.

Thus in effect, on matters related to race, the Racial Contract prescribes for its signatories an inverted epistemology, an epistemology of ignorance, a particular pattern of localized and global cognitive dysfunctions (which are psychologically and socially functional), producing the ironic outcome that whites will in general be unable to understand the world they themselves have made. Part of what it means to be constructed as "white" (the metamorphosis of the sociopolitical contract), part of what it requires to achieve Whiteness, successfully to become a white person (one imagines a ceremony with certificates attending the successful rite of passage: "Congratulations, you're now an official white person!"), is a cognitive model that precludes self-transparency and genuine understanding of social realities. To a significant extent, then, white signatories will live in an invented delusional world, a racial fantasyland, a "consensual hallucination," to quote William Gibson's famous characterization of cyberspace, though this particular hallucination is located in real space. There will be white mythologies, invented Orients, invented Africas, invented Americas, with a correspondingly fabricated population, countries that never were, inhabited by people who never were—Calibans and Tontos, Man Fridays and Sambos—but who attain a virtual reality through their existence in travelers' tales, folk myth, popular and highbrow fiction, colonial reports, scholarly theory, Hollywood cinema, living in the white imagination and determinedly imposed on their alarmed real-life counterparts. One could say then, as a general rule, that

white misunderstanding, misrepresentation, evasion, and self-deception on matters related to race are among the most pervasive mental phenomena of the past few hundred years, a cognitive and moral economy psychically required for conquest, colonization, and enslavement. And these phenomena are in no way *accidental,* but *prescribed* by the terms of the Racial Contract, which requires a certain schedule of structured blindnesses and opacities in order to establish and maintain the white polity. . . .

It would be a fundamental error, then . . . to see racism as anomalous, a mysterious deviation from European Enlightenment **humanism.** Rather, it needs to be realized that, in keeping with the Roman precedent, *European humanism usually meant that only Europeans were human.* European moral and political theory, like European thought in general, developed within the framework of the Racial Contract and, as a rule, took it for granted. As Edward Said points out in *Culture and Imperialism,* we must not see culture as "antiseptically quarantined from its worldly affiliations." But this occupational blindness has in fact infected most "professional humanists" (and certainly most philosophers), so that "as a result [they are] unable to make the connection between the prolonged and sordid cruelty of practices such as slavery, colonialist and racial oppression, and imperial subjection on the one hand, and the poetry, fiction, philosophy of the society that engages in these practices on the other."[3] By the nineteenth century, conventional white opinion casually assumed the uncontroversial validity of a hierarchy of "higher" and "lower," "master" and "subject" races, for whom, it is obvious, different rules must apply.

The modern world was thus expressly created as a *racially hierarchical* polity, globally dominated by Europeans. A 1969 *Foreign Affairs* article worth rereading today reminds us that as late as the 1940s the world "was still by and large a Western white-dominated world. The long-established patterns of white power and nonwhite non-power were still the generally accepted order of things. All the accompanying assumptions and mythologies about race and color were still mostly taken for granted. . . . [W]hite supremacy was a generally assumed and accepted state of affairs in the United States as well as in Europe's empires."[4] But statements of such frankness are rare or nonexistent in mainstream white opinion today, which generally seeks to rewrite the past so as to deny or minimize the obvious fact of global white domination.

Yet the United States itself, of course, is a white settler state on territory expropriated from its aboriginal inhabitants through a combination of military force, disease, and a "century of dishonor" of broken treaties.[5] The expropriation involved literal genocide (a word now unfortunately devalued by hyperbolic overuse) of a kind that some recent revisionist historians have argued needs to be seen as comparable to the Third Reich's. Washington, Father of the Nation, was, understandably, known somewhat differently to the Senecas as "Town Destroyer." In the Declaration of Independence, Jefferson characterized Native Americans as "merciless Indian Savages," and in the Constitution, blacks, of course, appear only obliquely, through the famous "60 percent solution." Thus, as Richard Drinnon concludes: "The Framers manifestly established a government under which non-Europeans were not men created equal—in the white polity . . . they were nonpeoples."[6] Though on a smaller scale and not always so ruthlessly (or, in the case of New Zealand, because of more successful indigenous resistance), what are standardly classified as the other white settler states—for example, Canada, Australia, New Zealand, Rhodesia, and South Africa—were all founded on similar policies: the extermination, displacement, and/or herding onto reservations of the aboriginal population. Pierre van den Berghe has coined the illuminating phrase "*Herrenvolk* democracies" to describe these polities, which captures perfectly the dichotomization of the Racial Contract. Their subsequent evolution has been somewhat different, but defenders of South Africa's system of apartheid often argued that U.S. criticism was hypocritical in light of its own history of jim crow, especially since de facto segregation remains sufficiently entrenched that even today, forty years after *Brown v. Board of Education,* two American sociologists can title their study *American Apartheid.*[7] The racist record of preliberation Rhodesia (now Zimbabwe)

and South Africa is well known; not so familiar may be the fact that the United States, Canada, and Australia all maintained "white" immigration policies until a few decades ago, and native peoples in all three countries suffer high poverty, infant mortality, and suicide rates.

Elsewhere, in Latin America, Asia, and Africa, large parts of the world were colonized, that is, formally brought under the rule of one or another of the European powers (or, later, the United States): the early Spanish and Portuguese empires in the Americas, the Philippines, and south Asia; the jealous competition from Britain, France, and Holland; the British conquest of India; the French expansion into Algeria and Indochina; the Dutch advance into Indonesia; the Opium Wars against China; the late nineteenth-century "scramble for Africa"; the U.S. war against Spain, seizure of Cuba, Puerto Rico, and the Philippines, and annexation of Hawaii. The pace of change this century has been so dramatic that it is easy to forget that less than a hundred years ago, in 1914, "Europe held a grand total of roughly 85 percent of the earth as colonies, protectorates, dependencies, dominions, and commonwealths. No other associated set of colonies in history was as large, none so totally dominated, none so unequal in power to the Western metropolis."[8]   One could say that the Racial Contract creates a transnational white polity, a virtual community of people linked by their citizenship in Europe at home and abroad (Europe proper, the colonial greater Europe, and the "fragments" of Euro-America, Euro-Australia, etc.), and constituted in opposition to their indigenous subjects. . . .

We live, then, in a world built on the Racial Contract. That we do is simultaneously quite obvious if you think about it (the dates and details of colonial conquest, the constitutions of these states and their exclusionary juridical mechanisms, the histories of official racist ideologies, the battles against slavery and colonialism, the formal and informal structures of discrimination, are all within recent historical memory and, of course, massively documented in other disciplines) and nonobvious, since most whites *don't* think about it or don't think about it as the outcome of a history of political oppression but rather as just "the way things are.". . .

The legacy of this world is, of course, still with us today, in the economic, political, and cultural domination of the planet by Europeans and their descendants. The fact that this racial structure, clearly political in character, and the struggle against it, equally so, have *not* for the most part been deemed appropriate subject matter for mainstream Anglo-American political philosophy and the fact that the very concepts hegemonic in the discipline are refractory to an understanding of these realities, reveal at best, a disturbing **provincialism** and an ahistoricity profoundly at odds with the radically foundational questioning on which philosophy prides itself and, at worst, a complicity with the terms of the Racial Contract itself.

NOTES

1. John Locke, *Two Treatises of Government*, p. 269.
2. Immanuel Kant, *Metaphysics of Morals*, pp. 230–232.
3. Edward W. Said, *Culture and Imperialism* (New York: Knopf, 1993), pp. xiv, xiii.
4. Harold R. Isaacs, "Color in World Affairs," *Foreign Affairs 47* (1969): 235, 246.
5. Helen Jackson, *A Century of Dishonor: A Sketch of the United States Government's Dealings with Some of the Indian Tribes* (1881; rpt. New York: Indian Head Books, 1993).
6. Richard Drinnon, *Facing West: The Metaphysics of Indian Hating and Empire-Building* (New York: Meridian, 1980), p. 102.
7. Douglas S. Massey and Nancy A. Denton, *American Apartheid: Segregation and the Making of the Underclass* (Cambridge: Harvard University Press, 1993).
8. Said, *Culture*, p. 8.

Questions for Thought

1. Do you agree with Mills that "white supremacy is the unnamed political system that has made the modern world what it is today"? Defend your answer.
2. Can you think of any differences between the social contract and the Racial Contract that Mills does not discuss?
3. In what ways, if any, do you think you have either benefited from or been harmed by the Racial Contract?
4. Which of your beliefs, if any, do you think have resulted from the "inverted epistemology" prescribed by the Racial Contract?
5. Do you agree with Mills's claim that "the modern world was thus expressly created as a racially hierarchical polity, globally dominated by Europeans"? Why or why not?
6. Do you believe that something like the Racial Contract governs the society in which you live? Defend your answer.

The Communist Manifesto 5

KARL MARX AND FRIEDRICH ENGELS

Karl Marx (1818–1883), the most famous proponent of revolutionary **socialism,** was born in the Rhineland city of Trier. Although many of Marx's maternal and paternal relatives were rabbis, his father, who was a lawyer, was forced to convert to Lutheranism in order to maintain his legal practice. After attending secondary school in Trier, Marx enrolled in the faculty of law at the University of Bonn in 1835. The following year, he transferred to the University of Berlin, where he studied law, history, philosophy, English, and Italian. He received his doctorate in 1841, having written his dissertation on the ancient Greek philosophers Democritus and **Epicurus.**

At the University of Berlin, Marx associated with a group of young thinkers who used the ideas of the most influential recent German philosopher, **G. W. F. Hegel,** to critique the German political and religious establishment. Since the universities were under government control, Marx's political activities made it impossible for him to obtain a position as a university lecturer. Instead, he began writing for the *Rheinische Zeitung,* a liberal businessman's newspaper published in Cologne, of which he soon became editor. It was during his tenure as editor of this newspaper that Marx first met Friedrich Engels, who was to become his lifelong friend, collaborator, and benefactor.

In May 1843, the Prussian government suppressed the *Rheinische Zeitung,* and Marx resigned as editor. Later that year, Marx married Jenny von Westphalen, to whom he had been engaged for several years, and moved to Paris. During his stay in Paris, he studied economics, wrote articles for a socialist journal, began his collaboration with Engels, and first espoused **communism** in a series of writings known as the "Economic and Philosophical Manuscripts of 1844."

Shortly after completing these writings, Marx was expelled from Paris by the French government. He spent the next three years living in Brussels, where he continued his economic studies and became involved with the workingmen's movement. It was at the request of one of the groups in this movement, the League of the Just, that Marx and Engels began work on one of their best-known writings, *The Communist Manifesto,* which was published in 1848. When a series of democratic revolutions occurred in several European countries that same year, Marx was able to return to Paris and then to Cologne, where he renewed publication of a newspaper, the *Neue Rheinische Zeitung.* The democratic revolutions were short-lived, however, and Marx fled from Cologne to Paris in 1849. Later that year, he was once again expelled from Paris, and he spent the remainder of his life exiled in London.

During his years in London, many of which were spent in relative poverty, Marx continued his journalistic activities, his economic studies, and his activism in the workingmen's movement. He was an occasional contributor to Horace Greeley's *New York Daily Tribune;* he spent many hours in the British Museum doing research for his monumental work on economics, *Das Capital;* and he was a dominant force in the International Working Men's Association, which was founded in London in 1864. In addition to his many intellectual and political interests, Marx was reportedly a devoted father who loved to play with his many children. Greatly saddened by the death of his wife, Marx died two years later on March 14, 1883. In addition to *Das Capital,* Marx's writings include *The Poverty of Philosophy* (1847), the *Grundrisse* (written in 1857–1858; published in 1939–1941), *A Contribution to the Critique of Political Economy* (1859), and *The Civil War in France* (1871).

Friedrich Engels (1820–1895), the son of a wealthy conservative textile manufacturer, was born in Barmen in the German Rhineland. After attending Elberfeld secondary school, Engels became a clerk in his father's office. Although he never received a university degree, Engels read widely in many fields. He also attended lectures at the University of Berlin, where he became part of a group of young Hegelian radicals, "The Free."

In 1842, Engels moved to Manchester, England, to complete his business apprenticeship in the branch office of his father's firm. While serving as a business agent for the firm, Engels became active in the trade union movement in England and traveled to Cologne, where he first met Karl Marx. He also wrote his first book, *The Condition of the Working Class in England in 1844.* Engels left his business position in 1844 to return to Europe and work actively with Marx. They collaborated on *The Communist Manifesto* in Brussels; then Engels moved to Baden, Germany, to take part in the democratic revolution of 1848.

When the revolution failed a year later, he fled to England, where he eventually moved to Manchester and reentered his father's business. Engels' father died in 1860, and Engels became a partner in the firm. Four years later, he married Elizabeth Burns. In 1869, he sold his partnership in the firm and moved to London in order to work more closely with Marx.

Like Marx, Engels was very active in the International Working Men's Association, serving as secretary for Spain, Portugal, and Italy on the General Council. He was also a tireless editor of Marx's manuscripts, being responsible for editing and publishing the second and third volumes of Marx's *Das Capital*. Finally, Engels was a staunch defender of communism in his own writings. These included *Herr Eugen Dühring's Umwälzung der Wissenschaft* (1878; *Herr Eugen Dühring's Revolution in Science*), *Die Entwicklung des Sozialismus von der Utopie zur Wissenschaft* (1883; translated as *Socialism: Utopian and Scientific*), *Der Ursprung der Familie, des Privateigentums und des Staats* (1884; *The Origin of the Family, Private Property and the State*), and *Ludwig Feuerbach und der Ausgang der klassischen deutschen Philosophie* (1888; *Ludwig Feuerbach and the Outcome of Classical German Philosophy*).

In the following excerpt from *The Communist Manifesto*, Marx and Engels set forth the principles and goals of communism in order to defend it against its critics. In this defense, they take a radically different view of the purpose and origin of government than did either Rousseau or Jefferson. Rather than resulting from a social contract or from the consent of the governed, Marx and Engels say that government, like every other social institution, is produced by economic conditions, specifically by class struggles in which one class tries to dominate all other classes. In the context of this class struggle, the ruling ideas of each age, including those ideas about the legitimacy and purpose of government, are the ideas held by the ruling class. Since the ruling class of modern capitalist society is the *bourgeoisie*—that is, those who control capital—Marx and Engels believe that the ideas and interests of the bourgeoisie dominate modern society.

Although bourgeois ideas and institutions dominate current society, Marx and Engels point out that they did not always do so, nor will they always continue to do so. They argue that the bourgeoisie and the economic institutions that gave rise to it were produced through a long course of development, one in which other classes and institutions that had been dominant fell by the wayside. They also claim that the capitalist system of production, which assured the ascendancy of the bourgeoisie, contains the seeds of its own destruction. The most important of these seeds is the class antagonism that necessarily exists between the bourgeoisie and the other principal class that is created by the capitalist economic system, the *proletariat.* The proletariat, in contrast to the bourgeoisie, is the class of workers who do not own capital but who subsist by selling their labor for wages. In modern capitalist society, according to Marx and Engels, these workers are subjected to "naked, shameless, direct, brutal exploitation"; they are commodities whose subsistence is dependent on unstable market conditions over which they have no control, commodities for whom work has lost all charm.

Marx and Engels predict that the opposition between the bourgeoisie and the proletariat will gradually escalate. As capital is accumulated into fewer and fewer hands, the middle class standing between the bourgeoisie and the proletariat will grow smaller and smaller until society is composed basically of two classes. Once this occurs, proletarians will be able to discern their common exploitation more clearly, and they will become more and more united in their attempt to overthrow the capitalistic system that is the source of this exploitation. On the other hand, economic competition in its various forms will fragment the bourgeoisie into warring factions, divided in the marketplace as well as on the battlefield. When this process of the organizing of the proletariat and the disorganizing of the bourgeoisie reaches a certain critical point, the proletariat will forcibly overthrow the governments and social institutions of modern capitalism and replace them with the radical alternatives of communism. Among the changes that Marx and Engels envision are the abolition of bourgeois private property (although the ownership of social goods will not be abolished), the rejection of class culture, the elimination of the subjection of women and children (as well as the family structure on which this subjection is based), and the overcoming of exploitation between individuals as well as between countries. In addition, everyone in society will be equally obligated to work, and free public education will be provided for all children. In short, the result will be what Marx elsewhere refers to as a "classless society." Interestingly, near the end of the selection, Marx and Engels claim that this revolution will lessen, and eventually eliminate, the need for political power. Since they believe that political power is principally an organized means whereby one class dominates another class, in a classless society there will be no need for political power. Indeed, in place of government as we now know it, there will be "an association, in which the free development of each is the condition for the free development of all."

Questions for Reading

1. What do Marx and Engels mean when they say that "the history of all hitherto existing society is the history of class struggles"? What evidence do they provide in support of this claim?
2. What are the essential differences between the bourgeoisie and the proletariat?
3. Why do Marx and Engels believe that the proletariat will be the "gravediggers" of the bourgeoisie? Through what process will the bourgeoisie be overthrown?
4. What are some of the economic predictions that Marx and Engels make in this selection?
5. What exactly do Marx and Engels mean when they say that bourgeois private property must be abolished? Why do they call for the abolition of bourgeois private property?
6. What are Marx and Engels' principal criticisms of the bourgeois family structure? What do they say about bourgeois marriage and sexual life?

MANIFESTO OF THE COMMUNIST PARTY

A SPECTER IS HAUNTING EUROPE—THE SPECTER of communism. All the powers of old Europe have entered into a holy alliance to exorcise this specter. . . .

Where is the party in opposition that has not been decried as communistic by its opponents in power? Where is the Opposition that has not hurled back the branding reproach of communism, against the more advanced opposition parties, as well as against its reactionary adversaries?

Two things result from this fact:

I. Communism is already acknowledged by all European powers to be itself a power.

II. It is high time that Communists should openly, in the face of the whole world, publish their views, their aims, their tendencies, and thus meet this nursery tale of the specter of communism with a manifesto of the party itself. . . .

I: Bourgeoisie and Proletariat[1]

The history of all previously existing society[2] is the history of class struggles.

This is the editor's revised version of a selection from the English language translation of Karl Marx and Friedrich Engels, Manifesto of the Communist Party, *London, 1888. This translation was originally edited by Engels.*

Freeman and slave, patrician and plebeian, lord and serf, guildmaster[3] and journeyman, in a word, oppressor and oppressed, have stood in constant opposition to one another. They have carried on an uninterrupted fight—now hidden, now open—a fight that each time ended, either in a revolutionary reconstitution of society at large, or in the common ruin of the contending classes.

In the earlier epochs of history, we find almost everywhere a complicated arrangement of society into various orders, a manifold gradation of social rank. In ancient Rome we have patricians, knights, plebeians, and slaves; in the Middle Ages, we find feudal lords, vassals, guild-masters, journeymen, apprentices, and serfs. In almost all of these classes, we again find subordinate gradations.

The modern bourgeois society that has sprouted from the ruins of feudal society has not done away with class antagonisms. It has merely established new classes, new conditions of oppression, new forms of struggle in place of the old ones.

However, our epoch, the epoch of the bourgeoisie, possesses this distinctive feature: It has simplified the class antagonisms. Society as a whole is more and more splitting up into two great hostile camps, into two great classes directly confronting each other—bourgeoisie and proletariat.

From the serfs of the Middle Ages sprang the chartered burghers of the earliest towns. The first elements of the bourgeoisie were developed from these burgesses. The discovery of America, the rounding of the Cape, opened up fresh ground for the rising bourgeoisie. The East-Indian and Chinese markets, the colonization of America and trade with the colonies, the increase in the means of exchange and in commodities generally—all of this gave commerce, navigation, and industry an impulse never before known. This in turn spurred the rapid development of the revolutionary element in the tottering feudal society.

The feudal system of industry, in which industrial production was monopolized by closed guilds, now no longer sufficed for the growing wants of the new markets. The manufacturing system took its place. The guild-masters were pushed aside by the manufacturing middle class; division of labor between the different corporate guilds vanished in the face of division of labor in each single workshop.

Meantime the markets kept ever growing, the demand ever rising. Even manufacture[4] no longer sufficed. Thereupon, steam and machinery revolutionized industrial production. The place of manufacture was taken by the giant, modern industry, while the industrial middle class was displaced by industrial millionaires—the leaders of whole industrial armies, the modern bourgeois.

Modern industry has established the world market, for which the discovery of America paved the way. This market has given an immense development to commerce, to navigation, to communication by land. This development has, in its turn, reacted on the extension of industry. And as industry, commerce, navigation, and railways extended, the bourgeoisie developed proportionally, increasing its capital and pushing into the background every class that remained from the Middle Ages. We see, therefore, how the modern bourgeoisie is itself the product of a long course of development, of a series of revolutions in the modes of production and of exchange.

Each step in the development of the bourgeoisie was accompanied by a corresponding political advance of that class. An oppressed class under the sway of the feudal nobility, it became an armed and self-governing association in the medieval commune.[5] . . . Then, in the period of manufacture proper, the bourgeoisie served either the semifeudal or the absolute monarchy as a counterpoise against the nobility, and was, in fact, the cornerstone of the great monarchies in general. Now, since the establishment of modern industry and of the world market, the bourgeoisie has at last conquered for itself, in the modern representative state, exclusive political sway. The executive of the modern state is but a committee for managing the common affairs of the whole bourgeoisie.

The bourgeoisie has in fact played a most revolutionary role in history. Wherever it has got the upper hand, the bourgeoisie has put an end to all feudal, patriarchal, idyllic relations. It has pitilessly torn asunder the motley feudal ties that bound man to his "natural superiors," and has left no other bond between man and man than naked self-interest, than callous "cash payment." It has drowned the most heavenly ecstasies of religious fervor, of chivalrous enthusiasm, of philistine sentimentalism, in the icy water of egotistical calculation. It has resolved personal worth into exchange value; and in place of the numberless indefeasible chartered freedoms, it has set up that single, unconscionable freedom—Free Trade. In summary, for exploitation that was veiled by religious and political illusions, it has substituted naked, shameless, direct, brutal exploitation.

The bourgeoisie has stripped of its halo every occupation hitherto honored and revered. It has converted the physician, the lawyer, the priest, the poet, and the man of science, into its paid wage-laborers. The bourgeoisie has torn away from the family its sentimental veil, and has reduced the family relation to a mere money relation. . . . It has been the first to show what man's activity can bring about. It has accomplished wonders far surpassing Egyptian pyramids, Roman aqueducts, and Gothic cathedrals; it has conducted expeditions that put in the shade all former migrations of nations and crusades.

The bourgeoisie cannot exist without constantly revolutionizing the instruments of production, and thereby the relations of production, and with them the whole relations of society. Whereas conservation of the old modes of production in unaltered form was the first condition of existence for all earlier industrial classes, constant revolutionizing of production, uninterrupted disturbance of all social conditions, everlasting uncertainty and agitation characterize the bourgeois epoch, distinguishing it from all earlier ones. All fixed, fast-frozen relations, with their train of ancient and venerable prejudices and opinions, are swept away; all new-formed relations become antiquated before they can ossify. All that is solid melts into air, all that is holy is profaned, and man is at last compelled to soberly face his real conditions of life and his relations with his kind.

The need of a constantly expanding market for its products chases the bourgeoisie over the whole surface of the globe. It must nestle everywhere, settle everywhere, establish connections everywhere.

Through its exploitation of the world market the bourgeoisie has given a cosmopolitan character to production and consumption in every country. To the great chagrin of reactionaries, it has drawn from under the feet of industry the national ground on which it stood. All traditional national industries have been destroyed or are daily being destroyed.

They are dislodged by new industries, whose introduction becomes a life and death question for all civilized nations. These new industries no longer work up indigenous raw material, they draw raw material from the remotest zones; their products are consumed, not only at home, but in every quarter of the globe. In place of the old wants, satisfied by the production of the country, we find new wants that can only be satisfied by the products of distant lands. In place of the old local and national seclusion and self-sufficiency, we have intercourse in every direction, universal interdependence of nations. And this is true of intellectual, as well as of material, production. The intellectual creations of individual nations become common property. National one-sidedness and narrow-mindedness become more and more impossible, and from the numerous national and local literatures there arises a world literature.

The bourgeoisie, by the rapid improvement of all instruments of production, by the immensely facilitated means of communication, draws all nations, even the most barbarian, into civilization. The cheap prices of its commodities are the heavy artillery with which it batters down all Chinese walls, with which it forces the barbarians' intensely obstinate hatred of foreigners to capitulate. It compels all nations, on pain of extinction, to adopt the bourgeois mode of production; it compels them to introduce what it calls civilization into their midst, *i.e.,* to become bourgeois themselves. In a word, it creates a world after its own image.

The bourgeoisie has subjected the country to the rule of the towns. It has created enormous cities, has greatly increased the urban population as compared with the rural, and has thus rescued a considerable part of the population from the idiocy of rural life. Just as it has made the country dependent on the towns, so it has made less-developed countries dependent on more-developed ones, nations of peasants on nations of bourgeois, the East on the West.

More and more the bourgeoisie keeps doing away with the scattered state of the population, of the means of production, and of property. It has agglomerated population, centralized means of production, and has concentrated property in a few hands. The necessary consequence of this was political centralization. Independent, or but loosely connected provinces, with separate interests, laws, governments and systems of taxation, became lumped together into one nation, with one government, one code of laws, one national class interest, one frontier and one customs tariff.

During its rule of barely one hundred years, the bourgeoisie has created more massive and more colossal productive forces than have all preceding generations together. The subjection of nature's forces to man and machinery, the application of chemistry to industry and agriculture, the creation of steam-navigation, railways, and electric telegraphs, the clearing of whole continents for cultivation, the canalization of rivers. What earlier century had even a presentiment that such productive forces slumbered in the lap of social labor?

Thus, we see that the means of production and of exchange, which served as the foundation for the growth of the bourgeoisie, were generated in feudal society. At a certain stage in the development of these means of production and of exchange, the conditions under which feudal society produced and exchanged, the feudal organization of agriculture and manufacturing industry, in a word, the feudal relations of property, became no longer compatible with the already developed productive forces. Rather, they became so many fetters that had to be burst asunder, and they were burst asunder. Into their place stepped free competition, accompanied by a social and political constitution adapted to it, and by the economic and political sway of the bourgeois class.

Now a similar movement is going on before our own eyes. Modern bourgeois society . . . is a society that has conjured up such gigantic means of production and of exchange that it is like the sorcerer who is no longer able to control the powers of the nether world that he has called up by his spells. For many past decades the history of industry and commerce is but the history of the revolt of modern productive forces against modern conditions of production, against the property relations that are the conditions for the existence of the bourgeoisie and of its rule. It is enough to mention the commercial crises that, by their periodical return, put the existence of the entire bourgeois society on trial, each time more threateningly. . . . The productive forces at the disposal of society no longer tend to further the development of the conditions of bourgeois property. On the contrary, they have become too powerful for these conditions, by which they are fettered, and no sooner do they overcome these fetters than they bring disorder into the whole of bourgeois society, endangering the existence of bourgeois property. The conditions of bourgeois society are too narrow to comprise the wealth created by them. And how does the bourgeoisie get over these crises? On the one hand it does so by enforced destruction of a mass of productive forces; on the other hand, by the conquest of new markets, as well as the more thorough exploitation of the old ones. That is to say, it gets over these crises by paving the way for more extensive and more destructive crises, and by diminishing the means whereby crises are prevented. Thus, the weapons with which the bourgeoisie felled feudalism to the ground are now turned against the bourgeoisie itself.

But not only has the bourgeoisie forged the weapons that bring death to itself; it has also called into existence the men who are to wield those weapons—the modern working class—the proletarians.

In the same proportion as the bourgeoisie, *i.e.,* capital, is developed, so is the proletariat, the modern working class (a class of laborers, who live only so long as they find work, and who find work only so long as their labor increases capital) developed. These laborers, who must sell themselves piecemeal, are a commodity, like every other article of commerce. Consequently they are exposed to all the vicissitudes of competition, to all the fluctuations of the market.

Owing to the extensive use of machinery and to division of labor, the work of the proletarians has lost all individual character, and, consequently, all charm for the workman. He becomes an appendage of the machine, and it is only the most simple, most monotonous, and most easily acquired task, that is required of him. Hence, the cost of production of a workman is restricted, almost entirely, to the means of subsistence that he requires for his maintenance, and for the propagation of his race. But the price of a commodity, and therefore also of labor, is equal to its cost of production. In proportion, therefore, as the repulsiveness of the work increases, the wage decreases. Nay more, in the same proportion that the use of machinery and division of labor increases, the burden of toil also increases, whether by prolongation of the working hours, by increase of the amount of work exacted in a given time, or by increased speed of the machinery, etc.

Modern industry has converted the little workshop of the patriarchal master into the great factory of the industrial capitalist. Masses of laborers, crowded into the factory, are organized like soldiers. As privates of the industrial army they are placed under the command of a perfect hierarchy of officers and sergeants. Not only are they slaves of the bourgeois class, and of the bourgeois state; they are daily and hourly enslaved by the machine, by the overseer, and, above all, by the individual bourgeois manufacturer himself. The more openly this despotism proclaims gain to be its end and aim, the pettier, the more hateful and the more embittering it is. . . .

No sooner has the laborer received his wages in cash, for the moment escaping exploitation by the manufacturer, than he is set upon by the other portions of the bourgeoisie, the landlord, the shopkeeper, the pawnbroker, etc. The lower strata of the middle class—the small tradespeople, shopkeepers, and retired tradesmen generally, the handicraftsmen and peasants—sink gradually into the proletariat. This is partly because their diminutive capital does not suffice for the scale on which modern industry is carried on, and is thus swamped in the competition with the large capitalists, partly because their specialized skill is rendered worthless by new methods of production. Thus the proletariat is recruited from all classes of the population.

The proletariat goes through various stages of development. With its birth begins its struggle with the bourgeoisie. At first the contest is carried on by individual laborers, then by the workers of a factory, then by the operatives of one trade, in one locality, against the individual bourgeois who directly exploits them. They direct their attacks not against the bourgeois conditions of production, but against the instruments of production themselves. They destroy imported wares that compete with their labor, they smash machinery to pieces, they set factories ablaze, and they seek to restore by force the vanished status of the workman of the Middle Ages. At this stage the laborers still form an incoherent mass scattered over the whole country, and broken up by their mutual competition. If anywhere they unite to form more compact bodies, this is not yet the consequence of their own active union. Rather, it results from the union of the bourgeoisie, which class, in order to attain its own political ends, is compelled to set the whole proletariat in motion, and is moreover still able to do so for a time. At this stage, therefore, the proletarians do not fight their enemies, but the enemies of their enemies—the remnants of absolute monarchy, the landowners, the nonindustrial bourgeois, and the petty bourgeoisie. Thus the whole historical movement is concentrated in the hands of the bourgeoisie; every victory so obtained is a victory for the bourgeoisie.

But with the development of industry the proletariat not only increases in number, it becomes concentrated in greater masses, its strength grows, and it feels that strength more. The various interests and conditions of life within the ranks of the proletariat are more and more equalized, in proportion as machinery obliterates all distinctions of labor and nearly everywhere reduces wages to the same low level. The growing competition among the bourgeois and the resulting commercial crises make the wages of the workers ever more fluctuating. The unceasing improvement of machinery, ever more rapidly developing, makes their livelihood more and more precarious; the collisions between individual workmen and individual bourgeois take more and more the character of collisions between two classes. Thereupon the workers begin to form combinations (trade unions) against the bourgeoisie; they join together in order to keep up the rate of wages; they found permanent associations in order to make provision beforehand for these occasional revolts. Here and there the conflict breaks out into riots.

Now and then the workers are victorious, but only for a time. The real fruit of their battles lies, not in the immediate results, but in the ever expanding union of the workers. This union is furthered by the improved means of communication which are created by modern industry, and which place the workers of different localities in contact with one another. It was just this contact that was needed to centralize the numerous local struggles, all of the same character, into one national struggle between classes. But every class struggle is a political struggle. And that union, which took the burghers of the Middle Ages, with their miserable highways, centuries to attain, can be achieved by the modern proletarians, thanks to railways, in a few years.

This organization of the proletarians into a class, and consequently into a political party, is continually being upset again by the competition between the workers themselves. But it ever rises up again, stronger, firmer, mightier. It compels legislative recognition of particular interests of the workers, by taking advantage of the divisions among the bourgeoisie itself. . . .

Altogether, collisions between the classes of the old society further the course of development of the proletariat in many ways. The bourgeoisie finds itself involved in a constant battle. At first it battles the **aristocracy**, later on, those portions of the bourgeoisie itself whose interests have become antagonistic to the progress of industry, and at all times the bourgeoisie of foreign countries. In all these battles it sees itself compelled to appeal to the proletariat, to ask for its help, and thus, to drag it into the political arena. The bourgeoisie itself, therefore, supplies the proletariat with its own elements of political and general education. In other words, it furnishes the proletariat with weapons for fighting the bourgeoisie.

Further, as we have already seen, entire sections of the ruling classes are, by the advance of industry, propelled into the proletariat, or are at least threatened in their conditions of existence. These also supply the proletariat with fresh elements of enlightenment and progress.

Finally, in times when the class struggle nears the decisive hour, the process of dissolution going on within the ruling class—in fact within the whole range of old society—assumes such a violent, glaring character, that a small section of the ruling class cuts itself adrift. This section then joins the revolutionary class, the class that holds the future in its hands. Just as, therefore, at an earlier period, a section of the nobility went over to the bourgeoisie, so now a portion of the bourgeoisie goes over to the proletariat. This is especially true of a portion of the bourgeois ideologists, who have raised themselves to the level of comprehending theoretically the historical movement as a whole.

Of all the classes that stand face to face with the bourgeoisie today, the proletariat alone is a really revolutionary class. The other classes decay and finally disappear in the face of modern industry; the proletariat is its special and essential product. . . .

The social conditions of the old society no longer exist for the proletariat. The proletarian is without property; his relation to his wife and children has no longer anything in common with bourgeois family relations; modern industrial labor, modern subjection to capital, the same in England as in France, in America as in Germany, has stripped him of every trace of national character. Law, morality, and religion, are to him so many bourgeois prejudices, behind which lurk in ambush just as many bourgeois interests.

All the preceding classes that got the upper hand sought to fortify their already acquired status by subjecting society at large to their conditions of appropriation. Proletarians cannot become masters of the productive forces of society, except by abolishing their own previous mode of appropriation, and thereby also every other previous mode of appropriation. They have nothing of their own to secure and to fortify; their mission is to destroy all previous securities for, and insurances of, individual property. All previous historical movements were movements of minorities, or in the interest of minorities. The proletarian movement is the self-conscious, independent movement of the immense majority, in the interest of the immense majority. The proletariat, the lowest stratum of our present society, cannot stir, cannot raise itself up, without the whole superincumbent strata of official society being sprung into the air. . . .

Hitherto, every form of society has been based, as we have already seen, on the antagonism of oppressing and oppressed classes. But in order to oppress a class, certain conditions must be assured to it under which it can, at least, continue its slavish existence. The serf, in the period of serfdom, raised himself to membership in the commune, just as the petty bourgeois, under the yoke of feudal absolutism, managed to develop into a bourgeois. The modern laborer, on the contrary, instead of rising with the progress of industry, sinks deeper and deeper below the conditions of existence of his own class. He becomes a pauper, and pauperism develops more rapidly than population and wealth. And here it becomes evident that the bourgeoisie is unfit any longer to be the ruling class in society and to impose its conditions of existence upon society as an overriding law. It is unfit to rule because it is incompetent to assure an existence to its slave within his slavery, because it cannot help letting him sink into such a state, that it has to feed him, instead of being fed by him. Society can no longer live under this bourgeoisie; in other words, its existence is no longer compatible with society.

The essential condition for the existence and domination of the bourgeois class is the formation and augmentation of capital; the condition for capital is wage-labor. Wage-labor rests exclusively on competition between the laborers. The advance of industry, whose involuntary promoter is the bourgeoisie, replaces the isolation of the laborers, due to competition, by their revolutionary combination, due to association. The development of modern industry, therefore, cuts from under its feet the very foundation on which the bourgeoisie produces and appropriates products. What the bourgeoisie therefore produces, above all, are its own gravediggers. Its fall and the victory of the proletariat are equally inevitable.

II: *Proletarians and Communists*

. . . The immediate aim of the Communists is the same as that of all the other proletarian parties: Formation of the proletariat into a class, overthrow of bourgeois supremacy, conquest of political power by the proletariat. The theoretical conclusions of the Communists are in no way based on ideas or principles that have been invented, or discovered, by this or that would-be universal reformer. They merely express, in general terms, actual relations springing from an existing class struggle, from a historical movement going on under our very eyes. The abolition of existing property relations is not at all a distinctive feature of communism.

All property relations in the past have continually been subject to historical change consequent upon the change in historical conditions. The French Revolution, for example, abolished feudal property in favor of bourgeois property.

The distinguishing feature of communism is not the abolition of property generally, but the abolition of bourgeois property. But modern bourgeois private property is the final and most complete expression of the system of producing and appropriating products that is based on class antagonisms, on the exploitation of the many by the few. For this reason, the theory of the Communists may be summed up in the single sentence: Abolition of private property.

We Communists have been accused of desiring to abolish the right of personally acquiring property as the fruit of a man's own labor, which property is alleged to be the groundwork of all personal freedom, activity and independence. Hard-won, self-acquired, self-earned property! Do you mean the property of the petty artisan and of the small peasant, a form of property that preceded the bourgeois form? There is no need to abolish that; the development of industry has to a great extent already destroyed it, and is still destroying it daily.

Or do you mean modern bourgeois private property? But does wage-labor create any property for the laborer? Not one bit. It creates capital, *i.e.,* the kind of property that exploits wage-labor, that cannot increase except upon condition of begetting a new supply of wage-labor for fresh exploitation. Property, in its present form, is based on the antagonism of capital and wage-labor. Let us examine both sides of this antagonism.

To be a capitalist, is to have . . . a social *status* in production. Capital is a collective product, and only by the united action of many members, nay, in the last resort, only by the united action of all members of society, can it be set in motion. Capital is therefore not a personal power, but a social power. When, therefore, capital is converted into common property, into the property of all members of society, personal property is not thereby transformed into social property. It is only the social character of the property that is changed. It loses its class character.

Let us now take wage-labor. The average price of wage-labor is the minimum wage, *i.e.,* that quantum of the means of subsistence that is absolutely essential to keep the laborer in bare existence as a laborer. What, therefore, the wage-laborer appropriates by means of his labor merely suffices to prolong and reproduce a bare existence. We by no means intend to abolish this personal appropriation of the products of labor, an appropriation that is made for the maintenance and reproduction of human life, and that leaves no surplus wherewith to command the labor of others. All that we want to do away with is the miserable character of this appropriation, under which the laborer lives merely to increase capital, and is allowed to live only insofar as the interest of the ruling class requires it.

In bourgeois society, living labor is but a means to increase accumulated labor. In Communist society, accumulated labor is but a means to widen, to enrich, and to promote the existence of the laborer.

In bourgeois society, therefore, the past dominates the present; in Communist society, the present dominates the past. In bourgeois society capital is independent and has individuality, while the living person is dependent and has no individuality. And the bourgeois says that the abolition of this state of things is the abolition of individuality and freedom! And it is right to do so. For the abolition of bourgeois individuality, bourgeois independence, and bourgeois freedom is undoubtedly aimed at.

Under the present bourgeois conditions of production, freedom means free trade, free selling and buying. But if selling and buying disappears, free selling and buying disappears also. This talk about free selling and buying, and all the other "brave words" of our bourgeoisie about freedom in general, have a meaning, if any, only in contrast with restricted selling and buying, with the fettered traders of the Middle Ages. But such talk has no meaning when opposed to the Communist abolition of buying and selling, of the bourgeois conditions of production, and of the bourgeoisie itself.

You are horrified at our intending to do away with private property. But in your existing society, private property is already done away with for nine-tenths of the population; its existence for the few is solely due to its non-existence in the hands of those nine-tenths. You reproach us, therefore, with intending to do away with a form of property, the necessary condition for whose existence is the nonexistence of any property for the immense majority of society. In a word, you reproach us with intending to do away with your property. Precisely so, that is just what we intend.

From the moment when labor can no longer be converted into capital, money, or rent, into a social power capable of being monopolized, *i.e.,* from the moment when individual property can no longer be transformed into bourgeois property, into capital, from that moment, you say, individuality vanishes.

You must, therefore, confess that by "individual" you mean no other person than the bourgeois, than the middle-class owner of property. This person must, indeed, be swept out of the way and made impossible.

Communism deprives no man of the power to appropriate the products of society; all that it does is to deprive him of the power to subjugate the labor of others by means of such appropriation.

It has been objected that if private property is abolished, all work will cease and universal laziness will overtake us. According to this, bourgeois society ought long ago to have gone to the dogs through sheer idleness; for those who work, acquire nothing, and those who acquire anything, do not work. The whole of this objection is but another expression of the **tautology:** There can no longer be any wage-labor when there is no longer any capital.

All objections urged against the Communist mode of producing and appropriating material products have, in the same way, been urged against the Communist modes of producing and appropriating intellectual products. Just as, to the bourgeois, the disappearance of class property is the disappearance of production itself, so the disappearance of class culture is to him identical with the disappearance of all culture.

That culture, the loss of which he laments, is, for the enormous majority, a mere training to act as a machine.

But don't wrangle with us so long as you apply, to our intended abolition of bourgeois property, the standard of your bourgeois notions of freedom, culture, law, etc. Your very ideas are but the outgrowth of the conditions of your bourgeois production and bourgeois property. Similarly, your juris-prudence is but the will of your class made into a law for all, a will whose essential character and direction are determined by the economic conditions of existence of your class. The selfish misconception that induces you to transform the social forms springing from your present mode of production and form of property into eternal laws of nature and of reason . . . is a misconception you share with every ruling class that has preceded you. What you see clearly in the case of ancient property, what you admit in the case of feudal property, you are of course forbidden to admit in the case of your own bourgeois form of property.

Abolition of the family! Even those most radically inclined flare up at this infamous proposal of the Communists. But on what foundation is the present form, the bourgeois form, of the family based? It is founded on capital, on private gain. In its completely developed form, this family exists only among the bourgeoisie. But this state of things finds its complement in the practical absence of the family among the proletarians and in public prostitution. The bourgeois family will vanish as a matter of course when its complement vanishes, and both will vanish with the vanishing of capital. Do you charge us with wanting to stop the exploitation of children by their parents? To this crime we plead guilty.

But, you will say, we destroy the most hallowed of relations when we replace home education by social public education. But is not your education also social? Is it not determined by the social conditions under which you educate, by the intervention of society, direct or indirect, by means of schools, etc.? The Communists have not invented the intervention of society in education; they do but seek to alter the character of that intervention and to rescue education from the influence of the ruling class.

As family ties among the proletarians become more and more torn asunder by the development of modern industry, as their children become more and more transformed into simple articles of commerce and instruments of labor, the bourgeois claptrap about family and education, about the sacred relationship between parent and child, grows more and more disgusting.

But you Communists would introduce community of women, screams the whole bourgeoisie in chorus.

The bourgeois sees in his wife a mere instrument of production. He hears that the instruments of production are to be held in common, and, naturally, he can come to no other conclusion than women will likewise be held in common. He has not the slightest clue that the real point at which we aim is to do away with the status of women as mere instruments of production.

Moreover, nothing is more ridiculous than the virtuous indignation of our bourgeois at the community of women, which they claim will be openly and officially established by the Communists. The Communists do not need to introduce community of women; it has existed almost from time immemorial. Our bourgeois, not content with having the wives and daughters of their proletarians at their disposal, not to speak of common prostitutes, take the greatest pleasure in seducing each other's wives.

Bourgeois marriage is in reality a system of wives in common. Thus, at the most, what the Communists might possibly be reproached with is that they desire to introduce an openly legalized community of women, in substitution for the hypocritically concealed community that already exists. For the rest, it is self-evident that the abolition of the present system of production must bring with it the abolition of the community of women springing from that system, *i.e.,* it will eliminate both public and private prostitution.

The Communists are further reproached with desiring to abolish countries and nationality. However, the workingmen have no country. We cannot take from them what they do not have. Still, since the proletariat must first acquire political supremacy, that is, it must first rise to be the leading class of the nation, thus constituting itself *the* nation, it is itself initially national—though not in the bourgeois sense of the word. National differences and antagonisms between peoples are vanishing gradually from day to day, owing to the development of the bourgeoisie, to freedom of commerce, to the world market, and to uniformity in the mode of production and in the conditions of life corresponding thereto.

The supremacy of the proletariat will cause national differences to vanish still faster. United action, of the leading civilized countries at least, is one of the first conditions for the emancipation of the proletariat.

In proportion as the exploitation of one individual by another is put to an end, the exploitation of one nation by another will also be put to an end. In proportion as the antagonism between classes within the nation vanishes, the hostility of one nation to another will come to an end.

The charges against communism made from a religious, a philosophical, and, generally, from an ideological standpoint, are not deserving of serious examination. Does it require deep **intuition** to comprehend that man's ideas, views, and conceptions, in a word, man's consciousness, changes with every change in the conditions of his material existence, in his social relations and in his social life? What else does the history of ideas prove, if not that intellectual production changes its character in proportion as material production is changed? The ruling ideas of each age have always been the ideas of its ruling class.

When people speak of ideas that revolutionize society, they do but express the fact that within the old society the elements of a new one have been created, and that the dissolution of the old ideas keeps even pace with the dissolution of the old conditions of existence.

When the ancient world was in its last throes, the ancient religions were overcome by Christianity. When Christian ideas succumbed in the eighteenth century to rationalist ideas, feudal society fought its death-battle with the then revolutionary bourgeoisie. The ideas of religious liberty and freedom of conscience merely gave expression to the sway of free competition within the domain of knowledge.

"Undoubtedly," it will be said, "religion, moral, philosophical and juridical ideas have been modified in the course of historical development. But religion, morality, philosophy, political science, and law constantly survived this change. Besides, there are eternal truths, such as Freedom, Justice, and so on, that are common to all states of society. But communism abolishes eternal truths; it abolishes all religion, and all morality, instead of constituting them on a new basis. It therefore acts in contradiction to all past historical experience."

What does this accusation reduce itself to? The history of all past society has consisted in the development of class antagonisms, antagonisms that assumed different forms at different epochs. But whatever form they may have taken, one fact is common to all past ages, that is, the exploitation of one part of society by the other. No wonder, then, that the social consciousness of past ages, despite all the multiplicity and variety it displays, moves within certain common forms, or general ideas, which cannot completely vanish except with the total disappearance of class antagonisms. The Communist revolution is the most radical rupture with traditional property relations; no wonder then that its development involves the most radical rupture with traditional ideas.

But let us have done with the bourgeois objections to communism. We have seen above that the first step in the revolution by the working class is to raise the proletariat to the position of ruling class, that is, to establish **democracy.** The proletariat will use its political supremacy to wrest, by degrees, all capital from the bourgeoisie, and to centralize all instruments of production in the hands of the state, *i.e.,* of the proletariat organized as the ruling class, while also increasing the total of productive forces as rapidly as possible.

Of course, in the beginning, this cannot be effected except by means of despotic inroads on the rights of property, and on the conditions of bourgeois production. In other words, it can only be effected by measures that at first appear economically insufficient and untenable, but that, in the course of the movement, outstrip themselves, necessitating further inroads upon the old social order. . . . These measures will of course be different in different countries. Nevertheless in the most advanced countries, the following steps will usually be necessary.

1. Abolition of private ownership of land, and the application of all rents of land to public purposes.

2. A heavy progressive or graduated income tax.

3. Abolition of all inheritance rights.

4. Confiscation of the property of all emigrants and rebels.

5. Centralization of credit in the hands of the state, by means of a national bank with state capital and an exclusive monopoly.

6. Centralization of the means of communication and transport in the hands of the state.

7. Extension of factories and instruments of production owned by the state, the bringing into cultivation of wastelands, and the improvement of the soil generally in accordance with a common plan.

8. Equal obligation of all to work. The establishment of industrial armies, especially for agriculture.

9. Combination of agriculture with manufacturing industries; the gradual abolition of the distinction between town and country, by means of a more equable distribution of the population throughout the country.

10. Free education for all children in public schools. Abolition of child factory labor in its present form. The combination of education with industrial production, etc.

When, in the course of development, class distinctions have disappeared, and all production has been concentrated in the hands of a vast association of the whole nation, the public power will lose its political character. Political power, properly so called, is merely the organized power of one class for oppressing another. If during its contest with the bourgeoisie the proletariat is compelled by the force of circumstances to organize itself as a class, if by means of a revolution the proletariat makes itself the ruling class, and thus forcefully eliminates the old conditions of production, then it will, along with these conditions, have eliminated the conditions for the existence of class antagonisms and of classes generally. Therefore, the proletariat will have abolished its own supremacy as a class. In place of the old bourgeois society, with its classes and class antagonisms, we will have an association, in which the free development of each is the condition for the free development of all. . . .

The Communists disdain to conceal their views and aims. They openly declare that their ends can be attained only by the forcible overthrow of all existing social conditions. Let the ruling classes tremble at a Communist revolution. The proletarians have nothing to lose but their chains. They have a world to win.

Workingmen of all countries, unite!

NOTES

1. The *bourgeoisie* is the class of modern capitalists, owners of the means of social production and employers of wage-labor; the *proletariat* is the class of modern wage-laborers, who, having no means of production of their own, are reduced to selling their labor power in order to live.—Engels.

2. That is, all *written* history. In 1837, the prehistory of society, the social organization existing previous to recorded history, was all but unknown. Since then Haxthausen has discovered common ownership of land in Russia, and Maurer proved it to be the social foundation from which all Teutonic races started in history. By and by, village communities were found to be, or to have been, the primitive form of society everywhere from India to Ireland. The inner organization of this primitive communistic society was laid bare, in its typical form, by Morgan's crowning discovery of the true nature of the *gens* and its relation to the *tribe*. With the dissolution of these primeval communities, society begins to be differentiated into separate and finally antagonistic classes. I have attempted to retrace this process of dissolution in *The Origin of the Family, Private Property, and the State.*—Engels.

3. Guild-master—that is, a full member of a guild—a master within, not a head of a guild.—Engels.

4. *Manufacture* refers to the system of production that came after the guild system but that still depended principally on direct human labor for power. It is to be distinguished from modern industry, which arose only when machinery driven by water and steam was introduced.—ED.

5. *Commune* was the name taken in France by the nascent towns even before they had won from their feudal lords and masters local self-government and political rights as the "Third Estate." Generally speaking, for the economic development of the bourgeoisie, England is here taken as the typical country; for its political development, France.—Engels.

Questions for Thought

1. To what extent do you believe that class struggle has moved history? What part, if any, has class struggle played in your own life?

2. Do you think that Marx and Engels would categorize you as a member of the bourgeoisie or as a member of the proletariat? What factors in your life would lead them to classify you in this way?

3. Given what you know about current economic conditions, which of the economic predictions made in this selection have come true? Which of them have not yet come true?

4. Do you believe that bourgeois private property should be abolished? Why or why not?

5. Which of the ten changes listed by Marx and Engels seem most desirable to you? Which of them seem least desirable?

6. How do your own views on the family, marriage, and sexual life compare with or differ from the views of Marx and Engels?

7. How does Marx and Engels' view on the origin and function of government differ from the views of Rousseau and Jefferson? Can you think of any similarities between the view of Marx and Engels and the views of Rousseau or Jefferson?

We Are Practical Revolutionaries   **6**

ERNESTO CHE GUEVARA

Ernesto Che Guevara (1928–1967) was born in Rosario, Argentina. Although his family was middle class and entrepreneurial, both of Guevara's parents were politically leftist in their thinking. Guevara thus spent many of his holidays traveling in Latin America and observing the abject poverty of most of the Latin American people. After receiving his M.D. from the University of Buenos Aires in 1953, Guevara went to Guatemala, which was governed by the socially progressive regime of Jacobo Arbenz. However, when the Arbenz regime was overthrown in 1954 by a CIA-supported coup, Guevara moved to Mexico, where he met Fidel and Raúl Castro. Guevara joined the Castros in their attempt to overthrow the Batista dictatorship in Cuba, serving first as a medical officer and eventually as commander of one of the most important guerrilla columns. When the revolutionary forces claimed victory in 1959, Guevara became a Cuban citizen and served the new government in several important positions, including the position of minister of industry. As a representative of the Cuban government, Guevara wrote and delivered many speeches in which he formulated and defended Cuba's new form of Marxism. In the mid-1960s, Guevara suddenly disappeared from public life so that he could better implement his revolutionary ideas. After traveling to the Congo, where he helped organize the Patrice Lumumba Battalion, Guevara went to Bolivia to lead a guerrilla group there. In October 1967, Guevara's group was attacked by a detachment of the Bolivian army. Guevara was wounded, captured, and then shot. Guevara's best-known writing was *La guerra de guerrillas* (1960), which was translated into English as *Guerrilla Warfare* in 1961. In the following selection, which is taken from *Venceremos! The Speeches and Writings of Ernesto Che Guevara,* Guevara describes the events leading up to one successful Marxist revolution, the overthrow of the Batista regime in Cuba. Although he acknowledges the importance of Marxist theory in this revolutionary movement, he emphasizes the fact that the revolution was practical rather than theoretical. Guevara also suggests that the revolution was marked by a transformation of consciousness as well as by a change of political systems. While the revolutionaries began with the theoretical assumption that the people would rise up in mass against the dictatorship and with a profound misunderstanding and mistrust of the **campesinos,** they came to realize both the necessity of prolonged guerrilla struggle and the importance of campesino participation.

Guevara attributes the success of the revolution to two factors. First, whereas the guerrillas were fighting for survival, land, and liberation, the government troops were fighting for a paycheck and pension. This difference in motivation meant that the guerrillas were willing to risk their lives, while the government troops generally were not. Second, because of the nature of the struggle and the goals of the revolution, the guerrillas were able to forge a unity among intellectuals, campesinos, and workers. Because of its oppressive nature, however, the Batista regime was never able to create such unity. Thus, the revolutionaries were able to overcome the much larger and better-equipped government army, and the people ultimately prevailed.

Questions for Reading

1. What, according to Guevara, were the principal causes of the Cuban Revolution?
2. Why, according to Guevara, did the Cuban Revolution succeed? What was his role in the revolution?
3. What is Guevara's attitude toward Marxism? What scientific analogies does he use to express his views on Marxism?
4. In what ways were the participants in the revolution changed during the struggle to overthrow the Batista regime?
5. Who were the campesinos, and why was participation of the campesinos crucial to the success of the revolution?

CUBA'S IS A UNIQUE REVOLUTION, WHICH SOME people maintain contradicts one of the most orthodox premises of the revolutionary movement, expressed by Lenin: "Without a revolutionary theory there is no revolutionary movement." It would be suitable to say that revolutionary theory, as the expression of a social truth, surpasses any declaration of it; that is to say, even if the theory is not known, the revolution can succeed if historical reality is interpreted correctly, and if the forces involved are utilized correctly. Every revolution always incorporates elements of very different tendencies, which nevertheless coincide in action and in the revolution's most immediate objectives.

It is clear that if the leaders have an adequate theoretical knowledge prior to the action, they can avoid trial and error whenever the adopted theory corresponds to the reality.

The principal actors of this revolution had no coherent theoretical criteria; but it cannot be said that they were ignorant of the various concepts of history, society, economics, and revolution which are being discussed in the world today.

Profound knowledge of reality, a close relationship with the people, the firmness of the liberator's objective, and the practical revolutionary experience gave to those leaders the chance to form a more complete theoretical concept.

The foregoing should be considered as introduction to the explication of this curious phenomenon which has intrigued the entire world: the Cuban Revolution. It is a deed worthy of study in contemporary world history: the how and the why of a group of men who, shattered by an army enormously superior in technique and equipment, first managed to survive, soon became strong, later became stronger than the enemy in the battle zones, still later moved into new zones of combat, and finally defeated that enemy on the battlefield, even though their troops were still very inferior in number.

Naturally, we who often do not show the requisite concern for theory will not run the risk of expounding the truth of the Cuban Revolution as though we were its masters. We will simply try to give the bases from which one can interpret this truth. In fact, the Cuban Revolution must be separated into two absolutely distinct stages: that of the armed action up to January 1, 1959, and the political, economic, and social transformations since then.

Even these two stages deserve further sub-divisions; however, we will not take them from the viewpoint of historical exposition, but from the viewpoint of the evolution of revolutionary thought of its leaders through their contact with the people. Incidentally, here one must introduce a general attitude toward one of the most controversial terms of the modern world: Marxism. When asked whether or not we are Marxists, our position is the same as that of a physicist or a biologist when asked if he is a "Newtonian," or if he is a "Pasteurian."

There are truths so evident, so much a part of people's knowledge, that it is now useless to discuss them. One ought to be "Marxist" with the same naturalness with which one is "Newtonian" in physics, or "Pasteurian" in biology, considering that if facts determine new concepts, these new concepts will never divest themselves of that portion of truth possessed by the older concepts they have outdated.

Such is the case, for example, of Einsteinian relativity or of Planck's "quantum" theory with respect to the discoveries of Newton. They take nothing at all away from the greatness of the learned Englishman. Thanks to Newton, physics was able to advance until it had achieved new concepts of space. The learned Englishman provided the necessary stepping-stones for them.

The advances in social and political science, as in other fields, belong to a long historical process whose links are connecting, adding up, molding, and constantly perfecting themselves. In the origin of peoples, there exist a Chinese, Arab, or Hindu mathematics. Today mathematics has no frontiers. In the course of history there was a Greek Pythagoras, an Italian Galileo, an English Newton, a German Gauss, a Russian Lobatchevsky, an Einstein, etc. Thus in the field of social and political sciences, from Democritus to Marx, a long series of thinkers added their original investigations and accumulated a body of experience and of doctrines.

The merit of Marx is in suddenly producing a qualitative change in the history of social thought. He interprets history, understands its dynamics, predicts the future, but in addition to predicting it (which would satisfy his scientific obligation), he expresses a revolutionary concept: The world must not only be interpreted, it must be transformed. Man ceases to be the slave and tool of his environment and converts himself into the architect of his own destiny. At that moment Marx puts himself in a position where he becomes the necessary target of all who have a special interest in maintaining the old—similar to Democritus before him, whose work was burned by Plato and his disciples, the ideologues of Athenian slave **aristocracy.** Beginning with the revolutionary Marx, a political group with concrete ideas establishes itself. Basing itself in the giants, Marx and Engels, and developing through successive steps with personalities like Lenin, Stalin, Mao Tse-tung, and the new Soviet and Chinese rulers, it establishes a body of doctrine and, let us say, examples to follow.

The Cuban Revolution takes up Marx at the point where he himself left science to shoulder his revolutionary rifle. And it takes him up at that point, not in a revisionist spirit, of struggling against that which follows Marx, of reviving "pure" Marx, but simply because up to that point Marx, the scientist, placed himself outside of the history he studied and predicted. From then on Marx the revolutionary could fight within history. We, practical revolutionaries, initiating our own struggle, simply fulfill laws foreseen by Marx, the scientist. We are simply adjusting ourselves to the predictions of the scientific Marx as we travel this road of rebellion, struggling against the old structure of power, supporting ourselves in the people for the destruction of this structure, and having the happiness of this people as the basis of our struggle. That is to say—and it is well to emphasize this once again—the laws of Marxism are present in the events of the Cuban Revolution, independently of what its leaders profess or fully know of those laws from the theoretical point of view. Those events began before the landing of the "Granma," and continued long after, and included the landing itself, the setting up of the second guerrilla column, the third and the fourth, the invasion of the Sierra de Cristal, the establishment of the second front, the general strike of April and its failure, the setback of the great offensive, and the invasion of Las Villas.

Each of those brief historical moments in the guerrilla warfare framed distinct social concepts and distinct appreciations of the Cuban reality; they outlined the thought of the military leaders of the Revolution—those who in time would also take their position as political leaders.

Before the landing of the "Granma," a mentality predominated that to some degree might be called "subjectivist": blind confidence in a rapid popular explosion; enthusiasm and faith in the power to liquidate the Batista regime by a swift, armed uprising combined with spontaneous revolutionary strikes and the subsequent fall of the dictator. The movement was the direct heir of the Orthodox party, and its main slogan was "Shame Against Money," that is to say, administrative honesty as the principal concern of the new Cuban Government. . . .

After the landing came the defeat, the almost total destruction of the forces, and their regrouping and integration as guerrillas. Characteristic of those few survivors, imbued with the spirit of struggle, was the understanding that to count upon spontaneous outbursts throughout the island was a deception, an illusion. They understood also that the fight would have to be a long one, and that it would need vast *campesino* participation. At this point, the *campesinos* entered the guerrilla war for the first time. Two forces—hardly important in terms of the number of combatants, but of great psychological value—were unveiled. First, the antagonism that the city people, who comprised the central guerrilla group, felt toward the *campesinos* was erased. The *campesinos* had distrusted the group and, above all, feared the barbarous reprisals of the government. Two facts revealed themselves at this stage, both very important for the interrelated factors: to the *campesinos,* the bestialities of the army and all the persecution would not be sufficient to put an end to the guerrilla war, even though the army was certainly capable of liquidating the *campesinos'* homes, crops, and families. To take refuge with those in hiding was a good solution. In turn, the guerrilla fighters learned the necessity, each time more pointed, of winning over the *campesino* masses, which required, obviously, that they be offered something they desired very much. And there was nothing that a *campesino* sought more than land.

After that came a nomadic stage in which the rebel army kept gaining zones of influence. It could not remain in these areas for any length of time, but then, neither could the enemy. As a result of a series of combats a rather fluid front was mapped. Then, on May 28, 1957, at Ubero, an attack was launched against a well-armed, well-situated garrison, which had ready access to reinforcements, due to its position by the sea and its airport. The rebel victory was very costly: some 30 per cent of the rebel forces were killed or wounded. But it showed that the forces could sweep down from the mountains and wage successful battles in the fields, that they could come after the enemy rather than wait for it to pursue them.

Shortly thereafter, the first segregation took place, and a second rebel column was organized. It went into combat immediately. The two columns attacked Estrada Palma the twenty-sixth of July, and five days later, Bueycito, which is thirty kilometers away. From then on the battles were more important. We were beginning to stand firm against enemy counter-attacks. We resisted all its attempts to penetrate the Sierra. And we maintained our vast front areas. . . .

Our successes became known, as they filtered through government censorship, and the people of Cuba began to look forward, for the first time, to a rebel victory. It is then that from Havana the idea of a nationwide struggle was discussed, specifically developing the idea of a general revolutionary strike.

The function of the rebel army would then be mainly one of an "irritating thorn," or catalyst, for the over-all struggle. In those days, our guerrillas became increasingly more daring and successful, and it is then that the heroic legend of Camilo Cienfuegos was born, as his column went into combat, successfully, in the lowlands of Oriente for the first time—under strict central orders.

Nevertheless, the general strike was badly organized and planned, for it did not take into account the workers' own struggle, their unity, or their concept of revolutionary activity. The general call for the strike was launched over a clandestine radio, but the specific date, to be kept secret until the last minute, was to be announced by word-of-mouth, and this manner of communication was not capable of reaching all of the people. The strike not only failed, but many valiant and dedicated revolutionary leaders were gunned down in the process. . . .

In any case, the failure of the strike made it clear that only through armed struggle could the government be toppled. It became imperative, therefore, that such a struggle be accelerated and intensified and that it lead to the final confrontation and defeat of the government forces on the field of battle.

By then, of course, we had established close bonds with the *campesinos.* In the liberated areas we had established a rebel administration, with civil and penal codes. We set up a judicial system, distributed foodstuffs, and levied taxes. Neighboring zones also felt our influence, and in the next two months we waged three major offensives, which caused a thousand deaths among the enemy, completely demoralizing it, which increased our strength from new volunteers by six hundred actual fighters.

It was then clear that we could not be defeated; every path in Oriente became a sieve for enemy casualties. All counteroffensives by the enemy failed. And then, Camilo Cienfuegos, leading column number two, and I, in charge of column number eight, named for another hero of our revolution, Antonio Maceo, were ordered to cross the province of Camaguey in order to establish ourselves in Las Villas and thus cut the enemy's communication lines. . . .

It may seem strange, incomprehensible, and even incredible that two columns of such small size [80 men in one, 140 in the other]—without communications, without mobility, without the most elemental arms of modern warfare—could fight against well-trained, and above all, well-armed troops. Basic was the characteristic of each group: The more uncomfortable the guerrilla fighter is, and the more he is initiated into the rigors of nature, the more he feels himself at home; his morale is higher; his sense of security, greater. At the same time he has learned to risk his life in every circumstance that might arise, to trust it to luck like a tossed coin. In general, as a result of this kind of combat, it matters little to the individual guerrilla whether or not he survives.

The enemy soldier in the Cuban example which at present concerns us, is the junior partner of the dictator; he is the man who gets the last crumbs left by a long line of profiteers that begins in Wall Street and ends with him. He is disposed to defend his privileges, but he is disposed to defend them only to the degree that they are important to him. His salary and his pension are worth some suffering and some dangers, but they are never worth his life: If the price of maintaining them will cost it, he is better off giving them up, that is to say, withdrawing from the face of guerrilla danger. From these two concepts and these two moralities springs the difference which would cause the crisis of December 31, 1958, Batista's downfall.

Meanwhile, the superiority of the rebel army became clearly evident, as did, with our arrival in Las Villas, the popularity of the 26th of July Movement with everyone: the revolutionary directorate, the second front of Las Villas, the Popular Socialist party, and even some small guerrilla bands of the Authentic Organization. This was due in great part to the magnetic personality of our leader, Fidel Castro, but also to the just cause of our revolutionary line.

Here ended the insurrection. But the men who arrived in Havana after two years of arduous struggle in the mountains and plains of Oriente, in the lowlands of Camaguey, and in the mountains, plains, and cities of Las Villas, were not the same men, ideologically, who landed on the beaches of Las Coloradoas, or who took part in the first phase of the struggle. Their distrust of the *campesino* had been converted into affection and respect for his virtues; their total ignorance of life in the country had been converted into a knowledge of the needs of our *guajiros;* their flirtations with statistics and with theory had been solidified by the cement which is practice.

With the banner of agrarian reform, the execution of which began in the Sierra Maestra, these men confronted imperialism. They knew that the agrarian reform was the basis upon which the new Cuba must build itself. They also knew that the agrarian reform would give land to all the dispossessed, and that it would dispossess its unjust possessors; and they knew that the greatest of the unjust possessors were also influential men in the State Department or in the government of the United States of America. But they had learned to conquer the difficulties with bravery, with audacity, and above all, with the support of the people; and they had now seen the future of liberation which awaited us on the other side of our sufferings.

To reach these conclusions, we traveled far and we changed a lot. As our armed struggle changed qualitatively in the course of the actual battle, so too did the social composition of the guerrillas and the ideological understanding of our leaders. This happened inevitably, because each battle, each confrontation, broadens, widens and therefore changes its participants. And this is the revolutionary process, to mature from each event. The *campesino* learns to believe in his own vigor. He gives the revolutionary army his capacity to suffer, his knowledge of the terrain, his love of the land, his hunger for the agrarian reform. The intellectual, of whatever type, throws in his mite, beginning to mold the theoretical framework on this knowledge. The worker contributes his sense of organization, of unity. Above all these, there is the rebel army, which proves to be much more than just an "irritating thorn," but on the contrary contributes the most important lesson, leading the masses to experience it, that all men can get rid of their fear of torment.

Never before was the concept of interaction so clear to us. We could feel with our bones how this concept deepened and matured in us, teaching us the value of armed insurrection, the strength that any man has when, with a weapon in his hand and the will to win in his heart, he confronts other men who are out to destroy him. And we learned from the *campesinos* that there is no limit to the efforts, to the sacrifices that we can all make when we are fighting for the destiny of the people.

Thus, when bathed in *campesino* sweat, with a horizon of mountains and clouds, beneath the radiant sun of the island, the rebel chief and his men entered Havana, a new "history climbed from the winter's garden with the feet of the people."

Questions for Thought

1. What do you think caused the Cuban Revolution? How do your views on this matter compare with or differ from the views of Guevara?
2. Do you think there were any similarities between the Cuban Revolution and the American Revolution? If so, what were they?
3. How does your attitude toward Marxism compare with or differ from Guevara's attitude?
4. Do you think that the revolutionary changes that took place in Cuba were positive or negative? Defend your answer.
5. Under what conditions, if any, do you think revolution would be justified?

7   In Defense of Democracy

JOHN DEWEY

John Dewey (1859–1952), the son of a grocer, was born in Burlington, Vermont. Dewey, who was described as a shy child who liked to read, attended public schools in his hometown before entering the University of Vermont in 1875. He graduated from the university in 1879 and spent the next three years of his life teaching high school, first in Pennsylvania and then in Burlington.

Having become interested in philosophy during his final semesters at the University of Vermont, Dewey continued his reading in philosophy while teaching. Then, after borrowing money from his aunt to pay tuition, he entered the philosophy graduate school at Johns Hopkins University in 1882 and received his Ph.D. two years later.

In the fall of 1884, Dewey accepted an academic position in philosophy and psychology at the University of Michigan. Aside from a visiting professorship at the University of Minnesota for one year, Dewey spent the next ten years teaching at Michigan. During this time, he became interested in issues in education and other areas of social concern. As his social and political views became more progressive, Dewey agreed to become editor of a weekly magazine with a socialist orientation. Although this magazine never reached publication, Dewey published several books on applied psychology and became an outspoken proponent of educational reform while still at the University of Michigan.

However, it was in his next job that Dewey developed the theories and wrote the books that first won him national acclaim. As chairman of the Department of Philosophy, Psychology, and Education at the University of Chicago, Dewey was able to fuse his theoretical concerns with his practical interest in educational reform. Perhaps the most concrete example of this fusion came when he established the University of Chicago's Laboratory School for testing the workability of educational and psychological theories. Also, through his participation in the activities of Hull House, a settlement house founded by Jane Addams in 1899, Dewey became intimately familiar with the social and economic problems faced by the poor. Out of these experiences, he became increasingly convinced that pure philosophical speculation was an empty, meaningless activity. The books that Dewey wrote during this time, such as *The School and Society* (1899) and *The Child and the Curriculum* (1902), were derived largely from his observations at the Laboratory School and were devoted to educational reform.

Despite Dewey's success and growing influence, friction with the president of the University of Chicago led to his resignation in 1904. Dewey then accepted a position as professor at Columbia University in New York City, and he was associated with Columbia for the remaining years of his life. Because he taught in the Columbia Teachers College, which served as a training center for teachers from many countries, Dewey's national recognition became international. This international stature grew in the 1920s, when he traveled to Mexico, Japan, and the Soviet Union to examine the educational techniques being employed in those countries. An activist in the true sense of the word, Dewey's influence was not confined to the area of educational reform. He was a cofounder and first president of the American Association of University Professors and a charter member of the first union for teachers in New York City. In addition, he helped establish the New School for Social Research in 1919 and the University-in-Exile in 1933. In 1937, Dewey headed a commission in Mexico City that exonerated Leon Trotsky of charges made during the Moscow trials, and he came to Bertrand Russell's defense when Russell was denied permission to teach at the City College of New York on the grounds that he was an atheist. Although Dewey disagreed with much of Russell's philosophy, he nevertheless helped edit a book of essays critical of the decision.

Both during his days of teaching at Columbia University and after his retirement in 1930, Dewey was a popular lecturer and a prolific writer. Some of his best-known later writings include *Democracy and Education* (1916), *Reconstruction in Philosophy* (1920), *Human Nature and Conduct* (1922), *Experience and Nature* (1925), *The Quest for Certainty* (1929), *Art as Experience* (1934), *Experience and Education* (1938), *Logic, the Theory of Inquiry* (1938), and *Freedom and Culture* (1939).

The following selection, which is taken from an essay titled "Democracy and Educational Administration," was read at a National Education Association convention in 1937. As should be evident, Dewey's audience consisted of a group of school administrators, and one of Dewey's chief aims in his address was to convince those administrators that teachers ought to have more freedom in the classroom. However, in order to support this rather specific proposal, Dewey examines the fundamental concepts of **democracy** and argues that democracy represents the best means of social interaction thus far devised.

One of Dewey's most important points is that democracy is more than a type of government—a government based on popular suffrage and recurring elections: it is also a way of life. The basic presupposition of this way of life is belief in the ability and intelligence of ordinary human beings, belief that when they are allowed to freely develop their talents, they can successfully resolve any social problem with which they are faced.

But in order for people to freely develop their talents, they must be allowed ample opportunity to do so. Thus, another of the presuppositions of the democratic way of life that Dewey discusses is the belief in equality. Dewey notes, however, that the democratic belief in equality is not belief in the equality of natural endowments but belief in the equality of opportunity. Unless everyone has an equal opportunity to express their views and to develop their talents, democracy cannot flourish.

As Dewey argues throughout his works, one of the keys to ensuring equal opportunity to all lies in the domain of education. A strong supporter of educational reform, Dewey believes that the public education system must promote equality of opportunity and the other fundamental beliefs of democracy. While other of his works focus on reforming the curriculum so that it prepares and encourages students to pursue the democratic way of life, in this particular essay Dewey is arguing that school administrators must allow teachers to pursue the democratic way of life in their classrooms.

Questions for Reading

1. What is the nature of the audience that Dewey is addressing in this essay? Of what is he trying to convince them?
2. How does Dewey define *democracy*?
3. How, according to Dewey, did political democracy develop? What are the basic characteristics of political democracy?
4. What does Dewey identify as the "foundation of democracy"?
5. Why does Dewey believe that schools play such an important role in society? What can schools do to promote democracy? What might they do to discourage democracy?
6. What, according to Dewey, is the proper role of the teacher in the classroom? What should be the role of the school administrator?

MY EXPERIENCE IN EDUCATIONAL ADMINISTRATION is limited. I should not venture to address a body of those widely experienced and continuously engaged in school administration about the details of the management of schools. But the topic suggested to me has to do with the relation of school administration to democratic ideals and methods; and to the general subject of the relation of education and democracy I have given considerable thought over many years. The topic suggested concerns a special phase of this general subject. I shall begin, then, with some remarks on the broad theme of democratic aims and methods. Much of what I shall say on this subject is necessarily old and familiar. But it seems necessary to rehearse some old ideas in order to have a criterion for dealing with the special subject.

In the first place, democracy is much broader than a special political form, a method of conducting government, of making laws and carrying on governmental administration by means of popular suffrage and elected officers. It is that, of course. But it is something broader and deeper than that. The political and governmental phase of democracy is a means, the best means so far found, for realizing ends that lie in the wide domain of human relationships and the development of human personality. It is, as we often say, though perhaps without appreciating all that is involved in the saying, a way of life, social and individual. The key-note of democracy as a way of life may be expressed, it seems to me, as the necessity for the participation of every mature human being in formation of the values that regulate the living of men together: which is necessary from the standpoint of both the general social welfare and the full development of human beings as individuals.

Universal suffrage, recurring elections, responsibility of those who are in political power to the voters, and the other factors of democratic government are means that have been found expedient for realizing democracy as the truly human way of living. They are not a final end and a final value. They are to be judged on the basis of their contribution to the end. It is a form of idolatry to erect means into the end which they serve. Democratic political forms are simply the best means that human wit has devised up to a special time in history. But they rest back upon the idea that no man or limited set of men is wise enough or good enough to rule others without their consent; the positive meaning of this statement is that all those who are affected by social institutions must share in producing and managing them. The two facts that each one is influenced in what he does and enjoys and in what he becomes by the institutions under which he lives, and that therefore he shall have, in a democracy, a voice in shaping them, are the passive and active sides of the same fact.

The development of political democracy came about through substitution of the method of mutual consultation and voluntary agreement for the method of subordination of the many to the few enforced from above. Social arrangements which involve fixed subordination are maintained by coercion. The coercion need not be physical. There

Reprinted from an address delivered to the National Education Association, February 22, 1937, and published under the title "Democracy and Educational Administration," in School and Society, *XLV (April 3, 1937), 457–467.*

have existed, for short periods, benevolent despotisms. But coercion of some sort there has been; perhaps economic, certainly psychological and moral. The very fact of exclusion from participation is a subtle form of suppression. It gives individuals no opportunity to reflect and decide upon what is good for them. Others who are supposed to be wiser and who in any case have more power decide the question for them and also decide the methods and means by which subjects may arrive at the enjoyment of what is good for them. This form of coercion and suppression is more subtle and more effective than is overt intimidation and restraint. When it is habitual and embodied in social institutions, it seems the normal and natural state of affairs. The mass usually become unaware that they have a claim to a development of their own powers. Their experience is so restricted that they are not conscious of restriction. It is part of the democratic conception that they as individuals are not the only sufferers, but that the whole social body is deprived of the potential resources that should be at its service. The individuals of the submerged mass may not be very wise. But there is one thing they are wiser about than anybody else can be, and that is where the shoe pinches, the troubles they suffer from.

The foundation of democracy is faith in the capacities of human nature, faith in human intelligence and in the power of pooled and cooperative experience. It is not belief that these things are complete but that if given a show they will grow and be able to generate progressively the knowledge and wisdom needed to guide collective action. Every autocratic and authoritarian scheme of social action rests on a belief that the needed intelligence is confined to a superior few, who because of inherent natural gifts are endowed with the ability and the right to control the conduct of others; laying down principles and rules and directing the ways in which they are carried out. It would be foolish to deny that much can be said of this point of view. It is that which controlled human relations in social groups for much the greater part of human history. The democratic faith has emerged very, very recently in the history of mankind. Even where democracies now exist, men's minds and feelings are still permeated with ideas about leadership imposed from above, ideas that developed in the long early history of mankind. After democratic political institutions

were nominally established, beliefs and ways of looking at life and of acting that originated when men and women were externally controlled and subjected to arbitrary power, persisted in the family, the church, business and the school, and experience shows that as long as they persist there, political democracy is not secure.

Belief in equality is an element of the democratic credo. It is not, however, belief in equality of natural endowments. Those who proclaimed the idea of equality did not suppose they were enunciating a psychological doctrine, but a legal and political one. All individuals are entitled to equality of treatment by law and in its administration. Each one is affected equally in quality if not in quantity by the institutions under which he lives and has an equal right to express his judgment, although the weight of his judgment may not be equal in amount when it enters into the pooled result to that of others. In short, each one is equally an individual and entitled to equal opportunity of development of his own capacities, be they large or small in range. Moreover, each has needs of his own, as significant to him as those of others are to them. The very fact of natural and psychological inequality is all the more reason for establishment by law of equality of opportunity, since otherwise the former becomes a means of oppression of the less gifted.

While what we call intelligence is distributed in unequal amounts, it is the democratic faith that it is sufficiently general so that each individual has something to contribute, whose value can be assessed only as it enters into the final pooled intelligence constituted by the contributions of all. Every authoritarian scheme, on the contrary, assumes that its value may be assessed by some *prior* principle, if not of family and birth, or race and color, or possession of material wealth, then by the position and rank a person occupies in the existing social scheme. The democratic faith in equality is the faith that each individual shall have the chance and opportunity to contribute whatever he is capable of contributing and that the value of his contribution be decided by its place and function in the organized total of similar contributions, not on the basis of prior status of any kind whatever.

I have emphasized in what precedes the importance of the effective release of intelligence in connection with personal experience in the democratic way of living. I have done so purposely because democracy is so often and so naturally associated in our minds with freedom of *action,* forgetting the importance of freed intelligence which is necessary to direct and to warrant freedom of action. Unless freedom of individual action has intelligence and informed conviction back of it, its manifestation is almost sure to result in confusion and disorder. The democratic idea of freedom is not the right of each individual to *do* as he pleases, even if it be qualified by adding "provided he does not interfere with the same freedom on the part of others." While the idea is not always, not often enough, expressed in words, the basic freedom is that of freedom of *mind* and of whatever degree of freedom of action and experience is necessary to produce freedom of intelligence. The modes of freedom guaranteed in the Bill of Rights are all of this nature: Freedom of belief and conscience, of expression of opinion, of assembly for discussion and conference, of the press as an organ of communication. They are guaranteed because without them individuals are not free to develop and society is deprived of what they might contribute.

What, it may be asked, have these things to do with school administration? There is some kind of government, of control, wherever affairs that concern a number of persons who act together are engaged in. It is a superficial view that holds government is located in Washington and Albany. There is government in the family, in business, in the church, in every social group. There are regulations, due to custom if not to enactment, that settle how individuals in a group act in connection with one another.

It is a disputed question of theory and practice just how far a democratic political government should go in control of the conditions of action within special groups. At the present time, for example, there are those who think the federal and state governments leave too much freedom of independent action to industrial and financial groups, and there are others who think the government is going altogether too far at the present time. I do not need to discuss this phase of the problem, much less try to settle it. But it must be pointed out that if the methods of regulation and administration in vogue in the conduct of secondary social groups are non-democratic, whether directly or indirectly or

both, there is bound to be an unfavorable reaction back into the habits of feeling, thought and action of citizenship in the broadest sense of that word. The way in which any organized social interest is controlled necessarily plays an important part in forming the dispositions and tastes, the attitudes, interests, purposes and desires, of those engaged in carrying on the activities of the group. For illustration, I do not need to do more than point to the moral, emotional and intellectual effect upon both employers and laborers of the existing industrial system. Just what the effects specifically are is a matter about which we know very little. But I suppose that every one who reflects upon the subject admits that it is impossible that the way in which activities are carried on for the greater part of the waking hours of the day; and the way in which the share of individuals are involved in the management of affairs in such a matter as gaining a livelihood and attaining material and social security, can not but be a highly important factor in shaping personal dispositions; in short, forming character and intelligence.

In the broad and final sense all institutions are educational in the sense that they operate to form the attitudes, dispositions, abilities and disabilities that constitute a concrete personality. The principle applies with special force to the school. For it is the main business of the family and the school to influence directly the formation and growth of attitudes and dispositions, emotional, intellectual and moral. Whether this educative process is carried on in a predominantly democratic or nondemocratic way becomes, therefore, a question of transcendent importance not only for education itself but for its final effect upon all the interests and activities of a society that is committed to the democratic way of life.

Since, as I have already said, it is the problem I wish to present rather than to lay down the express ways in which it is to be solved, I might stop at this point. But there are certain corollaries which clarify the meaning of the issue. Absence of participation tends to produce lack of interest and concern on the part of those shut out. The result is a corresponding lack of effective responsibility. Automatically and unconsciously, if not consciously, the feeling develops, "This is none of our affair; it is the business of those at the top; let that particular set of Georges do what needs to be done." The countries in which autocratic government prevails are just those in which there is least public spirit and the greatest indifference to matters of general as distinct from personal concern. Can we expect a different kind of psychology to actuate teachers? Where there is little power, there is correspondingly little sense of positive responsibility. It is enough to do what one is told to do sufficiently well to escape flagrant unfavorable notice. About larger matters, a spirit of passivity is engendered. In some cases, indifference passes into evasion of duties when not directly under the eye of a supervisor; in other cases, a carping, rebellious spirit is engendered. A sort of game is instituted between teacher and supervisor like that which went on in the old-fashioned schools between teacher and pupil. Other teachers pass on, perhaps unconsciously, what they feel to be arbitrary treatment received by them to their pupils.

The argument that teachers are not prepared to assume the responsibility of participation deserves attention, with its accompanying belief that natural selection has operated to put those best prepared to carry the load in the positions of authority. Whatever the truth in this contention, it still is also true that incapacity to assume the responsibilities involved in having a voice in shaping policies is bred and increased by conditions in which that responsibility is denied. I suppose there has never been an autocrat, big or little, who did not justify his conduct on the ground of the unfitness of his subjects to take part in government. I would not compare administrators to political autocrats. Upon the whole, what exists in the schools is more a matter of habit and custom than it is of any deliberate autocracy. But, as was said earlier, habitual exclusion has the effect of reducing a sense of responsibility for what is done and its consequences. What the argument for democracy implies is that the best way to produce initiative and constructive power is to exercise it. Power, as well as interest, comes by use and practice. Moreover, the argument from incapacity proves too much. If it is so great as to be a permanent bar, then teachers can not be expected to have the intelligence and skill that are necessary to execute the directions given to them. The delicate and difficult task of developing character and good judgment in the young needs every stimulus and inspiration possible. It is

impossible that the work should not be better done when teachers have that understanding of what they are doing that comes from having shared in forming its guiding ideas.

Classroom teachers are those who are in continuous direct contact with those taught. The position of administrators is at best indirect by comparison. If there is any work in the world that requires the conservation of what is good in experience so that it may become an integral part of further experience, it is that of teaching. I often wonder how much waste there is in the traditional system. There is some loss even at the best of the potential capital acquired by successful teachers. It does not get freely transmitted to other teachers who might profit by it. Is not the waste very considerably increased when teachers are not called upon to communicate their successful methods and results in a form by which it would have organic effect upon general school policies? Add to this waste what results when teachers are called upon to give effect in the classroom to courses of study they do not understand the reasons for, and the total loss mounts up so that it is a fair estimate that the absence of democratic methods is the greatest single cause of educational waste.

I conclude by saying that the present subject is one of peculiar importance at the present time. The fundamental beliefs and practices of democracy are now challenged as they never have been before. In some nations they are more than challenged. They are ruthlessly and systematically destroyed. Everywhere there are waves of criticism and doubt as to whether democracy can meet pressing problems of order and security. The causes for the destruction of political democracy in countries where it was nominally established are complex. But of one thing I think we may be sure. Wherever it has fallen it was too exclusively political in nature. It had not become part of the bone and blood of the people in daily conduct of life. Democratic forms were limited to Parliament, elections and combats between parties. What is happening proves conclusively, I think, that unless democratic habits of thought and action are part of the fiber of a people, political democracy is insecure. It can not stand in isolation. It must be buttressed by the presence of democratic methods in all social relationships. The relations that exist in educational institutions are second only in importance in this respect to those which exist in industry and business, perhaps not even to them.

I recur then to the idea that the particular question discussed is one phase of a wide and deep problem. I can think of nothing so important in this country at present as a rethinking of the whole problem of democracy and its implications.

Neither the rethinking nor the action it should produce can be brought into being in a day or year. The democratic idea itself demands that the thinking and activity proceed cooperatively. My utmost hope will be fulfilled if anything I have said plays any part, however small, in promoting cooperative inquiry and experimentation in this field of democratic administration of our schools.

Questions for Thought

1. How would you define *democracy*? Do you agree with Dewey that democracy represents the best means of social interaction thus far devised? Defend your answer.
2. To what extent do you think the schools you attended encouraged the democratic way of life? To what extent did they discourage it?
3. What exactly does "equality of opportunity" mean to you? Do you think equality of opportunity can exist where there is gross economic/class inequality? Why or why not?
4. Do you think that teachers should be permitted to teach sex education in the classroom? How do you think Dewey would respond to this question?
5. In what ways are Marx and Engel's views similar to the views of Dewey? In what ways are they different?

8   The Political Theory of Islam

ABU'L A'LA MAUDUDI

Abu'l A'la Maududi (1903–1979), Islamic philosopher and social reformer, was born in Aurangabad, India. He began his writing career as a journalist in 1920 and soon after became the editor of a daily Islamic newspaper published in India. In 1929, he published an important scholarly work on Islam, "Al-Jihad Fi-al-Islam" ("Holy War in Islam"). A prolific writer throughout his life, this was the first of more than sixty books that he would write on Islam. Because of this literary output, Maududi was awarded the first Faisal Award for Islamic Literature.

In 1938, Maududi moved to Punjab to direct Dar al-Islam, an Islamic research institute. He also served as the dean of the faculty of theology at Islamia College in Lahore for two years before founding an Islamic renaissance movement, the Jamaat-e-Islami Party, in 1941. A political activist who called for the establishment of an Islamic constitution, Maududi was arrested seven years later and imprisoned for twenty months. In 1953, he was sentenced to death for a political pamphlet that he wrote; however, after mass demonstrations of his behalf, his sentence was reduced to fourteen years' imprisonment. Maududi died of a heart attack on September 22, 1979, in Buffalo, New York, where he had traveled for medical treatment.

In the following selection, which was originally presented as a lecture to the Inter-Collegiate Muslim Brotherhood in 1939, Maududi describes and defends the basic principles of Islamic political theory. His purpose in doing so, as he tells us near the beginning, is to clear up several popular misunderstandings and distortions of the Islamic view. Thus, he attempts to do for Islamic political theory what Marx and Engels attempted to do for **communism** in the earlier selection from *The Communist Manifesto.* Maududi's position on the origin of government, however, differs radically from that of Marx and Engels. Whereas Marx and Engels believed that government is a product of this-worldly economic struggles, Maududi claims that Islamic political philosophy begins with the belief in the unity and absolute sovereignty of **Allah** or God. In the Islamic state, Allah is ruler and legislator, while the people are his "vice-regents"; that is, they are agents acting on behalf of Allah to establish his laws on earth. Since Maududi believes that Allah's laws were revealed to Muhammad and written in the **Qur'an,** he concludes that only governments based on these revealed laws are legitimate.

After initially pointing out that the Islamic state is diametrically opposed to Western secular democracies (the former is founded on the rule of God, while the latter are based on the rule of the people), Maududi nevertheless argues that the Islamic state is more democratic than are Western governments. Claiming that Western politicians are generally persons who "can dupe the masses by their wealth, power, and deceptive propaganda," he says that when elected, they become overlords who reflect regional and class interests rather than the will of the people. On the other hand, in the Islamic state, which he refers to as a "**theo-democracy**," vice-regency extends to the entire community of believers, each of whom has equal freedom to express his or her opinions. As Maududi says, "The entire Muslim population runs the state in accordance with the Book of God and the practice of His Prophet." Moreover, in the Islamic state, there is no discrimination based on family or race, and equal opportunity exists for all men. In response to the objection that human freedom is restricted by Islamic law and tradition, Maududi argues that these restrictions are "divine limits" (**Hudud-Allah**) imposed by God and that divine limits are not incompatible with human freedom. Indeed, he believes that such limits provide the social structure and stability within which humans can freely interact and thus that they are "absolutely necessary in the interest of man himself."

While Maududi's account of the origin of the Islamic state differs greatly from Marx and Engels's account of the origin of government, there are several similarities between what Maududi says about the nature and purpose of government and what Marx and Engels say. Like Marx and Engels, Maududi believes that the purpose of government is to prevent exploitation, to safeguard liberty, and to institute a well-balanced system of social and economic justice. Moreover, in the Islamic state, as in the communist state, there is no realm that is purely personal or purely private. Rather, both communistic political theory and Islamic political theory maintain that in the ideal state, the opposition between the individual and society is overcome. In the Islamic state, as Maududi says, this means that "the purpose of an individual's life is the same as that of the life of the community, namely, the execution and enforcement of Divine Law and the acquisition of God's pleasure."

Questions for Reading

1. What, according to Maududi, is the origin of government?
2. What does Maududi mean when he says that the Islamic state is a "theo-democracy"? Why does he believe that such a state would be more democratic than Western democracies?
3. How does Maududi define the term *divine limits*? Why does he believe that such limits are not incompatible with human freedom?

4. In what ways, according to Maududi, is the Islamic state like the communist state? In what ways is it different?

5. How, according to Maududi, is the equilibrium between individualism and collectivism established in an Islamic state? What is his basic criticism of Western individualism?

WITH CERTAIN PEOPLE IT HAS BECOME A SORT of fashion to somehow identify Islam with one or the other systems of life in vogue at the time. So at this time also there are people who say that Islam is a **democracy,** and by this they mean to imply that there is no difference between Islam and the democracy as in vogue in the West. Some others suggest that Communism is but the latest and revised version of Islam and it is in the fitness of things that Muslims imitate the Communist experiment of Soviet Russia. Still some others whisper that Islam has the elements of dictatorship in it and we should revive the cult of "obedience to the **amir**" (the leader). All these people, in their misinformed and misguided zeal to serve what they hold to be the cause of Islam, are always at great pains to prove that Islam contains within itself the elements of all types of contemporary social and political thought and action. Most of the people who indulge in this prattle have no clear idea of the Islamic way of life. They have never made nor try to make a systematic study of the Islamic political order—the place and nature of democracy, social justice, and equality in it. Instead they behave like the proverbial blind men who gave altogether contradictory descriptions of an elephant because one had been able to touch only its tail, the other its legs, the third its belly and the fourth its ears only. Or perhaps they look upon Islam as an orphan whose sole hope for survival lies in winning the patronage and the sheltering care of some dominant creed. That is why some people have begun to present apologies on Islam's behalf. As a matter of fact this attitude emerges from an inferiority complex, from the belief that we as Muslims can earn no honour or respect unless we are able to show that our religion resembles the modern creeds and it is in agreement with most of the contemporary ideologies. These people have done a great disservice to Islam; they have reduced the political theory of Islam to a puzzle, a hotchpotch. They have turned Islam into a juggler's bag out of which can be produced anything that holds a demand! Such is the intellectual plight in which we are engulfed. Perhaps it is a result of this sorry state of affairs that some people have even begun to say that Islam has no political or economic system of its own and anything can fit into its scheme.

In these circumstances it has become essential that a careful study of the political theory of Islam should be made in a scientific way, with a view to grasp its real meaning, nature, purpose and significance. Such a systematic study alone can put an end to this confusion of thought and silence those who out of ignorance proclaim that there is nothing like Islamic political theory, Islamic social order and Islamic culture. I hope it will also bring to the world groping in darkness the light that it urgently needs, although it is not yet completely conscious of such a need. . . .

FIRST PRINCIPLE OF ISLAMIC POLITICAL THEORY

The belief in the Unity and the sovereignty of Allah is the foundation of the social and moral system propounded by the Prophet. It is the very starting-point of the Islamic political philosophy. The basic principle of Islam is that human beings must, individually and collectively, surrender all rights of overlordship, legislation and exercising of authority over others. No one should be allowed to pass orders or make commands *in his own right* and no one ought to accept the obligation to carry out such commands and obey such orders. None is entitled to make laws on his own authority and none is obliged to abide by them. This right vests in Allah alone:

"The Authority rests with none but Allah. He commands you not to surrender to any one save Him. This is the right way (of life)."[1]

From Sayyid Abu'l A'la Maududi, The Islamic Law and Constitution *(Lahore: Islamic Publications Ltd., 1960).*

"They ask: 'have we also got some authority?' Say: 'all authority belongs to God alone.'"[2]

"Do not say wrongly with your tongues that this is lawful and that is unlawful."[3]

"Whoso does not establish and decide by that which Allah hath revealed, such are disbelievers."[4]

According to this theory, sovereignty belongs to Allah. He alone is the law-giver. No man, even if he be a Prophet, has the right to order others *in his own right* to do or not to do certain things. The Prophet himself is subject to God's commands:

"I do not follow anything except what is revealed to me."[5]

Other people are required to obey the Prophet because he enunciates not his own but God's commands:

"We sent no messenger save that he should be obeyed *by Allah's leave*."[6]

"They are the people unto whom We gave the Scripture and Command and Prophethood."[7]

"It is not (possible) for any human being unto whom Allah has given the Scripture and the Wisdom and the Prophethood that he should have thereafter said unto mankind: Become slaves of *me instead of Allah;* but (what he said was) be ye faithful servants of the Lord."[8]

Thus the main characteristics of an Islamic state that can be deduced from these express statements of the Holy Qur'an are as follows:—

1. No person, class or group, not even the entire population of the state as a whole, can lay claim to sovereignty. God alone is the real sovereign; all others are merely His subjects;

2. God is the real law-giver and the authority of absolute legislation vests in Him. The believers cannot resort to totally independent legislation nor can they modify any law which God has laid down, even if the desire to effect such legislation or change in Divine laws is unanimous; and

3. An Islamic state must, in all respects, be founded upon the law laid down by God through His Prophet. The government which runs such a state will be entitled to obedience in its capacity as a political agency set up to enforce the laws of God and only in so far as it acts in that capacity. If it disregards the law revealed by God, its commands will not be binding on the believers.

THE ISLAMIC STATE: ITS NATURE AND CHARACTERISTICS

The preceding discussion makes it quite clear that Islam, speaking from the view-point of political philosophy, is the very antithesis of secular Western democracy. The philosophical foundation of Western democracy is the sovereignty of the people. In it, this type of absolute power of legislation—of the determination of values and of the norms of behaviour—rests in the hands of the people. Lawmaking is their prerogative and legislation must correspond to the mood and temper of their opinion. If a particular piece of legislation is desired by the masses, howsoever ill-conceived it may be from a religious and moral viewpoint, steps have to be taken to place it on the statute book; if the people dislike any law and demand its abrogation, howsoever just and rightful it might be, it has to be expunged forthwith. This is not the case in Islam. On this count, Islam has no trace of Western democracy. Islam, as already explained, altogether repudiates the philosophy of popular sovereignty and rears its polity on the foundations of the sovereignty of God and the viceregency (**khilafat**) of man.

A more apt name for the Islamic polity would be the "kingdom of God" which is described in English as a "theocracy." But Islamic theocracy is something altogether different from the theocracy of which Europe has had a bitter experience wherein a priestly class, sharply marked off from the rest of the population, exercises unchecked domination and enforces laws of its own making in the name of God, thus virtually imposing its own divinity and godhood upon the common people. Such a system of government is satanic rather than divine. Contrary to this, the theocracy built up by Islam is not ruled by any particular religious class but by the whole community of Muslims including the rank and file. The entire Muslim population runs the state in accordance with the Book of God and the practice of His Prophet. If I were permitted to coin a new term, I would describe this system of government as a "theo-democracy," that is to say a divine democratic government, because under it the Muslims have been given a limited popular sovereignty under the suzerainty of God. The executive under this system of government is constituted by the general will of the Muslims who have also the right to depose it. All administrative matters and all questions about which no explicit injunction is to be found in the *shari'ah* are settled by the consensus of opinion among the Muslims. Every Muslim who is capable and qualified to give a sound opinion on matters of Islamic law, is entitled to interpret the law of God when such interpretation becomes necessary. In this sense the Islamic polity is a democracy. But, as has been explained above, it is a theocracy in the sense that where an explicit command of God or His Prophet already exists, no Muslim leader or legislature, or any religious scholar, can form an independent judgment; not even all the Muslims of the world put together, have any right to make the least alteration in it.

Before proceeding further, I feel that I should put in a word of explanation as to why these limitations and restrictions have been placed upon popular sovereignty in Islam, and what is the nature of these limitations and restrictions. It may be said that God has, in this manner, taken away the liberty of human mind and intellect instead of safeguarding it as I was trying to prove. My reply is that God has retained the right of legislation in His own hand not in order to deprive man of his natural freedom but to safeguard that very freedom. His purpose is to save man from going astray and inviting his own ruin.

One can easily understand this point by attempting a little analysis of the so-called Western secular democracy. It is claimed that this democracy is founded on popular sovereignty. But everybody knows that the people who constitute a state do not all of them take part either in legislation or in its administration. They have to delegate their sovereignty to their elected representatives so that the latter may make and enforce laws on their behalf. For this purpose an electoral system is set up. But a divorce has been effected between politics and religion, and as a result of this secularisation, the society and particularly its politically active elements have ceased to attach much or any importance to morality and ethics. And this is also a fact that only those persons generally come to the top who can dupe the masses by their wealth, power, and deceptive propaganda. Although these representatives come into power by the votes of the common people, they soon set themselves up as an independent authority and assume the position of overlords

(*ilahs*). They often make laws not in the best interest of the people who raised them to power but to further their own sectional and class interests. They impose their will on the people by virtue of the authority delegated to them by those over whom they rule. This is the situation which besets people in England, America and in all those countries which claim to be the haven of secular democracy.

Even if we overlook this aspect of the matter and admit that in these countries laws are made according to the wishes of the common people, it has been established by experience that the great mass of the common people are incapable of perceiving their own true interests. It is the natural weakness of man that in most of the affairs concerning his life he takes into consideration only some one aspect of reality and loses sight of other aspects. His judgments are usually one-sided and he is swayed by emotions and desires to such an extent that rarely, if ever, can he judge important matters with the impartiality and objectivity of scientific reason. Quite often he rejects the plea of reason simply because it conflicts with his passions and desires. I can cite many instances in support of this contention but to avoid prolixity I shall content myself with giving only one example: the Prohibition Law of America. It had been rationally and logically established that drinking is injurious to health, produces deleterious effects on mental and intellectual faculties and leads to disorder in human society. The American public accepted these facts and agreed to the enactment of the Prohibition Law. Accordingly the law was passed by the majority vote. But when it was put into effect, the very same people by whose vote it had been passed, revolted against it. The worst kinds of wine were illicitly manufactured and consumed, and their use and consumption became more widespread than before. Crimes increased in number. And eventually drinking was legalised by the vote of the same people who had previously voted for its prohibition. This sudden change in public opinion was not the result of any fresh scientific discovery or the revelation of new facts providing evidence against the advantages of prohibition, but because the people had been completely enslaved by their habit and could not forgo the pleasures of self-indulgence. They delegated their own sovereignty to the evil spirit in them and set up their own desires and passions as their "*ilahs*" (gods) at whose call they all went in for the repeal of the very law they had passed after having been convinced of its rationality and correctness. There are many other similar instances which go to prove that man is not competent to become an absolute legislator. Even if he secures deliverance from the service of other *ilahs,* he becomes a slave to his own petty passions and exalts the devil in him to the position of a supreme Lord. Limitations on human freedom, provided they are appropriate and do not deprive him of all initiative, are absolutely necessary in the interest of man himself.[9]

That is why God has laid down those limits which, in Islamic phraseology, are termed 'divine limits' (*Hudud-Allah*). These limits consist of certain principles, checks and balances and specific injunctions in different spheres of life and activity, and they have been prescribed in order that man may be trained to lead a balanced and moderate life. They are intended to lay down the broad framework within which man is free to legislate, decide his own affairs and frame subsidiary laws and regulations for his conduct. These limits he is not permitted to overstep and if he does so, the whole scheme of his life will go awry.

Take for example man's economic life. In this sphere God has placed certain restrictions on human freedom. The right to private property has been recognised, but it is qualified by the obligation to pay **zakat** (poor dues) and the prohibition of interest, gambling and speculation. A specific law of inheritance for the distribution of property among the largest number of surviving relations on the death of its owner has been laid down and certain forms of acquiring, accumulating and spending wealth have been declared unlawful. If people observe these just limits and regulate their affairs within these boundary walls, on the one hand their personal liberty is adequately safeguarded and, on the other, the possibility of class war and domination of one class over another, which begins with capitalist oppression and ends in working-class dictatorship, is safely and conveniently eliminated.

Similarly in the sphere of family life, God has prohibited the unrestricted intermingling of the sexes and has prescribed **purdah,** recognised man's guardianship of woman, and clearly defined the rights and duties of husband, wife and children. The laws of divorce and separation have been clearly set forth, conditional polygamy has been permitted and

penalties for fornication and false accusations of adultery have been prescribed. He has thus laid down limits which, if observed by man, would stabilise his family life and make it a haven of peace and happiness. There would remain neither that tyranny of male over female which makes family life an inferno of cruelty and oppression, nor that satanic flood of female liberty and licence which threatens to destroy human civilisation in the West.

In like manner, for the preservation of human culture and society God has, by formulating the law of *Qisas* (Retaliation), commanding to cut off the hands for theft, prohibiting wine-drinking, placing limitations on uncovering one's private parts and by laying down a few similar permanent rules and regulations, closed the door of social disorder for ever. I have no time to present to you a complete list of all the divine limits and show in detail how essential each one of them is for maintaining equilibrium and poise in life. What I want to bring home to you here is that through these injunctions God has provided a permanent and immutable code of behaviour for man, and that it does not deprive him of any essential liberty nor does it dull the edge of his mental faculties. On the contrary, it sets a straight and clear path before him, so that he may not, owing to his ignorance and weaknesses which he inherently possesses, lose himself in the maze of destruction; and instead of wasting his faculties in the pursuit of wrong ends, he may follow the road that leads to success and progress in this world and the hereafter. If you have ever happened to visit a mountainous region, you must have noticed that in the winding mountain paths which are bounded by deep caves on the one side and lofty rocks on the other, the border of the road is barricaded and protected in such a way as to prevent travellers from straying towards the abyss by mistake. Are these barricades intended to deprive the wayfarer of his liberty? No, as a matter of fact, they are meant to protect him from destruction; to warn him at every bend of the dangers ahead and to show him the path leading to his destination. That precisely is the purpose of the restrictions (*hudud*) which God has laid down in His revealed Code. These limits determine what direction man should take in life's journey and they guide him at every turn and pass and point out to him the path of safety which he should steadfastly follow.

As I have already stated, this code, enacted as it is by God, is unchangeable. You can, if you like, rebel against it, as some Muslim countries have done. But you cannot alter it. It will continue to be unalterable till the last day. It has its own avenues of growth and evolution, but no human being has any right to tamper with it. Whenever an Islamic State comes into existence, this code would form its fundamental law and will constitute the mainspring of all its legislation. Everyone who desires to remain a Muslim is under an obligation to follow the Qur'an and the *Sunnah* which must constitute the basic law of an Islamic State.

The Purpose of the Islamic State

The purpose of the state that may be formed on the basis of the Qur'an and *Sunnah* has also been laid down by God. The Qur'an says:

> "We verily sent Our messengers with clear proofs, and revealed with them the Scripture and the Balance, that mankind may observe right measure; and We revealed iron, wherein is mighty power and (many) uses for mankind."[10]

In this verse steel symbolises political power and the verse also makes it clear that the mission of the prophets is to create conditions in which the mass of people will be assured of social justice in accordance with the standards enunciated by God in His Book which gives explicit instructions for a well-disciplined mode of life. In another place God has said:—

> "(Muslims are) those who, if We give them power in the land, establish the system of Salat (worship) and Zakat (poor dues) and enjoin virtue and forbid evil and inequity."[11]
>
> "You are the best community sent forth unto mankind; ye enjoin the Right conduct and forbid the wrong; and ye believe in Allah."[12]

It will readily become manifest to anyone who reflects upon these verses that the purpose of the state visualised by the Holy Qur'an is not negative but positive. The object of the state is not merely to prevent people from exploiting each other, to safeguard their liberty and to protect its subjects from foreign invasion. It also aims at evolving and developing that well-balanced system of social justice which has been set forth by God in His Holy Book. Its object is to eradicate all forms of evil and to encourage all types of virtue and excellence expressly mentioned by God in the Holy Qur'an. For this purpose political power will be made use of as and when the occasion demands; all means of propaganda and peaceful persuasion will be employed; the moral education of the people will also be undertaken; and social influence as well as the force of public opinion will be harnessed to the task.

The Islamic State Is Universal and All-Embracing

A state of this sort cannot evidently restrict the scope of its activities. Its approach is universal and all-embracing. Its sphere of activity is co-extensive with the whole of human life. It seeks to mould every aspect of life and activity in consonance with its moral norms and programme of social reform. In such a state no one can regard any field of his affairs as personal and private. Considered from this aspect the Islamic state bears a kind of resemblance to the Fascist and Communist states. But you will find later on that, despite its all-inclusiveness, it is something vastly and basically different from the modern totalitarian and authoritarian states. Individual liberty is not suppressed under it nor is there any trace of dictatorship in it. It presents the middle course and embodies the best that the human society has ever evolved. The excellent balance and moderation that characterise the Islamic system of government and the precise distinctions made in it between right and wrong elicit from all men of honesty and intelligence the admiration and the admission that such a balanced system could not have been framed by anyone but the Omniscient and All-Wise God.

The Islamic State Is an Ideological State

Another characteristic of the Islamic State is that it is an ideological state. It is clear from a careful consideration of the Qur'an and the *Sunnah* that the state in Islam is based on an ideology and its objective is to establish that ideology. State is an instrument of reform and must act likewise. It is a dictate of this very nature of the Islamic State that such a state should be run only by those who believe in the ideology on which it is based and in the Divine Law which it is assigned to administer. The administrators of the Islamic state must be those whose whole life is devoted to the observance and enforcement of this Law, who not only agree with its reformatory programme and fully believe in it but thoroughly comprehend its spirit and are acquainted with its details. Islam does not recognise any geographical, linguistic or colour bars in this respect. It puts forward its code of guidance and the scheme of its reform before all men. Whoever accepts this programme, no matter to what race, nation or country he may belong, can join the community that runs the Islamic state. But those who do not accept it are not entitled to have any hand in shaping the fundamental policy of the state. They can live within the confines of the State as non-Muslim citizens (*zimmis*). Specific rights and privileges have been accorded to them in the Islamic law. A *zimmi*'s life, property and honour will be fully protected, and if he is capable of any service, his services will also be made use of. He will not, however, be allowed to influence the basic policy of this ideological state. The Islamic state is based on a particular ideology and it is the community which believes in the Islamic ideology which pilots it. Here again, we notice some sort of resemblance between the Islamic and the Communist states. But the treatment meted out by the Communist states to persons holding creeds and ideologies other than its own bears no comparison with the attitude of the Islamic state. Unlike the Communist state, Islam does not impose its social principles on others by force, nor does it confiscate their properties or unleash a reign of terror by mass executions of the people and their transportation to the slave camps of Siberia. Islam does not want to eliminate its minorities; it wants to protect them and gives them the freedom to live according to their own culture. The generous and just treatment which Islam has accorded to non-Muslims in an Islamic State and the fine distinction drawn by it between justice and injustice and good and evil will convince all those who are not prejudiced against it, that the prophets sent by God accomplish their task in an altogether different manner—something radically different and diametrically opposed to the way of the false reformers who strut about here and there on the stage of history.

THE THEORY OF THE CALIPHATE AND THE NATURE OF DEMOCRACY IN ISLAM

I will now try to give a brief exposition of the composition and structure of the Islamic state. I have already stated that in Islam, God alone is the real sovereign. Keeping this cardinal principle in mind if we consider the position of those persons who set out to enforce God's law on earth, it is but natural to say that they should be regarded as representatives of the Supreme Ruler. Islam has assigned precisely this very position to them. Accordingly the Holy Qur'an says:—

> "Allah has promised to those among you who believe and do righteous deeds that He will assuredly make them to succeed (the present rulers) and grant them viceregency in the land just as He made those before them to succeed (others)."[13]

The verse illustrates very clearly the Islamic theory of state. Two fundamental points emerge from it.

1. The first point is that Islam uses the term 'viceregency' (*khilafat*) instead of sovereignty. Since, according to Islam, sovereignty belongs to God alone, anyone who holds power and rules in accordance with the laws of God would undoubtedly be the viceregent of the Supreme Ruler and will not be authorised to exercise any powers other than those delegated to him.

2. The second point stated in the verse is that the power to rule over the earth has been promised to *the whole community of believers;* it has not been stated that any particular person or class among them will be raised to that position. From this it follows that all believers are repositories of the caliphate. The caliphate granted by God to the faithful is the popular vice-regency and not a limited one. There is no reservation in favour of any family, class or race. Every believer is a caliph of God in his individual capacity. By virtue of this position he is individually responsible to God. The Holy Prophet has said: "Everyone of you is a ruler and everyone is answerable for his subjects." Thus one caliph is in no way inferior to another.

This is the real foundation of democracy in Islam. The following points emerge from an analysis of this conception of popular viceregency:

(*a*) A society in which everyone is a caliph of God and an equal participant in this caliphate, cannot tolerate any class divisions based on distinctions of birth and social position. All men enjoy equal status and position in such a society. The only criterion of superiority in this social order is personal ability and character. This is what has been repeatedly and explicitly asserted by the Holy Prophet:

> "No one is superior to another except in point of faith and piety. All men are descended from Adam and Adam was made of clay."
>
> "An Arab has no superiority over a non-Arab nor a non-Arab over an Arab; neither does a white man possess any superiority over a black man nor a black man over a white one, except in point of piety."

After the conquest of Mecca, when the whole of Arabia came under the dominion of the Islamic state, the Holy Prophet addressing the members of his own clan, who in the days before Islam enjoyed the same status in Arabia as the Brahmins did in ancient India, said:

> "O people of Qurayish! Allah has rooted out your haughtiness of the days of Ignorance and the pride of ancestry. O men, all of you are descended from Adam and Adam was made of clay. There is no pride whatever in ancestry; there is no merit in an Arab as against a non-Arab nor in a non-Arab as against an Arab. Verily the most meritorious among you in the eyes of God is he who is the most pious."

(*b*) In such a society no individual or group of individuals will suffer any disability on account of birth, social status, or profession that may in any way impede the growth of his faculties or hamper the development of his personality. Every one would enjoy equal opportunities of progress. The way would be left open for him to make as much progress as possible according to his inborn capacity and personal merits without prejudice to similar rights of other people. Thus, unrestricted scope for personal achievement has always been the hallmark of Islamic society. Slaves and their descendants were appointed as military officers and governors of provinces, and noblemen belonging to the highest families did not feel ashamed to serve under them. Cobblers who used to stitch and mend shoes rose in the social scale and became leaders of highest order (*imams*): Weavers and clothsellers became judges, *muftis* and jurists and to this day they are reckoned as the heroes of Islam. The Holy Prophet has said:

> "Listen and obey even if a negro is appointed as a ruler over you."

(*c*) There is no room in such a society for the dictatorship of any person or group of persons since everyone is a caliph of God herein. No person or group of persons is entitled to become an absolute ruler by depriving the rank and file of their inherent right of caliphate. The position of a man who is selected to conduct the affairs of the state is no more than this: that all Muslims (or, technically speaking, all caliphs of God) delegate their caliphate to him for administrative purposes. *He is answerable to God on the one hand and on the other to his fellow 'caliphs' who have delegated their authority to him.* Now, if he raises himself to the position of an irresponsible absolute ruler, that is to say a dictator, he assumes the character of a usurper rather than a caliph, because dictatorship is the negation of popular vicegerency. No doubt the Islamic state is an all-embracing state and comprises within its sphere all departments of life, but this all-inclusiveness and universality are based upon the universality of Divine Law which an Islamic ruler has to observe and enforce. The guidance given by God about every aspect of life will certainly be enforced in its entirety. But an Islamic ruler cannot depart from these instructions and adopt a policy of regimentation on his own. He cannot force people to follow or not to follow a particular profession; to learn or not to learn a special art; to use or not to use a certain script; to wear or not to wear a certain dress and to educate or not to educate their children in a certain manner. The powers which the dictators of Russia, Germany and Italy have appropriated or which Ataturk has exercised in Turkey have not been granted by Islam to its *Amir* (leader). Besides this, another important point is that in Islam *every individual is held personally answerable to God.* This personal responsibility cannot be shared by anyone else. Hence, *an individual enjoys full liberty to choose whichever path he likes and to develop his faculties in any direction that suits his natural gifts.* If the leader obstructs him or obstructs the growth of his personality, he will himself be punished by God for this tyranny. That is precisely the reason why there is not the slightest trace of regimentation in the rule of the Holy Prophet and of his rightly-guided caliphs; and

(*d*) In such a society every sane and adult Muslim, male or female, is entitled to express his or her opinion, for each one of them is the repository of the caliphate. God has made this caliphate conditional, not upon any particular standard of wealth or competence but only upon faith and good conduct. Therefore all Muslims have equal freedom to express their opinions.

Equilibrium Between Individualism and Collectivism

Islam seeks to set up, on the one hand, this superlative democracy and on the other it has put an end to that individualism which militates against the health of the body politic. The relations between the individual and the society have been regulated in such a manner that neither the personality of the individual suffers any diminution or corrosion, as it does in the Communist and Fascist social system, nor is the individual allowed to exceed his bounds to such an extent as to become harmful to the community, as happens in the Western democracies. In Islam, the purpose of an individual's life is the same as that of the life of the community, namely, the execution and enforcement of Divine Law and the acquisition of God's pleasure. Moreover, Islam has, after safeguarding the rights of the individual, imposed upon him certain duties towards the community. In this way requirements of individualism and collectivism have been so well harmonised that the individual is afforded the fullest opportunity to develop his potentialities and is thus enabled to employ his developed faculties in the service of the community at large. These are, briefly, the basic principles and essential features of the Islamic political theory.

NOTES

1. *Al-Qur'an*, 12: 40.
2. Ibid., 3: 154.
3. Ibid., 16: 116.
4. Ibid., 5: 44.
5. Ibid., 6: 50.
6. Ibid., 4: 64.
7. Ibid., 7: 90.
8. Ibid., 3: 79.
9. The question, however, is: Who is to impose these restrictions? According to the Islamic view, it is only Allah, the Creator, the Nourisher, the All-Knowing, Who is entitled to impose restrictions on human freedom and not *any man*. No man is entitled to do so. If any man arbitrarily imposes restrictions on human freedom, that is despotism pure and simple. In Islam there is no place for such despotism.—TRANS.
10. *Al-Qur'an*, 57: 25.
11. Ibid., 22: 41.
12. Ibid., 3: 110.
13. Ibid., 24: 55.

Questions for Thought

1. How do Maududi's views on the origin of government differ from the views of Marx and Engels? How do they differ from Dewey's views?
2. What do you think is the appropriate relationship between religion and government? How do your views compare with or differ from the views of Maududi?
3. What is Maududi's discussion of the Prohibition law in the United States intended to prove? Can you think of other examples that might support his position?
4. Do you agree with Maududi that "divine limits" are not incompatible with human freedom? Why or why not?
5. To what extent do you consider yourself to be an individual? To what extent do you consider yourself to be a member of the community? Where would you draw the boundary between individualism and community?

9   Who Is Your Mother? Red Roots of White Feminism

PAULA GUNN ALLEN

Paula Gunn Allen (b. 1939), who identifies strongly with her Laguna Pueblo and Sioux heritage, was born in Cubero, New Mexico. She earned her bachelor's and master's degrees in English from the University of Oregon and her Ph.D. in American studies from the University of New Mexico. Allen has taught at the University of California at Berkeley, the University of New Mexico, San Francisco State University, and Fort Lewis College. Allen's final academic position was at the University of California at Los Angeles, where she taught English, Creative Writing, and American Indian Studies. She retired from that position in 1999.

After receiving her degrees in English, Allen turned her attention to Native American studies in the early 1970s. Around the same time, she discovered *Black Elk Speaks,* the book that she credits with introducing her to the concept of the sacred hoop. (A selection from *Black Elk Speaks* is included in Chapter 6 of this text.) This concept of the sacred hoop, the recognition of the circle of life and the interconnectedness of all living things within it, became a central theme in Allen's teaching and writing. It also provided the title for the collection of essays from which the following selection is taken.

In addition to *The Sacred Hoop: Recovering the Feminine in American Indian Traditions* (1986), Allen has published several volumes of poetry, including *The Blind Lion* (1974), *Coyote's Daylight Trip* (1978), *A Cannon Between My Knees* (1981), *Shadow Country* (1982), and *Skin and Bones* (1988), as well as a novel, *The Woman Who Owned the Shadows* (1983). She has also edited two important texts devoted to preserving and disseminating the wisdom of Native American women, *Spider Woman's Granddaughters: Traditional Tales and Contemporary Writing by Native American Women* (1989) and *Grandmothers of the Light: A Medicine Woman's Sourcebook* (1991). Her other writings include *Studies of American Indian Literature: Critical Essays and Course Designs* (1983), *Women in American Indian Mythology* (1994), *As Long as the Rivers Flow: The Stories of Nine Native Americans* (1996), and *Off the Reservation: Reflections on Boundary-Busting, Border-Crossing Loose Cannons* (1998).

In the following essay, Allen describes the values and political principles that guide Native American tribal systems and contrasts these values and political principles with those that underlie European-derived models of government. She claims that tribal systems value tradition, that they emphasize the central importance of female power, and that they promote "**autonomy** of individuals, cooperation, human dignity, and egalitarian distribution of status, goods, and services." European-derived models, on the other hand, deny the importance of tradition and the power of women, and they create a hierarchical ordering of the members of society that necessarily restricts autonomy and leads to economic inequality.

On the basis of this contrast, Allen argues that the contemporary ideals of freedom and tolerance are not derived principally from European models, as is often claimed, but rather from the pluralistic democracies that already existed on this continent when the Europeans arrived. Citing what she calls the "Indianization" of American culture, she also claims that other recent social advances, such as more permissive child-rearing practices, are derived from Native American traditions as well. Finally, Allen concludes that the American dream of liberty and justice for all, the dream that is intimately connected to our conception of legitimate government, will be realized only by rejecting European-derived models of government and following the guidance of Native American values and political principles.

Questions for Reading

1. What does Allen mean by the term *gynocratic*? On what basis does she claim that many Native American tribal systems are gynocratic?
2. What, according to Allen, are the essential differences between European-derived models of government and Native American tribal systems?
3. Why does Allen believe that tradition is so important? How is tradition maintained among her people?
4. How, according to Allen, are Native American women generally portrayed in popular culture and "miseducation"? What were the lives of Native American women really like?
5. What does Allen mean by "Indianization"? What examples of the Indianization of American culture does she cite?

AT LAGUNA PUEBLO IN NEW MEXICO, "WHO is your mother?" is an important question. At Laguna, one of several of the ancient Keres **gynocratic** societies of the region, your mother's identity is the key to your own identity. Among the Keres, every individual has a place within the universe—human and nonhuman—and that place is defined by clan membership. In turn, clan membership is dependent on matrilineal descent. Of course, your mother is not only that woman whose womb formed and released you—the term refers in every individual case to an entire generation of women whose psychic, and consequently physical, "shape" made the psychic existence of the following generation possible. But naming your own mother (or her equivalent) enables people to place you precisely within the universal web of your life, in each of its dimensions: cultural, spiritual, personal, and historical.

Among the Keres, "context" and "matrix" are equivalent terms, and both refer to approximately the same thing as knowing your derivation and place. Failure to know your mother, that is, your position and its attendant traditions, history, and place in the scheme of things, is failure to remember your significance, your reality, your right relationship to earth and society. It is the same as being lost—isolated, abandoned, self-estranged, and alienated from your own life. This importance of tradition in the life of every member of the community is not confined to Keres Indians; all American Indian Nations place great value on traditionalism.

The Native American sense of the importance of continuity with one's cultural origins runs counter to contemporary American ideas: in many instances, the immigrants to America have been eager to cast off cultural ties, often seeing their antecedents as backward, restrictive, even shameful. Rejection of tradition constitutes one of the major features of American life, an attitude that reaches far back into American colonial history and that now is validated by virtually every cultural institution in the country. Feminist practice, at least in the cultural artifacts the community values most, follows this cultural trend as well.

The American idea that the best and the brightest should willingly reject and repudiate their origins leads to an allied idea—that history, like everything in the past, is of little value and should be forgotten as quickly as possible. This all too often causes us to reinvent the wheel continually. We find ourselves discovering our collective pasts over and over, having to retake ground already covered by women in the preceding decades and centuries. The Native American view, which highly values maintenance of traditional customs, values, and perspectives, might result in slower societal change and in quite a bit less social upheaval, but it has the advantage of providing a solid sense of identity and lowered levels of psychological and interpersonal conflict.

Contemporary Indian communities value individual members who are deeply connected to the traditional ways of their people, even after centuries of concerted and brutal effort on the part of the American government, the churches, and the corporate system to break the connections between individuals and their tribal world. In fact, in the view of the traditionals, rejection of one's culture—one's traditions, language, people—is the result of colonial oppression and is hardly to be applauded. They believe that the roots of oppression are to be found in the loss of tradition and memory because that loss is always accompanied by a loss of a positive sense of self. In short, Indians think it is important to remember, while Americans believe it is important to forget.

The traditional Indians' view can have a significant impact if it is expanded to mean that the sources of social, political, and philosophical thought in the Americas not only should be recognized and honored by Native Americans but should be embraced by American society. If American society judiciously modeled the traditions of the various Native Nations, the place of women in society would become central, the distribution of goods and power would be egalitarian, the elderly would be respected, honored, and protected as a primary social and cultural resource, the ideals of physical beauty would be considerably enlarged (to include "fat," strong-featured women, gray-haired, and wrinkled individuals, and others who in contemporary American culture are viewed as "ugly"). Additionally, the destruction of the biota, the life sphere, and the natural resources of the planet would be curtailed, and the spiritual nature of human and nonhuman life would become a primary organizing principle of human society. And if the traditional tribal systems that are emulated included pacifist ones, war would cease to be a major method of human problem solving.

RE-MEMBERING CONNECTIONS AND HISTORIES

The belief that rejection of tradition and of history is a useful response to life is reflected in America's amazing loss of memory concerning its origins in the matrix and context of Native America. America does not seem to remember that it derived its wealth, its values, its food, much of its medicine, and a large part of its "dream" from Native America. It is ignorant of the genesis of its culture in this Native American land, and that ignorance helps to perpetuate the longstanding European and Middle Eastern monotheistic, hierarchical, patriarchal cultures' oppression of women, gays, and lesbians, people of color, working class, unemployed people, and the elderly. Hardly anyone in America speculates that the constitutional system of government might be as much a product of American Indian ideas and practices as of colonial American and Anglo-European revolutionary fervor.

Even though Indians are officially and informally ignored as intellectual movers and shapers in the United States, Britain, and Europe, they are peoples with ancient tenure on this soil. During the ages when tribal societies existed in the Americas largely untouched by patriarchal oppression, they developed elaborate systems of thought that included science, philosophy, and government based on a belief in the central importance of female energies, autonomy of individuals, cooperation, human dignity, human freedom, and egalitarian distribution of status, goods, and services. Respect for others, reverence for life, and, as a byproduct, pacifism as a way of life; importance of kinship ties in the customary ordering of social interaction; a sense of the sacredness and mystery of existence; balance and harmony in relationships both sacred and secular were all features of life among the tribal confederacies and nations. And in those that lived by the largest number of these principles, gynarchy was the norm rather than the exception. Those systems are as yet unmatched in any contemporary industrial, agrarian, or postindustrial society on earth.

As we have seen in previous essays, there are many female gods recognized and honored by the tribes and Nations. Femaleness was highly valued, both respected and feared, and all social institutions reflected this attitude. Even modern sayings, such as the Cheyenne statement that a people is not conquered until the hearts of the women are on the ground, express the Indians' understanding that without the power of woman the people will not live, but with it, they will endure and prosper.

Indians did not confine this belief in the central importance of female energy to matters of worship. Among many of the tribes (perhaps as many as 70 percent of them in North America alone), this belief was reflected in all of their social institutions. The Iroquois Constitution or White Roots of Peace, also called the Great Law of the Iroquois, codified the Matrons' decision-making and economic power:

> The lineal descent of the people of the Five Fires [the Iroquois Nations] shall run in the female line. Women shall be considered the progenitors of the Nation. They shall own the land and the soil. Men and women shall follow the status of their mothers. (Article 44)

> The women heirs of the chieftainship titles of the League shall be called Oiner or Otinner [Noble] for all time to come. (Article 45)

> If a disobedient chief persists in his disobedience after three warnings [by his female relatives, by his male relatives, and by one of his fellow council members, in that order], the matter shall go to the council of War Chiefs. The Chiefs shall then take away the title of the erring chief *by order of the women in whom the title is vested*. When the chief is deposed, the women shall notify the chiefs of the League . . . and the chiefs of the League shall sanction the act. The women will then select another of their sons as a candidate and the chiefs shall elect him. (Article 19) (Emphasis mine)[1]

The Matrons held so much policy-making power traditionally that once, when their position was threatened, they demanded its return and consequently the power of women was fundamental in shaping the Iroquois Confederation sometime in the sixteenth or early seventeenth century. It was women

> who fought what may have been the first successful feminist rebellion in the New World. The year was 1600, or thereabouts, when these tribal feminists decided that they had had enough of unregulated warfare by their men. Lysistratas among the Indian women proclaimed a boycott on lovemaking and childbearing. Until the men conceded them the power to decide upon war and peace, there would be no more warriors. Since the men believed that the women alone knew the secret of childbirth, the rebellion was instantly successful.

> In the constitution of Deganawidah the founder of the Iroquois Confederation of Nations had said: "He caused the body of our mother, the woman, to be of great worth and honor. He purposed that she shall be endowed and entrusted with the birth and upbringing of men, and that she shall have the care of all that is supplanted by which life is sustained and supported and the power to breathe is fortified: *and moreover that the warriors shall be her assistants.*"

> The footnote of history was curiously supplied when Susan B. Anthony began her "Votes for Women" movement two and a half centuries later. Unknowingly the feminists chose to hold their founding convention of latter-day suffragettes in the town of Seneca [Falls], New York. The site was just a stone's throw from the old council house where the Iroquois women had plotted their feminist rebellion. (Emphasis mine)[2]

Beliefs, attitudes, and laws such as these became part of the vision of American feminists and of other human liberation movements around the world. Yet feminists too often believe that no one has ever experienced the kind of society that empowered women and made that empowerment the basis of its rules of civilization. The price the feminist community must pay because it is not aware of the recent presence of gynarchical societies on this continent is unnecessary confusion, division, and much lost time.

THE ROOT OF OPPRESSION IS LOSS OF MEMORY

An odd thing occurs in the minds of Americans when Indian civilization is mentioned: little or nothing. As I write this, I am aware of how far removed my version of the roots of American feminism must seem to those steeped in either mainstream or radical versions of feminism's history. I am keenly aware of the lack of image Americans have about our continent's recent past. I am intensely conscious of popular notions of Indian women as beasts of burden, squaws, traitors, or, at best, vanished denizens of a long-lost wilderness. How odd, then, must my contention seem that the gynocratic tribes of the American continent provided the basis for all the dreams of liberation that characterize the modern world.

We as feminists must be aware of our history on this continent. We need to recognize that the same forces that devastated the gynarchies of Britain and the Continent also devastated the ancient African civilizations, and we must know that those same materialistic, antispiritual forces are presently engaged in wiping out the same gynarchical values, along with the peoples who adhere to them, in Latin America. I am convinced that those wars were and continue to be about the imposition of patriarchal civilization over the holistic, pacifist, and spirit-based gynarchies they supplant. To that end the wars of imperial conquest have not been solely or even mostly waged over the land and its resources, but they have been fought within the bodies, minds, and hearts of the people of the earth for dominion over them. I think this is the reason traditionals say we must remember our origins, our cultures, our histories, our mothers and grandmothers, for without that memory, which implies continuance rather than nostalgia, we are doomed to engulfment by a paradigm that is fundamentally inimical to the vitality, autonomy, and self-empowerment essential for satisfying, high-quality life.

The vision that impels feminists to action was the vision of the Grandmothers' society, the society that was captured in the words of the sixteenth-century explorer Peter Martyr nearly five hundred years ago. It is the same vision repeated over and over by radical thinkers of Europe and America, from François Villon to John Locke, from William Shakespeare to Thomas Jefferson, from Karl Marx to Friedrich Engels, from Benito Juarez to Martin Luther King, from Elizabeth Cady Stanton to Judy Grahn, from Harriet Tubman to Audre Lorde, from Emma Goldman to Bella Abzug, from Malinalli to Cherríe Moraga, and from Iyatiku to me. That vision as Martyr told it is of a country where there are "no soldiers, no gendarmes or police, no nobles, kings, regents, prefects, or judges, no prisons, no lawsuits . . . . All are equal and free," or so Friedrich Engels recounts Martyr's words.[3]

Columbus wrote:

> Nor have I been able to learn whether they [the inhabitants of the islands he visited on his first journey to the New World] held personal property, for it seemed to me that whatever one had, they all took shares of. . . . They are so ingenuous and free with all they have, that no one would believe it who has not seen it; of anything that they possess, if it be asked of them, they never say no; on the contrary, they invite you to share it and show as much love as if their hearts went with it.[4]

At least that's how the Native Caribbean people acted when the whites first came among them; American Indians are the despair of social workers, bosses, and missionaries even now because of their deeply ingrained tendency to spend all they have, mostly on others. In any case, as the historian William Brandon notes,

> the Indian *seemed* free, to European eyes, gloriously free, to the European soul shaped by centuries of toil and tyranny, and this impression operated profoundly on the process of history and the development of America. Something in the peculiar character of the Indian world gave an impression of classlessness, of propertylessness, and that in turn led to an impression, as H. H. Bancroft put it, of "humanity unrestrained . . . in the exercise of liberty absolute."[5]

A FEMINIST HEROINE

Early in the women's suffrage movement, Eva Emery Dye, an Oregon suffragette, went looking for a heroine to embody her vision of feminism. She wanted a historical figure whose life would symbolize the strengthened power of women. She found Sacagawea (or Sacajawea) buried in the journals of Lewis and Clark. The Shoshoni teenager had traveled with the Lewis and Clark expedition, carrying her infant son, and on a small number of occasions acted as translator.[6]

Dye declared that Sacagawea, whose name is thought to mean Bird Woman, had been the guide to the historic expedition, and through Dye's work Sacagawea became enshrined in American memory as a moving force and friend of the whites, leading them in the settlement of western North America.[7]

But Native American roots of white feminism reach back beyond Sacagawea. The earliest white women on this continent were well acquainted with tribal women. They were neighbors to a number of tribes and often shared food, information, child care, and health care. Of course little is made of these encounters in official histories of colonial America, the period from the Revolution to the Civil War, or on the evermoving frontier. Nor, to my knowledge, has either the significance or incidence of intermarriage between Indian and white or between Indian and Black been explored. By and large, the study of Indian-white relations has been focused on government and treaty relations, warfare, missionization, and education. It has been almost entirely documented in terms of formal white Christian patriarchal impacts and assaults on Native Americans, though they are not often characterized as assaults but as "civilizing the savages." Particularly in organs of popular culture and miseducation, the focus has been on what whites imagine to be degradation of Indian women ("squaws"), their equally imagined love of white government and white conquest ("princesses"), and the horrifying, misleading, fanciful tales of "bloodthirsty, backward primitives" assaulting white Christian settlers who were looking for life, liberty, and happiness in their chosen land.

But, regardless of official versions of relations between Indians and whites or other segments of the American population, the fact remains that great numbers of apparently "white" or "Black" Americans carry notable degrees of Indian blood. With that blood has come the culture of the Indian, informing the lifestyles, attitudes, and values of their descendants. Somewhere along the line—and often quite recently—an Indian woman was giving birth to and raising the children of a family both officially and informally designated as white or Black—not Indian. In view of this, it should be evident that one of the major enterprises of Indian women in America has been the transfer of Indian values and culture to as large and influential a segment of American immigrant populations as possible. Their success in this endeavor is amply demonstrated in the Indian values and social styles that increasingly characterize American life. Among these must be included "permissive" child-rearing practices, for . . . imprisoning, torturing, caning, strapping, starving, or verbally abusing children was considered outrageous behavior. Native Americans did not believe that physical or psychological abuse of children would result in their edification. They did not believe that children are born in sin, are congenitally predisposed to evil, or that a good parent who wishes the child to gain salvation, achieve success, or earn the respect of her or his fellows can be helped to those ends by physical or emotional torture.

The early Americans saw the strongly protective attitude of the Indian people as a mark of their "savagery"—as they saw the Indian's habit of bathing frequently, their sexual openness, their liking for scant clothing, their raucous laughter at most things, their suspicion and derision of authoritarian structures, their quick pride, their genuine courtesy, their willingness to share what they had with others less fortunate than they, their egalitarianism, their ability to act as if various lifestyles were a normal part of living, and their granting that women were of equal or, in individual cases, of greater value than men.

Yet the very qualities that marked Indian life in the sixteenth century have, over the centuries since contact between the two worlds occurred, come to mark much of contemporary American life. And those qualities, which I believe have passed into white culture from Indian culture, are the very ones that fundamentalists, immigrants from Europe, the

Middle East, and Asia often find the most reprehensible. Third- and fourth-generation Americans indulge in growing nudity, informality in social relations, egalitarianism, and the rearing of women who value autonomy, strength, freedom, and personal dignity—and who are often derided by European, Asian, and Middle Eastern men for those qualities. Contemporary Americans value leisure almost as much as tribal people do. They find themselves increasingly unable to accept child abuse as a reasonable way to nurture. They bathe more than any other industrial people on earth—much to the scorn of their white cousins across the Atlantic, and they sometimes enjoy a good laugh even at their own expense (though they still have a less developed sense of the ridiculous than one might wish).

Contemporary Americans find themselves more and more likely to adopt a "live and let live" attitude in matters of personal sexual and social styles. Two-thirds of their diet and a large share of their medications and medical treatments mirror or are directly derived from Native American sources. Indianization is not a simple concept, to be sure, and it is one that Americans often find themselves resisting; but it is a process that has taken place, regardless of American resistance to recognizing the source of many if not most of American's vaunted freedoms in our personal, family, social, and political arenas.

This is not to say that Americans have become Indian in every attitude, value, or social institution. Unfortunately, Americans have a way to go in learning how to live in the world in ways that improve the quality of life for each individual while doing minimal damage to the biota, but they have adapted certain basic qualities of perception and certain attitudes that are moving them in that direction.[8]

AN INDIAN-FOCUSED VERSION OF AMERICAN HISTORY

American colonial ideas of self-government came as much from the colonists' observations of tribal governments as from their Protestant or Greco-Roman heritage. Neither Greece nor Rome had the kind of pluralistic **democracy** as that concept has been understood in the United States since Andrew Jackson, but the tribes, particularly the gynarchical tribal confederacies, did. It is true that the *oligarchic*

form of government that colonial Americans established was originally based on Greco-Roman systems in a number of important ways, such as its restriction of citizenship to propertied white males over twenty-one years of age, but it was never a form that Americans as a whole have been entirely comfortable with. Politics and government in the United States during the Federalist period also reflected the English common law system as it had evolved under patriarchal feudalism and monarchy—hence the United States' retention of slavery and restriction of citizenship to propertied white males.

The Federalists did make one notable change in the feudal system from which their political system derived on its Anglo side. They rejected blooded **aristocracy** and monarchy. This idea came from the Protestant Revolt to be sure, but it was at least reinforced by colonial America's proximity to American Indian nonfeudal confederacies and their concourse with those confederacies over the two hundred years of the colonial era. It was this proximity and concourse that enabled the revolutionary theorists to "dream up" a system in which all local polities would contribute to and be protected by a central governing body responsible for implementing policies that bore on the common interest of all. It should also be noted that the Reformation followed Columbus's contact with the Americas and that his and Martyr's reports concerning Native Americans' free and easy egalitarianism were in circulation by the time the Reformation took hold.

The Iroquois feudal system, like that of several in the vicinity of the American colonies, is remarkably similar to the organization of the federal system of the United States. It was made up of local, "state," and federal bodies composed of executive, legislative, and judicial branches. The Council of Matrons was the executive: it instituted and determined general policy. The village, tribal (several villages), and Confederate councils determined and implemented policies when they did not conflict with the broader Council's decisions or with theological precepts that ultimately determined policy at all levels. The judicial was composed of the men's councils and the Matron's council, who sat together to make decisions. Because the matrons were the ceremonial center of the system, they were also the prime policymakers.

Obviously, there are major differences between the structure of the contemporary American government and that of the Iroquois. Two of those differences were and are crucial to the process of just government. The Iroquois system is spirit-based, while that of the United States is secular, and the Iroquois Clan Matrons formed the executive. The female executive function was directly tied to the ritual nature of the Iroquois politic, for the executive was lodged in the hands of the Matrons of particular clans across village, tribe, and national lines. The executive office was hereditary, and only sons of eligible clans could serve, at the behest of the Matrons of their clans, on the councils at the three levels. Certain daughters inherited the office of Clan Matron through their clan affiliations. No one could impeach or disempower a Matron, though her violation of certain laws could result in her ineligibility for the Matron's council. For example, a woman who married *and took her husband's name* could not hold the title Matron.

American ideas of social justice came into sharp focus through the commentaries of Iroquois observers who traveled in France in the colonial period. These observers expressed horror at the great gap between the lifestyles of the wealthy and the poor, remarking to the French philosopher Montaigne, who would heavily influence the radical communities of Europe, England, and America, that "they had noticed that in Europe there seemed to be two moities, consisting of the rich 'full gorged' with wealth, and the poor, starving 'and bare with need and povertie.' The Indian tourists not only marveled at the division, but marveled that the poor endured 'such an injustice, and that they took not the others by the throte, or set fire on their house.'"[9] It must be noted that the urban poor eventually did just that in the French Revolution. The writings of Montaigne and of those he influenced provided the theoretical framework and the vision that propelled the struggle for liberty, justice, and equality on the Continent and later throughout the British empire.

The feminist idea of power as it ideally accrues to women stems from tribal sources. The central importance of the clan Matrons in the formulation and determination of domestic and foreign policy as well as in their primary role in the ritual and ceremonial life of their respective Nations was the single most important attribute of the Iroquois, as of the Cherokee and Muskogee, who traditionally inhabited the southern Atlantic region. The latter peoples were removed to what is now Oklahoma during the Jackson administration, but prior to the American Revolution they had regular and frequent communication with and impact on both the British colonizers and later the American people, including the African peoples brought here as slaves.

Ethnographer Lewis Henry Morgan wrote an account of Iroquoian matriarchal culture, published in 1877,[10] that heavily influenced Marx and the development of communism, particularly lending it the idea of the liberation of women from patriarchal dominance. The early socialists in Europe, especially in Russia, saw women's liberation as a central aspect of the socialist revolution. Indeed, the basic ideas of socialism, the egalitarian distribution of goods and power, the peaceful ordering of society, and the right of every member of society to participate in the work and benefits of that society, are ideas that pervade American Indian political thought and action. And it is through various channels—the informal but deeply effective Indianization of Europeans, and christianizing Africans, the social and political theory of the confederacies feuding and then intertwining with European dreams of liberty and justice, and, more recently, the work of Morgan and the writings of Marx and Engels—that the age-old gynarchical systems of egalitarian government found their way into contemporary feminist theory.

When Eva Emery Dye discovered Sacagawea and honored her as the guiding spirit of American womanhood, she may have been wrong in bare historical fact, but she was quite accurate in terms of deeper truth. The statues that have been erected depicting Sacagawea as a Matron in her prime signify an understanding in the American mind, however unconscious, that the source of just government, of right ordering of social relationships, the dream of "liberty and justice for all" can be gained only by following the Indian Matrons' guidance. For, as Dr. Anna Howard Shaw said of Sacagawea at the National American Woman's Suffrage Association in 1905:

> Forerunner of civilization, great leader of men, patient and motherly woman, we bow our hearts to do you honor! . . . May we the daughters of

an alien race . . . learn the lessons of calm endurance, of patient persistence and unfaltering courage exemplified in your life, in our efforts to lead men through the Pass of justice, which goes over the mountains of prejudice and conservatism to the broad land of the perfect freedom of a true republic; one in which men and women together shall in perfect equality solve the problems of a nation that knows no caste, no race, no sex in opportunity, in responsibility or in justice! May 'the eternal womanly' ever lead us on![11]

NOTES

1. The White Roots of Peace, cited in *The Third Woman: Minority Women Writers of the United States,* ed. Dexter Fisher (Boston: Houghton Mifflin, 1980), p. 577. Cf. Thomas Sanders and William Peek, eds., *Literature of the American Indian* (New York: Glencoe Press, 1973), pp. 208–239. Sanders and Peek refer to the document as "The Law of the Great Peace."

2. Stan Steiner, *The New Indians* (New York: Dell, 1968), pp. 219–220.

3. William Brandon, *The Last Americans: The Indian in American Culture* (New York: McGraw-Hill, 1974), p. 294.

4. Brandon, *Last Americans*, p. 6.

5. Brandon, *Last Americans*, pp. 7–8. The entire chapter "American Indians and American History" (pp. 1–23) is pertinent to the discussion.

6. Ella E. Clark and Margot Evans, *Sacagawea of the Lewis and Clark Expedition* (Berkeley: University of California Press, 1979), pp. 93–98. Clark details the fascinating, infuriating, and very funny scholarly escapade of how our suffragette foremothers created a feminist hero from the scant references to the teenage Shoshoni wife of the expedition's official translator, Pierre Charbonneau.

7. The implications of this maneuver did not go unnoticed by either whites or Indians, for the statues of the idealized Shoshoni woman, the Native American matron Sacagawea, suggest that American tenure on American land, indeed, the right to be on this land, is given to whites by her. While that implication is not overt, it certainly is suggested in the image of her that the sculptor chose: a tall, heavy woman, standing erect, nobly pointing the way westward with upraised hand. The impression is furthered by the habit of media and scholar of referring to her as "the guide." Largely because of the popularization of the circumstances of Sacagawea's participation in the famed Lewis and Clark expedition, Indian people have viewed her as a traitor to her people, likening her to Malinalli (La Malinche, who acted as interpreter for Cortés and bore him a son) and Pocahontas, that unhappy girl who married John Rolfe (not John Smith) and died in England after bearing him a son. Actually none of these women engaged in traitorous behavior. Sacagawea led a long life, was called Porivo (Chief Woman) by the Comanches, among whom she lived for more than twenty years, and in her old age engaged her considerable skill at speaking and manipulating white bureaucracy to help in assuring her Shoshoni people decent reservation holdings.

8. A full discussion is impossible here but an examination of American child-rearing practices, societal attitudes toward women and exhibited by women (when compared to the same in Old World cultures) as well as the foodstuffs, medicinal materials, countercultural and alternative cultural systems, and the deeply Indian values these reflect should demonstrate the truth about informal acculturation and cross-cultural connections in the Americas.

9. Brandon, *Last Americans*, p. 6.

10. Lewis Henry Morgan, *Ancient Society or Researches in the Lines of Human Progress from Savagery Through Barbarism to Civilization* (New York, 1877).

11. Clark and Evans, *Sacagawea*, p. 96.

Questions for Thought

1. What do you think are the most important differences between European-derived models of government and Native American tribal systems?

2. How important is tradition in your life? Which of your ancestral traditions do you consider most sacred?

3. Can you think of specific examples from popular culture in which Native American women are depicted in the negative manner that Allen describes? Can you think of specific examples in which their lives are portrayed more realistically?

4. Do you think that Indianization, as Allen describes it, represents positive change? Why or why not?

5. What arguments, if any, can you think of to defend European-derived models of government against Allen's criticisms?

Where Do Our Obligations to Society End?

On Liberty   **10**

JOHN STUART MILL

John Stuart Mill (1806–1873), an influential nineteenth-century English philosopher, was born in London. His father, James Mill, was a Scottish philosopher, historian, and economist who belonged to a group of philosophical radicals and reformers that included the economist David Ricardo and the utilitarian Jeremy Bentham. The younger Mill received most of his education from his father and his father's friends. Even though he never attended school, Mill began studying Greek at age three and Latin four years later. By age thirteen, he had read most of the Greek and Latin classics, and he had intensively studied logic, mathematics, history, and political economy. Mill was also thoroughly grounded in the reformist politics of his father. When he was seventeen, Mill was already writing articles for the *Westminster Review* and actively working for social change. He was arrested during this time for distributing pamphlets on contraception.

After spending fourteen months in France in 1820–1821, Mill returned to England to study law with John Austin. He soon gave this up, however, and took a position in the East India Company as a junior clerk under his father. Mill worked for the East India Company for the next thirty-five years, retiring only when the company was dissolved.

In 1826, Mill suffered from a severe state of depression that lasted for several months, a state that he attributed to his overly analytical education. Believing that this education had stunted his emotional growth, Mill turned to art, music, and poetry as a remedy for his malady. In 1830, he met Harriet Taylor, the wife of a wealthy merchant, who further contributed to his emotional growth. Although she remained with her husband, Taylor was Mill's intellectual companion and intimate friend until her husband died in 1849. Then, two years after her husband's death, Taylor and Mill were married. When his wife died in Avignon, France, seven years later, Mill bought a house near her grave.

Although Mill published two books in the 1840s, most of his best-known works were published after his wife's death. These included *On Liberty* (1859), *Considerations on Representative Government* (1861), *Utilitarianism* (1863), *On the Subjection of Women* (1869), and *Autobiography* (1873). In addition to his writing, Mill served for one term as a member of the House of Commons from 1865 to 1868. One of Mill's legislative proposals, which did not pass, was to extend voting rights to women. Mill died in Avignon on May 8, 1873, after a brief illness.

In the following selection from *On Liberty*, Mill focuses specifically on the question that serves as the heading for the second section of this chapter, the question of where our obligations to society end. He begins by noting that this question, the question of civil or social liberty, has a long history. Initially, it was raised in a political context in which the interests of the ruler or rulers were not identical with the interests of the subjects. In this context, the purpose of civil or social liberty was to protect the people from their own rulers. However, with the advent of modern democratic government, this political context changed. Mill notes that this radical change of political context led some people to argue that social liberty was no longer needed, for they believed that tyranny was not possible in a **democracy.** But Mill observes that the people elected in a democratic government do not always represent the interests of the people who elect them; moreover, although democracy is a type of self-government, "the 'self-government' spoken of is not the government of each by himself, but of each by all the rest." This leaves open the possibility for what Mill calls "tyranny of the majority"—that is, the possibility that those elected by majority vote may try to oppress the minority members of society. But even if the likelihood of governmental oppression were reduced in a democratic society, Mill notes that individuals also need protection against "social tyranny," against the tendency of society to coerce conformity to its norms and values by powerful means other than governmental regulation. Given that tyranny of the majority and social tyranny are both real possibilities in a democracy, Mill claims that social liberty is just as necessary in a democratic society as it was in earlier nondemocratic societies.

Having argued that social liberty is still necessary, Mill goes on to discuss the limits of such liberty. When, Mill asks, is the government or society justified in restricting individual freedom? Noting that this important question has received no clear-cut answer, Mill proposes a principle to establish the boundary between the sphere of legitimate government interference and the sphere of individual freedom. This principle, which Mill believes to be justified by considerations of utility, is that governmental authority should extend only to those actions that are harmful to others, but not to those actions that concern only the individual. As Mill clearly says, "Over himself, over his own body and mind, the individual is sovereign."

In explaining this principle, Mill notes that society is certainly justified in prohibiting actions that directly harm others and even in requiring certain actions that, if left undone, would bring injury to others. Moreover, while Mill rejects the social contract theory of the origin of government, he believes that anyone who receives the protection of society owes something in return. Thus, each person can be required to contribute his or her fair share toward paying the costs of maintaining social programs for the common good. Mill argues that beyond these areas of legitimate government control, however, there is the proper sphere of human freedom. This sphere consists of "all that portion of a person's life and conduct which affects only himself or, if it also affects others, only with their free, voluntary, and undeceived consent and participation." As the qualifying clause in this statement clearly indicates, Mill believes that his principle applies only to adult members of society who have full control of their mental faculties. Under Mill's principle, these members should be guaranteed certain individual freedoms, such as freedom of thought, conscience, expression, pursuits, and assembly, as long as these do not directly harm other nonconsenting members of society. Mill concludes that only a society that fully implements this principle can be said truly to be free.

Questions for Reading

1. What does Mill mean by *civil* or *social liberty*?
2. Why does Mill think that social liberty is still needed in democratic societies? What exactly does Mill mean by "tyranny of the majority"?
3. What principle does Mill propose for determining the limit of social liberty? What reasons does Mill give for accepting this principle?
4. Under Mill's principle, what sorts of actions are prohibited, and what sorts of actions are required? What are our general obligations to society?
5. What exactly does Mill mean by *social tyranny*? How, according to Mill, is such tyranny instituted?
6. What, according to Mill, are some of the reasons people give for not accepting his principle? How does Mill respond to these objections?

INTRODUCTION

THE SUBJECT OF THIS ESSAY IS NOT THE SO-called "liberty of the will," which is so unfortunately contrasted with the misnamed doctrine of philosophical necessity. Rather, the subject is civil or social liberty, that is, the nature and limits of the power that can be legitimately exercised by society over the individual. This question, which is seldom stated and hardly ever discussed in general terms, profoundly influences the practical controversies of the age by its latent presence, and will likely soon be recognized as the vital question of the future. It is so far from being new that, in a certain sense, it has divided mankind almost from the remotest ages. However, in the stage of progress into which the more civilized portions of the species have now entered, it presents itself under new conditions and requires a different and more fundamental treatment.

The struggle between liberty and authority is the most conspicuous feature in the portions of history with which we are earliest familiar, particularly in the case of Greece, Rome, and England. But in old times this contest was between subjects, or some classes of subjects, and the government. Liberty meant protection against the tyranny of the political rulers. The rulers were conceived (except in some of the popular governments of Greece) as being in a position that was necessarily antagonistic to the people whom they ruled. They consisted of a governing One, or a governing tribe or caste, and they derived their authority from inheritance or conquest. In all events, they did not hold their authority at the pleasure of the governed. . . . Their power was regarded as necessary, but also as highly dangerous; it was seen as a weapon that they would attempt to use against their subjects, no less than against external enemies. To prevent the weaker members of the community from being preyed upon by innumerable vultures, it was needful that there should be an animal of prey stronger than the rest, commissioned to keep them down. But as the king of the vultures would be no less bent upon preying on the flock than any of the minor harpies, it was indispensable to be in a perpetual attitude of defense against his beak and claws. The aim, therefore, of patriots was to set limits to the power that the ruler should be suffered to exercise over the community; and this limitation was what they meant by liberty. It was attempted in two ways. The first way was by obtaining recognition of certain immunities called political liberties or rights, the infringement of which by the ruler was to be regarded as a breach of duty. Moreover, if the ruler did infringe upon these rights, specific resistance or general rebellion was held to be justifiable. A second (and generally a later) way was the establishment of constitutional checks by which the consent of the community, or of a body of some sort supposed to represent its interests, was made a necessary condition to some of the more important acts of the governing power. To the first of these modes of limitation, the ruling power, in most European countries, was compelled, more or less, to submit. It was not so with the second; and, to attain this, or, when already in some degree possessed, to attain it more completely, became everywhere the principal object of the lovers of liberty. And so long as mankind was content to combat one enemy by another, and to be ruled by a master on condition of being guaranteed more or less efficaciously against his tyranny, they did not carry their aspirations beyond this point.

However, in the progress of human affairs, a time came when men ceased to think it a necessity of nature that their governors should be an independent power opposed in interest to themselves. It appeared to them to be much better that the various magistrates of the state should be their tenants or delegates, revocable at their pleasure. In that way alone, it seemed, could they have complete security that the powers of government would never be abused to their disadvantage. By degrees this new demand for elective and temporary rulers became the prominent object of the exertions of the popular party, wherever any such party existed, and superseded, to a considerable extent, the previous efforts to limit the power of rulers. As the struggle proceeded for making the ruling power emanate from the periodical choice of the ruled, some persons began to think that too much importance had been attached to the limitation of the power itself. *That* (it might seem) was a resource against rulers whose interests were habitually opposed to those of the people. What was now wanted was that the

This is the editor's revised version of a selection from John Stuart Mill, On Liberty, *London, 1859.*

rulers should be identified with the people, that their interest and will should be the interest and will of the nation. The nation did not need to be protected against its own will. There was no fear of its tyrannizing over itself. Let the rulers be effectually responsible to it, promptly removable by it, and it could afford to trust them with power of which it could itself dictate the use to be made. Their power was but the nation's own power, concentrated and in a form convenient for exercise. . . .

But, in political and philosophical theories as well as in persons, success discloses faults and infirmities which failure might have concealed from observation. The notion that the people have no need to limit their power over themselves might seem axiomatic, when popular government was a thing only dreamed about, or read of as having existed at some distant period of the past. . . . In time, however, a democratic republic came to occupy a large portion of the earth's surface and it made itself felt as one of the most powerful members of the community of nations.[1] Elective and responsible government then became subject to the observations and criticisms which wait upon a great existing fact. It was now perceived that such phrases as "self-government," and "the power of the people over themselves," do not express the true state of the case. The "people" who exercise the power are not always the same people with those over whom it is exercised; and the "self-government" spoken of is not the government of each by himself, but of each by all the rest. The will of the people, moreover, practically means the will of the most numerous or the most active *part* of the people—the majority, or those who succeed in making themselves accepted as the majority. The people, consequently, *may* desire to oppress a part of their number, and precautions are as much needed against this as against any other abuse of power. The limitation, therefore, of the power of government over individuals loses none of its importance when the holders of power are regularly accountable to the community, that is, to the strongest party therein. This view of things . . . has had no difficulty in establishing itself; and in political speculations "the tyranny of the majority" is now generally included among the evils against which society requires to be on its guard.

Like other tyrannies, the tyranny of the majority was at first . . . held in dread chiefly as operating through the acts of the public authorities. But reflecting persons perceived that when society is itself the tyrant—society collectively over the separate individuals who compose it—its means of tyrannizing are not restricted to the acts which it may do by the hands of its political functionaries. Society can and does execute its own mandates. And if it issues wrong mandates instead of right ones, or any mandates at all in things with which it ought not to meddle, it practices a social tyranny more formidable than many kinds of political oppression. Although this social tyranny is not usually upheld by such extreme penalties, it leaves fewer means of escape, penetrating much more deeply into the details of life and enslaving the soul itself. Protection, therefore, against the tyranny of the magistrate is not enough. Protection is also needed against the tyranny of the prevailing opinion and feeling, against the tendency of society to impose, by other means than civil penalties, its own ideas and practices as rules of conduct on those who dissent from them. Such rules of conduct fetter the development and, if possible, prevent the formation of any individuality not in harmony with the ways of society, and compel all characters to fashion themselves upon the model of its own. There is a limit to the legitimate interference of collective opinion with individual independence; and to find that limit, and maintain it against encroachment, is as indispensable to a good condition of human affairs as is protection against political despotism.

But though this proposition is not likely to be contested in general terms, the practical question where to place the limit—how to make the fitting adjustment between individual independence and social control—is a subject on which nearly everything remains to be done. All that makes existence valuable to anyone depends on the enforcement of restraints upon the actions of other people. Some rules of conduct, therefore, must be imposed: by law in the first place, and by opinion on many things that are not fit subjects for the operation of law. What these rules should be is the principal question in human affairs. But if we except a few of the most obvious cases, it is a question on which least progress has been made in resolving. No two ages, and scarcely any two countries, have decided it alike; and the decision of one age or country is a wonder to another. Yet the people of any given age and country no more suspect any difficulty in it than if it were a subject on which mankind had always agreed. The rules which obtain among themselves appear to them self-evident and self-justifying. This all but universal illusion is one of the examples of the magical influence of custom, which is not only, as the proverb says, a second nature, but which is continually mistaken for the first. The effect of custom in preventing any misgiving about the rules of conduct which mankind impose on one another is all the more complete, because the subject is one on which it is not generally considered necessary that reasons should be given, either by one person to others or by each to himself. People are accustomed to believe, and have been encouraged to believe by some who aspire to the character of philosophers, that their feelings on subjects of this nature are better than reasons and render reasons unnecessary. The practical principle which guides them to their opinions on the regulation of human conduct is the feeling in each person's mind that everybody should be required to act as he, and those with whom he sympathizes, would like them to act. No one, indeed, acknowledges to himself that his standard of judgment is his own liking. But an opinion on a point of conduct, not supported by reasons, can only count as one person's preference; and if the reasons, when given, are a mere appeal to a similar preference felt by other people, it is still only many people's liking instead of one. To an ordinary man, however, his own preference, thus supported, is not only a perfectly satisfactory reason but the only one he generally has for any of his notions of morality, taste, or propriety, except for those that are expressly written in his religious creed. . . .

The likings and dislikings of society, or of some powerful portion of it, is thus the main thing that has practically determined the rules laid down for general observance, under the penalties of law or opinion. And in general, those who have been in advance of society in thought and feeling have left this condition of things unassailed in principle, however they may have come into conflict with it in some of its details. They have occupied themselves in inquiring what things society ought to like or dislike, rather than in questioning whether its likings or dislikings should be a law to individuals. They preferred endeavoring to alter the feelings of mankind on the particular points on which they were themselves heretical, instead of making common cause in defense of freedom with heretics generally. . . .

In England, from the peculiar circumstances of our political history, the yoke of . . . law is lighter than in most other countries of Europe; and there is considerable jealousy of direct interference by the legislative or the executive power with private conduct. This is not so much from any just regard for the independence of the individual as it is from the still subsisting habit of looking on the government as representing an opposite interest to the public. The majority has not yet learned to feel the power of the government as their power, or its opinions as their opinions. When they do so, individual liberty will probably be as much exposed to invasion from the government as it already is from public opinion. But, as yet, there is a considerable amount of feeling ready to be called forth against any extension of the law to control individuals in things for which they have not hitherto been controlled. However, there is very little discrimination as to whether the matter is, or is not, within the legitimate sphere of legal control. Thus, while this feeling is highly salutary on the whole, it is perhaps quite as often misplaced as well grounded in the particular instances of its application. There is, in fact, no recognized principle by which the propriety or impropriety of government interference is customarily tested. People decide according to their personal preferences. Some, whenever they see any good to be done, or evil to be remedied, would willingly instigate the government to undertake the business, while others prefer to bear almost any amount of social evil rather than add one to the departments of human interests amenable to governmental control. . . .

The object of this essay is to assert one very simple principle that can legitimately govern, in all cases, the dealings of society with the individual in matters of compulsion and control. It applies equally whether the means of control used be physical force in the form of legal penalties or the moral coercion of public opinion. That principle is that the sole end for which mankind are warranted, individually or collectively, in interfering with the liberty of action of any of their number is self-protection. In other words, the only purpose for which power can be rightfully exercised over any member of a civilized community, against his will, is to prevent harm to others. His own good, either physical or moral, is not a sufficient warrant. He cannot rightfully be compelled to do or forbear because it will be better for him to do so, because it will make him happier, because, in the opinions of others, to do so would be wise or even right. These are good reasons for remonstrating with him, or reasoning with him, or persuading him, or entreating him, but not for compelling him or visiting him with any evil in case he do otherwise. To justify that, the conduct from which it is desired to deter him must be calculated to produce evil to someone else. The only part of the conduct of anyone for which he is amenable to society is that which concerns others. In the part that merely concerns himself, his independence is, of right, absolute. Over himself, over his own body and mind, the individual is sovereign.

It is, perhaps, hardly necessary to say that this doctrine is meant to apply only to human beings in the maturity of their faculties. We are not speaking of children or of young persons below the age that the law may fix as that of manhood or womanhood. Those who are still in a state to require being taken care of by others must be protected against their own actions as well as against external injury. . . .

It is proper to state that I forgo any advantage that my argument could derive from the idea of abstract right as a thing independent of utility. I regard utility as the ultimate appeal on all ethical questions; but it must be utility in the largest sense, grounded on the permanent interests of man as a progressive being. Those interests, I contend, authorize the subjection of individual spontaneity to external control only in respect to those actions of each that concern the interest of other people. If anyone does an act hurtful to others, there is a *prima facie* case for punishing him by law or, where legal penalties are not safely applicable, by general disapprobation. There are also many positive acts for the benefit of others that he may rightfully be compelled to do. These include giving evidence in a court of justice, bearing his fair share in the common defense or in any other joint work that is necessary to the interest of the society from which he enjoys protection, and performing certain acts of individual beneficence, such as saving a fellow creature's life or interposing to protect the defenseless against ill usage—things which whenever it is obviously a man's duty to do he may rightfully be made responsible to society for not doing. A person may cause evil to others not only by his actions but also by his inaction, and in either case he is justly accountable to them for the injury. The latter case, it

is true, requires a much more cautious exercise of compulsion than the former. To make anyone answerable for doing evil to others is the rule; to make him answerable for not preventing evil is, comparatively speaking, the exception. Yet there are many cases clear enough and grave enough to justify that exception. In all things which regard the external relations of the individual, he is *de jure* amenable to those whose interests are concerned, and, if need be, to society as their protector. . . .

But there is a sphere of action in which society, as distinguished from the individual, has, if any, only an indirect interest—a sphere comprehending all that portion of a person's life and conduct which affects only himself or, if it also affects others, only with their free, voluntary, and undeceived consent and participation. . . . This, then, is the appropriate region of human liberty. It comprises, first, the inward domain of consciousness, demanding liberty of conscience in the most comprehensive sense, liberty of thought and feeling, absolute freedom of opinion and sentiment on all subjects, practical or speculative, scientific, moral, or theological. The liberty of expressing and publishing opinions may seem to fall under a different principle, since it belongs to that part of the conduct of an individual which concerns other people. However, being almost of as much importance as the liberty of thought itself and resting in great part on the same reasons, it is practically inseparable from it. Secondly, the principle requires liberty of tastes and pursuits, of framing the plan of our life to suit our own character, of doing what we like, subject to such consequences as may follow. Such liberty should be without impediment from our fellow creatures, so long as what we do does not harm them, even though they should think our conduct foolish, perverse, or wrong. Thirdly, from this liberty of each individual follows the liberty, within the same limits, of combination among individuals; freedom to unite for any purpose not involving harm to others, the persons combining being supposed to be of full age and not forced or deceived.

No society in which these liberties are not generally respected is free, whatever may be its form of government; and none is completely free in which they do not exist absolute and unqualified. The only freedom that deserves the name is the freedom to pursue our own good in our own way, so long as we do not attempt to deprive others of theirs or impede their efforts to obtain it. Each is the proper guardian of his own health, whether bodily *or* mental and spiritual. Mankind are greater gainers by suffering each other to live as seems good to themselves than by compelling each to live as seems good to the rest. . . .

OF THE LIMITS TO THE AUTHORITY OF SOCIETY OVER THE INDIVIDUAL

What, then, is the rightful limit to the sovereignty of the individual over himself? Where does the authority of society begin? How much of human life should be assigned to individuality, and how much to society?

Each will receive its proper share if each has that which more particularly concerns it. To individuality should belong the part of life in which it is chiefly the individual that is interested; to society should belong the part that chiefly interests society.

Though society is not founded on a contract, and though no good purpose is answered by inventing a contract in order to deduce social obligations from it, everyone who receives the protection of society owes a return for the benefit. The fact of living in society renders it indispensable that each should be bound to observe a certain line of conduct toward the rest. This conduct consists, first, in not injuring the interests of one another, or rather certain interests which, either by express legal provision or by tacit understanding, ought to be considered as rights. Secondly, each person must bear his share (to be fixed on some equitable principle) of the labors and sacrifices incurred for defending the society or its members from injury and molestation. These conditions society is justified in enforcing at all costs to those who endeavor to withhold fulfillment. Nor is this all that society may do. The acts of an individual may be hurtful to others or wanting in due consideration for their welfare, without going to the length of violating any of their constituted rights. The offender may then be justly punished by opinion, though not by law. As soon as any part of a person's conduct affects prejudicially the interests of others, society has jurisdiction over it, and the question whether the general welfare will or will not be promoted by interfering with it becomes open to discussion. But there is no room for entertaining any such question when a person's conduct affects the interests of no persons besides himself, or needs not affect them unless they like (all the persons concerned being of full age and the ordinary amount of understanding). In all such cases, there should be perfect freedom, legal and social, to do the action and stand the consequences. . . .

The distinction here pointed out between the part of a person's life that concerns only himself and that which concerns others, many persons will refuse to admit. How (it may be asked) can any part of the conduct of a member of society be a matter of indifference to the other members? No person is an entirely isolated being; it is impossible for a person to do anything seriously or permanently hurtful to himself without mischief reaching at least to his near connections, and often far beyond them. If he injures his property, he does harm to those who directly or indirectly derived support from it, and usually diminishes, by a greater or less amount, the general resources of the community. If he deteriorates his bodily or mental faculties, he not only brings evil upon all who depended on him for any portion of their happiness, but disqualifies himself from rendering the services which he owes to his fellow creatures generally, perhaps becoming a burden on their affection or benevolence. And if such conduct were very frequent hardly any offense that is committed would detract more from the general sum of good. Finally, if by his vices or follies a person does no direct harm to others, he is nevertheless (it may be said) injurious by his example; and he ought to be compelled to control himself for the sake of those whom the sight or knowledge of his conduct might corrupt or mislead.

And even (it will be added) if the consequences of misconduct could be confined to the vicious or thoughtless individual, ought society to abandon to their own guidance those who are manifestly unfit for it? If protection against themselves is confessedly due to children and persons under age, is not society equally bound to afford it to persons of mature years who are equally incapable of self-government? If gambling, drunkenness, incontinence, idleness, and uncleanliness are as injurious to happiness, and as great a hindrance to improvement, as many or most of the acts prohibited by law, why (it may be asked) should law, so far as is consistent with practicability and social convenience, not endeavor to repress these also? And as a supplement to the unavoidable imperfections of law, ought not opinion at least organize a powerful police against these vices and visit rigidly with social penalties those who are known to practice them? There is no question here (it may be said) about restricting individuality, or impeding the trial of new and original experiments in living. The only things it is sought to prevent are things that have been tried and condemned from the beginning of the world until now—things which experience has shown not to be useful or suitable to any person's individuality. There must be some length of time and amount of experience after which a moral or prudential truth may be regarded as established; and it is merely desired to prevent generation after generation from falling over the same precipice that has been fatal to their predecessors.

I fully admit that the mischief which a person does to himself may seriously affect, both through their sympathies and their interests, those nearly connected with him and, in a minor degree, society at large. When, by conduct of this sort, a person is led to violate a distinct and assignable obligation to any other person or persons, the case is taken out of the self-regarding class and becomes amenable to moral disapprobation in the proper sense of the term. If, for example, a man, through intemperance or extravagance, becomes unable to pay his debts, or, having undertaken the moral responsibility of a family, becomes from the same cause incapable of supporting or educating them, he is deservedly reprobated and might be justly punished. But this is because of the breach of duty to his family or creditors, not for the extravagance. If the resources that ought to have been devoted to them had been diverted from them for the most prudent investment, the moral culpability would have been the same. . . . Again, in the frequent case of a man who causes grief to his family by addiction to bad habits, he deserves reproach for his unkindness or ingratitude. But so he may for cultivating habits not in themselves vicious, if they are painful to those with whom he passes his life, or who from personal ties are dependent on him for their comfort. Whoever fails in the consideration generally due to the interests and feelings of others—not being compelled by some more imperative duty, or justified by allowable self-preference—is a subject of moral disapprobation for that failure, but not for the cause of it, nor for the errors, merely personal to himself, that may have remotely led to it. In like manner, when a person disables himself, by conduct purely self-regarding, from the performance of some definite duty incumbent on him to the public, he is guilty of a social offense. No person ought to be punished simply for being drunk; but a soldier or a policeman should be punished for being drunk on duty. Whenever, in short, there is a definite damage, or a definite risk of damage, either to an individual or to the public, the case is taken out of the province of liberty and placed in that of morality or law.

But with regard to the merely contingent or, as it may be called, constructive injury which a person causes to society by conduct that neither violates any specific duty to the public, nor occasions perceptible hurt to any assignable individual except himself, the inconvenience is one that society can afford to bear for the sake of the greater good of human freedom. If grown persons are to be punished for not taking proper care of themselves, I would rather it were for their own sake than under pretense of preventing them from impairing their capacity or rendering to society benefits which society does not pretend it has a right to exact. But I cannot consent to argue the point as if society had no means of bringing its weaker members up to its ordinary standard of rational conduct, except waiting till they do something irrational, and then punishing them, legally or morally, for it. Society has had absolute power over them during all the early portion of their existence; it has had the whole period of childhood and nonage in which to try whether it could make them capable of rational conduct in life. The existing generation is master both of the training and the entire circumstances of the generation to come. It cannot indeed make them perfectly wise and good, because it is itself so lamentably deficient in goodness and wisdom; and its best efforts are not always, in individual cases, its most successful ones. But it is perfectly well able to make the rising generation, as a whole, as good as, and a little better than, itself. If society lets any considerable number of its members grow up mere children, incapable of being acted on by rational consideration of distant motives, society has itself to blame for the consequences. Society is armed, not only with all the powers of education, but also with the ascendancy which the authority of a received opinion always exercises over the minds who are least fitted to judge for themselves; and it is aided by the *natural* penalties which cannot be prevented from falling on those who incur the distaste or the contempt of those who know them. Let not society pretend that it needs, besides all this, the power to issue commands and enforce obedience in the personal concerns of individuals in which, on all principles of justice and policy, the decision ought to rest with those who are to abide the consequences. Nor is there anything that tends more to discredit and frustrate the better means of influencing conduct than a resort to the worse. If there be among those whom it is attempted to coerce into prudence or temperance any of the material of which vigorous and independent characters are made, they will infallibly rebel against the yoke. No such person will ever feel that others have a right to control him in his concerns, such as they have to prevent him from injuring them in theirs; and it easily comes to be considered a mark of spirit and courage to fly in the face of such usurped authority and do with ostentation the exact opposite of what it enjoins. . . . With respect to what is said of the necessity of protecting society from the bad example set to others by the vicious or the self-indulgent, it is true that a bad example may have a pernicious effect, especially the example of doing wrong to others with impunity to the wrongdoer. But we are now speaking of conduct which, while it does no wrong to others, is supposed to do great harm to the agent himself. I do not see how those who believe this can think otherwise than that the example, on the whole, must be more salutary than hurtful. Indeed, if it displays the misconduct, it displays also the painful or degrading consequences which, if the conduct is justly censured, must be supposed to be in all or most cases attendant on it.

But the strongest of all the arguments against the interference of the public with purely personal conduct is that, when it does interfere, the odds are that it interferes wrongly and in the wrong place. On questions of social morality, of duty to others, the opinion of the public, that is, of an overruling majority, though often wrong, is likely to be still oftener right. This is so because on such questions they are only required to judge of their own interests, of the manner in which some mode of conduct that, if allowed to be practiced, would affect themselves. But the opinion of a similar majority, imposed as a law on the minority, on questions of self-regarding conduct is quite as likely to be wrong as right. For in these cases public opinion means, at the best, some people's opinion of what is good or bad for other people, while very often it does not even mean that. For the public, with the most perfect indifference, passes over the pleasure or convenience of those whose conduct they censure and considers only their own preference. There are many people who consider as an injury to themselves any conduct for which they have a distaste, and resent it as an outrage to their feelings. For example, a religious bigot, when charged with disregarding the religious feelings of others, has been known to retort that they disregard his feelings by persisting in their abominable worship or creed. But there is no parity between the feeling of a person for his own opinion and the feeling of another who is offended at his holding it, no more than between the desire of a thief to take a purse and the desire of the right owner to keep it.

NOTE

1. Mill is here referring to the United States of America.—ED.

Questions for Thought

1. How would you define *civil* or *social liberty*? How does civil liberty differ from personal freedom?
2. Have you ever been subjected to what Mill calls "tyranny of the majority"? If so, under what circumstances?
3. Do you think that Mill's principle for determining the legitimate limits of government interference should be accepted? Why or why not?
4. Can you think of any currently existing governmental laws or regulations that would not be legitimate according to Mill's principle? If so, do you think these laws or regulations should be repealed? Defend your answer.
5. If your best friend were contemplating suicide, do you think that you would be justified in intervening? Why or why not? How do you think Mill would respond to this question?

11   Principles of Nonviolence

MOHANDAS K. GANDHI

Mohandas K. Gandhi (1869–1948), also known as Mahatma ("Great-Souled"), led the Indian movement for independence from British rule. Gandhi was raised in a deeply religious home, and his parents taught him to value pacifism and the sanctity of all living things (**ahimsa**) above all else. After studying law in England, he went to South Africa to seek work. Shocked by the separatist policies he found there, Gandhi led a series of protests against the South African government. In 1919, he returned to India to work on human rights issues in his native country. He became head of the Indian National Congress and led a famous march to the sea in 1930 to protest a British-imposed tax. Although Gandhi was arrested many times in both South Africa and India, he consistently advocated a policy of nonviolence. In 1947, he successfully negotiated with the British for Indian independence. However, just a few months after his people had won their independence, Gandhi was killed by an assassin's bullet.

In the following excerpts from his writings, which were arranged in sutra form by D. S. Sarma, Gandhi assumes, as did Mill, that individuals are justified in resisting the unjust policies of a government. Gandhi insists, however, that such resistance must be governed by what he calls **satyagraha,** the term that he coined to refer to nonviolent Indian resistance to segregation and racism in South Africa. Gandhi states that satyagraha is not merely passive resistance, for it is the result of an active decision to resist oppression. Moreover, whereas passive resistance has sometimes included acts of violence, Gandhi claims that satyagraha excludes violence in any form. Rather, satyagraha is the use of "soul force" or "truth force," not bodily force, to bring about social change. Indeed, Gandhi argues that in order to actualize satyagraha in his or her life, a person must eliminate all vestiges of anger or ill will through self-analysis and self-purification. Once this is done, the person will no longer resist violence with violence. As Gandhi says, "A satyagrahi will always try to overcome evil by good, anger by love, untruth by truth, himsa by ahimsa." Rejecting concern for the body and bodily pleasures, the satyagrahi becomes a force for social change that cannot ultimately be defeated.

Questions for Reading

1. What does Gandhi mean by *satyagraha*? How does satyagraha differ from civil disobedience?
2. Why, according to Gandhi, have historians failed to note the role that satyagraha has played in world history?
3. What are Gandhi's views on the relationship of the soul to the body? What is the connection between these views and the practice of satyagraha?
4. How is the concept of truth used in this selection?
5. Why, according to Gandhi, will satyagraha ultimately succeed in achieving its objectives?

53

I SEE SO MUCH MISAPPREHENSION ABOUT *satyagraha* amongst us, as well as amongst Englishmen that, though I have said and written much about it, I think it proper to say something even at the risk of repetition.

Satyagraha was a word coined in South Africa to name a certain movement. First, even the Gujarati word for the great movement that our countrymen in South Africa were carrying on was "passive resistance." Once I happened to address a meeting of Europeans in connection with the movement, and on that occasion the European president of the meeting said there was nothing active in the power of the Indians—who were voteless and unarmed—to offer passive resistance, which could only be a weapon of the weak. He was my friend. He expressed these views without meaning any insult to us, but I felt humiliated. I was conscious that the nature of the fight that the Indians were offering in South Africa was not the result of their weakness. They had purposely decided on that sort of agitation. I took the earliest opportunity to correct my friend's views and demonstrate to him that it was beyond the power of weak men to put up a fight of the nature the Indians in South Africa were doing. They were exhibiting greater courage than that required of a soldier.

Whilst I was in England, in connection with the same movement, I saw that the suffragist women were burning buildings and whipping officers and calling their agitation "passive resistance," and the people also called it so. In the agitation of the Indians in South Africa there was no room for these violent acts. I thus saw that to let our movement be known by the name of "passive resistance" was fraught with dangers. I could not find an English word that could correctly express our movement. In the meeting of Europeans above referred to I called our movement one of "soul force." But I did not dare to make the word current as expressive of our movement. Some capable Englishmen could see the imperfectness of the words "passive resistance," but they could not suggest a better phrase. I now see that "Civil Resistance" is the phrase which can correctly express our movement. Some time ago I somehow hit upon this phrase, and so I have now been using it in English. "Civil Resistance" expresses much more than is conveyed by the phrase "Civil Disobedience," though it expresses much less than *satyagraha*.

I also saw that in South Africa, truth and justice were our only weapons, that the force we were putting forth was not brute force but soul force, be it ever so little. This force is not found to be within the power of brutes, and as truth ever contains soul force, the South African agitation began to be known in our vernacular by the name of *satyagraha*.

That *satyagraha* is thus based on purity is no exaggeration. We can now understand that *satyagraha* is not merely Civil Disobedience. At times, it may be *satyagraha* not to offer Civil Disobedience. When it appears to us to be our duty to offer Civil Disobedience—when not to offer it seems to us derogatory to our manliness and to our soul—then only Civil Disobedience can be *satyagraha*.

This *satyagraha* can be offered not only against Government but against family and society. In short, *satyagraha* may be used as between husband and wife, [between] father and son, and between friends. We may use this weapon in any sphere of life and to get redress of any grievance. The weapon purifies the one who uses it as well as the one against whom it is used. A good use of the weapon can never be undesirable and it is ever infallible. If *satyagraha* is converted into *duragraha* and thus becomes fruitful of evil results, *satyagraha* cannot be blamed.

This sort of *satyagraha* consciously or unconsciously appears to be used mostly in families. That is to say, if a son finds that his father is unjust to him, he does not put up with the injustice, and he pays the penalty with pleasure. In the end he succeeds in winning over his callous father and in having justice from him. But a deadening inertia prevents us from carrying *satyagraha* beyond the family sphere. And I have therefore thought the use of *satyagraha* in the political and social sphere to be a new experiment. Tolstoy in one of his letters drew attention to the fact that this was a new experiment.

There are some who believe that *satyagraha* may be used only in the religious sphere. My wide experience points to a contrary conclusion. We may use it in other spheres and spiritualize them, and by so doing we hasten the victory and are saved many a false thing. I am firmly of the opinion that *satyagraha* contains the observance of the manifest laws of economics, and therefore I believe *satyagraha* to be a practical affair. *Satyagraha* being, as I have shown above, a new weapon, it may take time to be understood and accepted by the people—and things pregnant with results great and good do take time—but when it pervades the land, then political and social reforms, which today take very long to be achieved, will be obtained in comparatively less time, the gulf that separates rulers and the ruled will be bridged over, and trust and love will take the place of distrust and estrangement.

There is only one thing needful for a wide propagation of *satyagraha*. If the leaders understand it correctly and put it before the people, I am sure the people are ready to welcome it. To understand its true beauty one should have unflinching faith in Truth and nonviolence. Truth does not require to be explained. I do not mean to enter here into a minute explanation of nonviolence. It means, in brief, that we should not be actuated by spite against him from whom we seek to obtain justice, that we should never think of obtaining anything from him by any violence to his person, but by pure civility. If we can trust ourselves to be equal to only this much nonviolence, the required reforms can be easily achieved.

When the whole nation adopts *satyagraha* as an eternal weapon, all our movements will take a new form. We shall be spared much of the hubbub and stump oratory, much of the petition making and passing of resolutions, and much of our mean selfishness. I see nothing in which lies social, economic, and political advancement of the nation so much as in *satyagraha*.

Satyagraha differs from Passive Resistance as the North Pole from the South. The latter has been conceived as a weapon of the weak and does not exclude the use of physical force or violence for the purpose of gaining one's end. Whereas, the former has been conceived as a weapon of the strongest and excludes the use of violence in any shape or form. . . .

Satyagraha is utter self-effacement, greatest humiliation, greatest patience, and brightest faith. It is its own reward. . . .

54

Its [*satyagraha*'s] root meaning is holding on to Truth, hence Truth force. I have called it Love force or Soul force. I discovered in the earliest stages that pursuit of Truth did not admit of violence being inflicted on one's opponent, but that he must be weaned from error by patience and sympathy. For, what appears to be Truth to the one may appear to be error to the other. And patience means self-suffering. So the doctrine came to mean vindication of Truth, not by infliction of suffering on the opponent, but on oneself.

When I refuse to do a thing that is repugnant to my conscience, I use soul force. For instance, the government of the day has passed a law which is applicable to me. I do not like it. If, by using violence, I force the government to repeal the law, I am employing what may be termed body force. If I do not obey the law, and accept the penalty for its breach, I use soul force. It involves sacrifice of self.

Soul force begins when man recognizes that body force, be it ever so great, is nothing compared to the force of the soul within, which pervades not only him but all creation.

55

The fact that there are so many men still alive in the world shows that it is based not on the force of arms but on the force of truth or love. Therefore, the greatest and most unimpeachable evidence of the success of this force is to be found in the fact that, in spite of the wars of the world, it still lives on.

Thousands, indeed tens of thousands, depend for their existence on a very active working of this force. Little quarrels of millions of families in their daily lives disappear before the exercise of this force. Hundreds of nations live in peace. History does not and cannot take note of this fact.

56

History is really a record of every interruption of the even working of the force of love or of the soul. Two brothers quarrel, one of them repents and reawakens the love that was lying dormant in him, the two again begin to live in peace; nobody takes note of this.

But if the two brothers, through the intervention of solicitors or for some other reason, take up arms or go to law—which is another form of the exhibition of brute force—their doings would be immediately noticed in the press, they would be the talk of their neighbors and would probably go down in history.

And what is true of families and communities is true of nations. There is no reason to believe that there is one law for families and another for nations. History, then, is a record of interruptions in the course of nature. Soul force, being natural, is not noted in history.

57

I have more than once dilated in my writings on the limits of *satyagraha*. *Satyagraha* presupposes self-discipline, self-control, self-purification, and a recognized social status in the person offering it. A *satyagrahi* must never forget the distinction between evil and the evil-doer. He must not harbor ill will or bitterness against the latter. He may not even employ needlessly offensive language against the evil person, however unrelieved his evil might be. For it should be an article of faith with every *satyagrahi* that there is no one so fallen in this world but can be converted by love. A *satyagrahi* will always try to overcome evil by good, anger by love, untruth by truth, *himsa* by *ahimsa*. *There is no other way of purging the world of evil.* Therefore, a person who claims to be a *satyagrahi* always tries by close and prayerful self-introspection and self-analysis to find out whether he is himself completely free from the taint of anger, ill will and such other human infirmities, whether he is not himself capable of those very evils against which he is out to lead a crusade. In self-purification and penance lies half the victory of a *satyagrahi*. A *satyagrahi* has faith that the silent and undemonstrative action of truth and love produces far more permanent and abiding results than speeches or such other showy performances. . . .

60

It is a fundamental principle of *satyagraha* that the tyrant whom the *satyagrahi* seeks to resist has power over his body and material possessions, but he can have no power over the soul. The soul can remain unconquered and unconquerable even when the body is imprisoned. The whole science of *satyagraha* was born from a knowledge of this fundamental truth.

61

Defeat has no place in the dictionary of nonviolence.

The path of a *satyagrahi* is beset with insurmountable difficulties. But in true *satyagraha* there is neither disappointment nor defeat. As truth is all-powerful, *satyagraha* can never be defeated.

There is no time limit for a *satyagrahi*, nor is there a limit to his capacity for suffering. Hence, there is no such thing as defeat in *satyagraha*. The so-called defeat may be the dawn of victory. It may be the agony of birth. . . .

64

The triumph of *satyagraha* consists in meeting death in the insistence on Truth.

65

From the standpoint of pure Truth, the body too is a possession. It has been truly said that desire for enjoyment creates bodies for the soul. When this desire vanishes, there remains no further need for the body, and man is free from the vicious cycle of births and deaths. The soul is omnipresent; why should she care to be confined within the cagelike body or do evil and even kill for the sake of that cage? We thus arrive at the ideal of total renunciation and learn to use the body for the purposes of service so long as it exists, so much so that service, and not bread, becomes with us the staff of life. We eat and drink, sleep and wake, for service alone. Such an attitude of mind brings us real happiness and the beatific vision in the fullness of time. . . .

70

The man who is saturated with the spirit of nonviolence has never any quarrel with a single individual. His opposition is directed to a system, to the evil in man, not against the man himself.

Questions for Thought

1. Can you think of anyone other than Gandhi who has promoted and/or practiced *satyagraha*?
2. Do you think that *satyagraha* is an effective way of bringing about social change? Why or why not?
3. Do you think that what Gandhi says about the movement of world history is accurate? How do Gandhi's views on this issue compare with or differ from the views of Marx and Engels?
4. Can you think of anything in contemporary society that ought to be changed? If so, what strategies would you use to change it?
5. Do you agree with Gandhi that it takes more courage to practice *satyagraha* than it does to be a soldier? Defend your answer.

12   Letter from Birmingham Jail

MARTIN LUTHER KING JR.

Martin Luther King Jr. (1929–1968) was a leader in the American civil rights movement from 1955 until his assassination in Memphis, Tennessee, in 1968. King, who was born in Atlanta, Georgia, received his Ph.D. from Boston University in 1955. While serving as pastor of the Dexter Avenue Baptist Church in Montgomery, Alabama, King became an outspoken critic of the segregation that existed throughout the South. Starting with the bus boycott in Montgomery in the mid-1950s, King urged the use of nonviolent protest as a means of bringing about social change. After his initial focus on segregation in transportation and public facilities, King turned his attention to voting rights, economic justice, and military conflict. He strongly criticized the Vietnam War and the economic inequality that existed in the United States. By the end of his life, King had realized that the triple evils of racism, economic exploitation, and militarism could be overcome only by a radical transformation of the social and economic order. Having been the target of racial slurs and racist attacks many times during his life, he was killed by an assassin's bullet on April 4, 1968.

In addition to being a powerful force behind the enactment of civil rights and voting rights legislation, King became an internationally known advocate of social and economic justice. He was chosen *Time* magazine's "Man of the Year" in 1963, and he was awarded the Nobel Peace Prize a year later. King was also known as a forceful orator. His "I Have a Dream" speech, which was delivered at the March on Washington in 1963, is considered a classic. While King's activities did not allow him much time for purely theoretical analysis, his writings demonstrate a wide knowledge of philosophical and theological theories and issues. His principal works are *Stride Toward Freedom* (1958), *Strength to Love* (1963), *Why We Can't Wait* (1964), and *Where Do We Go from Here: Chaos or Community?* (1967).

The "Letter from Birmingham Jail" was written on April 16, 1963, in response to a statement from white clergymen criticizing King's presence and civil rights activities in Birmingham, Alabama. In this powerful letter, King not only defends his presence and activities in Birmingham but also provides a powerful philosophical defense of nonviolent direct action as a method of confronting injustice, as well as an impassioned critique of the silence and apathy of white moderates and the white church.

Noting that "injustice anywhere is a threat to justice everywhere," King argues that we must be prepared to confront racism and injustice wherever it arises. Noting that oppressors never voluntarily stop oppressing others, King argues that we must take direct action to create tension that brings oppression and injustice to the surface so that it can be dealt with. He also draws a clear-cut distinction between just and unjust laws and argues that we have a duty to disobey laws that are unjust. Finally, he critiques the view that time itself will eventually conquer evil by noting that time is neutral and that injustice can be overcome only when people act decisively to end it. Like Gandhi in the preceding selection, King argues that this decisive activity must be nonviolent and guided by love.

Toward the end of his letter, King expresses his great disappointment with white moderates and with the white church and its leadership. King argues that, in calling for patience and moderation, white moderates fail to realize the extent of racial injustice and the urgency of the movement to overcome it. While only a few of the white churches lined up with the racist opponents of the struggle for equality, most of the others "remained silent behind the anesthetizing security of the stained-glass windows." In opposition to such apathy, King calls on modern Christians to follow the example of those very early Christians who, in living according to the true meaning of the gospel, resisted oppression and injustice even to the point of death.

Questions for Reading

1. How does King describe the racial climate of Birmingham, Alabama, in 1963?
2. What are the four basic steps of any nonviolent campaign? How, according to King, were these steps followed in Birmingham?
3. How does King respond to those who have asked him to be patient, to wait?
4. What are the essential differences between a just law and an unjust law? What leads King to make this distinction?
5. Why, according to King, have some people accused him of being an extremist? How does King respond to this accusation?
6. What are King's basic criticisms of white moderates and the white church?

April 16, 1963

MY DEAR FELLOW CLERGYMEN:

While confined here in the Birmingham city jail, I came across your recent statement calling my present activities "unwise and untimely." Seldom do I pause to answer criticism of my work and ideas. If I sought to answer all the criticisms that cross my desk, my secretaries would have little time for anything other than such correspondence in the course of the day, and I would have no time for constructive work. But since I feel that you are men of genuine good will and that your criticisms are sincerely set forth, I want to try to answer your statement in what I hope will be patient and reasonable terms.

I think I should indicate why I am here in Birmingham, since you have been influenced by the view which argues against "outsiders coming in." I have the honor of serving as president of the Southern Christian Leadership Conference, an organization operating in every southern state, with headquarters in Atlanta, Georgia. We have some eighty-five affiliated organizations across the South, and one of them is the Alabama Christian Movement for Human Rights. Frequently we share staff, educational and financial resources with our affiliates. Several months ago the affiliate here in Birmingham asked us to be on call to engage in a nonviolent direct-action program if such were deemed necessary. We readily consented, and when the hour came we lived up to our promise. So I, along with several members of my staff, am here because I was invited here. I am here because I have organizational ties here.

But more basically, I am in Birmingham because injustice is here. Just as the prophets of the eighth century B.C. left their villages and carried their "thus saith the Lord" far beyond the boundaries of their home towns, and just as the Apostle Paul left his village of Tarsus and carried the gospel of Jesus Christ to the far corners of the Greco-Roman world, so am I compelled to carry the gospel of freedom beyond my own home town. Like Paul, I must constantly respond to the Macedonian call for aid.

Moreover, I am cognizant of the interrelatedness of all communities and states. I cannot sit idly by in Atlanta and not be concerned about what happens in Birmingham. Injustice anywhere is a threat to justice everywhere. We are caught in an inescapable network of mutuality, tied in a single garment of destiny. Whatever affects one directly, affects all indirectly. Never again can we afford to live with the narrow, provincial "outside agitator" idea. Anyone who lives inside the United States can never be considered an outsider anywhere within its bounds.

You deplore the demonstrations taking place in Birmingham. But your statement, I am sorry to say, fails to express a similar concern for the conditions that brought about the demonstrations. I am sure that none of you would want to rest content with the superficial kind of social analysis that deals merely with effects and does not grapple with underlying causes. It is unfortunate that demonstrations are taking place in Birmingham, but it is even more unfortunate that the city's white power structure left the Negro community with no alternative.

In any nonviolent campaign there are four basic steps: collection of the facts to determine whether injustices exist; negotiation; self-purification; and direct action. We have gone through all these steps in Birmingham. There can be no gainsaying the fact that racial injustice engulfs this community. Birmingham is probably the most thoroughly segregated city in the United States. Its ugly record of

brutality is widely known. Negroes have experienced grossly unjust treatment in the courts. There have been more unsolved bombings of Negro homes and churches in Birmingham than in any other city in the nation. These are the hard, brutal facts of the case. On the basis of these conditions, Negro leaders sought to negotiate with the city fathers. But the latter consistently refused to engage in good-faith negotiation.

Then, last September, came the opportunity to talk with leaders of Birmingham's economic community. In the course of the negotiations, certain promises were made by the merchants—for example, to remove the stores' humiliating racial signs. On the basis of these promises, the Reverend Fred Shuttlesworth and the leaders of the Alabama Christian Movement for Human Rights agreed to a moratorium on all demonstrations. As the weeks and months went by, we realized that we were the victims of a broken promise. A few signs, briefly removed, returned; the others remained.

As in so many past experiences, our hopes had been blasted, and the shadow of deep disappointment settled upon us. We had no alternative except to prepare for direct action, whereby we would present our very bodies as a means of laying our case before the conscience of the local and the national community. Mindful of the difficulties involved, we decided to undertake a process of self-purification. We began a series of workshops on nonviolence, and we repeatedly asked ourselves: "Are you able to accept blows without retaliating?" "Are you able to endure the ordeal of jail?" We decided to schedule our direct-action program for the Easter season, realizing that except for Christmas, this is the main shopping period of the year. Knowing that a strong economic-withdrawal program would be the by-product of direct action, we felt that this would be the best time to bring pressure to bear on the merchants for the needed change.

Then it occurred to us that Birmingham's mayoral election was coming up in March, and we speedily decided to postpone action until after election day. When we discovered that the Commissioner of Public Safety, Eugene "Bull" Connor, had piled up enough votes to be in the run-off, we decided again to postpone action until the day after the run-off so that the demonstrations could not be used to cloud the issues. Like many others, we waited to see

Mr. Connor defeated, and to this end we endured postponement after postponement. Having aided in this community need, we felt that our direct-action program could be delayed no longer.

You may well ask: "Why direct action? Why sit-ins, marches and so forth? Isn't negotiation a better path?" You are quite right in calling for negotiation. Indeed, this is the very purpose of direct action. Nonviolent direct action seeks to create such a crisis and foster such a tension that a community which has constantly refused to negotiate is forced to confront the issue. It seeks so to dramatize the issue that it can no longer be ignored. My citing the creation of tension as part of the work of the nonviolent-resister may sound rather shocking. But I must confess that I am not afraid of the word "tension." I have earnestly opposed violent tension, but there is a type of constructive, nonviolent tension which is necessary for growth. Just as Socrates felt that it was necessary to create a tension in the mind so that individuals could rise from the bondage of myths and half-truths to the unfettered realm of creative analysis and objective appraisal, so must we see the need for nonviolent gadflies to create the kind of tension in society that will help men rise from the dark depths of prejudice and racism to the majestic heights of understanding and brotherhood.

The purpose of our direct-action program is to create a situation so crisis-packed that it will inevitably open the door to negotiation. I therefore concur with you in your call for negotiation. Too long has our beloved Southland been bogged down in a tragic effort to live in monologue rather than dialogue.

One of the basic points in your statement is that the action that I and my associates have taken in Birmingham is untimely. Some have asked: "Why didn't you give the new city administration time to act?" The only answer that I can give to this query is that the new Birmingham administration must be prodded about as much as the outgoing one, before it will act. We are sadly mistaken if we feel that the election of Albert Boutwell as mayor will bring the millennium to Birmingham. While Mr. Boutwell is a much more gentle person than Mr. Connor, they are both segregationists, dedicated to maintenance of the status quo. I have hope that Mr. Boutwell will be reasonable enough to see the futility of massive resistance to desegregation. But he will not see this without pressure from devotees of civil rights. My friends, I must say to you that we have not made a single gain in civil rights without determined legal and nonviolent pressure. Lamentably, it is an historical fact that privileged groups seldom give up their privileges voluntarily. Individuals may see the moral light and voluntarily give up their unjust posture; but, as Reinhold Niebuhr has reminded us, groups tend to be more immoral than individuals.

We know through painful experience that freedom is never voluntarily given by the oppressor; it must be demanded by the oppressed. Frankly, I have yet to engage in a direct-action campaign that was "well timed" in the view of those who have not suffered unduly from the disease of segregation. For years now I have heard the word "Wait!" It rings in the ear of every Negro with piercing familiarity. This "Wait" has almost always meant "Never." We must come to see, with one of our distinguished jurists, that "justice too long delayed is justice denied."

We have waited for more than 340 years for our constitutional and God-given rights. The nations of Asia and Africa are moving with jet-like speed toward gaining political independence, but we still creep at horse-and-buggy pace toward gaining a cup of coffee at a lunch counter. Perhaps it is easy for those who have never felt the stinging darts of segregation to say, "Wait." But when you have seen vicious mobs lynch your mothers and fathers at will and drown your sisters and brothers at whim; when you have seen hate-filled policemen curse, kick and even kill your black brothers and sisters; when you see the vast majority of your twenty million Negro brothers smothering in an air-tight cage of poverty in the midst of an affluent society; when you suddenly find your tongue twisted and your speech stammering as you seek to explain to your six-year-old daughter why she can't go to the public amusement park that has just been advertised on television, and see tears welling up in her eyes when she is told that Fun-town is closed to colored children, and see ominous clouds of inferiority beginning to form in her little mental sky, and see her beginning to distort her personality by developing an unconscious bitterness toward white people; when you have to concoct an answer for a five-year-old son who is asking: "Daddy, why do white people treat colored people so mean?"; when you take a cross-country drive and find it necessary to sleep night after night in the uncomfortable corners of your automobile because no motel will accept you; when you are humiliated day in and day out by nagging signs reading "white" and "colored"; when your first name becomes "nigger," your middle name becomes "boy" (however old you are) and your last name becomes "John," and your wife and mother are never given the respected title "Mrs."; when you are harried by day and haunted by night by the fact that you are a Negro, living constantly at tiptoe stance, never quite knowing what to expect next, and are plagued with inner fears and outer resentments; when you are forever fighting a degenerating sense of "nobodiness"—then you will understand why we find it difficult to wait. There comes a time when the cup of endurance runs over, and men are no longer willing to be plunged into the abyss of despair. I hope, sirs, you can understand our legitimate and unavoidable impatience.

You express a great deal of anxiety over our willingness to break laws. This is certainly a legitimate concern. Since we so diligently urge people to obey the Supreme Court's decision of 1954 outlawing segregation in the public schools, at first glance it may seem rather paradoxical for us consciously to break laws. One may well ask: "How can you advocate breaking some laws and obeying others?" The answer lies in the fact that there are two types of laws: just and unjust. I would be the first to advocate obeying just laws. One has not only a legal but a moral responsibility to obey just laws. Conversely, one has a moral responsibility to disobey unjust laws. I would agree with St. Augustine that "an unjust law is no law at all."

Now, what is the difference between the two? How does one determine whether a law is just or unjust? A just law is a man-made code that squares with the moral law or the law of God. An unjust law is a code that is out of harmony with the moral law. To put it in the terms of St. Thomas Aquinas: An unjust law is a human law that is not rooted in eternal law and natural law. Any law that uplifts human personality is just. Any law that degrades human personality is unjust. All segregation statutes are unjust because segregation distorts the soul and damages the personality. It gives the segregator a false sense of superiority and the segregated a false sense of inferiority. Segregation, to use the terminology of the Jewish philosopher Martin Buber, substitutes an "I–it" relationship for an "I–thou" relationship and ends up relegating persons to the status of things. Hence segregation is not only politically, economically and sociologically unsound, it is morally wrong and sinful. Paul Tillich has said that sin is separation. Is not segregation an existential expression of man's tragic separation, his awful estrangement, his terrible sinfulness? Thus it is that I can urge men to obey the 1954 decision of the Supreme Court, for it is morally right; and I can urge them to disobey segregation ordinances, for they are morally wrong.

Let us consider a more concrete example of just and unjust laws. An unjust law is a code that a numerical or power majority group compels a minority group to obey but does not make binding on itself. This is *difference* made legal. By the same token, a just law is a code that a majority compels a minority to follow and that it is willing to follow itself. This is *sameness* made legal.

Let me give another explanation. A law is unjust if it is inflicted on a minority that, as a result of being denied the right to vote, had no part in enacting or devising the law. Who can say that the legislature of Alabama which set up that state's segregation laws was democratically elected? Throughout Alabama all sorts of devious methods are used to prevent Negroes from becoming registered voters, and there are some counties in which, even though Negroes constitute a majority of the population, not a single Negro is registered. Can any law enacted under such circumstances be considered democratically structured?

Sometimes a law is just on its face and unjust in its application. For instance, I have been arrested on a charge of parading without a permit. Now, there is nothing wrong in having an ordinance which requires a permit for a parade. But such an ordinance becomes unjust when it is used to maintain segregation and to deny citizens the First-Amendment privilege of peaceful assembly and protest.

I hope you are able to see the distinction I am trying to point out. In no sense do I advocate evading or defying the law, as would the rabid segregationist. That would lead to anarchy. One who breaks an unjust law must do so openly, lovingly, and with a willingness to accept the penalty. I submit that an individual who breaks a law that conscience tells him is unjust, and who willingly accepts the penalty of imprisonment in order to arouse the conscience of the community over its injustice, is in reality expressing the highest respect for law.

Of course, there is nothing new about this kind of civil disobedience. It was evidenced sublimely in the refusal of Shadrach, Meshach and Abednego to obey the laws of Nebuchadnezzar, on the ground that a higher moral law was at stake. It was practiced superbly by the early Christians, who were willing to face hungry lions and the excruciating pain of chopping blocks rather than submit to certain unjust laws of the Roman Empire. To a degree, academic freedom is a reality today because Socrates practiced civil disobedience. In our own nation, the Boston Tea Party represented a massive act of civil disobedience.

We should never forget that everything Adolf Hitler did in Germany was "legal" and everything the Hungarian freedom fighters did in Hungary was "illegal." It was "illegal" to aid and comfort a Jew in Hitler's Germany. Even so, I am sure that, had I lived in Germany at the time, I would have aided and comforted my Jewish brothers. If today I lived in a Communist country where certain principles dear to the Christian faith are suppressed, I would openly advocate disobeying that country's antireligious laws.

I must make two honest confessions to you, my Christian and Jewish brothers. First, I must confess that over the past few years I have been gravely disappointed with the white moderate. I have almost reached the regrettable conclusion that the Negro's great stumbling block in his stride toward freedom is not the White Citizen's Counciler or the Ku Klux Klanner, but the white moderate, who is more devoted to "order" than to justice; who prefers a negative peace which is the absence of tension to a positive peace which is the presence of justice; who constantly says: "I agree with you in the goal you seek, but I cannot agree with your methods of direct action"; who paternalistically believes he can set the timetable for another man's freedom; who lives by a mythical concept of time and who constantly advises the Negro to wait for a "more convenient season." Shallow understanding from people of good will is more frustrating than absolute misunderstanding from people of ill will.

Lukewarm acceptance is much more bewildering than outright rejection.

I had hoped that the white moderate would understand that law and order exist for the purpose of establishing justice and that when they fail in this purpose they become the dangerously structured dams that block the flow of social progress. I had hoped that the white moderate would understand that the present tension in the South is a necessary phase of the transition from an obnoxious negative peace, in which the Negro passively accepted his unjust plight, to a substantive and positive peace, in which all men will respect the dignity and worth of human personality. Actually, we who engage in nonviolent direct action are not the creators of tension. We merely bring to the surface the hidden tension that is already alive. We bring it out in the open, where it can be seen and dealt with. Like a boil that can never be cured so long as it is covered up but must be opened with all its ugliness to the natural medicines of air and light, injustice must be exposed, with all the tension its exposure creates, to the light of human conscience and the air of national opinion before it can be cured.

In your statement you assert that our actions, even though peaceful, must be condemned because they precipitate violence. But is this a logical assertion? Isn't this like condemning a robbed man because his possession of money precipitated the evil act of robbery? Isn't this like condemning Socrates because his unswerving commitment to truth and his philosophical inquiries precipitated the act by the misguided populace in which they made him drink hemlock? Isn't this like condemning Jesus because his unique God-consciousness and never-ceasing devotion to God's will precipitated the evil act of crucifixion? We must come to see that, as the federal courts have consistently affirmed, it is wrong to urge an individual to cease his efforts to gain his basic constitutional rights because the quest may precipitate violence. Society must protect the robbed and punish the robber.

I had also hoped that the white moderate would reject the myth concerning time in relation to the struggle for freedom. I have just received a letter from a white brother in Texas. He writes: "All Christians know that the colored people will receive equal rights eventually, but it is possible that you are in too great a religious hurry. It has taken

Christianity almost two thousand years to accomplish what it has. The teachings of Christ take time to come to earth." Such an attitude stems from a tragic misconception of time, from the strangely irrational notion that there is something in the very flow of time that will inevitably cure all ills. Actually, time itself is neutral; it can be used either destructively or constructively. More and more I feel that the people of ill will have used time much more effectively than have the people of good will. We will have to repent in this generation not merely for the hateful words and actions of the bad people but for the appalling silence of the good people. Human progress never rolls in on wheels of inevitability; it comes through the tireless efforts of men willing to be co-workers with God, and without this hard work, time itself becomes an ally of the forces of social stagnation. We must use time creatively, in the knowledge that the time is always ripe to do right. Now is the time to make real the promise of **democracy** and transform our pending national elegy into a creative psalm of brotherhood. Now is the time to lift our national policy from the quicksand of racial injustice to the solid rock of human dignity.

You speak of our activity in Birmingham as extreme. At first I was rather disappointed that fellow clergymen would see my nonviolent efforts as those of an extremist. I began thinking about the fact that I stand in the middle of two opposing forces in the Negro community. One is a force of complacency, made up in part of Negroes who, as a result of long years of oppression, are so drained of self-respect and a sense of "somebodiness" that they have adjusted to segregation; and in part of a few middle-class Negroes who, because of a degree of academic and economic security and because in some ways they profit by segregation, have become insensitive to the problems of the masses. The other force is one of bitterness and hatred, and it comes perilously close to advocating violence. It is expressed in the various black nationalist groups that are springing up across the nation, the largest and best-known being Elijah Muhammad's Muslim movement. Nourished by the Negro's frustration over the continued existence of racial discrimination, this movement is made up of people who have lost faith in America, who have absolutely repudiated Christianity, and who have concluded that the white man is an incorrigible "devil."

I have tried to stand between these two forces, saying that we need emulate neither the "do-nothingism" of the complacent nor the hatred and despair of the black nationalist. For there is the more excellent way of love and nonviolent protest. I am grateful to God that, through the influence of the Negro church, the way of nonviolence became an integral part of our struggle.

If this philosophy had not emerged, by now many streets of the South would, I am convinced, be flowing with blood. And I am further convinced that if our white brothers dismiss as "rabble-rousers" and "outside agitators" those of us who employ non-violent direct action, and if they refuse to support our nonviolent efforts, millions of Negroes will, out of frustration and despair, seek solace and security in black-nationalist ideologies—a development that would inevitably lead to a frightening racial nightmare.

Oppressed people cannot remain oppressed forever. The yearning for freedom eventually manifests itself, and that is what has happened to the American Negro. Something within has reminded him of his birthright of freedom, and something without has reminded him that it can be gained. Consciously or unconsciously, he has been caught up by the *Zeitgeist,* and with his black brothers of Africa and his brown and yellow brothers of Asia, South America and the Caribbean, the United States Negro is moving with a sense of great urgency toward the promised land of racial justice. If one recognizes this vital urge that has engulfed the Negro community, one should readily understand why public demonstrations are taking place. The Negro has many pent-up resentments and latent frustrations, and he must release them. So let him march; let him make prayer pilgrimages to the city hall; let him go on freedom rides—and try to understand why he must do so. If his repressed emotions are not released in nonviolent ways, they will seek expression through violence; this is not a threat but a fact of history. So I have not said to my people: "Get rid of your discontent." Rather, I have tried to say that this normal and healthy discontent can be channeled into the creative outlet of nonviolent direct action. And now this approach is being termed extremist.

But though I was initially disappointed at being categorized as an extremist, as I continued to think about the matter I gradually gained a measure of satisfaction from the label. Was not Jesus an extremist for love: "Love your enemies, bless them that curse you, do good to them that hate you, and pray for them which despitefully use you, and persecute you." Was not Amos an extremist for justice: "Let justice roll down like waters and righteousness like an ever-flowing stream." Was not Paul an extremist for the Christian gospel: "I bear in my body the marks of the Lord Jesus." Was not Martin Luther an extremist: "Here I stand; I cannot do otherwise, so help me God." And John Bunyan: "I will stay in jail to the end of my days before I make a butchery of my conscience." And Abraham Lincoln: "This nation cannot survive half slave and half free." And Thomas Jefferson: "We hold these truths to be self-evident, that all men are created equal . . ." So the question is not whether we will be extremists, but what kind of extremists we will be. Will we be extremists for hate or for love? Will we be extremists for the preservation of injustice or for the extension of justice? In that dramatic scene on Calvary's hill three men were crucified. We must never forget that all three were crucified for the same crime—the crime of extremism. Two were extremists for immorality, and thus fell below their environment. The other, Jesus Christ, was an extremist for love, truth and goodness, and thereby rose above his environment. Perhaps the South, the nation and the world are in dire need of creative extremists.

I had hoped that the white moderate would see this need. Perhaps I was too optimistic; perhaps I expected too much. I suppose I should have realized that few members of the oppressor race can understand the deep groans and passionate yearnings of the oppressed race, and still fewer have the vision to see that injustice must be rooted out by strong, persistent and determined action. I am thankful, however, that some of our white brothers in the South have grasped the meaning of this social revolution and committed themselves to it. They are still all too few in quantity, but they are big in quality. Some—such as Ralph McGill, Lillian Smith, Harry Golden, James McBride Dabbs, Ann Braden and Sarah Patton Boyle—have written about our struggle in eloquent and prophetic terms. Others have marched with us down nameless streets of the South. They have languished in filthy, roach-infested jails, suffering the abuse and brutality of policemen who view them as "dirty nigger-lovers." Unlike so many of their moderate brothers and sisters, they have recognized the urgency of the moment and sensed the need for powerful "action" antidotes to combat the disease of segregation.

Let me take note of my other major disappointment. I have been so greatly disappointed with the white church and its leadership. Of course, there are some notable exceptions. I am not unmindful of the fact that each of you has taken some significant stands on this issue. I commend you, Reverend Stallings, for your Christian stand on this past Sunday, in welcoming Negroes to your worship service on a nonsegregated basis. I commend the Catholic leaders of this state for integrating Spring Hill College several years ago. But despite these notable exceptions, I must honestly reiterate that I have been disappointed with the church. I do not say this as one of those negative critics who can always find something wrong with the church. I say this as a minister of the gospel, who loves the church; who was nurtured in its bosom; who has been sustained by its spiritual blessings and who will remain true to it as long as the cord of life shall lengthen.

When I was suddenly catapulted into the leadership of the bus protest in Montgomery, Alabama, a few years ago, I felt we would be supported by the white church. I felt that the white ministers, priests and rabbis of the South would be among our strongest allies. Instead, some have been outright opponents, refusing to understand the freedom movement and misrepresenting its leaders; all too many others have been more cautious than courageous and have remained silent behind the anesthetizing security of stained-glass windows.

In spite of my shattered dreams, I came to Birmingham with the hope that the white religious leadership of this community would see the justice of our cause and, with deep moral concern, would serve as the channel through which our just grievances could reach the power structure. I had hoped that each of you would understand. But again I have been disappointed.

I have heard numerous southern religious leaders admonish their worshipers to comply with a desegregation decision because it is the law, but I have longed to hear white ministers declare: "Follow this decree because integration is morally right and because the Negro is your brother." In the midst of blatant injustices inflicted upon the Negro, I have watched white churchmen stand on the sideline and mouth pious irrelevancies and sanctimonious trivialities. In the midst of a mighty struggle to rid our nation of racial and economic injustice, I have heard many ministers say: "Those are social issues, with which the gospel has no real concern." And I have watched many churches commit themselves to a completely otherworldly religion which makes a strange, un-Biblical distinction between body and soul, between the sacred and the secular.

I have traveled the length and breadth of Alabama, Mississippi and all the other southern states. On sweltering summer days and crisp autumn mornings I have looked at the South's beautiful churches with their lofty spires pointing heavenward. I have beheld the impressive outlines of her massive religious-education buildings. Over and over I have found myself asking: "What kind of people worship here? Who is their God? Where were their voices when the lips of Governor Barnett dripped with words of interposition and nullification? Where were they when Governor Wallace gave a clarion call for defiance and hatred? Where were their voices of support when bruised and weary Negro men and women decided to rise from the dark dungeons of complacency to the bright hills of creative protest?"

Yes, these questions are still in my mind. In deep disappointment I have wept over the laxity of the church. But be assured that my tears have been tears of love. There can be no deep disappointment where there is not deep love. Yes, I love the church. How could I do otherwise? I am in the rather unique position of being the son, the grandson and the great-grandson of preachers. Yes, I see the church as the body of Christ. But, oh! How we have blemished and scarred that body through social neglect and through fear of being nonconformists.

There was a time when the church was very powerful—in the time when the early Christians rejoiced at being deemed worthy to suffer for what they believed. In those days the church was not merely a thermometer that recorded the ideas and principles of popular opinion; it was a thermostat that transformed the mores of society. Whenever the early Christians entered a town, the people in power became disturbed and immediately sought to convict the Christians for being "disturbers of the peace" and "outside agitators." But the Christians pressed on, in the conviction that they were "a colony of heaven," called to obey God rather than man. Small in number, they were big in commitment. They were too God-intoxicated to be "astronomically intimidated." By their effort and example they brought an end to such ancient evils as infanticide and gladiatorial contests.

Things are different now. So often the contemporary church is a weak, ineffectual voice with an uncertain sound. So often it is an archdefender of the status quo. Far from being disturbed by the presence of the church, the power structure of the average community is consoled by the church's silent—and often even vocal—sanction of things as they are.

But the judgment of God is upon the church as never before. If today's church does not recapture the sacrificial spirit of the early church, it will lose its authenticity, forfeit the loyalty of millions, and be dismissed as an irrelevant social club with no meaning for the twentieth century. Every day I meet young people whose disappointment with the church has turned into outright disgust.

Perhaps I have once again been too optimistic. Is organized religion too inextricably bound to the status quo to save our nation and the world? Perhaps I must turn my faith to the inner spiritual church, the church within the church, as the true *ekklesia* and the hope of the world. But again I am thankful to God that some noble souls from the ranks of organized religion have broken loose from the paralyzing chains of conformity and joined us as active partners in the struggle for freedom. They have left their secure congregations and walked the streets of Albany, Georgia, with us. They have gone down the highways of the South on tortuous rides for freedom. Yes, they have gone to jail with us. Some have been dismissed from their churches, have lost the support of their bishops and fellow ministers. But they have acted in the faith that right defeated is stronger than evil triumphant. Their witness has been the spiritual salt that has preserved the true meaning of the gospel in these troubled times. They have carved a tunnel of hope through the dark mountain of disappointment.

I hope the church as a whole will meet the challenge of this decisive hour. But even if the church does not come to the aid of justice, I have no despair about the future. I have no fear about the outcome of our struggle in Birmingham, even if our motives are at present misunderstood. We will reach the goal of freedom in Birmingham and all over the nation, because the goal of America is freedom. Abused and scorned though we may be, our destiny is tied up with America's destiny. Before the pilgrims landed at Plymouth, we were here. Before the pen of Jefferson etched the majestic words of the Declaration of Independence across the pages of history, we were here. For more than two centuries our forebears labored in this country without wages; they made cotton king; they built the homes of their masters while suffering gross injustice and shameful humiliation—and yet out of a bottomless vitality they continued to thrive and develop. If the inexpressible cruelties of slavery could not stop us, the opposition we now face will surely fail. We will win our freedom because the sacred heritage of our nation and the eternal will of God are embodied in our echoing demands.

Before closing I feel impelled to mention one other point in your statement that has troubled me profoundly. You warmly commended the Birmingham police force for keeping "order" and "preventing violence." I doubt that you would have so warmly commended the police force if you had seen its dogs sinking their teeth into unarmed, nonviolent Negroes. I doubt that you would so quickly commend the policemen if you were to observe their ugly and inhumane treatment of Negroes here in the city jail; if you were to watch them push and curse old Negro women and young Negro girls; if you were to see them slap and kick old Negro men and young boys; if you were to observe them, as they did on two occasions, refuse to give us food because we wanted to sing our grace together. I cannot join you in your praise of the Birmingham police department.

It is true that the police have exercised a degree of discipline in handling the demonstrators. In this sense they have conducted themselves rather "nonviolently" in public. But for what purpose? To preserve the evil system of segregation. Over the past few years I have consistently preached that nonviolence demands that the means we use must be as pure as the ends we seek. I have tried to make clear that it is wrong to use immoral means to attain moral ends. But now I must affirm that it is just as wrong, perhaps even more so, to use moral means to preserve immoral ends. Perhaps Mr. Connor and his policemen have been rather nonviolent in public, as was Chief Pritchett in Albany, Georgia, but they have used the moral means of nonviolence to maintain the immoral end of racial injustice. As T. S. Eliot has said: "The last temptation is the greatest treason: To do the right deed for the wrong reason."

I wish you had commended the Negro sit-inners and demonstrators of Birmingham for their sublime courage, their willingness to suffer and their amazing discipline in the midst of great provocation. One day the South will recognize its real heroes. They will be the James Merediths, with the noble sense of purpose that enables them to face jeering and hostile mobs, and with the agonizing loneliness that characterizes the life of the pioneer. They will be old, oppressed, battered Negro women, symbolized in a seventy-two-year-old woman in Montgomery, Alabama, who rose up with a sense of dignity and with her people decided not to ride segregated buses, and who responded with ungrammatical profundity to one who inquired about her weariness: "My feets is tired, but my soul is at rest." They will be the young high school and college students, the young ministers of the gospel and a host of their elders, courageously and nonviolently sitting in at lunch counters and willingly going to jail for conscience's sake. One day the South will know that when these disinherited children of God sat down at lunch counters, they were in reality standing up for what is best in the American dream and for the most sacred values in our Judeo-Christian heritage, thereby bringing our nation back to those great wells of democracy which were dug deep by the founding fathers in their formulation of the Constitution and the Declaration of Independence.

Never before have I written so long a letter. I'm afraid it is much too long to take your precious time. I can assure you that it would have been much shorter if I had been writing from a comfortable desk, but what else can one do when he is alone in a narrow jail cell, other than write long letters, think long thoughts and pray long prayers?

If I have said anything in this letter that overstates the truth and indicates an unreasonable impatience, I beg you to forgive me. If I have said anything that understates the truth and indicates my having a patience that allows me to settle for anything less than brotherhood, I beg God to forgive me.

I hope this letter finds you strong in the faith. I also hope that circumstances will soon make it possible for me to meet each of you, not as an integrationist or a civil-rights leader but as a fellow clergyman and a Christian brother. Let us all hope that the dark clouds of racial prejudice will soon pass away and the deep fog of misunderstanding will be lifted from our fear-drenched communities, and in some not too distant tomorrow the radiant stars of love and brotherhood will shine over our great nation with all their scintillating beauty.

Yours for the cause of Peace and Brotherhood,
MARTIN LUTHER KING, JR.

Questions for Thought

1. How would you describe the racial climate of the city in which you live today?
2. Do you agree with King that we have the right to disobey unjust laws? Why or why not?
3. Can you think of any present-day laws that would be unjust according to King's criteria?
4. Have you ever labeled someone an extremist? If so, in what context? Do you consider yourself to be an extremist? Why or why not?
5. Do you think that King's criticisms of white moderates and the white church are still relevant today? Defend your answer.
6. What are some of the analogies or metaphors that King uses? How effective do you think his use of analogy and metaphor are?
7. Toward the end of his letter, King asks the following question: "Is organized religion too inextricably bound to the status quo to serve our nation and the world?" How would you answer this question?

13   Power and Racism

STOKELY CARMICHAEL

Stokely Carmichael (1941–1998) was born in Port of Spain, Trinidad. His parents immigrated to the United States in 1952. In 1960, Carmichael joined CORE (the Congress of Racial Equality) and became involved with the Freedom Rides that were organized to protest segregation on public buses in the South. Carmichael then entered Howard University, from which he earned a degree in philosophy in 1964. In 1966, he became chairperson of the Student Nonviolent Coordinating Committee (SNCC), and he later served as prime minister of the Black Panther Party. He was coauthor of the book *Black Power: The Politics of Black Liberation*.

In 1969, after becoming further disillusioned with the racist attitudes that still prevailed in many areas of the United States, Carmichael and his then wife, Miriam Makeba, emigrated to Guinea. In Guinea, Carmichael founded the All-African People's Revolutionary Party, became an aide to Guinea's prime minister, and later changed his name to Kwame Toure to honor African socialist leaders Kwame Nkrumah and Ahmed Sekoe Toure. Dedicated to the struggle for civil and human rights throughout his life, Carmichael always answered his telephone with the greeting, "Ready for the revolution!"

In the following article, which was written in 1966 when he was chairperson of SNCC, Carmichael suggests that the pervasive racism that existed in the United States at that time seriously undermined governmental authority. He explains how the concept of black power represents a necessary response to this pervasive racism. At the same time, Carmichael criticizes the civil rights movement, which had adopted a philosophy of non-violence, for operating from a position of weakness. He also criticizes the struggle for integration as a subterfuge for the maintenance of white supremacy.

In place of nonviolence and integration, Carmichael calls for the acquisition of political and economic power. After describing the movement to attain voting rights in the South and acknowledging its ultimate failure, Carmichael argues that racism can be overcome only by shaking the very foundations of the American economy. Progressive people, blacks as well as whites, must learn to recognize the United States as an "octopus of exploitation" whereby "a powerful few have been maintained and enriched at the expense of the poor and voiceless colored masses." By recognizing that racism and hypocrisy extend to the very core of political and economic life in the United States, it may be possible to slay this octopus of exploitation and replace it with a new society in which "the spirit of community and humanistic love prevail."

Questions for Reading

1. What does Carmichael mean by "black power"? What leads him to defend this concept?
2. What does Carmichael mean when he says the United States is an "octopus of exploitation"? What reasons does he give for making this claim?
3. What is the point of Carmichael's remarks about Tarzan? What analogy does he use in connection with these remarks?
4. What does Carmichael mean by "psychological equality"? How does he believe that such equality is to be attained?
5. What are some of the changes that Carmichael is seeking? Why does he reject the call for integration?

ONE OF THE TRAGEDIES OF THE STRUGGLE against racism is that up to now there has been no national organization which could speak to the growing militancy of young black people in the urban ghetto. There has been only a civil rights movement, whose tone of voice was adapted to an audience of liberal whites. It served as a sort of buffer zone between them and angry young blacks. None of its so-called leaders could go into a rioting community and be listened to. In a sense, I blame ourselves—together with the mass media—for what has happened in Watts, Harlem, Chicago, Cleveland, and Omaha.[1] Each time the people in those cities saw Martin Luther King get slapped, they became angry; when they saw four little black girls bombed to death, they were steaming.[2] We had nothing to offer that they could see, except to go out and be beaten again.

We helped build their frustration. For too many years, black Americans marched and had their heads broken and got shot. They were saying to the country, "Look, you guys are supposed to be nice guys and we are only going to do what we are supposed to do—why do you beat us up, why don't you give us what we ask, why don't you straighten yourselves out?" After years of this, we are at almost the same point—because we demonstrated from a position of weakness. We cannot be expected any longer to march and have our heads broken in order to say to whites: Come on, you're nice guys. For you are not nice guys. We have found you out.

An organization which claims to speak for the needs of a community—as does the Student Nonviolent Coordinating Committee—must speak in the tone of that community, not as somebody

Stokely Carmichael, *"What We Want,"* The New York Review of Books, *September 22, 1966. Copyright 1966 by the Student Nonviolent Coordinating Committee.*

else's buffer zone. This is the significance of Black Power as a slogan. For once, black people are going to use the words they want to use—not just the words whites want to hear. And they will do this no matter how often the press tries to stop the use of the slogan by equating it with racism or separatism. An organization which claims to be working for the needs of a community—as SNCC does—must work to provide that community with a position of strength from which to make its voice heard. This is the significance of black power beyond the slogan.

Black power can be clearly defined for those who do not attach the fears of white America to their questions about it. We should begin with the basic fact that black Americans have two problems: they are poor and they are black. All other problems arise from this two-sided reality: lack of education, the so-called apathy of black men. Any program to end racism must address itself to that double reality.

Almost from its beginning, SNCC sought to address itself to both conditions with a program aimed at winning political power for impoverished Southern blacks. We had to begin with politics because black Americans are a propertyless people in a country where property is valued above all. We had to work for power, because this country does not function by morality, love, and non-violence, but by power. Thus we determined to win political power, with the idea of moving on from there into activity that would have economic effects. With power, the masses could *make or participate in making* the decisions which govern their destinies, and thus create basic change in their day-to-day lives.

But if political power seemed to be the key to self-determination, it was also obvious that the key had been thrown down a deep well many years earlier. Disenfranchisement, maintained by racist terror, made it impossible to talk about organizing for political power in 1960. The right to vote had to be won, and SNCC workers devoted their energies to this from 1961 to 1965. They set up voter registration drives in the Deep South. They created pressure for the vote by holding mock elections in Mississippi in 1963 and by helping to establish the Mississippi Freedom Democratic Party (MFDP) in 1964. That struggle was eased, though not won, with the passage of the 1965 Voting Rights Act.

SNCC workers could then address themselves to the question: "Who can we vote for, to have our needs met—how do we make our vote meaningful?"

SNCC had already gone to Atlantic City for recognition of the Mississippi Freedom Democratic Party by the Democratic convention and been rejected; it had gone with the MFDP to Washington for recognition by Congress and been rejected. In Arkansas, SNCC helped thirty Negroes to run for School Board elections; all but one were defeated, and there was evidence of fraud and intimidation sufficient to cause their defeat. In Atlanta, Julian Bond ran for the state legislature and was elected—twice—and unseated—twice. In several states, black farmers ran in elections for agricultural committees which make crucial decisions concerning land use, loans, etc. Although they won places on a number of committees, they never gained the majorities needed to control them. . . .

Ultimately, the economic foundations of this country must be shaken if black people are to control their lives. The colonies of the United States—and this includes the black ghettos within its borders, north and south—must be liberated. For a century, this nation has been like an octopus of exploitation, its tentacles stretching from Mississippi and Harlem to South America, the Middle East, southern Africa, and Vietnam; the form of exploitation varies from area to area but the essential result has been the same—a powerful few have been maintained and enriched at the expense of the poor and voiceless colored masses. This pattern must be broken. As its grip loosens here and there around the world, the hopes of black Americans become more realistic. For racism to die, a totally different America must be born.

This is what the white society does not wish to face; this is why that society prefers to talk about integration. But integration speaks not at all to the problem of poverty, only to the problem of blackness. Integration . . . means the man who "makes it," leaving his black brothers behind in the ghetto as fast as his new sports car will take him. It has no relevance to the Harlem wino or to the cottonpicker making three dollars a day. As a lady I know in Alabama once said, "the food that Ralph Bunche eats doesn't fill my stomach."

Integration, moreover, speaks to the problem of blackness in a despicable way. As a goal, it has been based on complete acceptance of the fact that *in order to have* a decent house or education, blacks must move into a white neighborhood or send their children to a white school. This reinforces, among both black and white, the idea that "white" is automatically better and "black" is by definition inferior. This is why integration is a subterfuge for the maintenance of white supremacy. It allows the nation to focus on a handful of Southern children who get into white schools, at great price, and to ignore the 94 percent who are left behind in unimproved all-black schools. Such situations will not change until black people have power—to control their own school boards, in this case. Then Negroes become equal in a way that means something, and integration ceases to be a one-way street. Then integration doesn't mean draining skills and energies from the ghetto into white neighborhoods; then it can mean white people moving from Beverly Hills into Watts, white people joining the Lowndes County Freedom Organization. Then integration becomes relevant.[3]

In April 1966, before the furor over black power, Christopher Jencks wrote in a *New Republic* article on white Mississippi's manipulation of the anti-poverty program:

> The war on poverty has been predicated on the notion that there is such a thing as a community which can be defined geographically and mobilized for a collective effort to help the poor. This theory has no relationship to reality in the Deep South. In every Mississippi county there are two communities. Despite all the pious platitudes of the moderates on both sides, these two communities habitually see their interests in terms of conflict rather than cooperation. Only when the Negro community can muster enough political, economic and professional strength to compete on somewhat equal terms, will Negroes believe in the possibility of true cooperation and whites accept its necessity. En route to integration, the Negro community needs to develop greater independence—a chance to run its own affairs and not cave in whenever "the man" barks. . . . Or so it seems to me, and to most of the knowledgeable people with whom I talked in Mississippi. To OEO, this judgment may sound like black nationalism. . . .

Mr. Jencks, a white reporter, perceived the reason why America's anti-poverty program has been a sick farce in both North and South. In the South, it is clearly racism which prevents the poor from running their own programs; in the North, it more often seems to be politicking and bureaucracy. But the results are not so different. . . . Behind it all is a federal government which cares far more about winning the war on the Vietnamese than the war on poverty; which has put the poverty program in the hands of self-serving politicians and bureaucrats rather than the poor themselves; which is unwilling to curb the misuse of white power but quick to condemn black power.

To most whites, black power seems to mean that the Mau Mau are coming to the suburbs at night. The Mau Mau are coming, and whites must stop them. Articles appear about plots to "get Whitey," creating an atmosphere in which "law and order must be maintained." Once again, responsibility is shifted from the oppressor to the oppressed. Other whites chide, "Don't forget—you're only 10 percent of the population; if you get too smart, we'll wipe you out." If they are liberals, they complain, "What about me?—don't you want my help any more?" These are people supposedly concerned about black Americans, but today they think first of themselves, of their feelings of rejection. Or they admonish, "You can't get anywhere without coalitions," without considering the problems of coalition with whom?; on what terms? (coalescing from weakness can mean absorption, betrayal); when? Or they accuse us of "polarizing the races" by our calls for black unity, when the true responsibility for polarization lies with whites who will not accept their responsibility as the majority power for making the democratic process work.

White America will not face the problem of color, the reality of it. The well-intended say: "We're all human, everybody is really decent, we must forget color." But color cannot be "forgotten" until its weight is recognized and dealt with. White America will not acknowledge that the ways in which this country sees itself are contradicted by being black—and always have been. Whereas most of the people who settled this country came here for freedom or for economic opportunity, blacks were brought here to be slaves. When the Lowndes County Freedom Organization chose the black panther as its symbol, it was christened by the press "the Black Panther Party"—but the Alabama Democratic Party, whose symbol is a rooster, has never been called the White Cock Party. No one ever talked about "white power" because power in this country *is* white. All this adds up to more than merely identifying a group phenomenon by some catchy name or adjective. The furor over that black panther reveals the problems that white America has with color and sex; the furor over "black power" reveals how deep racism runs and the great fear which is attached to it.

Whites will not see that I, for example, as a person oppressed because of my blackness, have common cause with other blacks who are oppressed because of blackness. This is not to say that there are no white people who see things as I do, but that it is black people I must speak to first. It must be the oppressed to whom SNCC addresses itself primarily, not to friends from the oppressing group.

From birth, black people are told a set of lies about themselves. We are told that we are lazy—yet I drive through the Delta area of Mississippi and watch black people picking cotton in the hot sun for fourteen hours. We are told, "If you work hard, you'll succeed"—but if that were true, black people would own this country. We are oppressed because we are black—not because we are ignorant, not because we are lazy, not because we're stupid (and got good rhythm), but because we're black.

I remember that when I was a boy, I used to go to see Tarzan movies on Saturday. White Tarzan used to beat up the black natives. I would sit there yelling, "Kill the beasts, kill the savages, kill 'em!" I was saying: Kill *me*. It was as if a Jewish boy watched Nazis taking Jews off to concentration camps and cheered them on. Today, I want the chief to beat hell out of Tarzan and send him back to Europe. But it takes time to become free of the lies and their shaming effect on black minds. It takes time to reject the most important lie: that black people inherently can't do the same things white people can do, unless white people help them.

The need for psychological equality is the reason why SNCC today believes that blacks must organize in the black community. Only black people can convey the revolutionary idea that black people are able to do things themselves. Only they can help create in the community an aroused and continuing black consciousness that will provide the basis for political strength. In the past, white allies have furthered white supremacy without the whites involved realizing it—or wanting it, I think. Black people must do things for themselves; they must get poverty money they will control and spend themselves, they must conduct tutorial programs themselves so that black children can identify with black people. This is one reason Africa has such importance: The reality of black men ruling their own nations gives blacks elsewhere a sense of possibility, of power, which they do not now have.

This does not mean we don't welcome help, or friends. But we want the right to decide whether anyone is, in fact, our friend. In the past, black Americans have been almost the only people whom everybody and his momma could jump up and call their friends. We have been tokens, symbols, objects—as I was in high school to many young whites, who liked having "a Negro friend." We want to decide who is our friend, and we will not accept someone who comes to us and says: "If you do X, Y, and Z, then I'll help you." We will not be told whom we should choose as allies. We will not be isolated from any group or nation except by our own choice. We cannot have the oppressors telling the oppressed how to rid themselves of the oppressor.

I have said that most liberal whites react to "black power" with the question, What about me?, rather than saying: Tell me what you want me to do and I'll see if I can do it. There are answers to the right question. One of the most disturbing things about almost all white supporters of the movement has been that they are afraid to go into their own communities—which is where the racism exists—and work to get rid of it. They want to run from Berkeley to tell us what to do in Mississippi; let them look instead at Berkeley. They admonish blacks to be nonviolent; let them preach nonviolence in the white community. They come to teach me Negro history; let them go to the suburbs and open up freedom schools for whites. Let them work to stop America's racist foreign policy; let them press this government to cease supporting the economy of South Africa.

There is a vital job to be done among poor whites. We hope to see, eventually, a coalition between poor blacks and poor whites. That is the only coalition which seems acceptable to us, and we see such a coalition as the major internal instrument of change in American society. . . . It is purely academic today to talk about bringing poor blacks and whites together, but the job of creating a poor-white power bloc must be attempted. The main responsibility for it falls upon whites. Black and white can work together in the white community where possible; it is not possible, however, to go into a poor Southern town and talk about integration. Poor whites everywhere are becoming more hostile—not less—partly because they see the nation's attention focused on black poverty and nobody coming to them.[4] . . .

Black people do not want to "take over" this country. They don't want to "get Whitey"; they just want to get him off their backs, as the saying goes. It was for example the exploitation by Jewish landlords and merchants which first created black resentment toward Jews—not Judaism. The white man is irrelevant to blacks, except as an oppressive force. Blacks want to be in his place, yes, but not in order to terrorize and lynch and starve him. They want to be in his place because that is where a decent life can be had.

But our vision is not merely of a society in which all black men have enough to buy the good things of life. When we urge that black money go into black pockets, we mean the communal pocket. We want to see money go back into the community and used to benefit it. We want to see the cooperative concept applied in business and banking. We want to see black ghetto residents demand that an exploiting landlord or storekeeper sell them, at minimal cost, a building or a shop that they will own and improve cooperatively; they can back their demand with a rent strike, or a boycott, and a community so unified behind them that no one else will move into the building or buy at the store. The society we seek to build among black people, then, is not a capitalist one. It is a society in which the spirit of community and humanistic love prevail. The word love is suspect; black expectations of what it might produce have been betrayed too often. But those were expectations of a response from the white community, which failed us. The love we seek to encourage is within the black community, the only American community where men call each other "brother" when they meet. We can build a community of love only where we have the ability and power to do so: among blacks.

As for white America, perhaps it can stop crying out against "black supremacy," "black nationalism," "racism in reverse," and begin facing reality. The reality is that this nation, from top to bottom, is racist; that racism is not primarily a problem of "human relations" but of an exploitation maintained—either actively or through silence—by society as a whole. Camus and Sartre have asked, can a man condemn himself? Can whites, particularly liberal whites, condemn themselves? Can they stop blaming us, and blame their own system? Are they capable of the shame which might become a revolutionary emotion?

We have found that they usually cannot condemn themselves, and so we have done it. But the rebuilding of this society, if at all possible, is basically the responsibility of whites—not blacks. We won't fight to save the present society, in Vietnam or anywhere else. We are just going to work, in the way *we* see fit, and on goals *we* define, not for civil rights but for all our human rights.

NOTES

1. When Carmichael wrote this article, all of these cities had just experienced periods of urban rioting, resulting in much death and destruction.—ED.

2. Carmichael is referring to the bombing of the Sixteenth Street Baptist Church in Birmingham, Alabama on September 15, 1963. Four young girls, Addie Mae Collins, Denise McNair, Carole Robertson, and Cynthia Wesley, were killed by the explosion.—ED.

3. One might still wonder today, four decades after this was written, whether the type of meaningful integration that Carmichael envisions has been realized on a broad scale.—ED.

4. Recent attacks on affirmative action programs, as well as increased incidences of hate crimes throughout the United States, suggest that this problem still exists. Of course, in many places today, much of the resentment is directed toward recent immigrants rather than African Americans.—ED.

Questions for Thought

1. Do you think that black power is an important political concept? Why or why not?
2. How do you think Carmichael would respond to Gandhi's notion of *satyagraha*?
3. Can you think of any historical examples that might support Carmichael's claim that the United States is "an octopus of exploitation"? Can you think of any evidence that might refute this claim?
4. To what extent do you think contemporary society is racist? Do you believe that it is more racist or less racist than when Carmichael wrote this article?
5. How would you define *integration*? Do you agree with Carmichael's criticisms of the value of integration? Why or why not?
6. How does the "totally different America" envisioned by Carmichael compare with or differ from the society in which you currently live? How would you describe an ideal society?

14   Feminism: A Transformational Politic

BELL HOOKS

bell hooks (b. 1952) is the pseudonym of Gloria Watkins, a writer, speaker, and teacher who grew up in Kentucky. hooks, who received her B.A. from Stanford University, her M.A. from the University of Wisconsin, and her Ph.D. from the University of California, Santa Cruz, is currently a professor of English and women's studies at the City College of New York. She has also taught in the Department of African-American Studies at Yale University and at Oberlin College.

hooks has published extensively in progressive periodicals, including *Aurora, Catalyst, Discourse, Sage,* and *Zeta.* Her books include *Ain't I a Woman: Black Women and Feminism* (1981), *Feminist Theory: From Margin to Center* (1984), *Talking Back: Thinking Feminist, Thinking Black* (1989), *Yearning: Race, Gender, and Cultural Politics* (1990), *Black Looks: Race and Representation* (1992), *Sisters of the Yam: Black Women and Self-recovery* (1993), *Outlaw Culture: Resisting Representations* (1994), *Teaching to Transgress: Education as the Practice of Freedom* (1994), *Art on My Mind: Visual Politics* (1995), *Killing Rage: Ending Racism* (1996), *Reel to Real: Race, Sex, and Class at the Movies* (1996), *Bone Black: Memories of Girlhood* (1997), *Words of Passion: A Writing Life* (1997), *Talking About Revolution* (1998), *Remembered Rapture: The Writer at Word* (1999), *Feminism Is for Everybody: Passionate Politics* (2000), *Where We Stand: Class Matters* (2000), *All About Love: New Visions* (2001), *Salvation: Black People and Love* (2001), *Communion: The Female Search for Love* (2002), *Rock My Soul: Black People and Self-Esteem* (2003), and *A Woman's Mourning Song* (2005). hooks has also written three books for children.

In the following excerpt from *Talking Back*, hooks, like Carmichael, characterizes the United States as a country in which racist and economic exploitation runs rampant, a country in which a few people (mainly white males) dominate and oppress everyone else. Unlike Carmichael, however, hooks believes that it is feminism, not the politics of black power, that holds the promise of self-transformation and social change. But in order for this promise to be realized, she claims that feminism must be redefined. Whereas feminists have traditionally focused solely on the domination of women by men, hooks argues that sexist oppression is interlocked with both racist oppression and class oppression and that sexist oppression can be overcome only by overcoming these other types of oppression as well.

In addition to arguing these general points about feminist theory, hooks makes several important points about feminist practice. First, she notes that self-transformation is the starting point of social transformation and that small-group discussions (or consciousness-raising sessions) are the best means of realizing self-transformation. Second, she argues that men as well as women must understand and embrace feminism if it is to be an agent of social change. Finally, she says that more effort should be extended to showing the positive benefits of feminist revolution, to documenting that it is indeed an act of love. As she says, "When women and men understand that working to eradicate patriarchal domination is a struggle rooted in the longing to make a world where everyone can live fully and freely, then we know our work to be a gesture of love."

Questions for Reading

1. How does hooks describe life in the modern world?
2. With which of the traditional assumptions of feminism does hooks disagree? What reasons does she give for rejecting these assumptions?
3. Within what context, according to hooks, did the paradigm of domination likely arise? What role, if any, did women have in constructing this paradigm?
4. How does hooks describe a small-group consciousness-raising session? Why does she believe that such a setting is the most effective setting for self-transformation?
5. What, according to hooks, are some of the benefits of undergoing feminist self-transformation?

WE LIVE IN A WORLD IN CRISIS—A WORLD governed by politics of domination, one in which the belief in a notion of superior and inferior, and its concomitant ideology—that the superior should rule over the inferior—effects the lives of all people everywhere, whether poor or privileged, literate or illiterate. Systematic dehumanization, worldwide famine, ecological devastation, industrial contamination, and the possibility of nuclear destruction are realities which remind us daily that we are in crisis. Contemporary feminist thinkers often cite sexual politics as the origin of this crisis. They point to the insistence on difference as the factor which becomes the occasion for separation and domination and suggest that differentiation of status between females and males globally is an indication that patriarchal domination of the planet is the root of the problem. Such an assumption has fostered the notion that elimination of sexist oppression would necessarily lead to the eradication of all forms of domination. It is an argument that has led influential Western white women to feel that feminist movement should be *the* central political agenda for females globally. Ideologically, thinking in this direction enables Western women, especially privileged white women, to suggest that racism and class exploitation are merely the offspring of the parent system: **patriarchy.** Within feminist movement in the West, this has led to the assumption that resisting patriarchal domination is a more legitimate feminist action than resisting racism and other forms of domination. Such thinking prevails despite radical critiques made by black women and other women of color who question this proposition. To speculate that an oppositional division between men and women existed in early human communities is to

From bell hooks, Talking Back: thinking feminist, thinking black, *South End Press, 1989. Reprinted by permission of South End Press.*

impose on the past, on these non-white groups, a worldview that fits all too neatly within contemporary feminist paradigms that name man as the enemy and woman as the victim.

Clearly, differentiation between strong and weak, powerful and powerless, has been a central defining aspect of gender globally, carrying with it the assumption that men should have greater authority than women, and should rule over them. As significant and important as this fact is, it should not obscure the reality that women can and do participate in politics of domination, as perpetrators as well as victims—that we dominate, that we are dominated. If focus on patriarchal domination masks this reality or becomes the means by which women deflect attention from the real conditions and circumstances of our lives, then women cooperate in suppressing and promoting false consciousness, inhibiting our capacity to assume responsibility for transforming ourselves and society.

Thinking speculatively about early human social arrangement, about women and men struggling to survive in small communities, it is likely that the parent-child relationship with its very real imposed survival structure of dependency, of strong and weak, of powerful and powerless, was a site for the construction of a paradigm of domination. While this circumstance of dependency is not necessarily one that leads to domination, it lends itself to the enactment of a social drama wherein domination could easily occur as a means of exercising and maintaining control. This speculation does not place women outside the practice of domination, in the exclusive role of victim. It centrally names women as agents of domination, as potential theoreticians, and creators of a paradigm for social relationship wherein those groups of individuals designated as "strong" exercise power both benevolently and coercively over those designated as "weak."

Emphasizing paradigms of domination that call attention to woman's capacity to dominate is one way to deconstruct and challenge the simplistic notion that man is the enemy, woman is the victim; the notion that men have always been the oppressors. Such thinking enables us to examine our role as women in the perpetuation and maintenance of systems of domination. To understand domination, we must understand that our capacity as women and men to be either dominated or dominating is a point of connection, of commonality. Even though I speak from the particular experience of living as a black woman in the United States, a white-supremacist, capitalist, patriarchal society, where small numbers of white men (and honorary "white men") constitute ruling groups, I understand that in many places in the world oppressed and oppressor share the same color. I understand that right here in this room, oppressed and oppressor share the same gender. Right now as I speak, a man who is himself victimized, wounded, hurt by racism and class exploitation is actively dominating a woman in his life—that even as I speak, women who are ourselves exploited, victimized, are dominating children. It is necessary for us to remember, as we think critically about domination, that we all have the capacity to act in ways that oppress, dominate, wound (whether or not that power is institutionalized). It is necessary to remember that it is first the potential oppressor within that we must resist—the potential victim within that we must rescue—otherwise we cannot hope for an end to domination, for liberation.

This knowledge seems especially important at this historical moment when black women and other women of color have worked to create awareness of the ways in which racism empowers white women to act as exploiters and oppressors. Increasingly this fact is considered a reason we should not support feminist struggle even though sexism and sexist oppression is a real issue in our lives as black women (see, for example, Vivian Gordon's *Black Women, Feminism, Black Liberation: Which Way?*).

It becomes necessary for us to speak continually about the convictions that inform our continued advocacy of feminist struggle. By calling attention to interlocking systems of domination—sex, race, and class—black women and many other groups of women acknowledge the diversity and complexity of female experience, of our relationship to power and domination. The intent is not to dissuade people of color from becoming engaged in feminist movement. Feminist struggle to end patriarchal domination should be of primary importance to women and men globally not because it is the foundation of all other oppressive structures but because it is that form of domination we are most likely to encounter in an ongoing way in everyday life.

Unlike other forms of domination, sexism directly shapes and determines relations of power in our private lives, in familiar social spaces, in that most intimate context—home—and in that most intimate sphere of relations—family. Usually, it is within the family that we witness coercive domination and learn to accept it, whether it be domination of parent over child, or male over female. Even though family relations may be, and most often are, informed by acceptance of a politic of domination, they are simultaneously relations of care and connection. It is this convergence of two contradictory impulses—the urge to promote growth and the urge to inhibit growth—that provides a practical setting for feminist critique, resistance, and transformation.

Growing up in a black, working-class, father-dominated household, I experienced coercive adult male authority as more immediately threatening, as more likely to cause immediate pain than racist oppression or class exploitation. It was equally clear that experiencing exploitation and oppression in the home made one feel all the more powerless when encountering dominating forces outside the home. This is true for many people. If we are unable to resist and end domination in relations where there is care, it seems totally unimaginable that we can resist and end it in other institutionalized relations of power. If we cannot convince the mothers and/or fathers who care not to humiliate and degrade us, how can we imagine convincing or resisting an employer, a lover, a stranger who systematically humiliates and degrades?

Feminist effort to end patriarchal domination should be of primary concern precisely because it insists on the eradication of exploitation and oppression in the family context and in all other intimate relationships. It is that political movement which most radically addresses the person—the personal—citing the need for transformation of self, of relationships, so that we might be better able to act in a revolutionary manner, challenging and resisting domination, transforming the world outside the self. Strategically, feminist movement should be a central component of all other liberation struggles because it challenges each of us to alter our person, our personal engagement (either as victims or perpetrators or both) in a system of domination.

Feminism, as liberation struggle, must exist apart from and as a part of the larger struggle to eradicate domination in all its forms. We must understand that patriarchal domination shares an ideological foundation with racism and other forms of group oppression, that there is no hope that it can be eradicated while these systems remain intact. This knowledge should consistently inform the direction of feminist theory and practice. Unfortunately, racism and class elitism among women has frequently led to the suppression and distortion of this connection so that it is now necessary for feminist thinkers to critique and revise much feminist theory and the direction of feminist movement. This effort at revision is perhaps most evident in the current widespread acknowledgment that sexism, racism, and class exploitation constitute interlocking systems of domination—that sex, race, and class, and not sex alone, determine the nature of any female's identity, status, and circumstance, the degree to which she will or will not be dominated, the extent to which she will have the power to dominate.

While acknowledgment of the complex nature of woman's status (which has been most impressed upon everyone's consciousness by radical women of color) is a significant corrective, it is only a starting point. It provides a frame of reference which must serve as the basis for thoroughly altering and revising feminist theory and practice. It challenges and calls us to re-think popular assumptions about the nature of feminism that have had the deepest impact on a large majority of women, on mass consciousness. It radically calls into question the notion of a fundamentally common female experience which has been seen as the prerequisite for our coming together, for political unity. Recognition of the inter-connectedness of sex, race, and class highlights the diversity of experience, compelling redefinition of the terms for unity. If women do not share "common oppression," what then can serve as a basis for our coming together?

Unlike many feminist comrades, I believe women and men must share a common understanding—a basic knowledge of what feminism is—if it is ever to be a powerful mass-based political movement. In *Feminist Theory: from margin to center,* I suggest that defining feminism broadly as "a movement to end sexism and sexist oppression" would enable us to have a common political goal. We would then have a basis on which to build solidarity. Multiple and contradictory definitions of feminism create confusion and undermine the effort to construct feminist movement so that it addresses everyone. Sharing a common goal does not imply that women and men will not have radically divergent perspectives on how that goal might be reached. Because each individual starts the process of engagement in feminist struggle at a unique level of awareness, very real differences in experience, perspective, and knowledge make developing varied strategies for participation and transformation a necessary agenda.

Feminist thinkers engaged in radically revisioning central tenets of feminist thought must continually emphasize the importance of sex, race and class as factors which *together* determine the social construction of femaleness, as it has been so deeply ingrained in the consciousness of many women active in feminist movement that gender is the sole factor determining destiny. However, the work of education for critical consciousness (usually called consciousness-raising) cannot end there. Much feminist consciousness-raising has in the past focused on identifying the particular ways men oppress and exploit women. Using the paradigm of sex, race, and class means that the focus does not begin with men and what they do to women, but rather with women working to identify both individually and collectively the specific character of our social destiny.

Imagine a group of women from diverse backgrounds coming together to talk about feminism. First they concentrate on working out their status in terms of sex, race, and class, using this as the standpoint from which they begin discussing patriarchy or their particular relations with individual men. Within the old frame of reference, a discussion might consist solely of talk about their experiences as victims in relationship to male oppressors. Two women—one poor, the other quite wealthy—might describe the process by which they have suffered physical abuse by male partners and find certain commonalities that might serve as a basis for bonding. Yet if these same two women engaged in a discussion of class, not only would the social

construction and expression of femaleness differ, so too would their ideas about how to confront and change their circumstances. Broadening the discussion to include an analysis of race and class would expose many additional differences even as commonalities emerged.

Clearly the process of bonding would be more complex, yet this broader discussion might enable the sharing of perspectives and strategies for change that would enrich rather than diminish our understanding of gender. While feminists have increasingly given "lip service" to the idea of diversity, we have not developed strategies of communication and inclusion that allow for the successful enactment of this feminist vision.

Small groups are no longer the central place for feminist consciousness-raising. Much feminist education for critical consciousness takes place in Women's Studies classes or at conferences that focus on gender. Books are a primary source of education which means that already masses of people who do not read have no access. The separation of grassroots ways of sharing feminist thinking across kitchen tables from the spheres where much of that thinking is generated, the academy, undermines feminist movement. It would further feminist movement if new feminist thinking could be once again shared in small group contexts, integrating critical analysis with discussion of personal experience. It would be useful to promote anew the small group setting as an arena for education for critical consciousness, so that women and men might come together in neighborhoods and communities to discuss feminist concerns.

Small groups remain an important place for education for critical consciousness for several reasons. An especially important aspect of the small group setting is the emphasis on communicating feminist thinking, feminist theory, in a manner that can be easily understood. In small groups, individuals do not need to be equally literate or literate at all because the information is primarily shared through conversation, in dialogue which is necessarily a liberatory expression. (Literacy should be a goal for feminists even as we ensure that it not become a requirement for participation in feminist education.) Reforming small groups would subvert the appropriation of feminist thinking by a select group of academic women and men, usually white, usually from privileged class backgrounds.

Small groups of people coming together to engage in feminist discussion, in dialectical struggle, make a space where the "personal is political" as a starting point for education for critical consciousness can be extended to include politicization of the self that focuses on creating understanding of the ways sex, race, and class together determine our individual lot and our collective experience. It would further feminist movement if many well-known feminist thinkers would participate in small groups, critically re-examining ways their works might be changed by incorporating broader perspectives. All efforts at self-transformation challenge us to engage in ongoing, critical self-examination and reflection about feminist practice, about how we live in the world. This individual commitment, when coupled with engagement in collective discussion, provides a space for critical feedback that strengthens our efforts to change and make ourselves anew. It is in this commitment to feminist principles in our words and deeds that the hope of feminist revolution lies.

Working collectively to confront difference, to expand our awareness of sex, race, and class as interlocking systems of domination, of the way we reinforce and perpetuate these structures, is the context in which we learn the true meaning of solidarity. It is this work that must be the foundation of feminist movement. Without it, we cannot effectively resist patriarchal domination; without it, we remain estranged and alienated from one another. Fear of painful confrontation often leads women and men active in feminist movement to avoid rigorous critical encounter, yet if we cannot engage dialectically in a committed, rigorous, humanizing manner, we cannot hope to change the world. True politicization—coming to critical consciousness—is a difficult, "trying" process, one that demands that we give up set ways of thinking and being, that we shift our paradigms, that we open ourselves to the unknown, the unfamiliar. Undergoing this process, we learn what it means to struggle and in this effort we experience the dignity and integrity of being that comes with revolutionary change. If we do not change our consciousness, we cannot change our actions or demand change from others.

Our renewed commitment to a rigorous process of education for critical consciousness will determine the shape and direction of future feminist movement. Until new perspectives are created, we cannot be living symbols of the power of feminist thinking. Given the privileged lot of many leading feminist thinkers, both in terms of status or class, and race, it is harder these days to convince women of the primacy of this process of politicization. More and more, we seem to form select interest groups composed of individuals who share similar perspectives. This limits our capacity to engage in critical discussion. It is difficult to involve women in new processes of feminist politicization because so many of us think that identifying men as the enemy, resisting male domination, gaining equal access to power and privilege is the end of feminist movement. Not only is it not the end, it is not even the place we want revitalized feminist movement to begin. We want to begin as women seriously addressing ourselves, not solely in relation to men, but in relation to an entire structure of domination of which patriarchy is one part. While the struggle to eradicate sexism and sexist oppression is and should be the primary thrust of feminist movement, to prepare ourselves politically for this effort we must first learn how to be in solidarity, how to struggle with one another.

Only when we confront the realities of sex, race, and class, the ways they divide us, make us different, stand us in opposition, and work to reconcile and resolve these issues will we be able to participate in the making of feminist revolution, in the transformation of the world. Feminism, as Charlotte Bunch emphasizes again and again in *Passionate Politics,* is a transformational politics, a struggle against domination wherein the effort is to change ourselves as well as structures. Speaking about the struggle to confront difference, Bunch asserts:

> A crucial point of the process is understanding that reality does not look the same from different people's perspectives. It is not surprising that one way feminists have come to understand

about differences has been through the love of a person from another culture or race. It takes persistence and motivation—which love often engenders—to get beyond one's **ethnocentric** assumptions and really learn about other perspectives. In this process and while seeking to eliminate oppression, we also discover new possibilities and insights that come from the experience and survival of other peoples.

Embedded in the commitment to feminist revolution is the challenge to love. Love can be and is an important source of empowerment when we struggle to confront issues of sex, race, and class. Working together to identify and face our differences—to face the ways we dominate and are dominated—to change our actions, we need a mediating force that can sustain us so that we are not broken in this process, so that we do not despair.

Not enough feminist work has focused on documenting and sharing ways individuals confront differences constructively and successfully. Women and men need to know what is on the other side of the pain experienced in politicization. We need detailed accounts of the ways our lives are fuller and richer as we change and grow politically, as we learn to live each moment as committed feminists, as comrades working to end domination. In reconceptualizing and reformulating strategies for future feminist movement, we need to concentrate on the politicization of love, not just in the context of talking about victimization in intimate relationships, but in a critical discussion where love can be understood as a powerful force that challenges and resists domination. As we work to be loving, to create a culture that celebrates life, that makes love possible, we move against dehumanization, against domination. In *Pedagogy of the Oppressed,* Paulo Freire evokes this power of love, declaring:

> I am more and more convinced that true revolutionaries must perceive the revolution, because of its creative and liberating nature, as an act of love. For me, the revolution, which is not possible without a theory of revolution—and therefore science—is not irreconcilable with love. . . . The distortion imposed on the word "love" by the capitalist world cannot prevent the revolution from being essentially loving in character, nor can it prevent the revolutionaries from affirming their love of life.

That aspect of feminist revolution that calls women to love womanness, that calls men to resist dehumanizing concepts of masculinity, is an essential part of our struggle. It is the process by which we move from seeing ourselves as objects to acting as subjects. When women and men understand that working to eradicate patriarchal domination is a struggle rooted in the longing to make a world where everyone can live fully and freely, then we know our work to be a gesture of love. Let us draw upon that love to heighten our awareness, deepen our compassion, intensify our courage, and strengthen our commitment.

Questions for Thought

1. What do you think the term *feminism* means? How does your definition compare with or differ from that of hooks?
2. In what ways is hooks' critique of life in the United States similar to the critique of Carmichael? In what ways, if any, is it different?
3. Do you agree with hooks' claim that self-transformation is a prerequisite of social change? Why or why not?
4. How does the household in which you grew up compare with or differ from the household in which hooks grew up? To what extent did the politics of domination exist in your own household?
5. Can you think of any reasons for favoring a feminist revolution? If such a revolution took place, how do you think society would differ from the society in which you now live?

Socialist Feminism: Our Bridge to Freedom   15

NELLIE WONG

Essayist and poet Nellie Wong (b. 1934) grew up in Oakland's Chinatown, where she found herself constantly torn between her Chinese heritage and American culture. Following the traditional role model for a Chinese-American woman of the time, Wong worked in her family's Chinese restaurant, went to business school, became a secretary, and got married. Feeling constricted by this traditional role, however, she began breaking out of it when she enrolled at San Francisco State College at the age of thirty-two. At San Francisco State, Wong pursued a degree in creative writing and gradually found her voice as a poet. In addition, she discovered and became active in the women's and labor movements that were thriving in San Francisco at the time. She was a founding member of Unbound Feet, an Asian-American women's writing and performing group, and the first organizer of the Women Writer's Union in San Francisco.

Wong's essays and poems have been published in numerous journals and anthologies, including *Breaking Silence: An Anthology of Asian American Poets, This Bridge Called My Back: Writings by Radical Women of Color, Women Poets of the World, Heresies,* and the *Iowa Review.* She has also authored three collections of poetry, *Dreams in Harrison Railroad Park* (1977), *The Death of Long Steam Lady* (1986), and *Stolen Moments* (1997), and she was coeditor of the important anthology *Voices of Color* (1999). In addition, Wong was featured in the documentary film *Mitsuye and Nellie, Asian American Poets,* and her poem "Song of Farewell" was chosen by the San Francisco Arts Commission to be inscribed in concrete on a municipal transit platform in the middle of the Embarcadero roadway in San Francisco. Wong held the position of senior analyst in the University of California at San Francisco Affirmative Action/Equal Opportunity Office until her retirement in 1998. Still living in San Francisco, Wong continues to speak at conferences on issues of race, gender, class, war, literature, labor, and community organizing.

In the following essay, which is a revised version of a speech originally presented at the conference "Common Differences: Third World Women and Feminist Perspectives" held in 1983 at the University of Illinois, Urbana-Champaign, Wong examines the problems of race, sex, sexuality, and class struggle that pervade modern society. While describing her own experiences with economic exploitation and her personal journey toward political awareness, Wong argues that socialist feminism is the only vehicle that will allow these problems to be resolved. Until they are resolved, she finds the legitimacy of government to be problematic. For this reason, she calls on all the exploited groups in society to unite to resist government coercion and oppression. Believing that women of color are the most oppressed group under capitalism, she suggests that they are best equipped to lead the movement toward liberation, a movement through which "worldwide socialism will break the stranglehold of worldwide imperialism."

Questions for Reading

1. How does Wong begin and conclude her essay?
2. What does Wong mean by "socialist feminism"? Why does she believe that feminism without socialism is inadequate?

3. What are some of the social problems that lead Wong to conclude that capitalism must be overthrown? How do her life experiences support this conclusion?

4. Who were Merle Woo and Henry Noble? What point is Wong trying to make in discussing their lives?

5. Why does Wong believe that women of color are best suited to lead a socialist feminist revolution?

We work for enough to live each day,
   Without a day off, like the labor laws say.
The price of noodles, 12 hours' work don't pay,
   So, change our working conditions. Hey!

(Refrain)
Fellow workers, get it together,
   For prosperity in our land,
Fellow workers, rise up together,
   To right things by our hand.

When we get our monthly paychecks,
   Our monthly worries merely grow,
Most of it goes for some rice and the rent—
   Our private debts we still owe.

Lifeless, as if they were poisoned,
   Are those fine young men,
Who once promised to work hard for us—
   Oh, revive your lost bravery again.

SONG OF FACTORY WOMEN, FEBRUARY 1973[1]

THIS SONG ILLUSTRATES ONLY ONE OF MANY working-class struggles being waged by women throughout the world. It shows that Korean women workers recognize their multi-issue oppression; their low wages won't pay for the price of noodles, their monthly paychecks do not alleviate their ongoing private debts, and they must take action into their own hands, independent from the men in their lives who act as if they were "poisoned" by their government's anti-labor stance. South Korea's leading exports are textiles, shoes, and electronic goods—industries with a mostly female work force.[2] A primarily female work force has helped maintain Korea's economic growth. However, women workers are the lowest-paid and work under the bleakest conditions. Sister workers in the Philippines, Singapore, Japan, Hong Kong, and Taiwan also suffer long hours, unpaid overtime, and sexual harassment. The conditions of Korea's women workers are typical of the majority of Asia's industrial workers.

Women continue to be a part of the ongoing liberation movements throughout the world. In 1982, during International Women's Day, I spoke at a public forum sponsored by the Anti-Family Protection Act Coalition in Los Angeles, California, where I paid tribute to international working women:

Women workers started the Russian Revolution.

Women workers sparked the shipyard strikes in Poland.

Women workers and housewives marched by the thousands to protest the inhumane, antiwoman repression in Iran.

Women workers protested the sexist antiworker conditions in textile factories in Korea.

Women militants fought the Kisaeng tourism/prostitution in Korea.

Women workers formed a 100-year marriage resistance in Kwangtung, China.

Women fighters, young and old, fought in liberation struggles in Vietnam, Nicaragua, Cuba, El Salvador, South Africa, Lebanon.

Women workers are fighting to end nuclear testing in the Marshall Islands.

And in the United States, women continue to participate on all political fronts, from reproductive rights to union organizing, for social, economic, political, racial, and sexual equality.

Diné and Hopi women, mostly grandmothers and mothers, in 1986 were leading the resistance to the U.S. government's forced "relocation" from Big Mountain, Arizona, of people from ancestral homelands in an area jointly held by the Navajo and Hopi nations. Giant energy corporations such as Peabody

Coal, Kerr McGee, and Exxon want unhampered access to the estimated 44 billion tons of high-grade coal and deposits of oil, natural gas, and uranium found on and around Big Mountain.[3]

The resistance of women is nothing new; however, it must be seen in the context of political, social, and economic conditions in which the total emancipation of women, as a sex, is hampered. The liberation of women cannot be relegated to simply overthrowing the **patriarchy** because male chauvinism is not eternal, any more than racism, anti-Semitism, or anti-gay bigotry is eternal. They are all products of the historical development of private property, where a few had everything, and most had virtually nothing (Hill 1984, 19). Resistance to the patriarchal institutions of private property has always existed. Opposition to the current epoch's patriarchal institution—capitalism—is, by definition, socialist. Without overthrowing the economic system of capitalism, as socialists and communists organize to do, we cannot liberate women *and* everybody else who is also oppressed.

Socialist feminism is our bridge to freedom. By feminism, I mean the political analysis and practice to free *all* women. No woman, because of her race, class, sexuality, age, or disability, is left out. Feminism, the struggle for women's equal rights, is inseparable from socialism—but is not identical to socialism. Socialism is an economic system which reorganizes production, redistributes wealth, and redefines state power so that the exploiters are expropriated and workers gain hegemony. Feminism, like all struggles for liberation from a specific type of bondage, is a reason for socialism, a catalyst to organize for socialism, and a benefit of socialism. At the same time, feminism is decisive to socialism. Where male supremacy functions, socialism cannot, because true socialism, by definition, connotes a higher form of human relations that can't possibly exist under capitalism. Revolutionary Trotskyist feminism sees the most oppressed sections of the working class as decisive to revolution—working women and particularly working women of color. This is the theory which integrates socialism and feminism.

Socialist feminism is a radical, disciplined, and all-encompassing solution to the problems of race, sex, sexuality, and class struggle. Socialist feminism lives in the battles of all people of color, in the lesbian and gay movement, and in the class struggle.

Revolutionary feminism also happens to be an integral part, a cornerstone, of every movement. It objectively answers the ideological search of black women and men. It is the political foundation of the new revolutionary vanguard: socialist feminist people of color.[4]

As a Chinese American working woman, I had been searching for many years to arrive at the heart and soul of my own liberation struggle. As a long-time office worker, I was laid off after eighteen and one-half years' service with Bethlehem Steel Corporation, the second-largest steelmaker in the United States. As a Chinese American, one of seven children of Cantonese immigrants, I questioned over and over why our lives were shaped by racism and sexism and our oppression as workers in this country. Historically, our lives as Chinese Americans are linked to those of other Asians, all people of color—of blacks who have been enslaved, and who are still fighting for their civil rights; of Japanese Americans who were incarcerated during World War II; and of other groups of workers who were brought in to build America.

I did not have the opportunity to attend college immediately after I graduated from high school. Economics, and the Confucianist and feudal ideology pervasive in the Chinese American community, dictated my taking a secretarial job at the age of seventeen. As a young office worker, I learned that my secretarial career was supposed to be temporary—that if I met the "right" man, got married, and had children, I would become a "real" woman fulfilling what society ordained; and that in itself, life as a woman worker had no value, particularly when that woman worker took shorthand, typed, and filed for a living.

My feminist consciousness began to take hold when I got married and when I began college in my mid-thirties while still working full time. Silenced most of my life, I began to articulate my experiences through creative writing courses. My seemingly personal and private deprivation and angst as a Chinese American working woman began to express itself in a social milieu—with other women, other Asian Americans, other people of color, other feminists, and other workers. What I had thought was personal and private was truly political, social, and public. What a jolt it was to realize what I had learned from a capitalist bourgeois society—through the public school system and the workplace—that as a woman-of-color worker, I was simply an individual left to my own capacities and wiles! What a revelation, as long in coming as it was, to learn that workers everywhere were connected to one another—that it was our labor that provided wealth for a few, and that a class analysis of our lives was essential to find the root causes of our multifaceted oppression.

My development to integrate all parts of me— my gender, my ethnicity, my class, and my worker status—grew by leaps and bounds when I joined Radical Women and the Freedom Socialist party, two socialist feminist organizations which integrated the study of class, race, sex, and sexuality as interlocking roots of the capitalist system. Not only did we study, but we were consistently active in the democratic movements for radical social change.

To speak seriously as one who is committed to building a socialist feminist society at home and abroad takes real change; it takes examining one's attitudes which have been shaped by a powerful capitalist system through the institutions of the state, the schools, the media, the church, and monogamous marriage. I had absorbed "my place." I had kept silent because I was Asian and a woman, and I had been determined not to appear too smart because I wouldn't be able to attract and hold a man.

Attending college at night as an adult, being married, working full-time, and organizing and socializing with feminists and radicals brought me to socialist feminism: the belief that unless every woman, every lesbian and gay man, every worker, and every child is free, none of us is free. Such is the beauty and triumph of radical, social knowledge. Such is the basis upon which I have committed myself to working for a socialist feminist society. Such is the foundation upon which the leadership of all the oppressed is being built.

Socialist feminism is the viable alternative to capitalism and world imperialism, which use sexism, racism, colonialism, heterosexism, **homophobia,** and class oppression to keep us down. Although revolutions waged in Soviet Russia, Cuba, Vietnam, Nicaragua, and China have brought about changes, oppression against women, sexual minorities, and workers still exists. While we can learn from the gains made by women in countries where revolutions have taken place, many inequalities still exist,

and nowhere have women achieved total liberation. Gay oppression and racism still exist in these countries, and there are far too few democratic freedoms. For example, abortion rights are denied in Nicaragua, as the influence of the Catholic church dominates in Latin America. In China, feminism— at least officially—is deemed to be a product of decadent, bourgeois capitalist society.

While true socialism is to be strived for in each context, socialism cannot exist within a single country but must be a worldwide system, supplanting world capitalism. The nations of the world are wholly interdependent, and without an international system of socialism, countries can share only their poverty, rather than the world's wealth. Worldwide socialism will break the stranglehold of worldwide imperialism. It will end the exploitation of one country for the profit of another country's capitalist class. And that is why the U.S., as the most powerful capitalist country in the world, dominates the global market, and why there is a need for a socialist feminist revolution in the U.S. Socialism alone is not the answer. Feminism alone is not the answer. There won't be a socialist revolution in this country without socialist feminists in the lead, and there won't be true emancipation of women without a socialist overthrow of capitalism. Socialism without feminism is a contradiction in terms.[5]

Our oppression as workers is rooted in the capitalist system. As women workers of color, we get the message, loud and clear, that if we only pull ourselves up by our own bootstraps, we will "succeed" as members of a capitalist society, and miraculously, our multi-issue oppressions as women and people of color will disappear. Within the women's movement, bourgeois feminist ideology teaches us that if we take the path of *partial* resistance, we might just make it to the executive boardroom. And if we do, we can become one of the bosses to stifle worker militance, and to uphold the profit-seeking status quo. Or radical feminist ideology teaches us that if we just overthrow the patriarchy, women will truly be free. Radical feminism does not take into account the oppression of gay men and men of color.

Multi-issue feminism is necessary to fight back and win against all forms of oppression. As my Asian American comrade Emily Woo Yamasaki says, "I cannot be an Asian American on Monday, a woman on Tuesday, a lesbian on Wednesday, a worker/student on Thursday, and a political radical on Friday. I am all these things every day." We are discriminated against as *workers* on the economic plane, as racial *minorities* on the economic and social planes, and as women on all three planes—economic, social, and domestic/family. We must cope with the world and with men as a unique category of people—women-of-color workers. We have been subjected to humiliations and brutalities unknown to most whites or even to men of color.

Feminism, in general, and socialist feminism, in particular, do have a vibrant history of militant struggle in this country. Today, increasing numbers of women of color and their allies are calling for an end to racism, sexism, and homophobia. Black women, Chicanas and Latinas, Native American women, and Asian/Pacific women have already demonstrated to the world their capacity for taking upon their shoulders the responsibility for social leadership. This talent and drive stem directly from the triple oppression unique to our position.

Women leaders have emerged from the radical movements of the 1950s, 1960s, and 1970s. In 1955, a black woman, Rosa Parks, refused to move to the back of the bus, inspiring the Montgomery Bus Boycott. In 1974, a Jewish woman, Clara Fraser, walked out on strike at Seattle City Light to protest unfair working conditions. Clara won a seven-year fight against the public utility based on a historic suit of political ideology and sex discrimination. Her fight and victory inspired a class-action suit against the utility by many more women workers who were fed up with sexism and racism on the job!

In 1982, a Chinese-Korean American lesbian, Merle Woo, was fired from her job as a lecturer in Asian American Studies at the University of California, Berkeley, for openly criticizing the right-wing moves of the Ethnic Studies Department. Merle was fired unfairly, though she received outstanding student evaluations and had been promised Security of Employment when she was first hired. Her firing, based on the pretext of an arbitrary rule limiting lecturers' employment to four years, was imposed upon two thousand lecturers throughout the university system. Although the Public Employment Relations Board (PERB) had ruled that Merle and other affected lecturers were to be rehired with back pay, the university

appealed the decision. Merle then filed a federal complaint charging discrimination based on race, sex, sexuality, and political ideology and abridgement of her First Amendment free-speech rights, which were the real reasons she was fired. In 1984, she was reinstated at the university. Merle fought back by organizing with the Merle Woo Defense Committee, composed of people of various communities who believed in the necessity of unifying around all of the issues.[6]

Henry Noble, a Jewish socialist feminist man, also fought an employment-rights case in Seattle. After several years with the Hutchinson Cancer Research Center, Henry's hours were reduced to 75 percent time. Why? Because he actively and successfully organized a union with his primarily female coworkers.

The workplace, where workers—people of color and white—often work side by side, offers a social arena in which the struggle against multi-issue oppressions can take place. Clearly, class analysis and action strike at the heart of capitalist exploitation of workers, whose rights are denied as workers, as women, and as people of color. The economy of capitalism could not have survived as long as it has if it did not depend on sexism and racism to split workers apart, and on the immense profits from paying people of color and women low, low wages. After all, combined, we represent the majority of workers, and that adds up to a lot of profits![7]

Our politics and strategies must be forged through political action independent of the twin parties of capitalism, the Republicans and the Democrats. It was two Democratic presidents—Roosevelt and Truman—who signed Executive Order 9066 and dropped the first atomic bombs on the Japanese cities of Hiroshima and Nagasaki during World War II. Militarism engenders profits. Defense contracts and the manufacture of guns, airplanes, and bombs perpetuate the warmongering drive of the capitalists, both Republicans and Democrats. A labor party could further our multi-issue political struggle, and that labor party must be led by women of color, lesbians, and feminist men. Its program would express the interests and needs of workers and their allies. It would provide an effective alternative and challenge to the boss-party politics dominating the electoral arena. It would be democratic. Anyone could join who agreed with the program, and it would be ruled by the will of the majority, not the labor bureaucrats.

But whether the road taken is via a labor party or some other organization or a combination of strategies for struggle, solidarity and victory will be realized only through the understanding that in unity there is strength. There must be solidarity and mutual aid between all the oppressed for the genuine liberation of any one group. But that unity can come about only if it is based solidly on the demands of the most oppressed strata. We need the unity of blacks, Native Americans, Jews, Chicanos, Latinos, Asian Americans, Puerto Ricans, the working class, the elderly, youth, women, sexual minorities, the disabled—all of the oppressed groups—to win our liberation.

And it is women, especially women of color, who are equipped by our bottommost socioeconomic position to serve as the vanguard on the way to solidarity. We must because nobody needs revolutionary social change as much as we—working women of all races and orientations—need it to survive. We can honor and support the revolutionary and working-class struggles throughout the world by building a socialist feminist revolution here on the soil of the United States. The American revolution will be decisive to international socialism because when U.S. capitalism is dismantled, world capitalism will be dismantled, along with its tyrannical and oppressive forms of institutionalized racism, sexism, and homophobia, and its global greed for profits. While we fight for a socialist feminist society, however, we must, at the same time, fight for reforms under capitalism. Reforms alone, though, are not enough, for they provide only a band-aid solution to the tremendous political, social, and economic problems that we face.

Radical labor history and women's history have taught us that women workers/leaders of all races will lead the way for our total emancipation, as shown in this poem titled "A Woman":

> I am a woman
> and if I live
> I fight and
> if I fight
> I contribute to
> the liberation
> of all Women
> and so victory
> is born even in the darkest hours.[8]

A new song of factory women, under a vibrant socialist feminist society, might go like this:

> We work for enough to live each day.
>   With three days off, like the labor laws say.
> The price of noodles, 15 minutes' work will pay.
>   So, our working conditions are better. Hey!

(Refrain)

> Fellow workers, get it together,
>   For prosperity in our land,
> Fellow workers, rise up together,
>   We've made things right with our hand.

> When we get our monthly paychecks,
>   Our monthly worries do not grow,
> Some of it goes for some rice and the rent—
>   Our private debts are part of the old.

> Spirited as they smile and work with us,
>   Are those fine young men,
> Who promise to work and keep fighting back—
>   Oh, our bravery is revived again.

> Sisters, brothers, we now have time,
>   To write and paint and dance together,
> Our backs no longer ache from working all day,
>   We love our children, with them we learn and play.

NOTES

1. "Change Our Working Conditions," *Connexions: An International Women's Quarterly* 6 (fall 1982): 13.

2. Ibid.

3. Debra O'Gara and Guerry Hoddersen, "Diné Elders Resist Eviction from Big Mountain," *The Freedom Socialist* 9 (1986).

4. Monica Hill, "Patriarchy, Class and the Left," *Discussion Bulletin* (of Freedom Socialist party, Los Angeles, California) 1, no. 1 (February 1984): 19–21.

5. Ibid., p. 21.

6. In June 1986, Merle Woo was terminated with no consideration for reappointment from her position as a visiting lecturer in the Graduate School of Education, University of California, Berkeley. Woo has filed a grievance with the American Federation of Teachers (AFT) based on UC's violation of her settlement agreement and the Academic Personnel Manual.

7. Hill, "Patriarchy, Class and the Left," p. 19.

8. "Good News for Women," *Asian Women's Liberation* 2 (April 1980): 19.

Questions for Thought

1. How do your own life experiences compare with or differ from those of Wong? Do any of your life experiences support her conclusion that capitalism ought to be overthrown?
2. What are some of the examples of women struggling against oppression that are provided by Wong? Can you think of other examples?
3. Wong says that "unless every woman, every lesbian and gay man, every worker, and every child is free, none of us is free." What evidence, if any, does she give to support this claim? Do you believe that this statement is true? Why or why not?
4. How effective is Wong's strategy of beginning and ending this essay with the lyrics to a song? What role, if any, does music have in promoting social change? Can you think of specific examples of songs that have inspired change?
5. How do Wong's views compare with or differ from the views of hooks?

On the Duty of Civil Disobedience   16

HENRY DAVID THOREAU

Henry David Thoreau (1817–1862), the third child of a pencil maker, was born in Concord, Massachusetts. At age eleven, he began attending Concord Academy, where he excelled academically. This earned Thoreau admission to Harvard University, which he attended from 1833 to 1837. During his sophomore year at Harvard, Thoreau became acquainted with Ralph Waldo Emerson, the essayist and poet who was the dominant force behind New England **Transcendentalism**. Emerson soon became Thoreau's spiritual guide and literary benefactor.

When Thoreau graduated from Harvard, he obtained a teaching job at his old grammar school, but he resigned two weeks after he started. Then, after working in his father's pencil-making business for a short while, Thoreau and his brother John opened a small, progressive school. The school closed three years later, however, when John fell ill and eventually died from the effects of lockjaw (tetanus).

With the closing of the school, Thoreau turned his attention to writing. The first issue of *The Dial*, a Transcendentalist journal founded by Emerson, was published in 1840. It included a poem and an essay written by Thoreau, who continued to contribute to *The Dial* until it ceased publication in 1844. Also in 1840, Thoreau fell in love with Ellen Sewall, who was visiting Concord. Although he proposed marriage to her and she initially accepted, her parents convinced her to break off the engagement. Thoreau remained single for the rest of his life.

After a brief stay in New York, where he attempted to widen his literary audience, Thoreau returned to Concord in 1843. During the next four years, Thoreau made the life choices that were to be the source of his greatest fame. Becoming more and more enamored with nature, he decided to try an experiment in simple, natural living. Choosing a site next to Walden Pond, a lake on nearby property owned by Emerson, Thoreau built a small cabin in 1845. While living there for the next two years, he wrote *A Week on the Concord and Merrimack Rivers* (published in 1849) and many of the notes that were later incorporated into his best-known book, *Walden; or, Life in the Woods* (published in 1854). Also while living there, Thoreau was arrested for refusing to pay his poll taxes, and he spent a night in jail in July 1846. This night in jail, as well as the philosophy of civil resistance that led to it, were later described and defended in Thoreau's most influential essay, "Resistance to Civil Government" (later retitled "Civil Disobedience"), most of which is reprinted here.

Upon leaving Walden Pond in 1847, Thoreau returned to his father's pencil business, eventually taking it over when his father died. He also became a surveyor, a collector of biological specimens, and the author of several series of magazine articles devoted to the description of nature. Following the philosophy that he laid down in "Civil Disobedience," he actively worked for the abolition of slavery, helping escaping slaves on the Underground Railroad and championing the cause of the radical abolitionist John Brown. Thoreau died of tuberculosis two months before his forty-fifth birthday.

In the following essay, Thoreau describes what he considers to be the proper role of government, arguing, as does Mill in the first selection in this section, that governmental authority over the individual must be limited. However, whereas Mill bases his principle concerning the limitation of governmental authority on utility, Thoreau appeals to what he believes to be a higher law, the law of individual conscience. According to Thoreau, whenever a government engages in any activity that violates the dictates of conscience, the legitimacy of that government is called into question. In such cases, we are not only justified in denying allegiance to the government but also morally required to make sure that we do not directly or indirectly contribute to furthering the governmental action.

When he wrote his essay, Thoreau believed that the invasion of Mexico, the existence of slavery, and the treatment of Native Americans were unjust and thus undermined the authority of the U.S. government. He believed that every citizen of the United States had a moral duty to do nothing to help perpetuate these injustices. Noting that voting was usually an ineffective response to injustice, Thoreau also called on everyone of conscience to work actively to eliminate such injustices. He says specifically that one should not pay taxes to support such governmental policies and that, generally, one should let his or her life be "a counter-friction to stop the machine." In another statement of defiance, Thoreau adds that "under a government which imprisons any unjustly, the true place for a just man is also a prison."

Near the end of his essay, Thoreau notes, as did Mill, that the emergence of democratic government seems to have increased the respect for individual liberty. However, like Carmichael and hooks, Thoreau believes that democratic government, at least in its present form, does not go far enough in respecting freedom. For this reason, Thoreau envisions a state in which the independence and power of the individual will be fully realized, a state in which there will be equal justice for all. Only such a state would deserve full allegiance from a person of conscience.

Questions for Reading

1. Where, according to Thoreau, does the authority of the state end? Upon what grounds can one refuse allegiance to the state?
2. What were the policies of the U.S. government in Thoreau's time that led him to refuse allegiance to the state?
3. Why did Thoreau spend a night in jail? What insights did he draw from this experience?
4. What is Thoreau's attitude toward voting?
5. Near the end of his essay, Thoreau raises the following question: "Is a democracy, such as we know it, the last improvement possible in government?" How does Thoreau answer this question?

I HEARTILY ACCEPT THE MOTTO— "THAT GOV-ernment is best which governs least"—and I should like to see it acted up to more rapidly and systematically. Carried out, it finally amounts to this, which also I believe—"That government is best which governs not at all." And when men are prepared for it that will be the kind of government they will have. Government is at best but an expedient; but most governments are usually, and all governments are sometimes, inexpedient. The objections which have been brought against a standing army, and they are many and weighty, and deserve to prevail, may also at last be brought against a standing government. The standing army is only an arm of the standing government. The government itself, which is only the mode which the people have chosen to execute their will, is equally liable to be abused and perverted before the people can act through it. Witness the present Mexican war, the work of comparatively few individuals using the standing government as their tool; for, in the outset, the people would not have consented to this measure.

This American government—what is it but a tradition, though a recent one, endeavoring to transmit itself unimpaired to posterity, but each instant losing some of its integrity? It has not the vitality and force of a single living man; for a single man can bend it to his will. It is a sort of wooden gun to the people themselves. But it is not the less necessary for this; for the people must have some complicated machinery or other, and hear its din, to satisfy that idea of government which they have. Governments show thus how successfully men can be imposed on, even impose on themselves, for their own advantage. It is excellent, we must all allow. Yet this government never of itself furthered any enterprise, but by the alacrity with which it got out of its way. *It* does not keep the country free. *It* does not settle the West. *It* does not educate. The character inherent in the American people has done all that has been accomplished; and it would have done somewhat more, if the government had not sometimes got in its way. For government is an expedient by which men would fain succeed in letting one another alone; and, as has been said, when it is most expedient, the governed are most let alone by it. . . .

But, to speak practically and as a citizen, unlike those who call themselves no-government men, I ask for, not at once no government, but *at once* a better government. Let every man make known what kind of government would command his respect, and that will be one step toward obtaining it.

After all, when power is once in the hands of the people, the practical reason why a majority are permitted to rule, and for a long period continue to do so, is not because they are most likely to be in the right, nor because this seems fairest to the minority, but because they are physically the strongest. But a government in which the majority rule in all cases cannot be based on justice, even as far as men understand it. Can there not be a government in which majorities do not virtually decide right and wrong, but conscience? In which majorities decide only those questions to which the rule of expediency is applicable? Must the citizen ever for a moment, or in the least degree, resign his conscience to the legislator? Why has every man a conscience, then? I think that we should be men first and subjects afterward. It is not desirable to cultivate a respect for the law, so much as for the right. The only obligation that I have a right to assume is to do at any time what I think right. It is truly enough said that a corporation has no conscience; but a corporation of conscientious men is a corporation *with* a conscience. Law never made men a whit more just; and, by means of their respect for it, even the well-disposed are daily made the agents of injustice. A common and natural result of an undue respect for law is that you may see a file of soldiers—colonel, captain, corporal, privates, powder-monkeys—all marching in admirable order over hill and dale to the wars, against their wills, their common sense and consciences. This makes it very steep marching indeed, and produces a palpitation of the heart. They have no doubt that it is a damnable business in which they are concerned; they are all peaceably inclined. Now, what are they? Men at all? Or small movable forts and magazines, at the service of some unscrupulous man in power? Visit the Navy-Yard, and behold a marine, such a man as an American government can make, or such as it can make a man with its black arts—a mere shadow and reminiscence of humanity. . . .

The mass of men serve the state thus, not as men mainly, but as machines, with their bodies. They are the standing army, and the militia, jailors, constables,

This is the editor's revised version of a selection from The Writings of Henry David Thoreau, *Boston, 1906.*

posse comitatus, etc. In most cases there is no free exercise whatever of the judgment or of the moral sense; but they put themselves on a level with wood and earth and stones; and wooden men can perhaps be manufactured that will serve the purpose as well. Such command no more respect than men of straw or a lump of dirt. They have the same sort of worth only as horses and dogs. Yet such as these even are commonly esteemed good citizens. Others—as most legislators, politicians, lawyers, ministers, and office-holders—serve the state chiefly with their heads; and, as they rarely make any moral distinctions, they are as likely to serve the Devil, without *intending* it, as God. A very few, as heroes, patriots, martyrs, reformers in the great sense, and *men,* serve the state with their consciences also, and so necessarily resist it for the most part; and they are commonly treated as enemies by it. A wise man will only be useful as a man, and will not submit to be "clay," and "stop a hole to keep the wind away." . . .

How does it become a man to behave toward this American government today? I answer that he cannot without disgrace be associated with it. I cannot for an instant recognize that political organization as *my* government which is the *slave's* government also.

All men recognize the right of revolution; that is, the right to refuse allegiance to, and to resist, the government, when its tyranny or its inefficiency is great and unendurable. But almost all say that such is not the case now. But such was the case, they think, in the Revolution of 1775. If one were to tell me that this was a bad government because it taxed certain foreign commodities brought to its ports, it is most probable that I should not make an ado about it, for I can do without them. All machines have their friction; and possibly this does enough good to counterbalance the evil. At any rate, it is a great evil to make a stir about it. But when the friction comes to have its machine, and oppression and robbery are organized, I say, let us not have such a machine any longer. In other words, when a sixth of the population of a nation which has undertaken to be the refuge of liberty are slaves, and a whole country is unjustly overrun and conquered by a foreign army, and subjected to military law, I think that it is not too soon for honest men to rebel and revolutionize. What makes this duty the more urgent is the fact that the country so overrun is not our own, but ours is the invading army. . . .

Practically speaking, the opponents to a reform in Massachusetts are not a hundred thousand politicians in the South, but a hundred thousand merchants and farmers here, who are more interested in commerce and agriculture than they are in humanity, and are not prepared to do justice to the slave and to Mexico, *cost what it may.* I quarrel not with far-off foes, but with those who, near at home, cooperate with, and do the bidding of, those far away, and without whom the latter would be harmless. We are accustomed to say that the mass of men are unprepared; but improvement is slow, because the few are not materially wiser or better than the many. It is not so important that many should be as good as you, as that there be some absolute goodness somewhere, for that will leaven the whole lump. There are thousands who are *in opinion* opposed to slavery and to the war, and who yet in effect do nothing to put an end to them. Esteeming themselves children of Washington and Franklin, they sit down with their hands in their pockets, and say that they know not what to do, and do nothing. They even postpone the question of freedom to the question of free-trade, while quietly reading the prices-current along with the latest news from Mexico, after dinner, and, it may be, fall asleep over them both. What is the price-current of an honest man and patriot today? They hesitate, and they regret, and sometimes they petition; but they do nothing in earnest and with effect. They will wait, well disposed, for others to remedy the evil, that they may no longer have it to regret. At most, they give only a cheap vote, and a feeble countenance and God-speed, to the right, as it goes by them. There are nine hundred and ninety-nine patrons of virtue to one virtuous man. But it is easier to deal with the real possessor of a thing than with the temporary guardian of it.

All voting is a sort of gaming, like checkers or backgammon, with a slight moral tinge to it, a playing with right and wrong, with moral questions; and betting naturally accompanies it. The character of the voters is not staked. I cast my vote, perchance, as I think right; but I am not vitally concerned that that right should prevail. I am willing to leave it to the majority. Its obligation, therefore, never exceeds that of expediency. Even voting *for the right* is *doing* nothing for it. It is only expressing to men feebly your desire that it should prevail. A wise man will not leave the right to the mercy of chance, nor wish it to prevail through the power of the majority. There is but little virtue in the action of masses of men. When the majority shall at length vote for the abolition of slavery, it will be because they are indifferent to slavery, or because there is but little slavery left to be abolished by their vote. *They* will then be the only slaves. Only *his* vote can hasten the abolition of slavery who asserts his own freedom by his vote. . . .

It is not a man's duty, as a matter of course, to devote himself to the eradication of any, even the most enormous wrong; he may still properly have other concerns to engage him. But it is his duty, at least, to wash his hands of it, and, if he no longer gives any thought to it, he should not support it practically. If I devote myself to other pursuits and contemplations, I must first see, at least, that I do not pursue them sitting upon another man's shoulders. I must get off him first, that he may pursue his contemplations too. See what gross inconsistency is tolerated. I have heard some of my townsmen say, "I should like to have them order me out to help put down an insurrection of the slaves, or to march to Mexico—see if I would go." And yet these very men have each, directly by their allegiance and indirectly, at least, by their money, furnished a substitute. The soldier who refuses to serve in an unjust war is applauded by those who do not refuse to sustain the unjust government that makes the war. He is applauded by those whose own act and authority he disregards and sets at naught, as if the state were penitent to the degree that it hired one to scourge it while it sinned, but not to the degree that it left off sinning for a moment. Thus, under the name of Order and Civil Government, we are all made at last to pay homage to and support our own meanness. After the first blush of sin comes its indifference; and from immoral it becomes, as it were, *un*moral. . . .

How can a man be satisfied to entertain an opinion merely, and enjoy *it*? Is there any enjoyment in it, if his opinion is that he is aggrieved? If you are cheated out of a single dollar by your neighbor, you do not rest satisfied with knowing that you are cheated, or with saying that you are cheated, or even with petitioning him to pay you your due. You take effectual steps at once to obtain the full amount and see that you are never cheated again. Action from principle, the perception and the performance of right, changes things and relations; it is essentially revolutionary, and does not consist wholly with anything which was. It not only divides states and churches, it divides families; yes, it divides the *individual*, separating the diabolical in him from the divine.

Unjust laws exist. Shall we be content to obey them, or shall we endeavor to amend them, and obey them until we have succeeded, or shall we transgress them at once? Men generally, under such a government as this, think that they ought to wait until they have persuaded the majority to alter them. They think that, if they should resist, the remedy would be worse than the evil. But it is the fault of the government itself that the remedy *is* worse than the evil. *It* makes it worse. Why is it not more apt to anticipate and provide for reform? Why does it not cherish its wise minority? Why does it cry and resist before it is hurt? Why does it not encourage its citizens to be on the alert to point out its faults, and *do* better than it would have them? Why does it always crucify Christ, excommunicate Copernicus and Luther, and pronounce Washington and Franklin rebels? . . .

If the injustice is part of the necessary friction of the machine of government, let it go, let it go: perchance it will wear smooth. Certainly the machine will wear out. If the injustice has a spring, or a pulley, or a rope, or a crank, exclusively for itself, then perhaps you may consider whether the remedy will not be worse than the evil. But if it is of such a nature that it requires you to be the agent of injustice to another, then, I say, break the law. Let your life be a counter friction to stop the machine. What I have to do is to see, at any rate, that I do not lend myself to the wrong that I condemn. . . .

I do not hesitate to say that those who call themselves Abolitionists should at once effectually withdraw their support, both in person and property, from the government of Massachusetts and not wait till they constitute a majority of one, before they suffer the right to prevail through them. I think that it is enough if they have God on their side, without waiting for that other one. Moreover, any man more right than his neighbors constitutes a majority of one already.

I meet this American government, or its representative, the state government, directly, and face to face, once a year—no more—in the person of its tax-gatherer. This is the only mode in which a man situated as I am necessarily meets it; and it then says distinctly, "Recognize me." The simplest, most effectual, and, in the present posture of affairs, the most indispensable mode of treating with it on this head, of expressing your little satisfaction with and love for it, is to deny it then. My civil neighbor, the tax-gatherer, is the very man I have to deal with—for it is, after all, with men and not with parchment that I quarrel—and he has voluntarily chosen to be an agent of the government. How shall he ever know well what he is and does as an officer of the government, or as a man, until he is obliged to consider whether he shall treat me, his neighbor, for whom he has respect, as a neighbor and well-disposed man, or as a maniac and disturber of the peace. . . . I know this well, that if one thousand, if one hundred, if ten men whom I could name—if ten *honest* men only—yes, if *one* HONEST man, in this State of Massachusetts, *ceasing to hold slaves,* were actually to withdraw from this co-partnership and be locked up in the county jail, it would be the abolition of slavery in America. For it matters not how small the beginning may seem to be: what is once well done is done forever. . . .

Under a government that imprisons any unjustly, the true place for a just man is also a prison. The proper place today, the only place which Massachusetts has provided for her freer and less desponding spirits, is in her prisons, to be put out and locked out of the State by her own act, as they have already put themselves out by their principles. It is there that the fugitive slave, and the Mexican prisoner on parole, and the Indian come to plead the wrongs of his race should find them; on that separate, but more free and honorable ground, where the State places those who are not *with* her, but *against* her. That is the only house in a slave State in which a free man can abide with honor. If any think that their influence would be lost there, that their voices would no longer afflict the ear of the State, or that they would not be as an enemy within its walls, they do not know by how much truth is stronger than error, or by how much more eloquently and effectively one can combat injustice who has experienced a little in his own person. Cast your whole vote, not a strip of paper merely, but your whole influence. A minority is powerless while it conforms to the majority; it is not even a minority then; but it is irresistible when it clogs by its whole weight. If

the alternative is to keep all just men in prison, or give up war and slavery, the State will not hesitate which to choose. If a thousand men were not to pay their tax-bills this year, that would not be as violent and bloody a measure as it would be to pay them, and enable the State to commit violence and shed innocent blood. This is, in fact, the definition of a peaceable revolution, if any such is possible. If the tax-gatherer, or any other public officer, asks me, as one has done, "But what shall I do?" my answer is, "If you really wish to do anything, resign your office." When the subject has refused allegiance, and the officer has resigned his office, then the revolution is accomplished. But even suppose blood should flow. Is there not a sort of blood shed when the conscience is wounded? Through this wound a man's real manhood and immortality flow out, and he bleeds to an everlasting death. I see this blood flowing now.

I have contemplated the imprisonment of the offender, rather than the seizure of his goods—though both will serve the same purpose—because they who assert the purest right, and consequently are most dangerous to a corrupt State, commonly have not spent much time in accumulating property. To such the State renders comparatively small service, and a slight tax is wont to appear exorbitant, particularly if they are obliged to earn it by special labor with their hands. If there were one who lived wholly without the use of money, the State itself would hesitate to demand it of him. But the rich man, not to make any invidious comparison, is always sold to the institution that makes him rich. Absolutely speaking, the more money, the less virtue; for money comes between a man and his objects, and obtains them for him; and it was certainly no great virtue to obtain it. . . .

When I converse with the freest of my neighbors, I perceive that, whatever they may say about the magnitude and seriousness of the question, and their regard for the public tranquillity, the long and the short of the matter is that they cannot spare the protection of the existing government. They also dread the consequences to their property and families of disobedience to it. For my own part, I should not like to think that I ever rely on the protection of the State. But, if I deny the authority of the State when it presents its tax-bill, it will soon take and waste all my property, and so harass me and my children without end. This is hard. This makes it impossible for a man to live honestly, and at the same time comfortably, in outward respects. It will not be worth the while to accumulate property that would be sure to go again. You must hire or squat somewhere, and raise but a small crop, and eat that soon. You must live within yourself, and depend upon yourself always tucked up and ready for a start, and not have many affairs. A man may grow rich in Turkey even, if he will be in all respects a good subject of the Turkish government. Confucius said: "If a state is governed by the principles of reason, poverty and misery are subjects of shame; if a state is not governed by the principles of reason, riches and honors are the subjects of shame." No, until I want the protection of Massachusetts to be extended to me in some distant Southern port where my liberty is endangered, or until I am bent solely on building up an estate at home by peaceful enterprise, I can afford to refuse allegiance to Massachusetts, as well as her right to my property and life. It costs me less in every sense to incur the penalty of disobedience to the State than it would to obey. I would feel as if I were worth less in that case. . . .

I have paid no poll-tax for six years. I was put into a jail once on this account, for one night. And as I stood considering the walls of solid stone, two or three feet thick, the door of wood and iron, a foot thick, and the iron grating which strained the light, I could not help being struck with the foolishness of that institution which treated me as if I were mere flesh and blood and bones, to be locked up. I wondered that it should have concluded at length that this was the best use it could put me to, and had never thought to avail itself of my services in some way. I saw that, if there was a wall of stone between me and my townsmen, there was a still more difficult one to climb or break through before they could get to be as free as I was. I did not for a moment feel confined, and the walls seemed a great waste of stone and mortar. I felt as if I alone of all my townsmen had paid my tax. They plainly did not know how to treat me, but behaved like persons who are underbred. In every threat and in every compliment there was a blunder, for they thought that my chief desire was to stand on the other side of that stone wall. I could not but smile to see how industriously they locked the door on

my meditations, which followed them out again without let or hindrance, and *they* were really all that was dangerous. As they could not reach me, they had resolved to punish my body; just as boys, if they cannot come at some person against whom they have spite, will abuse his dog. I saw that the State was half-witted, that it was timid as a lone woman with her silver spoons, that it did not know its friends from its foes, and I lost all my remaining respect for it and pitied it.

Thus the State never intentionally confronts a man's sense, intellectual or moral, but only his body, his senses. It is not armed with superior wit or honesty, but with superior physical strength. I was not born to be forced. I will breathe after my own fashion. Let us see who is the strongest. What force has a multitude? They only can force me who obey a higher law than I. They force me to become like themselves. I do not hear of *men* being *forced* to live this way or that by masses of men. What sort of life to live would that be? When I meet a government that says to me, "Your money or your life," why should I be in haste to give it my money? It may be in a great strait, and not know what to do: I cannot help that. It must help itself; do as I do. It is not worth the while to snivel about it. I am not responsible for the successful working of the machinery of society. I am not the son of the engineer. I perceive that, when an acorn and a chestnut fall side by side, the one does not remain inert to make way for the other, but both obey their own laws, and spring and grow and flourish as best they can, till one, perchance, overshadows and destroys the other. If a plant cannot live according to its nature, it dies; and so a man.

The night in prison was novel and interesting enough. The prisoners in their shirt-sleeves were enjoying a chat and the evening air in the doorway, when I entered. But the jailer said, "Come, boys, it is time to lock up"; and so they dispersed, and I heard the sound of their steps returning into the hollow apartments. My room-mate was introduced to me by the jailer as "a first-rate fellow and a clever man." When the door was locked, he showed me where to hang my hat, and how he managed matters there. The rooms were whitewashed once a month; and this one, at least, was the whitest, most simply furnished, and probably the neatest apartment in the town. He naturally wanted to know where I came from, and what brought me there; and, when I had told him, I asked him in my turn how he came there, presuming him to be an honest man, of course. And, as the world goes, I believe he was. "Why," said he, "they accuse me of burning a barn; but I never did it." As near as I could discover, he had probably gone to bed in a barn when drunk and smoked his pipe there; and so a barn was burnt. He had the reputation of being a clever man; he had been there some three months waiting for his trial to come on; and he would have to wait as much longer. But he was quite domesticated and contented, since he got his board for nothing and thought that he was well treated.

He occupied one window, and I the other; and I saw that if one stayed there long, his principal business would be to look out the window. I had soon read all the tracts that were left there, examined where former prisoners had broken out and where a grate had been sawed off, and heard the history of the various occupants of that room. For I found that even here there was a history and a gossip that never circulated beyond the walls of the jail. Probably this is the only house in the town where verses are composed, which are afterward printed in a circular form, but not published. I was shown quite a long list of verses which were composed by some young men who had been detected in an attempt to escape, who avenged themselves by singing them.

I pumped my fellow-prisoner as dry as I could, for fear I should never see him again; but at length he showed me which was my bed and left me to blow out the lamp.

It was like traveling into a far country, such as I had never expected to behold, to lie there for one night. It seemed to me that I never had heard the town-clock strike before, or the evening sounds of the village; for we slept with the windows open, which were inside the grating. It was to see my native village in the light of the Middle Ages. Our Concord was turned into a Rhine stream, and visions of knights and castles passed before me. They were the voices of old burghers that I heard in the streets. I was an involuntary spectator and auditor of whatever was done and said in the kitchen of the adjacent village-inn—a wholly new and rare experience to me. It was a closer view of my native town. I was fairly inside of it. I never had seen its institutions before. This is one of its peculiar institutions; for it is a shire town. I began to comprehend what its inhabitants were about.

In the morning our breakfasts were put through the hole in the door, in small oblong-square tin pans, made to fit, and holding a pint of chocolate, with brown bread, and an iron spoon. When they called for the vessels again, I was green enough to return what bread I had left; but my comrade seized it and said that I should lay that up for lunch or dinner. Soon after he was let out to work at haying in a neighboring field, whither he went every day, and would not be back till noon; so he bade me good-day, saying that he doubted if he should see me again.

When I came out of prison—for some one interfered and paid that tax—I did not perceive that great changes had taken place on the common, such as he observed who went in a youth and emerged a tottering and gray-headed man. Yet a change had to my eyes come over the scene—the town, the State, and country—greater than any that mere time could effect. I saw yet more distinctly the State in which I lived. I saw to what extent the people among whom I lived could be trusted as good neighbors and friends. I saw that their friendship was for summer weather only, that they did not greatly propose to do right, that they were a distinct race from me by their prejudices and superstitions, as the Chinamen and Malays are, that in their sacrifices to humanity they ran no risks, not even to their property, that after all they were not so noble but treated the thief as he had treated them, and that they hoped, by a certain outward observance, by a few prayers, and by walking in a particular straight though useless path from time to time, that they could save their souls. This may be to judge my neighbors harshly, for I believe that many of them are not aware that they have such an institution as the jail in their village.

It was formerly the custom in our village when a poor debtor came out of jail, for his acquaintances to salute him, looking through their fingers, which were crossed to represent the grating of a jail window, "How do ye do?" My neighbors did not thus salute me, but first looked at me, and then at one another, as if I had returned from a long journey. I was put into jail as I was going to the shoemaker's to get a shoe that was mended. When I was let out the next morning, I proceeded to finish my errand, and, having put on my mended shoe, joined a huckleberry party who were impatient to put themselves under my conduct. In half an hour—for the horse was soon tackled—I was in the midst of a huckleberry field, on one of our highest hills, two miles off, and then the State was nowhere to be seen.

This is the whole history of "My Prisons."

I have never declined paying the highway tax, because I am as desirous of being a good neighbor as I am of being a bad subject; and as for supporting schools, I am doing my part to educate my fellow-countrymen now. It is for no particular item in the tax-bill that I refuse to pay it. I simply wish to refuse allegiance to the State, to withdraw and stand aloof from it effectually. I do not care to trace the course of my dollar, if I could, till it buys a man or a musket to shoot with—the dollar is innocent—but I am concerned to trace the effects of my allegiance. In fact, I quietly declare war with the State, after my fashion, though I will still make what use and get what advantage of her I can, as is usual in such cases. . . .

I do not wish to quarrel with any man or nation. I do not wish to split hairs, to make fine distinctions, or to set myself up as better than my neighbors. I seek rather, I may say, even an excuse for conforming to the laws of the land. I am but too ready to conform to them. Indeed, I have reason to suspect myself on this head; and each year, as the tax-gatherer comes round, I find myself disposed to review the acts and position of the general and State governments, and the spirit of the people, to discover a pretext for conformity. . . .

Seen from a lower point of view, the Constitution, with all its faults, is very good; the law and the courts are very respectable. Even this State and this American government are, in many respects, very admirable and rare things, to be thankful for, such as a great many have described them. But seen from a point of view a little higher, they are what I have described them; seen from a higher still, and the highest, who shall say what they are, or that they are worth looking at or thinking of at all?

However, the government does not concern me much, and I shall bestow the fewest possible thoughts on it. It is not many moments that I live under a government, even in this world. If a man is thought-free, fancy-free, imagination-free, . . . unwise rulers or reformers cannot fatally interrupt him.

I know that most men think differently from myself; but those whose lives are by profession devoted to the study of these or kindred subjects content me as little as any. Statesmen and legislators, standing so completely within the institution, never distinctly and nakedly behold it. They speak of moving society, but have no resting-place without it. They may be men of a certain experience and discrimination, and have no doubt invented ingenious and even useful systems, for which we sincerely thank them; but all their wit and usefulness lie within certain not very wide limits. They are wont to forget that the world is not governed by policy and expediency. . . . The lawyer's truth is not Truth, but consistency or a consistent expediency. Truth is always in harmony with herself, and is not concerned chiefly to reveal the justice that may consist with wrong-doing. . . .

They who know of no purer sources of truth, who have traced up its stream no higher, stand, and wisely stand, by the Bible and the Constitution, and drink at it there with reverence and humility; but they who behold where it comes trickling into this lake or that pool, gird up their loins once more and continue their pilgrimage toward its fountainhead. . . .

The authority of government, even such as I am willing to submit to—for I will cheerfully obey those who know and can do better than I, and in many things even those who neither know nor can do so well—is still an impure one. To be strictly just, it must have the sanction and consent of the governed. It can have no pure right over my person and property but what I concede to it. The progress from an absolute to a limited monarchy, from a limited monarchy to a **democracy,** is a progress toward a true respect for the individual. . . . Is a democracy, such as we know it, the last improvement possible in government? Is it not possible to take a step further towards recognizing and organizing the rights of man? There will never be a really free and enlightened State until the State comes to recognize the individual as a higher and independent power, from which all its own power and authority are derived, and treats him accordingly. I please myself with imagining a State at last that can afford to be just to all men, that can treat the individual with respect as a neighbor. Such a State even would not think it inconsistent with its own repose if a few were to live aloof from it, neither meddling with it nor embraced by it, but who fulfilled all the duties of neighbors and fellow-men. A State which bore this kind of fruit and suffered it to drop off as fast as it ripened, would prepare the way for a still more perfect and glorious State, which also I have imagined, but not yet anywhere seen.

Questions for Thought

1. What do you think Thoreau means when he says, "That government is best which governs not at all"? Do you agree with this statement? Why or why not?
2. Can you think of current governmental policies that Thoreau would have found troubling? If so, what do you think should be done about them?
3. Do you agree with Thoreau's claim that one is justified in breaking unjust laws? What about his refusal to pay taxes?
4. Do you believe that democracy as we know it is the last improvement possible in government? Why or why not?
5. In what ways are Thoreau's views on governmental authority like the views of Mill? In what ways are they different?

17   Anarchism: What It Really Stands For

EMMA GOLDMAN

Emma Goldman (1869–1940), an early defender of women's rights and birth control, was born in Kovno, Russia. Although she had little formal education, Goldman read widely and joined a radical student circle in St. Petersburg. In 1885, she immigrated to the United States, settling in Rochester, New York. In Rochester and later in New Haven, Connecticut, Goldman worked in clothing factories and associated with a number of socialist and anarchist groups. She moved to New York City in 1889, where she continued her political activities. In 1893, Goldman was arrested for inciting a riot by speaking to striking workers and telling them to take food "by force" if necessary. When released from jail, she embarked on a series of lecture tours in the United States and Europe.

In 1906, Goldman co-founded the anarchist journal *Mother Earth* with her close friend Alexander Berkman. She served as editor of the journal until it was suppressed by the government in 1917, and she continued to lecture on a variety of topics. These included **anarchism,** free love, birth control, and European drama. She was arrested and briefly jailed in 1916 for one of her lectures on birth control. An opponent of U.S. involvement in World War I, Goldman worked against the military draft once it was instituted. Because of her efforts against the war, she was arrested again in 1917 and sentenced to two years in prison. When she was released in September 1919, Goldman was declared a "subversive alien" and deported to Russia.

Two years later, after having become disenchanted with the Soviet government, Goldman left Russia. She traveled around Europe, residing at various times in Germany, Sweden, England, and France. During this time, Goldman continued to lecture, authored two books describing her negative experiences in Russia, and wrote her autobiography *Living My Life,* which was published in 1931. Goldman's last political cause was to oppose the rise of fascism in Spain. She died in Toronto, Canada, on May 14, 1940, where she had moved to continue her work against Spanish fascism. In addition to her autobiography, Goldman's writings include *Anarchism and Other Essays* (1910), *The Social Significance of Modern Drama* (1914), *My Disillusionment in Russia* (1923), and *My Further Disillusionment in Russia* (1924).

In the following essay from *Anarchism and Other Essays,* Goldman describes and defends the philosophy of anarchism. Like Thoreau in the preceding essay, Goldman calls for a radical decrease of governmental interference in human lives. Indeed, she seems to take this demand a step further than Thoreau; for aside from a slogan stating that the best government is that which "governs not at all," Thoreau's essay supports a limited form of government. Goldman, however, argues that "all forms of government rest on violence, and are therefore wrong and harmful, as well as unnecessary." She thus calls for the abolition of government and the establishment of a new society that recognizes unrestricted individual liberty.

Realizing that anarchism has been misunderstood and distorted by its opponents, Goldman spends a large portion of her essay arguing against certain objections to the anarchist position. First, against those who claim that anarchism represents a beautiful but impractical ideal, she says that this is so only if the practical is defined in terms of that which already exists or is realizable under present conditions. From the standpoint of present economic and social realities, anarchism is indeed impractical. However, Goldman believes that these realities, which are morally bankrupt, can and must be overthrown. Through revolutionary direct action, economic and social realities can be altered so that they are compatible with anarchism.

Second, against those who say that anarchism represents violence and destruction, Goldman argues that anarchism is the only philosophy that combats the most pervasive form of violence in our society, the violence that results from ignorance and the conflict between individual freedom and social instincts. According to Goldman, such ignorance and conflict have been maintained by three oppressive social institutions—religion, property, and government—each of which is predicated on violence against the individual. With the emergence of anarchism, these sources of violence would be eliminated. Thus, in place of a social order founded on violence against the individual, anarchism will produce a social order that will "guarantee to every human being free access to the earth and full enjoyment of the necessities of life, according to individual desires, tastes, and inclinations." In such a social order, Goldman believes that violent behavior will be greatly reduced, if not totally eliminated.

Questions for Reading

1. How does Goldman define *anarchism*?
2. What, according to Goldman, are the two principal objections to anarchism? How does she respond to each of these objections?
3. Why does Goldman reject religion?
4. What are Goldman's principal criticisms of property and centralized production? How would economic conditions in an anarchist society differ from economic conditions today?
5. What are the four defenses of government against which Goldman argues?
6. How, according to Goldman, will anarchism be produced? Why does she think that voting is an ineffective means of social change?

Anarchy

Ever reviled, accursed, ne'er understood,
    Thou art the grisly terror of our age.
"Wreck of all order," cry the multitude,
    "Art thou, and war and murder's endless rage."
O, let them cry. To them that ne'er have striven
    The truth that lies behind a word to find,
To them the word's right meaning was not given.
    They shall continue blind among the blind.
But thou, O word, so clear, so strong, so pure,
    Thou sayest all which I for goal have taken.
I give thee to the future! Thine secure
    When each at least unto himself shall waken.
Comes it in sunshine? In the tempest's thrill?
    I cannot tell—but it the earth shall see!
I am an Anarchist! Wherefore I will
    Not rule, and also ruled I will not be!
              JOHN HENRY MACKAY

THE HISTORY OF HUMAN GROWTH AND DE-velopment is at the same time the history of the terrible struggle of every new idea heralding the approach of a brighter dawn. In its tenacious hold on tradition, the Old has never hesitated to make use of the foulest and cruelest means to stay the advent of the New, in whatever form or period the latter may have asserted itself. Nor need we retrace our steps into the distant past to realize the enormity of opposition, difficulties, and hardships placed in the path of every progressive idea. The rack, the thumbscrew, and the knout are still with us; so are the convict's garb and the social wrath, all conspiring against the spirit that is serenely marching on.

Anarchism could not hope to escape the fate of all other ideas of innovation. Indeed, as the most revolutionary and uncompromising innovator, Anarchism must needs meet with the combined ignorance and venom of the world it aims to reconstruct.

To deal even remotely with all that is being said and done against Anarchism would necessitate the writing of a whole volume. I shall therefore meet only two of the principal objections. In so doing, I shall attempt to elucidate what Anarchism really stands for.

The strange phenomenon of the opposition to Anarchism is that it brings to light the relation between so-called intelligence and ignorance. And yet this is not so very strange when we consider the relativity of all things. The ignorant mass has in its favor that it makes no pretense of knowledge or tolerance. Acting, as it always does, by mere impulse, its reasons are like those of a child. "Why?" "Because." Yet the opposition of the uneducated to Anarchism deserves the same consideration as that of the intelligent man.

What, then, are the objections? First, Anarchism is impractical, though a beautiful ideal. Second, Anarchism stands for violence and destruction, hence it must be repudiated as vile and dangerous. Both the intelligent man and the ignorant mass judge not from a thorough knowledge of the subject, but either from hearsay or false interpretation.

A practical scheme, says Oscar Wilde, is either one already in existence, or a scheme that could be carried out under the existing conditions; but it is exactly the existing conditions that one objects to, and any scheme that could accept these conditions is wrong and foolish. The true criterion of the practical, therefore, is not whether the latter can keep intact the wrong or foolish; rather is it whether the scheme has vitality enough to leave the stagnant waters of the old, and build, as well as sustain, new life. In the light of this conception, Anarchism is indeed practical. More than any other idea, it is helping to do away with the wrong and foolish; more than any other idea, it is building and sustaining new life. The emotions of the ignorant man are continuously kept at a pitch by the most blood-curdling stories about Anarchism. Not a thing too outrageous to be employed against this philosophy and its exponents. Therefore Anarchism represents to the unthinking what the proverbial bad man does to the child,—a black monster bent on swallowing everything; in short, destruction and violence.

Destruction and violence! How is the ordinary man to know that the most violent element in society is ignorance; that its power of destruction is the very thing Anarchism is combating? Nor is he aware that Anarchism, whose roots, as it were, are part of nature's forces, destroys, not healthful tissue, but parasitic growths that feed on the life's essence of

---

From Emma Goldman, Anarchism and Other Essays, *Mother Earth Publishing Association, 1911.*

society. It is merely clearing the soil from weeds and sagebrush, that it may eventually bear healthy fruit.

Someone has said that it requires less mental effort to condemn than to think. The widespread mental indolence, so prevalent in society, proves this to be only too true. Rather than to go to the bottom of any given idea, to examine into its origin and meaning, most people will either condemn it altogether, or rely on some superficial or prejudicial definition of non-essentials.

Anarchism urges man to think, to investigate, to analyze every proposition; but that the brain capacity of the average reader be not taxed too much, I also shall begin with a definition, and then elaborate on the latter.

ANARCHISM:—The philosophy of a new social order based on liberty unrestricted by man-made law; the theory that all forms of government rest on violence, and are therefore wrong and harmful, as well as unnecessary.

The new social order rests, of course, on the materialistic basis of life; but while all Anarchists agree that the main evil today is an economic one, they maintain that the solution of that evil can be brought about only through the consideration of *every phase* of life,—individual, as well as the collective; the internal, as well as the external phases.

A thorough perusal of the history of human development will disclose two elements in bitter conflict with each other; elements that are only now beginning to be understood, not as foreign to each other, but as closely related and truly harmonious, if only placed in proper environment: the individual and social instincts. The individual and society have waged a relentless and bloody battle for ages, each striving for supremacy, because each was blind to the value and importance of the other. The individual and social instincts—the one a most potent factor for individual endeavor, for growth, aspiration, self-realization; the other an equally potent factor for mutual helpfulness and social well-being.

The explanation of the storm raging within the individual, and between him and his surroundings, is not far to seek. The primitive man, unable to understand his being, much less the unity of all life, felt himself absolutely dependent on blind, hidden forces ever ready to mock and taunt him. Out of that attitude grew the religious concepts of man as

a mere speck of dust dependent on superior powers on high, who can only be appeased by complete surrender. All the early sagas rest on that idea, which continues to be the *Leitmotiv* of the biblical tales dealing with the relation of man to God, to the State, to society. Again and again the same motif, *man is nothing, the powers are everything.* Thus Jehovah would only endure man on condition of complete surrender. Man can have all the glories of earth, but he must not become conscious of himself. The State, society, and moral laws all sing the same refrain: Man can have all the glories of earth, but he must not become conscious of himself.

Anarchism is the only philosophy which brings to man the consciousness of himself; which maintains that God, the State, and society are non-existent, that their promises are null and void, since they can be fulfilled only through man's subordination. Anarchism is therefore the teacher of the unity of life; not merely in nature, but in man. There is no conflict between the individual and the social instincts, any more than there is between the heart and the lungs: the one the receptacle of a precious life essence, the other the repository of the element that keeps the essence pure and strong. The individual is the heart of society, conserving the essence of social life; society is the lungs which are distributing the element to keep the life essence—that is, the individual—pure and strong.

"The one thing of value in the world," says Emerson, "is the active soul; this every man contains within him. The soul active sees absolute truth and utters truth and creates." In other words, the individual instinct is the thing of value in the world. It is the true soul that sees and creates the truth alive, out of which is to come a still greater truth, the re-born social soul.

Anarchism is the great liberator of man from the phantoms that have held him captive; it is the arbiter and pacifier of the two forces for individual and social harmony. To accomplish that unity, Anarchism has declared war on the pernicious influences which have so far prevented the harmonious blending of individual and social instincts, the individual and society.

Religion, the dominion of the human mind; Property, the dominion of human needs; and Government, the dominion of human conduct, represent the stronghold of man's enslavement and all the horrors it entails. Religion! How it dominates man's mind, how it humiliates and degrades his soul. God is everything, man is nothing, says religion. But out of that nothing God has created a kingdom so despotic, so tyrannical, so cruel, so terribly exacting that naught but gloom and tears and blood have ruled the world since gods began. Anarchism rouses man to rebellion against this black monster. Break your mental fetters, says Anarchism to man, for not until you think and judge for yourself will you get rid of the dominion of darkness, the greatest obstacle to all progress.

Property, the dominion of man's needs, the denial of the right to satisfy his needs. Time was when property claimed a divine right, when it came to man with the same refrain, even as religion, "Sacrifice! Abnegate! Submit!" The spirit of Anarchism has lifted man from his prostrate position. He now stands erect, with his face toward the light. He has learned to see the insatiable, devouring, devastating nature of property, and he is preparing to strike the monster dead.

"Property is robbery," said the great French Anarchist Proudhon. Yes, but without risk and danger to the robber. Monopolizing the accumulated efforts of man, property has robbed him of his birthright, and has turned him loose a pauper and an outcast. Property has not even the timeworn excuse that man does not create enough to satisfy all needs. The A B C student of economics knows that the productivity of labor within the last few decades far exceeds normal demand. But what are normal demands to an abnormal institution? The only demand that property recognizes is its own gluttonous appetite for greater wealth, because wealth means power; the power to subdue, to crush, to exploit, the power to enslave, to outrage, to degrade. America is particularly boastful of her great power, her enormous national wealth. Poor America, of what avail is all her wealth, if the individuals comprising the nation are wretchedly poor? If they live in squalor, in filth, in crime, with hope and joy gone, a homeless, soulless army of human prey. It is generally conceded that unless the returns of any business venture exceed the cost, bankruptcy is inevitable. But those engaged in the business of producing wealth have not yet learned even this simple lesson. Every year the cost of production in human life is growing larger (50,000 killed, 100,000 wounded in America

last year); the returns to the masses, who help to create wealth, are ever getting smaller. Yet America continues to be blind to the inevitable bankruptcy of our business of production. Nor is this the only crime of the latter. Still more fatal is the crime of turning the producer into a mere particle of a machine, with less will and decision than his master of steel and iron. Man is being robbed not merely of all products of his labor, but of the power of free initiative, of originality, and the interest in, or desire for, the things he is making.

Real wealth consists in things of utility and beauty, in things that help to create strong, beautiful bodies and surroundings inspiring to live in. But if man is doomed to wind cotton around a spool, or dig coal, or build roads for thirty years of his life, there can be no talk of wealth. What he gives to the world is only gray and hideous things, reflecting a dull and hideous existence,—too weak to live, too cowardly to die. Strange to say, there are people who extol this deadening method of centralized production as the proudest achievement of our age. They fail utterly to realize that if we are to continue in machine subserviency, our slavery is more complete than was our bondage to the King. They do not want to know that centralization is not only the death-knell of liberty, but also of health and beauty, of art and science, all these being impossible in a clocklike, mechanical atmosphere.

Anarchism cannot but repudiate such a method of production: its goal is the freest possible expression of all the latent powers of the individual. Oscar Wilde defines a perfect personality as "one who develops under perfect conditions, who is not wounded, maimed, or in danger." A perfect personality, then, is only possible in a state of society where man is free to choose the mode of work, the conditions of work, and the freedom to work. One to whom the making of a table, the building of a house, or the tilling of the soil, is what the painting is to the artist and the discovery to the scientist,—the result of inspiration, of intense longing, and deep interest in work as a creative force. That being the ideal of Anarchism, its economic arrangements must consist of voluntary productive and distributive associations, gradually developing into free communism, as the best means of producing with the least waste of human energy. Anarchism, however, also recognizes the right of the individual, or numbers of individuals, to arrange at all times for other forms of work, in harmony with their tastes and desires.

Such free display of human energy being possible only under complete individual and social freedom, Anarchism directs its forces against the third and greatest foe of all social equality; namely, the State, organized authority, or statutory law,—the dominion of human conduct.

Just as religion has fettered the human mind, and as property, or the monopoly of things, has subdued and stifled man's needs, so has the State enslaved his spirit, dictating every phase of conduct. "All government in essence," says Emerson, "is tyranny." It matters not whether it is government by divine right or majority rule. In every instance its aim is the absolute subordination of the individual.

Referring to the American government, the greatest American Anarchist, David Thoreau, said: "Government, what is it but a tradition, though a recent one, endeavoring to transmit itself unimpaired to posterity, but each instance losing its integrity; it has not the vitality and force of a single living man. Law never made man a whit more just; and by means of their respect for it, even the well disposed are daily made agents of injustice."

Indeed, the keynote of government is injustice. With the arrogance and self-sufficiency of the King who could do no wrong, governments ordain, judge, condemn, and punish the most insignificant offenses, while maintaining themselves by the greatest of all offenses, the annihilation of individual liberty. Thus Ouida is right when she maintains that "the State only aims at instilling those qualities in its public by which its demands are obeyed, and its exchequer is filled. Its highest attainment is the reduction of mankind to clockwork. In its atmosphere all those finer and more delicate liberties, which require treatment for spacious expansion, inevitably dry up and perish. The State requires a taxpaying machine in which there is no hitch, an exchequer in which there is never a deficit, and a public, monotonous, obedient, colorless, spiritless, moving humbly like a flock of sheep along a straight high road between two walls."

Yet even a flock of sheep would resist the chicanery of the State, if it were not for the corruptive, tyrannical, and oppressive methods it employs to serve its purposes. Therefore Bakunin repudiates the State as synonymous with the surrender of the liberty of the individual or small minorities,—the destruction of social relationship, the curtailment, or complete denial even, of life itself, for its own aggrandizement. The State is the altar of political freedom and, like the religious altar, it is maintained for the purpose of human sacrifice.

In fact, there is hardly a modern thinker who does not agree that government, organized authority, or the State, is necessary *only* to maintain or protect property and monopoly. It has proven efficient in that function only.

Even George Bernard Shaw, who hopes for the miraculous from the State under Fabianism, nevertheless admits that "it is at present a huge machine for robbing and slave-driving of the poor by brute force." This being the case, it is hard to see why the clever prefacer wishes to uphold the State after poverty shall have ceased to exist.

Unfortunately there are still a number of people who continue in the fatal belief that government rests on natural laws, that it maintains social order and harmony, that it diminishes crime, and that it prevents the lazy man from fleecing his fellows. I shall therefore examine these contentions.

A natural law is that factor in man which asserts itself freely and spontaneously without any external force, in harmony with the requirements of nature. For instance, the demand for nutrition, for sex gratification, for light, air, and exercise, is a natural law. But its expression needs not the machinery of government, needs not the club, the gun, the handcuff, or the prison. To obey such laws, if we may call it obedience, requires only spontaneity and free opportunity. That governments do not maintain themselves through such harmonious factors is proven by the terrible array of violence, force, and coercion all governments use in order to live. Thus Blackstone is right when he says, "Human laws are invalid, because they are contrary to the laws of nature."

Unless it be the order of Warsaw after the slaughter of thousands of people, it is difficult to ascribe to governments any capacity for order or social harmony. Order derived through submission and maintained by terror is not much of a safe guaranty; yet that is the only "order" that governments have ever maintained. True social harmony grows naturally out of solidarity of interests. In a society where those who always work never have anything, while those who never work enjoy everything, solidarity of interests is non-existent; hence social harmony is but a myth. The only way organized authority meets this grave situation is by extending still greater privileges to those who have already monopolized the earth, and by still further enslaving the disinherited masses. Thus the entire arsenal of government—laws, police, soldiers, the courts, legislatures, prisons,—is strenuously engaged in "harmonizing" the most antagonistic elements in society.

The most absurd apology for authority and the law is that they serve to diminish crime. Aside from the fact that the State is itself the greatest criminal, breaking every written and natural law, stealing in the form of taxes, killing in the form of war and capital punishment, it has come to an absolute standstill in coping with crime. It has failed utterly to destroy or even minimize the horrible scourge of its own creation.

Crime is naught but misdirected energy. So long as every institution of today, economic, political, social, and moral, conspires to misdirect human energy into wrong channels; so long as most people are out of place doing the things they hate to do, living a life they loathe to live, crime will be inevitable, and all the laws on the statutes can only increase, but never do away with, crime. What does society, as it exists to-day, know of the process of despair, the poverty, the horrors, the fearful struggle the human soul must pass on its way to crime and degradation. Who that knows this terrible process can fail to see the truth in these words of Peter Kropotkin: "Those who will hold the balance between the benefits thus attributed to law and punishment and the degrading effect of the latter on humanity; those who will estimate the torrent of depravity poured abroad in human society by the informer, favored by the Judge even, and paid for in clinking cash by governments, under the pretext of aiding to unmask crime; those who will go within prison walls and there see what human beings become when deprived of liberty, when subjected to the care of brutal keepers, to coarse, cruel words, to a thousand stinging, piercing humiliations, will agree with us that the entire apparatus of prison and punishment is an abomination which ought to be brought to an end." The deterrent influence of law on the lazy man is too absurd to merit consideration. If society were only relieved of the waste and expense of keeping a lazy class, and the equally great expense of the paraphernalia of protection this lazy class requires, the social tables would contain an abundance for all, including even the occasional lazy individual. Besides, it is well to consider that laziness results either from special privileges, or physical and mental abnormalities. Our present insane system of production fosters both, and the most astounding phenomenon is that people should want to work at all now. Anarchism aims to strip labor of its deadening, dulling aspect, of its gloom and compulsion. It aims to make work an instrument of joy, of strength, of color, of real harmony, so that the poorest sort of a man should find in work both recreation and hope.

To achieve such an arrangement of life, government, with its unjust, arbitrary, repressive measures, must be done away with. At best it has but imposed one single mode of life upon all, without regard to individual and social variations and needs. In destroying government and statutory laws, Anarchism proposes to rescue the self-respect and independence of the individual from all restraint and invasion by authority. Only in freedom can man grow to his full stature. Only in freedom will he learn to think and move, and give the very best in him. Only in freedom will he realize the true force of the social bonds which knit men together, and which are the true foundation of a normal social life.

But what about human nature? Can it be changed? And if not, will it endure under Anarchism?

Poor human nature, what horrible crimes have been committed in thy name! Every fool, from king to policeman, from the flatheaded parson to the visionless dabbler in science, presumes to speak authoritatively of human nature. The greater the mental charlatan, the more definite his insistence on the wickedness and weaknesses of human nature. Yet, how can any one speak of it today, with every soul in prison, with every heart fettered, wounded, and maimed?

John Burroughs has stated that experimental study of animals in captivity is absolutely useless. Their character, their habits, their appetites undergo a complete transformation when torn from their soil in field and forest. With human nature caged in a narrow space, whipped daily into submission, how can we speak of its potentialities?

Freedom, expansion, opportunity, and, above all, peace and repose, alone can teach us the real dominant factors of human nature and all its wonderful possibilities.

Anarchism, then, really stands for the liberation of the human mind from the dominion of religion; the liberation of the human body from the dominion of property; liberation from the shackles and restraint of government. Anarchism stands for a social order based on the free grouping of individuals for the purpose of producing real social wealth; an order that will guarantee to every human being free access to the earth and full enjoyment of the necessities of life, according to individual desires, tastes, and inclinations. This is not a wild fancy or an aberration of the mind. It is the **conclusion** arrived at by hosts of intellectual men and women the world over; a conclusion resulting from the close and studious observation of the tendencies of modern society: individual liberty and economic equality, the twin forces for the birth of what is fine and true in man.

As to methods, Anarchism is not, as some may suppose, a theory of the future to be realized through divine inspiration. It is a living force in the affairs of our life, constantly creating new conditions. The methods of Anarchism therefore do not comprise an iron-clad program to be carried out under all circumstances. Methods must grow out of the economic needs of each place and clime, and of the intellectual and temperamental requirements of the individual. The serene, calm character of a Tolstoy will wish different methods for social reconstruction than the intense, overflowing personality of a Michael Bakunin or a Peter Kropotkin. Equally so it must be apparent that the economic and political needs of Russia will dictate more drastic measures than would England or America. Anarchism does not stand for military drill and uniformity; it does, however, stand for the spirit of revolt, in whatever form, against everything that hinders human growth. All Anarchists agree in that, as they also agree in their opposition to the political machinery as a means of bringing about the great social change.

"All voting," says Thoreau, "is a sort of gaming, like checkers, or backgammon, a playing with right and wrong; its obligation never exceeds that of expediency. Even voting for the right thing is doing nothing for it. A wise man will not leave the right to the mercy of chance, nor wish it to prevail through the power of the majority." A close examination of the machinery of politics and its achievements will bear out the logic of Thoreau.

What does the history of parliamentarism show? Nothing but failure and defeat, not even a single reform to ameliorate the economic and social stress of the people. Laws have been passed and enactments made for the improvement and protection of labor. Thus it was proven only last year that Illinois, with the most rigid laws for mine protection, had the greatest mine disasters. In States where child labor laws prevail, child exploitation is at its highest, and though with us the workers enjoy full political opportunities, capitalism has reached the most brazen zenith.

Even were the workers able to have their own representatives, for which our good Socialist politicians are clamoring, what chances are there for their honesty and good faith? One has but to bear in mind the process of politics to realize that its path of good intentions is full of pitfalls: wire-pulling, intriguing, flattering, lying, cheating; in fact, chicanery of every description, whereby the political aspirant can achieve success. Added to that is a complete demoralization of character and conviction, until nothing is left that would make one hope for anything from such a human derelict. Time and time again the people were foolish enough to trust, believe, and support with their last farthing aspiring politicians, only to find themselves betrayed and cheated.

It may be claimed that men of integrity would not become corrupt in the political grinding mill. Perhaps not; but such men would be absolutely helpless to exert the slightest influence on behalf of labor, as indeed has been shown in numerous instances. The State is the economic master of its servants. Good men, if such there be, would either remain true to their political faith and lose their economic support, or they would cling to their economic master and be utterly unable to do the slightest good. The political arena leaves one no alternative, one must either be a dunce or a rogue.

The political superstition is still holding sway over the hearts and minds of the masses, but the true lovers of liberty will have no more to do with it.

Instead, they believe with Stirner that man has as much liberty as he is willing to take. Anarchism therefore stands for direct action, the open defiance of, and resistance to, all laws and restrictions, economic, social, and moral. But defiance and resistance are illegal. Therein lies the salvation of man. Everything illegal necessitates integrity, self-reliance, and courage. In short, it calls for free, independent spirits, for "men who are men, and who have a bone in their backs which you cannot pass your hand through."

Universal suffrage itself owes its existence to direct action. If not for the spirit of rebellion, of the defiance on the part of the American revolutionary fathers, their posterity would still wear the King's coat. If not for the direct action of a John Brown and his comrades, America would still trade in the flesh of the black man. True, the trade in white flesh is still going on; but that, too, will have to be abolished by direct action. Trade-unionism, the economic arena of the modern gladiator, owes its existence to direct action. It is but recently that law and government have attempted to crush the trade-union movement, and condemned the exponents of man's right to organize to prison as conspirators. Had they sought to assert their cause through begging, pleading, and compromise, trade-unionism would today be a negligible quantity. In France, in Spain, in Italy, in Russia, nay even in England (witness the growing rebellion of English labor unions), direct, revolutionary, economic action has become so strong a force in the battle for industrial liberty as to make the world realize the tremendous importance of labor's power. The General Strike, the supreme expression of the economic consciousness of the workers, was ridiculed in America but a short time ago. Today every great strike, in order to win, must realize the importance of the solidaric general protest.

Direct action, having proven effective along economic lines, is equally potent in the environment of the individual. There a hundred forces encroach upon his being, and only persistent resistance to them will finally set him free. Direct action against the authority in the shop, direct action against the authority of the law, direct action against the invasive, meddlesome authority of our moral code, is the logical, consistent method of Anarchism.

Will it not lead to a revolution? Indeed, it will. No real social change has ever come about without a revolution. People are either not familiar with their history, or they have not yet learned that revolution is but thought carried into action.

Anarchism, the great leaven of thought, is today permeating every phase of human endeavor. Science, art, literature, the drama, the effort for economic betterment, in fact every individual and social opposition to the existing disorder of things, is illumined by the spiritual light of Anarchism. It is the philosophy of the sovereignty of the individual. It is the theory of social harmony. It is the great, surging, living truth that is reconstructing the world, and that will usher in the Dawn.

Questions for Thought

1. How would you define the term *anarchism?* How does your definition compare with or differ from Goldman's definition?
2. Do you agree with Goldman's attitude toward religion? If not, what could you say to try to convince her to change her mind?
3. How do your views on property compare with or differ from the views of Goldman?
4. Do you believe that government is necessary? If so, what are its principal functions? If not, why not?
5. What are the principal areas of agreement between Goldman and Thoreau? Can you think of any ways in which their views differ?

Chapter 6

Religion

Introductory Remarks

IN THE INTRODUCTION TO THE LAST CHAPTER, I mentioned three dangers associated with the path of thinking about politics: the danger of disagreement, the danger of disloyalty, and the danger of dullness. As you now prepare to journey down the final philosophical path in this text—the path of thinking about religion—I should warn you that these same dangers are to be found on this path as well. Like political dialogue, religious dialogue often seems to be marked by endless argument and confrontation. While recent ecumenical movements have tried to move beyond this state of affairs, they have had little success. Thus, there still remains much disagreement, not only between different religions (consider, for example, recent confrontations among Jews, Christians, and Muslims in the Middle East) but also between differing divisions of the same religion.

Moreover, while an increasing number of my students have been reared in a purely secular environment and thus are able to discuss religion without facing the fear of disloyalty, others have grown up within a strong religious tradition that prohibits questioning certain assumptions. If you fall into this latter category, then the danger of disloyalty may be even more worrisome on the path of thinking about religion than on the path of thinking about politics.

Finally, just as many people find political thinking and discussion to be terribly dull, others feel the same way about religion. I believe one reason for this is that, at least in Judaism and Christianity, much thinking about religion has taken the form of debates about detailed ritualistic observance or about abstract theological questions. The *Mishnah* is filled with seemingly endless rabbinical opinion about how to meet the requirements of biblical commandments, whereas the writings of Christian apologists are often devoted to the formulation and defense of abstract theological doctrines.

If you get beyond such theological debates, however, the path of thinking about religion becomes existentially exciting. Indeed, like the path of thinking about politics, the path of thinking about religion can be a path of personal and social transformation. In examining religious literature, you will find numerous examples of radical personal transformation. Consider, for example, the case of Prince Gautama, who gave up a life of luxury to become the Buddha, or the case of the New Testament writer Paul, who went from being an adamant persecutor of members of the early Christian sect to one of its foremost defenders and missionaries. Moreover, history offers a large number of social transformations as well, from Zarathustra's religious transformation of ancient Persian society and culture to the Islamic Revolution in Iran in the early 1980s. The possibility of achieving personal and/or social transformation through religious experience is a motif that occurs in several of the selections found in this chapter.

Overview of Selections

As with the path of thinking about politics, there are numerous questions that could be addressed on the path of thinking about religion. In this chapter, I have gathered a number of writings from various times and cultures that focus on two of these questions. The selections in the first part deal more or less directly with the general question of the nature of religious belief. As you no doubt know, people claiming to be religious often disagree on the content of religious belief. Jews and Muslims insist on the indivisibility of the one God, many Christians accept the doctrine of the Trinity, certain Hindus believe in a multiplicity of gods, and Jains and Theravadan Buddhists often do not believe in any gods at all. But in addition to this and countless other differences related to content, religious thinkers often disagree on the nature of religious belief itself. By describing either their own religious experiences or the religious experiences of others, the writers in the first section offer us their views about what constitutes the nature of genuine religious belief.

In addition to providing accounts of the nature of genuine religious belief, the last two selections in the first part criticize certain religious doctrines and practices. In doing so, they suggest that these religious doctrines and practices are harmful in some way. A distinguishing feature of the selections in the second part is that they focus explicitly on this question of whether religious belief is beneficial or harmful. The first three writers argue that religious belief, at least in some form, is absolutely essential to individual and social well-being, whereas the fourth author claims that religion comprises an important sphere of human thinking. The next two authors express a more ambivalent attitude about the value of religion, while the last two authors maintain that religious belief is overwhelmingly harmful.

In the first selection of the chapter, the noted Christian writer Aurelius Augustinus describes certain aspects of the path that led him to embrace Christian doctrine. Finding that it was impossible to rationally resolve doubts about the existence of evil, Augustinus says that these doubts were overcome by a mystical vision in which he experienced the invisible nature of God. This powerful vision left him longing to be in the presence of God, a longing that he believes can be fulfilled only by humbling oneself and submitting to Christ Jesus. In a somewhat similar vein, Black Elk, in the second selection, describes part of the great vision that he received from the spirit world, while explaining how this vision became a source of personal and social healing. Unlike Augustinus, however, Black Elk stresses the importance of religious ceremonies for activating the healing power of his vision. For Black Elk, visions and religious ceremonies allow one to establish a personal relationship with the spirit world, without the mediation of Christ Jesus.

In the third selection, the Christian philosopher Thomas Aquinas follows a path far removed from that of either Augustinus or Black Elk. Whereas many of the insights of both Augustinus and Black Elk were derived from powerful religious experiences, Aquinas believes that most religious beliefs can be accepted on the basis of reason. In this brief selection, he provides five arguments for one of the fundamental Christian beliefs, the belief in the existence of God.

Next, the Danish philosopher Søren Kierkegaard describes Abraham as the true religious hero for having unswerving faith in God, even when God commanded him to sacrifice his only son. For Kierkegaard, it is such faith, not reason or experience, which is the essential element of genuine religious belief.

In contrast to all four of the earlier writers, Martin Buber, in the fifth selection, says that belief in God results from a type of relationship that is most fully realized in our interaction with other people. Buber describes two essential ways in which we relate to the world, the relationship of I-It and the relationship of I-Thou. In the latter type of relationship, humans are able to move beyond the objectifying attitude of the I-It and to mutually embrace one another with the totality of their being. Buber believes that traces of the eternal Thou (or God) are found in all genuine I-Thou relationships.

In the next selection, Gustavo Gutiérrez suggests that genuine religious belief is necessarily tied to a sincere effort to promote economic and social justice. Although Gutiérrez is a Catholic priest, he criticizes certain traditional Christian doctrines and practices while offering a version of Christianity, a theology of liberation, which recognizes the plight of the poor and engages in the revolutionary movement to end poverty and injustice.

In the final writing of the first section, Starhawk agrees with Gutiérrez that genuine religious belief is connected with efforts to promote economic and social justice. However, in opposition to him, she argues that such justice cannot be achieved within the confines of Christian tradition. After recounting a brief history of the persecution of witches by the Christian church, Starhawk goes on to contrast witchcraft, which she believes encourages independence and the development of spiritual and economic power, with the hierarchical and authoritarian structure of Christianity.

The selections in the second section focus more directly on the question of whether religious belief is beneficial or harmful to the individual and/or society. In the first selection, William James defends the adoption and value of religious belief against those who argue that we should accept only those beliefs that are warranted by scientific evidence. While not denying the value of science, James claims that science is unable to answer many of the important questions of life and that we are justified in using our passional nature, our will to believe, in order to arrive at satisfactory answers to such questions.

Next, Joseph Campbell describes the crucial role that mythology has played, and must continue to play, in the life of the individual and society. Noting that traditional myths and religions have lost their effectiveness in the modern world, Campbell says that a new mythology must emerge if the future well-being of the individual and society is to be assured.

Carol Christ, in the third selection, agrees with Campbell about the importance of mythology. Like Campbell, she also believes that traditional mythology and religion is no longer effective, especially in the lives of women. As the title to her essay suggests, she argues that women need the imagery and symbolism of the Goddess (that is, myths and rituals affirming the sacredness of the female principle) if they are to overcome the negative portrayal and treatment of women associated with patriarchal religious beliefs and practices.

In the fourth selection, Alfred North Whitehead examines the conflict that often exists between science and religion. Claiming that science and religion are two important spheres of human thinking, Whitehead argues that this conflict need not lead to the rejection of either science or religion. Rather, he argues that the interplay between scientific and religious thinking can lead to progress in both spheres.

Kwasi Wiredu, in the fifth selection, also examines the relationship between religious belief, which he refers to as the "spiritistic outlook," and scientific or rational knowledge. Focusing specifically on traditional African religion, Wiredu argues that prescientific religious thinking, the type of thinking that "tends to construct explanations of natural phenomena in terms of the activities of the gods and kindred spirits," is inferior in many respects to scientific thinking. For this reason, he believes that the advancement of African culture requires that rational inquiry displace prescientific religious thinking.

In the next two selections, Antony Flew and Lin Yutang raise several interesting questions concerning the nature and value of religious belief. First, Flew philosophically analyzes the language used to express religious beliefs. After showing how religious claims are often qualified when they are found to be incompatible with empirical evidence, he argues that such qualifications tend to make such claims so weak that they become empty or meaningless. Next, in a brief account of his personal journey from Christianity to paganism, Lin Yutang suggests that the theological beliefs of Christianity are less satisfying than the philosophy of paganism. Lin claims that Christianity devalues earthly existence, and he believes that it encourages people to remain immature and psychologically dependent. However, Lin does not totally reject religion, for he says that being pagan need not mean being nonreligious.

While also focusing on Christianity, Bertrand Russell, in the final selection, portrays religion as a disease born of fear, a disease that has been the source of endless human misery. He claims that Christianity has been the opponent of both intellectual and moral progress, and that it has endorsed psychologically unhealthy views on sex. Finally, Russell argues that Christianity has promoted intolerance, thus undermining social harmony.

As you read and discuss these selections, keep in mind that their ultimate value will lie in the role that they may play in your own psychological and spiritual development. Indeed, this can be said for all the selections in this text. As I suggested in earlier introductory remarks, if the path of philosophical reflection is not to be a path of lifeless abstractions, then it must be linked to self-analysis and personal growth.

Contemporary Applications

On the first day of an Aristotle seminar that I took at Tulane University, the professor stated that each graduate student would be responsible for teaching the class once during the semester. Knowing that certain of Aristotle's texts were much more difficult than others, I chose one of the easier readings to teach. Unfortunately, another student in the class chose the same reading. In an attempt at fairness, the professor suggested that we flip a coin to decide which of us would get to do that particular reading. This seemed to be a reasonable solution, and I was getting ready to call "tails." However, the other student who had chosen that particular reading, a Muslim student from Iran, politely declined to participate. Without realizing it, the professor had asked him to violate one of his fundamental religious beliefs. For in the religion of Islam, as I learned from conversing with the student after class, gambling in any form is taboo.

This incident clearly shows the importance of having a basic understanding of the religious beliefs of others. If we are to live together peaceably, we must know enough about people's beliefs so that we do not unintentionally tread on them. Although the incident in the Aristotle seminar was amicably resolved (I chose a different reading), religious misunderstandings and intolerance have been, and still are, the source of much violence and conflict.

While some of the readings in this chapter (as in preceding chapters) will help you understand a few of the specific beliefs of different religions, they are more directly related to broader questions concerning the source and value of religious belief. Consider the content of my conversation with my fellow student at Tulane. After asking him why he had refused to participate in the coin toss, I could have asked him why he had adopted the particular religious beliefs that he had. Why these beliefs and not others?

In the wonderful PBS television series *The Power of Myth,* Bill Moyers asked Joseph Campbell (a selection from Campbell's first book is included in this chapter) what he thought about faith. Campbell replied that he did not need faith because he had "experience." What do you think Campbell meant by this reply?

When I was a student at McGill University, I awoke from my sleep one night to the sight of a female figure with glowing golden hair that was dressed in a glowing white robe. The figure never said a word; she merely pointed her finger toward me before vanishing from my sight. What did this experience mean? Was this apparition a spiritual messenger, perhaps an angel, who had brought me a divine message? Or was she simply a figment of my imagination?

Being somewhat familiar with the Bible, I knew that people had often claimed to see angels, burning bushes that did not burn, or dead bones come to life. And I knew that these visions were claimed to be the source of religious insight or revelation. (I now know that such visions are common in religions other than Judaism and Christianity.) But I also knew someone who had taken LSD and who had religious visions that convinced him that he was the resurrected Jesus. Furthermore, I had a friend who worked at the state mental hospital and who told me stories of numerous patients suffering from religious delusions, patients who often claimed to be visited by angels, demons, or other spiritual beings. In light of all this, what was I to make of my experience? Or to broaden the question, what are we to make of the religious visions or experiences of others, such as those of Augustinus and Black Elk, that are described in selections included in this chapter?

After thinking about these questions for a while, you may decide that experience is not the most reliable source of religious belief. But if you do come to this **conclusion,** then you will have to try to discover some other more reliable source (unless, of course, you are willing to admit that religious beliefs are unfounded). In reading the selections in the first part of this chapter, you will discover at least three other candidates that might serve as this more reliable source: reason, faith, and relationship. However, as with experience, these sources are certainly not immune from philosophical investigation. Consider, for example, the following questions:

Which religious beliefs, if any, can be rationally proven?
Which religious beliefs, if any, can be rationally refuted?

If there is overwhelming scientific evidence against a religious belief, must this belief be rejected?

What exactly do we mean when we say that we accept a belief on the basis of faith?

Is faith any more reliable than experience?

What can we say or do when two people accept contradictory beliefs, both claiming that their beliefs are justified by faith?

How can my relationships with other people serve as a source of religious belief?

When someone speaks of having a "personal relationship" with God, what exactly are they claiming?

Is the claim to have a relationship with God merely delusion, wishful thinking, or the product of human arrogance?

While these are interesting and difficult questions, the principal question addressed by the readings in the second part of the chapter is perhaps even more challenging. Is religious belief beneficial or harmful? If you stop to think about this question, you can no doubt think of evidence that supports both sides of this issue. There are many examples of stories in which religious belief inspired positive personal and social transformations, but there are also stories of wars, persecutions, and attempted genocide that were inspired by religious belief.

In my own life, religion has certainly been a double-edged sword. While I have personally benefited from reading those gems of wisdom that are embedded in the sacred literature of many different religions, I have also seen how this literature can be used to justify segregation, intolerance, and even murder.

When I was a young boy, I attended a fundamentalist church in South Carolina, a church whose members claimed that they were following the teachings of Christ. It was a tumultuous time in the South, a time in which segregation laws were being challenged, a time in which some people would go to any extreme to prevent those laws from being overturned. I still vividly remember the words of one of the songs we sang in vacation Bible school:

Jesus loves the little children
All the children of the world
Black and yellow, red and white
They're all precious in His sight
Jesus loves the little children of the world.

One would think that anyone teaching children to sing such a song would be opposed to segregation, that they would realize that the Christian brotherhood they spoke about so often was not restricted to people with the same color of skin as them. But such was not the case. Just as the Bible had earlier been used to justify slavery, it was now used to justify segregation. Indeed, one of my Sunday school teachers, a deacon in the church, was also a local leader in the Ku Klux Klan, a restaurant owner who vowed that no "nigger" would ever step foot in his restaurant.

My own experience demonstrates clearly to me that religion can be used in ways that harm people. But then there is the other side of the coin. Weren't Dr. King and other civil rights leaders using religion to promote positive social change? (Notice how many times religious beliefs are appealed to in the "Letter from Birmingham Jail" reprinted in the last chapter.) And can't religion be used to promote other desirable goals, such as the empowerment of women or the liberation of people from oppressive political and economic structures? These are certainly claims made by Carol Christ and Gustavo Gutiérrez in selections included in this chapter. As you read these and the other selections in this chapter, ask yourself the following questions:

What are some of the benefits of religion to your life and/or to the society in which you live?

What are some of the harms of religion to your life and/or to the society in which you live?

Are some religious beliefs more beneficial and/or harmful than other religious beliefs?

Would your life and/or society be better off if there were no religious beliefs?

What Is the Nature of Religious Belief?

Confessions on the Nature of God   1

AURELIUS AUGUSTINUS

Aurelius Augustinus (354–430 C.E.), popularly known as Saint Augustine, was born in the small town of Tagaste in North Africa. Augustinus' father was a pagan who encouraged his son to pursue an academic career as a means to obtaining a government position; his mother was a pious Christian who urged him to follow a spiritual path. In his early life, Augustinus moved in the more secular direction championed by his father. He received a standard Roman education, which emphasized rhetoric. At age nineteen, he read Cicero's treatise *Hortensius* and developed a marked interest in philosophy and the pursuit of wisdom. He also led a rather licentious life, living for several years with a mistress who bore him a son. During this time, he was a follower of the dualistic philosophy of **Manichaeanism,** which claimed to represent true Christianity but that was labeled heretical by official Church doctrine.

In the year 386, Augustinus converted to orthodox Christianity, a conversion that he describes in decidedly mystical terms in his *Confessions*. He left his mistress and moved to Milan, where he obtained a professorship in rhetoric. There he listened to the sermons of Ambrose, the bishop of Milan, who was the leading Christian apologist of his day. He also became familiar with the teachings of **Neoplatonism,** a pagan philosophy that both Ambrose and Augustinus saw as being compatible with Christian doctrine.

In the early 390s, Augustinus left Milan and returned to North Africa, where he settled into a semimonastic life in the city of Hippo. He was ordained a priest and became the bishop of Hippo in 395. Holding this position for the rest of his life, Augustinus devoted most of his time to Church business. He delivered numerous sermons, and he wrote hundreds of pamphlets and letters in which he elaborated and defended Church doctrine. This work culminated in his monumental apologetical work *De civitate Dei* (*The City of God*), on which he worked from 413 to 426. His other major writings include *Confessiones* (ca. 400; *The Confessions*), *De doctrina Christiana* (397–428; *Christian Instruction*), and *De Trinitate* (400–416; *On the Trinity*). His death coincided with the end of Roman civilization in Africa. When Augustinus died in Hippo in 430, the Vandals were massing to storm the city.

In the following selection from his *Confessions,* Augustinus describes the religious path that delivered him from certain problems and doubts that he had about Christian doctrine. Although Augustinus says that he never doubted the existence of God, he claims he was initially troubled by his inability to get beyond certain vague physical images of God and by what philosophers have called the "problem of evil." Simply stated, the problem of evil concerns how evil could have originated in a universe created by an incorruptible, all-knowing, all-powerful God. It was this problem that led the Manichaeans to posit the existence of two primary deities—the Father of Greatness, who was the source of everything good in the universe, and the Prince of Darkness, who was responsible for the existence of evil. By the time Augustinus wrote *The Confessions,* he had rejected this heretical solution to the problem of evil; but he was also skeptical of the attempt to blame the origin of evil on human disobedience. Since God, the creator of humans, is both all-knowing and all-powerful, Augustinus believed that the attempt to blame evil on human disobedience failed to exonerate God from ultimate responsibility for the existence of evil.

In the midst of these doubts, Augustinus says that he experienced a religious vision that allowed him to discern the true nature of God and to resolve the problem of evil. Augustinus describes this vision both as an intense light that differed from any other light that he had ever seen and as a voice from God that led him into the innermost region of his being. As he says, "I entered and with my soul's eye, such as it was, saw above that same eye of my soul the immutable light higher than my mind." Elsewhere, Augustinus describes this insight as an inward ascendancy whereby he moves progressively from experience of external bodies, to experience of the soul, the soul's "inward force," the power of reasoning, the light of reason, and finally to the vision of the invisible nature of God.

For Augustinus, this vision of God confirmed his rejection of the Manichaean belief in the existence of a god of darkness, and it reaffirmed his belief that God is incorruptible, all-knowing, and all-powerful. It also provided him with a solution to the problem of evil. Augustinus's solution is, simply put, that evil does not exist, at least not from the perspective of God. Seen as a whole, everything that God created is good; things appear to be evil to us only because we see things from a limited perspective.

Near the end of this selection, Augustinus says that while he had received a powerful vision into the nature of God, he was unable to keep this vision before his mind. Reverting to everyday experience, he was left with a longing to be in the full presence of God. Following orthodox Christian doctrine at this point, Augustinus claims that this is possible only through the mediation of Christ Jesus. Those who humble themselves and submit to Christ will ultimately be lifted up into the presence of God.

Questions for Reading

1. How does Augustinus describe the nature of God?
2. What, according to philosophers, is the problem of evil? How is this problem dealt with in the selection from the Bible reprinted in Chapter 2? Why does Augustinus reject this solution?
3. How does Augustinus attempt to resolve the problem of evil?

4. What was the nature of the religious vision that Augustinus experienced? What theological conclusions did Augustinus draw from his vision?
5. What seems to be Augustinus' attitude toward the body in the present selection?
6. How, according to Augustinus, is one lifted up into the presence of God?

I

BY NOW MY EVIL AND SINFUL YOUTH WAS BE-hind me, and I was passing into early manhood. But as I grew older, it became even more shameful that I could not imagine any **substance** except that which can be seen by the eyes. I did not think of you, O God, under the figure of a human body. For from the time that I began to understand anything of philosophy, I had always rejected that idea; and I rejoiced to find that this idea had also been rejected by our spiritual mother, your Catholic Church. But I did not know how else to conceive of you.

As a mere man with many limitations, I was trying to conceive of you, the supreme, sole and true God; and with all my heart I believed that you were incorruptible, incapable of being injured, and unchangeable. For although I did not know why or how, I saw plainly and certainly that what can be corrupted is inferior to what cannot, that what cannot receive injury is superior to what can, and that what is unchangeable is better than things subject to change. My heart passionately cried out against all my imaginings, and I tried with one blow to eliminate from my mind's eye all those unclean images that buzzed around it. However, these images were only expelled for a moment, and in the twinkling of an eye they gathered again thick about me, flew against my face, and clouded my vision. So, although I did not think of you as having a human body, and I did think of you as being incorruptible, incapable of being injured, and unchangeable, I was still forced to view you as something physical occupying space, whether infused in the world, or diffused infinitely beyond it. For it seemed to me that anything that did not occupy space would be absolutely nothing; it would not even be a void. . . .

Then I was so gross-hearted—not even being clear about my own self—that I thought that whatever was not extended in space (that is, whatever was not diffused, condensed, swelled out, or did not or could not receive some of these qualities) was absolutely nothing. My mind searched for such images as my eyes normally see, and I did not yet realize that the mental act by which I formed those very images did not itself occupy space, although it could not have formed the images unless it had itself been something great. Also I endeavored to conceive of you, life of my life, as penetrating the whole mass of the universe, extending beyond it throughout immeasurable space, bounding the earth, the heaven, and all other things, but being bounded by nothing. For the body of air that is above the earth does not hinder the light of the sun from passing through and penetrating it, not by bursting or cutting, but by filling it wholly. Similarly, I thought that the bodies of heaven, air, sea, earth and everything else, from the greatest to the smallest, was permeated by your presence, while your secret inspiration governed all things that you had created, both inwardly and outwardly.

This was what I held, for I was unable to think of anything else. However, it was false. For if this were true, a greater part of the earth would contain a greater portion of you, while a smaller part would contain a smaller portion. All things would be full of you in the sense that the body of an elephant would contain more of you than the body of a sparrow—the difference being determined by how much larger the body of the elephant is, that is, by how much more space it occupies. On this view, you would be making yourself present to the world in fragments, larger fragments in larger bodies, smaller fragments in smaller bodies; and that is not the case. However, you had not yet enlightened my darkness.

This is the editor's revised version of a selection from Edward Bouverie Pusey's nineteenth-century translation of The Confessions of Saint Augustine.

II

In opposition to the Manichees, those deceived deceivers and word-spinners who did not speak your word, the argument proposed by Nebridius was sufficient. When we heard the argument long ago while we were still in Carthage, we were staggered by it. Nebridius observed that the Manichees suggest that there is a reign of darkness that is in conflict with you, and against which you must do battle. But what could that reign of darkness do to you, if you refused to fight against it? If the Manichees answered, "it would do some harm to you," then you would be subject to injury and corruption. But if they said, "it would do no harm to you," then there would be no reason why you should fight against it. . . . So if they affirmed of you, whatever you were, that your substance was incorruptible, then all their beliefs would be false and abominable. However, if they affirmed that you were corruptible, that very statement itself, without debate, would prove to be false and revolting.

This argument of Nebridius thus sufficed against those who deserved to be vomited out of my overly full stomach. For they had no means of escape from this dilemma, without thinking and speaking horrible blasphemies about you.

III

But although I firmly believed that you—our Lord and true God, who made our souls, our bodies, and all other things—were absolutely incorruptible and unalterable, yet I did not clearly and without difficulty understand the cause of evil. Still, whatever the cause might be, I knew that I could not allow it to persuade me to believe the immutable God to be mutable. Otherwise I was in danger of becoming the evil whose origin I was seeking. I sought out the origin of evil, then, free from anxiety, for I was certain that what the Manichees said was not true. With all my heart I rejected their beliefs, because my inquiry into the origin of evil demonstrated that they were filled with evil, for they preferred to think that your substance suffered evil, rather than believing that their substance committed it.

So I tried hard to understand something else I had heard, namely, that free-will was the cause of our doing evil and that your just judgment was the reason that we suffered evil. But I could not follow clearly this line of reasoning. When I endeavored to draw my mind's eye out of that deep pit, I was again plunged back in. No matter how often I tried, the result was the same. But this raised me a little into your light, for I now knew that I had a will, as surely as I knew that I lived. And I knew that when I willed to do or not to do something, it was surely I, and I alone, who willed to do or not to do it. I was also coming to realize that the cause of my sin resided there.

Still, I believed that whatever happened against my will, I suffered rather than did; and I judged these things not to be my fault, but my punishment. Moreover, holding that you were just, I speedily confessed that I was not being unjustly punished. But then I asked, "Who made me? Was it not my God, who is not only good, but goodness itself? How then did I derive the power to will evil rather than good, which would make it just for me to be punished? Who put this power in me? Who planted within me this seed of bitterness, seeing that I was wholly formed by my most sweet God? If the devil were the author, where did the devil come from? If he were a good angel who became a devil because of his own perverse will, where did this perverse will that made him a devil come from, since an angel is wholly made by a Creator who is pure goodness?" By such thoughts I was again sunk down and choked; yet I was not brought down to the hell of that error where no one confesses to you—the error that you suffer evil rather than that man does it.

IV

I now tried to discover other truths, as I had previously established that the incorruptible is better than the corruptible, and that, whatever you are, you must be incorruptible. For there has never been a soul, nor will there ever be one, who is able to conceive any thing better than you, the supreme and highest good. But since the incorruptible is certainly superior to the corruptible, as I had already ascertained, then if you were not incorruptible, I could have conceived of something higher than my God. But seeing the superiority of the incorruptible to the corruptible, I should have looked for you there, deducing from that truth the origin of evil—that is, the source of a corruption that can by no means impair your substance. For corruption in no way impairs our God—whether by will, necessity, or chance—because He is God. What he wills is good, and he is himself that same good; but to be corrupted is not good. Nor can you be forced against your will to do anything, since your will is not greater than your power. It would only be greater if you were greater than yourself, for the will and power of God is God Himself. And what can be unforeseen by you, since you know all things? No nature exists which you do not know. And why should we keep saying, "that substance which is God is not corruptible," since if it were corruptible, it would not be God?

V

I searched for the origin of evil, but I searched in a flawed way, not seeing the flaw in my very search. I now set before my mind's eye the whole of creation—everything that we can see in it, such as sea, earth, air, stars, trees, mortal creatures, and everything that we cannot see, such as the firmament of heaven, angels, and all the spiritual beings. But I imagined all of these to be bodies, each occupying its own place; and I made one great mass of your creation, distinguishing within it different kinds of bodies—some physical bodies, and some the kind of bodies that I imagined for spirits. And I made this mass huge, not as huge as it is (since I could not know its exact size), but as huge as I thought appropriate. Yet, despite its great size, I still thought of it as finite in every direction. But you, Lord, I imagined to be infinite in all directions, surrounding and penetrating every part of your creation, which, though finite, is still full of you, the infinite. I visualized you as a boundless sea, everywhere, and in every direction, through unmeasured space. And I saw your creation as a sponge, huge, but finite, a sponge that needs, in all its parts, to be filled from your immeasurable sea. And I said, "behold God. Behold what God has created." God is good, yes, most mightily and incomparably better than everything else, and he, the good, created everything good. See how he surrounds and fulfils everything. What is evil then, and from where did it creep into creation? What is its root, and what its seed? . . .

From where indeed does evil come, seeing that God, the good, has created all things good? Indeed he, who is the greatest and highest good, has created these lesser goods; still both creator and created are good. What is the origin of evil? Or, was there some evil matter from which God made, formed, and ordered creation, leaving something in it that he did not convert into good? But why did he do so? Seeing that he is almighty, did he not have the power to transform and change the whole, so that no evil remained in it? Lastly, why would he make any thing at all out of this matter, rather than destroying it altogether? Could it have possibly existed against his will? Or if it had existed from eternity, why did God allow it to exist so long in its unordered state, before deciding to create something from it? Or if he suddenly decided to create something, would not the Almighty have destroyed this evil matter, so that he alone would exist as the true, supreme, and infinite good? Since he was good and it was not good for him to create something that was not good, then couldn't he have destroyed that evil matter and replaced it with good matter, from which he could then have created all things. For he would not be almighty, if he could not create something good without the aid of matter which he himself had not created.

Such thoughts revolved in my miserable heart and I was burdened with the most gnawing worries, fearing that I might die before I had found the truth. Yet the faith in your Christ, our Lord and Savior, taught within the Catholic Church, was firmly fixed in my heart, though in many respects this faith was as yet unformed, fluctuating from the rule of doctrine. Nonetheless, my mind did not forsake it, but rather drank more and more of it with each passing day. . . .

VII

But I was still searching for the origin of evil and I could see no answer. Yet, you did not allow any fluctuations in my thinking to carry me away from the faith whereby I believed that you existed, that your substance was unchangeable, and that you cared for and would judge men. My faith also assured me that in Christ, your Son our Lord, and in your holy scriptures, which were commended by the authority of your Catholic Church, you had fixed the path of salvation by which man can attain the future life after death. These things being safe and immovably settled in my mind, I anxiously sought out the origin of evil. What pangs my teeming heart suffered, what groans, O my God! Yet even then and there your ears were open, but I knew it not.

As I vehemently continued my seeking in silence, those silent struggles of my soul were strong cries pleading for your mercy. You knew what I suffered, but no man did. For, how could my tongue express this suffering in words for the ears of even my closest friends? Did the whole tumult of my soul, which neither time nor utterance could adequately express, reach them? Yet the whole of my turmoil reached your hearing. It roared out from the groaning of my heart; my desire was before you, and the light of my eyes was not with me. For that was within me, while I was still focused on externals. The light of my eyes was not situated in space, but I was focusing on things contained in space. I found no resting-place there. These external things did not receive me . . . , nor did they allow me to turn within, where it might be well enough with me. For I was superior to these external things, but inferior to you. You are my true joy if I remain subject to you, but you have made the inferior things that you created below me subject to me. To remain in your image, to serve you while ruling my body—this was the true mean, the middle ground in which I would find health and safety.

But when in pride I rose in opposition to you, running against the Lord with the thick neck of my shield, even these inferior things were set above me. They oppressed me, and there was no respite or breathing space anywhere. Wherever I turned, they filled my sight, and images of them pervaded my thinking, preventing me from turning back toward you. It was as if they were saying to me, "Where are you going, you unworthy and defiled man?" All these things had grown out of my wound, for you humble the proud like one that is wounded. And through my own swelling conceit I was separated from you, as though my pride-swollen face had closed up my eyes.

VIII

But you, Lord, abide forever. Yet you are not angry with us forever, because you pity our dust and ashes.

So, it was pleasing in your sight to reform my deformities. By inward goads you roused me, so that I would be ill at ease until you were manifested to my inward sight. Thus, my swelling was abated by your invisible healing hand, and the troubled and bedimmed sight of my mind was improved each day by the stinging ointment of health-producing sorrow. . . .

X

Being admonished in this way to return to myself, I was able, with you as my guide and helper, to enter into my most inward self. I entered, and with the eye of my soul (such as it was), I beheld the unchangeable light that was above the eye of my soul, above my mind. It was not ordinary light, which all flesh may see, nor was it a greater light of the same kind whose brightness had been magnified so that it filled all space with its greatness. Your light was not like this; it differed absolutely from all such light. Nor was it above my soul, as oil is above water or heaven is above earth. It was above my soul, because it made me; and I was below it, because I was made by it. He who knows the truth, knows that light; and he who knows that light, knows eternity. Love knows it. O truth who is eternity, love who is truth, eternity who is love—you are my God! To you I sigh night and day. When I first knew you, you lifted me up so that I could see that there was something to see, and yet realize that I was not then ready to see it. And you shocked the weakness of my sight by radiating your beams of light upon me most strongly, and I trembled with love and awe. I then perceived myself to be far distanced from you, in the region of unlikeness; and it seemed as if I heard your voice from on high saying: "I am the food of grown men; grow, and you will feed upon me. And you will not transform me into you, like the food that your body eats, but you will be transformed into me."

And I learned that for iniquity you chasten man. Indeed, you made my soul waste away like a moth caught in a spider's web. And I asked, "Is truth therefore nothing, since it is not diffused through finite or infinite space?" And you cried to me from afar: "Yet verily, I AM who I AM." I heard this as one hears with one's heart, and this left no room for doubt. I would have found it easier to doubt my own existence than to doubt the existence of that truth, which is clearly seen and understood by those things which are made.

XI

And I contemplated the other things below you. I perceived that it is not the case that they absolutely are, nor is it the case that they absolutely are not. They are, because they come from you; but they are not, because they are not what you are. For that which absolutely is, is that which remains unchangeable. . . .

XII

And it became clear to me that corruptible things are good. If they were absolutely good, they could not be corrupted. Also, if they were not good at all they could not be corrupted, for there would be nothing in them that might corrupt. For corruption does injury, but injury only occurs if it diminishes goodness. Thus, either corruption does not injure, which is impossible, or (which is most certainly the case) everything that is corrupted is deprived of good. But if something were deprived of all good, it would cease to be. For if something existed that could no longer be corrupted, it would be in a better state than before, because it would be permanently incorruptible. And what is more preposterous than to affirm that something becomes better by losing all its good? Therefore, if things are deprived of all good, they will no longer be. Therefore, as long as something exists, it is good; and whatsoever is, is good. That evil, then, into whose origin I have been inquiring, is not any substance. For if it were a substance, it would be good. For either it would be an incorruptible substance and thus an absolute good, or it would be a corruptible substance which, unless it were good, could not be corrupted. Thus, I saw and clearly perceived that you made all things good, and that there is no substance that you did not make. But since you did not make all things equal, all things are good when viewed individually; but when viewed together, they are very good. For our God made all things very good.

XIII

For you evil does not exist at all. Indeed, not only for you, but also for your creation as a whole, because there is nothing outside of your creation that could break in and corrupt the order that you have created for it. But in the various parts of your creation, some things, because they conflict with other things, are taken to be evil. However, these same things are in harmony with other things, and everything is good when considered individually. . . .

Far be it from me to say, "These things should not be." For if I saw nothing but the parts that conflict with one another, I might indeed long for something better; but even for these I should still praise you. That you are to be praised is shown by all things—by the earth, dragons, and deeps; by fire, hail, snow, ice, and stormy wind, all of which fulfill your word; by mountains, hills, fruitful trees, and cedars; by beasts, cattle, creeping things, and flying fowls; by all people, princes, and judges of the earth; by young men and maidens, old men and young, all of whom praise your name. Moreover from the heavens, all these praise you, our God—your angels and all your hosts; the sun, moon, and all the stars and light; the Heaven of heavens, and the waters that are above the heavens.

Surveying all this, I no longer longed for individual things to be better, because I conceived of your creation as a whole. With a sounder judgment I now realized that while higher things are better than lower things, everything together is better than higher things alone. . . .

XVI

My own experience had shown me that there is nothing strange in the fact that bread, which is pleasant to a healthy palate, is loathsome to one distempered, and that light, which is offensive to sore eyes, is delightful to eyes that are healthy. Your justice displeases the wicked. They are even more displeased by the viper and worms, which you have created good to inhabit the inferior portions of your creation. In such places the wicked themselves are also well suited, to the extent that they are unlike you, although they become suited to higher places if they grow more like to you.

And I inquired what wickedness is. I discovered that it is not a substance. Rather, wickedness is a perversion of the will. It is a perversion whereby the will turns towards lower things and away from you, O God, who are the highest substance, thereby denying its own inner life and lusting greedily for external things.

XVII

And I marveled to find that at last I loved you, not a phantasm of you. Yet I was not stable in the enjoyment of my God. By your beauty, I was lifted up to you; but I was soon borne down from you by my own weight, sinking with sorrow into inferior things. This weight was my sexual habit. Yet there dwelled with me a remembrance of you; and I did not have the slightest doubt that you were the one to whom I should cleave, although my nature was not yet such as could cleave to you. For the body that is corruptible weighs down the soul, and our earthly habitation weighs down the mind that muses upon many things. . . .

I was now examining why I admired the beauty of celestial or terrestrial bodies, as well as on what grounds I was able to judge soundly on things mutable, pronouncing, "This ought to be thus, this not." In examining the source of my own judgments about these things, I found the unchangeable and genuine eternity of truth that transcends my constantly changing mind. And thus by degrees, I ascended from bodies to the soul, which perceives through the bodily senses. From there I ascended to the soul's inward faculty, to which the bodily senses represent external things, this being the limit beyond which the faculties of beasts cannot reach. Then again I ascended to the reasoning faculty, which has the power to judge what is referred to it by the senses of the body. This faculty, realizing that it was itself mutable, raised itself up to its own understanding, thereby drawing my thoughts away from the power of habit. In this manner it was able to withdraw itself from those legions of contradictory phantasms, so that it might find the light that suffused it. At this point, without hesitation, it cried out, "The unchangeable is to be preferred to the changeable." At this moment it also knew that unchangeable, for unless it had known the unchangeable in some way, it would have had no sure ground by which to prefer the unchangeable to the changeable. And thus with the flash of one trembling glance, it arrived at That Which Is. Then I saw your invisible things that are understood by the things that are made. But I did not possess the strength to keep my gaze fixed. Rather, because of my weakness, I returned to my old habits, carrying with me only a loving memory and a longing for something of which I had, as it were, caught the fragrance, but was not yet able to eat.

XVIII

I then searched for a way to obtain sufficient strength to enjoy you. But I did not find it until I embraced that mediator between God and men, the Man Christ Jesus, who is over all things. . . . He was calling unto me saying, "I am the way, the truth, and the life." He mixed with flesh the food that I was unable to eat, for "the Word was made flesh." Through him, your wisdom, whereby you created all things, can provide milk to nourish our infant souls.

Questions for Thought

1. Do you think Augustinus' description of the nature of God is accurate? If so, why? If not, how would you describe the nature of God?

2. Do you think that the existence of evil is problematic? If so, how would you attempt to resolve it?

3. Can you think of other people who have claimed to have religious visions? If so, how did their visions compare with or differ from Augustinus' vision?

4. Have you ever had a religious vision that compares, in any way, with Augustinus' vision?

5. Do you believe, as Augustinus does, that one can be lifted up into the presence of God? If so, how? If not, why not?

The Powers of the Bison and the Elk   2

BLACK ELK

Black Elk (1863–1950), a **Lakota** holy man, was born on the Little Powder River. His father, also known as Black Elk, fought against the U.S. forces that successfully usurped Native land after gold was discovered on it in the 1860s. Later his family joined Crazy Horse in his attempt to avoid reservation life, but they were eventually forced to move to the reservation. However, after Crazy Horse's murder by government soldiers, Black Elk's family and many others fled to Canada, where they joined Sitting Bull, Gall, and their followers, who had earlier avoided reservation life by fleeing across the border. Eventually, harsh winters and near starvation drove them back to the reservation in the United States.

Having experienced a series of visions beginning at age five, Black Elk gained a wide reputation as a healer. These visions, which he interpreted as the source of his healing power, allowed him not only to discover the remedies for illnesses but also to predict certain aspects of the future. In Paris, recovering from an illness he developed while traveling with Buffalo Bill's Wild West Show, Black Elk had a powerful vision of the suffering of his people. In 1890, not long after he had returned to his people, between 200 and 300 of them were massacred by government troops at Chankpe Opi Wakpala (Wounded Knee Creek) in South Dakota.

After having witnessed the frozen bodies of the massacred people, Black Elk settled on the Pine Ridge Reservation, where he died in 1950 at the age of eighty-seven. Eighteen years earlier, he had recounted the story of his life and the life of his people to John G. Neihardt. The resulting book, *Black Elk Speaks,* is a classic work of Native American spiritualism. A second book recording Black Elk's religious insights, *The Sacred Pipe: Black Elk's Account of the Seven Rites of the Oglala Sioux,* was published in 1953.

In "The Powers of the Bison and the Elk," which is taken from *Black Elk Speaks,* Black Elk describes two of the ceremonies that were performed to activate the healing powers of his great vision. Black Elk points out that these ceremonies were symbolic and that they were necessary to understand the meaning of his vision. As he says in two places, "[T]he power in the ceremony was in understanding what it meant; for nothing can live well except in a manner that is suited to the way the sacred Power of the World lives and moves." Black Elk also insists that it is the power of the "outer world," that is, spiritual power, that cures people and that he is only a medium through which this power passes.

Like the earlier selections from Benally and Ed (Eagle Man) McGaa, this selection gives us a glimpse into other aspects of Native American spirituality. While the ceremonies recognize the sacredness of the bison and the elk, other statements imply a belief in the sacredness of all life. The ceremonies also affirm the significance of the four directions, of the circle (especially as represented by the nation's hoop), and of the spiritual powers of both women and men.

Questions for Reading

1. What was the significance of Black Elk's vision for his life and beliefs?
2. Why was it important that Black Elk perform the bison and elk ceremonies? How did the bison ceremony compare with and differ from the elk ceremony?
3. Why was Black Elk reluctant to reveal the nature of his vision? Why did he finally decide to describe it?
4. What, according to Black Elk, was the source of his power? Under what conditions might he lose his power?
5. What is the significance of the circle or the hoop in this selection?

I THINK I HAVE TOLD YOU, BUT IF I HAVE NOT, you must have understood, that a man who has a vision is not able to use the power of it until after he has performed the vision on earth for the people to see. You remember that my great vision came to me when I was only nine years old, and you have seen that I was not much good for anything until after I had performed the horse dance near the mouth of the Tongue River during my eighteenth summer. And if the great fear had not come upon me, as it did, and forced me to do my duty, I might have been less good to the people than some man who had never dreamed at all, even with the memory of so great a vision in me. But the fear came, and if I had not obeyed it, I am sure it would have killed me in a little while.

It was even then only after the **heyoka** ceremony, in which I performed my dog vision, that I had the power to practice as a medicine man, curing sick people; and many I cured with the power that came through me. Of course it was not I who cured. It was the power from the outer world, and the visions and ceremonies had only made me like a hole through which the power could come to the two-leggeds. If I thought that I was doing it myself, the hole would close up and no power could come through. Then everything I could do would be foolish. There were other parts of my great vision that I still had to perform before I could use the power that was in those parts. If you think about my great vision again, you will remember how the red man turned into a bison and rolled, and that the people found the good red road after that. If you will read again what is written, you will see how it was.

To use the power of the bison, I had to perform that part of my vision for the people to see. It was during the summer of my first cure that this was done. I carried the pipe to Fox Belly, a wise and good old medicine man, and asked him to help me do this duty. He was glad to help me, but first I had to tell him how it was in that part of my vision. I did not tell him all my vision, only that part. I had never told any one all of it, and even until now nobody ever heard it all. Even my old friend, Standing Bear, and my son here have heard it now for the first time when I have told it to you. Of course there was very much in the vision that even I cannot tell when I try hard, because very much of it was not for words. But I have told what can be told.

It has made me very sad to do this at last, and I have lain awake at night worrying and wondering if I was doing right; for I know I have given away my power when I have given away my vision, and maybe I cannot live very long now. But I think I have done right to save the vision in this way, even though I may die sooner because I did it; for I know the meaning of the vision is wise and beautiful and good; and you can see that I am only a pitiful old man after all.

Well, I told Fox Belly all that he needed to know that he might help me. And when he had heard even so little, he said: "My boy, you had a great vision, and I can see that it is your duty to help the people walk the red road in a manner pleasing to the Powers."

This ceremony was not a long one, but it had great meaning, because it made a picture of the relation between the people and the bison, and the power was in the meaning.

First we made a sacred place like a bison wallow at the center of the nation's hoop, and there we set up the sacred tepee. Inside this we made the circle of the four quarters. Across the circle from south to north we painted a red road, and Fox Belly made little bison tracks all along on both sides of it, meaning that the people should walk there with the power and endurance of the bison, facing the great white cleansing wind of the world. Also, he placed at the north end of the road the cup of water, which is the gift of the west, so that the people, while leaning against the great wind with the endurance of bison, would be going toward the water of life.

I was painted red all over like the man of my vision before he turned into a bison. I wore bison horns, and on the left horn hung a piece of the day-break-star herb, which bears the four-rayed flower of understanding. On the left side of my body I wore a single eagle feather, which was for my people, hanging on the side of the bison and feeding there.

One Side had come over to help me in this ceremony too. He was painted red all over, and he carried the drum and the pipe, and wherever I went, he followed, as the people follow the bison. We stood inside the tepee at the south end of the good red road, and Fox Belly sang like this:

Revealing this, they walk.
A sacred herb—revealing it, they walk.
Revealing this, they walk.
The sacred life of bison—revealing it, they walk.
Revealing this, they walk.
A sacred eagle feather—revealing it, they walk.
Revealing them, they walk.
The eagle and the bison—like relatives they walk.

Then, after we had walked the red road, One Side and I went out of the tepee and the people flocked around us, and the sick came with scarlet offerings to be cured. We went all around among the people, acting like bison and making the sounds they make. Then we returned to the tepee, and there the people brought their little children to us, and to each I gave a little of the water of life from the wooden cup, that their feet might know the good red road that leads to health and happiness.

It is from understanding that power comes; and the power in the ceremony was in understanding what it meant; for nothing can live well except in a manner that is suited to the way the sacred Power of the World lives and moves.

After this, I went on curing sick people, and I was busy doing this. I was in doubt no longer. I felt like a man, and I could feel the power with me all the time.

It was during the next summer, when I was in my twentieth year (1883), that I performed the elk ceremony, as a duty to that part of my great vision. You will remember how the pipe and the bison were in the east and the elk in the south.

This ceremony of the elk was to represent the source of life and the mystery of growing.

I sent a pipe to Running Elk, who was Standing Bear's uncle and a good and wise old man. He came and was willing to help me. We set up a sacred tepee at the center as before. I had to use six elks and four virgins. The elks are of the south, but the power that they represented in my vision is nourished by the four quarters and from the sky and the earth; so there were six of them. The four virgins represented the life of the nation's hoop, which has four quarters; so there were four virgins. Running Elk chose two of the elks, and I, who stood between the Power of the World and the nation's hoop, chose the four others, for my duty was to the life of the hoop on earth. The six elk men wore complete elk hides on their backs and over their heads. Their limbs were painted black from the knee and elbow down, and yellow from there up; for the growing power is rooted in mystery like the night, and reaches lightward. Seeds sprout in the darkness of the ground before they know the summer and the day. In the night of the womb the spirit quickens into flesh. The four virgins wore scarlet dresses, and each had a single eagle feather in her braided hair; for out of the woman the people grows, and the eagle feather again was for the people as in the bison ceremony. The faces of the virgins were painted yellow, the color of the south, the source of life. One had a daybreak star in red upon her forehead. One had a crescent moon in blue, for the power of woman grows with the moon and comes and goes with it. One had the sun upon her forehead; and around the mouth and eyebrows of the fourth a big blue circle was painted to mean the nation's hoop. On the back of each of the elk men was painted the nation's hoop, for upon the backs of men the nation is carried, and in the center of each hoop hung a single eagle feather for the people. They had yellow masks upon their faces, for behind the woman's power of life is hidden the power of man. They all carried flowering sticks cut from the sacred rustling tree (the cottonwood) with leaves left at the top, and the sticks were painted red. The woman is the life of the flowering tree, but the man must feed and care for it. One of the virgins also carried the flowering stick, another carried the pipe which gives peace, a third bore the herb of healing and the fourth held the sacred hoop; for all these powers together are woman's power.

Of course, before any of this was done, those who were to take part were purified in the sweat lodge as always.

We were all inside the sacred tepee, and Running Elk sang this song:

Advancing to the quarters,
Advancing to the quarters,
They are coming to behold you.
Advancing to the quarters,
Advancing to the quarters,
They are coming to behold you.

Then the elk men all made the elk sound, *unh, unh, unh.* Running Elk then sang again:

Singing, I send a voice as I walk.
Singing, I send a voice as I walk.
A sacred hoop I wear as I walk.

It was time now to come out of the sacred tepee: first came the virgin with the pipe; next she who bore the flowering stick, then the one who held the herb; and last, the bearer of the nation's hoop. The four virgins stood abreast, facing the west. Then we six elk men came out, snorting and stamping our feet. We stopped abreast, behind the virgins, who now held up the sacred things they carried, offering them to the thunder beings. When they had done this, they walked abreast to the north, while we elk men danced around them in a circle, and there they offered their sacred objects to the great white cleansing wind. In the same way we went to the east and to the south, the virgins making the offering at each place, and we elk men dancing around them in a circle all the while.

From the south, the four virgins turned straight north, following the good red road to the center of the village where the sacred tepee stood, and we elk men followed, dancing around them, for the power of the man encircles and protects the power of the woman.

The four maidens entered the tepee: first, she with the sacred hoop; then she who bore the flowering stick; next, the one who held the cleansing herb; and after her, the bearer of the pipe.

When they had all entered, we elk men followed into the tepee.

This was the ceremony, and as I said before, the power of it was in the understanding of its meaning; for nothing can live well except in a manner suited to the way the Power of the World lives and moves to do its work.

Questions for Thought

1. Have you ever had what you considered to be a spiritual vision or dream? If so, what significance did it have for you?
2. How do the religious ceremonies of Black Elk compare with or differ from other religious ceremonies with which you are familiar?
3. What do you think Black Elk means by the "power of the outer world"? Do you think that it is possible for people to be cured by this power? Why or why not?
4. What does the term *heyoka* mean? (Hint: You can find a definition in the glossary.) Can you think of heyoka-like figures in other religions?
5. In what ways was Black Elk's vision like the vision of Augustinus? In what ways was it different?

Whether God Exists   3

THOMAS AQUINAS

Thomas Aquinas (1225–1274), an Italian Dominican theologian, was born in the family castle of Roccasecca, located midway between Rome and Naples. After spending his first five years at the castle, Aquinas, as was customary at the time for the youngest son of a prominent family, was given into the care of monks in the hopes that he himself would pursue the monastic life. He lived and studied at the Benedictine abbey of Monte Cassino until 1239, when he was sent to Naples to study at the university there. While at the university, Thomas was introduced to the works of Aristotle and attracted to the Dominicans, an order of priests that had been confirmed by Pope Honorarius III in 1216. After he joined the Dominican order in 1244, he was sent to Rome and then to Paris.

When Aquinas's mother learned that he had joined a mendicant order, she sent her eldest son to bring him home, by force if necessary. His brother captured him and took him to one of the family castles. However, after several attempts to persuade Aquinas to renounce the order failed (including hiring a prostitute to attempt to seduce him), he was released. He rejoined the Dominicans in Naples before returning to Paris.

While in Paris, Aquinas studied philosophy and theology before moving to Cologne in 1248 to study with Albert the Great. He returned to Paris in 1252, where he completed advanced theological training and began teaching at the University of Paris. Beginning in 1259, Aquinas spent several years teaching and working in a number of Dominican monasteries near Rome. Returning again to Paris in 1268, he resumed his teaching at the University of Paris, where he remained until he was called back to Italy in 1272. He taught and preached in Naples until the end of 1273, when poor health forced his retirement. On a journey to attend a Church council during the first part of 1274, Aquinas's poor health was exacerbated when he suffered a head injury during the trip. In March 1274, he died in the monastery at Fossanova, which was situated near the castle in which he was born.

Aquinas was a prolific writer and defender of the Catholic Church who, since 1567, has been considered one of the doctors, or officially sanctioned theologians, of the Church. Some of his better-known works include *De Ente et Essentia* (1253; *On Being and Essence*), *De Principiis Naturae* (1253), *Quaestiones Disputatae de Veritate* (1256–1259; translated as *Truth*), *Summa de Veritate Catholicae Fidei Contra Gentiles* (1259–1264; translated as *On the Truth of the Catholic Faith*), *Quaestiones Disputatae de Potentia Dei* (1265; translated as *On the Power of God*), *De Regno* (1265–1266; *On Kingship*), *Compendium Theologiae* (1265–1269; *Compendium of Theology*), *Summa Theologiae* (1265–1273; *The Summa Theologica*), *Quaestiones Disputatae de Spiritualibus Creaturis* (1267; translated as *On Spiritual Creatures*), *Quaestiones Disputata de Anima* (1269; translated as *The Soul*), *Quaestiones Disputatae de Virtutibus* (1269–1272; translated as *The Virtues in General*), *De Unitate Intellectus* (1270; *The Unicity of the Intellect*), *De Substantiis Separatis* (1271; *Treatise on Separate Substances*), and *De Aeternitate Mundi* (1271; *On the Eternity of the World*).

In the following selection from his massive *Summa Theologica* (the English translation fills twenty-two volumes), Aquinas attempts to defend certain religious beliefs by means of rational argumentation. While Aquinas admits elsewhere that some religious beliefs, such as the Catholic doctrine of the Trinity, cannot be based on reason—he accepts the doctrine on the basis of revelation instead—he does believe that most religious beliefs can be rationally defended. In this excerpt, he attempts to refute two arguments that attempt to prove the nonexistence of God while providing five arguments offering proof that God exists.

The first **premise** in each argument for God's existence makes a claim about something that is found in the natural world. In the first argument, the claim is that motion, that is, movement or change from potentiality to actuality, exists. The second argument begins with the observation that efficient causality exists, while the third begins with the recognition that some things in the universe have possible existence (i.e., they come to be and pass away) and that others have necessary existence. In the fourth argument, the first premise is that there are gradations of being (e.g., hot, hotter, hottest), while the fifth argument starts with the claim that all natural beings act with purpose and not by chance.

Aquinas rationally examines each of these premises, and in each case his line of reasoning leads to the postulation of the existence of God. For example, in the first argument, he says that every change from potentiality to actuality must be produced by something that already possesses the actuality that is to be produced. In other words, a thing cannot change itself; it must be changed by something else. In searching for the initial cause of the movement from potentiality to actuality, we may be led backward through a series of intermediate causes. However, Aquinas argues that this series cannot go on to infinity and that we must ultimately arrive at a first unmoved cause that puts everything else into motion. This first unmoved cause is God. As should be obvious, this argument (and each of the others that follow it) exhibits a level of rational abstraction that is far removed from the type of religious experience that Black Elk describes in the preceding selection.

Questions for Reading

1. What are the basic assumptions in the two arguments that call into question God's existence?
2. How does Aquinas respond to these two arguments?
3. What is the logical structure of Aquinas' first way of proving the existence of God? In what respect does his second way differ from his first way?
4. What, if anything, does Aquinas' third way of proving God's existence have in common with his fourth way?
5. Why does Aquinas believe that all natural bodies act for some purpose? How does he use this assumption to prove the existence of God?

OBJECTION 1. It has been argued that God does not exist on the following grounds. If one of a pair of contraries were infinite, the other would be altogether destroyed. But the word "God" means that He is infinite goodness. If, therefore, God existed, there could be no evil. But there is evil in the world. Therefore God does not exist.

Objection 2. It has been further argued that it is superfluous to suppose that what can be accounted for by a few principles has been produced by many. But it seems that everything that appears in the world can be accounted for by other principles, even if God did not exist. For all natural things can be reduced to one principle, namely, nature or natural causes, while all things that happen intentionally can be reduced to another principle, namely, human reason or will. Therefore there is no need to suppose God's existence. . . .

This is the editor's revised version of a selection from Saint Thomas Aquinas, Summa Theologica, *translated by the Fathers of Dominican Province, New York: Benziger Brothers, 1911.*

To such objections I answer that: The existence of God can be proved in five ways.

The first and more manifest way is the argument from motion.[1] It is certain and evident to our senses that some things are in motion. Whatever is in motion is moved by something else. For nothing can be in motion unless it has a potentiality for that towards which it is being moved, whereas a thing moves inasmuch as it is in act. By "motion" we mean nothing else than the change of something from a state of potentiality into a state of actuality. But nothing can be changed from potentiality to actuality, except by something already in a state of actuality. For example, fire, which is actually hot, makes wood, which is potentially hot, to be actually hot. Thereby fire moves and changes wood from potentiality to actuality. Yet, it is not possible that the same thing at the same moment should be in a state of actuality and potentiality from the same point of view, but only from different points of view. What is actually hot cannot simultaneously be potentially hot; still, it is simultaneously potentially cold. It is therefore impossible that, from the same point of view and in the same way, anything should be both moved and mover, that is, that it should move itself. Therefore, whatever is in motion must be put in motion by something else. If that by which it is put in motion were itself put in motion, then this also must have been put in motion by something else, and that by something else again. This cannot go on to infinity. For if it did, there would be no first mover, and, consequently, no other mover—seeing that subsequent movers only move inasmuch as they are put in motion by the first mover; as the staff only moves because it is put in motion by the hand. Therefore it is necessary to arrive at a First Mover, put in motion by no other. Everyone understands that this First Mover is God.

The second way is from the nature of efficient causation. In the world of sensible things we find that there is an order of efficient causality. There is no case known (neither is it, indeed, possible) in which a thing is found to be the **efficient cause** of itself. For if it were the efficient cause of itself, it would be prior to itself, which is impossible. Now in tracing the chain of efficient causes, one cannot go on to infinity. For in all such chains of efficient causality, the first is the cause of the intermediate cause, and the intermediate is the cause of the ultimate cause or effect, whether the intermediate causes are several, or only one. To take away the cause is to take away the effect. Therefore, if there were no first cause among efficient causes, there would be neither intermediate cause nor ultimate cause. But if it were possible to go on to infinity in the chain of efficient causes, there would be no first efficient causes, no intermediate efficient causes, no ultimate effects—all of which is plainly false. Therefore it is necessary to put forward a First Efficient Cause, to which everyone gives the name of God.

The third way, which is taken from possibility and necessity, runs thus. We find in nature things that may possibly either exist or not exist, since they are found to be generated and then to be corrupted. Consequently, they can come into being and then cease to exist. It is impossible for these things to always exist, for that which can someday cease to exist must at some time have not existed. Therefore, if everything could cease to exist, then at one time there could have been nothing in existence. If this were true, even now there would be nothing in existence, because that which does not exist begins to exist only by means of something already existing. Therefore, if at one time nothing existed, it would have been impossible for anything to have begun to exist, and even now nothing would be in existence—which is absurd. Therefore, not all beings are merely possible; there must exist something the existence of which is necessary. Every necessary thing either has its necessity caused by something else or it does not. It is impossible to go on to infinity in necessary things which have their necessity caused by something else, as has been already proved in regard to efficient causes. Therefore we cannot but postulate the existence of some being having of itself its own necessity, a being that does not receive its necessity from something else, but rather causes in others their necessity. This all men speak of as God.

The fourth way is taken from the gradation to be found in things. Among beings there are some more and some less good, true, noble, and the like. But "more" and "less" are predicated of particular things, insofar as they resemble in their different ways something that is in the degree of "most." For example, a thing is said to become hotter when it more nearly resembles that which is hottest. Since this is the case, there must be something that is truest, something that is best, something that is noblest, and, ultimately, something that is uttermost being. For the truer things are, the more truly they exist. What is most complete in any genus is the cause of everything in that genus. For instance, fire, which is the most complete form of heat, is the cause whereby all things are made hot. Therefore there must also be something that is to all beings the cause of their being, goodness, and every other perfection; and this we call God.

The fifth way is taken from the governance of the world. We see that things that lack intelligence, such as natural bodies, act for some purpose. This fact is evident from their acting always, or nearly always, in the same way, so as to obtain the best result. Hence it is plain that it is not by chance that they achieve their purpose, but rather by design. Whatever lacks intelligence cannot fulfill some purpose, unless it is directed by some being endowed with intelligence and knowledge—as an archer shoots an arrow to its mark. Therefore some intelligent being exists by whom all natural things are directed towards a definite purpose; and this being we call God.

Reply to Objection 1. As Augustine says: *Since God is wholly good, He would not allow any evil to exist in His works, unless His omnipotence and goodness were such as to bring good even out of evil.* This is part of the infinite goodness of God, that He should allow evil to exist, only to produce good out of it.

Reply to Objection 2. Since nature works out its determinate end under the direction of a higher agent, whatever is done by nature must be traced back to God as to its first cause. In a like manner, whatever is done designedly must also be traced back to some higher cause other than human reason or will. For these can suffer change and are defective, and things that are capable of change and of defect must be traced back to an immovable and self-necessary first principle.

NOTE

1. In this selection, Aquinas follows Aristotle in using the term "motion" to signify the movement or change from potentiality to actuality, not from one place to another. An example of motion in this sense is the movement or change that occurs when an acorn, which is potentially an oak tree, actually becomes an oak tree. Movement from one place to another, which we might call "locomotion" in order to avoid confusion, is produced by efficient causality, which is discussed in the second way of proving God's existence.—ED.

Questions for Thought

1. Of the two attempts to prove that God does not exist, which one do you find more convincing, and why? Can you think of other arguments that might prove God's nonexistence?

2. In several of his ways of proving God's existence, Aquinas says that "one cannot go back to infinity." What exactly does Aquinas mean by this? Why does he think that this statement is true?

3. On the basis of the several conclusions that he draws in his five ways of proving the existence of God, how would you describe Aquinas' conception of God? How does Aquinas' conception of God or deity compare with or differ from your own?

4. Why does Aquinas believe that the actions of natural bodies can be categorized as purposeful? Do you agree with him on this point? Why or why not?

5. What are the essential differences between Aquinas' views on the nature of religious belief and the views of Black Elk? Can you think of any point on which the two would agree?

A Panegyric upon Abraham   **4**

SØREN KIERKEGAARD

Søren Kierkegaard (1813–1855), the youngest child of a successful wool merchant, was born in Copenhagen, Denmark. His father was fifty-six when Kierkegaard was born, and, having retired from business, he provided much of his son's early education, which included a decidedly pietist element. However, after briefly attending the University of Copenhagen, Kierkegaard rebelled against his strict upbringing by leading a life of debauchery for several years. Then, at age twenty-five, three months before his father's death, Kierkegaard experienced a religious conversion and was reconciled with his father.

This change of lifestyle led Kierkegaard back to the University of Copenhagen, where he completed his studies in 1841. That same year, he became a Lutheran pastor and preached his first sermon. He also broke off his engagement with Regina Olsen, the daughter of a treasury official, to whom he had proposed marriage the preceding year. Later realizing that he was as unsuited for the ministry as he was for marriage, Kierkegaard withdrew from the church and devoted his time to writing.

For the rest of his life, Kierkegaard wrote prolifically, often using pseudonyms to represent conflicting philosophical perspectives. In his writings, he became a staunch critic of both modern culture and the Lutheran Church and a defender of the solitary, authentic individual. Although he withdrew from society for the most part, he did become involved in two public disputes. In the first dispute, he attacked a popular Copenhagen satirical paper, *The Corsair,* for its poor journalistic standards. As a result, Kierkegaard became one of its favorite targets. In his second dispute, he wrote a series of bitter attacks against the Lutheran Church for its willingness to compromise Christian beliefs with state power. This latter dispute led Kierkegaard to refuse the Church sacrament as he lay on his deathbed. He died on November 11, 1855, a month after suddenly falling ill from a spinal disease.

Kierkegaard's important works include *Enten-Eller* (1843; *Either/Or*), *Gentagelsen* (1843; *Repetition*), *Frygt og Baeven* (1843; *Fear and Trembling*), *Begrebet Angest* (1844; *The Concept of Dread*), *Filosofiske Smuler eller en Smule Filosofi* (1844; translated as *Philosophical Fragments*), *Stadier paa Livets Vej* (1845; *Stages on Life's Way*), *Afsluttende uvidenskabeligt Efterskrift til de filosofiske Smuler* (1846; translated as *Concluding Unscientific Postscript*), and *Sygdommen til Døden* (1849; *The Sickness Unto Death*). His *Journals,* which were published posthumously, have also influenced later writers.

In the following excerpt from *Fear and Trembling,* Kierkegaard portrays the ancient Jewish patriarch Abraham as the ideal religious hero. While admitting that other types of heroism exist, Kierkegaard says that Abraham's greatness lay in the fact that he loved God more than he loved himself or other human beings and that he expected the impossible, never doubting God, even when God commanded him to sacrifice his only son, Isaac.

For Kierkegaard, as should be obvious from his description of Abraham, faith is the only path to religious belief. Kierkegaard praises Abraham for leaving "his earthly understanding behind," for believing in God's promises even when there was overwhelming evidence that

God was not going to fulfill them. Never having second thoughts, never attempting to plead with God to change His mind, Abraham's unwavering faith ultimately led him to the altar where he was fully prepared to carry out God's command to kill his son.

In other writings, Kierkegaard expands on these claims. He argues that reason can never produce religious belief and that Christianity, the religion that he considers most satisfying, makes no logical sense. Indeed, Kierkegaard claims that Christianity is based on a **paradox,** that of God becoming man. Since Kierkegaard, like most Western philosophers, believes that God and humanity are mutually exclusive categories, he says that we cannot rationally understand how one being can be God and man at the same time. However, rather than rejecting Christianity because it cannot be rationally understood or explained, Kierkegaard embraces Christianity on the basis of a "leap of faith."

Questions for Reading

1. At the beginning of this selection, Kierkegaard claims that if there were "no eternal consciousness in man," life would be nothing but despair. What exactly does Kierkegaard mean by this statement?
2. What, according to Kierkegaard, are the basic types of heroism? Why does he believe that Abraham represents the highest type?
3. What does Kierkegaard say about the nature of youth? Why does he believe that although Abraham lived for 130 years, he never became old?
4. Why, according to Kierkegaard, did God command Abraham to kill Isaac? How did Abraham respond to this command?
5. How is the concept of faith understood in this selection?

IF THERE WERE NO ETERNAL CONSCIOUSNESS in a man, if at the foundation of all there lay only a wildly seething power which writhing with obscure passions produced everything that is great and everything that is insignificant, if a bottomless void never satiated lay hidden beneath all—what then would life be but despair? If such were the case, if there were no sacred bond which united mankind, if one generation arose after another like the leafage in the forest, if the one generation replaced the other like the song of birds in the forest, if the human race passed through the world as the ship goes through the sea, like the wind through the desert, a thoughtless and fruitless activity, if an eternal oblivion were always lurking hungrily for its prey and there was no power strong enough to wrest it from its maw— how empty then and comfortless life would be! But therefore it is not thus, but as God created man and woman, so too He fashioned the hero and the poet or orator. The poet cannot do what that other does, he can only admire, love and rejoice in the hero. Yet he too is happy, and not less so, for the hero is as it were his better nature, with which he is in love, rejoicing in the fact that this after all is not himself, that his love can be admiration. He is the genius of recollection, can do nothing except call to mind what has been done, do nothing but admire what has been done; he contributes nothing of his own, but is jealous of the entrusted treasure. He follows the option of his heart, but when he has found what he sought, he wanders before every man's door with his song and with his oration, that all may admire the hero as he does, be proud of the hero as he is. This is his achievement, his humble work; this is his faithful service in the house of the hero. If he thus remains true to his love, he strives day and night against the cunning of oblivion which would trick him out of his hero, then he has completed his work, then he is gathered to the hero, who has loved him just as faithfully, for the poet is as it were the hero's better nature, powerless it may be as a memory is, but also transfigured as a memory is. Hence no one shall be forgotten who was great, and though time tarries long, though a cloud of misunderstanding takes the hero away, his lover comes nevertheless, and the longer the time that has passed, the more faithfully will he cling to him.

No, not one shall be forgotten who was great in the world. But each was great in his own way, and each in proportion to the greatness of that which he *loved*. For he who loved himself became great by himself, and he who loved other men became great by his selfless devotion, but he who loved God became greater than all. Everyone shall be remembered, but each became great in proportion to his *expectation*. One became great by expecting the possible, another by expecting the eternal, but he who expected the impossible became greater than all. Everyone shall be remembered, but each was great in proportion to the greatness of that with which he *strove*. For he who strove with the world became great by overcoming the world, and he who strove with himself became great by overcoming himself, but he who strove with God became greater than all. So there was strife in the world, man against man, one against a thousand, but he who strove with God was greater than all. So there was strife upon earth: there was one who overcame all by his power, and there was one who overcame God by his impotence. There was one who relied upon himself and gained all, there was one who secure in his strength sacrificed all, but he who believed God was greater than all. There was one who was great by reason of his power, and one who was great by reason of his wisdom, and one who was great by reason of his hope, and one who was great by reason of his love; but Abraham was greater than all, great by reason of his power whose strength is impotence, great by reason of his wisdom whose secret is foolishness, great by reason of his hope whose form is madness, great by reason of the love which is hatred of oneself.

By faith Abraham went out from the land of his fathers and became a sojourner in the land of promise. He left one thing behind, took one thing with him: he left his earthly understanding behind and took faith with him—otherwise he would not have wandered forth but would have thought this unreasonable. By faith he was a stranger in the land of promise, and there was nothing to recall what was dear to him, but by its novelty everything tempted his soul to melancholy yearning—and yet he was God's select, in whom the Lord was well pleased! Yea, if he had been disowned, cast off from God's grace, he could have comprehended it better; but now it was like a mockery of him and of his faith. There was in the world one too who lived in banishment[1] from the fatherland he loved. He is not forgotten, nor his Lamentations when he sorrowfully sought and found what he had lost. There is no song of Lamentations by Abraham. It is human to lament, human to weep with them that weep, but it is greater to believe, more blessed to contemplate the believer.

By faith Abraham received the promise that in his seed all races of the world would be blessed. Time passed, the possibility was there, Abraham believed; time passed, it became unreasonable, Abraham believed. There was in the world one who had an expectation, time passed, the evening drew nigh, he was not paltry enough to have forgotten his expectation, therefore he too shall not be forgotten. Then he sorrowed, and sorrow did not deceive him as life had done, it did for him all it could, in the sweetness of sorrow he possessed his delusive expectation. It is human to sorrow, human to sorrow with them that sorrow, but it is greater to believe, more blessed to contemplate the believer. There is no song of Lamentations by Abraham. He did not mournfully count the days while time passed, he did not look at Sarah with a suspicious glance, wondering whether she were growing old, he did not arrest the course of the sun, that Sarah might not grow old, and his expectation with her. He did not sing lullingly before Sarah his mournful lay. Abraham became old, Sarah became a laughing-stock in the land, and yet he was God's elect and inheritor of the promise that in his seed all the races of the world would be blessed. So were it not better if he had not been God's elect? What is it to be God's elect? It is to be denied in youth the wishes of youth, so as with great pains to get them fulfilled in old age. But Abraham believed and held fast the expectation. If Abraham had wavered, he would have given it up. If he had said to God, "Then perhaps it is not after all Thy will that it should come to pass, so I will give up the wish. It was my only wish, it was my bliss. My soul is sincere, I hide no secret malice because

Thou didst deny it to me"—he would not have been forgotten, he would have saved many by his example, yet he would not be the father of faith. For it is great to give up one's wish, but it is greater to hold it fast after having given it up, it is great to grasp the eternal, but it is greater to hold fast to the temporal after having given it up.

Then came the fullness of time. If Abraham had not believed, Sarah surely would have been dead of sorrow, and Abraham, dulled by grief, would not have understood the fulfillment but would have smiled at it as at a dream of youth. But Abraham believed, therefore he was young; for he who always hopes for the best becomes old, and he who is always prepared for the worst grows old early, but he who believes preserves an eternal youth. Praise therefore to that story! For Sarah, though stricken in years, was young enough to desire the pleasure of motherhood, and Abraham, though gray-haired, was young enough to wish to be a father. In an outward respect the marvel consists in the fact that it came to pass according to their expectation, in a deeper sense the miracle of faith consists in the fact that Abraham and Sarah were young enough to wish, and that faith had preserved their wish and therewith their youth. He accepted the fulfillment of the promise, he accepted it by faith, and it came to pass according to the promise and according to his faith—for Moses smote the rock with his rod, but he did not believe.

Then there was joy in Abraham's house, when Sarah became a bride on the day of their golden wedding.

But it was not to remain thus. Still once more Abraham was to be tried. He had fought with that cunning power which invents everything, with that alert enemy which never slumbers, with that old man who outlives all things—he had fought with Time and preserved his faith. Now all the terror of the strife was concentrated in one instant. "And God tempted Abraham and said unto him, Take Isaac, thine only son, whom thou lovest, and get thee into the land of Moriah, and offer him there for a burnt offering upon the mountain which I will show thee."

So all was lost—more dreadfully than if it had never come to pass! So the Lord was only making sport of Abraham! He made miraculously the preposterous actual, and now in turn He would annihilate it. It was indeed foolishness, but Abraham did not laugh at it like Sarah when the promise was announced. All was lost! Seventy years of faithful expectation, the brief joy at the fulfillment of faith. Who then is he that plucks away the old man's staff, who is it that requires that he himself shall break it? Who is he that would make a man's gray hairs comfortless, who is it that requires that he himself shall do it? Is there no compassion for the venerable oldling, none for the innocent child? And yet Abraham was God's elect, and it was the Lord who imposed the trial. All would now be lost. The glorious memory to be preserved by the human race, the promise in Abraham's seed—this was only a whim, a fleeting thought which the Lord had had, which Abraham should now obliterate. That glorious treasure which was just as old as faith in Abraham's heart, many, many years older than Isaac, the fruit of Abraham's life, sanctified by prayers, matured in conflict—the blessing upon Abraham's lips, this fruit was now to be plucked prematurely and remain without significance. For what significance had it when Isaac was to be sacrificed? That sad and yet blissful hour when Abraham was to take leave of all that was dear to him, when yet once more he was to lift up his head, when his countenance would shine like that of the Lord, when he would concentrate his whole soul in a blessing which was potent to make Isaac blessed all his days—this time would not come! For he would indeed take leave of Isaac, but in such a way that he himself would remain behind; death would separate them, but in such a way that Isaac remained its prey. The old man would not be joyful in death as he laid his hands in blessing upon Isaac, but he would be weary of life as he laid violent hands upon Isaac. And it was God who tried him. Yea, woe, woe unto the messenger who had come before Abraham with such tidings! Who would have ventured to be the emissary of this sorrow? But it was God who tried Abraham.

Yet Abraham believed, and believed for this life. Yea, if his faith had been only for a future life, he surely would have cast everything away in order to hasten out of this world to which he did not belong. But Abraham's faith was not of this sort, if there be such a faith; for really this is not faith but the furthest possibility of faith which has a presentiment of its object at the extremest limit of the horizon, yet is separated from it by a yawning abyss within which despair carries on its game. But Abraham believed precisely for this life, that he was to grow old in the land, honored by the people, blessed in his generation, remembered forever in Isaac, his dearest thing in life, whom he embraced with a love for which it would be a poor expression to say that he loyally fulfilled the father's duty of loving the son, as indeed is evinced in the words of the summons, "the son whom thou lovest." Jacob had twelve sons, and one of them he loved; Abraham had only one, the son whom he loved.

Yet Abraham believed and did not doubt; he believed the preposterous. If Abraham had doubted —then he would have done something else, something glorious; for how could Abraham do anything but what is great and glorious! He would have marched up to Mount Moriah, he would have cleft the fire-wood, lit the pyre, drawn the knife—he would have cried out to God, "Despise not this sacrifice, it is not the best thing I possess, that I know well, for what is an old man in comparison with the child of promise; but it is the best I am able to give Thee. Let Isaac never come to know this, that he may console himself with his youth." He would have plunged the knife into his own breast. He would have been admired in the world, and his name would not have been forgotten; but it is one thing to be admired, and another to be the guiding star which saves the anguished.

But Abraham believed. He did not pray for himself, with the hope of moving the Lord—it was only when the righteous punishment was decreed upon Sodom and Gomorrha that Abraham came forward with his prayers.

We read in those holy books: "And God tempted Abraham, and said unto him, Abraham, Abraham, where art thou? And he said, Here am I." Thou to whom my speech is addressed, was such the case with thee? When afar off thou didst see the heavy dispensation of providence approaching thee, didst thou not say to the mountains, Fall on me, and to the hills, Cover me? Or if thou wast stronger, did not thy foot move slowly along the way, longing as it were for the old path? When a call was issued to thee, didst thou answer, or didst thou not answer perhaps in a low voice, whisperingly? Not so Abraham: joyfully, buoyantly, confidently, with a loud voice, he answered, "Here am I." We read further: "And Abraham rose early in the morning"—as

though it were to a festival, so he hastened, and early in the morning he had come to the place spoken of, to Mount Moriah. He said nothing to Sarah, nothing to Eleazar. Indeed who could understand him? Had not the temptation by its very nature exacted of him an oath of silence? He cleft the wood, he bound Isaac, he lit the pyre, he drew the knife. My hearer, there was many a father who believed that with his son he lost everything that was dearest to him in the world, that he was deprived of every hope for the future, but yet there was none that was the child of promise in the sense that Isaac was for Abraham. There was many a father who lost his child; but then it was God, it was the unalterable, the unsearchable will of the Almighty, it was His hand took the child. Not so with Abraham. For him was reserved a harder trial, and Isaac's fate was laid along with the knife in Abraham's hand. And there he stood, the old man, with his only hope! But he did not doubt, he did not look anxiously to the right or to the left, he did not challenge heaven with his prayers. He knew that it was God the Almighty who was trying him, he knew that it was the hardest sacrifice that could be required of him; but he knew also that no sacrifice was too hard when God required it—and he drew the knife.

Who gave strength to Abraham's arm? Who held his right hand up so that it did not fall limp at his side? He who gazes at this becomes paralyzed. Who gave strength to Abraham's soul, so that his eyes did not grow dim, so that he saw neither Isaac nor the ram? He who gazes at this becomes blind.—And yet rare enough perhaps is the man who becomes paralyzed and blind, still more rare one who worthily recounts what happened. We all know it—it was only a trial.

If Abraham when he stood upon Mount Moriah had doubted, if he had gazed about him irresolutely, if before he drew the knife he had by chance discovered the ram, if God had permitted him to offer it instead of Isaac—then he would have betaken himself home, everything would have been the same, he has Sarah, he retained Isaac, and yet how changed! For his retreat would have been a flight, his salvation an accident, his reward dishonor, his future perhaps perdition. Then he would have borne witness neither to his faith nor to God's grace, but would have testified only how dreadful it is to march out to Mount Moriah. Then Abraham would not have been forgotten, nor would Mount Moriah, this mountain would then be mentioned, not like Ararat where the Ark landed, but would be spoken of as a consternation, because it was here that Abraham doubted.

Venerable Father Abraham! In marching home from Mount Moriah thou hadst no need of a panegyric which might console thee for thy loss; for thou didst gain all and didst retain Isaac. Was it not so? Never again did the Lord take him from thee, but thou didst sit at table joyfully with him in thy tent, as thou dost in the beyond to all eternity. Venerable Father Abraham! Thousands of years have run their course since those days, but thou hast need of no tardy lover to snatch the memorial of thee from the power of oblivion, for every language calls thee to remembrance—and yet thou dost reward thy lover more gloriously than does any other; hereafter thou dost make him blessed in thy bosom; here thou dost enthral his eyes and his heart by the marvel of thy deed. Venerable Father

Abraham! Second Father of the human race! Thou who first wast sensible of and didst first bear witness to that prodigious passion which disdains the dreadful conflict with the rage of the elements and with the powers of creation in order to strive with God; thou who first didst know that highest passion, the holy, pure and humble expression of the divine madness which the pagans admired—forgive him who would speak in praise of thee, if he does not do it fittingly. He spoke humbly, as if it were the desire of his own heart, he spoke briefly, as it becomes him to do, but he will never forget that thou hadst need of a hundred years to obtain a son of old age against expectation, that thou didst have to draw the knife before retaining Isaac; he will never forget that in a hundred and thirty years thou didst not get further than to faith.

NOTE

1. It is evident from the sequel that Jeremiah is meant.—TRANS.

Questions for Thought

1. Do you agree with Kierkegaard's claim that if there were no eternal consciousness in man, life would be despair? Why or why not?
2. Why do you think God commanded Abraham to kill Isaac? Under what conditions, if any, would you be willing to kill your only child?
3. What do you think Kierkegaard means by "faith"? Do you agree with Kierkegaard that faith is necessary for religious belief? Do you think Black Elk would have agreed with this claim?
4. Can you think of any problems that might arise from basing religious belief on faith?
5. How do Kierkegaard's views on the nature of Christianity compare with or differ from Augustinus's views? How do they compare with or differ from Aquinas's views?

5   I and Thou

MARTIN BUBER

Martin Buber (1878–1965), Jewish philosopher and religious writer, was born in Vienna. Raised by his paternal grandparents, Buber spent his childhood in Lvov, Galicia. Later he studied philosophy and art history at the Universities of Vienna, Zurich, Leipzig, and Berlin before receiving his Ph.D. from Vienna in 1904. Prior to completing his doctorate, Buber had become very active in the newly founded Zionist movement, serving as editor of its official journal, *Die Welt,* from 1901 to 1904. He also helped start the Jüdischer Verlag publishing house in 1902. In 1916, Buber founded a monthly German Jewish journal, *Die Jude,* for which he served as editor until it folded in 1924. Thereafter, he became professor of Jewish philosophy and ethics at the University of Frankfurt. He was also active in the cultural life of the Jüdische Lehrhaus, an institute to provide free adult Jewish education, which he had co-founded with Franz Rosenzweig in 1920.

Fleeing Nazi ascendancy in Germany, Buber emigrated to Palestine in 1938, where he became a professor of social philosophy at the Hebrew University in Jerusalem. He also became a dominant leader in the Yihud movement, a small group of Jews who advocated Arab-Jewish cooperation and the establishment of a binational Arab-Jewish state. When the nation of Israel was created in 1948, however, he reluctantly endorsed its existence while nonetheless remaining sympathetic to the plight of the Arab peoples in the region.

Buber, who was married to the popular German author Paula Winkler, was a prolific writer and translator. He translated many Jewish tales into German, and he completed a German translation of the Hebrew Bible in 1962. In addition, he wrote many essays devoted to Jewish nationalism and Jewish religion. His best-known philosophical writings include *Ich und Du* (1923; *I and Thou*), *Die Frage an den Einzelnen* (1936; translated in a collection of his essays titled *Between Man and Man*), *Der Glaube der Propheten* (1950; *The Prophetic Faith*), and *Bilder von Gut und Bose* (1952; translated as *Good and Evil: Two Interpretations*). Buber died in Jerusalem in 1965.

In the following excerpt from *I and Thou,* Buber claims that there are two essential ways in which humans can exist in the world—in the attitude of "I-It" or in the attitude of "I-Thou." In the attitude of I-It, everything in the world is experienced as a thing that occupies space and time, as one thing bounded by other things. Moreover, since Buber believes that the I or self exists only in relation, taking its form from that to which it is related, he claims that in the I-It relation the self is experienced as an internal thing that does not differ in any essential respect from external things. Just as the world is fragmented into a collection of separate things, the self is experienced as a collection of mental states that lack totality. As Buber puts it, "The primary word *I-It* can never be spoken with the whole being."

While Buber believes that the attitude of I-It is necessary for continued human survival, he claims that it does not represent our most significant way of relating to the world. Indeed, the attitude of I-It is a one-way relation, a relation in which other beings are treated as a means for obtaining what we desire, a relation in which there is no possibility of discovering God. The attitude of I-Thou, on the other hand, represents a way of relating to the world in which there is mutual recognition between the self and that to which it is related. If I relate to another person as Thou, I no longer experience that person as one thing among others or as a bundle of qualities, but I meet him or her as a unique, all-consuming presence. As Buber says, "He is *Thou* and fills the heavens. . . . All else lives in *his* light." Moreover, in this attitude, I no longer experience myself as a collection of mental states, but I speak and act with my whole being. The relation of I-Thou is thus a direct meeting in which two beings mutually embrace each other with the totality of their being. Buber believes that it is through such relationships that one can discern the trace of the eternal Thou or God.

Having described the nature of the I-Thou attitude, Buber notes that there are three spheres in which relation can arise. We can establish a relation with nature, with other people, and with spiritual beings. While the I-Thou attitude can be realized to some extent in each of these spheres, Buber claims that it is in our life with other humans that it is most fully realized. For this reason, it is in our unique, authentic relationships with other people that we most fully discover the traces of the Eternal Thou or God. As Buber says, "The relation to humans is the authentic simile of the relation to God—in it truthful address receives truthful reply."

Questions for Reading

1. What does Buber mean by an *I-It* relation?
2. How does an *I-Thou* relation differ from an *I-It* relation? What does Buber mean when he says that "the primary word *I-Thou* can only be spoken with the whole being"?
3. What, according to Buber, are the three spheres in which relation can arise? Why does he believe that the *I-Thou* relation can be fully realized in only one of these spheres?
4. How does one's perception of the world change when one moves from an *I-It* relation to an *I-Thou* relation?
5. What claims does Buber make about the Eternal *Thou* or God in this selection?

TO MAN THE WORLD IS TWOFOLD, DEPENDING upon his twofold attitude.

The attitude of man is twofold, depending upon the twofold nature of the fundamental words that he can speak.

The fundamental words are not single words, but paired words.

The one fundamental word is the word-pair *I-Thou*.

The other fundamental word is the word-pair *I-It*; whereby without changing the fundamental word, *He* or *She* can be substituted for *It*.

Thus, the *I* of man is also twofold. For the *I* of the fundamental word *I-Thou* is not the same as the *I* of the fundamental word *I-It*.

Fundamental words do not predicate anything beyond themselves but, being spoken, they bring about a way of existing.

Fundamental words are spoken with one's being.

When *Thou* is spoken, the *I* of the word-pair *I-Thou* is spoken along with it. When *It* is spoken, the *I* of the word-pair *I-It* is spoken along with it.

The fundamental word *I-Thou* can only be spoken with one's whole being. The fundamental word *I-It* can never be spoken with one's whole being.

There is no *I* by itself, but only the *I* of the fundamental word *I-Thou* and the *I* of the fundamental word *I-It*.

When a man says *I*, he means one of these two. The *I* that he means is present when he says *I*. Also, when he says *Thou* or *It*, the *I* of one or the other of these fundamental words is present.

Being *I* and saying *I* are one and the same. When one says *I*, one of the fundamental words is also spoken. Whoever speaks a fundamental word enters into the word and takes a stand therein.

The life of human beings is not encompassed by transitive verbs alone.

It does not consist solely of activities that aim at an object. I observe something. I experience something. I imagine something. I desire something. I feel something. I think something. The life of

This is the editor's translation of selections from Ich und Du *by Martin Buber, Köln: Verlag Jakob Hegner, 1966.*

human beings does not consist solely of all this and of things like this.

All this and things like this establish the realm of *It*. But the realm of *Thou* has another ground.

When one speaks *Thou*, one has no thing as object. For where one thing is, another thing is; every *It* is bounded by another *It*. *It* exists, only when limited by another *It*. But when *Thou* is spoken, no thing exists. *Thou* has no bounds.

When one speaks *Thou*, one has no thing, one has nothing. But one enters into relation.

It is said that man *experiences* his world. What does this mean? Man experiences the surface of things and finds out about them. He gains knowledge, an experience, of their inner character. He learns what things are.

But it is not by experiences alone that man spends time in the world. Experiences bring him only into a world of *It*, a world consisting of *It* and *It* and *It*, of *He* and *He*, of *She* and *She*, and *It* again.

I experience something. If one adds "inner" experiences to "outer" experiences, nothing changes. . . . Inner things are just like outer things. Nothing but things and things!

I experience something. If one adds "hidden" experiences to "disclosed" experiences, nothing changes. One is so sure of one's wisdom, so sure that one has the key with which one can pry open a hidden compartment in things. Oh secrecy without secret, oh increase of information! It, it, it!

One who experiences has no part in the world. For the experience is "in him," and not between him and the world.

The world has no part in the experience. It lets itself be experienced, but it does not concern itself; for it does nothing to the experience, and nothing happens to it because of the experience.

As experience, the world belongs to the fundamental word *I-It*. The fundamental word *I-Thou* endows the world with relation.

There are three spheres in which the world of relation arises.

The first is our life with nature. There the relation pulsates in darkness, below the level of speech. Creatures stir among us, but they are incapable of coming to us; and our saying *Thou* to them adheres to the threshold of speech.

The second is our life with humans. There the relation is manifest and takes the form of speech. We can give and receive the *Thou*.

The third is our life with spiritual beings. There the relation is cloaked in clouds, but reveals itself; it is without speech, but begets speech. We hear no *Thou*, but still we feel called upon to answer—composing, thinking, acting. We speak the fundamental word with our being, without being able to say *Thou* with our mouth. But how are we permitted to include what lies outside speech into the world of the fundamental word?

In each sphere, in its own way, through each unfolding that is present to us, we glimpse the border of the eternal *Thou*. In each sphere, in its own way, we hear a whisper of the eternal *Thou*. In each *Thou* we address the eternal *Thou*. . . .

If I stand face to face with a human being as my *Thou*, saying the fundamental word *I-Thou* to him, he is not a thing among things; he does not exist as a thing.

Neither is this human being *He* or *She*, bounded by another *He* or *She*, a specific point within the network of space and time. Nor is he a character that one can experience or describe, or a loose bundle of attributes that can be labeled. Rather, without neighbor and seamless, he is Thou and fills the circle of heaven. It is not that nothing else exists other than him, but everything else lives in *his* light.

Just as the melody is not composed of the tones, or the verse of the words, or the statue of the lines—they must be torn and ruptured if their unity is to be shattered into such multiplicity—so it is with the man to whom I say *Thou*. I can extract from him the tint of his hair or his speech or his kindliness; indeed, I must continually do so. But when I do, he is no longer *Thou*. . . .

I do not find the man to whom I say *Thou* in a time and place. I can put him in a particular time and place—indeed I must continually do so—but when I do so, he is only a *He* or a *She*, i.e., an *It*, and no longer my *Thou*.

As long as the heaven of the *Thou* rests over me, the winds of causation cower at my heels, and the whirl of fate is stilled.

I do not experience the man to whom I say *Thou*. Rather, I stand in relation to him, in the sanctity of the fundamental word. Not until I step out of it, do I experience him again. Experience is far removed from *Thou*. . . .

—What, then, does one experience of *Thou*?
—Nothing even. For one does not *experience* it.
—What, then, does one know of *Thou*?
—Only everything. For one does not know anything singular about it.

I encounter the *Thou* by grace—I do not find it through searching. But saying the fundamental word to it is an act of my being, my essential nature.

The *Thou* meets me. But I step into immediate relation with it. Hence, the relation is choosing and being chosen, action and passion, rolled into one. . . .

The fundamental word *I-Thou* can only be spoken with the whole being. The amassing and merging of the whole being can never happen because of me nor can it happen without me. From the *Thou*, *I* become; by saying *Thou*, *I* become.

All real living is meeting.

The relation to the *Thou* is direct. No conceptual scheme, no previous knowledge, no fantasy, stands between *I* and *Thou*. Indeed, the memory itself is transformed as it rushes out of its singularity into wholeness. No purpose, no greed, no anticipation, stands between *I* and *Thou*. Indeed, longing itself is transformed as it rushes out of its dream into the appearance. Every means is a hindrance. Only when every means has disintegrated does the meeting commence. . . .

The world of *It* exists in the context of space and time. The world of *Thou* does not exist in the context of space and time.

After the events of the relational process have run their course, the particular *Thou must* become an *It*. Through entering into the relational process, a particular *It* may become a *Thou*.

These are the two basic privileges of the world of *It*. They move man to view the world of *It* as the world in which he has to live, and as the world in which it is comfortable to live. Indeed, they move

man to view the world of *It* as a world that puts forward all kinds of incentives, arousals, activities and perceptions. In this solid and conducive chronicle, the moments of the *Thou* appear as odd lyrical-dramatic episodes, seductive and magical to be sure, but pulling us to perilous extremes, unfastening the well-tried context, leaving behind more questions than contentment, shattering security—even alienating and gratuitous. Indeed, since one must return from these moments back to "the world," why not remain in it? Why not call to order that which stands across from us and send it "home" to the objective sphere? If at times one finds oneself about to say *Thou* to father, wife, or companion, why not say *Thou* and mean *It*? Indeed, producing the sound *Thou* with the vocal chords is by no means speaking the uncanny fundamental word; yes, even whispering an amorous *Thou* with the soul is harmless, as long as one means nothing more serious than to experience and to use.

One cannot live in the naked present. Life would be quickly consumed if precautions were not taken to overcome the present rapidly and thoroughly. However, one can live in the naked past; indeed, only in doing so can life be arranged. One needs only to fill each moment with experiencing and using, and the moment burns no longer.

And in all the gravity of truth, I say to you: without *It*, one cannot live. However, if one lives with *It* alone, one is not fully human. . . .

The prolonged lines of relations intersect in the eternal *Thou*.

Each particular *Thou* is a view through to the eternal *Thou*. Through each particular *Thou* the fundamental word speaks to the eternal *Thou*. . . . The aboriginal *Thou* is realized in each particular *Thou* but consummated in none. It is consummated solely in the immediate relation with the *Thou* which, by its essence, cannot become *It*. . . .

In the relation to God, there is unconditional exclusiveness and unconditional inclusiveness. One who steps into the absolute relation is no longer concerned with anything particular, neither things nor beings, neither the earth nor heaven; but everything is enclosed in the relation. For to step into the pure relation is not to put everything aside, but to see everything in the *Thou*; it is not to renounce the world, but to ground it. To look away from the world does not help one to God; to gaze at the world does not help one to God. But one who looks at the world in Him stands in His presence. "Here is the world; there is God"—this is the saying of *It*. "God is in the world"—that is another saying of *It*. However, to discard or leave behind nothing at all, to comprehend all the world in Him, gives the world its due and its truth; finding nothing next to God but everything in Him—that is the quintessential relation.

One does not find God if one remains in the world, one does not find God if one transcends the world. Rather, when one goes out to meet one's *Thou* with one's whole being, carrying to it all the being of the world, one finds Him for whom one cannot search. . . .

There are three spheres in which the world of relation is built.

The first is our life with nature, in which the relation adheres to the threshold of speech.

The second is our life with humans, in which the relation takes the form of speech.

The third is our life with spiritual beings, in which the relation is without speech, but begets speech.

In each sphere, in each act of relation, through each unfolding that is present to us, we glimpse the border of the eternal *Thou*. In each sphere, in its own way, we hear a whisper of the eternal *Thou*. In each *Thou* we address the eternal *Thou*. . . .

Of the three spheres there is one, our life with humans, that stands out. It is here that language is perfected, as a succession of speech and response. It is here alone that the word formed in language meets its reply. It is only here that the fundamental word goes out and comes back in the same form—the address and the reply speak with the same tongue. *I* and *Thou* stand not merely in relation, but also in firm "sincerity." The moments of relation are here, and only here, conjoined through the element of speech in which they are immersed. It is here that what faces us has blossomed into the full actuality of the *Thou*. Thus, it is here alone that, as inescapable actuality, there is gazing and being gazed upon, knowing and being known, loving and being loved. . . .

The relation to humans is the authentic simile of the relation to God—in it truthful address receives truthful reply.

Questions for Thought

1. Can you think of examples of interactions in your own life that could be labeled *I-It* interactions?
2. Do you think you have related to another human being on the *I-Thou* level? If so, how would you describe that relation?
3. What do you think Buber means when he says that an *I-Thou* relation can help us glimpse the eternal *Thou*? Do you think you have ever glimpsed the eternal *Thou*? If so, how would you describe what you encountered?
4. Under what conditions, if any, would you be justified in treating another person as an *It*? What are the implications of treating someone as an *It*?
5. Do you think Buber would agree with Kierkegaard's claim that faith is the basis of religious belief? Explain your response.

Involvement in the Liberation Process   6

GUSTAVO GUTIÉRREZ

Gustavo Gutiérrez (b. 1928), a priest and theologian who was born in Lima, Peru, is one of the leading proponents of liberation theology. After receiving his M.A. from the University of Louvain and his M.Th. from the Institut Catholique de Lyon, Gutiérrez became a professor of theology at the Universidad Catolica de Lima and the director of the Instituto Bartolome de la Casas. He also became parish priest in one of the poorest areas of Lima. His experiences while ministering to the needs of the people in Rimac, a slum area of Lima, led him to reexamine many of the presuppositions of his formal theological education. Gutiérrez, who holds honorary degrees from several universities, has been a principal professor at the Pontifical University of Peru, and a visiting professor at numerous universities in both North America and Europe.

Beginning with his *La pastoral de la iglesia de America Latina,* which was published in 1969, Gutiérrez has written prolifically in his attempt to reawaken and defend the Catholic Church's role in serving the poor and in resisting political and economic oppression. His writings include *Teología de la liberación prospectivos* (1971; translated as *A Theology of Liberation: History, Politics, and Salvation* [1973]), *Religión, instrumento de liberación?* (1973), *Praxis of Liberation and Christian Faith* (1974), *Teología desde el reverso de la historia* (1977), *La fuerza histórica de los pobres* (1983; translated as *The Power of the Poor in History*), *We Drink from Our Wells: The Spiritual Journey of a People* (1984), *Hablar de Dios desde el sufrimiento del inocente: Una reflexión sobre el libro de Job* (1986; translated as *On Job: God-Talk and the Suffering of the Innocent* [1987]), *The God of Life* (1991), and *Las Casas: In Search of the Poor of Jesus Christ* (1993). Some of his more important writings were collected in *Gustavo Gutiérrez: Essential Writings* (1996).

Gutiérrez, who has been described as a "priest in the great tradition of Tutu," was named a member of the Legion of Honor by the French government in 1993. He has taken his message on behalf of the poor to audiences in numerous countries, and he has been the recipient of more than a dozen honorary degrees.

In the following essay, which is taken from *The Power of the Poor in History,* Gutiérrez raises some of the same concerns about the contemporary Church that King does toward the end of "Letter from Birmingham Jail" (reprinted in the last chapter). Like King, Gutiérrez notes that the Church has traditionally been a force that upheld the status quo and obstructed the path of those who worked to eliminate injustice. However, whereas King only holds out hope that the revolutionary and liberating power of the gospel might find expression in the lives of some Christians, Gutiérrez argues that the Latin American Church itself is on the verge of affirming and living this revolutionary and liberating power.

In defending this new movement within the Latin American Church, Gutiérrez points to two important biblical themes as justification: the recurring claim that creation and salvation go hand in hand, and the promises of messianic peace that are found throughout the Bible. Gutiérrez argues that both of these themes are incompatible with the commonly held belief that the Church should minister only to spiritual needs and not to social and political needs. Rather, as he forcefully says, Christ's "salvific work embraces all dimensions of human existence." Thus, Gutiérrez believes that, in order to fulfill its true mission, the Church must align itself with the oppressed peoples who are suffering from "institutionalized violence" and actively work to create a world from which injustice and oppression have been eliminated. For Gutiérrez, faith or religious vision that is divorced from the struggle to help the poor and oppressed masses is misguided.

Questions for Reading

1. Why does Gutiérrez believe that the Latin American Church is in crisis?
2. What does Gutiérrez mean by "institutionalized violence"? What is his attitude toward violence in general?

3. Why does Gutiérrez believe that personal spiritual change or salvation is insufficient? Which gospel messages does he use to support this claim?
4. What suggestions does Gutiérrez make for transforming the Church?
5. How is the concept of liberation used in this selection?

INTRODUCTION

THE LATIN AMERICAN CHURCH IS IN CRISIS. Some may try to tone down this fact or offer various interpretations of it, but that does not change the essential fact. The reality is clear enough and it cannot be hidden away or talked out of existence. We must face up to it boldly if we do not want to live in an imaginary world.

The scope and seriousness of the situation is of enormous proportions. Long gone is the era when the church could handle questions and problems by appealing to its doctrines and distinctions. Today it is the church itself that is being called into question. It is being called into question by many Christians who experience in their daily lives the terrible distance that separates the church from its roots in the gospel and its lack of harmony with the real world of Latin America. It is also being called into question by many who are far away from it—many more than our traditional pastoral outlook is willing to admit— who see it as an obstructive force in the effort to construct a more just society. And now it is even being called into question by those who are associated with the existing "order," and who look with discomfort on the initiatives being undertaken by some dynamic segments in the church.[1]

So let us grant that the church is living through a time of crisis and a moment of judgment (which is what crisis means). The ecclesial community is confronted with "happenings" and with Christ, the Lord of history, through them. And we might well raise Cardinal Suhard's old question: Does all this represent *growth* or *decline* for the church in Latin America? To pose this question aright, we must adjust our theological perspective and spell out what we really mean by "growth" and "decline" when it comes to the church. But even if we do that, there is a danger that our anxiety-ridden question will drive us to focus on the dry bones of numerical statistics or to dull our disquiet in some new form of triumphalism.

There is every indication that the coming years will provide us with very different ways of viewing the church, that we shall view its presence in ways that are quite different from those that we have been accustomed to in the past or that we might formulate today. But for the present we are faced with a more modest task: to recognize and acknowledge the emergence of a new situation that is full of promise and uncertainty, and that is leading us to a new ecclesial awareness under the impulse of the Spirit.

At the opening of the second session of Vatican II, when the shadow of John XXIII still cast a bright glow over the church, Pope Paul VI spoke of the church's desire and duty of coming at last to a full understanding of its true nature.[2] And a year later he spoke once again of the need for the church to deepen its awareness of the mission it must carry out in the world. The council faced up to this task; and the church has continued to do this, often in unexpected ways, in the years following the end of the council. Going beyond the strict letter of its documents, the council opened up perspectives that have not ceased to provoke wondrous surprise, fear, or alarm—depending on one's point of view.

In line with this spirit, the church of Latin America has sought to find its place. Accustomed to being a docile link in the chain of Christianity, the Christian community of Latin America has nevertheless begun to show an awareness of itself, to examine its presence on this continent, and to raise its voice above a whisper. There has been no lack of opposition and misunderstanding from those who regard this as insubordination pure and simple.

The documents issuing from Medellín and groups of involved bishops, priests, religious, and lay persons bear witness to this new development. Even clearer witness is provided by the gestures, initiatives, crises, experiences, and ferment of ideas that lie behind these same documents, as well as by the specific commitments they have prompted.

The church in Latin America is particularly rich in problems. But that is not a wholly negative state of

From Gustavo Gutiérrez, The Power of the Poor in History, *Orbis Books, 1983. Reprinted by permission of Orbis Books.*

affairs. If it shows the required courage, the very gravity of the problems it faces may enable it to get quickly to the heart of the matter. It can slough off the atavistic encumbrances that have plagued its gospel message and its ecclesial structures. It can frankly ask itself the most essential questions: What does being Christian mean? How can the church truly be the church in the new circumstances that surround it?

In coming to this new ecclesial awareness, we can distinguish two vital aspects. Inseparable in practice, they may be studied separately for the sake of greater clarity. These two aspects are (1) our new understanding of the Latin American situation, and (2) the quest for new ways in which the people of God might exert its presence therein.

CONFRONTING THE REAL SITUATION OF LATIN AMERICA

The self-awareness of the Christian community is conditioned historically by the world of which it is a part, and by its way of viewing this world.

Moving Out of the Ghetto

We need not begin from scratch to work up our own private vision of reality. In the case of Latin America, which is what concerns us here, we must rather become really involved in the way that the people of Latin America see themselves and their course in history. Thus we must start by opening our ears and listening to them—which presupposes that we are willing to move out of our own narrow world.

From the past right up to today, the Christian community in Latin America has lived largely in its own ghetto world. Born at a time when the Catholic Church was leading a Counter-Reformation movement, the Latin American church has always been marked by an attitude of defense. This defensive posture has led it to engage in silent retreat on numerous occasions, to act as a quiet refuge for all those who felt fearful and in need of protection as they tried to follow God's lead. This posture was reinforced by the occasional attacks from liberal and anticlerical factions during the period that followed political independence in the last century. It was further reinforced by the harsh criticism of more recent social movements, which have sought

to introduce radical social change and which have regarded the church as an obstacle to such change.

All this led the church to solidify its ties with established authority, thus enjoying the latter's support and forming a common front against their presumed enemies. It also led it to create and maintain costly educational institutions, social services, and charitable works that were practically duplicates of those in the world around it. It was a futile, perhaps last-ditch effort to prolong an outdated brand of Christianity in a society that no longer evinced religious oneness and that had clearly and openly entered a period of ideological **pluralism.** The church thus became an easy and compliant prey for those who used it to protect their own selfish interests and the established order, in the name of the "Christian West."

Probing the Real Causes

Moving out of the ghetto is one aspect of a broader attitude: opening up to the world. It involves sharing, in a more positive and unreserved way, the vision that Latin Americans have of their situation. It also involves contributing in an effective way to the elaboration and development of this vision, and committing ourselves wholeheartedly to the activities it entails.

Recent years have been critical ones in this respect. We have come out of a long period when ignorance about the real Latin American situation prevailed, and we have also left behind the brief period when false optimism was promoted by vested interests. We are abandoning the sketchy and hazy views of the past for an overall, integrated understanding of our real situation.

The true face of Latin America is emerging in all its naked ugliness. It is not simply or primarily a question of low educational standards, a limited economy, an unsatisfactory legal system, or inadequate legal institutions. What we are faced with is a situation that takes no account of the dignity of human beings, or their most elemental needs, that does not provide for their biological survival, or their basic right to be free and autonomous. Poverty, injustice, alienation, and the exploitation of human beings by other human beings combine to form a situation that the Medellín conference did not hesitate to condemn as "institutionalized violence."[3]

This phrase might well seem strange in a pronouncement by the hierarchy.[4] But it should be emphasized that it is not something thrown in as an aside, for the whole Medellín document on peace is focused on this concept.[5] It is a commonplace for all experts on Latin America, and a reality that is known and experienced daily by most of those who live in Latin America. It is only within this real context that one can honestly raise the complex question of the moral rightness or wrongness of putting down violence. No double standard will do. We cannot say that violence is all right when the oppressor uses it to maintain or preserve "order," but wrong when the oppressed use it to overthrow this same "order."[6]

The most important change in our understanding of the Latin American situation, however, has to do with its deeper, underlying causes. These are now seen in the context of a broader historical process. It is becoming ever more clear that underdevelopment, in a total sense, is primarily due to economic, political, and cultural dependence on power centers that lie outside Latin America. The functioning of the capitalist economy leads simultaneously to the creation of greater wealth for the few and greater poverty for the many. Acting in complicity with these outside power centers, the **oligarchies** of each nation in Latin America operate through various mechanisms to maintain their dominion over the internal affairs of their own countries.

This new awareness of the Latin American situation shines through various documents in varying degrees of clarity. It finds authoritative and clear-cut expression in the Medellín document on peace, which forthrightly speaks of "internal colonialism" and "external neocolonialism."[7] In Latin America these are the ultimate causes of the violence that is committed against the most basic human rights.

Our new vision, attentive to structural factors, will help Christians to avoid the fallacy of proposing a personal change detached from concrete conditions, as a necessary prerequisite to any social transformation. If any of us remain wedded to this fallacy, in the name of some hazy **humanism** or disembodied spiritualism, we shall only prove to be accomplices in the continuing postponement of the radical changes that are necessary. Such changes call for simultaneous work on both persons and structures, for they condition each other mutually.

Involvement in the Liberation Process

When we characterize the Latin American situation as one of dependence and unfair domination, we are naturally led to talk about liberation, and to participate in the process that will lead to it. We are in fact dealing with a term that expresses the new stance adopted by Latin Americans, a stance that is gradually taking concrete shape in official documents. It is recapitulated forcefully in the Medellín conference and in the Thirty-Sixth Episcopal Assembly of Peru. Expressions such as "development" and "integration," with their attendant retinue of international alliances, agencies, and experts, are relegated to the shadows; for they involve a different vision of the Latin American situation.

But to stress the need for liberation presupposes far more than simply differences in our analyses of the situation. At a deeper level, it means that we see the ongoing development of humanity in a particular perspective, and in terms of a specific philosophy and theology of history. It means that we see it as a process of human emancipation, aiming toward a society where men and women are truly free from servitude, and where they are the active shapers of their own destiny. Such a process does not lead us simply to a radical transformation of structures—to a revolution. It goes much further, implying the perduring creation of a wholly new way for men and women to be human.

There is an urgent need for Christians to involve themselves in the work of liberating this oppressed continent, by establishing real solidarity with the oppressed persons who are the chief victims. The first step is for the church as a whole to break its many ties with the present order, ties that it has maintained overtly or covertly, wittingly or unwittingly, up to now. This will not be an easy task, for it will mean abandoning outworn traditions, suspicions, viewpoints, advantages, and privileges, as well as the forces of inertia. It will also mean accepting the fact that the future cast of the church will be radically different from the one we know today. It will mean incurring the wrath of the groups in power—with all the risks that entails. Above all, it will mean believing in the revolutionary and liberating power of the gospel—believing in the Lord—and authentic faith, a faith that goes beyond the mere recitation and acceptance of codified truths. This will not be easy. We know it, of course, and we have said it countless times. But perhaps we have not been sufficiently aware of the fears and vacillations of the vast majority of the Christian community in Latin America. Perhaps we have not realized how much they bore ironic witness to this truth.

One manifestation of our break with injustice and exploitation, which the present economic and social structures foist upon the vast majority of our people under the guise of law, should come from the bishops. They must turn to the oppressed, declaring their solidarity with them and their desire to join with them in their struggle. This is what they must do instead of what they have done in the past, when they turned to those in power and called for necessary reforms while implying that their own position need not be affected by such change.[8]

CREATING A NEW ECCLESIAL PRESENCE

At Vatican II the church affirmed a desire to render service. The concrete forms that this pledge takes must necessarily be based on the world in which the Christian community is present.

Present Inadequacies

A better awareness of the harsh realities in Latin America goes hand in hand with a clearer realization that the church's structures are inadequate for the world in which it lives. They show up as outdated and lacking in vitality when confronted with new questions, and in one way or another seem to be tied up with the unjust order we wish to eradicate. This fact is the chief source of the misunderstandings, frictions, crises, and desertions that we witness.

Those who want to shape their lives to the demands of the gospel find it increasingly difficult to accept vague, romantic appeals to "fellowship" and "Christian unity" that do not take account of the causes underlying the present state of affairs, or of the concrete conditions required for the construction of a just society. Such vague appeals forget that the catholicity, the universality, of the church is not something attained once for all time, or something to be maintained at any price. It must be won continuously, by courageous effort and open-eyed struggle. Wittingly or unwittingly, these appeals

seem designed to palliate the real tensions that do and should exist, and ultimately to maintain the status quo. The frank and decisive stands taken by the hierarchy and other sectors of the church in the last few years have been welcome breaths of fresh air. They will undoubtedly help to separate the wheat from the chaff. They will identify the real Christian among all those who call themselves Christians.

Vatican II proclaims that the church, like Christ, must carry out its work of redemption "in poverty and under oppression." But this is not the image presented by the Latin American church as a whole. Quite the contrary. Once upon a time we may not have been clearly aware of this, but that time is past. Today the church feels the sharp pangs of its tragic inconsistency; it is aware of its disloyalty to the gospel, its failure to confront the real situation in Latin America.

This has given rise to letters, declarations, new forms of commitment, and even "protest movements" in the church. All these things can easily become grist for the sensation-seeking media. But altogether apart from their transitory news value, their sometimes ambiguous doctrinal roots, and the misleading commentaries they provoke, they have a much deeper significance, and we must try to probe it. They betoken the concern many Christians have with the form that the church's presence in Latin America now takes. They reveal a hidden vitality, a spirit that refuses to be bound to the cold letter of the law. If we do not pay heed to the message they contain, we may one day find ourselves in an atmosphere of general indifference, longing wistfully for those "hotheads" who had used unconventional means to express their desire for change in the church and for fidelity to the gospel.

The most vital sectors of the people of God in Latin America are thus committed to a search for two things: (1) the theological bases that will ground their activity on a continent caught up in a process of liberation; and (2) new ecclesial structures that will allow them to live a true life of faith in accordance with Latin Americans' growing awareness of their own specific historical destiny.

A Theology of Human Liberation

We have suggested that an authentic presence in Latin America presupposes a concern on the part of the church for the specifically political dimensions of that presence. Would such a concern mean the church was falling prey to some sort of aberrant temporalism, and abandoning its spiritual mission? After all, this is what frightens many persons of good will (and ill will).

The gospel, these persons say, is first and foremost a message of eternal salvation; building the earth is a task for human beings on this earth. The first task belongs to the church, the second task belongs to temporal society. The most they will admit is that the church may lay down certain ethical dictates for the work of building civil society—so long as they do not openly question the interests of those who hold the reins of economic and political power.

But a closer look at reality, such as I have outlined above, has wrought a profound change in the life and outlook of the whole church. Although I cannot discuss the process in detail here, I can point out that the church has restored its ties with the Christian tradition of antiquity and has rediscovered that salvation embraces all humanity, and each individual. It will be worth our while to spell out briefly the theological notions that form the basis for this new outlook on the part of the church.

Concrete reflection on human existence has carried contemporary theology far beyond the scholastic and essentialist outlook that was based on distinguishing various orders and levels. At the same time that it was renewing its contact with its roots in the Bible, theology was moving toward the notion that humankind had but one vocation; or, to put it more exactly, that all human beings shared the same single vocation. Thus we do not have two juxtaposed histories, one sacred and the other profane. There is only one single process of human development, definitively and irreversibly assumed by Christ, the Lord of history. His salvific work embraces all the dimensions of human existence. Two major biblical themes clearly illustrate this viewpoint: the relationship between creation and salvation, and the messianic promises.

In the rather simplistic catechetics of the past, creation was presented as the explanation for the existing world. This is not incorrect, but it is incomplete. In the Bible, creation is not a stage prior to the work of salvation; it is the first salvific activity. "Before the world was made, he chose us in Christ" (Eph. 1:4). Creation is inserted in the salvation process, in God's self-communication. The religious experience of Israel is primarily history, but this history is simply the prolongation of God's creative activity. That is why the Psalms praise **Yahweh** simultaneously as Creator and Savior (see Ps. 136). The God who transformed chaos into cosmos is the same as the one who acts in salvation history. The redemptive work of Christ, in turn, is presented in the context of creation (see John 1). Creation and salvation have a christological import; in Christ all have been created and all have been saved (see Col. 1:15–20).

Thus when we say that men and women fulfill themselves by carrying on the work of creation through their own labors, we are asserting that they are operating within the framework of God's salvific work from the very first. Subduing the earth, as Genesis bids them do, is a salvific work. To work in the world and transform it is to save it. Inasmuch as it is a humanizing factor that transforms nature, work tends to build a society that is more just and more worthy of humankind—as Marx clearly saw. The Bible helps us to appreciate the deeper reaches of this effort. Building the earthly city is not simply a humanizing phase prior to evangelization, as theology used to put it. Building the earthly city actually immerses human beings in the salvation process that touches all humanity. Every obstacle that degrades or alienates the work of men and women in building a humane society is an obstacle to the work of salvation.

A second major theme of the Bible echoes this same thinking. The messianic promises, the events that announce and accompany the coming of the Messiah, are not isolated happenings. Like the first theme, the thread of messianism runs through the whole Bible. It is actively present in the history of Israel, and thus has its proper place in the historical development of God's people.

The prophets proclaim a reign of peace. But peace presupposes the establishment of justice, the defense of the rights of the poor, the punishment of oppressors, and a life free from the fear of enslavement. A benighted spiritualization has often caused us to forget the human power imbedded in the messianic promises and the transforming effect they might have on unjust social structures. The conquest of poverty and the abolition of exploitation are signs of the Messiah's arrival and presence. According to the book of Isaiah, the kingdom will become a reality when "they shall not build for others to live in, or plant for others to eat" (Isa. 65:22)—when everyone profits from their own labor. To work for a just world where there is no servitude, oppression, or alienation is to work for the advent of the Messiah. The messianic promises establish a close tie between the kingdom of God and living conditions that are worthy of human beings. God's kingdom and social injustice are incompatible.

The message to be gleaned from these two biblical themes is clear. Salvation embraces all, as *Populorum Progressio* (21) reminds us. Preaching the gospel message is not preaching escape from the world. On the contrary, the word of God deepens and fortifies our involvement in history. Concretely, this involvement means solidarity with the oppressed of Latin America and participation in their struggle for emancipation. And this solidarity and participation involve the realization that salvation history is a continuing process of liberation. It is through encounters with the poor and the exploited that we shall encounter the Lord (see Matt. 25:31ff). To be a Christian in our day is to involve ourselves creatively in the different phases of humanity's liberation process. Faith opens up infinite horizons to our human effort, giving dynamic vitality to our active presence in history.

These are some of the theological notions that implicitly or explicitly underlie the new Christian statements coming from Latin America. Only against this backdrop can we properly understand the efforts of certain Christian groups to be authentically present in the world of Latin America. Theirs is not a suspect temporalism; theirs is a desire, though undoubtedly flawed and imperfect, to be wholly loyal to the word of the Lord.

New Ecclesial Structures

There was a time when the vitality or decrepitude of the Latin American church was measured by the number of its priests. You simply calculated the number of faithful per priest and made your analysis on that basis. If you were at all in touch with the actual situation, you made mention of the disturbing geographical distance between the priests and most of their faithful. The scarcity of vocations seemed to be the major obstacle to be overcome if the underdeveloped church were to grow. Today, few still view the matter that way. The problem of priests has other, more delicate, facets. Everything seems to indicate that the lifestyle of the priest, which had remained static for centuries, is about to undergo a profound transformation in the near future. But even more important is the fact that it is merely one symptom of the broader and graver crisis afflicting the Christian community.

The older approach to this whole problem had a markedly clerical cast, which tended to minimize the problematical nature of the situation. Its gravest error was undoubtedly the type of solution it suggested for the church's problems. It was felt we could move out of the past by making efforts to modernize certain ecclesiastical structures or to inaugurate certain pastoral adaptations. Basically it is that whole approach that is today being called into question.

From now on we shall have to attack this issue with greater boldness, with the fortitude that Scripture enjoins on Christ's disciples (see Acts 4:31). That fortitude must induce us to carry out not halfway reforms that gloss over our fears and trepidations, but a transformation far more radical than anything we know today. The times demand of us a creative spark that will allow us to work up and create new ecclesial structures and new ways for the Christian community to be present to the world. The alarmed reaction of certain factions in the church that rise up in protest against those who would explore the signs of the times is no solution.

One solid line of endeavor for the Latin American church in this quest will be for it to assert its own distinctive personality. We have lived in a state of dependence that has not allowed us to fully develop our own qualities up to now. As a church, we have been a mirror image rather than a fountainhead, in the terms of Father de Lima Vas. We have been mirroring the European church—uncritically borrowing our theology, institutions, canon law, spirituality, and lifestyle. We have not been a creative fountainhead for new activities that would fit in with a world in revolution, for ecclesial structures that would be appropriate for a Third World church, or for ideas that would allow us to strike deep roots in our own reality. Working free of the colonial mentality is undoubtedly one of the major tasks confronting the

Christian community of Latin America. It will also be one way in which we can make a genuine contribution to the universal church.

Another solid line of endeavor will be our commitment to genuine poverty. This is an area where Christians offer ample witness to the contrary. We often confuse making a vow of poverty with living a life of poverty. We often confuse possession of absolute essentials with comfortable ensconcement in the world. We often confuse instruments for service with power leverage. We need an honest, clear-headed reform that will put an end to the discrepancy between our preaching and our practice. We must live in a church that is not only open to the poor but poor itself. Only in this way can we radically change the present face of the Christian community.

In this context, the episcopal conference at Medellín may represent for the Latin American church what Vatican II was for the whole church. It was not an end point but a point of departure. It was not only a forum for documents that sum up the ecclesial community's present awareness of this moment in history, but also a stimulus to push on further and to put life into our words. All this will not be done without difficulty. We shall always feel light-headed impulses that will prompt us to sensation-seeking postures rather than deep commitments. But the greatest threat will be the temptation to immobility and a preference for changes that do not really change the existing situation. We are more bound to the old structures than we realize.

Vatican II, and, one hopes, the Medellín conference, opened up the floodgates and allowed long-dammed waters to flow freely. When the flood is over, we shall realize that it has done more cleansing than destroying. Right now, however, our task is not to anxiously protect the texts of Vatican II and Medellín from erroneous interpretations, or to provide erudite commentaries. The important thing for us is to expound them in our deeds—to verify their truth in our daily Christian life.

The church is experiencing the effects of living in a world that is undergoing profound and decisive changes. The church itself must set out on uncharted roads, turn down new byways, without knowing what risks and obstacles will be encountered. It is not easy to believe that the Spirit will lead us to the whole truth (see John 16:13). It is not easy to set out without consulting a road map in advance. But today that is what the Christian community in Latin America must do.

Some may well complain that the positions expressed in these documents do not offer any responses or solutions. That may be true. But we must not forget that those who change the course of history are usually those who pose a new set of questions, rather than those who offer solutions.

NOTES

1. This alarm is clearly reflected in an article by Alberto Lleras Camargo that was published in the North American magazine *Vision* (September 29, 1968). In line with a similar article on the Medellín conference that was published in a Peruvian periodical, Lleras Camargo pejoratively labels one group of participating bishops "progressivists" and "radicals."

2. Address at the opening of the second session of Vatican Council II (September 29, 1965).

3. See the Medellín Document on Peace, in *Between Honesty and Hope* (Maryknoll, N.Y.: Maryknoll, 1970).

4. The expression was not retracted, as some uninformed commentators had hoped. Nor is it derived from Marxist sociology, as these same persons opined. The basic notion and the term itself can be found before Medellín in various statements issued by lay apostolic groups.

5. The idea is present at the very beginning of the Document on Peace and is developed throughout (see numbers 1 and 14, for example).

6. See the interesting article by Gonzalo Arroyo, "Violencia institucionalizada en Amèrica Latina," *Mensaje*, November 1968. The author concludes on a forceful note: "Have we Christians, who profess belief in the rewards of peace, done more than talk about global structural changes? Have we devoted all our energy to eliminating institutionalized injustice? If we are not doing that today, we have no right to cast the first stone!" (p. 544).

7. See the Document on Peace.

8. In this connection it is interesting to note the section directed to "our fellow peasants and laborers" in a statement of the Peruvian Episcopal Assembly, January 1969. Citing the Medellín document on peace, they state that they "will do everything in our power to foster and promote your grassroots organizations, so that you may reclaim your rights and obtain authentic justice" (Justice and Peace Commission, 2.4.2). In another section they stress that their forthright denunciation of abuses and injustices will be accompanied by "concrete action in solidarity with the poor and the oppressed" (ibid., 2.4.6).

Questions for Thought

1. Do you agree with Gutiérrez's claim that the Christian church has traditionally been a force that obstructed the path of those who struggled against social and political injustice? Defend your answer.
2. What do you think the term *spiritual salvation* means? Do you agree with Gutiérrez that personal salvation is insufficient? Why or why not?
3. In what ways, if any, do you think the Church should be changed? How do your views on this matter compare with or differ from the views of Gutiérrez?
4. How would you describe the proper role of the Church (or religion) in modern society?
5. Do you think Gutiérrez would agree with Kierkegaard's claim that Abraham represented the highest type of hero? Explain your answer.

7   Witchcraft and Women's Culture

STARHAWK

Starhawk (b. 1951), whose birth name was Miriam Samos, is an American witch, feminist, and peace activist who has taught at several colleges in the San Francisco Bay Area. Having been taught witchcraft as a college student, she practiced as a solitary for several years before forming her first coven, Compost. She later formed another coven, Honeysuckle (which was composed solely of women), and became the first national president of the Covenant of the Goddess (a church in the Bay Area). Starhawk also founded Reclaiming, a feminist collective in San Francisco that offers classes, workshops, and public rituals in witchcraft and that participates in peace activities and demonstrations. Starhawk describes Reclaiming as a "community of women and men working to unify spirit and politics."

Starhawk holds an M.A. in psychology from Antioch West University, and she travels widely in North America and Europe giving lectures and workshops. She has also been active in movements for social change for over thirty years. In this capacity, she has helped organize numerous antinuclear actions, traveled to Nicaragua with Witness for Peace, and helped with the training for recent actions in the antiglobalization movement.

Starhawk's first book, *The Spiral Dance: A Rebirth of the Ancient Religion of the Great Goddess* (1979), was based on the Faery tradition of witchcraft. Her other books include *Dreaming the Dark* (1982), *Truth or Dare: Encounters of Power, Authority, and Mystery* (1988), *The Earth Path: Grounding Your Spirit in the Rhythms of Nature* (2004), and two novels, *The Fifth Sacred Thing* (1993) and *Walking to Mercury* (1997). She is also coauthor of *The Pagan Book of Living and Dying* (1997), *Circle Round: Raising Children in the Goddess Tradition* (1998), and *The Twelve Wild Swans: A Journey into Magic, Healing and Action* (2000). Starhawk has also participated in a recording of ritual chants, recorded the guided meditation *Way to the Well*, and worked to help make the recently released documentary film, *Sign of Our Times*.

In the following essay, which was first discussed at the 1977 meetings of the American Academy of Religion, Starhawk discusses the history and philosophy of witchcraft. Focusing on the history of northern Europe, she notes that traces of the ancient practice of witchcraft can be found in many places. She also observes that the old tradition of witchcraft initially coexisted with the newer religion of Christianity. But this peaceful coexistence ended in the Middle Ages, when the persecution of witches and the distortion of the meaning of witchcraft became widespread. Because of this persecution and the later emphasis on science during the Age of Reason, much of the traditional wisdom was lost. Starhawk believes, however, that the present era is marked by a reawakening of awareness of the Great Goddess and a renewed interest in the "craft of the wise."

After presenting this brief history of witchcraft, Starhawk contrasts the philosophy and rituals of witchcraft with those of the Judeo-Christian tradition. In opposition to a transcendent Father God, witchcraft recognizes the existence of an immanent Earth Mother. In opposition to **dualisms** between God and nature and between spirit and flesh, witchcraft recognizes the interconnectedness and sacredness of all life. In opposition to dogma and dependence, witchcraft contains no set of doctrines and recognizes the **autonomy** of each practitioner. Finally, in opposition to "the formless, abstracted *agape* of the early Christians," witchcraft emphasizes the passionate, personal, uniting love that individual humans feel for other individuals.

Questions for Reading

1. What literary device does Starhawk use to open her essay?
2. Why, according to Starhawk, were witches persecuted during the Middle Ages? What were some of the claims that were used to justify this persecution?
3. What are the essential philosophical or religious differences between witchcraft and Christianity? Why does Starhawk believe that witchcraft is the preferable religion?
4. What does the Goddess symbolize within the tradition of witchcraft? What is the role of the Horned God?
5. Which psychological or spiritual qualities are most valued by witchcraft? How is love viewed in this religion?
6. What, according to Starhawk, is the structure and purpose of a coven? What are the principal benefits of belonging to a coven?

THE UNHEWN STONES ARE NEWLY RISEN. Within their circle, an old woman raises a flint knife and points it toward the bright full moon. She cries out, a wail echoed by her clan folk as they begin the dance. They circle wildly around the central fire, feeling the power rise within them until they unite in ecstatic frenzy. The priestess cries again, and all drop to the earth, exhausted but filled with a deep sense of peace. A cup of ale is poured into the fire, and the flames leap up high. "Blessed be the mother of all life," the priestess says, "May She be generous to Her children."

The birth is a difficult one, but the midwife has brought many women through worse. Still, she is worried. She has herbs to open the womb and stop the blood, herbs to bring sleep, and others to bring forgetfulness of pain. But now her baskets are almost empty. This year she could not go gathering at the proper times of the moon and sun. The new priest and his spies are everywhere—if she were to be caught digging simples in the moonlight it would be sure proof of witchcraft, not just against herself but against her daughters and sisters and her daughter's daughters. As she pours out the last of her broth for the laboring woman, the midwife sighs. "Blessed Tana, Mother of mothers," she breathes softly, "When will the old ways return?"

The child is in a state of shock. Her memories of the last three days are veiled in a haze of smoke and noise that seem to swirl toward this climax of acrid smells and hoarse shouting. The priest's grip is clawlike as he forces her to watch the cruel drama in the center of the square. The girl's eyes are open, but her mind has flown far away, and what she sees is not the scene before her: her mother, the stake, the flames. She is running through the open field behind their cottage, smelling only clean wind, seeing only clear sky. The priest looks down at her blank face and crosses himself in fear. "Devil's spawn!" he spits on the ground. "If I had my way, we'd hold to custom and burn you too!"

It is the night of the full moon. Nine women stand in a circle, on a rocky hill above the city. The western sky is rosy with the setting sun; in the east the moon's face begins to peer above the horizon. Below, electric lights wink on the ground like fallen stars. A young woman raises a steel knife and cries out, a wail echoed by the others as they begin the dance. They circle wildly around a cauldron of smoldering herbs, feeling the power rise within them until they unite in ecstasy. The priestess cries again, and all drop to the earth, exhausted, but filled with an overwhelming sense of peace. The woman pours out a cup of wine onto the earth, refills it and raises it high. "Hail, Tana, Mother of mothers!" she cries. "Awaken from your long sleep, and return to your children again!"

From earliest times,[1] women have been witches, *wicce,* "wise ones"—priestesses, diviners, midwives, poets, healers, and singers of songs of power. Woman-centered culture, based on the worship of the Great Goddess, underlies the beginnings of all civilization. Mother Goddess was carved on the walls of paleolithic caves, and painted in the shrines of the earliest cities, those of the Anatolian plateau. For her were raised the giant stone circles, the henges of the British Isles, the dolmens and cromlechs of the later Celtic countries, and for her the great passage graves of Ireland were dug. In her honor, sacred dancers leaped the bulls in Crete and composed lyric hymns within the colleges of the holy isles of the Mediterranean. Her **mysteries** were celebrated in secret rites at Eleusis, and her initiates included some of the finest minds of Greece. Her priestesses discovered and tested the healing herbs and learned the secrets of the human mind and body that allowed them to ease the pain of childbirth, to heal wounds and cure diseases, and to explore the realm of dreams and the unconscious. Their knowledge of nature enabled them to tame sheep and cattle, to breed wheat and corn from grasses and weeds, to forge ceramics from mud and metal from rock, and to track the movements of moon, stars, and sun.

Witchcraft, "the craft of the wise," is the last remnant in the west of the time of women's strength and power. Through the dark ages of persecution, the covens of Europe preserved what is left of the mythology, rituals, and knowledge of the ancient matricentric (mother-centered) times. The great centers of worship in Anatolia, Malta, Iberia, Brittany, and Sumeria are now only silent stones and works of art we can but dimly understand. Of the mysteries of Eleusis, we have literary hints; the poems of Sappho survive only in fragments. The great collections of early literature and science were destroyed by patriarchal forces—the library of Alexandria burnt by Caesar, Charlemagne's collection of lore burnt by his son Louis "the Pious," who was offended at its "paganism." But the craft remains, in spite of all efforts to stamp it out, as a living tradition of Goddess-centered worship that traces its roots back to the time before the triumph of **patriarchy.**

The old religion of witchcraft before the advent of Christianity was an earth-centered, nature-oriented worship that venerated the Goddess, the source of life, as well as her son-lover-consort, who was seen as the Horned God of the hunt and animal life. Earth, air, water, fire, streams, seas, wells, beasts, trees, grain, the planets, sun, and most of all, the moon, were seen as aspects of deity. On the great seasonal festivals—the solstices and equinoxes, and the eves of May, August, November, and February,—all the countryside would gather to light huge bonfires, feast, dance, sing, and perform the rituals that assured abundance throughout the year.

When Christianity first began to spread, the country people held to the old ways, and for hundreds of years the two faiths coexisted quite peacefully. Many people followed both religions, and country priests in the twelfth and thirteenth centuries were frequently upbraided by church authorities for dressing in skins and leading the dance at the pagan festivals.

But in the thirteenth and fourteenth centuries, the church began persecution of witches, as well as Jews and "heretical" thinkers. Pope Innocent the VIII, with his Bull of 1484, intensified a campaign of torture and death that would take the lives of an estimated 9 million people, perhaps 80 percent of whom were women.

The vast majority of victims were not coven members or even necessarily witches. They were old widows whose property was coveted by someone else, young children with "witch blood," midwives who furnished the major competition to the male-dominated medical profession, free-thinkers who asked the wrong questions.

An enormous campaign of propaganda accompanied the witch trials as well. Witches were said to have sold their souls to the devil, to practice obscene and disgusting rites, to blight crops and murder children. In many areas, the witches did worship a Horned God as the spirit of the hunt, of animal life and vitality, a concept far from the power of evil that was the Christian devil. Witches were free and open about sexuality—but their rites were "obscene" only to those who viewed the human body itself as filthy and evil. Questioning or disbelieving any of the slander was itself considered proof of witchcraft or heresy, and the falsehoods that for hundreds of years could not be openly challenged had their effect. Even today, the word *witch* is often automatically associated with "evil."

With the age of reason in the eighteenth century, belief in witches, as in all things psychic and supernatural, began to fade. The craft as a religion was forgotten; all that remained were the wild stories of broomstick flights, magic potions, and the summoning of spectral beings.

Memory of the true craft faded everywhere except within the hidden covens. With it, went the memory of women's heritage and history, of our ancient roles as leaders, teachers, healers, seers. Lost, also, was the conception of the Great Spirit, as manifest in nature, in life, in woman. Mother Goddess slept, leaving the world to the less than gentle rule of the God-Father.

The Goddess has at last stirred from sleep, and women are reawakening to our ancient power. The feminist movement, which began as a political, economic, and social struggle, is opening to a spiritual dimension. In the process, many women are discovering the old religion, reclaiming the word *witch* and, with it, some of our lost culture.

Witchcraft, today, is a kaleidoscope of diverse traditions, rituals, theologies, and structures. But underneath the varying forms is a basic orientation common to all the craft. The outer forms of religion—the particular words said, the signs made, the names used—are less important to us than the inner forms, which cannot be defined or described but must be felt and intuited.

The craft is earth religion, and our basic orientation is to the earth, to life, to nature. There is no dichotomy between spirit and flesh, no split between Godhead and the world. The Goddess is manifest in the world; she brings life into being, *is* nature, *is* flesh. Union is not sought outside the world in some heavenly sphere or through dissolution of the self into the void beyond the senses. Spiritual union is found in life, within nature, passion, sensuality—through being fully human, fully one's self.

Our great symbol for the Goddess is the moon, whose three aspects reflect the three stages in women's lives and whose cycles of waxing and waning coincide with women's menstrual cycles. As the new moon or crescent, she is the Maiden, the Virgin—not chaste, but belonging to herself alone, not bound to any man. She is the wild child, lady of the woods, the huntress, free and untamed—Artemis, Kore, Aradia, Nimue. White is her color. As the full moon, she is the mature woman, the sexual being, the mother and nurturer, giver of life, fertility, grain, offspring, potency, joy—Tana, Demeter, Diana, Ceres, Mari. Her colors are the red of blood and the green of growth. As waning or dark moon, she is the old woman, past menopause, the hag or crone that is ripe with wisdom, patroness of secrets, prophecy, divination, inspiration, power—Hecate, Ceridwen, Kali, Anna. Her color is the black of night.

The Goddess is also earth—Mother Earth, who sustains all growing things, who is the body, our bones and cells. She is air—the winds that move in the trees and over the waves, breath. She is the fire of the hearth, of the blazing bonfire and the fuming volcano; the power of transformation and change. And she is water—the sea, original source of life; the rivers, streams, lakes and wells; the blood that flows in the rivers of our veins. She is mare, cow, cat, owl, crane, flower, tree, apple, seed, lion, sow, stone, woman. She is found in the world around us, in the cycles and seasons of nature, and in mind, body, spirit, and emotions within each of us. Thou art Goddess. I am Goddess. All that lives (and all that is, lives), all that serves life, is Goddess.

Because witches are oriented to earth and to life, we value spiritual qualities that I feel are especially important to women, who have for so long been conditioned to be passive, submissive and weak. The craft values independence, personal strength, *self*—not petty selfishness but that deep core of strength within that makes us each a unique child of the Goddess. The craft has no dogma to stifle thought, no set of doctrines that have to be believed. Where authority exists, within covens, it is always coupled with the freedom every covener has, to leave at any time. When self is valued—in ourselves—we can see that self is everywhere.

Passion and emotion—that give depth and color and meaning to human life—are also valued. Witches strive to be in touch with feelings, even if they are sometimes painful, because the joy and pleasure and ecstasy available to a fully alive person make it worth occasional suffering. So-called negative emotion—anger—is valued as well, as a sign that something is wrong and that action needs to be taken. Witches prefer to handle anger by taking action and making changes rather than by detaching ourselves from our feelings in order to reach some nebulous, "higher" state.

Most of all, the craft values love. The Goddess' only law is "Love unto all beings." But the love we value is not the airy flower power of the hippies or the formless, abstracted *agape* of the early Christians. It is passionate, sensual, personal love, *eros*, falling in love, mother-child love, the love of one unique human being for other individuals, with all their personal traits and idiosyncrasies. Love is not something that can be radiated out in solitary meditation—it manifests itself in relationships and interactions with other people. It is often said "You cannot be a witch alone"—because to be a witch is to be a lover, a lover of the Goddess and a lover of other human beings.

The coven is still the basic structure of the craft, and generally covens meet at the times of full moons and the major festivals, although some meet also on new moons and a few meet once a week. A coven is a small group, at most of thirteen members—for the thirteen full moons of the year. Its small size is important. Within the coven, a union, a merging of selves in a close bond of love and trust, takes place. A coven becomes an energy pool each member can draw on. But, because the group remains small, there is never the loss of identity and individuality that can happen in a mass. In a coven, each person's individuality is extremely important. Each personality colors and helps create the group identity, and each member's energy is vital to the working of the group.

Covens are separate and autonomous, and no one outside the coven has any authority over its functioning. Some covens may be linked in the same tradition—meaning they share the same rituals and symbology—but there is no hierarchy of rule. Elder witches can and do give advice, but only those within the coven may actually make decisions.

Covens are extremely diverse. There are covens of hereditary witches who have practiced rites unchanged for hundreds of years, and covens who prefer to make up their own rituals and may never do the same thing twice. There are covens of "perfect couples"—an even number of women and men permanently paired, and covens of lesbian feminists or of women who simply prefer to explore women's spirituality in a space removed from men. There are covens of gay men and covens that just don't worry about sexual polarities. A few covens are authoritarian—with a high priestess or high priest who makes most of the decisions. (Coveners, of course, always have the option of leaving.) Most are democratic, if not anarchic, but usually older or more experienced members—"elders"—assume leadership and responsibility. Actual roles in rituals are often rotated among qualified coveners.

Rituals also vary widely. A craft ritual might involve wild shouting and frenzied dancing, or silent meditation, or both. A carefully rehearsed drama might be enacted, or a spontaneous poetic chant carried on for an hour. Everyone may enter a deep trance and scry in a crystal ball—or they may pass around a bottle of wine and laugh uproariously at awful puns. The best rituals combine moments of intense ecstasy and spiritual union, with moments of raucous humor and occasional silliness. The craft is serious without being dry or solemn.

Whether formal or informal, every craft ritual takes place within a circle—a space considered to be "between the worlds," the human world and the realm of the Goddess. A circle can be cast, or created, in any physical space, from a moonlit hillside to the living room of a modern apartment. It may be outlined in stones, drawn in chalk or paint, or drawn invisibly with the point of a sword or ceremonial wand. It may be consecrated with incense, salt water, and a formal invocation to each of the four quarters of the universe, or created simply by having everyone join hands. The casting of the circle begins the ritual and serves as a transition into an expanded state of consciousness. The power raised by the ritual is contained within the circle so that it can reach a higher peak instead of dissipating.

The Goddess, and if desired, the Horned God (not all traditions of the craft relate to the male force) can be invoked once the circle is cast. An invocation may be set beforehand, written out and memorized, but in our coven we find the most effective invocations are those that come to us spontaneously, out of the inspiration of the season, the phase of the moon, and the particular mood and energy of the moment. Often we invoke the Goddess by chanting together a line or phrase repeated over and over: "Moon mother bright light of all earth sky, we call you" is an example. As we chant, we find rhythms, notes, melodies, and words seem to flow through us and burst out in complex and beautiful patterns.

Chanting, dancing, breathing, and concentrated will, all contribute to the raising of power, which is the essential part of a craft ritual. Witches conceive of psychic energy as having form and substance that can be perceived and directed by those with a trained awareness. The power generated within the circle is built into a cone form, and at its peak is released—to the Goddess, to reenergize the members of the coven, or to do a specific work such as a healing. When the cone is released, any scattered energy that is left is grounded, put back into the earth, by falling to the ground, breathing deeply, and relaxing. High-energy states cannot be maintained indefinitely without becoming a physical and emotional drain—any more than you could stay high on methedrine forever without destroying your body. After the peak of the cone, it is vital to let go of the power and return to a calm, relaxed state. Silent meditation, trance, or psychic work are often done in this part of the ritual.

Energy is also shared in tangible form—wine, cakes, fruit, cheesecake, brownies, or whatever people enjoy eating. The Goddess is invited to share with everyone, and a libation is poured to her first. This part of the ritual is relaxed and informally social, devoted to laughing, talking, sharing of news and any business that must be done.

At the end, the Goddess is thanked and bid farewell, and the circle is formally opened. Ending serves as a transition back into ordinary space and time. Rituals finish with a kiss and a greeting of "Merry meet, merry part, and merry meet again."

The underlying forms of craft rituals evolved out of thousands of years of experience and understanding of human needs and the potentials of human consciousness. That understanding, which is part of women's lost heritage, is invaluable, not just in the context of rituals and spiritual growth, but also for those working toward political and social change, because human needs and human energies behave the same in any context.

Witches understand that energy, whether it is psychic, emotional, or physical, always flows in cycles. It rises and falls, peaks and drops, and neither end of the cycle can be sustained indefinitely, any more than you could run forever without stopping. Intense levels of energy must be released and then brought down and grounded; otherwise the energy dissipates or even turns destructive. If, in a ritual, you tried to maintain a peak of frenzy for hours and hours, you would find that after a while the energy loses its joyful quality, and instead of feeling union and ecstasy, you begin to feel irritated and exhausted. Political groups that try to maintain an unremitting level of anger—a high-energy state—also run out of steam in precisely the same way. Releasing the energy and grounding out allows the power itself to work freely. It clears channels and allows you to rest and recharge and become ready for the next swing into an up cycle. Releasing energy does not mean losing momentum; rather, real movement, real change, happens in a rhythmic pattern of many beats, not in one unbroken blast of static.

Craft rituals also add an element of drama and fantasy to one's life. They allow us to act out myths and directly experience archetypes of symbolic transformation. They allow us, as adults, to recapture the joy of childhood make-believe, of dressing up, of pretending, of play. Magic, by Dion Fortune's definition, "the art of changing consciousness at will," is not so far removed from the creative fantasy states we enter so easily as children, when our dolls become alive, our bicycles become wild horses, ourselves arctic explorers or queens. Allowing ourselves, as adults, to play and fantasize with others, puts us in touch with the creative child within, with a deep and rich source of inspiration.

The craft also helps us open our intuitive and psychic abilities. Although witchcraft is commonly associated with magic and the use of extrasensory powers, not all covens put a great deal of stress on psychic training. Worship is more often the main focus of activity. However, any craft ritual involves some level of psychic awareness just in sensing the energy that is raised.

Ordinarily, the way into the craft is through initiation into an already established coven. However, because covens are limited in size and depend on some degree of harmony between personalities, it is often difficult to find one that is open to new members and that fits your preferences. In San Francisco, Los Angeles, and New York, covens often run open study groups and can be found through publications and open universities. In other areas of the country, it may be difficult to locate a practicing coven at all.

However, there is nothing to stop you from starting a coven or a *circle*—a term I use for a group whose members meet for rituals but are not formally initiated—on your own. Women, especially, are more and more joining together to explore a Goddess-oriented spirituality and to create rituals and symbols that are meaningful to us today. Starting your own circle requires imagination, creativity, and experimentation, but it is a tremendously exciting process. You will miss formal psychic training—but you may discover on your own more than anyone else could teach you. Much of what is written on the craft is biased in one way or another, so weed out what is useful to you and ignore the rest.

I see the next few years as being crucial in the transformation of our culture away from the patriarchal death cults and toward the love of life, of nature, of the female principle. The craft is only one path among the many opening up for women, and many of us will blaze new trails as we explore the uncharted country of our own interiors. The heritage, the culture, the knowledge of the ancient priestesses, healers, poets, singers, and seers were nearly lost, but a seed survived the flames that will blossom in a new age into thousands of flowers. The long sleep of Mother Goddess is ended. May She awaken in each of our hearts—Merry meet, merry part, and blessed be.

NOTE

1. This article is limited to the history of traditions that come from northern Europe. Southern and eastern Europe, Asia, India, Africa, and the Americas all have rich traditions of Goddess religions and **matricentric** cultures, but to even touch on them all would be impossible in a short essay. The history presented here is the "inner" or "mythic" history that provides a touchstone for modern witches. Like the histories of all peoples, its truth is intuited in the meaning it gives to life, even though it may be recognized that scholars might dispute some facets of the story.

Questions for Thought

1. Why do you think witches have been persecuted? Do you think they should have been persecuted? Defend your answer.
2. Which of the beliefs of witchcraft do you find most appealing? Which of them do you find least appealing?
3. Can you think of religions other than witchcraft in which the Goddess is the principal deity? What role, if any, does the Goddess play in Christianity?
4. Which psychological or spiritual qualities do you most value? How do your views on this matter compare with or differ from the views of Starhawk?
5. Why do craft rituals take place in a circle? If you were to create a religious ritual, what form would it take?

Is Religious Belief Beneficial or Harmful?

The Will to Believe   8

WILLIAM JAMES

William James (1842–1910), one of whose brothers was the novelist Henry James, was born in New York City. James' father, often described as an eccentric follower of the Swiss mystic Emanuel Swedenborg, was a true proponent of self-development who left his children free to make their own decisions on matters of belief. Although much of James' education was provided informally by his father and his father's friends (who included such **transcendentalist** writers as Ralph Waldo Emerson), he intermittently attended a variety of private educational institutions in the United States and abroad.

Because his family's wealth freed James from the necessity of seeking immediate employment (his grandfather had become rich by investing in the Erie Canal), he was able to pursue a variety of interests. In 1860, James studied painting for a year before deciding that his talents lay elsewhere. The following year, he entered the Lawrence Scientific School at Harvard University, where he studied chemistry, anatomy, and physiology. In 1864, he transferred to the Harvard Medical School, although he had no intention of practicing medicine. In 1865–1866, James volunteered for an expedition to Brazil with the well-known naturalist Louis Agassiz. Unfortunately, during this expedition he contracted smallpox, the first of a series of health problems that were to plague him in later life. After returning to medical school for a term, he spent the years 1867–1868 in Germany, recuperating and studying physiology.

James returned to the United States in 1868 and received his M.D. from Harvard the following year. However, still ill and suffering from an emotional crisis precipitated by doubts about human freedom, he spent the next three years living in his father's house. Then, in 1872, he was offered a job teaching physiology at Harvard. Displaying the breadth of his learning, he began teaching psychology in 1875 and philosophy in 1879. James remained affiliated with Harvard until 1907.

After marrying Alice Gibbens in 1878, James' health problems seemed to diminish, and he turned wholeheartedly to writing and lecturing. Contracting to write a textbook on psychology in 1880, James instead wrote a large two-volume work in theoretical psychology, *The Principles of Psychology,* which was published ten years later. Having written this definitive work in psychology, James then turned his attention to religion, writing diverse essays and lectures on the subject between 1893 and 1903. A collection of these were published in the widely read work *The Will to Believe and Other Essays in Popular Philosophy,* published in 1897. However, the culmination of James' focus on religion came in 1901–1902, when he delivered the Gifford Lectures at the University of Edinburgh in Scotland. These were published in 1902 under the title *The Varieties of Religious Experience.*

From this point to the end of his life, James devoted his energies more and more to describing and defending the views of **Pragmatism,** a method of philosophy that he had first identified in a lecture at the University of California in 1898. (While lecturing on pragmatism at Stanford University in 1906, James experienced the great earthquake that destroyed much of San Francisco.) When health problems returned, James was forced to give up lecturing in 1908. After unsuccessfully seeking a cure in Europe, he returned to the United States. He died at his country home in New Hampshire in 1910. In addition to the previously mentioned writings, James' works include *Pragmatism: A New Name for Some Old Ways of Thinking* (1907), *The Meaning of Truth: A Sequel to "Pragmatism"* (1909), *A Pluralistic Universe* (1909), *Some Problems of Philosophy: A Beginning of an Introduction to Philosophy* (1911), *Essays in Radical Empiricism* (1912), and *Memories and Studies* (1912).

In the following essay, James defends the adoption and value of religious beliefs against those who argue that we should accept only beliefs that are warranted by scientific evidence. While acknowledging the value of science, James argues that even scientific endeavor is not purely rational but depends to a certain extent on our volitions (or what he calls our "passional nature"). Moreover, he claims that there are certain beliefs—beliefs that are living, forced, and momentous—for which we are justified in using our passional nature to fill the vacuum that is left by reason. In other words, even though such beliefs cannot usually be justified on the basis of evidence, they can be— and James thinks they ought to be—justified by our will to believe.

Questions for Reading

1. What is the nature of the audience that James is addressing? What assumptions does he make about the beliefs of his audience?
2. How does James define the term *option*? What are the various kinds of options that he describes?
3. What, according to James, is Pascal's wager? What is his purpose in describing Pascal's wager in his essay?
4. On James' account, why do you believe what you believe?
5. What, according to James, are the two essential things that religion says? Why does he think that we are better off if we believe these two things?

I HAVE BROUGHT WITH ME TONIGHT SOMETHING like a sermon on justification by faith to read to you. I mean that it is an essay in justification *of* faith, a defense of our right to adopt a believing attitude in religious matters, in spite of the fact that our merely logical intellect may not have been convinced. Accordingly, "The Will to Believe" is the title of my paper.

I have long defended to my own students the lawfulness of voluntarily adopted faith. But as soon as they have gotten well-imbued with the logical spirit, they have as a rule refused to admit my

contention to be lawful philosophically, even though in point of fact they were themselves personally all the time chock-full of some faith or other. I am all the while, however, so profoundly convinced that my own position is correct that your invitation seems to me to be a good occasion to more clearly state my position. Perhaps your minds will be more open than the minds of those with whom I have hitherto had to deal. I will be as little technical as I can, although I must begin by setting up some technical distinctions that will help us in the end.

This is the editor's revised version of selected material from William James, The Will to Believe and Other Essays in Popular Philosophy, *New York, 1897.*

I

Let us give the name *hypothesis* to anything that may be proposed to our belief; and just as the electricians speak of live and dead wires, let us speak of any hypothesis as either *live* or *dead*. A live hypothesis is one that appeals as a real possibility to him to whom it is proposed. If I ask you to believe in the **Mahdi,** the notion makes no electric connection with your nature—it refuses to scintillate with any credibility at all. As a hypothesis it is completely dead. To an Arab, however (even if he is not one of the Mahdi's followers), the hypothesis is among the mind's possibilities: it is alive. This shows that the deadness and liveness in a hypothesis are not intrinsic properties, but relations to the individual thinker. They are measured by his willingness to act. The maximum of liveness in a hypothesis means willingness to act irrevocably. Practically, that means belief; but there is some believing tendency wherever there is willingness to act at all.

Next, let us call the decision between two hypotheses an *option*. Options may be of several kinds. They may be—1, *living* or *dead;* 2, *forced* or *avoidable;* 3, *momentous* or *trivial*. For our purposes we may call an option a *genuine* option when it is of the forced, living, and momentous kind.

1)   A living option is one in which both hypotheses are live ones. If I say to you, "Be a theosophist or be a Muslim," it is probably a dead option, because for you neither hypothesis is likely to be alive. But if I say, "Be an **agnostic** or be a Christian," it is otherwise. Trained as you are, each hypothesis makes some appeal, however small, to your belief.

2)   Next, if I say to you, "Choose between going out with your umbrella or without it," I do not offer you a genuine option. For it is not forced. You can easily avoid it by not going out at all. Similarly, if I say, "Either love me or hate me," . . . your option is avoidable. You may remain indifferent to me, neither loving nor hating. . . . But if I say, "Either accept this truth or go without it," I put you in a forced option, for there is no standing place outside of the alternative. Every dilemma based on a complete logical disjunction, where there is no possibility of not choosing, is an option of this forced kind.

3)   Finally, if I were Dr. Nansen and proposed to you to join my North Pole expedition, your option would be momentous. For this would probably be your only similar opportunity, and your choice now would either exclude you from the North Pole sort of immortality altogether or put at least the chance of it into your hands. He who refuses to embrace a unique opportunity loses the prize as surely as if he tried and failed. On the other hand, the option is trivial when the opportunity is not unique, when the stake is insignificant, or when the decision is reversible if it later prove unwise. Such trivial options abound in the scientific life. A chemist finds a hypothesis live enough to spend a year in its verification: he believes it to that extent. But if his experiments prove inconclusive either way, he abandons this hypothesis, no vital harm being done.

It will facilitate our discussion if we keep all these distinctions clearly in mind.

II

The next matter to consider is the actual psychology of human opinion. When we look at certain facts, it seems as if our passional and volitional nature lay at the root of all our convictions. When we look at other facts, however, it seems as if this nature can do nothing once the intellect has had its say. Let us consider the latter facts first.

Does it not seem preposterous on the face of it to talk of our opinions being modifiable at will? Can our will either help or hinder our intellect in its perceptions of truth? Can we, by just willing it, believe that Abraham Lincoln's existence is a myth, and that the portraits of him in McClure's Magazine are all of someone else? Can we, by any effort of our will, or by any amount of wishful thinking, believe ourselves well and about when we are roaring with rheumatism in bed? Can we by such means feel certain that the sum of two one-dollar bills in our pocket must be a hundred dollars? We can *say* any of these things, but we are absolutely impotent to believe them. And of just such things is the whole fabric of the truths in which we do believe made up—matters of fact, immediate or remote, as Hume said, and relations between ideas, which are either there or not there for us if we see them. At any rate, if they are not there, they cannot be put there by any action of our own.

In Pascal's *Pensées* or Thoughts, there is a cele-brated passage known in literature as Pascal's wager. In it he tries to force us into Christianity by reason-ing as if our concern with truth resembled our concern with the stakes in a game of chance. Translated freely his words are these: You must either believe or not believe that God exists. Which will you do? Your human reason cannot decide. A game is going on between you and the nature of things, which on the day of judgment will bring out either heads or tails. Weigh what your gains and your losses would be if you were to stake all you have on heads, or God's existence. If you win in such a case, you gain eternal beatitude; if you lose, you lose nothing at all. If there were an infinity of chances in this wager, with only one of these being for God, you still ought to stake your all on God. For though you surely risk a finite loss by this procedure, any finite loss is reason-able, even a certain finite loss, if there is the possibility of infinite gain. Go, then, and take holy water, and have masses said. Belief will come and stupefy your scruples. . . . Why should you not? At bottom, what have you to lose?

You probably feel that when religious faith expresses itself thus, in the language of the gaming table, it is put to its last trumps. Surely Pascal's own personal belief in masses and holy water had far different springs; and this celebrated page of his is but an argument for others, a last desperate snatch at a weapon against the hardness of the unbelieving heart. We feel that a faith in masses and holy water adopted willfully after such a mechanical calculation would lack the inner soul of faith's reality. And if we were ourselves the Deity, we would probably take particular pleasure in cutting off believers of this sort from their infinite reward. It is evident that unless there were some pre-existing tendency to believe in masses and holy water, the option offered by Pascal would not be a living option. Certainly no Turk ever took to masses and holy water on account of this line of reasoning; and even to us Protestants these means of salvation seem such foregone impos-sibilities that Pascal's logic, invoked for them specifically, leaves us unmoved. . . . No tendency to act on it exists in us to any degree.

The talk of believing by our volition seems, then, from one point of view, simply silly. From another point of view, it is worse than silly—it is vile. When one turns to the magnificent edifice of the physical sciences, and sees how it was reared; . . . what patience and postponement, what choking down of preference, what submission to the icy laws of outer fact are wrought into its very stones and mor-tar; how absolutely impersonal it stands in its vast augustness—then how besotted and contemptible seems every little sentimentalist who comes blowing his voluntary smoke-wreaths, pretending to decide things from out of his private dream! Can we wonder if those bred in the rugged and manly school of sci-ence should feel like spewing such subjectivism out of their mouths? The whole system of loyalties that is nourished in the schools of science goes dead against the toleration of such sentimentalists. So that it is only natural that those who have caught the scientific fever should pass over to the opposite extreme, and write sometimes as if the incorruptibly truthful intellect ought positively to prefer in its cup even bitterness and unacceptableness to the heart . . .

III

All this strikes one as healthy. . . . Free-will and sim-ple wishing do seem, in the matter of our credences, to be only fifth wheels to the coach. Yet if any one should thereupon assume that intellectual insight is what remains after wish and will and sentimental preference have taken wing, or that pure reason is what then settles our opinions, he would fly quite as directly in the teeth of the facts.

It is only our already dead hypotheses that our willing nature is unable to bring to life again. But what has made them dead for us is for the most part a previous action of our willing nature of an antago-nistic kind. When I say "willing nature," I do not mean only such deliberate volitions as may have set up habits of belief from which we cannot now escape. I mean all such factors of belief as fear and hope, prejudice and passion, imitation and partisan-ship, the circumpressure of our caste and set. As a matter of fact, we hardly know how or why we believe what we believe. . . . Here in this room, all of us believe in molecules and the conservation of energy, in democracy and necessary progress, in Protestant Christianity and the duty of fighting for the Monroe Doctrine—all for no reasons worthy of the name. We see into these matters with no more inner clarity, and probably with much less, than any disbeliever in them might possess. His unconventionality would probably have some grounds to show for its conclusions; but for us, not insight, but the *prestige* of the opinions, is what makes the spark shoot from them and light up our sleeping magazines of faith. Our reason is quite satisfied, in nine hundred and ninety-nine cases out of every thousand, if it can find a few arguments that will do to recite in case our credulity is criticized by someone else. Our faith is faith in someone else's faith, and in the greatest matters this is almost always the case. For instance, our belief in truth itself, that is, our belief that there is a truth and that our minds can know it—what is that but a passionate affirmation of desire, backed up by our social system? We want to have a truth; we want to believe that our experiments, studies and discussions must put us in a continually better and better position toward it. On this front, we agree to fight out our thinking lives. But if a **pyrrhonistic** skeptic asks us *how we know* all this, can our logic find a reply? No, certainly it cannot! There is just one volition against another—we are willing to go in for life on a trust or assumption that he, for his part, does not care to make.

As a rule we disbelieve all facts and theories for which we have no use. . . . Huxley belabors the bishops because there is no use for **sacerdotalism** in his scheme of life. Newman, on the contrary, goes over to Roman Catholicism and finds all sorts of good reasons for staying there, because a priestly system is for him an organic need and delight. Why do so few "scientists" even look at the evidence for what is called "telepathy"? Because they think, as a leading biologist once told me before he died, that even if such a thing were true, scientists ought to band together to keep it suppressed and concealed. It would undo the uniformity of Nature and all sorts of other things without which scientists cannot carry on their pursuits. But if this very man had been shown something which, as a scientist, he could *do* with telepathy, he might not only have examined the evidence, but even have found it good enough. This very law that the logicians would impose upon us—if I may give the name of logicians to those who would rule out our willing nature here—is based on nothing but their own natural wish to exclude all elements for which they, in their professional capacity as logicians, can find no use.

Evidently, then, our non-intellectual nature does influence our convictions. There are passional tendencies and volitions that run before and others that come after belief. It is only the latter that are too late for the fair; and they are not too late when the previous passional work has been already in their own direction. Pascal's argument, instead of being powerless, then seems a regular clincher. It is the last stroke needed to make our faith in masses and holy water complete. The state of things is evidently far from simple; and pure insight and logic, whatever they might do ideally, are not the only things that really do produce our creeds.

IV

Now that we have recognized this mixed-up state of affairs, our next duty is to ask whether it is simply reprehensible and pathological, or whether, on the contrary, we must treat it as a normal element in making up our minds. Briefly stated, the thesis I defend is this: *Our passional nature not only lawfully may, but must, decide an option between propositions, whenever it is a genuine option that cannot by its nature be decided on intellectual grounds. For to say, under such circumstances, "Do not decide, but leave the question open," is itself a passional decision— just like deciding yes or no—and is attended with the same risk of losing the truth.* The thesis thus abstractly expressed will, I trust, soon become quite clear. . . .

VIII

And now . . . let us go straight at our question. I have said, and now repeat, that as a matter of fact we do find our passional nature influencing us in our opinions. But what's more, there are some options between opinions in which this influence must be regarded both as an inevitable and as a lawful determinant of our choice.

I fear here that some of you in the audience will begin to scent danger and lend an inhospitable ear. Two first steps of passion you have indeed had to admit as necessary—we must think so as to avoid dupery, and we must think so as to gain truth. But you will probably consider that the surest path to those ideal consummations will not allow us to take any further passional steps.

Well, of course, I agree with this as far as the facts will allow. Wherever the option between losing truth and gaining it is not momentous, we can throw the chance of *gaining truth* away, and at any rate save ourselves from any chance of *believing falsehood,* by not making up our minds at all until we have objective evidence. In scientific questions, this is almost always the case; and even in human affairs in general, the need of acting is seldom so urgent that having a false belief to act on is better than having no belief at all. . . . Such options are not forced on us. On every account it is better not to make them, but to still keep weighing reasons pro and con with an unbiased hand. . . . Let us agree, then, that wherever there is no forced option, the dispassionately judicial intellect with no pet hypothesis at least saves us from dupery and ought to be the ideal.

The question next arises: Are there not somewhere forced options in our speculative questions, and can we (as men who may be interested at least as much in positively gaining truth as in merely escaping dupery) always wait with impunity until the coercive evidence arrives? It seems *a priori* improbable that the truth should be so nicely adjusted to our needs and powers as that. In the great boarding house of nature, the cakes and the butter and the syrup seldom come out so even and leave the plates so clean. Indeed, we should view them with scientific suspicion if they did.

IX

Moral questions immediately present themselves as questions whose solution cannot wait for sensible proof. A moral question is a question not of what sensibly exists, but of what is good, or would be good if it did exist. Science can tell us what exists. But to compare the *worth,* both of what exists and of what does not exist, we must not consult science, but what Pascal calls our heart. Science herself consults her heart when she lays it down that the infinite ascertainment of fact and correction of false belief are the supreme goods for man. Challenge this statement and science can only repeat it oracularly,

or else prove it by showing that such ascertainment and correction bring man all sorts of other goods that man's heart in turn declares to be good. The question of having or not having moral beliefs at all is decided by our will. . . .

Turn now from these wide questions of good to a certain class of questions of fact, questions concerning personal relations, states of mind between one man and another. For example, *Do you like me or not?* Whether you do or not depends, in countless instances, on whether I meet you half-way, on whether I am willing to assume that you must like me, and show you trust and expectation. The previous faith on my part in your liking's existence is in such cases what makes your liking come. But if I stand aloof and refuse to budge an inch until I have objective evidence of your liking, until you have done something apt, . . . ten to one your liking never comes. How many women's hearts are vanquished by the mere sanguine insistence of some man that they *must* love him! He will not consent to the hypothesis that they cannot. The desire for a certain kind of truth here brings about that special truth's existence; and so it is in innumerable cases of other sorts. Who gains promotions, boons, appointments, but the man in whose life they are seen to play the part of live hypotheses, who . . . sacrifices other things for their sake before they have come, and takes risks for them in advance? His faith acts on the powers above him as a claim and creates its own verification. . . .

There are, then, cases where a fact cannot come at all unless a preliminary faith exists in its coming. *And where faith in a fact can help create the fact,* it would be an insane logic that would say that faith running ahead of scientific evidence is the "lowest kind of immorality" into which a thinking being can fall. Yet such is the logic by which our scientific absolutists pretend to regulate their lives.

X

In truths dependent on our personal action, then, faith based on desire is certainly a lawful and possibly an indispensable thing.

But now, it will be said, these are all childish human cases and have nothing to do with great cosmic matters, like the question of religious faith.

Let us then pass on to that. Religions differ so much in their accidents that in discussing the religious question we must make it very generic and broad. What then do we now mean by the religious hypothesis? Science says things are; morality says some things are better than other things; and religion says essentially two things.

First, she says that the best things are the more eternal things, the overlapping things, the things in the universe that throw the last stone, so to speak, and say the final word. "Perfection is eternal." This phrase of Charles Secrétan seems a good way of putting this first affirmation of religion, an affirmation that obviously cannot yet be verified scientifically at all.

The second affirmation of religion is that we are better off even now if we believe her first affirmation to be true.

Now, let us consider what the logical elements of the situation are *in case the religious hypothesis in both its branches is really true.* . . . So, proceeding, we see, first, that religion offers itself as a *momentous* option. We are supposed to gain, even now, by our belief, and to lose by our nonbelief, a certain vital good. Secondly, religion is a *forced* option, so far as that good goes. We cannot escape the issue by remaining skeptical and waiting for more light, because, although we do avoid error in that way *if religion is untrue,* we lose the good, *if it is true,* just as certainly as if we positively chose to disbelieve. It is as if a man should hesitate indefinitely to ask a certain woman to marry him because he was not perfectly sure that she would prove an angel after he brought her home. Would he not cut himself off from that particular angel-possibility as decisively as if he went and married someone else? **Skepticism,** then, is not avoidance of option; it is an option of a certain particular kind of risk. *Better risk loss of truth than chance of error*—that is your faith-vetoer's exact position. He is actively playing his stake as much as the believer is; he is backing the field against the religious hypothesis, just as the believer is backing the religious hypothesis against the field. To preach skepticism to us as a duty until "sufficient evidence" for religion is found is, therefore, tantamount to telling us that, when in presence of the religious hypothesis, yielding to our fear of its being error is wiser and better than yielding to our hope that it may be true. It is not intellect against all passions, then; it is only intellect with one passion

laying down its law. And by what, pray tell, is the supreme wisdom of this passion warranted? Dupery for dupery, what proof is there that dupery through hope is so much worse than dupery through fear? I, for one, can see no proof; and I simply refuse obedience to the scientist's command to imitate his kind of option, in a case where my own stake is important enough to give me the right to choose my own form of risk. If religion is true but the evidence for it still insufficient, I do not wish, by putting your extinguisher upon my nature (which feels to me as if it had after all some business in this matter), to forfeit my sole chance in life of getting upon the winning side. That chance depends, of course, on my willingness to run the risk of acting as if my passional need of taking the world religiously might be prophetic and right.

All this is on the supposition that it really may be prophetic and right, and that, even to us who are discussing the matter, religion is a live hypothesis that may be true. Now, to most of us, religion comes in a still further way that makes a veto on our active faith even more illogical. The more perfect and more eternal aspect of the universe is represented in our religions as having personal form. The universe is no longer a mere *It* to us, but a *Thou,* if we are religious; and any relation that may be possible from person to person might be possible here. For instance, although in one sense we are passive portions of the universe, in another we show a curious **autonomy,** as if we were small active centers on our own account. We feel, too, as if the appeal of religion to us were made to our own active good-will, as if evidence might be forever withheld from us unless we met the hypothesis half-way. To take a trivial illustration: just as a man who in company of gentlemen made no advances, asked a warrant for every concession, and believed no one's word without proof, would cut himself off by such churlishness from all the social rewards that a more trusting spirit would earn—so here, one who shuts himself up in snarling logicality and tries to make the gods extort his recognition willy-nilly, or not get it at all, might cut himself off forever from his only opportunity of making the gods' acquaintance. This feeling, forced on us we know not whence, that by obstinately believing there are gods—although not to do so would be so easy both for our logic and our life—we are doing the universe the deepest service we can, seems part of the living essence of the religious hypothesis. If the hypothesis *were* true in all its parts, including this one, then pure intellectualism, with its veto on our making willing advances, would be an absurdity; and some participation of our sympathetic nature would be logically required. I, therefore, for one, cannot see my way to accepting the agnostic rules for truth-seeking, or to willfully agreeing to keep my willing nature out of the game. I cannot do so for the plain reason that *a rule of thinking that would absolutely prevent me from acknowledging certain kinds of truth if those kinds of truth were really there, would be an irrational rule.* That for me is the long and short of the formal logic of the situation, no matter what the kinds of truth might materially be. . . .

When I look at the religious question as it really puts itself to concrete men, and when I think of all the possibilities that it involves, both practically and theoretically, then this command that we put a stopper on our heart, instincts, and courage, and that we *wait*—acting of course meanwhile more or less as if religion were *not* true—until doomsday, or until such time as our intellect and senses working together may have raked in enough evidence—this command, I say, seems to me the queerest idol ever manufactured in the philosophic cave. . . . Indeed we *may* wait if we will—I hope you do not think that I am denying that—but if we do so, we do so at our peril as much as if we believed. In either case we *act,* taking our life in our hands.

Questions for Thought

1. What type of person is James arguing against in this essay? To what extent, if any, do you consider yourself to be this type of person?
2. Can you think of options in your own life that could be classified as living, forced, and momentous? Contrast these with other options that are dead, avoidable, and/or trivial.
3. Do you agree with James' account of how we derive our beliefs? Why or why not?
4. If you have religious beliefs, how do they compare with or differ from the two essential religious beliefs that James identifies?
5. Assuming that your best friend is **agnostic,** do you think that James' argument would convince him or her to become religious? Why or why not?

9   Myth and Society

JOSEPH CAMPBELL

Joseph Campbell (1904–1987), one of the world's foremost comparative mythologists, was born in New York City. Having been awakened to the power of myth when he discovered Native American folklore as a child, Campbell pursued this interest while studying literature at Columbia University, the University of Paris, and the University of Munich. He returned to the United States from his studies abroad in 1929, the year in which the Great Depression began.

Unable to find a job, Campbell spent the next five years living in a small hut in Woodstock, New York, where he continued his study of comparative mythology. In 1934, he obtained a position on the literature faculty at Sarah Lawrence College in Bronxville, New York, and he taught there until his retirement in 1972. Campbell was a prolific writer and editor, a popular lecturer, and the star of two PBS television/video series, *The Power of Myth* and *The Transformations of Myth Through Time*. Not limiting himself to the sphere of academia, Campbell befriended the film director George Lucas, and his writings inspired Lucas' film *Star Wars* and its sequels. Also, toward the end of his life, Campbell discovered the music of the Grateful Dead and participated in an innovative presentation with two of the band's members, Jerry Garcia and Mickey Hart. He died in Honolulu, Hawaii, where he had retired with his wife, the dancer Jean Erdman.

Campbell's writings include *The Masks of God* (a four-volume study of world mythology), *The Hero with a Thousand Faces, The Flight of the Wild Gander, Myths to Live By* (a collection of his essays), and several volumes of the multivolume *Historical Atlas of World Mythology*, which he did not live to complete. He was also the editor of many works. Among these were *The Portable Jung, The Portable Arabian Nights*, and *Myths, Dreams, and Religions*.

In the following excerpt from his first book *The Hero with a Thousand Faces*, Campbell discusses the crucial role that he thinks mythology has played, and must continue to play, in human life. After stating that there is "no final system for the interpretation of myths," Campbell says that myth has been interpreted in many diverse ways, from Frazer's negative evaluation that myths consist of crude, outdated attempts to explain natural phenomena to Coomaraswamy's positive claim that myth expresses humanity's profoundest metaphysical truths. While admitting that each of these explanations is true from a certain perspective, Campbell suggests that myth served two basic functions in the ancient world. It helped the individual fit into the community in which he or she lived, and it helped the community acknowledge and submit to the cycles of the natural world and the cosmos. Other ancient myths, however, had the seemingly contrary purpose of showing the individual how to escape from social roles and restraints in order to begin a quest for his or her inner essence. While ancient myths appear to guide the individual in opposite directions, Campbell says that the ultimate outcome of the ancient mythical journey was the discovery that one's inner essence is the same as the essence of the world. As he says, "Just as the way of social participation may lead in the end to a realization of the All in the individual, so that of exile brings the hero to the Self in all."

At the end of this selection, Campbell says that modern individuals and modern societies have moved outside the mythological realm. Quoting Nietzsche's line from *Thus Spoke Zarathustra* that "Dead are all the gods," Campbell says that the modern democratic emphasis on the self-determining individual, as well as the development of modern industry and modern science, have rendered ancient myth and traditional religion useless in the contemporary world. With this demise of ancient myth and traditional religion, Campbell believes that we have also lost the social harmony and individual wholeness that were produced by the ancient mythological journey. The modern secular state has become a battleground of competing economic and political forces, and the individual psyche has been fragmented. Realizing the impossibility of resurrecting outmoded myths and outdated religions, Campbell claims that these social and individual problems can be overcome only with the emergence of a new mythology that can "render the modern world spiritually significant." But the emergence of this mythology cannot be consciously controlled, nor will it be accomplished overnight. Until this mythology emerges, we are destined to live in an impoverished, chaotic world. Rather than ending on this pessimistic note, however, Campbell says that even in such a world, we can strive to be the creative hero who does everything possible to guide and save the society in which we live. The creative hero, as Campbell concludes, "shares the supreme ordeal—carries the cross of the redeemer—not in the bright moments of his tribe's great victories, but in the silences of his personal despair."

Questions for Reading

1. What does Campbell mean when he says that there is "no final system for the interpretation of myths"? Why does he choose the god Proteus to illustrate this point?
2. What, according to Campbell, were the principal functions of myth in ancient societies?
3. Why, according to Campbell, are ancient myth and traditional religion useless in modern society?
4. How does Campbell think the modern world can be made "spiritually significant"? What role does the hero play in this process?
5. What is the quotation from Nietzsche that Campbell cites? Why does Campbell choose this particular quotation?

1: THE SHAPESHIFTER

THERE IS NO FINAL SYSTEM FOR THE INTER-pretation of myths, and there will never be any such thing. Mythology is like the god Proteus, "the ancient one of the sea, whose speech is sooth." The god "will make assay, and take all manner of shapes of things that creep upon the earth, of water likewise, and of fierce fire burning."[1]

The life-voyager wishing to be taught by Proteus must "grasp him steadfastly and press him yet the more," and at length he will appear in his proper shape. But this wily god never discloses even to the skillful questioner the whole content of his wisdom. He will reply only to the question put to him, and what he discloses will be great or trivial, according to the question asked. "So often as the sun in his course stands high in mid heaven, then forth from the brine comes the ancient one of the sea, whose speech is sooth, before the breath of the West Wind he comes, and the sea's dark ripple covers him. And when he is got forth, he lies down to sleep in the hollow of the caves. And around him the seals, the brood of the fair daughter of the brine, sleep all in a flock, stolen forth from the grey sea water, and bitter is the scent they breathe of the deeps of the salt sea."[2] The Greek warrior-king Menelaus, who was guided by a helpful daughter of this old sea-father to the wild lair, and instructed by her how to wring from the god his response, desired only to ask the secret of his own personal difficulties and the whereabouts of his personal friends. And the god did not disdain to reply.

Mythology has been interpreted by the modern intellect as a primitive, fumbling effort to explain the world of nature (Frazer); as a production of poetical fantasy from prehistoric times, misunderstood by succeeding ages (Müller); as a repository of allegorical instruction, to shape the individual to his group (Durkheim); as a group dream, symptomatic of archetypal urges within the depths of the human psyche (Jung); as the traditional vehicle of man's profoundest metaphysical insights (Coomaraswamy); and as God's Revelation to His children (the Church). Mythology is all of these. The various judgments are determined by the viewpoints of the judges. For when scrutinized in terms not of what it is but of how it functions, of how it has served mankind in the past, of how it may serve today, mythology shows itself to be as amenable as life itself to the obsessions and requirements of the individual, the race, the age.

2: THE FUNCTION OF MYTH, CULT AND MEDITATION

In his life-form the individual is necessarily only a fraction and distortion of the total image of man. He is limited either as male or as female; at any given period of his life he is again limited as child, youth, mature adult, or ancient; furthermore, in his life-role he is necessarily specialized as craftsman, tradesman, servant, or thief, priest, leader, wife, nun, or harlot; he cannot be all. Hence, the totality—the fullness of man—is not in the separate member, but in the body of the society as a whole; the individual can be only an organ. From his group he has derived his techniques of life, the language in which he thinks, the ideas on which he thrives; through the past of that society descended the genes that built his body. If he presumes to cut himself off, either in deed or in thought and feeling, he only breaks connection with the sources of his existence.

The tribal ceremonies of birth, initiation, marriage, burial, installation, and so forth, serve to translate the individual's life-crises and life-deeds into classic, impersonal forms. They disclose him to himself, not as this personality or that, but as the warrior, the bride, the widow, the priest, the chieftain; at the same time rehearsing for the rest of the community the old lesson of the archetypal stages. All participate in the ceremonial according to rank and function. The whole society becomes visible to itself as an imperishable living unit. Generations of individuals pass, like anonymous cells from a living body; but the sustaining, timeless form remains. By an enlargement of vision to embrace this super-individual, each discovers himself enhanced, enriched, supported, and magnified. His role, however unimpressive, is seen to be intrinsic to the beautiful festival-image of man—the image, potential yet necessarily inhibited, within himself.

Social duties continue the lesson of the festival into normal, everyday existence, and the individual is validated still. Conversely, indifference, revolt—or exile—break the vitalizing connectives. From the standpoint of the social unit, the broken-off individual is simply nothing—waste. Whereas the man or woman who can honestly say that he or she has lived the role—whether that of priest, harlot, queen, or slave—*is* something in the full sense of the verb *to be*.

Rites of initiation and installation, then, teach the lesson of the essential oneness of the individual and the group; seasonal festivals open a larger horizon. As the individual is an organ of society, so is the tribe or city—so is humanity entire—only a phase of the mighty organism of the cosmos.

It has been customary to describe the seasonal festivals of so-called native peoples as efforts to control nature. This is a misrepresentation. There is much of the will to control in every act of man, and particularly in those magical ceremonies that are thought to bring rain clouds, cure sickness, or stay the flood; nevertheless, the dominant motive in all truly religious (as opposed to black-magical) ceremonial is that of submission to the inevitables of destiny—and in the seasonal festivals this motive is particularly apparent.

No tribal rite has yet been recorded which attempts to keep winter from descending; on the contrary: the rites all prepare the community to endure, together with the rest of nature, the season of the terrible cold. And in the spring, the rites do not seek to compel nature to pour forth immediately corn, beans, and squash for the lean community; on the contrary: the rites dedicate the whole people to the work of nature's season. The wonderful cycle of the year, with its hardships and periods of joy, is celebrated, and delineated, and represented as continued in the life-round of the human group.

Many other symbolizations of this continuity fill the world of the mythologically instructed community. For example, the clans of the American hunting tribes commonly regarded themselves as descended from half-animal, half-human, ancestors. These ancestors fathered not only the human members of the clan, but also the animal species after which the clan was named; thus the human members of the beaver clan were blood cousins of the animal beavers, protectors of the species and in turn protected by the animal wisdom of the wood folk. Or another example: The hogan, or mud hut, of the Navahos of New Mexico and Arizona, is constructed on the plan of the Navaho image of the cosmos. The entrance faces east. The eight sides represent the four directions and the points between. Every beam and joist corresponds to an element in the great hogan of the all-embracing earth and sky. And since the soul of man itself is regarded as identical in form with the universe, the mud hut is a representation of the basic harmony of man and world, and a reminder of the hidden life-way of perfection.

But there is another way—in diametric opposition to that of social duty and the popular cult. From the standpoint of the way of duty, anyone in exile from the community is a nothing. From the other point of view, however, this exile is the first step of the quest. Each carries within himself the all; therefore it may be sought and discovered within. The differentiations of sex, age, and occupation are not essential to our character, but mere costumes which we wear for a time on the stage of the world. The image of man within is not to be confounded with the garments. We think of ourselves as Americans, children of the twentieth century, Occidentals, civilized Christians. We are virtuous or sinful. Yet such designations do not tell what it is to be man, they denote only the accidents of geography, birth-date, and income. What is the core of us? What is the basic character of our being?

The **asceticism** of the medieval saints and of the yogis of India, the Hellenistic mystery initiations, the ancient philosophies of the East and of the West, are techniques for the shifting of the emphasis of individual consciousness away from the garments. The preliminary meditations of the aspirant detach his mind and sentiments from the accidents of life and drive him to the core. "I am not that, not that," he meditates: "not my mother or son who has just died; my body, which is ill or aging; my arm, my eye, my head; not the summation of all these things. I am not my feeling; not my mind; not my power of **intuition.**" By such meditations he is driven to his own profundity and breaks through, at last, to unfathomable realizations. No man can return from such exercises and take very seriously himself as Mr. So-and-so of Such-and-such a township, U.S.A.— Society and duties drop away. Mr. So-and-so, having discovered himself big with man, becomes in-drawn and aloof.

This is the stage of Narcissus looking into the pool, of the Buddha sitting contemplative under the tree, but it is not the ultimate goal; it is a requisite step, but not the end. The aim is not to *see,* but to realize that one *is,* that essence; then one is free to wander as that essence in the world. Furthermore: the world too is of that essence. The essence of oneself and the essence of the world: these two are one. Hence separateness, withdrawal, is no longer necessary. Wherever the hero may wander, whatever he may do, he is ever in the presence of his own essence—for he has the perfected eye to see. There is no separateness. Thus, just as the way of social participation may lead in the end to a realization of the All in the individual, so that of exile brings the hero to the Self in all.

Centered in this hub-point, the question of selfishness or altruism disappears. The individual has lost himself in the law and been reborn in identity with the whole meaning of the universe. For Him, by Him, the world was made. "O Mohammed," God said, "hadst thou not been, I would not have created the sky."

3: THE HERO TODAY

All of which is far indeed from the contemporary view; for the democratic ideal of the self-determining individual, the invention of the power-driven machine, and the development of the scientific method of research, have so transformed human life that the long-inherited, timeless universe of symbols has collapsed. In the fateful, epoch-announcing words of Nietzsche's Zarathustra: "Dead are all the gods."[3] One knows the tale; it has been told a thousand ways. It is the hero-cycle of the modern age, the wonder-story of mankind's coming to maturity. The spell of the past, the bondage of tradition, was shattered with sure and mighty strokes. The dream-web of myth fell away; the mind opened to full waking consciousness; and modern man emerged from ancient ignorance, like a butterfly from its cocoon, or like the sun at dawn from the womb of mother night.

It is not only that there is no hiding place for the gods from the searching telescope and microscope; there is no such society any more as the gods once supported. The social unit is not a carrier of religious content, but an economic-political organization. Its ideals are not those of the hieratic pantomime, making visible on earth the forms of heaven, but of the secular state, in hard and unremitting competition for material supremacy and resources. Isolated societies, dream-bounded within a mythologically charged horizon, no longer exist except as areas to be exploited. And within the progressive societies themselves, every last vestige of the ancient human heritage of ritual, morality, and art is in full decay.

The problem of mankind today, therefore, is precisely the opposite to that of men in the comparatively stable periods of those great coordinating mythologies which now are known as lies. Then all meaning was in the group, in the great anonymous forms, none in the self-expressive individual; today no meaning is in the group—none in the world: all is in the individual. But there the meaning is absolutely unconscious. One does not know toward what one moves. One does not know by what one is propelled. The lines of communication between the conscious and the unconscious zones of the human psyche have all been cut, and we have been split in two.

The hero-deed to be wrought is not today what it was in the century of Galileo. Where then there was darkness, now there is light; but also, where light was, there now is darkness. The modern hero-deed must be that of questing to bring to light again the lost Atlantis of the coordinated soul.

Obviously, this work cannot be wrought by turning back, or away, from what has been accomplished by the modern revolution; for the problem is nothing if not that of rendering the modern world spiritually significant—or rather (phrasing the same principle the other way round) nothing if not that of making it possible for men and women to come to full human maturity through the conditions of contemporary life. Indeed, these conditions themselves are what have rendered the ancient formulae ineffective, misleading, and even pernicious. The community today is the planet, not the bounded nation; hence the patterns of projected aggression which formerly served to co-ordinate the in-group now can only break it into factions. The national idea, with the flag as totem, is today an aggrandizer of the nursery ego, not the annihilator of an infantile situation. Its parody-rituals of the parade ground serve the ends of Holdfast, the tyrant dragon, not the God in whom self-interest is annihilate. And the numerous saints of this anticult—namely the patriots whose ubiquitous photographs, draped with flags, serve as official icons—are precisely the local threshold guardians (our demon Sticky-hair) whom it is the first problem of the hero to surpass.

Nor can the great world religions, as at present understood, meet the requirement. For they have become associated with the causes of the factions, as instruments of propaganda and self-congratulation. (Even Buddhism has lately suffered this degradation, in reaction to the lessons of the West.) The universal triumph of the secular state has thrown all religious organizations into such a definitely secondary, and finally ineffectual, position that religious pantomime is hardly more today than a sanctimonious exercise for Sunday morning, whereas business ethics and patriotism stand for the remainder of the week. Such a monkey-holiness is not what the functioning world requires; rather, a transmutation of the whole social order is necessary, so that through every detail and act of secular life the vitalizing image of the universal god-man who is actually immanent and effective in all of us may be somehow made known to consciousness.

And this is not a work that consciousness itself can achieve. Consciousness can no more invent, or even predict, an effective symbol than foretell or control tonight's dream. The whole thing is being worked out on another level, through what is bound to be a long and very frightening process, not only in the depths of every living psyche in the modern world, but also on those titanic battlefields into which the whole planet has lately been converted. We are watching the terrible clash of the Symplegades, through which the soul must pass—identified with neither side. But there is one thing we may know, namely, that as the new symbols become visible, they will not be identical in the various parts of the globe; the circumstances of local life, race, and tradition must all be compounded in the effective forms. Therefore, it is necessary for men to understand, and be able to see, that through various symbols the same redemption is revealed. "Truth is one," we read in the Vedas; "the sages call it by many names." A single song is being inflected through all the colorations of the human choir. General propaganda for one or another of the local solutions, therefore, is superfluous—or much rather, a menace. The way to become human is to learn to recognize the lineaments of God in all of the wonderful modulations of the face of man.

With this we come to the final hint of what the specific orientation of the modern hero-task must be, and discover the real cause for the disintegration of all of our inherited religious formulae. The center of gravity, that is to say, of the realm of mystery and danger has definitely shifted. For the primitive hunting peoples of those remotest human millenniums when the sabertooth tiger, the mammoth, and the lesser presences of the animal kingdom were the primary manifestations of what was alien—the source at once of danger, and of sustenance—the great human problem was to become linked psychologically to the task of sharing the wilderness with these beings. An unconscious identification took place, and this was finally rendered conscious in the half-human, half-animal, figures of the mythological totem-ancestors. The animals became the tutors of humanity. Through acts of literal imitation—such as today appear only on the children's playground (or in the madhouse)—an effective annihilation of the human ego was accomplished and society achieved a cohesive organization. Similarly, the tribes supporting themselves on plant-food became cathected to the plant; the life-rituals of planting and reaping were identified with those of human pro-creation, birth, and progress to maturity. Both the plant and the animal worlds, however, were in the end brought under social control. Whereupon the great field of instructive wonder shifted—to the skies—and mankind enacted the great pantomime of the sacred moon-king, the sacred sun-king, the hieratic, planetary state, and the symbolic festivals of the world-regulating spheres.

Today all of these mysteries have lost their force; their symbols no longer interest our psyche. The notion of a cosmic law, which all existence serves and to which man himself must bend, has long since passed through the preliminary mystical stages represented in the old astrology, and is now simply accepted in mechanical terms as a matter of course. The descent of the Occidental sciences from the heavens to the earth (from seventeenth-century astronomy to nineteenth-century biology), and their concentration today, at last, on man himself (in twentieth-century anthropology and psychology), mark the path of a prodigious transfer of the focal point of human wonder. Not the animal world, not the plant world, not the miracle of the spheres, but man himself is now the crucial mystery.

Man is that alien presence with whom the forces of **egoism** must come to terms, through whom the ego is to be crucified and resurrected, and in whose image society is to be reformed. Man, understood however not as "I" but as "Thou": for the ideals and temporal institutions of no tribe, race, continent, social class, or century, can be the measure of the inexhaustible and multifariously wonderful divine existence that is the life in all of us.

The modern hero, the modern individual who dares to heed the call and seek the mansion of that presence with whom it is our whole destiny to be atoned, cannot, indeed must not, wait for his community to cast off its slough of pride, fear, rationalized avarice, and sanctified misunderstanding. "Live," Nietzsche says, "as though the day were here." It is not society that is to guide and save the creative hero, but precisely the reverse. And so every one of us shares the supreme ordeal—carries the cross of the redeemer—not in the bright moments of his tribe's great victories, but in the silences of his personal despair.

NOTES

1. *Odyssey*, IV, 401, 417–18, translation by S. H. Butcher and Andrew Lang (London, 1879).
2. Ibid., IV, 400–406.
3. Nietzsche, *Thus Spake Zarathustra*, 1.22.3.

Questions for Thought

1. Do you agree with Campbell that "there is no final system for the interpretation of myths"? What might be some of the theological implications of accepting this claim?
2. What do you think the function of myth was in ancient society? What function, if any, does myth play in your own life?
3. Do you agree with Campbell that ancient myth and traditional religion are useless in modern society? If so, why? If not, how would you try to convince him that he is mistaken on this point?
4. What, if anything, makes you own life "spiritually significant"?
5. What do you think Campbell means by the "modern creative hero"? Do you believe that you are heroic in Campbell's sense of the term? Why or why not?
6. How would you classify Campbell's religious beliefs? How would you classify your own religious beliefs?

Why Women Need the Goddess   **10**

CAROL P. CHRIST

Carol P. Christ (b. 1945), who received advanced degrees from Stanford University and Yale University, has been very active in feminist, peace, and Goddess movements for many years. She is former co-chair of the women and religion section of the American Academy of Religion, and she has taught at Harvard Divinity School, Columbia University, Pomona College, and San Jose State University. In 1987, experiencing a glass ceiling in her field and burned out by many years of feminist activism, she resigned from her tenured full professorship at San Jose State and moved to Greece. She currently spends much of her time writing and making rituals on the island of Lesbos, where she also teaches workshops and leads Goddess pilgrimages at the Ariadne Institute for the Study of Myth and Ritual.

Of the work of the Ariadne Institute, which she also directs, Christ says the following: "In traveling to Crete, we seek to connect to ancient women, to a time and place where women were at home in their bodies, honored and revered, subordinate to none. We seek knowledge of a time when women and men came together freely without specters of domination and control, self-loathing and shame, that have marred the relation of the sexes for thousands of years. . . . We seek to heal the wounds of patriarchy, violence, and war. We hope to participate in the creation of ecologically balanced, peaceful cultures in which every woman and man, every creature and every living thing is respected and revered for its unique contribution to the web of life."

Coeditor of the influential anthologies *Womanspirit Rising: A Feminist Reader in Religion* (1979) and *Weaving the Visions: New Patterns in Feminist Spirituality* (1989), Christ is also the author of *Diving Deep and Surfacing: Women Writers on Spiritual Quest* (1980), *Laughter of Aphrodite* (1987), *Odyssey with the Goddess* (1995), *Rebirth of the Goddess* (1998), and *She Who Changes: Re-Imagining the Divine in the World* (2003). The following essay, which was the keynote address at the University of California at Santa Cruz Extension conference "The Great Goddess Re-Emerging," was originally published in *Heresies* (Spring 1978).

In this essay, Christ describes several aspects of the emerging Goddess movement and explains the significance of this movement for women's psychological and spiritual development. In doing so, she contrasts the beliefs and practices of the Goddess movement with certain beliefs and practices of patriarchal religion as represented by the Judeo-Christian tradition. Unlike Gutiérrez, Christ believes that this tradition is beyond redemption and that it symbolizes oppression and not liberation, especially in the case of women.

In contrast to the paternalistic symbolism of God the Father, Christ argues that the Goddess symbolizes "the newfound beauty, strength, and power of women." Specifically, she claims that the symbolism of the Goddess has four important implications for the lives of women. First, unlike the Judeo-Christian tradition, it validates female power as both beneficent and effective. Second, it affirms the body, especially the female body, as well as the cycles of life and nature. Third, it provides a positive valuation of the will while at the same time offering a model of the will that differs from the egocentric model associated with patriarchal thinking. Finally, the symbolism of the Goddess revalues women's bonds and heritage, especially the bond between mother and daughter. In short, Christ claims that the symbol of the Goddess is a powerful psychological and political tool in the struggle for liberation and self-affirmation.

Questions for Reading

1. What does Christ mean by the "Goddess"? Does she think that the Goddess physically exists?
2. What are Christ's main criticisms of the Judeo-Christian tradition?
3. Why does Christ believe that symbols are so important? How do the moods and motivations associated with the symbolism of God the Father differ from those associated with the symbolism of the Goddess?
4. What, according to Christ, are the four important implications of the Goddess symbol for women?
5. Why does Christ believe that it is important for people, especially women, to affirm the value of the body and the will?
6. Which Greek myth does Christ describe in her essay? Why does she choose this particular myth to discuss?

At the close of Ntosake Shange's stupendously successful broadway play "For Colored Girls Who Have Considered Suicide When the Rainbow Is Enuf," a tall beautiful black woman rises from despair to cry out, "I found God in myself and I loved her fiercely."[1] Her discovery is echoed by women around the country who meet spontaneously in small groups on full moons, solstices, and equinoxes to celebrate the Goddess as symbol of life and death powers and waxing and waning energies in the universe and in themselves.[2]

> It is the night of the full moon. Nine women stand in a circle, on a rocky hill above the city. The western sky is rosy with the setting sun; in the east the moon's face begins to peer above the horizon. . . . The woman pours out a cup of wine onto the earth, refills it and raises it high. "Hail, Tana, Mother of mothers!" she cries. "Awaken from your long sleep, and return to your children again!"[3]

What are the political and psychological effects of this fierce new love of the divine in themselves for women whose spiritual experience has been focused on the male God of Judaism and Christianity? Is the spiritual dimension of feminism a passing diversion, an escape from difficult but necessary political work? Or does the emergence of the symbol of Goddess among women have significant political and psychological ramifications for the feminist movement?

To answer this question, we must first understand the importance of religious symbols and rituals in human life and consider the effect of male symbolism of God on women. According to anthropologist Clifford Geertz, religious symbols shape a cultural ethos, defining the deepest values of a society and the persons in it. "Religion," Geertz writes, "is a system of symbols which act to produce powerful, pervasive, and long-lasting moods and motivations"[4] in the people of a given culture. A "mood" for Geertz is a psychological attitude such as awe, trust, and respect, while a "motivation" is the *social* and *political* trajectory created by a mood that transforms mythos into ethos, symbol system into social

Carol Christ, "Why Women Need the Goddess: Phenomenological, Psychological, and Political Reflections." First appeared in Heresies No. 5, "The Great Goddess," Spring 1978. Reprinted by permission of the author. Carol P. Christ (Ph.D. Yale) is the author of six books, including Rebirth of the Goddess, that have helped to establish the study of women and religion in North America and Europe.

and political reality. Symbols have both psychological and political effects, because they create the inner conditions (deep-seated attitudes and feelings) that lead people to feel comfortable with or to accept social and political arrangements that correspond to the symbol system.

Because religion has such a compelling hold on the deep psyches of so many people, feminists cannot afford to leave it in the hands of the fathers. Even people who no longer "believe in God" or participate in the institutional structure of patriarchal religion still may not be free of the power of the symbolism of God the Father. A symbol's effect does not depend on rational assent, for a symbol also functions on levels of the psyche other than the rational. Religion fulfills deep psychic needs by providing symbols and rituals that enable people to cope with limit situations[5] in human life (death, evil, suffering) and to pass through life's important transitions (birth, sexuality, death). Even people who consider themselves completely secularized will often find themselves sitting in a church or synagogue when a friend or relative gets married, or when a parent or friend has died. The symbols associated with these important rituals cannot fail to affect the deep or unconscious structures of the mind of even a person who has rejected these symbolisms on a conscious level—especially if the person is under stress. The reason for the continuing effect of religious symbols is that the mind abhors a vacuum. Symbol systems cannot simply be rejected, they must be replaced. Where there is not any replacement, the mind will revert to familiar structures at times of crisis, bafflement, or defeat.

Religions centered on the worship of a male God create "moods" and "motivations" that keep women in a state of psychological dependence on men and male authority, while at the same time legitimating the *political* and *social* authority of fathers and sons in the institutions of society.

Religious symbol systems focused around exclusively male images of divinity create the impression that female power can never be fully legitimate or wholly beneficent. This message need never be explicitly stated (as, for example, it is in the story of Eve) for its effect to be felt. A woman completely ignorant of the myths of female evil in biblical religion nonetheless acknowledges the anomaly of female power when she prays exclusively to a male God.

She may see herself as like God (created in the image of God) only by denying her own sexual identity and affirming God's transcendence of sexual identity. But she can never have the experience that is freely available to every man and boy in her culture, of having her full sexual identity affirmed as being in the image and likeness of God. In Geertz' terms, her "mood" is one of trust in male power as salvific and distrust of female power in herself and other women as inferior or dangerous. Such a powerful, pervasive, and long-lasting "mood" cannot fail to become a "motivation" that translates into social and political reality.

In *Beyond God the Father,* feminist theologian Mary Daly detailed the psychological and political ramifications of father religion for women. "If God in 'his' heaven is a father ruling his people," she wrote, "then it is the 'nature' of things and according to divine plan and the order of the universe that society be male dominated. Within this context, a *mystification of roles* takes place: The husband dominating his wife represents God 'himself.' The images and values of a given society have been projected into the realm of dogmas and 'Articles of Faith,' and these in turn justify the social structures which have given rise to them and which sustain their plausibility."[6]

Philosopher Simone de Beauvoir was well aware of the function of patriarchal religion as legitimater of male power. As she wrote, "Man enjoys the great advantage of having a god endorse the code he writes; and since man exercises a sovereign authority over women it is especially fortunate that this authority has been vested in him by the Supreme Being. For the Jew, Mohammedans, and Christians, among others, man is Master by divine right; the fear of God will therefore repress any impulse to revolt in the downtrodden female."[7]

This brief discussion of the psychological and political effects of God religion puts us in an excellent position to begin to understand the significance of the symbol of Goddess for women. In discussing the meaning of the Goddess, my method will first be phenomenological. I will isolate a meaning of the symbol of the Goddess as it has emerged in the lives of contemporary women. I will then discuss its psychological and political significance by contrasting the "moods" and "motivations" engendered by Goddess symbols with those engendered by

Christian symbolism. I will also correlate Goddess symbolism with themes that have emerged in the women's movement, in order to show how Goddess symbolism undergirds and legitimates the concerns of the women's movement, much as God symbolism in Christianity undergirded the interests of men in **patriarchy.** I will discuss four aspects of Goddess symbolism here: the Goddess as affirmation of female power, the female body, the female will, and women's bonds and heritage. There are, of course, many other meanings of the Goddess that I will not discuss here.

The sources for the symbol of the Goddess in contemporary spirituality are traditions of Goddess worship and modern women's experience. The ancient Mediterranean, pre-Christian European, native American, Mesoamerican, Hindu, African, and other traditions are rich sources for Goddess symbolism. But these traditions are filtered through modern women's experiences. Traditions of Goddesses' subordination to Gods, for example, are ignored. Ancient traditions are tapped selectively and eclecticly, but they are not considered authoritative for modern consciousness. The Goddess symbol has emerged spontaneously in the dreams, fantasies, and thoughts of many women around the country in the past several years. Kirsten Grimstad and Susan Rennie reported that they were surprised to discover widespread interest in spirituality, including the Goddess, among feminists around the country in the summer of 1974.[8] *WomanSpirit* magazine, which published its first issue in 1974 and has contributors from across the United States, has expressed the grass roots nature of the women's spirituality movement. In 1976, a journal, *Lady Unique,* devoted to the Goddess emerged. In 1975, the first women's spirituality conference was held in Boston and attended by 1,800 women. In 1978, a University of Santa Cruz course on the Goddess drew over 500 people. Sources for this essay are these manifestations of the Goddess in modern women's experiences as reported in *WomanSpirit, Lady Unique,* and elsewhere, and as expressed in conversations I have had with women who have been thinking about the Goddess and women's spirituality.

The simplest and most basic meaning of the symbol of Goddess is the acknowledgment of the legitimacy of female power as a beneficent and independent power. A woman who echoes Ntosake

Shange's dramatic statement, "I found God in myself and I loved her fiercely," is saying "Female power is strong and creative." She is saying that the divine principle, the saving and sustaining power, is in herself, that she will no longer look to men or male figures as saviors. The strength and independence of female power can be intuited by contemplating ancient and modern images of the Goddess. This meaning of the symbol of Goddess is simple and obvious, and yet it is difficult for many to comprehend. It stands in sharp contrast to the paradigms of female dependence on males that have been predominant in Western religion and culture. The internationally acclaimed novelist Monique Wittig captured the novelty and flavor of the affirmation of female power when she wrote, in her mythic work *Les Guerilleres,*

> There was a time when you were not a slave, remember that. You walked alone, full of laughter, you bathed bare-bellied. You say you have lost all recollection of it, remember . . . you say there are not words to describe it, you say it does not exist. But remember. Make an effort to remember. Or, failing that, invent.[9]

While Wittig does not speak directly of the Goddess here, she captures the "mood" of joyous celebration of female freedom and independence that is created in women who define their identities through the symbol of Goddess. Artist Mary Beth Edelson expressed the political "motivations" inspired by the Goddess when she wrote,

> The ascending archetypal symbols of the feminine unfold today in the psyche of modern Every woman. They encompass the multiple forms of the Great Goddess. Reaching across the centuries we take the hands of our Ancient Sisters. The Great Goddess alive and well is rising to announce to the patriarchs that their 5,000 years are up—Hallelujah! Here we come.[10]

The affirmation of female power contained in the Goddess symbol has both psychological and political consequences. Psychologically, it means the defeat of the view engendered by patriarchy that women's power is inferior and dangerous. This new "mood" of affirmation of female power also leads to new "motivations"; it supports and undergirds women's trust in their own power and the power of other women in family and society.

If the simplest meaning of the Goddess symbol is an affirmation of the legitimacy and beneficence of female power, then a question immediately arises, "Is the Goddess simply female power writ large, and if so, why bother with the symbol of Goddess at all? Or does the symbol refer to a Goddess 'out there' who is not reducible to a human potential?" The many women who have rediscovered the power of Goddess would give three answers to this question: (1) The Goddess is divine female, a personification who can be invoked in prayer and ritual; (2) the Goddess is symbol of the life, death, and rebirth energy in nature and culture, in personal and communal life; and (3) the Goddess is symbol of the affirmation of the legitimacy and beauty of female power (made possible by the new becoming of women in the women's liberation movement). If one were to ask these women which answer is the "correct" one, different responses would be given. Some would assert that the Goddess definitely is *not* "out there," that the symbol of a divinity "out there" is part of the legacy of patriarchal oppression, which brings with it the authoritarianism, hierarchicalism, and dogmatic rigidity associated with biblical monotheistic religions. They might assert that the Goddess symbol reflects the sacred power within women and nature, suggesting the connectedness between women's cycles of menstruation, birth, and menopause, and the life and death cycles of the universe. Others seem quite comfortable with the notion of Goddess as a divine female protector and creator and would find their experience of Goddess limited by the assertion that she is not *also* out there as well as within themselves and in all natural processes. When asked what the symbol of Goddess means, feminist priestess Starhawk replied, "It all depends on how I feel. When I feel weak, she is someone who can help and protect me. When I feel strong, she is the symbol of my own power. At other times I feel her as the natural energy in my body and the world."[11] How are we to evaluate such a statement? Theologians might call these the words of a sloppy thinker. But my deepest **intuition** tells me they contain a wisdom that Western theological thought has lost.

To theologians, these differing views of the "meaning" of the symbol of Goddess might seem to threaten a replay of the trinitarian controversies. Is there, perhaps, a way of doing theology, which would not lead immediately into dogmatic controversy, which would not require theologians to say definitively that one understanding is true and the others are false? Could people's relation to a common symbol be made primary and varying interpretations be acknowledged? The diversity of explications of the meaning of the Goddess symbol suggests that symbols have a richer significance than any explications of their meaning can express, a point literary critics have long insisted on. This phenomenological fact suggests that theologians may need to give more than lip service to a theory of symbol in which the symbol is viewed as the primary fact and the meanings are viewed as secondary. It also suggests that a *thea*logy[12] of the Goddess would be very different from the *theo*logy we have known in the West. But to spell out this notion of the primacy of *symbol* in thealogy in contrast to the primacy of the *explanation* in theology would be the topic of another paper. Let me simply state that women, who have been deprived of a female religious symbol system for centuries, are therefore in an excellent position to recognize the power and primacy of symbols. I believe women must develop a theory of symbol and thealogy congruent with their experience at the same time as they "remember and invent" new symbol systems.

A second important implication of the Goddess symbol for women is the affirmation of the female body and the life cycle expressed in it. Because of women's unique position as menstruants, birth-givers, and those who have traditionally cared for the young and the dying, women's connection to the body, nature, and this world has been obvious. Women were denigrated because they seemed more carnal, fleshy, and earthy than the culture-creating males.[13] The misogynist anti*body* tradition in Western thought is symbolized in the myth of Eve who is traditionally viewed as a sexual temptress, the epitome of women's carnal nature. This tradition reaches its nadir in the *Malleus Maleficarum* (*The Hammer of Evil-Doing Women*), which states, "All witchcraft stems from carnal lust, which in women is insatiable."[14] The Virgin Mary, the positive female image in Christianity, does not contradict Christian denigration of the female body and its powers. The Virgin Mary is revered because she, in her perpetual virginity, transcends the carnal sexuality attributed to most women.

The denigration of the female body is expressed in cultural and religious taboos surrounding menstruation, childbirth, and menopause in women. While menstruation taboos may have originated in a perception of the awesome powers of the female body,[15] they degenerated into a simple perception that there is something "wrong" with female bodily functions. Menstruating women were forbidden to enter the sanctuary in ancient Hebrew and premodern Christian communities. Although only Orthodox Jews still enforce religious taboos against menstruant women, few women in our culture grow up affirming their menstruation as a connection to sacred power. Most women learn that menstruation is a curse and grow up believing that the bloody facts of menstruation are best hidden away. Feminists challenge this attitude to the female body. Judy Chicago's art piece "Menstruation Bathroom" broke these menstrual taboos. In a sterile white bathroom, she exhibited boxes of Tampax and Kotex on an open shelf, and the wastepaper basket was overflowing with bloody tampons and sanitary napkins.[16] Many women who viewed the piece felt relieved to have their "dirty secret" out in the open.

The denigration of the female body and its powers is further expressed in Western culture's attitudes toward childbirth.[17] Religious iconography does not celebrate the birthgiver, and there is no theology or ritual that enables a woman to celebrate the process of birth as a spiritual experience. Indeed, Jewish and Christian traditions also had blood taboos concerning the woman who had recently given birth. While these religious taboos are rarely enforced today (again, only by Orthodox Jews), they have secular equivalents. Giving birth is treated as a disease requiring hospitalization, and the woman is viewed as a passive object, anesthetized to ensure her acquiescence to the will of the doctor. The women's liberation movement has challenged these cultural attitudes, and many feminists have joined with advocates of natural childbirth and home birth in emphasizing the need for women to control and take pride in their bodies, including the birth process.

Western culture also gives little dignity to the postmenopausal or aging woman. It is no secret that our culture is based on a denial of aging and death, and that women suffer more severely from this denial than men. Women are placed on a pedestal and considered powerful when they are young and beautiful, but they are said to lose this power as they age. As feminists have pointed out, the "power" of the young woman is illusory, since beauty standards are defined by men, and since few women are considered (or consider themselves) beautiful for more than a few years of their lives. Some men are viewed as wise and authoritative in age, but old women are pitied and shunned. Religious iconography supports this cultural attitude towards aging women. The purity and virginity of Mary and the female saints is often expressed in the iconographic convention of perpetual youth. Moreover, religious mythology associates aging women with evil in the symbol of the wicked old witch. Feminists have challenged cultural myths of aging women and have urged women to reject patriarchal beauty standards and to celebrate the distinctive beauty of women of all ages.

The symbol of Goddess aids the process of naming and reclaiming the female body and its cycles and processes. In the ancient world and among modern women, the Goddess symbol represents the birth, death, and rebirth processes of the natural and human worlds. The female body is viewed as the direct incarnation of waxing and waning, life and death, cycles in the universe. This is sometimes expressed through the symbolic connection between the twenty-eight-day cycles of menstruation and the twenty-eight-day cycles of the moon. Moreover, the Goddess is celebrated in the triple aspect of youth, maturity, and age, or maiden, mother, and crone. The potentiality of the young girl is celebrated in the nymph or maiden aspect of the Goddess. The Goddess as mother is sometimes depicted giving birth, and giving birth is viewed as a symbol for all the creative, life-giving powers of the universe.[18] The life-giving powers of the Goddess in her creative aspect are not limited to physical birth, for the Goddess is also seen as the creator of all the arts of civilization, including healing, writing, and the giving of just law. Women in the middle of life who are not physical mothers may give birth to poems, songs, and books, or nurture other women, men, and children. They too are incarnations of the Goddess in her creative, life-giving aspect. At the end of life, women incarnate the crone aspect of the Goddess. The wise old woman, the woman who knows from experience what life is about, the woman whose closeness to her own death gives her a distance and perspective on the problems of life, is celebrated as the third aspect of the Goddess. Thus, women learn to value youth, creativity, and wisdom in themselves and other women.

The possibilities of reclaiming the female body and its cycles have been expressed in a number of Goddess-centered rituals. Hallie Mountainwing and Barbry My Own created a summer solstice ritual to celebrate menstruation and birth. The women simulated a birth canal and birthed each other into their circle. They raised power by placing their hands on each other's bellies and chanting together. Finally they marked each other's faces with rich, dark menstrual blood saying, "This is the blood that promises renewal. This is the blood that promises sustenance. This is the blood that promises life."[19] From hidden dirty secret to symbol of the life power of the Goddess, women's blood has come full circle. Other women have created rituals that celebrate the crone aspect of the Goddess. Z. Budapest believes that the crone aspect of the Goddess is predominant in the fall, especially at Halloween, an ancient holiday. On this day, the wisdom of the old woman is celebrated, and it is also recognized that the old must die so that the new can be born.

The "mood" created by the symbol of the Goddess in triple aspect is one of positive, joyful affirmation of the female body and its cycles and acceptance of aging and death as well as life. The "motivations" are to overcome menstrual taboos, to return the birth process to the hands of women, and to change cultural attitudes about age and death. Changing cultural attitudes toward the female body could go a long way toward overcoming the spirit-flesh, mind-body **dualisms** of Western culture, since, as Ruether has pointed out, the denigration of the female body is at the heart of these dualisms. The Goddess as symbol of the revaluation of the body and nature thus also undergirds the human potential and ecology movements. The "mood" is one of affirmation, awe, and respect for the body and nature, and the "motivation" is to respect the teachings of the body and the rights of all living beings.

A third important implication of the Goddess symbol for women is the positive valuation of will in a Goddess-centered ritual, especially in Goddess-centered ritual magic and spellcasting in womanspirit and feminist witchcraft circles. The basic notion behind ritual magic and spellcasting is energy as power. Here the Goddess is a center or focus of power and energy; she is the personification of the energy that flows between beings in the natural and human worlds. In Goddess circles, energy is raised by chanting or dancing. According to Starhawk, "Witches conceive of psychic energy as having form and substance that can be perceived and directed by those with a trained awareness. The power generated within the circle is built into a cone form, and at its peak is released—to the Goddess, to reenergize the members of the coven, or to do a specific work such as healing."[20] In ritual magic, the energy raised is directed by willpower. Women who celebrate in Goddess circles believe they can achieve their wills in the world.

The emphasis on the will is important for women, because women traditionally have been taught to devalue their wills, to believe that they cannot achieve their will through their own power, and even to suspect that the assertion of will is evil. Faith Wildung's poem "Waiting," from which I will quote only a short segment, sums up women's sense that their lives are defined not by their own will, but by waiting for others to take the initiative.

Waiting for my breasts to develop
Waiting to wear a bra
Waiting to menstruate
. . .
Waiting for life to begin, Waiting—
Waiting to be somebody
. . .
Waiting to get married
Waiting for my wedding day
Waiting for my wedding night
. . .
Waiting for the end of the day
Waiting for sleep. Waiting . . .[21]

Patriarchal religion has enforced the view that female initiative and will are evil through the juxtaposition of Eve and Mary. Eve caused the fall by asserting her will against the command of God, while Mary began the new age with her response to God's initiative, "Let it be done to me according to thy word" (Luke 1:38). Even for men, patriarchal religion values the passive will subordinate to divine initiative. The classical doctrines of sin and grace view sin as the prideful assertion of will and grace as the obedient subordination of the human will to the divine initiative or order. While this view of will might be questioned from a human perspective, Valerie Saiving has argued that it has particularly deleterious consequences for women in Western culture. According to Saiving, Western culture encourages males in the assertion of will, and thus it may make some sense to view the male form of sin as an excess of will. But since culture discourages females in the assertion of will, the traditional doctrines of sin and grace encourage women to remain in their form of sin, which is self-negation or insufficient assertion of will.[22] One possible reason the will is denigrated in a patriarchal religious framework is that both human and divine will are often pictured as arbitrary, self-initiated, and exercised without regard for other wills.

In a Goddess-centered context, in contrast, the will is valued. *A woman is encouraged to know her will, to believe that her will is valid, and to believe that her will can be achieved in the world,* three powers traditionally denied to her in patriarchy. In a Goddess-centered framework, a woman's will is not subordinated to the Lord God as king and ruler, nor to men as his representatives. Thus a woman is not reduced to waiting and acquiescing in the wills of others as she is in patriarchy. But neither does she adopt the egocentric form of will that pursues self-interest without regard for the interests of others.

The Goddess-centered context provides a different understanding of the will than that available in the traditional patriarchal religious framework. In the Goddess framework, will can be achieved only when it is exercised in harmony with the energies and wills of other beings. Wise women, for example, raise a cone of healing energy at the full moon or solstice when the lunar or solar energies are at their high points with respect to the earth. This discipline encourages them to recognize that not all times are propitious for the achieving of every will. Similarly, they know that spring is a time for new beginnings in work and love, summer a time for producing external manifestations of inner potentialities, and fall or winter times for stripping down to the inner core and extending roots. Such awareness of waxing and waning processes in the universe discourages arbitrary ego-centered assertion of will, while at the same time encouraging the assertion of individual will in cooperation with natural energies and the

energies created by the wills of others. Wise women also have a tradition that whatever is sent out will be returned and this reminds them to assert their wills in cooperative and healing rather than egocentric and destructive ways. This view of will allows women to begin to recognize, claim, and assert their wills without adopting the worst characteristics of the patriarchal understanding and use of will. In the Goddess-centered framework, the "mood" is one of positive affirmation of personal will in the context of the energies of other wills or beings. The "motivation" is for women to know and assert their wills in cooperation with other wills and energies. This of course does not mean that women always assert their wills in positive and life-affirming ways. Women's capacity for evil is, of course, as great as men's. My purpose is simply to contrast the differing attitudes toward the exercise of will *per se,* and the female will in particular, in Goddess-centered religion and in the Christian God-centered religion.

The fourth and final aspect of Goddess symbolism that I will discuss here is the significance of the Goddess for a revaluation of woman's bonds and heritage. As Virginia Woolf has said, "Chloe liked Olivia," a statement about a woman's relation to another woman, is a sentence that rarely occurs in fiction. Men have written the stories, and they have written about women almost exclusively in their relations to men.[23] The celebrations of women's bonds to each other, as mothers and daughters, as colleagues and coworkers, as sisters, friends, and lovers, is beginning to occur in the new literature and culture created by women in the women's movement. While I believe that the revaluing of each of these bonds is important, I will focus on the mother-daughter bond, in part because I believe it may be the key to the others.

Adrienne Rich has pointed out that the mother-daughter bond, perhaps the most important of woman's bonds, "resonant with charges . . . the flow of energy between two biologically alike bodies, one of which has lain in amniotic bliss inside the other, one of which has labored to give birth to the other,"[24] is rarely celebrated in patriarchal religion and culture. Christianity celebrates the father's relation to the son and the mother's relation to the son, but the story of mother and daughter is missing. So, too, in patriarchal literature and psychology the mothers and the daughters rarely exist. Volumes have been written about the oedipal complex, but little has been written about the girl's relation to her mother. Moreover, as de Beauvoir has noted, the mother-daughter relation is distorted in patriarchy because the mother must give her daughter over to men in a male-defined culture in which women are viewed as inferior. The mother must socialize her daughter to become subordinate to men, and if her daughter challenges patriarchal norms, the mother is likely to defend the patriarchal structures against her own daughter.[25]

These patterns are changing in the new culture created by women in which the bonds of women to women are beginning to be celebrated. Holly Near has written several songs that celebrate women's bonds and women's heritage. In one of her finest songs she writes of an "old-time woman" who is "waiting to die." A young woman feels for the life that has passed the old woman by and begins to cry, but the old woman looks her in the eye and says, "If I had not suffered, you wouldn't be wearing those jeans/Being an old-time woman ain't as bad as it seems."[26] This song, which Near has said was inspired by her grandmother, expresses and celebrates a bond and a heritage passed down from one woman to another. In another of Near's songs, she sings of a "a hiking-boot mother who's seeing the world/For the first time with her own little girl." In this song, the mother tells the drifter who has been traveling with her to pack up and travel alone if he thinks "traveling three is a drag" because "I've got a little one who loves me as much as you need me/And darling, that's loving enough."[27] This song is significant because the mother places her relationship to her daughter above her relationship to a man, something women rarely do in patriarchy.[28]

Almost the only story of mothers and daughters that has been transmitted in Western culture is the myth of Demeter and Persephone that was the basis of religious rites celebrated by women only, the Thesmophoria, and later formed the basis of the Eleusian **mysteries,** which were open to all who spoke Greek. In this story, the daughter, Persephone, is raped away from her mother, Demeter, by the God of the underworld. Unwilling to accept this state of affairs, Demeter rages and withholds fertility from the earth until her daughter is returned to her. What is important for women in this story is that a mother

fights for her daughter and for her relation to her daughter. This is completely different from the mother's relation to her daughter in patriarchy. The "mood" created by the story of Demeter and Persephone is one of celebration of the mother-daughter bond, and the "motivation" is for mothers and daughters to affirm the heritage passed on from mother to daughter and to reject the patriarchal pattern where the primary loyalties of mother and daughter must be to men.

The symbol of Goddess has much to offer women who are struggling to be rid of the "powerful, pervasive, and long-lasting moods and motivations" of devaluation of female power, denigration of the female body, distrust of female will, and denial of the women's bonds and heritage that have been engendered by patriarchal religion. As women struggle to create a new culture in which women's power, bodies, will, and bonds are celebrated, it seems natural that the Goddess would reemerge as symbol of the newfound beauty, strength, and power of women.

NOTES

1. From the original cast album, Buddah Records, 1976.

2. See Susan Rennie and Kristen Grimstad, "Spiritual Explorations Cross-Country," *Quest* 1, no. 4 (1975), 49–51; and *WomanSpirit* magazine.

3. See Starhawk, "Witchcraft and Women's Culture," in this volume.

4. "Religion as a Cultural System," in William L. Lessa and Evon Z. Vogt, eds., *Reader in Comparative Religion*, 2nd ed. (New York: Harper and Row, 1972), p. 206.

5. Geertz, p. 210.

6. Boston: Beacon Press, 1974, p. 13, italics added.

7. *The Second Sex*, trans. H. M. Parshley (New York: Alfred A. Knopf, 1953).

8. See Grimstad and Rennie.

9. *Les Guerilleres*, trans. David LeVay (New York: Avon Books, 1971), p. 89. Also quoted in Morgan MacFarland, "Witchcraft: The Art of Remembering," *Quest* 1, no. 4 (1975), 41.

10. "Speaking for Myself," *Lady Unique* 1, 1976, 56.

11. Personal communication.

12. A term coined by Naomi Goldenberg to refer to reflection on the meaning of the symbol of Goddess.

13. This theory of the origins of the Western dualism is stated by Rosemary Ruether in *New Woman: New Earth* (New York: Seabury Press, 1975), and elsewhere.

14. Heinrich Kramer and Jacob Sprenger (New York: Dover, 1971), p. 47.

15. See Rita M. Gross, "Menstruation and Childbirth as Ritual and Religious Experience in the Religion of the Australian Aborigines," in *The Journal of the American Academy of Religion*, 45, no. 4 (1977), supplement 1147–1181.

16. *Through the Flower* (New York: Doubleday and Company, 1975), plate 4, pp. 106–107.

17. See Adrienne Rich, *Of Woman Born* (New York: Bantam Books, 1977), Chapters 6 and 7.

18. See James Mellaart, *Earliest Civilizations of the Near East* (New York: McGraw-Hill, 1965), p. 92.

19. Barbry My Own, "Ursa Maior: Menstrual Moon Celebration," in Anne Kent Rush, ed., *Moon, Moon* (Berkeley, Calif., and New York: Moon Books and Random House, 1976), pp. 374–387.

20. Starhawk, "Witchcraft and Women's Culture."

21. In Judy Chicago, pp. 213–217.

22. "The Human Situation: A Feminine View," in *Journal of Religion* 40 (1960), 100–112.

23. *A Room of One's Own* (New York: Harcourt Brace Jovanovich, 1928), p. 86.

24. Rich, p. 226.

25. De Beauvoir, pp. 448–449.

26. "Old Time Woman," lyrics by Jeffrey Langley and Holly Near, from *Holly Near: A Live Album*, Redwood Records, 1974.

27. "Started Out Fine," by Holly Near from *Holly Near: A Live Album*.

28. Rich, p. 223.

Questions for Thought

1. How do you think Gutiérrez would respond to Christ's criticisms of the Judeo-Christian tradition? What is your response to these criticisms?

2. What moods and motivations do you associate with the symbolism of God the Father? What moods and motivations do you associate with the symbolism of the Goddess?

3. What do you think is the most adequate symbol of divinity? Defend your answer.

4. Do you believe that it is important to affirm the value of the body and the will? Why or why not?

5. What is the nature and purpose of the rituals described in Christ's essay? Have you participated in religious rituals? If so, what was the nature and purpose of the rituals in which you participated?

6. How do Christ's criticisms of Christianity compare with or differ from the criticisms of Starhawk?

11   Religion and Science

ALFRED NORTH WHITEHEAD

Alfred North Whitehead (1861–1947), British philosopher and mathematician, was born at Ramsgate on the Isle of Thanet in England. His father was an Anglican priest who taught Whitehead at home until he was fourteen. He was then sent to the Sherborne School in Dorset, an ancient public school with a reputation for excellence. At Sherborne, Whitehead became a student leader and excelled in his studies, especially in mathematics. This earned him a mathematics scholarship from Trinity College of Cambridge University, in which he enrolled in 1880.

At Cambridge, Whitehead again excelled academically. This earned him election into the "Apostles," an elite discussion group. It also earned him a fellowship in mathematics, followed by a lectureship, which he held until 1910. During the years of his lectureship,

Whitehead married Evelyn Willoughby Wade, taught and then collaborated with Bertrand Russell, and wrote several works on mathematics. The most famous of these mathematical works, the three-volume *Principia Mathematica* (1903), was coauthored by Russell.

Realizing that he would not be able to obtain a professorship at Cambridge, Whitehead moved to London in 1910. After writing an introductory text on mathematics, he was given a teaching position at the University of London in 1911. Three years later, Whitehead became a professor of applied mathematics at the Imperial College of Science and Technology. While in London, Whitehead served on the governing board of several schools, and he delivered a series of lectures calling for educational reform. Despite the emotional trauma that he experienced when his youngest son was killed in battle, he also managed to finish two books dealing with the philosophy of science, *Enquiry Concerning the Principles of Natural Knowledge* (1919) and *The Concept of Nature* (1920).

In 1924, Whitehead was offered a chair in philosophy at Harvard University, and he moved to the United States. Although he was sixty-three when he accepted the position at Harvard, he taught there for the next thirteen years. He was a popular teacher and speaker who gave guest lectures in many universities. In 1928, he delivered the prestigious Gifford Lectures at the University of Edinburgh, and these lectures served as the basis for his most influential work on **metaphysics,** *Process and Reality* (1929). His other published works include *Science and the Modern World* (1925), *Religion in the Making* (1926), and *Adventures of Ideas* (1933).

Remaining a British subject, Whitehead was elected to the British Academy in 1931 and awarded the Order of Merit in 1945. In his last wishes, he asked that his body be cremated, that there be no funeral, and that his unpublished letters and manuscripts be destroyed. When he died in 1947, his widow Evelyn Whitehead saw to it that these wishes were followed.

In the following selection from *Science and the Modern World,* Whitehead examines the relationship between science and religion. He notes that science and religion have comprised two important spheres of human thinking that have historically been in conflict with each other. From the early Christian belief that the world was going to end within a generation, to the theological text written in 535 C.E. claiming that the earth was flat on the basis of biblical evidence, to the modern Christian denial of the theory of evolution, Whitehead says that religious thinkers have often been at odds with scientific theories and findings.

While scientists have often used this conflict as a reason for rejecting religious thinking and theologians have often used it as a reason for rejecting scientific thinking, Whitehead says that neither of these moves is justified. Although he believes that we should accept nothing in either sphere without good evidence for doing so, he says that the conflict between science and religion can motivate us to think more deeply in each of these spheres. In order to see that this is the case, Whitehead says that we must recognize that both science and religion have developed over time and that they will continue to do so. Once we recognize this, instead of seeing the clash between science and religion as a justification for choosing one of these spheres of thinking and rejecting the other, we can view the conflict as "a sign that there are wider truths and finer perspectives within which a reconciliation of a deeper religion and a more subtle science will be found."

Whitehead believes that most of the obstacles to such a reconciliation between science and religion come from theologians rather than scientists. While modern scientists have embraced change as part of the scientific method, theologians have begrudgingly accepted change only when change could no longer be effectively resisted. Adopting a siege mentality, religious thinkers have equated the death of particular religious images or beliefs with the death of religion itself. Moreover, Whitehead believes that the churches still rely on two outdated and inappropriate motivations for religious belief— the appeal to the fear of an all-powerful, vindictive God who will punish us if we do not believe and the appeal to the usefulness of religion in helping to ensure social order and ethical conduct. In opposition to these motivations for religious belief, Whitehead claims that the purpose of religion is to provide us with a vision that inspires us to live a life of adventure. Religion is, as he says, "the vision of something which stands beyond, behind, and within, the passing flux of immediate things; . . . something that gives meaning to all that passes, and yet eludes apprehension; . . . something which is the ultimate ideal, and the hopeless quest."

Questions for Reading

1. Why does Whitehead believe that science and religion have often been in conflict? What examples of this conflict does he cite?
2. How does Whitehead suggest that we view the conflict between religion and science? What proposal does he make for resolving this conflict?
3. How does Whitehead explain the gradual decline of religious influence in the Western world? What is his attitude toward this decline?
4. What, according to Whitehead, is the true purpose of religion?
5. In Whitehead's view, what can religion give us that science cannot?

THE DIFFICULTY IN APPROACHING THE QUES-tion of the relations between Religion and Science is, that its elucidation requires that we have in our minds some clear idea of what we mean by either of the terms, "religion" and "science." Also I wish to speak in the most general way possible, and to keep in the background any comparison of particular creeds, scientific or religious. We have got to understand the type of connection which exists between the two spheres, and then to draw some definite conclusions respecting the existing situation which at present confronts the world.

The *conflict* between religion and science is what naturally occurs to our minds when we think of this subject. It seems as though, during the last half-century, the results of science and the beliefs of religion had come into a position of frank disagreement, from which there can be no escape, except by abandoning either the clear teaching of science, or the clear teaching of religion. This **conclusion** has been urged by controversialists on either side. Not by all controversialists, of course, but by those trenchant intellects which every controversy calls out into the open. The distress of sensitive minds, and the zeal for truth, and the sense of the importance of the issues, must command our sincerest sympathy. When we consider what religion is for mankind, and what science is, it is no exaggeration to say that the future course of history depends upon the decision of this generation as to the relations between them. We have here the two strongest general forces (apart from the mere impulse of the various senses) which influence men, and they seem to be set one against the other—the force of our religious intuitions, and the force of our impulse to accurate observation and logical deduction.

From Alfred North Whitehead, Science and the Modern World, *Macmillan Publishing Company, 1925.*

A great English statesman once advised his countrymen to use large-scale maps, as a preservative against alarms, panics, and general misunderstanding of the true relations between nations. In the same way in dealing with the clash between permanent elements of human nature, it is well to map our history on a large scale, and to disengage ourselves from our immediate absorption in the present conflicts. When we do this, we immediately discover two great facts. In the first place, there has always been a conflict between religion and science; and in the second place, both religion and science have always been in a state of continual development. In the early days of Christianity, there was a general belief among Christians that the world was coming to an end in the lifetime of people then living. We can make only indirect inferences as to how far this belief was authoritatively proclaimed; but it is certain that it was widely held, and that it formed an impressive part of the popular religious doctrine. The belief proved itself to be mistaken, and Christian doctrine adjusted itself to the change. Again in the early Church individual theologians very confidently deduced from the Bible opinions concerning the nature of the physical universe. In the year A.D. 535, a monk named Cosmas wrote a book which he entitled, *Christian Topography*. He was a traveled man who had visited India and Ethiopia; and finally he lived in a monastery at Alexandria, which was then a great centre of culture. In this book, basing himself upon the direct meaning of Biblical texts as construed by him in a literal fashion, he denied the existence of the antipodes, and asserted that the world is a flat parallelogram whose length is double its breadth.

In the seventeenth century the doctrine of the motion of the earth was condemned by a Catholic tribunal. A hundred years ago the extension of time demanded by geological science distressed religious people, Protestant and Catholic. And today the doctrine of evolution is an equal stumbling-block. These are only a few instances illustrating a general fact.

But all our ideas will be in a wrong perspective if we think that this recurring perplexity was confined to contradictions between religion and science; and that in these controversies religion was always wrong, and that science was always right. The true facts of the case are very much more complex, and refuse to be summarised in these simple terms.

Theology itself exhibits exactly the same character of gradual development, arising from an aspect of conflict between its own proper ideas. This fact is a commonplace to theologians, but is often obscured in the stress of controversy. I do not wish to overstate my case; so I will confine myself to Roman Catholic writers. In the seventeenth century a learned Jesuit, Father Petavius, showed that the theologians of the first three centuries of Christianity made use of phrases and statements which since the fifth century would be condemned as heretical. Also Cardinal Newman devoted a treatise to the discussion of the development of doctrine. He wrote it before he became a great Roman Catholic ecclesiastic; but throughout his life, it was never retracted and continually reissued.

Science is even more changeable than theology. No man of science could subscribe without qualification to Galileo's beliefs, or to Newton's beliefs, or to all his own scientific beliefs of ten years ago.

In both regions of thought, additions, distinctions, and modifications have been introduced. So that now, even when the same assertion is made today as was made a thousand, or fifteen hundred years ago, it is made subject to limitations or expansions of meaning, which were not contemplated at the earlier epoch. We are told by logicians that a proposition must be either true or false, and that there is no middle term. But in practice, we may know that a proposition expresses an important truth, but that it is subject to limitations and qualifications which at present remain undiscovered. It is a general feature of our knowledge, that we are insistently aware of important truths; and yet that the only formulations of these truths which we are able to make presuppose a general standpoint of conceptions which may have to be modified. I will give you two illustrations, both from science: Galileo said that the earth moves and that the sun is fixed; the Inquisition said that the earth is fixed and the sun moves; and Newtonian astronomers, adopting an absolute theory of space, said that both the sun and the earth move. But now we say that any one of these three statements is equally true, provided that you have fixed your sense of "rest" and "motion" in the way required by the statement adopted. At the date of Galileo's controversy with the Inquisition, Galileo's way of stating the facts was, beyond question, the fruitful procedure for the sake of scientific research. But in itself it was not more true than the formulation of the Inquisition. But at that time the modern concepts of relative motion were in nobody's mind; so that the statements were made in ignorance of the qualifications required for their more perfect truth. Yet this question of the motions of the earth and the sun expresses a real fact in the universe; and all sides had got hold of important truths concerning it. But with the knowledge of those times, the truths appeared to be inconsistent.

Again I will give you another example taken from the state of modern physical science. Since the time of Newton and Huyghens in the seventeenth century there have been two theories as to the physical nature of light. Newton's theory was that a beam of light consists of a stream of very minute particles, or corpuscles, and that we have the sensation of light when these corpuscles strike the retinas of our eyes. Huyghens' theory was that light consists of very minute waves trembling in an all-pervading ether, and that these waves are traveling along a beam of light. The two theories are contradictory. In the eighteenth century Newton's theory was believed, in the nineteenth century Huyghens' theory was believed. Today there is one large group of phenomena which can be explained only on the wave theory, and another large group which can be explained only on the corpuscular theory. Scientists have to leave it at that, and wait for the future, in the hope of attaining some wider vision which reconciles both.

We should apply these same principles to the questions in which there is a variance between science and religion. We would believe nothing in either sphere of thought which does not appear to us to be certified by solid reasons based upon the critical research either of ourselves or of competent authorities. But granting that we have honestly taken this precaution, a clash between the two on points of detail where they overlap should not lead us hastily to abandon doctrines for which we have solid evidence. It may be that we are more interested in one set of doctrines than in the other. But, if we have any sense of perspective and of the history of thought, we shall wait and refrain from mutual anathemas.

We should wait: but we should not wait passively, or in despair. The clash is a sign that there are wider truths and finer perspectives within which a reconciliation of a deeper religion and a more subtle science will be found.

In one sense, therefore, the conflict between science and religion is a slight matter which has been unduly emphasised. A mere logical contradiction cannot in itself point to more than the necessity of some readjustments, possibly of a very minor character on both sides. Remember the widely different aspects of events which are dealt with in science and in religion respectively. Science is concerned with the general conditions which are observed to regulate physical phenomena; whereas religion is wholly wrapped up in the contemplation of moral and **aesthetic** values. On the one side there is the law of gravitation, and on the other the contemplation of the beauty of holiness. What one side sees, the other misses; and vice versa.

Consider, for example, the lives of John Wesley and of Saint Francis of Assisi. For physical science you have in these lives merely ordinary examples of the operation of the principles of physiological chemistry, and of the dynamics of nervous reactions: for religion you have lives of the most profound significance in the history of the world. Can you be surprised that, in the absence of a perfect and complete phrasing of the principles of science and of the principles of religion which apply to these specific cases, the accounts of these lives from these divergent standpoints should involve discrepancies? It would be a miracle if it were not so.

It would, however, be missing the point to think that we need not trouble ourselves about the conflict between science and religion. In an intellectual age there can be no active interest which puts aside all hope of a vision of the harmony of truth. To acquiesce in discrepancy is destructive of candour, and of moral cleanliness. It belongs to the self-respect of intellect to pursue every tangle of thought to its final unravelment. If you check that impulse, you will get no religion and no science from an awakened thoughtfulness. The important question is, In what spirit are we going to face the issue? There we come to something absolutely vital.

A clash of doctrines is not a disaster—it is an opportunity. I will explain my meaning by some illustrations from science. The weight of an atom of nitrogen was well known. Also it was an established scientific doctrine that the average weight of such atoms in any considerable mass will be always the same. Two experimenters, the late Lord Rayleigh and the late Sir William Ramsay, found that if they obtained nitrogen by two different methods, each equally effective for that purpose, they always observed a persistent slight difference between the average weights of the atoms in the two cases. Now I ask you, would it have been rational of these men to have despaired because of this conflict between chemical theory and scientific observation? Suppose that for some reason the chemical doctrine had been highly prized throughout some district as the foundation of its social order:—would it have been wise, would it have been candid, would it have been moral, to forbid the disclosure of the fact that the experiments produced discordant results? Or, on the other hand, should Sir William Ramsay and Lord Rayleigh have proclaimed that chemical theory was now a detected delusion? We see at once that either of these ways would have been a method of facing the issue in an entirely wrong spirit. What Rayleigh and Ramsay did was this: They at once perceived that they had hit upon a line of investigation which would disclose some subtlety of chemical theory that had hitherto eluded observation. The discrepancy was not a disaster: it was an opportunity to increase the sweep of chemical knowledge. You all know the end of the story: finally argon was discovered, a new chemical element which had lurked undetected, mixed with the nitrogen. But the story has a sequel which forms my second illustration. This discovery drew attention to the importance of observing accurately minute differences in chemical substances as obtained by different methods. Further researches of the most careful accuracy were undertaken. Finally another physicist, F. W. Aston, working in the Cavendish Laboratory at Cambridge in England, discovered that even the same element might assume two or more distinct forms, termed *isotopes,* and that the law of the constancy of average atomic weight holds for each of these forms, but as between the different isotopes differs slightly. The research has effected a great stride in the power of chemical theory, far transcending in importance the discovery of argon from which it originated. The moral of these stories lies on the surface, and I will leave to you their application to the case of religion and science.

In formal logic, a contradiction is the signal of a defeat: but in the evolution of real knowledge it marks the first step in progress towards a victory. This is one great reason for the utmost toleration of variety of opinion. Once and forever, this duty of toleration has been summed up in the words, "Let both grow together until the harvest." The failure of Christians to act up to this precept, of the highest authority, is one of the curiosities of religious history. But we have not yet exhausted the discussion of the moral temper required for the pursuit of truth. There are short cuts leading merely to an illusory success. It is easy enough to find a theory, logically harmonious and with important applications in the region of fact, provided that you are content to disregard half your evidence. Every age produces people with clear logical intellects, and with the most praiseworthy grasp of the importance of some sphere of human experience, who have elaborated, or inherited, a scheme of thought which exactly fits those experiences which claim their interest. Such people are apt resolutely to ignore, or to explain away, all evidence which confuses their scheme with contradictory instances. What they cannot fit in is for them nonsense. An unflinching determination to take the whole evidence into account is the only method of preservation against the fluctuating extremes of fashionable opinion. This advice seems so easy, and is in fact so difficult to follow.

One reason for this difficulty is that we cannot think first and act afterwards. From the moment of birth we are immersed in action, and can only fitfully guide it by taking thought. We have, therefore, in various spheres of experience to adopt those ideas which seem to work within those spheres. It is absolutely necessary to trust to ideas which are generally adequate, even though we know that there are subtleties and distinctions beyond our ken. Also apart from the necessities of action, we cannot even keep before our minds the whole evidence except under the guise of doctrines which are incompletely harmonised. We cannot think in terms of an indefinite multiplicity of detail; our evidence can acquire its proper importance only if it comes before us marshalled by general ideas. These ideas we inherit—they form the tradition of our civilisation. Such traditional ideas are never static. They are either fading into meaningless formulae, or are gaining power by the new lights thrown by a more delicate apprehension. They are transformed by the urge of critical reason, by the vivid evidence of emotional experience, and by the cold certainties of scientific perception. One fact is certain, you cannot keep them still. No generation can merely reproduce its ancestors. You may preserve the life of a flux of form, or preserve the form amid an ebb of life. But you cannot permanently enclose the same life in the same mould.

The present state of religion among the European races illustrates the statements which I have been making. The phenomena are mixed. There have been reactions and revivals. But on the whole, during many generations, there has been a gradual decay of religious influence in European civilisation. Each revival touches a lower peak than its predecessor, and each period of slackness a lower depth. The average curve marks a steady fall in religious tone. In some countries the interest in religion is higher than in others. But in those countries where the interest is relatively high, it still falls as the generations pass. Religion is tending to degenerate into a decent formula wherewith to embellish a comfortable life. A great historical movement on this scale results from the convergence of many causes. I wish to suggest two of them . . . for consideration.

In the first place for over two centuries religion has been on the defensive, and on a weak defensive. The period has been one of unprecedented intellectual progress. In this way a series of novel situations have been produced for thought. Each such occasion has found the religious thinkers unprepared. Something, which has been proclaimed to be vital, has finally, after struggle, distress, and anathema, been modified and otherwise interpreted. The next generation of religious apologists then congratulates the religious world on the deeper insight which has been gained. The result of the continued repetition of this undignified retreat, during many generations, has at last almost entirely destroyed the intellectual authority of religious thinkers. Consider this contrast: when Darwin or Einstein proclaim theories which modify our ideas, it is a triumph for science. We do not go about saying that there is another defeat for science, because its old ideas have been abandoned. We know that another step of scientific insight has been gained.

Religion will not regain its old power until it can face change in the same spirit as does science. Its principles may be eternal, but the expression of those principles requires continual development. This evolution of religion is in the main a disengagement of its own proper ideas from the adventitious notions which have crept into it by reason of the expression of its own ideas in terms of the imaginative picture of the world entertained in previous ages. Such a release of religion from the bonds of imperfect science is all to the good. It stresses its own genuine message. The great point to be kept in mind is that normally an advance in science will show that statements of various religious beliefs require some sort of modification. It may be that they have to be expanded or explained, or indeed entirely restated. If the religion is a sound expression of truth, this modification will only exhibit more adequately the exact point which is of importance. This process is a gain. In so far, therefore, as any religion has any contact with physical facts, it is to be expected that the point of view of those facts must be continually modified as scientific knowledge advances. In this way, the exact relevance of these facts for religious thought will grow more and more clear. The progress of science must result in the unceasing codification of religious thought, to the great advantage of religion.

The religious controversies of the sixteenth and seventeenth centuries put theologians into a most unfortunate state of mind. They were always attacking and defending. They pictured themselves as the garrison of a fort surrounded by hostile forces. All such pictures express half-truths. That is why they are so popular. But they are dangerous. This particular picture fostered a pugnacious party spirit which really expresses an ultimate lack of faith. They dared not modify, because they shirked the task of disengaging their spiritual message from the associations of a particular imagery.

Let me explain myself by an example. In the early medieval times, Heaven was in the sky, and Hell was underground; volcanoes were the jaws of Hell. I do not assert that these beliefs entered into the official formulations: but they did enter into the popular understanding of the general doctrines of Heaven and Hell. These notions were what everyone thought to be implied by the doctrine of the future state. They entered into the explanations of the influential exponents of Christian belief. For example, they occur in the *Dialogues* of Pope Gregory, the Great, a man whose high official position is surpassed only by the magnitude of his services to humanity. I am not saying what we ought to believe about the future state. But whatever be the right doctrine, in this instance the clash between religion and science, which has relegated the earth to the position of a second-rate planet attached to a second-rate sun, has been greatly to the benefit of the spirituality of religion by dispersing these medieval fancies.

Another way of looking at this question of the evolution of religious thought is to note that any verbal form of statement which has been before the world for some time discloses ambiguities; and that often such ambiguities strike at the very heart of the meaning. The effective sense in which a doctrine has been held in the past cannot be determined by the mere logical analysis of verbal statements, made in ignorance of the logical trap. You have to take into account the whole reaction of human nature to the scheme of thought. This reaction is of a mixed character, including elements of emotion derived from our lower natures. It is here that the impersonal criticism of science and of philosophy comes to the aid of religious evolution. Example after example can be given of this motive force in development. For example, the logical difficulties inherent in the doctrine of the moral cleansing of human nature by the power of religion rent Christianity in the days of Pelagius and Augustine—that is to say, at the beginning of the fifth century. Echoes of that controversy still linger in theology.

So far, my point has been this: that religion is the expression of one type of fundamental experiences of mankind: that religious thought develops into an increasing accuracy of expression, disengaged from adventitious imagery: that the interaction between religion and science is one great factor in promoting this development.

I now come to my second reason for the modern fading of interest in religion. This involves the ultimate question which I stated in my opening sentences. We have to know what we mean by religion. The churches, in their presentation of their answers to this query, have put forward aspects of religion which are expressed in terms either suited to the emotional reactions of bygone times or directed to excite modern emotional interests of nonreligious character. What I mean under the first heading is that religious appeal is directed partly to excite that instinctive fear of the wrath of a tyrant which was inbred in the unhappy populations of the arbitrary empires of the ancient world, and in particular to excite that fear of an all-powerful arbitrary tyrant behind the unknown forces of nature. This appeal to the ready instinct of brute fear is losing its force. It lacks any directness of response, because modern science and modern conditions of life have taught us to meet occasions of apprehension by a critical analysis of their causes and conditions. Religion is the reaction of human nature to its search for God. The presentation of God under the aspect of power awakens every modern instinct of critical reaction. This is fatal; for religion collapses unless its main positions command immediacy of assent. In this respect the old phraseology is at variance with the psychology of modern civilisations. This change in psychology is largely due to science, and is one of the chief ways in which the advance of science has weakened the hold of the old religious forms of expression. The non-religious motive which has entered into modern religious thought is the desire for a comfortable organisation of modern society. Religion has been presented as valuable for the ordering of life. Its claims have been rested upon its function as a sanction to right conduct. Also the purpose of right conduct quickly degenerates into the formation of pleasing social relations. We have here a subtle degradation of religious ideas, following upon their gradual purification under the influence of keener ethical intuitions. Conduct is a by-product of religion—an inevitable by-product, but not the main point. Every great religious teacher has revolted against the presentation of religion as a mere sanction of rules of conduct. Saint Paul denounced the Law, and Puritan divines spoke of the filthy rags of righteousness. The insistence upon rules of conduct marks the ebb of religious fervour. Above and beyond all things, the religious life is not a research after comfort. I must now state, in all diffidence, what I conceive to be the essential character of the religious spirit.

Religion is the vision of something which stands beyond, behind, and within, the passing flux of immediate things; something which is real, and yet waiting to be realised; something which is a remote possibility, and yet the greatest of present facts; something that gives meaning to all that passes, and yet eludes apprehension; something whose possession is the final good, and yet is beyond all reach; something which is the ultimate ideal, and the hopeless quest.

The immediate reaction of human nature to the religious vision is worship. Religion has emerged into human experience mixed with the crudest fancies of barbaric imagination. Gradually, slowly, steadily the vision recurs in history under nobler form and with clearer expression. It is the one element in human experience which persistently shows an upward trend. It fades and then recurs. But when it renews its force, it recurs with an added richness and purity of content. The fact of the religious vision, and its history of persistent expansion, is our one ground for optimism. Apart from it, human life is a flash of occasional enjoyments lighting up a mass of pain and misery, a bagatelle of transient experience.

The vision claims nothing but worship; and worship is a surrender to the claim for assimilation, urged with the motive force of mutual love. The vision never overrules. It is always there, and it has the power of love presenting the one purpose whose fulfilment is eternal harmony. Such order as we find in nature is never force—it presents itself as the one harmonious adjustment of complex detail. Evil is the brute motive force of fragmentary purpose, disregarding the eternal vision. Evil is overruling, retarding, hurting. The power of God is the worship He inspires. That religion is strong which in its ritual and its modes of thought evokes an apprehension of the commanding vision. The worship of God is not a rule of safety—it is an adventure of the spirit, a flight after the unattainable. The death of religion comes with the repression of the high hope of adventure.

Questions for Thought

1. Can you think of examples that demonstrate the conflict between science and religion? How would you explain the origin of this conflict?
2. Do you agree with Whitehead's claim that both religion and science have been in a state of continual development? If so, why? If not, why not?
3. Do you agree with Whitehead that the influence of religion has declined? If not, why not? If so, how would you explain this decline?
4. How do you think Whitehead would respond to Christians who reject the theory of evolution? How would you respond to them?
5. How do Whitehead's views about religion compare with or differ from Campbell's views?

12   How Not to Compare African Thought with Western Thought

KWASI WIREDU

Kwasi Wiredu (b. 1931) was born in the West African country of Ghana. He received his undergraduate education at the University of Ghana, where he later taught philosophy for twenty-three years. His graduate work in philosophy was completed at Oxford University. At Oxford, he studied with Gilbert Ryle, P. F. Strawson, and

Stuart Hampshire. Wiredu has held visiting professorships at the University of California, Los Angeles; at Carleton College in Minnesota; at the University of Richmond; and at Duke University. He currently teaches philosophy at the University of South Florida.

Wiredu has published numerous articles on **epistemology, metaphysics,** and traditional African philosophy. He received the 1982 Ghana National Book Award for his first book, *Philosophy and an African Culture,* which was published by Cambridge University Press in 1980. His other books include *Conceptual Decolonization in African Philosophy: Four Essays by Kwasi Wiredu* (1995), and *Cultural Universals and Particulars: An African Perspective* (1996). He is also coeditor of the text *Person and Community: Ghanaian Philosophical Studies, I* (1992).

In the following essay, which first appeared in *Ch'indaba,* Wiredu contrasts traditional African thinking with modern scientific thinking. He argues that much of traditional African thinking, which offers spiritualistic explanations of natural phenomena, is based on superstition and is decidedly inferior to modern scientific thinking. Citing the institution of funerals in Ghana as one example of how traditional African thinking leads to harmful consequences in the lives of the believers, Wiredu concludes that cultural progress in Africa requires that this prescientific, spiritualistic outlook be displaced by the method of rational inquiry.

Wiredu points out, however, that not all African thinking is traditional thinking and that not all Western thinking is scientific thinking. Noting the similarities of traditional African thinking and Christianity, he argues that the type of prescientific, spiritualistic outlook that is prevalent in many spheres of African thought was once the dominant type of thinking in the West and that many vestiges of this type of thinking can still be found in the West today. Because of the failure of anthropologists to acknowledge the existence of this sphere of traditional thought in the West that is comparable to traditional African thought, they have mistakenly compared modern Western thinking, which emphasizes the importance of observation and evidence, with traditional African thinking, which often explains natural phenomena by appealing to the activities of gods and kindred spirits. One upshot of this faulty comparison, according to Wiredu, is the belief that Western thinking is superior to African thinking. While admitting that the domain of rational inquiry is wider in the West than it is in Africa, Wiredu concludes that the domain of rational inquiry is not a specifically Western domain and that, in the West as in Africa, "the realms of religion, morals, and politics remain strongholds of irrationality."

Questions for Reading

1. What, according to Wiredu, are the basic presuppositions of traditional African thinking? How does traditional African thinking differ from modern scientific thinking?
2. What evidence does Wiredu provide to show that the basic presuppositions of traditional African thinking can be found in the West? Why does he think that traditional African thinking and Christianity have much in common?
3. What, according to Wiredu, are some of the undesirable consequences of comparing traditional African thought with modern Western thought?
4. In what ways does Africa lag behind the West in the cultivation of rational inquiry? What examples does Wiredu give to show that this is indeed the case?
5. What is Wiredu's attitude toward "folk thought"? What is his discussion of the Akans conception of personhood intended to show?

MANY WESTERN ANTHROPOLOGISTS AND EVEN non-anthropologists have often been puzzled by the virtual ubiquity of references to gods and all sorts of spirits in traditional African explanations of things. One Western anthropologist, Robin Horton, has suggested that this failure of understanding is partly attributable to the fact that many Western anthropologists "have been unfamiliar with the theoretical thinking of their own culture."[1] I suggest that a very much more crucial reason is that they have also apparently been unfamiliar with the folk thought of their own culture.

Western societies too have passed through a stage of addiction to spiritistic explanations of phenomena. What is more, significant residues of this tradition remain a basic part of the mental make-up of a large mass of the not-so-sophisticated sections of Western populations. More importantly still, elements of the spiritistic outlook are, in fact, deeply embedded in the philosophical thought of many contemporary Westerners—philosophers and even scientists.

Obviously it is a matter of first rate philosophical importance to distinguish between traditional, i.e, pre-scientific, spiritistic thought and modern scientific thought by means of a clearly articulated criterion (or set of criteria). Indeed, one of the most influential and fruitful movements in recent Western philosophy, namely the logical positivist movement, may be said to have been motivated by the quest for just such a criterion. Also anthropologically and psychologically it is of interest to try to understand how traditional modes of thought function in the total context of life in a traditional society. Since African societies are among the closest approximations in the modern world to societies in the pre-scientific stage of intellectual development, the interest which anthropologists have shown in African thought is largely understandable.

Unfortunately instead of seeing the basic non-scientific characteristics of African traditional thought as typifying traditional thought in general, Western anthropologists and others besides have tended to take them as defining a peculiarly African way of thinking. The ill effects of this mistake have been not a few.

One such effect is that the really interesting cross-cultural comparisons of modes of thought have tended not to be made. If one starts with the recognition that all peoples have some background of traditional thought—and remember by *traditional* thought here I mean pre-scientific thought of the type that tends to construct explanations of natural phenomena in terms of the activities of gods and kindred spirits—then the interesting and anthropologically illuminating comparison will be to see in what different ways spiritistic categories are employed by various peoples in the attempt to achieve a coherent view of the world. In such specific differences will consist the real peculiarities of, say, African traditional thought in contradistinction from, say, Western traditional thought. Such comparisons may well turn out to hold less exotic excitement for the Western anthropologist than present practice would seem to suggest. In the absence of any such realization, what has generally happened is that not only the genuine distinguishing features of African traditional thought but also its basic non-scientific, spiritistic, tendencies have been taken as a basis for contrasting Africans from Western peoples. One consequence is that many Westerners have gone about with an exaggerated notion of the differences in nature between Africans and the peoples of the West. I do not imply that this has necessarily led to anti-African racism. Nevertheless, since in some obvious and important respects, traditional thought is inferior to modern, science-oriented thought, some Western liberals have apparently had to think hard in order to protect themselves against conceptions of the intellectual inferiority of Africans as a people.

Another ill effect relates to the self-images of Africans themselves. Partly through the influence of Western anthropology and partly through insufficient critical reflection on the contemporary African situation, many very well placed Africans are apt to identify African thought with *traditional* African thought. The result has not been beneficial to the movement for modernization, usually championed by the very same class of Africans. The mechanics of this interplay of attitudes is somewhat subtle. To begin with, these Africans have been in the habit of calling loudly, even stridently, for the cultivation of

From Kwasi Wiredu, "How Not to Compare African Thought with Western Thought." First appeared in Ch'indaba.
Published by permission of the author.

an African authenticity or personality. True, when such a call is not merely a political slogan, it is motivated by a genuine desire to preserve the indigenous culture of peoples whose confidence in themselves has been undermined by colonialism. But it was a certain pervasive trait of this same culture that enabled sparse groups of Europeans to subjugate large masses of African populations and keep them in colonial subjection for many long years and which even now makes them a prey to neo-colonialism. I refer to the *traditional* and non-literate character of the culture, with its associated technological under-development. Being traditional is, of course, not synonymous with being non-literate. A culture can be literate and yet remain traditional i.e., non-scientific, as the case of India, for example, proves. India has a long tradition of written literature, yet it was not until comparatively recent times that the scientific spirit made any appreciable inroads into the Indian way of life. But, of course, a culture cannot be both scientific and non-literate, for the scientific method can only flourish where there can be recordings of precise measurements, calculations and, generally, of observational data. If a culture is both non-scientific and non-literate, then in some important respects it may be said to be backward in a rather deep sense. We shall in due course note the bearing of the non-literate nature of the traditional African culture on the question of just what African philosophy is.

What is immediately pertinent is to remark that unanalyzed exhortations to Africans to preserve their indigenous culture are not particularly useful—indeed, they can be counterproductive. There is an urgent need in Africa today for the kind of analysis that would identify and separate the backward aspects of our culture—I speak as an anxious African—from those aspects that are worth keeping. That such desirable aspects exist is beyond question, and undoubtedly many African political and intellectual leaders are deeply impregnated by this consideration. Yet the analytical dimension seems to be lacking in their enthusiasm. So we have, among other distressing things, the frequent spectacle of otherwise enlightened Africans assiduously participating in the pouring of libation to the spirits of our ancestors on ceremonial occasions, or frantically applauding imitation of the frenzied dancing of "possessed" fetish priests—all this under the

impression that in so doing they are demonstrating their faith in African culture.

In fact, many traditional African institutions and cultural practices, such as the ones just mentioned, are based on superstition. By "superstition" I mean a rationally unsupported belief in entities of any sort. The attribute of being superstitious attaches not to the content of a belief but to its mode of entertainment. Purely in respect of content the belief, for example, in abstract entities in semantic analysis common among many logistic **ontologists** in the West is not any more brainy than the traditional African belief in ancestor spirits. But logisticians are given to arguing for their ontology. I happen to think their arguments for abstract entities wrong-headed;[2] but it is not open to me to accuse them of superstition. When, however, we come to the traditional African belief in ancestor spirits—and this, I would contend, applies to traditional spiritistic beliefs everywhere—the position is different. That our departed ancestors continue to hover around in some rarefied form ready now and then to take a sip of the ceremonial schnapps is a proposition that I have never known to be rationally defended. Indeed, if one were to ask a traditional elder, "unspoilt" by the scientific orientation, for the rational justification of such a belief, one's curiosity would be quickly put down to intellectual arrogance acquired through Western education.

Yet the principle that one is not entitled to accept a proposition as true in the absence of any evidential support is not Western in any but an episodic sense. The Western world happens to be the place where, as of now, this principle has received its most sustained and successful application in certain spheres of thought, notably in the natural and mathematical sciences. But even in the Western world there are some important areas of belief wherein the principle does not hold sway. In the West just as anywhere else the realms of religion, morals and politics remain strongholds of irrationality. It is not uncommon, for example, to see a Western scientist, fully apprised of the universal reign of law in natural phenomena, praying to God, a spirit, to grant rain and a good harvest and other things besides. Those who are tempted to see in such a thing as witchcraft the key to specifically *African* thought—there is no lack of such people among foreigners as well as Africans themselves—ought to be reminded that there are numbers of white men in today's London who proudly proclaim themselves to be witches. Moreover, if they would but read, for example, Treyor-Roper's historical essay on "Witches and Witchcraft,"[3] they might conceivably come to doubt whether witchcraft in Africa has ever attained the heights to which it reached in Europe in the sixteenth and seventeenth centuries.

It should be noted, conversely, that the principle of rational evidence is not entirely inoperative in the thinking of the traditional African. Indeed, no society could survive for any length of time without conducting a large part of their daily activities by the principle of belief according to the evidence. You cannot farm without some rationally based knowledge of soils and seeds and of meteorology; and no society can achieve any reasonable degree of harmony in human relations without a *basic* tendency to assess claims and allegations by the method of objective investigation. The truth, then, is that rational knowledge is not the preserve of the modern West[4] nor is superstition a peculiarity of the African peoples.

Nevertheless, it is a fact that Africa lags behind the West in the cultivation of rational inquiry. One illuminating (because fundamental) way of approaching the concept of "development" is to measure it by the degree to which rational methods have penetrated thought habits. In this sense, of course, one cannot compare the development of peoples in absolute terms. The Western world is "developed," but only relatively. Technological sophistication is only an aspect, and that not the core, of development. The conquest of the religious, moral and political spheres by the spirit of rational inquiry remains, as noted earlier, a thing of the future even in the West. From this point of view the West may be said to be still underdeveloped. The quest for development, then, should be viewed as a continuing world-historical process in which all peoples, Western and non-Western alike, are engaged.

There are at least two important advantages in looking at development in this way. The first is that it becomes possible to see the movement towards modernization in Africa not as essentially a process in which Africans are unthinkingly jettisoning their own heritage of thought in the pursuit of Western ways of life, but rather as one in which Africans in common with all other peoples seek to attain a specifically *human* destiny—a thought that should assuage the qualms of those among thoughtful Africans who are wont to see modernization as a foreign invasion. The relation between the concepts of development and modernization ought to be obvious. Modernization is the application of the results of modern science for the improvement of the conditions of human life. It is only the more visible side of development; it is the side that is more immediately associated with the use of advanced technology and novel techniques in various areas of life such as agriculture, health education and recreation. Because modernization is not the whole of development there is a need to view it always in a wider human perspective. Many should link the modernization of the conditions of his life with the modernization of all aspects of his thinking. It is just the failure to do this that is responsible for the more unlovable features of life in the West. Moreover, the same failure bedevils attempts at development in Africa. Rulers and leaders of opinion in Africa have tended to think of development in terms of the visible aspects of modernization—in terms of large buildings and complex machines, to the relative neglect of the more intellectual foundations of modernity. It is true that African nations spend every year huge sums of money on institutional education. But it has not been appreciated that education ought to lead to the cultivation of a rational[5] outlook on the world on the part of the educated and, through them, in the traditional folk at large. Thus it is that even while calling for modernization, influential Africans can still be seen to encourage superstitious practices such as the pouring of libation to spirits in the belief that in this kind of way they can achieve development without losing their Africanness. The second advantage of seeing development in the way suggested above is that the futility of any such approach becomes evident. To develop in any serious sense, we in Africa must break with our old uncritical habits of thought; that is we must advance past the stage of traditional thinking.

Lest these remarks appear rather abstract, let us consider a concrete situation. Take the institution of funerals in Ghana, for example. Owing to all sorts of superstitions about the supposed career of the spirits of departed relatives, the mourning of the dead takes the form of elaborate and, consequently, expensive and time consuming social ceremonies. When a person dies there has first to be a burial ceremony on the third day; then on the eighth day there is a funeral celebration at which customary rites are performed; then forty days afterwards there is a fortieth day celebration (*adaduanan*). Strictly, that is not the end. There are such occasions as the eightieth day and first anniversary celebrations. All these involve large alcohol-quaffing gatherings. Contrary to what one might be tempted to think, the embracing of Christianity by large sections of Ghanaian population has not simplified funeral celebrations; on the contrary, it has brought new complications. Christianity too teaches of a whole hierarchy of spirits, started from the Supreme Threefold Spirit down to the angels both good and refractory down further to the lesser spirits of deceased mortals. Besides, conversion to Christianity in our lands has generally not meant the exchange of the indigenous religion for the new one, but rather an amalgamation of both, which is made more possible by their common spiritistic orientation. Thus, in addition to all the traditional celebrations, there is nowadays the neo-Christian Memorial Service, replete with church services and extended refreshments, a particularly expensive phase of the funeral process. The upshot is that if a close relation of a man, say his father, died, then unless he happens to be rich, he is in for very hard financial times indeed. He has to take several days off work, and he has to borrow respectable sums of money to defray the inevitable expenses.

The extent of the havoc that these funeral habits have wrought on the national economy of Ghana has not been exactly calculated, but it has become obvious to public leaders that it is enormous and that something needs urgently to be done about it. However, the best that these leaders have seemed capable of doing so far has been to exhort the people to reform their traditional institutions in general and cut down on funeral expenses in particular. These appeals have gone unheeded; which is not surprising, if one recalls that these leaders themselves are often to be seen ostentatiously taking part in ceremonies, such as the pouring of libation, which are based on the same sort of beliefs as those which lie behind the funeral practices. It has so far apparently been lost upon our influential men that

while the underlying beliefs retain their hold, any verbal appeals are wasted on the populace.

The ideal way to reform backward customs in Africa must, surely, be to undermine their superstitious belief-foundations by fostering in the people—at all events, in the new generation of educated Africans—the spirit of rational inquiry in all spheres of thought and belief. Even if the backward beliefs in question were *peculiarly* African, it would be necessary to work for their eradication. But my point is that they are not African in any intrinsic, inseparable sense; and the least that African philosophers and foreign well-wishers can do in this connection is to refrain, in this day and age, from serving up the usual congeries of unargued conception about gods, ghosts, and witches in the name of *African philosophy*. Such a description is highly unfortunate. If at all deserving of the name "philosophy," these ideas should be regarded not as a part of African philosophy simply, but rather as a part of *traditional* philosophy in Africa.

This is not verbal cavilling. The habit of talking of African philosophy as if all African philosophy is *traditional* carries the implication, probably not always intended, that modern Africans have not been trying, or worse still, ought not to try, to philosophize in a manner that takes account of present day development in human knowledge, logical, mathematical, scientific, literary, etc. Various causes have combined to motivate this attitude. African nationalists in search of an African identity, Afro-Americans in search of their African roots and Western foreigners in search of exotic diversion—all demand an African philosophy that shall be fundamentally different from Western philosophy, even if it means the familiar witches' brew. Obviously, the work of contemporary African philosophers trying to grapple with the modern philosophical situation cannot satisfy such a demand.

The African philosopher writing today has no tradition of written philosophy in his continent[6] to draw upon. In this respect, his plight is very much unlike that of say, the contemporary Indian philosopher. The latter can advert his mind to any insights that might be contained in a long-standing Indian heritage of written philosophical meditations; he has what he might legitimately call *classical* Indian philosophers to investigate and profit by. And if he is broad-minded, he will also study Western philosophy and try in his own philosophizing to take cognizance of the intellectual developments that have shaped the modern world. Besides all this, he has, as every people have, a background of unwritten folk philosophy which he might examine for whatever it may be worth. Notice that we have here three levels of philosophy: we have spoken of a folk philosophy, a written traditional[7] philosophy and a modern philosophy. Where long-standing written sources are available folk philosophy tends not to be made much of. It remains in the background as a sort of diffused, immanent, component of community thought habits whose effect on the thinking of the working philosopher is largely unconscious.[8] Such a fund of community thought is not the creation of any specifiable set of philosophers; it is the common property of all and sundry, thinker and non-thinker alike, and it is called a *philosophy* at all only by a quite liberal acceptation of the term. Folk thought, as a rule, consists of bald assertions without argumentative justification, but philosophy in the narrower sense must contain not just theses. Without argumentation and clarification, there is, strictly, no philosophy.

Of course, folk thought can be comprehensive and interesting on its own account. Still its non-discursiveness remains a drawback. For example, according to the conception of a person found among the Akans of Ghana, (the ethnic group to which the present writer belongs), a person is constituted by *nipakua* (a body) and a combination of the following entities conceived as spiritual **substances**:[9] (1) *okra* (soul, approximately), that whose departure from a man means death, (2) *sunsum,* that which gives rise to a man's character, (3) *ntoro,* something passed on from the father which is the basis of inherited characteristics and, finally, (4) *mogya,* something passed on from the mother which determines a man's clan identity and which at death becomes the *saman* (ghost). This last entity seems to be the one that is closest to the material aspect of a person; literally, *mogya* means blood. Now, in the abstract, all this sounds more interesting, certainly more imaginative, than the thesis of some Western philosophers that a person consists of a soul and body. The crucial difference, however, is that the Western philosopher

tries to argue for this thesis, clarifying his meaning and answering objections, known or anticipated; whereas the transmitter of folk conceptions merely says: "This is what our ancestors said."[10] For this reason folk conceptions tend not to develop with time. Please note that this is as true in the West and elsewhere as it is in Africa.

But in Africa, where we do not have even a written traditional philosophy, anthropologists have fastened on our folk world-views and elevated them to the status of a continental philosophy. They have then compared this "philosophy" with Western (written) philosophy. In other, better placed, parts of the world, if you want to know the philosophy of the given people, you do not go to aged peasants or fetish priests or court personalities; you go to the individual thinkers, in flesh, if possible, and in print. And as any set of individuals trying to think for themselves are bound to differ among themselves, you would invariably find a variety of theories and doctrines, possibly but not necessarily, sharing substantial affinities. Since the reverse procedure has been the only one that has seemed possible to anthropologists, it is not surprising that misleading comparisons between African traditional thought and Western scientific thought have resulted. My contention, which I have earlier hinted at, is that African traditional thought should in the first place only be compared with Western folk thought. For this purpose, of course, Western anthropologists will first have to learn in detail about the folk thought of their own peoples. African folk thought may be compared with Western philosophy only in the same spirit in which Western folk thought may be compared also with Western philosophy, that is, only in order to find out the marks which distinguish folk thought in general from individualized philosophizing. Then, if there be any who are anxious to compare African philosophy with Western philosophy, they will have to look at the philosophy that Africans are producing today.

Naturally Western anthropologists are not generally interested in contemporary African philosophy. Present day African philosophers have been trained in the Western tradition, in the continental or Anglo-American style, depending on their colonial history. Their thinking, therefore, is unlikely to hold many peculiarly African novelties for anyone knowledgeable in Western philosophy. For this very same reason, African militants and our Afro-American brothers are often disappointed with the sort of philosophy syllabus that is taught at a typical modern department of philosophy in Africa. They find such a department mainly immersed in the study of Logic, Epistemology, Metaphysics, Ethics, Political Philosophy, etc., as these have been developed in the West, and they question why Africans should be so engrossed in the philosophy of their erstwhile colonial oppressors.

The attentive reader of this discussion should know the answer by now: The African philosopher has no choice but to conduct his philosophical inquiries in relation to the philosophical writings of other peoples, for his own ancestors left him no heritage of philosophical writings. He need not—to be sure, he must not—restrict himself to the philosophical works of his particular former colonial oppressors, but he must of necessity study the written philosophies of other lands, because it would be extremely injudicious for him to try to philosophize in self-imposed isolation from all modern currents of thought, not to talk of longer-standing nourishment for the mind. In the ideal, he must acquaint himself with the philosophies of all the peoples of the world, compare, contrast, critically assess them and make use of whatever of value he may find in them. In this way it can be hoped that a tradition of philosophy as a discursive discipline will eventually come to be established in Africa which future Africans and others too can utilize. In practice the contemporary African philosopher will find that it is the philosophies of the West that will occupy him the most, for it is in that part of the world that modern developments in human knowledge have gone farthest and where, consequently, philosophy is in closest touch with the conditions of the modernization which he urgently desires for his continent. In my opinion, the march of modernization is destined to lead to the universalization of philosophy everywhere in the world.

The African philosopher cannot, of course, take the sort of cultural pride in the philosophical achievements of Aristotle or Hume or Kant or Frege or Husserl of which the Western student of philosophy may permit himself. Indeed an African needs a certain level-headedness to touch some of these thinkers at all. Hume,[11] for example, had absolutely no respect for black men. Nor was Marx,[12] for another instance, particularly progressive in this respect. Thus any partiality the African philosopher may develop for these thinkers must rest mostly on considerations of truth-value.

As regards his own background of folk thought, there is a good reason why the African philosopher should pay more attention to it than would seem warranted in other places. Africans are a much oppressed and disparaged people. Some foreigners there have been who were not even willing to concede that Africans as a traditional people were capable of any sort of coherent[13] world-view. Those who had the good sense and the patience and industry to settle down and study traditional African thought were often, especially in the 19th and early 20th centuries, colonial anthropologists who sought to render the actions and attitudes of our forefathers intelligible to the colonial rulers so as to facilitate their governance. Although some brilliant insights were obtained, there were also misinterpretations and straightforward errors. Africans cannot leave the task of correction to foreign researchers alone. Besides, particularly in the field of morality, there are non-superstition-based conceptions from which the modern Westerner may well have something to learn. The exposition of such aspects of African traditional thought specially befits the contemporary African philosopher.

Still, in treating of their traditional thought, African philosophers should be careful not to make hasty comparisons.[14] Also they should approach their material critically; this last suggestion is particularly important since all peoples who have made any breakthrough in the quest for modernization have done so by going beyond folk thinking. It is unlikely to be otherwise in Africa. I should like to repeat, however, that the process of sifting the elements of our traditional thought and culture calls for a good measure of analytical circumspection lest we exchange the good as well as the bad in our traditional ways of life for dubious cultural imports. It should be clear from the foregoing discussion that the question of how African thought may appropriately be compared with Western thought is not just an important academic issue but also one of great existential urgency.

NOTES

1. Robin Horton, "African Traditional Thought and Western Science," in *Rationality*, ed. Bryan Wilson (Oxford: Basil Blackwell). Originally published in *Africa* 37, nos. 1 & 2 (1967).

2. My reasons for this remark will be found in my series of articles on "Logic and Ontology," *Second Order: An African Journal of Philosophy* 2, no. 1 (January 1973) and no. 2 (July 1973); 3, no. 2 (July 1974); 4, no. 1 (January 1975).

3. *Encounter* 28, no. 5 (May 1967) and no. 6 (June 1967).

4. Note that "the West" and "Western" are used in a cultural, rather than ideological sense in this discussion.

5. I am aware that my insistence in the overriding value of rationality will be found jarring by those Westerners who feel that the claims of rationality have been pushed too far in their countries and that the time is overdue for a return to "Nature" and the exultation in feeling, **intuition** and immediacy. No doubt the harsh individualism of Western living might seem to lend support to this point of view. But in my opinion the trouble is due to too little rather than too much rationality in social organization. This, however, is too large a topic to enter into here.

6. The Arab portions of Africa are, of course, an exception, though even there what we have is the result of the interaction between indigenous thought and Greek influences.

7. "Traditional" here still has the prescientific connotation. Of course, if one should speak of *traditional* British **empiricism,** for example, that connotation would be absent.

8. Since such effects do, in fact, occur, this threefold stratification should not be taken as watertight.

9. See, for example, W. E. Abraham, *The Mind of Africa* (Chicago: University of Chicago Press, 1967).

10. However, the circumstances that in Africa, for example, our traditional thought tends not to be elaborately argumentative should be attributed not to any intrinsic lack of the discursive spirit in our ancestors but rather to the fact that their thoughts were not written down.

11. Hume was able to say in his *Essays* (London: George Routledge & Sons, Ltd), footnote on pages 152 and 153 in the course of the essay on "National Characters": "I am apt to suspect the Negroes to be naturally inferior to the Whites. There scarcely ever was a civilized nation of that complexion, nor any individual, eminent either in action or speculation. . . . In Jamaica, indeed they talk of one Negro as a man of parts and learning; but it is likely that he is admired for slender accomplishments, like a parrot who speaks a few words plainly." Obviously considerable maturity is required in the African to be able to contemplate impartially Hume's disrespect for Negroes and his philosophical insights, deploring the former and acknowledging and assimilating the latter. A British philosopher, Michael Dummett, was recently placed in a not altogether dissimilar situation when, himself a passionate opponent of racialism, he discovered in the course of writing a monumental work on Frege (*Frege: Philosophy of Language*, Duckworth, London, 1973)—a work that he had, indeed, suspended for quite some time in order to throw himself heart and soul into the fight against racial discrimination in his own country, Britain—that his subject was a racialist of some sort. (See his own remarks in his preface to the above-mentioned book.) It would have argued a lack of balance in him if he had scrapped the project on the discovery. In any event he went ahead to complete the work and put all students of the philosophy of logic in his debt.

12. Marx is known once, in a burst of personal abuse of Lassalle, in a letter to Engels, to have animadverted: "This combination of Jewry and Germany with a fundamental Negro streak. . . . The fellow's self assertiveness is Negro too." Quoted in J. Hampden Jackson, *Marx, Proudhon and European Socialism* (London: English Universities Press, 1951), p. 144. It is sometimes understandable for a man to chide his own origins, but to condemn a downtrodden people like this is more serious. Would that black men everywhere had more of the self assertiveness which Marx here deprecates. The Akans of Ghana have a proverb which says: "If the truth happens to lie in the most private part of your own mother's anatomy, it is no sin to extract it with your corresponding organ." African enthusiasts of Marx, (or of Hume, for that matter) may perhaps console themselves with the following less delicate adaptation of this proverb. "If the truth happens to lie in the mouth of your racial traducer it is no pulillanimity to take it from there."

13. Coherent thought is not necessarily scientific thought. Traditional thought can display a high degree of coherence; and certainly African traditional thought is not lacking in coherence.

14. I ought perhaps to point out that the kind of comparison between African thought and Western thought that has been criticized in this discussion is the sort which seeks to characterize the given varieties of thinking as wholes. My remarks do not necessarily affect the comparison of isolated propositions.

Questions for Thought

1. How effective is the example of the institution of funerals in Ghana in supporting Wiredu's claim that modern scientific thinking is superior to traditional prescientific thinking? Can you think of other examples that might support this claim?
2. Do you agree with Wiredu's conclusion that progress in both Africa and the West depends on displacing traditional prescientific thought with the method of rational inquiry? Why or why not?
3. Can you think of examples of "folk thought" found in the West? How do you think Western folk thought compares with or differs from African folk thought?
4. To what extent, if any, are your own views based on folk thought or tradition?
5. In what ways are Wiredu's views on the relationship of science and religion similar to Whitehead's views? In what ways are they different?

Theology and Falsification   13

ANTONY FLEW

Antony Garrard Newton Flew (b. 1923), the son of a Methodist minister, was born in London. He attended St. Faith's Preparatory School in Cambridge from 1930 to 1936 and Kingsworth School in Bath from 1936 to 1941. Following this, he studied Japanese at the School of Oriental and African Studies in London before joining the British Air Force as an intelligence officer in 1943. Flew's military career ended after World War II, and he resumed his studies, this time at St. John's College of Oxford University. At Oxford, Flew studied with Gilbert Ryle, and he was awarded the University Prize in Philosophy. He earned his B.A. in 1947 and his M.A. in 1949. Many years later, in 1974, he was awarded a doctoral degree from the University of Keele.

During his long teaching career, Flew held full-time positions at four universities. He was Lecturer in Philosophy at Christ Church, Oxford, from 1949 to 1950, Lecturer in Moral Philosophy at the University of Aberdeen from 1950 to 1954, Professor of Philosophy at the University of Keele from 1954 to 1974, and Professor of Philosophy at the University of Reading from 1973 to 1982. Upon his retirement from the University of Reading, Flew taught part-time at York University in Toronto for three years. Over the course of his career, Flew also held the position of visiting professor at several universities, including New York University, Swarthmore College, the University of Pittsburgh, the University of Southern California, the University of California, San Diego, and the Australian National University.

A prolific writer, Flew has published over seventy articles and pamphlets on a wide variety of subjects, edited numerous anthologies, and authored more than twenty books. His books include *A New Approach to Psychical Research* (1953), *Hume's Philosophy of Belief* (1961), *God and Philosophy* (1966), *Crime or Disease?* (1973), *Thinking About Thinking* (1975), *The Presumption of Atheism, and Other Philosophical Essays on God, Freedom and Immortality* (1976), *Darwinian Evolution* (1984), *The Logic of Mortality* (1987), *Equality in Liberty and Justice* (1989), and *Atheistic Humanism* (1993).

Flew, who has defended atheism in many of his lectures and writings, recently created a stir when he stated that he had perhaps been mistaken in doing so. While this change in his position seems to be evolving still, Flew apparently now endorses a type of **deism.** However, he has made it abundantly clear that his views on God are still far removed from the views of theistic religions such as Christianity and Islam. Not only does Flew continue to reject the possibility of miracles and any sort of supernatural revelation, he made the following provocative statement in a recent interview: "I'm thinking of a God very different from the God of the Christian and far and away from the God of Islam, because both are depicted as omnipotent Oriental despots, cosmic Saddam Husseins."

In the following selection from *New Essays in Philosophical Theology*, an anthology that was originally published in 1955, Flew raises important questions about the language of religious belief. After recounting John Wisdom's tale of the gardener—a tale that describes a hypothetical conversation about a gardener between a believer and a nonbeliever —Flew says that the believer's statements about the gardener in this tale are characteristic of many theological statements concerning God. While the believer maintains belief in the gardener throughout the conversation, his or her belief is gradually qualified when the nonbeliever provides evidence that calls that belief into question. At first the believer maintains the existence of a physical gardener; when the physical gardener fails to appear, however, the believer revises his belief to claim that the gardener is invisible. When equipment that was set up to detect an invisible gardener fails to do so, the believer then maintains that the gardener is intangible. And so goes the conversation. Wisdom's point, with which Flew fully agrees, is that in the end so many qualifications have been made that the claim about the gardener's existence has become vacuous. Just so, when people talk about the existence of God, something similar occurs.

Flew goes on to analyze other statements about God, statements such as "God loves us as a father loves his children." This statement, like the one about the existence of God, often gets qualified when someone points out that children suffer and die from terrible diseases, natural disasters, and so on, events against which a human father would surely protect his children if it were in his power to do so. In order to maintain belief in the statement about God's love, the believer then has to qualify it by saying something like "God's love differs from human love." But when he or she does this, what exactly is the believer now asserting?

According to Flew, a statement has meaning only if its denial admits of falsification— that is, only if there is some evidence that would count against the statement, evidence that could potentially make the believer deny the statement's truth. Yet, with many assertions about God, this is not the case. No matter how many suffering children one encounters, no matter how much evidence there is against the statement that "God loves us as a father loves his children," the believer still affirms the truth of that statement. However, Flew claims that since such a statement does not admit the possibility of falsification, it is not truly an assertion. Flew concludes by asking the believer this question: "What would have to occur or to have occurred to constitute for you a disproof of the love of, or existence of, God?"

Questions for Reading

1. What, according to Flew, takes place in Wisdom's tale of the gardener? How does the tale end?
2. What exactly does Flew mean when he claims that "a fine brash hypothesis may thus be killed by inches, the death by a thousand qualifications"?
3. Why does Flew introduce statements such as "God has a plan"?
4. How is the concept of falsification used in this selection?
5. With what question does Flew conclude? What significance does this question have for Flew?

Let us begin with a parable. It is a parable developed from a tale told by John Wisdom in his haunting and revelatory article "Gods."[1] Once upon a time two explorers came upon a clearing in the jungle. In the clearing were growing many flowers and many weeds. One explorer says, "Some gardener must tend this plot." The other disagrees, "There is no gardener." So they pitch their tents and set a watch. No gardener is ever seen. "But perhaps he is an invisible gardener." So they set up a barbed-wire fence. They electrify it. They patrol with blood-hounds. (For they remember how H. G. Wells' *The Invisible Man* could be both smelt and touched though he could not be seen.) But no shrieks ever suggest that some intruder has received a shock. No movements of the wire ever betray an invisible climber. The bloodhounds never give cry. Yet still the Believer is not convinced. "But there is a gardener, invisible, intangible, insensible to electric shocks, a gardener who has no scent and makes no sound, a gardener who comes secretly to look after the garden which he loves." At last the **Skeptic** despairs, "But what remains of your original assertion? Just how does what you call an invisible, intangible, eternally elusive gardener differ from an imaginary gardener or even from no gardener at all?"

In this parable we can see how what starts as an assertion, that something exists or that there is some **analogy** between certain complexes of phenomena, may be reduced step by step to an altogether different status, to an expression perhaps of a "picture preference."[2] The Skeptic says there is no gardener. The Believer says there is a gardener (but invisible, etc.). One man talks about sexual behavior. Another man prefers to talk of Aphrodite (but knows that there is not really a superhuman person additional to, and somehow responsible for, all sexual phenomena).[3] The process of qualification may be checked at any point before the original assertion is completely withdrawn and something of that first assertion will remain. . . . Mr. Wells' invisible man could not, admittedly, be seen, but in all other respects he was a man like the rest of us. But though the process of qualification may be, and of course usually is, checked in time, it is not always judiciously

so halted. Someone may dissipate his assertion completely without noticing that he has done so. A fine brash hypothesis may thus be killed by inches, the death by a thousand qualifications.

And in this, it seems to me, lies the peculiar danger, the endemic evil, of theological utterance. Take such utterances as "God has a plan," "God created the world," "God loves us as a father loves his children." They look at first sight very much like assertions, vast cosmological assertions. Of course, this is no sure sign that they either are, or are intended to be, assertions. But let us confine ourselves to the cases where those who utter such sentences intend them to express assertions. (Merely remarking parenthetically that those who intend or interpret such utterances as crypto-commands, expressions of wishes, disguised ejaculations, concealed ethics, or as anything else but assertions, are unlikely to succeed in making them either properly orthodox or practically effective.)

Now to assert that such and such is the case is necessarily equivalent to denying that such and such is not the case.[4] Suppose then that we are in doubt as to what someone who gives vent to an utterance is asserting, or suppose that, more radically, we are skeptical as to whether he is really asserting anything at all, one way of trying to understand (or perhaps it will be to expose) his utterance is to attempt to find what he would regard as counting against, or as being incompatible with, its truth. For if the utterance is indeed an assertion, it will necessarily be equivalent to a denial of the negation of that assertion. And anything which would count against the assertion, or which would induce the speaker to withdraw it and to admit that it had been mistaken, must be part of (or the whole of) the meaning of the negation of that assertion. And to know the meaning of the negation of an assertion, is as near as makes no matter, to know the meaning of that assertion.[5] And if there is nothing which a putative assertion denies then there is nothing which it asserts either—and so it is not really an assertion. When the Skeptic in the parable asked the Believer, "Just how does what you call an invisible, intangible, eternally elusive gardener differ from an imaginary gardener or even from no gardener at all?" he was suggesting that the Believer's earlier statement had been so eroded by qualification that it was no longer an assertion at all.

Now it often seems to people who are not religious as if there was no conceivable event or series of events the occurrence of which would be admitted by sophisticated religious people to be a sufficient reason for conceding "There wasn't a God after all" or "God does not really love us then." Someone tells us that God loves us as a father loves his children. We are reassured. But then we see a child dying of inoperable cancer of the throat. His earthly father is driven frantic in his efforts to help, but his Heavenly Father reveals no obvious sign of concern. Some qualification is made—God's love is "not a merely human love" or it is "an inscrutable love," perhaps—and we realize that such sufferings are quite compatible with the truth of the assertion that "God loves us as a father (but, of course, . . .)." We

are reassured again. But then perhaps we ask: what is this assurance of God's (appropriately qualified) love worth, what is this apparent guarantee really a guarantee against? Just what would have to happen not merely (morally and wrongly) to tempt but also (logically and rightly) to entitle us to say "God does not love us" or even "God does not exist"? I therefore put to you the simple central questions, "What would have to occur or to have occurred to constitute for you a disproof of the love of, or the existence of, God?"

NOTES

1. P.A.S., 1944–1945, reprinted as Chapter X of *Logic and Language*, Vol. I (Blackwell, 1951), and in his *Philosophy and Psychoanalysis* (Blackwell, 1953).
2. Cf. J. Wisdom, "Other Minds," *Mind*, 1940; reprinted in his *Other Minds* (Blackwell, 1952).
3. Cf. Lucretius, *De Rerum Natura*, II, 655–660.
4. For those who prefer symbolism: $p \equiv \sim\sim p$.
5. For by simply negating $\sim p$ we get p: $\sim\sim p \equiv p$.

Questions for Thought

1. With which of the discussants in the tale of the gardener do you agree? How would you respond to the other discussant's claims or questions?
2. Do you accept any of the statements about God, such as "God has a plan," that Flew cites? If so, how would you defend them against Flew's critique?
3. Can you think of other statements about God that would be vacuous according to Flew's analysis?
4. Do you agree with Flew's statement that "if there is nothing which a putative assertion denies then there is nothing which it asserts either"? Defend your answer.
5. How would you respond to the question with which Flew concludes his article?
6. How do Flew's concerns about religious belief compare with and differ from the concerns of Wiredu?

---

14   Why I Am a Pagan

LIN YUTANG

Lin Yutang (1895–1976) was born in Changchow, China. After attending St. John's College, Harvard University, and the University of Leipzig (from which he received his Ph.D. in 1923), Lin returned to China, where he became a professor of English philology at Peking (Beijing) National University. He later taught at National Amoy University and served as chancellor of Nanyang University in Singapore. Lin also briefly worked in the Ministry of Foreign Affairs of the Chinese government and headed the arts and letters division of UNESCO in Paris. Lin, who resided in the

United States for thirty years and was a critic of the Chinese Communist Revolution, died in Hong Kong.

Throughout his career, Lin was a prolific editor, translator, essayist, and novelist. He edited and translated many anthologies of Chinese literature and philosophy and compiled a Chinese-English modern-usage dictionary. His other writings include *My Country and My People* (1935), *A History of the Press and Public Opinion in China* (1936), *Confucius Saw Nancy, and Essays About Nothing* (1937), *The Importance of Living* (1937), *Moment in Peking: A Novel of Contemporary Chinese Life* (1939), *On the Wisdom of America* (1950), *The Secret Name* (1958), *The Importance of Understanding* (1960), and *The Pleasures of a Nonconformist* (1962).

In the following selection, which is excerpted from *The Importance of Living*, Lin describes the personal journey that leads him from Christianity to paganism. He also contrasts pagan belief with Christian belief, while providing several reasons for preferring the former. In one of his most powerful contrasts, Lin says that Christians have the security of a wise father watching over them, but that such belief promotes immaturity and dependence. Pagans, on the other hand, are like orphans—less secure than Christians but much more independent.

Lin also argues that the pagan world is simpler than the Christian world and in many ways less arrogant. Whereas Christianity is characterized by a complex theology of sin and redemption, paganism rejects theology as irrelevant to human existence. Whereas Christianity believes that morality requires the threat of eternal reward or punishment, paganism affirms that virtue is its own reward. And whereas Christianity expresses its arrogance by believing in human immortality and God's concern for humankind, paganism accepts the natural cycles of life and death. However, Lin stresses that while being pagan means being non-Christian, it does not mean being atheistic or godless. Although pagans would find any claim to know the true nature of God to be another example of Christian arrogance, they do recognize the existence of divine mystery. Indeed, in a provocative statement near the end of the selection, Lin suggests that the path of the pagan is closer to the path of primitive Christianity than is the path of later Christian revelation and theology.

Questions for Reading

1. What, according to Lin, is a pagan?
2. What events in Lin's life led him to become a pagan?
3. How, according to Lin, does pagan belief differ from Christian belief? Which Christian beliefs does Lin find most problematic?
4. Lin claims that he has no feeling of sin. What do you think he means by sin, and why does he not feel sinful?
5. Why does Lin reject the concept of revelation?

RELIGION IS ALWAYS AN INDIVIDUAL, PERsonal thing. Every person must work out his own views of religion, and if he is sincere, God will not blame him, however it turns out. Every man's religious experience is valid for himself, for . . . it is not something that can be argued about. But the story of an honest soul struggling with religious problems, told in a sincere manner, will always be of benefit to other people. That is why, in speaking about religion, I must get away from generalities and tell my personal story.

I am a pagan. The statement may be taken to imply a revolt against Christianity; and yet "revolt" seems a harsh word and does not correctly describe the state of mind of a man who has passed through a very gradual evolution, step by step, away from Christianity, during which he clung desperately, with love and piety, to a series of tenets which, against his will, were slipping away from him. Because there was never any hatred, therefore it is impossible to speak of a rebellion.

As I was born in a pastor's family and at one time prepared for the Christian ministry, my natural emotions were on the side of religion during the entire struggle rather than against it. In this conflict of emotions and understanding, I gradually arrived at a position where I had, for instance, definitely renounced the doctrine of redemption, a position which could most simply be described as that of a pagan. It was, and still is, a condition of belief concerning life and the universe in which I feel natural and at ease, without having to be at war with myself. The process came as naturally as the weaning of a child or the dropping of a ripe apple on the ground; and when the time came for the apple to drop, I would not interfere with its dropping. In Taoistic phraseology, this is but to live in the **Tao,** and in Western phraseology it is but being sincere with oneself and with the universe, according to one's lights. I believe no one can be natural and happy unless he is intellectually sincere with himself, and to be natural is to be in heaven. To me, being a pagan is just being natural.

"To be a pagan" is no more than a phrase, like "to be a Christian." It is no more than a negative statement, for, to the average reader, to be a pagan means only that one is not a Christian; and since "being a Christian" is a very broad and ambiguous term, the meaning of "not being a Christian" is equally ill-defined. It is all the worse when one defines a pagan as one who does not believe in religion or in God, for we have yet to define what is meant by "God" or by the "religious attitude toward life." Great pagans have always had a deeply reverent attitude toward nature. We shall therefore have to take the word in its conventional sense and mean by it simply a man who does not go to church

(except for an **aesthetic** inspiration, of which I am still capable), does not belong to the Christian fold, and does not accept its usual, orthodox tenets.

On the positive side, a Chinese pagan, the only kind of which I can speak with any feeling of intimacy, is one who starts out with this earthly life as all we can or need to bother about, wishes to live intently and happily as long as his life lasts, often has a sense of the poignant sadness of this life and faces it cheerily, has a keen appreciation of the beautiful and the good in human life wherever he finds them, and regards doing good as its own satisfactory reward. I admit, however, he feels a slight pity or contempt for the "religious" man, who does good in order to get to heaven and who, by implication, would not do good if he were not lured by heaven or threatened with hell. If this statement is correct, I believe there are a great many more pagans in this country than are themselves aware of it. The modern liberal Christian and the pagan are really close, differing only when they start out to *talk* about God.

I think I know the depths of religious experience, for I believe one can have this experience without being a great theologian like Cardinal Newman— otherwise Christianity would not be worth having or must already have been horribly misinterpreted. As I look at it at present, the difference in spiritual life between a Christian believer and a pagan is simply this: the Christian believer lives in a world governed and watched over by God, to whom he has a constant personal relationship, and therefore in a world presided over by a kindly father; his conduct is also often uplifted to a level consonant with this consciousness of being a child of God, no doubt a level which is difficult for a human mortal to maintain consistently at all periods of his life or of the week or even of the day; his actual life varies between living on the human and the truly religious levels.

On the other hand, the pagan lives in this world like an orphan, without the benefit of that consoling feeling that there is always someone in heaven who cares and who will, when that spiritual relationship called prayer is established, attend to his private personal welfare. It is no doubt a less cheery world; but there is the benefit and dignity of being an orphan who by necessity has learned to be independent, to take care of himself, and to be more mature, as all orphans are. It was this feeling rather than any intellectual belief—this feeling of dropping into a world without the love of God—that really scared me till the very last moment of my conversion to paganism; I felt, like many born Christians, that if a personal God did not exist the bottom would be knocked out of this universe.

And yet a pagan can come to the point where he looks on that perhaps warmer and cheerier world as at the same time a more childish, I am tempted to say a more adolescent, world; useful and workable, if one keeps the illusion unspoiled, but no more and no less justifiable than a truly Buddhist way of life; also a more beautifully coloured world but consequently less solidly true and therefore of less worth. For me personally, the suspicion that anything is coloured or not solidly true is fatal. There is a price one must be willing to pay for truth; whatever the consequences, let us have it. This position is comparable to and psychologically the same as that of a murderer: if one has committed a murder, the best thing he can do next is to confess it. That is why I say it takes a little courage to become a pagan. But, after one has accepted the worst, one is also without fear. Peace of mind is that mental condition in which you have accepted the worst. (Here I see for myself the influence of Buddhist or Taoist thought.)

Or I might put the difference between a Christian and a pagan world like this: the pagan in me renounced Christianity out of both pride and humility, emotional pride and intellectual humility, but perhaps on the whole less out of pride than of humility. Out of emotional pride because I hated the idea that there should be any other reason for our behaving as nice, decent men and women than the simple fact that we are human beings; theoretically, and if you want to go in for classifications, classify this as a typically humanist thought. But more out of humility, of intellectual humility, simply because I can no longer, with our astronomical knowledge, believe that an individual human being is so terribly important in the eyes of that Great Creator, living as the individual does, an infinitesimal speck on their earth, which is an infinitesimal speck of the solar system, which is again an infinitesimal speck of the universe of solar systems. The audacity of man and his presumptuous arrogance are what stagger me. What right have we to conceive of the character of a Supreme Being, of whose work we can see only a millionth part, and to postulate about His attributes?

The importance of the human individual is undoubtedly one of the basic tenets of Christianity. But let us see what ridiculous arrogance that leads to in the usual practice of Christian daily life.

Four days before my mother's funeral there was a pouring rain, and if it continued, as was usual in July in Changchow, the city would be flooded, and there could be no funeral. As most of us came from Shanghai, the delay would have meant some inconvenience. One of my relatives—a rather extreme but not an unusual example of a Christian believer in China—told me that she had faith in God, Who would always provide for His children. She prayed, and the rain stopped, apparently in order that a tiny family of Christians might have their funeral without delay. But the implied idea that, but for us, God would willingly subject the tens of thousands of Changchow inhabitants to a devastating flood, as was often the case, or that He did not stop the rain because of them but because of us who wanted to have a conveniently dry funeral, struck me as an unbelievable type of selfishness. I cannot imagine God providing for such selfish children.

There was also a Christian pastor who wrote the story of his life, attesting to many evidences of the hand of God in his life, for the purpose of glorifying God. One of the evidences adduced was that, when he had got together 600 silver dollars to buy his passage to America, God lowered the rate of exchange on the day this so very important individual was to buy his passage. The difference in the rate of exchange for 600 silver dollars could have been at most ten or twenty dollars, and God was willing to rock the bourses in Paris, London, and New York in order that this curious child of His might save ten or twenty dollars. Let us remind ourselves that this way of glorifying God is not at all unusual in any part of Christendom.

Oh, the impudence and conceit of man, whose span of life is but three-score and ten! Mankind as an aggregate may have a significant history, but man as an individual, in the words of Su Tungp'o, is no more than a grain of millet in an ocean or an insect *fuyu* born in the morning and dying at eve, as compared with the universe. The Christian will not be humble. He will not be satisfied with the aggregate immortality of this great stream of life, of which he is already a part, flowing on to eternity, like a mighty stream which empties into the great sea and changes and yet does not change. The clay vessel will ask of the potter, "Why hast thou cast me into this shape and why hast thou made me so brittle?" The clay vessel is not satisfied that it can leave little vessels of its own kind when it cracks up. Man is not satisfied that he has received this marvellous body, this almost divine body. He wants to live for ever! And he will not let God alone. He must say his prayers and he must pray daily for small personal gifts from the Source of All Things. Why can't he let God alone?

There was once a Chinese scholar who did not believe in Buddhism, and his mother who did. She was devout and would acquire merit for herself by mumbling, *"Namu omitabha!"* a thousand times day and night. But every time she started to call Buddha's name, her son would call, "Mamma!" The mother became annoyed. "Well," said the son, "don't you think Buddha would be equally annoyed, if he could hear you?"

My father and mother were devout Christians. To hear my father conduct the evening family prayers was enough. And I was a sensitively religious child. As a pastor's son I received the facilities of missionary education, profited from its benefits, and suffered from its weaknesses. For its benefits I was always grateful and its weaknesses I turned into my strength. For according to Chinese philosophy there are no such things in life as good and bad luck.

I was forbidden to attend Chinese theatres, never allowed to listen to Chinese minstrel singers, and entirely cut apart from the great Chinese folk tradition and mythology. When I entered a missionary college, the little foundation in classical Chinese given me by my father was completely neglected. Perhaps it was just as well—so that later, after a completely Westernized education, I could go back to it with the freshness and vigorous delight of a child of the West in an Eastern wonderland. The complete substitution of the fountain pen for the writing brush during my college and adolescent period was the greatest luck I ever had and preserved for me the freshness of the Oriental mental world unspoiled, until I should become ready for it. If Vesuvius had not covered up Pompeii, Pompeii would not be so well preserved, and the imprints of carriage-wheels on her stone pavements would not be so clearly marked to-day. The missionary college education was my Vesuvius.

Thinking was always dangerous. More than that, thinking was always allied with the devil. The conflict during the collegiate-adolescent period, which, as usual, was my most religious period, between a heart which felt the beauty of the Christian life and a head which had a tendency to reason everything away, was taking place. Curiously enough, I can remember no moments of torment or despair, of the kind that drove Tolstoy almost to suicide. At every stage I felt myself a unified Christian, harmonious in my belief, only a little more liberal than the last, and accepting some fewer Christian doctrines. Anyway, I could always go back to the Sermon on the Mount. The poetry of a saying like "Consider the lilies of the field" was too good to be untrue. It was that and the consciousness of the inner Christian life that gave me strength.

But the doctrines were slipping away terribly. Superficial things first began to annoy me. The "resurrection of the flesh," long disproved when the expected second coming of Christ in the first century did not come off and the Apostles did not rise bodily from their graves, was still there in the Apostles' Creed. This was one of those things.

Then, enrolling in a theological class and initiated into the holy of holies, I learned that another article in the creed, the virgin birth, was open to question, different deans in American theological seminaries holding different views. It enraged me that Chinese believers should be required to believe categorically in this article before they could be baptized, while the theologians of the same church regarded it as an open question. It did not seem sincere and somehow it did not seem right.

Further schooling in meaningless commentary scholarship as to the whereabouts of the "water gate" and such minutiae completely relieved me of responsibility to take such theological studies seriously, and I made a poor showing in my grades. My professors considered that I was not cut out for the Christian ministry, and the bishop thought I might as well leave. They would not waste their instruction on me. Again this seems to me now a blessing in disguise. I doubt, if I had gone on with it and put on the clerical garb, whether it would have been so easy for me to be honest with myself later on. But this feeling of rebellion against the discrepancy of the beliefs required of the theologian and of the average convert was the nearest kind of feeling to what I may call a "revolt."

By this time I had already arrived at the position that the Christian theologians were the greatest enemies of the Christian religion. I could never get over two great contradictions. The first was that the theologians had made the entire structure of the Christian belief hang upon the existence of an apple. If Adam had not eaten an apple, there would be no original sin, and if there were no original sin, there would be no need of redemption. That was plain to me, whatever the symbolic value of the apple might be. This seemed to be preposterously unfair to the teachings of Christ, who never said a word about the original sin or the redemption. Anyway, from pursuing literary studies, I feel, like all modern Americans, no consciousness of sin and simply do not believe in it. All I know is that if God loves me only half as much as my mother does, He will not send me to Hell. That is a final fact of my inner consciousness, and for no religion could I deny its truth.

Still more preposterous another proposition seemed to me. This was the argument that, when Adam and Eve ate an apple during their honeymoon, God was so angry that He condemned their posterity to suffer from generation to generation for that little offence but that, when the same posterity murdered the same God's only Son, God was so delighted that He forgave them all. No matter how people explain and argue, I cannot get over this simple untruth. This was the last of the things that troubled me.

Still, even after my graduation, I was a zealous Christian and voluntarily conducted a Sunday school at Tsing Hua, a non-Christian college at Peking, to the dismay of many faculty members. The Christmas meeting of the Sunday school was a torture to me, for here I was passing on to the Chinese children the tale of herald angels singing upon a midnight clear when I did not believe it myself. Everything had been reasoned away, and only love and fear remained: a kind of clinging love for an all-wise God which made me feel happy and peaceful and suspect that I should not have been so happy and peaceful without that reassuring love—and fear of entering into a world of orphans.

Finally my salvation came. "Why," I reasoned with a colleague, "if there were no God, people would not do good and the world would go topsy-turvy."

"Why?" replied my Confucian colleague. "We should lead a decent human life simply because we are decent human beings," he said.

This appeal to the dignity of human life cut off my last tie to Christianity, and from then on I was a pagan.

It is all so clear to me now. The world of pagan belief is a simpler belief. It postulates nothing, and is obliged to postulate nothing. It seems to make the good life more immediately appealing by appealing to the good life alone. It better justifies doing good by making it unnecessary for doing good to justify itself. It does not encourage men to do, for instance, a simple act of charity by dragging in a series of hypothetical postulates—sin, redemption, the cross, laying up treasure in heaven, mutual obligation among men on account of a third-party relationship in heaven—all so unnecessarily complicated and roundabout, and none capable of direct proof. If one accepts the statement that doing good is its own justification, one cannot help regarding all theological baits to right living as redundant and tending to cloud the lustre of a moral truth. Love among men should be a final, absolute fact. We should be able just to look at each other and love each other without being reminded of a third party in heaven. Christianity seems to me to make morality appear unnecessarily difficult and complicated and sin appear tempting, natural, and desirable. Paganism, on the other hand, seems alone to be able to rescue religion from theology and restore it to its beautiful simplicity of belief and dignity of feeling.

In fact, I seem to be able to see how many theological complications arose in the first, second, and third centuries and turned the simple truths of the Sermon on the Mount into a rigid, self-contained structure to support a priestcraft as an endowed institution. The reason was contained in the word *revelation*—the revelation of a special mystery or divine scheme given to a prophet and kept by all apostolic succession, which was found necessary in all religions, from Mohammedanism and Mormonism to the Living Buddha's Lamaism and Mrs. Eddy's Christian Science, in order for each of them to handle exclusively a special, patented monopoly of salvation. All priestcraft lives on the common staple food of revelation. The simple truths of Christ's teaching on the Mount must be adorned, and the lily He so marvelled at must be gilded. Hence we have the "first Adam" and the "second Adam," and so on and so forth.

But Pauline logic, which seemed so convincing and unanswerable in the early days of the Christian era, seems weak and unconvincing to the more subtle modern critical consciousness; and in this discrepancy between the rigorous Asiatic **deductive** logic and the more pliable, more subtle appreciation of truth of the modern man, lies the weakness of the appeal to the Christian revelation or any revelation for the modern man. Therefore, only by a return to paganism and renouncing the revelation can one return to primitive (and for me more satisfying) Christianity.

It is wrong, therefore, to speak of a pagan as an irreligious man: irreligious he is only as one who refuses to believe in any special variety of revelation. A pagan always believes in God but would not like to say so, for fear of being misunderstood. All Chinese pagans believe in God, the most commonly met with designation in Chinese literature being the term *chaowu,* or the Creator of Things. The only difference is that the Chinese pagan is honest enough to leave the Creator of Things in a halo of mystery, toward whom he feels a kind of awed piety and reverence. What is more, that feeling suffices for him. Of the beauty of this universe, the clever artistry of the myriad things of this creation, the mystery of the stars, the grandeur of heaven, and the dignity of the human soul he is equally aware. But that again suffices for him. He accepts death as he accepts pain and suffering and weighs them against the gift of life and the fresh country breeze and the clear mountain moon and he does not complain. He regards bending to the will of Heaven as the truly religious and pious attitude and calls it "living in the Tao." If the Creator of Things wants him to die at seventy, he gladly dies at seventy. He also believes that "heaven's way always goes round" and that there is no permanent injustice in this world. He does not ask for more.

Questions for Thought

1. Would you classify yourself as a pagan? Why or why not?
2. Can you think of any important differences between pagan belief and Christian belief that Lin has overlooked?
3. In what ways, if any, are Lin's criticisms of Christianity similar to the criticisms made by Starhawk and Carol Christ?
4. What do you think sin is? Do you feel sinful? If so, why do you think you feel this way?
5. Do you think that revelation is an important religious concept? Why or why not?
6. How do you think Lin would respond to the question of whether religion is beneficial or harmful?

15   Has Religion Made Useful Contributions to Civilization?

BERTRAND RUSSELL

Bertrand Arthur William Russell (1872–1970), British nobleman, philosopher, mathematician, and social activist, was born in Trelleck, Wales. Both of Russell's parents, who were freethinkers and atheists, died before he was five, and he went to live in the household of his paternal grandparents. When his grandfather Lord John Russell, the initiator of the Reform Bill of 1832 and a prime minister under Queen Victoria, died two years later, Russell and his brother were raised by their grandmother. Lady Russell, who was a politically liberal Puritan, hired a series of governesses to educate the boys according to strict, exacting standards. Despite his puritanical upbringing, Russell had religious doubts by age eleven, and he eventually became one of the most outspoken critics of Christianity.

Russell studied mathematics and philosophy at Trinity College of Cambridge University from 1890 to 1894. The year he graduated, Russell married Alys Pearsall Smith, a Quaker from Philadelphia, who was the first of his four wives. The next several years were extremely productive for Russell. By the turn of the century, he had been appointed a fellow at Trinity College, lectured on mathematics in the United States, studied economics in Germany, and published the first of his many books, *German Social Democracy* (1896).

In the first decade of the twentieth century, this diverse and productive lifestyle continued. Russell wrote a book on Leibniz, worked on *Principia Mathematica* with Alfred North Whitehead, wrote his first popular essay on religion, unsuccessfully ran for Parliament as a proponent of women's suffrage, was elected a fellow of the Royal Society, and fell out of love with his first wife. From 1910 through 1916, Russell lectured in philosophy at Trinity College, where Ludwig Wittgenstein was one of his students. When he was dismissed from this position and jailed for six months because of his outspoken opposition to World War I, Russell used the time in prison to write his *Introduction to Mathematical Philosophy* (1919) and to begin work on *The Analysis of Mind* (1921).

In 1919, Russell met Dora Black, who was to become his second wife two years later. In 1920, he traveled to both China and the Soviet Union and published a book that was strongly critical of the Soviet regime. This was followed by two more unsuccessful attempts to win a seat in Parliament and by several books devoted to the popularization of science and philosophy. The late 1920s was an especially productive period for Russell. He and his wife, Dora, started the experimental Beacon Hill School; he published several influential books on social and religious questions, such as *On Education, Especially in Early Childhood* (1926), *Why I Am Not a Christian* (1927), and *Marriage and Morals* (1929), and he wrote an important work, *The Analysis of Matter,* that analyzed the fundamental concepts and principles of physical science.

After divorcing his second wife in 1935 and marrying his third wife a year later, Russell moved to the United States in 1938, where he taught at the University of Chicago and the University of California at Los Angeles. Russell was offered a professorship at City College of New York in 1940; however, in an often-cited case of judicial misconduct, his appointment was annulled by a judge who expressed concern about Russell's moral and religious convictions. He then signed a five-year contract at the Barnes Foundation in Philadelphia and taught there from 1941 through 1943. When his contract was suddenly terminated, Russell successfully sued for wrongful dismissal and returned to England, where he was reappointed to a lectureship at Trinity College.

With the publication of his widely read *History of Western Philosophy* in 1945, Russell's fame grew rapidly. He appeared on a number of BBC radio broadcasts and was awarded the Order of Merit in 1949 and the Nobel Prize for literature in 1950. After his fourth marriage in 1952, Russell's political activism became even more pronounced. He delivered a famous radio broadcast condemning nuclear weapons tests in 1954, and he was cofounder and first president of the Campaign for Nuclear Disarmament. In 1961, when he was eighty-nine years old, Russell was imprisoned for a week for leading a sit-in to protest nuclear weapons. Throughout the 1960s, he was also a vocal opponent of the Vietnam War and was one of the organizers of an international war crimes tribunal to call attention to American military misconduct. Toward the end of his life, Russell published his *Autobiography,* which many critics consider a classic in that genre.

As should be obvious from the preceding account of his life, Russell was a prolific writer. He was reportedly one of the few philosophers who could write quickly and clearly, usually without the need of revision. Some of his important writings that have not been previously mentioned include *Our Knowledge of the External World* (1914), *Principles of Social Reconstruction* (1916), *What I Believe* (1925), *Sceptical Essays* (1927), *Education and the Social Order* (1932), *Power: A New Social Analysis* (1938), *An Inquiry into Meaning and Truth* (1940), *Human Knowledge, Its Scope and Limits* (1948), *Authority and the Individual* (1949), *Unpopular Essays* (1950), and *New Hopes for a Changing World* (1951).

In the following essay from *Why I Am Not a Christian,* Russell does not express the ambivalence toward religious belief that Whitehead does. On the contrary, Russell opens his essay with a clear and forceful condemnation of religion. As he bluntly says, "I regard it [religion] as a disease born of fear and as a source of untold misery to the human race." Russell spends the remainder of his essay chronicling what he considers to be the faults of religion, focusing especially on Christianity.

Russell begins by saying that the Christian church has always opposed progress on both an intellectual and a moral level. Like Whitehead, Russell points out that the church has done everything possible to thwart the advance of scientific knowledge. Moreover, Russell adds, the church has supported ethical codes that interfere with human happiness. At different times in its history, the church has endorsed slavery and opposed almost all movements toward economic justice. And the church has consistently espoused an attitude toward sex that is psychologically unhealthy and morally problematic. This attitude has led to the oppression of women and to an unreasonable opposition to both birth control and sex education.

Russell continues his polemic against Christianity by arguing that, contrary to the claims of Christian apologists, the church has done much to undermine social harmony. By divorcing personal righteousness from beneficent action, the church has succeeded in excluding the social virtues from the sphere of moral concern. By emphasizing the immortality of the individual soul, Christianity has made humans more egotistic. By attacking sex and parenthood, the church has promoted the breakup of families for the sake of creed. And by insisting on the exclusivity of the Christian God and Christian dogma, the church has not only undermined the tolerance necessary for the existence of social harmony, but has also engaged in and encouraged fierce persecution. As should be obvious from this summary, Russell believes that religion has been overwhelmingly harmful to human existence.

Questions for Reading

1. What, according to Russell, is the worst feature of Christianity? What are some of the other Christian beliefs that he criticizes?
2. What leads Russell to claim that the Christian church has ignored the teachings of Christ?
3. How does Russell describe the church's reaction to science?
4. On what grounds does Russell claim that Christianity has undermined social harmony? What are some of the examples that he cites in support of this claim?
5. What, according to Russell, are the three impulses embodied in religion? What impact do these impulses have on human life?
6. What seems to be Russell's position on the education of children? How does his position differ from the church's position?

MY OWN VIEW ON RELIGION IS THAT OF LUCRETIUS. I regard it as a disease born of fear and a source of untold misery to the human race. I cannot, however, deny that it has made some contributions to civilization. It helped in early days to fix the calendar, and it caused Egyptian priests to chronicle eclipses with such care that in time they became able to predict them. These two services I am prepared to acknowledge, but I do not know of any others.

The word *religion* is used nowadays in a very loose sense. Some people, under the influence of extreme Protestantism, employ the word to denote any serious personal convictions as to morals or the nature of the universe. This use of the word is quite un-historical. Religion is primarily a social phenomenon. Churches may owe their origin to teachers with strong individual convictions, but these teachers have seldom had much influence upon the churches that they founded, whereas churches have had enormous influence upon the communities in which they flourished. To take the case that is of most interest to members of Western civilization: the teaching of Christ, as it appears in the Gospels, has had extraordinarily little to do with the ethics of Christians. The most important thing about Christianity, from a social and historical point of view, is not Christ but the church, and if we are to judge of Christianity as a social force we must not go to the Gospels for our material. Christ taught that you should give your goods to the poor, that you should not fight, that you should not go to church, and that you should not punish adultery. Neither Catholics nor Protestants have shown any strong desire to follow His teaching in any of these respects. Some of the Franciscans, it is true, attempted to teach the doctrine of apostolic poverty, but the Pope condemned them, and their doctrine was declared heretical. Or, again, consider such a text as "Judge not, that ye be not judged," and ask yourself what influence such a text has had upon the Inquisition and the Ku Klux Klan.

What is true of Christianity is equally true of Buddhism. The Buddha was amiable and enlightened; on his deathbed he laughed at his disciples for supposing that he was immortal. But the Buddhist priesthood—as it exists, for example, in Tibet—has been obscurantist, tyrannous, and cruel in the highest degree.

There is nothing accidental about this difference between a church and its founder. As soon as absolute truth is supposed to be contained in the sayings of a certain man, there is a body of experts to interpret his sayings, and these experts infallibly acquire power, since they hold the key to truth. Like any other privileged caste, they use their power for their own advantage. They are, however, in one respect worse than any other privileged caste, since it is their business to expound an unchanging truth, revealed once for all in utter perfection, so that they become necessarily opponents of all intellectual and moral progress. The church opposed Galileo and Darwin; in our own day it opposes Freud. In the days of its greatest power it went further in its opposition to the intellectual life. Pope Gregory the Great wrote to a certain bishop a letter beginning: "A report has reached us which we cannot mention without a blush, that thou expoundest grammar to certain friends." The bishop was compelled by pontifical authority to desist from this wicked labor, and Latinity did not recover until the Renaissance. It is not only intellectually but also morally that religion is pernicious. I mean by this that it teaches ethical codes which are not conducive to human happiness. When, a few years ago, a plebiscite was taken in Germany as to whether the deposed royal houses should still be allowed to enjoy their private property, the churches in Germany officially stated that it would be contrary to the teaching of Christianity to deprive them of it. The churches, as everyone knows, opposed the abolition of slavery as long as they dared, and with a few well-advertised exceptions they oppose at the present day every movement toward economic justice. . . .

CHRISTIANITY AND SEX

The worst feature of the Christian religion, however, is its attitude toward sex—an attitude so morbid and so unnatural that it can be understood only when taken in relation to the sickness of the civilized world at the time the Roman Empire was decaying. We sometimes hear talk to the effect that Christianity improved the status of women. This is one of the grossest perversions of history that it is possible to make. Women cannot enjoy a tolerable position in society where it is considered of the utmost importance that they should not infringe a very rigid moral code. Monks have always regarded Woman primarily as the temptress; they have thought of her mainly as the inspirer of impure lusts. The teaching of the church has been, and still is, that virginity is best, but that for those who find this impossible marriage is permissible. "It is better to marry than to burn," as St. Paul brutally puts it. By making marriage indissoluble, and by stamping out all knowledge of the *ars amandi,* the church did what it could to secure that the only form of sex which it permitted should involve very little pleasure and a great deal of pain. The opposition to birth control has, in fact, the same motive: if a woman has a child a year until she dies worn out, it is not to be supposed that she will derive much pleasure from her married life; therefore birth control must be discouraged.

The conception of Sin which is bound up with Christian ethics is one that does an extraordinary amount of harm, since it affords people an outlet for their sadism which they believe to be legitimate, and even noble. Take, for example, the question of the prevention of syphilis. It is known that, by precautions taken in advance, the danger of contracting this disease can be made negligible. Christians, however, object to the dissemination of knowledge of this fact, since they hold it good that sinners should be punished. They hold this so good that they are even willing that punishment should extend to the wives and children of sinners. There are in the world at the present moment many thousands of children suffering from congenital syphilis who would never have been born but for the desire of Christians to see sinners punished. I cannot understand how doctrines leading to this fiendish cruelty can be considered to have any good effects upon morals.

It is not only in regard to sexual behavior but also in regard to knowledge on sex subjects that the attitude of Christians is dangerous to human welfare. Every person who has taken the trouble to study the question in an unbiased spirit knows that the artificial ignorance on sex subjects which orthodox Christians attempt to enforce upon the young is extremely dangerous to mental and physical health, and causes in those who pick up their knowledge by the way of "improper" talk, as most children do, an attitude that sex is in itself indecent and ridiculous. I do not think there can be any defense for the view that knowledge is ever undesirable. I should not put barriers in the way of the acquisition of knowledge by anybody at any age. But in the particular case of sex knowledge there are much weightier arguments in its favor than in the case of most other knowledge. A person is much less likely to act wisely when he is ignorant than when he is instructed, and it is ridiculous to give young people a sense of sin because they have a natural curiosity about an important matter.

Every boy is interested in trains. Suppose we told him that an interest in trains is wicked; suppose we kept his eyes bandaged whenever he was in a train or on a railway station; suppose we never allowed the word "train" to be mentioned in his presence and preserved an impenetrable mystery as to the means by which he is transported from one place to another. The result would not be that he would cease to be interested in trains; on the contrary, he would become more interested than ever but would have a morbid sense of sin, because this interest had been represented to him as improper. Every boy of active intelligence could by this means be rendered in a greater or less degree neurasthenic. This is precisely what is done in the matter of sex; but, as sex is more interesting than trains, the results are worse. Almost every adult in a Christian community is more or less diseased nervously as a result of the taboo on sex knowledge when he or she was young. And the sense of sin which is thus artificially implanted is one of the causes of cruelty, timidity, and stupidity in later life. There is no rational ground of any sort or kind for keeping a child ignorant of anything that he may wish to know, whether on sex or on any other matter. And we shall never get a sane population until this fact is recognized in early education, which is impossible so long as the churches are able to control educational politics.

Leaving these comparatively detailed objections on one side, it is clear that the fundamental doctrines of Christianity demand a great deal of ethical perversion before they can be accepted. The world, we are told, was created by a God who is both good and omnipotent. Before He created the world He foresaw all the pain and misery that it would contain; He is therefore responsible for all of it. It is useless to argue that the pain in the world is due to sin. In the first place, this is not true; it is not sin that causes rivers to overflow their banks or volcanoes to erupt. But even if it were true, it would make no difference. If I were going to beget a child knowing that the child was going to be a homicidal maniac, I should be responsible for his crimes. If God knew in advance the sins of which man would be guilty, He was clearly responsible for all the consequences of those sins when He decided to create man. The usual Christian argument is that the suffering in the world is a purification for sin and is therefore a good thing. This argument is, of course, only a rationalization of sadism; but in any case it is a very poor argument. I would invite any Christian to accompany me to the children's ward of a hospital, to watch the suffering that is there being endured, and then to persist in the assertion that those children are so morally abandoned as to deserve what they are suffering. In order to bring himself to say this, a man must destroy in himself all feelings of mercy and compassion. He must, in short, make himself as cruel as the God in whom he believes. No man who believes that all is for the best in this suffering world can keep his ethical values unimpaired, since he is always having to find excuses for pain and misery.

THE OBJECTIONS TO RELIGION

The objections to religion are of two sorts—intellectual and moral. The intellectual objection is that there is no reason to suppose any religion true; the moral objection is that religious precepts date from a time when men were more cruel than they now are and therefore tend to perpetuate inhumanities which the moral conscience of the age would otherwise outgrow.

To take the intellectual objection first: there is a certain tendency in our practical age to consider that it does not much matter whether religious teaching is true or not, since the important question is whether it is useful. One question cannot, however, well be decided without the other. If we believe the Christian religion, our notions of what is good will be different from what they will be if we do not believe it. Therefore, to Christians, the effects of Christianity may seem good, while to unbelievers they may seem bad. Moreover, the attitude that one ought to believe such and such a proposition, independently of the question whether there is evidence in its favor, is an attitude which produces hostility to evidence and causes us to close our minds to every fact that does not suit our prejudices.

A certain kind of scientific candor is a very important quality, and it is one which can hardly exist in a man who imagines that there are things which it is his duty to believe. We cannot, therefore, really decide whether religion does good without investigating the question whether religion is true. To Christians, Mohammedans, and Jews the most fundamental question involved in the truth of religion is the existence of God. In the days when religion was still triumphant the word "God" had a perfectly definite meaning; but as a result of the onslaughts of Rationalists the word has become paler and paler, until it is difficult to see what people mean when they assert that they believe in God. Let us take, for purposes of argument, Matthew Arnold's definition: "A power not ourselves that makes for righteousness." Perhaps we might make this even more vague and ask ourselves whether we have any evidence of purpose in the universe apart from the purposes of living beings on the surface of this planet.

The usual argument of religious people on this subject is roughly as follows: "I and my friends are persons of amazing intelligence and virtue. It is hardly conceivable that so much intelligence and virtue could have come about by chance. There must, therefore, be someone at least as intelligent and virtuous as we are who set the cosmic machinery in motion with a view to producing Us." I am sorry to say that I do not find this argument so impressive as it is found by those who use it. The universe is large; yet, if we are to believe Eddington, there are probably nowhere else in the universe beings as intelligent as men. If you consider the total amount of matter in the world and compare it with the amount forming the bodies of intelligent beings, you will see that the latter bears an almost infinitesimal proportion to the former. Consequently, even if it is enormously improbable that the laws of chance will produce an organism capable of intelligence out of a casual selection of atoms, it is nevertheless probable that there will be in the universe that very small number of such organisms that we do in fact find.

Then again, considered as the climax to such a vast process, we do not really seem to me sufficiently marvelous. Of course, I am aware that many divines are far more marvelous than I am, and that I cannot wholly appreciate merits so far transcending my own. Nevertheless, even after making allowances under this head, I cannot but think that Omnipotence operating through all eternity might have produced something better. And then we have to reflect that even this result is only a flash in the pan. The earth will not always remain habitable; the human race will die out, and if the cosmic process is to justify itself hereafter it will have to do so elsewhere than on the surface of our planet. And even if this should occur, it must stop sooner or later. The second law of thermo-dynamics makes it scarcely possible to doubt that the universe is running down, and that ultimately nothing of the slightest interest will be possible anywhere. Of course, it is open to us to say that when that time comes God will wind up the machinery again; but if we do say this, we can base our assertion only upon faith, not upon one shred of scientific evidence. So far as scientific evidence goes, the universe has crawled by slow stages to a somewhat pitiful result on this earth and is going to crawl by still more pitiful stages to a condition of universal death. If this is to be taken as evidence of purpose, I can only say that the purpose is one that does not appeal to me. I see no reason, therefore, to believe in any sort of God, however vague and however attenuated. I leave on one side the old metaphysical arguments, since religious apologists themselves have thrown them over.

THE SOUL AND IMMORTALITY

The Christian emphasis on the individual soul has had a profound influence upon the ethics of Christian communities. It is a doctrine fundamentally akin to that of the Stoics, arising as theirs did in communities that could no longer cherish political hopes.

The natural impulse of the vigorous person of decent character is to attempt to do good, but if he is deprived of all political power and of all opportunity to influence events, he will be deflected from his natural course and will decide that the important thing is to be good. This is what happened to the early Christians; it led to a conception of personal holiness as something quite independent of beneficent action, since holiness had to be something that could be achieved by people who were impotent in action. Social virtue came therefore to be excluded from Christian ethics. To this day conventional Christians think an adulterer more wicked than a politician who takes bribes, although the latter probably does a thousand times as much harm. The medieval conception of virtue, as one sees in their pictures, was of something wishy-washy, feeble, and sentimental. The most virtuous man was the man who retired from the world; the only men of action who were regarded as saints were those who wasted the lives and substance of their subjects in fighting the Turks, like St. Louis. The church would never regard a man as a saint because he reformed the finances, or the criminal law, or the judiciary. Such mere contributions to human welfare would be regarded as of no importance. I do not believe there is a single saint in the whole calendar whose saintship is due to work of public utility. With this separation between the social and the moral person there went an increasing separation between soul and body, which has survived in Christian **metaphysics** and in the systems derived from Descartes. One may say, broadly speaking, that the body represents the social and public part of a man, whereas the soul represents the private part. In emphasizing the soul, Christian ethics has made itself completely individualistic. I think it is clear that the net result of all the centuries of Christianity has been to make men more egotistic, more shut up in themselves, than nature made them; for the impulses that naturally take a man outside the walls of his ego are those of sex, parenthood, and patriotism or herd instinct. Sex the church did everything it could to decry and degrade; family affection was decried by Christ himself and by the bulk of his followers; and patriotism could find no place among the subject populations of the Roman Empire. The polemic against the family in the Gospels is a matter that has not received the attention it deserves. The church treats the

Mother of Christ with reverence, but He Himself showed little of this attitude. "Woman, what have I to do with thee?" (John ii, 4) is His way of speaking to her. He says also that He has come to set a man at variance against his father, the daughter against her mother, and the daughter-in-law against her mother-in-law, and that he that loveth father and mother more than Him is not worthy of Him (Matt. x, 35–37). All this means the breakup of the biological family tie for the sake of creed—an attitude which had a great deal to do with the intolerance that came into the world with the spread of Christianity.

This individualism culminated in the doctrine of the immortality of the individual soul, which was to enjoy hereafter endless bliss or endless woe according to circumstances. The circumstances upon which this momentous difference depended were somewhat curious. For example, if you died immediately after a priest had sprinkled water upon you while pronouncing certain words, you inherited eternal bliss; whereas, if after a long and virtuous life you happened to be struck by lightning at a moment when you were using bad language because you had broken a bootlace, you would inherit eternal torment. I do not say that the modern Protestant Christian believes this, nor even perhaps the modern Catholic Christian who has not been adequately instructed in theology; but I do say that this is the orthodox doctrine and was firmly believed until recent times. The Spaniards in Mexico and Peru used to baptize Indian infants and then immediately dash their brains out: by this means they secured that these infants went to Heaven. No orthodox Christian can find any logical reason for condemning their action, although all nowadays do so. In countless ways the doctrine of personal immortality in its Christian form has had disastrous effects upon morals, and the metaphysical separation of soul and body has had disastrous effects upon philosophy.

SOURCES OF INTOLERANCE

The intolerance that spread over the world with the advent of Christianity is one of its most curious features, due, I think, to the Jewish belief in righteousness and in the exclusive reality of the Jewish God. Why the Jews should have had these peculiarities I do not know. They seem to have developed during the captivity as a reaction against the attempt to absorb the Jews into alien populations. However that may be, the Jews, and more especially the prophets, invented emphasis upon personal righteousness and the idea that it is wicked to tolerate any religion except one. These two ideas have had an extraordinarily disastrous effect upon Occidental history. The church has made much of the persecution of Christians by the Roman State before the time of Constantine. This persecution, however, was slight and intermittent and wholly political. At all times, from the age of Constantine to the end of the seventeenth century, Christians were far more fiercely persecuted by other Christians than they ever were by the Roman emperors. Before the rise of Christianity this persecuting attitude was unknown to the ancient world except among the Jews. If you read, for example, Herodotus, you find a bland and tolerant account of the habits of the foreign nations he visited. Sometimes, it is true, a peculiarly barbarous custom may shock him, but in general he is hospitable to foreign gods and foreign customs. He is not anxious to prove that people who call Zeus by some other name will suffer eternal perdition and ought to be put to death in order that their punishment may begin as soon as possible. This attitude has been reserved for Christians. It is true that the modern Christian is less robust, but that is not thanks to Christianity; it is thanks to the generations of freethinkers, who, from the Renaissance to the present day, have made Christians ashamed of many of their traditional beliefs. It is amusing to hear the modern Christian telling you how mild and rationalistic Christianity really is and ignoring the fact that all its mildness and rationalism is due to the teaching of men who in their own day were persecuted by all orthodox Christians. Nobody nowadays believes that the world was created in 4004 B.C.; but not so very long ago **skepticism** on this point was thought an abominable crime. My great-great-grandfather, after observing the depth of the lava on the slopes of Etna, came to the **conclusion** that the world must be older than the orthodox supposed and published this opinion in a book. For this offense he was cut by the county and ostracized from society. Had he been a man in humbler circumstances, his punishment would doubtless have been more severe. It is no credit to the orthodox that they do not now believe all the absurdities that were believed 150 years ago. The gradual emasculation of the Christian doctrine has been effected in spite of the most vigorous resistance, and solely as the result of the onslaughts of freethinkers.

THE DOCTRINE OF FREE WILL

The attitude of the Christians on the subject of natural law has been curiously vacillating and uncertain. There was, on the one hand, the doctrine of free will, in which the great majority of Christians believed; and this doctrine required that the acts of human beings at least should not be subject to natural law. There was, on the other hand, especially in the eighteenth and nineteenth centuries, a belief in God as the Lawgiver and in natural law as one of the main evidences of the existence of a Creator. In recent times the objection to the reign of law in the interests of free will has begun to be felt more strongly than the belief in natural law as affording evidence for a Lawgiver. Materialists used the laws of physics to show, or attempt to show, that the movements of human bodies are mechanically determined, and that consequently everything that we say and every change of position that we effect fall outside the sphere of any possible free will. If this be so, whatever may be left for our unfettered volitions is of little value. If, when a man writes a poem or commits a murder, the bodily movements involved in his act result solely from physical causes, it would seem absurd to put up a statue to him in the one case and to hang him in the other. There might in certain metaphysical systems remain a region of pure thought in which the will would be free; but, since that can be communicated to others only by means of bodily movement, the realm of freedom would be one that could never be the subject of communication and could never have any social importance.

Then, again, evolution has had a considerable influence upon those Christians who have accepted it. They have seen that it will not do to make claims on behalf of man which are totally different from those which are made on behalf of other forms of life. Therefore, in order to safeguard free will in man, they have objected to every attempt at explaining the behavior of living matter in terms of physical and chemical laws. The position of Descartes, to the effect that all lower animals are automata, no longer finds favor with liberal theologians. The doctrine of continuity makes them inclined to go a step further still and maintain that even what is called dead matter is not rigidly governed in its behavior by unalterable laws. They seem to have overlooked the fact that, if you abolish the reign of law, you also abolish the possibility of miracles, since miracles are acts of God which contravene the laws governing ordinary phenomena. I can, however, imagine the modern liberal theologian maintaining with an air of profundity that all creation is miraculous, so that he no longer needs to fasten upon certain occurrences as special evidence of Divine intervention.

Under the influence of this reaction against natural law, some Christian apologists have seized upon the latest doctrines of the atom, which tend to show that the physical laws in which we have hitherto believed have only an approximate and average truth as applied to large numbers of atoms, while the individual electron behaves pretty much as it likes. My own belief is that this is a temporary phase, and that the physicists will in time discover laws governing minute phenomena, although these laws may differ very considerably from those of traditional physics. However that may be, it is worth while to observe that the modern doctrines as to minute phenomena have no bearing upon anything that is of practical importance. Visible motions, and indeed all motions that make any difference to anybody, involve such large numbers of atoms that they come well within the scope of the old laws. To write a poem or commit a murder (reverting to our previous illustration), it is necessary to move an appreciable mass of ink or lead. The electrons composing the ink may be dancing freely around their little ballroom, but the ballroom as a whole is moving according to the old laws of physics, and this alone is what concerns the poet and his publisher. The modern doctrines, therefore, have no appreciable bearing upon any of those problems of human interest with which the theologian is concerned.

The free-will question consequently remains just where it was. Whatever may be thought about it as a matter of ultimate metaphysics, it is quite clear that nobody believes in it in practice. Everyone has always believed that it is possible to train character;

everyone has always known that alcohol or opium will have a certain effect on behavior. The apostle of free will maintains that a man can by will power avoid getting drunk, but he does not maintain that when drunk a man can say "British Constitution" as clearly as if he were sober. And everybody who has ever had to do with children knows that a suitable diet does more to make them virtuous than the most eloquent preaching in the world. The one effect that the free-will doctrine has in practice is to prevent people from following out such common-sense knowledge to its rational conclusion. When a man acts in ways that annoy us we wish to think him wicked, and we refuse to face the fact that his annoying behavior is a result of antecedent causes which, if you follow them long enough, will take you beyond the moment of his birth and therefore to events for which he cannot be held responsible by any stretch of imagination.

No man treats a motorcar as foolishly as he treats another human being. When the car will not go, he does not attribute its annoying behavior to sin; he does not say, "You are a wicked motorcar, and I shall not give you any more petrol until you go." He attempts to find out what is wrong and to set it right. An analogous way of treating human beings is, however, considered to be contrary to the truths of our holy religion. And this applies even in the treatment of little children. Many children have bad habits which are perpetuated by punishment but will probably pass away of themselves if left unnoticed. Nevertheless, nurses, with very few exceptions, consider it right to inflict punishment, although by so doing they run the risk of causing insanity. When insanity has been caused it is cited in courts of law as a proof of the harmfulness of the habit, not of the punishment. (I am alluding to a recent prosecution for obscenity in the State of New York.)

Reforms in education have come very largely through the study of the insane and feeble-minded, because they have not been held morally responsible for their failures and have therefore been treated more scientifically than normal children. Until very recently it was held that, if a boy could not learn his lessons, the proper cure was caning or flogging. This view is nearly extinct in the treatment of children, but it survives in the criminal law. It is evident that a man with a propensity to crime must be stopped, but so must a man who has hydrophobia

and wants to bite people, although nobody considers him morally responsible. A man who is suffering from plague has to be imprisoned until he is cured, although nobody thinks him wicked. The same thing should be done with a man who suffers from a propensity to commit forgery; but there should be no more idea of guilt in the one case than in the other. And this is only common sense, though it is a form of common sense to which Christian ethics and metaphysics are opposed.

To judge of the moral influence of any institution upon a community, we have to consider the kind of impulse which is embodied in the institution and the degree to which the institution increases the efficacy of the impulse in that community. Sometimes the impulse concerned is quite obvious, sometimes it is more hidden. An Alpine club, for example, obviously embodies the impulse to adventure, and a learned society embodies the impulse toward knowledge. The family as an institution embodies jealousy and parental feeling; a football club or a political party embodies the impulse toward competitive play; but the two greatest social institutions—namely, the church and the state—are more complex in their psychological motivation. The primary purpose of the state is clearly security against both internal criminals and external enemies. It is rooted in the tendency of children to huddle together when they are frightened and to look for a grown-up person who will give them a sense of security. The church has more complex origins. Undoubtedly the most important source of religion is fear; this can be seen in the present day, since anything that causes alarm is apt to turn people's thoughts to God. Battle, pestilence, and shipwreck all tend to make people religious. Religion has, however, other appeals besides that of terror; it appeals especially to our human self-esteem. If Christianity is true, mankind are not such pitiful worms as they seem to be; they are of interest to the Creator of the universe, who takes the trouble to be pleased with them when they behave well and displeased when they behave badly. This is a great compliment. We should not think of studying an ants' nest to find out which of the ants performed their formicular duty, and we should certainly not think of picking out those individual ants who were remiss and putting them into a bonfire. If God does this for us, it is a compliment to our importance; and it is even a pleasanter compliment if he awards to the good among us everlasting happiness in heaven. Then there is the comparatively modern idea that cosmic evolution is all designed to bring about the sort of results which we call good—that is to say, the sort of results that give us pleasure. Here again it is flattering to suppose that the universe is controlled by a Being who shares our tastes and prejudices.

THE IDEA OF RIGHTEOUSNESS

The third psychological impulse which is embodied in religion is that which has led to the conception of righteousness. I am aware that many freethinkers treat this conception with great respect and hold that it should be preserved in spite of the decay of dogmatic religion. I cannot agree with them on this point. The psychological analysis of the idea of righteousness seems to me to show that it is rooted in undesirable passions and ought not to be strengthened by the *imprimatur* of reason. Righteousness and unrighteousness must be taken together; it is impossible to stress the one without stressing the other also. Now, what is "unrighteousness" in practice? It is in practice behavior of a kind disliked by the herd. By calling it unrighteousness, and by arranging an elaborate system of ethics around this conception, the herd justifies itself in wreaking punishment upon the objects of its own dislike, while at the same time, since the herd is righteous by definition, it enhances its own self-esteem at the very moment when it lets loose its impulse to cruelty. This is the psychology of lynching, and of the other ways in which criminals are punished. The essence of the conception of righteousness, therefore, is to afford an outlet for sadism by cloaking cruelty as justice.

But, it will be said, the account you have been giving of righteousness is wholly inapplicable to the Hebrew prophets, who, after all, on your own showing, invented the idea. There is truth in this: righteousness in the mouths of the Hebrew prophets meant what was approved by them and **Yahweh.** One finds the same attitude expressed in the Acts of the Apostles, where the Apostles began a pronouncement with the words "For it seemed good to the Holy Ghost, and to us" (Acts 15:28).

This kind of individual certainty as to God's tastes and opinions cannot, however, be made the basis of any institution. That has always been the difficulty with which Protestantism has had to contend: a new prophet could maintain that his revelation was more authentic than those of his predecessors, and there was nothing in the general outlook of Protestantism to show that this claim was invalid. Consequently Protestantism split into innumerable sects, which weakened one another; and there is reason to suppose that a hundred years hence Catholicism will be the only effective representative of the Christian faith. In the Catholic Church inspiration such as the prophets enjoyed has its place; but it is recognized that phenomena which look rather like genuine divine inspiration may be inspired by the Devil, and it is the business of the church to discriminate, just as it is the business of an art connoisseur to know a genuine Leonardo from a forgery. In this way revelation becomes institutionalized at the same time. Righteousness is what the church approves, and unrighteousness is what it disapproves. Thus the effective part of the conception of righteousness is a justification of herd antipathy.

It would seem, therefore, that the three human impulses embodied in religion are fear, conceit, and hatred. The purpose of religion, one may say, is to give an air of respectability to these passions, provided they run in certain channels. It is because these passions make, on the whole, for human misery that religion is a force for evil, since it permits men to indulge these passions without restraint, where but for its sanction they might, at least to a certain degree, control them.

I can imagine at this point an objection, not likely to be urged perhaps by most orthodox believers but nevertheless worthy to be examined. Hatred and fear, it may be said, are essential human characteristics; mankind always has felt them and always will. The best that you can do with them, I may be told, is to direct them into certain channels in which they are less harmful than they would be in certain other channels. A Christian theologian might say that their treatment by the church is analogous to its treatment of the sex impulse, which it deplores. It attempts to render concupiscence innocuous by confining it within the bounds of matrimony. So, it may be said, if mankind must inevitably feel hatred, it is better to direct this hatred against those who are really harmful, and this is precisely what the church does by its conception of righteousness. To this contention there are two replies—one comparatively superficial; the other going to the root of the matter. The superficial reply is that the church's conception of righteousness is not the best possible; the fundamental reply is that hatred and fear can, with our present psychological knowledge and our present industrial technique, be eliminated altogether from human life.

To take the first point first. The church's conception of righteousness is socially undesirable in various ways—first and foremost in its depreciation of intelligence and science. This defect is inherited from the Gospels. Christ tells us to become as little children, but little children cannot understand the differential calculus, or the principles of currency, or the modern methods of combating disease. To acquire such knowledge is no part of our duty, according to the church. The church no longer contends that knowledge is in itself sinful, though it did so in its palmy days; but the acquisition of knowledge, even though not sinful, is dangerous, since it may lead to pride of intellect, and hence to a questioning of the Christian dogma. Take, for example, two men, one of whom has stamped out yellow fever throughout some large region in the tropics but has in the course of his labors had occasional relations with women to whom he was not married; while the other has been lazy and shiftless, begetting a child a year until his wife died of exhaustion and taking so little care of his children that half of them died from preventable causes, but never indulging in illicit sexual intercourse. Every good Christian must maintain that the second of these men is more virtuous than the first. Such an attitude is, of course, superstitious and totally contrary to reason. Yet something of this absurdity is inevitable so long as avoidance of sin is thought more important than positive merit, and so long as the importance of knowledge as a help to a useful life is not recognized. The second and more fundamental objection to the utilization of fear and hatred in the way practiced by the church is that these emotions can now be almost wholly eliminated from human nature by educational, economic, and political reforms. The educational reforms must be the basis, since men who feel hate and fear will also admire these emotions and wish to perpetuate them, although this admiration and wish will probably be unconscious, as it is in the ordinary Christian. An education designed to eliminate fear is by no means difficult to create. It is only necessary to treat a child with kindness, to put him in an environment where initiative is possible without disastrous results, and to save him from contact with adults who have irrational terrors, whether of the dark, of mice, or of social revolution. A child must also not be subject to severe punishment, or to threats, or to grave and excessive reproof. To save a child from hatred is a somewhat more elaborate business. Situations arousing jealousy must be very carefully avoided by means of scrupulous and exact justice as between different children. A child must feel himself the object of warm affection on the part of some at least of the adults with whom he has to do, and he must not be thwarted in his natural activities and curiosities except when danger to life or health is concerned. In particular, there must be no taboo on sex knowledge, or on conversation about matters which conventional people consider improper. If these simple precepts are observed from the start, the child will be fearless and friendly.

On entering adult life, however, a young person so educated will find himself or herself plunged into a world full of injustice, full of cruelty, full of preventable misery. The injustice, the cruelty, and the misery that exist in the modern world are an inheritance from the past, and their ultimate source is economic, since life-and-death competition for the means of subsistence was in former days inevitable. It is not inevitable in our age. With our present industrial technique we can, if we choose, provide a tolerable subsistence for everybody. We could also secure that the world's population should be stationary if we were not prevented by the political influence of churches which prefer war, pestilence, and famine to contraception. The knowledge exists by which universal happiness can be secured; the chief obstacle to its utilization for that purpose is the teaching of religion. Religion prevents our children from having a rational education; religion prevents us from removing the fundamental causes of war; religion prevents us from teaching the ethic of scientific co-operation in place of the old fierce doctrines of sin and punishment. It is possible that mankind is on the threshold of a golden age; but, if so, it will be necessary first to slay the dragon that guards the door, and this dragon is religion.

Questions for Thought

1. What do you think is the worst feature of Christianity? What do you think is the best feature of Christianity?
2. Do you agree with Russell's claim that the Christian church has ignored the teachings of Christ? If so, in what way or ways has it done so?
3. How do Russell's views on the relation between science and religion compare with or differ from the views of Whitehead?
4. Do you think Christianity has undermined social harmony? Defend your answer.
5. How does Russell's account of the impulses embodied in religion compare with and differ from Lin Yutang's account?
6. Do you agree with what Russell says about the education of children? Why or why not?
7. What do you think are the three greatest harms of religion? What do you think are the three greatest benefits?

Glossary

Abhidhamma The third section of the *Tripitaka* or *Three Baskets,* the sacred writings of Theravada Buddhism.

Academic philosophy A term that refers to the form of philosophy that dominated Plato's Academy from the fourth century B.C.E. Unlike the philosophy of Plato himself, academic philosophy was skeptical in nature. Hume praises this school of philosophy for maintaining theoretical skepticism while admitting that practical life requires that human beings take positions on many matters.

Advaita A Sanskrit word that translates as "nonduality." It refers to any school of Hindu thought that accepts the sameness or identity of the Atman and Brahman.

Aesthetic Pertaining to a sense of beauty or good taste; concerned with emotion and sensation rather than intellect or reason.

Aesthetics The branch of philosophy that deals with taste and the study of beauty in the arts and elsewhere.

Agape Nonerotic love. This term, which is used by New Testament writers to refer to the kind of love that Jesus urges, is criticized by Starhawk for being too abstract and impersonal.

Agni The Hindu god of fire who serves as the channel through which offerings can be made to the other gods; one of the three chief deities of the *Vedas,* he is ever-young, since the fire is relit every day, but also immortal.

Agnostic Refers generally to the claim that we cannot know certain types of knowledge; in religion, it refers specifically to the claim that we cannot know whether God exists.

Aha'ánáoo'níłʼ One of the four categories of knowledge in Navajo philosophy. Translated as "the gathering of family," this type of knowledge focuses on family ties and emotional connections. It is associated with the yellow evening twilight.

Ahimsa The Sanskrit word that literally means "nonkilling." It is the most important moral term in the religion or philosophy of Jainism, and it is an important concept in the writings of Gandhi.

Allah The Islamic name for the Supreme Being or God.

Amir A prince or political leader in certain Islamic countries; often written as *emir.*

Analogy Generally refers to any partial likeness or similarity that is used for the purpose of comparison; in logic, the term refers to a type of inductive argumentation in which one argues from the likeness of two things in several respects to their likeness in another respect.

Anarchism   The political philosophy that governmental authority in any form is coercive and thus illegitimate; Goldman says that anarchism is the philosophy of a new social order based on liberty unrestricted by manmade law.

Anatman   Literally, "without an Atman"; the Buddhist doctrine of "no self" or "no soul," which implies that living beings lack a spiritual essence.

Anaxagoras   An ancient Greek philosopher who believed that the universe was produced, through a process of separation, from an undifferentiated mixture containing an infinite number of "seeds" or "germs." He was the first philosopher to choose Athens as his home.

Androcentric   Describes something that is centered or focused on men, usually to the neglect or exclusion of women.

Apollo   The ancient Greek god of the sun, music, and the intellect who represented logic and order.

A posteriori   Refers to any knowledge claim or truth that is derived from sense experience.

Apperception   In Leibniz's philosophy, another term for consciousness. According to Leibniz, all Monads have unconscious perceptions, but only some of them have consciousness or apperception.

A priori   Refers to any knowledge claim or truth that can be known or proved independently of experience. Most philosophers believe that *a priori* knowledge claims are necessarily true.

A propos   With reference to.

Arahatship   The state of attaining sainthood in Buddhism; the ideal state of Theravada Buddhism.

Ariosto, Ludivico   Italian writer who lived from 1474 to 1533; he is best known for his *Orlando Furioso*, an epic comic poem that expresses the ideals of the Renaissance.

Aristocracy   A form of government ruled by an elite class of persons who hold exceptional rank; government by the best or most capable people in the state.

Ars Amandi   A Latin phrase that refers to the sexual arts; the study of erotic techniques.

Asceticism   The practice of self-denial, of not allowing oneself pleasure, often for religious reasons.

Atman   In Hinduism, one's spiritual essence or soul. Given Hindu beliefs about reincarnation, this essence or soul is not restricted to human beings.

Autonomy   Another word for freedom of thought or action. An autonomous thought is one that is not determined by external factors.

Avidya   In Hinduism, the state of ignorance or not-knowing that prevents one from achieving *moksha*.

Bad faith   An existentialist term that characterizes someone who denies either their facticity or their transcendence. It is sometimes equated with self-deception.

Behaviorism   A school of psychology founded by the American psychologist J. B. Watson. Behaviorists maintain that the subject matter of psychology should be the outward, objectively observable behavior of living organisms and that this behavior is fully determined by environmental factors, such as stimulus-response conditioning.

Bik'ehgo da'iináanii   One of the four categories of knowledge in Navajo philosophy. Translated as "that which gives direction to life," this type of knowledge emphasizes character development and moral deliberation. It is associated with the dawn.

Boshongo   One of the groups of Bantu peoples of central and southern Africa.

Bourgeoisie   In Marxist theory, the class of modern capitalists who own the means of production and who employ wage laborers.

Brahma   The Hindu god who is viewed as creator of this world and countless others. In the lengthy epic poem, the *Mahabharata,* Brahma is one member of a triumvirate of gods: Brahma (the creator), Vishnu (the preserver), and Shiva (the destroyer).

Brahman   In the Upanishads, the all-pervading divine essence that constitutes all reality. One achieves spiritual salvation or liberation when one realizes the basic identity between one's spiritual essence (one's Atman) and Brahman.

Brahmin   A member of the highest level of the varna system in Hinduism. The traditional role of a brahmin is to serve as holy man and teacher.

Bumba   The creator god of the Boshongo people.

Caliphate   Originally the name given to a state or government ruled by a caliph, an Islamic ruler who claimed succession from Muhammed. Maududi claims that the true caliphate resides in all believers.

Campesino   A native of a Latin American rural area, especially a farmer or farm laborer.

Categorical imperative   Kant's term for a moral law or command that is given to us by reason and that is universal and unqualified. Kant claims that there is only one categorical imperative: "Act only on that maxim whereby thou canst at the same time will that it should become a universal law." In other words, Kant claims that the ultimate moral law is that in all cases we should act in such a way that we would want everyone else to act.

Chaowu   A term found in Chinese literature that means the "creator of things."

Chih   In the philosophy of Mencius, a term that means wisdom or right decision.

Chronos (Kronos)   According to Greek mythology, one of the Titans, the first race of gods; he is said to have wrested power from his father Uranus by castrating him, a fate that later befell Chronos when he was castrated by his son Zeus.

Cogito   The shortened form of Descartes' *Cogito Ergo Sum*—"I think, therefore I am." This was Descartes' indubitable, self-evident truth, which served as the foundation of all other knowledge claims.

Collectivism   The socialist principle that says that all economic activity should be under the control of the people as a whole rather than a privileged class.

Communism   An economic system in which the means and modes of production are held in common rather than being individually or privately owned.

Conclusion   In logical argumentation, any claim that is supported by other claims.

Confucians   The philosophical followers of Kung Fu-tzu (Kung the master) who lived in China from 551 to 479 B.C.E. Kung Fu-tzu's name was Latinized to "Confucius."

Contractarianism   Refers to any philosophical theory that justifies political arrangements or moral principles by appealing to a social contract that is either explicitly or implicitly agreed to.

Contractualist   Someone who believes that moral values and/or political rights are based on an agreement or contract between persons.

Conversation of Gestures   Mead's term for the rudimentary form of communication in which the acts or gestures of one participant in a conversation modifies the acts or gestures of the other participant, and vice versa; it is the internalization of the conversation of gestures that, according to Mead, gives rise to the self.

Cosmology   The branch of philosophy or astronomy that deals with the origin, fundamental structure, and evolution of the universe.

Deductive   A type of argument in which the truth of the premises is claimed to guarantee the truth of the conclusion. A famous example of a deductive argument is "All men are mortal; Socrates is a man; therefore Socrates is mortal."

Deism   Belief in God that is based on reasoning about the natural world. Most Deists believe that God created the universe as well as natural laws to govern its operation, thus denying the existence of miracles.

De jure   By legal right.

Democracy   A term derived from the ancient Greeks that literally means "rule by the people."

Deracination   Literally, "to be plucked up by the roots"; the conscious rejection of racial identification or classification.

De se   A Latin term meaning "of himself or herself"; Anderson uses this term in referring to first person knowledge about oneself.

Drylongso   An African American term that refers to the ordinary, everyday aspects of life.

Dualism   The philosophical position that two distinct kinds of substances make up reality. The most commonly accepted philosophical dualism is that between mind (or soul) and body.

Efficient cause   One of the four causes or necessary elements in things that, according to Aristotle, explain change. The efficient cause is the motivation or force of movement that produces change.

Egoism   In ethics, the view that moral values are ultimately determined by self-interest; generally, the disposition to judge things according to one's own personal interests without considering the interests of others.

Embryology   The study of embryos; the branch of biology that studies the formation and early development of living organisms.

Empirical   Refers to something known or validated by experience or experiment.

Empiricism   The theory that all knowledge, except for certain tautological truths of logic and mathematics, is derived from sense experience. Empiricists also hold that, with the exception of the tautological truths of logic and mathematics, all knowledge claims must ultimately be verified by sense experience.

Encompassing   Jaspers' term for the ultimate, indefinite limits of being, which surround, envelop, and permeate everything that exists. While the encompassing surpasses conceptualization and explanation, it can be experienced as the horizon that limits the infinite possibilities of *Existenz,* or authentic existence.

Endymion   In Greek mythology, a handsome young mortal who was loved by a moon goddess and whose youth and beauty were preserved by eternal sleep.

En-soi   Literally, "in itself"; this term is used by existentialist writers, such as Jean-Paul Sartre and Simone de Beauvoir, to refer to the nonhuman aspect of being, an aspect that is devoid of conscious choice and freedom.

Entelechy   In Aristotle's metaphysics, the condition of a thing whose essence is fully actualized. Leibniz says that Monads may be referred to as Entelechies since they have in themselves a certain perfection.

Epicurus   Ancient Greek philosopher who lived from 341 to 270 B.C.E. Epicurus taught that everything that exists is a combination of atoms and that the highest good is pleasure, that is, freedom from disturbance or pain.

Epistemology   The branch of philosophy that examines the nature of knowledge and tries to determine its origin and limits.

Eros   From the ancient Greek god of carnal love, this term refers to physical or sexual love. Eros is one of the types of love that, according to Starhawk, is promoted by the religion of witchcraft.

Esse   A Latin term meaning "to be or to exist."

Ethnocentric   Believing in the cultural superiority of one's own ethnic group.

Ethnography   The branch of anthropology that deals with the scientific study and description of individual cultures.

Existentialism   A modern philosophical movement centered in France and Germany that takes the description and analysis of concrete human existence as its starting point and that emphasizes human freedom and responsibility.

Existenz   Jaspers' term for authentic human existence. According to Jaspers, our *Existenz,* our genuine self, is nonobjective and unique.

Facticity   The existentialist term for those things about a person that cannot be changed, for example, the year in which one was born.

Final cause   One of the four causes or necessary elements in things that, according to Aristotle, explain change. The final cause is the goal or purpose of the process of change.

Forms   Plato's term for the perfect entities that occupy the world of Being. According to Plato, things existing in the everyday world of sense experience, a world that he designates as the world of Becoming, are imperfect copies of the Forms.

Fourth World   A term used to refer to indigenous peoples as a global group.

Genealogy   A term that is used philosophically to refer to the method of tracing the cultural origin and development of a concept or practice in order to evaluate it; this method, which was first used by the German philosopher Friedrich Nietzsche in the nineteenth century, has become popular within certain contemporary philosophical movements.

Guajiros   The Cuban term for peasants.

Gynocentric   Focused solely on women; concerned with only women.

Gynocratic   A combination of *gynarchy,* government by women, and *democratic.* Allen uses the term to refer to Native American systems of government that fuse pluralistic democracy with a recognition of the central importance of the power of women; the opposite of phallocratic.

Háá'ayįįh, sihasin dóó hodílzin   One of the four categories of knowledge in Navajo philosophy. Translated as "rest, contentment, and respect for creation," this type of knowledge focuses on the interconnectedness of all life and reverence for nature. It is associated with darkness.

Hades   In Greek mythology, the underworld where the spirits of the dead go.

Hedonism   The philosophical doctrine that pleasure is the ultimate good in life.

Hedonistic calculus   Bentham's term for his system of computation that allows one to determine the amounts of pleasure or pain caused by an action or law. As a utilitarian, Bentham believes that this hedonistic calculus can be used to make moral decisions and to justify social rules or principles.

Hegel, Georg Wilhelm Friedrich   A German idealist philosopher (1770–1831) who was extremely influential during the first half of the nineteenth century. Hegel is best known for his attempt to systematically explain all knowledge and history and for his use of the dialectical method in doing so.

Hermeneutics   The art or practice of interpretation; used especially in connection with biblical interpretation.

Heteronomy   The opposite of autonomy; the belief that one's actions are caused by external factors over which one has no control.

Heyoka   The sacred clown, or contrary, in Lakota culture whose powers came from the thunder beings (*Wakinyan*) in the west. The heyoka acted in opposite or unexpected ways (for example, speaking backward). His antics, which were considered holy, were intended to make people laugh, to lighten their burdens.

Hodiernal   Of or belonging to the present.

Homophobia   Literally, "fear of persons having the same sex as oneself." It is often claimed that hatred or prejudice directed against homosexuals results from homophobia.

Hózhǫ́   The Navajo term for harmony or the "Beauty Way of Life." According to Navajo philosophy, this is the ultimate goal of knowing and living.

Hsin-hsin   The Chinese term *hsin* is often translated as "mind"; hsin-hsin refers to the ability to find joy, delight, or happiness in the present moment.

Hudud-Allah   Literally, "divine limits." Maududi says that these restrictions, which are placed on humans by Allah and stated in the Qur'an, provide the necessary framework within which freedom and democracy can be realized.

Humanism   A philosophy or attitude that focuses on human beings and human culture rather than on God or theology. According to Sartre, existentialism is a type of humanism.

Idealism   The metaphysical position that there are no material objects, only minds and their ideas.

Imam   In the largest branch of Islam (Sunni), the term refers to the prayer leader in a mosque; in the other principal branch of Islam (Shi'ite), the term refers to certain spiritual leaders who were the legitimate successors of Muhammed.

Immanence   The opposite of transcendence; the lack of ability or opportunity to make conscious choices or decisions.

Immanent knowledge   Schopenhauer's term for knowledge that is confined to the realm of possible experience, that is, knowledge about the way things appear to us. This type of knowledge is contrasted with transcendental knowledge.

Impression   Hume's term for a perceptual datum or sensual image that is more vivid than an idea. One example that Hume gives is the impression or sensual experience of pain as opposed to the idea of pain.

Indigenismo   Refers to any movement or policy that attempts to address the problems of the indigenous population of a country; critics often see such movements or policies as paternalistic attempts to subdue and/or assimilate indigenous populations.

Inductive   A type of argument in which the truth of the premises is claimed to provide probability, but not certainty, for the truth of the conclusion. Generalizations, arguments by analogy, causal arguments, and statistical inductions are subcategories of inductive argumentation.

Infantile sexuality   Freud's term for the sexual development that takes place during the first few years in the life of an infant.

Innate ideas   Ideas or knowledge that we are born with, for example, the idea of God. Most rationalists believe that we have innate ideas, whereas most empiricists do not.

In rebus   A Latin phrase that means "in cases, things, or matters."

Inter alia   A Latin phrase that means "among other things."

Intuition   Immediate knowledge, attained without the use of reasoning or analysis. According to Bergson, we have intuitive knowledge of our own self as it flows through time.

Jen   In Chinese philosophy, a term that refers to inner goodness or perfection. It is sometimes translated as "love," "benevolence," or "universal kindness." Whereas Confucius suggested that jen was extremely hard to attain and thus that only a few human beings were capable of realizing it, Mencius took the more "democratic" view that jen, as humane conduct, was within the grasp of most human beings.

Karma   The fruits or consequences of one's actions that determine one's lot in future lives; that which binds us to the endless cycle of birth, life, and rebirth. This concept is found in Hinduism, Buddhism, and Jainism, although it is explained somewhat differently in each religion.

K'é   The Navajo word for love or reverence. It implies the recognition of the inherent value of others, a recognition that is the basis of caring, love, and esteem.

Khilafat Vice-regency; Maududi's term for the proper political role of humans who are to serve as vice-regents or deputies of Allah.

Lakota One of the groups of Native Americans that formerly occupied most of the Great Plains; the language spoken by this group.

Last man Nietzsche's term for the ultimate follower of the herd—that is, for a human being in whom the possibility of creativity has been completely extinguished. He contrasts the last man with the *Übermensch,* or superman.

Li In Chinese thought, a term that refers to the observance of rites. However, in Confucian philosophy, li, which is often translated as "propriety," also refers to the outward, behavioral expression of jen or inner goodness. Occasionally the term is translated as "etiquette."

Libertarianism A political philosophy that advocates the maximization of individual rights and liberty, and the minimization of the role of the state.

Libido Freud's term for psychosexual energy originating in the "it"; the libido powers our urges and desires, serving as the basic fuel of our actions.

Lingua franca Any language or medium of communication that allows speakers of different languages to communicate with one another.

Logical positivism A twentieth-century philosophical movement originating in Vienna. The logical positivists emphasized the primacy of scientific thinking and claimed that all meaningful statements must be either tautological or verifiable through experience.

Mahayana One of the two main branches of Buddhism. Mahayana, which literally means "greater vehicle," originated around the first century B.C.E. It is the version of Buddhism most frequently found in Japan, China, Vietnam, Tibet, and Korea.

Mahdi In Shi'ite Islam, the "guided one," that is, the messianic figure who, according to Shi'ite belief, will one day appear on earth and guide the world into an era of justice.

Mana A term that refers to an impersonal, invisible, force or power that is thought to pervade nature. In the nineteenth century, R. H. Codrington discovered this term during missionary work in Melanesia, and he argued that the experience of *mana,* of an impersonal, invisible natural force, was the experience that served as the origin of religious belief.

Manichaeanism A religion founded by the Persian prince Mānī in the third century C.E. Mānī, who saw himself as fulfilling the teachings of Zarathustra, the Buddha, and Jesus, taught the dualistic view that there were two gods. One of these gods, the Father of Greatness, was the source of all the good in the world, whereas the other god, the Prince of Darkness, was the source of evil.

Mantras The first and oldest parts of the Vedas; more generally, the term may refer to any chant or sacred verse.

Manumission Emancipation; freedom from slavery or bondage.

Master morality Nietzsche's term for any morality, such as that of Aristotle, that is created by people holding positions of privilege and power. According to Nietzsche, the basic moral distinction found in such a morality is that between good (or noble) and bad (or base).

Materialism The philosophical doctrine that only physical matter and the properties of physical matter exist.

Matricentric A society or cultural practice that is centered on the mother.

Maxim Kant's term for the rule or intention that governs an act.

Maya A Sanskrit term that means unreality or false knowledge. In the Upanishads, *maya* is that which stands between us and liberation—that is, that which keeps us from realizing the sameness of Atman and Brahman.

Meta-ethical relativism The doctrine that there is no single universally valid moral code and that moral truth and justifiability, if they exist, are contingent on cultural and/or historical factors.

Metaphysical imperialism Valadez's term for the forced imposition of a dominant culture's vision of reality on another culture.

Metaphysics The branch of philosophy that deals with questions concerning the ultimate nature of reality. Metaphysics is often divided into ontology, the study of being, and cosmology, the study of the cosmos or universe. Typical metaphysical questions include the following: What is real? What is the origin of what is real? How does change occur?

Mishnah A collection of Jewish oral laws compiled by Judah ha Nasi in the second century C.E.

Misogyny The extreme dislike or hatred of women. Often misogyny is claimed to be the foundation of sexism.

Mitakuye Oyasin Literally, "we are all related." In the philosophy of the Lakota, this term, which is used as a greeting and in ceremonies, points to the interconnectedness of all life forms.

Mohists The philosophical followers of Mo-tzu, a Chinese thinker who lived during the fifth century B.C.E. Mo-tzu was originally a Confucian, but he later broke with Confucian doctrines. Mo-tzu's own philosophy emphasized universal benevolence and love.

Moksha In Hindu thought, a term that means liberation or release, usually liberation from the cycle of reincarnation. According to Hinduism, *moksha* is the goal of one's religious or spiritual journey.

Monad Leibniz's term for the ultimate components of reality. According to Leibniz, a Monad is a "spiritual atom" that does not directly interact with other Monads but expresses the universe from its own perspective.

Monism The metaphysical position that reality is one; sometimes the term is also applied to the position that there is only one type of substance.

Mores A sociological term that refers to the unquestioned assumptions or traditions of a social group that embody and/or determine the moral views of that group.

Mysteries Secret religious cults in ancient Greece that were connected with agriculture and often taught that the soul was immortal and would be reborn. The Mysteries of the goddess Demeter and the god Dionysus were celebrated at Eleusis for over a thousand years.

Naturalism The philosophical position that all phenomena can be understood and explained by natural causes and laws and that there is no need to resort to moral, religious, or supernatural factors.

Neoplatonism A school of Greek philosophy founded by Ammonius Saccas in the third century C.E. Claiming that their beliefs were derived from Plato, the neoplatonists espoused a syncretistic view that combined Greek philosophy with elements of Oriental mysticism and concepts derived from Judaism and Christianity.

Nihigáál One of the four categories of knowledge in Navajo philosophy. Translated as "sustenance," this type of knowledge focuses on self-reliance and on becoming a contributing member of one's community. It is associated with the blue twilight.

Nihilism The belief that nothing has value, that life has no meaning; more specifically, it refers to a nineteenth-century Russian political philosophy that advocated the violent overthrow of social and political institutions to make way for a new social order.

Nirvana The spiritual goal in Buddhism; literally, the word means "extinguished" and refers to the cessation of *tanha,* or desire.

Nominalism The metaphysical view that only particular things are real and that universals are abstractions or linguistic constructions having no real existence.

Normative moral relativism The doctrine that it is wrong to pass judgment on others who have values that differ from one's own or to try to make others change their moral values; according to Wong, normative moral relativism may be either extreme or qualified.

Nous The Greek word for mind or reason.

Object-cathexes   *Cathexis* is Freud's term for the investment or buildup of sexual energy that requires discharge or release; an *object-cathexis* is any object that has been imbued with this investment or build-up of sexual energy.

Oedipus complex   Freud's term for the tendency in early childhood to experience sexual desires towards one's parent of the opposite sex, the female version of which is sometimes labeled the "Electra complex"; according to Freud, the process of working through the Oedipus complex initiates development of the "over-I," and if this process is not completed, serious psychological problems will arise.

Oglala   One of the groups of Native Americans who formerly inhabited most of the Great Plains; Black Elk was an Oglala holy man.

Oligarchy   A form of government in which power is held by a few persons or a privileged class; a society ruled by a wealthy elite.

OM   First found in the Upanishads, this became the most sacred word or sound in Hinduism. Often used in meditational chants, the word also serves to introduce or conclude important papers and books.

Ontocentrism   The belief that the conception of reality held by the group within which you reside is superior to all other conceptions of reality.

Ontologist   Someone who studies ontology.

Ontology   The branch of metaphysics that studies the nature of being or existence as such.

Paradox   A logical puzzle that defies rational explanation or solution; an apparently self-contradictory conclusion drawn from premises that initially seem to be acceptable. Kierkegaard says that the traditional conception of Christ as being both fully human and fully divine is paradoxical.

Pathos   The power or quality of something to evoke a feeling of pity or compassion.

Patriarchy   A social group or culture in which the father is the head of the family or social unit and in which descent is determined by the male line; more generally, any institution in which power is held by and transferred through males.

Percipi   A Latin term meaning to be perceived.

Petrarch, Francesco   Italian poet and scholar who lived from 1304 to 1374; he is best known for his *Canzoniere*, a collection of love poems, and for reinitiating humanistic studies in Italy.

Phallocratic   A social system or conceptual scheme that is based on the primacy and maintenance of the power of men and that either denies the power of women or relegates it to the background; the opposite of gynocratic.

Phenomena   In Kantian philosophy, the term refers to appearances—that is, to the way things seem to us. Kant contrasts phenomena with noumena, or things in themselves.

Phenomenology   Refers specifically to a twentieth-century philosophical movement founded by Edmund Husserl that says that philosophy should focus on the study of phenomena or the way things appear to consciousness; more generally, it refers to a methodology that focuses on description rather than explanation.

Philosophes   A group of popular eighteenth-century French intellectuals or philosophers; Rousseau and Voltaire are the best-known members of the group.

Phylogeny   The evolutionary development and history of a kind of organism; also refers to the evolutionary development of an organ or other part of an organism.

Physicalist   Someone who accepts the doctrine of physicalism, the belief that all meaningful statements, other than those of logic and mathematics, must refer to observable properties of spatiotemporal things or events; for example, a physicalist would argue that all meaningful statements about the mind are actually statements about events in the brain.

Pleasure principle   Freud's term for our most fundamental striving toward pleasure and/or away from pain; this principle, which governs the workings of the "it," demands immediate gratification.

Plenum   In modern science, the term refers to a space in which a gas is contained at a pressure greater than atmospheric pressure; in Leibniz's philosophy it refers to any completely filled space.

Pluralism   The metaphysical position that there are many nonreducible substances. An early pluralist was the ancient Greek philosopher Empedocles, who said that there were four nonreducible elements in the universe: earth, air, fire, and water.

Pluralist   Someone who believes in metaphysical or political pluralism. A pluralist society is one in which diversity is allowed and encouraged, in which minority groups are allowed to fully participate while still maintaining their cultural differences.

Pragmatism   A modern American philosophical movement founded by C. S. Peirce and popularized by William James and John Dewey. Pragmatists maintain that the meaning of propositions lies in their observable consequences and that the truth of a proposition is determined by practical considerations or workability.

Praxis   A term that refers to practical application as opposed to mere theory.

Premise   In logical argumentation, an assumed claim that is used to support some other claim.

Prima facie   Literally, "at first glance"; refers to something that is given or self-evident.

Process philosophy   Refers to any philosophical theory that claims that reality is always changing and that the different components of reality are interrelated or interconnected.

Proletariat   In Marxist theory, the class of modern wage laborers or workers who, having no means of production of their own, are reduced to selling their labor in order to survive.

Provincialism   Literally, being able to see things only from the perspective of one's own province; being limited in perspective or narrow minded.

Pseudo-proposition   Ayer's term for a statement or proposition that is grammatically correct and appears to be meaningful but that is actually meaningless since it cannot be empirically verified. Ayer claims that as they are commonly used, the statements "God exists" and "the soul exists" are pseudo-propositions.

Psychoanalysis   The psychological theory and method of treatment developed by Freud that employs such techniques as free association and dream analysis to recover forgotten or repressed desires or memories that are the root of a person's psychological problems.

Purdah   Derived from the Persian word for a veil or curtain, *purdah* refers to the Muslim practice of secluding women behind veils and/or in private apartments.

Purusha   In Hinduism, this term refers to the primal person, the "all," from which the concrete universe is produced; Purusha, the immortal Person, is often identified with Atman, the imperishable Self.

Pyrrhonism   A school of radical skepticism founded by the ancient Greek philosopher Pyhho around 300 B.C.E.

Pyrrhonistic   Refers to an extreme form of skepticism.

Quantum mechanics   A theory of the mechanics or movement of atoms, molecules, and so on that accepts and incorporates Heisenberg's uncertainty principle—that is, the principle that measuring either of two related quantities, such as the position or momentum of a particle, produces uncertainty in the measurement of the other.

Quietism   A Christian philosophy that attempts to annihilate the will through passive contemplation and mystical experience. This is one of the philosophies that Sartre contrasts with existentialism.

Qur'an   Often transcribed as "Koran," this is the basic sacred literature of Islam. It is traditionally believed to be the literal word of God (Allah), which was revealed to Muhammed in the seventh century C.E.

Raison d'être   A French term that means reason or justification for being/existing.

Raja   A ruler or "king" in India.

Rationalism   The philosophical position that knowledge or truth is not derived from the senses but from rational intuition plus deductive reasoning.

Rawlsian   Refers to the philosophy of the North American philosopher John Rawls (1921–2002). According to Mills, Rawls', book *A Theory of Justice* (1971) is to be credited for "the revival of social contract theory, and indeed postwar political philosophy in general."

Reality principle   Freud's term for the principle, governing the "I," that takes into account both the desires of the "it" and the practicalities of the external world; in a properly functioning psyche, the reality principle overrules and moderates the pleasure principle that holds sway in the "it," thereby substituting deferred gratification for immediate gratification.

Recollection   Plato's doctrine that we are born with all genuine knowledge and that learning consists of remembering what we already know.

Reincarnation   The belief that one has been, or can be, reborn into another body. The Hindu doctrine of *samsara* is one example of a philosophical belief in reincarnation, as is Plato's belief in the transmigration of the soul.

Relativism   The philosophical position that there is no absolute knowledge, no single correct view of reality.

Repression   Freud's term for the process through which the "I" rids itself of potentially harmful desires by driving them underground into the unconscious.

Sacerdotalism   The methods or practices of the priesthood; the belief that priests act as mediators between God and humans.

Samsara   In Indian thought, the cycle of birth, life, and death to which one is bound until one achieves *moksha* or liberation.

Sangha   The order or society of Buddhist monks.

Satyagraha   Gandhi's term for the active practice of nonviolence to bring about social or political change. Gandhi is careful to distinguish this term, which is sometimes translated as "soul force" or "love force," from passive resistance.

Schleiermacher, Friedrich Daniel Ernst   Perhaps the greatest systematic Protestant theologian (1768–1834) of the nineteenth century. He is best known for his defense of faith as the vehicle of religious belief and for his claim that Christianity is based on a feeling of absolute dependence.

Shari'ah   An Arabic word meaning "path," which refers to Islamic law; all of Allah's commandments concerning human activities.

Shudra   The lowest class of the classical Hindu *varna* system. *Shudras* are servants whose sole duty in life is to take care of the needs of others.

Skandhas   In Buddhism, the five processes that make something what it is. These processes, some physical and some mental, are constantly changing.

Skepticism   Fear or doubt about the possibility of knowledge.

Slave morality   Nietzsche's term for any morality, such as that of early Christianity, that is created by people who are subservient and powerless. According to Nietzsche, the basic moral distinction found in such a morality is that between good and evil, where "good" refers to the virtues of the powerless, such as meekness, while "evil" refers to the virtues of those in power, such as pride.

Socialism   A theory or social system in which the means of production and the goods produced by them are owned and controlled collectively rather than privately.

Soma   One of the deities of the Vedas who was the lord of medicinal plants. The term *soma* is also used for the moon and for a sacred plant in ancient India that was the source of a favorite drink of the gods.

Somatophobia   Literally, "fear of the body." According to Spelman, somatophobia characterizes much of Western philosophy.

Sophists   Wandering teachers in ancient Greece who taught philosophy and rhetoric for pay. Many of the Sophists denied the existence of absolute knowledge or goodness, and they appeared as opponents of Socrates in several of Plato's dialogues.

Subjective idealism   The name given to Berkeley's philosophical position that there are only finite minds, God's mind, and ideas.

Substance   From Greek words meaning "to stand under," substance refers to the ultimate reality of a thing that underlies its sensible properties or characteristics.

Sunnah   Literally, "custom"; the body of traditional Islamic law, much of which is based on the teachings and practices of Muhammed. Maududi claims that in an Islamic state, every Muslim has an obligation to follow the Qur'an and the Sunnah.

Superman   One translation of Nietzsche's term *Übermensch*. In Nietzsche's philosophy, the superman is the creative individual who has broken from the herd and followed his or her own unique path.

Surrealism   A twentieth-century movement in literature, the arts, and philosophy that was spearheaded by the French poet and critic André Breton. Surrealists attempted to liberate the unconscious in order to totally transform political, cultural, and philosophical values.

Sutra   A Sanskrit word meaning "row." It refers to any collection of sayings that are devoted to the same topic. One of the best known of the sutras is the *Kama Sutra*, whose topic is sexual positions and relationships.

Tanha   The Buddha's term for the cause of suffering and pain; often translated as "desire," tanha must be overcome or eliminated if one is to achieve Nirvana, or enlightenment.

Tao   One of the most important concepts of Chinese philosophy, the term is often translated as "the Way." In Taoism, the term refers to the ultimate principle or nature of the universe, a principle or nature that cannot be encompassed by logical or rational categories.

Taoism   An ancient Chinese philosophy or religion whose founder was traditionally claimed to be Lao-tzu, a legendary figure from the sixth century B.C.E. According to Taoism, the ultimate goal in life is to harmonize oneself with the Tao, the ultimate "Way" or nature of the universe.

Tathāgata   An early, honorary title of the Buddha. The meaning is not universally agreed on, but one possible meaning is "one who has fully realized the ultimate."

Tautology   A statement that is logically or necessarily true. One example of a tautology is the statement "Either it is going to rain or it is not."

Theo-democracy   Maududi's term for a true Islamic government; the term was coined to distinguish such governments from Western secular democracies and to suggest that genuine human freedom can result only from submission to Allah.

Theravada   Literally, the "Way of the Elders." One of the two principal branches of Buddhism. Many scholars believe that the practices and beliefs of Theravada most closely resemble the practices and beliefs of the Buddha and his earliest followers. Today Theravada is found mainly in Sri Lanka and the countries of Southeast Asia (Laos, Thailand, Myanmar, and Cambodia).

Theseus   A hero in Greek mythology who slew the Minotaur and liberated the Athenians from their yearly tribute of young men and women to Minos.

Thing-in-itself   Kant and Schopenhauer's term for the way a thing actually is as opposed to the way it appears to us.

Transcendence   Those aspects of one's existence that are consciously chosen. This term may also refer to the ability and opportunity to make conscious choices in one's life. As such, it is contrasted with the term *immanence*, which refers to the lack of ability or opportunity to make such choices.

Transcendental   A term used by Vasconcelos (and earlier by Kant) to refer to the categories or basic rules of human knowledge; it is the element of knowing that is contributed by the human intellect.

Transcendentalism   Any philosophy that maintains that knowledge of reality is to be attained through intuitive or spiritual sources rather than empirical sources. Transcendentalism in the United States flourished in New England during the middle part of the nineteenth century. Its best-known proponents were Ralph Waldo Emerson and Henry David Thoreau.

Transcendentalist   A proponent of transcendentalism.

Transcendental knowledge   Schopenhauer's term for knowledge that passes beyond the bounds of possible experience and that attempts to determine the nature of things as they are in themselves and not merely as they appear to us.

Trope   Any figure of speech, such as metaphor or irony, that uses words in other than their literal sense.

Universalism   Wong's term for the belief that there is a single universally valid moral code; this position is often termed "absolutism."

Untermenschen   A German term that refers to people what are subordinate to other people; it often carries the connotation of being subhuman.

Upanishads   The most philosophical parts of the sacred literature of Hinduism. The probable literal meaning of the term is "near sitting," which indicates that these writings originated from philosophical discussions about the Vedas between students and their gurus (teachers).

Utilitarianism   The ethical theory proposed by Jeremy Bentham and popularized by John Stuart Mill that considers utility or usefulness as the ultimate criterion of moral worth. For Mill and Bentham, that action is right which brings about the greatest amount of happiness for the greatest number of people.

Vaihinger, Hans   German philosopher and Kant scholar who lived from 1852 to 1933; in his best-known work *Philosophie des Als Ob* (1911; *Philosophy of the As-If*), he argues that reality cannot be truly known but that human beings construct systems of thought and act as if reality corresponds to these constructions.

Varna   A term that literally means "color" and that refers to the fourfold hierarchical ordering in Hindu society. In this ordering, the four classes are holy men (Brahmin), warriors (Kshatriya), merchants (Vaishya), and servants (Shudra). This term is often confused with the term *caste,* but the caste system in India is much more extensive than the four classes represented by the term *varna.*

Vedas   The most sacred texts of Hinduism.

Vicious circle   In logic, a mistake in reasoning that occurs when the premise used to support a conclusion is then itself supported by the conclusion. An example of this would be to appeal to a statement in the Qur'an to prove the existence of Allah and to then turn around and use the existence of Allah to prove the reliability of the Qur'an.

Vijñānavāda   Mentalism; an Indian philosophical doctrine that only the mind has reality.

Wakan Tanka   Literally, "father" or "grandfather." This is one of the words used to address the Lakota great spirit or supreme deity.

Weltanschauung   A German term meaning "worldview," or the way the world appears. In philosophy, the term often carries the sense of a comprehensive worldview in comparison or contrast with another comprehensive worldview.

Wotan   Teutonic father-god who is associated with fire and the sun and who is always striving to achieve new heights of power and wisdom.

Wu Wei   A Taoist concept that is often translated as "actionless activity." It refers to the Taoist belief that the ideal life is a life that follows the movement of the Tao without struggling against it.

Yahweh   The god who revealed himself to Moses in the form of a burning bush that was not consumed and who became the god of the Israelites. In the Hebrew text, the term is written without vowels as *YHWH*.

Yama   Hindu god of death and lord of the underworld.

Yang   Literally, the "bright or sunny side of a hill"; in Chinese thought, yang is the positive force in nature that is associated with heaven and the male, among other things. Life requires a combination of yang and yin (negative force).

Yi   In Chinese thinking, a word that refers to economic and social justice. For Mencius, the term *yi,* or justice, refers to an internal state or virtue, which is the source or foundation of justice in society.

Yin   Literally, the "dark side of a hill"; in Chinese thought, yin is the negative force in nature that is associated with the earth and the female, among other things. This force should not be viewed as bad or evil, for in Chinese thought yin is just as essential as yang (positive force). Indeed, a harmonious existence requires a balance of both.

Yoga   One of the philosophical systems of Hinduism; more generally, a Hindu discipline or system of physical and mental exercises designed to lead to heightened awareness and ultimately to *moksha.*

Yu   One of the three ancient legendary heroes of China (along with Yao and Shun). In fourth-century B.C.E. Chinese history, it was believed that the world began with a great flood and was made inhabitable by the work of these three heroes. In order to prevent further flooding, Yu supposedly built dams and mountains.

Yüeh   In its modern sense, the word refers to the Chinese dialect spoken in the Kwangtung Province in southern China; as used by Mencius, it seems to refer to a geographical area in southern China.

Zakat   The poor tax or almsgiving that constitutes one of the five duties required of devout Muslims. It is viewed as a religious tax collected for the benefit of the poor, orphans, and travelers.

Zeus   The Greek god of the heavens who, according to Greek mythology, castrated his father Chronos; he is often depicted brandishing a thunderbolt, his principal weapon, which he hurls at those who displease him.

Zimmi   The term for a non-Muslim citizen of an Islamic state.

Zionism   A movement founded in the nineteenth century that initially aimed at the reestablishment of a Jewish state in Palestine and that is now dedicated to the development of Israel.

Zoroastrianism   An ancient religion founded by the priest Zarathustra (latinized into Zoroaster) around the tenth century B.C.E. Zoroastrians worship one god, Ahura Mazda, and see the earth as a battleground between the forces of good and evil. It is believed that the eschatology of Zoroastrianism influenced other Middle Eastern religions, such as postexilic Judaism, Christianity, and Islam.